Principles of Marketing

Seventh Canadian Edition

Philip Kotler
Northwestern University

Gary Armstrong
University of North Carolina

Peggy H. Cunningham
Queen's University

PEARSON

Prentice
Hall

Toronto

Library and Archives Canada Cataloguing in Publication

Kotler, Philip
    Principles of marketing / Philip Kotler, Gary Armstrong,
Peggy H. Cunningham.—7th Canadian ed.

Includes index.
ISBN-13: 978-0-13-202001-5
ISBN-10: 0-13-202001-7

1. Marketing—Textbooks. 2. Marketing—Management—Textbooks.
I. Armstrong, Gary II. Cunningham, Margaret H. III. Title.

HF5415.K636 2008   658.8   C2006-905141-0

ISBN-13: 978-0-13-202001-5
ISBN-10: 0-13-202001-7

Editor-in-Chief: Gary Bennett
Acquisitions Editor: Don Thompson
Marketing Manager: Eileen Lasswell
Developmental Editor: Joanne Scattolon
Production Editor: Jen Handel
Copy Editor: Audrey Dorsch
Proofreader: Dawn Hunter
Production Coordinator: Andrea Falkenberg
Composition: Gerry Dunn
Photo and Permissions Research: Lisa Brant
Art Director: Julia Hall
Interior and Cover Design: Anthony Leung

  3 4 5   12 11 10 09 08
Printed and bound in Hong Kong.
GCC/03

PEARSON

Prentice
Hall

About the Authors

As a team, Philip Kotler, Gary Armstrong, and Peggy Cunningham provide a blend of skills uniquely suited to writing an introductory marketing text. Professor Kotler is one of the world's leading authorities on marketing. Professors Armstrong and Cunningham are award-winning teachers of undergraduate business students. Together, they make the complex world of marketing practical, approachable, and enjoyable.

Philip Kotler is one of the world's leading authorities on marketing. He is the S. C. Johnson & Son Distinguished Professor of International Marketing at the Kellogg School of Management, Northwestern University. He received his master's degree at the University of Chicago and his Ph.D. at MIT, both in economics. Dr. Kotler is author of Marketing Management, now in its twelfth edition and the most widely used marketing textbook in graduate schools of business. He has authored more than 20 other successful books and more than one hundred articles in leading journals. He is the only three-time winner of the coveted Alpha Kappa Psi award for the best annual article published in the Journal of Marketing. He was named the first recipient of two major awards: the Distinguished Marketing Educator of the Year Award given by the American Marketing Association and the Philip Kotler Award for Excellence in Health Care Marketing presented by the Academy for Health Care Services Marketing. Other major honors include the 1978 Paul Converse Award of the AMA, honoring his original contribution to marketing, the European Association of Marketing Consultants and Sales Trainers Prize for Marketing Excellence, the 1995 Sales and Marketing Executives International (SMEI) Marketer of the Year award, the 2002 Academy of Marketing Science Distinguished Educator Award, and honorary doctoral degrees from Stockholm University, the University of Zurich, Athens University of Economics and Business, DePaul University, the Cracow School of Business and Economics, Groupe H.E.C. in Paris, the Budapest School of Economic Science and Public Administration, and the University of Economics and Business Administration in Vienna.

Professor Kotler has been a consultant to many major U.S. and foreign companies in the areas of marketing strategy and planning, marketing organization, and international marketing. He has been Chairman of the College of Marketing of the Institute of Management Sciences, a Director of the American Marketing Association, a Trustee of the Marketing Science Institute, a Director of the MAC Group, a member of the Yankelovich Advisory Board, and a member of the Copernicus Advisory Board, and a member of the Advisory Board of the Drucker Foundation. He has traveled extensively throughout Europe, Asia, and South America, advising and lecturing to many companies about global marketing opportunities.

Gary Armstrong is Crist W. Blackwell Distinguished Professor of Undergraduate Education in the Kenan-Flagler Business School at the University of North Carolina at Chapel Hill. He holds undergraduate and masters degrees in business from Wayne State University in Detroit, and he received his Ph.D. in marketing from Northwestern University. Dr. Armstrong has contributed numerous articles to leading business journals. As a consultant and researcher, he has worked with many companies on marketing research, sales management, and marketing strategy. But Professor Armstrong's first love is teaching. His Blackwell Distinguished Professorship is the only permanent endowed professorship for distinguished undergraduate teaching at the University of North Carolina at Chapel Hill. He has been very active in the teaching and administration of Kenan-Flagler's undergraduate program. His recent administrative posts include Chair of the Marketing Faculty, Associate Director of the Undergraduate Business Program, Director of the Business Honors Program, and others. He works closely with business student groups and has received several campus-wide and Business School teaching awards. He is the only repeat recipient of the school's highly regarded Award for Excellence in Undergraduate Teaching, which he won three times. In 2004, Professor Armstrong received the UNC Board of Governors Award for Excellence in Teaching, the highest teaching honor bestowed at the University of North Carolina at Chapel Hill.

Peggy Cunningham is the Marie Shantz Teaching Associate Professor of Marketing at Queen's University School of Business. She received her undergraduate degree from Queen's University, completed her MBA at the University of Calgary, and earned her Ph.D. in marketing from Texas A&M University. She was the founding Director of Queen's new MBA program for students with undergraduate business degrees. She has considerable international experience and has been a visiting professor at universities and government training programs in France, Germany, China, the U.K., and the U.S. Her prior industry experience and current consulting practice help her to bring the perspective of the practitioner to the study of marketing. She conducts research in the fields of social alliances, corporate social responsibility, marketing ethics, relationship marketing, and cause-related marketing. Her work is published in a number of journals, including the *Journal of the Academy of Marketing Science* and the *California Management Review.* She is also the Canadian co-author with Philip Kotler of *Marketing Management,* Canadian Twelfth Edition, and *Marketing: An Introduction.* She is a devoted teacher who tries to inspire her students to realize their full and unique potential. In recognition of these efforts, she has received several teaching and service awards, including the PriceWaterhouseCoopers Leaders in Management Education Award (2004), the Frank Knox award for teaching excellence, a Queen's campus-wide award granted by undergraduate students, and the Academy of Marketing Science Outstanding Teacher in 2001. She has applied her love of teaching to a wide range of courses, including marketing management and strategy, branding, principles of marketing, services marketing, international marketing, marketing ethics, and customer relationship management.

Brief Contents

Contents

Preface

Welcome to the Seventh Canadian Edition of *Principles of Marketing*!

Our goal has always been to offer the most current, applied, resourceful, and exciting text for the introductory marketing course. That's why it continues to be one of the most widely used introductory marketing texts in Canada.

Quality without Question

We've pored over every book page, figure, table, exercise, illustration, example, and reference. We've included the latest concepts and practices to keep the text fresh and timely. And we've reviewed hundreds of pages of feedback from marketing instructors and students to make sure that this book responds to your needs.

New to this edition, we solicited feedback in the form of technical reviews from experts in several areas of marketing to ensure we have integrated the most current data and examples.

We think you will agree that the seventh Canadian edition is the best yet, and that it offers the highest level of **Quality without Question**.

The Seventh Canadian Edition Builds on Several Major Themes

- **Building and managing profitable customer relationships.** Creating value *for* customers in order to capture value *from* customers in return. Today's marketers must be good at *creating customer value* and *managing customer relationships*. Leading marketing companies understand the marketplace and customer needs, design customer-driven marketing strategies that create customer value, develop marketing programs that deliver value and satisfaction, and build strong customer relationships. In return, they capture value from customers in the form of sales, profits, and customer equity.

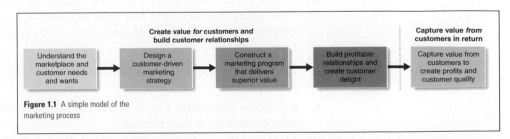

Figure 1.1 A simple model of the marketing process

- **Marketers must also excel at partner relationship management.** They must work closely with partners inside and outside the company to jointly build profitable customer relationships. Successful marketers are now partnering effectively with other company departments to build strong company value chains. And they are joining with outside partners to build effective supply chains and effective customer-focused alliances.

- **Building and managing strong brands to create brand equity.** Well-positioned brands with strong brand equity provide the basis upon which to build profitable customer relationships. Today's marketers must know how to position their brands and manage them well.

- **Harnessing marketing technologies in this digital age.** Digital and high-tech marketing developments are dramatically changing both buyers and marketers. Today's marketers must know how to leverage new information, communication, and transportation technologies to connect more effectively with customers and marketing partners in this digital age.

- **Marketing in a socially responsible way around the globe.** As technological developments make the world an increasingly smaller place, marketers must market their brands globally and in socially responsible ways.

Real Marketing

The seventh Canadian edition includes new and expanded material on a wide range of topics, including the following:

- Measuring and managing return on marketing
- Managing customer relationships
- Positioning and positioning maps
- Value-based pricing
- Database marketing
- Buzz marketing and experiential marketing
- Environmental sustainability
- Supplier development and supply chain management
- Marketing and diversity
- Socially responsible marketing
- New marketing technologies
- Global marketing

316   **Part 3**   Designing a Customer-Driven Marketing Strategy and Marketing Mix

REAL MARKETING   **8.2**

WestJet's Value Proposition: "Less for Much Less"

WestJet transformed itself into a national airline using a classic "less for less" value proposition.

Principles of Marketing features real-world examples that show concepts in action and reveal the drama of modern marketing. Every chapter-opening vignette and Real Marketing highlight has been replaced or significantly updated to deliver on our promise of offering the most current and exciting text.

Learn how...

- **NASCAR** creates high-octane, totally involving, very profitable customer relationships.

- **Mountain Equipment Co-op** aligns ethics and social responsibility with a savvy relationship marketing strategy.

- **McDonald's** reversed its fortunes by aligning itself with the new marketplace realities and now has customers and stockholders alike humming its catchy "I'm lovin' it" jingle.

- **RFID technology**—embedding tiny "smart chips" in the products you buy— gives us an exciting glimpse into the future of supply chain management.

- The **Dove Campaign for Real Beauty** was born using the insights from powerful marketing research.

- **Steinway** proves that when it comes to its pianos, price is nothing, the Steinway experience is everything.

- The **Art Gallery of Ontario** adopts segmentation, target marketing, and positioning to better market itself in the increasingly competitive non-profit sector.

- **Whole Foods Market** thrives by positioning away from behemoth Wal-Mart rather than trying to compete head to head.

- **lululemon** rose from being a small Vancouver-based retailer to a company that is making its brand known on the world stage.

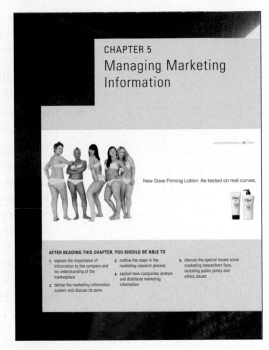

- **McCain** continues to prove that Canadian companies can be a dominant force in the global food industry.

Supplements

New and Improved Resources for Instructors

Instructor's Resources Centre: Instructor resources are password protected and available for download via **www.pearsoned.ca.** For your convenience, many of these resources are also available on the **Instructor's Resource CD-ROM.**

- **Instructor's Manual:** View this resource chapter-by-chapter or download the entire manual as a zip file.

- **TestGen:** Computerized test item file for building tests and exams. Compatible with PC or Macintosh computers.

- **MyTest (online only):** MyTest from Pearson Canada is a powerful assessment-generation program that helps instructors easily create and print quizzes, tests, exams, as well as homework or practice handouts. Questions and tests can all be authored online, allowing instructors ultimate flexibility and the ability to efficiently manage assessments at anytime, from anywhere. Included in MyMarketingLab.

- **PowerPoints:** When it comes to PowerPoints, Pearson Canada knows one size does not fit all. That's why we offer instructors more than one option.

  - **PowerPoint BASIC:** This simple presentation includes basic outlines and key points from each chapter. BASIC was designed for instructors who prefer to customize PowerPoints and who want to be spared from having to strip out embedded files or other media-rich features. The BASIC PowerPoints are also available to students in MyMarketingLab.

  - **PowerPoint MEDIA RICH (on IRCD only):** This media-rich alternative includes basic outlines and key points from each chapter, plus advertisements and images from the text, discussion questions, weblinks, and embedded video snippets from the accompanying video library. It's the best option if you want a complete presentation solution. Instructors can further customize this presentation using the Image Library featured on the Instructor's Resource CD-ROM.

- **Image Library (on IRCD only):** Access many of the images, ads, and illustrations featured in the text. Ideal for PowerPoint customization.

- **Instructor's Resource CD-ROM (IRCD):** Includes Instructor's Manual, TestGen, PowerPoints BASIC, PowerPoints MEDIA RICH, and Image Library.

- **CBC/Pearson Education Canada Video Library:** Pearson Canada and the CBC have worked together to bring you seven segments from such notable CBC programs as *Venture, Marketplace,* and *Undercurrents.* Designed specifically to complement the text, this case collection is an excellent tool for bringing students into contact with the world outside the classroom. These programs have extremely high production quality, present substantial content, and have been chosen to relate directly to chapter topics. (Please contact your Pearson Education Canada sales representative for details. These videos are subject to availability and terms negotiated upon adoption of the text.)

- **Prentice Hall Video Library:** Featuring 18 exciting segments, *all new* to this edition and filmed in 2003 or 2004. All segments are available online as well as in VHS or DVD formats. Here are the videos filmed in 2004:

  - American Express and the modern marketing environment
  - The NFL and the importance of social responsibility
  - Song Airlines and smart pricing strategies
  - Eaton's approach to B2B issues, including buyer behaviour
  - Reebok's retailing and wholesaling policies
  - Wild Planet's strategies in consumer markets

- **MyMarketingLab:** This site delivers all classroom resources for instructors and students in one place: **www.pearsoned.ca/mymarketinglab**. All instructor resources are organized by learning objective so you can customize your lecture more conveniently than ever before. MyMarketingLab is available with WebCT, Blackboard, or standalone, bringing all resources together into one exciting new online resource for instructors and students. Resources include the following:

  - Diagnostic Tests for student review—this quizzing can be monitored by you, and results reveal which learning objectives students are struggling with so you can customize your review and assessment
  - Personalized Study Plan based on each student's results in the diagnostic test offers remediation by learning objective to help students focus on the concepts they find most challenging
  - Case-based adaptive questions—scenario-based questioning to give you a chance to apply what you have learned and practice your critical thinking skill
  - Ability to mark homework, quizzes, and tests automatically and have them automatically populate in your grade book
  - Link to eText
  - Case Pilot to aid in analyzing cases
  - Glossary Flashcards for quick and fun study of marketing terms
  - MyTest

- **AdCritic.com:** Pearson Canada and AdAge are bringing the most current ads and commentary from advertising experts into your classroom. Only Pearson Canada can offer students 16 weeks of access to a special AdCritic.com site that includes AdAge's encyclopedia of articles at a deeply discounted rate. A limited number of access codes are available at a special price only when shrink-wrapped with a Pearson Canada text, so be sure and specify the appropriate package with your local bookstore in advance. Please visit **www.prenhall.com/marketing** for a tour of the AdCritic site.

New and Improved Resources for Students

- **MyMarketingLab:** This site delivers all classroom resources for students in one place: **www.pearsoned.ca/mymarketinglab**. An access code is packaged with your text. Resources include the following:
  - Diagnostic quizzing for review—Pretest and Exit Test
  - Personalized Study Plan based on your results in the diagnostic test offering you remediation by learning objective to help you focus on the concepts you find most challenging
  - Marketing Toolkit: Interactive modules to aid in review of understanding key concepts
  - Link to eText
  - Case Pilot to aid in analyzing cases
  - Glossary Flashcards for quick and fun study of marketing terms

MyMarketingLab is also available through WebCT or Blackboard.

- **Companion Website:** This site contains student quizzes and the text glossary. You can reach the Companion Website by going to **www.pearsoned.ca/kotler**.

Acknowledgments for the Seventh Canadian Edition

Many reviewers at other colleges and universities provided expert comments and suggestions. We are indebted to the following colleagues who reviewed for this edition:

Sergio Carvalho, University of Manitoba

June Cotte, University of Western Ontario

Timothy Dewhirst, University of Saskatchewan

Sarah Holding, Malaspina University-College

Lea Katsanis, Concordia University

Shirley Lichti, Wilfrid Laurier University

Jooseop Lim, Concordia University

Miguel Morales, Saint Mary's University

Susan E. Reid, Bishop's University

F.H. Rolf Seringhaus, Wilfrid Laurier University

Elaine Sprague, University of British Columbia

Keith Wallace, Kwantlen University College

David Williams, University of Saskatchewan

Mehdi Zahaf, Lakehead University

We also owe a great deal to the people at Pearson Education Canada who helped develop this book. Acquisitions Editor Laura Forbes always provided a smile and energetic support for this edition as well as ably managing the many facets of this complex revision project. Developmental Editors Pam Voves and Joanne Scattolon were a joy to work with and provided constant support, insights, and timely, detailed feedback. We also owe thanks to Jennifer Handel, Production Editor. Her patience with a never-ending list of changes and her willingness to consult about these changes was much appreciated. Audrey Dorsch, Copy Editor, brought a keen eye for errors and inconsistencies, and her work made this a better quality product. Proofreader Dawn Hunter contributed greatly to the value of the final text with her enthusiastic eyes and inquisitive mind. Krista Cunningham was an invaluable resource in the development of this edition. Her research and experience in the area of brand management helped us provide rich and relevant content. We would also like to thank many of the behind-the-scenes members of the Pearson Canada team: Andrea Falkenberg, Production Coordinator; Anthony Leung, Designer; and Gerry Dunn, Composition Specialist. Additional thanks go to Marketing Manager Eileen Lasswell for her initiative and creative eye.

Finally, we owe many thanks to our families—Kathy, Betty, KC, Keri, Delaney, Mandy, Matt, and Molly; Nancy, Amy, Melissa, and Jessica; Paul and Krista—for their constant support and encouragement. To them, we dedicate this book.
Philip Kotler
Gary Armstrong
Peggy Cunningham

CHAPTER 1

Marketing: Managing Profitable Customer Relationships

AFTER STUDYING THIS CHAPTER, YOU SHOULD BE ABLE TO

1. define marketing and outline the steps in the marketing process

2. explain the importance of understanding customers and the marketplace, and identify the five core marketplace concepts

3. identify the key elements of a customer-driven marketing strategy and discuss the marketing management orientations that guide marketing strategy

4. discuss customer relationship management, and identify strategies for creating value *for* customers and capturing value *from* customers in return

5. describe the major trends and forces that are changing the marketing landscape in this age of relationships

A Great Way to Learn and Instruct Online

The Pearson Education Canada Companion Website is easy to navigate and is organized to correspond to the chapters in this textbook. Whether you are a student in the classroom or a distance learner you will discover helpful resources for in-depth study and research that empower you in your quest for greater knowledge and maximize your potential for success in the course.

[www.pearsoned.ca/kotler]

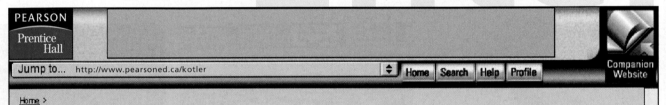

PEARSON Prentice Hall

Jump to... | http://www.pearsoned.ca/kotler | ⬍ | Home | Search | Help | Profile

Companion Website

Home ›

Companion Website

Principles of Marketing, Seventh Canadian Edition, by Kotler/Armstrong/Cunningham

Student Resources

The modules in this section provide students with tools for learning course material. These modules include:

- Chapter Objectives
- PowerPoint Express
- Glossary
- Chapter Quiz
- Internet Exercises
- Digital Connections
- Company Weblinks
- CBC Video Cases
- Video Shorts Exercises
- Case Pilot
- Comprehensive Cases
- Virtual Library
- Measuring and Forecasting Demand
- Careers in Marketing

In the quiz modules students can send answers to the grader and receive instant feedback on their progress through the Results Reporter. Coaching comments and references to the textbook may be available to ensure that students take advantage of all available resources to enhance their learning experience.

Instructor Resources

A link to this book on the Pearson online catalogue (www.pearsoned.ca) provides instructors with additional teaching tools. Downloadable PowerPoint Presentations and an Instructor's Manual are just some of the materials that may be available. The catalogue is password protected. To get a password, simply contact your Pearson Education Canada Representative or call Faculty Sales and Services at 1-800-850-5813.

Previewing the Concepts

Welcome to the exciting world of marketing! In this chapter, to start you off, we will introduce you to the basic concepts. We'll start with a simple question: What *is* marketing? Simply put, marketing is managing profitable customer relationships. The aim of marketing is to create value for customers and to capture value in return. Chapter 1 is organized around five steps in the marketing process—from understanding customer needs and designing customer-driven marketing strategies and programs to building customer relationships and capturing value for the firm. Understanding these basic concepts, and forming your own ideas about what they really mean to you, will give you a solid foundation for all that follows.

To set the stage, let's first look at NASCAR Canada. The entity was born in June of 2004, when the National Association of Stock Car Auto Racing (NASCAR) entered a partnership with TSN, Canada's Sports Leader. Although NASCAR is broadcast to 150 countries in 23 languages, Canada has the largest NASCAR fan base outside of the U.S. Despite its short history of operation, NASCAR Canada has already become a high-octane national marketing phenomenon. How? By creating value for its millions of fans. In return, NASCAR captures value from these fans, both for itself and for its many new Canadian sponsors. Read on and see how NASCAR does it.

When you first read about NASCAR just a few lines earlier, did you instantly think of tobacco-spitting American rednecks and run-down racetracks? Think again! Six million Canadians are NASCAR fans, and thanks to the fact that NASCAR is a great marketing organization, these numbers are bound to grow. For fans from around the world, NASCAR is a lot more than stock car races. It's a high-octane, totally involving experience.

As for the stereotypes, throw them away. NASCAR is the number one televised motorsport in Canada. TSN's coverage of the 2005 Daytona 500 was the most-watched motorsport race in TSN's 21-year history. Canadian NASCAR fans come from all across the country. People living in Ontario make up the highest percentage of the audience at 39 percent, with Quebec taking second place with 24 percent. British Columbia makes up 12 percent of the market, with Alberta, at 11 percent, running close behind.

In the United States, NASCAR is now the second-highest-rated regular season sport on TV—only the NFL draws more viewers. NASCAR fans are young, affluent, and decidedly family oriented. The combined North American fan base is more than 80 million strong—four of every ten people in Canada and the United States regularly watch or attend NASCAR events. Most important, fans are passionate about NASCAR. As NASCAR Canada's website proclaims, its fans are the most brand conscious among all professional sports fans, and they are three times more likely to purchase the products of NASCAR sponsors compared with companies not involved in the sport. An ardent NASCAR fan spends nearly $700 a year on NASCAR-related clothing, collectibles, and other items. It's not surprising that firms as diverse as Procter and Gamble, Lilydale Incorporated (based in Edmonton, it is Canada's fastest-growing brand of fresh chicken), and the Canadian romance novel giant Harlequin Enterprises Limited have signed licensing agreements with the ultra-popular auto-racing organization. Under the new agreement, Harlequin is publishing women's fiction titles with NASCAR plotlines and the NASCAR brand on the covers.

What's NASCAR's secret? Its incredible success results from a single-minded focus: creating lasting customer relationships. For fans, the NASCAR relationship develops through a careful blend of live racing events, abundant media coverage, and compelling websites.

Each year, Canadian fans flock south of the border to experience the adrenalin-charged, heart-stopping excitement of NASCAR racing firsthand by attending national tours to some two dozen tracks around the country. Six events are being planned for launch in Canada by 2007.

At these events, fans hold tailgate parties, camp and cook out, watch the cars roar around the track, meet the drivers, and swap stories with other NASCAR enthusiasts. Track facilities even include RV parks next to and right inside the racing oval.

Marvels one sponsor, "[In] what other sport can you drive your beat-up RV or camper into the stadium and sit on it to watch the race?" NASCAR really cares about its customers and goes out of its way to show them a good time. For example, rather than fleecing fans with overpriced food and beer, NASCAR tracks encourage fans to bring their own. Such actions mean that NASCAR might lose a sale today, but it will keep the customer tomorrow.

To further the customer relationship, NASCAR makes the sport a wholesome family affair. The environment is safe for kids—uniformed security guards patrol the track to keeps things in line. The family atmosphere extends to the drivers, too. Unlike the aloof and often distant athletes in other sports, NASCAR drivers seem like regular guys. Like Paul Tracy, the darling of Canadian racing, who began to compete in NASCAR in 2006, they are friendly and readily available to mingle with fans and sign autographs. Fans view drivers as good role models, and the long NASCAR tradition of family involvement creates the next generation of loyal fans.

Can't make it to the track? No problem. That is where TSN comes in with well-orchestrated coverage and in-car cameras that put fans in the middle of the action, giving them vicarious thrills that keep them glued to the screen.

NASCAR also delivers the NASCAR experience through its engaging websites. TSN's NASCAR site (www.tsn.ca/auto_racing/nascar/) and NASCAR.com serve up a glut of information and entertainment—in-depth news, driver bios, background information, online games, community discussions, and merchandise. True die-hard fans can subscribe to TrackPass to get up-to-the-minute standings, race video, streaming audio from the cars, and access to a host of archived audio and video highlights.

TrackPass with PitCommand even delivers a real-time data feed, complete with the GPS locations of cars and data from drivers' dashboards.

But a big part of the NASCAR experience is the feeling that the sport itself is personally accessible. Anyone who knows how to drive feels that he or she, too, could be a champion NASCAR driver. As 48-year police officer Ed Sweat puts it, "Genetics did not bless me with the height of a basketball player, nor was I born to have the bulk of a lineman in the NFL. But ... on any given Sunday, with a rich sponsor, the right car, and some practice, I could be draftin' and passin', zooming to the finish line, trading paint with Tony Stewart!"

Ultimately, all of this fan enthusiasm translates into financial success for NASCAR and for its sponsors. Just ask dental hygienist Jenny German, an ardent fan of NASCAR driver Jeff Gordon. According to one account, "She actively seeks out any product he endorses."

Because of such loyal fan relationships, NASCAR Canada and NASCAR have attracted more than 250 big-name sponsors, from Wal-Mart and Home Depot to Canadian Tire and Sun Media. In all, corporations spend more than US$1 billion a year for NASCAR sponsorships and promotions. Nextel is shelling out US$750 million over the next ten years to be a NASCAR sponsor and to put its name on the Nextel Cup series. "Other sponsors eagerly pay up to US$15 million per year to sponsor a top car and to get their corporate colors and logos emblazoned on team uniforms and on the hoods or side panels of team cars. Or they pay US$3 million to US$5 million a year to become the 'official' (fill-in-the-blank) of NASCAR racing."

So if you're still thinking of NASCAR as rednecks and moonshine, you'd better think again. NASCAR is a premier marketing organization that knows how to create customer value that translates into deep and lasting customer relationships. "Better than any other sport," says a leading sports marketing executive, "NASCAR listens to its fans and gives them what they want." In turn, fans reward NASCAR and its sponsors with deep loyalty and the promise of lasting profits.[1]

Today's successful companies have one thing in common: Like NASCAR Canada, they are strongly customer focused and heavily committed to marketing. These companies share a passion for satisfying customer needs in well-defined target markets. They motivate everyone in the organization to help build lasting customer relationships through superior customer value and satisfaction. As co-founder Bernie Marcus of Home Depot asserted, "All of our people understand what the Holy Grail is. It's not the bottom line. It's an almost blind, passionate commitment to taking care of customers."

What Is Marketing?

Marketing, more than any other business function, deals with customers. Although we will soon explore more-detailed definitions of marketing, perhaps the simplest definition is this one: Marketing is managing profitable customer relationships. The twofold goal of marketing is to attract new customers by promising superior value and to keep and grow current customers by delivering satisfaction.

Wal-Mart has become the world's largest retailer, and the world's largest company, by delivering on its promise, "Always low prices. Always!" At Disney theme parks, "imagineers" work wonders in their quest to "make a dream come true today." Dell leads the personal computer industry by consistently making good on its promise to "be direct." Dell Canada makes it easy for customers to custom design their own computers and have them delivered quickly to their doorsteps or desktops. Provigo, a supermarket chain owned by Loblaws that operates mainly in Quebec, now has 110 outlets and employees 5700 people. It has built its business by providing "quality, variety, and freshness throughout its stores," along with the promise to make the lives of its customers easier by offering quick, courteous service aligned with its customers' needs. The company also knows it is important to be involved in its customers' communities and it focuses on providing financial assistance to the families of children who have physical or developmental challenges. These and other highly successful companies know that if they take care of their customers, market share and profits will follow.

Sound marketing is critical to the success of every organization. In 2005, Canada's top five firms[2] (ranked according to profitability), EnCana, Royal Bank of Canada, Manulife Financial, Bank of Nova Scotia, and Imperial Oil, make extensive use of marketing. But so do not-for-profit organizations, such as universities, hospitals, museums, symphony orchestras, and even churches.

You already know a lot about marketing—it's all around you. You see the results of marketing in the abundance of products in your nearby shopping mall. You see marketing in the advertisements that fill your TV screen, spice up your magazines, stuff your mailbox, or enliven your webpages. At home, at school, where you work, and where you play, you see marketing in almost everything you do. Yet, there is much more to marketing than meets the consumer's casual eye. Behind it all is a massive network of people and activities competing for your attention and purchases.

This book will give you a complete and formal introduction to the basic concepts and practices of today's marketing. In this chapter, we begin by defining marketing and the marketing process.

Marketing Defined

What *is* marketing? Many people think of marketing only as selling and advertising. And no wonder—every day we are bombarded with television commercials, direct-mail offers, sales calls, and Internet pitches. However, selling and advertising are only the tip of the marketing iceberg.

Today, marketing must be understood not in the old sense of making a sale—"telling and selling"—but in the new sense of *satisfying customer needs* in a socially responsible and ethical manner. If the marketer does a good job of understanding consumer needs; develops products that provide superior value; and prices, distributes, and promotes them effectively and ethically, these products will sell very easily. Thus, selling and advertising are only part of a larger "marketing mix"—a set of marketing tools that work together to satisfy customer needs and build lasting customer relationships.

In 2004, the American Marketing Association offer revised its definition of **marketing:** "Marketing is an organizational function and a set of processes for creating,

Marketing
An organizational function and a set of processes for creating, communicating, and delivering value to customers and for managing customer relationships in ways that benefit the organization and its stakeholders.

communicating, and delivering value to customers and for managing customer relationships in ways that benefit the organization and its stakeholders."[3] Thus, though the focus of marketing is on customers and profitability, marketers must also recognize the needs and rights of other groups affected by marketing decisions—the firm's stakeholders. Stakeholder groups include employees, unions, customers, members of the distribution channel, competitors, activists, government, and the press. Thus, broadly defined, marketing is a social and managerial process by which individuals and groups obtain what they need and want through creating and exchanging value with others. See how EnCana, Canada's most profitable company in 2005, captures the essence of this definition in its vision statement and in the comments of its chair, Gwyn Morgan:[4]

> EnCana was born in Calgary in 2002 with the merging of two major oil and gas companies. Right from its inception, it had a lofty mission: "Our vision is to create a truly great company—one where quality work is the norm; where we stretch and strive to be the best we can be; and where great things are accomplished." In describing the firm's journey towards greatness, Gwyn Morgan stressed, "All along the way, we are guided by clearly articulated principles—business principles that help us achieve our vision, moral principles that provide an inner compass guiding our behaviour, and team principles that define what we can expect of each other.... True success can only be attained if EnCana is a company respected by our competitors and admired by our stakeholders. A company which understands that sustained shareholder value can only be delivered by people of strong character.... A company which understands that our success is measured through both our behaviour and our bottom line."

Business principles, moral principles, and principles of teamwork have helped make EnCana Canada's most profitable company.

Figure 1.1 A simple model of the marketing process

The Marketing Process

Figure 1.1 presents a simple five-step model of the marketing process. In the first four steps, companies work to understand consumers, create customer value, and build strong customer relationships. In the final step, companies reap the rewards of creating superior customer value. By creating value *for* consumers, they in turn capture value *from* consumers in the form of sales, profits, and long-term customer equity.[5]

In this and the next chapter, we will examine the steps of this simple model of marketing. In this chapter, we will review each step but focus more on the customer relationship steps—understanding consumers, building customer relationships, and capturing value from customers. In Chapter 2, we'll look more deeply into the second and third steps—designing marketing strategies and constructing marketing programs.

Understanding the Marketplace and Consumer Needs

As a first step, marketers need to understand customer needs and wants and the marketplace within which they operate. We now examine five core customer and marketplace concepts: *needs, wants,* and *demands; marketing offers (products, services,* and *experiences); value* and *satisfaction; exchanges* and *relationships;* and *markets.*

Customer Needs, Wants, and Demands

Needs
States of felt deprivation.

Wants
The form human needs take as shaped by culture and individual personality.

Demands
Human wants that are backed by buying power.

The most basic concept underlying marketing is that of human needs. Human **needs** are states of felt deprivation. They include basic *physical* needs for food, clothing, warmth, and safety; *social* needs for belonging and affection; and *individual* needs for knowledge and self-expression. These needs were not created by marketers; they are a basic part of the human makeup.

Wants are the form human needs take as they are shaped by culture and individual personality. A Canadian *needs* food but *wants* organic produce from Loblaws. Wants are shaped by one's society as well as by marketing programs. They are described in terms of objects that will satisfy needs. When backed by buying power, wants become **demands**. Given that their wants and resources, people demand products with benefits that add up to the most value and satisfaction. For example, while people need liquids to survive, they often want bottled water. Over the past two decades, Canadian demand for bottled water has grown. By the year 2000, more than 700 million litres were consumed. Given that we are a country blessed with lots of fresh, almost free, water, this trend is surprising. However, when newspaper headlines draw attention to situations such as the one in Walkerton, where deadly *E.coli* bacteria contaminated the town's water supply, and marketers advertise the taste, purity, and lifestyle associated with the drinking of branded, bottled water, many people changed their habits and switched from tap water to bottled water. As a CBC poll revealed, people often have trouble explaining why they want certain alternatives. Though some believe that bottled water is cleaner, chemical free, and better for you, others know that there is little difference between bottled and tap water. As one woman noted, "It's this mental block that I have that drinking [bottled] water is better than tap water."[6]

Outstanding marketing companies go to great lengths to learn about and understand their customers' needs, wants, and demands. They conduct consumer research and analyze mountains of customer data. Their people at all levels—including top management—stay close to customers. For example, top executives from Wal-Mart spend two days each week visiting stores and mingling with customers. Harley-Davidson's chair and CEO regularly mounts his Harley and rides with customers to get feedback and ideas.

At consumer products giant Procter & Gamble, top executives even visit with ordinary consumers in their homes and on shopping trips. "We read the data and look at the charts," says one P&G executive, "but to shop [with consumers] and see how the woman is changing retailers to save 10 cents on a loaf of bread [so she can] spend it on things that are more important—that's important to us to keep front and center." Says P&G's CEO, "When the consumer is boss, when you try to win the consumer value equation, when you try to make the consumer's life better, then you're focused externally … and it's an absolutely huge difference."[7]

Marketing Offers—Products, Services, and Experiences

Marketing offer

Some combination of products, services, information, or experiences offered to a market to satisfy a need or want.

Consumers' needs and wants are fulfilled through a **marketing offer**—some combination of products, services, information, or experiences offered to a market to satisfy a need or want. Marketing offers are not limited to physical *products*. They also include *services*—activities or benefits offered for sale that are essentially intangible and do not result in the ownership of anything. Examples include banking, airline, hotel, tax preparation, and home repair services. More broadly, marketing offers also include other entities, such as *persons*, *places*, *organizations*, *information*, and *ideas*.

Many sellers make the mistake of paying more attention to the specific products they offer than to the benefits and experiences produced by these products. These sellers suffer from "marketing myopia." They are so taken with their products that they focus only on existing wants and lose sight of underlying customer needs.[8] They forget that a product is only a tool to solve a consumer problem. A manufacturer of quarter-inch drill bits may think that the customer needs a drill bit. But what the customer *really* needs is a quarter-inch hole. These sellers will have trouble if a new product comes along that serves the customer's need better or less expensively. The customer will have the same *need* but will *want* the new product.

Smart marketers look beyond the attributes of the products and services they sell. By orchestrating several services and products, they create *brand experiences* for consumers. For example, Disney World is an experience; so is a ride on a Harley-Davidson motorcycle. You experience a visit to the Bank of Nova Scotia or to Sony's playstation.com website. And you don't just watch a NASCAR race; you immerse yourself in the NASCAR experience. "What consumers really want [are offers] that dazzle their senses, touch their hearts, and stimulate their minds," declares one expert. "They want [offers] that deliver an experience."[9]

How can you help protect the prairie and the penguin?

Simple. Visit www.earthshare.org and learn how the world's leading environmental groups are working together under one name. And how easy it is for you to help protect the prairies and the penguins and the planet.

One environment. One simple way to care for it. **Earth Share**

Products do not have to be physical objects. Here, the "product" is an idea: "how easy it is for you to help protect the prairies and the penguins and the planet."

Customer Value and Satisfaction

Consumers usually face a broad array of products and services that might satisfy a given need. How do they choose among these many marketing offers? Customers form expectations about the value and satisfaction that various marketing offers will deliver and they buy accordingly. Satisfied customers buy again and tell others about their good experiences. Dissatisfied customers often switch to competitors and disparage the product to others.

Marketers must be careful to set the right level of expectations. If they set expectations too low, they may satisfy those who buy but fail to attract enough buyers. If they raise expectations too high, buyers will be disappointed. Customer value and customer satisfaction are key building blocks for developing and managing customer relationships. We will revisit these core concepts later in the chapter.

Exchanges and Relationships

Exchange
The act of obtaining a desired object from someone by offering something in return.

Marketing occurs when people decide to satisfy needs and wants through exchange relationships. **Exchange** is the act of obtaining a desired object from someone by offering something in return. In the broadest sense, the marketer tries to bring about a response to some marketing offer. The response may be more than simply buying or trading products and services. A political candidate, for instance, wants votes, a church wants membership, and a social action group wants idea acceptance.

Marketing consists of actions taken to build and maintain desirable exchange *relationships* with target audiences involving a product, a service, an idea, or other object. Beyond simply attracting new customers and creating transactions, the goal is to retain customers and grow their business with the company. Marketers want to build strong relationships by consistently delivering superior customer value. We will expand on the important concept of customer relationship management later in the chapter.

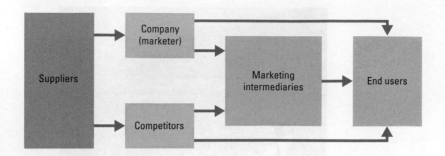

Figure 1.2 Elements of a modern marketing system

Markets

Market
The set of actual and potential buyers of a product or service.

The concepts of exchange and relationships lead to the concept of a market. A **market** is the set of actual and potential buyers of a product. These buyers share a particular need or want that can be satisfied through exchange relationships.

Marketing means managing markets to bring about profitable customer relationships. However, creating these relationships takes work. Sellers must search for buyers, identify their needs, design good marketing offers, set prices for them, promote them, and store and deliver them. Activities such as product development, research, communication, distribution, pricing, and service are core marketing activities.

Although we normally think of marketing as being carried on by sellers, buyers also carry on marketing. Consumers do marketing when they search for the goods they need at prices they can afford. Company purchasing agents do marketing when they track down sellers and bargain for good terms.

Figure 1.2 shows the main elements in a modern marketing system. In the usual situation, marketing involves serving a market of final consumers in the face of competitors. The company and the competitors send their respective offers and messages to consumers, either directly or through marketing intermediaries. All of the actors in the system are affected by major environmental forces (demographic, economic, physical, technological, political/legal, social/cultural).

Each party in the system adds value for the next level. All of the arrows represent relationships that must be developed and managed. Thus, a company's success at building profitable relationships depends not only on its own actions but also on how well the entire system serves the needs of final consumers. Wal-Mart cannot fulfill its promise of low prices unless its suppliers provide merchandise at low costs. And Ford cannot deliver high quality to car buyers unless its dealers provide outstanding service.

Designing a Customer-Driven Marketing Strategy

Marketing management
The art and science of choosing target markets and building profitable relationships with them.

Once it fully understands consumers and the marketplace, marketing management can design a customer-driven marketing strategy. We define **marketing management** as the art and science of choosing target markets and building profitable relationships with them. The marketing manager's aim is to find, attract, keep, and grow target customers by creating, delivering, and communicating superior customer value.

To design a winning marketing strategy, the marketing manager must answer two important questions: *What customers will we serve? (What's our target market?)*

and *How can we serve these customers best? (What's our value proposition?)* We will discuss these marketing strategy concepts briefly here, and then look at them in more detail in the next chapter.

Selecting Customers to Serve

The company must first decide *who* it will serve. It does this by dividing the market into segments of customers (*market segmentation*) and selecting which segments it will go after (*target marketing*). Some people think of marketing management as finding as many customers as possible and increasing demand. But marketing managers know that they cannot serve all customers in every way. By trying to serve all customers, they may not serve any customers well. Instead, the company wants to select only customers that it can serve well and profitably. For example, Holt Renfrew and Harry Rosen stores profitably target affluent professionals; Dollar Stores profitably target families with more modest means.

Some marketers may even seek *fewer* customers and reduced demand. For example, many power companies have trouble meeting demand during peak usage periods. The summer of 2005 was exceptionally warm in Ontario, thus Ontario Power Generation practised **demarketing** to encourage customers to reduce their use of power by turning up the thermostat in their houses when they were not home and delaying the operation of appliances, such as dishwashers, until the evening after the peak demand period.

Thus, marketing managers must decide which customers they want to target, and decide on the level, timing, and nature of their demand. Simply put, marketing management is *customer management* and *demand management*.

Demarketing
Marketing to reduce demand temporarily or permanently; the aim is not to destroy demand but only to reduce or shift it.

Choosing a Value Proposition

The company must also decide how it will serve targeted customers—how it will *differentiate and position* itself in the marketplace. A company's *value proposition* is the set of benefits or values it promises to deliver to consumers to satisfy their needs. Porsche promises driving performance and excitement: "What a dog feels like when its leash breaks." Tide laundry detergent promises powerful, all-purpose cleaning, whereas Gain "cleans and freshens like sunshine." Altoids positions itself as "the curiously strong mint."

Such value propositions differentiate one brand from another. They answer the customer's question "Why should I buy your brand rather than a competitor's?" Companies must design strong value propositions that give them the greatest advantage in their target markets.

Marketing Management Orientations

Marketing management wants to design strategies that will build profitable relationships with target consumers. But what *philosophy* should guide these marketing strategies? What weight should be given to the interests of customers, the organization, and society? Very often, these interests conflict.

There are five alternative philosophies under which organizations design and carry out their marketing strategies: the *production, product, selling, marketing,* and *societal marketing concepts*. These are not progressive marketing stages as some marketing scholars contend; they are orientations that different companies use (see Real Marketing 1.1).

REAL MARKETING

The Eras of Marketing—Getting It Right

The history of marketing practice and the emergence of the discipline of marketing has long been disputed. Many believe that people practised marketing in the earliest days of antiquity. (For example, the stoppers in huge clay jars of wine were marked with symbols [brands] identifying the wine maker.) In contrast, others say we are using modern ideas to interpret primitive practices of the past. They believe that marketing as a practice only emerged during the Industrial Revolution. There is more consensus, however, that the development of marketing as a discipline for academic study and research emerged in the early twentieth century. Rooted in economics, marketing emerged as an academic discipline in universities, such as the Ohio State University and Northwestern University in the United States, and Queen's University in Canada, from the turn of the century to 1920.

A focal point of controversy is an article written by Robert Keith. In 1960, he published an article in the *Journal of Marketing* describing what he believed to be distinct eras of increasingly sophisticated marketing practice—the production era (1869–1930), the sales era (1930–1950), and the marketing era (1950 onward). He used his experiences at the Pillsbury Company as the basis of his contention but suggested that his experience was typical of the evolution of marketing overall. Other scholars, including two Canadian academics, Brian Jones and Alan Richardson, attacked his analysis and showed that different firms simultaneously exhibited very different orientations or combined orientations throughout their past.

If you examine the early history of catalogues used by Canadian department stores, you can also see that, rather than passing through distinct eras, many of the practices used by modern marketers were rooted in the practices of businesses operating in the 1800s and 1900s. In the late nineteenth century, Canada's population grew dramatically, but it was geographically dispersed. Department store growth accompanied this population growth. They used mail-order catalogues to reach Canada's diverse peoples.

History of Canadian Catalogues—Selected Marketing Milestones

1882
The first mail-order catalogue was introduced in Canada by Carsley's, a department store located in Montreal. Mail-order catalogues were first used by retailers in France and the United States. Carsley's was so successful in adapting the practice to Canada that by 1894, its "immense mail-order department [was] one of the wonders of the establishment." The first Eaton's catalogue, called "The Wishing Book" was distributed at the Toronto exhibition. The company founder, Timothy Eaton, saw the catalogue as a tool to eventually reach a national audience through high-quality service: "This catalogue is destined to go wherever the maple leaf grows, throughout the vast Dominion. We have the facilities for filling mail orders satisfactorily, no matter how far the letter has to come and the goods have to go."

1895
Simpson's, also based in Toronto, introduced its first full catalogue and offered free samples to help build trust and sales.

1896
The Hudson's Bay Company's Winnipeg office published a catalogue on the eve of the British company's 226th anniversary.

1898
Regional specialization began as Eaton's developed catalogues designed for the western market—its Klondike Catalogue (1898) and the Settlers' Catalogue (1903). Scroggie's introduced French-language catalogues (1908).

1900
Eaton's catalogue featured both domestic and international products including the Eaton Beauty doll, produced by Armand Marseille, Germany.

1910
Department stores and their catalogues increased the use of private brands to promote customer loyalty. Eaton brands included "EATON," "Eatonia," "Acme," "Cravinette," "Edgerite," "Imperial," "Foundation," "Multiplex," "Braemore," "Lady Fair," "Birkdale," and "Renown."

1910
Competition heated up between national chains and local stores. Smaller, local department stores, such as J. Flanagan's in Moncton, Christie Grand in Winnipeg (1914), Cairns in Saskatoon (1916), Ramsey's in Edmonton (1916), and Pryce-Jones in Calgary (1911), issued their own catalogues, not only to sell goods but also to promote their own stores and remind patrons to shop locally.

1915

With the growth of the west, improved distribution was needed. Eaton's established a distribution centre in Saskatoon, and Simpson's built an eight-storey warehouse in Regina in 1916.

1920s

Regional segmentation grew. Eaton's opened a regional mail-order headquarters in Moncton (1920). Dupuis Frères, a Montreal department store established in 1868, issued a French-language catalogue, recognizing that the French-Canadian population constituted a distinct segment of the buying population (1922). It used religious and nationalistic themes to promote its merchandise. The Vancouver-based department store chain Army and Navy opened a mail-order business headquartered in Regina (1925). Eaton's and Simpson's launched French-language versions of their catalogues (1928).

1923

Simpson's signed an agreement with the post office so that its catalogues could be distributed to all post office boxes on rural routes. Rural mail delivery was first introduced in 1908, and this service enabled the first truly national direct marketing initiatives.

1930s

As the Depression deepened across the country, many national catalogue marketers were forced to reduce the size of their catalogues and lay off staff. Local businesses increasingly resented the mail-order companies that competed with them for sales.

1935

Eaton's began using celebrity endorsers in its catalogues. Radio had built interest in hockey, and the Toronto Maple Leaf legends King Clancy, Lorne Chabot, and Red Horner used their growing fame to endorse products in the Eaton's catalogue.

1940s

Catalogue marketers reflected important socioeconomic trends. They demonstrated their support for the Canadian war effort by sending orders and free goods (such as cigarettes) to troops overseas.

1946 onward

During the postwar period, the variety of goods increased dramatically as did the purchasing power of Canadians. In particular, electrification of rural Canada increased demand for electric appliances. The baby boom gave rise to the identification of children and teenagers as specific target markets in the 1950s and '60s. In 1953, Simpson's merged with the American Sears and the first Simpsons-Sears catalogue was issued. Eaton's restructured in response to strong competition from Simpsons-Sears. By 1955, it had fourteen department stores, forty-two branch stores, six foreign buying offices, four mail-order warehouses, four factories, and 299 order offices. The emergence of ecommerce in the 1990s allowed Canadians to shop from companies next door or around the world. Eaton's, once Canada's largest department store chain, couldn't successfully position itself within this competitive market and closed its doors in 1999. Sears emerged as the most successful department store catalogue in Canada.

Sources: For a fuller explanation of the controversies surrounding the periodization of marketing history, see Stanley C. Hollander, Kathleen M. Rassuli, D.G. Brian Jones, and Laura Farlow Dix (2005), "Periodization in Marketing History," *Journal of Macromarketing,* 25 (1): pp. 32–41. Other sources: Shirley Lavertu, Marguerite Sauriol, and John Willis, "Before e-commerce: A history of Canadian Mail-Order Catalogues," www.civilization.ca/cpm/catalog/cat0000e.html; D.G. Brian Jones and Alan J. Richardson, "The Myth of the Marketing Revolution," (forthcoming *Journal of Macromarketing*); Robert J. Keith (1960), "The marketing revolution," *Journal of Marketing* 24 (3): 35–38.

Porsche targets affluent buyers with promises of driving excitement: "What a dog feels like when the leash breaks."

The Production Concept

Production concept
The idea that consumers will favour products that are available and highly affordable.

The **production concept** holds that consumers will favour products that are available and highly affordable. Therefore, management should focus on improving production and distribution efficiency. This philosophy is useful when the demand for a product exceeds the supply or when the product's cost is too high and improved productivity is needed to bring it down.

The production concept, however, can lead to marketing myopia. Companies run a major risk of focusing too narrowly on their own operations and losing sight of the real objective—satisfying customer needs and building customer relationships.

The Product Concept

Product concept
The idea that consumers will favour products that offer the most in quality, performance, and features, and that the organization should therefore devote its energy to making continuous product improvements.

The **product concept** holds that consumers will favour products that offer the most in quality, performance, and innovative features. Under this concept, marketing strategy focuses on making continuous product improvements. Some manufacturers believe that if they can build a better mousetrap, the world will beat a path to their door. But they are often rudely shocked. Buyers may well be looking for a better solution to a mouse problem but not necessarily for a better mousetrap. The solution might be a chemical spray, for example. Furthermore, a better mousetrap will not sell unless the manufacturer designs, packages, and prices it attractively; places it in convenient distribution channels; brings it to the attention of people who need it; and convinces buyers that it is a better product.

Thus, the product concept also can lead to marketing myopia. For instance, Kodak assumed that consumers wanted photographic film rather than a way to capture and share memories. Thus, it initially overlooked the challenge of digital cameras. Although it now leads the digital camera market in sales, it has yet to make significant profits from this business.[10]

The Selling Concept

Selling concept
The idea that consumers will not buy enough of the firm's products unless it undertakes a large-scale selling and promotion effort.

Many companies follow the **selling concept**, which holds that consumers will not buy enough of the firm's products unless it undertakes a large-scale selling and promotion effort. The concept is typically practised with unsought goods—those that buyers do not normally think of, such as insurance or blood donations. These industries must be good at tracking down prospects and selling them on product benefits.

Other firms practise the selling concept when they face overcapacity. Their aim is to sell what they make rather than make what the market wants. This is a risky strategy because it focuses on creating sales transactions rather than on building long-term, profitable customer relationships.

The Marketing Concept

Marketing concept
The marketing management philosophy that holds that achieving organizational goals depends on knowing the needs and wants of target markets and delivering the desired satisfactions better than competitors do.

The **marketing concept** holds that achieving organizational goals depends on knowing the needs and wants of target markets and delivering the desired satisfactions better than competitors do. Under the marketing concept, customer focus and value are the *paths* to sales and profits.

Instead of a product-centred "make and sell" philosophy, the marketing concept is a customer-centred "sense and respond" philosophy. It views marketing not as "hunting" but as "gardening." The job is not to find the right customers for your product, but to find the right products for your customers.

Figure 1.3 contrasts the selling concept and the marketing concept. The selling concept takes an *inside-out* perspective. It starts with the factory, focuses on the company's existing products, and calls for heavy selling and promotion to obtain profitable sales. It focuses primarily on customer conquest—getting short-term sales with little concern about who buys or why.

In contrast, the marketing concept takes an *outside-in* perspective. In the words of one Ford executive, "If we're not customer driven, our cars won't be either." The marketing concept starts with a well-defined market, focuses on customer needs, and integrates all the marketing activities that affect customers. In turn, it yields profits by creating lasting relationships with the right customers through ethical means of creating customer value and satisfaction.

Implementing the marketing concept often means more than simply responding to customers' stated desires and obvious needs. *Customer-driven* companies research current customers deeply to learn about their desires, gather new product and service ideas, and test proposed product improvements. Such customer-driven marketing usually works well when a clear need exists and when customers know what they want.

In many cases, however, customers *don't* know what they want or even what is possible. For example, twenty years ago, how many consumers would have thought to ask for cellphones, fax machines, home copiers, twenty-four-hour online buying,

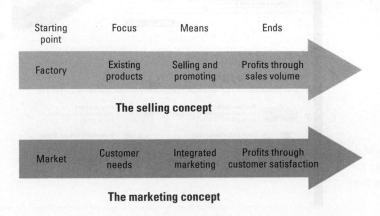

Starting point	Focus	Means	Ends
Factory	Existing products	Selling and promoting	Profits through sales volume

The selling concept

| Market | Customer needs | Integrated marketing | Profits through customer satisfaction |

The marketing concept

Figure 1.3 The selling and marketing concepts contrasted

DVD players, satellite navigation systems in their cars, or wearable PCs? Such situations call for *customer-driving* marketing—understanding customer needs even better than customers themselves do and creating products and services that will meet existing and latent needs, now and in the future.

As Sony's visionary leader, Akio Morita, puts it: "Our plan is to lead the public with new products rather than ask them what kinds of products they want. The public does not know what is possible, but we do." And according to an executive at 3M, "Our goal is to lead customers where they want to go before *they* know where they want to go."[11]

The Societal Marketing Concept

Societal marketing concept

A principle of enlightened marketing that holds that a company should make good marketing decisions by considering consumers' wants, the company's requirements, consumers' long-run interests, and society's long-run interests.

The **societal marketing concept** questions whether the marketing concept overlooks possible conflicts between consumer *short-run wants* and consumer *long-run welfare*. Is a firm that satisfies the immediate needs and wants of target markets always doing what's best for consumers in the long run? The societal marketing concept holds that marketing strategy should deliver value to customers and other stakeholders affected by marketing decisions and practices in a way that maintains or improves both the consumer's *and the society's* well-being.

Consider the fast-food industry. You may see today's giant fast-food chains as offering tasty and convenient food at reasonable prices. Yet many consumer groups have voiced concerns. Critics point out that hamburgers, fried chicken, french fries, and most other fast foods are high in fat and salt. Meals are now "super-sized," leading consumers to overeat and contributing to a national obesity epidemic. Thus, in satisfying short-term consumer wants, the chains may be successful, but in terms of long-term results, they may be harming consumer health and causing environmental problems in the long run. A whopping 46 percent of Canadians are overweight, and children's obesity rates have tripled in only twenty years. To address this concern, some leading chains, such as Wendy's Restaurants of Canada, are working to better follow the societal marketing concept. In 2004, Wendy's began promoting healthy options as part of its menus. On its webpage titled

Wendy's is following the societal marketing concept as it works to educate consumers and offer them healthier choices.

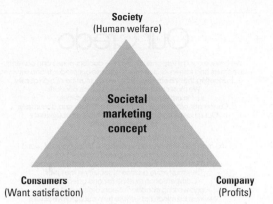

Figure 1.4 Three considerations underlying the societal marketing concept

"Nutrition Facts," Wendy's notes that it now offers Combos with a choice of sides, at no extra charge. Consumers who want to make healthier choices can now have a fresh side salad or Caesar side salad instead of fries. They can choose bottled water, orange or apple juice, or a diet soft drink instead of a regular soft drink. Similar tactics are being followed with regard to kids' meals. Children can choose mandarin oranges instead of fries, and they are offered a choice of juices, partly skimmed white milk, or low-fat chocolate milk instead of a Jr. Frosty™ or a soft drink. The chain's website provides loads of information not just about reducing fat and calories but also about a host of nutrition-related topics designed to help people cope with dietary problems, such as diabetes, allergies, or gluten sensitivity.[12]

As Figure 1.4 shows, companies should balance three considerations in setting their marketing strategies: company profits, consumer wants, *and* society's interests.

Preparing a Marketing Plan and Program

The company's marketing strategy outlines which customers the company will serve and how it will create value for these customers. Next, the marketer constructs a marketing program that will actually deliver the intended value to target customers. The marketing program builds customer relationships by transforming the marketing strategy into action. It consists of the firm's *marketing mix*, the set of marketing tools the firm uses to implement its marketing strategy.

The major marketing mix tools are classified into four broad groups, called the *four Ps* of marketing: product, price, place, and promotion. To deliver on its value proposition, the firm must first create a need-satisfying marketing offer (product). It must decide how much it will charge for the offer (price) and how it will make the offer available to target consumers (place). Finally, it must communicate with target customers about the offer and persuade them of its merits (promotion). We will explore marketing programs and the marketing mix in much more detail in the next chapter.

Building Customer Relationships

The first three steps in the marketing process—understanding the marketplace and customer needs, designing a customer-driven marketing strategy, and constructing marketing programs—all lead up to the fourth and most important step: building profitable customer relationships.

Our Credo

We believe our first responsibility is to the doctors, nurses and patients,
to mothers and fathers and all others who use our products and services.
In meeting their needs everything we do must be of high quality.
We must constantly strive to reduce our costs
in order to maintain reasonable prices.
Customers' orders must be serviced promptly and accurately.
Our suppliers and distributors must have an opportunity
to make a fair profit.

We are responsible to our employees,
the men and women who work with us throughout the world.
Everyone must be considered as an individual.
We must respect their dignity and recognize their merit.
They must have a sense of security in their jobs.
Compensation must be fair and adequate,
and working conditions clean, orderly and safe.
We must be mindful of ways to help our employees fulfill
their family responsibilities.
Employees must feel free to make suggestions and complaints.
There must be equal opportunity for employment, development
and advancement for those qualified.
We must provide competent management,
and their actions must be just and ethical.

We are responsible to the communities in which we live and work
and to the world community as well.
We must be good citizens — support good works and charities
and bear our fair share of taxes.
We must encourage civic improvements and better health and education.
We must maintain in good order
the property we are privileged to use,
protecting the environment and natural resources.

Our final responsibility is to our stockholders.
Business must make a sound profit.
We must experiment with new ideas.
Research must be carried on, innovative programs developed
and mistakes paid for.
New equipment must be purchased, new facilities provided
and new products launched.
Reserves must be created to provide for adverse times.
When we operate according to these principles,
the stockholders should realize a fair return.

Johnson & Johnson

Johnson & Johnson's Credo stresses putting people before profits. J&J's quick product recall following a tragic Tylenol tampering incident some years ago cost the company US$240 million in earnings but strengthened consumer confidence and loyalty.

Customer Relationship Management

Customer relationship management (CRM) is perhaps the most important concept of modern marketing. Until recently, CRM has been defined narrowly as a customer data management activity. By this definition, it involves managing detailed information about individual customers and carefully managing customer "touchpoints" in order to maximize customer loyalty. We will discuss this narrower CRM activity in Chapter 5, dealing with marketing information.

More recently, however, customer relationship management has taken on a broader meaning. In this broader sense, **customer relationship management** is the overall process of building and maintaining profitable customer relationships by delivering superior customer value and satisfaction. It deals with all aspects of acquiring, keeping, and growing customers. Kraft Canada has taken the lead in CRM practices for the North American operation.

Customer relationship management (CRM)
The overall process of building and maintaining profitable customer relationships by delivering superior customer value and satisfaction.

Relationship Building Blocks: Customer Value and Satisfaction

The key to building lasting customer relationships is to create superior customer value and satisfaction. Satisfied customers are more likely to be loyal customers and to give the company a larger share of their business.

Customer perceived value
The difference between total customer value and total customer cost.

Customer Value Attracting and retaining customers can be a difficult task. Customers often face a bewildering array of products and services from which to choose. A customer buys from the firm that offers the highest **customer perceived value**—the customer's evaluation of the difference between all the benefits and all the costs of a marketing offer relative to those of competing offers.

For example, FedEx customers gain a number of benefits. The most obvious is fast and reliable package delivery. However, by using FedEx, customers also may receive some status and image values. Using FedEx usually makes both the package sender and the receiver feel more important. When deciding whether to send a package via FedEx, customers will weigh these and other perceived values against the money, effort, and psychological costs of using the service. Moreover, they will compare the value of using FedEx against the value of using other shippers—UPS, Purolator, or Canada Post. They will select the service that gives them the greatest perceived value.

Customers often do not judge product values and costs accurately or objectively. They act on *perceived* value. For example, does FedEx really provide faster, more reliable express delivery? If so, is this better service worth the higher prices that FedEx charges? Major competitors argue that their services are comparable, and their prices are much lower. However, judging by market share, most consumers perceive otherwise.[13]

Customer satisfaction

The extent to which a product's perceived performance matches a buyer's expectations.

Customer Satisfaction **Customer satisfaction** depends on the product's perceived performance relative to a buyer's expectations. If the product's performance falls short of expectations, the customer is dissatisfied. If performance matches expectations, the customer is satisfied. If performance exceeds expectations, the customer is highly satisfied or delighted.

Outstanding marketing companies go out of their way to keep important customers satisfied. Highly satisfied customers make repeat purchases and tell others about their good experiences with the product. The key is to match customer expectations with company performance. Smart companies aim to *delight* customers by promising only what they can deliver, then delivering *more* than they promise (see Real Marketing 1.2).[14]

However, although the customer-centred firm seeks to deliver high customer satisfaction relative to competitors, it does not attempt to *maximize* customer satisfaction. A company can always increase customer satisfaction by lowering its price or increasing its services. But this may result in lower profits. Thus, the purpose of marketing is to generate customer value profitably. This requires a very delicate balance: The marketer must continue to generate more customer value and satisfaction but not "give away the house."

Is FedEx's service worth the higher price? FedEx thinks so. Its ads promise that if you need reliability, speed, and peace of mind, "Relax, it's FedEx."

REAL MARKETING

Customer Relationships: Delighting Customers

Top-notch marketing companies know that delighting customers involves more than simply opening a complaint department, smiling a lot, and being nice. These companies set very high standards for customer satisfaction and often make seemingly outlandish efforts to achieve them. Consider the following example:

> A man bought his first new Lexus, LS 430—an $85 000 piece of machinery. He could afford a Mercedes, a Jaguar, or a Cadillac, but he bought the Lexus. As he started to drive it home, he luxuriated in the smell of the leather interior and the glorious handling. He tried all of the car's options—the lights, the windshield washer, the gizmo cup holder that popped out of the centre console, the seat heater that warmed his bottom on a cold winter morning. On a whim, he turned on the radio. His favourite classical music station came on in splendid quadraphonic sound that ricocheted around the interior. He pushed the second button; it was his favourite news station. The third button brought his favourite talk station that kept him awake on long trips. The fourth button was set to his daughter's favourite rock station. In fact, every button was set to his specific tastes. The customer knew the car was smart, but was it psychic? No. The mechanic at Lexus had noted the radio settings on his trade-in and duplicated them on the new Lexus. The customer was delighted. This was his car now—through and through! No one told the mechanic to do it. It's just part of the Lexus philosophy: Delight a customer and continue to delight that customer, and you will have a customer for life. What the mechanic did cost Lexus nothing. Not one red cent. Yet it solidified the relationship that could be worth high six figures to Lexus in customer lifetime value. Such relationship-building passions in dealerships around the country have made Lexus the nation's top-selling luxury vehicle.

Studies show that going to extremes to keep customers happy, although sometimes costly, goes hand in hand with good financial performance. Delighted customers come back again and again. Thus, in today's highly competitive marketplace, companies can well afford to lose money on one transaction if it helps to cement a profitable long-term customer relationship.

For companies interested in delighting customers, exceptional value and service are more than a set of policies or actions—they are a companywide attitude, an important part of the overall company culture. Employees at Sheridan Nurseries, which operates at ten locations in southern Ontario, pride themselves in their team approach to customer service. One customer couldn't believe the service she received when she left a message on the firm's website about a faulty product. When she posted the message, she didn't actually even expect an answer. To her delight, the message was answered promptly. When the problem couldn't be resolved immediately, the customer service representative followed up over a three-month period until the customer was completely satisfied.

WestJet is well known for its low fares and prompt arrivals. But its friendly and often funny flight staff goes to great lengths to delight customers. Satisfied customers aren't hesitant to post their compliments online. Just see what Dave Graubard said in 2005 on the Airline Forum, "Last week [I] flew WestJet from Calgary to Ft. McMurray via Edmonton both directions. Excellent flights on new 737-700 aircraft.... Professional and fun flight attendants, ontime flights and comfortable seats.... I always fly WestJet when I'm in Canada and wish they were tied to a US airline to link up with."

Four Seasons Hotels, long known for its outstanding service, tells its employees the story of Ron Dyment, a doorman in Toronto, who forgot to load a departing guest's briefcase into his taxi. The doorman called the guest, a lawyer in Washington, D.C., and learned that he desperately needed the briefcase for a meeting the following morning. Without first asking for approval from management, Dyment hopped on a plane and returned the briefcase. The company named Dyment Employee of the Year.

There's no simple formula for taking care of customers, but neither is it a mystery. According to the CEO of L.L. Bean, "A lot of people have fancy things to say about customer service ... but it's just a day-in, day-out, ongoing, never-ending, unremitting, persevering, compassionate kind of activity." For the companies that do it well, it's also very rewarding.

Sources: Examples and quotes are from Denny Hatch and Ernie Schell, "Delight Your Customers," *Target Marketing,* April 2002, pp. 32–39; Sheridan Nurseries example was a personal experience of the author; WestJet quote from Skytrax Airline Forum, Dave Graubard, 23 September 2005, www.airlinequality.com/Forum/westjet.htm; Dana James, "Lighting the Way," *Marketing News,* April 1, 2002, pp. 1, 11; Patricia Sellers, "Companies That Serve You Best," *Fortune,* May 31, 1993, pp. 74–88; Chip R. Bell and Ron Zemke, "Service Magic," *Executive Excellence,* May 2003, p. 13; and Fiona Haley, "Fast Talk," *Fast Company,* December 2003, p. 57. Also see "Lexus Retains Best-Selling Luxury Brand Title for Fourth Year in a Row," www.lexus.com/about/press_releases/index.html (accessed January 5, 2004); and "Lexus Awards and Accolades," www.lexus.com (accessed June 2004).

Customer Relationship Levels and Tools

Companies can build customer relationships at many levels, depending on the nature of the target market. At one extreme, a company with many low-margin customers may seek to develop *basic relationships* with them. For example, Procter & Gamble does not phone or call on all of its Tide customers to get to know them personally. Instead, P&G creates relationships through brand-building advertising, sales promotions, a toll-free customer response number, and its Tide FabricCare Network website (www.Tide.com).

At the other extreme, in markets with few customers and high margins, sellers want to create *full partnerships* with key customers. For example, P&G customer teams work closely with Wal-Mart, Safeway, and other large retailers. Between these two extreme situations, other levels of customer relationships are appropriate.

Today, most leading companies are developing customer loyalty and retention programs. Beyond offering consistently high value and satisfaction, marketers can use specific marketing tools to develop stronger bonds with consumers. For example, many companies now offer *frequency marketing programs* that reward customers who buy frequently or in large amounts. Airlines offer frequent-flier programs, hotels give room upgrades to their frequent guests, and supermarkets give patronage discounts to "very important customers."

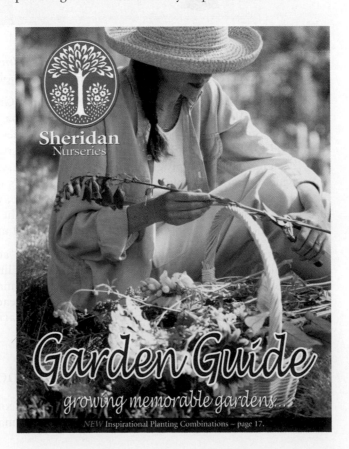

Sheridan Nurseries delights its customers with its exceptional service provided by its knowledgeable staff.

Harley-Davidson sponsors the Harley Owners Group (H.O.G.), which gives Harley owners "an organized way to share their passion and show their pride." The worldwide club now numbers more than 1300 local chapters and 800 000 members.

Other companies sponsor *club marketing programs* that offer members special discounts and create member communities. For example,[15]

Harley-Davidson sponsors the Harley Owners Group (H.O.G.), which gives Harley riders "an organized way to share their passion and show their pride." H.O.G membership benefits include two magazines (*Hog Tales* and *Enthusiast*), a *H.O.G. Touring Handbook,* a roadside assistance program, a specially designed insurance program, theft reward service, a travel center, and a "Fly & Ride" program enabling members to rent Harleys while on vacation. The company also maintains an extensive H.O.G. website, which offers information on H.O.G. chapters, rallies, events, and benefits. The worldwide club now numbers more than 1300 local chapters and 800 000 members.

To build customer relationships, companies can add structural ties as well as financial and social benefits. A business marketer might supply customers with special equipment or online linkages that help them manage their orders, payroll, or inventory. For example, McKesson Corporation, a leading pharmaceutical wholesaler, has set up an online system to help small pharmacies manage their inventories, their order entry, and their shelf space.

The Changing Nature of Customer Relationships

Dramatic changes are occurring in the ways in which companies are relating to their customers. Yesterday's companies focused on mass marketing to all customers at arm's length. Today's companies are building more direct and lasting relationships with more carefully selected customers. Here are some important trends in the way companies are relating to their customers.

Relating with More Carefully Selected Customers

Few firms today still practise true mass marketing—selling in a standardized way to any customer who comes along. Today, most marketers realize that they don't want relationships with every customer. Instead, companies now are targeting fewer, more profitable customers.

At the same time that companies are finding new ways to deliver more value *to* customers, they are also beginning to assess carefully the value *of* customers to the firm. Called *selective relationship management*, many companies now use customer profitability analysis to weed out losing customers and target winning ones for pampering. Once they identify profitable customers, firms can create attractive offers and special handling to capture these customers and earn their loyalty.

But what should the company do with unprofitable customers? If it can't turn them into profitable ones, it may even want to "fire" customers that are too unreasonable or that cost more to serve than they are worth. For example, the banking industry has led the way in assessing customer profitability. After decades of casting a wide net to lure as many customers as possible, many banks are now mining their vast databases to identify winning customers and cut out losing ones.

Banks now routinely calculate customer value based on such factors as an account's average balances, account activity, services usage, branch visits, and other variables. A bank's customer service reps use such customer ratings when deciding how much—or how little—leeway to give a customer who wants, say, a lower credit-card interest rate. Profitable customers often get what they want; for customers whose accounts lose money for the bank, the service representatives rarely budge.

This sorting-out process, of course, has many risks. For one, future profits are hard to predict. A high school student on his or her way to a MBA and a plum job on Bay Street might be unprofitable now but worth courting for the future. Still, most banks believe that the benefits outweigh the risks.[16]

Relating for the Long Term

Just as companies are being more selective about which customers they choose to serve, they are serving chosen customers in a deeper, more lasting way. Today's companies are going beyond designing strategies to *attract* new customers and create *transactions* with them. They are using customer relationship management to *retain* current customers and build profitable, long-term *relationships* with them. The new view is that marketing is the science and art of finding, retaining, *and* growing profitable customers.

Why the new emphasis on retaining and growing customers? In the past, growing markets and an upbeat economy meant a plentiful supply of new customers. However, companies today face some new marketing realities. Changing demographics, more sophisticated competitors, and overcapacity in many industries mean that there are fewer customers to go around. Many companies are now fighting for shares of flat or fading markets.

As a result, the costs of attracting new consumers are rising. In fact, on average, it costs five to ten times as much to attract a new customer as it does to keep a current customer satisfied. Sears found that it costs twelve times more to attract a customer than to keep an existing one. Given these new realities, companies now go all out to keep profitable customers.[17]

Relating Directly

Beyond connecting more deeply with their customers, many companies are also connecting more *directly*. In fact, direct marketing is booming. Consumers can now buy virtually any product without going to a store—by telephone, mail-order catalogues, kiosks, and online. Business purchasing agents routinely shop on the Web for items ranging from standard office supplies to high-priced, high-tech computer equipment.

Some companies sell *only* via direct channels—firms such as Dell, Expedia, and Amazon.com, to name only a few. Other companies use direct connections to supplement their other communications and distribution channels. For example, Sony sells Playstation consoles and game cartridges through retailers, supported by millions of dollars of mass-media advertising. However, Sony uses its www.PlayStation.com website to build relationships with game players of all ages. The site offers information about the latest games, news about events and promotions, game guides and support, and even online forums in which game players can swap tips and stories.

Some marketers have hailed direct marketing as the "marketing model of the next century." They envision a day when all buying and selling will involve direct connections between companies and their customers. Others, although agreeing that direct marketing will play a growing and important role, see it as just one more way to approach the marketplace. We will take a closer look at the world of direct marketing in Chapters 16 and 17.

Partner Relationship Management

When it comes to creating customer value and building strong customer relationships, today's marketers know that they can't go it alone. They must work closely with a variety of marketing partners. In addition to being good at *customer relationship management*, marketers must also be good at **partner relationship management**. Major changes are occurring in how marketers partner with others inside and outside the company to jointly bring more value to customers.

Partner relationship management

Working closely with partners in other company departments and outside the company to jointly bring greater value to customers.

Partners Inside the Company

Traditionally, marketers have been charged with understanding customers and representing customer needs to different company departments. The old thinking was that marketing is done only by marketing, sales, and customer support people. However, in today's more connected world, the marketing department no longer has sole ownership of customer interactions. Every functional area can interact with customers, especially electronically. The new thinking is that every employee must be customer focused. David Packard, co-founder of Hewlett-Packard, wisely said, "Marketing is far too important to be left only to the marketing department."[18]

Today, rather than letting each department go its own way, firms are linking all departments in the cause of creating customer value. Rather than assigning only sales and marketing people to customers, they are forming cross-functional customer teams. For example, Procter & Gamble assigns "customer development teams" to each of its major retailer accounts. These teams—consisting of sales and marketing people, operations specialists, market and financial analysts, and others—coordinate the efforts of many P&G departments toward helping the retailer be more successful.

Marketing Partners Outside the Firm

Changes are also occurring in how marketers connect with their suppliers, channel partners, and even competitors. Most companies today are networked companies, relying heavily on partnerships with other firms.

Marketing channels consist of distributors, retailers, and others who connect the company to its buyers. The *supply chain* describes a longer channel, stretching from raw materials to components to final products that are carried to final buyers. For example, the supply chain for personal computers consists of suppliers of computer chips and other components, the computer manufacturer, and the distributors, retailers, and others who sell the computers.

Through *supply chain management*, many companies today are strengthening their connections with partners all along the supply chain. They know that their fortunes rest not just on how well they perform. Success at building customer relationships also rests on how well their entire supply chain performs against competitors' supply chains. These companies don't just treat suppliers as vendors and distributors as customers. They treat both as partners in delivering customer value. On the one hand, for example, Lexus works closely with carefully selected suppliers to improve quality and operations efficiency. On the other hand, it works with its franchise dealers to provide top-grade sales and service support that will bring customers in the door and keep them coming back.

Beyond managing the supply chain, today's companies are also discovering that they need *strategic* partners if they hope to be effective. In the new, more competitive global environment, going it alone is going out of style. *Strategic alliances* are booming across almost all industries and services. For example, Dell Computer recently ran advertisements telling how it partners with Microsoft and Intel to provide customized ebusiness solutions. And Volkswagen is working jointly with Archer Daniels Midland to develop biodiesel fuel. Sometimes, even competitors work together for mutual benefit:

> Hewlett-Packard (HP) recently partnered with Apple Computer to bring to market HP-branded iPods, manufactured by Apple, as part of HP's effort to broaden its presence in consumer electronics. "By partnering with Apple, we have the opportunity to add value by integrating the world's largest digital music offering into HP's larger digital entertainment strategy," says HP chair and CEO Carly Fiorina. Adds Apple CEO Steve Jobs, "Apple's goal is to get iPods and iTunes into the hands of every music lover around the world, and partnering with HP, an innovative consumer company, is going to help us do just that."[19]

As Jim Kelly, former CEO at UPS, puts it, "The old adage 'If you can't beat 'em, join 'em,' is being replaced by 'Join 'em and you can't be beat.'"[20]

Capturing Value from Customers

The first four steps in the marketing process involve building customer relationships by creating and delivering superior customer value. The final step involves capturing value in return, in the form of current and future sales, market share, and profits. By creating superior customer value, the firm creates highly satisfied customers who stay loyal and buy more. This, in turn, means greater long-run returns for the firm. Here, we discuss the outcomes of creating customer value: *customer loyalty and retention, share of market and share of customer*, and *customer equity*.

Creating Customer Loyalty and Retention

Good customer relationship management creates customer delight. In turn, delighted customers remain loyal and talk favourably to others about the company and its products. Studies show big differences in the loyalty of customers who are

Customer lifetime value
The value of the entire stream of purchases that the customer would make over a lifetime of patronage.

less satisfied, somewhat satisfied, and completely satisfied. Even a slight drop from complete satisfaction can create an enormous drop in loyalty. Thus, the aim of customer relationship management is to create not just customer satisfaction, but customer delight.[21]

Companies are realizing that losing a customer means losing more than a single sale. It means losing the entire stream of purchases that the customer would make over a lifetime of patronage. For example, here is a dramatic illustration of **customer lifetime value**:

> Stew Leonard, who operates a highly profitable three-store supermarket, says that he sees US$50 000 flying out of his store every time he sees a sulking customer. Why? Because his average customer spends about $100 a week, shops 50 weeks a year, and remains in the area for about 10 years. If this customer has an unhappy experience and switches to another supermarket, Stew Leonard's has lost US$50 000 in revenue. The loss can be much greater if the disappointed customer shares the bad experience with other customers and causes them to defect. To keep customers coming back, Stew Leonard's has created what the *New York Times* has dubbed the "Disneyland of Dairy Stores," complete with costumed characters, scheduled entertainment, a petting zoo, and animatronics throughout the store. From its humble beginnings as a small dairy store in 1969, Stew Leonard's has grown at an amazing pace. It's built 29 additions onto the original store, which now serves more than 250 000 customers each week. This legion of loyal shoppers is largely a result of the store's passionate approach to customer service. Rule #1 at Stew Leonard's—The customer is always right. Rule #2—If the customer is ever wrong, reread rule #1![22]

Stew Leonard is not alone in assessing customer lifetime value. Lexus estimates that a single satisfied and loyal customer is worth US$600 000 in lifetime sales. The customer lifetime value of a Taco Bell customer exceeds US$12 000.[23] Thus, working to retain and grow customers makes good economic sense. In fact, a company can lose money on a specific transaction but still benefit greatly from a long-term relationship.

This means that companies must aim high in building customer relationships. Customer delight creates an emotional relationship with a product or service, not just a rational preference. L.L. Bean, long known for its outstanding customer service and high customer loyalty, preaches the following "golden rule": Sell good merchandise, treat your customers like human beings, and they'll always come back for more." Hanging on to customers is "so basic, it's scary," claims one marketing executive. "We find out what our customers' needs and wants are, and then we overdeliver."[24]

Growing Share of Customer

Share of customer
The portion of the customer's purchasing that a company gets in its product categories.

Beyond simply retaining good customers to capture customer lifetime value, good customer relationship management can help marketers to increase their **share of customer**—the share they get of the customer's purchasing in their product categories. Many marketers are now spending less time figuring out how to increase share of market and more time trying to grow share of customer. Thus, banks want to increase "share of wallet." Supermarkets and restaurants want to get more "share of stomach." Car companies want to increase "share of garage" and airlines want greater "share of travel."

To increase share of customer, firms can leverage customer relationships by offering greater variety to current customers. Or they can train employees to cross-sell and up-sell in order to market more products and services to existing customers. For example, Amazon.com, is highly skilled at leveraging relationships with its 35 million customers to increase its share of each customer's purchases. Originally

To keep customers coming back, Stew Leonard's has created the "Disneyland of dairy stores." Rule 1—the customer is always right. Rule 2—if the customer is ever wrong, reread rule 1!

an online bookseller, Amazon now offers customers music, videos, gifts, toys, consumer electronics, office products, home improvement items, lawn and garden products, apparel and accessories, and an online auction. In addition, based on each customer's purchase history, the company recommends related books, CDs, or videos that might be of interest. In this way, Amazon.com captures a greater share of each customer's leisure and entertainment budget.

Building Customer Equity

We can now see the importance of not just acquiring customers, but of keeping and growing them as well. Customer relationship management takes a long-term view. Companies want not only to create profitable customers but also to "own" them for life, capture their customer lifetime value, and earn a greater share of their purchases.

What Is Customer Equity?

Customer equity

The total combined customer lifetime values of all of the company's customers.

The ultimate aim of customer relationship management is to produce high **customer equity**.[25] Customer equity is the combined discounted customer lifetime values of all of the company's current and potential customers. Clearly, the more loyal the firm's profitable customers, the higher the firm's customer equity. Customer equity may be a better measure of a firm's performance than are current sales or market share. Whereas sales and market share reflect the past, customer equity suggests the future. Consider Cadillac:

> In the 1970s and 1980s, Cadillac had some of the most loyal customers in the industry. To an entire generation of car buyers, the name "Cadillac" defined luxury. Cadillac's share of the luxury car market reached a whopping 51 percent in 1976. Based on market share and sales, the brand's future looked rosy. However, measures of customer equity would have painted a bleaker picture. Cadillac customers were getting older (average age 60) and average customer

To increase customer lifetime value and customer equity, Cadillac's highly successful Break Through ads target a younger generation of consumers.

lifetime value was falling. Many Cadillac buyers were on their last car. Thus, although Cadillac's market share was good, its customer equity was not. Compare this with BMW. Its more youthful and vigorous image didn't win BMW the early market share war. However, it did win BMW younger customers with higher customer lifetime values. The result: Cadillac now captures only about a 15 percent market share, lower than BMW's. And BMW's customer equity remains much higher—it has more customers with a higher average customer lifetime value. Thus, market share is not the answer. We should care not just about current sales but also about future sales. Customer lifetime value and customer equity are the name of the game.[26]

Building the Right Relationships with the Right Customers

Companies should manage customer equity carefully. They should view customers as assets that need to be managed and maximized. But not all customers, not even all loyal customers, are good investments. Surprisingly, some loyal customers can be unprofitable, and some disloyal customers can be profitable. Which customers should the company acquire and retain? "Up to a point, the choice is obvious: Keep the consistent big spenders and lose the erratic small spenders," says one expert. "But what about the erratic big spenders and the consistent small spenders? It's often unclear whether they should be acquired or retained, and at what cost."[27]

The company can classify customers according to their potential profitability and manage its relationships with them accordingly. Figure 1.5 classifies customers into one of four relationship groups, according to their profitability and projected loyalty.[28] Each group requires a different relationship management strategy. "Strangers" show low profitability and little projected loyalty. There is little fit between the company's offerings and their needs. The relationship management strategy for these customers is simple: don't invest anything in them.

"Butterflies" are profitable but not loyal. There is a good fit between the company's offerings and their needs. However, like real butterflies, we can enjoy them for only a short while and then they're gone. An example is stock market investors who trade shares often and in large amounts, but who enjoy hunting out the best deals without building a regular relationship with any single brokerage company. Efforts to convert butterflies into loyal customers are rarely successful. Instead, the company should enjoy the butterflies for the moment. It should use promotional

	Short-term customers	Long-term customers
High profitability	**Butterflies** Good fit between company's offerings and customer's needs; high profit potential	**True Friends** Good fit between company's offerings and customer's needs; highest profit potential
Low profitability	**Strangers** Little fit between company's offerings and customer's needs; lowest profit potential	**Barnacles** Limited fit between company's offerings and customer's needs; low profit potential

Potential profitability

Projected loyalty

Figure 1.5 Customer relationship groups

Source: Reprinted by permission of *Harvard Business Review*. Adapted from "The Management of Customer Loyalty" by Werner Relnartz and V. Kumar, July 2002, p. 93. Copyright © by the president and fellow of Harvard College; all rights reserved.

blitzes to attract them, create satisfying and profitable transactions with them, and then cease investing in them until the next time around.

"True friends" are both profitable and loyal. There is a strong fit between their needs and the company's offerings. The firm wants to make continuous relationship investments to delight these customers and nurture, retain, and grow them. It wants to turn true friends into "true believers," who come back regularly and tell others about their good experiences with the company.

"Barnacles" are highly loyal but not very profitable. There is a limited fit between their needs and the company's offerings. An example is smaller bank customers who bank regularly but do not generate enough returns to cover the costs of maintaining their accounts. Like barnacles on the hull of a ship, they create drag. Barnacles are perhaps the most problematic customers. The company might be able to improve their profitability by selling them more, raising their fees, or reducing service to them. However, if they cannot be made profitable, they should be "fired."

The point here is an important one: Different types of customers require different relationship management strategies. The goal is to build the *right relationships* with the *right customers*.[29]

The New Marketing Landscape

As the world spins into the first decade of the twenty-first century, dramatic changes are occurring in the marketplace. Richard Love of Hewlett-Packard observes, "The pace of change is so rapid that the ability to change has now become a competitive advantage." Yogi Berra, the legendary New York Yankees catcher, summed it up more simply when he said, "The future ain't what it used to be." As the marketplace changes, so must those who serve it.

In this section, we examine the major trends and forces that are changing the marketing landscape and challenging marketing strategy. We look at four major developments: the new digital age, rapid globalization, the call for more ethics and social responsibility, and the growth in not-for-profit marketing.

The Digital Age

The recent technology boom has created a digital age. The explosive growth in computer, telecommunications, information, transportation, and other technologies has had a major impact on the ways companies bring value to their customers.

Now, more than ever before, we are all connected to one another and to things near and far in the world around us. Where it once took weeks or months to travel across Canada, we can now travel around the globe in only hours or days. Where it once took days or weeks to receive news about important world events, we now see them as they are occurring through live satellite broadcasts. Where it once took weeks to correspond with others in distant places, they are now only moments away by phone or the Internet.

The technology boom has created exciting new ways to learn about and track customers, and to create products and services tailored to individual customer needs. Technology is also helping companies to distribute products more efficiently and effectively. And it's helping them to communicate with customers in large groups or one to one.

Through videoconferencing, marketing researchers at a company's headquarters in Vancouver can look in on focus groups in Winnipeg or Paris without ever stepping onto a plane. With only a few clicks of a mouse button, a direct marketer can tap into online data services to learn anything from what car you drive to what you read to what flavour of ice cream you prefer. Or, using today's powerful computers, marketers can create their own detailed customer databases and use them to target individual customers with offers designed to meet their specific needs.

Technology has also brought a new wave of communication and advertising tools—ranging from cellphones, fax machines, CD-ROM, and interactive TV to video kiosks at airports and shopping malls. Marketers can use these tools to zero in on selected customers with carefully targeted messages. Through ecommerce, customers can learn about, design, order, and pay for products and services—without ever leaving home. Then, through the marvels of express delivery, they can receive their purchases in less than twenty-four hours. From virtual reality displays that test new products to online virtual stores that sell them, the technology boom is affecting every aspect of marketing.

The Internet

Internet
A vast public web of computer networks that connect users of all types all around the world to one another and to an amazingly large information repository.

The technology that has most profoundly affected business and marketing is the **Internet**. Today, the Internet links individuals and businesses of all types to one another and to information all around the world. It allows anytime, anywhere connections to information, entertainment, and communication. Companies are using the Internet to build closer relationships with customers and marketing partners. Beyond competing in traditional marketplaces, they now have access to exciting new market*spaces*.

Internet usage surged in the 1990s with the development of the user-friendly World Wide Web. As Industry Canada notes, "Canada is well-positioned to be a leader in the New Economy, given its sophisticated infrastructure, its highly connected population and its early Electronic Commerce policy initiatives." Internet usage by Canadian business has grown dramatically from 63.4 percent of businesses using the Internet in 2000 to 81.6 percent using it in 2004. The Internet is truly a global phenomenon—the number of Internet users worldwide reached 972 million in 2005 and they are expected to approach 1.5 billion by 2007.[30] This growing and diverse Internet population means that all kinds of people are now going to the Web for information and to buy products and services.

> If consumer e-commerce looks promising, business-to-business e-commerce is just plain booming. Canadian business-to-business transactions were projected to reached $15 billion in 2005, compared with only $3 billion in consumer purchases. It seems that almost every business has set up shop on the Web. Companies large and small have moved quickly to exploit the power of the Internet.[31]

Thus, the technology boom is providing exciting new opportunities for marketers. We will explore the impact of the new digital age in more detail in Chapter 17.

The Internet has had a major impact on the ways marketers connect with and bring value to their customers.

Rapid Globalization

As they are redefining their relationships with customers and partners, marketers are also taking a fresh look at the ways in which they connect with the broader world around them. In an increasingly smaller world, many marketers are now connected *globally* with their customers and marketing partners.

Today, almost every company, large or small, is touched in some way by global competition. A neighbourhood florist buys its flowers from Mexican nurseries, while a large Canadian electronics manufacturer competes in its home markets with giant Japanese rivals. A fledgling Internet retailer finds itself receiving orders from all over the world at the same time that a Canadian consumer-goods producer introduces new products into emerging markets abroad.

North American firms have been challenged at home by the skilful marketing of European and Asian multinationals. Companies such as Toyota, Siemens, Nestlé, Sony, and Samsung have often outperformed their North American counterparts. Similarly, Canadian companies in a wide range of industries have found new opportunities abroad. Firms as varied as engineering firm SNC Lavalin; Montreal-based Forensic Technology, a marketer of crime-solving technology; or toymaker Mega Bloks Inc. have developed truly global operations, making and selling their products worldwide. Coca-Cola offers a mind-boggling 300 different brands in more than 200 countries.

Today, companies are not only trying to sell more of their locally produced goods in international markets, but they also are buying more supplies and components abroad. For example, Alfred Sung, one of Canada's top fashion designers, may choose cloth woven from Australian wool with designs printed in Italy. He will design a dress and email the drawing to a Hong Kong agent, who will place the order with a Chinese factory. Finished dresses will be air-freighted to Toronto, where they will be redistributed to department and specialty stores around the country.

Coca-Cola is a truly global operation, offering more than 300 different brands in more than 200 countries, including BPM Energy drink in Ireland, Mare Rosso Bitter in Spain, Sprite Ice Cube in Belgium, Fanta in Chile, and NaturAqua in Hungary.

Thus, managers in countries around the world are increasingly taking a global, not just a local, view of the company's industry, competitors, and opportunities. They are asking: What is global marketing? How does it differ from domestic marketing? How do global competitors and forces affect our business? To what extent should we "go global"? We will discuss the global marketplace in more detail in Chapter 18.

The Call for More Ethics and Social Responsibility

As the new definition of marketing indicates, marketers are being called upon to take greater responsibility for the social and environmental impact of their actions. As the worldwide consumerism and environmentalism movements mature and become even more vocal, companies are facing tougher demands. Some companies resist these movements, budging only when forced by legislation or organized consumer outcries. More forward-looking companies, however, readily accept their responsibilities to the world around them. They view socially responsible actions as an opportunity to do well by doing good. They seek ways to profit by serving the best long-run interests of their customers and communities.

Some companies—such as Ben & Jerry's, Timberland, Saturn, EnCana, and others—are practising "caring capitalism" and distinguishing themselves by being more civic-minded and caring. They are building social responsibility and action into their company value and mission statements. For example, consider Ben & Jerry's, a division of Unilever. Its mission statement challenges all employees, from top management to the ice cream scoopers in each store, to include concern for individual and community welfare in their day-to-day decisions.[32] We will revisit the relationship between marketing and social responsibility in greater detail in Chapter 4.

As not-for-profit organizations like World Vision Canada increasingly use marketing techniques, marketing professionals, such as Caroline Riseboro, are drawn to the sector.

The Growth of Not-for-Profit Marketing

In the past, marketing has been most widely applied in the for-profit business sector. In recent years, however, marketing also has become a major part of the strategies of many not-for-profit organizations, such as universities, hospitals, museums, symphony orchestras, and even churches. Organizations as diverse as the Sierra Club of Canada, the Heart and Stroke Foundation, and the Ivey School at the University of Western Ontario are using marketing techniques to build better relationships with key stakeholders, such as donors, volunteers, and prospective students and alumni. They are hiring experienced marketers from the for-profit sector to help them accomplish their mission. Consider the experience of Caroline Riseboro, who went to work for World Vision Canada:

> When Caroline decided to leave one of Canada's largest advertising agencies to accept a job with World Vision Canada, many of her colleagues thought she was crazy. However, Caroline wanted to use her marketing skills to give back to society. She certainly had a chance to put them to work. Selling an intangible product to people with only a limited marketing budget is the first obvious challenge. The more subtle hurdle, however, is the fierce competition for a small share of consumers' discretionary income. As Caroline noted, "It's not easy to convince Canadians to forego a daily latte to give a needy child overseas the opportunity for an education.... Try highlighting the benefits of self-sacrifice; it's not so sexy of a sell." Non-profit marketers also need impeccable ethics. Donors constantly look for assurance that their charitable dollars are not being wasted on needless marketing expenses. Thus, as Caroline has learned if you can successfully market charitable giving, you can market just about anything.[33]

Government agencies have also shown an increased interest in marketing. For example, the Canadian military has a marketing plan to attract recruits, and provincial and federal government agencies are now designing *social marketing campaigns* to encourage energy conservation and concern for the environment or to discourage smoking, excessive drinking, and drug use. According to *Strategy Magazine*, public sector advertising is annually among the top three categories of television advertisers in English Canada.[34]

So, What Is Marketing? Pulling It All Together

At the start of this chapter, Figure 1.1 (page 7) presented a simple model of the marketing process. Now that we've discussed all of the steps in the model, Figure 1.6 presents an expanded model that will help you pull it all together. What is marketing? Simply put, marketing is the process building profitable customer relationships by creating value for customers and capturing value in return.

The first four steps of the marketing process focus on creating value for customers. The company first gains a full understanding of the marketplace by researching consumer needs and managing marketing information. It then designs a customer-driven marketing strategy based on the answers to two simple questions. The first question is "What consumers will we serve?" (market segmentation and targeting). Good marketing companies know that they cannot serve all customers in every way. Instead, they need to focus their resources on the customers they can serve best and most profitably. The second marketing strategy question is "How can

Figure 1.6 An expanded model of the marketing process

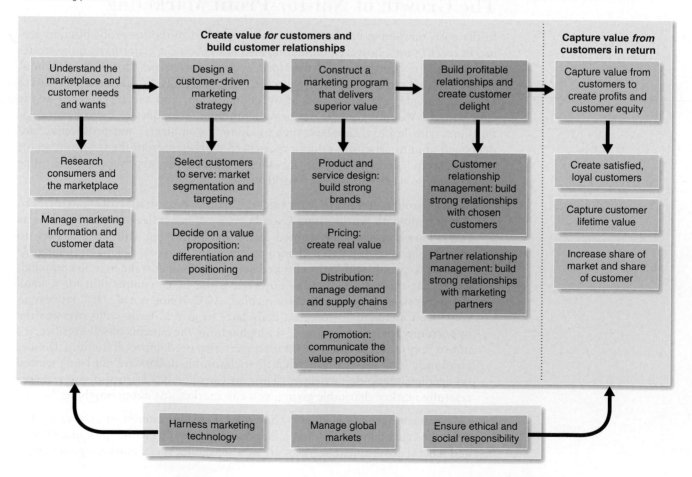

we best serve targeted customers?" (differentiation and positioning). Here, the marketer outlines a value proposition that spells out what values the company will deliver in order to win target customers.

With its marketing strategy decided, the company now constructs a marketing program—consisting of the four marketing mix elements, or the four Ps—that transforms the marketing strategy into real value for customers. The company develops product offers and creates strong brand identities for them. It prices these offers to create real customer value and distributes the offers to make them available to target consumers. Finally, the company designs promotion programs that communicate the value proposition to target consumers and persuade them to act on the marketing offer.

Perhaps the most important step in the marketing process involves building value-laden, profitable relationships with target customers. Throughout the process, marketers practise customer relationship management to create customer satisfaction and delight. In creating customer value and relationships, however, the company cannot go it alone. It must work closely with marketing partners both inside the company and throughout the marketing system. Thus, beyond practising good customer relationship management, firms must also practise good partner relationship management.

The first four steps in the marketing process create value *for* customers. In the final step, the company reaps the rewards of its strong customer relationships by capturing value *from* customers. Delivering superior customer value creates highly satisfied customers who will buy more and will buy again. This helps the company to capture customer lifetime value and greater share of customer. The result is increased long-term customer equity for the firm.

Finally, in the face of today's changing marketing landscape, companies must take into account three additional factors. In building customer and partner relationships, they must harness marketing technology, take advantage of global opportunities, and ensure that they act in an ethical and socially responsible way.

Figure 1.6 provides a good roadmap to future chapters of the text. Chapters 1 and 2 introduce the marketing process, with a focus on building customer relationships and capturing value from customers. Chapters 3 and 4 address the first steps of the marketing process—understanding the marketing environment, and understanding the impact marketing has on society and the ethical concerns associated with marketing practice. Chapter 5 focuses on managing marketing information. Chapter 6 and Chapter 7 are designed to help you understand consumer behaviour and business buying behaviour respectively. In Chapter 8, we look more deeply into the two major marketing strategy decisions: selecting which customers to serve (segmentation and targeting) and deciding on a value proposition (differentiation and positioning). Chapters 9 through 16 discuss the marketing mix variables, one by one. Chapter 17 and 18 explore special marketing factors: marketing technology in this new digital age, and global marketing.

Reviewing the Concepts

Today's successful companies share a strong customer focus and a heavy commitment to marketing. The goal of marketing is to build and manage profitable customer relationships.

1. **Define marketing and outline the steps in the marketing process.**

Marketing is an organizational function and a set of processes for creating, communicating, and delivering value to customers and for managing customer relationships in ways that benefit the organization and its stakeholders.

The marketing process involves five steps. The first four steps create value *for* customers. First, marketers need to understand the marketplace and customer needs and wants. Next, marketers design a customer-driven marketing strategy with the goal of getting, keeping, and growing target customers. In the third step, marketers construct a marketing program that actually delivers superior value. All of these steps form the basis for the fourth step, building profitable customer relationships and creating customer delight. In the final step, the company reaps the rewards of strong customer relationships by capturing value *from* customers.

2. **Explain the importance of understanding customers and the marketplace, and identify the five core marketplace concepts.**

Outstanding marketing companies go to great lengths to learn about and understand their customers' needs, wants, and demands. This understanding helps them to design want-satisfying marketing offers and build value-laden customer relationships by which they can capture customer lifetime value and greater share of customer. The result is increased long-term customer equity for the firm.

The core marketplace concepts are *needs, wants,* and *demands; marketing offers (products, services, and experiences); value* and *satisfaction; exchange* and *relationships;* and *markets. Wants* are the form taken by human needs when shaped by culture and individual personality. When backed by buying power, wants become *demands.* Companies address needs by putting forth a *value proposition,* a set of benefits that they promise to consumers to satisfy their needs. The value proposition is fulfilled through a *marketing offer* that delivers customer value and satisfaction, resulting in long-term exchange relationships with customers.

3. **Identify the key elements of a customer-driven marketing strategy and discuss marketing management orientations that guide marketing strategy.**

To design a winning marketing strategy, the company must first decide *who* it will serve. It does this by divid-ing the market into segments of customers (*market segmentation*) and selecting which segments it will cultivate (*target marketing*). Next, the company must decide *how* it will serve targeted customers (how it will *differentiate and position* itself in the marketplace).

Marketing management can adopt one of five competing market orientations. The *production concept* holds that management's task is to improve production efficiency and bring down prices. The *product concept* holds that consumers favour products that offer the most in quality, performance, and innovative features; thus, little promotional effort is required. The *selling concept* holds that consumers will not buy enough of the organization's products unless it undertakes a large-scale selling and promotion effort. The *marketing concept* holds that achieving organizational goals depends on determining the needs and wants of target markets and delivering the desired satisfactions more effectively and efficiently than competitors do. The *societal marketing concept* holds that generating customer satisfaction *and* long-run societal well-being are the keys to both achieving the company's goals and fulfilling its responsibilities.

4. **Discuss customer relationship management, and identify strategies for creating value *for* customers and capturing value *from* customers in return.**

Broadly defined, *customer relationship management* is the process of building and maintaining profitable customer relationships by delivering superior customer value and satisfaction. The aim of customer relationship management is to produce high *customer equity,* the total combined customer lifetime values of all of the company's customers. The key to building lasting relationships is the creation of superior *customer value* and *satisfaction.*

Companies want not only to acquire profitable customers but also to build relationships that will keep them and grow "share of customer." Different types of customer require different customer relationship management strategies. The marketer's aim is to build the *right relationships* with the *right customers.* In return for creating value *for* targeted customers, the company captures value *from* customers in the form of profits and customer equity.

In building customer relationships, good marketers realize that they cannot go it alone. They must work closely with marketing partners inside and outside the company. In addition to being good at customer relationship management, they must also be good at *partner relationship management.*

5. Describe the major trends and forces that are changing the marketing landscape in this age of relationships.

As the world spins into the twenty-first century, dramatic changes are occurring in the marketing arena. The boom in computer, telecommunications, information, transportation, and other technologies has created exciting new ways to learn about and track customers, and to create products and services tailored to individual customer needs. In an increasingly smaller world, many marketers are now connected *globally* with their customers and marketing partners. Today, almost every company, large or small, is touched in some way by global competition. Today's marketers are also re-examining their ethical and societal responsibilities.

Marketers are being called upon to take greater responsibility for the social and environmental impact of their actions. Finally, in the past, marketing has been most widely applied in the for-profit business sector. In recent years, however, marketing also has become a major part of the strategies of many not-for-profit organizations, such as colleges, hospitals, museums, symphony orchestras, and even churches.

As discussed throughout the chapter, the major new developments in marketing can be summed up in a single word: *relationships*. Today, marketers of all kinds are taking advantage of new opportunities for building relationships with their customers, their marketing partners, and the world around them.

Reviewing the Key Terms

Customer equity   27
Customer lifetime value   26
Customer perceived value   18
Customer relationship management   18
Customer satisfaction   19
Demands   7
Demarketing   11

Exchange   9
Internet   30
Market   10
Marketing   5
Marketing concept   15
Marketing management   10
Marketing offer   8
Needs   7

Partner relationship management   24
Product concept   14
Production concept   14
Selling concept   15
Share of customer   26
Societal marketing concept   16
Wants   7

Discussing the Concepts

1. The concepts of needs, wants, and demand are very important to understanding marketing. Find a copy of an advertisement or promotion and use it illustrate how these three concepts are related.

2. "Customer value and satisfaction" is one unit of the five core marketplace concepts used in understanding the marketplace and consumer needs. What are the other four core marketplace concepts? Of the five core concepts is there one concept that stands out as being more important than any of the others? Support your answer.

3. Contrast the following two marketing management orientations: "The Selling Concept" and "The Marketing Concept." Can you name a market or market category where "The Selling Concept" is still the more popular marketing management orientation?

4. Customer loyalty and retention programs are important in building customer relationships and customer equity. Discuss why a national grocery chain, such as Sobey's or Costco, would choose a "club" program over a "frequency" program.

5. "Today, most marketers realize that they don't want to connect with just any customers." Do you agree with that statement? Why? Which company would be more likely to follow this creed, Wal-Mart or Porsche? When formulating your answer, also think about why ethics is important when managing customer relationships.

6. Does it make sense that working with other departments in an organization may bring greater value to customers? Create a short description of how working with your human resources department could generate increased customer value.

7. The fifth and final step in the marketing process is to capture value and generate profits and customer equity for the organization. Name the four customer-value-creation steps in this marketing process that result in creation of value for the organization. Is the marketing process iterative?

Applying the Concepts

1. This chapter discusses the concepts of customer value and satisfaction. Building on this knowledge, is it logical to assume that if you increase the perceived customer value for a product that there is a corresponding increase in customer satisfaction? Under what conditions might this not occur?

2. A cellphone company spends $148.50 in total costs to acquire a new user. On average, this new user spends $60 a month for calling and related services, and the cellphone company generates an 18 percent profit margin in each of the twenty-five months that the user is expected to stay with the service. What is the customer lifetime value of this user to the cellphone company?

Focus on Technology

A CFO.com article by John Berry, eCFO, discusses the concept of Customer Lifetime Value (although in the article it is referred to as Lifetime Customer Value).* Berry describes how Convergys, a billing, customer, and employee care solutions provider, developed technology that enabled a US$2.1 billion-in-revenue company to report a 16 percent increase in operating income from its Customer Management Group. A large portion of this increase came from "winning new business from old customers" and was directly related to the "lifetime value modeling index" technology Convergys created. Bob Lento, VP of Sales for Convergys said, "This lifetime value modeling index is an empirical validation of our own instinctive belief that there is potential to grow existing client relationships significantly." The table shows the index that Convergys developed for their customer.

1. What is the basic premise on which CLV rests?

2. State your own opinion on the value of CLV.

3. The example includes nonoperation measures. Does this make sense? Why?

The CLV Rating System Developed by Convergys

Index	Measures	Weight
Average revenue score	Current and projected spending	15%
Revenue change score	Year-to-year actual spending	15%
Profitability score	Customer contribution margin	20%
Current relationship	Signed contract length, total years as client	10%
Technology entanglement	Systems integration, reporting, Convergys Web-assisted service, e-mail	20%
Share of client	Outsource potential	10%
Partnership	Level of contact, referenceable future value	10%

* See "Lifetime Customer Value," CFO.com, September 15, 2001, www.cfo.com/Article?article-4899.

Focus on Ethics

According to the National Longitudinal Survey of Children and Youth, more than one-third of Canadian children aged 2 to 11 are overweight, and of these, about half could be considered obese. As a brother, sister, aunt or uncle, you know that a considerable amount of food advertising is directed at children from the ages of 6 to 11. A recent Kaiser Foundation report reviewed the findings of forty studies on the role of the media in fuelling the rapid growth of childhood obesity. The report concluded that the majority of research finds a direct link between the amount of time children spend interacting with the media and their body weight. "The report cites studies showing that the typical American child sees about 40,000 ads a year on television, and that the majority of ads aimed at children are for sweets, cereal, soda and fast food."*

Place yourself in the role of a brand manager of a food product (sweet snack) with a primary target market of children aged 6 to 11. In a telephone interview, you are asked the following questions by a reporter from the *Globe and Mail* in response to the Kaiser Foundation report. How would you respond?

1. Do food ads children are exposed to on TV influence them to make unhealthy food choices?

2. Do cross promotions between your product and popular TV and movie characters encourage children to buy and eat high-calorie foods?

3. Would you support government regulation directed at regulating food ads for children aged 6 to 11?

* See "Making a Meal of Couch Potatoes and Doughnuts," *Marketing Week*, March 25, 2004, p. 28; and www.kff.org/entmedia/7030.cfm.

Video Case
Subaru

Building strong, profitable relationships with customers is the key to good marketing. Companies build brands by delighting customers and reinforcing good relationships with each interaction and through every touchpoint. But how do you maintain ties with customers who make a purchase only once every five or ten years? For Subaru, the answer is simple: by providing satisfying experiences with each service visit between purchases.

The goal of Subaru's Stellar Performer Dealers is to provide an exceptional dealer experience with every visit. Working with their customers, these dealers take an in-depth look at the way they do business and what they can do to better serve their customers and improve their long-term relationships. Those relationships give Subaru an edge when the time comes for a customer to make the next car purchase decision.

After viewing the video featuring Subaru of America, answer the following questions about building profitable customer relationships.

1. How does Subaru's research help the company and its dealers build stronger customer relationships?

2. How has your experience with dealer service affected your satisfaction with your car? How could that experience be improved to enhance your relationship with the brand and the company? If you were in the market for new car, what impact would your relationship have on your purchase decision?

3. What is Subaru's value proposition?

4. How is Subaru's approach to creating relationships with customers similar to Lexus's approach? How is it different?

Online Media Resources

Video Short
Log on to your Companion Website at www.pearsoned.ca/kotler to view the video segment related to the Video Case above.

CBC CBC Video Case
Please refer to Appendix 2 to read a CBC Video Case for this chapter, and log on to your Companion Website at www.pearsoned.ca/kotler to view the corresponding video segment.

Case Pilot
Log on to your Companion Website at www.pearsoned.ca/kotler to sharpen your case analysis skills and take the Case Pilot Challenge!

Company Case
Office Depot: "Thank You for Calling..."

"Thank you for calling Office Depot. All of our customer service representatives are busy serving other customers. Please stay on the line, and you will be connected to the next available agent."

"Thank you for calling Office Depot. Your call may be monitored and recorded for use in customer service representative training."

Steve Haine switched the telephone receiver to his right hand and glanced at his watch. He'd been on hold for almost ten minutes and had listened as the automated system repeated the pair of messages about every minute during that period.

Normally, Steve, a marketing professor at a well-known university, would have hung up long ago rather

than spending his valuable time on hold just to register a complaint. However, he'd spent this Monday morning making a presentation on customer service to a group of middle and top managers at a major corporation's local manufacturing plant. As a part of the presentation, he'd discussed complaint handling. Now, he was interested in seeing how Office Depot would react to his story.

A Botched Delivery
Steve's story had begun earlier in the afternoon. Upon returning from his presentation, he'd phoned his wife, Dana, to confirm their plans for the evening. Dana was

an independent insurance salesperson who worked out of their home.

Steve noted that the phone rang more than the usual number of times before Dana picked up. "Hi," he began after she answered. "Just got back from the presentation and wanted to check in with you about tonight."

"Listen," Dana barked, and Steve immediately detected from the tone of her voice that he had called at a bad time. "I've got a delivery man stuck in the driveway and don't have time to talk now. I'm so mad. Call back later."

"Okay," Steve answered, realizing Dana had already hung up. He knew it was very unusual for Dana to be so upset, so something must have really gotten to her.

Steve wondered about Dana's statement that someone was stuck in the driveway. He and Dana lived in a neighbourhood characterized by its rolling hills and trees. Their house sat on the side of a heavily wooded hill. Their driveway was almost forty metres long, curving to the left and rising about four metres from the street entrance to the parking area. From the parking area, there were fifteen steps leading to a deck on the front of the house and to the front door. The left-hand turn and incline made the driveway appear steeper than it really was, and it was not unusual for delivery trucks to have some problems negotiating the driveway.

About an hour-and-a-half later, Steve called Dana again. "Hi," she responded after recognizing Steve's voice. "I'm sorry if I snapped at you earlier, but I was so mad."

"Who was the delivery from?" Steve asked.

"Office Depot. Two small packages for you."

"Oh. That must be my new pen and the refills. Wow, I just ordered them on Friday at the Office Depot website! You remember that I lost my good Cross pen at the conference I attended in Tampa last week. After I got back, I went to Office Max, Staples, and Office Depot to buy a new pen, but none of them had my pen. So I went to the Cross website to find the pen's model name and then ordered it from the Office Depot website. The pen only cost $25, and I also ordered two refills. The total bill was just over $30, and I paid an additional $5.95 for delivery. I just assumed Office Depot would mail the pen to me within the three to five business days its website indicates. Anyway, that's what the packages are, and I'm sorry I contributed to a bad time for you."

"Well, you don't know the half of it," Dana responded. "I was working in the office when the telephone rang. It was the delivery person. He announced that he was from Office Depot and had a delivery. He was at the bottom of the driveway and said he could not make it up the driveway. I couldn't imagine what we were getting from Office Depot, but I told him I would meet him at the driveway at the bottom of the stairs. When I got to the bottom of the stairs, I saw his truck. He was only a metre into the driveway, at the curve. I looked at him and he looked at me. Then, he rolled down his window and stuck out his arm with the two small packages and a clipboard with a form for me to sign. I continued to look at him and realized that he was not going to get out of his truck. Finally, I understood that I was going to have to walk down the driveway and take the packages!"

"You mean he didn't get out of the truck?"

"No! He wasn't willing to get out of the truck and walk the twenty-five metres to bring me the packages, which must have weighed about 225 grams in total!"

"Well, I can understand your being upset. We've delivery people all the time who don't want to drive up the driveway. But they always just walk the package up to the house and either give it to us or leave it at the door."

"Yes, but that's not all the story," Dana continued. "As I walked back up the driveway with the packages, I heard the truck backing out and then heard a scraping sound. I turned around and saw that the driver had backed at the wrong angle and the right-hand rear wheel had gone off the driveway. The truck had bottomed out on the driveway's edge. He was stuck."

"You're kidding!"

"No, I couldn't believe it. He wasn't far enough into the driveway to get stuck, but somehow he had. So, over the next hour I made several trips to and from the house to bring him boards from your shop and other things so he could try to get some leverage and get out. None of his attempts worked. Finally, I had to go back up to the office and get him a phone book so he could call a tow truck. I had to call three companies before I could find one that could come. The truck came finally and pulled him out."

"Why did you have to make the calls?" Steve asked.

"The driver didn't speak English very well, and I thought I could communicate our location better than he could."

"What a nightmare!" Steve exclaimed. "I know how busy you are and to have to spend an hour with this lazy guy and make trips for him up and down the driveway must have really gotten to you. I can understand you didn't have time to talk to me when I called."

"Well, just don't order anything else from Office Depot!"

The Calls

After his call to Dana, Steve thought about the situation. He had just spent the morning telling the managers that complaints were valuable. Despite being busy, he decided to share this story with Office Depot.

First, he'd gone to the Office Depot website. After some looking, he found a "contact us" link that contained a toll-free number to speak to a customer service representative. After a brief wait and several recorded messages, he got a representative. Steve told her the story, but realized during the conversation that her job was only to assist with orders. Steve told the representative that he wanted to share his story with someone who could deal with his complaint. The representative informed him that he would need to call corporate headquarters and gave him the toll-free number.

When Steve called the number, the Office Depot operator answered, then transferred him to the customer service line, and the wait and recorded messages began.

The Complaint

Steve shifted his weight, switched hands again, and looked out his office window. He was just about to give up, despite his good intentions, when a real person finally answered his call.

"Hello, my name is Iris. Thank you for calling Office Depot. How may I help you?"

"Hello, Iris. My name's Steve Haine. I've a story I want to relate to you."

Iris asked Steve for his order number but he didn't have it. However, using his name and street address she found his order and the related information. Steve then told Iris his story, interrupted only by her asking

incredulously, "You mean he didn't get out of the truck? He just rolled down the window and handed the packages out for your wife to come get them?"

"Yes, that's correct," Steve answered. He went on to complete recounting the event and then concluded, "Iris, I'm a marketing professor. I wanted to share this story with you, hoping that it will help you improve your customer service. I'm not asking for my money back, and I don't want to tell you how to run your business. But if I worked in customer service at Office Depot, I'd follow up on this situation and take some steps to keep this kind of thing from happening again."

"I've made notes on your call, Mr. Haine. Thank you for calling," Iris concluded.

Steve hung up the phone and wondered what, if anything, Office Depot would do with his complaint. He reflected on the topics he'd covered in his presentation that morning, topics such as customer perceived value, customer satisfaction, customer relationship management, customer lifetime value, and customer equity. He hoped Iris had taken good notes; but, if she hadn't, he hoped his call had been recorded!

Questions for Discussion

1. What marketing orientation or approach does Office Depot appear to be using now? How does Office Depot create value for its customers? Describe two things it could do to move it more toward implementing the marketing concept.

2. Are Steve and Dana Haine the "right" customers for Office Depot? What could Office Depot do to build relationships with customers like Steve and Dana?

3. What customer satisfaction problems do you see in the case?

4. How do the concepts of customer lifetime value and customer equity come into play in this case?

5. If you were in charge of Office Depot's customer service operation and learned of Steve's story, what steps would you take?

CHAPTER 2

Company and Marketing Strategy: Partnering to Build Customer Relationships

AFTER STUDYING THIS CHAPTER, YOU SHOULD BE ABLE TO

1. explain companywide strategic planning and its four steps

2. discuss how to design business portfolios and develop growth strategies

3. explain marketing's role in strategic planning and how marketing works with its partners to create and deliver customer value

4. describe the elements of a customer-driven marketing strategy and mix, and the forces that influence them

5. list the marketing management functions, including the elements of a marketing plan, and discuss the importance of measuring and managing return on marketing

Previewing the Concepts

In the first chapter, we explored the marketing process by which companies create value for consumers in order to capture value in return. In this chapter, we'll dig more deeply into steps two and three of the marketing process—designing customer-driven marketing strategies and constructing marketing programs. But first we'll examine marketing's role in the broader organization. Marketing contributes to and is guided by the company's overall strategic plan. First, marketing urges a whole-company philosophy that puts customers at the centre. Then, under the overall strategic plan, marketers work with other company functions to design marketing strategies for delivering value to carefully targeted customers. Finally, marketers develop "marketing mixes"—consisting of product, price, distribution, and promotion tactics—to carry out these strategies profitably.

Let's look first at the Walt Disney Company. Known for its wholesome family entertainment, theme parks, and family films, the company has woven its special "Disney magic" to create and fulfill fantasies for people around the world. But what you may not know is that the Walt Disney Company has now grown and diversified. As you read on, think about all the strategic planning challenges facing Disney today.

When you think of the Walt Disney Company, you probably think first of theme parks and animated films. And no wonder. Since the release of its first Mickey Mouse cartoon more than eighty years ago, it has perfected the art of movie animation. From pioneering films, such as *Snow White and the Seven Dwarfs*, *Fantasia*, and *Pinocchio*, to more recent features, such as *The Lion King*, *Toy Story*, *Monsters, Inc.*, *Finding Nemo*, *Pirates of the Caribbean*, and *the Chronicles of Narnia*, Disney has brought pure magic to the theatres, living rooms, and hearts and minds of audiences around the world.

But perhaps nowhere is the Disney magic more apparent than at the company's premier theme parks. Each year, more than 40 million people flock to the Disney World resort alone, making it the world's number-one tourist attraction. What brings so many people to Disney World? Part of the answer lies in its many attractions found in the resort's four major theme parks—Magic Kingdom, Epcot, Disney-MGM Studios, and Disney's Animal Kingdom. But these attractions reveal only part of the Disney World value proposition. In fact, what visitors like best is the park's sparkling cleanliness and the friendliness of Disney World employees. Thus, the real "Disney magic" lies in the company's obsessive dedication to its mission to "make people happy" and to "make a dream come true."

The company orients all of its people—from the executive in the corner office, to the monorail driver—around the customer's experience. On their first day, all new Disney World employees report for a three-day motivational course at Disney University in Orlando, where they learn about the hard work of making fantasies come true. They learn that they are in the entertainment business—"cast members" in the Disney World "show." The job of each cast member is to enthusiastically serve Disney's "guests."

Before they receive their "theme costumes" and go "on stage," employees take courses titled Traditions I and Traditions II, in which they learn the Disney language, history, and culture. They are taught to be enthusiastic, helpful, and *always* friendly. They learn to do good deeds, such as volunteering to take pictures of guests, so that the whole family can be in the picture. Cast members are taught never to say, "It's not my job." When a guest asks a question—whether it's "Where's the nearest restroom?" or "What are the names of Snow White's seven dwarfs?"—they need to know the answer. If they see a piece of trash on the ground, they pick it up. Disney's customer-delight mission and marketing have become legendary. Its theme parks are so highly regarded for outstanding customer service that many leading corporations send managers to Disney University to learn how Disney does it.

You might be surprised to learn, however, that theme parks are only a small part of a much bigger Disney story. Parks and resorts account for only about 30 percent of today's Walt Disney Company empire. In recent years, Disney has become a real study in strategic planning. Throughout the 1990s, seeking growth, Disney diversified rapidly, transforming itself into a $32 billion international media and entertainment colossus. Beyond its theme parks, the Walt Disney Company now owns or has a major stake in all of the following:

- A major television and radio network—ABC—along with ten company-owned television stations, seventy-two radio stations, and thirteen international broadcast channels

- Nineteen cable networks (including the Disney Channel, Toon Disney, SOAPnet, ESPN, A&E, the History Channel, Lifetime Television, E! Entertainment, and ABC Family)

- Four television production companies, eight movie and theatrical production companies, and a distribution company (including Walt Disney Pictures, Touchstone Pictures, Hollywood Pictures, Miramax Films, Dimension Films, and Buena Vista Productions). Many of the shows it produces, such as *Lost, Grey's Anatomy* and *Desperate Housewives*, target adults 18–49 (the age group for which advertisers pay a premium)

- Five publishing groups (including Hyperion Books, Disney Educational Productions, and Disney Press)

- Five music labels (Walt Disney Records, Hollywood Records, Buena Vista Records, Mammoth Records, and Lyric Street Records)

- Nineteen Internet groups (including Disney Online, Disney's Blast, ABC.com, ESPN.com, FamilyFun.com, NASCAR.com, NBA.com, and NFL.com)

- Disney Interactive (which develops and markets computer software, video games, and CD-ROMS)

- Disney Consumer Products Worldwide (Disney brand and character products ranging from toys, apparel, and books to breakfast foods, personal care items, stationery, home furnishings, interactive games, and electronics)

- The Disney Store—550 retail store locations (sixteen in Canada) carrying Disney-related merchandise

- Anaheim Sports (the Mighty Ducks of Anaheim National Hockey League team)

- Disney Cruise Lines

In addition to diversification, Disney's second strategic priority is global expansion. The firm is working to create and expand relationships with millions of new consumers around the world. China has become an important market for Disney. It has the world's largest population and one of the fastest-growing economies. Disney's animated characters are popular throughout the country; *Mickey Mouse Magazine* is the number-one children's magazine in China, and 2005 marked a major milestone for Disney with its successful opening of Hong Kong Disneyland.

Disney's ability to leverage technology provides the third leg of its long-term growth strategy. As new generations of consumers embrace devices as varied as video games, personal video players, and broadband-based devices, Disney will be there to provide original and compelling content to meet this growing demand. Its groundbreaking partnership with Apple to provide ABC and Disney Channel content on the Apple iPod is one example of Disney's commitment to serve consumers through the use of new technology.

Though its strategy is impressive, managing Disney's diverse portfolio of businesses has become a real *Monsters, Inc.* During the last half of the 1980s, the smaller, more focused Disney experienced soaring sales and profits. Revenues grew at an average rate of 23 percent annually; net income grew at 50 percent a year. In contrast, the new and more complex Disney has struggled for growth and profitability. While in 1997 its revenues increased by 59 percent, in 2005 they went up by 19 percent. For the past three years, however, its profit margins have hovered around 6 percent, its stock price has been recovering, and it seems to be back on the path to profitable growth. One thing seems certain—creating just the right blend of businesses to make up the new Magic Kingdom won't be easy. It will take masterful strategic planning—along with some big doses of the famed "Disney magic"—to give the modern Disney story a happily-ever-after ending.[1]

Marketing strategies and programs operate within the context of broader, company-wide strategic plans. Thus, to understand the role of marketing within an organization, we must first understand the organization's overall strategic planning process. Like Disney, all companies must look ahead and develop long-term strategies to meet the changing conditions in their industries and ensure long-term survival.

In this chapter, we look first at the organization's overall strategic planning. Next, we discuss how marketers, guided by the strategic plan, work closely with others inside and outside the firm to serve consumers. We then examine marketing strategy and planning—how marketers choose target markets, position their marketing offers, develop a marketing mix, and manage their marketing programs. Finally, we look at the important step of measuring and managing return on marketing investment.

Companywide Strategic Planning: Defining Marketing's Role

Strategic planning

The process of developing and maintaining a strategic fit between the organization's goals and capabilities, and its changing marketing opportunities. It involves defining a clear company mission, setting supporting objectives, designing a sound business portfolio, and coordinating functional strategies.

The hard task of selecting an overall company strategy for long-run growth and profitability is called *strategic planning*. Each company must find the game plan that makes the most sense given its specific situation, opportunities, objectives, and resources. This is the focus of **strategic planning**—the process of developing and maintaining a strategic fit between the organization's goals and capabilities and its changing marketing opportunities.

Strategic planning sets the stage for the rest of the planning in the firm. Companies usually prepare annual plans and long-range plans. These plans are strategic in that they are crafted to grow and transform the company's current businesses in their rapidly evolving environments and to develop new businesses to meet the market needs anticipated in the future.

At the corporate level, the company starts the strategic planning process by defining its overall purpose and mission (see Figure 2.1). This mission then is turned into detailed supporting objectives that guide the whole company. Next, headquarters decides what portfolio of businesses and products is best for the company and how much support to give each one. In turn, each business and product develops detailed marketing and other departmental plans that support the companywide plan. Thus, marketing planning occurs at the market, business-unit, and product levels. It supports company strategic planning with more detailed plans for specific marketing opportunities.[2]

Defining a Market-Oriented Mission

An organization exists to accomplish something. At first, it has a clear purpose or mission, but over time its mission may become unclear as the organization grows, adds new products and markets, or faces new conditions in the environment. When management senses that the organization is drifting, it must renew its search for purpose. It is time to ask: What is our business? Who are our consumers and what do they value? What should our business be? These simple-sounding questions are among the most difficult the company will ever have to answer. Successful companies continuously raise these questions and answer them carefully and completely.

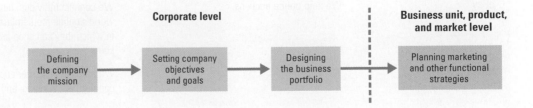

Figure 2.1 Steps in strategic planning

Mission statement
A statement of the organization's purpose—what it wants to accomplish in the larger environment.

Many organizations develop formal mission statements that answer these questions. A **mission statement** is a statement of the organization's purpose—what it wants to accomplish in the larger environment. A clear mission statement acts as an "invisible hand" that guides people in the organization. Studies have shown that firms with well-crafted mission statements have better organizational and financial performance.[3]

Some companies define their missions myopically in product or technology terms ("We make and sell furniture" or "We are a chemical-processing firm"). But mission statements should be *market oriented* and defined in terms of consumer needs. Products and technologies eventually become outdated, but basic market needs may last forever.

A market-oriented mission statement defines the business in terms of satisfying basic customer needs. For example, RBC Financial Group isn't just a bank—it strives to "always earn the right to be our clients' first choice." Likewise, Chapters.Indigo.ca sees itself not as a book company, but as a Canadian ecommerce company that serves as a destination for online shoppers. By building relationships with its customers, it can serve a variety of their online shopping needs—everything from books to gardening items—in a secure, high-service environment.[4] Table 2.1 provides several other examples of product-oriented versus market-oriented business definitions.

Management should avoid making its mission too narrow or too broad. A pencil manufacturer that says it is in the communication equipment business is stating its mission too broadly. Missions should be *realistic*. Singapore Airlines would be deluding itself if it adopted the mission to become the world's largest airline. Missions should also be *specific*. Many mission statements are written for public relations purposes and lack specific, workable guidelines. Such generic statements sound good but provide little real guidance or inspiration.

Missions should fit the *market environment*. The Girl Scouts of U.S.A. would not recruit successfully in today's environment with its former mission: "to prepare

Table 2.1 Market-Oriented Business Definitions

Company	Product-Oriented Definition	Market-Oriented Definition
M·A·C Cosmetics	We make cosmetics.	We sell lifestyle and self-expression, tolerance of diversity, and a platform for the outrageous.
Zellers	We run discount stores.	We offer products and services that deliver superior style and value to Canadians.
Canadian Tire	We sell tools and home-improvement items.	We provide advice and solutions that transform ham-handed people into Mr. and Ms. Fixits.
Amazon.ca	We sell books, videos, CDs, toys, consumer electronics, hardware, housewares, and other products.	We make the Internet buying experience fast, easy, and enjoyable—we're the place where you can find and discover anything you want to buy online.
Disney	We run theme parks.	We create fantasies—a place where families can dream together.
eBay	We hold online auctions.	We connect individual buyers and sellers in the world's online marketplace, a unique Web community in which they can shop around, have fun, and get to know each other.
Nike	We sell shoes.	We help people experience the emotion of competition, winning, and crushing competitors.

young girls for motherhood and wifely duties." Today, its mission is to be the place "where girls grow strong." The organization should base its mission on its *distinctive competencies*. Finally, mission statements should be *motivating*. A company's mission should not be stated as making more sales or profits—profits are only a reward for undertaking a useful activity. A company's employees need to feel that their work is significant and that it contributes to people's lives. For example, Walt Disney Company's aim is to "make people happy."

Setting Company Objectives and Goals

The company's mission needs to be turned into detailed supporting objectives for each level of management. Each manager should have objectives and be responsible for reaching them. For example, Monsanto operates in many businesses, including agriculture, pharmaceuticals, and food products. The company defines its mission as creating "abundant food and a healthy environment." It seeks to help feed the world's exploding population while at the same time sustaining the environment.

This mission leads to a hierarchy of objectives, including business objectives and marketing objectives. Monsanto's overall objective is to build profitable customer relationships by creating environmentally better products and getting them to market faster at lower costs. For its part, the agricultural division's objective is to increase agricultural productivity and reduce chemical pollution. It does this by researching new pest- and disease-resistant crops that produce higher yields without chemical spraying. But research is expensive and requires improved profits to plow back into research programs. So improving profits becomes another major Monsanto objective. Profits can be improved by increasing sales or reducing costs. Sales can be increased by improving the company's share of the North American market, by entering new foreign markets, or both. These goals then become the company's current marketing objectives.

Marketing strategies and programs must be developed to support these marketing objectives. To increase its market share, Monsanto might increase its products' availability and promotion. To enter new foreign markets, the company may cut prices and target large farms abroad. These are its broad marketing strategies. Each broad marketing strategy must then be defined in greater detail. For example, increasing the product's promotion may require more salespeople and more

The Girl Scouts' mission is to be a place "Where Girls Grow Strong."

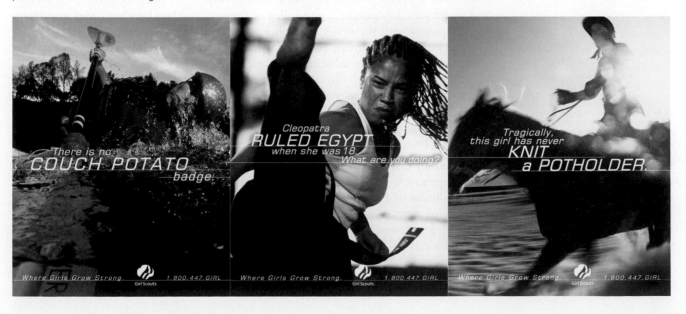

advertising; if so, both requirements will have to be spelled out. In this way, the firm's mission is translated into a set of objectives for the current period.

Designing the Business Portfolio

Business portfolio

The collection of businesses and products that make up the company.

Guided by the company's mission statement and objectives, management now must plan its **business portfolio**—the collection of businesses and products that make up the company. Some firms have relatively simple portfolios in terms of the number of businesses they run. EnCana, for example, headquartered in Calgary, is North America's leading natural gas producer. Its only other business is a closely related one, oil. Saskatchewan Wheat Pool, on the other hand, has a much more complex portfolio of businesses. It is an integrated, diversified business, fully or partially owning more than twenty affiliated companies, which process and market everything from fish, fertilizer, cattle, and ethanol to malt, canola oil, doughnuts, and newspapers.

The best business portfolio is the one that best fits the company's strengths and weaknesses to opportunities in the environment. Business portfolio planning involves two steps. First, the company must analyze its *current* business portfolio and decide which businesses should receive more, less, or no investment. Second, it must shape the *future* portfolio by developing strategies for growth and downsizing.

Analyzing the Current Business Portfolio

Portfolio analysis

The process by which management evaluates the products and businesses making up the company.

The major activity in strategic planning is business **portfolio analysis**, whereby management evaluates the products and businesses making up the company. The company will want to put strong resources into its more profitable businesses and phase down or drop its weaker ones.

Management's first step is to identify the key businesses making up the company. These can be called the strategic business units. A *strategic business unit* (SBU) is a unit of the company that has a separate mission and objectives and that can be planned independently from other company businesses. An SBU can be a company division, a product line within a division, or sometimes a single product or brand.

The next step in business portfolio analysis calls for management to assess the attractiveness of its various SBUs and decide how much support each deserves. Most companies are well advised to "stick to their knitting" when designing their business portfolios. It's usually a good idea to focus on adding products and businesses that fit closely with the firm's core philosophy and competencies.

The purpose of strategic planning is to find ways in which the company can best use its strengths to take advantage of attractive opportunities in the environment. So most standard portfolio-analysis methods evaluate SBUs on two important dimensions—the attractiveness of the SBU's market or industry and the strength of the SBU's position in that market or industry. The best-known portfolio-planning method was developed by the Boston Consulting Group, a leading management consulting firm.[5]

Growth-share matrix

A portfolio-planning method that evaluates a company's strategic business units in terms of its market growth rate and relative market share.

The Boston Consulting Group Approach Using the Boston Consulting Group (BCG) approach, a company classifies all its SBUs according to the **growth-share matrix** shown in Figure 2.2. On the vertical axis, *market growth rate* provides a measure of market attractiveness. On the horizontal axis, *relative market share* serves as a measure of company strength in the market. The growth-share matrix defines four types of SBUs.

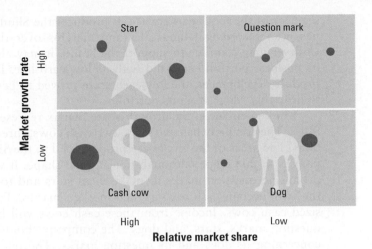

Figure 2.2 The BCG growth-share matrix

SBUs are classified as stars, cash cows, question marks, or dogs. International packaged goods firm, Unilever, whose Canadian operations are headquartered in Toronto, has a diverse range of businesses and brands. The BCG matrix is a useful tool that can help its managers think about the investment it should make in its major businesses.

Stars. Stars are high-growth, high-share businesses or products. They often need heavy investment to finance their rapid growth. Eventually their growth will slow down, and they will turn into cash cows. Over the past few years, Unilever has expanded its Dove business unit. While just a few years ago, this unit produced and marketed only bar soap, today the Dove business consists of a full range of personal care products that includes shampoos, conditioners, and styling products; face care products, such as its Essential Nutrients™; and body products, such as its body washes and anti-perspirants. This line of products commands a large share of the market and has been growing rapidly, largely because of its "Real Beauty" campaign.

Cash cows. Cash cows are low-growth, high-share businesses or products. These established and successful SBUs need less investment to hold their market share. Thus, they produce a lot of cash that the company uses to pay its bills and to support other SBUs that need investment. Unilever built its business around its spreads business. In Canada, the major brand within this business is Becel, which holds the largest market share of any Canadian margarine. The brand generates a lot of cash for the company, which it uses to support this brand as well as other initiatives, such as new product development.

Question marks. Question marks are low-share business units in high-growth markets. They require a lot of cash to hold their share, let alone increase it. Management has to think hard about which question marks it should try to build into stars and which should be phased out. Within its personal care division, Unilever has a number of shampoo businesses. Its ThermaSilk line of products has been struggling. Though the specialty shampoo category is growing, this brand has not done well and holds only a small share of the marketplace. In an attempt to turn the business from a question mark into a star, the Thermasilk brand may be dropped in favour of an entirely new line, Sunsilk, based on a similar technology and formulation. The Sunsilk line, however, is a colour-coded line designed to resolve hair problems such as frizziness, dryness, or split ends. Sunsilk has become the fastest-growing brand in Europe and was introduced into Canada in 2006, using a significant advertising campaign and promotional support.[6]

Dogs. Dogs are low-growth, low-share businesses and products. They may generate enough cash to maintain themselves but do not promise to be large sources of cash. Unilever has retained a single business unit in the increasingly competitive diet segment of the food marketplace. It produces the SlimFast brand, and the product has been recording falling sales and margins over the past few years. Though Unilever may continue to support the brand, it may also consider deleting it from its business portfolio as it did with its low-carb line. Despite heavy investment in product development, the low-carb craze proved to be a fad and Unilever decided to drop this "dog" from its portfolio.

The ten circles in the growth-share matrix represent a company's ten current SBUs. The company has two stars, two cash cows, three question marks, and three dogs. The areas of the circles are proportional to the SBU's dollar sales. This company is in fair shape, although not in good shape. It wants to invest in the more promising question marks to make them stars and to maintain the stars so that they will become cash cows as their markets mature. Fortunately, it has two good-sized cash cows. Income from these cash cows will help finance the company's question marks, stars, and dogs. The company should take some decisive action concerning its dogs and its question marks. The picture would be worse if the company had no stars, if it had too many dogs, or if it had only one weak cash cow.

Once it has classified its SBUs, the company must determine what role each will play in the future. One of four strategies can be pursued for each SBU. The company can invest more in the business unit in order to *build* its share. Or it can invest just enough to *hold* the SBU's share at the current level. It can *harvest* the SBU, milking its short-term cash flow regardless of the long-term effect. Finally, the company can *divest* the SBU by selling it or phasing it out and using the resources elsewhere.

As time passes, SBUs change their positions in the growth-share matrix. Each SBU has a life cycle. Many SBUs start out as question marks and move into the star category if they succeed. They later become cash cows as market growth falls, then finally die off or turn into dogs toward the end of their life cycle. The company needs to add new products and units continuously so that some of them will become stars and, eventually, cash cows that will help finance other SBUs.

Problems with Matrix Approaches   The BCG and other formal methods revolutionized strategic planning. However, such approaches have limitations. They can be difficult, time-consuming, and costly to implement. Management may find it difficult to define SBUs and measure market share and growth. In addition, these approaches focus on classifying *current* businesses but provide little advice for *future* planning.

Formal planning approaches can also place too much emphasis on market-share growth or growth through entry into attractive new markets. Using these approaches, many companies plunged into unrelated and new high-growth businesses that they did not know how to manage—with very bad results. At the same time, these companies were often too quick to abandon, sell, or milk to death their healthy mature businesses. As a result, many companies that diversified too broadly in the past now are narrowing their focus and getting back to the basics of serving one or a few industries that they know best.

Because of such problems, many companies have dropped formal matrix methods in favour of more customized approaches that are better suited to their specific situations. Unlike former strategic-planning efforts, which rested mostly in the hands of senior managers at company headquarters, today's strategic planning has been decentralized. Increasingly, companies are placing responsibility for strategic planning in the hands of cross-functional teams of managers who are close to their markets. Some teams even include customers and suppliers in their strategic-planning processes.

Developing Strategies for Growth and Downsizing

Beyond evaluating current businesses, designing the business portfolio involves finding businesses and products the company should consider in the future. Companies need growth if they are to compete more effectively, satisfy their stakeholders, and attract top talent. "Growth is pure oxygen," states one executive. "It creates a vital, enthusiastic corporation where people see genuine opportunity." At the same time, a firm must be careful not to make growth itself an objective. The company's objective must be "profitable growth."

Marketing has the main responsibility for achieving profitable growth for the company. Marketing must identify, evaluate, and select market opportunities and lay down strategies for capturing them. One useful device for identifying growth opportunities is the **product/market expansion grid**, shown in Figure 2.3.[7] We apply it here to Tim Hortons (see Real Marketing 2.1).

Tim Hortons' strategy is deceptively simple and has long been founded on **market penetration**. It works to open a critical mass of outlets in a predefined geographic region and then it supports them with advertising. Increased awareness and the building of strong brand equity in turn builds requests for new franchises—which is how Tim Hortons plans to continue expansion in both Quebec and western Canada. It also works to train people who come into Tim Hortons first thing in the morning for coffee and breakfast to return several times during the rest of the day. To that end, Hortons routinely upgrades and refurbishes its outlets, adding double drive-throughs and establishing satellite outlets in settings such as hospitals and retail stores—bringing the restaurant to the consumer instead of the other way around. "Wherever you are," says one top manager, "there's a coffee and a doughnut waiting for you."

Second, the firm explores possibilities for **market development**—identifying and developing new markets for its current products. For instance, managers could review new *demographic markets*. Perhaps new groups—such as senior consumers or ethnic groups—could be encouraged to visit Tim Hortons coffee shops for the first time or to buy more from them. Managers also could review new *geographical markets*. Tim Hortons has recently moved south of the border.

Third, Tim Hortons' management focuses on **product development**—offering modified or new products to current markets. Hortons introduced cappuccino, bagels, sandwiches, and soup to get consumers to see it as more than a doughnut shop.

Fourth, Hortons might consider **diversification**. It could start up or buy businesses outside of its current products and markets. For example, it might consider adding gas bars to complement its drive-through services. It could leverage its strong brand name onto products like sportswear that fit with its friendly, relaxed image. However, it must take care: Companies that diversify too broadly into unfamiliar products or industries can lose their market focus.

Product/market expansion grid
A portfolio-planning tool for identifying company growth opportunities through market penetration, market development, product development, or diversification.

Market penetration
A strategy for company growth by increasing sales of current products to current market segments without changing the product.

Market development
A strategy for company growth by identifying and developing new market segments for current company products.

Product development
A strategy for company growth by offering modified or new products to current market segments.

Diversification
A strategy for company growth through starting up or acquiring businesses outside the company's current products and markets.

	Existing products	New products
Existing markets	Market penetration	Product development
New markets	Market development	Diversification

Figure 2.3 The product/market expansion grid

REAL MARKETING

2.1

Tim Hortons: Where Things Are Really Perking

*C*anadians, it appears, *always have time for Tim Hortons.* Founded in 1964, the firm recently celebrated its fortieth anniversary. Generations of competitors have come and gone, but none have managed to defeat Hortons, headquartered in Oakville, Ontario. In fact, it has become a Canadian icon. Throughout its history, Hortons' marketing savvy has turned this once simple doughnut shop into a giant with 2651 outlets that generated $996 million in revenues in 2005. Today, Tim Hortons rivals McDonald's Canada for the number-one spot in terms of fast-food sales. If you narrow the marketplace to sales of Canadian coffee and baked goods, it controls a whopping 70 percent of the market. In recognition of its marketing prowess, *Strategy* magazine named it "Marketer of the Year" in 2002.

The dominance of the chain can be seen in these facts: one of every three cups of coffee sold in Canada comes from Tim Hortons, and 68 percent of Canadians identify Tim Hortons as their "most often" coffee brand. Forty-five percent of its customers visit the company's stores five to ten times each and every week, and every day Canadians dunk millions of Tim

Tim Hortons doesn't advertise until it has enough outlets in a region to justify the expense. It knows advertising has more impact when people can see its outlets in their daily travels.

Hortons doughnuts. Employing more than 55 000 people, Tim Hortons is one of Canada's largest employers.

Tim Hortons works relentlessly to build its brand, which has become an idealized image of the Canadian national character: friendly, neighbourly, unpretentious, gently playful, frugal, trustworthy, and, yes, clean. It brings this brand image to life by featuring real people in its ads—both customers and employees. "Tim Hortons never fakes it," notes Philippe Garneau, a partner at Toronto's Garneau Würstlin Philp Brand Engineering. Tim Hortons communicates its brand image through its "true stories" television vignettes, which are based on the best of hundreds of suggestions the company receives from its customers every year. Each story exemplifies the emotional relationship the customer has with Tim Hortons and portrays how Hortons fits into customers' daily lives.

The doughnut chain's long-running "Roll up the Rim to Win" promotion has become a beloved part of Canadian slang, and sketches set at Hortons are shown weekly on the comedy news show *Air Farce*. Some of the approximately $3 million a year that Hortons spends on advertising is also focused on its new products—bagels, sandwiches, and soup—to get consumers to see Tim Hortons as more than a doughnut shop. New products have also increased revenues for both the corporation and its franchisees.

As impressive as these figures are, one has to wonder what else Tim Hortons has done to achieve this success—after all, it really offers fairly standard products, such as coffee and baked goods. Hortons' strategy is deceptively simple. First, it has followed one consistent product and positioning strategy throughout its history. Its promise of "Always Fresh" is never broken, and it makes this promise concrete in many ways. For example, its new interactive digital menus identify products just as they are being taken out of the oven. Next, it builds outlets in focal areas until there are enough outlets in the area to justify advertising. As Patti Jameson, director of corporate communications, notes, "Advertising is a lot more relevant to people when they actually see the stores on the street."

Having the physical presence of a retail outlet made brand messages more relevant and meaningful.

Given Tim Hortons' track record, it's hard to imagine how it could expand any further (if your town is anything like mine). There seems to be an outlet on the corner of every major intersection. Yet even an institution needs to be willing to change and grow. And change is exactly what Hortons has done in recent years. In a bid to broaden its appeal and attract more women and young people, the chain has recently branched out into new product lines, such as iced cappuccino. It also retooled its lunchtime offerings, offering Tim's Own brand of soups and sandwiches.

The firm isn't about to stop there. Since Hortons believes that the breakfast category is underdeveloped in the U.S. and that Americans are poorly served by current "morning destinations," it sees tremendous opportunity south of the border. In 2006, it operated 310 outlets in the United States. "In the U.S., they don't have high expectations for morning destinations.... People will grab a coffee from a gas station in the morning, [but] we're promising that consistent experi-ence. No one else is really doing everyday morning coffee and baked goods very well." Two television spots and a series of radio ads each portray Tim Hortons as the real reason morning people are so chip-per. The tag line is: "Morning people. Where do they come from?" Although success in the highly competi-tive U.S. market is far from guaranteed, if the history of professional hockey offers any indication, then Americans may also soon be claiming this Canadian institution as their own.

Sources: Wendy's 2004 Summary Annual Report to Shareholders; Terry Poulton, Special Report: Top Clients 2002, "Long Live the Double Double," *Strategy*, July 29, 2002, p. 19; Natalie Bahadur, "Tim Hortons Plans Aggressive Roll-Out," *Strategy*, March 29, 1999, p. 7; Lesley Daw, "More Than Just a Doughnut Shop," *Marketing Magazine,* December 20/27, 1999, www.marketingmag.ca/; Scott Gardiner, "In Praise of Saint Timmy," *Marketing Magazine,* August 21, 2000, www.marketingmag.ca; Laura Pratt, "Roll Up the Rim Major Player for Tim Hortons," *Strategy*, May 22, 2000, p. 22; Craig Saunders, "Tim Hortons Issues Wakeup Call," *Strategy*, February 14, 2000, p. 25; Sinclair Stewart, "Top Client, Retail–Restaurants: Tim Hortons Brews Up Fresh Ideas," *Strategy*, August 2, 1999, p. 7; Sinclair Stewart, "Tim Hortons Brews New U.S. Campaign," *Strategy*, September 27, 1999, p. 3.

Downsizing

Reducing the business portfolio by eliminating products or business units that are not profitable or that no longer fit the company's overall strategy.

Companies must not only develop strategies for *growing* their business portfolios but also strategies for **downsizing** them. There are many reasons that a firm might want to abandon products or markets. The market environment might change, making some of the company's products or markets less profitable. The firm may have grown too fast or entered areas where it lacks experience. This can occur when a firm enters too many foreign markets without the proper research or when a company introduces new products that do not offer superior customer value. Finally, some products or business units simply age and die. One marketing expert summarizes the problem this way:

Companies spend vast amounts of money and time launching new brands, leveraging existing ones, and acquiring rivals. They create line extensions and brand extensions, not to mention channel extensions and sub-brands, to cater to the growing number of niche segments in every market.... Surprisingly, most businesses do not examine their brand portfolios from time to time to check if they might be selling too many brands, identify weak ones, and kill unprofitable ones. They tend to ignore loss-making brands rather than merge them with healthy brands, sell them off, or drop them. Consequently, most portfolios have become [jammed] with loss-making and marginally profitable brands. Moreover, the surprising truth is that most brands don't make money for companies. Many corporations generate fewer than 80 to 90 percent of their profits from fewer than 20 percent of the brands they sell, while they lose money or barely break even on many of the other brands in their portfolios.[8]

When a firm finds brands or businesses that are unprofitable or that no longer fit its overall strategy, it must carefully prune, harvest, or divest them. Weak busi-nesses usually require a disproportionate amount of management attention. Managers should focus on promising growth opportunities, not fritter away energy trying to salvage fading ones.

Planning Marketing: Partnering to Build Customer Relationships

The company's strategic plan establishes what kinds of businesses the company will be in and its objectives for each. Then, within each business unit, more detailed planning takes place. The major functional departments in each unit—marketing, finance, accounting, purchasing, operations, information systems, human resources, and others—must work together to accomplish strategic objectives.

Marketing plays a key role in the company's strategic planning in several ways. First, marketing provides a guiding *philosophy*—the marketing concept—that suggests that company strategy should revolve around building profitable relationships with important consumer groups. Second, marketing provides *inputs* to strategic planners by helping to identify attractive market opportunities and by assessing the firm's potential to take advantage of them. Finally, within individual business units, marketing designs *strategies* for reaching the unit's objectives. Once the unit's objectives are set, marketing's task is to help carry them out profitably.

Customer value and satisfaction are important ingredients in the marketer's formula for success. However, as we noted in Chapter 1, marketers alone cannot produce superior value for customers. Although it plays a leading role, marketing can be only a partner in attracting, keeping, and growing customers. In addition to *customer relationship management*, marketers must also practise *partner relationship management*. They must work closely with partners in other company departments to form an effective *value chain* that serves the customer. Moreover, they must partner effectively with other companies in the marketing system to form a competitively superior *value-delivery network*. We now take a closer look at the concepts of a company value chain and value-delivery network.

Partnering with Other Company Departments

Value chain
The series of departments that carry out value-creating activities to design, produce, market, deliver, and support a firm's products.

Each company department can be thought of as a link in the company's **value chain**.[9] That is, each department carries out value-creating activities to design, produce, market, deliver, and support the firm's products. The firm's success depends not only on how well each department performs its work but also on how well the activities of various departments are coordinated.

For example, Wal-Mart's goal is to create customer value and satisfaction by providing shoppers with the products they want at the lowest possible prices. Marketers at Wal-Mart play an important role. They learn what customers need and stock the store's shelves with the desired products at unbeatable low prices. They prepare advertising and merchandising programs and assist shoppers with customer service. Through these and other activities, Wal-Mart's marketers help deliver value to customers.

However, the marketing department needs help from the company's other departments. Wal-Mart's ability to offer the right products at low prices depends on the purchasing department's skill in developing the needed suppliers and buying from them at low cost. Wal-Mart's information technology department must provide fast and accurate information about which products are selling in each store. And its operations people must provide effective, low-cost merchandise handling.

A company's value chain is only as strong as its weakest link. Success depends on how well each department performs its work of adding customer value and on how well the activities of various departments are coordinated. At Wal-Mart, if purchasing can't wring the lowest prices from suppliers, or if operations can't distribute merchandise at the lowest costs, then marketing can't deliver on its promise of lowest prices.

Wal-Mart's ability to offer the right products at low prices depends on the contributions of people in all of the company's departments—marketing, purchasing, information systems, and operations.

Ideally, then, a company's different functions should work in harmony to produce value for consumers. But, in practice, departmental relations are full of conflicts and misunderstandings. The marketing department takes the consumer's point of view. But when marketing tries to develop customer satisfaction, it can cause other departments to do a poorer job *in their terms*. Marketing department actions can increase purchasing costs, disrupt production schedules, increase inventories, and create budget headaches. Thus, the other departments may resist the marketing department's efforts.

Yet marketers must find ways to get all departments to "think consumer" and to develop a smoothly functioning value chain. Marketing management can best gain support for its goal of customer satisfaction by working to understand the company's other departments. Marketing managers need to work closely with managers of other functions to develop a system of functional plans under which the different departments can work together to accomplish the company's overall strategic objectives.

Jack Welch, General Electric's highly regarded former CEO, told his employees: "Companies can't give job security. Only customers can!" He emphasized that all General Electric employees, regardless of their department, have an impact on customer satisfaction and retention. His message: "If you are not thinking customer, you are not thinking."[10]

Partnering with Others in the Marketing System

In its quest to create customer value, the firm needs to look beyond its own value chain and into the value chains of its suppliers, distributors, and, ultimately, customers. Consider McDonald's. People do not swarm to McDonald's only because they love the chain's hamburgers. Consumers flock to the McDonald's *system*, not just to its food products. Throughout the world, McDonald's finely tuned system delivers a high standard of what the company calls QSCV—quality, service, cleanliness, and value. McDonald's is effective only to the extent that it successfully partners with its franchisees, suppliers, and others to jointly deliver exceptionally high customer value.[11]

See how Canadian Tire uses partnerships with suppliers to enhance customer value:

Canadian Tire recently entered into an agreement with NAPA Canada, a distributor of automotive replacement parts. Using parts-ordering and automated-inventory technology, Napa now supplies Canadian Tire stores with emergency parts and automotive products not normally kept in stock. The agreement allows Canadian Tire to continue grow its automotive product and service organization without adding the infrastructure and inventory costs associated with low-volume products while allowing Canadian Tire to significantly enhance the services it offers automotive customers.[12]

Value-delivery network
The network made up of the company, suppliers, distributors, and ultimately customers who "partner" with one another to improve the performance of the entire system.

More companies today are partnering with the other members of the supply chain to improve the performance of the customer **value-delivery network**. For example, Honda has designed a program for working closely with its suppliers to help them reduce their costs and improve quality. When Honda chose Magna Donnelly Corporation to supply all of the mirrors for its cars, it sent engineers swarming over the supplier's plants, looking for ways to improve its products and operations. This helped Magna Donnelly reduce its costs by 2 percent in the first year. As a result of its improved performance, its sales to Honda grew from $5 million annually to more than $60 million in less than 10 years. In turn, Honda gained an efficient, low-cost supplier of quality components. And Honda customers received greater value in the form of lower-cost, higher-quality cars.[13]

Increasingly in today's marketplace, competition no longer takes place between individual competitors. Rather, it takes place between the entire value-delivery networks created by these competitors. Thus, Honda's performance against Toyota depends on the quality of Honda's overall value-delivery network versus Toyota's. Even if Honda makes the best cars, it might lose in the marketplace if Toyota's dealer network provides more customer-satisfying sales and service.

Toyota and its dealers must work together to sell cars. Toyota makes good cars and builds the brand; dealerships like Modern Toyota bring value to customers and communities.

Marketing Strategy and the Marketing Mix

The strategic plan defines the company's overall mission and objectives. Marketing's role and activities are shown in Figure 2.4, which summarizes the major activities involved in managing marketing strategy and the marketing mix.

Marketing strategy
The marketing logic by which the business unit hopes to achieve its marketing objectives.

Consumers stand in the centre. The goal is to build strong and profitable customer relationships. Next comes **marketing strategy**—the marketing logic by which the company hopes to achieve these profitable relationships. Through market segmentation, targeting, and positioning, the company decides which customers it will serve and how. It identifies the total market, then divides it into smaller segments, selects the most promising segments, and focuses on serving and satisfying customers in these segments.

Guided by marketing strategy, the company designs a marketing mix made up of factors under its control—product, price, place, and promotion. To find the best marketing strategy and mix, the company engages in marketing analysis, planning, implementation, and control. Through these activities, the company watches and adapts to the actors and forces in the marketing environment.

We will now look briefly at each activity. Then, in later chapters, we will discuss each one in more depth.

Customer-Centred Marketing Strategy

As we emphasized throughout Chapter 1, to succeed in today's competitive marketplace, companies need to be customer centred. They must win customers from competitors, then keep and grow them by delivering greater value. But before it can satisfy consumers, a company must first understand their needs and wants. Thus, sound marketing requires a careful customer analysis.

Companies know that they cannot profitably serve all consumers in a given market—at least not all consumers in the same way. There are too many different kinds of consumers with too many different kinds of needs. And most companies

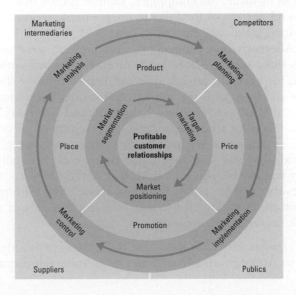

Figure 2.4 Managing marketing strategy and the marketing mix

are in a position to serve some segments better than others. Thus, each company must divide up the total market, choose the best segments, and design strategies for profitably serving chosen segments. This process involves three steps: *market segmentation*, *target marketing*, and *market positioning*.

Market Segmentation

The market consists of many types of customers, products, and needs. The marketer has to determine which segments offer the best opportunity for achieving company objectives. Consumers can be grouped and served in various ways based on geographic, demographic, psychographic, and behavioural factors. The process of dividing a market into distinct groups of buyers with different needs, characteristics, or behaviour who might require separate products or marketing programs is called **market segmentation**.

Every market has segments, but not all ways of segmenting a market are equally useful. For example, Tylenol would gain little by distinguishing between male and female users of pain relievers if both respond the same way to marketing efforts. A **market segment** consists of consumers who respond in a similar way to a given set of marketing efforts. In the car market, for example, consumers who want the biggest, most comfortable car regardless of price make up one market segment. Customers who care mainly about price and operating economy make up another segment. It would be difficult to make one car model that was the first choice of consumers in both segments. Companies are wise to focus their efforts on meeting the distinct needs of individual market segments.

Target Marketing

After a company has defined market segments, it can enter one or many segments of a given market. **Target marketing** involves evaluating each market segment's attractiveness and selecting one or more segments to enter. A company should target segments in which it can profitably generate the greatest customer value and sustain it over time.

A company with limited resources might decide to serve only one or a few special segments or "market niches." Such "nichers" specialize in serving market segments that major competitors overlook or ignore. For example, Arm & Hammer has a lock on the baking soda corner of most consumer goods categories, including toothpaste, deodorizers, and others. Oshkosh Truck has found its niche as the world's largest producer of airport rescue trucks and front-loading concrete mixers. And in its niche, the Philippines, Jollibee proves that small can be beautiful. It captures 65 percent of the Filipino burger market, dominating McDonald's and other fast-food giants (see Real Marketing 2.2).

Alternatively, a company might choose to serve several related segments—perhaps those with different kinds of customers but with the same basic wants. The GAP, for example, targets male and female clothing shoppers, kids, and female lingerie shoppers with the same casual-themed merchandise in different outlets: the original GAP, GAPkids and babyGAP, and GAPbody. Or a large company might decide to offer a complete range of products to serve all market segments. Most companies enter a new market by serving a single segment, and if this proves successful, they add segments. Large companies eventually seek full market coverage. They want to be the General Motors of their industry. GM says that it makes a car for every "person, purse, and personality." The leading company normally has different products designed to meet the special needs of each segment. See how Sun-Rype Products Ltd. evolved:[14]

> Headquartered in Kelowna, B.C., the firm's modern-day performance reflects its use of product-based and geographic segmentation. It began as a regional

---

Market segmentation
Dividing a market into distinct groups of buyers who have distinct needs, characteristics, or behaviour and who might require separate products or marketing mixes.

Market segment
A group of consumers who respond in a similar way to a given set of marketing efforts.

Target marketing
The process of evaluating each market segment's attractiveness and selecting one or more segments to enter.

REAL MARKETING | 2.2

Jollibee vs. McDonald's: Small Can Be Beautiful

When someone says "fast-food restaurant," what's the first name that comes to mind? Chances are its McDonald's, the world's largest food service organization. McDonald's holds a 43 percent share of the U.S. fast-food burger market, many times the share of its nearest competitor. Ask the same question in the Philippines, however, and the first name uttered will likely be Jollibee. That's right, Jollibee. In the grand scheme of global commerce, Jollibee Foods Corporation isn't exactly a household name. But in its niche, the Philippines, it's king of the burger market. "If McDonald's is the Goliath of fast food," notes one industry analyst, "Jollibee is its Filipino David."

At first glance, the rivalry between Jollibee and McDonald's looks like no contest. McDonald's has more than 30 000 outlets in more than 100 countries, more than 3000 of them in Asia alone, and more than US$50 billion in annual system-wide sales. By comparison, Jollibee has only about 400 restaurants, contributing about US$516 million in annual revenues. Its sales equal less than half of the US$1.3 billion or more that McDonald's spends annually just on U.S. advertising. When the first golden arches went up in Manila in

Market nicher Jollibee is king of the burger market in the Philippines. The Jollibee burger is similar to "what a Filipino mother would cook at home."

1981, everyone assumed that McDonald's would dominate in the Philippines as it has everywhere else.

But despite these lopsided numbers, in the Philippines, small Jollibee has humbled the global giant. Jollibee captures a 65 percent share of the Philippines' hamburger market, more than half of the fast-food market as a whole, and about twice McDonald's sales in the country. Its revenues are growing rapidly and profitably. What's Jollibee's secret? Smart niching. Whereas McDonald's exports largely standardized fare to consumers around the world, Jollibee is relentlessly local—it concentrates on serving the unique tastes of Filipino consumers.

In many ways, Jollibee's operations mirror those of McDonald's: both offer cleanliness, fast service, and convenient locations. Jollibee's Champ burger competes with the Big Mac, and its peach-mango pie replicates McDonald's apple version. However, in contrast to the fairly bland fare that McDonald's serves so successfully worldwide, Jollibee's menu and flavours are specially suited to Filipino tastes. The local chain cooks up sweet, spicy burgers and serves seasoned chicken and spaghetti with sweet sauce, the way Filipinos like it. It serves these meals with rice or noodles, not french fries. "We've designed these products, which are really all-American delights, to suit the Filipino palate," says Jollibee's marketing vice-president. Some items, however, are uniquely Filipino. For example, Jollibee's Palabok Fiesta meal, featuring bihon noodles topped with pork-shrimp sauce and garnished with flaked smoked fish, is very popular in the Philippines. Most Americans wouldn't like it because it smells of fish.

Beyond its special understanding of the Filipino palate, Jollibee has also mastered the country's culture and lifestyle. "What happens in the normal Filipino family is that weekends are especially for children," notes a Philippine business analyst, "and parents try to ask their children where they want to eat." Jollibee lures kids with in-store play activities and a cast of captivating characters. Its hamburger-headed Champ, complete with boxing gloves, goes head-to-head with McDonald's Hamburglar. And its massive orange-jacketed Jolly Bee character and a blonde spaghetti-haired girl named Hetti are better known and loved in the Philippines than Ronald McDonald.

The well-known Jolly Bee character epitomizes the Filipino spirit of lighthearted, everyday happiness. Like Filipino working people, explains Jollibee CEO Tony Tan, "the bee hops around and produces sweet things for life, and is happy even though it is busy." Indeed, the company's "jolliness is infectious," says the analyst. It's "as much a part of [the chain's] success as its recipes. Jollibee's staff outsmile McDonald's by a huge stretch. [They recently] started greeting customers with a gesture adopted from the sign language of the deaf—a vertical stroke for 'bee' and hands shovelling towards the heart for 'happy'—which kids have now started using on playgrounds. Jollibee staff call customers and one another 'sir' and 'mom,' which is at once casual and respectful in the Philippines.... Everyone at Jollibee projects fun."

Jollibee has some additional advantages in this seemingly unfair rivalry. Although much smaller in global terms than McDonald's, Jollibee concentrates most of its limited resources within the Philippines, where its restaurants outnumber McDonald's two to one. But its primary advantage comes from simply doing a better job of giving Filipino consumers what they want. Notes the analyst, "The Jollibee burger is similar to what a Filipino mother would cook at home."

So, small can be beautiful. Jollibee has shown that, through smart niching, small players can compete effectively against industry giants.

Sources: See "Happy Meals for McDonald's Rival," *Business Week,* July 29, 1996, p. 77; Cris Prystay and Sanjay Kumar, "Asia Bites Back," *Asian Business,* January 1997, pp. 58–60; Dominic Jones and Nicholas Bradbury, "Blue Chips of the Future," *Euromoney,* December 1998, pp. 99–102; "McDonald's Sales Momentum Continues," McDonald's press release, February 17, 2004, www.mcdonalds.com/corp/news/fnpr/fpr_03052004.html; Rizzarene S. Manrique, "Special Report: Industry Report (Hotels and Restaurants):[8]," *BusinessWorld,* March 3, 2004, p. 1; "Retail Brief Jollibee Foods Corporation," *Wall Street Journal,* February 18, 2004, p. 1; "Good Food, Family and Happiness," *BusinessWorld,* February 24, 2004, p. 1; and "Our Company: The Jollibee Phenomenon," www.jollibee.com.ph/corporate/phenomenon.htm (accessed November 2004).

player, and thus it's not surprising that the Sun-Rype brand is the number-one player, with a 55 percent share of the pure apple juice category in Western Canada. Over the years, however, Sun-Rype has added other related products—more juice varieties and other fruit-based products, such as its Fruit to Go and Energy to Go products. Sun-Rype learned to stick to strategies based on its core competencies the hard way. In the mid-1990s, Sun-Rype strayed from its apple-and-fruit-based strengths and tried coffee-flavoured snack bars and granola-type bars. Because the products were outside of Sun-Rype's realm of expertise, their lives were short. "We're now focused on our core competencies of fruit-based juices and snacks," stressed marketing vice-president Cameron Johnston. While diversifying from juices to fruit-based snacks was

Sun-Rype's strategy has been one of leveraging its core competencies to expand its product and geographic markets.

a wise fiscal and consumer move, over-diversifying to coffee and grain snacks was a mistake." With its product strategy now firmly entrenched, Sun-Rype is expanding its share of central and eastern Canadian marketplaces, and its Fruit to Go and Energy to Go bars command a 31 percent share of this broader market.

Market Positioning

After a company has decided which market segments to enter, it must decide what positions it wants to occupy in those segments. A product's *position* is the place the product occupies relative to competitors in consumers' minds. Marketers want to develop unique market positions for their products. If a product is perceived to be exactly like others on the market, consumers would have no reason to buy it.

Market positioning is arranging for a product to occupy a clear, distinctive, and desirable place relative to competing products in the minds of target consumers. Thus, marketers plan positions that distinguish their products from competing brands and give them the greatest strategic advantage in their target markets. For example, Saturn is "a different kind of company, different kind of car"; the Hummer is "like nothing else"; and Toyota's hybrid Prius provides "a lifetime of fresh air with every purchase." The luxurious Bentley promises "18 handcrafted feet of shameless luxury." Such deceptively simple statements form the backbone of a product's marketing strategy.

Market positioning
Arranging for a product to occupy a clear, distinctive, and desirable place relative to competing products in the minds of target consumers.

Toyota's Prius is "a revelation brilliantly disguised as a car." The Hummer is "like nothing else—need is a very subjective word."

In positioning its product, the company first identifies possible competitive advantages upon which to build the position. To gain competitive advantage, the company must offer greater value to target consumers. It can do this either by charging lower prices than competitors do or by offering more benefits to justify higher prices. But if the company positions the product as *offering* greater value, it must then *deliver* that greater value. Thus, effective positioning begins with actually *differentiating* the company's marketing offer so that it gives consumers more value. Once the company has chosen a desired position, it must take strong steps to deliver and communicate that position to target consumers. The company's entire marketing program should support the chosen positioning strategy.

Developing the Marketing Mix

Marketing mix
The set of controllable tactical marketing tools—product, price, place, and promotion—that the firm blends to produce the response it wants in the target market.

Once the company has decided on its overall marketing strategy, it is ready to begin planning the details of the marketing mix, one of the major concepts in modern marketing. The **marketing mix** is the set of controllable, tactical marketing tools that the firm blends to produce the response it wants in the target market. The marketing mix consists of everything the firm can do to influence the demand for its product. The many possibilities can be collected into four groups of variables known as the "four *Ps*": *product*, *price*, *place*, and *promotion*. Figure 2.5 shows the particular marketing tools under each *P*.

Product means the goods-and-services combination the company offers to the target market. Thus, a Ford Taurus product consists of nuts and bolts, spark plugs, pistons, headlights, and thousands of other parts. Ford offers several Taurus styles and dozens of optional features. The car comes fully serviced and with a comprehensive warranty that is as much a part of the product as the tailpipe.

Price is the amount of money customers have to pay to obtain the product. Ford calculates suggested retail prices that its dealers might charge for each Taurus. But Ford dealers rarely charge the full sticker price. Instead, they negotiate the price with each customer, offering discounts, trade-in allowances, and credit terms. These actions adjust prices for the current competitive situation and bring them into line with the buyer's perception of the car's value.

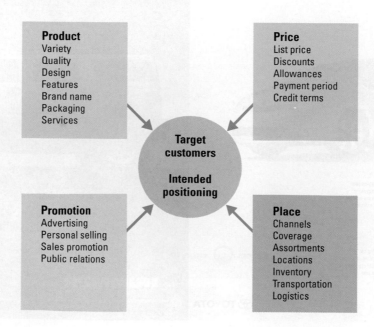

Figure 2.5 The four *Ps* of the marketing mix

Place includes company activities that make the product available to target consumers. Ford partners with a large body of independently owned dealerships that sell the company's many different models. Ford selects its dealers carefully and supports them strongly. The dealers keep an inventory of Ford automobiles, demonstrate them to potential buyers, negotiate prices, close sales, and service the cars after the sale.

Promotion means activities that communicate the merits of the product and persuade target customers to buy it. Ford spends more than US$2.2 billion each year on advertising, just less than US$755 per car sold, to tell consumers about the company and its many products.[15] Dealership salespeople assist potential buyers and persuade them that Ford is the best car for them. Ford and its dealers offer special promotions—sales, cash rebates, low financing rates—as added purchase incentives.

An effective marketing program blends all of the marketing mix elements into a coordinated program designed to achieve the company's marketing objectives by delivering value to consumers. The marketing mix constitutes the company's tactical tool kit for establishing strong positioning in target markets.

Some critics feel that the four Ps may omit or underemphasize certain important activities. For example, they ask, "Where are services?" Just because they don't start with a P doesn't justify omitting them. The answer is that services, such as banking, airline, and retailing services, are products too. We might call them *service products*. "Where is packaging?" the critics might ask. Marketers would answer that they include packaging as just one of many product decisions. All said, as Figure 2.5 suggests, many marketing activities that might appear to be left out of the marketing mix are subsumed under one of the four Ps. The issue is not whether there should be four, six, or ten Ps so much as what framework is most helpful in designing marketing programs.

There is another concern, however, that is valid. It holds that the four Ps concept takes the seller's view of the market, not the buyer's view. From the buyer's viewpoint, in this age of customer relationships, the four Ps might be better described as the four Cs:[16]

4Ps	4Cs
Product	Customer solution
Price	Customer cost
Place	Convenience
Promotion	Communication

Thus, while marketers see themselves as selling products, customers see themselves as buying value or solutions to their problems. And customers are interested in more than just the price; they are interested in the total costs of obtaining, using, and disposing of a product. Customers want the product and service to be as conveniently available as possible. Finally, they want two-way communication. Marketers would do well to think through the four Cs first and then build the four Ps on that platform.

Managing the Marketing Effort

In addition to being good at the *marketing* in marketing management, companies also need to pay attention to the *management*. Managing the marketing process requires the four marketing management functions shown in Figure 2.6—*analysis*, *planning*, *implementation*, and *control*. The company first develops companywide

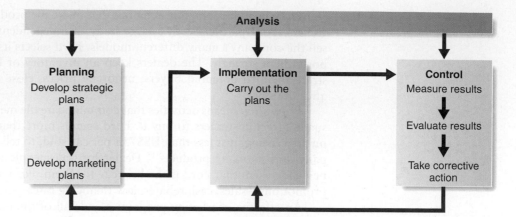

Figure 2.6 Marketing analysis, planning, implementation, and control

strategic plans, and then translates them into marketing and other plans for each division, product, and brand. Through implementation, the company turns the plans into actions. Control consists of measuring and evaluating the results of marketing activities and taking corrective action where needed. Finally, marketing analysis provides information and evaluations needed for all of the other marketing activities.

Marketing Analysis

Managing the marketing function begins with a complete analysis of the company's situation. The company must analyze its markets and marketing environment to find attractive opportunities and avoid environmental threats. It must analyze company strengths and weaknesses as well as current and possible marketing actions to determine which opportunities it can best pursue. Marketing provides input to each of the other marketing management functions. We discuss marketing analysis more fully in Chapter 3.

Marketing Planning

Through strategic planning, the company decides what it wants to do with each business unit. Marketing planning involves deciding on marketing strategies that will help the company attain its overall strategic objectives. A detailed marketing plan is needed for each business, product, or brand. What does a marketing plan look like? Our discussion focuses on product or brand plans.

Table 2.2 outlines the major sections of a typical product or brand plan. (See Appendix 2 for a sample marketing plan.) The plan begins with an executive summary, which quickly overviews major assessments, goals, and recommendations. The main section of the plan presents a detailed analysis of the current marketing situation as well as potential threats and opportunities. It next states major objectives for the brand and outlines the specifics of a marketing strategy for achieving them.

A *marketing strategy* consists of specific strategies for target markets, positioning, the marketing mix, and marketing expenditure levels. In this section, the planner explains how each strategy responds to the threats, opportunities, and critical issues spelled out earlier in the plan. Additional sections of the marketing plan lay out an action program for implementing the marketing strategy along with the details of a supporting marketing budget. The last section outlines the controls that will be used to monitor progress and take corrective action.

Table 2.2 Contents of a Marketing Plan

Section	Purpose
Executive summary	Presents a brief summary of the main goals and recommendations of the plan for management review, helping top management to find the plan's major points quickly. A table of contents should follow the executive summary.
Current marketing situation	Describes the target market and company's position in it, including information about the market, product performance, competition, and distribution. This section includes:
	• A *market description* that defines the market and major segments, then reviews customer needs and factors in the marketing environment that may affect customer purchasing.
	• A *product review,* that shows sales, prices, and gross margins of the major products in the product line.
	• A review of *competition,* which identifies major competitors and assesses their market positions and strategies for product quality, pricing, distribution, and promotion.
	• A review of *distribution,* which evaluates recent sales trends and other developments in major distribution channels.
Threats and opportunities analysis	Assesses major threats and opportunities that the product might face, helping management to anticipate important positive or negative developments that might have an impact on the firm and its strategies.
Objectives and issues	States the marketing objectives that the company would like to attain during the plan's term and discusses key issues that will affect their attainment. For example, if the goal is to achieve a 15 percent market share, this section looks at how this goal might be achieved.
Marketing strategy	Outlines the broad marketing logic by which the business unit hopes to achieve its marketing objectives and the specifics of target markets, positioning, and marketing expenditure levels. It outlines specific strategies for each marketing-mix element and explains how each responds to the threats, opportunities, and critical issues spelled out earlier in the plan.
Action programs	Spells out how marketing strategies will be turned into specific action programs that answer the following questions: *What* will be done? *When* will it be done? *Who* is responsible for doing it? *How* much will it cost?
Budgets	Details a supporting marketing budget that is essentially a projected profit-and-loss statement. It shows expected revenues (forecasted number of units sold and the average net price) and expected costs (of production, distribution, and marketing). The difference is the projected profit. Once approved by higher management, the budget becomes the basis for materials buying, production scheduling, personnel planning, and marketing operations.
Controls	Outlines the control that will be used to monitor progress and allow higher management to review implementation results and spot products that are not meeting their goals.

Note: Log on to your Companion Website at www.pearsoned.ca/kotler to view a full marketing plan. See also the Comprehensive Case in Appendix 1 on the Rocky Mountain Soap Company to practise developing a plan for the company.

Marketing Implementation

Planning good strategies is only a start toward successful marketing. A brilliant marketing strategy counts for little if the company fails to implement it properly. **Marketing implementation** is the process that turns marketing *plans* into marketing *actions* in order to accomplish strategic marketing objectives. Implementation involves day-to-day, month-to-month activities that effectively put the marketing plan to work. Whereas marketing planning addresses the *what* and *why* of marketing activities, implementation addresses the *who, where, when,* and *how.*

Marketing implementation
The process that turns marketing strategies and plans into marketing actions in order to accomplish strategic marketing objectives.

Many managers think that "doing things right" (implementation) is as important as, or even more important than, "doing the right things" (strategy). The fact is that both are critical to success, and companies can gain competitive advantages through effective implementation. One firm can have essentially the same strategy as another, yet win in the marketplace through faster or better execution. Still, implementation is difficult—it is often easier to think up good marketing strategies than it is to carry them out.

In an increasingly connected world, people at all levels of the marketing system must work together to implement marketing strategies and plans. At Black & Decker, for example, marketing implementation for the company's power tool products requires day-to-day decisions and actions by thousands of people both inside and outside the organization. Marketing managers make decisions about target segments, branding, packaging, pricing, promoting, and distributing. They talk with engineering about product design, with manufacturing about production and inventory levels, and with finance about funding and cash flows. They also connect with outside people, such as advertising agencies to plan ad campaigns and the media to obtain publicity support. The sales force urges Home Depot, Wal-Mart, and other retailers to advertise Black & Decker products, provide ample shelf space, and use company displays.

Successful marketing implementation depends on how well the company blends its people, organizational structure, decision and reward systems, and company culture into a cohesive action program that supports its strategies. At all levels, the company must be staffed by people who have the needed skills, motivation, and personal characteristics. The company's formal organization structure plays an important role in implementing marketing strategy; so do its decision and reward systems. For example, if a company's compensation system rewards managers for short-run profit results, they will have little incentive to work toward long-run market-building objectives.

Finally, to be successfully implemented, the firm's marketing strategies must fit with its company culture—the system of values and beliefs shared by people in the organization. A study of America's most successful companies found that these companies have almost cultlike cultures built around strong, market-oriented missions. At companies such as Wal-Mart, Dell, Microsoft, Nordstrom, Citicorp, Procter & Gamble, and Walt Disney, "employees share such a strong vision that they know in their hearts what's right for their company."[17]

Marketing Department Organization

The company must design a marketing organization that can carry out marketing strategies and plans. If the company is very small, one person might do all of the research, selling, advertising, customer service, and other marketing work. As the company expands, a marketing department emerges to plan and carry out marketing activities. In large companies, this department contains many specialists. Thus, Black & Decker has product and market managers, sales managers and salespeople, market researchers, advertising experts, and many other specialists.

Modern marketing departments can be arranged in several ways. The most common form of marketing organization is the *functional organization*. Under this organization, different marketing activities are headed by a functional specialist—a sales manager, advertising manager, marketing research manager, customer service manager, or new-product manager. A company that sells across the country or internationally often uses a *geographic organization*. Its sales and marketing people are assigned to specific countries, regions, and districts. Geographic organization allows salespeople to settle into a territory, get to know their customers, and work with a minimum of travel time and cost.

Companies with many very different products or brands often create a *product management organization*. Using this approach, a product manager develops and implements a complete strategy and marketing program for a specific product or brand. Product management first appeared at Procter & Gamble in 1929. A new company soap, Camay, was not doing well, and a young P&G executive was assigned to give his exclusive attention to developing and promoting this product. He was successful, and the company soon added other product managers.[18] Since then, many firms, especially consumer products companies, have set up product management organizations.

For companies that sell one product line to many different types of markets and customers that have different needs and preferences, a *market* or *customer management organization* might be best. A market management organization is similar to the product management organization. Market managers are responsible for developing marketing strategies and plans for their specific markets or customers. This system's main advantage is that the company is organized around the needs of specific customer segments.

Large companies that produce many different products flowing into many different geographic and customer markets usually employ some *combination* of the functional, geographic, product, and market organization forms. This ensures that each function, product, and market receives its share of management attention. However, it can also add costly layers of management and reduce organizational flexibility. Still, the benefits of organizational specialization usually outweigh the drawbacks.

Marketing organization has become an increasingly important issue in recent years. As we discussed in Chapter 1, many companies are finding that today's marketing environment calls for less focus on products, brands, and territories and more focus on customers and customer relationships. More and more companies are shifting their brand management focus toward *customer management*—moving away from managing just product or brand profitability and toward managing customer profitability and customer equity.[19] And many companies now organize their marketing operations around major customers. For example, companies such as Procter & Gamble, Black & Decker, and Newell Rubbermaid have large teams, or even whole divisions, set up to serve large customers like Wal-Mart, Loblaws, or Home Depot.

Marketing Control

Marketing control
The process of measuring and evaluating the results of marketing strategies and plans, and taking corrective action to ensure that objectives are achieved.

Because many surprises occur during the implementation of marketing plans, the marketing department must practise constant marketing control. **Marketing control** involves evaluating the results of marketing strategies and plans and taking corrective action to ensure that objectives are attained. Marketing control involves four steps. Management first sets specific marketing goals. It then measures its performance in the marketplace and evaluates the causes of any differences between expected and actual performance. Finally, management takes corrective action to close the gaps between its goals and its performance. This may require changing the action programs or even changing the goals.

Operating control involves checking ongoing performance against the annual plan and taking corrective action when necessary. Its purpose is to ensure that the company achieves the sales, profits, and other goals set out in its annual plan. It also involves determining the profitability of different products, territories, markets, and channels.

Strategic control involves looking at whether the company's basic strategies are well matched to its opportunities. Marketing strategies and programs can quickly become outdated, and each company should periodically reassess its overall

Marketing audit
A comprehensive, systematic, independent, and periodic examination of a company's environment, objectives, strategies, and activities to determine problem areas and opportunities and to recommend a plan of action to improve the company's marketing performance.

approach to the marketplace. A major tool for such strategic control is a marketing audit. The **marketing audit** is a comprehensive, systematic, independent, and periodic examination of a company's environment, objectives, strategies, and activities to determine problem areas and opportunities. The audit provides good input for a plan of action to improve the company's marketing performance.[20]

The marketing audit covers *all* major marketing areas of a business, not just a few trouble spots. It assesses the marketing environment, marketing strategy, marketing organization, marketing systems, marketing mix, and marketing productivity and profitability. The audit is normally conducted by an objective and experienced outside party. The findings may come as a surprise—and sometimes as a shock—to management. Management then decides which actions make sense and how and when to implement them.

The Marketing Environment

Managing the marketing function would be hard enough if the marketer had to deal only with the controllable marketing mix variables. But the company operates in a complex marketing environment, consisting of uncontrollable forces to which the company must adapt. The environment produces both threats and opportunities. The company must carefully analyze its environment so that it can avoid the threats and take advantage of the opportunities.

The company's marketing environment includes forces close to the company that affect its ability to serve consumers, such as other company departments, channel members, suppliers, competitors, and publics. It also includes broader demographic and economic forces, political and legal forces, technological and ecological forces, and social and cultural forces. Marketers need to consider all of these forces in the process of building and maintaining profitable relationships with customers and marketing partners. We will examine the marketing environment more fully in Chapter 3.

Measuring and Managing Return on Marketing

Return on marketing (or marketing ROI)
The net return from a marketing investment divided by the costs of the marketing investment.

Marketing managers must ensure that their marketing dollars are being well spent. In the past, many marketers spent freely on big advertising campaigns and other expensive marketing programs, often without thinking carefully about the financial returns on their spending. They believed that marketing produces intangible outcomes, which do not lend themselves readily to measures of productivity or return. "Many believe marketing is essentially creative and that, consequently, its financial returns are not measurable," notes one analyst. "Measuring and managing the effectiveness of marketing investments in generating profitable returns has long been a problem for corporations," says a marketing productivity consultant. "Marketing is perhaps the only remaining function within an organization not held to strict financial performance requirements."[21]

But all that is changing. Given today's tighter economy and shrinking budgets, marketers face growing pressures to show that they are adding value in line with their costs. Many companies now view marketing as an investment rather than an expense. They expect marketers to account for results, in terms of both market impact and profits. In response, marketers are developing better measures of *return on marketing*. **Return on marketing** (or *marketing ROI*) is the net return from a

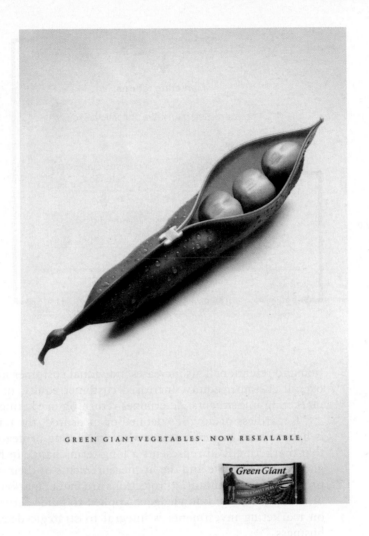

GREEN GIANT VEGETABLES. NOW RESEALABLE.

The outcomes of marketing programs are often intangible and measuring these results can be difficult. For example, how would you measure the "return on marketing" for an ad like this one?

marketing investment divided by the costs of the marketing investment. It measures the profits generated by investments in marketing activities.

Measuring the sometimes intangible outcomes of marketing programs can be difficult. For example, how would you measure the "return on marketing" for an ad like this one?

It's true that marketing returns are difficult to measure. One recent study found that 68 percent of marketing executives have difficulty measuring the ROI of their marketing programs. In another study of marketing professionals, 73 percent of those surveyed felt there are no adequate return on marketing measurement tools available.[22] "There's a reason why companies aren't keeping closer tabs on their marketing ROI: It's tough to measure, more so than for other business expenses," says one analyst. "You can imagine buying a piece of equipment, ... and then measuring the productivity gains that result from the purchase," he says. "But in marketing, benefits like advertising impact aren't easily put into dollar returns. It takes a leap of faith to come up with a number."[23]

A company can assess return on marketing in terms of standard marketing performance measures, such as brand awareness, sales, or market share. Increasingly, however, marketers are using customer-centred measures of marketing impact, such as customer acquisition, customer retention, and customer lifetime value. Figure 2.7 views marketing expenditures as investments that produce returns in the form of more profitable customer relationships.[24] Marketing investments result in improved customer value and satisfaction, which in turn increases customer attrac-

Figure 2.7 Return on marketing

Adapted from Roland T. Rust, Katherine N. Lemon, and Valarie A. Zeithaml, "Return on Marketing: Using Customer Equity to Focus Marketing Strategy," *Journal of Marketing*, January 2004, p. 112.

tion and retention. This increases individual customer lifetime values and the firm's overall customer equity. Increased customer equity, in relation to the cost of the marketing investments, determines return on marketing.

Regardless of how it's defined or measured, the return on marketing concept is here to stay. In a recent survey of marketing professionals, 70 percent asserted that marketing ROI represents a long-term change in how they do business. "All good marketers live and die by measurements of their results," states a marketing productivity consultant. "Projections are made, marketing is delivered, results are measured, and the knowledge is applied to guide future marketing.... The return on marketing investments is integral to strategic decisions at [all levels] of the business."[25]

Reviewing the Concepts

In Chapter 1, we defined marketing and outlined the steps in the marketing process. In this chapter, we examined companywide strategic planning and marketing's role in the organization. Then, we looked more deeply into marketing strategy and the marketing mix, and reviewed the major marketing management functions. So you've had a pretty good overview of the fundamentals of modern marketing. In future chapters, we'll expand on these fundamentals.

1. **Explain companywide strategic planning and its four steps.**

Strategic planning sets the stage for the rest of the company's planning. Marketing contributes to strategic planning, and the overall plan defines marketing's role in the company. Although formal planning offers a variety of benefits to companies, not all companies use it or use it well.

Strategic planning involves developing a strategy for long-run survival and growth. It consists of four steps: defining the company's mission, setting objectives and goals, designing a business portfolio, and developing functional plans. *Defining a clear company mission* begins with drafting a formal mission statement, which should be market oriented, realistic, specific, motivating, and consistent with the market environment. The mission is then transformed into detailed *supporting goals and objectives* to guide the entire company. Based on those goals and objectives, headquarters designs a *business portfolio*, deciding which businesses and products should receive more or fewer resources. In turn, each business and product unit must develop *detailed marketing plans* in line with the companywide plan.

2. **Discuss how to design business portfolios and develop growth strategies.**

Guided by the company's mission statement and objectives, management plans its *business portfolio*, or the collection of businesses and products that make up the company. The firm wants to produce a business portfolio that best fits its strengths and weaknesses to opportunities in the environment. To do this, it must analyze and adjust its *current* business portfolio and develop growth and downsizing strategies for adjusting the *future* portfolio. The company might use a formal portfolio-planning method. But many companies are now designing more-customized portfolio-planning approaches that better suit their unique situations. The *product/market expansion grid* suggests four possible growth paths: market penetration, market development, product development, and diversification.

3. **Explain marketing's role in strategic planning and how marketing works with its partners to create and deliver customer value.**

Under the strategic plan, the major functional departments—marketing, finance, accounting, purchasing, operations, information systems, human resources, and others—must work together to accomplish strategic objectives. Marketing plays a key role in the company's strategic planning by providing a *marketing-concept philosophy* and *inputs* regarding attractive market opportunities. Within individual business units, market-

ing designs *strategies* for reaching the unit's objectives and helps to carry them out profitably.

Marketers alone cannot produce superior value for customers. A company's success depends on how well each department performs its customer value-adding activities and how well the departments work together to serve the customer. Thus, marketers must practise *partner relationship management*. They must work closely with partners in other company departments to form an effective *value chain* that serves the customer. And they must partner effectively with other companies in the marketing system to form a competitively superior *value-delivery network*.

4. **Describe the elements of a customer-driven marketing strategy and mix, and the forces that influence them.**

Consumers' relationships are at the centre of marketing strategy and programs. Through market segmentation, target marketing, and market positioning, the company divides the total market into smaller segments, selects segments it can best serve, and decides how it wants to bring value to target consumers. It then designs a *marketing mix* to produce the response it wants in the target market. The marketing mix consists of product, price, place, and promotion decisions.

5. **List the marketing management functions, including the elements of a marketing plan, and discuss the importance of measuring and managing return on marketing.**

To find the best strategy and mix and to put them into action, the company engages in marketing analysis, planning, implementation, and control. The main components of a *marketing plan* are the executive summary, current marketing situation, threats and opportunities, objectives and issues, marketing strategies, action programs, budgets, and controls. To plan good strategies is often easier than to carry them out. To be successful, companies must also be effective at *implementation*—turning marketing strategies into marketing actions.

Much of the responsibility for implementation goes to the company's marketing department. Marketing departments can be organized in one or a combination of ways: *functional marketing organization, geographic organization, product management organization*, or *market management organization*. In this age of customer relationships, more and more companies are now changing their organizational focus from product or territory management to customer-relationship management. Marketing organizations carry out *marketing control*, both operating control and strategic control. They use *marketing audits* to determine marketing opportunities and problems and to recommend short-run and long-run actions to improve overall marketing performance.

Marketing managers must ensure that their marketing dollars are being well spent. Today's marketers face growing pressures to show that they are adding value in line with their costs. In response, marketers are developing better measures of *return on marketing* (or *marketing ROI*). Increasingly, they are using customer-centred measures of marketing impact as a key input into their strategic decision making.

Reviewing the Key Terms

Business portfolio   48
Diversification   51
Downsizing   53
Growth-share matrix   48
Market development   51
Market penetration   51
Market positioning   61
Market segment   58

Market segmentation   58
Marketing audit   68
Marketing control   67
Marketing implementation   65
Marketing mix   62
Marketing strategy   57
Mission statement   46
Portfolio analysis   48

Product development   51
Product/market expansion grid   51
Return on marketing   68
Strategic planning   45
Target marketing   58
Value chain   54
Value-delivery network   56

Discussing the Concepts

1. Which of the following two terms do you think best describes the process of developing and maintaining a fit between the organization's goals and capabilities and its changing marketing opportunities: strategic planning or corporate planning. Why?

2. The BCG growth-share matrix identifies four classifications of SBU's: stars, cash cows, question marks, and dogs. Briefly discuss why management may find it difficult to dispose of a "question mark."

3. Discuss each of the three steps that a company must perform in choosing the best market segments and designing strategies to maximize profitability in selected segments.

4. This chapter discusses a useful strategy tool for identifying growth opportunities. Discuss the differences between the four options that compose the product/market expansion grid. Which option would a smaller company pursue if it decided to enter an existing market served by many large, well-known competitors? Assume the product being introduced by this smaller company is a new offering for the organization, but this new product offers a number of unique features.

5. Do you think that the "four Ps" marketing mix framework does an adequate job of describing marketer responsibilities in preparing and managing marketing programs? Why? Do you see any issues with this framework in relation to service products?

Applying the Concepts

1. In a small group, discuss whether the following statement from Burton Snowboards North America, manufacturer and marketer of a leading snowboard brand, meets the five criteria of a good mission statement:

"Burton Snowboards is a rider-driven company solely dedicated to creating the best snowboarding equipment on the planet."

2. Ansoff's product/market expansion grid is a portfolio-planning tool used to identify potential growth opportunities for companies. The four opportunities defined by the grid are market penetration, market development, product development, and diversification. Cite one example for each of these four possible growth opportunities that have occurred in the PC industry during the past few years.

3. During the past few years, Nike has successfully entered the golfing market with a line of clubs, balls, bags, footwear, and apparel for men, women, and kids. Most visibly, Nike has enlisted the services of Tiger Woods to promote its golf products. Prepare a brief marketing plan for Nike's golfing products line for the coming year. In preparing the plan, consider who Nike is targeting and how it positions its golfing products in its target markets. For more information, visit www.nikegolf.com.

Focus on Technology

AT&T Natural Voices designs text-to-speech (T2S) software. These T2S software engines convert written language into speech that sounds amazingly real. AT&T has partnered with many companies to improve the customer value network and increase sales. One of the partner companies that sells AT&T Natural Voices directly to customers over the Internet is NextUp. If you have not used or experienced a T2S engine before, you can get a free demonstration at www.nextup.com/nvdemo.html. Just follow these simple directions: (A) paste any sentence of less than thirty words into the demonstration space provided, (B) select a language, (C) select a voice, and (D) click "Go."

Now suppose that you are a member of a new-product marketing team in a firm that has developed T2S technology. You have been asked by the company CEO to present some possible applications for the university undergraduate education market.

1. In a small team, brainstorm at least three applications for the university undergraduate education market.

2. The T2S engine that you demo'ed was developed by AT&T. Why, do you think, did AT&T seek out a partner (NextUp.com) to co-market this product, rather than marketing the product itself?

3. Are there other companies with which AT&T could have partnered? Which ones?

Focus on Ethics

Even new companies with revolutionary products fail if they do not develop a marketing strategy that is sound. One such company that failed was the original Napster. In 1999, Shawn Fanning developed peer-to-peer (P2P) software that allows users to share music, movies, and games with others over the Internet. Fanning went on to found Napster, a company that created a firestorm of controversy around the questions "What is fair use, and what is piracy?" Napster was at the centre of major lawsuits between the P2P software enablers on one side and global recording companies on the other. Napster argued that its software only facilitates the private, noncommercial use of previously owned recorded musical works. The Recording Industry Association of America (RIAA) stated that Napster "launched a service that enables and facilitates the piracy of music on an unprecedented scale."*

1. Assuming that Napster knew its software was used to share copyrighted material on the Internet, possibly illegally, should it have proceeded with the P2P software?

2. Though this Napster situation was unique, what should an organization do if it has a promising technology or product that potentially infringes on others' legal rights? Can you think of an organization that has recently experienced a similar situation?

3. In your opinion, has file sharing and downloading of music over the Internet decreased, remained the same, or increased since the RIAA's legal action against Napster? Why?

*See Steven V. Brull, "Commentary: The Record Industry Can't Stop the Music," *BusinessWeek Online*, May 15, 2000, www.businessweek.com/2000/00-20/b3681181.htm.

Video Case

Starbucks

Today, with more than 7500 stores, it might seem as though there is a Starbucks on almost every street corner in every town across the United States and in many cities abroad. But less than twenty years ago, Starbucks was just getting started, boasting only fifteen stores. Starbucks has achieved this phenomenal growth by sticking closely to its winning formula: the Starbucks experience. Plush armchairs, frothy lattes, soothing music, and indulgent treats encourage customers to return again and again.

Starbucks' growth has not been limited to its stores. In addition, the coffee house has explored new retail channels, introduced new products, and sought opportunities for international growth. But without baristas, extending the Starbucks experience to these new ventures can be tricky. As Starbucks expands its product line and global reach, the company will have to stay true to its original formula to keep things perking.

After watching the video featuring Starbucks, answer the following questions about strategic planning:

1. List several businesses and products that are included in Starbucks' business portfolio. Analyze the portfolio using the Boston Consulting Group Approach.

2. How does Starbucks' entry into the grocery market affect the company's relationships with its customers?

3. Is it possible to convey the "Starbuck's experience" through new retail channels?

4. How did Starbucks successfully make the transition from a nicher to a mainstream marketer? What can the company do to maintain its small company feel as it expands?

Online Media Resources

Video Short
Log on to your Companion Website at www.pearsoned.ca/kotler to view the video segment related to the Video Case above.

CBC ⊕ CBC Video Case
Please refer to Appendix 2 to read a CBC Video Case for this chapter, and log on to your Companion Website at www.pearsoned.ca/kotler to view the corresponding video segment.

Case Pilot
Log on to your Companion Website at www.pearsoned.ca/kotler to sharpen your case analysis skills and take the Case Pilot Challenge!

Company Case

Trap-Ease America: The Big Cheese of Mousetraps

Conventional Wisdom

One April morning, Martha House, president of Trap-Ease America, entered her office in Costa Mesa, California. She paused for a moment to contemplate the Ralph Waldo Emerson quote that she had framed and hung near her desk:

> "If a man [can] ... make a better mousetrap than his neighbor ... the world will make a beaten path to his door."

Perhaps, she mused, Emerson knew something that she didn't. She *had* the better mousetrap—Trap-Ease—but the world didn't seem all that excited about it.

The National Hardware Show

Martha had just returned from the National Hardware Show in Chicago. Standing in the trade show display booth for long hours and answering the same questions hundreds of times had been tiring. Yet, all the hard work had paid off. Each year, National Hardware

Show officials held a contest to select the best new product introduced at that year's show. The Trap-Ease had won the contest this year, beating out more than 300 new products.

Such notoriety was not new for the Trap-Ease mousetrap, however. *People* magazine had run a feature article on the trap, and the trap had been the subject of numerous talk shows and articles in various popular press and trade publications.

Despite all of this attention, however, the expected demand for the trap had not materialized. Martha hoped that this award might stimulate increased interest and sales.

Background

A group of investors had formed Trap-Ease America in January after it had obtained worldwide rights to market the innovative mousetrap. In return for marketing rights, the group agreed to pay the inventor and patent holder, a retired rancher, a royalty fee for each trap sold. The group then hired Martha to serve as president and to develop and manage the Trap-Ease America organization.

Trap-Ease America contracted with a plastics-manufacturing firm to produce the traps. The trap consisted of a square, plastic tube measuring about 15 centimetres long and four centimetres in diameter. The tube bent in the middle at a 30-degree angle, so that when the front part of the tube rested on a flat surface, the other end was elevated. The elevated end held a removable cap into which the user placed bait (cheese, dog food, or some other aromatic tidbit). The front end of the tube had a hinged door. When the trap was "open," this door rested on two narrow "stilts" attached to the two bottom corners of the door. (See Exhibit 1.)

The simple trap worked very efficiently. A mouse, smelling the bait, entered the tube through the open end. As it walked up the angled bottom toward the bait, its weight made the elevated end of the trap drop downward. This action elevated the open end, allowing the hinged door to swing closed, trapping the mouse. Small teeth on the ends of the stilts caught in a groove on the bottom of the trap, locking the door closed. The user could then dispose of the mouse while it was still alive, or the user could leave it alone for a few hours to suffocate in the trap.

Martha believed the trap had many advantages for the consumer when compared with traditional spring-loaded traps or poisons. Consumers could use it safely and easily with no risk of catching their fingers while loading it. It posed no injury or poisoning threat to

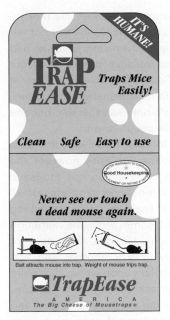

Exhibit 1

children or pets. Furthermore, with Trap-Ease, consumers avoided the unpleasant mess they often encountered with the violent spring-loaded traps. The Trap-Ease created no clean-up problem. Finally, the user could reuse the trap or simply throw it away.

Martha's early research suggested that women were the best target market for the Trap-Ease. Men, it seemed, were more willing to buy and use the traditional, spring-loaded trap. The targeted women, however, did not like the traditional trap. These women often stayed at home and took care of their children. Thus, they wanted a means of dealing with the mouse problem that avoided the unpleasantness and risks that the standard trap created in the home.

To reach this target market, Martha decided to distribute Trap-Ease through national grocery, hardware, and drug chains such as Safeway, Kmart, Hechingers, and CB Drug. She sold the trap directly to these large retailers, avoiding any wholesalers or other intermediaries.

The traps sold in packages of two, with a suggested retail price of US$2.49. Although this price made the Trap-Ease about five to ten times more expensive than smaller, standard traps, consumers appeared to offer little initial price resistance. The manufacturing cost for the Trap-Ease, including freight and packaging costs, was about 31 cents per unit. The company paid an additional 8.2 cents per unit in royalty fees. Martha priced the traps to retailers at 99 cents per unit (two units to a package) and estimated that, after sales and volume discounts, Trap-Ease would produce net revenue from retailers of 75 cents per unit.

To promote the product, Martha had budgeted approximately US$60 000 for the first year. She planned to use US$50 000 of this amount for travel costs to visit trade shows and to make sales calls on retailers. She planned to use the remaining US$10 000 for advertising. So far, however, because the mousetrap had generated so much publicity, she had not felt that she needed to do much advertising. Still, she had placed advertising in *Good Housekeeping* (after all, the trap had earned the *Good Housekeeping* Seal of Approval) and in other "home and shelter" magazines. Martha was the company's only salesperson, but she intended to hire more salespeople soon.

Martha had initially forecast Trap-Ease's first-year sales at five million units. Through April, however, the company had only sold several hundred thousand units. Martha wondered if most new products got off to such a slow start, or if she was doing something wrong. She had detected some problems, although none seemed overly serious. For one, there had not been enough repeat buying. For another, she had noted that many of the retailers upon whom she called kept their sample mousetraps on their desks as conversation pieces—she wanted the traps to be used and demonstrated. Martha wondered if consumers were also buying the traps as novelties rather than as solutions to their mouse problems.

Martha knew that the investor group believed that Trap-Ease America had a "once-in-a-lifetime chance" with its innovative mousetrap, and she sensed the group's impatience with the company's progress so far. She had budgeted approximately US$250 000 in administrative and fixed costs for the first year (not including marketing costs). To keep the investors happy, the company needed to sell enough traps to cover those costs and make a reasonable profit.

Back to the Drawing Board

In these first few months, Martha had learned that marketing a new product was not an easy task. Some customers were very demanding. For example, one national retailer had placed a large order with instructions that Trap-Ease America was to deliver the order to the loading dock at one of the retailer's warehouses between 1:00 and 3:00 p.m. on a specified day. When the truck delivering the order arrived after 3 p.m., the retailer refused to accept the shipment. The retailer told Martha it would be a year before she got another chance.

As Martha sat down at her desk, she realized she needed to rethink her marketing strategy. Perhaps she had missed something or made some mistake that was causing sales to be so slow. Glancing at the quotation again, she thought that perhaps she should send the picky retailer and other customers a copy of Emerson's famous quote.

Questions for Discussion

1. Martha and the Trap-Ease America investors believe they face a once-in-a-lifetime opportunity. What information do they need to evaluate this opportunity? How do you think the group would write its mission statement? How would *you* write it?

2. Has Martha identified the best target market for Trap-Ease? What other market segments might the firm target?

3. How has the company positioned the Trap-Ease for the chosen target market? Could it position the product in other ways?

4. Describe the current marketing mix for Trap-Ease. Do you see any problems with this mix?

5. Who is Trap-Ease America's competition?

6. How would you change Trap-Ease's marketing strategy? What kinds of control procedures would you establish for this strategy?

CHAPTER 3
The Marketing Environment

AFTER STUDYING THIS CHAPTER, YOU SHOULD BE ABLE TO

1. describe the environmental forces that affect the company's ability to serve its customers

2. explain how changes in the demographic and economic environments affect marketing decisions

3. identify the major trends in the firm's natural and technological environments

4. explain the key changes in the political and cultural environments

5. discuss how companies can react to the marketing environment

Previewing the Concepts

In Part 1 (Chapters 1 and 2), you learned about the basic concepts of marketing and the steps in the marketing process for building profitable relationships with targeted consumers. In Part 2, we'll look more deeply into the first step of the marketing process—understanding the marketplace and consumer needs and wants. In this chapter, you'll discover that marketing does not operate in a vacuum but rather in a complex and changing environment. Other *actors* in this environment—suppliers, intermediaries, customers, competitors, publics, and others—may work with or against the company. Major environmental *forces*—demographic, economic, natural, technological, political, and cultural—shape marketing opportunities, pose threats, and affect the company's ability to serve customers and develop lasting relationships with them. To understand marketing, and to develop effective marketing strategies, you must first understand the context in which marketing operates.

First, we'll look at a marketing icon, McDonald's. Ray Kroc spotted an important shift in consumer lifestyles and bought a small chain of restaurants that he built into the vast McDonald's fast-food empire. But while the shifting marketing environment brought opportunities for McDonald's, it has also created challenges.

*I*n 1955, Ray Kroc, a 52-year-old salesman of milk-shake mixing machines, discovered a string of seven restaurants owned by Richard and Maurice McDonald. Kroc saw the McDonald brothers' fast-food concept as a perfect fit for increasingly on-the-go, time-squeezed, family-oriented lifestyles. Kroc bought the small chain for US$2.7 million, and the rest is history.

McDonald's grew quickly to become the world's largest fast-food restaurant. Its more than 31 000 restaurants worldwide now serve 47 million customers each day, racking up sales of more than US$50 billion annually. There are more than 1375 McDonald's in Canada including traditional restaurants and nontraditional restaurants, such as Wal-Mart McDonald's. Approximately 65 percent of all McDonald's Canada restaurants are owned and operated by Canadian entrepreneurs. McDonald's is a major business in Canada. It employs more than 77 000 people and is one of the largest employers of Canadian youth. McDonald's Canada has a network of more than 120 Canadian suppliers. In 2003 alone, McDonald's purchased almost 90 percent of the supplies used in its Canadian operations—more than $638 million worth of food and paper goods—from Canadian suppliers.

The Golden Arches are one of the world's most familiar symbols, and other than Santa Claus, no character in the world is more recognizable than Ronald McDonald. "By making fast food respectable for middle-class families," says an industry analyst, "the Golden Arches did for greasy spoons what Holiday Inn did for roadside motels in the 1950s and what Sam Walton later did for the discount retail store."

But just as the changing marketplace has provided opportunities for McDonald's, it has also presented challenges. In fact, over the past decade, the once-shiny Golden Arches have lost some of their lustre, as the company has struggled to address shifting consumer lifestyles. Although McDonald's is still North America's most-visited fast-food chain, its sales growth began to slump, and its market share fell. In 2002, the company posted its first-ever quarterly loss.

What happened? For one thing, McDonald's appears to have fumbled on the fundamentals. For years it has regularly rated rock-bottom in customer surveys on food and service quality. But perhaps more damaging, in this age of obesity lawsuits and $5 lattes, McDonald's seemed a bit out of step with the times. "When I was a teenager, it was much more acceptable within my peer level to eat here," says one twenty-six-year-old customer about his local McDonald's. "But now, it comes off as uncultured, unclassy, and uncool."

Today's consumers want more choices. They're looking for fresher, better-tasting food and more upscale atmospheres. As a result, McDonald's has been losing share to what the industry calls "fast-casual" restaurants. Competitors such as Tim Hortons, Swiss Chalet, Boston Pizza, and Mövenpick offer more imaginative meals in more fashionable surroundings. And for busy consumers who'd rather "eat-out-in," even the local supermarket offers a full selection of prepared, ready-to-serve gourmet meals to go.

Many North Americans are seeking healthier eating options, and 63 percent of fast-food patrons complained in a recent survey that there are too few healthy menu choices. Thirty-six percent said they don't eat at fast-food restaurants as much because they worry about their health. As the market leader, McDonald's often bears the brunt of such criticism. In a recent, unsuccessful lawsuit, the parents of two teenage girls even charged that McDonald's was responsible for their children's obesity and related health problems, including diabetes. Films, such as *Super Size Me*, singled out McDonald's, and made the restaurants seem less attractive places to either eat or work.

Reacting to these challenges, in early 2003, McDonald's announced a turnaround plan to better align the company with the new marketplace realities. McDonald's revised its vision and aimed at being Canada's "best" quick service restaurant experience. The plan included the following initiatives:

Back to Basics—McDonald's is now refocusing on what made it successful: consistent products and reliable service. Management is pouring money back into existing stores, speeding up service, training employees, and monitoring restaurants to make sure they stay bright and clean.

If You Can't Lick 'Em, Join 'Em—To compete better with the likes of Starbucks and to expand its customer base, McDonald's recently reintroduced *McCafe*, a chain of upscale coffee shops. McCafe offers leather seating, a knowledgeable staff, and espresso in porcelain cups, along with made-to-order drinks, gourmet sandwiches, and Internet access.

What's On Your Plate—Working with pediatricians, dietetic associations, and the Society for Nutrition Education, McDonald's has designed a children's nutrition education program called *What's On Your Plate*. The program features Willie Munchright, a purple clay animation character, who goes on television, online, and into the classroom to teach children how to maintain a balanced diet and enjoy a healthy lifestyle. Willie reminds kids that "it takes all different kinds of foods to build stronger dudes."

Improving the Fare—McDonald's is working to make its menu and its customers healthier. For example, it recently phased out its "super size" option and introduced a "Go Active! Adult Happy Meal" featuring an entrée salad, a bottle of Dasani water, and a "stepometer," which measures physical activity by tracking daily steps. It now offers all-white-meat chicken in McNuggets, low-fat "milk jugs," and apple slices. In early January 2005, McDonald's Restaurants of Canada introduced a new line of toasted deli sandwiches.

The company also runs ads in such publications as *O, the Oprah Magazine* and *Marie Claire,* recommending its salads, milks, and juices along with exercise tips for women and children who care about nutrition. And McDonald's "Real Life Choices" campaign helps consumers fit the foods they love into any of three lifestyles: "watching calories," "watching fat," and "watching carbohydrates." Says a nationally renowned nutritionist who helped develop the program, "I teamed up with McDonald's to show consumers how to enjoy the McDonald's food they love, without compromising their diets." Even the harshest McDonald's critics, although still skeptical, applaud these actions.

McDonald's efforts to realign itself with the changing marketing environment appear to be paying off. By early 2004, the company was posting steady, even startling, sales and profit increases, and customers and stockholders alike were humming the chain's catchy new jingle, "I'm lovin' it." By 2006, stock analysts saw "tasty prospects" for McDonalds as its sales in North America and Europe continued to rise. Former McDonald's CEO Jim Cantalupo, summed it up this way: "Ray Kroc used to say he didn't know what we would be selling in the year 2000, but whatever it was we would be selling the most of it. He recognized early on that consumer needs change and we want to change with it."[1]

Marketing environment
The actors and forces outside marketing that affect marketing management's ability to build and maintain successful relationships with target customers.

Marketers need to be good at building relationships with customers, others in the company, and external partners. To do this effectively, they must understand the major environmental forces that surround all of these relationships. A company's **marketing environment** consists of the actors and forces outside marketing that affect marketing management's ability to build and maintain successful relationships with target customers. Successful companies know the vital importance of constantly watching and adapting to the changing environment.

As we move further into the twenty-first century, both consumers and marketers wonder what the future will bring. The environment continues to change rapidly. More than any other group in the company, marketers must be the trend trackers and opportunity seekers. Although every manager in an organization needs to observe the outside environment, marketers have two special aptitudes. They have disciplined methods—marketing intelligence and marketing research—for collecting information about the marketing environment. They also spend more time in the customer and competitor environments. By carefully studying the environment, marketers can adapt their strategies to meet new marketplace challenges and opportunities.

The marketing environment is made up of a *microenvironment* and a *macroenvironment*. The **microenvironment** consists of the actors close to the company that affect its ability to serve its customers—the company, suppliers, marketing intermediaries, customer markets, competitors, and publics. The **macroenvironment** consists of the larger societal forces that affect the microenvironment—demographic, economic, natural, technological, political, and cultural forces. We look first at the company's microenvironment.

Microenvironment
The actors close to the company that affect its ability to serve its customers—the company, suppliers, marketing intermediaries, customer markets, competitors, and publics.

Macroenvironment
The larger societal forces that affect the microenvironment—demographic, economic, natural, technological, political, and cultural forces.

The Company's Microenvironment

Marketing management's job is to build relationships with customers by creating customer value and satisfaction. However, marketing managers cannot do this alone. Figure 3.1 shows the major actors in the marketer's microenvironment. Marketing success will require building relationships with other company departments, suppliers, marketing intermediaries, customers, competitors, and various publics, which combine to make up the company's value delivery network.

The Company

In designing marketing plans, marketing management takes other company groups into account—groups such as top management, finance, research and development (R&D), purchasing, operations, and accounting. All these interrelated groups form the internal environment. Top management sets the company's mission, objectives, broad strategies, and policies. Marketing managers make decisions within the strategies and plans made by top management.

Marketing managers must also work closely with other company departments. Finance is concerned with finding and using funds to carry out the marketing plan. The R&D department focuses on designing safe and attractive products. Purchasing worries about getting supplies and materials, whereas operations is responsible for producing and distributing the desired quality and quantity of products. Accounting

Figure 3.1 Actors in the microenvironment

has to measure revenues and costs to help marketing know how well it is achieving its objectives. Together, all of these departments have an impact on the marketing department's plans and actions. Under the marketing concept, all of these functions must "think consumer." They should work in harmony to provide superior customer value and satisfaction.

Suppliers

Suppliers form an important link in the company's overall customer value delivery system. They provide the resources needed by the company to produce its goods and services. Supplier problems can seriously affect marketing. Marketing managers must watch supply availability—supply shortages or delays, labour strikes, and other events can cost sales in the short run and damage customer satisfaction in the long run. Marketing managers also monitor the price trends of their key inputs. Rising supply costs may force price increases that can harm the company's sales volume.

Most marketers today treat their suppliers as partners in creating and delivering customer value. Canadian Tire, as the example outlining its agreement with NAPA in Chapter 2 showed, goes to great lengths to work with its suppliers. It invests heavily in technology to increase the efficiency of its ordering system. Supplier relationships are particularly important since, as part of its 2005–2009 strategic plan, Canadian Tire plans to increase the number of products it sources globally in order to maintain product margins, increase sales, and improve the customer value. It has extensive policies with regard to the management of supplier relationships, including policies stipulating that its suppliers must adhere to the same principles of ethics and social responsibility as Canadian Tire does itself.[2]

Marketing Intermediaries

Marketing intermediaries
Firms that help the company to promote, sell, and distribute its goods to final buyers; they include resellers, physical distribution firms, marketing service agencies, and financial intermediaries.

Marketing intermediaries help the company to promote, sell, and distribute its goods to final buyers. They include resellers, physical distribution firms, marketing services agencies, and financial intermediaries. *Resellers* are distribution channel firms that help the company find customers or make sales to them. These include wholesalers and retailers, who buy and resell merchandise. Selecting and partnering with resellers is not easy. No longer do manufacturers have many small, independent resellers from which to choose. They now face an increasingly consolidated retail market with large and growing reseller organizations, such as Loblaws, Wal-Mart, Home Depot, Costco, and Future Shop. These organizations frequently have enough power to dictate terms or even shut the manufacturer out of large markets.

Physical distribution firms help the company to stock and move goods from their points of origin to their destinations. Working with warehouse and transportation firms, a company must determine the best ways to store and ship goods, balancing factors such as cost, delivery, speed, and safety. *Marketing services agencies* are the marketing research firms, advertising agencies, media firms, and marketing consulting firms that help the company target and promote its products to the right markets. When the company decides to use one of these agencies, it must choose carefully because these firms vary in creativity, quality, service, and price. *Financial intermediaries* include banks, credit companies, insurance companies, and other businesses that help finance transactions or insure against the risks associated with the buying and selling of goods. Most firms and customers depend on financial intermediaries to finance their transactions.

Like suppliers, marketing intermediaries form an important component of the company's overall value delivery system. In its quest to create satisfying customer relationships, the company must do more than just optimize its own performance. It must partner effectively with marketing intermediaries to optimize the performance of the entire system.

Thus, today's marketers recognize the importance of working with their intermediaries as partners rather than simply as channels through which they sell their products. For example, Coca-Cola has a ten-year deal with Wendy's that makes it the fast-food chain's exclusive soft drink provider. In the deal, Coca-Cola provides Wendy's with much more than just soft drinks. It also pledges powerful marketing support.

Along with the soft drinks, Wendy's gets a cross-functional team of 50 Coke employees who are dedicated to understanding the finer points of Wendy's business. It also benefits from Coke dollars spent in joint marketing campaigns. Bigger still is the staggering amount of consumer research that Coca-Cola provides its partners. Coke ... goes to great lengths to understand beverage drinkers—and to make sure its partners can use those insights. The company has also analyzed the demographics of every zip code in the [United States] and used the information to create a software program called Solver. By answering questions about their target audience, Wendy's franchise owners can determine which Coke brands are preferred by the customers in their area. Coca-Cola also has even studied the design of drive-through menu boards to better understand which layouts, fonts, letter sizes, colours, and visuals induce consumers to order more food and drink. Such intense partnering efforts have earned Coca-Cola a 68 percent share of the U.S. fountain soft drink market, compared with a 22 percent share for Pepsi.[3]

Coca-Cola provides Wendy's with much more than just soft drinks. It also pledges powerful marketing support.

Customer and Consumer Markets

The company needs to study five types of markets closely. *Consumer markets* consist of individuals and households that buy goods and services for personal consumption. *Business markets* buy goods and services for further processing or for use in their production process, whereas *reseller markets* buy goods and services to resell at a profit. *Government markets* are made up of government agencies that buy goods and services to produce public services or transfer the goods and services to others who need them. Buyers in these three markets are usually referred to as customers. Finally, *international markets* consist of these buyers in other countries, including consumers, producers, resellers, and governments (buyers may be consumers or customers). Each market type has special characteristics that call for careful study by the seller.

Competitors

The marketing concept states that to be successful, a company must provide greater customer value and satisfaction than its competitors do. Thus, marketers must do more than simply adapt to the needs of target consumers. They also must gain strategic advantage by positioning their offerings strongly against competitors' offerings in the minds of consumers.

No single competitive marketing strategy is best for all companies. Each firm should consider its own size and industry position compared with those of its competitors. Large firms with dominant positions in an industry can use certain strategies that smaller firms cannot afford. But being large is not enough. There are winning strategies for large firms, but there are also losing ones. And small firms can develop strategies that give them better rates of return than large firms enjoy.

Publics

Public

Any group that has an actual or a potential interest in or impact on an organization's ability to achieve its objectives.

The company's marketing environment also includes various publics. A **public** is any group that has an actual or potential interest in or impact on an organization's ability to achieve its objectives. We can identify seven types of publics:

- *Financial publics* influence the company's ability to obtain funds. Banks, investment houses, and stockholders are the major financial publics.

- *Media publics* carry news, features, and editorial opinion. They include newspapers, magazines, and radio and television stations.

- *Government publics*. Management must take government developments into account. Marketers must often consult the company's lawyers on issues of product safety, truth in advertising, and other matters.

- *Citizen-action publics*. A company's marketing decisions may be questioned by consumer organizations, environmental groups, minority groups, and others. Its public relations department can help it stay in touch with consumer and citizen groups.

- *Local publics* include neighbourhood residents and community organizations. Large companies usually appoint a community relations officer to deal with the community, attend meetings, answer questions, and contribute to worthwhile causes.

- *General public*. A company needs to be concerned about the general public's attitude toward its products and activities. The public's image of the company affects its buying.

- *Internal publics* include workers, managers, volunteers, and the board of directors. Large companies use newsletters and other means to inform and motivate

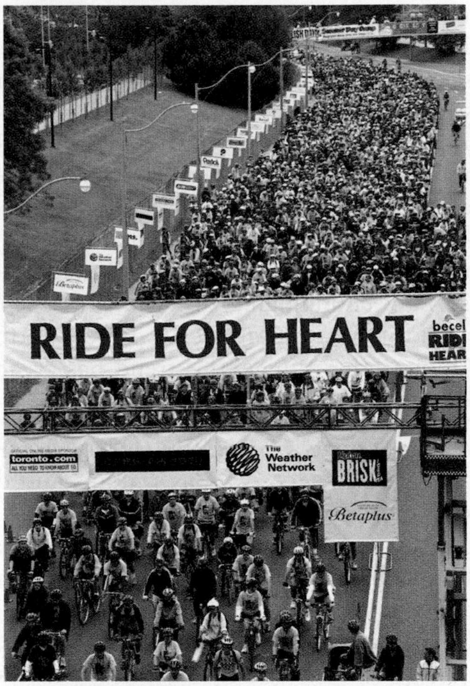
RIDE FOR HEART
The Weather Network
Betaplus

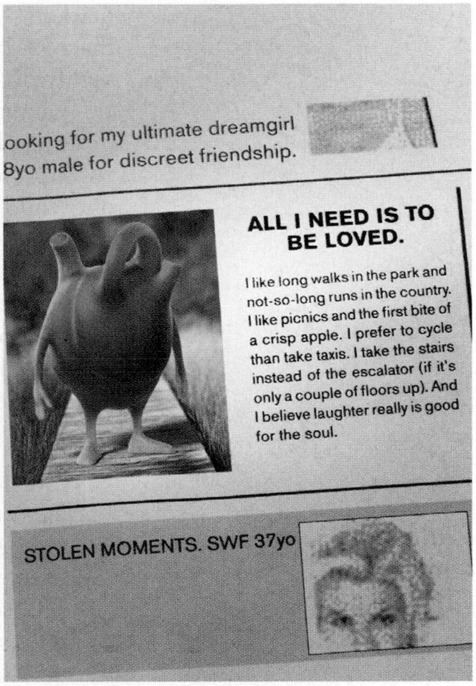
8yo male for discreet friendship.
ALL I NEED IS TO BE LOVED.
I like long walks in the park and not-so-long runs in the country. I like picnics and the first bite of a crisp apple. I prefer to cycle than take taxis. I take the stairs instead of the escalator (if it's only a couple of floors up). And I believe laughter really is good for the soul.
STOLEN MOMENTS. SWF 37yo

The Unilever Canada Foundation supports causes and community publics. Unliever's Becel brand supports heart health with its advertising and its active involvement in the annual Becel "Ride for Heart" which engages both employees and the general public.

their internal publics. When employees feel good about their company, this positive attitude spills over to external publics.

A company can prepare marketing plans for these major publics as well as for its customer markets. Suppose the company wants a specific response from a particular public, such as goodwill, favourable word of mouth, or donations of time or money. The company would have to design an offer to this public that is attractive enough to produce the desired response.

The Company's Macroenvironment

The company and all of the other actors operate in a larger macroenvironment of forces that shape opportunities and pose threats to the company. Figure 3.2 shows the six major forces in the company's macroenvironment. In the remaining sections of this chapter, we examine these forces and show how they affect marketing plans.

Demographic Environment

Demography
The study of human populations in terms of size, density, location, age, gender, race, occupation, and other statistics.

Demography is the study of human populations in terms of size, density, location, age, gender, race, occupation, and other statistics. The demographic environment is of major interest to marketers because it involves people, and people make up

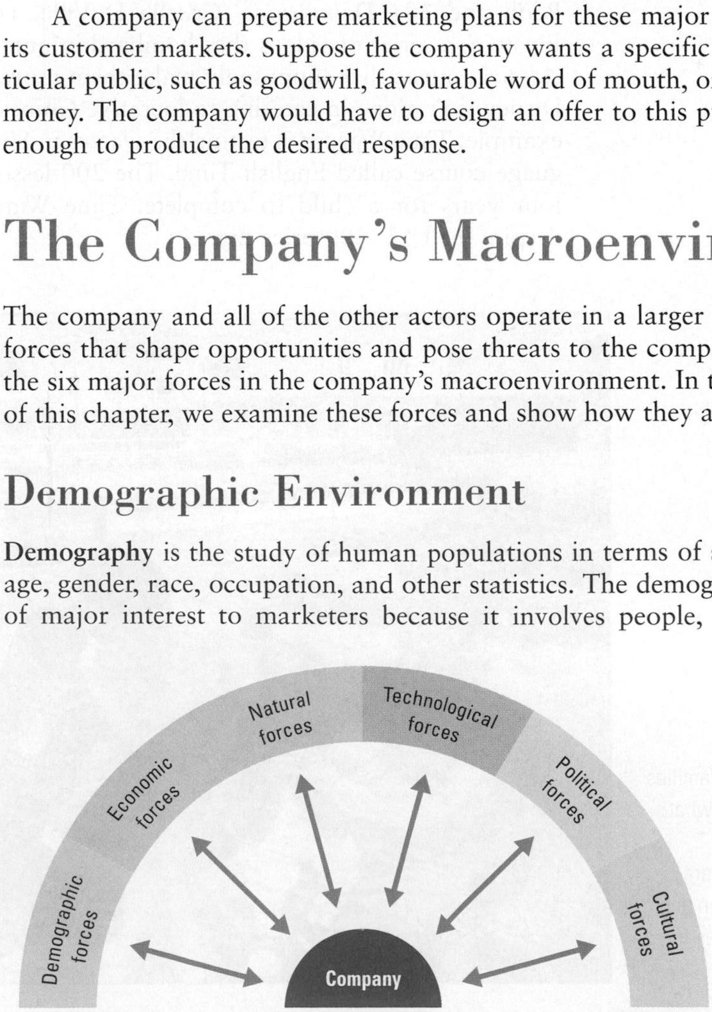
Demographic forces
Economic forces
Natural forces
Technological forces
Political forces
Cultural forces
Company

Figure 3.2 Major forces in the company's macroenvironment

markets. The world population is growing at an explosive rate. It now totals more than 6.4 billion and will exceed 8.1 billion by the year 2030.[4] The world's large and highly diverse population poses both opportunities and challenges.

Changes in the world demographic environment have major implications for business. For example, consider China. Twenty-five years ago, to curb its skyrocketing population, the Chinese government passed regulations limiting families to one child each. As a result, Chinese children—known as "little emperors and empresses"—are being showered with attention and luxuries under what's known as the "six-pocket syndrome." As many as six adults—two parents and four doting grandparents—may be indulging the whims of each child. Parents in the average Beijing household now spend about 40 percent of their income on their cherished only child. Among other things, this trend has created huge market opportunities for children's educational products:

> In China's increasingly competitive society, parents these days are desperate to give Junior an early edge. "Today's moms and dads are … looking to supplement a kid's education starting from Day Zero," says one marketer. That's creating opportunities for companies peddling educational offerings aimed at kids. Disney, for example, began in China in 1994 with Mandarin versions of Mickey Mouse and Donald Duck comic books. A year later, it introduced children's books. Today, with more than 10 million comics and 2.7 million books sold, it's moving full speed into educational products. Magic English, a US$225 Disney package that includes workbooks, flash cards, and twenty-six videodisks, has been phenomenally successful since it was introduced two years ago. Disney launched interactive educational CD-ROMs featuring the likes of Winnie the Pooh and *101 Dalmations'* Cruella DeVille. Disney has begun selling Baby Einstein, a series of videos that bombard infants and toddlers with images and classical music that supposedly make them more receptive to learning later on. Disney isn't alone in catering to lucrative Chinese coddled-kiddies market. For example, Time Warner is testing the waters in Shanghai with an interactive language course called English Time. The 200-lesson, 40-CD set takes as long as four years for a child to complete. Time Warner is expecting strong sales, despite the US$3300 price tag.[5]

Chinese regulations limiting families to one child have resulted in what's known as the "six-pocket syndrome." Chinese children are being showered with attention and luxuries, creating opportunities for marketers.

Thus, marketers keep close track of demographic trends and developments in their markets, both at home and abroad. They track changing age and family structures, geographic population shifts, educational characteristics, and population diversity. Here we discuss the most important demographic trends in Canada.

Changing Age Structure of the Canadian Population

According to Statistics Canada, the population of Canada is expected to exceed 33 million by 2011. However, the growth rate of Canada's population has slowed. The single most important demographic trend in Canada is the changing age structure of the population: The Canadian population is getting *older*. As revealed by 2001 census data, the median age rose to 37.6 years as a result of the aging of the largest demographic segment, the baby boomers, and a very low number of births during the 1990s.[6] The combination of these two trends may mean future labour shortages. To better understand this, there is a 1:4 ratio for the number of people aged 15 to 24 entering the workforce for every one person aged 55 to 64. Table 3.1 shows the changing age distribution of the Canadian population as of 2005. Here, we discuss the three largest age groups—the baby boomers, Generation X, and Generation Y—and their impact on today's marketing strategies.

The Baby Boomers   The post–World War II baby boom, which began in 1947 and ran through 1966, produced 9.8 million **baby boomers** in Canada. Although there was a baby boom in both Canada and the U.S., Canadian marketers have to recognize that our baby boom was unique. It started later than the American version (1947 versus 1946) and lasted longer (the American boom ended in 1964; the Canadian boom continued until 1966). While the American baby boom resulted in 3.5 children per family, the Canadian boom produced an average of 4 children. Furthermore, the baby boom was not a worldwide phenomenon. Among the other developed countries, only Australia and New Zealand experienced the same expansion in the birth rate. In Europe, there was no baby boom, and in Japan, the birth rate declined during our baby boom years, which explains why these countries have a higher proportion of older people in their societies.[7]

Baby boomers
The 9.8 million Canadians born during the baby boom, following World War II and lasting until the mid-1960s.

Table 3.1 Canadian Population by Age Group (2005)

Cohort	Year of birth	Age in 2005	Population (in millions)	Percentage of Population
Pre-WW1	Before 1914	92+	0.1	0.5
WW1	1914–1919	86–91	0.3	1
1920s	1920–1929	76–85	1.5	4
Depression	1930–1939	66–75	2.2	7
WW2	1940–1945	60–65	1.5	5
Baby boom	1947–1966	40–59	9.7	30
Baby bust	1967–1979	26–39	6.8	21
Children of the boomers	1980–1995	10–25	6.5	20
Children of the baby bust cohorts	1996 on	0–9	3.6	11

Sources: Adapted from Statistics Canada, "Population by Sex and Age Group, 2002," www.statcan.ca/english/Pgdb/demo10a.htm and "Shifts in the population size of various age groups," www12.statcan.ca/english/census01/Products/Analytic/companion/age/population.cfm (accessed January 10, 2006).

In Canada, the baby boomers have become one of the largest forces shaping the marketing environment. The fact that Linda Cook was recently named CEO of Shell Canada Ltd. at age 44 is important not only because she is one of the few women to attain such a position, but also because it is an indication of the power that baby boomers, in general, are now wielding in Canadian business. The boomers have presented a moving target, creating new markets as they grew through infancy to pre-adolescence, teenagehood, young adulthood, and now middle age. The baby boomers account for a third of the population but make up 40 percent of the workforce and earn more than half of all personal income.

Baby boomers cut across all walks of life. But marketers have typically paid the most attention to the small upper crust of the boomer generation—its more educated, mobile, and wealthy segments. These segments have gone by many names. In the 1980s, they were called "yuppies" (young urban professionals), "yummies" (young upwardly mobile mommies), and "DINKs" (dual-income, no-kids couples). In the 1990s, however, yuppies and DINKs gave way to a new breed, with such names as "DEWKs" (dual earners with kids) and "MOBYs" (mother older, baby younger). Now, to the chagrin of many in this generation, they are acquiring such titles as "WOOFs" (well-off older folks), "ZOOMERS" (extremely busy and active older couples), or even "GRUMPIES" (just what the name suggests).

The youngest boomers are now in their late thirties; the oldest are in their late fifties. The maturing boomers are experiencing the pangs of midlife and rethinking the purpose and value of their work, responsibilities, and relationships. They are approaching life with a new stability and reasonableness in the way they live, think, eat, and spend. As they continue to age, they will create a large and important seniors market.[8]

Boomers are also reaching their peak earning and spending years. Thus, they constitute a lucrative market for new housing and home remodelling, financial services, travel and entertainment, eating out, health and fitness products, and high-priced cars and other luxuries. It would be a mistake to think of the boomers as aging and staid. Many boomers are rediscovering the excitement of life and have the means to play it out. For example, the median age of a Harley-Davidson buyer is 44.6 years, squarely in the middle of the boomer age range.[9]

Active baby boomers constitute a lucrative market. Some 56 percent of adults who've taken adventure-based vacations during the past five years come from this cohort.

It would be a mistake to think of the boomers as aging and staid. The personal watercraft industry has now virtually abandoned young adult consumers in favour of targeting middle-aged boomers.

Generation X
The 7 million Canadians born between 1967 and 1976 in the "birth dearth" following the baby boom.

Generation X The baby boom was followed by a "birth dearth," creating another generation of 7 million Canadians born between 1967 and 1976. Author Douglas Coupland calls them **Generation X**, because they lie in the shadow of the boomers and lack obvious distinguishing characteristics. Others call them the "baby busters," the "yiffies"—young, individualistic, freedom-minded few—or the "generation caught in the middle" (between the larger baby boomers and Generation Ys).

The Generation Xers are defined as much by their shared experiences as by their age. Increasing divorce rates and higher employment for their mothers made them the first generation of latchkey kids. Having grown up during times of recession and corporate downsizing, they have developed a more cautious economic outlook. They care about the environment and respond favourably to socially responsible companies. Although they seek success, they are less materialistic; they prize experience, not acquisition. They are cautious romantics who want a better quality of life and are more interested in job satisfaction than in sacrificing personal happiness and growth for promotion.

As a result, the Gen Xers are a more skeptical bunch, cynical about frivolous marketing pitches that promise easy success. Says one marketer, "Marketing to Gen Xers is difficult, and it's all about word of mouth. You can't tell them you're good, and they have zero interest in a slick brochure that says so. You have to rely on somebody they know and trust to give you instant credibility. They have a lot of 'filters' in place."[10] Once labelled as "the MTV generation" and as body-piercing slackers who whined about "McJobs," the Gen Xers have now grown up and are beginning to take over. The Gen Xers are poised to displace the lifestyles, culture, and materialistic values of the baby boomers. By the year 2010, they will have overtaken the baby boomers as a primary market for almost every product category.[11]

With so much potential, many companies, like the vibrant, Canadian-based retailer Aritzia are focusing on a segment of GenX consumers—forward-thinking, fashion-conscious women aged 15 to 35. Founded in Vancouver in 1984, the company today has over twenty stores located in Vancouver, Toronto, Calgary, Edmonton, and Ottawa. The company has plans to expand into the United

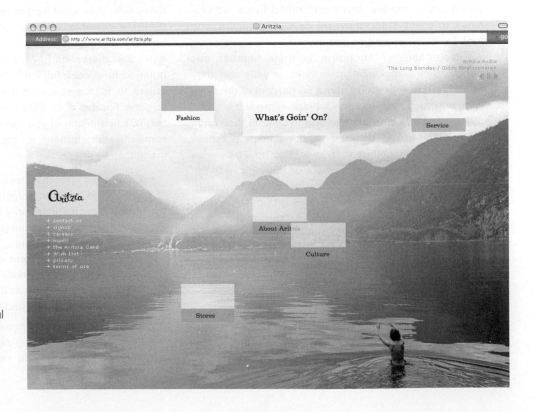

Aritzia, a vibrant Canadian-based retailer, has been highly successful in serving a segment of the Gen X marketplace—women aged 15 to 35 who are focused on urban high style.

REAL MARKETING   3.1

The Teen Market: Youth Will Be Served

According to Statistics Canada, there were an estimated 2 081 000 teens aged 15 to 19 in 2001 (the year of the last census). Care has to be used when using the term "teen," however, since older teens are turned off by the label. To them "teen" means a younger person or tween. Teenagers are focused on issues that affect their lives—postsecondary education, violence in schools, quality of high school education, the environment, poverty, and gun control, to list a few.

Gone are the days when kids saved up their pennies for candy and ice cream at the corner soda fountain. Today's teens are big spenders. A study by Youth Culture Research, suggests that Canadian teenagers have a disposable income of almost $20 billion. Teen girls, a group that represents approximately 8 percent of all Canadian women, are the most closely watched consumer group in the Canadian market. According to Canada's *Marketing Magazine*, the average disposable income of a Canadian teenage girl is $131 a week. Despite this sum, 50 percent of teens are concerned about lack of money, and their limited funds are precious to them. Thus, they are careful shoppers who look for value as well as quality.

Nonetheless, "shopping is their number one hobby." Teens make 54 mall visits a year and they intend to buy something about 50 percent of the time. With so much cash to spend, teens represent a lucrative market for companies willing to cater to their often fickle, trend-driven tastes. The items teens purchase reflect their own self-images as well as how they wish others to perceive them. The act of buying can therefore be one of independence or conformity, self-expression or socialization. For this group, "newness" is often associated with coolness. It's not surprising that hair and make-up product manufacturers describe female Canadian teenagers as fickle consumers. They are in constant pursuit of the latest trends to express themselves and like to experiment with numerous products. Their paradoxical need for acceptance and individuality leads them to go for bold colours, glitter, and shiny or glossy cosmetics.

To tap into this vast market of potential new customers, all kinds of companies are targeting teens with new or modified products. Some of these products are naturals for the teen market, such as action movies, acne creams, teen magazines, cellphones, and *NSync. A single form of any product rarely appeals to all teens since they are highly segmented demographically and psychographically. Thus, firms tailor their products to meet the preferences of distinct subgroups. For example, the store Bluenotes carries six private labels for each type of teen out there: preppy, skater, rocker, hip hopper, and so on.

Since teens are heavy users of text messaging and wireless phones, advertisers are itching to forge agreements with wireless phone companies, such as Bell Mobility, Telus Mobility, Microcell, and Rogers AT&T Wireless. Roman Bodnarchuk, founder of N5R, a Toronto-based consulting firm that specializes in loyalty marketing, explains why teens and young adults have been attracted to this technology. "BlackBerries are cool, but very expensive. And wireless laptops are not that portable. And besides, email is too slow for these kids, they want instant response. Text messaging (SMS) is portable, it's silent—making communication possible during science class—and cheap." He also notes that marketers have to be teen savvy if they are going to be successful. Teens have come up with a language to fit the space limitations of the tiny phone screens. For example, POS means parents over shoulder; TOY is thinking of you. Here are some examples of companies attempting to cash in on the hot teen market:

- *Caboodles:* Canadian teen cosmetic manufacturer Caboodles has been hugely successful in reaching the teen segment not only in Canada but also internationally. Its sales were just shy of $52 million in North America, though the Canadian market makes up just 9 percent of the overall business. The company also markets its popular line to teens in countries as diverse as Italy, Australia, Germany, China, Greece, Dubai, and Guam.
- *Wildseed:* Cellphone manufacturer Wildseed has spent years conducting research to develop cellphones for teens. The research shows that for

teenagers, a desirable cellphone is not about smaller, lighter, sleeker. What teens want from a cellphone ranges from the concrete (music, messaging, and games) to the abstract (style, personality, and individuality). As a result, Wildseed phones have "smart skins"—replaceable faceplates with computer chips that allow teens to individualize the phone's functions and appearance to match their personalities. For example, skateboarders can choose graffiti-splattered faceplates that come with edgy urban ringer tones and gritty icons. A Wildseed marketer quotes one seventeen-year-old customer as saying, "I want to be in charge of my wireless phone, change the screens, have new ringtones. That is what is so cool about skins. I can change my phone every day."

- *Fuel:* Who says boys don't read? Not the publishers of new *Fuel* magazine! It is distributed through 2500 Canadian schools and has a circulation of 100 000. While lifestyle magazines, such as *Seventeen,* have long been aimed at teenage girls, similar publications for boys have been startlingly absent. Research revealed, however, that the interests and tastes of the two genders were very different. "Boys were complaining about how they hated seeing tampon ads in the magazine. The more we tested, the more we found that what boys and girls liked and didn't like were at odds with each other." *Fuel* is taking advantage of this insight to break new ground.

- *Avon:* Avon recently launched a new beauty business called *mark,* in celebration of young women making their mark in the world today. The new brand targets young women 16–24. To sell *mark,* Avon has signed on a corps of young women as independent sales representatives (parental consent required), who market the brand to their peer group while at the same time creating their own entrepreneurial business opportunity. *Mark* is sold through magalogs, the www.meetmark.com website, and "social beauty parties." Can a company known for its appeal to middle-American women sell successfully to young women? Avon thinks so. The new brand is distinctly more upscale and trendier than Avon's traditional look. "This is very much not just another brand," says Avon's chief executive, Andrea Jung.

- *Hot Topic:* Clothing retailer Hot Topic targets the 17 percent of high school students who consider themselves "alternative teens." The store carries an assortment of items you just won't find at Abercrombie & Fitch. The merchandise reflects a variety of music-related lifestyles, including street, retro-influenced lounge, punk, club, and gothic wear. Rather than khakis and tank tops, the store stocks pinstripe fishnet stockings, pink fur pants, feather boas, blue hair dye, black nail polish, and Morbid Makeup. Teens can buy T-shirts from TV shows such as *SpongeBob SquarePants*, Kermit the Frog underwear, and licensed concert apparel from rockers such as Eminem, Marilyn Manson, Tool, and Linkin Park. Whereas Gap, American Eagle, and other teen retailers have recently reported flat or declining sales, Hot Topic's sales are, well, hot. Sales have increased an average of more than 30 percent annually for the past three years.

To target young women, Avon launched a new beauty business, *mark,* offering more upscale and trendier products through "social beauty parties" and *meet mark* magalogs like this one.

Sources: Examples adapted from information found in "Teens Spent $175 Billion in 2003," press release, Teenage Research Unlimited, January 9, 2004, www.teenresearch.com; Michèle Parent, "Selling Cosmetics to Canadian Teens," Industry Canada, August 20, 2002, http://strategis.ic.gc.ca/epic/internet/inimr-ri.nsf/

en/gr107630e.htm; Leslie Earnest, "California: Hot Topic Results Suit It to a Tee," *The Los Angeles Times,* March 5, 2003, p. C2; Leslie Earnest, Sally Beatty, "Avon Set to Sell to Teens," *Wall Street Journal,* October 17, 2002, p. B1; Deborah Netburn, "The New Avon Ladies," *Los Angeles Times,* March 21, 2004, p. E.4; "Teens Audience Profile," The Health Communication Unit Ontario Ministry of Health and Long-Term Care, www.thcu.ca/infoandresources/teensaudienceprofile.htm#top (accessed January 22, 2006); Brad Smith, "Personalization: Bigger Than Games?" *Wireless Week,* January 15, 2004, p. 15; and Jean Halliday, "Automakers Mix It up to Chase Young Buyers," *Automotive News,* April 26, 2004, p. 28B. Susan Henrich, "R u redi 4 Text Marketing?" *National Post,* March 17, 2003, www.nationalpost.com; Eve Lazarus, "Caboodles Rules," *Marketing Magazine,* January 20, 2003, www.marketingmag.ca; Kathleen Martin, "Boys Read," *Marketing Magazine,* January 20, 2003, www.marketingmag.ca/magazine/current/youth_report/article.jsp?content=20030120_23991.

States. Aritzia prides itself on its ability to connect its customers to the energy of the culture. Aritzia brings its customers the most sought-after urban high-style brands for young women. Popular brands—7 For All Mankind, Habitual, Rock and Republic, and Adidas by Stella McCartney—share space with the firm's own exclusive lines like Talula, Talula Babaton, TNA, Wilfred, and Community.[12]

Such urban professionals, aged 25 to 40, are more likely to live in a loft, an apartment, or a townhouse than a house in the suburbs. They are skeptical, impatient, and highly mobile. They like trends but not gimmicks, and they gravitate to the cool and casual.

Generation Y
The 6.9 million children of the Canadian baby boomers, born between 1977 and 1994.

Generation Y Both the baby boomers and the Gen Xers will one day be passing the reins to the latest demographic group, **Generation Y**. Also called the "echo boom," the children of the baby boomers now represent approximately 20 percent of the Canadian population. Ranging in age from preteens to mid-twenties, the echo boomer generation is still forming its buying preferences and behaviours.

After years of bust, markets for teen's toys and games, clothes, furniture, and food have enjoyed a boom. Designers and retailers have created new lines, new products, and even new stores devoted to children and teens—Tommy Hilfiger, DKNY, Gap, Talbots, Pottery Barn, and Eddie Bauer, to name just a few (see Real Marketing 3.1 on page 90). New media appeared that cater specifically to this market: *Time*, *Sports Illustrated*, and *People* have all started new editions for kids and teens. Banks have offered banking and investment services for young people, including investment camps.[13]

Generation Y oldsters are now graduating from university and are moving up in their careers. Like the trailing edge of Generation X ahead of them, one distinguishing characteristic of Generation Y is their utter fluency and comfort with computer, digital, and Internet technology. About nine out of ten teens have a home computer, 50 percent have Internet access, and more than 50 percent of teens 12 to 17 own a mobile phone. In all, they are an impatient, now-oriented bunch. "Blame it on the relentless and dizzying pace of the Internet, twenty-four-hour cable news cycles, cellphones, and TiVo for creating the on-demand, gotta-get-it-now universe in which we live," says one observer. "Perhaps nowhere is the trend more pronounced than among the Gen Y set."[14]

Generation Y represents an attractive target for marketers. Even the automobile industry is aggressively targeting this generation of future care buyers.

Automakers are using music, online contests, and race cars to lure Generation Y as they approach their key vehicle-buying years. For example, Honda's Civic Tour targets a core segment of 15- to 25-year-olds. It consists of a 38-stop music tour, featuring the band Dashboard Confessional. Honda will pay for the first 100 000 downloads at http://civictour.honda.com of one of the band's songs, to be performed live at one of three concerts. In a similar effort, Audi kicked off an online contest in conjunction with its sponsorship of singer David Bowie's North American "Reality Tour." Visitors to the website were asked to "mash up" two of Bowie's songs into one to win an Audi TT coupe. Whereas Audi's traditional buyers are in their late

To lure the Gen Y set as they approach their key vehicle-buying years, Honda's 38-stop Civic Tour features bands like Dashboard Confessional.

thirties to early fifties, the contest targets twenty-somethings. The promotion's goals are to build brand awareness and "bring Audi to a whole new generation," says an Audi marketer.[15]

Generational Marketing Do marketers have to create separate products and marketing programs for each generation? Some experts caution that each generation spans decades of time and many socioeconomic levels. For example, marketers often split the baby boomers into three smaller groups—leading boomers, core boomers, and trailing boomers—each with its own beliefs and behaviours. Similarly, they split Generation Y into Gen Y adults, Gen Y teens, and Gen Y kids. Thus, marketers need to form more precise age-specific segments within each group. More important, defining people by their birth date may be less effective than segmenting them by their lifestyle or life stage.

Others warn that marketers have to be careful about turning off one generation each time they craft a product or message that appeals effectively to another. "The idea is to try to be broadly inclusive and at the same time offer each generation something specifically designed for it," notes one expert. "Tommy Hilfiger has big brand logos on his clothes for teenagers and little pocket polo logos on his shirts for baby boomers. It's a brand that has a more inclusive than exclusive strategy."[16]

Changing Canadian Households

When one uses the term *household,* a stereotype of the typical family living in the suburbs with its two children may leap to mind. However, this stereotype is far from accurate. The 2001 census suggests that "Canada is a place of loners and shrinking families, where lovers have increasingly lost interest in a walk down the aisle, the young adults like to shack up with mom and dad, and the eldest citizens are more often living the solitary life." In other words, the 2001 census suggests a number of new paradoxes. On one hand, there is a growing "crowded nest" syndrome. About 41 percent of young Canadians aged 20 to 29 now live with their parents. There are 8.3 million families in Canada, but fewer have children than in years past. Married or common-law couples with children now represent only 44 percent of all families, compared with 49 percent just ten years earlier. Although married couples still constitute the majority of Canadian parents, their numbers continue to drop. Thirty percent of parents now live in common-law arrangements. Another trend is that one in five of Canada's children lives in a single-parent household. As a result of these trends, the average Canadian household shrank to 2.6 people in 2001 from 2.9 people in 1981.[17]

Responsibility for household tasks and the care of children is also changing. There are now more dual-income families as more and more women enter the workforce. Today, women account for more than 48 percent of the workforce. The employment rate of women with children has grown particularly sharply in the past two decades, especially for those with preschool-aged children. More than 60 percent of women with children under age three were employed, more than double the figure in 1976. Human Resources Development Canada, however, reports that women earn an average annual salary of $45 820, 79.3 percent of men's average salary of $58 250.[18]

Geographic Shifts in Population

The population of Canada is expected to grow by approximately 4 percent between 2001 and 2006. As Table 3.2 shows, however, growth rates across all provinces and territories are not uniform. The populations of Newfoundland and Labrador, Saskatchewan, and Yukon decreased during the 1998–2002 period, while the populations of the other provinces and territories grew.[19]

Canadians are a mobile people with itchy feet. For more than a century, Canadians have been moving from rural to urban areas. The urban areas show a faster pace of living, more commuting, higher incomes, and greater variety of goods and services than can be found in the small towns and rural areas that dot Canada. Moreover, each year about 12 people in 1000 swap provinces. For the past few years, Alberta and Ontario have been the top two choices when it came to inter-

Table 3.2 Canada's Population

	1998 (thousands)	2002 (thousands)	Change (%)
Canada	30 248.4	31 414.0	3.9
Newfoundland and Labrador	545.3	531.6	−2.5
Prince Edward Island	136.9	139.9	2
Nova Scotia	936.1	944.8	0.8
New Brunswick	753.3	756.7	0.5
Quebec	7 323.6	7 455.2	2
Ontario	11 387.4	12 068.3	5.9
Manitoba	1 137.9	1 150.8	1
Saskatchewan	1 024.9	1 011.8	−1
Alberta	2 906.8	3 113.6	7.1
British Columbia	3 997.1	4 141.3	3.6
Yukon	31.5	29.9	−5
Northwest Territories	41.1	41.4	0
Nunavut	26.4	28.7	8.7

Source: Adapted from Statistics Canada, "Population, Provinces and Territories," www.statcan.ca/english/Pgdb/demo02.htm (extracted May 14, 2003).

provincial moves. Recent research has shown that interprovincial moves and income are correlated. People who moved from one province to another tended to increase their earnings, especially if they moved away from a "have not" province. The effects were especially strong for men and younger people.[20]

Canada's cities are changing as well. Canadian cities are often surrounded by large suburban areas. Statistics Canada calls these combinations of urban and suburban populations "Census Metropolitan Areas" (CMAs). About 50 percent of Canada's population lives in the top 25 CMAs. Marketers also track the relative growth of these markets to see which areas are expanding and which ones are contracting.

Population shifts interest marketers because people in different regions buy differently. For example, 46 percent of people classified as "serious technology users" reside in Ontario, compared with 18 percent who live in British Columbia and the 6 percent who live in Atlantic Canada.[21]

The shift in where people live has also caused a shift in where they work. For example, the migration toward metropolitan and suburban areas has resulted in a rapid increase in the number of people who "telecommute"—work at home or in a remote office and conduct their business by phone, fax, modem, or the Internet.

This trend, in turn, has created a booming SOHO (small office/home office) market. Fifteen percent of Canadian households report that they have a home office. In addition to commuters, it estimated that there were 618 000 home-based businesses in Canada. Typically, home-based business operators are male (60.3 percent) and between the ages of 25 and 54 (76.4 percent). Many (31 percent) are highly educated. The top five industries for home-based businesses are professional, scientific, and technical services (17.8 percent); agriculture (12.1 percent); trade (10.2 percent); health care and social assistance (9.2 percent); and construction (8.3 percent).[22]

Many marketers are actively courting the home office segment. One example is FedEx Kinko's Office and Print Centers:

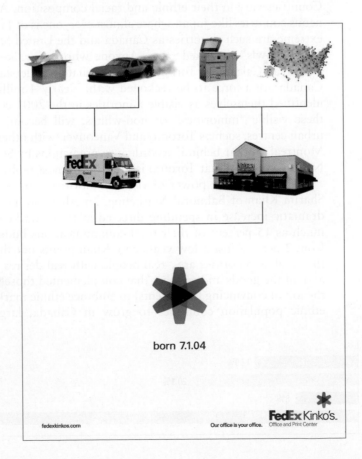

To serve the burgeoning small office/home office market, FedEx Kinkos has reinvented itself as the well-appointed office outside the home. New ads proclaim, "Our office is your office."

Founded in the 1970s as a campus photocopying business, Kinko's was bought by FedEx in 2004. It's locations were renamed FedEx Kinko's Office and Print Centers. As the new name suggests, FedEx Kinko's is now much more than a self-service copy shop. Serving primarily small office/home office customers, it has reinvented itself as the well-appointed office outside the home. New ads proclaim, "Our office is your office." Where once there were only copy machines, FedEx Kinko's 1200 centres now offer a full range of business services, including binding and finishing, colour copying and printing, document management, shipping services, computer rental, T-Mobile HotSpot wireless Internet connections, and much more. People can come to a FedEx Kinko's store to do all their office jobs: They can copy, send and receive faxes, use various programs on the computer, go on the Internet, order stationery and other printed supplies, ship packages, and even rent a conference room or conduct a teleconference. As more and more people join the work-at-home trend, FedEx Kinko's offers an escape from the isolation of the home office.[23]

A Better-Educated and More White-Collar Population

Figure 3.3 shows Canada's working-age population (those aged 25 to 64) is becoming better educated. As of 2004, people with university degrees or post-secondary certificates equal 59.1 percent of the population. Eight percent have some post-secondary education. Those with a high-school education equal 20.1 percent. However, 12.9 percent of the population has less than high-school education. People with higher education tend to have higher incomes, thus the demand for higher-quality products ranging from books to computers to cars is also increasing.[24]

Increasing Diversity

Countries vary in their ethnic and racial composition. At one extreme are homogeneous countries like Japan where almost everyone is of Japanese descent. At the other extreme are such countries as Canada and the United States whose populations are "salad bowls" of mixed races. Anyone who has walked the streets of Vancouver, Montreal, Calgary, or Toronto will immediately understand that visible minorities in Canada are a force to be reckoned with. Nearly 4 million (14 percent) Canadians identified themselves as visible minorities in the 2001 census. In less than 10 years, these visible "minorities" or non-whites, will become the "majorities" in major urban centres, such as Toronto and Vancouver, with other cities, such as Calgary and Montreal, not far behind, according to predictions by Statistics Canada. The United Nations reported that Toronto is the world's most multicultural city.

The purchasing power of visible minorities is huge, so it is not surprising that Sharifa Khan of Balmoral Marketing, an ethnic ad agency in Toronto, has seen a dramatic increase in spending directed at these markets. Many clients allocate as much as 15 percent of their total communications budget to ethnic marketing, up from 2 percent just a few years ago. Khan points out that once her clients realized that visible minorities are "real people with real desires to own a home, a nice car, and all the goods and services that complemented those things they desired it made the job of convincing [her clients] to embrace ethnic marketing a lot easier."[25] As the ethnic population continues to grow in Canada, large companies, from Sears,

Figure 3.3 Education profile of Canadians

Source: Adapted from "A Profile of Education in Canada," Canadian Council on Social Development, 2004, www.ccsd.ca/factsheets/education.

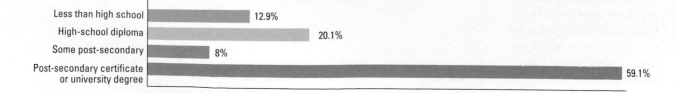

Less than high school — 12.9%
High-school diploma — 20.1%
Some post-secondary — 8%
Post-secondary certificate or university degree — 59.1%

McDonald's, and Air Canada to Levi Strauss, Procter & Gamble, and General Mills, feature people from different backgrounds in their ads and can now target specially designed products and promotions to one or more of these groups. They can use a variety of media vehicles introduced to serve ethnic marketplaces. There are 18 television networks, 49 radio stations, and 190 newspapers and magazines available to reach various ethnic populations. Though there are approximately 200 different visible minorities living in Canada, only 12 groups are growing significantly and have well-developed media that target their communities: Chinese, Caribbean (predominantly Jamaican), South Asian (India, Pakistan, Tamil, Bangladesh), Korean, Hispanic, Italian, Greek, Portuguese, Ukrainian, Polish, Filipinos, and First Nations.[26] It must be remembered, however, that visible minorities often read the same media, such as daily newspapers, as other Canadians.

Marketers must avoid negative stereotypes when it comes to serving ethnic markets. Seventeen percent of immigrants hold university degrees, compared with 11 percent of people born in Canada. Immigrants are also more likely to hold managerial or professional jobs and have more stable family lives than people born in Canada.

Targeting ethnic consumers involves far more than mere tokenism, as many ethnic marketing specialists warn. Merely placing a person from a visible minority in an advertisement is not sufficient evidence that one is an ethnic marketer. Communicating in the consumer's native language is often mandatory, but marketers must also face the challenge of not alienating sophisticated second-generation individuals. The TD Bank recently demonstrated the power of providing information in potential customers' native language. The bank launched a Chinese Green Info Line to target potential Chinese investors. More than 300 callers per month take advantage of the service, which has generated considerable investments. Wal-Mart now runs television spots targeting South Asian, Cantonese, Mandarin, Spanish, Portuguese, and Italian communities. Telus and Nokia use print advertising to target consumers from various ethnic backgrounds in Toronto and Vancouver. Professor Ashwin Joshi of Schulich School of Business at York University in Toronto, notes that IKEA is another marketer that is sensitive to the needs of consumers from different

Firms such as Telus know the importance of cultural sensitivity and building meaningful connections with people of different ethnic backgrounds.

ethnic backgrounds. For example, through its extensive links with people of South Asian origins, it developed insights that it used to shape its marketing practices. IKEA learned that religion plays a key role for this community and that it is not uncommon for the different religious groups to have sacred places in their homes where they place their religious artifacts. This led IKEA to specifically design furniture to house these artifacts. IKEA also takes pride in participating in key festivals, such as Diwali and Idd, by having the appropriate items (e.g., candle holders made of clay) on sale during the time of these events.[27]

The diversity in the Canadian marketplace isn't restricted to ethnic markets. People's sexual orientation is another point of diversity, and there is growing tolerance of alternative lifestyles in Canada. For example, more than 1 million people attend lesbian and gay pride events in Toronto. For the first time, the 2001 census collected data on gay and lesbian couples. It counted a total of 34 200 same-sex common-law couples, representing 0.5 percent of all couples.[28] Since homosexual consumers tend to be cosmopolitan and professional, with high incomes, they are desirable target markets for everything from technology products and health and beauty products to travel, fashion, entertainment, and financial services. It is not surprising that in 2001 the City of Toronto ran a campaign aimed at attracting more gay and lesbian tourists. A new company, Hudson Nuptials, targets gay couples who want to take advantage of Canada's new laws legalizing gay marriage. It makes all the arrangements and provides intimate destination wedding experiences for same-sex couples seeking to get married in Toronto. Despite the growing importance of this market, until recently few national advertisers targeted this audience explicitly. One reason is the lack of research on this market. Another reason is the dearth of middle-of-the-road media directed at these consumers. Additionally, some marketers feared that advertising in gay media or at gay events would cause a backlash from heterosexual consumers.

These things are changing. Several research firms, including Environics, have started gathering information on the market. A growing body of media is directed at the gay community, including electronic media, such as PrideNet (www.pridenet.com). People who have experience advertising to the gay community, such as Tom Blackmore, a partner in the Toronto-based advertising agency Robins Blackmore, say that clients who have used creative materials that are relevant to this audience have experienced remarkable successes from their campaigns. The one mistake that marketers can make with respect to this audience is doing nothing. "It is a market that people have ignored for way too long," Blackmore explains.[29]

Diversity goes beyond ethnicity or sexual preferences. For example, 12.4 percent of the Canadian population has some form of disability. This group has considerable spending power as well as great need for tailored products and services. Not only do they value services that make daily life easier, such as online grocery shopping from sites such as www.GroceryGateway.com, but they are also a growing market for travel, sports, and other leisure-oriented products. The Canadian Abilities Foundation provides a wealth of information ranging from products and services to housing and travel advice on its EnableLink website. Consider the following example:[30]

> In the past, Volkswagen has targeted people with disabilities who want to travel. For example, one recent marketing campaign for its EuroVan touted the vehicle's extra-wide doors, high ceilings, and overall roominess, features that accommodate most wheelchair lifts and make driving more fun for people with disabilities. Volkswagen even modified its catchy tag line "Drivers Wanted" to appeal to motorists with disabilities, coining the new slogan "All Drivers Wanted." Volkswagen also teams each year with the non-profit organization VSA arts to sponsor its "Driving Force" competition, designed to identify promising young artists with physical, cognitive, or mental disabilities.

driving force

A National Juried Exhibit for Young Artists with Disabilities, Ages 16-25

For the third year, VSA *arts* and Volkswagen of America, Inc. have partnered to recognize and showcase young artists with disabilities, ages 16-25, who are living in the United States. This collaboration supports these artists at a critical time; many are deciding whether to pursue the arts as a career. The award validates and helps finance that decision.

These 15 finalists are motivated by an intense desire and dedication to practice fine art. Art is their primary motivation - to use the arts as a way to understand the past, the unique contributions of all artists, the boundaries that define us, and the personal philosophies that influence their work. Self-directed by this inherent need to create, many of these artists employ the arts as personal exploration. Their work becomes a profound search for identity and a way to share their unique perspectives.

Volkswagen targets people with disabilities by teaming each year with the non-profit organization VSA arts to sponsor its "Driving Force" competition, designed to identify promising young artists with physical, cognitive, or mental disabilities.

Proclaims a VW spokesperson, "Volkswagen believes that the 'heartware' is equally as important as the 'hardware.' For people with disabilities, the automobile provides both freedom of mobility and self-expression."

As the population in Canada grows more diverse, respecting diversity may be the key to economic survival for many companies. Thus, successful marketers will continue to diversify their marketing programs to take advantage of opportunities in fast-growing segments.

Economic Environment

Economic environment
Factors that affect consumer buying power and spending patterns.

Markets require buying power as well as people. The **economic environment** consists of factors that affect consumer purchasing power and spending patterns. Nations vary greatly in their levels and distribution of income. Some countries have *subsistence economies*—they consume most of their own agricultural and industrial output. These countries offer few market opportunities. At the other extreme are *industrial economies*, which constitute rich markets for many different kinds of goods. Marketers must pay close attention to major trends and consumer spending patterns both across and within their world markets. The following are some of the major economic trends in Canada.

Changes in Income

During the 1990s, the baby boom generation moved into its prime wage-earning years, and the number of small families headed by dual-career couples continued to increase. They bought and bought, seemingly without caution, amassing record levels of debt. It was fashionable to describe yourself as 'born to shop.' Thus, along with rising incomes in some segments came increased financial burdens. Repaying debts added to increased household and family expenses, and the need to save for their children's tuition payments and their own retirements made more and more families feel financially squeezed. They spent more carefully and sought greater value in the products and services they bought. *Value marketing* became the watchword for many marketers.

Marketers should pay attention to *income distribution* as well as average income. Income distribution in Canada is still very skewed. At the top are *upper-class* consumers, whose spending patterns are not affected by current economic events and who are a major market for luxury goods. You might see some of these people frequenting the Second Cup coffee shop in upscale Rockcliffe Park, nestled close to the Ottawa River. There is also a comfortable *middle class,* which is somewhat careful about its spending but can still afford the good life some of the time. The *working class* must stick close to the basics of food, clothing, and shelter, and must try hard to save. Finally, the *underclass* (persons on welfare and many retirees) must count their pennies even when making the most basic purchases. People within Canada's lowest income segment are often found on Aboriginal reserves. Of the 4400 communities ranked by income by Statistics Canada, the bottom 200 are almost all Aboriginal. Education rates are low, unemployment is high, and individual incomes may be as low as $4000 per year. One observer noted, "Reserves, especially in Western Canada, are somewhere between Mexico and Somalia in terms of standard of living. The disparity between the reserves and the rest of Canada is immense. It should be a major embarrassment."[31]

This distribution of income has created a two-tiered market. Many companies are aggressively targeting the affluent. Other companies are now tailoring their marketing offers to two different markets—the affluent and the less affluent. For example, Walt Disney Company (www.disney.com) markets two distinct Winnie-the-Pooh bears:

> The original line-drawn figure appears on fine china, pewter spoons, and pricey kids' stationery found in upscale specialty and department stores such as Nordstrom and Bloomingdale's. The plump, cartoon-like Pooh, clad in a red shirt and a goofy smile, adorns plastic key chains, polyester bed sheets, and animated videos. It sells in Wal-Mart stores and five-and-dime shops. Except at Disney's own stores, the two Poohs do not share the same retail shelf. [Thus, Disney offers both] upstairs and downstairs Poohs, hoping to land customers on both sides of the [income] divide.[32]

Changing Consumer Spending Patterns

Table 3.3 shows the proportion of total expenditures made by the average Newfoundland and Labrador household in 2004 for major categories of goods and services. Tables for other provinces can be found at www40.statcan.ca/101/cst01/famil16a.htm. Food, housing, and transportation use up most household income (44 percent). This compares with 48 percent in 2001. Consumer spending patterns have changed considerably in the past 50 years. In 1947, spending on the basics (food, clothing, housing, fuel) accounted for 69 cents out of every dollar. What expenditures account for the other 21 cents no longer spent on the basics? Canadians are spending more on two categories—what Statistics Canada refers to as personal goods and services; and recreation, entertainment, education, and cultural services.[33]

However, consumers at different income levels have different spending patterns. Some of these differences were noted over a century ago by Ernst Engel, who studied how people shifted their spending as their income rose. He found that as family income rises, the percentage spent on food declines, the percentage spent on housing remains constant (except for utilities such as gas, electricity, and public services,

Engel's laws
Differences noted more than a century ago by Ernst Engel in how people shift their spending across food, housing, transportation, health care, and other goods and services categories as family income rises.

Table 3.3 2004 Average Newfoundland and Labrador Household Expenditures

Canada 2004		Household characteristics
Estimated number of households		11 952 550
	Average Expenditure per Household $	**Households Reporting Expenditures %**
Total expenditures	63 636	100.0
Total current consumption	45 436	100.0
Food	6 910	100.0
Shelter	12 200	99.9
Household operation	2 920	100.0
Household furnishings and equipment	1 870	92.8
Clothing	2 506	98.2
Transportation	8 626	93.7
Health care	1 690	97.0
Personal care	897	99.4
Recreation	3 678	97.4
Reading materials and other printed matter	283	79.6
Education	1 078	41.2
Tobacco products and alcoholic beverages	1 495	83.5
Games of chance (net amount)	264	70.3
Miscellaneous	1 020	82.4
Personal income taxes	12 902	92.9
Personal insurance payments and pension contributions	3 645	81.7
Gifts of money and contributions	1 652	75.2

Source: "Average Household Expenses, Provinces and Territories," adapted from Statistics Canada website www40.statcan.ca/101/cst01/famil16a.htm (last modified December 12, 2005).

which decrease), and both the percentage spent on other categories and that devoted to savings increase. **Engel's laws** generally have been supported by later studies.

Changes in such major economic variables as income, cost of living, interest rates, and savings and borrowing patterns have a large impact on the marketplace. Companies watch these variables by using economic forecasting. Businesses do not have to be wiped out by an economic downturn or caught short in a boom. With adequate warning, they can take advantage of changes in the economic environment.

Natural Environment

Natural environment
Natural resources that are needed as inputs by marketers or that are affected by marketing activities.

The **natural environment** involves the natural resources that are needed as inputs by marketers or that are affected by marketing activities. Environmental concerns have grown steadily during the past three decades. In many cities around the world, air and water pollution have reached dangerous levels. World concern continues to mount about the possibilities of global warming, and many environmentalists fear that we soon will be buried in our own trash.

Marketers should be aware of trends in the natural environment. The first involves growing *shortages of raw materials*. Air and water may seem to be infinite resources, but some groups see long-run dangers. Air pollution chokes many of the world's large cities. Great Lakes water levels are low, causing problems in many Canadian interior port cities, and water shortages are already a big problem in some parts of the United States and the world. Renewable resources, such as forests and food, also have to be used wisely. Nonrenewable resources, such as oil, coal, and various minerals, pose a serious problem. Firms making products that require these scarce resources face large cost increases, even if the materials do remain available.

A second environmental trend is *increased pollution*. Industry will almost always damage the quality of the natural environment. Consider the disposal of chemical and nuclear wastes; the dangerous mercury levels in the ocean; the quantity of chemical pollutants in the soil and food supply; and the littering of the environment with nonbiodegradable bottles, plastics, and other packaging materials.

A third trend is *increased government intervention* in natural resource management. The governments of different countries vary in their concern and efforts to promote a clean environment. Some, like the German government, vigorously pursue environmental quality. Others, especially many poorer nations, do little about pollution, largely because they lack the needed funds or political will. Even the richer nations lack the vast funds and political accord needed to mount a worldwide environmental effort. The general hope is that companies around the world will accept more social responsibility, and that less expensive devices can be found to control and reduce pollution.

The Canadian government passed the *Environmental Protection Act* in 1989. This act established stringent pollution-control measures as well as the means for their enforcement, including fines as high as $1 million if regulations are violated. In the United States, the Environmental Protection Agency (EPA) was created in 1970 to set and enforce pollution standards and to conduct pollution research. Thus, companies doing business in Canada and the U.S. can expect strong controls from government and pressure groups. Instead of opposing regulation, marketers should help develop solutions to the material and energy problems facing the world.

UPS's fleet of 70 000 boxy brown trucks now includes some 1800 alternative-fuel vehicles, 2500 low-emissions vehicles, and a growing number of electric vehicles, including zero-emission Dodge fuel cell-powered vans like this one.

Concern for the natural environment has spawned the so-called green movement. Today, enlightened companies go beyond what government regulations dictate. They are developing *environmentally sustainable* strategies and practices in an effort to create a world economy that the planet can support indefinitely. They are responding to consumer demands with ecologically safer products, recyclable or biodegradable packaging, recycled materials and components, better pollution controls, and more energy-efficient operations.

3M runs a Pollution Prevention Pays program that helps prevent pollution at the source—in products and manufacturing processes. Between 1975 and 2002, the program prevented 777 713 tonnes of pollutants and saved US$894 million. McDonald's has a long-standing rainforest policy and a commitment to purchasing recycled products and energy-efficient restaurant construction techniques. And UPS's fleet of 70 000 boxy brown trucks now includes some 1800 alternative-fuel vehicles, 2500 low-emissions vehicles, and a growing number of electric vehicles. Loblaw (www.Loblaw.com) began its G.R.E.E.N. program in 1989; today, it is one of the most successful environmental businesses in the world. More than 100 new products have been launched since the program's inception, while manufacturing changes have helped make dozens of other products environmentally friendly. More and more, companies are recognizing the link between a healthy economy and a healthy ecology.[34]

Technological environment

Forces that create new technologies, creating new product and market opportunities.

Technological Environment

The **technological environment** is perhaps the most dramatic force now shaping our destiny. Technology has released such wonders as antibiotics, organ transplants, laptop computers, and the Internet. It also has released such horrors as nuclear missiles, chemical weapons, and assault rifles. It has released such mixed blessings as the automobile, television, and credit cards. Our attitude toward technology depends on whether we are more impressed with its wonders or its blunders. For example, what would you think about having tiny transmitters implanted in all of the products you buy that would allow for tracking products from their point of production though use and disposal? On the one hand, it would provide many advantages. On the other hand, it could be a bit scary. Either way, it's already happening (see Real Marketing 3.2).

The technological environment changes rapidly. Think of all of today's common products that were not available 100 years ago, or even 30 years ago. John A. Macdonald did not know about automobiles, airplanes, radios, or the electric light. William Lyon Mackenzie King did not know about xerography, synthetic detergents, or Earth satellites. And John Diefenbaker did not know about personal computers, MP3 players, or the Internet.

New technologies create new markets and opportunities. However, every new technology replaces an older technology. Transistors hurt the vacuum-tube industry, xerography hurt the carbon-paper business, the auto hurt the railroads, and compact discs hurt phonograph records. When old industries fought or ignored new technologies, their businesses declined. Thus, marketers should watch the technological environment closely. Companies that do not keep up with technological change soon will find their products outdated. And they will miss new product and market opportunities.

The United States leads the world in research and development (R&D) spending. Total U.S. R&D spending reached an estimated US$291 billion in 2004.[35] Canada, in comparison, spends approximately $24 billion per year for R&D.[36] Japan leads both countries when it comes to the proportion of GDP spent on R&D. Canada ranks fifteenth in the world in research and development spending as a percentage of all products and services, but knowing the importance of R&D to economic growth, the Canadian government is aiming to be among the top five research-intensive countries in the world.[37]

REAL MARKETING

3.2

Tiny Transmitters in Every Product.
Is This Great Technology, or What?

*E*nvision a world in which every product contains a tiny transmitter, loaded with information. Imagine a time when we could track every item electronically—anywhere in the world, at any time, automatically. Producers could track the precise flow of goods up and down the supply chain, ensuring timely deliveries and lowering inventory and distribution costs. Retailers could track real-time merchandise movements in their stores, helping them manage inventories, keep shelves full, and automatically reorder goods.

And picture the futuristic new world that such technology would create for consumers:

As you stroll through the aisles of your supermarket, you pluck a six-pack of your favourite beverage from the shelf. Shelf sensors detect your selection and beam an ad to the screen on your shopping cart, offering special deals on

salty snacks that might go great with your beverage. When you reach the shampoo section, electronic readers scan your cart and note that you haven't made the usual monthly purchase of your favourite brand. "Did you forget the shampoo?" asks the screen. As your shopping cart fills, scanners detect that you might be buying for a dinner party; the screen suggests a wine that complements the meal you've planned. After shopping, you bag your groceries and leave the store. Exit scanners automatically total up your purchases and charge them to your credit card. At home, readers track what goes into and out of your pantry, automatically updating your shopping list when stocks run low. To plan your Sunday dinner, you scan the Butterball turkey you just purchased. An embedded transmitter chip yields serving instructions and recipes for several side dishes. You pop the bird into your "smart oven," which fol-

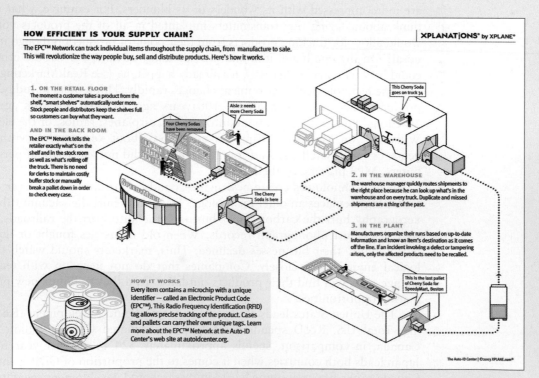

Imagine a time when we could track every item electronically—anywhere in the world, at any time, automatically. RFID technology might soon make this a reality.

lows instructions coded on the chip and cooks the turkey to perfection. Is this great technology, or what?

Seem far-fetched? Not really. In fact, it might soon become a reality with the backing of such marketing heavyweights as Wal-Mart, Home Depot, Target, Albertson's, Procter & Gamble, Coca-Cola, IBM, and Gillette.

This futuristic technology is exploding onto today's marketing scene, boosted by the rapid development of tiny, affordable radio-frequency identification (RFID) transmitters—or smart chips—that can be embedded in all of the products you buy. The transmitters are so small that several would fit on the head of a pin. Yet they can be packed with coded information that can be read and rewritten at any point in the supply chain.

RFID technology (also called Auto-ID) provides producers and retailers with amazing new ways to track inventories, trends, and sales. They can use embedded chips to follow products—everything from ice cream and cat food to tires, insulation, and jet engines—step by step from factories to warehouses to retail shelves to recycling centres.

The smart chips make today's bar code systems seem badly outmoded. Whereas bar codes must be visible to be read, embedded RFID chips can be read in any location. Bar codes identify only a product's manufacturer. In contrast, the chips can identify each individual product item and can carry codes that, when paired with a database containing the details, reveal an almost endless supply of information. Thus, beyond identifying an item as a litre of Nielsen 2% skim milk, an embedded smart chip can identify that *specific* litre of milk—its manufacture date, expiration date, location in the supply chain, and a storehouse of other product-specific information.

Although it may seem futuristic, Auto-ID technology is already in use. Every time consumers flash an ExxonMobil Speed-Pass card to purchase gas at the pump or breeze through an automated toll booth, they're using an RFID chip. In addition, Auto-ID technology is being tested and implemented by a number of big companies. For example, Gillette recently launched two RFID pilot projects. The first project uses embedded transmitters to track products from the factory to grocery store shelves. Gillette hopes that the technology will improve service to its retail customers while at the same time reducing its inventories from between 5 percent to 25 percent. In the second project, Gillette has installed readers on shelves in selected Wal-Mart and Tesco stores. It claims that retailers lose more than US$30 billion a year in sales because shelves aren't fully stocked. The shelf readers track Gillette's razors as they come and go, and prompt store staff to restock when quantities dwindle.

Other large manufacturers and retailers are adding fuel to the RFID fire. Procter & Gamble plans to have the chips on products in broad distribution as soon as 2008. By 2010, P&G will be able to link shopper loyalty card information with data about the products they buy. Mega-retailers, such as Wal-Mart and Target, have already ordered their top suppliers to be RFID-capable.

Even smaller retailers are putting smart chips to work. Fashion retailer Prada recently installed the chips in its store in New York City. Based on scans of items in customers' hands, video screens show personalized product demonstrations and designer sketches. In dressing rooms, readers identify each item of clothing a customer tries it on and offer additional size, colour, and design information through interactive touch screens.

With innovations like these, you'd think most consumers would welcome the tiny transmitters. But many consumer advocates worry about invasion of privacy issues. If companies can link products to specific consumers and track consumer buying and usage, they fear, marketers would gain access to too much personal information. Says one analyst, "Backers of the technology appear torn between the urge to hype its huge potential and fear that consumers will get spooked."

To counter these concerns, Auto-ID technology proponents point out that the transmitters have limited range, most under six metres. So reading chips inside consumers' homes or tracking them on the move would be nearly impossible. The Auto-ID industry is also working to address consumer privacy concerns. Among other things, it is drafting a privacy policy that includes giving customers the option of permanently disabling the chips at checkout. And according to an RFID consultant, the basic mission is not to spy on consumers. It's to serve them better. "It's not Orwellian. That is absolutely, positively not the vision of Auto-ID," she says. "The vision is for … brand manufacturers and retailers to be able to have right-time, right-promotion, real-time eye-to-eye [contact] with the consumer."

In coming years, as smart chips appear on more and more products, RFID technology will no doubt bring significant benefits to both marketers and the customers they serve. "The idea of someone using tiny radio transmitters to influence consumer purchase behaviour was once only the stuff of paranoid delusions," says the analyst. "But in the not-so-distant future, it could become the basis of a new generation of marketing."

▶

Sources: Jack Neff, "A Chip Over Your Shoulder?" *Advertising Age,* April 22, 2002, p. 4; "Business: The Best Thing Since the Bar-Code: The IT Revolution," *The Economist,* February 8, 2003, p. 57–58; "Gillette, Michelin Begin RFID Pilots," *Frontline Solutions,* March 2003, p. 8; "RFID Benefits Apparent," *Chain Store Age,* March 2003, p. 63; Faith Keenan, "If Supermarket Shelves Could Talk," *Business Week,* March 31, 2003, pp. 66–67; Jack Neff, "P&G Products to Wear Wire," *Advertising Age,* December 15, 2004, pp. 1, 32; Greg Lindsey, "Prada's High-Tech Misstep," *Business 2.0,* March 2004, pp. 72–75; Kevin Higgins "Brave New RFID World," *Food Engineering,* January 2004, p. 81; Robert Spiegel, "RFID Report," *Supply Chain Management Review,* April 2004, pp. 17–18; and information accessed online at www.autoidlabs.org, July 2004.

To accomplish this aim, Industry Canada and the National Research Council are funding new efforts to foster increased research. Other government-backed initiatives include the Canada Foundation for Innovation, which awards funds to help post-secondary educational institutions, research hospitals, and non-profit institutions modernize their research infrastructure and equip themselves for state-of-the-art research.

Scientists today are researching a wide range of promising new products and services, ranging from practical solar energy, electric cars, and cancer cures to voice-controlled computers and genetically engineered food crops. Today's research usually is carried out by research teams rather than by lone inventors, such as Alexander Graham Bell. Many companies are adding marketing people to R&D teams to try to obtain a stronger marketing orientation. Scientists also speculate on fantasy products, such as flying cars, three-dimensional televisions, and space colonies. The challenge in each case is not only technical but also commercial—to make *practical, affordable* versions of these products.

As products and technology become more complex, the public needs to know that these are safe. Canada has a complex web of departments and regulations devoted to issues associated with product safety. For example, Agriculture and Agri-Food Canada and the Canadian Food Inspection Agency monitor the safety of food products. The Department of Justice Canada oversees the *Consumer Packaging and Labelling Act,* the *Food and Drug Act,* and the *Hazardous Products Act.* Health Canada also has a food safety and product safety division. Transport Canada governs vehicle recalls.

The technological environment is a dramatic force that creates new markets and opportunities.

Political Environment

Political environment
Laws, government agencies, and pressure groups that influence and limit various organizations and individuals in a given society.

Marketing decisions are strongly affected by developments in the political environment. The **political environment** consists of laws, government agencies, and pressure groups that influence or limit various organizations and individuals in a given society.

Legislation Regulating Business

Even the most liberal advocates of free-market economies agree that the system works best with at least some regulation. Well-conceived regulation can encourage competition and ensure fair markets for goods and services. Thus, governments develop *public policy* to guide commerce—sets of laws and regulations that limit business for the good of society as a whole. Almost every marketing activity is subject to a wide range of laws and regulations.

Increasing Legislation Legislation affecting business around the world has increased steadily over the years. Canada has many laws covering such issues as competition, fair trade practices, environmental protection, product safety, truth in advertising, packaging and labelling, pricing, and other important areas (see Table 3.4). The European Commission has been active in establishing a new framework of laws covering competitive behaviour, product standards, product liability, and commercial transactions for the nations of the European Union.

Several countries have gone further than Canada in passing strong consumerism legislation. For example, Norway bans several forms of sales promotion—trading stamps, contests, premiums—as being inappropriate or unfair ways of promoting products. Thailand requires food processors selling national brands to market low-price brands also, so that low-income consumers can find economy brands on the shelves. In India, food companies must obtain special approval to launch brands that duplicate those already existing on the market, such as additional soft drinks or new brands of rice.

Understanding the public-policy implications of a particular marketing activity is not a simple matter. For example, in Canada, many laws are created at the federal, provincial, and municipal levels, and these regulations often overlap. Moreover, regulations are constantly changing—what was allowed last year may now be prohibited, and what was prohibited may now be allowed. Marketers must work hard to keep up with changes in regulations and their interpretations.

Business legislation has been enacted for a number of reasons. The first is to *protect companies* from each other. Although business executives may praise competition, they sometimes try to neutralize it when it threatens them. So laws are passed to define and prevent unfair competition.

The second purpose of government regulation is to *protect consumers* from unfair business practices. Some firms, if left alone, would make shoddy products, tell lies in their advertising, and deceive consumers through their packaging and pricing. Unfair business practices have been defined and are enforced by various agencies.

The third purpose of government regulation is to *protect the interests of society* against unrestrained business behaviour. Profitable business activity does not always create a better quality of life. Regulation arises to ensure that firms take responsibility for the social costs of their production or products.

Changing Government Agency Enforcement International marketers will encounter dozens, or even hundreds, of agencies set up to enforce trade policies and regulations. In Canada, several federal agencies, such as Health Canada, the Canadian Food Inspection Agency, Industry Canada, and the Canadian Environmental Assessment Agency, have been established. Because such government

Table 3.4 Major Federal Legislation Affecting Marketing

The *Competition Act* is a major legislative act affecting the marketing activities of companies in Canada. Specific sections and the relevant areas are

- Section 34: Pricing—Forbids suppliers to charge different prices to competitors purchasing like quantities of goods (price discrimination). Forbids price-cutting that lessens competition (predatory pricing).

- Section 36: Pricing and Advertising—Forbids advertising prices that misrepresent the "usual" selling price (misleading price advertising).

- Section 38: Pricing—Forbids suppliers to require subsequent resellers to offer products at a stipulated price (resale price maintenance).

- Section 33: Mergers—Forbids mergers by which competition is, or is likely to be, lessened to the detriment of the interests of the public.

Other selected acts that have an impact on marketing activities are

- *National Trade Mark and True Labelling Act*—Established the term *Canada Standard,* or *CS*, as a national trademark; requires certain commodities to be properly labelled or described in advertising for the purpose of indicating material content or quality.

- *Consumer Packaging and Labelling Act*—Provides a set of rules to ensure that full information is disclosed by the manufacturer, packer, or distributor. Requires that all prepackaged products bear the quantity in French and English in metric as well as traditional Canadian standard units of weight, volume, or measure.

- *Motor Vehicle Safety Act*—Establishes mandatory safety standards for motor vehicles.

- *Food and Drug Act*—Prohibits the advertisement and sale of adulterated or misbranded foods, cosmetics, and drugs.

- *Personal Information Protection and Electronic Documents Act*—Establishes rules to govern the collection, use, and disclosure of personal information that recognize the right of privacy of individuals. The law recognizes the needs of organizations to collect, use, or disclose personal information for appropriate purposes. (For full details of the act, see www.privcom.gc.ca/legislation/02_06_01_e.asp.)

agencies have some discretion in enforcing the laws, they can have a major impact on a company's marketing performance. At times, the staffs of these agencies have appeared to be overly eager and unpredictable. Some of the agencies sometimes have been dominated by lawyers and economists who lacked a practical sense of how business and marketing work.

New laws and their enforcement will continue to increase. Business executives must watch these developments when planning their products and marketing programs. Marketers need to know about the major laws protecting competition, consumers, and society. They need to understand these laws at the local, provincial, national, and international levels.

Increased Emphasis on Ethics and Socially Responsible Actions

Written regulations cannot possibly cover all potential marketing abuses, and existing laws are often difficult to enforce. However, beyond written laws and regulations, business is also governed by social codes and rules of professional ethics.

Socially Responsible Behaviour Changing Government Agency Enforcement Enlightened companies encourage their managers to look beyond what the regulatory system allows and simply "do the right thing." These socially responsible firms actively seek out ways to protect the long-run interests of their consumers and the environment. The recent rash of business scandals and increased concerns about the environment have created fresh interest in the issues of ethics and social responsibility. More companies are now developing policies, guidelines, and other responses to complex social responsibility issues. For example, 45 percent of Fortune 250 companies issued environmental, social, or sustainability reports in 2001, up from 35 percent in 1998.[38]

The boom in ecommerce and Internet marketing has created a new set of social and ethical issues. Online privacy issues are the primary concern. For example, website visitors often provide extensive personal information that might leave them open to abuse by unscrupulous marketers. Moreover, both Intel and Microsoft have been accused of covert, high-tech computer chip and software invasions of customers' personal computers to obtain information for marketing purposes.[39]

Throughout the text, we present Real Marketing exhibits that summarize the main public policy, ethical, and social responsibility issues surrounding major marketing decisions. In Chapter 4, we discuss a broad range of societal marketing issues in greater depth.

Cultural Environment

Cultural environment
Institutions and other forces that affect society's basic values, perceptions, preferences, and behaviours.

The **cultural environment** is made up of institutions and other forces that affect a society's basic values, perceptions, preferences, and behaviours. People grow up in a particular society that shapes their basic beliefs and values. They absorb a worldview that defines their relationships with others. The following cultural characteristics can affect marketing decision making.

Persistence of Cultural Values

People in a given society hold many beliefs and values. Their core beliefs and values have a high degree of persistence. For example, many Canadians believe in cultural diversity (versus assimilation), respect for human rights, democracy, gender equality, stability of government, the rule of law, sustainable development, social support for the underprivileged, universal health care, a love of nature, hard work, getting married, giving to charity, and being honest.[40] These beliefs shape more specific attitudes and behaviours found in everyday life. *Core* beliefs and values are passed on from parents to children and are reinforced by schools, churches, business, and government.

Secondary beliefs and values are more open to change. Believing in marriage is a core belief; believing that people should get married early in life is a secondary belief. Marketers have some chance of changing secondary values but little chance of changing core values. For example, family-planning marketers could argue more effectively that people should get married later than that they should not get married at all.

Shifts in Secondary Cultural Values

Although core values are fairly persistent, cultural swings do take place. Consider the impact of popular music groups, movie personalities, and other celebrities on young people's hairstyling and clothing norms. Marketers want to predict cultural shifts in order to spot new opportunities or threats. Several firms offer "futures" forecasts in this connection, such as the Yankelovich Monitor, Market Facts' BrainWaves Group, and the Trends Research Institute.

The Yankelovich Monitor has tracked consumer value trends for years. At the dawn of the twenty-first century, it looked back to capture lessons from the past decade that might offer insight into the 2000s.[41] Yankelovich maintains that the "decade drivers" for the 2000s will primarily come from the baby boomers and

Generation Xers. The baby boomers will be driven by four factors in the 2000s: "adventure" (fuelled by a sense of youthfulness), "smarts" (fuelled by a sense of empowerment and willingness to accept change), "intergenerational support" (caring for younger and older, often in nontraditional arrangements), and "retreading" (embracing early retirement with a second career or phase of their work life). Gen Xers will be driven by three factors: "redefining the good life" (being highly motivated to improve their economic well-being and remain in control), "new rituals" (returning to traditional values but with a tolerant mindset and active lifestyle), and "cutting and pasting" (balancing work, play, sleep, family, and other aspects of their lives).

The major cultural values of a society are expressed in people's views of themselves and others, as well as in their views of organizations, society, nature, and the universe.

People's Views of Themselves People vary in their emphasis on serving themselves versus serving others. Some people seek personal pleasure, wanting fun, change, and escape. Others seek self-realization through religion, recreation, or the avid pursuit of careers or other life goals. People use products, brands, and services as a means of self-expression, and they buy products and services that match their views of themselves.

Yankelovich Monitor recently discovered a conflicted consumer segment whose purchases are motivated by self-views of both duty and fun:[42]

> The Yankelovich Monitor has identified a paradoxical consumer segment motivated equally by duty and fun. Comprising more than one-third of the population, these folks want to have their cake and rely on it, too. "Duty and Fun" consumers agree that "duty should always come before pleasure" *and* say that they "try to have as much fun as they can now and let the future take care of itself." Their split personalities indicate an internal struggle that affects everyday life and buying. To reach these conflicted consumers, marketers must give them something that makes them smile at the register, while offering sound payment options, guarantees, testimonials, and other forms of assurance. For example, PetSmart permits shoppers to bring their pets shopping, allowing duty and fun to happily coexist. And with its hybrid Prius, Toyota merges a respected company brand (duty) and leading-edge technology (fun), turning what could have been a fuddy-duddy failure into a ride for those sold on dutiful fun.

People's Views of Others Recently, observers have noted a shift from a "me society" to a "we society" in which more people want to be with and serve others.[43]

> After years of serious "nesting"—staying close to the security and creature comforts of home and hearth—Canadians are finally starting to tiptoe out of their homes to hang out in the real world. The nesting instinct has gone in and out of fashion before. When the first big wave hit in the early '80s, trend watchers coined the term "cocooning" to describe the surge of boomers buying their first homes and filling them up with oversize furniture and fancy gadgets. The dot-com boom set off another round, partly fuelled by cool home gizmos like plasma TVs and PlayStations. Though many expected 9/11 to send people even deeper into nesting mode, sociologists say it actually got people out looking for companionship. Marketers are beginning to address the shift. The Running Room, for example, creates communities for people wanting to walk or run with others. And no less a nesting icon than Home Depot is expanding its gardening business, testing out landscape-supply stores.

More and more, people want to get out of the house and be with others. This trend suggests a greater demand for "social support" products and services that improve direct communication between people, such as health clubs and family vacations.

PetSmart serves the conflicted "duty and fun" segment by permitting customers to bring their pets shopping, allowing duty and fun to happily coexist.

People's Views of Organizations   People have differing attitudes toward corporations, government agencies, trade unions, universities, and other organizations. By and large, people are willing to work for major organizations, and they expect them, in turn, to carry out society's work. Canadians increasingly desire greater autonomy and personal freedom in the workplace, however. If they can't control their work, many are turning to self-employment as a means of achieving the autonomy desired.[44] Since the late 1980s, there has been a sharp decrease in confidence in and loyalty toward business and political organizations and institutions. Waves of company downsizings in the 1990s bred further cynicism and distrust. And recent corporate scandals at Enron, WorldCom, Tyco International, and other large companies have resulted in a further loss of confidence in big business. Many people today see work not as a source of satisfaction but as a required chore to earn money to enjoy their nonwork hours. These trends suggest that organizations need to find new ways to win consumer and employee confidence.

People's Views of Society   People differ in their attitudes toward their society: nationalists defend it, reformers want to change it, and malcontents want to leave it. Canadians increasingly want to have intense and energetic lives lived in a more ethical world.[45] People's orientation to their society influences their consumption patterns, levels of savings, and attitudes toward the marketplace. For example, more and more Canadians have a sense of national pride. Some companies, such as Zellers, responded with "made-in-Canada" themes and promotions. Others, such as Petro-Canada, Clearly Canadian, Molson Canadian, and Upper Canada Brewing Company, made national identity part of their branding strategy.

People's Views of Nature   People vary in their attitudes toward the natural world. Some feel ruled by it, others feel in harmony with it, and still others seek to master it. A long-term trend has been people's growing mastery over nature through technology and the belief that nature is bountiful. More recently, however, people have recognized that nature is finite and fragile, that it can be destroyed or spoiled by human activities.

This renewed love of all things natural has created a sizable "lifestyles of health and sustainability" (LOHAS) market for everything from natural, organic, and nutritional products to renewable energy and alternative medicine. Business has responded by offering more products and services catering to these interests. Tour operators are offering more wilderness adventures, and retailers are offering more fitness gear and apparel. Marketing communicators are using appealing natural backgrounds in advertising their products. And food producers have found growing markets for natural and organic foods. Canadian organic retail sales have been growing by a whopping 20 percent a year. Chains specializing in organic foods like Planet Organic, headquartered in Port Coquitlam, B.C., are springing up. Approximately one in twenty fruit and vegetable farms in Canada considers itself to be an organic producer, and Canada is among the top five world producers of organic grains and oilseeds. Most of Canada's organically grown products are exported to the United States, Europe, and Japan. The worldwide market is huge and sales of organic products are estimated at $20 billion.[46]

People's Views of the Universe   Finally, people vary in their beliefs about the origin of the universe and their place in it. Although many Canadians have religious beliefs, attendance at religious services has been dropping off gradually through the years. A recent Statistics Canada survey shows Canadians' continuing slide out the doors of the country's churches, temples, and synagogues. In 1946, 67 percent of adult Canadians regularly attended religious services, but by 2001, the figure had dropped to 20 percent. Yann Martel, Canadian author of the acclaimed *Life of Pi*,

Marketers are responding to changes in people's view of the natural environment by offering more natural and organic products. White Wave's Silk soymilk has found success in the $25 billion industry.

noted in an interview that Canadians and Americans are going in opposite directions with regard to religion. "America is a very religious, almost puritanical country. In Canada, secularism is triumphant, and to talk noncynically, nonironically about religion is strange," he says. Only 30 percent of Canadians report religion is very important to them, compared with 59 percent of Americans. The statistics would be even more skewed if it were not for the growing number of devout Muslim, Sikh, and Hindu immigrants now living in Canada. Canadian marketers have to use caution when picking up lifestyle ads from the United States. While showing people in religious settings may draw attention from American consumers, they may strike Canadians as inappropriate.[47]

Responding to the Marketing Environment

Someone once observed, "There are three kinds of companies: those who make things happen, those who watch things happen, and those who wonder what's happened."[48] Many companies view the marketing environment as an uncontrollable element to which they must react and adapt. They passively accept the marketing environment and do not try to change it. They analyze the environmental forces and design strategies that will help the company avoid the threats and take advantage of the opportunities the environment provides.

Other companies take a *proactive* stance toward the marketing environment. Rather than simply watching and reacting, these firms take aggressive actions to affect the publics and forces in their marketing environment. Such companies hire lobbyists to influence legislation affecting their industries and stage media events to gain favourable press coverage. They run advertorials (ads expressing editorial points of view) to shape public opinion. They press lawsuits and file complaints with regulators to keep competitors in line, and they form contractual agreements to better control their distribution channels.

Often, companies can find positive ways to overcome seemingly uncontrollable environmental constraints. For example,

> Cathay Pacific Airlines ... determined that many travelers were avoiding Hong Kong because of lengthy delays at immigration. Rather than assuming that this was a problem they could not solve, Cathay's senior staff asked the Hong Kong government how to avoid these immigration delays. After lengthy discussions, the airline agreed to make an annual grant-in-aid to the government to hire more immigration inspectors—but these reinforcements would service primarily the Cathay Pacific gates. The reduced waiting period increased customer value and thus strengthened [Cathay's competitive advantage].[49]

Marketing management cannot always control environmental forces. In many cases, it must settle for simply watching and reacting to the environment. For example, a company would have little success trying to influence geographic population shifts, the economic environment, or major cultural values. But whenever possible, smart marketing managers will take a *proactive* rather than *reactive* approach to the marketing environment.

Reviewing the Concepts

In this chapter and the next three chapters, you'll examine the environments of marketing and how companies analyze these environments to better understand the marketplace and consumers. Companies must constantly watch and manage the *marketing environment* in order to seek opportunities and ward off threats. The marketing environment comprises all the actors and forces influencing the company's ability to transact business effectively with its target market.

1. Describe the environmental forces that affect the company's ability to serve its customers.

The company's *microenvironment* consists of other actors close to the company that combine to form the company's value delivery network or that affect its ability to serve its customers. It includes the company's *internal environment*—its several departments and management levels—as it influences marketing decision making. *Marketing-channel firms*—suppliers and marketing intermediaries, including resellers, physical distribution firms, marketing services agencies, and financial intermediaries—cooperate to create customer value. Five types of customer *markets* include consumer, business, reseller, government, and international markets. *Competitors* vie with the company in an effort to serve customers better. Finally, various *publics* have an actual or potential interest in or impact on the company's ability to meet its objectives.

The *macroenvironment* consists of larger societal forces that affect the entire microenvironment. The six forces making up the company's macroenvironment include demographic, economic, natural, technological, political, and cultural forces. These forces shape opportunities and pose threats to the company.

2. Explain how changes in the demographic and economic environments affect marketing decisions.

Demography is the study of the characteristics of human populations. Today's *demographic environment* shows a changing age structure, shifting family profiles, geographic population shifts, a better-educated and more white-collar population, and increasing diversity. The *economic environment* consists of factors that affect buying power and patterns. The economic environment is characterized by more consumer concern for value and shifting consumer spending patterns. Today's squeezed consumers are seeking greater value—just the right combination of good quality and service at a fair price. The distribution of income also is shifting. The rich have grown richer, the middle class has shrunk, and the poor have remained poor, leading to a two-tiered market. Many companies now tailor their marketing offers to two different markets—the affluent and the less affluent.

3. Identify the major trends in the firm's natural and technological environments.

The *natural environment* shows three major trends: shortages of certain raw materials, higher pollution levels, and more government intervention in natural resource management. Environmental concerns create marketing opportunities for alert companies. The marketer should watch for four major trends in the *technological environment*: the rapid pace of technological change, high R&D budgets, the concentration by companies on minor product improvements, and increased government regulation. Companies that fail to keep up with technological change will miss out on new product and marketing opportunities.

4. Explain the key changes in the political and cultural environments.

The *political environment* consists of laws, agencies, and groups that influence or limit marketing actions. The political environment has undergone three changes that affect marketing worldwide: increased legislation regulating business, strong government agency enforcement, and greater emphasis on ethics and socially responsible actions. The *cultural environment* is made up of institutions and forces that affect a society's values, perceptions, preferences, and behaviours. The environment shows long-term trends toward a "we society," a lessening trust of institutions, increasing patriotism, greater appreciation for nature, a new spiritualism, and the search for more meaningful and enduring values.

5. Discuss how companies can react to the marketing environment.

Companies can passively accept the marketing environment as an uncontrollable element to which they must adapt, avoiding threats and taking advantage of opportunities as they arise. Or they can take a *proactive* stance, working to change the environment rather than simply reacting to it. Whenever possible, companies should try to be proactive rather than reactive.

Reviewing the Key Terms

Discussing the Concepts

1. List the six actors in the company's microenvironment. Next, go to Research in Motion's website at www.rim.net. Click on the Investors button, and then on the Annual Report link in the left-hand column. In the annual report, how many of the six microenvironment actors can you find? Briefly describe each.

2. List the six larger macroenvironmental forces. Go to the ATCO Group's website at www.atco.com. Atco is an Alberta-based corporation actively engaged worldwide in power generation, utilities, and global enterprises. Click on the Investor Relations bar at the top of the page and select Financial Reports from the menu. Find the most recent annual report. In the annual report, find and briefly describe as many of the six macroenvironmental forces as you can.

3. The text lists seven types of publics that may affect a company's ability to achieve its objectives. Assume you are a marketing manager for an automobile company. You have been charged with repositioning an SUV model that was once identified as a "fuel guzzler." The model has been redesigned with a superefficient,

nonpolluting hybrid engine. Which of the seven types of publics would have the greatest impact on your establishing the new "fuel-efficient" positioning?

4. A wag once said, "You can watch the size of the Cadillac market shrink by just reading the obituaries." In the context of the external environmental forces discussed in the chapter, what did this person mean? What has Cadillac done to counter this trend? From an environmental management perspective, are Cadillac's actions reactive or proactive? Why?

5. Discuss the primary reasons why a company would hire a lobbyist in Ottawa. Would it make sense for the same company to also hire lobbyist at the provincial level? Why?

6. There's an old saying that "two good marketing people can't make up for one bad technology decision." Is it a certainty that a company will lose out on new opportunities if it does not keep up with new technology? Explain your position. Can you think of an industry where technology may not play an important role?

Applying the Concepts

1. Manic Panic (www.manicpanic.com) is one of the more popular brands at Hot Topic (see Real Marketing 3.1 on page 90–91). Tish and Snooky, two sisters from the Bronx, opened their shop in New York's East Village business district because, "there was no other store or company that catered to ... musicians, punks, Goths, club-kids, performers, dancers, models and just about

anyone who likes a little wild style." Using the macroenvironmental forces and recent trends as the basis for your answer, explain why you believe Manic Panic has been successful. Would your answers be the same if you were explaining the success of SoulDaisy (www.souldaisy.com/index.html), founded in 2000 by Vancouver clothing designer Shainin Hudda? Why?

Focus on Technology

The U.S. Federal Trade Commission (FTC) recently hosted a public workshop on Radio Frequency Identification (RFID) to discuss all of the technology's applications as well as its potential pitfalls. At the workshop, one speaker commented that RFID "promises to reform, if not revolutionize, many corners of the marketplace." As we discussed in the chapter, RFID is already a part of many consumers' daily lives. And, as companies like Wal-Mart and Gillette embrace the technology, RFID is truly changing the way suppliers and retailers work together.

At the FTC workshop, Simon Langford, Manager of RFID Strategy for Wal-Mart, offered his thoughts on the benefits of RFID. Review his presentation online at

www.ftc.gov/bcp/workshops/rfid/langford.pdf and answer the following questions:

1. How does RFID help strengthen Wal-Mart's relationships with its many partners?

2. What are some of the benefits for Wal-Mart? For Wal-Mart's suppliers?

3. How does RFID technology increase value and satisfaction for Wal-Mart's customers?

4. How might consumer privacy concerns affect the widespread acceptance of RFID technology?

Focus on Ethics

In *Imperfect Alternatives: Choosing Institutions in Law, Economics and Public Policy,* Neil Komesar discusses who should make the rules governing major public policy, including environmental concerns, nonrenewable resource conservation, and information privacy. He asks who should decide when it comes to making the rules on these tough issues. Should we let the private sector (business) make the rules, and let it be sorted out in the market? Should we leave it to the courts, who are charged with interpreting the laws? Or should government agencies be primarily responsible?

1. In small groups, choose one of the three issues above (environmental concerns, nonrenewable resources, or information privacy) and present three reasons that the private sector is the best institution to make the rules.

2. Have you heard these arguments used by business before? Are these good arguments?

3. Are you convinced that the private sector is suited to establish the rules? If not, which of the other institutions would you select?

Video Case
American Express

You might think that the explosion of media outlets—everything from cable channels and Internet sites to interactive retail stores and electronic billboards—has made it easier for marketers to reach consumers. But, in many cases, all of the new choices have resulted in fragmented market access, with few good mainstream options for reaching the masses. Even more challenging for marketers, customers themselves are choosing when and how they want to interact with marketers and retailers. In this new marketing environment, marketers are seeking new ways to break through the clutter and build lasting relationships with consumers.

The marketers at American Express face a special challenge when trying to reach out to customers. Credit card companies are notorious for contributing to the marketing clutter by bombarding consumers with offers. Just stop and think—how many credit card

offers did you receive in the mail last week? To break through, American Express first creates credit cards that meet the differing needs of specific consumer groups based on income and spending habits. Then the credit card giant creates advertisements and promotions targeting each group.

After viewing the video featuring American Express, answer the following questions about the marketing environment.

1. Is American Express taking a proactive approach to managing its marketing environment? How?

2. Select one of the demographic trends detailed in the chapter and discuss how that trend impacts American Express's core customers and, in turn, the company's marketing efforts.

Online Media Resources

Video Short
Log on to your Companion Website at **www.pearsoned.ca/kotler** to view the video segment related to the Video Case on page 116.

CBC ✦ CBC Video Case
Please refer to Appendix 2 to read a CBC Video Case for this chapter, and log on to your Companion Website at **www.pearsoned.ca/kotler** to view the corresponding video segment.

Case Pilot
Log on to your Companion Website at **www.pearsoned.ca/kotler** to sharpen your case analysis skills and take the Case Pilot Challenge!

Company Case
Prius: Leading a Wave of Hybrids

North Americans love their cars. Until the recent rapid escalation in gas prices, SUVs sold briskly, and one of the biggest spectator sports is stockcar racing. Thus, it might not appear logical that a small, hybrid, sluggish vehicle would sell well in the North American market. Despite such expectations, Toyota successfully introduced the Prius in Canada in July 2001, first selling the car in Toronto and Ottawa before rolling it out nationally. During the same period, Honda introduced the Insight. The Prius, whose name means "to go before," was targeted at Canadians who wanted or needed a vehicle but who were also concerned about the environment. Soon after launch, the cars virtually flew out of dealer showrooms, even if consumers weren't quite sure how to pronounce it (PREE-us, not PRY-us). Given Toyota's success with the Prius and Honda's with the Insight, other automotive companies have plans to introduce hybrids of some sort.

Hybrid vehicles have both a gas engine and an electric motor. When starting up or at very low speeds (under 24 kph), the auto runs on the electric motor. At roughly 24 kph, the gas engine kicks in. This means that the auto gets power from only the battery at low speeds, and from both the gas engine and electric motor during heavy acceleration. Once up to speed, the gas engine sends power directly to the wheels and, through the generator, to the electric motor or battery. When braking, energy from the slowing wheels—energy that is wasted in a conventional car—is sent back through the electric motor to charge the battery. At a stop, the gas engine shuts off, saving fuel. When the driver presses the accelerator, the electric motor kicks in. When starting up and operating at low speeds, the auto does not make noise, which seems eerie to some drivers and to pedestrians who don't hear it coming!

The original Prius was a small, cramped compact with a dull design. It had a four-cylinder gas engine and

a 33-kilowatt electric motor. It went from 0 to 100 kph in a woeful 14.5 seconds. But it got 5.6 litres per 100 km. The 2004 Prius is a much spiffier-looking car that can hit 100 kph in 10.5 seconds and get 4.3 litres per 100 km. Its top speed is 170 kph. Although that sounds like a big improvement, in actual driving it isn't so exciting. One test driver referred to the Prius as labouring its way to 60 in 10.5 seconds; then taking another 10.5 seconds to get to 80, and then he didn't have enough time in the day to get to 100 kph. The car ran a 400-metre track in 18 seconds at 124 kph; so the test driver concluded that you could drag race any school bus, confident of victory. But you'd better watch out for SUVs—they can blow you off the road! A muscle car, the Prius isn't.

In a continent where getting everywhere quickly seems to be the mantra, why would the Prius be so successful? For the first model, the answer lies in Toyota's clever marketing campaign. To begin with, it wasn't aimed at the mass market. Instead, Toyota thought that the first hybrid buyers would be "techies" and early adopters (people who are highly likely to buy something just because it's new). The company was right. Once Toyota identified the target market, it was able to educate the *right* consumers two years before introduction. The company established a website to distribute information and sent ebrochures to 40 000 likely buyers just before the introduction. The press was also excited about the technology. Auto magazines, and even general interest media, ran articles describing, enthusing, or belittling the hybrids. All of this coverage helped Toyota sell 1800 cars immediately.

In all, Toyota spent US$15 million in 2002 touting the Prius. There were print ads in magazines, such as *Newsweek* and *Vanity Fair*, as well as an Internet-based advertising campaign. In the United States, television advertising was placed on channels such as Discovery, the History Channel, the Learning Channel, and MSNBC. Such ads were deemed too expensive for the smaller Canadian marketplace. Here Toyota relied more on promotions and environment-related sponsorships. Ads running before the actual introduction used the tagline "A car that sometimes runs on gas power and sometimes runs on electric power, from a company that always runs on brain power." These ads helped to position Toyota as an "environmentally concerned" company and more subtly stressed the technology aspect of the car. After all, Americans love technology and are quick adopters of it.

After introduction, the ads appealed more to emotion with taglines such as "When it sees red, it charges"—a reference to the recharging of the battery at stoplights. Such ads are based on ambiguity where the headline attracts attention because its meaning is not clear. The consumer must process the information in the ad in order to interpret it. The result is higher ad impact and longer ad recall. Toyota also took advantage of the environmental appeal by sending out green seed cards shaped like Toyota's logo to prospective buyers on Earth Day. They also wrapped some Priuses in green and gave away cars at Earth Day events.

Though US$15 million in advertising may sound like a lot, it's really just a drop in the bucket compared with the US$190 million that Toyota spent overall to market cars and trucks in 2002. For the first six months of introduction, Toyota sold close to 5000 cars, which is quite good given the newness of the technology, the dull design, and the lack of muscle.

Much of the Prius's success is based on correct identification of the target market. Many early purchasers were attracted by the technology, began to modify cars, and shared their experiences through chat rooms, such as Priusenvy.com. The object of attachment was the computer system. One owner in Philadelphia was able to add cruise control (an option not offered by Toyota) by wiring in a few switches in the car's computer system. The founder of the Priusenvy.com website figured out how to use the car's dashboard display screen to show files from his laptop, play video games, and look at images taken by a camera mounted on the rear of his car. One Austrian consumer installed a sniffer—a device on the car's computer network that monitors electronic messages. With the sniffer, he could hook up add-ons such as a MiniDisc Player, an MP3 player, a laptop computer, and a TV tuner.

Even though the Internet played a major part in the Prius launch, Toyota does not sell the car from its website. Buyers go to **www.prius.toyota.com** online to look at colours and decide on options, such as CD players and floor mats. After that, the dealers get involved, but it takes specially trained salespeople to explain and promote the Prius. One of the most common questions dealers are asked is "Does it have to be plugged in?" The answer is no; you push a button and it starts. But if you want the high fuel efficiency of the car—nearly four litres per 100 km—you have to operate it correctly, and many Prius owners haven't done that. Therefore, Toyota is planning to launch an educational campaign aimed at salespeople and consumers. It will also put an operating manual in the glove compartment of each new car.

By 2004, Toyota had skimmed off the market of techies and early adopters and needed to launch a new version of its car to appeal to a wider market. To launch the new Prius, Toyota spent more than US$40 million spread over media in more consumer-oriented magazines and TV. It seems to have worked, as Prius sales increased rapidly.

The new Prius is a sleek, Asian-inspired design that comes in seven colours, such as salsa red pearl or tidal and pearl. The most popular colour is silver metallic with a grey/burgundy interior. Once inside the Prius, you find a stubby switch to engage reverse or drive and a push button that turns everything on. An eighteen-centimetre energy monitor touch screen displays fuel consumption, outside temperature, and battery charge level. It also explains whether you're running on gas, electricity, regenerated energy, or a combination of these. There are also screens to show how much electricity you have stored and to arrange your air conditioning, audio, and satellite navigation system. The interior is roomy and practical, with plenty of rear legroom. There are many storage space cubbyholes and shelves in the front, as well as a deep dashboard that leaves ample space for maps, books, and even your lunch. The CD player holds six discs. In all, it's quite an improvement over the 2000 model.

In the summer of 2004, gasoline prices began to rise. As a result, buyers moved toward smaller SUVs, cars, and hybrids. Sales of full-sized SUVs, such as the Ford Excursion and Expedition and the Lincoln Navigator, fell during the first four months of the year followed by a sharp drop in April. Sales of GM's Hummer tanked by 25 percent. Even rental car companies started to respond to this trend. In July 2004, Discount Car and Truck Rentals added the Toyota Prius to its lineup of vehicles, first in its Toronto market, but then to its 240 locations across Canada. It plans to add other models of hybrid cars and trucks as soon as these low-emission vehicles become available.

At the same time, demand for Priuses increased. By June 2004, waiting lists for the Prius often stretched to six months or more and some dealers had quit taking deposits. Spots on dealers' waiting lists were being auctioned on eBay for US$500 and some dealers tacked as much as $5000 to the car's Canadian sticker price of $29 900. At the same time, automotive companies were trying to move the gas-guzzlers by offering incentives. As inventory levels dropped and waiting lists lengthened, Toyota increased monthly production from 7500 vehicles per month to 10 000 and eventually to 15 000. Toyota President Fujio Cho announced that the increased production should alleviate the shortages. But he made it clear that Toyota has no plans at present to start production at a second plant.

Toyota and Honda are not the only companies in the hybrid market. Though the Japanese created new cars, Ford began production of a hybrid model of the Escape SUV, giving consumers a choice of a hybrid or regular model. To promote the hybrid, Ford began an environmental print campaign built around fuel efficiency, emissions, and other environmental concerns. Later in 2004, the campaign broadened to include TV. GM is following a similar strategy, putting hybrid technology in vehicles that use the most gas. GM claims that each of its hybrid buses (sold to cities) will provide the fuel savings of 8000 hybrid cars. It has also developed a hybrid model of its Silverado truck that will hit the market in late 2004 or early 2005. By 2007, GM expects to be making 1 million hybrids of some sort. Analysts believe that U.S. automakers need to get into the hybrid market because of the internal learning curve—"the quicker you get into the game, the quicker you get the real-world experience at developing and marketing these vehicles."

Clearly Toyota is the leader in hybrid sales with the Prius. Its Lexus division introduced a Lexus SUV hybrid in the fall of 2004, moving hybrids up to the luxury car level. Dealers received more than 9000 prepaid, advance orders for the 2006 model. Thus, Toyota has a big jump on North American automakers who have only dabbled in this market. If gas prices remain high or rise even higher, Toyota will be very well-placed to take advantage of the scramble for hybrid cars. By the end of April 2006, Toyota reached a major milestone. Worldwide cumulative sales of the Prius had passed the half-million mark with 504,700 units sold. Perhaps Mr. Cho would decide that a second plant is needed after all.

Questions for Discussion

1. What microenvironmental factors affected the introduction and relaunch of the Toyota Prius? How well has Toyota dealt with these factors?

2. Outline the major macroenvironmental factors— demographic, economic, natural, technological, political and cultural—that affected the introduction and relaunch of the Toyota Prius. How well has Toyota dealt with each of these factors?

3. Evaluate Toyota's marketing strategy so far. What has Toyota done well? How might it improve its strategy?

4. GM's marketing director for new ventures, Ken Stewart, says, "If you want to get a lot of hybrids on the road, you put them in vehicles that people are buying now." This tends to summarize the U.S. automakers' approach to hybrids. Would you agree with Mr. Stewart? Why or why not?

Sources: Kevin Ransom, "Ford, GM Get Rolling on Hybrid Debuts," *Adweek,* August 2, 2004, p. 6; "Testing Toyota's Hybrid Car," *GP,* June 7, 2004; Kevin A. Wilson, "Hyped Hybrid," *Autoweek,* June 28, 2004; Norihiko Shirouzu and Jeffrey Ball, "Revolution Under the Hood," *Wall Street Journal,* May 12, 2004, p. B.1; and Sholnn Freeman, "Auto Watch: Hot for a Hybrid Car? Cool Your Engines," *Wall Street Journal,* June 13, 2004, p. 4; Bernadette Johnson, "Toyota unveils first gas/electric hybrid," *Strategy,* July 17, 2000, p. 4; "discount plugs in to electric cars," *Marketing Daily,* July 22, 2004; "Worldwide Toyota Prius Sales Top 500,000 Mark," *Carscoop,* June 7, 2006, http://carscoop. blogspot.com/2006/06/worldwide-toyota-prius-sales-top.html.

Chapter 4

Marketing and Society: Social Responsibility and Marketing Ethics

AFTER STUDYING THIS CHAPTER YOU SHOULD BE ABLE TO

1. understand marketing's multiple responsibilities, and identify the major social and ethical criticisms of marketing

2. define *consumerism* and *environmentalism* and explain how they affect marketing strategies

3. describe the principles of socially responsible marketing

4. explain the role of ethics in marketing

Previewing the Concepts

In this chapter, we'll focus on marketing as a social institution. Since many marketing decisions have social and ethical implications, we introduce this topic early in the book so that you become increasingly aware of how marketers can influence our values and behaviours for better or worse. First, we'll look at some common criticisms of marketing as it affects individual consumers, other businesses, and society as a whole. Then, we'll examine consumerism and consumer-based legislation, environmentalism, and other citizen and public actions to keep marketing in check. Finally, we'll see how companies themselves can benefit from proactively pursuing socially responsible and ethical practices. You'll see that social responsibility and ethical actions are more than just the right thing to do; they're also good for business.

*B*efore moving on, let's visit the concept of social responsibility in business. There is a lot of debate about what the duties and obligations of businesses should be. Should business organizations and the marketing people working within them just serve the shareholders or owners of the firm by maximizing profits, obeying the law, and using resources wisely? Or do they have a wider set of responsibilities that includes serving the interests of all stakeholders—groups that are affected by corporate actions, such as customers, employees, suppliers, distributors, regulators, and members of the community at large?

More and more marketers today are taking a stakeholder perspective of social responsibility. While marketers see themselves first and foremost as customer advocates, they also know that marketing is pervasive in today's society. Thus, they are responsible for the impact their actions and marketing programs have on a wide group of stakeholders. Over the past twenty-five years, companies such as Ben & Jerry's and The Body Shop have reflected their sensitivity to ethics and social responsibility by using pioneering ideas like "values-led business" or "caring capitalism"—putting "principles ahead of profits." But *can* a company dedicated to doing good still do well? *Can* it successfully serve a "triple bottom line"—simultaneously being economically, socially, and environmentally responsible? Organizations such as Mountain Equipment Co-op have demonstrated that aligning these goals is not only possible, it is an inspirational business model.

Corporate social revolutionaries—people such as Ben Cohen and Jerry Greenfield, who founded Ben & Jerry's Homemade Ice Cream, or Anita Roddick, who gave birth to

The Body Shop International—pioneered the concept of "values-led business" or "caring capitalism." Their mission: use business to make the world a better place. Ben & Jerry's Homemade, for example, bought only hormone-free milk and cream from local dairy farms and used only organic fruits and nuts to make its ice cream, which it sold in environmentally friendly containers. From the start, Ben & Jerry's donated a whopping 7.5 percent of pre-tax profits to support projects that exhibited "creative problem solving and hopefulness ... relating to children and families, disadvantaged groups, and the environment." In a similar fashion, Anita Roddick put "passion before profits," and had a similar mission: "To dedicate our business to the pursuit of social and environmental change." The firm's natural-ingredient-based cosmetics were formulated without any animal testing, and supplies were often sourced from developing countries. The Body Shop, which now operates in forty-seven countries, donates a percentage of profits each year to animal-rights groups, women's causes, homeless shelters, Amnesty International, AIDS research, Save the Rain Forest, and other social causes. Today, these two companies have been acquired by multinationals (Unilever owns Ben & Jerry's and L'Oréal bought The Body Shop in early 2006). Both parents, however, allow these businesses to operate relatively independently and they both still pursue their social mission. Both companies have been criticized, however, for not being genuine and authentic in their efforts, or for having only a limited impact on the social issues they promote themselves as addressing. *Globe and Mail* reporter Jon Entine, for example, says that instead of focusing on the efforts of such "New Age" companies, we should look at the efforts of major corporations who have the financial resources to have a real impact on social issues. Such companies have found that they can improve their bottom lines while doing good by selling "quality products, treating employees, vendors and franchisees with integrity and upgrading their environmental practices."

The experiences of the 1980s revolutionaries taught the socially responsible business movement some hard lessons. The result is a new generation of activist entrepreneurs—not social activists with big hearts who hate capitalism, but well-trained business managers and company builders with a passion for a cause.

Mountain Equipment Co-op (MEC) is one such organization. Its logo has become a Canadian national icon despite the fact that it has shunned traditional marketing tactics like mass media advertising. MEC was born in Vancouver in 1971 to fill a set of unmet needs for quality outdoor equipment at affordable prices. But just filling a need alone didn't make MEC what is has become today. It filled this need in a distinct and unique fashion. As the company's website notes, "MEC's operations are driven by our members' needs and values rather than the financial drive to maximize profit.... Our core purpose has always been to support people in achieving the benefit of self-propelled, wilderness-oriented recreation." Furthermore, its vision for itself as it pictures the future is to provide "leadership for a just world, and action for a healthy planet." MEC, therefore, sets aside 0.4 percent of its sales revenues to fund environmental projects each and every year.

Unlike traditional retailers, MEC is a member-owned cooperative. Throughout its history, MEC has consistently offered a narrow set of products and has placed considerable attention on the quality of its products and services. While recognizing that it is a retailer that survives by promoting "consumption," it works to do so in an environmentally responsible manner, trying to be "green" in what it does. MEC prides itself on building ecologically friendly stores: it reduces energy consumption, recuperates on-site groundwater, uses recycled building materials whenever possible, and even cultivates small rooftop gardens designed to filter smoggy air and reduce the building's heating and cooling costs. Even when it replaces a store, as it did in Ottawa, MEC works to be sensitive to environmental issues. Thus, it worked hard so that 86 percent of the previous building that stood on MEC's Ottawa site was recycled, and most of it was used in the new building.

Another of MEC's initiatives is its Ecological Footprint Calculator. This educational tool was developed to encourage members to think more about the sustainability of their day-to-day life choices and provoke discussion about social values and thoughtful

consumption. MEC also encourages its members to use their gear to the full extent of its life. To help them do this, MEC has member education programs on the use and care of its products. It has a product repair program and a gear reuse program in addition to its recycling and donation programs for used equipment. It is also working to expand its rental programs for those who only need gear occasionally.

While MEC certainly focused on customer needs, quality products, and high service, it also grew into the realization that many stakeholder groups were critically connected to its long-term success. It is a values-led organization that knows the power of having a motivated network of top-quality suppliers. It is energized by its employees and it is committed to people and their communities. This orientation is exemplified in its statement of values:

- We conduct ourselves ethically and with integrity.
- We show respect for others in our words and actions.
- We act in the spirit of community and cooperation.
- We respect and protect our natural environment.
- We strive for personal growth and continual learning, and adventure.

MEC also knows that simply working to make a one-time sale to a customer isn't enough. Developing lifetime relationships with its members has been another touchstone of the cooperative. As part of its vision, MEC sets the goal of having MEC members purchase most of their needs for outdoor activities from MEC. It sends members catalogues twice yearly. Each is filled with high-quality information as well as products. It also sends out newsletters and is beginning to rely more and more on its website (www.mec.ca) and ecommerce capabilities to maintain the link with the 2 million people who have paid $5 for their lifetime membership.

Such relationships are critical since MEC has no doubt that its best marketers are the members themselves. Member-generated word-of-mouth communication has long worked to help the company grow. And grow it has. In 2005, its sales were $197 million. MEC currently operates stores in Vancouver, Victoria, Calgary, Edmonton, Winnipeg, Toronto, Ottawa, Montreal, and Halifax. But no matter what it does today or in the future, MEC tries to take the high road and be an exemplar of ethics, integrity, and environmental responsibility in its undertakings.[1]

Canadians wish more companies shared MEC's perspective. A recent *Maclean's* survey of Canadian attitudes revealed that 45 percent of Canadians have a more negative view of the business community than in previous surveys and expressed a general concern about the ethics, morality, and social responsibility of business leaders. In the light of recent business scandals in the United States and Canada, Canadians today are demanding more of business and marketing. Consider the results of a recent poll:[2]

- 88 percent of Canadians believe that business should do more than simply make a profit, create jobs, and obey laws.
- 53 percent of Canadians think that a key differentiator for a company is social responsibility, far ahead of either brand reputation or financial success.
- 52 percent of Canadians have punished a specific company they viewed as not behaving responsibly.
- Slightly more than 50 percent of recent North American MBA grads said they would accept a lower salary to work for a socially responsible company.
- The Jantzi Social Index of 60 socially responsible companies showed a 5 percent higher return on investment than the TSE 300 in 2000.

Such trends are important to responsible marketers, who constantly strive to discover what consumers want and to respond with marketing offers that give satisfaction and value to buyers and profit to the producer. They adhere to the *marketing concept,* which is a philosophy of creating customer value while making a profit. It is a win–win philosophy of mutual gain.

Suncor, a Calgary-based integrated energy company employing more than 3400 people, is a good example of a company that remains profitable while fulfilling a values-led mission. Its website proclaims,

Today, we see social responsibility as encompassing every area of our business. It's reflected in the kind of workplace opportunities we provide and in how healthy and safe we make that workplace for our employees, our contractors and all others who may be affected by our operations. It comes to life in the way we communicate and interact with stakeholders and in our recognition of the economic and special needs of neighbouring communities. It is made visible by the encouragement we provide to community growth and involvement—whether that means supporting an employee in volunteer efforts, or providing financial help to a community project through the Suncor Energy Foundation.[3]

Not all marketers follow the marketing concept, however. In fact, some companies use questionable marketing practices, and some marketing actions that seem innocent in themselves strongly affect the larger society. Consider the sale of fast-food products, for example. On the face of it, companies should be free to sell hamburgers and french fries and people should be free to buy them. But this private transaction involves larger questions of public policy. For example, if people

Responding to consumer concerns about today's fat-laden fast food, McDonald's cut the "super size" option from its menu and introduced healthier fare, such as its Go Active Happy Meal.

overconsume these and other fat-laden products, they become obese, harming their health and maybe shortening their own lives. The health problems associated with obesity places a financial burden on the person's family and on society at large. Illness may cause them to be a less productive member of the workforce, causing harm to their firms and the firms' insurance agencies. Finally, their habits may influence those of their children, beginning another cycle of poor nutrition. Recent studies show that a whopping 46 percent of Canadians are overweight or obese, and that obesity rates in children have tripled in only twenty years. Thus, the marketing of fast-food products has sparked substantial debate and negotiation in recent years.[4]

This chapter examines the social effects of private marketing practices. We examine several questions: What are the most frequent social criticisms of marketing? What steps have private citizens taken to curb marketing ills? What steps have legislators and government agencies taken to curb marketing ills? What steps have enlightened companies taken to carry out socially responsible and ethical marketing?

Social and Ethical Criticisms of Marketing

Marketing is often criticized. Some of the criticism is justified; much is not. It cannot be denied, however, that marketers must understand the ethical and social issues associated with their profession and work to resolve these issues. There are ethical issues associated with every aspect of marketing practice.

Ethicists use two sets of criteria to determine whether an action is ethical or unethical: (1) principles and duties (such as the duty to avoid harm), and (2) whether the consequences of an action are beneficial or harmful to individuals and society. Social critics claim that certain marketing practices hurt individual consumers, society as a whole, and other business firms. These topics are explored in the next sections.

Marketing's Impact on Individual Consumers

Consumers have many concerns about how well the marketing system serves their interests. Surveys usually show that consumers hold mixed or even slightly unfavourable attitudes toward marketing practices. Consumers, consumer advocates, government agencies, and other critics have accused marketing of harming consumers through high prices, deceptive practices, high-pressure selling, shoddy or unsafe products, planned obsolescence, and poor service to disadvantaged consumers.

High Prices

Many critics charge that the marketing system causes prices to be higher than they would be under more "sensible" systems. They point to three factors—*high costs of distribution, high advertising and promotion costs,* and *excessive markups.*

High Costs of Distribution A long-standing charge is that greedy intermediaries mark up prices beyond the value of their services. Critics charge either that there are too many intermediaries, that intermediaries are inefficient and poorly run, or that they provide unnecessary or duplicate services. As a result, distribution costs too much, and consumers pay for these excessive costs in the form of higher prices.

How do retailers answer these charges? They argue that intermediaries do work that would otherwise have to be done by manufacturers or consumers.

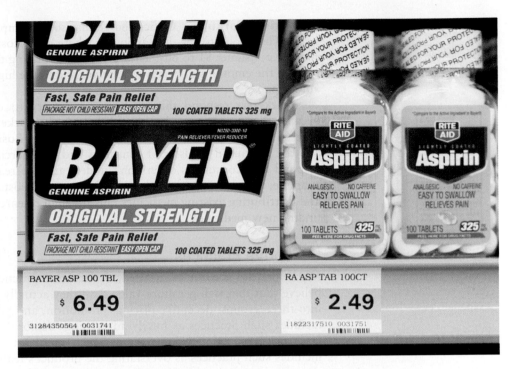

A heavily promoted brand of Aspirin sells for much more than a virtually identical non-branded or store-branded product. Critics charge that promotion adds only psychological value to the product rather than functional value.

Markups reflect services that consumers themselves want—more convenience, larger stores and assortment, longer store hours, return privileges, and others. Moreover, the costs of operating stores keep rising, forcing retailers to raise their prices. In fact, they argue, retail competition is so intense that margins are actually quite low. For example, after taxes, supermarket chains are typically left with anywhere from a bare 1 percent to 10 percent profit on their sales, depending on what product category is examined. If some resellers try to charge too much relative to the value they add, other resellers will step in with lower prices. Low-price stores, such as the Dollar Store, Zellers, Wal-Mart, Best Buy, and other discounters, pressure their competitors to operate efficiently and keep their prices down.

High Advertising and Promotion Costs   Modern marketing is accused of pushing up prices because of heavy advertising and sales promotion. For example, a dozen tablets of a heavily promoted brand of pain reliever sell for the same price as 100 tablets of less-promoted brands. Differentiated products—cosmetics, detergents, toiletries—include promotion and packaging costs that can amount to 40 percent or more of the manufacturer's price to the retailer. Critics charge that much of the packaging and promotion adds only psychological value to the product rather than functional value. Retailers use additional promotions—advertising, displays, and sweepstakes—that add several cents to retail prices.

Marketers respond that consumers can usually buy functional versions of products at lower prices. However, they *want* and are willing to pay more for products that also provide psychological benefits—that make them feel wealthy, attractive, or special. Brand name products may cost more, but branding gives buyers assurances of consistent quality. Heavy advertising adds to product costs but adds value by informing millions of potential buyers of the availability and merits of a brand. If consumers want to know what is available on the market, they must expect manufacturers to spend large sums of money on advertising. Also, heavy advertising and promotion may be necessary for a firm to match competitors' efforts. The business would lose "share of mind" if it did not match competitive spending. At the same time, companies are cost conscious about promotion and try to spend their money wisely.

Excessive Markups   Critics charge that some companies mark up goods excessively. They point to the drug industry, where a pill costing five cents to make may cost the consumer $1 to buy. They point to the pricing tactics of funeral homes that prey on the emotions of bereaved relatives and to the high charges for television and auto repair.

Marketers respond that most businesses try to deal fairly with consumers because they want repeat business. When shady marketers take advantage of consumers, they should be reported to the police, Better Business Bureau (www.bbb.org), and the provincial ministry of consumer and commercial relations. Marketers also respond that consumers often don't understand the reason for high markups. For example, pharmaceutical markups must cover the costs of purchasing, promoting, and distributing existing medicines plus the high research and development costs of finding new medicines.

Deceptive Practices

Marketers are sometimes accused of deceptive practices that lead consumers to believe that they will get more value than they actually do. Deceptive practices fall into three groups: deceptive pricing, promotion, and packaging. *Deceptive pricing* includes such practices as falsely advertising "factory" or "wholesale" prices or a large price reduction from a phoney high retail list price. *Deceptive promotion* includes such practices as overstating the product's features or performance, luring the customer to the store for a bargain that is out of stock, or running rigged contests. *Deceptive packaging* includes exaggerating package contents through subtle design, not filling the package to the top, using misleading labelling, or describing size in misleading terms. The Competition Bureau acts as a watchdog to prevent such practices. Here are a few examples of the cases it brought to the courts in 2005:[5]

- Sears Canada Inc. was ordered to pay $487 000, under the *Competition Act*'s Deceptive Marketing Practices provisions. Sears was found guilty of making false or misleading claims regarding savings available to consumers when they advertised discounts on certain tires across Canada.

- Criminal charges were laid against JD Marvel Products Inc., CDN MailOrder Exchange Inc. (CMOE) and their president, John Dragan, for engaging in deceptive marketing practices that targeted Canadian and U.S. consumers, mainly seniors, after the Competition Bureau received a total of 5700 complaints. The companies offered a wide range of consumer products through mail order, advertising inserts, coupons, catalogues and the Internet. The Bureau found that products were not delivered in the advertised time period of two to five weeks, that some products were never delivered, and that the performance of some of the products was not as advertised.

- The Labatt Brewing Company was convicted and fined $250 000 by the Competition Bureau for price maintenance on discount beer sold by nine Quebec independent retailers. Between March 2004 and April 2005, some of Labatt's sales representatives attempted, either by agreement, threat, promise or similar means, to influence upward or discourage the reduction of the price at which the retailers sold the products.

Other deceptive practices are more subtle. Everyone's received an envelope claiming "You have won $10 000 000!" or a pop-up webscreen promising free goods or discounted prices. These sweepstakes companies have come under the gun for their deceptive communication practices. Publishers Clearing House, for example, recently paid heavily to settle claims that its high-pressure tactics had misled consumers into believing that they had won prizes when they hadn't.[6]

Sweepstakes promoter Publishers Clearing House recently paid heavily to settle claims that its high-pressure tactics had misled consumers into believing that they had won prizes that they hadn't.

Telemarketing fraud is another practice that hurts consumers and the marketing profession.

According to PhoneBusters, the national reporting centre for telemarketing fraud, deceptive telemarketing has cost Canadians approximately $40 million since 1995.[7] The Canadian Marketing Association (CMA) has partnered with government to develop initiatives aimed at preventing and combating this crime.

Since deceptive practices hurt the reputation of all marketers, the CMA works to develop codes of ethics and standards of good practice so that industry can regulate itself better. It works with policymakers to strengthen the *Competition Act*. Deceptive practices have led to industry self-regulation standards as well as legislation and other consumer protection actions. The *Competition Act* forbids many of the practices. Advertising Standards Canada has published several guidelines listing deceptive practices. The toughest problem is defining what is "deceptive."

Marketers argue that most companies avoid deceptive practices because such practices harm their business in the long run. If consumers do not get what they expect, they will switch to more reliable products. In addition, consumers usually protect themselves from deception. Most consumers recognize a marketer's selling intent and are careful when they buy, sometimes to the point of not believing completely true product claims.

High-Pressure Selling

Salespeople are sometimes accused of high-pressure selling that persuades people to buy goods they had no intention of buying. It is often said that encyclopedias, insurance, real estate, cars, and jewellery are *sold*, not *bought*. Salespeople are trained to deliver smooth, canned talks to entice purchase. They sell hard because sales contests promise big prizes to those who sell the most.

Marketers know that buyers often can be talked into buying unwanted or unneeded things. Laws require door-to-door salespeople to announce that they are selling a product. Buyers in most provinces also have a "three-day cooling-off period" in which they can cancel a contract after rethinking it. In addition, when they feel that undue selling pressure has been applied, consumers can complain to the Better Business Bureau or to their provincial ministry regulating commerce.

But in most cases, marketers have little to gain from high-pressure selling. Such tactics may work in one-time selling situations for short-term gain. However, most selling involves building long-term relationships with valued customers. High-pressure or deceptive selling can do serious damage to such relationships. For example, imagine a Procter & Gamble account manager trying to pressure a Wal-Mart buyer, or an IBM salesperson trying to browbeat a General Electric information technology manager. It simply wouldn't work.

Shoddy or Unsafe Products

Another criticism is that products lack the quality they should have. One complaint is that many products are not made well and that many services are not performed well.

A second complaint is that many products deliver little benefit. For example, some consumers are surprised to learn that many of the "healthy" foods being marketed today—from cholesterol-free salad dressings and low-fat frozen dinners to high-fibre bran cereals—may have little nutritional value. In fact, they may even be harmful. The fast-food industry and manufacturers of fatty snacks are also coming under increasing scrutiny as claims are made about the addictive nature of these foods and their effect on the waistlines of Canadian consumers. It has even been suggested that a tax be placed on such items. The argument goes that if fast food is as harmful to our health as tobacco products, why shouldn't it be taxed in a similar way? Certainly the Canadian government is concerned about the spiralling costs of health care caused by the marketing of harmful products. Companies like Kraft Foods Canada are taking this issue seriously. It is cutting down on portion sizes, developing more nutritious products, and halting in-school marketing to children.[8]

A third complaint concerns product safety. Product safety has been a problem for several reasons, involving issues such as manufacturer indifference, increased production complexity, poorly trained labour, and poor quality control. For years, Consumers Union—the non-profit testing and information organization that publishes the *Consumer Reports* magazine and website (www.consumer.org)—has reported various hazards in tested products: electrical dangers in appliances, carbon-monoxide poisoning from room heaters, injury risks from lawn mowers, and faulty automobile design, among many others. The organization's testing and other activities have helped consumers make better buying decisions and encouraged businesses to eliminate product flaws (see Real Marketing 4.1).

However, most manufacturers *want* to produce quality goods. The way a company deals with product quality and safety problems can damage or help its reputation. Companies selling poor-quality or unsafe products risk damaging conflicts with consumer groups and regulators. More fundamentally, unsafe products can result in product liability suits and large awards for damages. Moreover, consumers who are unhappy with a firm's products may avoid future purchases and talk other consumers into doing the same. Consider what happened to Bridgestone/Firestone following its recent recall of 6.5 million flawed Firestone tires (400 000 tires were recalled in Canada). Product liability and safety concerns have driven the company to the edge of bankruptcy:[9]

Profits have disappeared, and both customers and tire dealers alike are fleeing the Firestone make. Ford, the tire maker's biggest customer, recently announced plans to replace another 13 million Firestone tires that it believes are unsafe. "You have a serious risk of the Firestone brand imploding," warns an industry analyst. How bad will the financial hit get? Cutting ties with Ford will cost the company 4 percent of its US$7.5 billion in revenues—about 40 percent of its sales to car companies. Mounting damages awards from rollover suits and legal bills could easily top the company's US$463 million legal reserve.

Thus, quality missteps can have severe consequences. Today's marketers know that customer-driven quality results in customer satisfaction, which in turn creates profitable customer relationships.

REAL MARKETING

When *Consumer Reports* Talks, Buyers Listen

For almost seventy years, Consumers Union (CU) has given buyers the lowdown on everything from SUVs and luggage to candy bars and lawn sprinklers. The non-profit product-testing organization's mission is summed up by its motto: Test, Inform, Protect. CU's magazine, *Consumer Reports*, is one of North America's most-read magazines. It reaches more than 4 million subscribers and—as dog-eared library copies will attest—has several times that many borrowers. CU's website (www.consumerreports.org) is the Web's largest paid-subscriber site, with more than 1.6 million users and more than 6.4 million subscribers to its newsletter.

One of world's the largest consumer organizations, Consumers Union is also one of the most influential. When it raved about Saucony's Jazz 3000 sneaker, sales doubled, leading to shortages.

Although some may view *Consumer Reports* as a deadly dull shoppers' guide to major household appliances, the magazine does a lot more than rate cars and refrigerators. It has looked at almost anything consumable—from mutual funds, home mortgages, and public health policies to retirement communities and prostate surgery. When a recent Consumers Union study found that that less than one-third of consumers trust ecommerce websites, the organization launched Consumer WebWatch (www.consumerwebwatch.org). The project's mission is "to investigate, inform, and improve the credibility of information published on the World Wide Web." The site gives ratings on everything from the disclosure of transaction fees and business partnerships to the publication of privacy policies and the labelling of pop-up ads.

The magazine is rarely harsh or loud. Instead, it's usually understated, and it can even be funny. The very first issue, in 1936, noted that Lifebuoy soap was itself so smelly that it simply overwhelmed your BO with LO. And what reader didn't delight to find in a 1990 survey of soaps that the most expensive bar, Eau de Gucci, at 31 cents per handwashing, wound up dead last in a blind test?

To avoid even the appearance of bias, CU has a strict no-ads, no-freebies policy. It buys all of its product samples on the open market and anonymously. CU's steadfast editorial independence has made *Consumer Reports* the bible of consumerism. "We're very single-minded about who we serve," says Rhoda Karpatkin, CU's recently retired president. "We serve the consumer."

A visit to CU's maze of labs confirms the thoroughness with which CU's testers carry out their

For almost seventy years, under its mission to "test, inform, protect," Consumers Union has given buyers the lowdown on everything from cars to candy bars.

mission. A chemist performs a cholesterol extraction test on a small white blob in a beaker—a ground-up piece of turkey enchilada, you are told. Elsewhere you find the remains of a piston-driven machine called Fingers, which added 1 + 1 on pocket calculators hundreds of thousands of times or until the calculators failed, whichever came first. You watch suitcases bang into one another inside a huge contraption—affectionately dubbed the "Mechanical Gorilla"—that looks like a three-metre-wide clothes dryer.

Next door, self-cleaning ovens are being tested, their interiors coated with a crusty substance—called "Monster Mash" by staffers—which suggests month-old chili sauce. The recipe includes tapioca, cheese, lard, grape jelly, tomato sauce, and cherry pie filling—mixed well and baked one hour at 218°C. If an oven's self-cleaning cycle doesn't render the resulting residue into harmless-looking ash, five million readers will be so informed.

From the start, Consumers Union has generated controversy. The second issue dismissed the Good Housekeeping Seal of Approval as nothing more than a fraudulent ploy by publisher William Randolph Hearst to reward loyal advertisers. Good Housekeeping responded by accusing CU of prolonging the Depression. To the business community, *Consumer Reports* was at first viewed as a clear threat to business. However, the controversy has more often helped than hurt subscriptions. Through the years, only thirteen makers of panned products have filed suit against CU, challenging findings unfavourable to their products. To this day Consumers Union has never lost or settled a libel suit.

Sources: Portions adapted from Doug Stewart, "To Buy or Not to Buy, That Is the Question at Consumer Reports," *Smithsonian*, September 1993, pp. 34–43. Other quotes and information from Robin Finn, "Still Top Dog, Consumers' Pitt Bull to Retire," *New York Times*, October 5, 2000, p. B2; Barbara Quint, "Consumers Union Launches Consumer WebWatch," *Information Today*, June 2002, p. 48; and the Consumers Union website, www.consumersunion.org, and the *Consumer Reports* website at www.consumerreports.org (accessed August 2002).

Planned Obsolescence

Critics have charged that some producers follow a program of planned obsolescence, causing their products to become obsolete before they actually should need replacement. For example, critics charge that some producers continually change consumer concepts of acceptable styles to encourage more and earlier buying. An obvious example is constantly changing clothing fashions.

Other producers are accused of holding back attractive functional features, then introducing them later to make older models obsolete. Critics claim that this occurs in the consumer electronics and computer industries. For example, Intel and Microsoft have been accused in recent years of holding back their next-generation computer chips and software until demand is exhausted for the current generation. Still other producers are accused of using materials and components that will break, wear, rust, or rot sooner than they should. One writer put it this way: "The marvels of modern technology include the development of a soda can which, when discarded, will last forever—and a ... car, which, when properly cared for, will rust out in two or three years."[10]

Marketers respond that consumers *like* style changes. They get tired of the old goods and want a new look in fashion or a new design in cars. No one has to buy the new look, and if too few people like it, it will simply fail. Companies that withhold new features run the risk that a competitor will introduce the new feature and steal the market.

For example, consider personal computers. Some consumers grumble that the consumer electronics industry's constant push to produce "faster, smaller, cheaper" models means that they must continually buy new machines just to keep up. Their old computers then enter landfills and present a major disposal problem. Others, however, can hardly wait for the latest model to arrive.

There was a time not so long ago when planned obsolescence was a troubling ghost in the machine. That was then. In today's topsy-turvy world of personal computers, obsolescence is not only planned, it is extolled by marketers as a principal virtue. Moreover, there has been hardly a peep from consumers, who dutifully line up to buy each new generation of faster, more powerful machines, eager to embrace the promise of simpler, happier, and more productive lives. Today's computer chips are no longer designed to wear out; in fact, they will last for decades or longer. Even so, hapless consumers now rush back to the store ever more quickly, not to replace broken parts but to purchase new computers that will allow them to talk longer, see more vivid colours, or play cooler games.[11]

Thus, companies do not design their products to break down earlier, because they do not want to lose customers to other brands. Instead, they seek constant improvement to ensure that products will consistently meet or exceed customer expectations. Much of so-called planned obsolescence is the working of the competitive and technological forces in a free society—forces that lead to ever-improving goods and services.

Poor Service to Disadvantaged Consumers

Finally, the marketing system has been accused of poorly serving disadvantaged consumers. Critics claim that the urban poor often have to shop in smaller stores that carry inferior goods and charge higher prices. A Consumers Union study compared the food shopping habits of low-income consumers and the prices they pay relative to middle-income consumers in the same city. The study found that the poor do pay more for inferior goods. The results suggested that the presence of large national chain stores in low-income neighbourhoods made a big difference in keeping prices down. However, the study also found evidence of "redlining"—a type of economic discrimination in which major chain retailers avoid placing stores in disadvantaged neighbourhoods.[12]

Similar redlining charges have been levelled at the home insurance, consumer lending, and banking industries. Most recently, home and auto insurers have been accused of assigning higher premiums to people with poor credit ratings. The insurers claim that individuals with bad credit tend to make more insurance claims, and that this justifies charging them higher premiums. However, critics and consumer advocates have accused the insurers of a new form of redlining. Says one writer, "This is a new excuse for denying coverage to the poor, elderly, and minorities."[13]

Clearly, better marketing systems must be built to service disadvantaged consumers. Moreover, low-income people and other vulnerable groups clearly need consumer protection. Industry Canada's Consumer Connection webpage (http://strategis.ic.gc.ca/epic/internet/inoca-bc.nsf/vwGeneratedInterE/Home) provides advice to Canadian consumers on everything from how to manage their money more effectively to how to avoid fraud.

Marketing's Impact on Society as a Whole

The marketing system has been accused of adding to several "evils" in society at large. Advertising has been a special target.

False Wants and Too Much Materialism

Critics, led by Emeritus Professor Rick Pollay of the University of British Columbia and organizations such as Adbusters, have charged that the marketing system in general, and advertising in particular, urges too much interest in material possessions. Although Pollay recognized that many of the consequences of advertising were unintended, he damned advertising for undermining family values, reinforcing negative stereotypes, and creating a class of perpetually dissatisfied consumers.[14] Advertising encourages people to judge themselves and others by what they *own* rather than by who they *are*. To be considered successful, some people believe they must own a large home, two cars, and the latest high-tech gadgets.

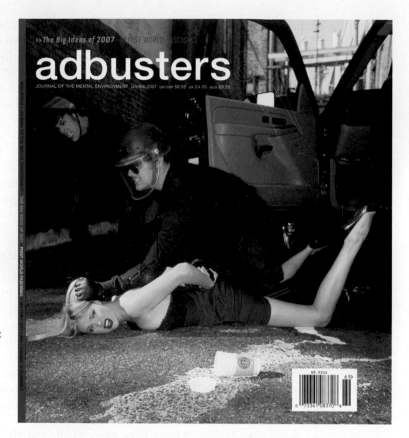

AdBusters magazine is a major critic of marketing's negative influence on our physical and cultural environments. Based in Vancouver, British Columbia, it has audiences around the world.

Today, even though many social scientists have noted a reaction against the opulence and waste of the previous decades and a return to more basic values and social commitment, our infatuation with material things continues. Though the Professional Marketing Research Association of Canada has done studies that indicate that Canadians are less materialistic than our American neighbours, it's hard to escape the notion that what many North Americans really value is stuff. We build more shopping malls than high schools. We save less and spend more. Nearly two-thirds of adults agree that wearing "only the best designer clothing" conveys status. Even more feel this way about owning expensive jewellery. Big homes are back in vogue, which means North Americans have more space to fulfill their acquisitive fantasies, from master bathrooms doubling as spas and gyms to fully wired home entertainment centres.[15]

Marketing critics do not view this interest in material things as a natural state of mind but rather as a matter of false wants created by marketing. Businesses hire advertisers to stimulate people's desires for goods, and advertisers use the mass media to create materialistic models of the good life. People work harder to earn the necessary money. Their purchases increase the output of North American industry, and industry in turn uses advertisers to stimulate more desire for the industrial output. Thus, marketing is seen as creating false wants that benefit industry more than they benefit consumers. A number of activist groups are starting to take action against overconsumption. See what public school students from in Ottawa, Ontario, did to support this cause:

The students from St. Elizabeth School in Ottawa developed a program and promoted "Buy Nothing Day" on the last Friday of November. (See their website at www3.sympatico.ca/dalia/buy0/index.htm.) The site notes that each North American produces on the average about 1.7 kg of garbage each day, much of which results from "careless" purchases and our shopping addiction. The students ask, "Do you think you could go through a day without shopping?" to

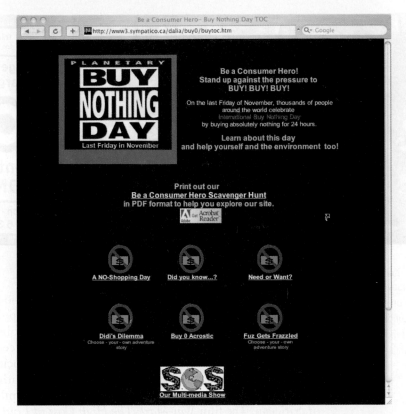

The students from St. Elizabeth School in Ottawa developed a program and promoted "Buy Nothing Day" using their website. They encourage Ottawa retailers and consumers to consider the impact that overconsumption has on the planet.

encourage people to stop shopping for just one day and think about the impact overconsumption has on the planet. Buy Nothing Day was the brainchild of Vancouver, B.C., artist Ted Dave in 1991. Supported by the Media Foundation and *Adbusters*, the movement has been adopted by activists around the world. In response to their campaign, the students note that one store in Ottawa did something really cool to celebrate the day. The Arbour Environmental Store stayed closed, put a poster of International Buy Nothing Day in their window and gave their employees a paid day off.[16]

These criticisms overstate the power of business to create needs, however. People have strong defences against advertising and other marketing tools. Marketers are most effective when they appeal to existing wants rather than when they attempt to create new ones. Furthermore, people seek information when making important purchases and often do not rely on single sources. Even minor purchases that can be affected by advertising messages lead to repeat purchases only if the product performs as promised. Finally, the high failure rate of new products shows that companies are not able to control demand.

On a deeper level, our wants and values are influenced not only by marketers but also by family, peer groups, religion, ethnic background, and education. If North Americans are highly materialistic, these values arose out of basic socialization processes that go much deeper than business and mass media alone could produce. Moreover, some social critics even see materialism as a positive and rewarding force:

When we purchase an object, what we really buy is meaning. Commercialism is the water we swim in, the air we breathe, our sunlight and our shade.... Materialism is a vital source of meaning and happiness in the modern world.... We have not just asked to go this way, we have demanded. Now most of the world is lining up, pushing and shoving, eager to elbow into the mall. Getting and spending has become the most passionate, and often the most imaginative, endeavour of modern life. Though this is dreary and depressing to some, as doubtless it should be, it is liberating and democratic to many more.[17]

In response to lane-clogging traffic congestion like that above, London now levies a congestion charge. The charge has reduced congestion by 40 percent and raised money to shore up the city's public transportation system.

Too Few Social Goods

Business has been accused of overselling private goods at the expense of public goods. As private goods increase, they require more public services that are usually not forthcoming. For example, an increase in automobile ownership (private good) requires more highways, traffic controls, parking spaces, and police services (public goods). The overselling of private goods results in "social costs." For cars, the social costs include traffic congestion, air pollution, and deaths and injuries from car accidents. The world's largest retailer, Wal-Mart, has recently been the target of this type of criticism. The film *Wal-Mart: The High Cost of Low Price* by Robert Greenwald, for example, accuses the retailer of making profits at the expense of communities and its workers (you can view the film trailer at www.walmartmovie.com/). Moreover, since Wal-Marts tend to be built in the edges of communities, critics claim taxpayers must cover the cost of new infrastructure (roads, water, and electricity) to service the stores. In its never-ending pursuit of low prices, the giant retailer has also been accused of driving its domestic suppliers out of business while it sources its goods from less developed countries.

A way must be found to restore a balance between private and public goods. One option is to make producers bear the full social costs of their operations. The government could require automobile manufacturers to build cars with better pollution-control systems. Take-out food suppliers could be forced to pay a "litter tax." Labour standards for stores like Wal-Mart could be strictly enforced. Many claim, however, that this would create higher business costs. Only producers that could support the sum of the private and social costs would survive.

A second option is to make consumers pay the social costs. For example, many cities around the world, such as London, England, are starting to charge "congestion tolls" in an effort to reduce traffic congestion. To unclog its streets, drivers are charged a levy of $8 per day per car to drive in an twenty-one-square-kilomtre area downtown. The charge has not only reduced traffic congestion by 40 percent, it raises money to shore up London's public transportation system.[18]

Cultural Pollution

Critics charge the marketing system with creating *cultural pollution*. Our senses are being assaulted constantly by advertising. Commercials interrupt serious programs; pop-up ad boxes interfere with our Internet searches, pages of ads obscure printed matter; billboards mar beautiful scenery. These interruptions continuously pollute people's minds with messages of materialism, sex, power, or status. Although most people do not find advertising overly annoying (some even think it is the best part of television programming), critics call for sweeping changes.

Marketers answer the charges of "commercial noise" with these arguments. First, they hope that their ads reach primarily the target audience. But because of mass-communication channels, some ads are bound to reach people who have no interest in the product and are therefore bored and annoyed. People who buy magazines addressed to their interests—such as *Harrowsmith* or *Canadian Business*— rarely complain about the ads because the magazines advertise products of interest. Second, ads make it possible for consumers to receive commercial television and radio free of charge and keep down the costs of magazines and newspapers. Many people think commercials are a small price to pay for these benefits. Finally, today's consumers have alternatives. For example, they can zip and zap TV commercials or avoid them altogether on many cable or satellite channels. Thus, to hold consumer attention, advertisers are making their ads more entertaining and informative.

Too Much Political Power

Another criticism is that business wields too much political power. Oil, tobacco, auto, and pharmaceutical firms lobby governments to promote their interests against the public interest. Advertisers are accused of holding too much power over the mass media, limiting their freedom to report independently and objectively. One critic has asked, "How can [most magazines] afford to tell the truth about the scandalously low nutritional value of most packaged foods ... when these magazines are being subsidized by such advertisers as General Foods, Kellogg's, Nabisco, and General Mills? ... The answer is *they cannot and do not.*"[19]

North American industries promote and protect their interests. They have a right to representation in Parliament and the mass media, although their influence can become too great. Fortunately, many powerful business interests once thought to be untouchable have been tamed in the public interest. For example, Petro-Canada was formed to give Canadians greater control over the oil industry.

Marketing's Impact on Other Businesses

Critics charge that a company's marketing practices can harm other companies and reduce competition. Three problems are involved: acquisitions of competitors, marketing practices that create barriers to entry, and unfair competitive marketing practices.

Critics claim that firms are harmed and competition reduced when companies expand by acquiring competitors rather than by developing their own new products. In virtually every major industry—retailing, entertainment, financial services, utilities, transportation, automobiles, telecommunications—the number of major competitors is shrinking. Consider the glut of acquisitions in the food industry during just the past few years: "The consolidation frenzy led to Unilever's buying Bestfoods, Philip Morris's snatching Nabisco, General Mills' swallowing Pillsbury, Kellogg's taking over Keebler, and PepsiCo's seizing of Quaker Oats."[20]

Acquisition is a complex subject. Acquisitions can sometimes be good for society. The acquiring company may gain economies of scale that lead to lower costs and lower prices. A well-managed company may take over a poorly managed company and improve its efficiency. An industry that was not very competitive may become more competitive after the acquisition. But acquisitions also can be harmful and, therefore, are regulated by the government.

Critics have charged that marketing practices bar new companies from entering an industry. Large companies can use patents and heavy promotional spending, and can tie up suppliers or dealers to keep out or drive out competitors. However, even people opposed to mergers among Canada's banks recognize that there are economic advantages to doing global business on a large scale. Some barriers that limit competition could be challenged by existing and new laws. For example, some critics have proposed a progressive tax on advertising spending to reduce the role of selling costs as a major barrier to entry.

Finally, some firms have used unfair competitive marketing practices with the intention of hurting or destroying other firms. They may set their prices below costs, threaten to cut off business with suppliers, or discourage the buying of a competitor's products. Regulation to prevent predatory pricing has been part of Canada's competition law for more than fifty years. Section 50(1)(c) of the *Competition Act* deals with this issue. In many cases, however, it is difficult to prove that the intent or action was really predatory. In recent years, Air Canada, Bell Canada, all of Canada's major oil companies, and even Canada Post have all been accused of predatory practices. Microsoft is another firm that has been battling this charge.

Competitors and regulators in both North America and Europe have accused giant Microsoft of predatory "bundling" practices, as was the case when it bundled its Internet Explorer browser into its Windows software. Bundling is the term used to describe Microsoft's practice of continually adding new features to Windows, the operating system installed on more than 90 percent of desktop computers. Because customers are essentially locked in to Windows, it's easy for the company to get them to use its other software—even if competitors make better products. That dampens competition, reduces choice, and could retard innovation. Microsoft's bundling practices sparked an antitrust suit by the U.S. government when the first mover in the industry, Netscape, saw its market share plummet as it tried to sell what Microsoft began to give away. The European Commission also took dramatic steps to stop what it saw as predatory bundling by Microsoft. It ordered Microsoft to offer a version of Windows with its media-playing software stripped out and it fined Microsoft more than US$600 million for using its "near monopoly" in the Windows operating system to squeeze out rivals in other types of software.[21]

Citizen and Public Actions to Regulate Marketing

Because some people view business as the cause of many economic and social ills, grassroots movements have arisen from time to time to keep business in line. The two major movements are *consumerism* and *environmentalism*.

Consumerism

The first consumer movements took place in the early 1900s and in the mid-1930s. Both were sparked by an upturn in consumer prices. Another movement began in the 1960s. Consumers had become better educated; products had become more complex and hazardous; and people were questioning the status quo. Many accused big business of wasteful and unethical practices. Canadian journalist Naomi Klein and her book *No Logo*, published in 2000, exemplify this movement. She worked to bring attention to the power of brands as cultural tools that turn people into walking billboards and that exploit workers in the world's poorest countries in their pursuit of profit. Today many consumer groups have been organized, and several consumer laws have been passed. The consumer movement has spread beyond North America and has become global in nature. Protestors, fearing negative outcomes on consumers and manufacturers alike, have disrupted conferences held by the World Trade Organization (WTO). Though the demonstrations were peaceful at the 2002 talks held in Kananaskis, outside of Calgary, they have degraded to violence in other areas.[22]

Consumerism
An organized movement of citizens and government agencies to improve the rights and power of buyers in relation to sellers.

But what is the consumer movement? **Consumerism** is an organized movement of citizens and government agencies to improve the rights and power of buyers in relation to sellers. It must be remembered that both parties have rights. Traditional *sellers' rights* include

- the right to introduce any product in any size and style, provided it is not hazardous to personal health or safety; or, if it is, to include proper warnings and controls
- the right to charge any price for the product, provided no discrimination exists among similar kinds of buyers
- the right to spend any amount to promote the product, provided it is not defined as unfair competition
- the right to use any product message, provided it is not misleading or dishonest in content or execution
- the right to use any buying incentive schemes, provided they are not unfair or misleading

The Consumers' Association of Canada (CAC; www.consumer.ca/) has acted as a consumer advocate and has provided information to Canadian consumers for more than fifty years. This volunteer-based, non-governmental organization was founded in 1947. With offices in every province, the association lobbies government to secure consumer rights in areas of food, health care, environment, consumer products and services, regulated industries (phone, electricity, telecommunications, and cable), financial institutions, taxation, trade, and other issues of concern to Canadians facing complex buying decisions. The association establishes annual priorities. Recent issues include concern about the high cost of insurance, the failure of the government to protect JetsGo passengers when the airline declared bankruptcy, the subsidization of Canada's dairy industry and the high prices consumers pay as a result, and the impact of Internet drug sales to American consumers. The association has also outlined the following as fundamental consumer rights:[23]

- *The right to safety.* Consumers have the right to be protected against the marketing of goods that are hazardous to health or life.
- *The right to be informed.* Consumers must be protected against fraudulent, deceitful, or grossly misleading information, advertising, labelling, or other practices. They are to be given the facts needed to make an informed choice.
- *The right to choose.* Consumers have the right to choose, wherever possible, among a variety of products and services at competitive prices. In industries where competition is not workable and government regulation is substituted, consumers must be assured of satisfactory quality and service at fair prices.
- *The right to be heard.* It is important that consumers' voices be heard. Thus, they must receive full and sympathetic consideration in the formulation of government policy, and fair and expeditious treatment in its administrative tribunals.
- *The right to redress against damage.* Consumers have the right to seek redress from a supplier of goods and services for any loss or damage suffered because of bad information, or faulty products or performance, and shall have easy and inexpensive access to settlement of small claims.
- *The right to consumer education.* Canadian consumers have the right to be educated as school children so that they will be able to act as informed consumers through their lives. Adults also have the right to consumer education.

Each proposed right has led to more specific proposals by consumerists. The right to be informed, for example, includes the right to know the true interest on a loan (truth in lending), the true cost per unit of a brand (unit pricing), the ingredients in a product (ingredient labelling), the nutrition in foods (nutritional labelling), product freshness (open dating), and the true benefits of a product (truth in advertising).

The Consumers' Association of Canada publishes this handbook to better inform consumers so they can make wise decisions and better understand their rights.

In addition to the CAC, the Office of Consumer Affairs, a branch of Industry Canada, publishes a number of online resources to help Canadians protect themselves and become wise shoppers. It contains tips on everything from "advance fee scams" to how to handle door-to-door sales and how to file a complaint if they have concerns about a sales or marketing practice. Better Business Bureaus also offer tips to consumers to protect themselves from fraud or shady business practices.

Environmentalism

Whereas consumerists consider whether the marketing system is efficiently serving consumer wants, environmentalists are concerned with marketing's effects on the environment and with the costs of serving consumer needs and wants. **Environmentalism** is an organized movement of concerned citizens, businesses, and government agencies to protect and improve people's living environment.

Many environmentalists are not against marketing and consumption; they simply want people and organizations to operate with more care for the environment. The marketing system's goal, they assert, should not be to maximize consumption, consumer choice, or consumer satisfaction, but rather to maximize life quality. And "life quality" means not only the quantity and quality of consumer goods and services, but also the quality of the environment. Environmentalists want environmental costs included in both producer and consumer decision making.

In response to these concerns, the Canadian government has undertaken a number of initiatives to improve the environment. It froze production levels of chlorofluorocarbons (CFCs), the major cause of ozone layer depletion, and Canada's environment ministers established a voluntary program intended to reduce excessive packaging. Despite a heated debate, the Kyoto Accord was endorsed in 2002. (To be aligned with the protocol, industrialized countries must cut their greenhouse gas emissions to below 1990 levels within 10 years.)[24]

Marketers cannot ignore the urgency of environmental issues or be blind to the fact that governments are increasingly willing to take action and pass regulations

Environmentalism
An organized movement of concerned citizens and government agencies to protect and improve people's living environment.

restricting marketing practices. All parts of the marketing mix are affected. Advertisers are accused of adding to the solid waste problem when they use direct mail or newspaper inserts. Manufacturers are criticized for making products that incorporate materials that increase pollution or cannot be recycled.[25] Distribution systems have been cited for adding to air pollution as trucks move products from the factory to the store. Critics claim that even when environmentally friendly products are available, they are priced too high for many consumers to afford.

Buying behaviour has changed as sensitivity to this issue has grown. The late 1980s saw the birth of a new product attribute—environmentally friendly. A recent survey conducted by the Grocery Product Manufacturers of Canada found that 80 percent of respondents said they would be willing to pay more for "green" products. Companies began to respond to these changes in demand. North American and European retailers are demanding more environmentally sensitive products: Wal-Mart has asked its suppliers to provide more of these products, and Loblaws has developed an entire line of products under its "Green" President's Choice label. Some people claim that "green marketing" is dead. If you think that is true, just consider some of the initiatives by the Canadian packaging industry:[26]

Canada's packaging industry worked so diligently to meet the goals established by the National Packaging Protocol, a voluntary agreement formulated to reduce the amount of packaging sent to landfills by 50 percent relative to what was sent to the trash in 1988, that it achieved the goals two years ahead of schedule. Thus, when Canada's major laundry detergent manufacturers introduced concentrated powders to the market, they not only reduced the amount of detergent that people used, they also resulted in a 40 percent reduction in packaging materials. This is only part of the commitment of the packaging industry, which has invested more than $2 billion in infrastructure to reduce, reuse, and recycle its packaging. Compared to a decade ago, there is almost no packaging produced in Canada that hasn't been improved from an environmental perspective. For example, the average glass container has 34 percent recycled content. Weights of containers have been reduced by at least 10 percent, saving fuel and shipping costs. Because the Canadian packaging industry had a jump on almost every other country in the world in designing better environmental packaging, there is strong export demand for Canadian packaging, especially in the U.S. It's a good initiative when you can sell more by using less.

Members of the Packaging Association of Canada (PAC) have worked to reduce the amount of packaging going into landfills and have gained international marketing opportunities in return.

Members of the Packaging Association of Canada (PAC) have worked to reduce the amount of packaging going into landfills and have gained international marketing opportunities in return.

As modern environmentalism evolved, responses by firms and the marketing profession were first driven by the actions of environmental groups and concerned consumers, then by new government laws and regulations. More recent is a movement whereby companies themselves are accepting responsibility for minimizing harm to the environment. They are shifting from resistance to prevention, and more and more companies are adopting policies of **environmental sustainability**—developing strategies that both sustain the environment and produce profits for the company. According to one strategist, "The challenge is to develop a *sustainable global economy:* an economy that the planet is capable of supporting indefinitely.... [It's] an enormous challenge—and an enormous opportunity."[27]

Figure 4.1 shows a grid that companies can use to gauge their progress toward environmental sustainability. At the most basic level, a company can practise *pollution prevention*. Instead of cleaning up waste after it has been created, pollution prevention means eliminating or minimizing waste before it is created. Companies emphasizing prevention have developed ecologically safer products, recyclable and biodegradable packaging, better pollution controls, and more energy-efficient operations. Rodeo Fine Homes, headquartered in Markham, Ontario, found that such policies can also give them a competitive advantage as well. It proposed the first environmentally sensitive subdivision in Newmarket, Ontario. The homes will be built using geothermal heating systems; they will heat water using solar power; and they will limit water use by using two-flush system toilets. For each lot, $1000 will be allocated for the building of community trails. Competition for development land in the Toronto area is fierce, and Rodeo's proposal won out over those of competitors even though its bid price for the land was lower than competitors. "We haven't invented anything," says Rodeo president Vince Maccarato. "We research and we found out that these technologies can achieve [these environmental] criteria."[28]

At the next level, companies can practise *product stewardship*—minimizing not just pollution from production but all environmental impacts throughout the full product life cycle. Many companies are adopting *design for environment (DFE)* practices, which involve thinking ahead to design products that are easier to recover, reuse, or recycle. DFE not only helps to sustain the environment, it can be highly profitable for the company. An example is Xerox Corporation's Equipment Remanufacture and Parts Reuse Program, which converts end-of-life office equipment into new products and parts:

Environmental sustainability
A management approach that involves developing strategies that both sustain the environment and produce profits for the company.

Figure 4.1 The environmental sustainability grid

Source: Stuart L. Hart, "Beyond Greening: Strategies for a Sustainable World," *Harvard Business Review*, January–February 1997, p. 74. Copyright © 1997 by the President and Fellows of Harvard College; all rights reserved. Reprinted by permission of *Harvard Business Review.*

	Internal	External
Tomorrow	**New environmental technology** Is the environmental performance of our products limited by our existing technology base? Is there potential to realize major improvements through new technology?	**Sustainability vision** Does our corporate vision direct us toward the solution of social and environmental problems? Does our vision guide the development of new technologies, markets, products, and processes?
Today	**Pollution prevention** Where are the most significant waste and emission streams from our current operations? Can we lower costs and risks by eliminating waste at the source or by using it as useful input?	**Product stewardship** What are the implications for product design and development if we assume responsibility for a product's entire life cycle? Can we add value or lower costs while simultaneously reducing the impact of our products?

Xerox starts by including reuse considerations in its design process to maximize end-of-life potential of products and parts. Its machines contain fewer parts and are designed for easy disassembly. Parts are designed for durability over multiple product life cycles and are coded with disposition instructions. As a result, equipment returned to Xerox at end-of-life can be remanufactured, reusing 70 to 90 percent (by weight) of old machine components, while still meeting performance standards for equipment made with all new parts. Xerox's program prevents more than 150 million pounds of waste from entering landfills each year. And it reduces the amount of raw material and energy needed to produce new parts. Xerox estimates that its savings in raw materials, labour, and waste disposal in the first year of the program alone ranged between US$350 million and US$450 million. Today, 100 percent of Xerox equipment is designed with remanufacturing and reuse in mind.[29]

At the third level, companies look to the future and plan for *new environmental technologies*. Many organizations that have made good sustainability headway are still limited by existing technologies. To develop fully sustainable strategies, they will need to develop new technologies. Bioniche, a small biotechnology company located in Belleville, Ontario, for example, is testing a new drug that will prevent cattle from shedding *E.coli* bacteria that contaminates water supplies and prevent tragedies such as the one that took place in Walkerton, Ontario, where seven people died a result of water contamination.

Finally, companies can develop a *sustainability vision*, which serves as a guide to the future. It shows how the company's products and services, processes, and policies must evolve and what new technologies must be developed to get there. This vision of sustainability provides a framework for pollution control, product stewardship, and environmental technology.

Most companies today focus on the lower-left quadrant of the grid in Figure 4.1, investing most heavily in pollution prevention. Some forward-looking companies practise product stewardship and are developing new environmental technologies. Few companies have well-defined sustainability visions. Emphasizing only one or a few cells in the environmental sustainability grid in Figure 4.1 can be short sighted. Investing only in the bottom half of the grid puts a company in a good position today but leaves it vulnerable in the future. In contrast, a heavy emphasis on the top half suggests that a company has good environmental vision but lacks the skills needed to implement it. Thus, companies should work at developing all four:

Hewlett-Packard (H-P) has evolved through three distinct phases of environmental sustainability over the past two decades. In the 1980s, it focused mostly on pollution control and prevention, with an eye on reducing emissions from existing manufacturing processes. In the 1990s, the focus shifted to product stewardship—on developing global processes for regulatory compliance, customer inquiry response systems, information management, public policy shaping, product take-back programs, green packaging, and integrating "design for environment" and life-cycle analysis into product development. Today, sustainability is about developing technologies that actually contribute a positive impact to environmental challenges. Pollution prevention and product stewardship have become baseline market expectations. To be an environmental leader in the twenty-first century, H-P knows that it needs to integrate environmental sustainability into its fundamental vision and strategy. "At H-P," says the company, "we believe that environmentally sustainable development is not an option, it's an imperative."[30]

Businesses alone cannot improve the environment. Consumers must also change their habits and government is there to help with new products and promotional programs. The Government of Ontario, for example, is working to promote a culture of conservation and is giving provincial residents the tools they need to make intelligent choices about electricity. It recently proposed legislation that would result in the installation smart meters in all homes and businesses by 2010. Smart metering, combined with a pricing structure that reflects the cost of power production at certain times of day and year, will allow consumers to make informed decisions about their electricity use, enabling them to save money while reducing the strain on the power system at peak periods.[31]

Environmentalism creates some special challenges for global marketers. As international trade barriers come down and global markets expand, environmental issues are having a growing impact on international trade. Countries in North America, Western Europe, and other developed regions are developing stringent environmental standards. However, environmental policies vary widely from country to country, and uniform worldwide standards are not expected for many years. Although countries such as Canada, Denmark, Germany, Japan, and the United States have fully developed environmental policies and high public expectations, other major countries, such as China, India, Brazil, and Russia, are only in the early stages of developing such policies. Thus, international companies are finding it difficult to develop standard environmental practices that work around the world. Instead, they are creating general policies and then translating these into tailored programs to meet local regulations and expectations.

Public Actions to Regulate Marketing

Citizen concerns about marketing practices usually will lead to public attention and legislative proposals. New bills will be debated—many will be defeated, others will be modified, and a few will become workable laws (see Figure 4.2). Canada's privacy law—the *Personal Information Protection and Electronic Documents Act*—is one example of a heavily debated proposal that became a law. The new Do-Not-Call Registry for telemarketers, which became law in November 2005, is another example.

Many of the laws that affect marketing are listed in Chapter 6. The task is to translate these laws into the language that marketing executives understand as they make decisions about competitive relations, products, price, promotion, and channels of distribution.

Figure 4.2 Major marketing decision areas that may be called into question under the law

Selling decisions
Bribing?
Stealing trade secrets?
Disparaging customers?
Misrepresenting?
Disclosure of customer rights?
Unfair discrimination?

Product decisions
Product additions and deletions?
Patent protection?
Product quality and safety?
Product warranty?

Advertising decisions
False advertising?
Deceptive advertising?
Bait-and-switch advertising?
Promotional allowances and services?

Packaging decisions
Fair packaging and labelling?
Excessive cost?
Scarce resources?
Pollution?

Channel decisions
Exclusive dealing?
Exclusive territorial distributorships?
Tying agreements?
Dealer's rights?

Price decisions
Price-fixing?
Predatory pricing?
Price discrimination?
Minimum pricing?
Price increases?
Deceptive pricing?

Competitive relations decisions
Anticompetitive acquisition?
Barriers to entry?
Predatory competition?

Business Actions Toward Socially Responsible Marketing

Today, most companies have grown to accept their environmental and social responsibility, seeing this as a way to serve consumer needs better. They may oppose certain pieces of legislation as inappropriate ways to solve certain problems, but they recognize their greater role in society and consumers' right to information and protection.

Enlightened Marketing

Enlightened marketing
A marketing philosophy holding that a company's marketing should support the best long-run performance of the marketing system; its five principles are consumer-oriented marketing, innovative marketing, value marketing, sense-of-mission marketing, and societal marketing.

The philosophy of **enlightened marketing** holds that a company's marketing should support the best long-run performance of the marketing system. Enlightened marketing consists of five principles: *consumer-oriented marketing, innovative marketing, value marketing, sense-of-mission marketing,* and *societal marketing.*

Consumer-Oriented Marketing

Consumer-oriented marketing
A philosophy of enlightened marketing that holds that the company should view and organize its marketing activities from the consumer's point of view.

Consumer-oriented marketing means that the company should view and organize its marketing activities from the consumer's point of view. It should work hard to sense, serve, and satisfy the needs of a defined group of customers. Consider this example:

> Montreal-based Walsh Integrated Environmental Systems Inc. was founded by David Walsh, right after he graduated from business school, when he realized what a huge waste management problem hospitals faced. Disposing of biohazardous waste costs twenty times as much as getting rid of regular waste, and can result in bills of more than $450 000 per year. Yet Walsh also saw that other materials, from pop cans to newspapers, were thrown in the bio-

The City of Toronto encourages consumers to change habits, such as pesticide use, that harm the environment.

hazardous containers. Walsh's new business developed a system called the Waste Tracker, which allows hospital staff to track the waste from each department, identify how much is biohazardous, and uncover who is misusing the system. Today his company serves more than 300 Canadian and U.S. hospitals, and he has expanded his services to include a quality support system that helps hospitals monitor the cleanliness of their rooms and labs as well as control their waste.[32]

Every successful company that we've discussed in this text has had this in common: an all-consuming passion for delivering superior value to carefully chosen customers. Only by seeing the world through its customers' eyes can the company build lasting and profitable customer relationships.

Innovative Marketing

Innovative marketing
A principle of enlightened marketing that requires that a company seek real product and marketing improvements.

The principle of **innovative marketing** requires that the company continuously seek real product and marketing improvements. The company that overlooks new and better ways to do things will eventually lose customers to another company that has found a better way. An excellent example of an innovative marketer is Samsung:

Less than a decade ago, Samsung was a copycat consumer electronics brand you bought off a shipping pallet at Costco if you couldn't afford a Sony. But today, the brand holds a high-end, cutting-edge aura. In 1996, Samsung Electronics made an inspired decision. It turned its back on cheap knock-offs and hired a crop of fresh, young designers, who unleashed a torrent of new products—not

In less than a decade, Samsung has given its brand a cutting-edge image by unleashing a torrent of new products—not humdrum, me-too products, but innovative and stylish products, targeted to high-end users.

humdrum, me-too products, but innovative and stylish products, targeted to high-end users. Samsung called them "lifestyle works of art"—from brightly coloured cellphones and elegantly thin DVD players to flat-panel TV monitors that hung on walls like paintings. Every new product had to pass the "Wow!" test: if it didn't get a "Wow!" reaction during market testing, it went straight back to the design studio. It abandoned low-end distributors and supported the innovative new products with a US$400 million marketing campaign. Samsung is now the world's fastest-growing brand.[33]

Customer-Value Marketing

Customer-value marketing
A principle of enlightened marketing that holds that a company should put most of its resources into value-building marketing investments.

According to the principle of **customer-value marketing**, the company should put most of its resources into value-building marketing investments. Many things marketers do—one-shot sales promotions, minor packaging changes, advertising puffery—may raise sales in the short run but add less *value* than would actual improvements in the product's quality, features, or convenience. Enlightened marketing calls for building long-run consumer loyalty by continually improving the value consumers receive from the firm's marketing offer.

Sense-of-Mission Marketing

Sense-of-mission marketing
A principle of enlightened marketing that holds that a company should define its mission in broad social terms rather than narrow product terms.

Sense-of-mission marketing means that the company should define its mission in broad *social* terms rather than narrow *product* terms. When a company defines a social mission, employees feel better about their work and have a clearer sense of direction. For example, defined in narrow product terms, Mountain Equipment Co-op sells high-quality outdoor gear. However, the organization states its mission more broadly as one of "social and environmental leadership."[34] Reshaping the basic task of selling consumer products into the larger mission of serving the interests of consumers, employees, the environment, and others in the organization's various "communities" gives MEC a vital sense of purpose. Like MEC, many companies today are undertaking socially responsible actions or even building social responsibility into their underlying missions.

Societal Marketing

Societal marketing
A principle of enlightened marketing that holds that a company should make marketing decisions by considering consumers' wants, the company's requirements, consumers' long-run interests, and society's long-run interests.

Following the principle of **societal marketing**, an enlightened company makes marketing decisions by considering consumers' wants and interests, the company's requirements, and society's long-run interests. The company is aware that neglecting consumer and societal long-run interests is a disservice to consumers and society. Alert companies and organizations view societal problems as opportunities. This is just what Hockey Canada did.

Canadians have a reputation for being polite, reserved and well mannered—unless of course they are watching their children wobbling around a hockey rink. In towns and cities across Canada, parents seem to have gone mad. They scream at their kids, hurl insults at rival teams, and beat refs to within an inch of their lives. For many kids, such behaviour was destroying Canada's best-loved game, so Hockey Canada decided to call a penalty shot. In a series of funny but provocative ads, it reverses the roles of parent and kid. One spot shows a man pulled over for a traffic violation. As the officer is writing up the ticket, the man's ten-year-old son is losing it in the back seat, furious because his spineless dad won't stand up to the cop. In another, a girl berates her father in front of his golf buddies as he tries to sink a putt. The breakthrough campaign has made us all aware of the problem and caused us to take a fresh look at our behaviour.[35]

Hockey Canada saw the bad behaviour of hockey parents as an opportunity to take action to improve the hockey experience for kids. Their irreverent campaign made parents everywhere re-examine their behaviour.

A societally oriented marketer wants to design products that are not only pleasing but also beneficial. Examples of products that create immediate consumer satisfaction as well as long-term social benefits abound. Philips Lighting's Earth Light compact fluorescent light bulb provides good lighting at the same time that it gives long life and energy savings. Toyota's gas-electric hybrid Prius gives both a quiet ride and fuel efficiency. Maytag's front-loading Neptune washer provides superior cleaning along with water savings and energy efficiency. President's Choice "Too Good to Be True" soup mixes, developed for people with special dietary needs, have been welcomed by consumers who want good-tasting, high-fibre, low-fat, easy-to-prepare, healthful food. And Herman Miller's office chairs are not only attractive and functional but also environmentally responsible:

> Herman Miller, one of the world's largest office furniture makers, has received numerous awards for environmentally responsible products and business practices. More than a decade ago, the company formed a Design for the Environment team responsible for infusing the company's design process with its environmental values. The team carries out "cradle-to-cradle" life cycle analyses on the company's products, including everything from how much of a product can be made from recycled materials to how much of the product itself can be recycled at the end of its useful life. For example, the team redesigned the company's chairs for the lowest possible ecological impact and high recyclability. Recently, Herman Miller introduced the Mirra chair, which is made from 42 percent recycled materials and is 96 percent recyclable. The frames need no paint or other finish. No ozone-depleting materials are used. Chairs are shipped partially assembled, thus reducing the packaging and energy needed to ship them. Finally, materials schematics are embedded in the bottoms of chair seats to help recycle chairs at the ends of their lives. Herman Miller chairs have won awards for design and function *and* for environmental responsibility. And it inspired future models of environmentally friendly chairs.[36]

Companies should try to turn all of their products into such desirable products. They should avoid the temptation to market pleasing products that may sell very well but may end up hurting the consumer and the environment. The product

Herman Miller's Design for the Environment team is responsible for infusing the company's design process with its environmental values. For example, its Mirra chair is made from 42 percent recycled materials and is 96 percent recyclable.

opportunity, therefore, is to add long-run benefits without reducing the product's pleasing qualities.

Marketing Ethics

Conscientious marketers face many moral dilemmas. Each area of marketing practice has ethical issues associated with it. Table 4.1 outlines just a few of the ethical issues marketers may face when fulfilling their roles. When facing these dilemmas, the best thing to do is often unclear. Because not all managers have fine moral sensitivity, companies need to develop *corporate marketing ethics policies*—broad guidelines that everyone in the organization must follow. These policies should cover distributor relations, advertising standards, customer service, pricing, and product development, as well as general ethical standards.

The finest guidelines cannot resolve all the difficult ethical situations the marketer faces. Table 4.2 lists some difficult ethical situations that marketers could face during their careers. If marketers choose immediate sales-producing actions in all these cases, their marketing behaviour may well be described as immoral or even amoral. If they refuse to go along with *any* of the actions, they may be ineffective as marketing managers and unhappy because of the constant moral tension. Managers need a set of principles that will help them to determine the moral importance of each situation and decide how far they can go in good conscience.

But *what* principle should guide companies and marketing managers on issues of ethics and social responsibility? One philosophy is that such issues are decided by the free market and legal system. Under this principle, companies and their managers are not responsible for making moral judgments. Companies can in good conscience do whatever the system legally allows.

A second philosophy puts responsibility not in the system but in the hands of individual companies and managers. This more enlightened philosophy suggests that a company should have a "social conscience." Companies and managers should apply high standards of ethics and morality when making corporate decisions, regardless of "what the system allows." History provides an endless list of examples of company actions that were legal and allowed but were highly irresponsible.

Table 4.1 Ethical Issues Associated with Marketing Practice

Marketing Element	Examples of Ethical Issues
Marketing Research	Invalid and/or unreliable research studies (agencies conducting research studies using inappropriate methods or measures)
	Invasion of consumer's privacy
	Disguising sales as research
	Failure to ensure voluntary and informed participation (pressuring consumers to comply through high-pressure tactics or high-value incentives)
	Failure to respect the confidentiality of respondents (revealing respondents' individual identities)
	Competitive intelligence gathering using unethical tactics (hiring competitors' employees, dumpster diving, spying)
Segmentation and Target Marketing	Redlining: discriminating against poor or disadvantaged consumers
	Targeting inappropriate products to vulnerable audiences (diet pills to anorexic women, violent video games to children)
Positioning	Making socially undesirable products desirable (promoting use of disposable cleaning devices that add to the landfill crisis versus reusable ones)
	Positioning on questionable benefits (the objectification of women in advertising and the suggestion that alcohol consumption makes males more sexually attractive, when alcohol may diminish sexual function and rape and physical abuse have been found to be associated with drinking)
Product	Failure to market products that are safe for the intended use (lead in children's' toys)
	Product testing (animal testing, failure to test sufficiently to reveal safety concerns)
	Marketing socially controversial products (cigarettes, firearms)
Packaging and Labelling	Actual size vs. apparent size (using design elements to make packages look larger than they are)
	Inadequate efforts with regard to product recalls
	Nutritional information (is information displayed in a fashion that can and will be processed?)
	Unclear or misleading labelling (use of terms such as "lite," "healthy," etc., that are ambiguous and may imply benefits not actually associated with the product)
	Excessive or environmentally unfriendly packaging (use of double and triple packaging that does little to protect the product but adds to the waste stream, use of harmful dyes, failure to use recycled materials)
Pricing	Price collusion: the illegal practice of forming price agreements with competitors
	Negative option billing: sending unrequested goods and billing consumers for them
	Prejudice in negotiated prices: research has demonstrated that women and racial minorities pay more in negotiated price situations, such as car buying
	Price discrimination: charging different segments different prices that are not based on cost (e.g., charging high prices in low-income neighbourhoods)
Advertising	Sex-role stereotyping in advertising (always showing women in domestic roles, not using women's voices in voice-overs in advertising)
	Dehumanizing images and portraying people as products: showing body parts versus the whole human being
	Bait-and-switch advertising: enticing consumers into retail establishments with offers of low-priced goods and then switching them to higher-priced alternatives
Sales and Channel Management	High-pressure sales tactics
	Unfairly disparaging competitors' goods
	Channel loading: pressuring channel members to take unneeded inventory at the end of a sales period to make the firm's sales numbers look better for reporting purposes

Table 4.2 Some Morally Difficult Situations in Marketing

1. You work for a fast-food company and up until now have not been convinced that eating fast food leads to obesity for many people, especially children. However, recent public policy debates now leave no doubt in your mind about the link between overconsumption of these foods and health problems. What do you do?

2. Your R&D department has changed one of your products slightly. It is not really "new and improved," but you know that putting this statement on the package and in advertising will increase sales. What do you do?

3. You have been asked to add a stripped-down model to your line that could be advertised to attract customers to the store. The product won't be very good, but salespeople will be able to switch buyers up to higher-priced units. You are asked to give the green light for this stripped-down version. What do you do?

4. You are considering hiring a product manager who just left a competitor's company. She would be more than happy to tell you all the competitor's plans for the coming year. What do you do?

5. One of your top dealers in an important territory has recently had family troubles, and his sales have slipped. It looks like it will take him some time to straighten out his family trouble. Meanwhile, you are losing many sales. Legally, you can terminate the dealer's franchise and replace him. What do you do?

6. You have a chance to win a big account that will mean a lot to you and your company. The purchasing agent hints that a "gift" would influence the decision. Your assistant recommends sending a fine colour television set to the buyer's home. What do you do?

7. You have heard that a competitor has a new product feature that will make a big difference in sales. The competitor will demonstrate the feature in a private dealer meeting at the annual trade show. You can easily send a snooper to this meeting to learn about the new feature. What do you do?

8. You have to choose between three ad campaigns outlined by your agency. "A" is a soft-sell, honest information campaign. "B" uses sex-loaded emotional appeals and exaggerates the product's benefits. "C" involves a noisy, irritating commercial that is sure to gain audience attention. Pretests show that the campaigns are effective in the following order: C, B, and A. What do you do?

9. You are interviewing a capable woman applicant for a job as a salesperson. She is better qualified than the men just interviewed. Nevertheless, you know that some of your important customers prefer dealing with men, and you will lose some sales if you hire her. What do you do?

10. You are a sales manager in an encyclopedia company. Your competitor's salespeople are getting into homes by pretending to take a research survey. After they finish the survey, they switch to their sales pitch. This technique seems to be very effective. What do you do?

Consider this example:

Prior to the [United States] *Pure Food and Drug Act*, the advertising for a diet pill promised that a person taking this pill could eat virtually anything at any time and still lose weight. Too good to be true? Actually the claim was quite true; the product lived up to its billing with frightening efficiency. It seems that the primary active ingredient in this "diet pill" was tapeworm larvae. These larvae would develop in the intestinal tract and, of course, be well fed; the pill taker would in time, quite literally, starve to death.[37]

Each company and marketing manager must work out a philosophy of socially responsible and ethical behaviour. Under the social marketing concept, companies and managers must look beyond what is legal and allowed, and develop standards based on personal integrity, corporate conscience, and long-run consumer welfare.

A clear and responsible philosophy will help the company deal with knotty issues such as the one faced recently by 3M:

> In late 1997, a powerful new research technique for scanning blood kept turning up the same odd result: tiny amounts of a chemical 3M had made for nearly forty years were showing up in blood drawn from people living all across North America. If the results held up, it meant that virtually all North Americans may be carrying some minuscule amount of the chemical, called perfluorooctane sulfonate (PFOS), in their systems.
>
> Even though they had yet to come up with definitive answers—and they insisted that there was no evidence of danger to humans—the company reached a drastic decision. In mid-2000, although under no mandate to act, 3M decided to phase out products containing PFOS and related chemicals, including its popular Scotchgard fabric protector. This was no easy decision. Since there was as yet no replacement chemical, it meant a potential loss of US$500 million in annual sales.
>
> 3M's voluntary actions drew praise from regulators. "3M deserves great credit for identifying the problem and coming forward," says an Environmental Protection Agency administrator. "It took guts," comments another government scientist. "The fact is that most companies ... go into anger, denial, and the rest of that stuff. [We're used to seeing] decades-long arguments about whether a chemical is really toxic." For 3M, however, it shouldn't have been all that difficult a decision—it was simply the right thing to do.[38]

As with environmentalism, the issue of ethics provides special challenges for international marketers. Business standards and laws vary widely from one country to the next. For example, whereas bribes and kickbacks are illegal for North American firms, they are standard business practice in many South American countries. When firms give a covert payment to a government official to obtain a concession, they are no longer just committing an unethical act, they are committing an illegal one, violating the Canada's *Corruption of Foreign Public Officials Act* (1998).

One recent study found that companies from some nations were much more likely to use bribes when seeking contracts in emerging-market nations. The most flagrant bribe-paying firms were from Russia and China, with Taiwan and South Korea close behind. The least corrupt were companies from Australia, Sweden, Switzerland, Austria, and Canada.[39] The question arises as to whether a company must lower its ethical standards to compete effectively in countries with lower standards. In one study, two researchers posed this question to chief executives of large international companies and got a unanimous response: No.[40]

Many professional associations and firms have developed codes of ethics to better manage ethical issues related to marketing. For example, the Canadian Direct Marketing Association has a code to regulate the practices of its members; excerpts are given in Table 4.3 on page 152. Companies are also developing programs to teach managers about important ethics issues and help them find the proper responses. They hold ethics workshops and seminars and set up ethics committees. Further, most major North American companies have appointed high-level ethics officers to champion ethics issues and to help resolve ethics problems and concerns facing employees. Under the new Canadian privacy laws, companies must also appoint privacy officers to keep an eye on this important issue within their organizations.

PricewaterhouseCoopers (PwC) is a good example. In 1996, PwC established an ethics office and comprehensive ethics program, headed by a high-level chief ethics officer. The ethics program begins with a code of conduct, called "The Way We Do Business." PwC employees learn about the code of conduct and about how to handle thorny ethics issues in a comprehensive ethics training program, called "Navigating the Grey." The program also includes an ethics help line and continuous communications at all levels. "Ethics is in everything we say and do," says PwC's CEO, Samuel DiPiazza. In recent years, the PwC training program involved

PricewaterhouseCoopers established a comprehensive ethics program, which begins with a code of conduct, called "The Way We Do Business." Says PwC's CEO, "Ethics is in everything we say and do."

40 000 employees, and the help line received more than 1000 calls from people asking for guidance in working through difficult ethics dilemmas.[41]

Many companies have developed innovative ways to educate employees about ethics:

Ontario Power Generation Inc. and Imperial Oil have appointed high-level ethics officers to champion ethics issues and to help resolve ethics problems and concerns facing employees. Nynex created a new position of vice-president of ethics, supported by a dozen full-time staff and a million-dollar budget. Since 1991, the ethics department has trained some 95 000 employees. This training includes sending 22 000 managers to full-day workshops that include case studies on ethical actions in marketing, finance, and other business functions.[42]

Citicorp has developed an ethics board game, which teams of employees use to solve hypothetical quandaries. General Electric employees can tap into

Table 4.3 Excerpts from the Canadian Marketing Association's Code of Ethics & Standards of Practice

B. PURPOSE OF CODE OF ETHICS AND STANDARDS OF PRACTICE

Marketers acknowledge that the establishment and maintenance of high standards of practice are a fundamental responsibility to the public, essential to winning and holding public confidence, and the foundation of a successful and independent information-based marketing industry in Canada.

H. OVERARCHING ETHICAL PRINCIPLES

H1 Personal Information Practices

Marketers must promote responsible and transparent personal information management practices in a manner consistent with the provisions of the Personal Information Protection and Electronic Documents Act (Canada) and/or applicable provincial legislation and the 10 privacy principles detailed in Section J of this Code.

H2 Truthfulness

Marketing communications must be clear and truthful. Marketers must not knowingly make a representation to a consumer or business that is false or misleading.

H3 Campaign Limitations

H3.1   Marketers must not participate in any campaign involving the disparagement or exploitation of any person or group on the grounds of race, colour, ethnicity, religion, national origin, gender, sexual orientation, martial status or age.

H3.3   Marketers must not participate in the dissemination of any material that unduly, gratuitously and without merit exploits sex, horror, mutilation, torture, cruelty, violence or hate, except where required to do so by law, such as a common carrier.

H3.4   Marketers must not knowingly exploit the credulity, lack of knowledge or inexperience of any consumer, taking particular care when dealing with vulnerable consumers. The term "vulnerable consumer" includes, but is not limited to children, teenagers, people with disabilities, the elderly and those for whom English or French is not their first language.

I. ACCURACY OF REPRESENTATION

I.1 Marketers must not misrepresent a product, service, or marketing program and must not mislead by statement, or manner of demonstration or comparison.

I4 Support for Claims

Test or survey data referred to in any marketing communication must be reliable, accurate, and current and must support the specific claim being made. Marketers must be able to substantiate the basis for any performance claim or comparison and must not imply a scientific, factual, or statistical basis where none exists.

I5 Disguise

I5.1   Marketers must not engage in marketing communications in the guise of one purpose when the intent is a different purpose.

I5.2   Marketers must not claim to be carrying out a survey or research when their real purpose is to sell a product or service or to raise funds.

I6 Testimonials

Testimonials and endorsements must be:

a.   authorized by the person or organization quoted;

b.   genuine and related to the experience of the person or organization quoted, both at the time made and at the time of the marketing communication.

I9 Price Claims

I9.1   Terms such as "regular price," "suggested retail value," "manufacturer's list price," and "fair market value," must represent prices at which the item has been sold in the relevant marketplace in substantial quantity or for a substantial period of time.

I14 Disclosures

I14.1   Prior to a consumer buying opportunity, marketing offers must provide all the information necessary for a reasonable consumer or business to make an informed purchase decision.

Precise disclosures will vary by product or service being marketed, but must include the

a.   exact nature of what is being offered;

b.   price, including all additional charges such as delivery or handling costs;

c. terms of payment;

d. consumer or business' commitment and any ongoing obligation in placing an order; and

e. delivery arrangements including shipping terms and delivery times.

I15 Fulfilment Practices

I15.1 *Shipment:* Goods offered shall be shipped within 30 days of the receipt of a properly completed order, or within any shorter period that may be prescribed by applicable law or within the time limit stated in the original agreement.

I15.2 *Delay:* If the delivery will be delayed, the customer or business must be advised within 30 days of the receipt of the order, or within any shorter period that may be prescribed by applicable law or within the time limit stated in the original agreement.

J. PROTECTION OF PERSONAL PRIVACY

All consumer marketers must abide by the *Personal Information Protection and Electronics Documents Act* (PIPEDA), and/or applicable provincial privacy laws and the following ten Privacy Principles from the National Standard of Canada and five additional requirements as outlined in this section.

J1 Ten Privacy Principles:

1. Accountability: An organization is responsible for personal information under its control and shall designate an individual or individuals who are accountable for the organization's compliance with the following principles.

2. Identifying Purposes: The purposes for which personal information is collected shall be identified by the organization at or before the time the information is collected.

3. Consent: The knowledge and consent of the individual are required for the collection, use or disclosure of personal information, except where inappropriate.

4. Limiting Collection: The collection of personal information shall be limited to that which is necessary for the purposes identified by the organization. Information shall be collected by fair and lawful means.

5. Limiting Use, Disclosure, and Retention: Personal information shall not be used or disclosed for purposes other than those for which it was collected, except with the consent of the individual or as required by the law. Personal information shall be retained only as long as necessary for fulfilment of those purposes.

6. Accuracy: Personal information shall be as accurate, complete, and up-to-date as is necessary for the purposes for which it is to be used.

7. Safeguards: Personal information shall be protected by security safeguards appropriate to the sensitivity of the information.

8. Openness: An organization shall make readily available to individuals specific information about its policies and practices relating to the management of personal information.

9. Individual Access: Upon request, an individual shall be informed of the existence, use and disclosure of his or her personal information and shall be given access to that information. An individual shall be able to challenge the accuracy and completeness of the information and have it amended as appropriate.

10. Challenging Compliance: An individual shall be able to address a challenge concerning compliance with the above principles to the designated individual or individuals for the organization's compliance.

K. SPECIAL CONSIDERATIONS IN MARKETING TO CHILDREN

K1 Age

For purposes of this Code, the term *child* refers to someone who has not reached his or her thirteenth birthday.

K2 Responsibility

Marketing to children imposes a special responsibility on marketers. Marketers must recognize that children are not adults and that not all marketing techniques are appropriate for children.

K3 Consent

When marketing to persons between 13 years and the age of majority, marketers are strongly cautioned that children may be exposed to these communications, and in such cases, these interactions with children are governed by the following guidelines concerning consent.

K3.1 Except as provided below under Section K4 of this Code, *Contests Directed to Children*, all marketing interactions directed to children that include the collection, transfer and requests for personal information require the express consent of the child's parent or guardian.

Source: Canadian Marketing Association, "Code of Ethics and Standards of Practice," effective January 1, 2007, www.the-cma.org/regulatory/codeofethics.cfm (accessed September 2006).

specially designed software on their personal computers to get answers to ethical questions. At Texas Instruments, employees are treated to a weekly column on ethics over an electronic news service. One popular feature: a kind of "Dear Abby" mailbag, answers provided by the company's ethics officer, ... that deals with the troublesome issues employees face most often.[43]

Still, written codes and ethics programs do not ensure ethical behaviour. Ethics and social responsibility require a total corporate commitment. They must be a component of the overall corporate culture. According to PwC's DiPiazza, "I see ethics as a mission-critical issue ... deeply imbedded in who we are and what we do. It's just as important as our product development cycle or our distribution system.... It's about creating a culture based on integrity and respect, not a culture based on dealing with the crisis of the day.... We ask ourselves every day, 'Are we doing the right things?'"[44]

Canada's 74 000 charities and non-profit organizations are not immune to questions of ethics. Though few question the importance of these worthy causes, there has been growing criticism about some of the fundraising methods they use. Two major concerns have surfaced. More charities are using lotteries to raise funds. These not only add to the pressures on people to gamble, but they may often jeopardize the welfare of the non-profit. Use of professional telemarketers is another source of ethical concern. They raise funds on the part of non-profit organizations, but the charity may only see a small portion of the money raised. In the face of growing public scrutiny, non-profits have to be as ethically aware and socially responsible as their for-profit counterparts.

The future holds many challenges and opportunities for marketing managers in this millennium. Technological advances in every area, from telecommunications, information technology, and the Internet to health care and entertainment, provide abundant marketing opportunities. However, forces in the socioeconomic, cultural, and natural environments increase the limits under which marketing can be carried out. Companies that are able to create new values in a socially responsible way will have a world to conquer.

Reviewing the Concepts

In this chapter, we've closed with many important concepts involving marketing's sweeping impact on individual consumers, other businesses, and society as a whole. You learned that responsible marketers discover what consumers want and respond with the right products, priced to give good value to buyers and profit to the producer. A marketing system should sense, serve, and satisfy consumer needs and improve the quality of consumers' lives. In working to meet consumer needs, marketers may take some actions that are not to everyone's liking or benefit. Marketing managers should be aware of the main *criticisms of marketing*.

1. **Understand marketing's multiple responsibilities, and identify the major social and ethical criticisms of marketing.**

Marketing's *impact on individual consumer welfare* has been criticized for its high prices, deceptive practices, high-pressure selling, shoddy or unsafe products, planned obsolescence, and poor service to disadvantaged consumers. Marketing's *impact on society* has been criticized for creating false wants and too much materialism, too few social goods, cultural pollution, and too much political power. Critics have also criticized marketing's *impact on other businesses* for harming competitors and reducing competition through acquisitions, practices that create barriers to entry, and unfair competitive marketing practices.

2. **Define** *consumerism* **and** *environmentalism* **and explain how they affect marketing strategies.**

   Concerns about the marketing system have led to *citizen action movements*. *Consumerism* is an organized social movement intended to strengthen the rights and power of consumers relative to sellers. Alert marketers view it as an opportunity to serve consumers better by providing more consumer information, education, and protection. *Environmentalism* is an organized social movement seeking to minimize the harm done to the environment and quality of life by marketing practices. The first wave of modern environmentalism was driven by environmental groups and concerned consumers; the second wave was driven by government, which passed laws and regulations governing industrial practices affecting the environment. Now, in the twenty-first century, the first two environmentalism waves are merging into a third and stronger wave in which companies are accepting responsibility for minimizing environmental harm. Companies now are adopting policies of *environmental sustainability*—developing strategies that both sustain the environment and produce profits for the company.

3. **Describe the principles of socially responsible marketing.**

   Many companies originally opposed these social movements and laws, but most of them now recognize a need for positive consumer information, education, and protection. Some companies have followed a policy of *enlightened marketing*, which holds that a company's

marketing should support the best long-run performance of the marketing system. Enlightened marketing consists of five principles: *consumer-oriented marketing*, *innovative marketing*, *value marketing*, *sense-of-mission marketing*, and *societal marketing*.

4. **Explain the role of ethics in marketing.**

   Increasingly, companies are responding to the need to provide company policies and guidelines to help their managers deal with questions of *marketing ethics*. Of course, even the best guidelines cannot resolve all of the difficult ethical decisions that individuals and firms must make. But there are some principles that marketers can choose among. One principle states that such issues should be decided by the free market and legal system. A second and more enlightened principle puts responsibility not in the system but in the hands of individual companies and managers. Each firm and marketing manager must develop a philosophy of socially responsible and ethical behaviour. Under the societal marketing concept, managers must look beyond what is legal and allowable and develop standards based on personal integrity, corporate conscience, and long-term consumer welfare.

   Because business standards and practices vary among countries, the issue of ethics poses special challenges for international marketers. The growing consensus among today's marketers is that it is important to make a commitment to a common set of shared standards worldwide.

Reviewing the Key Terms

Consumerism   137
Consumer-oriented marketing   143
Customer-value marketing   145
Enlightened marketing   143
Environmental sustainability   140

Environmentalism   138
Innovative marketing   144
Sense-of-mission marketing   145
Societal marketing   145

Discussing the Concepts

1. Many firms, such as Molson, Canada Trust, Procter & Gamble, Bell Canada, and Imperial Oil, have been practising cause-related marketing as a means of fulfilling their social responsibilities. Cause-related marketing is the practice of associating a for-profit firm's products or services with a non-profit cause. Although the primary purpose of the program is the accomplishment of marketing objectives, the non-profit also achieves significant benefits from these campaigns. Describe some of the cause-related campaigns you

   have seen. Do you think they are a legitimate means for firms to fulfill part of their social responsibility?

2. Marketing receives much criticism, some justified and much not. Which of the major criticisms of marketing discussed in the chapter do you think are most justified? Which are least justified?

3. You have been invited to appear along with an economist on a panel assessing marketing practices in the soft-drink industry. You are surprised when the

economist opens the discussion with a long list of criticisms of marketing, focusing on the unnecessarily high marketing costs and deceptive promotional practices. Abandoning your prepared comments, you set out to defend marketing, in general, and the soft-drink industry, in particular. How would you respond to the economist's attack?

4. Comment on the state of consumers' rights on the Internet and in ecommerce. Design a "Bill of Rights" that would protect consumers while they shop for products and services on the Internet. Consider such issues as government regulation, ease and convenience of use, warranties, guarantees and return policies, privacy, security, and cost-efficient commerce.

Applying the Concepts

1. Suppose you are a key person in the marketing department of your organization. You recently learned that your company is marketing an unsafe product, which has already resulted in a few consumer injuries. Publicly acknowledging the problem would damage your brand's image and would require an expensive product recall. However, you believe that you could quietly introduce an improved version of the product, avoiding both the recall and the harmful publicity. What would you do?

2. In a small group, search the Internet for companies that have included a discernable societal marketing goal in their mission/vision statements. Record and share these mission statements. Rewrite the following

Focus on Technology

Retail check-out scanners have been around for almost a generation. They save time for the consumer and are an integral part of the retailer's supply chain management system. But according to recent reports, whether intentionally or unintentionally, one out of thirty scanner prices is wrong. Half of the incorrect prices are too high and the other half are too low. The Competition Bureau did a study on price scanners, and it found that they were almost 100 percent accurate. However, it did find human errors in terms of updating databases or having prices entered into the scanning system that did not match prices on the shelves.

5. What is the basic philosophy supporting enlightened marketing? List and briefly describe each of the five principles of enlightened marketing. Cite several examples of firms that practise enlightened marketing.

6. Compare the marketing concept, discussed in Chapter 1, with the principle of societal marketing. Should all marketers adopt the societal marketing concept? Why or why not?

7. You are the marketing manager for a small firm that makes kitchen appliances. While conducting field tests, you discover a design flaw in one of your most popular models that could potentially cause harm to a small number of consumers. However, a product recall would likely bankrupt your company, leaving all of the employees (including you) jobless. What would you do?

Dell mission statement, incorporating a more societal marketing focus.

"Dell's mission is to be the world's most successful computer company, delivering the best customer experience in markets we serve."

3. Recent public concerns over children and the Internet resulted the *Children's Online Privacy Protection Act* (COPPA). Among other things, this act requires websites that are visited by children under the age of 13 to post a privacy policy detailing any personally identifiable information collected from those children. Do some research and answer the question: What consumer need is being met by COPPA?

1. How trusting are consumers of electronic scanning?

2. Do you believe some retailers intentionally mismark items? Why would they do this? Is it easy or difficult to prove that an item is intentionally mismarked?

3. Would Radio Frequency Identification (RFID) help to fix this problem? Why or why not?

Sources: See Price Scanning Report 1996–1999, Competition Bureau Fair Business Practices Branch, www.competitionbureau.gc.ca/internet /index.cfm?itemID=1288&lg=e; "Check that list twice: Scanner mistakes can add up," CBC Marketplace, March 29, 2000 (www.cbc.ca/consumers/ market/files/money/scanners/index.html); www.ftc.gov/reports/scanner2/ scanner2.htm; and www.ftc. gov/reports/scanner1/scanners.htm.

Focus on Ethics

A *whistle-blower* is a person who reports illegal or unethical behaviour to the public, to the government, or to those in positions of authority. If there ever was a whistle-blower poster-person, it's Sherron Watkins, of Houston, Texas. As you may recall, this ex-vice president of corporate development at Enron wrote a memo to Kenneth Lay, Enron's chairman and CEO, alerting him to the company's financial improprieties. Watkins' story is one of concern for a company she helped build and compassion for fellow employees. Visit www.time.com/time/personoftheyear/2002/ and read the *Time* website article selecting Watkins and two other whistle-blowers as "Time Magazine Person of the Year 2002." Then visit http://fl1.findlaw.com/news.findlaw.com/hdocs/docs/enron/empltr2lay82001.pdf and read the now-famous Watkins' memo. Respond to the following questions:

1. Did Sherron Watkins do the right thing in going to Kenneth Lay rather than to the media? Explain?

2. In the memo, is Watkins clear about Enron's alleged illegal financial dealings?

3. If you had been Kenneth Lay and had received Watkins' letter, what would you have done?

4. Do you think there is adequate protection for whistle-blowers?

Sources: See www.telltheboard.com/questions/ definitions.html; and http://news.findlaw.com/hdocs/docs/ enron/empltr2lay82001.pdf.

Video Case
NFL

When you think of the NFL, you probably think first of Monday night football and the Super Bowl. Since 1920, the league has brought professional football to fans across the United States and around the world. You may also know that the league provides more than just athletic entertainment for fans. The NFL also strives to have a positive impact on communities across America. So, in 1974, the league formed a partnership with the United Way. Today, that partnership had grown into a charitable enterprise that generates funds and services for more than 30 million people each year.

The benefit to the community and to the United Way is clear, but the NFL benefits from its charitable efforts as well. In addition to connecting more deeply with fans through community outreach and player volunteer efforts, the NFL sponsors a series of ad campaigns featuring the United Way that reminds fans that football players are regular people who want to do good in the communities where they work and live.

After viewing the video featuring the NFL, answer the following questions about marketing and social responsibility:

1. Why do you think the NFL partners with the United Way? How does the United Way benefit? How does the NFL benefit?

2. Make a list of criticisms about the NFL's marketing efforts. Does the NFL's partnership with the United Way lessen any of those concerns?

Online Media Resources

Video Short
Log on to your Companion Website at www.pearsoned.ca/kotler to view the video segment related to the Video Case above.

CBC ⊕ CBC Video Case
Please refer to Appendix 2 to read a CBC Video Case for this chapter, and log on to your Companion Website at www.pearsoned.ca/kotler to view the corresponding video segment.

Case Pilot
Log on to your Companion Website at www.pearsoned.ca/kotler to sharpen your case analysis skills and take the Case Pilot Challenge!

Company Case
Vitango: Fighting Malnutrition

Imagine teaching an elementary school class in which students are constantly inattentive and falling asleep—not because they are bored but because they are malnourished. In many countries, this is not an unusual problem. Two billion people around the globe suffer from anemia—an iron deficiency. Iron deficiency leads to reduced resistance to disease, lowers learning ability in children, and contributes to the death of one out of five pregnant mothers. Two hundred million children do not get enough vitamin A. As a result, 250 000 of them go blind each year; vitamin A deficiency is also a contributing factor in the deaths of 2.2 million children under five each year from diarrhea. Many malnourished children suffer from zinc deficiency, which leads to growth failure and infections. Close to 2 billion people do not get enough iodine, and iodine deficiency is the leading cause of preventable mental retardation in the world. If only they used the ordinary table salt found in homes and restaurants all across North America, this wouldn't happen.

What can businesses do about this deplorable situation? Quite a bit. Companies such as Coca-Cola and Procter & Gamble have invested millions of dollars in research on micronutrients. They are learning how to fortify everyday food and beverages with additional minerals and vitamins to wipe out deficiencies and keep schoolchildren around the world alert and mentally prepared for school.

Fortified foods are common in North America. Iodine has been added to ordinary table salt for decades; milk contains vitamin D and calcium; and cornflakes list all the micronutrients found in them on the box. A quick check of your pantry reveals that many drinks and other foods have vitamins and minerals added to them. Thus, adding micronutrients to foods is not new or unusual in this country.

What are new are the efforts of companies to identify specific deficiencies and to develop new technologies for adding micronutrients to foodstuffs in order to eliminate or reduce the deficiencies in specific countries. A good example is a Coca-Cola beverage product called Vitango in Botswana.

Coca-Cola spent years developing a powdered beverage that, when mixed with water, looks and tastes like a sweeter version of Hi-C. (Hi-C is a fruit punch that is one of Coca-Cola's largest selling brands. It is made with real fruit juice and contains 100 percent of the recommended daily intake of vitamin C per serv-ing.) The beverage is fortified with 12 vitamins and with minerals that are chronically lacking in the diets of people in developing countries. Coke tested this product in Botswana in Project Mission. Every day for eight weeks, nurses visited schools where they mixed the beverage and passed out paper cups of the "new Hi-C." At the end of the test period, levels of iron and zinc in the children's blood levels had grown. Some parents noted that their children had become more attentive at school. After the Botswana tests, Coca-Cola also ran tests in Peru to determine how well the nutrients are absorbed into the bloodstream.

Coca-Cola, however, is not yet ready to launch Vitango. One issue is the powdered product form. Given the impurities of much of the water in Africa, Coca-Cola wants to package Vitango in a ready-to-drink formula, not in the powdered version now available. That will require reformulation that could actually drive down the price.

P&G has also developed micronutrient-enriched drinks for distribution in developing countries. In the 1990s, P&G developed its own proprietary technology for iron, vitamin A, and iodine fortification, which it called GrowthPlus. GrowthPlus was the basic ingredient in a product called Nutridelight that P&G launched in the Philippines. Unfortunately, it didn't sell well—primarily because it was priced at 50 percent above the market price of other powdered drinks.

More recently, P&G has launched another product, Nutristar, in Venezuela. Sold at most food stores, it contains eight vitamins and five minerals, comes in flavours such as mango and passion fruit, and promises to produce "taller, stronger, and smarter kids." To date, Nutristar is doing quite well. One reason is that it's available at McDonald's, where it is chosen by consumers with about half of all Happy Meals sold. P&G is also offering free samples in schools.

The major problem with both Coca-Cola's and P&G's nutritional products is price. These products were expensive to develop because of long lead times, the need to enlist the help of nutritional experts around the world, and the need to develop products that appeal to the local population's tastes. If offered at "reasonable" prices, they would be out of the reach of the world's desperately poor, the group that needs them most. Consider P&G's Vitango. The poor people in other countries are *not* eating at McDonald's. In countries such as Botswana, they are barely existing on cornmeal and rice. They simply cannot afford to buy fortified sweetened drinks or, for that matter, any sweetened drinks.

How can P&G and Coca-Cola market such products without pricing them too high for the intended market? Learning its lesson in the Philippines, P&G priced Nutristar about 25 percent higher than other powdered drinks and 30 percent below carbonated soft drinks. Even so, that's still too high for the poverty-stricken. Coca-Cola originally planned to sell Vitango for about 20 cents for a 225 millilitre liquid serving but then realized that this price was too high. That's part of the reason for continuing developmental work on the product.

One solution to the pricing problem is to work with governments, but many of them are too poor to be able to afford the products. Or they lack the resources to educate their people on the merits of fortified foods. Enter GAIN—the Global Alliance for Improved Nutrition—an international consortium set up by the Bill and Melinda Gates charitable foundation. GAIN offers companies assistance in lobbying for favourable tariffs and tax rates and for speedier regulatory review of new products in targeted countries. It also gives local governments money to increase the demand for fortified foods, including large-scale public relations campaigns or a government "seal of approval." This program received $70 million over five years beginning in May 2002. Such actions should help Coca-Cola and P&G by educating target populations about the value of fortified foods and beverages so that they will buy such products.

Of course, Coca-Cola and P&G can work with governments on their own, but their actions may be distrusted. After all, these are "for-profit" organizations whose motives may be suspect. GAIN has the advantage that it's a not-for-profit.

Though GAIN seems like a wonderful resource for helping malnourished people, it does have its critics. They point out that selling or giving away fortified foods does not solve the underlying problem of poverty. Nor does it teach people good nutritional habits. Moreover, in addition to their vitamins and minerals, many of the "fortified" foods also contain overly large amounts of fat, sugar, and salt. So, for example, whereas the foods might help reduce iron deficiency, they could also lead to obesity. Some observers claim that it would be better to teach people how to grow fruits and vegetables. The

problem is that people will die from malnutrition before poverty is eliminated or trees bear fruit.

Other issues must also be addressed. A fortified beverage, such as Vitango, will help in dealing with malnutrition but can't eliminate it. People will still need to eat a variety of other foods, which makes education very important. Remember that these products contain no juice. They are intended as supplements, not as substitutes for a proper diet. Lack of understanding about how to use products has landed other companies, such as Nestlé with its infant formula, in trouble when they were used inappropriately.

Given all these problems, why would Coca-Cola and P&G develop these products in the first place? One answer is future sales and profits. Products such as Nutristar and Vitango could create a basis from which to launch other Coca-Cola or P&G products, such as snack foods or juice drinks. As sales of carbonated beverages around the world have slowed, these fortified drinks pose a growth opportunity for the companies. Another answer is goodwill, and not just goodwill for the companies involved. By helping other nations of the world, North American corporations can help to lower the disparities between rich and poor countries.

Questions for Discussion

1. Which of the textbook's criticisms of marketing's impact on individual consumers, if any, are found in the cases of Vitango and Nutristar?

2. Which of the criticisms of marketing's impact on society as a whole are found in the Vitango and Nutristar case?

3. Could Vitango and Nutristar be considered enlightened marketing? Why or why not?

4. Are the development and marketing of such products as fortified foods and beverages ethical and socially responsible?

5. How should Coca-Cola proceed with the marketing of Vitango?

Sources: Jill Bruss, "Reaching the World," *Beverage Industry,* December 2001, p. 281; Rance Crain, "U.S. Marketers Must Develop Products to Help Third World," *Advertising Age,* December 3, 2001, p. 20; Betsy McKay, "Drinks for Developing Countries," *Wall Street Journal,* November 27, 2001, pp. B1, B6; and Rachel Zimmerman, "Gates Fights Malnutrition with Cheese, Ketchup Incentives," *Wall Street Journal,* May 9, 2002, p. B1.

CHAPTER 5

Managing Marketing Information

campaignforrealbeauty.ca 🐦 Dov

New Dove Firming Lotion. As tested on real curves

Previewing the Concepts

In Chapter 3, you learned about the complex and changing marketing environment. In this chapter, we'll continue our exploration of how marketers go about understanding the marketplace and consumers. We'll look at how companies develop and manage information about important marketplace elements—about customers, competitors, products, and marketing programs. We'll examine marketing information systems designed to give managers the right information, in the right form, at the right time to help them make better marketing decisions. This is an era in which marketers are working to develop and maintain lasting relationships with their customers. Without detailed information about what customers want and need today and in the future, building relationships is next to impossible.

We'll also take a close look at the marketing research process and at some special marketing research considerations. In some cases, information is gathered by firms themselves through their daily interactions with key customers and competitors. In other cases, organizations hire market research agencies that specialize in different types of markets and different types of research techniques. No matter what the case, however, companies must know what questions to ask and how to manage and interpret the mountains of marketing information. Failure to effectively manage this task has resulted in some of the largest marketing blunders ever. Take the case of Coca-Cola's ill-considered decision some years ago to introduce New Coke. The company based its decision on substantial marketing research, yet the new product fizzled badly. In contrast, other brands have used the insights gleaned from marketing research to re-invent themselves. See what Unilever Canada did with Dove.

*D*ove, the world's top cleansing brand, was born in 1957 as a beauty soap bar that was clinically proven to be milder than other leading soaps. It was especially suitable for dry, sensitive skin. Research revealed that 50 percent of women have dry skin; so the bar soon became popular. It wasn't long before it became the world's number one cleansing brand. It is sold in more than 80 countries and generates annual sales revenues of more than $5 billion. In North America alone, more than one billion showers are taken with Dove products each year. Dove beauty soap still racks up double-digit growth, and it outsells all other skin care bars combined.

Why, you might wonder, would such a successful brand spend much on marketing research? The impetus for the project came from the need to extend the meaning of the Dove brand beyond bar soap. Over the years, a number of extensions had been launched to take advantage of the powerful Dove brand name. In February 2003, for example, the Dove name was put onto a new line of hair care prod-

ucts. In July of the same year, a line of face care products was also launched bearing the Dove name.

The brand team at Unilever Canada quickly realized that consumers were confused about the brand and the tried and true associations linking the name with bar soap were outdated. The positioning just wasn't sufficient to link all the products bearing the Dove name. As Erin Iles, the head of the Dove brand team noted, "The brand was a bar of soap with a quarter of moisturizing cream. People trusted it and saw it as an honest brand, but they also saw it as a bit of a boring brand. That's fine when your product mix is a bar of soap. But as soon as your product mix includes moisturizers that sell for $16 and toners and shampoos, it can't be this boring brand that lives in your shower that you don't think about. We really needed to make it a beauty brand."

The Dove team needed solid research and a lot of insight before this repositioning task could be undertaken. While other companies were using thin, perfect, airbrushed models to peddle their lines of beauty products, this didn't seem right for Dove. For the Dove team, the first question became "how women's self-esteem is affected by body image." As part of its primary data-gathering initiative, a global survey was commissioned by Unilever. The company also undertook ethnographic research. The term comes from a branch of anthropology that deals with the scientific description of specific human cultures. Thus, to understand women's culture and how they thought about beauty, researchers would go shopping with women and spend time in their homes talking about the meaning of beauty and deciphering what they consider beautiful.

The research uncovered the fact that only 2 percent of women—only 1 percent in Canada—consider themselves beautiful. Despite this finding, women feel pressured to be beautiful. Sixty-three percent of women strongly agree that women today are expected to be more attractive than their mother's generation. Even more troubling, was other secondary data (published research undertaken by others) that showed that girls as young as nine years old were dissatisfied with their body image, and girls as young as seven expressed the desire to be thinner.

Paradoxically, Dove's research also suggested that all women want to be beautiful in their own unique way, not in a fashion dictated by Hollywood movies or fashion magazines. In fact, 36 percent of Canadian women surveyed described themselves as "natural," but very few viewed themselves as "sexy," "stunning," or "gorgeous." Although many of the women's responses referred to physical aspects of beauty, they also rated kindness, happiness, confidence, dignity, and humour as powerful, inner components of beauty. As Dr. Susie Orbach, one of the chief researchers on the project, noted, "What's interesting is women explaining the notion of beauty in a much broader sense." If the research team hadn't designed the study to ask the right questions and if they hadn't really probed to get to the heart of what makes women feel beautiful, they would have missed the insights that later made the "Campaign for Real Beauty" such a success.

The research initiative led the Dove marketers to the conclusion that it was time to change the definition of beauty. Although the research itself is fascinating, it is how Unilever used the insight that is really exceptional. From the beginning of the repositioning effort, the Dove team had women look at themselves and open a dialogue on what beauty is. This desire for dialogue could be seen in the marketing campaign that followed the research efforts. Take the most visible and striking example—the large billboards and print "tick-box" ads that featured images of everyday women along with two choices consumers can use to interpret their beauty (for example, "Fab? or Fat?," "Bald? or Beautiful?"). People could record their votes by phone or on the website. Another example was the *Beyond Compare Photo Tour*. Renowned photographers from around the world were asked to contribute pictures of women they considered beautiful. As the exhibit toured the country, Dove again asked women what they thought of the photographs and what they said about beauty. This again created an opportunity for the brand team to learn even more deeply about what women considered as beauty.

The research and resulting marketing campaign won Unilever Canada a number of awards, including the 2005 Media Innovation Award, a Cassie Award, a *Marketing Magazine* Promo Gold award, and *Strategy Magazine*'s 2004 Marketer of the Year. Even more important than the awards, however, is the fact that packaged goods giant Unilever and the Dove marketing and research teams imbued the brand with the kind of cultural relevance usually reserved for "lifestyle" brands like MINI or Apple. The campaign has been extended to young girls who are also concerned about their looks. It was this rendition of the campaign, developed by the Toronto office of Ogilvy & Mather, that viewers saw nestled in the U.S. broadcast of the 2006 Super Bowl. "There were questions about whether to put something like that on the Super Bowl..." said Janet Kestin, creative director of Ogilvy & Mather in Toronto. "But of course, there are tons of women who watch, too. According to *Advertising Age* magazine, the 2006 Super Bowl attracted an audience comprising 44 per cent women." This research-driven campaign has certainly been a touchdown with women of all ages![1]

To produce superior value and satisfaction for customers—the keys to building strong relationships—companies need information at almost every turn. As the Dove case illustrates, good products and marketing programs begin with solid information on consumer needs and wants. Information about trends and evolving attitudes allowed Dove to strongly position its products in the minds of women and thereby build a stronger relationship with them. Companies also need an abundance of information on competitors, resellers, and other actors and forces in the marketplace.

With the recent explosion of information technologies, companies can now generate information in great quantities. In fact, today's managers often receive too much information. One study found that with all the companies offering data, and with all the information now available through supermarket scanners, large retailers typically now have the equivalent of 515 km of bookshelves of information on their products. Wal-Mart, the largest retailer of all, has more than three and a half times that much information in its data warehouse. Thus, running out of information is not a problem, but seeing through the "data smog" is. "In this oh-so-overwhelming Information age," comments one observer, "it's all too easy to be buried, burdened, and burned out by data overload."[2]

Despite this data glut, marketers frequently complain that they lack enough information of the *right* kind. One recent study found that although half of the managers surveyed said they couldn't cope with the volume of information coming at them, two-thirds wanted even more. The researcher concluded that, "despite the volume, they're still not getting what they want."[3] Thus, most marketing managers don't need *more* information, they need *better* information.

A former CEO at Unilever once said that if Unilever only knew what it knows, it would double its profits. The meaning is clear: Many companies sit on rich information but fail to manage and use it well.[4] Companies must design effective marketing information systems that give managers the right information, in the right form, at the right time to help them make better marketing decisions.

A **marketing information system (MIS)** consists of people, equipment, and procedures to gather, sort, analyze, evaluate, and distribute needed, timely, and accurate information to marketing decision makers. Figure 5.1 shows that the MIS begins and ends with information users—marketing managers, internal and external partners, and others—who need marketing information. First, it interacts with these information users to *assess information needs*. Next, it *develops needed information* from internal company databases, marketing intelligence activities, and marketing research. Then it helps users to analyze information to put it in the right form for making marketing decisions and managing customer relationships. Finally, the MIS *distributes* the marketing information and helps managers *use* it in their decision making.

Marketing information system (MIS)
People, equipment, and procedures to gather, sort, analyze, evaluate, and distribute needed, timely, and accurate information to marketing decision makers.

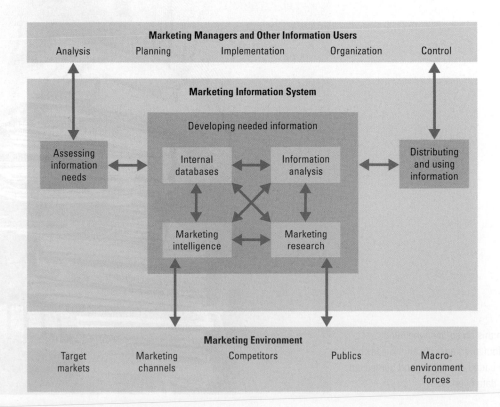

Figure 5.1 The marketing information system

Assessing Marketing Information Needs

The marketing information system primarily serves the company's marketing and other managers. However, it may also provide information to external partners, such as suppliers, resellers, or marketing services agencies. For example, Wal-Mart gives Procter & Gamble and other key suppliers access to information on customer buying patterns and inventory levels. And Dell creates tailored Premium Pages for large customers, giving them access to product design, order status, and product support and service information. In designing an information system, the company must consider the needs of all of these users.

A good marketing information system balances the information users would *like* to have against what they really *need* and what is *feasible* to offer. The company begins by interviewing managers to find out what information they would like. Some managers will ask for whatever information they can get without thinking carefully about what they really need. Too much information can be as harmful as too little. Other managers may omit things they ought to know, or they may not know to ask for some types of information they should have. For example, managers might need to know that a competitor plans to introduce a new product during the coming year. Because they do not know about the new product, they do not think to ask about it. The MIS must monitor the marketing environment in order to provide decision makers with information they should have to make key marketing decisions.

"In this oh-so-overwhelming Information age, it's all too easy to be buried, burdened, and burned out by data overload."

Sometimes the company cannot provide the needed information, either because it is not available or because of MIS limitations. For example, a brand manager might want to know how competitors will change their advertising budgets next year and how these changes will affect industry market shares. The information on planned budgets probably is not available. Even if it is, the company's MIS may not be advanced enough to forecast resulting changes in market shares.

Finally, the costs of obtaining, processing, storing, and delivering information can mount quickly. The company must decide whether the benefits of having additional information are worth the costs of providing it, and both value and cost are often hard to assess. By itself, information has no worth; its value comes from its *use*. In many cases, additional information will do little to change or improve a manager's decision, or the costs of the information may exceed the returns from the improved decision. Marketers should not assume that additional information will always be worth obtaining. Rather, they should weigh carefully the costs of getting more information against the benefits resulting from it.

Developing Marketing Information

Marketers can obtain the needed information from *internal data, marketing intelligence*, and *marketing research*.

Internal Data

Internal databases
Electronic collections of information obtained from data sources within the company.

Many companies build extensive **internal databases**, electronic collections of information obtained from data sources within the company. Marketing managers can readily access and work with information in the database to identify marketing opportunities and problems, strengthen relationships with customers, plan programs, and evaluate performance. Nintendo Canada, for example, has a database of about 175 000 Canadian consumers. To maintain an active relationship with these consumers, Nintendo sends them a monthly newsletter that provides updates on new products and games. Amazon.ca is another company that uses its database to build relationships and enhance the value it brings to its customers. When a consumer searches for a book on the Amazon.ca website, the company not only

Amazon.ca uses its vast database to build relationships with customers and add value to their online purchasing experience.

provides information on the book (such as availability, shipping time and price) but also posts reviews of the book from other readers. Amazon also offers information about other books that the customer might be interested in. Using the customer's purchasing history contained in the database, a computer program derives a list of books that have appealed to people with similar interests. Customers are also presented with a section entitled "customers who bought this item also bought" which is an electronic means of creating a community of readers where one person recommends a book to another. Finally, Amazon.ca also offers a kind of personalized promotion called "better together" by bundling the book with another book that might be of interest to the customer.

Information in the database can come from many sources. The accounting department prepares financial statements and keeps detailed records of sales, costs, and cash flows. Operations reports on production schedules, shipments, and inventories. The sales force reports on reseller reactions and competitor activities. The marketing department furnishes information on customer demographics, psychographics, and buying behaviour. And the customer service department keeps records of customer satisfaction or service problems. Research studies done for one department may provide useful information for several others.

Here is an example of how one company uses its internal database to make better marketing decisions:

> When the Hudson Bay Company and Zellers merged their loyalty programs, they created one of the most comprehensive and potentially far-reaching customer databases in Canada. The database contains information on more than 8.5 million members, which equates to approximately one third of Canada's adult population, according to the database managers. As one VP noted, "When someone's buying kids' clothing at either the Bay or at Zellers, we now have the data to tell us that." In fact, the data is so detailed that by matching the stock keeping unit number (the SKU number) with the purchase information, the database managers and the marketers who depend on it can determine not only what size the child is, but also make an informed guess about the sex and age of the purchasers' children. And the information goes far beyond kids' clothes. The stores carry a massive array of merchandise that is purchased by the 85 percent of the Canadian population who comes through their doors every year.[5]

Sometimes a firm's internal database isn't up to the task of taking a brand in a new direction. Thus, firms sometimes rely on the databases of marketing agencies, such as Montreal-based NewAd, rather than their own internal resources, as with the case with Old Spice.

> When Procter & Gamble wanted to breathe new life into its half-century-old brand, Old Spice, it went to NewAd. P&G wanted to attract and build relationships with younger male consumers. In 2004, NewAd had developed a database named "Target" as a tool to increase the effectiveness of its clients marketing and communications programs. To build the database, NewAd interviewed 12 000 people across Canada, focusing on those who frequented restaurants and bars. Subjects were asked questions about their lifestyles, preferences, and media habits. "For the Old Spice brand, the NewAd guys extracted a snapshot of the typical Red Zone buyer. First, they found the 18- to 34-year-old guys most likely to spend on personal care. Second, they determined that this group loved to go dancing. Then, they calculated their online habits." Finally came the insights that led to the Red Zone After Hours campaign, which is made up of dance events in bars, incorporates an online contest, and a televised dance competition. As part of the campaign, brand ambassadors who attend the events encourage men in the target group to participate in a dance-off. The perform-

The successful Old Spice Red Zone After Hours campaign was developed with the help of NewAd and its extensive database named "Target."

ances are filmed and uploaded to the brand's website. Visitors to the brand's website could then vote to select their favourite as finalists, who were flown to Toronto for a live dance-off at MuchMusic. It's been a powerful initiative. Old Spice sales have increased at a rate of 13 percent a year in a category where others manage only 1 percent annual growth.[6]

Internal databases usually can be accessed more quickly and cheaply than other information sources, but they also present some problems. Because internal information was collected for other purposes, it may be incomplete or in the wrong form for making marketing decisions. For example, sales and cost data used by the accounting department for preparing financial statements must be adapted for use in evaluating the value of a specific customer segment, sales force, or channel performance. Data also ages quickly; keeping the database current requires a major effort. In addition, a large company produces mountains of information, which must be well integrated and readily accessible so that managers can find it easily and use it effectively.

Because of the costs of updating and maintaining internal databases, many companies are buying services from other organizations. Rogers Publishing Ltd., for example, is the first magazine publisher to tap Canada Post Corp.'s vast database of 1.2 million people who register address changes to distribute a home decor magazine called *Chocolat*. Rogers knows that people who move are a prime market for new furniture or home decorations.[7]

Marketing Intelligence

Marketing intelligence
The systematic collection and analysis of publicly available information about competitors and developments in the marketing environment.

Marketing intelligence is the systematic collection and analysis of publicly available information about competitors and developments in the marketplace. The goal of marketing intelligence is to improve strategic decision making, assess and track competitors' actions, and provide early warning of opportunities and threats.

Competitive intelligence gathering has grown dramatically as more and more companies are now busily snooping on their competitors. Techniques range from quizzing the company's own employees and benchmarking competitors' products to researching the Internet, lurking around industry trade shows, and rooting through rivals' trash bins.

Much intelligence can be collected from people inside the company—executives, engineers and scientists, purchasing agents, and the sales force. The company can also obtain important intelligence information from suppliers, resellers, and key customers. Or it can get good information by observing competitors. It can buy and analyze competitors' products, monitor their sales, check for new patents, and examine various types of physical evidence. For example, one company regularly checks out competitors' parking lots—full lots might indicate plenty of work and prosperity; half-full lots might suggest hard times.

Some companies have even rifled through their competitors' garbage, which is legally considered abandoned property once it leaves the premises. In one garbage-snatching incident, Oracle was caught rifling through rival Microsoft's dumpsters. In another case, Procter & Gamble admitted to "dumpster diving" at rival Unilever's headquarters. The target was Unilever's hair-care products—including Salon Selectives, Finesse, Thermasilk, and Helene Curtis—which competed with P&G's own Pantene, Head & Shoulders, and Pert brands. "Apparently, the operation was a big success," notes an analyst. "P&G got its mitts on just about every iota of info there was to be had about Unilever's brands." However, when news of the questionable tactics reached top P&G managers, they were shocked. They immediately stopped the project, voluntarily informed Unilever, and set up negotiations to right whatever competitive wrongs had been done. Although P&G claims it broke no laws, the company reported that the dumpster raids "violated our strict guidelines regarding our business policies."[8]

Competitors may reveal intelligence information through their annual reports, business publications, trade show exhibits, press releases, advertisements, and webpages. The Internet is proving to be a vast new source of competitor-supplied information. Most companies now place volumes of information on their websites, providing details to attract customers, partners, suppliers, or franchisees. Using

Procter & Gamble admitted to "dumpster diving" at rival Unilever's Helene Curtis headquarters. When P&G's top management learned of the questionable practice, it stopped the project, voluntarily informed Unilever, and set up talks to right whatever competitive wrongs had been done.

Internet search engines, marketers can search specific competitor names, events, or trends and see what turns up.[9]

Even companies with the most basic technology can use it to gather intelligence, advises a competitive intelligence consultant. Keep tabs on your rivals' websites, and check to see if they have updated or altered their copy on any product lines. Have they redesigned the site or shifted its focus? What do search engines turn up on rivals? How is the press covering them? Your industry? Often, publicly accessible bulletin boards offer additional clues: Investors may log on to discuss rumours and tidbits of information. And keep watch for off-duty employees. They post, too. "Clients are often surprised that there's so much out there to know," says the consultant. "They're busy with their day-to-day operations and they don't realize how much information can be obtained with a few strategic keystrokes."

Intelligence seekers can also pore through any of thousands of online databases. Some are free. For example, you can search the System for Electronic Document Analysis and Retrieval (SEDAR) database for the documents and information filed by public companies and investment funds with the Canadian Securities Administrators. The Howard Ross Library of Management at McGill lists many resources for learning more about Canadian businesses, and Hoovers.com has a searchable website containing financial information on publicly traded Canadian and U.S. companies. And for a fee, companies can subscribe to any of more than 3000 online databases and information search services, such as Dialog, DataStar, LexisNexis, Dow Jones News Retrieval, UMI ProQuest, and Dun & Bradstreet's Online Access.

The intelligence game goes both ways. Facing determined marketing intelligence efforts by competitors, most companies are now taking steps to protect their own information. For example, Unilever has begun widespread competitive intelligence training. According to a former Unilever staffer, "We were told how to protect information, as well as how to get it from competitors. We were warned to always keep our mouths shut when traveling.... We were even warned that spies from competitors could be posing as drivers at the mini-cab company we used." Unilever even performs random checks on internal security. Says the former staffer, "At one [internal marketing] conference, we were set up when an actor was employed to infiltrate the group. The idea was to see who spoke to him, how much they told him, and how long it took to realize that no one knew him. He ended up being there for a long time."[10]

The growing use of marketing intelligence raises a number of ethical issues. Although most of the preceding techniques are legal, and some are considered to be shrewdly competitive, some may involve questionable ethics. Clearly, companies should take advantage of publicly available information. However, they should not stoop to snooping. With all the legitimate intelligence sources now available, a company does not have to break the law or accepted codes of ethics to get good intelligence.

Marketing Research

In addition to information about competitor and marketplace happenings, marketers often need formal studies of specific situations. For example, General Electric wants to know what appeals will be most effective in its corporate advertising campaign. Or Toshiba wants to know how many and what kinds of people or companies will buy its new superfast tablet PC. In such situations, marketing intelligence will not provide the detailed information needed. Managers will need marketing research.

Marketing research is the systematic design, collection, analysis, and reporting of data relevant to a specific marketing situation facing an organization. Companies

Marketing research
The systematic design, collection, analysis, and reporting of data relevant to a specific marketing situation facing an organization.

use marketing research in a wide variety of situations. For example, marketing research can help marketers understand customer satisfaction and purchase behaviour. It can help them assess market potential and market share, or to measure the effectiveness of pricing, product, distribution, and promotion activities.

Some large companies have their own research departments that work with marketing managers on marketing research projects. This is how Kraft, Citigroup, and many other corporate giants handle marketing research. In addition, these companies—like their smaller counterparts—frequently hire outside research specialists to consult with management on specific marketing problems and conduct marketing research studies. Sometimes firms simply purchase data collected by outside firms to aid in their decision making.

The marketing research process has four steps (see Figure 5.2): *defining the problem and research objectives, developing the research plan, implementing the research plan,* and *interpreting and reporting the findings.*

Defining the Problem and Research Objectives

Marketing managers and researchers must work closely together to define the problem and agree on research objectives. The manager best understands the decision for which information is needed; the researcher best understands marketing research and how to obtain the information.

Defining the problem and research objectives is often the hardest step in the research process. The manager may know that something is wrong, without knowing the specific causes. For example, in the Dove case, Unilever began with a broad problem statement, "How do women themselves define beauty?" and then designed a series of more specific questions to tap into this broader issue.

After the problem has been defined carefully, the manager and researcher must set the research objectives. A marketing research project might have one of three types of objectives. The objective of **exploratory research** is to gather preliminary information that will help define the problem and suggest hypotheses. The objective of **descriptive research** is to describe things, such as the market potential for a product or the demographics and attitudes of consumers who buy the product. The objective of **causal research** is to test hypotheses about cause-and-effect relationships. For example, would a 10 percent decrease in tuition at a private college result in an enrolment increase sufficient to offset the reduced tuition? Managers often start with exploratory research and later follow with descriptive or causal research.

The statement of the problem and research objectives guides the entire research process. The manager and researcher should put the statement in writing to be certain that they agree on the purpose and expected results of the research.

Developing the Research Plan

Once the research problems and objectives have been defined, researchers must determine the exact information needed, develop a plan for gathering it efficiently, and present the plan to management. The research plan outlines sources of existing data and spells out the specific research approaches, contact methods, sampling plans, and instruments that researchers will use to gather new data.

Exploratory research
Marketing research to gather preliminary information that will help define problems and suggest hypotheses.

Descriptive research
Marketing research to better describe marketing problems, situations, or markets, such as the market potential for a product or the demographics and attitudes of consumers.

Causal research
Marketing research to test hypotheses about cause-and-effect relationships.

Figure 5.2 The marketing research process

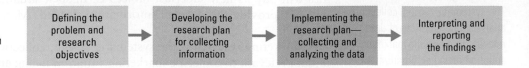

| Defining the problem and research objectives | Developing the research plan for collecting information | Implementing the research plan— collecting and analyzing the data | Interpreting and reporting the findings |

Research objectives must be translated into specific information needs. For example, suppose Campbell decides to conduct research on how consumers would react to the introduction of new heat-and-go microwavable cups for its SpaghettiOs. Such packaging has been successful for Campbell's soups—the company promotes its Soup at Hand brands as "sippable soup, anytime, anywhere." The containers would cost more but would allow consumers to heat their SpaghettiOs in a microwave oven and to eat them without using dishes. This research might call for the following specific information:

- The demographic, economic, and lifestyle characteristics of current SpaghettiOs users. (Busy working couples might find the convenience of the new packaging worth the price; families with children might want to pay less and wash the bowls.)
- Consumer-usage patterns for SpaghettiOs and related products: how much they eat, where, and when. (The new packaging might be ideal for adults eating lunch on the go, but less convenient for parents feeding lunch to several children.)
- Retailer reactions to the new packaging. (Failure to get retailer support could hurt sales of the new package.)
- Forecasts of sales of both new and current packages. (Will the new packaging create new sales or simply take sales from the current packaging? Will the package increase Campbell's profits?)

Campbell managers will need these and many other types of information to decide whether to introduce the new packaging.

The research plan should be presented in a *written proposal*. A written proposal is especially important when the research project is large and complex or when an outside firm carries it out. The proposal should cover the management problems addressed and the research objectives, the information to be obtained, and the way the results will help management decision making. The proposal also should include research costs.

To meet the manager's information needs, the research plan can call for gathering secondary data, primary data, or both, as was the case with the Dove repositioning project. **Secondary data** consist of information that already exists somewhere, having been collected for another purpose. **Primary data** consist of information collected for the specific purpose at hand.

Gathering Secondary Data

Researchers usually start by gathering secondary data. The company's internal database provides a good starting point. However, the company can also tap a wide assortment of external information sources, including commercial data services and government sources. (See Table 5.1.)

Companies can buy secondary data reports from outside suppliers.[11] For example, Information Resources, Inc., sells supermarket scanner purchase data from a panel of 70 000 households nationally, with measures of trial and repeat purchasing, brand loyalty, and buyer demographics. The *Monitor* service by Yankelovich sells information on important social and lifestyle trends. These and other firms supply high-quality data to suit a wide variety of marketing information needs.[12]

Using commercial **online databases**, marketing researchers can conduct their own searches of secondary data sources. General database services, such as Dialog and LexisNexis, put an incredible wealth of information at the keyboards of marketing decision makers. Beyond commercial websites offering information for a fee, almost every industry association, government agency, business publication, and news medium offers free information to those tenacious enough to find their web-

Secondary data
Information that already exists somewhere, having been collected for another purpose.

Primary data
Information collected for the specific purpose at hand.

Online databases
Computerized collections of information available from online commercial sources or via the Internet.

TABLE 5.1 Selected External Information Sources

FOR BUSINESS DATA:

Scott's Directories lists, on an annual basis, manufacturers, their products, and their North American Industry Classification (NAICS) codes, alphabetically as well as by city and region. The directory also provides the names and telephone and fax numbers of chief executives, as well as corporate information, such as annual sales. Directories come in four volumes: Ontario, Quebec, Atlantic Canada, and Western Canada.

SEDAR (www.sedar.com) has an extensive database that includes the financial filing information, annual reports, and company profiles for Canadian public companies.

Canadian Trade Index and Fraser's Canadian Trade Directory provide information on manufacturers of different product categories, manufacturing equipment, and supplies.

AC Nielsen Corporation (www.acnielsen.com) provides supermarket scanner data on sales, market share, and retail prices; data on household purchasing; and data on television audiences.

Information Resources, Inc. (www.infores.com) provides supermarket scanner data for tracking grocery product movement and new product purchasing data.

Arbitron (www.arbitron.com) provides local-market and Internet radio audience and advertising expenditure information, among other media and ad spending data.

Simmons Market Research Bureau (www.smrb.com) provides detailed analysis of consumer patterns in 400 product categories in selected markets.

Dun & Bradstreet (www.dnb.com) maintains a database containing information on more than 50 million individual companies around the globe.

ComScore Networks (www.comscore.com) provides consumer behaviour information and geodemographic analysis of Internet and digital media users around the world.

Thomson Dialog (http://library.dialog.com) offers access to ABI/INFORM, a database of articles from 800 publications and to reports, newsletters, and directories covering dozens of industries.

LexisNexis (www.lexisnexis.com) features articles from business, consumer, and marketing publications plus tracking of firms, industries, trends, and promotion techniques.

CompuServe (www.compuserve.com) provides access to databases of business and consumer demographics, government reports, and patent records, plus articles from newspapers, newsletters, and research reports.

Factiva (www.factiva.com) specializes in in-depth financial, historical, and operational information on public and private companies.

Hoovers Online (www.hoovers.com) provides business descriptions, financial overviews, and news about major companies around the world.

Canoe (www.canoe.ca) (Canadian Online Explorer) bills itself as Canada's leading news and information site.

CNN (www.cnn.com) reports U.S. and global news and covers the markets and news-making companies in detail.

American Demographics (www.demographics.com) reports on demographic trends and their significance for businesses.

FOR GOVERNMENT DATA:

Statistics Canada (www.statcan.ca) provides summary data on demographic, economic, social, and other aspects of the Canadian economy and society.

Industry Canada's Strategis website (www.strategis.ic.gc.ca) provides resources for Canadian businesses.

Western Economic Diversification Canada (www.wd.gc.ca) provides information for people starting or operating a business in Western Canada.

Ontario Ministry for Economic Development and Trade (www.ontariocanada.com/ontcan/en/home.jsp) and other provincial governments, have sites that provide information for small business development.

Stat-USA (www.stat-usa.gov), a Department of Commerce site, highlights statistics on U.S. business and international trade.

U.S. Census (www.census.gov) provides detailed statistics and trends about the U.S. population.

For Internet data: Interactive Advertising Bureau (www.iab.net) covers statistics about advertising on the Internet.

Jupiter Research (www.jupiterresearch.com) monitors Web traffic and ranks the most popular sites.

INFORMATION TO
change
the world

Dial g

Pharmaceutical, chemical and medical journals. Company financials. Patents and trademarks. Newspapers, newswires, trade publications and scholarly sources. Domain names. Engineering literature. Market research and brokerage reports.

One Company.   One Interface.   One Relationship.

www.dialog.com

THOMSON
DIALOG

Online database services, such as Dialog, put an incredible wealth of information at the keyboards of marketing decision makers. Dialog puts "information to change the world, or your corner of it," at your fingertips.

sites. There are so many websites offering data that finding the right ones can become an almost overwhelming task.

Secondary data can usually be obtained more quickly and at a lower cost than primary data. Also, secondary sources can sometimes provide data an individual company cannot collect on its own—information that either is not directly available or would be too expensive to collect. For example, it would be too expensive for Kraft Foods to conduct a continuing retail store audit to find out about the market shares, prices, and displays of competitors' brands. But it can buy the InfoScan service from Information Resources, Inc., which provides this information from thousands of scanner-equipped supermarkets.

Secondary data can also present problems. The needed information may not exist—researchers can rarely obtain all the data they need from secondary sources. For example, Campbell will not find existing information about consumer reactions to new packaging that it has not yet placed on the market. Even when data can be found, they might not be very usable. The researcher must evaluate secondary information carefully to make certain it is *relevant* (fits research project needs), *accurate* (reliably collected and reported), *current* (up-to-date enough for current decisions), and *impartial* (objectively collected and reported).

Primary Data Collection

Secondary data provide a good starting point for research and often help to define research problems and objectives. In most cases, however, the company must also collect primary data. Just as researchers must carefully evaluate the quality of secondary information, they also must take great care when collecting primary data. They need to make sure that it will be relevant, accurate, current, and unbiased.

TABLE 5.2 Planning Primary Data Collection

Research Approaches	Contact Methods	Sampling Plan	Research Instruments
Observation	Mail	Sampling unit	Questionnaire
Survey	Telephone	Sample size	Mechanical instruments
Experiment	Personal	Sampling procedure	Online

Table 5.2 shows that designing a plan for primary data collection calls for a number of decisions on *research approaches*, *contact methods*, *sampling plan*, and *research instruments*.

Research Approaches

Research approaches for gathering primary data include observation, surveys, and experiments. Here, we discuss each one in turn.

Observational research
The gathering of primary data by observing relevant people, actions, and situations.

Observational Research   Observational research involves gathering primary data by observing relevant people, actions, and situations. For example, a consumer packaged-goods marketer might visit supermarkets and observe shoppers as they browse the store, pick up and examine packages, and make buying decisions. Or a bank might evaluate possible new branch locations by checking traffic patterns, neighbourhood conditions, and the location of competing branches. Fisher-Price even set up an observation lab in which it could observe the reactions of little tots to new toys:

> The Fisher-Price Play Lab is a sunny, toy-strewn space where, since 1961, lucky kids have tested Fisher-Price prototypes. Today three boys and three girls—all 4-year-olds—speed through the front door. Two boys tug quietly, but firmly, for the wheel of a new radio-controlled race set—a brand-new offering. The girls skid to a stop near a small subdevelopment of dollhouses. And from behind the one-way glass, toy designers study the action intently, occasionally stepping out to join the play. At the Play Lab, creation and (attempted) destruction happily coexist. Over an 8-week session with these kids, designers will test dozens of toy concepts, sending out crude models, then increasingly sophisticated revisions, to figure out what gets kids worked up into a new-toy frenzy.[13]

Observational research can obtain information that people are unwilling or unable to provide. In some cases, observation may be the only way to obtain the needed information. In contrast, some things simply cannot be observed, such as feelings, attitudes and motives, or private behaviour. Long-term or infrequent behaviour is also difficult to observe. Because of these limitations, researchers often use observation along with other data collection methods.

As was the case with the Dove project, a wide range of companies now use *ethnographic research*. Ethnographic research involves sending trained observers to watch:[14]

> A girl walks into a bar and says to the bartender, "Give me a Diet Coke and a clear sight line to those guys drinking Miller Lite in the corner." No joke. The "girl" is Emma Gilding, corporate ethnographer at the Ogilvy & Mather ad agency. Her assignment is to hang out in bars across the country, watching guys in their native habitat as they knock back beers with their friends. As a videographer films the action, Gilding keeps tabs on how closely the guys stand to one another. She sees that high-fiving is out, fist-pounding is in. She eavesdrops

Fisher-Price set up an observation lab in which it could observe the reactions of little tots to new toys.

on stories, and observes how the mantle is passed from one speaker to another, as in a tribe around a campfire. Back at the office, a team of trained anthropologists and psychologists pored over more than 70 hours of footage from five similar nights in bars from across the country. One key insight: Miller is favoured by groups of drinkers, while its main competitor, Bud Lite, is a beer that sells to individuals. Miller drinkers felt more comfortable expressing affection for friends than did the Bud Lite boys. The result was a hilarious series of ads that cut from a Miller Lite drinker's weird experiences in the world—getting caught in the subway taking money from a blind musician's guitar case, or hitching a ride in the desert with a deranged trucker—to shots of him regaling friends with tales over a brew. The Miller Lite ads got high marks from audiences for their entertainment value and emotional resonance. Notes Miller's brand manager, "So much other research is done in isolation of social groups. But [ethnographic research] helped us to understand the Miller Lite drinker and his friends as genuine people."

Ethnographic research often yields the kinds of intimate details that just don't emerge from traditional focus groups. To glean greater insights into buying behaviour, one company even went so far as to set up an actual retail store that serves as an ethnographic lab. (See Real Marketing 5.1.)

Survey research
The gathering of primary data by asking people questions about their knowledge, attitudes, preferences, and buying behaviour.

Single-source data systems
Electronic monitoring systems that link consumers' exposure to television advertising and promotion (measured using television meters) with what they buy in stores (measured using store checkout scanners).

Survey Research   Survey research, the most widely used method for primary data collection, is the approach best suited for gathering *descriptive* information. A company that wants to know about people's knowledge, attitudes, preferences, or buying behaviour can often find out by asking them directly.

Some firms provide marketers with a more comprehensive look at buying patterns through **single-source data systems**. These systems start with surveys of huge consumer panels—carefully selected groups of consumers who agree to participate in ongoing research. Then, they electronically monitor survey respondents' purchases and exposure to various marketing activities. Combining the survey and monitoring information gives a better understanding of the link between consumer characteristics, attitudes, and purchase behaviour.

The major advantage of survey research is its flexibility—it can be used to obtain many different kinds of information in many different situations. However, survey research also presents some problems. Sometimes people are unable to answer survey questions because they cannot remember or have never thought about what they do and why. People may be unwilling to respond to unknown interviewers or about things they consider private. Respondents may answer survey questions even when they do not know the answer in order to appear smarter or more informed. Or they may try to help the interviewer by giving pleasing answers. Finally, busy people may not take the time, or they might resent the intrusion into their privacy.

Experimental research
The gathering of primary data by selecting matched groups of subjects, giving them different treatments, controlling related factors, and checking for differences in group responses.

Experimental Research Whereas observation is best suited for exploratory research and surveys for descriptive research, **experimental research** is best suited for gathering *causal* information. Experiments involve selecting matched groups of subjects, giving them different treatments, controlling unrelated factors, and checking for differences in group responses. Thus, experimental research tries to explain cause-and-effect relationships.

For example, before adding a new sandwich to its menu, McDonald's might use experiments to test the effects on sales of two different prices it might charge. It could introduce the new sandwich at one price in one city and at another price in another city. If the cities are similar, and if all other marketing efforts for the sandwich are the same, then differences in sales in the two cities could be related to the price charged.

REAL MARKETING | 5.1

Watching Consumers in Their Natural Settings

What's this—a young man sitting in his car writing feverishly in his black book. You know what he is up to, I bet! Maybe not if you didn't guess being part of a market research study run by Toronto-based In-Sync, one of Canada's most leading-edge research groups. The agency believes the best way to get to the heart of your target is through "auto ethnography" or empowering the targets to research themselves. Take a recent research study for a high-end car manufacturer. In-Sync used auto-ethnography to understand people's relationship to their own vehicle. "We charge them with exercises that direct them to become reflective of their needs and their relationship to a brand or product," says In-Sync partner Susan Bardwell. In the automobile study, eight people (who owned the client car or key competitive brands) were sent markers, stickers, instructions, and a black book filled with a series of self-reflective exercises (such as describing moods and personifying drivers using words and images) to complete within a week. Once these exercises were finished, respondents were interviewed about their answers. Research insights helped the manufacturer reposition their vehicle using messaging that wasn't about the technological genius of the car, as it was in the past, but about the relevance of the vehicle to its driver.

Let's look at another example. Microphones capture every word while cameras record the action. Observers, posted at every turn, document each move.

What's this—the runway at the Academy Awards? No, this is a retail store called Once Famous, and the observers there are scrutinizing consumers, not celebrities. The store is a unique ethnographic laboratory for studying consumer behaviour in a natural setting. Although designed to look and feel like an ordinary retail store, surveillance is everywhere at Once Famous. Ethnographers watch from behind mirrored glass, while salespeople interview would-be buyers. Five cameras track consumers as they prowl the store. Sensitive hidden microphones catch every utterance, from shoppers' questions to snide comments between friends. Later, researchers pore over the tapes and analyze each shopper's behaviour, looking for clues.

To guard against accusations of invasion of privacy, Once Famous posts a prominent sign, complete with flashing lights, to alert shoppers that the store is in "Testing Mode." Additional signs invite shoppers who don't wish to be observed to "kindly visit us when this sign has been removed." In fact, much of the time Once Famous is just a store like any other store—it doesn't stay in "test mode" all of the time and it even turns a profit on sales.

Once Famous is the work of FAME, a retail brand advertising agency. It's located in a heavy-traffic downtown area. Stocked with fancy pillows, knickknacks, and hand-made arts and crafts, the store attracts a variety of shoppers. Mingled with the store's regular inventory is an ever-changing assortment of clients' test products. For FAME and its clients, the store helps fill a big gap in everyone's understanding of that elusive species, the shopper. Retailers know from inventory records what is on the shelf, and they know from point-of-sale data what ends up in shopper's baskets. But they lack a true understanding of the mysterious, often fickle buying process that connects the shelf to the checkout counter. What causes a consumer to skip past one aisle but spend a half hour strolling down another? What leads a person to pick up a product, examine it, put it back, walk away, come back later, pick it up again, and then finally buy it? How do the offhand or pointed comments of friends, spouses, or sales staff affect the buying decision?

The data FAME collects at Once Famous help marketers understand more about consumers and how they interact with the wealth of sensory and social cues in a retail store. "We can get really close to customers at the point of decision making." Once Famous experiments have yielded interesting details on how people shop, including the different ways in which men and women decide what to buy. "Women find an object they like and visit it," says Jeri Quest, FAME's executive vice-president for strategic development. "Men look at how it's made, what's the construction." Men stand back and study things, but women can't wait to get their hands on merchandise. These differences may go as far back as childhood shopping experiences. Mothers are more likely to tell their sons to keep their hands to themselves while shopping. When they are adults, men are considerably less likely to pick up a product and get a closer look unless explicitly invited to. In contrast, daughters who shop with mom more are likely to learn her

approach to evaluating a product by experiencing it. As adults, women evaluate products based on the story they tell and what they may say about their owners.

Based on results like these, many retailers tailor their displays to appeal to men and women differently. Stores such as Sharper Image, which target men, provide details about design and construction and post signs encouraging shoppers to push buttons, test massage chairs, and ask questions. Pottery Barn, with its largely female audience, displays products in quaint groupings, allowing shoppers to visualize merchandise in their own homes, experience the products more intimately, and discover what those products might say about them. To gain these valuable insights, manufacturers and retailers pay anywhere from US$50 000 to US$200 000 to have their products stocked at Once Famous.

Once Famous may be the first research lab of its kind, but it won't be the last. Analysts predict a rise in the number of such detailed "retail ethnography" labs as the retail world grows more and more competitive. We'll be watching.

Sources: Samantha Yaffe, "Going Deep," *Strategy*, February 2005; Keyla Kokmen, "The Company Store," *City Pages Media*, June 5, 2002, www.citypages.com/databank/23/1122/article10444.asp; Erik Baard, "Going Retail with Market Research," *Wired News*, August 8, 2002, p.1; Bruce Horovitz, "Shop, You're on Candid Camera," *USA Today*, November 5, 2002, p. 1B; Timothy Henderson, "Shopping Guinea Pigs," *Stores*, December 2002, www.stores.org/archives/archives02.html; Stephanie Simon, "Shopping with Big Brother," *Los Angeles Times*, May 2, 2002, www.chicagotribune.com/technology/chi-020502shopping.story; Lynda Gutierrez, "Spy and Buy," *Plain Talk*, www.plainvanillashell.com/archiveoped.asp?id5324 (accessed May 2004); and information from www.fameretail.com (accessed March 2004).

Once Famous is an actual retail store that serves as an ethnographic lab to yield greater insights into buying behaviour.

Contact Methods

Information can be collected by mail, telephone, personal interview, or online. Table 5.3 shows the strengths and weaknesses of each of these contact methods.

Mail, Telephone, and Personal Interviewing *Mail questionnaires* can be used to collect large amounts of information at a low cost per respondent. Respondents may give more honest answers to more personal questions on a mail questionnaire than to an unknown interviewer in person or over the phone. Also, no interviewer is involved to bias the respondent's answers.

However, mail questionnaires are not very flexible—all respondents answer the same questions in a fixed order. Mail surveys usually take longer to complete, and the response rate—the number of people returning completed questionnaires—is often very low. Finally, the researcher often has little control over the mail questionnaire sample. Even with a good mailing list, it is hard to control *who* at the mailing address fills out the questionnaire.

Telephone interviewing is one of the best methods for gathering information quickly, and it provides greater flexibility than mail questionnaires. Interviewers can explain difficult questions and, depending on the answers they receive, skip some questions or probe on others. Response rates tend to be higher than with mail questionnaires, and interviewers can ask to speak to respondents with the desired characteristics or even by name. A 2004 survey by the Marketing Research and Intelligence Association (MRIA) revealed that 46 percent of Canadians had responded to a telephone survey at home versus 33 percent who had answered a mail survey in the past year. Responses to Internet questionnaires were the third most popular survey response method but accounted for only 12 percent of the responses.[15]

However, with telephone interviewing, the cost per respondent is higher than with mail questionnaires. Also, people may not want to discuss personal questions with an interviewer. The method introduces interviewer bias—the way interviewers talk, how they ask questions, and other differences may affect respondents' answers. Finally, different interviewers may interpret and record responses differently, and under time pressures some interviewers might even cheat by recording answers without asking questions.

Personal interviewing takes two forms—individual and group interviewing. *Individual interviewing* involves talking with people in their homes or offices, on the street, or in shopping malls. Such interviewing is flexible. Trained interviewers can

TABLE 5.3 Strengths and Weaknesses of Contact Methods

	Mail	Telephone	Personal	Online
Flexibility	Poor	Good	Excellent	Good
Quantity of data that can be collected	Good	Fair	Excellent	Good
Control of interviewer effects	Excellent	Fair	Poor	Fair
Control of sample	Fair	Excellent	Fair	Poor
Speed of data collection	Poor	Excellent	Good	Excellent
Response rate	Fair	Good	Good	Good
Cost	Good	Fair	Poor	Excellent

Source: Adapted with permission from *Marketing Research: Measurement and Method,* 7th ed., by Donald S. Tull and Del I. Hawkins. Copyright 1993 by Macmillan Publishing Company.

guide interviews, explain difficult questions, and explore issues as the situation requires. They can show subjects actual products, advertisements, or packages and observe reactions and behaviour. However, individual personal interviews may cost three to four times as much as telephone interviews.

Group interviewing consists of inviting six to ten people to talk with a trained moderator about a product, a service, or an organization. Participants normally are paid a small sum for attending. The moderator encourages free and easy discussion, hoping that group interactions will bring out actual feelings and thoughts. At the same time, the moderator "focuses" the discussion—hence the name **focus group interviewing**. Researchers and marketers watch the focus group discussions from behind one-way glass and comments are recorded in writing or on videotape for later study.

Focus group interviewing has become one of the major marketing research tools for gaining insight into consumer thoughts and feelings. However, focus group studies usually employ small sample sizes to keep time and costs down, and it may be hard to generalize from the results. Because interviewers have more freedom in personal interviews, the problem of interviewer bias is greater.

Today, many researchers are changing the way they conduct focus groups. Some are employing videoconferencing technology to connect marketers in distant locations with live focus group action. Using cameras and two-way sound systems, marketing executives in a far-off boardroom can look in and listen, even using remote controls to zoom in on faces and pan the focus group at will. Other researchers are changing the environments in which they conduct focus groups. To help consumers relax and to elicit more authentic responses, they are using settings that are more comfortable and more relevant to the products being researched. For example, they might conduct focus groups for cooking products in a kitchen setting, or focus groups for home furnishings in a living room setting. One research firm offers facilities that look just like anything from a living room or play room to a bar or even a courtroom.

Some firms are now going on site to conduct focus group sessions. Here's what one retailer did before designing a new line of products for students entering university:

> To hear firsthand from university-bound students about their concerns when shopping for their dorm rooms, and to get a sense from students of what life in

Focus group interviewing
Personal interviewing that involves inviting six to ten people to gather for a few hours with a trained interviewer to talk about a product, a service, or an organization. The interviewer "focuses" the group discussion on important issues.

Today, many researchers are employing videoconferencing and Internet technology to connect marketers with live focus group action. The ActiveGroup research firm lets marketers eavesdrop on focus groups from any location, no matter how distant. Says the company, "no travelling, no scheduling, no problems."

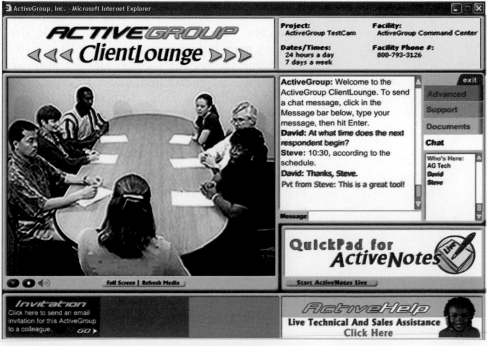

a dorm is like, Jump Associates was hired to conduct focus groups. But rather than inviting respondents to its research facilities, Jump sponsored a series of "game nights" at high school grads' homes, inviting incoming students as well as first-year students living in dorms. To get them talking about dorm life, Jump devised a board game that involved issues associated with going to university. The game naturally led to informal conversations—and questions. Jump researchers were on the sidelines to observe, while a video camera recorded the proceedings. The research paid off with a new product line designed for freshmen. Among the new offerings: Kitchen in a Box, which provides basic accessories for a budding dorm room cook.[16]

Online Marketing Research   Advances in communication technologies have resulted in a number of new high-tech contact methods. One is *computer-assisted telephone interviewing (CATI),* in which interviewers sit at computers, read questions on the screen, and type in respondents' answers. Another is *completely automated telephone surveys (CATS),* in which respondents are dialled by computer and asked prerecorded questions. They enter responses by voice or through the phone's buttons. Other high-tech contact methods include disks-by-mail and computer-based fax surveys.

The latest technology to hit marketing research is the Internet. Increasingly, marketing researchers are collecting primary data through **online (Internet) marketing research**—*Internet surveys, experiments,* and *online focus groups.*

Online (Internet) marketing research

Collecting primary data through Internet surveys and online focus groups.

Web research offers some real advantages over traditional surveys and focus groups. The most obvious advantages are speed and low costs. Online focus groups require some advance scheduling, but results are practically instantaneous. For example, one soft drink company recently conducted an online survey to test teenager opinions of new packaging ideas. The 10- to 15-minute Internet survey included dozens of questions along with 765 images of labels and bottle shapes. Some 600 teenagers participated over a three- to four-day period. Detailed analysis from the survey was available just five days after all the responses had come in—lightning quick compared with offline efforts.[17]

Internet research is also relatively low in cost. Participants can dial in for a focus group from anywhere in the world, eliminating travel, lodging, and facility costs. For surveys, the Internet eliminates most of the postage, phone, labour, and printing costs associated with other approaches. "A survey on the Internet is only 10 or 20 percent as expensive as mail, telephone, or in-person surveys," says one researcher. Moreover, notes another, sample size has little influence on costs. "There's not a huge difference between 10 and 10 000 on the Web," he says.

Online surveys and focus groups are also excellent for reaching the hard-to-reach—the often-elusive teen, single, affluent, and well-educated audiences. It's also good for reaching working mothers and other people who lead busy lives. They respond to it in their own space and at their own convenience. The Internet also works well for bringing together people from different parts of the country, especially those in higher-income groups who can't spare the time to travel to a central site.

Using the Internet to conduct marketing research does have some drawbacks. For one, restricted Internet access can make it difficult to get a broad cross-section of North Americans. Another major problem is controlling who's in the sample. "If you can't see a person with whom you are communicating," says a research executive, "how do know who they really are?"

Even when you reach the right respondents, online surveys and focus groups can lack the dynamics of more personal approaches. The online world is devoid of the eye contact, body language, and direct personal interactions found in traditional focus group research. And the Internet format—running, typed commentary, and online "emoticons" (punctuation marks that express emotion, such as :-) to signify

I have the power to send you back to the drawing board.
-Greenfield Online panelist

High-quality research begins with high-quality respondents – which is why more and more marketers demand that Greenfield Online field their research projects. When you use Greenfield Online for your research data needs, you get instant access to our robust panel of more than 1.7 million members that can help you keep your marketing strategies on track. Our panel has been pre-recruited and is made up of 100% opt-in members, resulting in higher response rates and better quality data for you. Power your research with our experience, our technology and our people.

Greenfield Online has partnered with some of the largest and most well-respected research firms in the industry, including the following and more: GfK Custom Research Inc., Taylor Nelson Sofres, ORC International, Directions For Decisions Inc., M/A/R/C Research, MORPACE International, Inc., Wirthlin Worldwide, MRSI, Harman Atchison Group, Directive Analytics, Rothstein-Tauber, Inc.

Ask that your research provider use Greenfield Online for your next project – or contact us directly at 1.866.899.1018.

Greenfield Online
Power your research™

Wilton, CT San Francisco, CA Beaconsfield, Bucks, UK

Companies are increasingly moving their research onto the Web. Greenfield online tells customers, "you get instant access to our robust panel of 1.7 million members that can help you keep your marketing strategies on track."

happiness)—greatly restricts respondent expressiveness. "You're missing all of the key things that make a focus group a viable method," says the executive. "You may get people online to talk to each other and play off each other, but it's very different to watch people get excited about a concept."

To overcome such sample and response problems, many online research firms use opt-in communities and respondent panels. Advances in technology—such as the integration of animation, streaming audio and video, and virtual environments—also help to overcome these limitations.

Perhaps the most explosive issue facing online researchers concerns consumer privacy. Though Canada's *Personal Information Protection and Electronic Documents Act* has been put in place to address these fears, they still remain. Some people fear that unethical researchers will use the email addresses and confidential responses gathered through surveys to sell products after the research is completed. They are concerned about the use of electronic agents (called Spambots or Spiders) that collect personal information without the respondents' consent. Despite these concerns, online research now accounts for 8 percent of all spending on quantitative marketing research, and most industry insiders predict healthy growth.[18]

Sampling Plan

Sample
A segment of the population selected for marketing research to represent the population as a whole.

Marketing researchers usually draw conclusions about large groups of consumers by studying a small sample of the total consumer population. A **sample** is a segment of the population selected to represent the population as a whole. Ideally, the sample should be representative so that the researcher can make accurate estimates of the thoughts and behaviours of the larger population.

Designing the sample requires three decisions. First, *who* is to be surveyed (what *sampling unit*)? The answer to this question is not always obvious. For example, to study the decision-making process for a family automobile purchase, should the researcher interview the husband, wife, other family members, dealership salespeople, or all of these? The researcher must determine what information is needed and who is most likely to have it.

Second, *how many* people should be surveyed (what *sample size*)? Large samples give more reliable results than small samples. It is not necessary to sample the entire target market or even a large portion to get reliable results, however. If well chosen, samples of less than 1 percent of a population can often give good reliability.

Third, *how* should the people in the sample be *chosen* (what *sampling procedure*)? Table 5.4 describes different kinds of samples. Using *probability samples*, each population member has a known chance of being included in the sample, and researchers can calculate confidence limits for sampling error. But when probability sampling costs too much or takes too much time, marketing researchers often take *nonprobability samples*, even though their sampling error cannot be measured. These varied ways of drawing samples have different costs and time limitations as well as different accuracy and statistical properties. Which method is best depends on the needs of the research project.

Research Instruments

In collecting primary data, marketing researchers have a choice of two main research instruments—the *questionnaire* and *mechanical devices*. The *questionnaire* is by far the most common instrument, whether administered in person, by phone, or online.

Questionnaires are very flexible—there are many ways to ask questions. *Closed-end questions* include all the possible answers, and subjects make choices among them. Examples include multiple-choice questions and scale questions. *Open-end questions* allow respondents to answer in their own words. In a survey of airline users, Southwest might simply ask, "What is your opinion of Southwest Airlines?" Or it might ask people to complete a sentence: "When I choose an airline, the most important consideration is...." These and other kinds of open-end questions often reveal more than closed-end questions because respondents are not limited in their

---

TABLE 5.4 Types of Samples

Probability Sample

Simple random sample	Every member of the population has a known and equal chance of selection.
Stratified random sample	The population is divided into mutually exclusive groups (such as age groups), and random samples are drawn from each group.
Cluster (area) sample	The population is divided into mutually exclusive groups (such as blocks), and the researcher draws a sample of the groups to interview.

Nonprobability Sample

Convenience sample	The researcher selects the easiest population members from which to obtain information.
Judgment sample	The researcher uses his or her judgment to select population members who are good prospects for accurate information.
Quota sample	The researcher finds and interviews a prescribed number of people in each of several categories.

answers. Open-end questions are especially useful in exploratory research, when the researcher is trying to find out *what* people think but not measuring *how many* people think in a certain way. Closed-end questions, on the other hand, provide answers that are easier to interpret and tabulate.

Researchers should also use care in the *wording* and *ordering* of questions. They should use simple, direct, unbiased wording. Questions should be arranged in a logical order. The first question should create interest if possible, and difficult or personal questions should be asked last so that respondents do not become defensive. A carelessly prepared questionnaire usually contains many errors. (See Table 5.5.)

Although questionnaires are the most common research instrument, researchers also use *mechanical instruments* to monitor consumer behaviour. Nielsen Media Research attaches *people meters* to television sets in selected homes to record who watches which programs. And retailers use *checkout scanners* to record shoppers' purchases.

Other mechanical devices measure subjects' physical responses. For example, eye cameras are used to study respondents' eye movements to determine at what points their eyes focus first and how long they linger on a given item. IBM is perfecting an "emotion mouse" that will figure out users' emotional states by measuring pulse, temperature, movement, and galvanic skin response. Using such inputs, an Internet marketer might offer a different screen display if it senses that the user is frustrated. Here's another new technology that captures information on consumers' emotional and physical responses:[19]

Machine response to facial expressions that indicate emotions will soon be a commercial reality. The technology discovers underlying emotions by capturing an image of a user's facial features and movements—especially around the eyes and mouth—and comparing the image against facial feature templates in a database. Hence, an elderly man squints at an ATM screen and the font size doubles almost instantly. A woman at a shopping center kiosk smiles at a travel ad, prompting the device to print out a travel discount coupon. Several users at another kiosk frown at a racy ad, leading a store to pull it.

TABLE 5.5 A "Questionable Questionnaire"

Suppose that a summer camp director had prepared the following questionnaire to use in interviewing the parents of prospective campers. How would you assess each question?

1. What is your income to the nearest hundred dollars? *People don't usually know their income to the nearest hundred dollars, nor do they want to reveal their income that closely. Moreover, a researcher should never open a questionnaire with such a personal question.*

2. Are you a strong or weak supporter of overnight summer camping for your children? *What do "strong" and "weak" mean?*

3. Do your children behave themselves well at a summer camp? Yes ( ) No ( ) *"Behave" is a relative term. Furthermore, are yes and no the best response options for this question? Besides, will people answer this honestly and objectively? Why ask the question in the first place?*

4. How many camps mailed literature to you last year? This year? *Who can remember this?*

5. What are the most salient and determinant attributes in your evaluation of summer camps? *What are salient and determinant attributes? Don't use big words on me!*

6. Do you think it is right to deprive your child of the opportunity to grow into a mature person through the experience of summer camping? *A loaded question. Given the bias, how can any parent answer yes?*

Implementing the Research Plan

The researcher next puts the marketing research plan into action. This involves collecting, processing, and analyzing the information. Data collection can be carried out by the company's marketing research staff or by outside firms. The data collection phase of the marketing research process is generally the most expensive and the most subject to error. Researchers should watch closely to make sure that the plan is implemented correctly. They must guard against problems with contacting respondents, with respondents who refuse to cooperate or who give biased answers, and with interviewers who make mistakes or take shortcuts.

Researchers must process and analyze the collected data to isolate important information and findings. They need to check data for accuracy and completeness and code it for analysis. The researchers then tabulate the results and compute averages and other statistical measures.

Interpreting and Reporting the Findings

The market researcher must now interpret the findings, draw conclusions, and report them to management. The researcher should not try to overwhelm managers with numbers and fancy statistical techniques. Rather, the researcher should present important findings that are useful in the major decisions faced by management.

However, interpretation should not be left only to the researchers. They are often experts in research design and statistics, but the marketing manager knows more about the problem and the decisions that must be made. The best research is meaningless if the manager blindly accepts faulty interpretations from the researcher. Similarly, managers may be biased—they might tend to accept research results that show what they expected and to reject those that they did not expect or hope for. In many cases, findings can be interpreted in different ways, and discussions between researchers and managers will help point to the best interpretations. Thus, as was the case on the Dove project, managers and researchers must work

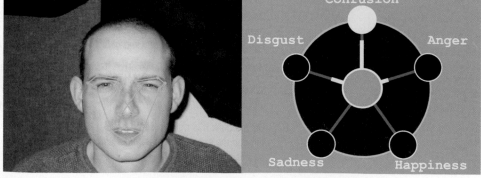

Mechanical measures of consumer response: Devices are in the works that will allow marketers to measure facial expressions and adjust their offers or communications accordingly.

together closely when interpreting research results, and both must share responsibility for the research process and resulting decisions.[20]

Analyzing Marketing Information

Information gathered in internal databases and through marketing intelligence and marketing research usually requires more analysis. And managers may need help in applying the information to their marketing problems and decisions. This help may include advanced statistical analysis to learn more about both the relationships within a set of data and their statistical reliability. Such analysis allows managers to go beyond means and standard deviations in the data and to answer questions about markets, marketing activities, and outcomes.

Information analysis might also involve a collection of analytical models that will help marketers make better decisions. Each model represents some real system, process, or outcome. These models can help answer the questions of *what if* and *which is best*. Marketing scientists have developed numerous models to help marketing managers make better marketing mix decisions, design sales territories and sales call plans, select sites for retail outlets, develop optimal advertising mixes, and forecast new-product sales.

Customer Relationship Management (CRM)

The question of how best to analyze and use individual customer data presents special problems. Most companies are awash in information about their customers. In

SAS offers CRM software that provides "a complete view of your customers." So you'll understand their needs, enhance their lifetime value, and achieve greater competitive advantage.

Customer relationship management (CRM)
The overall process of building and maintaining profitable customer relationships by delivering superior customer value and satisfaction.

fact, smart companies capture information at every possible customer *touchpoint*. These touchpoints include customer purchases, sales force contacts, service and support calls, website visits, satisfaction surveys, credit and payment interactions, market research studies—every contact between the customer and the company.

The trouble is that this information is usually scattered widely across the organization. It is buried deep in the separate databases and records of different company departments. To overcome such problems, many companies are now turning to **customer relationship management (CRM)** to manage detailed information about individual customers and carefully manage customer touch points in order to maximize customer loyalty. In recent years, there has been an explosion in the number of companies using CRM. The Canadian Marketing Association reports that 86 percent of Canadian companies practise CRM in some form. The retail sector is the largest adopter, followed closely by the financial services and technology sectors. North American companies spent an estimated US$50 billion in 2004 on CRM systems from companies such as Siebel Systems, Oracle, Microsoft, and SAS, and spending was expected to increase by 11.5 percent a year through 2007.[21]

CRM consists of sophisticated software and analytical tools that integrate customer information from all sources, analyze it in depth, and apply the results to build stronger customer relationships. CRM integrates everything that a company's sales, service, and marketing teams know about individual customers to provide a 360-degree view of the customer relationship.

CRM analysts develop *data warehouses* and use sophisticated *data mining* techniques to unearth the riches hidden in customer data. A data warehouse is a company-wide electronic database of finely detailed customer information that needs to be sifted through for gems. The purpose of a data warehouse is not just to gather information but to pull it together into a central, accessible location. Then, once the data warehouse brings the data together, the company uses high-powered data mining techniques to sift through the mounds of data and dig out interesting findings about customers. Such data systems can give a company a big competitive advantage.

By using CRM to understand customers better, companies can provide higher levels of customer service and develop deeper customer relationships. They can use CRM to pinpoint high-value customers, target them more effectively, cross-sell the company's products, and create offers tailored to specific customer requirements. Consider the following examples:[22]

- Grocery Gateway, the online grocery retailer headquartered in Toronto, uses its massive database to reward its clients at key points in the customer life cycle and even tailors these rewards to the individual. From the customers' point of view, they see a company who unexpectedly surprises them with free gifts. Grocery Gateway sends them gifts at key milestones, such as their twenty-fifth or fiftieth online order. The reward could be an electronic coupon they can apply to their next online order, or it may be a gift basket full of Grocery Gateway products, tailored to their wants and needs according to past purchases. Surprise is the key since the customer doesn't know what triggers the reward.

  "There are two mind-sets about marketing," says director of marketing Scott Robinson. "One is fostering an expectation and delivering on it. Then there's the unexpected customer appreciation tactics. We do both. It's a bizarre way of saying thanks a lot for your business, and we really value it."

- FedEx's CRM system has helped to cut costs, improve customer support, and use customer data to cross-sell and up-sell services to customers. The system gives every member of FedEx's 3300-person sales force a comprehensive view of every customer, detailing each one's needs and helping the rep to sort through the company's more than 220 services to find the best fit for each customer. For instance, if a customer who does a lot of international shipping calls to arrange a delivery, a sales rep will see a detailed customer history on his or her computer screen, assess the customer's needs, and determine the most appropriate offering on the spot. The CRM system will also help FedEx conduct promotions and qualify potential sales leads. The CRM software analyzes market segments, points out market "sweet spots," and calculates how profitable those segments will be to the company and to individual salespeople.

- Marks & Spencer—Britain's "most trusted retailer"—has one of the richest customer databases of any retailer in the world. The database contains demographic and purchasing information on more than 3 million M&S charge account customers, point-of-sale information from 10 million store transactions per week, and a wealth of data from external sources. The CRM system organizes this wealth of data and analyzes it to help Marks & Spencer make better decisions on everything from corporate branding to targeted communications and sales promotions. "We have a much better idea of what kinds of offers to put in front of different customers and when, and what tone of voice to use, based on their individual tastes, preferences, and behaviour," says Steven Bond, head of the retailer's Customer Insight Unit (CIU). For example, by identifying who shops and when—older customers tend to shop early to avoid the crowds, while younger male shoppers leave things until the last minute, for instance—M&S can align its product availability and marketing activity accordingly. Or a regular customer checking out of the store's food section might be enticed into the menswear department with a promotion personalized according to whether he or she is an "Egyptian cotton and silk tie" purchaser or has a lifestyle that demands no-iron shirts. CRM has put Marks & Spencer at the leading edge of customer analysis. This, in turn, creates more satisfied customers and more profitable customer relationships.

CRM benefits don't come without cost or risk, not only in collecting the original customer data but also in maintaining and mining it. An estimated half or more of all CRM efforts fail to meet their objectives. The most common cause of CRM failures is that companies mistakenly view CRM only as a technology and software solution.[23] But technology alone cannot build profitable customer relationships. "CRM is not a technology solution—you can't achieve … improved customer

Marks & Spencer's Customer Insight Unit uses the retailer's rich customer database to make better decisions on everything from corporate branding to targeted communications and sales promotions.

relationships by simply slapping in some software," says a CRM expert. Instead, CRM is just one part of an effective overall *customer relationship management strategy*. "Focus on the *R*," advises the expert. "Remember, a relationship is what CRM is all about."[24]

When it works, the benefits of CRM can far outweigh the costs and risks. Based on regular polls of its customers, Siebel Systems claims that customers using its CRM software report an average 16 percent increase in revenues and 21 percent increase in customer loyalty and staff efficiency. "No question that companies are getting tremendous value out of this," says a CRM consultant. "Companies [are] looking for ways to bring disparate sources of customer information together, then get it to all the customer touch points." The powerful new CRM techniques can unearth "a wealth of information to target that customer, to hit their hot button."[25]

Distributing and Using Marketing Information

Marketing information has no value until it is used to make better marketing decisions. Thus, the marketing information system must make the information available to the managers and others who make marketing decisions or deal with customers on a day-to-day basis. In some cases, this means providing managers with regular performance reports, intelligence updates, and reports on the results of research studies.

But marketing managers may also need nonroutine information for special situations and on-the-spot decisions. For example, a sales manager having trouble with a large customer may want a summary of the account's sales and profitability over the past year. Or a retail store manager who has run out of a best-selling product may want to know the current inventory levels in the chain's other stores. Increasingly, therefore, information distribution involves entering information into databases and making it available in a user-friendly and timely way.

Many firms use a company *intranet* to facilitate this process. The intranet provides ready access to research information, stored reports, shared work documents, contact information for employees and other stakeholders, and more. For example, iGo, a catalogue and Web retailer, integrates incoming customer service calls with up-to-date database information about customers' Web purchases and email inquiries. By accessing this information on the intranet while speaking with the customer, iGo's service representatives can get a well-rounded picture of each customer's purchasing history and previous contacts with the company.

In addition, companies are increasingly allowing key customers and value-network members to access account, product, and other data on demand through *extranets*. Suppliers, customers, resellers, and select other network members may access a company's extranet to update their accounts, arrange purchases, and check orders against inventories to improve customer service. For example, one insurance firm allows its 200 independent agents access to a Web-based database of claim information covering 1 million customers. This allows the agents to avoid high-risk customers and to compare claim data with their own customer databases. And Wal-Mart stores around the globe use the Retail Link system, which provides suppliers with up to two years' worth of data on how their products have sold in Wal-Mart stores.[26]

Thanks to modern technology, today's marketing managers can gain direct access to the information system at any time and from virtually any location. They can tap into the system while working at a home office, from a hotel room, or from the local Starbucks through a wireless network—any place where they can turn on a laptop and link up. Such systems allow managers to get the information they need directly and quickly and to tailor it to their own needs. From just about anywhere, they can obtain information from company or outside databases, analyze it using statistical software, prepare reports and presentations, and communicate directly with others in the network.

Other Marketing Information Considerations

This section discusses marketing information in two special contexts: marketing research in small businesses and non-profit organizations, and international marketing research. Finally, we look at public policy and ethics issues in marketing research.

Marketing Research in Small Businesses and Non-profit Organizations

Just like larger firms, small organizations need market information. Start-up businesses need information about their industries, competitors, potential customers, and reactions to new market offers. Existing small businesses must track changes in customer needs and wants, reactions to new products, and changes in the competitive environment.

Managers of small businesses and non-profit organizations often think that marketing research can be done only by experts in large companies with big research budgets. True, large-scale research studies are beyond the budgets of most small businesses. However, many of the marketing research techniques discussed in this chapter also can be used by smaller organizations in a less formal manner and at little or no expense.

Managers of small businesses and non-profit organizations can obtain good marketing information simply by *observing* things around them. For example, retailers can evaluate new locations by observing vehicle and pedestrian traffic. They can monitor competitor advertising by collecting ads from local media. They can evaluate their customer mix by recording how many and what kinds of customers shop in the store at different times. In addition, many small business managers routinely visit their rivals and socialize with competitors to gain insights.

Managers can conduct informal *surveys* using small convenience samples. The director of an art museum can learn what patrons think about new exhibits by conducting informal focus groups—inviting small groups to lunch and having discussions on topics of interest. Retail salespeople can talk with customers visiting the store; hospital officials can interview patients. Restaurant managers might make random phone calls during slack hours to interview consumers about where they eat out and what they think of various restaurants in the area. Bissell, a nicher in the carpet-cleaning industry, used a small convenience sample to quickly and cheaply test the market for its Steam Gun—a newly developed home-cleaning device that resembled a handheld vacuum cleaner.

> Bissell had only four weeks and a tight budget to get a feel for how consumers would respond to the new product. Aware that women with children often purchase such products, Bissell made a US$1500 donation to a local Parent Teacher Association (PTA) for the chance to make a presentation. After the presentation, it gave twenty interested women the Steam Gun to take home. Following a two-

week trial period, Bissell's marketing research director visited the mothers in their homes to watch them use product. This "research on a shoestring" yielded several interesting discoveries. First, Bissell learned that the women weren't sold on the cleaning ability of hot water used without chemicals. Second, it would have to change the product name. When roped into chores, children would arm themselves with the Steam Gun and take aim at their siblings. One child was quoted as saying, "Freeze, or I'll melt your face off!" Finally, Bissell found that the product had special appeal to those who were serious about cleaning. They used it to get into hard-to-reach places and blast off tough grime. Based on these findings, Bissell changed the name of the product to the Steam 'n Clean and focused on the cleaning power of super hot steam when promoting the product. The Steam 'n Clean was successfully launched through infomercials and in nationwide retail chains.[27]

Managers also can conduct their own simple *experiments*. For example, by changing the themes in regular fundraising mailings and watching the results, a non-profit manager can find out much about which marketing strategies work best. By varying newspaper advertisements, a store manager can learn the effects of things such as ad size and position, price coupons, and media used.

Small organizations can obtain most of the secondary data available to large businesses. In addition, the Conference Board of Canada, federal government, and provincial governments offer dozens of free publications that give advice on topics ranging from preparing a business plan to ordering business signs. Many business schools have entrepreneurship and small business consulting centres, and they may also conduct marketing research for small firms for no charge as part of class projects. The business sections at local libraries can also be a good source of information. Local newspapers often provide information on local shoppers and their buying patterns. Finally, small businesses can collect a considerable amount of information at very little cost on the Internet. They can scour competitor and customer websites and use Internet search engines to research specific companies and issues.

Bissell used a small convenience sample to quickly and cheaply test the market for its Steam 'n Clean home-cleaning device.

In summary, secondary data collection, observation, surveys, and experiments can all be used effectively by small organizations with small budgets. Although these informal research methods are less complex and less costly, they still must be conducted carefully. Managers must think carefully about the objectives of the research, formulate questions in advance, recognize the biases introduced by smaller samples and less skilled researchers, and conduct the research systematically.[28]

International Marketing Research

International marketing researchers follow the same steps as domestic researchers, from defining the research problem and developing a research plan to interpreting and reporting the results. However, these researchers often face more and different problems. Whereas domestic researchers deal with fairly homogenous markets within a single country, international researchers deal with differing markets in many different countries. These markets often vary greatly in their levels of economic development, cultures and customs, and buying patterns.

In many foreign markets, the international researcher sometimes has a difficult time finding good secondary data. Whereas North American marketing researchers can obtain reliable secondary data from dozens of domestic research services, many countries have almost no research services at all. Some of the largest international research services do operate in many countries. For example, AC Nielsen Corporation (owned by VNU NV, the world's largest marketing research company) has offices in more than 100 countries, from China to Chile. And 65 percent of the revenues of the world's 25 largest marketing research firms comes from outside their home countries.[29] However, most research firms operate in only a relative handful of countries. Thus, even when secondary information is available, it usually must be obtained from many different sources on a country-by-country basis, making the information difficult to combine or compare.

Because of the scarcity of good secondary data, international researchers often must collect their own primary data. Here again, researchers face problems not found domestically. For example, they may find it difficult simply to develop good samples. North American researchers can use current telephone directories, census tract data, and any of several sources of socioeconomic data to construct samples. However, such information is largely lacking in many countries.

Once the sample is drawn, the North American researcher usually can reach most respondents easily by telephone, by mail, on the Internet, or in person. Reaching respondents is often not so easy in other parts of the world. Researchers in Mexico cannot rely on telephone, Internet, and mail data collection—most data collection is door to door and concentrated in three or four of the largest cities. In some countries, few people have phones or personal computers (PCs). For example, whereas there are 690 phones and 652 PCs per 1000 people in Canada, there are only 117 phones and 54 PCs per 1000 people in Mexico. In Ghana, the numbers drop to 11 phones and 3 PCs per 1000 people. In some countries, the postal system is notoriously unreliable. In Brazil, for instance, an estimated 30 percent of the mail is never delivered. In many developing countries, poor roads and transportation systems make certain areas hard to reach, making personal interviews difficult and expensive.[30]

Cultural differences from country to country cause additional problems for international researchers. Language is the most obvious obstacle. For example, questionnaires must be prepared in one language and then translated into the languages of each country researched. Responses then must be translated back into the original language for analysis and interpretation. This adds to research costs and increases the risks of error.

Some of the largest research services have large international organizations. AC Nielsen has offices in more than 100 countries.

Translating a questionnaire from one language to another is anything but easy. Many idioms, phrases, and statements mean different things in different cultures. For example, a Danish executive noted, "Check this out by having a different translator put back into English what you've translated from English. You'll get the shock of your life. I remember [an example in which] 'out of sight, out of mind' had become 'invisible things are insane.'"[31]

Consumers in different countries also vary in their attitudes toward marketing research. People in one country may be very willing to respond; in other countries, nonresponse can be a major problem. Customs in some countries may prohibit people from talking with strangers. In certain cultures, research questions often are considered too personal. For example, in many Latin American countries, people may feel embarrassed to talk with researchers about their choices of shampoo, deodorant, or other personal care products. Similarly, in most Muslim countries, mixed-gender focus groups are taboo, as is videotaping female-only focus groups.[32]

Even when respondents are *willing* to respond, they may not be *able* to because of high functional illiteracy rates. And middle-class people in developing countries often make false claims in order to appear well-off. For example, in a study of tea consumption in India, more than 70 percent of middle-income respondents claimed that they used one of several national brands. However, the researchers had good reason to doubt these results—more than 60 percent of the tea sold in India is unbranded generic tea.

Despite these problems, the recent growth of international marketing has resulted in a rapid increase in the use of international marketing research. Global companies have little choice but to conduct such research. Although the costs and problems associated with international research may be high, the costs of not doing it—in terms of missed opportunities and mistakes—might be even higher. Once recognized, many of the problems associated with international marketing research can be overcome or avoided.

Public Policy and Ethics in Marketing Research

Most marketing research benefits both the sponsoring company and its consumers. Through marketing research, companies learn more about consumers' needs, resulting in more satisfying products and services and stronger customer relationships. However, the misuse of marketing research can also harm or annoy consumers. Two major public policy and ethics issues in marketing research are intrusions on consumer privacy and the misuse of research findings.

Intrusions on Consumer Privacy

Many consumers feel positively about marketing research and believe that it serves a useful purpose. In a 2004 survey by MRIA[33] (the Marketing Research and Intelligence Association that resulted from the merger between the Canadian Association of Marketing Research Organizations and the Professional Marketing Research Society), 87 percent of the respondents agreed that research surveys give people the opportunity to provide feedback to manufacturers and other organizations. The survey also demonstrated that Canadian participation levels in research surveys have significantly increased. In 1995, only 42 percent of Canadians noted they had participated in a survey in the past year. In 2004, this percentage had increased to 52 percent. Nonetheless, more than two-thirds of the survey respondents had refused on at least one occasion to participate in a survey during the previous year. Though a third of the people polled believe that research is an invasion of privacy, 56 percent think some questions are too personal, and only 44 percent agree that "companies that conduct research surveys can be trusted to protect my rights to privacy." Some practices have led to a mistrust of marketing research. Fifty-three percent of Canadians surveyed noted that they were contacted for an alleged research survey, which actually turned out to be an attempt to sell them a product or service. Called "mugging and sugging," this practice is most prevalent in Ontario.

A few consumers fear that researchers might use sophisticated techniques to probe our deepest feelings and then use this knowledge to manipulate our buying. Or they worry that marketers are building huge databases full of personal information about customers. Canada's *Personal Information Protection and Electronic Documents Act*, which came into full force in 2004, was designed to protect consumers from these concerns. Under its provisions, organizations must state the reasons why they are collecting the information. They must obtain consumers' consent before they can collect, use, or transfer information about an individual, and they must limit the information collected to the purpose they state at the beginning of the collection process. Moreover, every organization has to appoint a privacy officer to ensure compliance with the legislation and to field consumer inquiries and complaints. Organizations also have to ensure that the personal information they store is accurate and, upon request, they must inform an individual about the information they have on that individual and give him or her access to that information.[34] In addition to the federal legislation, the Internet Advertising and Marketing Bureau of Canada (IAMBC) scrutinizes the practices of Internet marketers. Without this protection, here is what you might face:

> Never heard of Acxiom? Chances are it's heard of you. It's the world's largest processor of consumer data, collecting and massaging more than a billion records a day. Acxiom's 5-acre data center manages 20 billion customer records. The company maintains a database on 96 percent of U.S. households that gives marketers a so-called real-time, 360-degree view of their customers. How? Acxiom provides a 13-digit code for every person, "so we can identify you wherever you go," says the company's demographics guru. Each person is placed into one of seventy lifestyle clusters, ranging from "Rolling Stones" and "Single City Struggles" to "Timeless Elders." Acxiom's catalogue offers

customers hundreds of lists, including a "pre-movers file," updated daily, of people preparing to change residences, as well as lists of people sorted by the frequency with which they use credit cards, the square footage of their homes, and their interest in the "strange and unusual." Its customers include nine of the country's top ten credit-card issuers, as well as nearly all the major retail banks, insurers, and automakers. Acxiom may even know things about you that you don't know yourself.[35]

Given such practices, it is not surprising that a recent survey found that 70 percent of Americans say that companies have too much of consumers' personal information, and 76 percent feel that their privacy has been compromised if a company uses the collected personal information to sell them products. These concerns have led to lower survey response rates in recent years.[36]

Banking is one industry where privacy has long been a concern, whether it is with regard to research or everyday transactions. RBC has been a leader in the area of privacy protection, believing that protecting confidentiality of personal and financial information is fundamental to the way it does business. In 2004, RBC and its agency, Longwoods International, won the Marketing Research and Intelligence Association award for the best integrated marketing research program for its work combining database and survey research to quantify the incremental sales impact and return on investment of its multi-channel marketing campaigns. RBC's commitment has not changed with the arrival of new technologies, such as the Internet and online services. Instead, it was extended to ensure that all clients' experiences with the bank were safe and secure. RBC was a strong supporter of industry privacy standards and related government regulation, playing an active role in the development of the Canadian Bankers Association's (CBA) *Privacy Model Code* and the Canadian Standards Association's (CSA) *Model for the Protection of Personal Privacy*. These models were the foundation upon which RBC tailored its own to meet the needs and expectations of its clients.[37]

In addition to protecting privacy, researchers increasingly need to provide value in exchange for information. For example, Amazon.com's customers do not mind if the firm builds a database of products they buy in order to provide future product recommendations. This saves time and provides value. Similarly, Bizrate users gladly complete surveys rating etail sites because they can view the overall ratings of others when making purchase decisions. The best approach is for researchers to ask only for the information they need, to use it responsibly to provide customer value, and to avoid sharing information without the customer's permission.

RBC has a long history of respecting privacy and protecting financial information, which it sees as fundamental to the way it does business whether in person or online. It played an active role in developing Canadian privacy standards. Its website lists its Ten Privacy Principles, which were designed to meet the needs and expectations of its clients.

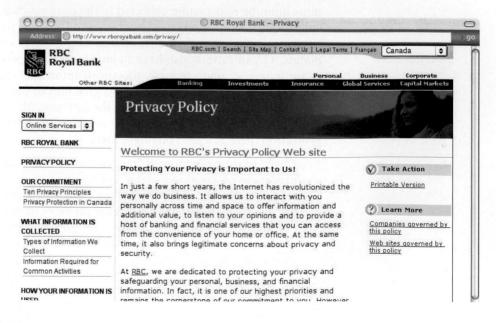

Misuse of Research Findings

Research studies can be powerful persuasion tools; companies often use study results as claims in their advertising and promotion. The results of other studies, however, appear to be little more than vehicles for pitching the sponsor's products. In fact, in some cases, the research surveys appear to have been designed just to produce the intended effect. Few advertisers openly rig their research designs or blatantly misrepresent the findings; most abuses tend to be subtle "stretches." Consider the following examples:[38]

- A study by Chrysler contends that North Americans overwhelmingly prefer Chrysler to Toyota after test driving both. However, the study included just 100 people in each of two tests. More importantly, none of the people surveyed owned a foreign car brand, so they appear to be favourably predisposed to North American brands.

- A Black Flag survey asked: "A roach disk ... poisons a roach slowly. The dying roach returns to the nest and after it dies is eaten by other roaches. In turn these roaches become poisoned and die. How effective do you think this type of product would be in killing roaches?" Not surprisingly, 79 percent said effective.

- A poll sponsored by the disposable diaper industry asked: "It is estimated that disposable diapers account for less than 2 percent of the trash in today's landfills. In contrast, beverage containers, third-class mail, and yard waste are estimated to account for about 21 percent of the trash in landfills. Given this, in your opinion, would it be fair to ban disposable diapers?" Again, not surprisingly, 84 percent said no.

Thus, subtle manipulations of the study's sample or the choice or wording of questions can greatly affect the conclusions reached.

In others cases, so-called independent research studies are actually paid for by companies with an interest in the outcome. Small changes in study assumptions or in how results are interpreted can subtly affect the direction of the results. For example, at least four widely quoted studies compare the environmental effects of using disposable diapers with those of using cloth diapers. The two studies sponsored by the cloth diaper industry conclude that cloth diapers are more environmentally friendly. Not surprisingly, the other two studies, sponsored by the paper diaper industry, conclude just the opposite. Yet both appear to be correct *given* the underlying assumptions used.

Recognizing that surveys can be abused, several associations—including the Marketing Research and Intelligence Association (MRIA) (see www.mria-arim.ca/STANDARDS/CODE2005.asp), the Canadian Marketing Association, and the American Marketing Association—have developed codes of research ethics and standards of conduct. In the end, however, unethical or inappropriate actions cannot simply be regulated away. Each company must accept responsibility for policing the conduct and reporting of its own marketing research to protect consumers' best interests and its own.

Reviewing the Concepts

In today's complex and rapidly changing marketplace, marketing managers need more and better information to make effective and timely decisions. This greater need for information has been matched by the explosion of information technologies for supplying information. Using today's new technologies, companies can now obtain great quantities of information, sometimes even too much. Yet marketers often complain that they lack enough of the *right* kind of information or have an excess of the *wrong* kind. In response, many companies are now studying their managers' information needs and designing information systems to help managers develop and manage market and customer information so that strong, valuable, and lasting customer relationships can be built and maintained.

1. **Explain the importance of information to the company and its understanding of the marketplace.**

   The marketing process starts with a complete understanding of the marketplace and consumer needs and wants. Thus, the company needs sound information in order to produce superior value and satisfaction for customers. The company also requires information on competitors, resellers, and other actors and forces in the marketplace. Increasingly, marketers are viewing information not only as an input for making better decisions but also as an important strategic asset and marketing tool essential for building customer relationships.

2. **Define the marketing information system and discuss its parts.**

   The *marketing information system (MIS)* consists of people, equipment, and procedures to gather, sort, analyze, evaluate, and distribute needed, timely, and accurate information to marketing decision makers. A well-designed information system begins and ends with users.

   The MIS first *assesses information needs.* The marketing information system primarily serves the company's marketing and other managers, but it may also provide information to external partners. Then, the MIS *develops information* from internal databases, marketing intelligence activities, and marketing research. *Internal databases* provide information on the company's own operations and departments. Such data can be obtained quickly and cheaply but often needs to be adapted for marketing decisions. *Marketing intelligence* activities supply everyday information about developments in the external marketing environment. *Market research* consists of collecting information relevant to a specific marketing problem faced by the company. Lastly, the MIS *distributes information* gathered from these sources to the right managers in the right form and at the right time.

3. **Outline the steps in the marketing research process.**

   The first step in the marketing research process involves *defining the problem and setting the research objectives,* which may be exploratory, descriptive, or causal research. The second step consists of *developing a research plan* for collecting data from primary and secondary sources. The third step calls for *implementing the marketing research plan* by gathering, processing, and analyzing the information. The fourth step consists of *interpreting and reporting the findings.* Additional information analysis helps marketing managers apply the information and provides them with sophisticated statistical procedures and models from which to develop more rigorous findings.

   Both *internal* and *external* secondary data sources often provide information more quickly and at a lower cost than primary data sources, and they can sometimes yield information that a company cannot collect by itself. However, needed information might not exist in secondary sources. Researchers must also evaluate secondary information to ensure that it is *relevant, accurate, current,* and *impartial.* Primary research must also be evaluated for these features. Each primary data collection method—*observational, survey,* and *experimental*—has its own advantages and disadvantages. Each of the various primary research contact methods—mail, telephone, personal interview, and online—also has its own advantages and drawbacks. Similarly, each contact method has its pluses and minuses.

4. Explain how companies analyze and distribute marketing information.

Information gathered in internal databases and through marketing intelligence and marketing research usually requires more analysis. This may include advanced statistical analysis or the application of analytical models that will help marketers make better decisions. To analyze individual customer data, many companies have now acquired or developed special software and analysis techniques—called *customer relationship management (CRM)*—that integrate, analyze, and apply the mountains of individual customer data contained in their databases.

Marketing information has no value until it is used to make better marketing decisions. Thus, the marketing information system must make the information available to the managers and others who make marketing decisions or deal with customers. In some cases, this means providing regular reports and updates; in other cases it means making nonroutine information available for special situations and on-the-spot decisions.

Many firms use company intranets and extranets to facilitate this process. Thanks to modern technology, today's marketing managers can gain direct access to the information system at any time and from virtually any location.

5. Discuss the special issues some marketing researchers face, including public policy and ethics issues.

Some marketers face special marketing research situations, such as those conducting research in small business, non-profit, or international situations. Marketing research can be conducted effectively by small businesses and non-profit organizations with limited budgets. International marketing researchers follow the same steps as domestic researchers but often face more and different problems. All organizations need to respond responsibly to major public policy and ethical issues surrounding marketing research, including issues of intrusions on consumer privacy and misuse of research findings.

Reviewing the Key Terms

Causal research   170
Customer relationship management   186
Descriptive research   170
Experimental research   176
Exploratory research   170
Focus group interviewing   179
Internal databases   165
Marketing information system   163
Marketing intelligence   167

Marketing research   169
Observational research   174
Online databases   171
Online (Internet) marketing research   180
Primary data   171
Sample   181
Secondary data   171
Single-source data systems   175
Survey research   175

Discussing the Concepts

1. Assume that you are a regional marketing manager for a cellular phone company. List at least three potential sources of internal data and discuss how these data would help you create cellular services that provide greater customer value and satisfaction.

2. In this chapter we define primary data and secondary data. Once secondary data, such as customer usage, is gathered and analyzed with the express purpose of making a pricing decision, is it still called secondary data, or is it primary data? Why?

3. Marketing research over the Internet has increased significantly in the past decade. Outline the strengths and weaknesses of marketing research conducted online.

4. Small businesses and non-profit organizations often lack the resources to conduct extensive market research. Assume that you are the director of fundraising for a small non-profit that is focused on a social issue. List three ways, using limited resources, that you could gather information about your primary donor group.

5. Conducting international marketing research is imperative for global firms. What basic problems might a Canadian toy manufacturer of stuffed polar bears, moose, and beavers face in conducting research in Asia? How might those issues differ from country to country?

Applying the Concepts

1. The Internet is now the largest source of secondary data available to a marketer. More and more sites with hundreds or even thousands of pages of information are being added on a daily basis. In a small group, count the number of clicks that it takes you to find the following items:

   • Alcan's net income for 2005

   • Number of Wal-Mart stores (all types) at close of the fiscal year

   • RBC's corporate vision and values statement

   • Cost per line to run an ad in the Report on Business section of the national addition of the *Globe and Mail*.

2. Imagine you are the owner of a small children's clothing store that specializes in upscale girl's fashions from size 2 to 6. You have found a potential new clothing line, but you are unsure whether the line will generate the sales needed to be profitable. Which type of research methodology (exploratory, descriptive, or causal) is best suited for answering your questions? Why?

3. Many consumer rights advocates argue that research data can be manipulated to support any conclusion. Assume you are attending a meeting where a car company's research for a fuel-efficient SUV is being presented. List five questions that you would ask that would test the interpretation and objectivity of the findings being presented.

Focus on Technology

If you were a Web marketer, you'd more than likely have heard of or used WebTrends analytic software. In mid-2004, NetIQ, a leading provider of systems management, security management, Windows administration, and web analytics solutions, introduced Version 7 of this popular product. WebTrends provides the marketer many valuable features. Go to www.netiq.com and read about the marketing benefits WebTrends.

1. From a marketing perspective, what is the primary purpose of WebTrends?

2. List and explain four of the marketing benefits of WebTrends.

3. Is WebTrends a marketing intelligence or marketing research product?

4. Does WebTrends collect primary or secondary data?

Focus on Ethics

TiVo Inc., a leading provider of digital video recorders and services, was founded on a single vision: "to create and continually enhance a new, easy, and much better, way to watch television." With more than 1 million subscribers, TiVo leads in an increasingly competitive market through its continual improvement and introduction of new services. While providing services, TiVo collects a great amount of viewing behaviour information, including each customer's recording and viewing history. In mid-2004, TiVo announced its intention to sell information about the viewing habits of its subscribers (excluding personal information) to advertisers and broadcasters.

1. Is TiVo acting ethically in selling this information? Is it acting legally in Canada and the U.S.?

2. Go to www.tivo.com and check out TiVo's privacy policy. What options does TiVo offer subscribers who are interested in protecting their privacy?

3. Consumer advocates assert that most TiVo subscribers are unaware of the information that the company collects. What steps, if any, would you recommend that TiVo take to inform subscribers about this practice?

Video Case
DDB Worldwide

DDB Worldwide, a global communications firm, has successfully mounted advertising campaigns for mega marketers including McDonald's, ExxonMobil, Johnson & Johnson, and Volkswagen. The agency strives to offer a unique approach to targeting, and communicating with a host of clients' consumers. As a result, DDB is one of the most decorated advertising agencies in the world.

The agency has also created some memorable campaigns, such as the humorous Rubberband Man commercials that aired for Office Max or the "Dude, You're Getting a Dell" series that DDB crafted for Dell. Although both campaigns won awards for creativity and humour, those traits alone don't make a campaign successful. Advertising is meant to connect with the customer, build brand meaning, and, ultimately, drive

sales. So, how does DDB ensure the success of its campaigns? Each campaign is based on extensive marketing research that helps DDB to understand each client's target customers.

After viewing the video featuring DDB Worldwide, answer the following questions about marketing research.

1. What marketing research techniques did DDB use to get to know JC Penney's core customer? Which technique uncovered the most useful information?

2. What other techniques might have helped DDB better understand JC Penney's target consumers?

3. How might DDB's marketing research approach differ if JC Penney were developing an online campaign to drive consumers to its website?

Online Media Resources

Video Short
Log on to your Companion Website at **www.pearsoned.ca/kotler** to view the video segment related to the Video Case above.

CBC ⊕ CBC Video Case
Please refer to Appendix 2 to read a CBC Video Case for this chapter, and log on to your Companion Website at **www.pearsoned.ca/kotler** to view the corresponding video segment.

Case Pilot
Log on to your Companion Website at **www.pearsoned.ca/kotler** to sharpen your case analysis skills and take the Case Pilot Challenge!

Company Case
Enterprise Rent-A-Car: Measuring Service Quality

Surveying Customers
Kevin Kirkman wheeled his shiny blue BMW coupe into his driveway, put the gearshift into park, set the parking brake, and got out to check his mailbox, as he did every day when he returned home. As he flipped through the deluge of catalogues and credit card offers, he noticed a letter from Enterprise Rent-A-Car. He wondered why Enterprise would be writing him.

The Wreck
Then he remembered. Earlier that month, Kevin had been involved in a wreck. As he was driving to work one rainy morning, another car had been unable to stop on the slick pavement and had plowed into his car as he

waited at a stoplight. Thankfully, neither he nor the other driver was hurt, but both cars had sustained considerable damage. In fact, he was not able to drive his car.

Kevin had used his cellphone to call the police, and while he was waiting for the officers to come, he had called his auto insurance agent. The agent had assured Kevin that his policy included coverage to pay for a rental car while he was having his car repaired. He told Kevin to have the car towed to a nearby auto repair shop and gave him the telephone number for the Enterprise Rent-A-Car office that served his area. The agent noted that his company recommended using Enterprise for replacement rentals and that Kevin's policy would cover up to $20 per day of the rental fee.

Once Kevin had checked his car in at the body shop and made the necessary arrangements, he telephoned the Enterprise office. Within 10 minutes, an Enterprise employee had driven to the repair shop and picked him up. They drove back to the Enterprise office, where Kevin completed the paperwork and rented a Ford Taurus. He drove the rental car for 12 days before the repair shop completed work on his car.

"Don't know why Enterprise would be writing me," Kevin thought. "The insurance company paid the $20 per day, and I paid the extra because the Taurus cost more than that. Wonder what the problem could be?"

Tracking Satisfaction

Kevin tossed the mail on the passenger's seat and drove up the driveway. Once inside his house, he opened the Enterprise letter to find that it was a survey to determine how satisfied he was with his rental. The survey itself was only one page long and consisted of 13 questions (see Exhibit 1).

Enterprise's executives believed that the company had become the largest rent-a-car company in the U.S. (in terms of number of cars, rental locations, and revenue) because of its laserlike focus on customer satisfaction and because of its concentration on serving the home-city replacement market. It aimed to serve customers like Kevin, who were involved in wrecks and suddenly found themselves without a car. While the more well-known companies, such as Hertz and Avis, battled for business in the cutthroat airport market, Enterprise quietly built its business by cultivating insurance agents and body-shop managers as referral agents so that when one of their clients or customers needed a replacement vehicle, they would recommend Enterprise. Although such replacement rentals accounted for about 80 percent of the company's business, it also served the discretionary market (leisure/vacation rentals), and the business market (renting cars to businesses for their short-term needs). It had also begun to provide on-site and off-site service at some airports.

Throughout its history, Enterprise had followed founder Jack Taylor's advice. Taylor believed that if the company took care of its customers and employees first, profits would follow. So the company was careful to track customer satisfaction.

About one in twenty randomly selected customers received a letter like Kevin's. An independent company mailed the letter and a postage-paid return envelope to the selected customers. Customers who completed the survey used the envelope to return it to the independent company. That company compiled the results and provided them to Enterprise.

Continuous Improvement

Meanwhile, back at Enterprise's St. Louis, Missouri, headquarters, the company's top managers were interested in taking the next steps in their customer-satisfaction program. Enterprise had used the percentage of customers who were completely satisfied to develop its Enterprise Service Quality index (ESQi). It used the survey results to calculate an overall average ESQi score for the company and a score for each individual branch. The company's branch managers believed in and supported the process.

However, top management believed that to really "walk the walk" on customer satisfaction, it needed to make the ESQi a key factor in the promotion process. The company wanted to take the ESQi for the branch or branches a manager supervised into consideration when it evaluated that manager for a promotion. Top management believed that such a process would ensure that its managers and all its employees would focus on satisfying Enterprise's customers.

The top managers realized, however, they had two problems in taking the next step. First, they wanted a better survey response rate. Although the company got a 25 percent response rate, which was good for this type of survey, it was concerned that it might still be missing important information. Second, it could take up to two months to get results back, and Enterprise believed it needed a process that would get the customer satisfaction information more quickly, at least on a monthly basis, so its branch managers could identify and take action on customer service problems quickly and efficiently.

Enterprise's managers wondered how they could improve the customer-satisfaction-tracking process.

Questions for Discussion

1. Analyze Enterprise's Service Quality Survey. What information is it trying to gather? What are its research objectives?

2. What decisions has Enterprise made with regard to primary data collection—research approach, contact methods, sampling plan, and research instruments?

3. In addition to or instead of the mail survey, what other means could Enterprise use to gather customer satisfaction information?

4. What specific recommendations would you make to Enterprise to improve the response rate and the timeliness of feedback from the process?

Source: Officials at Enterprise Rent-A-Car contributed to and supported development of this case.

Exhibit 1   Service Quality Survey

Please mark the box that best reflects your response to each question.

	Completely Satisfied	Somewhat Satisfied	Neither Satisfied Nor Dissatisfied	Somewhat Dissatisfied	Completely Dissatisfied
1. Overall, how satisfied were you with your recent car rental from Enterprise on January 1?	☐	☐	☐	☐	☐

2. What, if anything, could Enterprise have done better? (*Please be specific*) _____

_____

3a. Did you experience any problems during the rental process?	Yes ☐ No ☐		3b. If you mentioned any problems to Enterprise, did they resolve them to your satisfaction?	Yes ☐ No ☐ Did not mention ☐

	Excellent	Good	Fair	Poor	N/A
4. If you personally called Enterprise to reserve a vehicle, how would you rate the telephone reservation process?	☐	☐	☐	☐	☐

	Both at start and end of rental	Just at start of rental	Just at end of rental	Neither time
5. Did you go to the Enterprise office. . .	☐	☐	☐	☐

	Both at start and end of rental	Just at start of rental	Just at end of rental	Neither time
6. Did an Enterprise employee give you a ride to help with your transportation needs. . .	☐	☐	☐	☐

7. After you arrived at the Enterprise office, how long did it take you to:	Less than 5 minutes	5–10 minutes	11–15 minutes	16–20 minutes	21–30 minutes	More than 30 minutes	N/A
◆ pick up your rental car?	☐	☐	☐	☐	☐	☐	☐
◆ return your rental car?	☐	☐	☐	☐	☐	☐	☐

8. How would you rate the. . .	Excellent	Good	Fair	Poor	N/A
◆ timeliness with which you were either picked up at the start of the rental or dropped off afterwards?	☐	☐	☐	☐	☐
◆ timeliness with which the rental car was either brought to your location and left with you or picked up from your location afterwards?	☐	☐	☐	☐	☐
◆ Enterprise employee who handled your paperwork. . . at the START of the rental?	☐	☐	☐	☐	☐
at the END of the rental?	☐	☐	☐	☐	☐
◆ mechanical condition of the car?	☐	☐	☐	☐	☐
◆ cleanliness of the car interior/exterior?	☐	☐	☐	☐	☐

	Yes	No	N/A
9. If you asked for a specific type or size of vehicle, was Enterprise able to meet your needs?	☐	☐	☐

	Car repairs due to accident	All other car repairs/ maintenance	Car was stolen	Business	Leisure/ vacation	Some other reason
10. For what reason did you rent this car?	☐	☐	☐	☐	☐	☐

	Definitely will call	Probably will call	Might or might not call	Probably will not call	Definitely will not call
11. The next time you need to pick up a rental car in the city or area in which you live, how likely are you to call Enterprise?	☐	☐	☐	☐	☐

	Once—this was first time	2 times	3–5 times	6–10 times	11 or more times
12. Approximately how many times in total have you rented from Enterprise (including this rental)?	☐	☐	☐	☐	☐

	0 times	1 time	2 times	3–5 times	6–10 times	11 or more times
13. Considering *all rental companies,* approximately how many times *within the past year* have you rented a car in the city or area in which you live (including this rental)?	☐	☐	☐	☐	☐	☐

CHAPTER 6
Consumer Markets and Consumer Buyer Behaviour

AFTER STUDYING THIS CHAPTER, YOU SHOULD BE ABLE TO

1. define the consumer market and construct a simple model of consumer buyer behaviour

2. name the four major factors that influence consumer buyer behaviour

3. list and understand the major types of buying decision behaviour and the stages in the buyer decision process

4. describe the adoption and diffusion process for new products

Previewing the Concepts

In the previous chapter, you studied how marketers obtain, analyze, and use information to identify marketing opportunities and to assess marketing programs. In this and the next chapter, we'll continue with a closer look at the most important element of the marketing environment—customers. The aim of marketing is to somehow affect how customers think about and behave toward the organization and its marketing offers. To affect the whats, whens, and hows of buying behaviour, marketers must first understand the *whys*. In this chapter, we look at *final consumer* buying influences and processes. In the next chapter, we'll study the buying behaviour of *business customers*. You'll see that understanding buying behaviour is an essential but very difficult task.

To get a better sense of the importance of understanding consumer behaviour, let's look first at Harley-Davidson, maker of North America's top-selling heavyweight motorcycles. Who rides these big Harley "Hogs"? What moves them to abandon home and hearth for the open road, and flock to Harley rallies by the hundreds of thousands? *You* might be surprised, but Harley-Davidson knows *very* well.

Harley buyers are granitelike in their devotion to the brand. "You don't see people tattooing Yamaha on their bodies," observes the publisher of *American Iron*, an industry publication. And according to another industry insider, "For a lot of people, it's not that they want a motorcycle; it's that they want a Harley—the brand is that strong."

Each year, in early March, more than 500 000 Harley bikers rumble through the streets of Daytona Beach, Florida, to attend Harley-Davidson's Bike Week celebration. Bikers from Canada and the U.S. lounge on their low-slung Harleys, swap biker tales, and sport T-shirts proclaiming "I'd rather push a Harley than drive a Honda."

Riding such intense emotions, Harley-Davidson has rumbled its way to the top of the heavyweight motorcycle market. Harley's "Hogs" capture one-fifth of all North American bike sales and more than half of the heavyweight segment. For several years running, sales have outstripped supply and waiting lists may be up to two years for popular models. By 2005, the company had experienced nineteen straight years of record sales and income. Its brand has become a cultural icon and communities of consumption have been formed around the brand by its fans. As is the case with any subculture, members of these communities are united by a common language, symbols, attitudes, interests, and behaviours or lifestyles, and being part of the community adds meaning to these consumers' lives.

Although you may think of Harley as the quintessential American brand, it has a long history in Canada. Fred Deeley established the first Canadian dealership in 1917, making it the second-oldest Harley-Davidson dealership in the world. Today the firm acts as the sole distributor for all of Canada, and it is the only Harley distribution system not completely owned and controlled by the American parent. The firm's mission is to see the Harley-Davidson lifestyle as an increasing and permanent part of Canadian society. The firm has been recognized for its efforts and has been placed multiple times on the prestigious list of Canada's 50 Best-Managed Companies. Deeley Harley-Davidson Canada attributes its success to a continuous improvement culture, its commitment to innovation, and customer service excellence. It constantly works to forge new markets for its products. For example, women now make up 14 percent of all new motorcycle purchasers. It also prides itself on its desire to stay close to the customer through efforts such as "The Ride Home From Canada" program, which celebrated the Harley-Davidson 100th Anniversary. The 8400 km cross-country trek brought riders from across Canada. They rode together and raised funds for Muscular Dystrophy Canada.

Harley-Davidson's marketers spend a great deal of time thinking about customers and their buying behaviour. They want to know who their customers are, what they think and how they feel, and why they buy a Harley Fat Boy Softail rather than a Yamaha or a Kawasaki or a big Honda Gold Wing Premium. What is it that makes Harley buyers so fiercely loyal? These are difficult questions; even Harley owners themselves don't know exactly what motivates their buying. But Harley management puts top priority on understanding customers and what makes them tick.

Who rides a Harley? You might be surprised. It's no longer just the Hell's Angels crowd. Motorcycles are attracting a new breed of riders—older, more affluent, and better educated. Harley now appeals more to "rubbies" (rich urban bikers) than to rebels. "While the outlaw bad-boy biker image is what we might typically associate with Harley riders," says an analyst, "they're just as likely to be CEOs and investment bankers." The average Harley customer is a 46-year-old husband with a median household income of more than $80 000.

There's no doubt that Harley-Davidson is a brand icon. As Canadian marketing consultant Elliott Ettenberg notes, this status has been achieved, "Not because the quality is best in class ("Harleys don't leak ... they just mark their spot"). Not because it's the least expensive (the machines are premium priced out of the box but you can run them up $40 000 to $50 000 for a truly unique pig). Not because it operates in a niche marketplace (almost all its product offerings are premium priced in a commodity business). But because at HD, they view the sale of a Harley as the beginning, not the end, of the relationship. They understand that bonding between products and people are a by-product of people bonding with people who share common values. The product is a means to the end.

Take its Harley Owner's Group best customer program, affectionately known as HOG. Members sport Harley clothing and accessories, and buy items as diverse as Harley housewares, shoes, trinkets, wallets, credit cards and watches. HOG members are offered special rates on insurance. They can fly anywhere Harley operates and rent a Harley at a participating dealer in that location for $700 per week. They have their own magazine. In other words, Harley has become a significant part of their lives. They socialize weekly, raise money for charity through poker runs and ride together on weekend events. They are part of a brand community no matter what their socioeconomic status. They are bonded together through their sharing of the Harley brand values of freedom and individuality. This message is consistently and discreetly reinforced at every point of customer contact.

To build this type of relationship, Harley-Davidson first had to gain a better understanding of customers' deeper motivations. It conducted focus groups in which it invited bikers to make cut-and-paste collages of pictures that expressed their feelings about Harley-Davidsons. It then mailed out 16 000 surveys containing a typical battery of psychological, sociological, and demographic questions as well as subjective questions, such as "Is Harley more typified by a brown bear or a lion?"

The research revealed seven core customer types: adventure-loving traditionalists, sensitive pragmatists, stylish status seekers, laid-back campers, classy capitalists, cool-headed loners, and cocky misfits. However, all owners appreciated their Harleys for the same basic reasons. "It didn't matter if you were the guy who swept the floors of the factory or if you were the CEO at that factory, the attraction to Harley was very similar," says a Harley executive. "Independence, freedom, and power were the universal Harley appeals." Says another analyst, "It's much more than a machine.... It is part of their own self expression and lifestyle." As the Harley website's home page announces, "Thumbing the starter of a Harley-Davidson does a lot more than fire the engine. It fires the imagination."

Such strong emotions and motivations are captured in a classic Harley-Davidson advertisement. The ad shows a close-up of an arm, the bicep adorned with a Harley-Davidson tattoo. The headline asks, "When was the last time you felt this strongly about anything?" The ad copy outlines the problem and suggests a solution: "Wake up in the morning and life picks up where it left off.... What once seemed exciting has now become part of the numbing routine. It all begins to feel the same. Except when you've got a Harley-Davidson. Something strikes a nerve. The heartfelt thunder rises up, refusing to become part of the background. Suddenly things are different. Clearer. More real. As they should have been all along. Riding a Harley changes you from within. The effect is permanent. Maybe it's time you started feeling this strongly. Things are different on a Harley."[1]

Consumer buyer behaviour
The buying behaviour of final consumers—individuals and households who buy goods and services for personal consumption.

Consumer market
All the individuals and households who buy or acquire goods and services for personal consumption.

The Harley-Davidson example shows that many different factors affect consumer buyer behaviour. Buying behaviour is never simple, yet understanding it is the essential task of marketing management. First we explore the dynamics of the consumer market and consumer buyer behaviour. In Chapter 7, we examine business markets and the business buying process.

Consumer buyer behaviour refers to the buying behaviour of final consumers—individuals and households who buy goods and services for personal consumption. All of these final consumers combine to make up the **consumer market.** The North American consumer market consists of more than 327 million people (more than 32 million in Canada and more than 295 million in the U.S.) who consume many trillions of dollars' worth of goods and services each year, making it one of the most attractive consumer markets in the world. The world consumer market consists of almost 6.4 *billion* people.[2]

Consumers around the world vary tremendously in age, income, education level, and tastes. They also buy an incredible variety of goods and services. How these diverse consumers connect with each other and with other elements of the world around them affects their choices among various products, services, and companies. Here we examine the fascinating array of factors that affect consumer behaviour.

Model of Consumer Behaviour

Consumers make many buying decisions every day. Most large companies research consumer buying decisions in great detail to answer questions about what consumers buy, where they buy, how and how much they buy, when they buy, and why they buy. Marketers can study actual consumer purchases to find out what they buy, where, and how much. But learning about the *whys* of consumer buyer behaviour is not so easy—the answers are often locked deep within the consumer's head.

Penetrating the dark recesses of the consumer's mind is no easy task. Often, consumers themselves don't know exactly what influences their purchases. "Ninety-five percent of the thought, emotion, and learning [that drive our purchases] occur in the unconscious mind—that is, without our awareness," notes one consumer behaviour expert.[3]

The central question for marketers is: How do consumers respond to various marketing efforts the company might use? The starting point is the stimulus-response model of buyer behaviour shown in Figure 6.1. This figure shows that marketing and other stimuli enter the consumer's "black box" and produce certain responses. Marketers must figure out what is in the buyer's black box.

Marketing stimuli consist of the four *P*s: product, price, place, and promotion. Other stimuli include major forces and events in the buyer's environment: economic, technological, political, and cultural. All these inputs enter the buyer's black box, where they are turned into a set of observable buyer responses: product choice, brand choice, dealer choice, purchase timing, and purchase amount.

Figure 6.1 Model of buyer behaviour

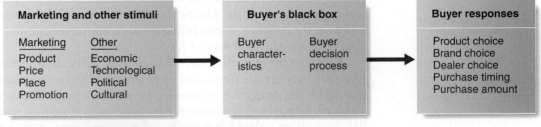

Factors influencing consumer behaviour

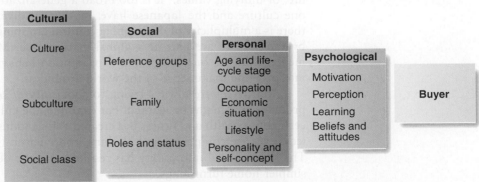

The marketer wants to understand how the stimuli are changed into responses inside the consumer's black box, which has two parts. First, the buyer's characteristics influence how he or she perceives and reacts to the stimuli. Second, the buyer's decision process itself affects the buyer's behaviour. We look first at buyer characteristics as they affect buying behaviour and then discuss the buyer decision process.

Characteristics Affecting Consumer Behaviour

Consumer purchases are influenced strongly by cultural, social, personal, and psychological characteristics, as shown in Figure 6.1. For the most part, marketers cannot control such factors, but they must take them into account.

Cultural Factors

Cultural factors exert a broad and deep influence on consumer behaviour. The marketer needs to understand the role played by the buyer's *culture*, *subculture*, and *social class*.

Culture

Culture

The set of basic values, perceptions, wants, and behaviours learned by a member of society from family and other important institutions.

Although **culture** does not determine behaviour, it is an important influence on a person's wants and behaviour. Human behaviour is largely learned. Growing up in a society, a child learns basic values, perceptions, wants, and behaviours from the family and other important institutions. For example, an American child normally learns or is exposed to the following values: achievement and success, activity and involvement, efficiency and practicality, progress, material comfort, individualism, freedom, humanitarianism, youthfulness, and fitness and health. In contrast, *Maclean's* magazine annual poll of Canadian values suggests that the majority of Canadians treasure freedom, the beauty of our natural landscape, our beliefs in respect, equality, and fair treatment, our flag, our social safety net, our international role, and our multicultural and multiracial makeup. We see ourselves as unique and distinctly different from Americans. One commonality between our two cultures, however, for better or worse, is that we are a consumer culture, and marketing practices reinforce this as a way of life.[4]

Every group or society has a culture, and cultural influences on buying behaviour may vary greatly from country to country. Failure to adjust to these differences can result in ineffective marketing or embarrassing mistakes. It should not be assumed, however, that culture is a homogeneous system of shared meaning, way of life, or unifying values.[5] It is too broad a generalization to say that Canadians have one culture and the Japanese have another. In diverse societies, such as Canada, there is a multiplicity of overlapping cultural groupings. These in turn are influenced by the fact we are part of a global marketplace. Marketing practices and global media influence our values and consumption behaviours and even affect how we interpret and make sense of the world around us.

Marketers are always trying to spot *cultural shifts* in order to discover new products that might be wanted. For example, the cultural shift toward greater concern about health and fitness has created a huge industry for health and fitness services, exercise equipment and clothing, more-natural foods, and a variety of diets. The shift toward informality has resulted in more demand for casual clothing and simpler home furnishings.

Subculture

Each culture contains smaller **subcultures**, or groups of people with shared value systems based on common life experiences and situations. Subcultures may result from differences in nationalities or ethnicity, religions, or geographic regions. Subcultures also form around brands and media vehicles. For example, the *Star Trek* series spawned the formation of a huge subculture that is worldwide. If you search Google for the *Star Trek* culture, you will find more than 11 million pages. Thus, many subcultures make up important market segments, and marketers often design products and marketing programs tailored to their needs. When reading the material on cultures and subcultures, however, one must be cautious not to over-generalize. Though marketers can benefit from the knowledge of these groupings and attitudes held by many within the group, they must not assume that the groups are homogeneous. There are always individuals within these categories who do not follow general trends characterizing the group.

Regionalism   Canada is a regional country, for example, so marketers may develop distinctive programs for the Atlantic provinces, Quebec, Central Canada, the Prairies, and B.C. The sheer size of the country and its varied geographic features and climate have certainly shaped regional character and personality. For example, Atlantic Canada is largely defined by its proximity to and historical relationship with the sea. Equally, the isolation imposed by the mountain barrier, along with the abundance and grandeur of British Columbia's natural environment, shaped the outlook of that region's residents. Immigration has also had a differential effect on the different regions within Canada. The economy of each region furthers these differences. The fate of regions linked to the rise and fall of commodities, such as fish, timber, wheat, minerals, or oil, has affected regional mindsets as well as economies. Perceived disparities in political power have also increased regionalism, especially in Quebec, Newfoundland and Labrador, and Alberta.[6]

Founding Nations   Canada had three founding nations: the English, French, and Aboriginal peoples (some include the Irish and Scottish as well, noting that the Canadian coat of arms reflects their founding nation status). The unique history and language of each of these nations has driven many of the cultural differences that result in different buying behaviours across Canada. The most recent census results (2001) reported that people noting their English language roots (anglophones) accounted for approximately 59 percent of the population, people whose mother tongue is French (francophones) made up approximately 23 percent of the population, and those reporting Aboriginal ancestry represented 4.4 percent of the total population. Canadian law, for example, makes it mandatory that nutritional information on food labels be bilingual. (See Real Marketing 6.1 on page 210 for more insight on marketing to French-Canadian consumers.)

Aboriginal Canadians are making their voices heard both in the political arena and in the marketplace. There are more than 983 000 Aboriginal Canadians, including Métis and Inuit. Among Canada's Aboriginal population, Cree is reported as the most common mother tongue. Not only do Native Canadians have distinct cultures that influence their values and purchasing behaviour, but they also have profoundly influenced the rest of Canada through their art, love of nature, and concern for the environment.

Banks have been particularly responsive to the unique needs of Aboriginal Canadians.[7] Scotiabank, for example, has maintained its relationship with Aboriginal people through its three on-reserve branches and twenty-four Aboriginal banking centres. It also uses a lot of grassroots marketing and public relations efforts, including its sponsorship of the Aboriginal Achievement Awards and ten annual scholarships of $2500 for young Aboriginal entrepreneurs. Publications, like *Windspeaker* magazine, can be used as vehicles to effectively advertise to Canada's Aboriginal peoples.

Windspeaker magazine is one tool promoted by the Aboriginal Multi-Media Society (AMMSA) to assist marketers who want to communicate with Canada's Aboriginal peoples effectively and efficiently.

Ethnic Consumers   According to Statistics Canada, roughly one out of every five people in Canada could be a member of a visible minority by 2017, when Canada celebrates its 150th anniversary. Two hundred thousand new immigrants come to Canada each year.[8] Thus, being sensitive to their cultural values is important, because 70 percent of the visible minority population were born outside Canada. According to Balmoral Marketing, an ethnic ad agency in Toronto, many firms are now spending as much as 15 percent of their total communications budget on ethnic marketing.[9] People with a Chinese background are still the largest group among visible minorities in Canada. According to a 2006 *Marketing Magazine* report, 3.74 percent of Canada's population is Chinese, with 40 percent of this group residing in Toronto and 31 percent living in Vancouver. The average Chinese household spends $63 500 each year, slightly higher than the Canadian average of $58 500. People of South Asian origin (currently 23 percent of visible minorities) may represent as large a marketplace by 2017. According to a recent survey, 50 percent of South Asians say their opinion of a company would improve if they saw the ads on South Asian TV, and 62 percent stated that they would look more positively on companies that sponsored community events. When asked for advice on how to communicate to ethnic markets, Chris Bhang, VP group account director, Allard Johnson Direct, speaking at the 2005 Canadian Marketing Association's Diversity Conference said, "Be colloquial, be creative but be relevant."

Madonna Lee, ethnic marketing manager at Rogers Wireless in Toronto seems to have mastered this advice. Rogers has been aiming at making its products and services more culturally relevant, and a 2006 campaign that ran in January over Chinese New Year, was an insightful example of how a company can better serve the $20 billion Chinese-Canadian marketplace. In the campaign, Rogers encouraged

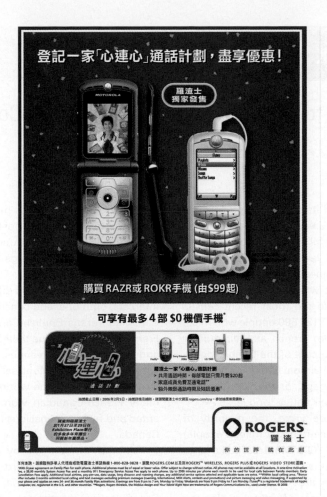

Rogers' insightful campaign targeting Canadians of Chinese origin has helped it build satisfaction and loyalty among people from this important marketplace.

consumers of Chinese origin to send a text message, "Kung Hci Fat Choy"—the international greeting meaning "congratulations and be prosperous"—for the Chinese New Year. Rogers' customers who sent the greeting to China, Taiwan, or Hong Kong could enter a contest to win a trip to one of those countries, and they could also download New Year's ring tones onto their cellphones. As Lee noted, Rogers' research showed that even though the younger second generation is fluent in English, "they feel respected if we communicate with them in their own language," and this helps promote increased customer loyalty.[10]

People who identified themselves as "black" in the 2001 census are Canada's third largest visible minority.[11] While some members of this group trace their ancestry back to Africa, many others have more recently immigrated from the Caribbean. See what Western Union did to attract Toronto's Caribbean community:

> One of Western Union's major strategies is to target communities, such as Toronto's Caribbean community, who find it important to keep in touch with people from their native countries. They may use Western Union to wire money back to family members. To reach this audience, Western Union has been an official sponsor of the Caribana festival for many years. Between 750 000 and one million people converge on Toronto for the Caribana festival each year, making it one of the largest cultural festivals. Since it is a Caribbean tradition to use a little towel, handkerchief, or scrap of cloth to wave to music, Western Union printed yellow and black handkerchiefs with their logo and gave them away to people to wave during the parade and other festivities. The idea gave Western Union an extremely high profile at the event and helped it communicate its product message effectively with this community.[12]

REAL MARKETING

Marketing to Quebec and French-Canadian Consumers

Quebec has long prided itself on being a "distinct society." Marketers must be aware of Quebec's uniqueness if they are to be successful in the province. Quebec is characterized by unique laws, a different mix of indigenous and national businesses and industries, and distinct attitudes and values when compared with the rest of Canada. According to the most recent census data, almost 6 million of the 7 125 580 people who make up Quebec's population claim French as their mother tongue (this equates to 81 percent of the Quebec population). This is compared with almost 600 000 who claim English as their native language, or the 700 000 who note another language as their native tongue.

Known for their *joie de vivre*, the majority of Quebec's population (52 percent, or 3.7 million people) lived in the Montreal area in 2001. Montreal has a large number of high-tech industries. As well as being the second-largest metropolitan area in Canada (behind Toronto and leading Vancouver), Montreal is also the second-largest French-speaking city in the world. One must not assume that the population of the Montreal region is homogeneous and made up only of francophones, however. Bilingualism is very common, and like other large Canadian cities, the population is diverse as a result of immigration, though Montreal does not receive as many immigrants as Toronto or Vancouver.

To protect its French culture and affirm the province's French-speaking identity, successive Quebec governments have passed legislation to ensure the use of French in the various areas of public life. Education in the province is also mostly in French, although it is also available in English.

Marketers who want to appeal to Quebec consumers need to do more than communicate in French, using dictionary translations of words. Language and the meanings derived from it are very cultural and context-based. Take a successful campaign by the Bank of Montreal that used the tag line, "Profitez." You wouldn't fully understand the campaign if you used only a dictionary-based interpretation of the word. Dictionaries say *profitez* equates to "profit from," "to profit," "to earn," or "something profitable." However, for Quebec consumers the meaning is more nuanced. They translate it as to "make the most of it," "enjoy," or "take advantage," and it is strongly associated with the enjoyment of life, meanings that make the campaign more powerful and rich.

Research has revealed differences in the activities, interests, opinions, and consumption habits of French-Canadian versus English-Canadian consumers. Many French Canadians value their European roots, their rich and diverse cultural venues, gourmet food, and fine wines. As a result, Montreal is known as one of the trendiest centres in the world. Research suggests that many French-Canadian women are more family oriented and fashion conscious than women in the rest of Canada.

A study undertaken by S.C. Johnson suggested that even attitudes toward cleaning vary between English and French Canada. Although many English Canadians just want to get the job done and see cleaning as a necessary evil, many people in Quebec get a sense of pride and accomplishment after they clean. Using this research, S.C. Johnson designed a highly successful campaign for its cleaning products that centred on the distinctly Québécois custom of July 1, Moving Day—the date on which people tend to move from one apartment to another because leases in Quebec traditionally expire on June 30.

Such differences are partly derived from culture; their Latin roots may make many French Canadians more emotional and impulsive. Demographic and socioeconomic differences also exist: education and income are both lower in Quebec than in Ontario. The legal environment is also different for marketers in Quebec. Besides strict language laws, there are stronger restrictions on advertising to children, for example. To be successful in French Canada, marketers must develop appeals that take these differences into account. For example, although many marketers are using national symbols to appeal to their customers, the separatist sentiments held by some Quebecers may make this an unwise choice for some marketers.

Quebec also has a distinct business and retail climate. Lavo Group, for example, is a packaged-goods manufacturer whose products rival those of Procter & Gamble and Colgate in the province. Many Québécois buy such Lavo products as La Parisienne laundry detergent and fabric softener instead of Tide and Downy, Hertel liquid cleanser instead of Mr. Clean, and Old Dutch powder cleanser instead of Comet. The financial services industry is also very different in Quebec than it is in the rest of Canada. Two players that are almost non-existent in English Canada, the Mouvement Desjardins (the federation of Quebec credit unions) and the National Bank, account for more than 60 percent of the province's financial services marketplace. Both organizations utilize integrated and Quebec-specific communications campaigns.

Quebec-based hardware chains Réno-Depot and RONA have many loyal customers in the province. When Home Depot entered Quebec in 2000, it had to compete with these companies—a completely different set of competitors than it had confronted in the rest of Canada. To help Home Depot gain acceptance, Montreal-based Cossette Communications developed an advertising campaign that appealed to Quebecers' unique sense of humour. Rather than creating ads with rational appeals that proclaimed Home Depot's high-

LE PETIT MEC

DICTIONNAIRE ILLUSTRÉ DU MATÉRIEL D'ACTIVITÉS DE GRANDE NATURE

M

MOUNTAIN EQUIPMENT CO-OP

MEC's respect for the Quebec culture, its long history of social and environment values, and the major investment it made in "francization" helped this B.C.-based retailer win over French Canadian consumers.

quality service, Cossette conducted qualitative research to uncover examples of realistic and believable bad shopping experiences of Quebec consumers. The campaign that resulted from this research features one commercial that shows a clerk literally running away from a client. In another commercial, a group of clerks chant, "It is not my department" despite customers' looks of dismay. The campaign not only created awareness of Home Depot, but it was also listed among Montrealers' favourite commercials in a recent survey.

For a long time, Quebec lagged the rest of Canada in terms of Internet adoption and usage. Today, however, more than 60 percent of Quebec adults are online. There are a growing number of French sites and online services, such as La Toile du Quebec (www.toile.qc.ca) and PetitMonde (www.petitmonde.com/), as well as the French versions of popular portals like Sympatico, Yahoo!, and MSN. Marketers have been quick to leverage this new interconnectivity. Volkswagen, Avon, L'Oréal, and La Senza are some of the Quebec-based companies that have jumped on the bandwagon. Not only are they building French versions of their company websites, they have intensified their email marketing campaigns in the province. The race is on to build databases to further this effort. Sympatico.ca, for example, has an opt-in email database of 700 000 French Canadians, comprising adults aged 25 to 49, most with families.

If marketers respect Quebec's unique laws with regard to contests and sweepstakes, they can utilize these tools to help build their databases. Sympatico.ca experienced phenomenal results when it ran a contest to meet Bryan Adams in Scotland. People had to register online, and Sympatico amassed 20 000 new Quebec subscribers as a result of this campaign. As their marketing manager noted, "French-speaking people love to play. And because they love to play, they tend to give their personal information freely—and by that I mean their postal code, age, and gender." Marketers have to tread softly, however. Quebecers still like to be wooed, especially when it comes to developing a one-to-one relationship. People from Quebec prefer more face-to-face interactions and personal contact than do people from the rest of the country.

Marketers must also be aware that Quebec has its own icons and unique media personalities. For example, Bell Canada's long-running Monsieur B campaign, which originated in 1992, is almost unknown in the rest of Canada. However, it has approached legendary status in the province, the way other advertising icons like the Green Giant, Aunt Jemima, and the lonely Maytag repairman have done in the rest of Canada. Jean-François Richard, vice-president, marketing communications at Bell in Montreal, notes, "I don't know of any

creative platform (anywhere) that has lasted so long and generated such results for so long for any advertiser!"

Because of all of these differences, many marketers develop unique programs designed just for the Quebec marketplace. Take the case of Mountain Equipment Co-op. Even though it has a very small annual budget of $40 000 devoted to the Montreal, Quebec City, and the French part of Ottawa markets, MEC tailors its campaigns to the unique perceptions of the French-speaking marketplace. For example, Louise Abrique, director of French marketing, had four staffers kayak down the St. Lawrence River with the new store's front door key for the grand opening of the Quebec City store. The event generated tremendous media coverage. She also developed "Le Petit MEC," a visual dictionary of more than 6000 words that translated all of the company's products into French. The glossary received a Mérite du français award from L'Office québécois de la langue française last year, garnering even more publicity. MEC, a western-based retailer, saw its membership jump from 75 000 to 200 000 in Quebec in just two years, and sales from the

Quebec City and Montreal stores are projected to make up 17 percent of MEC's national sales. What were the secrets to success? According to Louise Arbique, it's respect for the culture, MEC's long history of social and environment values, and the major investment it made in "francization." "Quebecers share MEC values," she says. "People really appreciate that they feel respected in their language and their culture, and we worked very hard to adapt MEC for the Quebecers."

Sources: Eve Lazarus, "Getting into Gear," *Marketing*, June 13, 2005; "Vive la difference: Does that mean I have to have a separate campaign?" *Strategy*, October 15, 2004; Nicolette Flemming, "The True Meaning of 'Profitez'," *Marketing*, June 10, 2002, p. 31; "Quebec success: Weather Network and Dairy Farmers of Canada hit the right formula," *Strategy*, October 15, 2004, p. 32; Bernadette Johnson, "Email Marketing Begins to Flourish in La Belle Province," *Strategy*, May 20, 2002, p. D10; Helena Katz, "Johnson Sharpens Its Quebec Strategy," *Marketing*, October 12, 1998, p. 3; Danny Kucharsky, "Monsieur B's Family," *Marketing*, June 11, 2001; Nathalie Fortier, "Building Success: How Cossette Poked Fun at Bad Customer Service to Give Home Depot a Firm Foundation in Quebec," *Marketing*, September 24, 2001; Tracey Arial, "Taking Aim at the Giants, *Marketing*, June 11, 2001.

Canada is increasingly becoming a multilingual society. Statistics Canada reports that one out of every six Canadians reported having a mother tongue other than English or French—in fact, more than 100 languages were reported in the 2001 census. Some marketers who resist ethnic marketing claim they don't know enough about these markets, fear that they may make a mistake, or say there are just too many languages to deal with to effectively tailor their campaigns.[13] They are neglecting a sizable market. Allophones, people who report a mother tongue other than English or French, exceed 5.3 million, or 18 percent of the population (up from 16.6 percent in the 1996 census). People who speak Mandarin or Cantonese form the third-most-common language group in Canada, followed by Italian, German, Punjabi, and Spanish.

Mature Consumers   Though age is a demographic variable, some researchers also contend that different age cohorts have distinct cultures. Median age in Canada, 37.6 years according to the 2001 census, is higher than ever before (median age is defined as the point where exactly one-half of the population is older, and the other half is younger). According to the 1996 census, the median age was 35.3. This increase in median age was the biggest census-to-census increase in a century. To see how rapidly the Canadian population has aged, it is interesting to note that the median age in Canada in 1966 (the year when the last of the baby boomers was born) was 25.4 years. Thus, today Canada's working-age population is dominated by older individuals, but there are regional variations. Nova Scotia and Quebec have the oldest populations. Each has a median age of 38.8 years. Alberta is the youngest, with a median age of 35.0. Because of high immigration rates, however, Canada's population is not aging as fast as the population of the United States.

The greying of Canada means that companies will have to do more than pay lip service to the idea of marketing to older people. Yet, businesses are not going to suddenly lose all interest in the 18–34 demographic. Instead, companies will have to learn to establish brands that attract older consumers without alienating younger ones. One example: a recent Pepsi commercial features a teenage boy in the middle of a mosh pit at a rock concert. He turns around to discover his father rocking nearby. People aren't considered over the hill at fifty anymore. Smart marketers will capitalize on this knowledge and create the image of an ageless society where people define themselves more by the activities they're involved in than by their age. For instance, university students can be twenty, thirty, or sixty years old.[14]

Mature consumers are better off financially than are younger consumer groups. Because mature consumers have more time and money, they are an ideal market for exotic travel, restaurants, high-tech home entertainment products, leisure goods and services, designer furniture and fashions, financial services, and health care services. Their desire to look as young as they feel also makes more-mature consumers good candidates for cosmetics and personal care products, health foods, fitness products, and other items that combat the effects of aging. The best strategy is to appeal to their active, multidimensional lives. For example, Kellogg aired a TV spot for All-Bran cereal in which individuals ranging in age from fifty-three to eighty-one are featured playing ice hockey, water skiing, running hurdles, and playing baseball, all to the tune of "Wild Thing."[15]

Social Class

Social classes

Relatively permanent and ordered divisions in a society whose members share similar values, interests, and behaviours.

Almost every society has some form of social class structure. **Social classes** are society's relatively permanent and ordered divisions. In some social systems, members of different classes are reared for certain roles and can change their social position only with great difficulty. In North America, however, the lines between social classes are not fixed and rigid; people can move to a higher social class or drop into a lower one.

According to the *Canadian Encyclopedia*, social class is understood in two ways. The first view examines social class based upon differences in occupation, income, education, wealth, status, and residence, and society is divided into categories such as upper, middle, and lower classes. The cost of entering the upper classes is going up. If the Barenaked Ladies were to write their famous song "If I Had a Million Dollars" today, they would need $10 million dollars to be rich. There are approximately 180 000 Canadians, or 58 065 Canadian families, who have socked away this cool sum. Marketers from organizations as diverse as financial institutions to luxury vacation providers scramble to serve this elite market. The gap between rich and poor is growing. The annual income of the top 1 percent of Canadian wage earners was $469 656 in 2000 (compared with $359 143 in 1990), while the annual income for the bottom 10 percent of working Canadians was $10 341 (compared with $10 260 in 1990).[16]

The second definition of social class is derived from ideas most often found in theories of socialism. Under this mode of thinking, social class is determined by whether people own the "means of production" (for example, land, resources, factories, etc.) or their "labour power" (for example, skill, strength, experience). People following the second view see society comprising two major classes, the "bourgeoisie" or middle class, and the "proletariat" or working class. In the socialist analysis, the middle class has most of the power. For example, although business people and professionals make up only 10 percent of the Canadian population, they account for 75 percent of those active in politics. Similarly, the poorest 20 percent of Canadians receive only 6.5 percent of total national income, while the richest 20 percent get 38.4 percent. Socialists therefore believe that the working class must win more power. No matter what system is used to understand the stratifications within society, the resulting system is often not always easy to apply. For example, where do managers belong? They may have a lot of power, but they often do not own things directly related to the business or production.[17]

Most Canadians see themselves as middle class, and we are less willing to think of ourselves in terms of social class than our neighbours south of the border. It is for this reason that the New Democratic Party no longer tries to appeal to "the working class" but to "ordinary Canadians." Marketers are interested in social class because people within a given social class may tend to share certain attitudes and lifestyles and may exhibit similar buying behaviour and product and brand preferences.

Social Factors

A consumer's behaviour also is influenced by social factors, such as the consumer's *small groups*, *family*, and *social roles* and *status*.

Groups

Group

Two or more people who interact to accomplish individual or mutual goals.

A person's behaviour is influenced by many small **groups**. Groups that have a direct influence and to which a person belongs are called *membership groups*. In contrast, *reference groups* serve as direct (face-to-face) or indirect points of comparison or reference in forming a person's attitudes or behaviour. People often are influenced by reference groups to which they do not belong. For example, an *aspirational group* is one to which the individual wishes to belong, as when a teenage hockey player hopes to play someday for the Calgary Flames. Marketers try to identify the reference groups of their target markets. Reference groups expose a person to new behaviours and lifestyles, influence the person's attitudes and self-concept, and create pressures to conform that may affect the person's product and brand choices.

The importance of group influence varies across products and brands. It tends to be strongest when the product is visible to others whom the buyer respects. Manufacturers of products and brands subjected to strong group influence must figure out how to reach **opinion leaders**—people within a reference group who, because of special skills, knowledge, personality, or other characteristics, exert influence on others. One expert calls them *the influentials*. "They drive trends, influence mass opinion and, most importantly, sell a great many products," he says.

Opinion leader

Person within a reference group who, because of special skills, knowledge, personality, or other characteristics, exerts influence on others.

Many marketers try to identify opinion leaders for their products and direct marketing efforts toward them. They use *buzz marketing* by enlisting or even creating opinion leaders to spread the word about their brands. L'Oréal Canada, for example, launched its Vibrantly Natural Colour Gel using buzz. A brightly painted semi-trailer

BzzAgent, a marketing consulting firm, helps its clients create buzz about their products. It has a volunteer army of 25 000 natural-born buzzers, who are given sample products. If they deem them authentically worth talking about, they begin the word of mouth communication so essential to buzz.

travelled to hot spots in Montreal, Toronto, and Vancouver. Each stop drew crowds of young women who not only sampled the product but also passed along the news to their friends. Some attempts to create buzz aren't so successful, however. In 2005, McDonalds offered to pay rappers $1 to $5 each time songs plugging its products were played on the radio according to *Advertising Age*. McDonald's effort was labelled an "unfortunate moment in advertising," however, and many decried the effort claiming it took away from the essence of hip hop culture, which is prized as an authentic, unprovoked, and uncontrolled commentary of society.[18]

Karl Moore, a marketing professor at McGill University and his colleague Laura Mingail, who has years of experience in the music industry, researched the history of buzz marketing. Buzz marketing was born when Russell Simmons' rap group Run DMC launched their 1986 song "My Adidas." After its release, the song quickly became a symbol of 1980s rap culture. More recently, McDonald's used the technique with its "I'm Lovin' It" campaign, in which it commissioned local urban market specialists across Canada to give street cred to the slogan prior to the official launch. Moore and Mingail note, "Buzz, the love child of strategic marketing and public relations, has been key in establishing street credibility for brands targeting the billion-dollar urban lifestyle market worldwide. This market is not an urban myth. It is arguably the top aspirational luxury lifestyle of the youth market. The same market that has been burning an increasing sum of money on items like Phat Farm polo T-shirts that cost $75 or more." To be successful using buzz, they offer several key pointers:

- Be exclusive—a successful buzz targeting urban youth should be perceived as privileged information.
- Be original—If you try to imitate other successful buzz tactics, you risk having your brand perceived as the "follower" as opposed to the "cool brand."
- Stay true to your brand: You can't go against your brand's heritage. If your brand is firmly established as a family brand or a commercial teen brand, it may be hard to create true street credibility.
- Know where that buzz comes from: Buzz is created by word of mouth, which has a strong effect on shaping first impressions of your brand. You'll have a hard time conveying the message that your brand is "cool" if the person passing on the message isn't a true tastemaker.
- Act locally: Celebrities doing marketing for the money don't create authentic buzz. Extensive databases are needed to tap each local market to determine the best buzz tactics.[19]

Family

Family members can strongly influence buyer behaviour. The family is the most important consumer buying organization in society, and it has been researched extensively. Marketers are interested in the roles and influence of the husband, wife, and children on the purchase of different products and services.

Husband–wife involvement varies widely by product category and by stage in the buying process. Buying roles change with evolving consumer lifestyles. In Canada and the United States, the wife traditionally has been the main purchasing agent for the family in the areas of food, household products, and clothing. But with 70 percent of women holding jobs outside the home and the willingness of husbands to do more of the family's purchasing, all this is changing. For example, in 1978 only 10 percent of males were classified as primary shoppers, but in 1998 the figure had risen to 17 percent. *Canadian Grocer* magazine estimates that 25 to 30 percent of men now grocery shop. Some males are forced into the role of shopper by demographic and lifestyle changes, such as late marriage and high divorce rates, but most

In 2006, Lowe's announced its entry into the Canadian market. Lowe's targets women shoppers, who initiate 80 percent of all home-improvement decisions. "Lure women, and they'll drag their Tim Allen tool guy husbands behind them."

take on the role as a result of being part of a time-pressed, two-income household. Whereas women make up just 40 percent of drivers, they now influence more than 80 percent of car-buying decisions. Men now account for about 40 percent of all food-shopping dollars. In all, North American women now make almost 85 percent of all purchases, spending US$6 trillion each year.[20]

Canadian families are changing and marketers need to be aware of these changes to be effective. First, people are staying single longer. For example, more than half of all Canadian men in their late twenties are single, whereas in the '70s, only one in five was. This helps explain why the men's personal care market has experienced double-digit growth and why 65 percent of men think boys should learn how to cook.

Second, there aren't as many kids. Fertility rates have fallen to an all-time low of 1.52 children per woman (compared with 2.08 in the United States). Third, according to Statistics Canada, these lower fertility rates, combined with higher divorce and separation rates, result in more smaller families, one-child couples, childless couples, single parents, and lone homeowners. In fact, today there are as many single-person households (2.98 million) as there are households with four or more persons (2.94 million).

What does this mean for marketers? Consider these examples. Many singles in need of companionship have adored pets and indulge them with everything from designer clothing to natural food pet food products. Appliance manufacturers can expect a boom in sales with increasing demand for individual units, but companies selling baby products, such as disposable diapers, or family products, such as minivans, may face troubled times. It's not surprising that minivan sales, for example, dropped by 14 percent in 2004.

Fourth, it should also be noted that when families have children, there is often only one child, and a lot of emotion and energy is now being fixated that single offspring. Not surprisingly, marketers are seeing a huge opportunity here. As one such parent notes, "We've spoiled him rotten. It's obscene. At one point he had all three popular gaming stations, PlayStation, Xbox, and Nintendo GameCube. Now he's also got a GameBoy handheld."

Fifth, despite the drop in birth rates, more and more families are experiencing a contrasting phenomena where cash-strapped, debt-laden adult children are staying home or returning home (41 percent of young adults ages 20 to 29 still living with their parents). Author Michael Adams, who is also the co-founder of research firm Environics in Toronto, says this generation of young Canadians is quite different from baby boomers at the same age who couldn't wait to get out on their own. "These kids in their twenties and mid-thirties have a significant connection to their parents. They are more like the old farm families, looking to have financial connections."

Finally, combine children staying at home with the fact that many baby boomer families also have their aged parents living with them, and you see households bursting at the seams. These "multi-generational" families are increasing in number, and nearly half a million grandparents live in households with their children and grandchildren. It's not surprising, therefore, that marketers will need more diversified strategies to reach the many new types of Canadian families.

Despite the different generations that may be sharing the same living space, the challenge, as Adams sees it, is that the traditional family unit is becoming increasingly atomized. "It used to be that the home was where people sat around the dinner table and spent time together, and that is not happening as much," he says. Technology, rather than making life simpler is making it more complex and is actually disconnecting household members. Children are in their rooms doing homework on their computers, teens are text messaging on their cellphones, and parents in two-income homes are using their BlackBerries. Despite this physical separation, the views of all family members, including children, are often listened to during major purchase decisions, such as those for cars or vacations.

People seeking more "quality time" together present a huge market for experiential opportunities, such as family day trips, a ski travel package, even simply going

Organizations targeting families, like the Family Channel, must be aware of the many changes affecting this group.

Canadian Tire Petroleum's new Q stores have been designed with Canada's time-strapped families in mind.

out for dinner. Combine this separation with how time-strapped many two-income families are today, and it's not surprising that 87 percent of Canadian men believe they should work less and spend more time with their family. New retail concepts are being born to address this need. Take, for example, Canadian Tire Petroleum's new Q stores, which sell groceries, caramel frappuccinos, and rotisserie chicken as well as gas. You can pick up milk for your child's morning cereal and a high-quality birthday card for your mother-in-law. Peter Kilty, Toronto-based president of Canadian Tire Petroleum says, "We talk about it as the ultimate convenience centre—it saves you time and makes your life easier. It's been designed with the customer in mind—they're time starved, they want quality products, they want them quickly and they want a great experience."[21]

Roles and Status

A person belongs to many groups—family, clubs, organizations. The person's position in each group can be defined in terms of both role and status. A *role* consists of the activities people are expected to perform according to the persons around them. Each role carries a *status* reflecting the general esteem given to it by society.

People usually choose products appropriate to their roles and status. Consider the various roles a working mother plays. In her company, she plays the role of a brand manager; in her family, she plays the role of wife and mother; at her favourite sporting events, she plays the role of avid fan. As a brand manager, she will buy the kind of clothing that reflects her role and status in her company. As a recreational tennis player, she might choose a medium-priced Wilson tennis racquet.

Personal Factors

A buyer's decisions also are influenced by personal characteristics, such as the buyer's *age* and *life-cycle stage*, *occupation*, *economic situation*, *lifestyle*, and *personality* and *self-concept*.

Age and Life-Cycle Stage

People change the goods and services they buy over their lifetimes. Tastes in food, clothes, furniture, and recreation are often age related. Buying is also shaped by the stage of the *family life cycle*—the stages through which families might pass as they mature over time. Marketers often define their target markets in terms of life-cycle stage and develop appropriate products and marketing plans for each stage.

Traditional family life-cycle stages include young singles and married couples with children. Today, however, marketers are increasingly catering to a growing number of alternative, nontraditional stages, such as unmarried couples, singles marrying later in life, childless couples, same-sex couples, single parents, extended parents (those with young adult children returning home), and others.

Sony recently overhauled its marketing approach in order to target products and services to consumers based on their life stages. It created a new unit called the Consumer Segment Marketing Division, which has identified seven life-stage segments. They include, among others, Gen Y (under 25), young professionals/DINKs (double income no kids, 25 to 34), families (35 to 54), and Zoomers (55 and over). A recent Sony ad aimed at Zoomers, people who have just retired or are close to doing so, shows a man living his dream by going into outer space. The ad deals not just with going into retirement, but with the psychological life-stage changes that go with it. "The goal is to get closer to consumers," says a Sony segment marketing executive.[22]

Occupation

A person's occupation affects the goods and services bought. Blue-collar workers tend to buy more rugged work clothes, whereas executives buy more business suits. Marketers try to identify the occupational groups that have an above-average interest in their products and services. A company can even specialize in making products needed by a given occupational group.

For example, Carhartt makes rugged, durable, no-nonsense work clothes. "From coats to jackets, bibs to overalls ... if the apparel carries the name Carhartt, the performance will be legendary." Its website carries real-life testimonials of hardworking Carhartt customers. One electrician, battling the cold in Canada's Arctic region, reports wearing Carhartt's lined Arctic bib overalls, Arctic jacket, and other clothing for more than two years without a single "popped button, ripped pocket seam, or stuck zipper."[23]

Sometimes moving from being associated with one occupation level to another can be challenging. See what Mark's Work Wearhouse is doing:[24]

Michael Strachan is the first marketing VP in Calgary-based Mark's Work Wearhouse's 28-year history (the firm owns L'Équipeur stores in Quebec). The retail chain is now owned by Canadian Tire. The chain is on a growth spurt, expanding from 320 stores across Canada to more than 400. His aim is to turn the store into a "Canadian super brand." To accomplish this aim, he must reinvent its brand image in the minds of Canadian consumers so it can compete more successfully against powerhouse competitors such as Wal-Mart and Costco. Strachan, a firm believer in extensive consumer research, began the journey with qualitative research that included customer exit interviews. Members of his marketing team also "physically went out and sat in the closets of a number of Canadians to try and understand how they thought about clothes and what they wanted in clothes." Next, more than 1000 English- and French-speaking Canadians between 30 and 55 were invited to attend focus groups in Vancouver, Edmonton, Toronto, Calgary, Montreal, and Quebec City. Though 95 percent of those interviewed were aware of the Mark's Work Wearhouse name, 66 percent thought of Mark's as primarily a blue-collar, workwear store. Although workwear continues to make up a healthy 25 percent of sales, Mark's now carries a much larger selection of items and is focused on men's and women's casual clothing. Thus, Strachan's job was to convince consumers "that we aren't about blue-collar clothes, but about clothes that work." This has become its major brand

Using thorough research and powerful advertising, Mark's Work Wearhouse has transformed itself into a Canadian superbrand using the slogan "clothes that work."

proposition and a company mantra "that's on every single thing from the smallest indoor sign to the biggest billboard."

Economic Situation

A person's economic situation will affect product choice. Marketers of income-sensitive goods watch trends in personal income, savings, and interest rates. If economic indicators point to a recession, marketers can take steps to redesign, reposition, and reprice their products closely. Some marketers target consumers who have lots of money and resources, charging prices to match. For example, Rolex positions it luxury watches as "a tribute to elegance, and object of passion, a symbol for all time." Other marketers target consumers with more modest means. Timex makes more affordable watches that "take a licking and keep on ticking."

Lifestyle

Lifestyle
A person's pattern of living as expressed in his or her activities, interests, and opinions.

People coming from the same subculture, social class, and occupation may have quite different lifestyles. **Lifestyle** is a person's pattern of living as expressed in his or her *psychographics*. It involves measuring consumers' major *AIO dimensions—activities* (work, hobbies, shopping, sports, social events), *interests* (food, fashion, family, recreation), and *opinions* (about themselves, social issues, business, products). Lifestyle captures something more than the person's social class or personality. It profiles a person's whole pattern of acting and interacting in the world.

Several research firms have developed lifestyle classifications. The most widely used is the SRI Consulting's *Values and Lifestyles (VALS)* typology (see Figure 6.2). VALS classifies people according to how they spend their time and money. It divides consumers into eight groups based on two major dimensions: primary motivation and resources. *Primary motivations* include ideals, achievement, and self-expression. According to SRI Consulting, consumers who are primarily motivated

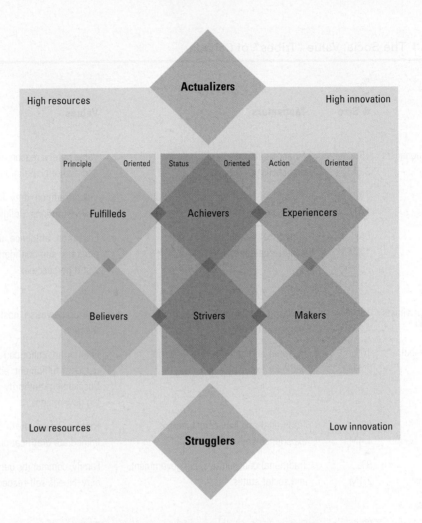

Figure 6.2 VALS™ lifestyle classifications

by ideals are guided by knowledge and principles. Consumers who are primarily motivated by *achievement* look for products and services that demonstrate success to their peers. Consumers who are primarily motivated by *self-expression* desire social or physical activity, variety, and risk.

Consumers within each orientation are further classified into those with *high resources* and those with *low resources*, depending on whether they have high or low levels of income, education, health, self-confidence, energy, and other factors. Consumers with either very high or very low levels of resources are classified without regard to their primary motivations (innovators, survivors). Innovators are people with so many resources that they exhibit all three primary motivations in varying degrees. In contrast, survivors are people with so few resources that they do not show a strong primary motivation. They must focus on meeting needs rather than fulfilling desires.

Michael Adams, president of Environics Research Group Ltd. (http://erg.environics.net), wrote *Sex in the Snow: Canadian Social Values at the End of the Millennium* to capture significant psychographic changes in the Canadian marketplace. His classification system begins with demographic factors as he divides the Canadian population along age-based lines into three groups: those over 50, baby boomers, and Generation Xers. Furthermore, he asserts that eleven value-based "tribes" exist within these broader groups. Table 6.1 provides descriptions of these groups.

Understanding lifestyle categories, such as VALS or the Tribes of Canada, can make or break a marketing initiative. See how Dose used lifestyle to build a brand:[25]

TABLE 6.1 The Social Value "Tribes" of Canada

Groups	% Pop. & Size	Motivators	Values	Exemplar
The Elders:				
Rational Traditionalists	15% 3.5M	Financial independence, stability, and security.	Value safety, reason, tradition, and authority. Religious.	Winston Churchill
Extroverted Traditionalists	7% 1.7M	Traditional communities and institutions.	Value tradition, duty, family, and institutions. Religious.	Jean Chrétien
Cosmopolitan Modernists	6% 1.4M	Traditional institutions. Nomadic, experience-seeking.	Education, affluence, innovation, progress, self-confidence, world perspective.	Pierre Trudeau
The Boomers:				
Disengaged Darwinists	18% 4.3M	Financial independence, stability, and security.	Self-preservation, nostalgia for the past.	Ralph Klein
Autonomous Rebels	10% 2.4M	Personal autonomy, self-fulfillment, and new experiences.	Egalitarian; abhor corruption; personal fulfillment; education. Suspicion of authority and big government.	Michael Moore (*Bowling for Columbine*)
Connected Enthusiasts	6% 1.4M	Traditional and new communities; experience-seeking.	Family, community, hedonism, immediate gratification.	Madonna
Anxious Communitarians	9% 2.1M	Traditional communities, big government, and social status.	Family, community, generosity, duty. Needs self-respect. Fearful.	Oprah Winfrey
The Gen-Xers:				
Aimless Dependents	8% 1.9M	Financial independence, stability, security.	Desire for independence. Disengagement. Fearful.	Eminem, Courtney Love, the Osbournes
Thrill-Seeking Materialists	7% 1.7M	Traditional communities, social status, experience-seeking.	Money, material possessions. recognition, living dangerously.	Richard Branson (Virgin Inc.), *Survivor* participants
Autonomous Postmaterialists	6% 1.4M	Personal autonomy and self-fulfillment.	Freedom, human rights, egalitarian, quality of life.	Naomi Klein (author of *No Logo*), Bono of U2
Social Hedonists	4% 9M	Experience-seeking, new communities.	Esthetics, hedonism, sexual freedom, instant gratification.	Samantha (Kim Cattrall's character on *Sex and the City*)
New Aquarians	4% 9M	Experience-seeking, new communities.	Ecologism, hedonism.	Phoebe (from *Friends*), Sarah McLachlan

Sources: Adapted from Michael Adams, *Sex in the Snow: Canadian Social Values at the End of the Millennium* (Toronto: Viking, 1997), pp. 203–217. See also Michael Adams, "The Demise of Demography," *Globe and Mail*, January 8, 1997, p. D5; and Ann Walmsley, "Canadian Specific," *Report on Business*, March 1997, pp. 15–16.

Watching a marketer undo a stereotype is a lot of fun. Only a few years ago, industry watchers announced the death knell of newspapers for youth, aged 18 to 34. Then came Dose, a lifestyle brand owned by CanWest that was launched in Calgary, Edmonton, Ottawa, Toronto, and Vancouver in April 2005. When it launched, it offered a free daily magazine, online service, and wireless portal. Its aims were lofty—to be "the most comprehensive free interactive service in the country." Dose promised "Because we're multi-platform, you'll find us where you work, play, study, shop, drink and eat. You also play a big part of Dose, so consider us a great way for your voice to be heard." The brand name was chosen after much debate, but Dose reflected the brand's evolving identity: compact, daily and necessary. Research undertaken before the launch revealed that youth don't like to be stereotyped, as skaters or hip-hop heads. Despite stereotypes to the contrary, they do care about politics. Their lives are fused seamlessly with multiple media (cellphones, Internet). They believe they are an underserved market and want content that's free and addresses their interests. While others underestimated the importance of news to this target audience, Dose discovered they wanted reliable, current information. By showing photos and providing bios of all its staff, the Dose website made it clear that the on-line paper is written by young people, for young people. It's certainly been a hit with 71 percent of 18 to 34s now aware of Dose. The road to success has been rocky, however. Today only the online version of Dose is published.

Lifestyle segmentation can also be used to understand how consumers use the Internet, computers, and other technology. Forrester developed its "Technographics" scheme, which segments consumers according to motivation, desire, and ability to invest in technology. The framework splits people into 10 categories, such as[26]

- *Fast Forwards:* the biggest spenders on computer technology. Fast Forwards are career focused, time strapped, driven, and top users of technology.

Dose is a lifestyle brand that has successfully done what seemed impossible—create a portal read and valued by the youth market.

- *New Age Nurturers:* also big spenders. However, they are focused on technology for home uses, such as family education and entertainment.
- *Mouse Potatoes:* consumers who are dedicated to interactive entertainment and willing to spend for the latest in "technotainment."
- *Techno-Strivers:* consumers who are up-and-coming believers in technology for career advancement.
- *Traditionalists:* small-town folks, suspicious of technology beyond the basics.

Delta Airlines used Technographics to better target online ticket sales. It created marketing campaigns for time-strapped Fast Forwards and New Age Nurturers, and eliminated Technology Pessimists (those skeptical of technology) from its list of targets. When used carefully, the lifestyle concept can help marketers understand changing consumer values and how they affect buying behaviour.

Personality and Self-Concept

Personality

The unique psychological characteristics that lead to relatively consistent and lasting responses to one's own environment.

Each person's distinct personality influences his or her buying behaviour. **Personality** refers to the unique psychological characteristics that lead to relatively consistent and lasting responses to one's own environment. Personality is usually described in terms of traits, such as self-confidence, dominance, sociability, autonomy, defensiveness, adaptability, and aggressiveness. Personality can be useful in analyzing consumer behaviour for certain product or brand choices. For example, coffee marketers have discovered that heavy coffee drinkers tend to be high on sociability. Thus, to attract customers, Starbucks and other coffeehouses create environments in which people can relax and socialize over a cup of steaming coffee.

The idea is that brands also have personalities, and that consumers are likely to choose brands whose personalities match their own. A *brand personality* is the specific mix of human traits that may be attributed to a particular brand. One researcher identified five brand personality traits:[27]

1. Sincerity (down-to-earth, honest, wholesome, and cheerful)
2. Excitement (daring, spirited, imaginative, and up-to-date)
3. Competence (reliable, intelligent, and successful)
4. Sophistication (upper class and charming)
5. Ruggedness (outdoorsy and tough)

The researcher found that a number of well-known brands tended to be strongly associated with one particular trait: Levi's with "ruggedness," MTV with "excitement," CNN with "competence," and Campbell's with "sincerity." Hence, these brands will attract persons who are high on the same personality traits.

Many marketers use a concept related to personality—a person's *self-concept* (also called *self-image*). The basic self-concept premise is that people's possessions contribute to and reflect their identities; that is, "we are what we have." Thus, in order to understand consumer behaviour, the marketer must first understand the relationship between consumer self-concept and possessions.

Psychological Factors

A person's buying choices are further influenced by four major psychological factors: *motivation, perception, learning,* and *beliefs and attitudes.*

Motivation

A person has many needs at any given time. Some are *biological,* arising from states of tension, such as hunger, thirst, or discomfort. Others are *psychological,* arising

Motive (drive)
A need that is sufficiently pressing to direct the person to seek satisfaction of the need.

from the need for recognition, esteem, or belonging. A need becomes a *motive* when it is aroused to a sufficient level of intensity. A **motive** (or **drive**) is a need that is sufficiently pressing to direct the person to seek satisfaction. Psychologists have developed theories of human motivation. Two of the most popular—the theories of Sigmund Freud and Abraham Maslow—have quite different meanings for consumer analysis and marketing.

Sigmund Freud assumed that people are largely unconscious about the real psychological forces shaping their behaviour. He saw the person as growing up and repressing many urges. These urges are never eliminated or under perfect control; they emerge in dreams, in slips of the tongue, in neurotic and obsessive behaviour, or ultimately in psychoses.

Freud's theory suggests that a person's buying decisions are affected by subconscious motives that even the buyer may not fully understand. Thus, an aging baby boomer who buys a sporty BMW 330Ci convertible might explain that he simply likes the feel of the wind in his thinning hair. At a deeper level, he may be trying to impress others with his success. At a still deeper level, he may be buying the car to feel young and independent again.

The term *motivation research* refers to qualitative research designed to probe consumers' hidden, subconscious motivations. Motivation researchers collect in-depth information from small samples of consumers to uncover the deeper motives for their product choices. The techniques range from sentence completion, word association, and inkblot or cartoon interpretation tests, to having consumers describe typical brand users or form daydreams and fantasies about brands or buying situations.

Well-known brands tend to be strongly associated with one particular trait: CNN stands for confidence and trust.

Many companies employ teams of psychologists, anthropologists, and other social scientists to carry out motivation research. One agency routinely conducts one-on-one, therapy-like interviews to delve into the inner workings of consumers. Another agency asks consumers to describe their favourite brands as animals or cars (say, Cadillacs versus Chevrolets) in order to assess the prestige associated with various brands. Still another agency has consumers draw figures of typical brand users. In one case, the agency asked 50 participants to sketch likely buyers of two different brands of cake mixes. Consistently, the group portrayed Pillsbury customers as apron-clad, grandmotherly types, whereas they pictured Duncan Hines purchasers as svelte, contemporary women.

Abraham Maslow sought to explain why people are driven by particular needs at particular times. Why does one person spend much time and energy on personal safety and another on gaining the esteem of others? Maslow's answer is that human needs are arranged in a hierarchy, as shown in Figure 6.3, from the most pressing at the bottom to the least pressing at the top. They include *physiological* needs, *safety* needs, *social* needs, *esteem* needs, and *self-actualization* needs.

A person tries to satisfy the most important need first. When that need is satisfied, it will stop being a motivator and the person will then try to satisfy the next most important need. For example, starving people (physiological need) will not take an interest in the latest happenings in the art world (self-actualization needs), nor in how they are seen or esteemed by others (social or esteem needs), nor even in whether they are breathing clean air (safety needs). But as each important need is satisfied, the next most important need will come into play.

Perception

A motivated person is ready to act. How the person acts is influenced by his or her own perception of the situation. All of us learn by the flow of information through our five senses: sight, hearing, smell, touch, and taste. However, each of us receives, organizes, and interprets this sensory information in an individual way. **Perception** is the process by which people select, organize, and interpret information to form a meaningful picture of the world.

People can form different perceptions of the same stimulus because of three perceptual processes: selective attention, selective distortion, and selective retention. People are exposed to a great amount of stimuli every day. For example, one analyst estimates that people are exposed to about 5000 ads every day.[28] It is impossible for a person to pay attention to all these stimuli. *Selective attention*—the

Perception

The process by which people select, organize, and interpret information to form a meaningful picture of the world.

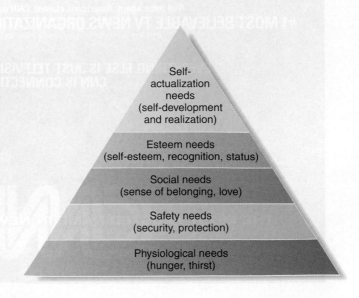

Figure 6.3 Maslow's hierarchy of needs

Source: From *Motivation and Personality* by Abraham H. Maslow. Copyright © 1970 by Abraham H. Maslow. Copyright 1954, 1987 by Harper & Row Publishers, Inc. Reprinted by permission of Addison-Wesley Educational Publishers Inc. Also see Barbara Marx Hubbard, "Seeking Our Future Potentials," *The Futurist*, May 1998, pp. 29–32.

Self-actualization needs (self-development and realization)

Esteem needs (self-esteem, recognition, status)

Social needs (sense of belonging, love)

Safety needs (security, protection)

Physiological needs (hunger, thirst)

tendency for people to screen out most of the information to which they are exposed—means that marketers have to work especially hard to attract the consumer's attention.

Even noticed stimuli do not always come across in the intended way. Each person fits incoming information into an existing mind-set. *Selective distortion* describes the tendency of people to interpret information in a way that will support what they already believe. For example, if you distrust a company, you might perceive even honest ads from the company as questionable. Selective distortion means that marketers must try to understand the mind-sets of consumers and how these will affect interpretations of advertising and sales information.

People also will forget much that they learn. They tend to retain information that supports their attitudes and beliefs. Because of *selective retention*, consumers are likely to remember good points made about a brand they favour and to forget good points made about competing brands. Because of selective exposure, distortion, and retention, marketers have to work hard to get their messages through. This fact explains why marketers use so much drama and repetition in sending messages to their market.

Interestingly, although most marketers worry about whether their offers will be perceived at all, some consumers worry that they will be affected by marketing messages without even knowing it—through *subliminal advertising*. In 1957, a researcher announced that he had flashed the phrases "Eat popcorn" and "Drink Coca-Cola" on a screen in a New Jersey movie theatre every five seconds for 1/300th of a second. He reported that although viewers did not consciously recognize these messages, they absorbed them subconsciously and bought 58 percent more popcorn and 18 percent more Coke. Suddenly advertisers and consumer-protection groups became intensely interested in subliminal perception. People voiced fears of being brainwashed, and California and Canada declared the practice illegal. Although the researcher later admitted to making up the data, the issue has not died. Some consumers still fear that they are being manipulated by subliminal messages.

Numerous studies by psychologists and consumer researchers have found no link between subliminal messages and consumer behaviour. It appears that subliminal advertising simply doesn't have the power attributed to it by its critics. Most advertisers scoff at the notion of an industry conspiracy to manipulate consumers

It's impossible for people to pay attention to the thousands of ads they're exposed to every day, so they screen most of them out.

through "invisible" messages. Says one industry insider: "[Some consumers believe we are] wizards who can manipulate them at will. Ha! Snort! Oh my sides! As we know, just between us, most of [us] have difficulty getting a 2 percent increase in sales with the help of $50 million in media and extremely liminal images of sex, money, power, and other [motivators] of human emotion. The very idea of [us] as puppeteers, cruelly pulling the strings of consumer marionettes, is almost too much to bear."[29]

Learning

Learning

Changes in an individual's behaviour arising from experience.

When people act, they learn. **Learning** describes changes in an individual's behaviour arising from experience. Learning theorists say that most human behaviour is learned. Learning occurs through the interplay of *drives*, *stimuli*, *cues*, *responses*, and *reinforcement*.

A *drive* is a strong internal stimulus that calls for action. A drive becomes a motive when it is directed toward a particular *stimulus object*. For example, a person's drive for self-actualization might motivate him or her to look into buying a digital camera. The consumer's response to the idea of buying a camera is conditioned by the surrounding cues. *Cues* are minor stimuli that determine when, where, and how the person responds. For example, the person might spot several camera brands in a shop window, hear of a special sale price, or discuss cameras with a friend. These are all cues that might influence a consumer's *response* to his or her interest in buying the product.

Suppose the consumer buys a Nikon digital camera. If the experience is rewarding, the consumer will probably use the camera more and more, and his or her response will be *reinforced*. Then, the next time the consumer shops for a camera, or for binoculars or some similar product, the probability is greater that he or she will buy a Nikon product. The practical significance of learning theory for marketers is that they can build up demand for a product by associating it with strong drives, using motivating cues, and providing positive reinforcement.

Beliefs and Attitudes

Belief

A descriptive thought that a person holds about something.

Through doing and learning, people acquire beliefs and attitudes. These, in turn, influence their buying behaviour. A **belief** is a descriptive thought that a person has about something. Beliefs may be based on real knowledge, opinion, or faith, and may or may not carry an emotional charge. Marketers are interested in the beliefs that people formulate about specific products and services, because these beliefs make up product and brand images that affect buying behaviour. If some of the beliefs are wrong and prevent purchase, the marketer will want to launch a campaign to correct them.

Attitude

A person's consistently favourable or unfavourable evaluations, feelings, and tendencies toward an object or idea.

People have attitudes regarding religion, politics, clothes, music, food, and almost everything else. **Attitude** describes a person's relatively consistent evaluations, feelings, and tendencies toward an object or idea. Attitudes put people into a frame of mind of liking or disliking things, of moving toward or away from them. Our digital camera buyer may hold attitudes such as "Buy the best," "The Japanese make the best electronics products in the world," and "Creativity and self-expression are among the most important things in life." If so, the Nikon camera would fit well into the consumer's existing attitudes.

Attitudes are difficult to change. A person's attitudes fit into a pattern, and to change one attitude may require difficult adjustments in many others. Thus, a company should usually try to fit its products into existing attitudes rather than attempt to change attitudes. Of course, there are exceptions in which the cost of trying to change attitudes may pay off handsomely:

By 1994, milk consumption had been in decline for 20 years. The general perception was that milk was unhealthy, outdated, just for kids, or good only with cookies and cake. To counter these notions, marketers throughout North America, such as the B.C. Dairy Foundation, the Quebec Milk Producers, and the National Fluid Milk Processors Education Program (MilkPEP) began campaigns aimed at changing attitudes. MilkPEP's famous ad campaign featured milk be-moustached celebrities and the tag line Got Milk? The long-running campaign has not only been wildly popular, it has been successful as well—not only did it stop the decline, milk consumption actually increased. Although initially the target market was women in their 20s, the campaign has been expanded to other target markets and has gained cult status with teens who collect the print ads featuring celebrities including music stars Hanson and LeAnn Rimes, supermodel Tyra Banks, and Kermit the Frog. A website (www.whymilk.com) is also used where young folks can make their own moustache, check out the latest Got Milk? ads, or get facts about "everything you ever need to know about milk." Travelling promotional events are also utilized, such as the search for the best teen bands and dancers. The best band will receive a recording contract, and the most talented dancer will spend next summer at the MTV Beach House. Teens can also enter a contest to sport a milk moustache in *Rolling Stone* magazine alongside a famous musician, and then follow the celebrity for a day as a roadie.[30]

We can now appreciate the many forces acting on consumer behaviour. The consumer's choice results from the complex interplay of cultural, social, personal, and psychological factors.

Attitudes are difficult to change, but the National Fluid Milk Processors' wildly popular milk moustache campaign succeeded in changing attitudes toward milk.

Types of Buying Decision Behaviour

Buying behaviour differs greatly for a tube of toothpaste, a tennis racquet, financial services, and a new car. More complex decisions usually involve more buying participants and more buyer deliberation. Figure 6.4 shows types of consumer buyer behaviour based on the degree of buyer involvement and the degree of differences among brands.[31]

Complex Buying Behaviour

Complex buying behaviour
Consumer buying behaviour in situations characterized by high consumer involvement in a purchase and significant perceived differences among brands.

Consumers undertake **complex buying behaviour** when they are highly involved in a purchase and perceive significant differences among brands. Consumers may be highly involved when the product is expensive, risky, purchased infrequently, and highly self-expressive. Typically, the consumer has much to learn about the product category. For example, a personal computer buyer may not know what attributes to consider. Many product features carry no real meaning: a "3.4GHz Pentium processor," "super VGA resolution," or "2GB SDRAM memory."

This buyer will pass through a learning process, first developing beliefs about the product, then attitudes, and then making a thoughtful purchase choice. Marketers of high-involvement products must understand the information-gathering and evaluation behaviour of high-involvement consumers. They need to help buyers learn about product-class attributes and their relative importance. They need to differentiate their brand's features, perhaps by describing the brand's benefits using print media with long copy. They must motivate store salespeople and the buyer's acquaintances to influence the final brand choice.

Dissonance-Reducing Buying Behaviour

Dissonance-reducing buying behaviour
Consumer buying behaviour in situations characterized by high involvement but few perceived differences among brands.

Dissonance-reducing buying behaviour occurs when consumers are highly involved with an expensive, infrequent, or risky purchase, but see little difference among brands. For example, consumers buying carpeting may face a high-involvement decision because carpeting is expensive and self-expressive. Yet buyers may consider most carpet brands in a given price range to be the same. In this case, because perceived brand differences are not large, buyers may shop around to learn what is available but buy relatively quickly. They may respond primarily to a good price or to purchase convenience.

After the purchase, consumers might experience *postpurchase dissonance* (after-sale discomfort) when they notice certain disadvantages of the purchased carpet brand or hear favourable things about brands not purchased. To counter such dissonance, the marketer's after-sale communications should provide evidence and support to help consumers feel good about their brand choices.

Figure 6.4 Four types of buying behaviour

Source: Adapted from Henry Assael, *Consumer Behaviour and Marketing Action* (Boston: Kent Publishing Company, 1987), p. 87. Copyright © 1987 by Wadsworth, Inc. Printed by permission of Kent Publishing Company, a division of Wadsworth, Inc.

	High involvement	Low involvement
Significant differences between brands	Complex buying behaviour	Variety-seeking buying behaviour
Few differences between brands	Dissonance-reducing buying behaviour	Habitual buying behaviour

Habitual Buying Behaviour

Habitual buying behaviour
Consumer buying behaviour in situations characterized by low consumer involvement and few significant perceived brand differences.

Habitual buying behaviour occurs under conditions of low consumer involvement and little significant brand difference. For example, take salt. Consumers have little involvement in this product category—they simply go to the store and reach for a brand. If they keep reaching for the same brand, it is out of habit rather than strong brand loyalty. Consumers appear to have low involvement with most low-cost, frequently purchased products.

In such cases, consumer behaviour does not pass through the usual belief-attitude-behaviour sequence. Consumers do not search extensively for information about the brands, evaluate brand characteristics, and make weighty decisions about which brands to buy. Instead, they passively receive information as they watch television or read magazines. Ad repetition creates *brand familiarity* rather than *brand conviction*. Consumers do not form strong attitudes toward a brand; they select the brand because it is familiar. Because they are not highly involved with the product, consumers may not evaluate the choice even after purchase. Thus, the buying process involves brand beliefs formed by passive learning, followed by purchase behaviour, which may or may not be followed by evaluation.

Because buyers are not highly committed to any brands, marketers of low-involvement products with few brand differences often use price and sales promotions to stimulate product trial. In advertising for a low-involvement product, ad copy should stress only a few key points. Visual symbols and imagery are important because they can be remembered easily and associated with the brand. Ad campaigns should include high repetition of short-duration messages. Television is usually more effective than print media because it is a low-involvement medium suitable for passive learning. Advertising planning should be based on classical conditioning theory, in which buyers learn to identify a certain product by a symbol repeatedly attached to it.

Variety-Seeking Buying Behaviour

Variety-seeking buying behaviour
Consumer buying behaviour in situations characterized by low consumer involvement but significant perceived brand differences.

Consumers undertake **variety-seeking buying behaviour** in situations characterized by low consumer involvement but significant perceived brand differences. In such cases, consumers often do a lot of brand switching. For example, when buying cookies, a consumer may hold some beliefs, choose a cookie brand without much evaluation, then evaluate that brand during consumption. But the next time, the consumer might pick another brand out of boredom or simply to try something different. Brand switching occurs for the sake of variety rather than because of dissatisfaction.

In such product categories, the marketing strategy may differ for the market leader and minor brands. The market leader will try to encourage habitual buying behaviour by dominating shelf space, keeping shelves fully stocked, and running frequent reminder advertising. Challenger firms will encourage variety seeking by offering lower prices, special deals, coupons, free samples, and advertising that presents reasons for trying something new.

The Buyer Decision Process

Now that we have looked at the influences that affect buyers, we are ready to look at how consumers make buying decisions. Figure 6.5 shows that the buyer decision process consists of five stages: *need recognition*, *information search*, *evaluation of alternatives*, *purchase decision*, and *postpurchase behaviour*. Clearly, the buying

Figure 6.5 Buyer decision process

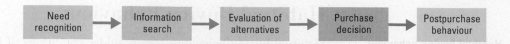

process starts long before actual purchase and continues long after. Marketers need to focus on the entire buying process rather than on just the purchase decision.

The figure suggests that consumers pass through all five stages with every purchase. But in more routine purchases, consumers often skip or reverse some of these stages. A woman buying her regular brand of toothpaste would recognize the need and go right to the purchase decision, skipping information search and evaluation. However, we use the model in Figure 6.5 because it shows all the considerations that arise when a consumer faces a new and complex purchase situation.

Need Recognition

Need recognition
The first stage of the buyer decision process, in which the consumer recognizes a problem or need.

The buying process starts with **need recognition**—the buyer recognizes a problem or need. The need can be triggered by *internal stimuli* when one of the person's normal needs—hunger, thirst, sex—rises to a level high enough to become a drive. A need can also be triggered by *external stimuli*. For example, an advertisement or a discussion with a friend might get you thinking about buying a new car. At this stage, the marketer should research consumers to find out what kinds of needs or problems arise, what brought them about, and how they led the consumer to this particular product.

Information Search

Information search
The stage of the buyer decision process in which the consumer is aroused to search for more information; the consumer may simply have heightened attention or may go into active information search.

An interested consumer may or may not search for more information. If the consumer's drive is strong and a satisfying product is near at hand, the consumer is likely to buy it then. If not, the consumer may store the need in memory or undertake an **information search** related to the need. For example, once you've decided you need a new car, at the least, you will probably pay more attention to car ads, cars owned by friends, and car conversations. Or you may actively look for reading material, phone friends, and gather information in other ways. The amount of searching you do will depend on the strength of your drive, the amount of information you start with, the ease of obtaining more information, the value you place on additional information, and the satisfaction you get from searching.

Consumers can obtain information from any of several sources. These include *personal sources* (family, friends, neighbours, acquaintances), *commercial sources* (advertising, salespeople, dealers, packaging, displays), *public sources* (mass media, consumer-rating organizations), and *experiential sources* (handling, examining, using the product). The relative influence of these information sources varies with the product and the buyer. Generally, the consumer receives the most information about a product from commercial sources—those controlled by the marketer. The most effective sources, however, tend to be personal. Commercial sources normally *inform* the buyer, but personal sources *legitimize* or *evaluate* products for the buyer.

As more information is obtained, the consumer's awareness and knowledge of the available brands and features increase. In your car information search, you may learn about the several brands available. The information might also help you to drop certain brands from consideration. A company must design its marketing mix to make prospects aware of and knowledgeable about its brand. It should carefully identify consumers' sources of information and the importance of each source.

Lakeport. Great Beer. Fair Prices.

Need recognition can be triggered by advertising. Lakeport Breweries was the first to recognize beer drinkers' need for a value-based product and triggered their need to search for a better priced products.

Evaluation of Alternatives

We have seen how the consumer uses information to arrive at a set of final brand choices. How does the consumer choose among the alternative brands? The marketer needs to know about **alternative evaluation**—that is, how the consumer processes information to arrive at brand choices. Unfortunately, consumers do not use a simple and single evaluation process in all buying situations. Instead, several evaluation processes are at work.

The consumer arrives at attitudes toward different brands through some evaluation procedure. How consumers go about evaluating purchase alternatives depends on the individual consumer and the specific buying situation. In some cases, consumers use careful calculations and logical thinking. At other times, the same consumers do little or no evaluating; instead they buy on impulse and rely on intuition. Sometimes consumers make buying decisions on their own; sometimes they turn to friends, consumer guides, or salespeople for buying advice.

Suppose you've narrowed your car choices to three brands. And suppose that you are primarily interested in four attributes—styling, operating economy, warranty, and price. By this time, you've probably formed beliefs about how each brand rates on each attribute. Clearly, if one car rated best on all the attributes, we could predict that you would choose it. However, the brands will no doubt vary in appeal. You might base your buying decision on only one attribute, and your choice would be easy to predict. If you wanted styling above everything else, you would buy the car that you think has the best styling. But most buyers consider several attributes, each with different importance. If we knew the importance weights that you assigned to each of the four attributes, we could predict your car choice more reliably.

Alternative evaluation
The stage of the buyer decision process in which the consumer uses information to evaluate alternative brands in the choice set.

Marketers should study buyers to find out how they actually evaluate brand alternatives. If they know what evaluative processes go on, marketers can take steps to influence the buyer's decision.

Purchase Decision

In the evaluation stage, the consumer ranks brands and forms purchase intentions. Generally, the consumer's **purchase decision** will be to buy the most preferred brand, but two factors can come between the purchase *intention* and the purchase *decision*. The first factor is the *attitudes of others*. If someone important to you thinks that you should buy the lowest-priced car, then the chances of your buying a more expensive car are reduced.

The second factor is *unexpected situational factors*. The consumer may form a purchase intention based on factors such as expected income, expected price, and expected product benefits. However, unexpected events may change the purchase intention. For example, the economy might take a turn for the worse, a close competitor might drop its price, or a friend might report being disappointed in your preferred car. Thus, preferences and even purchase intentions do not always result in actual purchase choice.

Postpurchase Behaviour

The marketer's job does not end when the product is bought. After purchasing the product, the consumer will be satisfied or dissatisfied and will engage in **postpurchase behaviour** of interest to the marketer. What determines whether the buyer is satisfied or dissatisfied with a purchase? The answer lies in the relationship between the *consumer's expectations* and the product's *perceived performance*. If the product falls short of expectations, the consumer is disappointed; if it meets expectations, the consumer is satisfied; if it exceeds expectations, the consumer is delighted.

The larger the gap between expectations and performance, the greater the consumer's dissatisfaction. This suggests that sellers should promise only what their brands can deliver so that buyers are satisfied. Some sellers might even understate product performance levels to boost later consumer satisfaction. For example, Boeing's salespeople tend to be conservative when they estimate the potential benefits of their aircraft. They almost always underestimate fuel efficiency—they promise a 5 percent savings that turns out to be 8 percent. Customers are delighted with better-than-expected performance; they buy again and tell other potential customers that Boeing lives up to its promises.

Almost all major purchases result in **cognitive dissonance**, or discomfort caused by postpurchase conflict. After the purchase, consumers are satisfied with the benefits of the chosen brand and are glad to avoid the drawbacks of the brands not bought. However, every purchase involves compromise. Consumers feel uneasy about acquiring the drawbacks of the chosen brand and about losing the benefits of the brands not purchased. Thus, consumers feel at least some postpurchase dissonance for every purchase.[32]

Why is it so important to satisfy the customer? Customer satisfaction is a key to building profitable relationships with consumers—to keeping and growing consumers and reaping their customer lifetime value. Satisfied customers buy a product again, talk favourably to others about the product, pay less attention to competing brands and advertising, and buy other products from the company. Many marketers go beyond merely *meeting* the expectations of customers—they aim to *delight* the customer. (See Real Marketing 6.2.)

Purchase decision
The buyer's decision about which brand to purchase.

Postpurchase behaviour
The stage of the buyer decision process in which consumers take further action after purchase, based on their satisfaction or dissatisfaction.

Cognitive dissonance
Buyer discomfort caused by postpurchase conflict.

REAL MARKETING

6.2

Lexus: Delighting Customers to Keep Them Coming Back

lose your eyes for a minute and picture a typical car dealership. Not impressed? Talk to a friend who owns a Lexus, and you'll no doubt get a very different picture. The typical Lexus dealership is ... well, anything but typical.

Lexus customers waiting for their cars to be serviced may lounge on an overstuffed sofa, watch a big-screen TV, surf the Internet, or sip lattes in the beverage area. One dealership is considering adding a manicure area, another has put in a putting machine so customers can brush up on their golf while waiting for an oil change, and a third offers its customers a fully furnished business centre complete with a fax machine and wireless Internet access.

Why all the special amenities? Lexus knows that good marketing doesn't stop with making the sale. Keeping customers happy *after* the sale is the key to building lasting relationships. Dealers across North America have a common goal: to delight customers and keep them coming back. Lexus believes that if you "delight the customer, and continue to delight the customer, you will have a customer for life." And Lexus understands just how valuable a customer can be—it estimates that the average lifetime value of a Lexus customer is more than US$600 000.

Despite the amenities, few Lexus customers spend much time hanging around the dealership. Lexus knows that the best dealership visit is the one that you don't have to make at all. So it builds customer-pleasing cars to start with—high-quality cars that need little servicing. In its "Lexus Covenant," the company vows that it will make "the finest cars ever built." In 2004, J.D. Power once again rated Lexus as the top brand for initial quality. The Lexus SC 430 model set the record for the fewest quality problems ever reported.

Right from the start of a relationship, Lexus aims to delight its customers. In Canada, it uses a sophisticated database to connect its dealership sales personnel with its more than 6600 customers to provide after sales service and invite them to Lexus events, such as a gala for new owners of Lexus vehicles. When a car does need to be serviced, Lexus goes out of its way to make it easy and painless. Most dealers will even pick up the car, and then return it when the maintenance is finished. And the car comes back spotless, thanks to a complimentary cleaning to remove bugs and road grime from the exterior and smudges from the leather interior. You might even be surprised to find that they've touched up a door ding to help restore the car to its fresh-from-the-factory lustre. "My wife will never buy another car except a Lexus," says one satisfied Lexus owner. "They come to our house, pick up the car, do an oil change, [spiff it up,] and bring it back. She's sold for life."

And when a customer does bring a car in, Lexus repairs it right the first time, on time. Dealers know that their well-heeled customers have money, "but what they don't have is time." So dealers are testing a system that uses three technicians instead of one for 50 000 km service checkups. The new system will cut a customer's wait in half. "I'm not in the car business," says one dealer. "I'm in the service business."

Beyond pampering customers with outstanding service, Lexus also creates special experiences that foster long-lasting relationships. Lexus Australia, for example, rewards loyal customers with VIP packages to the theatre. It gives them an opportunity to buy the

Lexus pledges to create the most satisfying ownership experience the world has ever seen.

▶

best seats at the Sydney Opera House. During inter-mission, customers can visit the exclusive Inner Circle VIP lounge and sip a complimentary glass of Domaine Chandon while opening their VIP gift pack of exclusive commemorative merchandise from the show.

Lexus uses the tagline "The Pursuit of Perfection." According to its website, from the very start, Lexus set out to "revolutionize the automotive experience with a passionate commitment the finest products, supported by dealers who create the most satisfying ownership experience the world has ever seen. We vow to value the customer as an important individual. To do things right the first time. And to always exceed expectations."

At Lexus, exceeding customer expectations some-times means fulfilling even seemingly outrageous cus-tomer requests. Dave Wilson, owner of several Lexus dealerships in Southern California, tells of an angry let-ter he received from a Lexus owner who spent US$374 to repair her car at his dealership. She'd owned four prior Lexus vehicles without a single problem. She said in her letter that she resented paying to fix her current one. Turns out, she thought they were maintenance free—as in get in and drive … and drive and drive. "She didn't think she had to do anything to her Lexus," says Wilson. "She had 60 000 miles on it, and never had the oil changed." Wilson sent back her US$374.

By all accounts, Lexus has lived up to its ambi-tious customer-satisfaction promise. It has created what appear to be the world's most satisfied car own-ers. Lexus regularly tops not just the J.D. Power qual-ity ratings, but also its customer-satisfaction ratings, and not just in the United States, but worldwide. In 2004, in the UK, Lexus achieved the highest J.D. Power customer-satisfaction score ever in the rating's 11-year history. Customer satisfaction translates into sales and customer loyalty. Lexus has become North America's number-one selling luxury car. And once a Lexus cus-tomer, always a Lexus customer—Lexus retains 84 per-cent of customers who've gone to the dealership for service.

Sources: Jean Halliday, "Dealers Improve Waiting Areas to Boost Loyalty," *Automotive News*, March 22, 2004, p. 38; Doron Levin, "Lexus Breaks the 'Rule' to Reign as Top Luxury Marque," *The Detroit News*, January 21, 2004; "J.D. Power and Associates and What Car? Report," press release, April 20, 2004; Steve Finlay, "At Least She Put Fuel in It," *Ward's Dealer Business*, August 1, 2003; "Lexus Roars for Loyal Customers," *B&T Magazine*, November 27, 2003; J.D. Power and Associates, "Lexus Dealers Repeat Top Ranking in Satisfaction with Vehicle Service," press release, October 25, 2001; "Keeping the Customer Satisfied," *The Derry Journal*, April 30, 2004; "Servco Lexus Customers Get a Sneak Peak at the All-New GX 470," *Servo Pacific*, April 2004; Mark Rechtin, "Lexus: Growth Won't Hurt Brand's Cachet," *Automotive News*, April 19, 2004, p. 49; "Lexus Sweeps Quality and Satisfaction Awards," Lexus press release, May 13, 2004; "Lexus Covenant," www.lexus.com/about/corporate/covenant.html (accessed January 2005); and "Lexus CRM Tool and Mailer," Actuent Solutions Inc., Case Studies, www.actuenthosting.com/clients/casestudies/1/ (accessed February 12, 2006).

A dissatisfied consumer responds differently. Bad word of mouth often travels farther and faster than good word of mouth. It can quickly damage consumer atti-tudes about a company and its products. But companies cannot simply rely on dis-satisfied customers to volunteer their complaints when they are dissatisfied. Most unhappy customers never tell the company about their problem. Therefore, a com-pany should measure customer satisfaction regularly. It should set up systems that *encourage* customers to complain. In this way, the company can learn how well it is doing and how it can improve.

But what should companies do about dissatisfied customers? At a minimum, most companies offer toll-free numbers and websites to handle complaints and inquiries. For example, over the past two decades, the Gerber help line (1-800-4-GERBER) has received more than 5 million calls. Help line staffers, most of them mothers or grandmothers themselves, handle customer concerns and provide baby care advice 24 hours a day, 365 days a year to more than 2400 callers a day. Customers can also log on to the Gerber website and enter a phone number, and a staffer will call them.

By studying the overall buyer decision, marketers may be able to find ways to help consumers move through it. For example, if consumers are not buying a new product because they do not perceive a need for it, marketing might launch adver-tising messages that trigger the need and show how the product solves customers' problems. If customers know about the product but are not buying because they hold unfavourable attitudes toward it, the marketer must find ways either to change the product or change consumer perceptions.

The Buyer Decision Process for New Products

We have looked at the stages buyers go through in trying to satisfy a need. Buyers may pass quickly or slowly through these stages, and some of the stages may even be reversed. Much depends on the nature of the buyer, the product, and the buying situation.

New product
A good, service, or idea that is perceived by some potential customers as new.

We now look at how buyers approach the purchase of new products. A **new product** is a good, service, or idea that is perceived by some potential customers as new. It may have been around for a while, but our interest is in how consumers learn about products for the first time and make decisions on whether to adopt them. We define the **adoption process** as "the mental process through which an individual passes from first learning about an innovation to final adoption," and *adoption* as the decision by an individual to become a regular user of the product.[33]

Adoption process
The mental process through which an individual passes from first hearing about an innovation to final adoption.

The Adoption Process

Consumers go through five stages in the process of adopting a new product:

- *Awareness:* The consumer becomes aware of the new product, but lacks information about it.
- *Interest:* The consumer seeks information about the new product.
- *Evaluation:* The consumer considers whether trying the new product makes sense.
- *Trial:* The consumer tries the new product on a small scale to improve his or her estimate of its value.
- *Adoption:* The consumer decides to make full and regular use of the new product.

This model suggests that the new-product marketer should think about how to help consumers move through these stages. A manufacturer of HDTVs (high-definition televisions) may discover that many consumers in the interest stage do not move to the trial stage because of uncertainty and the large investment. If these same consumers were willing to use HDTVs on a trial basis for a small fee, the manufacturer could consider offering a trial-use plan with an option to buy.

Individual Differences in Innovativeness

People differ greatly in their readiness to try new products. In each product area, there are "consumption pioneers" and early adopters. Other individuals adopt new products much later. People can be classified into the adopter categories shown in Figure 6.6. After a slow start, an increasing number of people adopt the new product. The number of adopters reaches a peak and then drops off as fewer non-adopters remain. Innovators are defined as the first 2.5 percent of the buyers to adopt a new idea (those beyond two standard deviations from mean adoption time); the early adopters are the next 13.5 percent (between one and two standard deviations); and so forth.

The five adopter groups have differing values. *Innovators* are venturesome—they try new ideas at some risk. *Early adopters* are guided by respect—they are opinion leaders in their communities and adopt new ideas early but carefully. The *early majority* are deliberate—although they rarely are leaders, they adopt new ideas before the average person. The *late majority* are skeptical—they adopt an

Figure 6.6 Adopter categorization on the basis of relative time of adoption of innovations

Source: Reprinted with the permission of The Free Press, a Division of Simon & Schuster, from *Diffusion of Innovations, Fifth Edition,* by Everett M. Rogers. Copyright © 2003 by The Free Press.

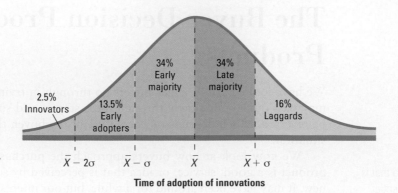

innovation only after a majority of people have tried it. Finally, *laggards* are tradition bound—they are suspicious of changes and adopt the innovation only when it has become something of a tradition itself.

This adopter classification suggests that an innovating firm should research the characteristics of innovators and early adopters and should direct marketing efforts toward them. In general, innovators tend to be relatively younger, better educated, and higher in income than later adopters and nonadopters. They are more receptive to unfamiliar things, rely more on their own values and judgment, and are more willing to take risks. They are less brand loyal and more likely to take advantage of special promotions, such as discounts, coupons, and samples.

Influence of Product Characteristics on Rate of Adoption

The characteristics of the new product affect its rate of adoption. Some products catch on almost overnight (Beanie Babies), whereas others take a long time to gain acceptance (HDTV). Five characteristics are especially important in influencing an innovation's rate of adoption. For example, consider the characteristics of HDTV in relation to the rate of adoption:

- *Relative advantage:* the degree to which the innovation appears superior to existing products. The greater the perceived relative advantage of using HDTV—say, in picture quality and ease of viewing—the sooner HDTVs will be adopted.

- *Compatibility:* the degree to which the innovation fits the values and experiences of potential consumers. HDTV, for example, is highly compatible with the lifestyles found in upper-middle-class homes. However, it is not very compatible with the programming and broadcasting systems currently available to consumers.

- *Complexity:* the degree to which the innovation is difficult to understand or use. HDTVs are not very complex and, therefore, once programming is available and prices come down, will take less time to penetrate North American homes than more complex innovations.

- *Divisibility:* the degree to which the innovation may be tried on a limited basis. HDTVs are still very expensive. To the extent that people can lease them with an option to buy, their rate of adoption will increase.

- *Communicability:* the degree to which the results of using the innovation can be observed or described to others. Because HDTV lends itself to demonstration and description, its use will spread faster among consumers.

This ad encourages trial by offering a coupon.

Other characteristics influence the rate of adoption, such as initial and ongoing costs, risk and uncertainty, and social approval. The new-product marketer has to research all these factors when developing the new product and its marketing program.

Consumer Behaviour Across International Borders

Understanding consumer behaviour is difficult enough for companies marketing within the borders of a single country. For companies operating in many countries, however, understanding and serving the needs of consumers can be daunting. Although consumers in different countries may have some things in common, their values, attitudes, and behaviours often vary greatly. International marketers must understand such differences and adjust their products and marketing programs accordingly.

Sometimes the differences are obvious. For example, in North America, where most people eat cereal regularly for breakfast, Kellogg focuses its marketing on persuading consumers to select a Kellogg brand rather than a competitor's brand. In France, however, where most people prefer croissants and coffee or no breakfast at all, Kellogg advertising simply attempts to convince people that they should eat cereal for breakfast. Its packaging includes step-by-step instructions on how to prepare cereal. In India, where many consumers eat heavy, fried breakfasts and many consumers skip the meal altogether, Kellogg's advertising attempts to convince buyers to switch to a lighter, more nutritious breakfast diet.

Often, differences across international markets are more subtle. They may result from physical differences in consumers and their environments. For example, Remington makes smaller electric shavers to fit the smaller hands of Japanese consumers and battery-powered shavers for the British market, where fewer bathrooms have electrical outlets. Other differences result from varying customs. In Japan, for example, where humility and deference are considered great virtues, pushy, hard-hitting sales approaches are considered offensive. Failing to understand such differences in customs and behaviours from one country to another can spell disaster for a marketer's international products and programs.

Marketers must decide on the degree to which they will adapt their products and marketing programs to meet the unique cultures and needs of consumers in various markets. On the one hand, they want to standardize their offerings in order to simplify operations and take advantage of cost economies. On the other hand, adapting marketing efforts within each country results in products and programs that better satisfy the needs of local consumers. The question of whether to adapt or standardize the marketing mix across international markets has created a lively debate in recent years.

Reviewing the Concepts

The North American consumer market consists of more than 327 million people who consume many trillions of dollars worth of goods and services each year, making it one of the most attractive consumer markets in the world. The world consumer market consists of more than 6.4 *billion* people. Consumers around the world vary greatly in age, income, education level, and tastes. Understanding how these differences affect *consumer buyer behaviour* is one of the biggest challenges marketers face.

1. Define the consumer market and construct a simple model of consumer buyer behaviour.

The *consumer market* consists of all the individuals and households who buy or acquire goods and services for personal consumption. The simplest model of consumer buyer behaviour is the stimulus–response model. According to this model, marketing stimuli (the four Ps) and other major forces (economic, technological, political, cultural) enter the consumer's "black box" and produce certain responses. Once in the black box, these inputs produce observable buyer responses, such as product choice, brand choice, purchase timing, and purchase amount.

2. Name the four major factors that influence consumer buyer behaviour.

Consumer buyer behaviour is influenced by four key sets of buyer characteristics: cultural, social, personal,

and psychological. Although many of these factors cannot be influenced by the marketer, they can be useful in identifying interested buyers and in shaping products and appeals to serve consumer needs better. *Culture* is the most basic determinant of a person's wants and behaviour. It includes the basic values, perceptions, preferences, and behaviours that a person learns from family and other important institutions. *Subcultures* are "cultures within cultures" that have distinct values and lifestyles and can be based on anything from age to ethnicity. People with different cultural and subcultural characteristics have different product and brand preferences. As a result, marketers may want to focus their marketing programs on the special needs of certain groups.

Social factors also influence a buyer's behaviour. A person's *reference groups*—family, friends, social organizations, professional associations—strongly affect product and brand choices. The buyer's age, life-cycle stage, occupation, economic circumstances, lifestyle, personality, and other *personal characteristics* influence his or her buying decisions. Consumer *lifestyles*—the whole pattern of acting and interacting in the world—are also an important influence on purchase decisions. Finally, consumer buyer behaviour is influenced by four major *psychological factors*—motivation, perception, learning, and beliefs and attitudes. Each of these factors provides a different perspective for understanding the workings of the buyer's black box.

3. **List and understand the major types of buying decision behaviour and stages in the buyer decision process.**

Buying behaviour may vary greatly across different types of products and buying decisions. Consumers undertake *complex buying behaviour* when they are highly involved in a purchase and perceive significant differences among brands. *Dissonance-reducing behaviour* occurs when consumers are more highly involved but see little difference among brands. *Habitual buying behaviour* occurs under conditions of low involvement and little significant brand difference. In situations characterized by low involvement but significant perceived brand differences, consumers engage in *variety-seeking buying behaviour.*

When making a purchase, the buyer goes through a decision process consisting of *need recognition, information search, evaluation of alternatives, purchase decision*, and *postpurchase behaviour.* The marketer's job is to understand the buyer's behaviour at each stage and the influences that are operating. During *need recognition*, the consumer recognizes a problem or need that could be satisfied by a product or service in the market. Once the need is recognized, the consumer is aroused to seek more information and moves into the *information search* stage. With information in hand, the

consumer proceeds to *alternative evaluation*, during which the information is used to evaluate brands in the choice set. From there, the consumer makes a *purchase decision* and actually buys the product. In the final stage of the buyer decision process, *postpurchase behaviour,* the consumer takes action based on satisfaction or dissatisfaction.

4. **Describe the adoption and diffusion process for new products.**

The product adoption process comprises five stages: awareness, interest, evaluation, trial, and adoption. Initially, the consumer must become aware of the new product. *Awareness* leads to *interest*, and the consumer seeks information about the new product. Once information has been gathered, the consumer enters the *evaluation* stage and considers buying the new product. Next, in the *trial* stage, the consumer tries the product on a small scale to improve his or her estimate of its value. If the consumer is satisfied with the product, he or she enters the *adoption* stage, deciding to use the new product fully and regularly.

With regard to diffusion of new products, consumers respond at different rates, depending on the consumer's characteristics and the product's characteristics. Consumers may be innovators, early adopters, early majority, late majority, or laggards. *Innovators* are willing to try risky new ideas; *early adopters*—often community opinion leaders—accept new ideas early but carefully; the *early majority*—rarely leaders—decide deliberately to try new ideas, doing so before the average person does; the *late majority* try an innovation only after a majority of people have adopted it; whereas *laggards* adopt an innovation only after it has become a tradition itself. Manufacturers try to bring their new products to the attention of potential early adopters, especially those who are opinion leaders.

Reviewing the Key Terms

Adoption process   237

Alternative evaluation   233

Attitude   228

Belief   228

Cognitive dissonance   234

Complex buying behaviour   230

Consumer buyer behaviour   204

Consumer market   204

Culture   206

Dissonance-reducing buying behaviour   230

Group   214

Habitual buying behaviour   231

Information search   232

Learning   228

Lifestyle   220

Motive (or drive)   225

Need recognition   232

New product   237

Opinion leader   214

Perception   226

Personality   224

Postpurchase behaviour   234

Purchase decision   234

Social classes   213

Subculture   207

Variety-seeking buying behaviour   231

Discussing the Concepts

1. Which of the following general characteristics affecting consumer behaviour would most influence the purchase of a new music CD: social class, age and life-cycle stage, or beliefs and attitudes?

2. A bank used SRI Consulting's Values and Lifestyles (VALS) research to profile customer segments that did not use any automated or electronic services. Based on your knowledge of the VALS classification system, speculate what might be the primary and secondary VALS types for this customer segment.

3. On a trip to Best Buy, suppose you overhear the following comment made in a conversation between two salespeople: "I think the sales director really knows our products and the market, and I've thought so for years." Is the salesperson expressing a belief or an attitude? Explain?

4. The vice-president of marketing for a regional dough-nut retailer says, "We believe our customers exhibit high-involvement buying behaviours." Do you agree? Why or why not?

5. Compare and contrast the consumer decision process someone might use in purchasing a new notebook computer at the Apple Canada website with that of purchasing a 454 g jar of Jif creamy-style peanut but-ter at Wal-Mart.

6. In a small group, discuss the following question: Who would be the better opinion leader for a high-technology cellular service, Stephen Harper or Bill Gates? Support your choice.

Applying the Concepts

1. You are the vice-president of marketing for a small soft-ware company that has developed new and novel spam-blocking software. You are charged with selecting a target market segment for the product launch. How would you use Rogers' *Diffusion of Innovations* frame-work to help you with this choice? (See Figure 6.6 on page 238.) What are some of the likely characteristics of this customer group?

2. In a small group, discuss how the buyer decision process for a university student would differ from that of a snowboarder in purchasing a backpack. How would you use this knowledge to develop an advertis-ing plan?

3. The chapter defines "alternative evaluation" as "how the consumer processes information to arrive at brand choices." Suppose, as discussed in the chapter, that you have narrowed your choice of new cars to brand A, B, or C. You have finalized the four most important new car attributes and their weights, and have created and filled in the evaluation matrix below. Which new car alternative will you more than likely select?

Attributes	Importance Weight	New Car Alternatives		
		Brand A	Brand B	Brand C
Styling	0.5	3	7	4
Operating Economy	0.2	6	5	7
Warranty	0.1	5	5	6
Price	0.2	8	7	8

Focus on Technology

Biometric technology is emerging from the 9/11 tragedy as one of the most important and accurate systems of per-sonal identification. Biometric systems discriminate based on measurement of a physical feature or repeatable behav-iour or action of the individual. They recognize individuals based on hand geometry, retinal scan, iris scan, fingerprint patterns, facial characteristics, DNA sequence characteris-tics, voice prints, and handwritten signature.

1. Name five situations where biometric technology would help with an issue or problem at your university or college. How would this technology help you as a student or personally?

2. In what situations might this technology help mar-keters to understand consumer buying or decision processes better? Explain.

Focus on Ethics

You are a marketer with a financial services firm in Canada. You've been tracking a product recently introduced into the United States. The product is Red Zone, a financial services product that provides consumers with information on their personal financial situations. Marketed directly to consumers via the Internet and direct mail, Red Zone is sold in the form of an annual prepaid membership for $79.95, after a 30-day free trial. To help attract subscribers, the company provides a "Free Red Zone Score" report along with the trial membership. Promotion focuses on the "Free Red Zone Score" with little mention of the Red Zone "trial membership." To the best of your knowledge, Red Zone's promotional language, ads, and order form were approved by its legal department. The "Free Red Zone Score" offer has great impact on the evaluation stage of the consumer decision process—it provides a 50-percent lift in membership trials over the basic offer.

Your research shows that a significant proportion of the paid members do not realize that they have signed a $79.95 Red Zone annual membership agreement that will be charged to their credit cards at the end of the 30-day free trial. When these unaware Red Zone members receive their monthly credit card bill and see the $79.95 charge, they often file complaints for a fraudulent charge with the credit card company. Moreover, they often followed up with a complaint to a state attorney general or the Better Business Bureau. Your boss, the marketing VP, has scheduled a meeting with you for tomorrow to ask for your recommendation about whether a product similar to Red Zone should be launched in the Canadian market by your firm.

1. Assess the consumer buying process for Red Zone. How do current promotion practices affect this buying process?

2. Would the current Red Zone promotion be legal in Canada? Is it ethical? Is it good business practice?

3. What will you recommend tomorrow? If you decide to launch the service, what would you do to prevent the service from experiencing the same criticisms as it has experienced in the United States?

Video Case
Wild Planet

We've all heard about the community outreach efforts of retailers such as Body Shop and Ben & Jerry's. But unlike the social activists of the past, today's values-led businesses are founded by well-trained business managers and company builders with a passion for a cause. The result is socially minded businesses with the know-how needed to target and connect with customers. For example, to make money and follow their values at the same time, the folks at Wild Planet have decided to market much more than just toys. They sell positive play experiences. Daniel Grossman started Wild Planet to create innovative products to "spark the imagination, promote creativity, and provide positive experiences without relying on violence."

Wild Planet appeals to consumers by pursuing its social mission of creating toys that do not rely on gender stereotypes or promote violence. And by getting to know its customers and their buying characteristics, the small toy retailer competes alongside megaretailers such as Toys "R" Us.

After viewing the video featuring Wild Planet, answer the following questions about consumer buying behaviour.

1. What characteristics of consumer behaviour are likely to influence Wild Planet's customers? Which characteristic do you think is most likely to motivate customers' purchases?

2. Visit Wild Planet's website and browse the information about the company as well as the products it offers. What demographic segment of consumers is the company targeting?

3. How does Wild Planet learn more about its customers' characteristics and buying behaviour?

Online Media Resources

Company Case
Weight? I'm on Atkins

Check out these startling facts: Statistics Canada data demonstrate that more than half of Canadians are overweight or obese, with almost 15 percent of the population falling in the category of "obese." Obesity leads to decreased life expectancy, limits quality of life, and diminishes national productivity. A conservative estimate of the total direct cost of overweight and obesity in Canada is $1.8 billion. Obesity isn't just a Canadian problem. The World Health Organization reports that overweight and obesity are increasing worldwide at an alarming rate, in both developed and developing countries to the extent that it is now a pandemic, affecting billions globally. For example, in the United States, the proportion of overweight or obese children increased from 8.9 percent in 1960 to 30.8 percent by 2000. Moreover, overweight children are likely to grow up to be overweight adults. The "weight growth spurt" in children could result in as many as 90 percent of the adult population being overweight in the future. As a result, this generation of children may be the first to die before their parents. That's an incredibly grim prospect.

Obesity is becoming the number-one killer in North America. Obesity-related ailments range from heart attacks to nineteen kinds of cancer, kidney disease, and diabetes. Overweight people are also prone to depression, other emotional upsets, and job loss (physical inability to perform at work). One study showed that children thought being overweight was as bad as having cancer, because they suffer from poor social interactions, low school achievement, lack of athletic prowess, and troubled family relationships.

Overweight children stay home from school four times as much as other children; are teased mercilessly; and have physical problems, such as sleep apnea, fatty liver, type 2 diabetes, or high cholesterol. The last two ailments were formerly associated mostly with middle-aged adults.

What's causing this epidemic? Fast-food restaurants have a lot to answer for here. The movie *Super Size Me* reported one man's attempt to live on fast food for a month. The result? He gained more than 11 kilograms. Every day, nearly one-third of North American children aged 4 to 19 eat fast food, likely packing on about three extra kilograms per child per year. Other restaurants with "all-you-can eat" meals encourage people to gorge themselves, and portions served in North America tend to be larger than they are in the rest of the world.

Besides overeating, we are becoming more sedentary. Many people hold office jobs and spend a great deal of time sitting down, talking on telephones, and typing on computers. Many drive everywhere (even to the gym) instead of walking. Major food processors prepare frozen, canned, and dried foods that are frequently low in protein and high in salt and fat. They've introduced all sorts of desserts and snackables and made them so convenient that you can eat, drive, and talk on your cellphone at the same time. The bottom line is that food is easier come by (we don't have to kill it, grow it, or cook it), so that it's easy to overeat.

What are North Americans doing about this? Many tackled their problem by following some kind of low-carb program. The favourites are the Atkins Diet and the South Beach Diet. Who has not had a colleague or friend declare, "I'm on Atkins," meaning "Don't serve me bread, potatoes, or pasta at your house"? The essence of Atkins, South Beach, and other low-carb diets is that a calorie is not just a calorie. Atkins believed the body switched from a carbohydrate-burning mechanism to a fat-burning machine when the quantity of carbohydrates was reduced. In the first two weeks of the Atkins Diet, dieters ingest almost no carbohydrates in order to stimulate the fat-burning process. Therefore, Atkins allows you to eat protein (meat, even bacon), eggs, and butter. Over the centuries, our bodies have been programmed to store fat. As the body shifts to fat-burning, it begins to reduce our stored fat.

Of course, the Atkins Diet flies in the face of conventional nutritional wisdom, which stresses low-fat diets. But is this diet really nonsense and pseudoscience, as one doctor called it? Doctors and nutritionists have to admit that people *do* lose weight on Atkins. An experiment at Harvard, in which participants were divided into low-fat diet groups, a low-carb group that got the same number of calories as the low-fat group, and a low-carb group that got 300 more calories per day. All participants were given their food for each day. At the end of a year, the low-fat group had lost 7.7 kilograms, the low-carb group 10.5 kilograms, and the low-carb group with the extra 300 calories 9 kilograms. These counterintuitive results contradict the theory that the best way to lose weight is to eat fewer calories and cut out fat. And they support Atkins' metabolic-advantage theory.

Atkins has had major effects on businesses—some good and some not-so-good. First, there's Atkins Direct, a catalogue company (founded by guess who?) that sells supplements and more than 100 approved foodstuffs, including bread. So, Atkins sells the book that stimulates the diet along with the foodstuffs and supplements to maintain the diet. Other businesses have jumped on the low-carb bandwagon. Publications such as *Low-Carb Living* and the *Low-Carb Energy* book have hit newsstands. In California there are even two low-carb supermarkets.

Restaurants, such as Burger King, McDonald's, T.G.I. Fridays, and Subway, have put low-carb alternatives on their menus. Frequently low-carb or bunless burgers (burgers with more lettuce and tomato in a box) show up on other restaurant's menus. Packaged-goods manufacturer Unilever developed a line of products called "Carb Options" but dropped the line because of low adoption. Anheuser Busch has been successful with Michelob Ultra, and Heinz has developed One Carb Ketchup. Pasta companies have introduced low-carb pasta. There are plenty of opportunities for companies to take advantage of the low-carb diet craze. That's just food processors and restaurants.

Rather than diet and follow the low-carb craze, some chose diet pills. Americans, in particular, like pills—take one and problems disappear. This requires no real effort—the medicine does it for you. Americans spend more than US$100 million a year on diet pills.

The best-known are Acutrim and Dexatrim, but there's no evidence that they work. There are also commercial weight-loss centres, such as Jenny Craig and Weight Watchers, that sell consultations, programs, books, and foodstuffs. Meal-replacement shakes, such as SlimFast and Shaklee, often show up at work at lunchtime.

Prescription drugs are like diet pills in that the customer expects the pill to do the work. Diet pills frequently hit the headlines: first because they are hailed as miracles and second because they create scandals. Drugs such as Redux and phen-fen were well publicized as causing ailments, such as pulmonary hypertension, heart valve disorders, and seizures. Last, there's surgery—bariatric surgery, such as stomach stapling, in which the stomach is stapled so that only a small amount of it is available for digestion. With smaller stomachs, people eat less. Such surgery is expensive and can lead to follow-up surgery for conditions such as abdominal hernias.

Although Atkins has "created" new businesses, it has also hurt other, older businesses. At the height of the Atkins Diet craze, fast-food sales dropped and makers of cereal and processed foods reported lower sales and revenue. Sales of Unilever's SlimFast went down, and Weight Watchers' slimming programs fell 6 percent. Bread makers lost revenues, and pasta makers have convened to discuss ploys to combat lower sales. In terms of helping people change their eating habits, this is good. But for employees and stockholders, it's bad.

Doctors and nutritionists have said for years that people should lose weight slowly and exercise. Many, however, want something that works fast—like those pills. They have also resisted exercise, even though just a little bit of it can go a long way. Swedish researchers have demonstrated that older adults who exercised only once a week were 40 percent less likely to die during a 12-year study than those who did nothing. Other research shows that people who say that they "exercise only occasionally" still had a 28 percent lower risk of dying in a 12-year study. Studies have also shown that exercise by aging adults helps to improve brain function. Finally, a study of teens in Texas high schools using physical education classes reported that feelings of sadness and the risk of suicide were lowered. Exercise is good for you not only physically but also mentally.

Business has also jumped on the exercise bandwagon. Exercise clinics and gyms like Good Life are springing up in local communities, and it's becoming a social outing to work out. People talk about their "workouts" at work, on lunch breaks, and among friends. One of my friends has even figured out that Friday and Saturday nights are urban-professional-singles night at her exercise club. Personal trainers and custom exercise programs have become more common. More exercise equipment is sold for home use. How many of you come from homes where there are used or (more likely) unused exercycles, tread mills, and weight stations?

Beyond the problem of real obesity, there's also another obesity-related problem. Eating disorders, such as anorexia and bulimia, are on the rise because of "perceived obesity." Anorexics starve themselves and bulimics binge eat and then purge themselves by vomiting. These two disorders affect 10 million American women and 1 million American men. The age of anorexics and bulimics is dropping to children 8 to 10 years old. Eating disorders are accompanied by stress and body image problems, and empowerment comes from being thin. Furthermore, psychological studies show that eating disorders lead to obsessiveness, dependency, overcontrolled hostility, assertiveness, locus of control, and lower self-esteem.

"Perceived obesity" is encouraged by cultural and social mores. Young women want to be as thin as the models they see every day in advertising. Thanks to television, magazines, movies, and the Internet, rail-thin girls and steroid-built beef-boys are being shoved into the faces of everyone. Babe Paley, wife of a CBS executive, has been quoted for years as saying, "A woman can never be too thin or too rich." If we follow that line of reasoning, then thin—even to the point of anorexia—is definitely beautiful. Some models starve themselves and take drugs to stay incredibly thin. Some obese people come to hate themselves because they don't meet society's expectations, and others regard them negatively.

Worse yet, obesity is not an equal opportunity ailment. Low-income people are more likely to be obese than the well-off. Obesity is highest among women reporting low income and lower levels of education, especially Aboriginal and black women.

Whether trends like the Atkins Diet are fads or permanent, it's clear that North Americans know that they need to lose weight; they know they need to exercise and change their eating habits. However, instead, of making these long-term changes, many go for the "latest popular thing."

Questions for Discussion

1. What social, cultural, and personal factors are associated with obesity? With eating disorders? What psychological factors?

2. How would obesity, diets, and exercise programs fit into VALS lifestyles? What groups are most likely to take advantage of which means of losing weight?

3. Why have so many consumers chosen Atkins or the South Beach Diet? How has the decision-making process affected their choice?

4. How has business capitalized on obesity and eating disorders? Is this desirable?

5. North Americans spend more than US$100 billion a year on ways to lose weight, but it doesn't happen. Next year, the same people will probably spend more. People appear not to care if they don't get the product they pay for. What social, cultural, and personal factors explain this? How does it benefit business?

Sources: Canadian Institutes of Health Research, "Obesity Research in Canada: Backgrounder," Shirley Bryan and Peter Walsh, "Physical Activity and Obesity in Canadian Women," Centre for Chronic Disease Prevention and Control, Health Canada, www.biomedcentral.com/1472-6874/4/S1/S6 (accessed August 25, 2004); Lori Widzinski, "Inside Out: Stories of Bulimia," *Library Journal*, June 1, 2003, p. 182; Susan McClelland, "Distorted Images," *Maclean's*, August 14, 2000, pp. 41–42; Rebecca L. Rogers and Trent A. Petrie, "Psychological Correlates of Anorexic and Bulimic Symptomatology," *Journal of Counseling and Development*, Vol. 79, No. 2, Spring 2001, pp. 178–188; "Kids Say Being Fat Is as Bad as Having Cancer," *Medical Post*, May 6, 2003, Vol. 39, Iss. 18; Tara Parker-Pope, "Health Matters: When It Comes to Exercise, a Little Bit Goes a Long Way," *Wall Street Journal*, August 9, 2004, p. R.5; Louise Witt, "Why We're Losing the War Against Obesity," *American Demographics*, December 2004, p. 27; Rachel Lehmann-Haupt, "La Vida Low Carb," *Folio,* March 2004, p. 58; Ann Brocklehurst, "The Lowdown on the Low-Carb Diet Wars," *Maclean's*, February 23, 2004, pp 38–39.

CHAPTER 7
Business Markets and Business Buyer Behaviour

"I've been using three different companies for **international,**
overnight and ground. Now I just call Brown."
It's all part of a simpler lifestyle I'm trying out."

Your world is complicated enough. Simplify it. Let Brown handle all your shipping. In return,

we'll give you the peace of mind that comes from using just one, perfectly integrated

shipping network. One company that can deliver international, overnight and ground

shipments to your customers, on time. Guaranteed. It's as simple as that.

INTERNATIONAL. OVERNIGHT. GROUND. SYNCHRONIZED.

WHAT CAN BROWN DO FOR YOU?™

UPS.com® 1-800-PICK-UPS®

**AFTER STUDYING THIS CHAPTER,
YOU SHOULD BE ABLE TO**

1. define the business market and
   explain how business markets differ
   from consumer markets

2. identify the major factors that
   influence business buyer behaviour

3. list and define the steps in the
   business buying decision process

4. compare the institutional and
   government markets and explain
   how institutional and government
   buyers make their buying decisions

Previewing the Concepts

In the previous chapter, you studied *final consumer* buying behaviour and factors that influence it. In this chapter, we'll do the same for *business customers*—those that buy goods and services for use in producing their own products and services or for resale to others.

To start, let's look at UPS (United Parcel Service). You probably know UPS as a neighbourhood small-package delivery company. It turns out, however, that a majority of UPS's business comes not from residential consumers but from large *business* customers. To succeed in its business-to-business markets, UPS must work closely with its business customers to become a strategic logistics partner.

ention UPS, and most people envision one of those familiar brown trucks with a friendly driver, rumbling around their neighbourhood dropping off parcels. That makes sense. UPS is the world's largest express carrier and package delivery company. In Canada, UPS first opened its doors for business in the basement of a Toronto hotel in 1975. Today, it employs more than 7435 people in Canada and 407 200 worldwide. UPS delivers to every address in Canada and the United States, and operates in more than 200 countries. In 2004 alone, the company's brown-clad drivers served more than 7.9 million customers daily delivering more than 3.6 billion packages and documents.

Whether you are a business or end consumer, the company's brown colour has come to mean something special. "We've been referred to for years as Big Brown," says a UPS marketing executive. "People love our drivers, they love our brown trucks, they love everything we do." Thus was born UPS's current "What Can Brown Do for You?" advertising theme.

Most of UPS's revenues come not from the residential customers who receive the packages, but from the *business* customers who send them. Whereas residential consumers might look to "Brown" simply for fast, friendly, low-cost package delivery, business customers usually have much more complex needs. Thus, in addition to package and document delivery, UPS is a leading provider of specialized transportation, logistics, capital, and ecommerce services. It provides services to help businesses track purchase orders, inventory, order status checks, invoices, payments, and returned merchandise. It provides timely information about packages—what's in them, where they're currently located, to whom they are going, when

they will get there, how much has been paid, and how much is owed.

Businesses must also be able to handle fluctuations in demand. Just think about the increase in demand for some products around Valentine's Day, for example. The holiday is big business in Canada. Consumers spend an estimated $20 million on flowers and $144 million on candy, mainly chocolates. What's more, most purchases are made at the last minute. Retailers must have these items in stock, and their suppliers must fulfill their needs during this critical time or the sales are lost. "While consumers celebrate the emotion of Valentine's Day, the business side is complex and potentially lucrative for companies that can take advantage of it," says Glenn Rice, president of UPS Canada. "For many Canadian companies, February 14 is an opportunity to increase sales following the quiet post-Christmas period. Getting product to market, in a cost effective and timely manner, allows companies to stay competitive. By working with UPS, our clients are assured their customers will 'feel the love' on Valentine's Day."

See what UPS does for deluxe chocolate manufacturer Hagensborg Foods Ltd. of Vancouver. Canadians are chocoholics, and demand surges on Valentine's Day to the extent that Hagensborg Foods Ltd. sees demand for its products jump by 35 percent in the weeks prior to February 14. "The weeks between Christmas and Valentine's Day are an incredibly busy time for us, as we ship our products to major grocery chains, department stores and gift-basket companies in Canada and the United States," says Robin Relph, president of Hagensborg Foods Ltd. "Our challenge is meeting this demand and keeping track of our shipments to customers." Being sure its chocolates are there on time and in perfect condition enables Hagensborg Foods Ltd. to maintain the long-term customer relationships that are so critical to its success.

Cupid also relies on UPS to get millions of roses and other flowers from countries such as Colombia and Ecuador to romantics across North America in time for Valentine's Day. To meet the demands of this holiday, UPS adds an additional 28 flights in the two weeks prior to February 14. Flowers are highly perishable. In a 24-hour period, flowers are cut, packed, and loaded onto a temperature-controlled UPS aircraft. They clear customs in Miami, and from there they are shipped to florists across Canada.

UPS knows that for many companies, all these work-a-day logistical concerns can be a nightmare. Moreover, most companies don't see these activities as strategic competencies that provide competitive advantage. Big Brown can show them how wrong they are. UPS handles the logistics, allowing its customers to focus on what they do best. It offers everything from ground and air package distribution, freight delivery (air, ocean, rail, and road), and mail services to inventory management, third-party logistics, international trade management, logistics management software and ecommerce solutions, and even financing. If it has to do with logistics, UPS can probably do it better than anyone can.

UPS has the resources to handle the logistics needs of just about any size business. It operates some 88 000 vehicles (package cars, vans, tractors, and motorcycles), 600 aircraft (making it the ninth-largest airline in the world), and more than 1000 warehouse facilities in 120 countries. It serves 90 percent of the world population and 99 percent of businesses in the Fortune 1000. UPS invests US$1 billion a year in information technology to support its highly synchronized, by-the-clock logistics services and to provide customers with information at every point in the process.

Beyond moving their packages around Canada, UPS can also help business customers to navigate the complexities of international shipping, with some 800 international flights per day to or from 466 international destinations. For example, although most residential customers don't need next-day air service to or from China, many businesses do seek help shipping to and from the burgeoning Asian manufacturing zones. UPS helps ensure the timely flow of crucial business documents, prototypes, high-value goods

(such as semiconductors), and emergency repair parts that wing their way across the Pacific every day. UPS even offers expedited customs services, with fast inspection and clearance processes that help get goods into the country quickly.

UPS also provides a wide range of financial services for its business customers. Its UPS Capital division will handle client's accounts receivable—UPS shippers can choose to be reimbursed immediately and have UPS collect payment from the recipient. Other financial services include credit cards for small businesses and programs to fund inventory, equipment leasing, and asset financing. UPS even bought a bank to underpin its financial operations.

To help its clients improve their own systems, UPS Consulting advises companies on redesigning their logistics systems to align them better with their business strategies. UPS Supply Chain Solutions helps customers to synchronize the flow of goods, funds, and information up and down their supply chains. UPS Logistics Technologies supplies software that improves customers' distribution efficiency, including street-level route optimization, territory planning, mobile delivery execution, real-time wireless dispatch, and GPS tracking.

So, what can Brown do for you? As it turns out, the answer depends on who you are. For its residential consumers, UPS uses those familiar brown trucks to provide simple and efficient package pickup and delivery services. But in its business-to-business markets, it develops deeper and more-involved customer relationships. The company's "What Can Brown Do for You?" ads feature a variety of business professionals discussing how UPS's broad range of services makes their jobs easier. But such ad promises have little meaning if not reinforced by actions. Says former UPS CEO Jim Kelly, "A brand can be very hollow and lifeless ... if the people and the organization ... are not 100 percent dedicated to living out the brand promise every day."

For UPS, that means that employees around the world must do more than just deliver packages from point A to point B for their business customers. They must roll up their sleeves and work hand in hand with customers to help solve their complex logistics problems. More than just providing shipping services, they must become strategic logistics partners.[1]

In one way or another, most companies must form strong relationships with other business firms. Relationships with suppliers, for example, help small firms like Toronto-based Cervélo Cycles (which has been making a huge name for itself on the international bicycle racing circuit) find the strongest, lightweight, high-performance components necessary for their leading-edge bicycle designs. As our opening example demonstrates, businesses also rely on relationships with service providers, such as UPS. Large companies, such as Nortel, Bombardier, SNC Lavalin (a major Canadian engineering company), Magna (a Canadian auto parts manufacturer), Alcan, and countless other firms, sell *most* of their products to other businesses. Even consumer-products companies, which make products used by final consumers, must first sell their products to retailers or other distributors. And they rely on the creative powers of their communications agencies (another type of important business-to-business relationship) to tell consumers about their products. See how important these business-to-business relationships have been to Nintendo Canada:

In 2004, Nintendo Canada, a Richmond, B.C.-based company, was named Marketer of the Year by the British Columbia chapter of the American Marketing Association. It took an amazing journey to get to this point. In 2002, Nintendo was a distant third in terms of market share, and it was bleeding money. Ron Bertram, general manager at Nintendo Canada, says the company took a serious look at itself, its customers, and its place in the industry. As a subsidiary of a large American firm, it couldn't control the marketing mix or product development, but it could control how it communicated the benefits of its products to different target audiences. To do this well, it had to build close working relationships with a public relations firm, an agency to develop its online communications programs, and another to help it build its brand through a television campaign. Like all firms selecting or reviewing its relationships with agencies, Nintendo sent out a call for bids outlining its goals and objectives in particular target markets. Agencies that made the short list then developed presentations, or "pitches," to demonstrate their skills with regard to helping Nintendo accomplish its objectives. Once an agency is selected, the two firms will work closely together to develop a communications campaign. Nintendo has multiple agency relationships. In 2004, Nintendo Canada's agency of record was Toronto's Leo Burnett. Its website, toomuchfun.ca, was created by Vancouver's Blast Radius, and its brand-building television campaign was created and produced by Alias, a Vancouver youth-marketing division of Cossette Communication-Marketing. In 2005, Nintendo wanted to give more punch to its online newsletter program. It compared the work of four agencies and finally chose Toronto-based Henderson Bas because of its challenging thinking, high-quality creative, and focus on Nintendo's bottom line. With the help of these important relationships, Nintendo has dramatically grown its business at a rate three times greater than growth in the overall marketplace.[2]

Business buyer behaviour

The buying behaviour of the organizations that buy goods and services for use in the production of other products and services or for the purpose of reselling or renting them to others at a profit.

Business buying process

The decision process by which business buyers determine which products and services their organizations need to purchase, and then find, evaluate, and choose among alternative suppliers and brands.

Business buyer behaviour refers to the buying behaviour of the organizations that buy goods and services for use in the production of other products and services that are sold, rented, or supplied to others. It also includes the behaviour of retailing and wholesaling firms that acquire goods for the purpose of reselling or renting them to others at a profit. In the **business buying process**, business buyers determine which products and services their organizations need to purchase, and then find, evaluate, and choose among alternative suppliers and brands. *Business-to-business (B-to-B) marketers* must do their best to understand business markets and business buyer behaviour.

Business Markets

The business market is *huge*. In fact, business markets involve far more dollars and items than do consumer markets. For example, think about the large number of business transactions involved in the production and sale of a single set of Goodyear tires. Various suppliers sell Goodyear the rubber, steel, equipment, and other goods that it needs to produce the tires. Goodyear then sells the finished tires to retailers, who in turn sell them to consumers. Thus, many sets of *business* purchases were made for only one set of *consumer* purchases. In addition, Goodyear sells tires as original equipment to manufacturers that install them on new vehicles, and as replacement tires to companies that maintain their own fleets of company cars, trucks, buses, or other vehicles.

Characteristics of Business Markets

In some ways, business markets are similar to consumer markets. Both involve people who assume buying roles and make purchase decisions to satisfy needs. However, business markets differ in many ways from consumer markets. The main differences, shown in Table 7.1 and discussed in the following sections, are in *market structure and demand*, the *nature of the buying unit*, and the *types of decisions and the decision process* involved.

Market Structure and Demand

The business marketer normally deals with *far fewer but far larger buyers* than the consumer marketer does. Even in large business markets, a few buyers often account for most of the purchasing. For example, when Goodyear sells replacement tires to final consumers, its potential market includes the owners of the millions of cars currently in use in North America and around the world. But Goodyear's fate in the business market depends on getting orders from one of only a handful of large automakers. Similarly, Black & Decker sells its power tools and outdoor equipment to tens of millions of consumers worldwide. However, it must sell these products through its major retail customers—Canadian Tire, Home Depot, Rona, and Wal-Mart.

Business markets are also *more geographically concentrated*. There are more than 2.2 million business establishments in Canada. About 58 percent of all Canadian businesses are located in Ontario and Quebec, concentrated in the metropolitan areas between Windsor and Quebec City (an area that also accounts for about one-third of Canada's population). Thirty-five percent of Canada's businesses are in the Western provinces; 6 percent are located in the Atlantic provinces. The

---

TABLE 7.1 Characteristics of Business Markets

Marketing Structure and Demand

Business markets contain *fewer but larger buyers*.

Business customers are *more geographically concentrated*.

Business buyer demand is *derived* from final consumer demand.

Demand in many business markets is *more inelastic*—not affected as much in the short run by price changes.

Demand in business markets *fluctuates more,* and more quickly.

Nature of the Buying Unit

Business purchases involve *more buyers*.

Business buying involves a *more professional purchasing effort*.

Types of Decisions and the Decision Process

Business buyers usually face *more complex buying decisions*.

The business buying process is *more formalized*.

In business buying, buyers and sellers work more closely together and build close long-run *relationships*.

provinces of Ontario and Quebec are home to the country's auto industry, while Canada's high-tech firms are clustered in Ottawa, Montreal, and Toronto. The petroleum industry calls Calgary and Edmonton home. New Brunswick attracts the telemarketing industry and is the location of many companies' call centres. Most agricultural output comes from a relatively few provinces.[3]

Derived demand

Business demand that ultimately comes from (derives from) the demand for consumer goods.

Business demand is **derived demand**—it ultimately derives from the demand for consumer goods. IBM and Dell buy Intel microprocessor chips because consumers buy personal computers (PCs). If consumer demand for PCs drops, so will the demand for computer chips.

Therefore, B-to-B marketers sometimes promote their products directly to final consumers to increase business demand. For example, Intel's long-running "Intel Inside" advertising campaign sells PC buyers on the virtues of Intel microprocessors. The increased demand for Intel chips boosts demand for the PCs containing them, and both Intel and its business partners win.

Similarly, DuPont promotes Teflon directly to final consumers as a key branded ingredient in many products—from nonstick cookware to stain-repellent, wrinkle-free clothing. You see Teflon Fabric Protector hangtags on clothing lines, such as Levi's Dockers, Donna Karan's menswear, and Ralph Lauren denim.[4] By making Teflon familiar and attractive to final buyers, DuPont also makes the products containing it more attractive.

Many business markets have *inelastic demand*; that is, total demand for many business products is not affected much by price changes, especially in the short run. A drop in the price of leather will not cause shoe manufacturers to buy much more leather unless it results in lower shoe prices that, in turn, will increase consumer demand for shoes.

Finally, business markets have more *fluctuating demand*. The demand for many business goods and services tends to change more—and more quickly—than the demand for consumer goods and services does. A small percentage increase in consumer demand can cause large increases in business demand. Sometimes a rise of only 10 percent in consumer demand can cause as much as a 200 percent rise in business demand during the next period.

Intel's long-running "Intel Inside" logo advertising campaign boosts demand for Intel chips and for the PCs containing them. Now, most computer markets feature a logo like this one in their ads.

Nature of the Buying Unit

Compared with consumer purchases, a business purchase usually involves *more decision participants* and a *more professional purchasing effort*. Often, business buying is done by trained purchasing agents who spend their working lives learning how to buy better. The more complex the purchase, the more likely that several people will participate in the decision-making process. Buying committees made up of technical experts and top management are common in the buying of major goods.

Beyond this, many companies are now upgrading their purchasing functions to "supply management" or "supplier development" functions. B-to-B marketers now face a new breed of higher-level, better-trained supply managers. These supply managers sometimes seem to know more about the supplier company than it knows about itself. Therefore, business marketers must have well-trained marketers and salespeople to deal with these well-trained buyers.

Types of Decisions and the Decision Process

Business buyers usually face *more complex* buying decisions than do consumer buyers. Purchases often involve large sums of money, complex technical and economic considerations, and interactions among many people at many levels of the buyer's organization. Because the purchases are more complex, business buyers may take longer to make their decisions. The business buying process also tends to be *more formalized* than the consumer buying process. Large business purchases usually call for detailed product specifications, written purchase orders, careful supplier searches, and formal approval.

Finally, in the business buying process, buyer and seller are often much *more dependent* on each other. Consumer marketers are often at a distance from their customers. In contrast, B-to-B marketers may roll up their sleeves and work closely with their customers during all stages of the buying process—from helping customers define problems, to finding solutions, to supporting after-sale operation. They often customize their offerings to individual customer needs.

In the short run, sales go to suppliers who meet buyers' immediate product and service needs. In the long run, however, B-to-B marketers keep a customer's sales by meeting current needs *and* by partnering with customers to help them solve their problems. In recent years, relationships between customers and suppliers have been changing from downright adversarial to close and chummy. In fact, many customer companies are now practising **supplier development**, systematically developing networks of supplier–partners to ensure an appropriate and dependable supply of products and materials that they will use in making their own products or resell to others. For example, Caterpillar no longer calls its buyers "purchasing agents"—they are managers of "purchasing and supplier development." And Wal-Mart doesn't have a "purchasing department," it has a "supplier development department." (See Real Marketing 7.1.) "Through appropriate supplier relationships management," says one manager, "both the buyer and supplier can ... deliver [more] value throughout each of their supply chains. Suppliers are an extension of our capabilities."[5]

Supplier development
Systematic development of networks of supplier–partners to ensure an appropriate and dependable supply of products and materials that they will use in making their own products or resell to others.

A Model of Business Buyer Behaviour

At the most basic level, marketers want to know how business buyers will respond to various marketing stimuli. Figure 7.1 shows a model of business buyer behaviour. In this model, marketing and other stimuli affect the buying organization and produce certain buyer responses. As with consumer buying, the marketing stimuli for business buying consist of the four Ps: product, price, place, and promotion. Other stimuli include major forces in the environment: economic, technological, political, cultural, and competitive. These stimuli enter the organization and are turned into

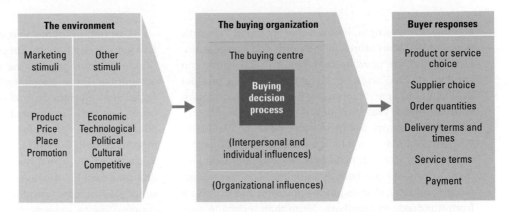

Figure 7.1 Model of business buyer behaviour

buyer responses: product or service choice; supplier choice; order quantities; and delivery, service, and payment terms. In order to design good marketing mix strategies, the marketer must understand what happens within the organization to turn stimuli into purchase responses.

Within the organization, buying activity consists of two major parts: the buying centre, made up of all the people involved in the buying decision, and the buying decision process. The model shows that the buying centre and the buying decision process are influenced by internal organizational, interpersonal, and individual factors as well as by external environmental factors.

REAL MARKETING   7.1

The Business Buying Process: Not Just "Purchasing," It's "Supplier Development"

*W*al-Mart sells more than a quarter of a trillion dollars' worth of goods each year. But before it can *sell* products to customers, it must first *purchase* them from suppliers. The giant retailer can't rely on spot purchases from suppliers who might not be available when needed. Wal-Mart must systematically develop a robust network of supplier–partners who will efficiently and reliably provide the tremendous volume of goods that it sells.

Some critics argue that Wal-Mart uses its massive size and buying power to force suppliers to accept razor-thin margins, sometimes even forcing them out of business. But if Wal-Mart were to do that to all of its suppliers, where would it obtain the huge supply of goods it needs to stock its store shelves around the world? Instead, for its own benefit, Wal-Mart must work with suppliers to make them more able.

These days, like Wal-Mart, most large businesses do more than "purchasing" in a narrow sense. Instead, they practise "supplier development," identifying, developing, and supporting suppliers to ensure a dependable supply of products and materials that they will use in making their own products or resell to others. They know that what's good for suppliers is also good for the company. So they partner with suppliers to help make them more effective.

Wal-Mart doesn't have a "purchasing department," it has a "supplier development department," which seeks out qualified suppliers and helps guide them through the complex Wal-Mart buying process. The department offers a Supplier Proposal Guide and maintains a website providing advice to suppliers wishing to do business with Wal-Mart. The retailer supports its suppliers in other ways. For example, it works actively with suppliers to test new products and marketing programs in its stores. And it lets major suppliers use its voluminous point-of-sale databases to analyze customers' regional buying habits. Procter &

▶

Gamble, for example, learned that its liquid Tide sells better at Wal-Mart stores in the north and northeastern U.S., while Tide powder sells better in the south and southwest. P&G uses such data to tailor its product availability to specific regions. By sharing information with suppliers, Wal-Mart helps them sell more products which, in turn, brings in more sales for Wal-Mart.

Like Wal-Mart, buyers in a wide range of industries are evolving from "purchasing" to "supplier development." Consider the heavily supplier-dependent automobile industry. Honda purchases parts and materials from hundreds of suppliers. More than a decade ago, Honda established a rigorous supplier relations program, which provides extensive supplier development and support. Honda doesn't just buy from its suppliers—it helps to train them as well. It offers more than 160 training classes for suppliers, on topics ranging from improving quality and reducing costs to developing front-line leadership. Honda also hosts twice-a-year events in which quality teams from as many as 100 suppliers meet to share ideas on improving manufacturing processes. "Our intent is to strengthen supplier business operations," says one Honda supplier executive. "The whole family organization is only as strong as the weakest link," says another. "So we have to perform together."

ChemStation does more than simply supply its customers with cleaning chemicals. "Our customers … think of us as more of a partner than a supplier."

Competitor Toyota also seeks out quality suppliers and helps to train them. For example, Toyota's Supplier Support Center spent three years teaching managers at supplier Ernie Green Industries about the Toyota Production System before issuing the first purchase order. Similarly, Toyota sent several consultants to supplier Summit Polymers' plant every day for four months to help Summit implement the Toyota system. Such supplier development activities have produced dramatic results. On average, Toyota has helped its suppliers increase productivity by 123 percent. Of course, Toyota expects to benefit in return. "We've grown quickly with … Toyota, and we're profitable," says Carl Code, a vice-president at Ernie Green Industries. "But it's no gravy train. They want suppliers to make enough money to stay in business, grow, and bring them innovation."

What does the shift from purchasing to supplier development mean for business-to-business marketers? It means that major business buyers are no longer looking only for "suppliers" from which to purchase goods and services. They are seeking "supplier–partners" with whom they can develop mutually beneficial supply relationships. But such relationships are a two-way street. Just as buyers are partnering with and supporting their suppliers, the suppliers must be worthy partners in return. They must work closely with the customers to better meet their supply needs.

For example, small industrial detergent maker ChemStation supplies thousands of products in hundreds of industries. ChemStation sells industrial cleaning chemicals to a wide variety of business customers, ranging from car washes to the U.S. Air Force. Whether a customer is washing down a fleet or a factory, a store or a restaurant, a distillery or an Army base, ChemStation comes up with the right cleaning solution every time.

But ChemStation does more than simply sell cleaning chemicals to its customers. It partners closely with them to custom design solutions to their unique cleaning problems. First, ChemStation works with each individual customer to concoct a soap formula specially designed for that customer. It has brewed special formulas for cleaning hands, mufflers, flutes, feathers, perfume vats, cosmetic eye makeup containers, yacht-making moulds, concrete trucks, oceangoing trawlers, and about anything else you can imagine. Next, ChemStation delivers the custom-made mixture to a tank installed at the customer's site. Finally, it maintains the tank by monitoring usage and automatically refilling the tank when supplies run low.

Partnering with an individual customer to find a full solution creates a lasting supplier–buyer relationship that helps ChemStation to lock out the competition. As noted in a recent issue of *Insights*, ChemStation's customer newsletter, "Our customers … oftentimes think of us as more of a partner than a supplier."

Sources: Katherine Zachary, "Honda Goes Beyond Philosophy in Supplier Efforts." *Ward's Auto World*, waw.wardsauto.com/ar/auto_honda_goes_beyond_2/index.htm (accessed July 1,

2003); Jeffrey H. Dyer and Nile W. Hatch, "Using Supplier Networks to Learn Faster," *MIT Sloan Management Review*, Spring 2004, pp. 77–84; "BJ's Knows … Our System Is Their Solution," *Insights*, March 2002, p. 1; Robert Sherefkin and Amy Wilson, "Why the Big 3 Can't Be Japanese," *Automotive News*, February 10, 2003; David Hannon, "Suppliers: Friend or Foe?" *Purchasing*, February 6, 2003, pp. 25–30; "Delphi: Parts Maker Helps Suppliers Shape Up," *InformationWeek*, April 19, 2004; information at www.chemstation.com (accessed January 2005); and "Supplier Information: Your Guide to Becoming a Wal-Mart Supplier," www.walmartstores.com (accessed January 2005).

Business Buyer Behaviour

The model in Figure 7.1 suggests four questions about business buyer behaviour: What buying decisions do business buyers make? Who participates in the buying process? What are the major influences on buyers? How do business buyers make their buying decisions?

Major Types of Buying Situations

There are three major types of buying situations.[6] At one extreme is the *straight rebuy*, which is a fairly routine decision. At the other extreme is the *new task*, which may call for thorough research. In the middle is the *modified rebuy*, which requires some research.

In a **straight rebuy**, the buyer reorders something without any modifications. It is usually handled on a routine basis by the purchasing department. Based on past

Straight rebuy

A business buying situation in which the buyer routinely reorders something without any modifications.

THE HIGHER THE TECHNOLOGY, THE MORE IMPORTANT THE SUPPORT.

FUJITSU

COMPUTERS, COMMUNICATIONS, MICROELECTRONICS

Business marketers often roll up their sleeves and work closely with their customers throughout the buying and consuming process. In this award-winning business-to-business ad, Fujitsu promises more than just high-tech products: "Our technology helps keep you moving upward. And our people won't let you down."

Modified rebuy
A business buying situation in which the buyer wants to modify product specifications, prices, terms, or suppliers.

New task
A business buying situation in which the buyer purchases a product or service for the first time.

Systems selling
Buying a packaged solution to a problem from a single seller, thus avoiding all the separate decisions involved in a complex buying situation.

Buying centre
All the individuals and units that participate in the business buying decision process.

buying satisfaction, the buyer simply chooses from the various suppliers on its list. "In" suppliers try to maintain product and service quality. They often propose automatic reordering systems so that the purchasing agent will save reordering time. "Out" suppliers try to offer something new or exploit dissatisfaction so that the buyer will consider them.

In a **modified rebuy**, the buyer wants to modify product specifications, prices, terms, or suppliers. The modified rebuy usually involves more decision participants than does the straight rebuy. The in suppliers may become nervous and feel pressured to put their best foot forward to protect an account. Out suppliers may see the modified rebuy situation as an opportunity to make a better offer and gain new business.

A company buying a product or service for the first time faces a **new-task** situation. In such cases, the greater the cost or risk, the larger the number of decision participants and the greater their efforts to collect information will be. The new-task situation is the marketer's greatest opportunity and challenge. The marketer not only tries to reach as many key buying influences as possible but also provides help and information.

The buyer makes the fewest decisions in the straight rebuy and the most in the new-task decision. In the new-task situation, the buyer must decide on product specifications, suppliers, price limits, payment terms, order quantities, delivery times, and service terms. The order of these decisions varies with each situation, and different decision participants influence each choice.

Many business buyers prefer to buy a packaged solution to a problem from a single seller. Instead of buying and putting all the components together, the buyer may ask sellers to supply the components *and* assemble the package or system. The sale often goes to the firm that provides the most complete system meeting the customer's needs. Thus, **systems selling** is often a key business marketing strategy for winning and holding accounts.

Sellers increasingly have recognized that buyers like this method and have adopted systems selling as a marketing tool. Systems selling is a two-step process. First, the supplier sells a group of interlocking products. For example, the supplier sells not only glue but also applicators and dryers. Second, the supplier sells a system of production, inventory control, distribution, and other services to meet the buyer's need for a smooth-running operation.

Systems selling is a key business marketing strategy for winning and holding accounts. For example, the Indonesian government requested bids to build a cement factory near Jakarta. A Canadian firm's proposal included choosing the site, designing the cement factory, hiring the construction crews, assembling the materials and equipment, and turning the finished factory over to the Indonesian government. A Japanese firm's proposal included all of these services, plus hiring and training workers to run the factory, exporting the cement through their trading companies, and using the cement to build some needed roads and new office buildings in Jakarta. Although the Japanese firm's proposal cost more, it won the contract. Clearly, the Japanese viewed the problem not as just building a cement factory (the narrow view of systems selling) but of running it in a way that would contribute to the country's economy. They took the broadest view of the customer's needs. This is true systems selling.[7]

Participants in the Business Buying Process

Who does the buying of the trillions of dollars' worth of goods and services needed by business organizations? The decision-making unit of a buying organization is called its **buying centre**: all the individuals and units that participate in the business decision-making process. The buying centre includes all members of the organiza-

Cardinal Health deals with a wide range of buying influences, from purchasing executives and hospital administrators to the surgeons who actually use its products.

tion who play a role in the purchase decision process. This group includes the actual users of the product or service, those who make the buying decision, those who influence the buying decision, those who do the actual buying, and those who control buying information.

The buying centre includes all members of the organization who play any of five roles in the purchase decision process.[8]

Users

Members of the buying organization who will actually use the purchased product or service.

Influencers

People in an organization's buying centre who affect the buying decision; they often help define specifications and also provide information for evaluating alternatives.

Buyers

The people who make an actual purchase.

Deciders

People in the organization's buying centre who have formal or informal power to select or approve the final suppliers.

Gatekeepers

People in the organization's buying centre who control the flow of information to others.

- **Users** are members of the organization who will use the product or service. In many cases, users initiate the buying proposal and help define product specifications.

- **Influencers** often help define specifications and also provide information for evaluating alternatives. Technical personnel are particularly important influencers.

- **Buyers** have formal authority to select the supplier and arrange terms of purchase. Buyers may help shape product specifications, but their major role is in selecting vendors and negotiating. In more complex purchases, buyers might include high-level officers participating in the negotiations.

- **Deciders** have formal or informal power to select or approve the final suppliers. In routine buying, the buyers are often the deciders, or at least the approvers.

- **Gatekeepers** control the flow of information to others. For example, purchasing agents often have authority to prevent salespersons from seeing users or deciders. Other gatekeepers include technical personnel and even personal secretaries.

The buying centre is not a fixed and formally identified unit within the buying organization. It is a set of buying roles assumed by different people for different purchases. Within the organization, the size and makeup of the buying centre will vary for different products and for different buying situations. For some routine purchases, one person—say a purchasing agent—may assume all the buying centre roles and serve as the only person involved in the buying decision. For more complex purchases, the buying centre may include twenty or thirty people from different levels and departments in the organization.

The buying centre concept presents a major marketing challenge. The business marketer must learn who participates in the decision, each participant's relative influence, and what evaluation criteria each decision participant uses. For example, the medical products and services group of Cardinal Health sells disposable surgical gowns to hospitals. It identifies the hospital personnel involved in this buying decision as the vice-president of purchasing, the operating room administrator, and the surgeons. Each participant plays a different role. The vice-president of purchasing analyzes whether the hospital should buy disposable gowns or reusable gowns. If analysis favours disposable gowns, then the operating room administrator compares competing products and prices and makes a choice. This administrator considers the gown's absorbency, antiseptic quality, design, and cost, and normally buys the brand that meets requirements at the lowest cost. Finally, surgeons affect the decision later by reporting their satisfaction or dissatisfaction with the brand.

The buying centre usually includes some obvious participants who are involved formally in the buying decision. For example, the decision to buy a corporate jet will probably involve the company's CEO, the chief pilot, a purchasing agent, some legal staff, a member of top management, and others formally charged with the buying decision. It may also involve less obvious, informal participants, some of whom may actually make or strongly affect the buying decision. Sometimes, even the people in the buying centre are not aware of all the buying participants. For example, the decision about which corporate jet to buy may actually be made by a corporate board member who has an interest in flying and who knows a lot about airplanes. This board member may work behind the scenes to sway the decision. Many business buying decisions result from the complex interactions of ever-changing buying centre participants.

Major Influences on Business Buyers

Business buyers are subject to many influences when they make their buying decisions. Some marketers assume that the major influences are economic. They think buyers will favour the supplier who offers the lowest price or the best product or the most service. They concentrate on offering strong economic benefits to buyers. However, business buyers actually respond to both economic and personal factors. Far from being cold, calculating, and impersonal, business buyers are human and social as well. They react to both reason and emotion.

Today, most B-to-B marketers recognize that emotion plays an important role in business buying decisions. For example, you might expect that an advertisement promoting large trucks to corporate fleet buyers would stress objective technical, performance, and economic factors. However, a recent ad for Volvo heavy-duty trucks shows two drivers arm-wrestling and claims, "It solves all your fleet problems. Except who gets to drive." It turns out that, in the face of an industry-wide driver shortage, the type of truck a fleet provides can help it to attract qualified drivers. The Volvo ad stresses the raw beauty of the truck and its comfort and roominess, features that make it more appealing to drivers. The ad concludes that Volvo trucks are "built to make fleets more profitable and drivers a lot more possessive."

When suppliers' offers are very similar, business buyers have little basis for strictly rational choice. Because they can meet organizational goals with any supplier, buyers can allow personal factors to play a larger role in their decisions. However, when competing products differ greatly, business buyers are more accountable for their choice and tend to pay more attention to economic factors. Figure 7.2 lists various groups of influences on business buyers—environmental, organizational, interpersonal, and individual.[9]

This Volvo truck ad mentions objective factors, such as efficiency and ease of maintenance. But it stresses more emotional factors, such as the raw beauty of the truck and its comfort and roominess, features that make "drivers a lot more possessive."

Environmental Factors

Business buyers are influenced heavily by factors in the current and expected *economic environment*, such as the level of primary demand, the economic outlook, and the cost of money. As economic uncertainty rises, business buyers cut back on new investments and attempt to reduce their inventories.

An increasingly important environmental factor is shortages in key materials. Many companies now are more willing to buy and hold larger inventories of scarce materials to ensure adequate supply. Business buyers also are affected by technological, political, and competitive developments in the environment. Culture and customs can strongly influence business buyer reactions to the marketer's behaviour and strategies, especially in the international marketing environment. (See Real Marketing 7.2.) The business marketer must watch these factors, determine how they will affect the buyer, and try to turn these challenges into opportunities.

Organizational Factors

Each buying organization has its own objectives, policies, procedures, structure, and systems, and the business marketer must understand these factors well. Questions

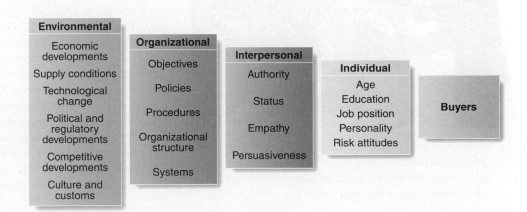

Figure 7.2 Major influences on business buyer behaviour

REAL MARKETING   7.2

International Marketing Manners: When In Rome, Do as the Romans Do

*P*icture this: Consolidated Amalgamation, Inc., thinks it's time that the rest of the world enjoyed the same fine products it has offered Canadian consumers for two generations. It dispatches Vice-President Harry E. Slicksmile to Europe, Africa, and Asia to explore the territory. Mr. Slicksmile stops first in London, where he makes short work of some bankers—he rings them up on the phone. He handles Parisians with similar ease: After securing a table at La Tour d'Argent, he greets his luncheon guest, the director of an industrial engineering firm, with the words, "Just call me Harry, Jacques."

In Germany, Mr. Slicksmile is a powerhouse. Whisking through a lavish, state-of-the-art marketing presentation, complete with flip charts and audio-visuals, he shows 'em that this Alberta boy *knows* how to make a buck. Heading on to Milan, Harry strikes up a conversation with the Japanese businessman sitting next to him on the plane. He flips his card onto the guy's tray and, when the two say good-bye, shakes hands warmly and clasps the man's right arm. Later,

for his appointment with the owner of an Italian packaging design firm, our hero wears his comfy corduroy sport coat, khaki pants, and Topsiders. Everybody knows Italians are zany and laid back.

Mr. Slicksmile next swings through Saudi Arabia, where he coolly presents a potential client with a multimillion-dollar proposal in a classy pigskin binder. His final stop is Beijing, China, where he talks business over lunch with a group of Chinese executives. After completing the meal, he drops his chopsticks into his bowl of rice and presents each guest with an elegant Tiffany's clock as a reminder of his visit.

A great tour, sure to generate a pile of orders, right? Wrong. Six months later, Consolidated Amalgamation has nothing to show for the trip but a stack of bills. Abroad, they weren't wild about Harry.

This hypothetical case has been exaggerated for emphasis. Canadians are seldom such dolts. We are used to dealing with ethnic diversity here at home. But experts say success in international business has a lot to do with knowing the territory and its people. By learning English and extending themselves in other ways, the world's business leaders have met North Americans more than halfway. In contrast, some businesspeople too often do little except assume that others will march to their music. They want things to be just the way they are at home when they travel. Fast. Convenient. Easy. So they may become rude and pushy, demanding that others change. Says one North American trade expert,. "I think more business would be done if we tried harder."

Poor Harry tried, all right, but in all the wrong ways. The British do not, as a rule, make deals over the phone as much as North Americans do. It's not so much a "cultural" difference as a difference in approach. A proper Frenchman neither likes instant familiarity—questions about family, church, or alma mater—nor refers to strangers by their first names. Harry's flashy presentation would likely have been a flop with the Germans, who dislike overstatement and showiness. When Harry Slicksmile grabbed his new Japanese acquaintance by the arm, the executive probably considered him disrespectful and presump-

Canadian companies must help their managers understand international customers and cultures. For example, Japanese people revere the business card as an extension of the self—they do not hand it out to others, they present it.

tuous. Japan, like many Asian countries, is a "no-contact culture" in which even shaking hands is a strange experience. Harry made matters worse by tossing his business card. Japanese people revere the business card as an extension of the self and as an indicator of rank. They do not *hand* it to people, they *present* it—with both hands. In addition, the Japanese are sticklers about rank. Unlike North Americans, they don't heap praise on subordinates in a room; they will praise only the highest-ranking official present.

Hapless Harry also goofed when he assumed that Italians are like Hollywood's stereotypes of them. The flair for design and style that has characterized Italian culture for centuries is embodied in the business-people of Milan and Rome. They dress beautifully and admire flair, but they blanch at garishness or impropriety in others' attire.

To the Saudi Arabians, the pigskin binder would have been considered vile. An American salesman who really did present such a binder was unceremoniously tossed out and his company was blacklisted from working with Saudi businesses. In China, Harry's casually dropping his chopsticks could have been misinter-preted as an act of aggression. Stabbing chopsticks into a bowl of rice and leaving them signifies death to the Chinese. The clocks Harry offered as gifts might have confirmed such dark intentions. To "give a clock" in Chinese sounds the same as "seeing someone off to his end."

Thus, to compete successfully in global markets, or even to deal effectively with international firms in their home markets, companies must help their managers to understand the needs, customs, and cultures of international business buyers.

Sources: Portions adapted from Susan Harte, "When in Rome, You Should Learn to Do What the Romans Do," *The Atlanta Journal-Constitution*, January 22, 1990, pp. D1, D6. Additional examples can be found in David A. Ricks, *Blunders in International Business Around the World* (Malden, MA: Blackwell Publishing, 2000); Terri Morrison, Wayne A. Conway, and Joseph J. Douress, *Dun & Bradstreet's Guide to Doing Business* (Upper Saddle River, NJ: Prentice Hall, 2000); James K. Sebenius, "The Hidden Challenge of Cross-Border Negotiations," *Harvard Business Review*, March 2002, pp. 76–85; Daniel Joseph, "Dangerous Assumptions," *Ceramic Industry*, January 2003, p. 120; and information at www.executiveplanet.com (accessed January 2005).

such as these arise: How many people are involved in the buying decision? Who are they? What are their evaluative criteria? What are the company's policies and limits on its buyers?

Interpersonal Factors

The buying centre usually includes many participants who influence each other, so *interpersonal factors* also influence the business buying process. However, it is often difficult to assess such interpersonal factors and group dynamics. Managers do not wear labels that identify them as important or unimportant buying centre participants, and powerful influencers are often buried behind the scenes. Nor does the highest-ranking buying centre participant always have the most influence. Participants may influence the buying decision because they control rewards and punishments, are well liked, have special expertise, or have a special relationship with other important participants. Interpersonal factors are often very subtle. Whenever possible, business marketers must try to understand these factors and design strategies that take them into account.

Individual Factors

Each participant in the business buying decision process brings in personal motives, perceptions, and preferences. These individual factors are affected by personal characteristics, such as age, income, education, professional identification, personality, and attitudes toward risk. Also, buyers have different buying styles. Some may be technical types who make in-depth analyses of competitive proposals before choosing a supplier. Other buyers may be intuitive negotiators who are adept at pitting the sellers against one another for the best deal.

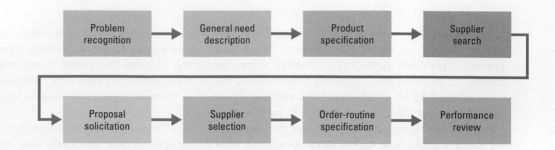

Figure 7.3 Stages of the business buying process

The Business Buying Process

Figure 7.3 lists the eight stages of the business buying process.[10] Buyers who face a new-task buying situation usually go through all stages of the buying process. Buyers making modified or straight rebuys may skip some of the stages. We will examine these steps for the typical new-task buying situation.

Problem Recognition

The buying process begins when someone in the company recognizes a problem or need that can be met by acquiring a specific product or service. **Problem recognition** can result from internal or external stimuli. Internally, the company may decide to launch a new product that requires new production equipment and materials. Or a machine may break down and need new parts. Perhaps a purchasing manager is unhappy with a current supplier's product quality, service, or prices. Externally, the buyer may get some new ideas at a trade show, see an ad, or receive a call from a salesperson who offers a better product or a lower price. In fact, in their advertising, business marketers often alert customers to potential problems and then show how their products provide solutions.

General Need Description

Having recognized a need, the buyer next prepares a **general need description** that describes the characteristics and quantity of the needed item. For standard items, this process presents few problems. For complex items, however, the buyer may have to work with others—engineers, users, consultants—to define the item. The team may want to rank the importance of reliability, durability, price, and other attributes desired in the item. In this phase, the alert business marketer can help the buyers define their needs and provide information about the value of different product characteristics.

Product Specification

The buying organization next develops the item's technical **product specifications**, often with the help of a value analysis engineering team. **Value analysis** is an approach to cost reduction in which components are studied carefully to determine if they can be redesigned, standardized, or made by less costly methods of production. The team decides on the best product characteristics and specifies them accordingly. Sellers, too, can use value analysis as a tool to help secure a new account. By showing buyers a better way to make an object, outside sellers can turn straight rebuy situations into new-task situations that give them a chance to obtain new business.

Problem recognition
The first stage of the business buying process in which someone in the company recognizes a problem or need that can be met by acquiring a good or a service.

General need description
The stage in the business buying process in which the company describes the general characteristics and quantity of a needed item.

Product specification
The stage of the business buying process in which the buying organization decides on and specifies the best technical product characteristics for a needed item.

Value analysis
An approach to cost reduction in which components are studied carefully to determine if they can be redesigned, standardized, or made by less costly methods of production.

Supplier Search

Supplier search
The stage of the business buying process in which the buyer tries to find the best vendors.

The buyer now conducts a **supplier search** to find the best vendors. The buyer can compile a small list of qualified suppliers by reviewing trade directories, doing a computer search, or phoning other companies for recommendations. Today, more and more companies are turning to the Internet to find suppliers. For marketers, this has levelled the playing field—the Internet gives smaller suppliers many of the same advantages as larger competitors.

The newer the buying task, and the more complex and costly the item, the greater the amount of time the buyer will spend searching for suppliers. The supplier's task is to get listed in major directories and build a good reputation in the marketplace. Salespeople should watch for companies in the process of searching for suppliers and make certain that their firm is considered.

Proposal Solicitation

Proposal solicitation
The stage of the business buying process in which the buyer invites qualified suppliers to submit proposals.

In the **proposal solicitation** stage of the business buying process, the buyer invites qualified suppliers to submit proposals. In response, some suppliers will send only a catalogue or a salesperson. However, when the item is complex or expensive, the buyer will usually require detailed written proposals or formal presentations from each potential supplier.

Business marketers must be skilled in researching, writing, and presenting proposals in response to buyer proposal solicitations. Proposals should be marketing documents, not just technical documents. Presentations should inspire confidence and should make the marketer's company stand out from the competition.

Supplier Selection

Supplier selection
The stage of the business buying process in which the buyer reviews proposals and selects a supplier or suppliers.

The members of the buying centre now review the proposals and select a supplier or suppliers. During **supplier selection**, the buying centre often will draw up a list of the desired supplier attributes and their relative importance. In one survey, purchasing executives listed the following attributes as most important in influencing the relationship between supplier and customer: quality products and services, on-time delivery, ethical corporate behaviour, honest communication, and competitive prices. Other important factors include repair and servicing capabilities, technical aid and advice, geographic location, performance history, and reputation. The members of the buying centre will rate suppliers against these attributes and identify the best suppliers.

Buyers may attempt to negotiate with preferred suppliers for better prices and terms before making the final selections. In the end, they may select a single supplier or a few suppliers. Many buyers prefer multiple sources of supplies to avoid being totally dependent on one supplier and to allow comparisons of prices and performance of several suppliers over time. Today's supplier development managers want to develop a full network of supplier–partners that can help the company bring more value to its customers.

Order-Routine Specification

Order-routine specification
The stage of the business buying process in which the buyer writes the final order with the chosen supplier(s).

The buyer now prepares an **order-routine specification**. It includes the final order with the chosen supplier or suppliers and lists items such as technical specifications, quantity needed, expected time of delivery, return policies, and warranties. In the case of maintenance, repair, and operating items, buyers may use *blanket contracts* rather than periodic purchase orders. A blanket contract creates a long-term relationship in which the supplier promises to resupply the buyer as needed at agreed prices for a set time period. A blanket order eliminates the expensive process of renegotiating a purchase each time that stock is required. It also allows buyers to write more, but smaller, purchase orders, resulting in lower inventory levels and carrying costs.

Blanket contracting leads to more single-source buying and to buying more items from that source. This practice locks the supplier in tighter with the buyer and makes it difficult for other suppliers to break in unless the buyer becomes dissatisfied with prices or service.

Performance Review

In this stage, the buyer reviews supplier performance. The buyer may contact users and ask them to rate their satisfaction. The **performance review** may lead the buyer to continue, modify, or drop the arrangement. The seller's job is to monitor the same factors used by the buyer to make sure that the seller is giving the expected satisfaction.

Performance review

The stage of the business buying process in which the buyer assesses the performance of the supplier and decides to continue, modify, or drop the arrangement.

We have described the stages that typically would occur in a new-task buying situation. The eight-stage model provides a simple view of the business buying decision process. The actual process is usually much more complex. In the modified rebuy or straight rebuy situation, some of these stages would be compressed or bypassed. Each organization buys in its own way, and each buying situation has unique requirements.

Different buying centre participants may be involved at different stages of the process. Although certain buying-process steps usually do occur, buyers do not always follow them in the same order, and they may add other steps. Often, buyers will repeat certain stages of the process. Finally, a customer relationship might involve many different types of purchases ongoing at a given time, all in different stages of the buying process. The seller must manage the total customer relationship, not just individual purchases.

Aurora, Ontario-based Magna International Inc., a leading global supplier of technologically advanced automotive systems, components, and complete modules, is well aware of the steps its customers go through when sourcing new parts or automotive systems. As of June 2006, Magna employed 84 000 people at 228 manufacturing divisions and 64 product development and engineering centres located throughout North and South America, Mexico, Europe and Asia. As one of the most diversified automotive suppliers in the world, Magna doesn't sell to the public, but does provide automotive systems and components to almost every original equipment manufacturer (OEM) across the globe. Its top customer is Daimler-Chrysler, but Magna also conducts business with almost every other automotive manufacturer firm in the world. Magna is recognized by these firms for its innovative technology, diverse capabilities, global presence, and unique culture. Magna delivers cost savings and a competitive-edge technologies to all of its customers. When marketing, Magna cannot appeal to the needs of just one type of person. It reaches a vast array of decision makers and product users—everyone from automotive design engineers and professional purchasing managers to the end consumer. To understand its clients' needs and help them meet their challenges, Magna must continue to build strong relationships with its customer base. As one analyst notes when describing Magna, "Building and keeping good relationships—it's what will separate a good company from a great one." Consider the story of how Magna came to the new Powerway technology, which it adopted as part of its ebusiness initiatives.

Relationships are two-way streets that can benefit both partners, especially if they collaborate on a number of efforts. Magna learned of Powerway through DaimlerChrysler, which was nudging some of its suppliers to use the system for certain collaboration functions. Magna didn't resent this little push. Instead, the company saw it as a way to work better with DaimlerChrysler. Says Ted Wozniak, Magna's CIO, "We didn't come at this the way a lot of suppliers do. We came at it with a partnership process." Furthermore, by listening to the cus-

Magna is the most diversified automotive supplier in the world. Working closely with its customers throughout their buying process, it designs, develops, and manufactures automotive systems, assemblies, modules, and components, and it engineers and even assembles complete vehicles for manufacturers of cars and light trucks around the world.

tomer and quickly responding to DaimlerChrysler's needs and new way of doing business, Magna got a jump on its competitors. Not only did the Powerway technology save Magna both time and money, it helped it consolidate a key relationship. Savings came through the elimination of a pile of paperwork and personal visits between Magna's plants and those of DaimlerChrysler.[11]

Business Buying on the Internet

During the past few years, advances in information technology have changed the face of the business-to-business marketing process. Online purchasing, often called *eprocurement*, is growing rapidly. In a recent survey, almost 75 percent of business buyers indicated that they use the Internet to make at least some of their purchases.[12] In addition to their own webpages on the Internet, companies are establishing extranets that link a company's communications and data with its regular suppliers and distributors.

Much online purchasing also takes place through online auctions and on public and private online trading exchanges (or emarketplaces). For example, public trading exchanges, such as the auto industry's Covisint exchange, offer a faster, more efficient way to buy, sell, trade, and exchange information B-to-B. The exchange handles billions of dollars in auto parts sales every year.[13]

Eprocurement gives buyers access to new suppliers, lowers purchasing costs, and hastens order processing and delivery. In turn, business marketers can connect with customers online to share marketing information, sell products and services, provide customer support services, and maintain ongoing customer relationships.

So far, most of the products bought online are MRO materials—maintenance, repair, and operations. General Electric, one of the world's biggest purchasers, plans to be buying *all* of its general operating and industrial supplies online within the

The RBC Financial Group has created an eprocurement system that offers benefits to its current and potential vendors as well as to the firm.

next few years. The actual dollar amount spent on these types of MRO materials pales in comparison to the amount spent for items such as airplane parts, computer systems, and steel tubing. Yet, MRO materials make up 80 percent of all business orders and the transaction costs for order processing are high. Thus, companies have much to gain by streamlining the MRO buying process on the Web. Service firms are also taking advantage of eprocurement. See what the RBC Financial Group has done:

> In 2005, the companies of RBC Financial Group announced a new opportunity for potential and existing RBC Financial Group vendors—an enterprise-wide eProcurement initiative using a secure Internet marketplace. RBC's eprocurement webpage notes, "Some would say electronic procurement or 'eProcurement' is plain old purchasing with a high-tech twist. It offers a lot more advantages and opportunities, though, for both buyers and suppliers." Vendors approved for RBC's eProcurement Initiative can upload a catalogue of goods and services. These catalogues can then be seen on the computer desktops of employees throughout all the companies of RBC Financial Group, creating an unrivalled selling opportunity for the vendor. The eProcurement network also provides fast transmission, order tracking and efficient processing of orders and payment of invoices, helping to eliminate delays or lost paper work.[14]

As the RBC example demonstrates, business-to-business eprocurement yields many benefits. First, it shaves transaction costs and results in more efficient purchasing for both buyers and suppliers. A Web-powered purchasing program eliminates the paperwork associated with traditional requisition and ordering procedures. On average, companies can trim the costs of purchased goods alone by 15 to 20 percent. For example, Owens Corning estimates that eprocurement has shaved 10 percent off its annual purchasing bill of US$3.4 billion.[15]

Plug into an entire industry.

covisint

Connect to the automotive industry from anywhere on earth through Covisint.

More than simply an e-marketplace, Covisint is an automotive business-to-business exchange, where everyone can increase efficiency, collaboration, visibility and grow new ideas. It's the next step in the electronic evolution of the automotive industry.

With its Web-based tools for product development, procurement and supply chain management, Covisint saves you time, saves you money and increases communication. Plug into Covisint and bring an entire industry to your desktop.

Accelerating the pace of business.
covisint.com

Public trading exchanges, such as the auto industry's Covisint exchange, offer "a faster, more efficient way to communicate, collaborate, buy, sell, trade, and exchange information—business to business. The exchange handles billions of dollars in auto parts sales every year.

Eprocurement reduces the time between order and delivery. Time savings are particularly dramatic for companies with many overseas suppliers. Adaptec, a leading supplier of computer storage, used an extranet to tie all of its Taiwanese chip suppliers together in a kind of virtual family. Now messages from Adaptec flow in seconds from its headquarters to its Asian partners, and Adaptec has reduced the time between the order and delivery of its chips from as long as 16 weeks to just 55 days—the same turnaround time for companies that build their own chips.

Finally, beyond the cost and time savings, eprocurement frees purchasing people to focus on more strategic issues. For many purchasing professionals, going online means reducing drudgery and paperwork and spending more time managing inventory and working creatively with suppliers. "That is the key," says the H-P executive. "You can now focus people on value-added activities. Procurement professionals can now find different sources and work with suppliers to reduce costs and to develop new products."

The rapidly expanding use of epurchasing, however, also presents some problems. For example, at the same time that the Web makes it possible for suppliers and customers to share business data and even collaborate on product design, it can also erode decades-old customer–supplier relationships. Many firms are using the Web to search for better suppliers.

Epurchasing can also create potential security disasters. More than 80 percent of companies say security is the leading barrier to expanding electronic links with customers and partners. Although email and home banking transactions can be protected through basic encryption, the secure environment that businesses need to carry out confidential interactions is still lacking. Companies are spending millions for research on defensive strategies to keep hackers at bay. Cisco Systems, for example, specifies the types of routers, firewalls, and security procedures that its partners must use to safeguard extranet connections. In fact, the company goes even further—it sends its own security engineers to examine a partner's defences and holds the partner liable for any security breach that originates from its computer.

Institutional and Government Markets

So far, our discussion of organizational buying has focused largely on the buying behaviour of business buyers. Much of this discussion also applies to the buying practices of institutional and government organizations. However, these two non-business markets have additional characteristics and needs. In this final section, we address the special features of institutional and government markets.

Institutional Markets

Institutional market
Schools, hospitals, nursing homes, prisons, and other institutions that provide goods and services to people in their care.

The **institutional market** consists of educational institutions, hospitals, nursing homes, prisons, and other institutions that provide goods and services to people in their care. Institutions differ from one another in their sponsors and in their objectives. For example, a firm selling adjustable beds to the institutional market in Toronto would want to consider how the needs of the private Shouldice Hernia Centre would differ from those of Princess Margaret Hospital and various private nursing homes.

Many institutional markets are characterized by low budgets and captive patrons. For example, hospital patients have little choice but to eat whatever food the hospital supplies. A hospital purchasing agent has to decide on the quality of food to buy for patients. Because the food is provided as a part of a total service package, the buying objective is not profit. Nor is strict cost minimization the goal—patients receiving poor-quality food will complain to others and damage the hospital's reputation. Thus, the hospital purchasing agent must search for institutional-food vendors whose quality meets or exceeds a certain minimum standard and whose prices are low.

Many marketers set up separate divisions to meet the special characteristics and needs of institutional buyers. For example, Heinz produces, packages, and prices its ketchup and other products differently to better serve the requirements of hospitals, schools, and other institutional markets.

Government Markets

Government market
Governmental units—federal, provincial or territorial, and local—that purchase or rent goods and services for carrying out the main functions of government.

The **government market** offers large opportunities for many companies, both big and small. In most countries, government organizations are major buyers of goods and services. The Government of Canada buys approximately $14 billion worth of goods and services every year from thousands of suppliers. There are more than 85 departments, agencies, Crown Corporations, and Special Operating Agencies. Public Works and Government Services Canada (PWGSC) is the government's largest purchasing organization, averaging 60 000 contracts totalling $10 billion annually. Provincial, territorial, and municipal governments also purchase a vast array of goods and services.[16] Government buying and business buying are similar in many ways. But there are also differences that must be understood by companies that wish to sell products and services to governments. To succeed in the government market, sellers must locate key decision makers, identify the factors that affect buyer behaviour, and understand the buying decision process.

Government organizations typically require suppliers to submit bids, and normally they award the contract to the lowest bidder. In some cases, the government unit will make allowance for the supplier's superior quality or reputation for completing contracts on time. Governments will also buy on a negotiated contract basis, primarily in the case of complex projects involving major R&D costs and risks, and in cases where there is little competition.

Government organizations tend to favour domestic suppliers over foreign suppliers. A major complaint of multinationals operating in Europe is that each country shows favouritism toward its nationals in spite of superior offers that are made by foreign firms. The European Economic Commission is gradually removing this bias.

Like consumer and business buyers, government buyers are affected by environmental, organizational, interpersonal, and individual factors. One unique thing about government buying is that it is carefully watched by outside publics, ranging from Parliament and the Senate to a variety of private groups interested in how the government spends taxpayers' money. For example, when selling to the federal government, vendor bids and contracts must comply with Canada's trade obligations under the North American Free Trade Agreement (NAFTA), the World Trade Organization Agreement on Government Procurement (WTO-AGP), and the Agreement on Internal Trade (AIT). Because their spending decisions are subject to public review, government organizations require considerable paperwork from suppliers, who often complain about excessive paperwork, bureaucracy, regulations, decision-making delays, and frequent shifts in procurement personnel.

Despite these challenges, selling to the government has many advantages. Government represents one of the largest markets in Canada, and 80 percent of federal contracts are tendered outside of Ottawa. Furthermore, the government is a good credit risk, and when exporting, it is a useful marketing tool to list the government as a customer. Finally, information about bidding opportunities in the federal government is widely available online through the Electronic Tendering System (MERX). There are even sometimes extra benefits associated with supplying government departments. In an effort to improve the competitiveness of Canadian businesses, products purchased by the government are evaluated for the potential to be marketed worldwide. For example, rations developed for the military by Magic Pan are now marketed to global institutions.[17]

Most governments provide would-be suppliers with detailed guides describing how to sell to the government. For example, the Government of Canada website provides a lot of detailed information on how to sell to the government. Various trade magazines and associations provide information on how to reach schools, hospitals, highway departments, and other government agencies.

Noneconomic criteria also play a growing role in government buying. Government buyers are asked to favour depressed business firms and areas; small business firms; minority-owned firms; and business firms that avoid race, gender, and age discrimination. Sellers need to keep these factors in mind when deciding to seek government business.

Many companies that sell to the government have not been marketing oriented for a number of reasons. Total government spending is determined by elected officials rather than by any marketing effort to develop this market. Government buying has emphasized price, making suppliers invest their effort in technology to bring costs down. When the product's characteristics are specified carefully, product differentiation is not a marketing factor. Nor do advertising or personal selling matter much in winning bids on an open-bid basis.

Several companies, however, including Bombardier, Nortel, and General Electric, however, have established separate government marketing departments to sell to governments worldwide. These companies anticipate government needs and projects, participate in the product specification phase, gather competitive intelligence, prepare bids carefully, and produce stronger communications to describe and enhance their companies' reputations. Other companies have set up customized marketing programs for government buyers. For example, Dell Computer has specific business units tailored to meet the needs of federal, provincial, and municipal buyers. Dell offers its customers tailor-made Premier.Dell.com Web pages that include special pricing, online purchasing, and service and support.

Reviewing the Concepts

Business markets and consumer markets are alike in some key ways. For example, both include people in buying roles who make purchase decisions to satisfy needs. But business markets also differ in many ways from consumer markets. For one thing, the business market is *enormous,* far larger than the consumer market. Within Canada alone, the business market includes organizations that annually purchase billions of dollars' worth of goods and services.

1. Define the business market and explain how business markets differ from consumer markets.

Business buyer behaviour refers to the buying behaviour of the organizations that buy goods and services for use in the production of other products and services that are sold, rented, or supplied to others. It also includes the behaviour of retailing and wholesaling firms that acquire goods for the purpose of reselling or renting them to others at a profit.

As compared with consumer markets, business markets usually have fewer, larger buyers who are more geographically concentrated. Business demand is *derived,* largely *inelastic,* and more *fluctuating.* More buyers are usually involved in the business buying decision, and business buyers are better trained and more professional than are consumer buyers. In general, business purchasing decisions are more complex, and the buying process is more formal than consumer buying.

2. Identify the major factors that influence business buyer behaviour.

Business buyers make decisions that vary with the three types of buying situations: *straight rebuys, modified rebuys,* and *new tasks.* The buying centre, which can consist of many different persons playing many different roles, is the decision-making unit of a buying organization. The business marketer needs to know the following: Who are the major participants? In what decisions do they exercise influence? What is their relative degree of influence? What evaluation criteria does each decision participant use? The business marketer also needs to understand the major environmental, organizational, interpersonal, and individual influences on the buying process.

3. List and define the steps in the business buying decision process.

The business buying decision process itself can be quite involved, with eight basic stages: (1) *problem recognition,* someone in the company recognizes a problem or need that can be met by acquiring a product or service; (2) *general need description,* the company determines the general characteristics and quantity of the needed item; (3) *product specification,* the buying organization decides on and specifies the best technical product characteristics for the needed item; (4) *supplier search,* the buyer seeks the best vendors; (5) *proposal solicitation,* the buyer invites qualified suppliers to submit proposals; (6) *supplier selection,* the buyer reviews proposals and selects a supplier or suppliers; (7) *order-routine specification,* the buyer writes the final order with the chosen supplier(s), listing the technical specifications, quantity needed, expected time of delivery, return policies, and warranties; and (8) *performance review,* the buyer rates its satisfaction with suppliers, deciding whether to continue, modify, or cancel them.

4. Compare the institutional and government markets and explain how institutional and government buyers make their buying decisions.

The *institutional market* comprises schools, hospitals, prisons, and other institutions that provide goods and services to people in their care. These markets are characterized by low budgets and captive patrons. The *government market,* which is vast, consists of government units—federal, provincial or territorial, and municipal—that purchase or rent goods and services for carrying out the main functions of government.

Government buyers purchase products and services for defence, education, public welfare, and other public needs. Government buying practices are highly specialized and specified, with open bidding or negotiated contracts characterizing most of the buying. Government buyers operate under the watchful eye of Parliament and many private watchdog groups. Hence, they tend to require more forms and signatures, and to respond more slowly and deliberately when placing orders.

Reviewing the Key Terms

Business buyer behaviour   251
Business buying process   251
Buyers   259
Buying centre   258
Deciders   259
Derived demand   253
Gatekeepers   259
General need description   264
Government market   270
Influencers   259
Institutional market   270
Modified rebuy   258
New task   258

Order-routine specification   265
Performance review   266
Problem recognition   264
Product specification   264
Proposal solicitation   265
Straight rebuy   257
Supplier development   254
Supplier search   265
Supplier selection   265
Systems selling   258
Users   259
Value analysis   264

Discussing the Concepts

1. How do the market structure and demand of the business markets for Intel's microprocessor chips differ from those of final consumer markets?

2. In general, how are decisions and the decision processes for business markets similar to those of consumer markets? How are they different?

3. In a buying centre purchasing process, which buying centre participant—a buyer, a decider, a gatekeeper, an influencer, a user—is most likely to make each of the following statements?

    - "This bonding agent had better be good. I have to put this product together."

    - "I specified this bonding agent on another job, and it worked for them."

    - "Without an appointment, no sales rep gets in to see Mr. Johnson."

    - "OK, it's a deal—we'll buy it."

    - "I'll place the order first thing tomorrow."

4. The chapter claims that the eight-step business buying process is similar to the five-step consumer buying process. How would you group the eight steps in the business buying process into the five steps in the consumer buying process?

5. List and explain three benefits and three drawbacks of business-to-business ecommerce.

6. Suppose that you own a small printing firm and have the opportunity to bid on a federal government contract that could bring a considerable amount of new business to your company. List three advantages and three disadvantages of working under contract with the federal government.

Applying the Concepts

1. Burst-of-Energy is a food product positioned in the extreme sports market as a performance enhancer. A distributor of the product has seen a change in the demand for the product (depicted in the figure at the right). The manufacturer has done nothing to generate this demand, but there have been a couple of reports that two popular celebrities were photographed with the product. Could something like this happen? Based on the demand chart, how would you characterize the demand for the product? Is it elastic or inelastic? Would you call this an example of fluctuating demand? Support your answers.

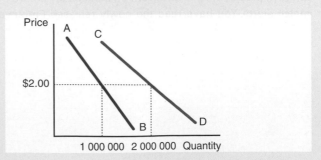

2. Suppose that you owned a small business that provides PC repair services to local businesses. In addition to the basic fix-it services you now provide, you are

thinking about offering new services. Applying the "systems-selling" concept, what additional services could you offer that would make a complete package or systems solution for your customers?

3. Form a small group and compare the similarities and differences between a buyer at a Veteran's Hospital and a buyer at a for-profit hospital, such as Shouldice Hernia Centre. Compare the buyers on the following four factors: environmental, organizational, interpersonal, and individual.

Focus on Technology

For small businesses, getting a contract with a division of the federal government can be both a blessing and a curse. The blessing comes in the form of welcome additional revenue. The curse comes with the unbelievable effort required to become a qualified federal government supplier. The government has been working, however, to simplify this process and make its procedures more transparent to small and large businesses. Public Works and Government Services Canada (PWGSC) is one of the main purchasing arms of the federal government. It awards some 60 000 contracts totalling $10 billion annually. There are two major online sources of information about selling to the federal government: Business Access Canada (formerly Contracts Canada) and the government electronic tendering service, known as MERX. Suppose that you are a small manufacturing company that specializes in the manufacture of hand-print biometric security systems.

1. Try to find a federal bid that is open for a security system. Which site was easiest to search? What frustrations did you experience using the site? Suggest one feature that would improve the usefulness of the site.

2. To bid for federal contracts, you often need to know your SIC or NAICS number and description. Find this for security systems.

Focus on Ethics

You are the senior buyer for a growing technology company based in Montreal. Your friends and business colleagues alike know that you are an avid golfer. You have just opened an invitation to attend the Bell Canadian Open. The invitation is from a supplier company that has been trying to sell you its new line of products for the past year. She wants to present you with a Champions Club pass that will provide you with upgraded food and beverage options, VIP washroom facilities, closed-circuit TVs, exclusive access to the Champions Club patio, and full grounds access for watching all the action! You know that these passes are valued at more than $1000. The supplier will also will pay for your travel, room, and meals, and you'll even get an opportunity to play in the pro-am event on Wednesday before the match starts. You have read the newly released Employee Manual and there is no reference or rule that specifically states that an employee cannot accept a fully paid trip from a vendor, although there are some vague restrictions on lunches and dinners paid for by suppliers.

1. Do you accept or decline the invitation?

2. Just because it is not specifically mentioned in the Employee Manual, would you be acting ethically if you accepted?

3. Do you think the supplier will expect "special" treatment in the next buying situation?

4. How would other company employees interpret your acceptance of this invitation?

Video Case
Eaton

You might not know about Eaton Corporation, but the company touches your life in many ways. Eaton's engine valves and torque converters are in your automobiles. More than three-quarters of new large commercial jets and all new military aircraft platforms rely on Eaton products to fly. And you'll find Eaton's products in the circuit breaker box in your home. So how come you've never heard of the company? Eaton is a business-to-business marketer, primarily selling its products to other businesses.

The company's success stems from its ability to create lasting relationships with its business customers. According to the company's website, Eaton works with customers and suppliers to "leverage collective strengths, capitalize on market positions, and provide an unparalleled combination of technologies and services." The company's rich understanding of its customers has made Eaton a US$8 billion dollar company.

After viewing the video featuring Eaton Corporation, answer the following questions about business buyer behaviour:

1. How do Eaton's business-to-business marketing efforts differ from those of companies targeting final customers?

2. Visit Eaton's website and review the pages detailing the products the company makes. How many products containing parts manufactured by Eaton play a role in your life? Do you think Eaton could or should market some of its products directly to final consumers to increase demand?

Online Media Resources

Video Short
Log on to your Companion Website at **www.pearsoned.ca/kotler** to view the video segment related to the Video Case above.

Case Pilot
Log on to your Companion Website at **www.pearsoned.ca/kotler** to sharpen your case analysis skills and take the Case Pilot Challenge!

Company Case
Kodak: Changing the Picture

Memories
"You press the button—we do the rest." With that simple slogan, George Eastman unveiled the first Kodak camera in 1888—yes, 1888, more than 119 years ago. In 1900, Kodak launched its famous Brownie cameras, which it priced at $1.00, opening the photography market to millions. Throughout the twentieth century, Kodak dominated the photography business. In the early 1960s, it introduced the first pocket camera, the Instamatic, and even smaller 110m cameras in the 1970s. In the 1990s, Kodak teamed with four other companies to develop and introduce the Advanced Photo System (APS), which allowed photographers to take three different-sized photos, including panoramic pictures, on one roll.

By 2000, Kodak was one of the most recognized and trusted brands in the world. Many people referred to the company as "Big Yellow." The company saw itself as being in the memory business, not in the photography business.

Going Negative
Despite its storied past, however, when Kodak President Daniel Carp assumed the role of CEO in

2000, he knew the company faced many new challenges that would require it to rethink and perhaps redesign its business strategy. The company's stock price, which had reached a historic peak of US$90 in 1997, had been plummeting. The company had begun to lay off workers.

Several factors were causing Kodak's problems. First, although Kodak had been the first company to produce a digital camera in 1976, it had been reluctant to develop the technology. Kodak, like many other companies, thought consumers would be slow to adopt digital technology. More importantly, however, it saw every digital camera that consumers purchased as another nail in the coffin of its core business—making film, photo-developing chemicals, and light-sensitive paper. Second, despite Kodak's dominance in traditional photography, many competitors, especially Fuji, were exposing flaws in Kodak's marketing and stealing market share. Third, the September 11, 2001, tragedy severely depressed vacation travel and the associated picture taking. Fourth, competition from an unexpected source—cellular phone manufacturers—surprised Kodak. Nokia introduced the first cellular phone with a built-in camera in November 2001.

Although many people thought such phones would only be toys, consumers began snapping them up such that in 2003 sales of camera phones from all makers topped 84 million units—twice the sales of conventional digital cameras. Finally, consumers who owned digital cameras or cellphone cameras were increasingly using their PCs to download and then print their own pictures on their printers, if they printed them at all. Analysts discovered that consumers printed only 2 percent of camera-phone pictures in North America versus 10 percent in Japan. Further, analysts predicted that the number of cellphones with cameras would jump from 6 percent in 2003, to 19 percent in 2004, to 42 percent in 2005.

The Proof Is in the Picture

Up through the 1980s, when consumers wanted to develop pictures, they took their film rolls to local drug stores, discount department stores, or photo shops. These stores sent film to regional labs run by Kodak and others, which produced the prints and returned them to the store for pickup. This process took many days. Then, with the development of the self-contained photo lab, retailers could place a machine directly in their store that would do all the photo processing. These photo labs allowed the retailers to offer faster

service—even one-hour service. As consumers demanded more one-hour photo developing, Kodak agreed that various large retailers could set up a national one-hour photo businesses. Kodak provided minilabs, which it bought from a Swiss manufacturer, that handled the photo developing on-site, collecting fees for leasing the equipment. Kodak sometimes even provided interest-free loans to retailers to help them implement the system.

Problems developed, however, when the minilabs proved to be unreliable. They broke down up to eleven times a month because of paper jams and software glitches. It often took two to three days to get the machines serviced, and when they were, the customers' film was exposed to light when the service people opened the machine.

As a result, some retailers, like Walgreen, the largest drug-store chain in the U.S., quietly began to install Fuji minilabs in some of its California stores. Fuji's machines, in addition to handling traditional film, also allowed consumers to make prints from their digital cameras memory devices, something Kodak's did not do. Kodak began selling kits to allow its minilabs to handle digital prints, but Walgreen officials believed Kodak's prints were lower quality. By early 2004, Fuji had 1500 minilabs in Walgreen's almost 4300 outlets.

Walgreen also approached Kodak about developing a Walgreen Internet site that would allow consumers to upload digital photos over the Web. Kodak would then store, and allow customers to order prints, which would then be mailed to them. Walgreen did not like Kodak's proposal as it minimized the Walgreen role and allowed Kodak to keep the pictures on its site, gaining an advantage in future customer orders. Despite these concerns, Walgreen was about to sign a deal with Kodak when two top officials, who favoured Kodak, retired. The company then nixed the deal and started developing its own website with Fuji, which was comfortable with a less prominent role. Walgreen launched its Web service in 2003, with Fuji carrying out the photo developing.

A New Development

Given all this, in early 2003, CEO Carp decided Kodak needed to re-evaluate its strategy. He hired Antonio Perez, who oversaw Hewlett-Packard's rise to dominance in inkjet printers, to be Kodak's new COO. Perez believes that Kodak's future is in digital imaging for consumers, businesses, and health care providers. As a result, in September 2003, Carp announced that

Kodak would make a historic shift in its strategy. The company would reduce its dependence on traditional film, boost investment in nonphotographic markets, and pursue digital markets, such as inkjet printers and high-end digital printing. These moves will put it in direct competition with entrenched competitors, such as H-P, Canon, Seiko Epson, and Xerox. Kodak indicated it would not make any long-term investments in traditional consumer film. At the time of this announcement, traditional film and photography accounted for 70 percent of Kodak's revenue and all of its operating profits. By 2006, the company said its traditional business would fall to 40 percent of revenues and one-half of earnings, while the digital business would provide 60 percent of revenue and one-half of earnings. As a part of the shift in strategy, Kodak announced in early 2004 that it would abandon its APS camera business and stop selling reloadable film cameras in Canada, the U.S., and Europe.

To grow Kodak's digital business, Carp and Perez will have to introduce new digital products and enter highly competitive new markets while maintaining its traditional film business, a highly profitable business it needs to fund its strategic changes. The company's goal is to increase revenues from US$13.3 billion in 2003 to US$16 billion in 2006 and US$20 billion by 2010.

Questions for Discussion

1. How are the market structure and demand, the nature of the buying unit, and the types of decisions and decision process different as Kodak moves from its focus on the consumer market to an increased focus on the commercial and health care markets?

2. What examples of the major types of buying situations do you see in the case?

3. How might the buying process change as Kodak moves to new products and new markets?

4. What marketing recommendations would you make to Kodak as it responds to the digital revolution?

Sources: Ravi Chandiramani, "Can Kodak Thrive Amid the Digital Revolution?" *Marketing,* July 3, 2003, p. 13; James Bandler, "Kodak Shifts Focus from Film, Betting Future on Digital Lines," *Wall Street Journal,* September 25, 2003, p. A1; Gregory Zuckerman and James Bandler, "Investors Seek to Rewind Kodak," *Wall Street Journal,* October 21, 2003, p. C1; "Business: Has Kodak Missed the Moment?" *The Economist,* January 3, 2004, p. 46; James Bandler, "Ending Era, Kodak Will Stop Selling Most Film Cameras," *Wall Street Journal,* January 14, 2004; James Bandler, "Kodak to Cut Staff Up to 21%, Amid Digital Push," *Wall Street Journal,* January 22, 2004, p. A1; "Kodak Changes the Picture," *Economist.com,* January 23, 2004, p. 1; James Bandler, "Losing Focus: As Kodak Eyes Digital Future, A Big Partner Starts to Fade," *Wall Street Journal,* January 23, 2004; Andy Reinhardt, Hiroko Tashiro, and Ben Elgin, "The Camera Phone Revolution," *Business Week,* April 12, 2004, p. 52; Faith Arner and Rachael Tiplady, "'No Excuse Not to Succeed'; How COO Antonio Perez Is Hustling Kodak Into the Digital Age," *Business Week,* May 10, 2004, p. 96.

CHAPTER 8

Segmentation, Targeting, and Positioning: Building the Right Relationships with the Right Customers

MASSIVE PARTY

in unexpected places

Celebrate the unexpected

Size Matters. Style Matters. Art Matters.

With installations and projects by artists including Bruno Billio, Shary Boyle, Alexander Irving, Laura Kikauka, John Marriott, Janet Morton, Max Streicher and Pearl Van Geest.

THURSDAY, APRIL 6, 2006 AT 8 PM
MUZIK
15 Saskatchewan Drive, Exhibition Place

TICKETS: (19+; ID required)
include open bar and hors d'oeuvres
$115 AGO Members
$125 Non-Members
($150 At the Door)

TO PURCHASE TICKETS:
call 416.979.6608 or visit
http://shop.ago.net/

Massive Party is a benefit for the Art Gallery of Ontario.

TRANS-FORMATION AGO

Massive Party is sponsored by:

globallive   **orion** SECURITIES INC.

ROGERS YAHOO! HI-SPEED INTERNET

Media Sponsor: Promotional Partner:

NOW   s·w·e·e·t·s·p·o·t·ca

With assistance from:
Creemore Springs Brewery
GIBSON & LYLE CATERING
Iceberg Vodka
SunOpta Inc.

AFTER STUDYING THIS CHAPTER, YOU SHOULD BE ABLE TO

1. define the three steps of target marketing: market segmentation, target marketing, and market positioning

2. list and discuss the major bases for segmenting consumer and business markets

3. explain how companies identify attractive market segments and choose a target marketing strategy

4. discuss how companies position their products for maximum competitive advantage in the marketplace

Previewing the Concepts

Now that you've learned what marketing is and about the importance of understanding consumers and the marketplace environment, you're ready to delve more deeply into marketing strategy and tactics. This chapter looks further into key marketing strategy decisions—how to divide up markets into meaningful customer groups (market segmentation), choose which customer groups to serve (target marketing), and create marketing offers that best serve targeted customers (positioning). Then, the chapters that follow explore the tactical marketing tools—the four Ps: product, place, price, and promotion—by which marketers bring these strategies to life.

As an opening example of segmentation, targeting, and position at work, let's look first at the Art Gallery of Ontario (AGO). Founded in 1900, the Art Gallery of Ontario is now the tenth-largest art museum in North America. It has a collection of more than 40 000 works, including the world's largest public collection of works by internationally renowned British sculptor Henry Moore. You may not think of an art gallery as a marketer, but increasingly the AGO and other non-profit entities are seeing the power of marketing tools such as segmentation, targeting, and positioning.

Though competition is stiff in the world of business, it is nothing compared with what is experienced in the not-for-profit sector. More and more charities are competing for limited funds. A recent Ipsos-Reid opinion poll showed that an overwhelming majority of Canadians recognize the importance of culture. Yet, when it comes to donations, statistics show they rank the arts low on their list of priorities. Canadians give the most dollars to religious organizations (49%), followed by health (20%), and social services (10%). Thus, knowing the marketplace for donors and being able to target critical segments with meaningful propositions is essential if the AGO is to survive and accomplish its goals.

Take a recent fundraising event held by the gallery. People driving across the Gardiner Expressway in Toronto saw two huge inflatable male figures by artist Max Streicher hover over Toronto's Canadian National Exhibition. They were there to draw attention to the dance floor at Muzik, a newly renovated party palace and the Art Gallery of Ontario's "Massive" party. On the floor could be found the "thirty- and forty-something BlackBerry crowd." One could spot Ben Mulroney among the attendees. Not the type of event you would expect an art gallery to hold. Why not? "Contemporary art is all about interpretation, getting the viewer stimulated, engaged, and this event was designed to do exactly that (ticket price: $125 per person).

Says one member of AGO's development staff, "It's an audience builder," and an integral part of the seduction of potential and future donors.

The 30 to 40 age group is one of the few segments with enough money to support cultural institutions that has not yet been exhausted by pleas for support. This is not the case with traditional supporters of the arts—Canada's wealthiest families. Hilary and Galen Weston, for example, have already given $10 million to the Royal Ontario Museum. Ken and Marilyn Thomson donated a staggering $70 million to the AGO. A $20 million donation by Four Seasons hotelier Isadore Sharp bought him naming rights to the Four Seasons Centre for the Performing Arts. However, with so many requests being aimed their way, this group is starting to suffer from donor fatigue.

The AGO knows that it cannot just send a mass mailing asking for support to Canada's general population. A 2004 survey undertaken by Statistics Canada showed that, though almost 6 million Canadians made donations to charities, the median donation was $230. However, a recent National Survey on Giving, Volunteering, and Participating (NSGVP) showed that less than 2 percent of the population make financial donations to the arts sector. The average donor was found to be over 45 (57 percent of donors), university educated (38 percent), and with a household income exceeding $50 000 (71 percent). Of even greater concern: although the value of donations is increasing, the number of donors has actually decreased. Thus, all arts organizations are scrambling in the search for new sources of funds. The up and coming age cohort of 30- to 40-year-old urban professionals may be that source.

Getting people aged 30 to 49 to support the AGO is not easy. First, many other major cultural institutions are courting this Prada-clad crowd. Second, as one long-time fundraiser puts it, "Cultural institutions aren't on their radar. They want cars, houses, big jewellery, private school for their children. If they're supporting art, they're putting it on their walls." Furthermore, the Me Generation is unphilanthropic relative to their wealth, says another industry insider. In addition, recent studies of this cohort have revealed that "this generation rejects their parents' value system. They want to do things their own way, and that often means not supporting the institutions their parents [supported]." Take the case of Ken Zuckerman, one of the attendees at the AGO's Massive party. He is a 43-year-old commercial and residential real-estate developer who cultivates an edgy image with his long, messy hair, beard stubble, untucked shirttails and blue-tinged glasses. At the event, he was enticed to help create art by donning lipstick and adding a big kiss to a canvas. He is a typical member of the AGO's new target market. Rather than passively giving to the gallery, potential donors in this cohort have a desire for interaction, involvement, and meaningful comment on art as well as on the AGO's tactics.

Thus, the AGO had to create a distinct position for its program to attract these younger donors. By naming the new program the "New Founders initiative" it immediately told potential patrons they won't be sitting in a room with their mothers' friends. Events associated with the New Founders initiative, like the Massive party, certainly aren't the stuffy cocktail parties usually associated with cultural fundraisers. Organizers and waiters wore wigs of fuzzy pink clown hair.

The goal of the program was to get 100 new philanthropists under the age of 50 who would be willing to donate at least $50 000. In return for their support, they would be invited to small dinner parties and exclusive tours of exhibitions before they open to the public. Because 120 New Founders have signed on so far, the program has been considered a resounding success. Says Bonnie Hillman, managing director of Arts & Communications, a public-relations and consulting firm that has worked closely with some Toronto arts institutions on fundraising efforts, "The institutions that have diversified their donor bases most are in the best shape now and will be in the future."[1]

Organizations today recognize that they cannot appeal to all people in the marketplace, or at least not to all buyers or donors in the same way. People are too varied in their needs, buying, and support practices. Moreover, the organizations themselves vary widely in their abilities to serve different segments of the market. Instead, an organization must identify the parts of the market that it can serve best and most profitably. It needs to design strategies to build the *right* relationships with the *right* people.

Thus, most organizations have moved away from mass marketing and toward *market segmentation and targeting*—identifying market segments, selecting one or more of them, and developing products and marketing programs tailored to each. Instead of scattering their marketing efforts (the "shotgun" approach), organizations are focusing on the buyers or donors who have greater interest in the values they create best (the "rifle" approach).

Companies have not always practised market segmentation and targeting. For most of the past century, major consumer products companies held fast to *mass marketing*—mass-producing, mass-distributing, and mass-promoting about the same product in about the same way to all consumers. Henry Ford typified this marketing strategy when he offered the Model T Ford to all buyers; they could have the car "in any colour as long as it is black." Similarly, Coca-Cola at one time produced only one drink for the whole market, hoping it would appeal to everyone.

However, many factors now make mass marketing more difficult. For example, the world's mass markets have slowly splintered into a profusion of smaller segments—the baby boomers here, the Gen Xers there; here the South Asian segment, there the Aboriginal Canadian segment; here working women, there single parents; here amateur hockey players, there professionals; here the Prairies, there the Atlantic provinces. Today, marketers find it very hard to create a single product or program that appeals to all of these diverse groups.

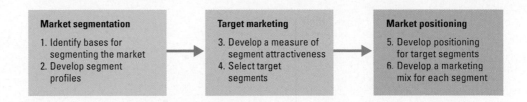

Figure 8.1 Steps in market segmentation, targeting, and positioning

Market segmentation

Dividing a market into smaller groups of buyers' distinct needs, characteristics, or behaviour that might require separate products or marketing mixes.

Target marketing

The process of evaluating each market segment's attractiveness and selecting one or more segments to enter.

Market positioning

Arranging for a product to occupy a clear, distinctive, and desirable place relative to competing products in the minds of target consumers.

Figure 8.1 shows the three major steps in target marketing. The first is **market segmentation**—dividing a market into smaller groups of buyers with distinct needs, characteristics, or behaviours who might require separate products or marketing mixes. The company identifies different ways to segment the market and develops profiles of the resulting market segments. The second step is **target marketing**—evaluating each market segment's attractiveness and selecting one or more of the market segments to enter. The third step is **market positioning**—setting the competitive positioning for the product and creating a detailed marketing mix. We discuss each of these steps in turn.

Market Segmentation

Markets consist of buyers, and buyers differ in one or more ways. They may differ in their wants, resources, locations, buying attitudes, and buying practices. Through market segmentation, companies divide large, heterogeneous markets into smaller segments that can be reached more efficiently and effectively with products and services that match their unique needs. In this section, we discuss four important segmentation topics: segmenting consumer markets, segmenting business markets, segmenting international markets, and segmenting markets effectively.

Before we go into these topics in detail, let's use a simple example so that you can see how a market could be segmented. Figure 8.2 illustrates a market for beverages. A marketer thinking about how to serve this market could divide people into many different subgroups. The subgroups would vary in size, position, and shape depending on how she decides to describe the needs and wants of people in the marketplace. Based on how she believes people respond to different offers, she decides to divide up the market based on two criteria—people's sensitivity to price (product cost), and their desire for a single product benefit: its ability to give them energy. Using these segmentation criteria, she discovers that there are three main groups in her marketplace. Group A is very sensitive to price (they want a low-cost beverage) and they don't care very much about whether their beverage gives them energy or not. This is a large group and one that might choose water as a means of satisfying their needs. The second group, group B, is smaller and is willing to pay a higher price, but wants a beverage that gives them some energy. This group might choose tea or coffee as a means of satisfying their thirst. Group C is much smaller, but people within this group put a high value on beverages that will energize them. If the marketer was working for a company like Red Bull, group C would be her target market. Though this market segment is smaller than the other segments, her firm could offer this group product benefits that closely align with their needs. The group's willingness to pay a price premium for her type of beverage would also allow the firm to make a profit. In this simple example, the marketer used only two criteria to segment the market. As you will see in the following section, she could have chosen many other criteria.

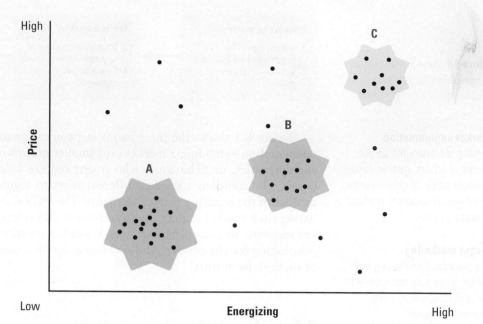

Figure 8.2 Understanding market segments: a hypothetical beverage market

Segmenting Consumer Markets

There is no single way to segment a market. A marketer has to try different segmentation variables, alone and in combination, to find the best way to view the market structure. Table 8.1 outlines the major variables that might be used in segmenting consumer markets. Here we look at the major *geographic*, *demographic*, *psychographic*, and *behavioural variables*.

Geographic Segmentation

Geographic segmentation
Dividing a market into different geographical units, such as nations, provinces, regions, counties, cities, or neighbourhoods.

Geographic segmentation calls for dividing the market into different geographical units, such as nations, regions, provinces, counties, cities, or even neighbourhoods. A company may decide to operate in one or a few geographical areas, or to operate in all areas but pay attention to geographical differences in needs and wants.

Many companies today are localizing their products, advertising, promotion, and sales efforts to fit the needs of individual regions, cities, and even neighbourhoods. For example, Parker Brothers offers localized versions of its popular Monopoly game for several major cities around the world, including Las Vegas in the United States, and Bath in southwest England. The Las Vegas version features a black board with The Strip rather than Boardwalk, hotel casinos, red Vegas dice, and custom pewter tokens, including blackjack cards, a wedding chapel, and a roulette wheel. Geographic segmentation is an important tool for Canadian marketers, especially when it comes to the province of Quebec. See what Rogers Video is currently doing as it builds outlets throughout the province.

Rogers sees Quebec as an attractive market because it knows that home video is a very large part of the Quebec lifestyle. Rogers marketers, however, must not only be aware of the language differences in the province, they also have to deal with a unique set of competitors when serving this geographic segment. Quebecor Media's giant SuperClub Vidéotron chain is well entrenched, as is Blockbuster and other players such as Club International. Rogers outlets in Quebec will have a special section devoted to Quebec cinema and will stock far more foreign-language fare than in the rest of Canada. Rogers' research has shown that Quebecers are bigger consumers of international cinema. Finally,

TABLE 8.1 Major Segmentation Variables for Consumer Markets

Geographic

World region or country	North America, Western Europe, Middle East, Pacific Rim, China, South East Asia, Latin America
Country region	Atlantic, Quebec, Ontario, Prairies, British Columbia, Territories
City or metro size	Under 5000; 5000–20 000, 20 000–50 000, 50 000–100 000; 100 000–250 000; 250 000–500 000; 500 000–1 000 000; 1 000 000–4 000 000; more than 4 000 000
Density	Urban, suburban, rural
Climate	Northern, Southern, Atlantic, Prairie, Mountain, West Coast

Demographic

Age	Under 6, 6–11, 12–19, 20–34, 35–49, 50–64, 65 and over
Gender	Male, female
Family size	1–2, 3–4, 5 and over.
Family life cycle	Young, single; young, married, no children; young, married with children; older, married with children; older, married, no children under 18; older, single; other
Income	Under $10 000; $10 000–$20 000; $20 000–$30 000; $30 000–$50 000; $50 000–$100 000; $100 000 and over
Occupation	Professional and technical; managers, officials, and proprietors; clerical; sales; craftspeople; supervisors; operatives; farmers; retired; students; homemakers; unemployed
Education	Grade school or less; some high school; high school graduate; college; some university, university graduate; post graduate
Religion	Catholic, Protestant, Jewish, Muslim, Hindu, other
Ethnic Origin	Aboriginal, British, French, South Asian, Chinese, German
Generation	Baby boomer, Generation X, Generation Y

Psychographic

Social class	Lower lowers, upper lowers, working class, middle class, upper middles, lower uppers, upper uppers
Lifestyle	Achievers, strivers, survivors
Personality	Compulsive, gregarious, authoritarian, ambitious

Behavioural

Occasions	Regular occasion; special occasion
Benefits	Quality, service, economy, convenience, speed
User status	Nonuser, ex-user, potential user, first-time user, regular user
User rates	Light user, medium user, heavy user
Loyalty status	None, medium, strong, absolute
Readiness stage	Unaware, aware, informed, interested, desirous, intending to buy
Attitude toward product	Enthusiastic, positive, indifferent, negative, hostile

Rogers' stores in the province will feature confectionery items exclusive to Quebec. To make its presence known, Rogers will use community-based marketing using tools like ads in community newspapers and local radio.[2]

Other companies are seeking to cultivate as-yet-untapped geographic territory. For example, many large companies are fleeing the fiercely competitive major cities and suburbs to set up shop in small towns. Hampton Inns, for instance, has opened a chain of smaller-format motels in towns too small for its standard-size units.

In contrast, other retailers are developing new store concepts that will give them access to higher-density urban areas. For example, Home Depot is introducing neighbourhood stores that look a lot like its traditional stores but at about two-thirds the size. It is placing these stores in high-density markets, such as southeast Calgary, which has been growing rapidly.[3]

Demographic Segmentation

Demographic segmentation
Dividing the market into groups based on demographic variables, such as age, sex, family size, family life cycle, income, occupation, education, religion, race, and nationality.

Demographic segmentation divides the market into groups based on variables such as age, gender, family size, family life cycle, income, occupation, education, religion, race, generation, and nationality. See how Telus used its understanding of ethnic background to target a unique segment:

South Asians, who represent a population of around 1 million (and one that is expected to double by 2017), will soon be Canada's largest visible minority group. In Toronto alone, the South Asian market is worth $12.6 billion a year, according to Mapinfo 2004 statistics. Some savvy marketers, like Telus, Canada's second largest phone company, have been working hard to meet their distinct needs. Telus is well-known for its use of animals, ranging from chameleons to bunnies in its advertising. But finding a spokescharacter that would resonate with the South Asian population wasn't easy. It finally chose hummingbirds and rainbow-coloured fish because they were consistent with the company's overall brand positioning, but were also meaningful to the Punjabi audience watching multicultural TV. The fish commercial carried a message about home networking, says Chris Neary, Telus's Vancouver-based marketing communications director, which was "particularly poignant for South Asians.

Using racial background as a segmentation variable, Telus saw the potential of the South Asian market. It worked with an advisory panel to ensure that its advertising communicated effectively with this important audience.

They tend to have large extended families with multiple computer users in the home and a fairly low understanding of what Telus offers in terms of IP-based services." Telus wants to build deep, on-going relationships with this segment, and to ensure that Telus doesn't use stereotypes when dealing with this group it utilizes a South Asian advisory panel that meets twice a year with senior executives. The panel assesses Telus' communications and new products, and discusses which sponsorships will best increase the company's profile within the community.[4]

Demographic factors are the most popular bases for segmenting customer groups. One reason is that consumer needs, wants, and usage rates often vary closely with demographic variables. Another is that demographic variables are easier to measure than most other types of variables. Even when market segments are first defined using other bases, such as benefits sought or behaviour, their demographic characteristics must be known in order to assess the size of the target market and to reach it efficiently.

Age and life-cycle segmentation

Dividing a market into different age and life-cycle groups.

Age and Life-Cycle Stage   Consumer needs and wants change with age. Some companies use **age and life-cycle segmentation**, offering different products or using different marketing approaches for different age and life-cycle groups. For example, for kids, Procter & Gamble sells Crest Spinbrushes featuring favourite children's characters. For adults, it sells more serious models, promising "a dentist-clean feeling twice a day." And Gap has branched out to target people at different life stages. In addition to its standard line of clothing, the retailer now offers baby Gap, Gap kids, and Gap Maternity.[5]

Marketers must be careful to guard against stereotypes when using age and life-cycle segmentation. For example, although some 70-year-olds require wheelchairs, others play tennis. Similarly, whereas some 40-year-old couples are sending their children off to university, others are just beginning new families. Thus, age is often a poor predictor of a person's life cycle, health, work or family status, needs, and buying power. Companies marketing to mature consumers usually employ positive images and appeals. For example, ads for Olay ProVital—designed to improve the elasticity and appearance the "maturing skin" of women over 50—feature attractive older spokeswomen and uplifting messages.

For kids, Procter & Gamble sells Crest Spinbrushes featuring favourite children's characters. For adults, it sells more serious models, promising "a dentist-clean feeling twice a day."

Gender segmentation
Dividing a market into different groups based on gender.

Gender   Gender segmentation has long been used in clothing, cosmetics, toiletries, and magazines. For example, Procter & Gamble was among the first with Secret, a brand of antiperspirant specially formulated for a woman's chemistry, packaged and advertised to reinforce the female image. More recently, even marketers of goods traditionally skewed toward males have noticed opportunities for targeting women.

Leatherman, which has traditionally targeted its multipurpose combination tool to men, now makes Leatherman Juice for women, hip and stylish tools offered in five vibrant colours. After research showed that Canadian Tire significantly trailed Home Depot in terms of its ability to appeal to women, the venerable retailer knew it had to take action because women make 90 percent of all home improvement decisions. Beginning with its new 5900-square-metre flagship in downtown Vancouver, it has begun designing stores from the ground up in large part with the female consumer in mind. In addition to increasing floor space, it's added female-oriented brands, such as Debbie Travis, and changed its merchandising so that consumers can find décor items in a single area. The strategy has been successful and sales in its newly designed outlets have outpaced those of more traditional stores.[6]

A growing number of websites also target women, such as Oxygen, iVillage, Lifetime, and WE. For example, Oxygen Media runs a website "designed for women by women" (www.oxygen.com). It appeals 18- to 34-year-old women with fresh and hip information, features, and exchanges on a wide variety of topics—from health and fitness, money and work, and style and home to relationships and self-discovery. The leading women's online community, iVillage (www.iVillage.com), offers "real solutions for real women" and entreats visitors to "join our community

Leatherman targets women with its "juice" tool in five vibrant colours, with ads like this one in *Cooking Light* magazine.

of smart, compassionate, real women." Various iVillage channels cover topics ranging from babies, food, fitness, pets, and relationships to careers, finance, and travel.[7]

Income segmentation

Dividing a market into different income groups.

Income   **Income segmentation** has long been used by the marketers of products and services such as automobiles, boats, clothing, cosmetics, financial services, and travel. Many companies target affluent consumers with luxury goods and convenience services. Stores such as Holt Renfrew focus on expensive jewellery, cosmetics, leather goods, and fine fashions. The Sutton Place Hotel, a five-star hotel in Vancouver, targets upscale travellers with promises of European flare, lavishly appointed guest rooms, innovative French continental cuisine, and complete beauty and fitness centres at its Vida Wellness Spa.

However, not all companies that use income segmentation target the affluent. For example, many retailers—such as the Dollar Store chain—successfully target lower-income groups. With their low-income strategies, the dollar stores are now the fastest growing retailers in North America. They have been so successful that giant discounters, such as Wal-Mart and Zellers, are now taking notice. Wal-Mart, for example, is testing "Pennies-n-Cents" sections in twenty Supercenters. "They are a major threat," says a retailing expert, "so much so that Wal-Mart will eventually have to buy one of these chains or start one."[8]

Psychographic Segmentation

Psychographic segmentation

Dividing a market into different groups based on social class, lifestyle, or personality characteristics.

Psychographic segmentation divides buyers into different groups based on social class, lifestyle, or personality characteristics. People in the same demographic group can have very different psychographic makeups.

In Chapter 6, we discussed how the products people buy reflect their *lifestyles*. Many marketers are also finding that age is a poor predictor of attitudes and purchase behaviour. Today, they are dealing with "ageless consumers." Boomers act younger than their predecessors, while their kids are more mature and responsible. As one marketing specialist notes, "The whole concept of segmenting the markets by age is passé." As a result, marketers often segment their markets by consumer lifestyles. Automotive and packaged goods marketers, such as Suzuki Canada, Toyota, Mitsubishi, Nissan, and Soyaworld, have used lifestyle insights to enable them to develop advertising that appeals to both teens and parents—something that was unheard of just a few year ago.[9] Pottery Barn is a retailer who understands lifestyle marketing. It sells more than just home furnishings; it sells an entire lifestyle—all that its customers aspire to be (see Real Marketing 8.1). One forward-looking grocery store found that segmenting its self-service meat products by lifestyle had a big payoff:

> Walk by the refrigerated self-service meat cases of most grocery stores and you'll usually find the offering grouped by type of meat. Pork is in one section, lamb is another, and chicken is in a third. However, a Nashville, Tennessee, Kroger supermarket decided to experiment and offer groupings of different meats by lifestyle. For instance, the store had a section called "Meals in Minutes," one called "Cookin' Lite," another, filled with prepared products like hot dogs and ready-made hamburger patties, called "Kids Love This Stuff," and one called "I Like to Cook." By focusing on lifestyle needs and not on protein categories, Kroger's test store encouraged habitual beef and pork buyers to consider lamb and veal as well. As a result, the 16-foot service case has seen a substantial improvement in both sales and profits.[10]

Marketers also have used *personality* variables to segment markets. For example, marketing for Honda motor scooters *appears* to target hip and trendy 22-year-olds. But it is *actually* aimed at a much broader personality group. One ad, for example, showed a delighted child bouncing up and down on his bed while the announcer says, "You've been trying to get there all your life." The ad reminds

REAL MARKETING

8.1

Pottery Barn: Oh, What a Lifestyle!

Shortly after Hadley MacLean got married, she and her husband, Doug, agreed that their old bed had to go. It was a mattress and box spring on a cheap metal frame, a relic of Doug's university days. But Hadley had never anticipated how tough it would be to find a new bed. "We couldn't find anything we liked, even though we were willing to spend the money," says Hadley, a 31-year-old marketing director. It turned out to be much more than just finding a piece of furniture at the right price. It was a matter of emotion: They needed a bed that meshed with their lifestyle—with who they are and where they are going.

Pottery Barn sells more than just home furnishings; it sells all that its customers aspire to be. It offers idyllic scenes of the perfect childhood at Pottery Barn Kids; trendy, fashion-forward self-expression at PBteen; and an upscale yet casual, family- and friend-focused lifestyle at its flagship Pottery Barn stores.

The couple finally ended up at Pottery Barn, where Doug fell in love with a mahogany sleigh bed that Hadley had spotted in the store's catalogue. The couple was so pleased with how great it looked in their Dutch Colonial home that they hurried back to the store for a set of end tables. And then they bought a quilt. And a mirror for the living room. And some stools for the dining room. "We got kind of addicted," Hadley confesses.

The MacLeans aren't alone. Pottery Barn, which moved into the Canadian market in the summer of 2001, has been successful throughout North America with its smart yet accessible product mix, seductive merchandising, and first-rate customer service. It is now a front-runner in the fragmented home furnishings and housewares industry—not just because of the products that it sells but also because of the connections that it makes with customers. Pottery Barn does more than just sell home furnishings. It sells an entire lifestyle.

Laura Alber, a tall, slim blond with pale-blue eyes and no makeup, could be the poster child for the Pottery Barn lifestyle. The 34-year-old mother of two says that she enjoys entertaining, describes herself as living "holistically," and has just bought the company's Westport sectional sofa, with its kid-resistant twill slipcovers. She also happens to be Pottery Barn's president. Moreover, she is obsessed with a towel. "Feel how great this is," says Alber, pulling a large white bath towel from a stack. "It's thick, it's got a beautiful dobby [the woven band a few inches from the towel's edge], it's highly absorbent, and it's [US]$24. I can say with great confidence that you can't top this." To some merchants, a towel is just a towel. But to Alber, the towel is a fluffy icon of the lifestyle to which Pottery Barn customers aspire: upscale but casual, active but laid back, family- and friend-focused, affluent but sensibly so.

Everyone at Pottery Barn works obsessively to understand the store's customers—who they are, how they live, and what they want out of life. To create a powerful lifestyle brand, says Celia Tejada, head of Pottery Barn's design and product development, you must first have a life. So staffers are encouraged to go to restaurants and notice how the tables are set. To scavenge flea markets for interesting artifacts. To cruise real-estate open houses and model homes, looking for new architectural and design trends. To entertain friends and note what products they wish that they had: a bigger platter, a nicer serving utensil, a better bowl for salsa—anything that may be a good addition to the lifestyle line.

Staffers then use their deep personal insights to develop products and store concepts that deliver the Pottery Barn lifestyle to customers. To pass muster, a potential new Pottery Barn product needs to pass the ultimate hurdle: "I ask my designers, 'Will you take it home or give it as a present to your best friends,'" Tejada says. "If they hesitate, I say, 'Throw it in the garbage.' Emotionally, it has to feel right."

Individual products or lines of merchandise aren't the only things inspired by the personal lives of Pottery Barn staffers. It's no coincidence that the first Pottery Barn Kids catalogue debuted simultaneously with the birth of Laura Alber's first child. The company's president was frustrated at trying to put together a good-looking nursery. She and her team developed a business plan for extending the Pottery Barn lifestyle to the bedrooms of newborns and young children.

There are now more than sixty Pottery Barn Kids stores, and more are planned for the future. As you might expect, Pottery Barn Kids delivers the ultimate kid lifestyle. Stores and catalogues create idyllic scenes of the perfect childhood, featuring themed bedrooms packed with accessories: fluttering curtains, cozy quilts, and stuffed animals.

The latest Pottery Barn sibling is PBteen, which targets the lifestyles of tweens and teens. The PBteen concept seems like a natural extension, but Pottery Barn staffers spent months trying to get inside the heads of their teenage customers. "Our designers [were] going to concerts, hanging out at schools, and watching MTV," says one VP. A contest asking kids to mail in snapshots of their rooms generated photographs that gave PBteen staffers a view into the real life-spaces of teenagers. Staffers pored over them like CIA analysts.

Regardless of which family member it targets, Pottery Barn gives customers an attainable and inspirational vision of what a really great lifestyle might look like. That may be the reason why, when *Condé Nast* magazine recently asked readers to name their favourite home-decorating magazine, an overwhelming number cited the Pottery Barn catalogue.

The Pottery Barn lifestyle suits the company as well as its customers in Canada and the United States. As one executive recently noted, "Our brand [embraces a lifestyle]. It's a state of mind. And customers can make it their own."

Sources: Adapted from Linda Tischler, "How Pottery Barn Wins with Style," *Fast Company*, June 2003, pp. 106–113. Additional information from Amy Merrick, "Child's Play for Furniture Retailers?—Amid Signs of a Baby Boom, the Big Chains Rush to Expand Offerings to Newborns, Kids," *Wall Street Journal*, September 25, 2002, p. B1; Charlyne Varkonyi Schaub, "Pottery Barn Tailoring Itself for Teens," *Sun-Sentinel*, May 9, 2003, accessed at www.sun-sentinel.com; "Williams-Sonoma, Inc.," *Hoover's Company Profiles,* Austin, May 15, 2003; "'Barns' Big Part of Williams-Sonoma Cash," *Home Textiles Today,* May 3, 2004, p. 1; and information at www.pbteen.com (accessed January 2005).

viewers of the euphoric feelings they got when they broke away from authority and did things their parents told them not to do. Thus, Honda is appealing to the rebellious, independent kid in all of us. As Honda notes on its webpage, "Fresh air, freedom, and flair—on a Honda scooter, every day is independence day!" In fact, more than half of Honda's scooter sales are to young professionals and older buyers—15 percent are purchased by the over-50 group. "My most stable [base of] customers [is] white males over 60," says one dealer. "They remember riding [motor scooters] when they were young."[11]

Behavioural Segmentation

Behavioural segmentation divides buyers into groups based on their knowledge, attitudes, uses, or responses to a product. Many marketers believe that behaviour variables are the best starting point for building market segments.

Occasions Buyers can be grouped according to occasions when they get the idea to buy, actually make their purchase, or use the purchased item. **Occasion segmentation** can help firms build up product usage. For example, orange juice is most

Behavioural segmentation
Dividing a market into groups based on consumer knowledge, attitude, use, or response to a product.

Occasion segmentation
Dividing the market into groups according to occasions when buyers get the idea to buy, actually make their purchase, or use the purchased item.

When Honda markets its Reflex and Elite scooters, it appeals to the rebellious, independent kid in all of us.

often consumed at breakfast, but orange growers have promoted drinking orange juice as a cool and refreshing drink at other times of the day. In contrast, Coca-Cola's "Coke in the Morning" advertising campaign attempts to increase Coke consumption by promoting the beverage as an early morning pick-me-up.

Some holidays, such as Mother's Day and Father's Day, were originally promoted partly to increase the sale of candy, flowers, cards, and other gifts. And many marketers prepare special offers and ads for holiday occasions. For example, Altoids offers a special "Love Tin," the "curiously strong valentine." Beatrice Foods runs special Thanksgiving and Christmas ads for Reddi-wip during November and December, months that account for 30 percent of all whipped cream sales. Butterball, on the other hand, advertises "Happy Thanksgrilling" during the summer to increase the demand for turkeys on non-Thanksgiving occasions.

Kodak, Konica, Fuji, and other camera makers use occasion segmentation in designing and marketing their one-time-use cameras. By mixing lenses, film speeds, and accessories, they have developed special disposable cameras for almost any picture-taking occasion, from underwater photography to taking baby pictures. The Kodak Water & Sport one-time-use camera is water resistant to 15 m deep and features a shock-proof frame, a sunscreen- and scratch-resistant lens, and 800-speed film. "It survives where your regular camera won't!" claims Kodak.[12]

Benefits Sought   A powerful form of segmentation is to group buyers according to the different *benefits* that they seek from the product. **Benefit segmentation** requires finding the major benefits people look for in the product class, the kinds of people who look for each benefit, and the major brands that deliver each benefit. For example, Procter & Gamble has identified several different laundry detergent segments. Each segment seeks a unique combination of benefits, from cleaning and bleaching to economy, fabric softening, fresh smell, strength or mildness, and lots of suds or only a few.

Benefit segmentation

Dividing the market into groups according to the different benefits that consumers seek from the product.

Altoids created a special "Love Tin"—a "curiously strong valentine."

The Champion athletic wear division of Sara Lee Corporation segments its markets according to benefits that different consumers seek from their activewear. For example, "fit and polish" consumers seek a balance between function and style—they exercise for results but want to look good doing it. "Serious sports competitors" exercise heavily and live in and love their activewear—they seek performance and function. By contrast, "value-seeking moms" have low sports interest and low activewear involvement—they buy for the family and seek durability and value. Thus, each segment seeks a different mix of benefits. Champion must target the benefit segment or segments that it can serve best and most profitably using appeals that match each segment's benefit preferences.

User Status   Markets can be segmented into groups of nonusers, ex-users, potential users, first-time users, and regular users of a product. For example, one study found that blood donors are low in self-esteem, low risk takers, and more highly concerned about their health; nondonors tend to be the opposite on all three dimensions. This suggests that social agencies should use different marketing approaches for keeping current donors and attracting new ones. A company's market position also influences its focus. Market share leaders focus on attracting potential users, whereas smaller firms focus on attracting current users away from the market leader.

Usage Rate   Markets can also be segmented into light, medium, and heavy product users. Heavy users are often a small percentage of the market but account for a high percentage of total consumption. Marketers usually prefer to attract one heavy user to their product or service rather than several light users.

For example, in the fast-food industry, heavy users make up only 20 percent of patrons but eat up about 60 percent of all the food served. A single heavy user, typically a single male in his 20s or 30s who doesn't know how to cook, might spend as much as $40 in a day at fast-food restaurants and visit them more than 20 times a month. Despite claims by some consumers that the fast-food chains are damaging their health, these heavy users are extremely loyal. "They insist they don't need saving," says one analyst, "protesting that they are far from the clueless fatties anti-fast-food activists make them out to be." Even the heaviest users "would have to be stupid not to know that you can't eat only burgers and fries and not exercise," he says.[13]

Interestingly, although fast-food companies, such as Burger King, McDonald's, and KFC, depend a lot on heavy users and do all they can to keep them satisfied with every visit, these companies often target light users with their ads and promotions. The heavy users "are in our restaurants already," says a Burger King marketer. The company's marketing dollars are more often spent trying to convince light users that they want a burger in the first place.

Loyalty Status A market can also be segmented by consumer loyalty. Consumers can be loyal to brands (Tide), stores (Loblaws), and companies (Ford). Buyers can be divided into groups according to their degree of loyalty. Some consumers are completely loyal—they buy one brand all the time. Others are somewhat loyal—they are loyal to two or three brands of a given product or favour one brand while sometimes buying others. Still other buyers show no loyalty to any brand. They either want something different each time they buy or they buy whatever's on sale.

A company can learn a lot by analyzing loyalty patterns in its market. It should start by studying its own loyal customers. For example, to better understand the needs and behaviour of its core soft drink consumers, Pepsi observed them in places where its products are consumed—in homes, in stores, in movie theatres, at sporting events, and at the beach. "We learned that there's a surprising amount of loyalty and passion for Pepsi's products," says Pepsi's director of consumer insights. "One fellow had four or five cases of Pepsi in his basement and he felt he was low on Pepsi and had to go replenish." The company used these and other study findings to pinpoint the Pepsi target market and develop marketing appeals.[14]

By studying its less loyal buyers, the company can detect which brands are most competitive with its own. If many Pepsi buyers also buy Coke, Pepsi can attempt to improve its positioning against Coke, possibly by using direct-comparison advertising. By looking at customers who are shifting away from its brand, the company can learn about its marketing weaknesses. As for nonloyals, the company may attract them by putting its brand on sale.

A company can learn a lot by analyzing loyalty patterns in its market. It should start by studying its own loyal customers.

Using Multiple Segmentation Bases

Marketers rarely limit their segmentation analysis to only one or a few variables. Rather, they are increasingly using multiple segmentation bases in an effort to identify smaller, better-defined target groups. Thus, a bank may not only identify a group of wealthy retired adults but also, within that group, distinguish several segments based on their current income, assets, savings and risk preferences, housing, and lifestyles.

One good example of multivariable segmentation is "geodemographic" segmentation. Several business information services—such as Claritas, Experian, Acxiom, and MapInfo—have arisen to help marketing planners link census information and consumer transaction data with consumer lifestyle patterns to better segment their markets down to postal codes, neighbourhoods, and even city blocks.

One of the leading lifestyle segmentation systems is the PRIZM "You Are Where You Live" system by Claritas. The PRIZM system marries a host of demographic factors—such as age, educational level, income, occupation, family composition, ethnicity, and housing—with buying transaction data and lifestyle information taken from consumer surveys. Using PRIZM, marketers can use where you live to paint a surprisingly precise picture of who you are and what you might buy.

You're a 36-year-old university graduate, and the price tag on your clothing testifies to your success. You drive a 3-year-old VW Jetta but have your eye on a new Honda Odyssey. You know your way around the gourmet section of your local market, buy fresh-ground coffee, and vacation at your time-share in Whistler. You're living out your own, individual version of the good life in the suburbs. You're unique—not some demographic cliché. Right? Wrong. You're

In marketing its Suave shampoo, Helene Curtis uses PRIZM to identify neighbourhoods with high concentrations of working women. Such women respond best to advertising messages suggesting that with Suave, looking great doesn't have to cost a fortune.

a prime example of PRIZM's "Kids & Cul-de-Sacs" cluster. If you consume, you can't hide from Claritas.[15]

PRIZM classifies you and everyone else into one of sixty-two unique neighbourhood types or "clusters." PRIZM clusters carry such exotic names as Blue Blood Estates, Money & Brains, Young Literati, New Eco-topias, Mobility Blues, Grey Power, and Hard Scrabble. "Those image-triggered nicknames save a lot of time and geeky technical research terms explaining what you mean," says one marketer. "It's the names that bring the clusters to life," says another.[16]

Regardless of what you call the categories, such systems can help marketers to segment people and locations into marketable groups of like-minded consumers. Each cluster exhibits unique characteristics and buying behaviour. For example, Blue Blood Estates neighbourhoods are suburban areas populated by elite, super-rich families. People in this cluster are more likely to belong to health clubs, take expensive trips, buy classical music, and read *Architectural Digest*.

Such segmentation provides a powerful tool for segmenting markets, refining demand estimates, selecting target markets, and shaping promotion messages. For example, in marketing its Suave shampoo, Unilever's Helene Curtis division uses PRIZM to identify neighbourhoods with high concentrations of working women. Such women respond best to advertising messages suggesting that with Suave, looking great doesn't have to cost a fortune.

With the burgeoning availability of data and computer power, geodemographic marketers are continually refining their techniques. More than just tracking major demographic shifts and adding new clusters or adjusting old ones, they are slicing and dicing geographic segments into ever-smaller patches of real estate that may include segments as small as a dozen or so households.[17]

Segmenting Business Markets

Consumer and business marketers use many of the same variables to segment their markets. Business buyers can be segmented geographically, demographically (industry, company size), or by benefits sought, user status, usage rate, and loyalty status. Yet, business marketers also use some additional variables, such as customer *operating characteristics*, *purchasing approaches*, *situational factors*, and *personal characteristics*. By going after segments instead of the whole market, companies can deliver just the right value proposition to each segment served and capture more value in return.

Almost every company serves at least some business markets. For example, you probably know American Express as a company that offers personal credit cards to consumers. But American Express, whose Canadian operations are located in Markham, Ontario, also targets businesses in three segments—merchants, corporations, and small businesses. It has developed distinct marketing programs for each segment. In the merchants segment, American Express focuses on convincing new merchants to accept the card and on managing relationships with those that already do. For larger corporate customers, the company offers a corporate card program, which includes extensive employee expense and travel management services. It also offers this segment a wide range of asset management, retirement planning, and financial education services. Finally, for small business customers, American Express has created the OPEN: Small Business Network, "the one place that's all about small business." Small business cardholders can access the network for everything from account and expense management software to expert small-business management advice and connecting with other small business owners to share ideas and get recommendations.[18]

Many companies set up separate systems for dealing with larger or multiple-location customers. For example, Steelcase, a major producer of office furniture,

This helps you buy what your small business needs.

This lets you track, organize, categorize, subdivide, examine, break down, cross-reference, combine and archive online what your small business spends.

Now you can access the Expense Management Report and many other online tools. But only if you have the American Express® Business Card. The Card with the savings, rewards and services of OPEN: The Small Business Network℠ behind it. **Apply now and get an instant decision. Visit OPEN.AMERICANEXPRESS.COM.**

For small business customers, American Express has created the OPEN: Small Business Network, "the one place that's all about small business."

first segments customers into 10 industries, including banking, insurance, and electronics. Next, company salespeople work with independent Steelcase dealers to handle smaller, local, or regional Steelcase customers in each segment. But many national, multiple-location customers, such as IBM, have special needs that may reach beyond the scope of individual dealers. So Steelcase uses national accounts managers to help its dealer networks handle its national accounts.

Within a given target industry and customer size, the company can segment by purchase approaches and criteria. As in consumer segmentation, many marketers believe that *buying behaviour* and *benefits* provide the best basis for segmenting business markets.[19]

Segmenting International Markets

Few companies have either the resources or the will to operate in all, or even most, of the countries that dot the globe. Although some large companies, such as Coca-Cola or Sony, sell products in more than 200 countries, most international firms focus on a smaller set. Take the case of SMART Technologies Inc., the winner of the 2005 Canada Export Award for Lifetime Achievement:

SMART Technologies Inc., the Calgary-based company with Ottawa manufacturing operations, was founded in 1987. It developed and marketed the world's first interactive whiteboard, and today is the world leader in its field with more than 97 percent of its revenues coming from international sales. As a small company, it had to use its resources wisely and carefully select its markets. "We sold in the United States for two years before we sold our first product in Canada," says David Martin, SMART's chair and co-CEO. SMART's interactive whiteboards and other products are used in every state, in schools, and by clients such as NASA, Boeing, Disney, and the U.S. Joint Chiefs of Staff. It also entered the United Kingdom and it now has 58 percent of the education market there. Recently, new market growth has come from countries such as Mexico and China.[20]

Operating in many countries presents new challenges. Different countries, even those that are close together, can vary greatly in their economic, cultural, and political makeup. Thus, just as they do within their domestic markets, international firms need to group their world markets into segments with distinct buying needs and behaviours.

Companies can segment international markets using one or a combination of several variables. They can segment by *geographic location*, grouping countries by regions, such as Western Europe, the Pacific Rim, the Middle East, or Africa. Geographic segmentation assumes that nations close to one another will have many common traits and behaviours. Although this is often the case, there are many exceptions. For example, although the United States and Canada have much in common, both differ culturally and economically from neighbouring Mexico. Even within a region, consumers can differ widely. For example, some U.S. marketers lump all Central and South American countries together. However, the Dominican Republic is no more like Brazil than Italy is like Sweden. Many Latin Americans don't even speak Spanish, including 140 million Portuguese-speaking Brazilians and the millions in other countries who speak a variety of indigenous dialects.

World markets can also be segmented on the basis of *economic factors*. For example, countries might be grouped by population income levels or by their overall level of economic development. A company's economic structure shapes its population's product and service needs and, therefore, the marketing opportunities it offers. Countries can be segmented by *political and legal factors*, such as the type and stability of government, receptivity to foreign firms, monetary regulations, and the amount of bureaucracy. Such factors can play a crucial role in a company's choice of which countries to enter and how. *Cultural factors* can also be used, grouping markets according to common languages, religions, values and attitudes, customs, and behavioural patterns.

Segmenting international markets on the basis of geographic, economic, political, cultural, and other factors assumes that segments should consist of clusters of countries. However, many companies use a different approach called **intermarket segmentation**. Using this approach, they form segments of consumers who have similar needs and buying behaviour even though they are located in different countries. For example, Mercedes-Benz targets the world's well-to-do, regardless of their country.

MTV targets the world's teenagers. The world's 560 million teens have a lot in common: They study, shop, and sleep. They are exposed to many of the same major issues: love, crime, homelessness, ecology, and working parents. In many ways, they have more in common with one another than with their parents. "Last year I was in 17 different countries," says one expert, "and it's pretty difficult to find anything that is different, other than language, among a teenager in Japan, a teenager in the UK, and a teenager in China." Says another, "Global teens in Buenos Aires, Beijing, and Bangalore swing to the beat of MTV while sipping Coke." MTV bridges the gap between cultures, appealing to what teens around the world have in common. Sony, Reebok, Nike, Swatch, and many other firms also actively target global teens.[21]

Intermarket segmentation
Forming segments of consumers who have similar needs and buying behaviour even though they are located in different countries.

Teens show surprising similarity no matter where in the world they live. For instance, these two teens could live almost anywhere. Thus, many companies target teenagers with worldwide marketing campaigns.

Segmenting Markets Effectively

Clearly, there are many ways to segment a market, but not all segmentations are effective. For example, buyers of table salt could be divided into blond and brunette customers. But hair colour obviously does not affect the purchase of salt. Furthermore, if all salt buyers bought the same amount of salt each month, believed that all salt is the same, and wanted to pay the same price, the company would not benefit from segmenting this market.

To be useful, market segments must be

- *Measurable:* The size, purchasing power, and profiles of the segments can be measured. Certain segmentation variables are difficult to measure. For example, there are 32.5 million left-handed people in the United States—almost equalling the entire population of Canada. Yet few products are targeted toward this left-handed segment. The major problem may be that the segment is hard to identify and measure. There are no data on the demographics of lefties, and neither Statistics Canada nor the U.S. Census Bureau keeps track of left-handedness in its surveys. Private data companies keep reams of statistics on other demographic segments but not on left-handers.

- *Accessible:* The market segments can be effectively reached and served. Suppose a fragrance company finds that heavy users of its brand are single men and women who stay out late and socialize a lot. Unless this group lives or shops at certain places and is exposed to certain media, its members will be difficult to reach.

- *Substantial:* The market segments are large or profitable enough to serve. A segment should be the largest possible homogenous group worth pursuing with a tailored marketing program. It would not pay, for example, for an automobile manufacturer to develop cars especially for people whose height is greater than 215 centimetres.

- *Differentiable:* The segments are conceptually distinguishable and respond differently to different marketing mix elements and programs. If married and unmarried women respond similarly to a sale on perfume, they do not constitute separate segments.

- *Actionable:* Effective programs can be designed for attracting and serving the segments. For example, although one small airline identified seven market segments, its staff was too small to develop separate marketing programs for each segment.

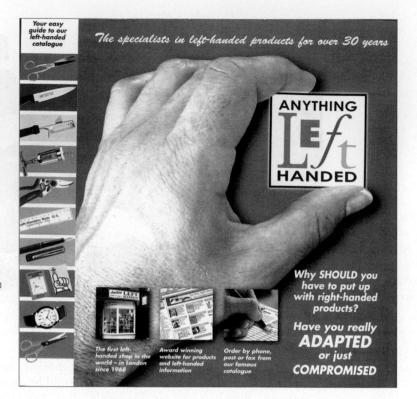

The "Leftie" segment can be hard to identify and measure. As a result, few companies tailor their offers to left-handers. However, some nichers, such as Anything Left-Handed in the UK, target this segment.

Target Marketing

Market segmentation reveals the firm's market segment opportunities. The firm now has to evaluate the various segments and decide how many and which segments it can serve best. We now look at how companies evaluate and select target segments.

Evaluating Market Segments

In evaluating different market segments, a firm must look at three factors: segment size and growth, segment structural attractiveness, and company objectives and resources. The company must first collect and analyze data on current segment sales, growth rates, and expected profitability for various segments. It will be interested in segments that have the right size and growth characteristics. But "right size and growth" is a relative matter. The largest, fastest-growing segments are not always the most attractive ones for every company. Smaller companies may lack the skills and resources needed to serve the larger segments. Or they may find these segments too competitive. Such companies may select segments that are smaller and less attractive, in an absolute sense, but that are potentially more profitable for them.

The company also needs to examine major structural factors that affect long-run segment attractiveness.[22] For example, a segment is less attractive if it already contains many strong and aggressive *competitors*. The existence of many actual or potential *substitute products* may limit prices and the profits that can be earned in a segment. The relative *power of buyers* also affects segment attractiveness. Buyers with strong bargaining power relative to sellers will try to force prices down, demand more services, and set competitors against one another—all at the expense of seller profitability. Finally, a segment may be less attractive if it contains *powerful suppliers* who can control prices or reduce the quality or quantity of ordered goods and services.

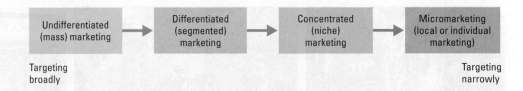

Figure 8.3 Target marketing strategies

Even if a segment has the right size and growth and is structurally attractive, the company must consider its own objectives and resources. Some attractive segments can be dismissed quickly because they do not mesh with the company's long-run objectives. Or the company may lack the skills and resources needed to succeed in an attractive segment. The company should enter only segments in which it can offer superior value and gain advantages over competitors.

Selecting Target Market Segments

Target market

A set of buyers sharing common needs or characteristics that the company decides to serve.

After evaluating different segments, the company must now decide which and how many segments it will target. A **target market** consists of a set of buyers who share common needs or characteristics that the company decides to serve.

Because buyers have unique needs and wants, a seller could potentially view each buyer as a separate target market. Ideally, then, a seller might design a separate marketing program for each buyer. However, although some companies do attempt to serve buyers individually, most face larger numbers of smaller buyers and do not find individual targeting worthwhile. Instead, they look for broader segments of buyers. More generally, target marketing can be carried out at several different levels. Figure 8.3 shows that companies can target very broadly (undifferentiated marketing), very narrowly (micromarketing), or somewhere in between (differentiated or concentrated marketing).

Undifferentiated Marketing

Undifferentiated (or mass) marketing

A market-coverage strategy in which a firm decides to ignore market segment differences and go after the whole market with one offer.

Using an **undifferentiated marketing** (or **mass marketing**) strategy, a firm might decide to ignore market segment differences and target the whole market with one offer. This mass-marketing strategy focuses on what is *common* in the needs of consumers rather than on what is *different*. The company designs a product and a marketing program that will appeal to the largest number of buyers.

As noted earlier in the chapter, most modern marketers have strong doubts about this strategy. Difficulties arise in developing a product or brand that will satisfy all consumers. Moreover, mass marketers often have trouble competing with more focused firms that do a better job of satisfying the needs of specific segments and niches.

Differentiated Marketing

Differentiated (or segmented) marketing

A market-coverage strategy in which a firm decides to target several market segments and designs separate offers for each.

Using a **differentiated marketing** (or **segmented marketing**) strategy, a firm decides to target several market segments and designs separate offers for each. Royal Bank of Canada (RBC) is Canada's largest bank and one of North America's leading diversified financial services companies. It provides a wide range of personal banking services for end consumers who need everything from chequing accounts and credit cards to wealth management services. For its business customers, it offers commercial banking, insurance, investment banking, and transaction processing services on a global basis. Gap Inc. has created three different retail store formats—Gap, Banana Republic, and Old Navy—to serve the varied needs of different fashion segments.

Estée Lauder offers dozens of different products aimed at carefully defined segments:

Gap has created three different retail store formats—Old Navy, GAP, and Banana Republic—to serve the varied needs of different fashion segments.

The four best-selling prestige perfumes in North America belong to Estée Lauder. So do seven of the top ten prestige makeup products and eight of the ten best-selling prestige skin care products. Estée Lauder is an expert in creating differentiated brands that serve the tastes of different market segments. There's the original Estée Lauder brand, which appeals to older women. Then there's Clinique, perfect for the middle-aged mom with a GMC Suburban and no time to waste. For the youthful crowd, there's the hip M.A.C. line (which Estée Lauder purchased from its Canadian founder). And, for the New Age type, there's upscale Aveda, with its aromatherapy line, and earthy Origins, which the company expects will become a US$1 billion brand. The company even offers downscale brands, such as Jane by Sassaby, for teens who shop at Wal-Mart.[23]

By offering product and marketing variations to segments, companies hope for higher sales and a stronger position within each market segment. Developing a stronger position within several segments creates more total sales than undifferentiated marketing across all segments. Estée Lauder's combined brands give it a much greater market share than any single brand could. The Estée Lauder and Clinique brands alone reap a combined 40 percent share of the prestige cosmetics market.

But differentiated marketing also increases the costs of doing business. A firm usually finds it more expensive to develop and produce, say, 10 units of 10 different products than 100 units of one product. Developing separate marketing plans for the separate segments requires extra marketing research, forecasting, sales analysis, promotion planning, and channel management. And trying to reach different market segments with different advertising increases promotion costs. Thus, the company must weigh increased sales against increased costs when deciding on a differentiated marketing strategy.

Concentrated Marketing

Concentrated (or niche) marketing

A market-coverage strategy in which a firm goes after a large share of one or a few segments or niches.

A third market-coverage strategy, **concentrated marketing** (or **niche marketing**), is especially appealing when company resources are limited. Instead of going after a small share of a large market, the firm goes after a large share of one or a few segments or niches. For example, Oshkosh Truck is the world's largest producer of airport rescue trucks and front-loading concrete mixers. Tetra sells 80 percent of the world's tropical fish food, and Steiner Optical captures 80 percent of the world's military binoculars market.

Through concentrated marketing, the firm achieves a strong market position because of its greater knowledge of consumer needs in the niches it serves and the special reputation it acquires. It can market more *effectively* by fine-tuning its products, prices, and programs to the needs of carefully defined segments. It can also market more *efficiently*, targeting its products or services, channels, and communications programs toward only consumers that it can serve best and most profitably.

Whereas segments are fairly large and normally attract several competitors, niches are smaller and may attract only one or a few competitors. Niching offers smaller companies an opportunity to compete by focusing their limited resources on serving niches that may be unimportant to or overlooked by larger competitors. Consider Apple Computer. Although it once enjoyed better than 13 percent of its market share, Apple is now a market nicher, capturing only about 3.5 percent of its market. Rather than competing head-on with other PC makers as they slash prices and focus on volume, Apple invests in research and development, making it the industry trendsetter. For example, when the company recently introduced iTunes, it captured more than 70 percent of the music download market. Such innovation has created a loyal base of consumers who are willing to pay more for Apple's cutting-edge products.[24]

Many companies start as nichers to get a foothold against larger, more resourceful competitors; then they grow into broader competitors. For example, WestJet was founded in 1996 to serve no-frills commuters and people travelling to visit friends and family in western Canada. Today it is a national carrier that competes directly with Air Canada in many key markets. In contrast, as markets change, some mega-marketers develop niche markets to create sales growth. For example, in recent years, Pepsi has introduced several niche products, such as Sierra Mist, Pepsi Blue, Mountain Dew Code Red, and Mountain Dew LiveWire. Initially, these brands combined accounted for barely 5 percent of Pepsi's overall soft-drink sales. However, Sierra Mist has now blossomed into Pepsi's fastest-growing beverage brand, and Code Red and LiveWire have revitalized the Mountain Dew brand. Says Pepsi-Cola North America's chief marketing officer, "The era of the mass brand has been over for a long time."[25]

Today, the low cost of setting up shop on the Internet makes it even more profitable to serve seemingly minuscule niches. Small businesses, in particular, are realizing riches from serving small niches on the Web. Here is a "Webpreneur" who achieved astonishing results:

Whereas Internet giants such as Amazon.com have yet to even realize a consistent profit, Steve Warrington is earning a six-figure income selling ostriches—and every product derived from them—online (www.ostrichesonline.com). Launched for next to nothing on the Web in 1996, Ostrichesonline.com now boasts that it sends newsletters to 43 000 subscribers and sells 20 000 ostrich products to more than 25 000 satisfied clients in more than 125 countries. The site tells visitors everything they ever wanted to know about ostriches and much, much more—it supplies ostrich facts, ostrich pictures, an ostrich farm

Some mega-marketers develop niche markets to create sales growth. For example, niche brands such as Code Red and LiveWire have revitalized Pepsi's Mountain Dew brand.

index, and a huge ostrich database and reference index. Visitors to the site can buy ostrich meat, feathers, leather jackets, videos, eggshells, and skin care products derived from ostrich body oil.[26]

Concentrated marketing can be highly profitable. At the same time, it involves higher-than-normal risks. Companies that rely on one or a few segments for all of their business will suffer greatly if the segment turns sour. Or larger competitors may decide to enter the same segment with greater resources. For these reasons, many companies prefer to diversify in several market segments.

Micromarketing

Micromarketing

The practice of tailoring products and marketing programs to the needs and wants of specific individuals and local customer groups—includes *local marketing* and *individual marketing*.

Differentiated and concentrated marketers tailor their offers and marketing programs to meet the needs of various market segments and niches. At the same time, however, they do not customize their offers to each individual customer. **Micromarketing** is the practice of tailoring products and marketing programs to suit the tastes of specific individuals and locations. Rather than seeing a customer in every individual, micromarketers see the individual in every customer. Lambertrand, a small company located in Sherbrooke, Quebec, is a micromarketer. Founded in 1993, the company designs and manufactures ready-to-wear women's clothing with a medieval/urban inspiration. Its sells garments through its own retail store as well as through eleven independent retailers across Ontario and Quebec. The company has sustained itself by focusing on differentiation achieved not only by its specialty apparel but also by its relentless commitment to innovation and creativity.[27]

Micromarketing includes *local marketing* and *individual marketing*.

Local marketing

Tailoring brands and promotions to the needs and wants of local customer groups—cities, neighbourhoods, and even specific stores.

Local Marketing   **Local marketing** involves tailoring brands and promotions to the needs and wants of local customer groups—cities, neighbourhoods, and even specific stores. Kraft, for example, helps supermarket chains identify the specific cheese assortments and shelf positioning that will optimize cheese sales in low-income, middle-income, and high-income stores and in different ethnic communities.

Local marketing has some drawbacks. It can drive up manufacturing and marketing costs by reducing economies of scale. It can also create logistics problems as companies try to meet the varied requirements of different regional and local markets. Further, a brand's overall image might be diluted if the product and message vary too much in different localities.

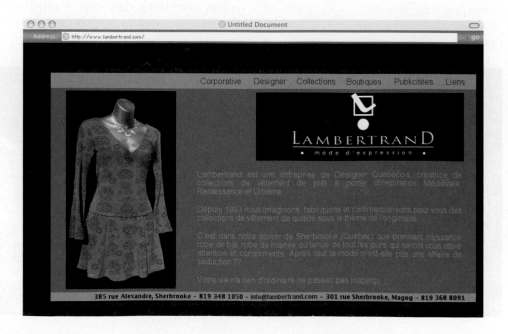

Lambertrand is a micromarketer. It sells specialty apparel with a medieval theme.

Still, as companies face increasingly fragmented markets, and as new supporting technologies develop, the advantages of local marketing often outweigh the drawbacks. Local marketing helps a company to market more effectively in the face of pronounced regional and local differences in demographics and lifestyles. It also meets the needs of the company's first-line customers—retailers—who prefer more fine-tuned product assortments for their neighbourhoods.

Individual marketing

Tailoring products and marketing programs to the needs and preferences of individual customers—also labelled "markets-of-one marketing," "customized marketing," and "one-to-one marketing."

Individual Marketing   In the extreme, micromarketing becomes **individual marketing**—tailoring products and marketing programs to the needs and preferences of individual customers. Individual marketing has also been labelled *one-to-one marketing, mass customization,* and *markets-of-one marketing.*

The widespread use of mass marketing has obscured the fact that for centuries consumers were served as individuals: The tailor custom-made the suit, the cobbler designed shoes for the individual, the cabinetmaker made furniture to order. Today, however, new technologies are permitting many companies to return to customized marketing. More powerful computers, detailed databases, robotic production and flexible manufacturing, and interactive communication media, such as email and the Internet—all have combined to foster "mass customization." *Mass customization* is the process through which firms interact one to one with masses of customers to design products and services tailor-made to individual needs.[28]

Dell creates custom-configured computers, Lenscrafters customizes eyewear, and Ford lets buyers "build a vehicle" from a palette of options. Hockey stick maker Branches Hockey lets customers choose from more than two-dozen options—including stick length, blade patterns, and blade curve—and turns out a customized stick in five days. Companies selling all kinds of products—from candy, clothing, and golf clubs to fire trucks—are customizing their offerings to the needs of individual buyers. Consider this example:

Looking to sweeten up a party or special celebration? Try the Customized M&M's section at the M&M's Brand Store site (http://shop.mms.com), where you can special order the tasty little candies in whatever combination of colours suits your fancy. The site lets you pick from a palette of 21 colours and order in 225 g or 2.5 kg customized bags. Mix up a patriotic combo of red and white for the chocolate lovers at your Canada Day celebration. Or special order a blend of your school colours for the next tailgate party. Send customized promotional tins or gift bags featuring your company colours to special customers. You can even print your very own M&Ms with personalized messages tailored to a special occasion. How about "boo" on your Halloween M&Ms, or "HO HO HO" at Christmas? Want to see your name on a batch of aqua-green M&Ms? No problem. Customized M&Ms are premium priced—nearly three times the cost of regular M&Ms. But business is booming, with sales doubling every year.[29]

Consumer goods marketers aren't the only ones going one to one. Business-to-business marketers are also finding new ways to customize their offerings. For example, BD, a major medical supplier, offers to customize almost anything for its hospital customers. It offers custom-designed labelling, individual packaging, customized quality control, customized computer software, and customized billing. And John Deere manufactures seeding equipment that can be configured in more than 2 million versions to individual customer specifications. The seeders are produced one at a time, in any sequence, on a single production line.

Particularly for small companies, mass customization provides a way to stand out against larger competitors:

Oshkosh Truck specializes in making fire, garbage, cement, and military trucks. Oshkosh is small—a tenth the size of larger rivals such as Paccar and Navistar International—and the truck industry is slumping. Yet Oshkosh has grown by

65 percent over the past five years; profits have more than doubled. What's the secret to Oshkosh's success? Mass customization—the ability to personalize its products and services to the needs of individual customers. For example, when firefighters order a truck from Oshkosh, it's an event. They travel to the plant to watch the vehicle, which may cost as much as US$800 000, take shape. The firefighters can choose from 19 000 options. A stripped-down fire truck costs US$130 000, but 75 percent of Oshkosh's customers order lots of extras, such as hideaway stairs, ladders, special doors, compartments, and firefighting foam systems for those difficult-to-extinguish fires. Some bring along paint chips so they can customize the colour of their fleet. Others are content just to admire the vehicles, down to the water tanks and hideaway ladders. "Some chiefs even bring their wives; we encourage it," says the president of Oshkosh's firefighting unit, Pierce Manufacturing. "Buying a fire truck is a very personal thing." Indeed, Pierce customers are in town so often the Holiday Inn renamed its lounge the Hook and Ladder. Through such customization and personalization, smaller Oshkosh has gained a big edge over its languishing larger rivals.[30]

Unlike mass production, which eliminates the need for human interaction, one to one has made relationships with customers more important than ever. Just as mass production was the marketing principle of the last century, mass customization is becoming a marketing principle for the twenty-first century. The world appears to be coming full circle—from the good old days when customers were treated as individuals, to mass marketing when nobody knew your name, and back again.

The move toward individual marketing mirrors the trend in consumer *self-marketing*. Increasingly, individual customers are taking more responsibility for determining which products and brands to buy. Consider two business buyers with two different purchasing styles. The first sees several salespeople, each trying to persuade him to buy his or her product. The second sees no salespeople but rather logs on to the Internet. She searches for information on available products; interacts electronically with various suppliers, users, and product analysts; and then makes up her own mind about the best offer. The second purchasing agent has taken more responsibility for the buying process, and the marketer has had less influence over her buying decision.

As the trend toward more interactive dialogue and less advertising monologue continues, self-marketing will grow in importance. As more buyers look up consumer reports, join Internet product discussion forums, and place orders via phone or online, marketers will have to influence the buying process in new ways. They will need to involve customers more in all phases of the product development and buying processes, increasing opportunities for buyers to practise self-marketing.

Choosing a Target Marketing Strategy

Companies need to consider many factors when choosing a target-marketing strategy. Which strategy is best depends on *company resources*. When the firm's resources are limited, concentrated marketing makes the most sense. The best strategy also depends on the degree of *product variability*. Undifferentiated marketing is more suited for uniform products, such as grapefruit or steel. Products that can vary in design, such as cameras and automobiles, are more suited to differentiation or concentration. The *product's life-cycle stage* also must be considered. When a firm introduces a new product, it may be practical to launch only one version, and undifferentiated marketing or concentrated marketing may make the most sense. In the mature stage of the product life cycle, however, differentiated marketing begins to make more sense.

Another factor is *market variability*. If most buyers have the same tastes, buy the same amounts, and react the same way to marketing efforts, undifferentiated marketing is appropriate. Finally, *competitors' marketing strategies* are important. When competitors use differentiated or concentrated marketing, undifferentiated marketing can be suicidal. Conversely, when competitors use undifferentiated marketing, a firm can gain an advantage by using differentiated or concentrated marketing.

Socially Responsible Target Marketing

Smart targeting helps companies to be more efficient and effective by focusing on the segments that they can satisfy best and most profitably. Targeting also benefits consumers—companies reach specific groups of consumers with offers carefully tailored to satisfy their needs. However, target marketing sometimes generates controversy and concern. The biggest issues usually involve the targeting of vulnerable or disadvantaged consumers with controversial or potentially harmful products. The diet industry, for example, has been accused of unfairly targeting insecure teens. In another case, a recent FTC study found that 80 percent of R-rated movies and 70 percent of video games with a mature rating were targeted to children under 17. Some critics have even called for a complete ban on advertising to children.[31] To encourage responsible advertising, the Canadian Marketing Association has published extensive children's advertising guidelines that recognize the special needs of child audiences. Other problems arise when the marketing of adult products spills over into the kid segment—intentionally or unintentionally.

Samantha Robertson finally got a cellphone for her ninth birthday. She was delighted and had been pleading with her parents every day for two months. She is typical of the most recent set of consumers targeted by cellphone companies—kids aged 8 to 12. Adoption is already widespread. According to a 2004 Statistics Canada survey, 17.5 percent of students in Canadian primary schools have cellphones. For some marketers, kids are a prime segment since other markets are saturated and parents are increasingly worried about the safety of their children. Companies as varied as the Walt Disney Co. and Bell Canada, with its new bright yellow Kittyphone, are aiming squarely at this market. However, serious questions are being asked about the safety of cellphones for children and the biological changes that they may cause which range from headaches and cancer to degenerative ear and brain diseases. Other scientists dismiss such concerns, pointing to research that shows no reason for worry. Though Health Canada has been mute on the topic, European countries have been issuing public warning to parents and in early 2005, the MYMO, a cellphone targeted at children, was pulled from the British market after a study showed prolonged use may be especially damaging to the underdeveloped skull tissue of very young children.[32]

The meteoric growth of the Internet and other carefully targeted direct media has raised fresh concerns about potential targeting abuses. The Internet allows increasing refinement of audiences and, in turn, more precise targeting. This might help makers of questionable products or deceptive advertisers to more readily victimize the most vulnerable audiences. Unscrupulous marketers can now send tailor-made deceptive messages directly to the computers of millions of unsuspecting consumers. Called "phishing" or "brand spoofing," it is the act of sending an email to a user falsely, claiming to be a legitimate enterprise in an attempt to scam the user into disclosing private information. For example, thousands of Canadians have received email messages that look like they come from legitimate financial institutions such as CIBC, RBC, Visa, or Caisse Desjardin, asking them for information such as credit card numbers, bank account information, social insurance numbers, and passwords so that their accounts can be updated. Rather than updating their accounts, the information is used for identity theft.

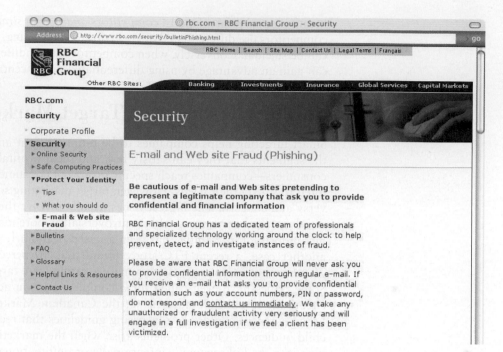

Legitimate financial institutions, such as RBC, never ask their customers for confidential information by email. To help protect their customers, RBC has posted warnings on their websites about practices called "phishing."

Not all attempts to target children, minorities, or other special segments draw such criticism. In fact, most provide benefits to targeted consumers. For example, Colgate makes a large selection of toothbrushes and toothpaste flavours and packages for children—such as Colgate Barbie Sparkling Bubble Fruit, Colgate Barnie Mild Bubble Fruit, and Colgate Looney Tunes Tazmanian Devil Wild Mint toothpastes, and Colgate Pokémon and Disney Monsters, Inc. character toothbrushes. Such products help make brushing teeth more fun and get children to brush longer and more often. And Nacara Cosmetiques markets cosmetics for "ethnic women who have a thirst for the exotic." The line is specially formulated to complement the darker skin tones of African women and dark-skinned women of Latin American, Indian, and Caribbean origins.

Thus, in target marketing, the issue is not really *who* is targeted but rather *how* and for *what*. Controversies arise when marketers attempt to profit at the expense of targeted segments—when they unfairly target vulnerable segments or target them with questionable products or tactics. Socially responsible marketing calls for segmentation and targeting that serve not just the interests of the company but also the interests of those targeted.

Most target marketing benefits both the marketer and the consumer. Nacara Cosmetiques markets cosmetics for "ethnic women who have a thirst for the exotic."

Positioning for Competitive Advantage

Product position

The way the product is defined by consumers on important attributes—the place the product occupies in consumers' minds relative to competing products.

Beyond deciding which segments of the market it will target, the company must decide what positions it wants to occupy in those segments. A **product's position** is the way the product is *defined by consumers* on important attributes—the place the product occupies in consumers' minds relative to competing products. Positioning involves implanting the brand's unique benefits and differentiation in customers' minds.

Tide is positioned as a powerful, all-purpose family detergent; Ivory Snow is positioned as the gentle detergent for fine washables and baby clothes; Sunlight is positioned as a product that gets dirt out so effectively, it is OK to have fun getting dirty. At Subway restaurants, you "Eat Fresh"; at Olive Garden restaurants, "When You're Here, You're Family." In the automobile market, the Toyota Echo and Ford Focus are positioned on economy, Mercedes and Cadillac on luxury, and Porsche and BMW on performance. Volvo positions powerfully on safety. And Toyota positions its fuel-efficient, hybrid Prius as a high-tech solution to the energy shortage. "How far will you go to save the planet?" it asks.

Consumers are overloaded with information about products and services. They cannot re-evaluate products every time they make a buying decision. To simplify the buying process, consumers organize products, services, and companies into categories and "position" them in their minds. A product's position is the complex set

CAPPUCCINO & TIRAMISU

WE LOVE WHEN YOU HATE TO LEAVE.

When you're here, you're Family.

At Olive Garden restaurants, "When You're Here, You're Family."

of perceptions, impressions, and feelings that consumers have for the product compared with competing products.

Consumers position products with or without the help of marketers. But marketers do not want to leave their products' positions to chance. They must *plan* positions that will give their products the greatest advantage in selected target markets, and they must design marketing mixes to create these planned positions.

Positioning Maps

In planning their positioning strategies, marketers often prepare *perceptual positioning maps,* which show consumer perceptions of their brands versus competing products on important buying dimensions. Figure 8.4 shows a positioning map for the large luxury sport utility vehicle market.[33] The position of each circle on the map indicates the brand's perceived positioning on two dimensions—price and orientation (luxury versus performance). The size of each circle indicates the brand's relative market share. Thus, customers view the market-leading Cadillac Escalade as a moderately priced, large luxury SUV with a balance of luxury and performance.

The original Hummer H1 is positioned as a very high performance SUV with a price tag to match. Hummer targets the H1 toward a small segment of well-off rugged individualists. According to the H1 website, "The H1 was built around one central philosophy: function. Every aspect of the H1 was created to allow it to go where cars and trucks just aren't supposed to go. [It] gives you an incredible sense of freedom and allows you to experience the world and your place in it."

By contrast, although also oriented toward performance, the Hummer H2 is positioned as a more luxury-oriented and more reasonably priced luxury SUV. The H2 is targeted toward a larger segment of urban and suburban professionals. "In a world where SUVs have begun to look like their owners, complete with love handles and mushy seats, the H2 proves that there is still one out there that can drop and give you twenty," says the H2 website. The H2 "strikes a perfect balance between interior comfort, on-the-road capability, and off-road capability."

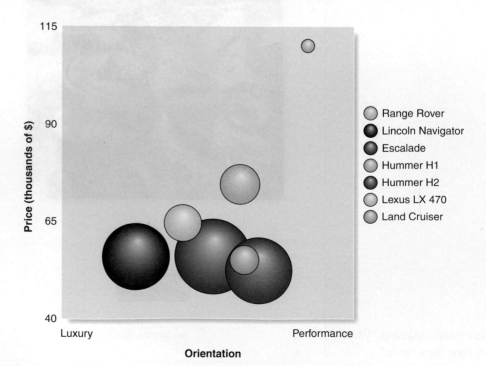

Figure 8.4 Positioning map: Large luxury SUVs

Choosing a Positioning Strategy

Some firms find it easy to choose their positioning strategy. For example, a firm well known for quality in certain segments will go for this position in a new segment if there are enough buyers seeking quality. But in many cases, two or more firms will go after the same position. Then, each will have to find other ways to set itself apart. Each firm must differentiate its offer by building a unique bundle of benefits that appeal to a substantial group within the segment.

The positioning task consists of three steps: identifying a set of possible competitive advantages upon which to build a position, choosing the right competitive advantages, and selecting an overall positioning strategy. The company must then effectively communicate and deliver the chosen position to the market.

Identifying Possible Competitive Advantages

Competitive advantage
An advantage over competitors gained by offering consumers greater value, either through lower prices or by providing more benefits that justify higher prices.

To build profitable relationships with target customers, marketers must understand customer needs better than competitors do and deliver more value. To the extent that a company can position itself as providing superior value, it gains **competitive advantage**. But solid positions cannot be built on empty promises. If a company positions its product as *offering* the best quality and service, it must then *deliver* the promised quality and service. Thus, positioning begins with actually *differentiating* the company's marketing offer so that it will give consumers superior value.

To find points of differentiation, marketers must think through the customer's entire experience with the company's product or service. An alert company can find ways to differentiate itself at every customer contact point. In what specific ways can a company differentiate itself or its market offer? It can differentiate along the lines of *product*, *services*, *channels*, *people*, or *image*.

Product differentiation takes place along a continuum. At one extreme we find physical products that allow little variation: chicken, steel, Aspirin. Yet even here some meaningful differentiation is possible. See how Maple Leaf Foods has positioned itself:

> The meat industry in both Canada and the world has been battered by challenges ranging from mad cow disease to allegations of uninspected meat. Toronto-based Maple Leaf Foods began to address these issues when it decided to incorporate consumer concerns in its core brand positioning efforts. It all started in 1999, when the Prime chicken brand was launched as part of the company's vision to transform itself into an aggressive and highly innovative food processor and packaged-goods manufacturer. Two years later, the company evolved Prime into Prime Naturally, vegetable-grain-fed chicken based on the insight that consumers were starting to understand how differentiation in product quality and safety offers them value at the meat counter. In 2002, Maple Leaf Foods created an overarching new corporate positioning and tag line, "We Take Care." The message is intended to give consumers greater confidence and assurance around taste delivery, family appeal and, ultimately, the safety of Maple Leaf products.[34]

At the other extreme are products that can be highly differentiated, such as automobiles, clothing, and furniture. Such products can be differentiated on features, performance, or style and design. Thus, Volvo provides new and better safety features; Whirlpool designs its dishwasher to run more quietly; Bose positions its speakers on their striking design characteristics. Similarly, companies can differentiate their products on such attributes as consistency, durability, reliability, or repairability.

Beyond differentiating its physical product, a firm can also differentiate the services that accompany the product. Some companies gain *services differentiation* through speedy, convenient, or careful delivery. See what Scotiabank has done:

Scotiabank's Rick White, VP brand and marketing management, helped Scotiabank rise from dead last to third place in the race for market share. Because his research showed that consumers often find banking a complicated, "necessary evil" and were truly feeling confused, he decided to position Scotiabank as the simple, helpful choice showing how friendly associates help frazzled customers find the money they need. He created an award-winning ad campaign to inform people about the new strategy. It is one thing to advertise friendly, surprisingly helpful service, but advertising alone certainly isn't enough. Rick also had to make sure the follow-through was there so that personnel in each branch made the promise a living reality.[35]

Installation can also differentiate one company from another, as can repair services. Many an automobile buyer will gladly pay a little more and travel a little farther to buy a car from a dealer that provides top-notch repair services. Some companies differentiate their offers by providing customer training service or consulting services—data, information systems, and advising services that buyers need. McKesson Corporation, a major drug wholesaler, consults with its 12 000 independent pharmacists to help them set up accounting, inventory, and computerized ordering systems. By helping its customers compete better, McKesson gains greater customer loyalty and sales.

Firms that practise *channel differentiation* gain competitive advantage through the way they design their channel's coverage, expertise, and performance. Amazon.com, Dell, and Avon set themselves apart with their high-quality direct channels. Caterpillar's success in the construction-equipment industry is based on superior channels. Its dealers worldwide are renowned for their first-rate service.

Scotiabank's positioning as the simple, helpful choice where frazzled customers find the help they need has helped the bank increase its market share.

Disney World people are known to be friendly and upbeat. Each employee is carefully trained to understand customers and to "make people happy."

Companies can gain a strong competitive advantage through *people differentiation*—hiring and training better people than their competitors do. Disney people are known to be friendly and upbeat. Singapore Airlines enjoys an excellent reputation largely because of the grace of its flight attendants. IBM offers people who make sure that the solution customers want is the solution they get: "People Who Get It. People Who Get It Done." People differentiation requires that a company select its customer-contact people carefully and train them well. For example, Disney trains its theme park people thoroughly to ensure that they are competent, courteous, and friendly—from the hotel check-in agents and monorail drivers to the ride attendants and the people who sweep Main Street USA. Each employee is carefully trained to understand customers and to "make people happy."

Even when competing offers look the same, buyers may perceive a difference based on company or brand *image differentiation*. A company or brand image should convey the product's distinctive benefits and positioning. Developing a strong and distinctive image calls for creativity and hard work. A company cannot develop an image in the public's mind overnight using only a few advertisements. If Fairmont Hotels—such as the Banff Springs or the Royal York—means quality, this image must be supported by everything the company says and does. Symbols—such as the McDonald's golden arches, the Prudential rock, the Nike swoosh, or Google's colourful logo—can provide strong company or brand recognition and image differentiation. The company might build a brand around a famous person, as Nike did with its Air Jordan basketball shoes and Tiger Woods golfing products. Some companies even become associated with colours, such as IBM (blue) or UPS (brown). The chosen symbols, characters, and other image elements must be communicated through advertising that conveys the company's or brand's personality.

Choosing the Right Competitive Advantages

Suppose a company is fortunate enough to discover several potential competitive advantages. It now must choose the ones on which it will build its positioning strategy. It must decide *how many* differences to promote and *which ones*.

How Many Differences to Promote?   Many marketers think that companies should aggressively promote only one benefit to the target market. Ad man Rosser Reeves, for example, said a company should develop a *unique selling proposition*

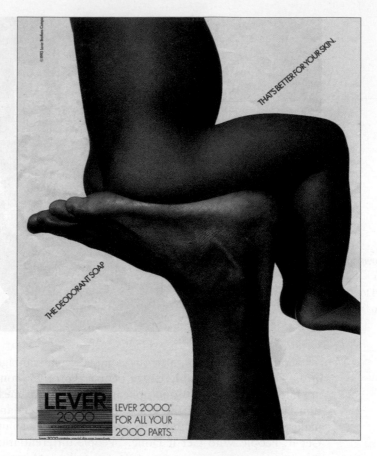

Unilever positioned its best-selling Lever 2000 soap on three benefits in one: cleansing, deodorizing, and moisturizing benefits. It's good "for all your 2000 parts."

(USP) for each brand and stick to it. Each brand should pick an attribute and tout itself as "number one" on that attribute. Buyers tend to remember number one better, especially in an overcommunicated society. Thus, Crest toothpaste consistently promotes its anticavity protection and Wal-Mart promotes low prices. A company that hammers away at one of these positions and consistently delivers on it probably will become best known and remembered for it.

Other marketers think that companies should position themselves on more than one differentiator. This may be necessary if two or more firms are claiming to be best on the same attribute. Today, in a time when the mass market is fragmenting into many small segments, companies are trying to broaden their positioning strategies to appeal to more segments. For example, Unilever introduced the first three-in-one bar soap—Lever 2000—offering cleansing, deodorizing, *and* moisturizing benefits. Clearly, many buyers want all three benefits. The challenge was to convince them that one brand can deliver all three. Judging from Lever 2000's outstanding success, Unilever easily met the challenge. However, as companies increase the number of claims for their brands, they risk disbelief and a loss of clear positioning.

Which Differences to Promote?   Not all brand differences are meaningful or worthwhile; not every difference makes a good differentiator. Each difference has the potential to create company costs as well as customer benefits. Therefore, the company must carefully select the ways in which it will distinguish itself from competitors. A difference is worth establishing to the extent that it satisfies the following criteria:

• *Important:* The difference delivers a highly valued benefit to target buyers.
• *Distinctive:* Competitors do not offer the difference, or the company can offer it in a more distinctive way.

- *Superior:* The difference is superior to other ways that customers might obtain the same benefit.
- *Communicable:* The difference is communicable and visible to buyers.
- *Pre-emptive:* Competitors cannot easily copy the difference.
- *Affordable:* Buyers can afford to pay for the difference.
- *Profitable:* The company can introduce the difference profitably.

Many companies have introduced differentiations that failed one or more of these tests. When Westin Stamford hotel in Singapore advertised that it is the world's tallest hotel, the distinction was not that important to most tourists—in fact, it turned many off. Polaroid's Polarvision, which produced instantly developed home movies, bombed too. Although Polarvision was distinctive and even pre-emptive, it was inferior to another way of capturing motion, namely, camcorders. Thus, choosing competitive advantages upon which to position a product or service can be difficult, yet such choices may be crucial to success.

Selecting an Overall Positioning Strategy

Value proposition
The full positioning of a brand—the full mix of benefits upon which it is positioned.

Consumers typically choose products and services that give them the greatest value. Thus, marketers want to position their brands on the key benefits that they offer relative to competing brands. The full positioning of a brand is called the brand's **value proposition**—the full mix of benefits upon which the brand is positioned. It is the answer to the customer's question "Why should I buy your brand?" Volvo's value proposition hinges on safety but also includes reliability, roominess, and styling, all for a price that is higher than average but seems fair for this mix of benefits.

Figure 8.5 shows possible value propositions upon which a company might position its products. In the figure, the five blue cells represent winning value propositions—positioning that gives the company competitive advantage. The orange cells, however, represent losing value propositions. The centre beige cell represents at best a marginal proposition. In the following sections, we discuss the five winning value propositions upon which companies can position their products: more for more, more for the same, the same for less, less for much less, and more for less.[36]

More for More   "More for more" positioning involves providing the most upscale product or service and charging a higher price to cover the higher costs. Fairmont Hotels, Mont Blanc writing instruments, Mercedes-Benz automobiles—each claims superior quality, craftsmanship, durability, performance, or style and

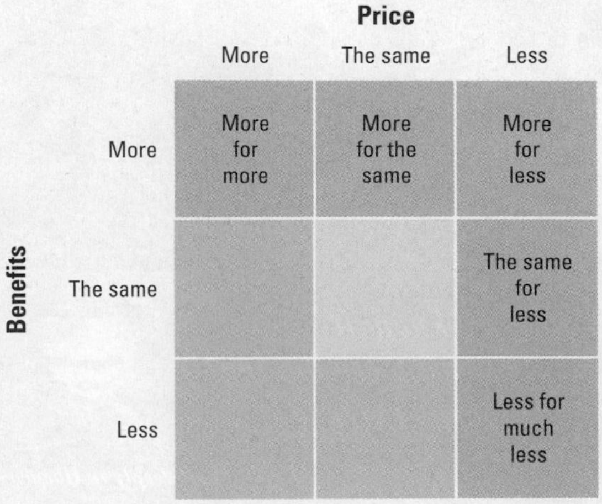

Figure 8.5 Possible value propositions

charges a price to match. Not only is the marketing offer high in quality, but it also gives prestige to the buyer. It symbolizes status and a loftier lifestyle. Often, the price difference exceeds the actual increment in quality.

Sellers offering "only the best" can be found in every product and service category, from hotels, restaurants, food, and fashion to cars and kitchen appliances. Consumers are sometimes surprised, even delighted, when a new competitor enters a category with an unusually high-priced brand. Starbucks coffee entered as a very expensive brand in a largely commodity category; Häagen-Dazs came in as a premium ice cream brand at a price never before charged.

In general, companies should be on the lookout for opportunities to introduce a "much-more-for-much-more" brand in any underdeveloped product or service category. Yet "more-for-more" brands can be vulnerable. They often invite imitators who claim the same quality but at a lower price. Luxury goods that sell well during good times may be at risk during economic downturns when buyers become more cautious in their spending.

More for the Same Companies can attack a competitor's more-for-more positioning by introducing a brand offering comparable quality but at a lower price. For example, Toyota introduced its Lexus line with a "more-for-the-same" value proposition. Its headline read: "Perhaps the first time in history that trading a $72 000 car for a $36 000 car could be considered trading up." It communicated the high quality of its new Lexus through rave reviews in car magazines and through a widely distributed videotape showing side-by-side comparisons of Lexus and Mercedes automobiles. It published surveys showing that Lexus dealers were providing customers with better sales and service experiences than were Mercedes dealerships.

Häagen-Dazs offers its superpremium ice cream at a price never before charged.

Many Mercedes owners switched to Lexus, and the Lexus repurchase rate has been 60 percent, twice the industry average.

The Same for Less   Offering "the same for less" can be a powerful value proposition—everyone likes a good deal. For example, Dell offers equivalent quality computers at a lower "price for performance." Discounts stores, such as Wal-Mart, and "category killers," such as Best Buy, Circuit City, and Sport Mart, also use this positioning. They don't claim to offer different or better products. Instead, they offer many of the same brands as department stores and specialty stores but at deep discounts based on superior purchasing power and lower-cost operations. Other companies develop imitative but lower-priced brands in an effort to lure customers away from the market leader. For example, AMD makes less expensive versions of Intel's market-leading microprocessor chips.

Less for Much Less   A market almost always exists for products that offer less and therefore cost less. Few people need, want, or can afford "the very best" in everything they buy. In many cases, consumers will gladly settle for less than optimal performance or give up some of the bells and whistles in exchange for a lower price. For example, many travellers seeking lodgings prefer not to pay for what they consider unnecessary extras, such as a pool, an attached restaurant, or mints on the pillow. Motel chains such as Motel 6 suspend some of these amenities and charge less accordingly.

"Less for much less" positioning involves meeting consumers' lower performance or quality requirements at a much lower price. For example, Family Dollar and Dollar General stores offer more affordable goods at very low prices. Sam's Club and Costco warehouse stores offer less merchandise selection and consistency, and much lower levels of service; as a result, they charge rock-bottom prices. Southwest Airlines, the most profitable air carrier in the United States, also practises less for much less positioning. It charges incredibly low prices by not serving food, not assigning seats, and not using travel agents. (See Real Marketing 8.2.)

More for Less   Of course, the winning value proposition would be to offer "more for less." Many companies claim to do this. For example, Dell Computer claims to have better products *and* lower prices for a given level of performance. Procter & Gamble claims that its laundry detergents provide the best cleaning *and* everyday low prices. In the short run, some companies can actually achieve such lofty positions. For example, when it first opened for business, Home Depot had arguably the best product selection, the best service, *and* the lowest prices compared with local hardware stores and other home improvement chains. Yet in the long run, companies will find it very difficult to sustain such best-of-both positioning. Offering more usually costs more, making it difficult to deliver on the "for less" promise. Companies that try to deliver both may lose out to more focused competitors. For example, facing determined competition from Lowe's stores, Home Depot must now decide whether it wants to compete primarily on superior service or on lower prices.

All said, each brand must adopt a positioning strategy designed to serve the needs and wants of its target markets. "More for more" will draw one target market, "less for much less" will draw another, and so on. Thus, in any market, there is usually room for many different companies, each successfully occupying different positions.

The important thing is that each company must develop its own winning positioning strategy, one that makes it special to its target consumers. Offering only "the same for the same" provides no competitive advantage, leaving the firm in the middle of the pack. Companies offering one of the three losing value propositions—"the same for more," "less for more," and "less for the same"—will inevitably fail. Customers soon realize that they've been underserved, tell others, and abandon the brand.

REAL MARKETING

WestJet's Value Proposition: "Less for Much Less"

In an industry beset by hard times, WestJet soars above its competition. Today, it is Canada's second-largest airline. In the wake of a global economic slump and the effects of increased terrorism, most airlines have suffered huge loses in recent years, or even declared bankruptcy. Yet even in these bleak times, WestJet rarely has gone into the red. What's the secret? WestJet is one of the most strongly and clearly positioned airlines in the world. It offers a classic "less-for-less" value proposition.

WestJet was founded in 1996 by Clive Beddoe, Mark Hill, Tim Morgan, and Donald Bell, four Calgary entrepreneurs who saw an opportunity to provide low-fare air travel across western Canada. They carefully researched other successful North American airlines and concluded that Southwest Airlines and Morris Air were the firms to mimic. As was the case with Southwest's successful model, the founders determined that WestJet would be employee owned. Today, WestJet employs about 5000 people, and 86 percent of these employees own shares in the company.

On February 29, 1996, the airline started flight operations to Vancouver, Kelowna, Calgary, Edmonton, and Winnipeg, with 220 employees and three aircraft. It carved out a successful niche with these short-haul flights and its low prices, combined with reliable service, and an off-the-wall sense of humour. To differentiate itself from other Canadian airlines, which it saw as look-alikes, it did not compete head-on for the coveted busi-ness traveller market to ensure profitability. Rather, it began specializing in serving what it calls as the VFR market (people visiting friends and relatives). It saw its main competitor as the family car and realized that if it could offer lower fares; people would choose to fly rather than drive to visit friends and relatives.

To offer low prices, WestJet worked to ensure its operating costs were low. It flew only one type of plane, which kept maintenance costs in check. It offers only basic in-flight service (no meals, no movies) and rapid turnaround at the gates to keep the planes in the air. The "less-for-less" philosophy is also evident in various service choices: they offer a single class of service, without ticket offices at points other than airports; they do not offer baggage transfer services with other airlines, in-flight meals, or frequent flier promotions. Nonetheless, in WestJet's case, "less service for less money" is defined as fewer amenities for a lower fare, *not* less customer service.

Over the years, the company continued to expand, first bringing more western cities into WestJet's world and then expanding nationally. To make noise in some of the new markets it was entering, it offered promotions that no other discount carrier had dared try, like the "Fly for a nickel" campaign it used when it began flying into Sudbury, Ontario.

Today, WestJet generates more than $1 billion in revenue and it is focused on growth. It is truly a national airline and has begun flying to key destina-

Sunny onboard and off. Daily flights to Orlando.

Enjoy great fares to one of our sunny Florida destinations, including Orlando, Tampa, Fort Myers, Fort Lauderdale and West Palm Beach. And with our comfy leather seats, live seatback TV from ExpressVu® and the newest Jets in North America, you'll be traveling in comfort and style.

Book now at **westjet.com** or **1 800 538 5696.**
Or call your travel agent.

WestJet transformed itself into a national airline using a classic "less for less" value proposition.

tions in the western and southern United States. Some analysts believe WestJet is making a major change in strategic direction and is consequently reshaping both its marketing strategies and brand positioning. Says one analyst, "They're going into markets that want more sophistication and more creature comforts."

Some experts wonder why WestJet is making such sweeping changes to a successful marketing style. Debi Andrus, a professor of marketing at the University of Calgary's Haskayne School of Business, for example, wonders, "Why not take that fun, folksy Canadian airline image and make it work as a fun, folksy North American airline image?" Andrus also wonders whether changing the brand to attract new customers in central Canada and the U.S. may turn off long-time customers, especially in western Canada. "It's going to be tough getting some people to accept an image change from the little

airline that could to the airline that's all grown up." Other analysts think these concerns are misplaced. Stuart Klaskin, a Miami-based strategic aviation consultant, believes WestJet's expansion strategy is bang on. He believes the low-cost market in the U.S. is stratified, with some consumers still demanding the absolute lowest price, while others want an additional level of comfort, such as leather seats and TV. Klaskin believes WestJet is on the leading edge of a new trend toward low-cost cross-border travel. WestJet may be on the verge of soaring even higher.

Sources: Norma Ramage, "WestJet on the Fly," *Marketing Magazine,* June 20, 2005; WestJet Fact Sheet, www.westjet.com (accessed April 2006); Peter Verburg, "Reach for the Bottom," *Canadian Business,* 2000; Helena Katz, "Peanuts and Pretzels Fly East," *Marketing,* March 6, 2000; Norma Ramage, "WestJet Fuels up Advertising Effort," *Marketing,* March 12, 2001.

Developing a Positioning Statement

Positioning statement
A statement that summarizes company or brand positioning—it takes this form: *To (target segment and need) our (brand) is (concept) that (point-of-difference).*

Company and brand positioning should be summed up in a **positioning statement**. The statement should follow this form: *To (target segment and need) our (brand) is (concept) that (point-of-difference).*[37] For example: *"To busy professionals who need to stay organized, Palm is an electronic organizer that allows you to back up files on your PC more easily and reliably than competitive products."* Sometimes a positioning statement is more detailed:

> To young, active soft-drink consumers who have little time for sleep, Red Bull is the soft drink that gives you more energy than any other brand because it has 80 mg of caffeine. With Red Bull, you can stay alert and keep going even when you haven't been able to get a good night's sleep.

Note that the positioning first states the product's membership in a category (Red Bull is a soft drink) and then shows its point-of-difference from other members of the category (its caffeine level). Placing a brand in a specific category suggests similarities that it might share with other products in the category. But the case for the brand's superiority is made on its points of difference. Sometimes marketers put a brand in a surprisingly different category before indicating the points of difference:

> Delissio is a frozen pizza whose crust rises when the pizza is heated. Instead of putting it in the frozen pizza category, the marketers positioned it in the delivered pizza category. Their ad shows party guests asking which pizza delivery service the host used. But, says the host, "It's not delivery, its Delissio!" This helped highlight Delissio's fresh quality and superior taste over the normal frozen pizza.

Communicating and Delivering the Chosen Position

Once it has chosen a position, the company must take strong steps to deliver and communicate the desired position to target consumers. All the company's marketing mix efforts must support the positioning strategy.

Positioning the company calls for concrete action, not just talk. If the company decides to build a position on better quality and service, it must first *deliver* that position. Designing the marketing mix—product, price, place, and promotion—involves working out the tactical details of the positioning strategy. Thus, a firm that seizes on a more-for-more position knows that it must produce high-quality products, charge a high price, distribute through high-quality dealers, and advertise in high-quality media. It must hire and train more service people, find retailers who have a good reputation for service, and develop sales and advertising messages that broadcast its superior service. This is the only way to build a consistent and believable more-for-more position.

Companies often find it easier to come up with a good positioning strategy than to implement it. Establishing a position or changing one usually takes a long time. In contrast, positions that have taken years to build can quickly be lost. Once a company has built the desired position, it must take care to maintain the position through consistent performance and communication. It must closely monitor and adapt the position over time to match changes in consumer needs and competitors' strategies. However, the company should avoid abrupt changes that might confuse consumers. Instead, a product's position should evolve gradually as it adapts to the ever-changing marketing environment.

Reviewing the Concepts

In this chapter, you've learned about the major elements of marketing strategy: segmentation, targeting, and positioning. Marketers know that they cannot appeal to all buyers in their markets, or at least not to all buyers in the same way. Buyers are too numerous, too widely scattered, and too varied in their needs and buying practices. Therefore, most companies today practise *target marketing*—identifying market segments, selecting one or more of them, and developing products and marketing mixes tailored to each.

1. Define the three steps of target marketing: market segmentation, target marketing, and market positioning.

Targeting marketing involves designing strategies to build the *right relationships* with the *right customers*. *Market segmentation* is the act of dividing a market into distinct groups of buyers with different needs, characteristics, or behaviours who might require separate products or marketing mixes. Once the groups have been identified, *targeting marketing* evaluates each market segment's attractiveness and selects one or more segments to serve. *Market positioning* consists of deciding how to best serve the target customer—setting the competitive positioning for the product and creating a detailed marketing plan.

2. List and discuss the major bases for segmenting consumer and business markets.

There is no single way to segment a market. Therefore, the marketer tries different variables to see which give the best segmentation opportunities. For consumer marketing, the major segmentation variables are geographic, demographic, psychographic, and behavioural. In *geographic segmentation,* the market is divided into different geographical units, such as nations, regions, provinces, counties, cities, or neighbourhoods. In *demographic segmentation,* the market is divided into groups based on demographic variables, including age, gender, family size, family life cycle, income, occupation, education, religion, race, generation, and nationality. In *psychographic segmentation,* the market is divided into different groups based on social class, lifestyle, or personality characteristics. In *behavioural segmentation,* the market is divided into groups based on consumers' knowledge, attitudes, uses, or responses to a product.

Business marketers use many of the same variables to segment their markets. But business markets also can be segmented by business consumer *demographics* (industry, company size), *operating characteristics, purchasing approaches, situational factors,* and *personal characteristics*. The effectiveness of segmentation analysis depends on finding segments that are *measurable, accessible, substantial, differentiable,* and *actionable*.

3. **Explain how companies identify attractive market segments and choose a target marketing strategy.**

To target the best market segments, the company first evaluates each segment's size and growth characteristics, structural attractiveness, and compatibility with company objectives and resources. It then chooses one of four target marketing strategies—ranging from very broad to very narrow targeting. The seller can ignore segment differences and target broadly using *undifferentiated (or mass) marketing.* This involves mass-producing, mass-distributing, and mass-promoting about the same product in about the same way to all consumers. Or the seller can adopt *differentiated marketing*—developing different market offers for several segments. *Concentrated marketing* (or *niche marketing)* involves focusing on only one or a few market segments. Finally, *micromarketing* is the

practice of tailoring products and marketing programs to suit the tastes of specific individuals and locations. Micromarketing includes *local marketing* and *individual marketing*. Which targeting strategy is best depends on company resources, product variability, product life-cycle stage, market variability, and competitive marketing strategies.

4. **Discuss how companies position their products for maximum competitive advantage in the marketplace.**

Once a company has decided which segments to enter, it must decide on its *market positioning* strategy—on which positions to occupy in its chosen segments. The positioning task consists of three steps: identifying a set of possible competitive advantages upon which to build a position, choosing the right competitive advantages, and selecting an overall positioning strategy. The brand's full positioning is called its *value proposition*—the full mix of benefits upon which the brand is positioned. In general, companies can choose from one of five winning value propositions upon which to position their products: more for more, more for the same, the same for less, less for much less, or more for less. Company and brand positioning are summarized in positioning statements that state the target segment and need, positioning concept, and specific points of difference. The company must then effectively communicate and deliver the chosen position to the market.

Reviewing the Key Terms

Discussing the Concepts

1. The chapter states that once we divide large, heterogeneous markets into smaller segments, we can reach them more efficiently and effectively. What does that statement mean? Why is this important to the marketer?

2. Briefly define each of the four sets of primary segmentation variables. If you could only use one of the four sets of variables to segment prospective students for the "part-time" MBA program at your university or college, which would it be? Why did you choose this variable?

3. The chapter discusses five requirements for effective segmentation. Suppose you are a product manager in a regional fast-food restaurant company. You are listening to a presentation on a new sandwich wrap idea (chicken breast and okra), and it is your turn to ask questions. Write five questions that you would ask the person presenting this product idea. Each question should be directed at one of the five segmentation requirements.

4. Is it a good idea for a small company to adopt a differentiated segmentation strategy? Explain.

5. In the context of marketing, what does the term "product positioning" mean? Why is it so important?

6. Using the value propositions presented in Figure 8.5 (page 313), describe the value proposition of Toys "R" Us. Is the Toys "R" Us value proposition clear? Is it appropriate?

Applying the Concepts

1. As discussed in the chapter, PRIZM is one of the leading lifestyle segmentation systems. Go to www.tetrad.com/pcensus/usa/prizmlst.html and review the 67 PRIZM clusters. Now identify a desirable cluster for each of the following retailers: Canadian Tire, Mountain Equipment Co-op, and Wal-Mart.

2. You are the product manager of a financial services product that is being sold directly to consumers over the Internet. The most important measure the company uses is customer acquisition cost. This is the cost associated with convincing a consumer to buy the service. You have been conducting tests with both a concentrated and an undifferentiated segmentation strategy, and the results are presented below. Which strategy is the best? Why?

Concentrated segmentation outcome

- Purchased 10 000 very targeted exposures on websites such as Yahoo Finance Canada and key-

words such as retirement planning, retirement savings, and RRSP.
- Paid $80 per thousand exposures.
- Obtained 400 clicks to the site, 40 trials, and 20 repeat customers.

Undifferentiated segmentation outcome

- Purchased 1 000 000 run-of-site exposures on websites.
- Paid $1.60 per thousand exposures.
- Obtained 2000 clicks to the site, 100 trials, and 40 repeat customers.

3. Assume that you are the marketing director for the school of business at your college or university, and that the dean has asked you to prepare a positioning statement for the business school. Write a positioning statement using the form presented in the chapter.

Focus on Technology

The chapter defines micromarketing as the practice of tailoring products and marketing programs to suit the tastes of specific individuals and locations. If you are a consumer-goods marketer, chances are good that you already have known the value of micromarketing in general and of SRC's Solocast in particular. Solocast is one of the many SRC desktop database engines that marketers can use to help them make better decisions. Suppose you are a women's clothing retailer and, based on buyer information that you have collected, you have a good idea of the personal lifestyle characteristics of your target market. According to SRC, Solocast will help you find more of your best target customers. You can get a better understanding of their habits—where they shop, what brands they prefer, and what types of communication would work best in reaching them.

Visit SRC's homepage at www.extendthereach.com and review the Solocast product. Now place yourself in the role of the women's clothing retailer.

1. Can you use Solocast to help find your next retail location?

2. Can you identify undetected segments of potential customers in your existing trade areas?

3. Can you use Solocast to reach your target more effectively?

Focus on Ethics

Electronic gaming continues to see rapid growth. In 2004 alone, it generated $914 million in sales revenues and the industry in Canada has been growing at a rate of 11 percent per year. In 2005, the Entertainment Software Association of Canada estimated that 35 percent of Canadian households owned a video game console. Video games have been criticized for their violent content and language and for their portrayal of women. Though the average age of Canadian video game players is 30, there is concern about the effects these games have on children. The five top best-selling games in Canada in 2004 were Grand Theft Auto: San Andreas; Halo 2; NHL 2005; Need for Speed: Underground 2; and NHL 2004. The top two best sellers are designated for mature audiences. To help parents determine what games were appropriate for their children, the "Commitment to Parents" national retailer code and "Ok To Play?—Check The Ratings" consumer education campaign were launched. It is the result of the collaborative efforts of the Retail Council of Canada, the Entertainment Software Association of Canada, and the Entertainment Software Rating Board (ESRB). The ESRB oversees rating system use by gaming software manufacturers. The ESRB has five age-based rating categories:

EC-Early Childhood (ages 3+), E-Everyone (ages 6+), T-Teen (ages 13+), M-Mature (ages 17+), and AO-Adults Only (ages 18 and older). More than 30 ESRB content descriptors provide consumers with more detail about the actual content in the game, including language, depictions of violence, suggestive themes, and type of humour. For a complete list of ratings and content descriptors, please visit www.esrb.org. Research published in 2005 suggests that 61 percent of parents are aware of the symbols and their meaning.

Sources: "Essential Facts," Entertainment Software Association of Canada, www.theesa.com/files/ESAC_Essential_Facts_2005.pdf (accessed July 2006); "About Commitment To Parents," Retail Council of Canada, www.retailcouncil.org/ctp/about_commitment.asp (accessed July 2006).

1. Do you believe that the marketers of mature video games unintentionally target children?

2. Do you think the rating system is an effective means of avoiding harm to children?

3. In general what do you think of the practice of targeting children? Are there markets where targeting children is appropriate?

Video Case
Procter & Gamble

With dozens of brands in the marketplace, Procter & Gamble offers an array of consumer products with dazzling success. In the United States alone, P&G offers seven brands of laundry detergent, three brands of deodorant, and two brands each of fabric softener, cosmetics, and disposable diapers. In each of these categories, P&G's products compete against each other, as well as with products offered by other companies, for share of the customer's wallet.

How does Procter and Gamble manage so many competing brands without cannibalizing its own profits? The company maximizes market penetration and sales by carefully segmenting markets, positioning products and brands, and targeting the right consumers. Together, P&G's portfolio of products meets the needs of a wide range of consumers. The result? Ninety-nine percent of all households in the United States use at least one P&G product.

After viewing the video featuring P&G, answer the following questions about segmentation, targeting, and positioning:

1. Visit P&G's website (www.PandG.com) and select two consumer products that compete in the same category. How are the two products positioned differently? Who is in the target market for each? List several P&G brands in other categories that target the same consumers.

2. What bases for segmentation does P&G use to differentiate the products you considered in the previous question?

3. According to the video, how does P&G position itself, as a company, in the marketplace?

Online Media Resources

Video Short
Log on to your Companion Website at
www.pearsoned.ca/kotler to view the
video segment related to the Video Case on
page 321.

CBC ✦ CBC Video Case
Please refer to Appendix 2 to read a
CBC Video Case for this chapter, and log
on to your Companion Website at
www.pearsoned.ca/kotler to view the
corresponding video segment.

Case Pilot
Log on to your Companion Website at
www.pearsoned.ca/kotler to sharpen
your case analysis skills and take the Case
Pilot Challenge!

Company Case
GM: Downsizing the Hummer

You probably know that the Hummer derives from what American soldiers informally call the "Humvee," which is an acronym for the formal designation, "High Mobility Multi-Purpose Wheeled Vehicle." In addition to seeing the TV ads, you've probably also seen the original nonmilitary Hummer, the H1, or its smaller offspring, the H2, around town. Canadian rental car companies offer them for those who want to be weekend warriors, and off-road tour operators promise people experiences of a lifetime around Banff.

The vehicle was born in 1979, when AM General, a specialty vehicle manufacturer, earned a contract from the U.S. Army to design the Humvee. TV coverage of the military build-up in advance of the Gulf War in 1991 introduced the public to the workhorse Humvee. In 1992, AM General, responding to the Humvee's notoriety, decided to introduce the first *civilian* version of the Humvee—the Hummer. Weighing in at 3220 kg, the Hummer featured a huge, 6.5 litre V-8, turbo-diesel engine that produced 195 horsepower and propelled the Hummer from 0 to 100 kph in a snail-like 18 seconds. However, the Hummer's purpose was not speed. AM General designed it, like its military parent, to take people off the beaten path—way off. The Hummer could plow through water to a depth of 76 cm and climb almost vertical, rocky surfaces. It even had a central tire inflation system that allowed the driver to inflate or deflate the vehicle's tires while on the move.

The advertising tag line dubbed the Hummer as "The world's most serious 4 x 4," and ad copy played up the vehicle's off-road capabilities and its military heritage. AM General targeted serious, elite road warriors who were willing to pay more than US$100 000 to have the toughest vehicle in the carpool. These people wanted to tell the world that they had been successful. To help buyers learn how to handle the Hummer in extreme off-road situations, AM General even offered a

Hummer Driving Academy, where drivers learned to handle 56 cm vertical walls, high water, 40 percent side slopes, and 60 percent inclines.

GM's Market Research

In 1998, GM was conducting market research using a concept vehicle that it described as rugged and militaristic. When the vehicle bore the GMC brand name (GM's truck division), the company found that consumers had a lukewarm reaction. However, when GM put the Hummer name on the vehicle, researchers found that it had the highest, most widespread appeal of any vehicle GM had *ever* tested. Armed with this insight, GM signed a 1999 agreement with AM General, giving it rights to the Hummer Brand. AM General also signed a seven-year contract to produce the Hummer H2 sport utility vehicle for GM.

Based on its research, GM believed that the H2, a smaller version of the Hummer, would appeal to rugged individualists and wealthy baby boomers who wanted the ability to go off-road and to "successful achievers," 30- and 40-something wealthy consumers who had jobs in investment banking and the like. GM believed that it could introduce the H2 in the luxury SUV market and compete successfully with brands such as the Lincoln Navigator or GM's own Cadillac Escalade. In July 2002 it launched the vehicle at a base sticker price of about US$49 000. It predicted that it could sell 19 000 H2s in 2002 (the 2003 model year) and then ramp up production to sell 40 000 units per year thereafter—a number that would make the H2 the largest seller in the luxury SUV market.

The Launch

Right on schedule in July 2002, GM introduced the 2003 Hummer 2. For the H2, GM targeted buyers with an average age of 42 and annual household incomes above US$125 000 versus H1 owners' averages of about 50 years old and household incomes above US$200 000.

GM and AM General designed and built the H2 in just 16 months, using GM's GMT 800 truck platform and a number of parts used in other GM models. The H2 was about the same size as the Chevy Tahoe, 13 cm narrower than the Hummer and about 32 kg lighter. However, it was about 635 kg heavier than other SUVs. It had a 316-horsepower engine that slurped almost 20 litres of gasoline every 100 km. It also featured a nine-speaker Bose stereo system. Buyers could upgrade the base model with a US$2575 luxury package that added heated leather front seats and a six-disc CD changer or with a US$2215 Adventure package that added air suspension, brush guards, and crossbars for the roof rack.

For promotion, GM used TV ads that broke on shows such as *CSI: Miami* that featured a well-dressed woman driving the H2 through an urban business district. The ad concluded with the line, "Threaten Men in a New Way." A later ad featured a young boy who builds a soap-box-derby-style racer that looks like a small Hummer. Although it was slower, he won the downhill race by going off-road and cutting across the paved, zig-zagged race course to edge out the typical race cars at the end.

The On-Road Test

At the H2's launch, auto analysts noted that it had a surprisingly smooth ride, but some questioned the quality of the interior furnishings and criticized the lack of storage space. The H2 sat only five people unless the owner installed an optional sixth seat in the back beside the spare tire. Further, they wondered if consumers would really spend so much for an off-the-road vehicle that studies showed only 10 percent of owners would *ever* take off the road. In addition, analysts noted the increasingly crowded luxury SUV market with pending entries from Porsche, BMW, Volvo, and Infiniti.

Despite the criticism, H2s roared out of the showrooms. Some buyers waited months to take delivery and even paid up to a US$10 000 price premium just to get one. GM was realizing profits of US$20 000 per vehicle. It reached its first-year target by selling 18 861 H2s by mid-2003. For calendar 2003, GM sold 35 259 H2s. Then, demand slowed, and GM began to offer $2000 dealer-cash incentives to try to reduce dealer inventories from an 80-day supply to a 45-day supply. Moreover, in early 2004, after five straight months of

sales declines, increasing gas prices seemed to be taking their toll on Hummer sales and pushing it toward the bottom in J.D. Power customer satisfaction ratings. H2 owners were forking out US$50 for gas every 515 km! Analysts thought GM would have to reduce its annual sales target to 30 000 H2s.

These events, however, did not deter GM from pursuing its long-term plan to sell 100 000 Hummer-branded vehicles a year. In mid-2003, it introduced the H2 Sport Utility Truck (SUT), an H2 with a pickup-truck-style cargo area in back replacing the enclosed area in the standard H2. The basic SUT's price was about US$1000 more than the base SUV.

In 2005, GM planned to introduce an even smaller Hummer, the H3 SUV. Priced in Canada in the $29 000 to $36 000 range, the company wanted the smaller, less menacing H3 to target drivers under 40. It believed the H3 would be especially appealing to young males, including teenagers.

GM wants to show that the smaller Hummers can retain the gesture, stance, and attitude of the larger Hummer. GM officials indicate that the typical Hummer owner makes more than US$200 000 a year and has two other vehicles he or she uses for routine driving. The Hummer is for fun. These officials believe that continued high gas prices will not affect Hummer sales. Hummer owners are proud and know that they will get attention. They own a Hummer because they want to and can afford it.

Some industry analysts, however, wonder if introducing more Hummers will dilute the brand's image and even steal sales from other GM vehicles. They argue that the decision to introduce smaller and lower-priced Hummers is a risky move, especially given the brand's aspirational nature.

Now What?

When GM was making its lofty sales projections, it did not expect the soaring gas prices that sent sales of sport utility vehicles into the tank through much of North America. In 2005, hurricanes Katrina and Rita and fears of gas shortages sent fuel prices soaring to well above $1 a litre across most of Canada and US$3 a gallon south of the border. "These ultra high gas prices are taking a toll on the larger, less fuel-efficient light trucks," said industry analyst Dennis DesRosiers, who heads DesRosiers Automotive Consultants Inc. in Richmond Hill, Ontario. The slide hit large SUVs, such as the Hummer, in particular, and sales in that category slumped by as much as 50 percent. The SUV slide may, however, be a regional phenomenon. As one Regina dealer noted, "Out here, [gas prices] are not top of mind." Carlos Gomes, a Bank of Nova Scotia economist, noted, however, that the mood of consumers is likely more buoyant in provinces that benefit from high oil prices, such as Alberta, than it is in Ontario and Quebec, which are the biggest markets for new vehicles.

SUV sales have been further hampered by the fact that they have long been targeted by environmental activists. With more and more evidence suggesting that global warming is a reality, these voices are gaining ground. For example, students in France target SUVs parked along the streets of Paris and paint signs on them to attack their owner's lack of environmental sensitivity. Sales of hybrids are on the rise and increased by 81 percent in North America in 2004. Though this represents less than 1 percent of the North American vehicle market, it is the fastest-growing segment. A report prepared by Booz Allen Hamilton projects that hybrids could reach 20 percent of new vehicle sales by 2010 and 80 percent by 2015. As 96 percent of the hybrids are produced by Japanese car makers, GM and the other North American car makers may be unable to play catch up.

Questions for Discussion

1. How has GM used the major segmentation variables for consumer markets in segmenting the SUV market?

2. What target-market decisions has GM made in selecting targets for the Hummer H2? How are those decisions different from AM General's target for the original Hummer?

3. How has GM attempted to position the H2 and the H3?

4. Why do you think some consumers will pay $40 000 or more for an off-road vehicle that 90 percent of them will never take off road?

5. Given rising oil prices and environmental concerns, should GM stop production of the Hummer, or should it continue to produce the vehicle but target it more precisely at niche marketplaces? If you select the latter option, what marketplaces would you suggest? How would you position the Hummer to these consumers?

Sources: Rosemary Barnes, "Popularity of Hummer Remains Unfazed by High Gasoline Prices," *KnightRidder/Tribune News*, June 5, 2004; David Welch, "A Bummer for the Hummer; Sales Are Way Down," *Business Week*, February 23, 2004, p. 49; Rick Dranz, "How Will Hummer Get Smaller? Check out H3T," *Automotive News*, December 15, 2003, p. 20; Dave Guilford, "Would a Small Hummer be Dumber?" *Automotive News*, October 13, 2003; Melanie Well, "Muscle Car," *Forbes*, July 22, 2002, p. 181; David Welch, "More Sport, Less Utility," *Business Week*, July 8, 2002, p. 110; Jean Halliday, "Of Hummers and Zen," *Advertising Age*, August 6, 2001, p. 29; Gregory L. White, "GM's New Baby Hummer Shares Its Toys With Chevy," *The Wall Street Journal*, April 10, 2001, p. B1; Greg Keenan, "SUV sales tank as gas soars," *Globe and Mail*, October 4, 2005; Jim Harris, "Bank on SUVs, Get Hammered by Gas Prices," Green Party of Canada, www.greenparty.ca/page110.html (accessed August 2006).

CHAPTER 9
Product, Services, and Branding Strategies

AFTER STUDYING THIS CHAPTER, YOU SHOULD BE ABLE TO

1. define *product* and the major classifications of products and services

2. describe the decisions that companies make regarding their individual products and services, product lines, and product mixes

3. discuss branding strategy—the decisions companies make in building and managing their brands

4. identify the four characteristics that affect the marketing of a service and the additional marketing considerations that services require

5. discuss two additional product issues: socially responsible product decisions and international product and services marketing

Previewing the Concepts

Now that you've had a good look at marketing strategy, we'll take a deeper look at the marketing mix—the tactical tools that marketers use to implement their strategies. In this and the next chapter, we'll study how companies develop and manage products and brands. Then, in the chapters that follow, we'll look at pricing, distribution, and marketing communication tools. The product is usually the first and most basic marketing consideration. We'll start with a seemingly simple question: What *is* a product? As it turns out, however, the answer is not so simple.

To begin, let's return to that seemingly simple question—what is a product? To bring this question to life, ask yourself to consider what you think of as athletic apparel. Perhaps a pair of comfy sweatpants and a T-shirt come to mind? As it turns out, to lululemon athletica customers, athletic apparel is more than comfortable and functional gear to sweat in—it's a statement about who they are.

uppose you've just joined a new gym and you're in the market for some new clothes to work out in. Where will you go? A mere five years ago, you likely would have driven to your local mall to the nearest SportChek, Athletes World, or Foot Locker. But, chances are, if you are a female in your twenties (or a very hip "new age" kind of guy), your answer might be different. The lululemon name and unique logo, which has been described as a "flippy hairdo" (it's actually a stylized letter A, which denotes the first letter of "Athletically Hip," one of the company's originally proposed names) have become famous in Canada. Lululemon stores are popping up everywhere in both Canada and around the globe, bringing their unique yoga-inspired clothing and philosophy to more and more satisfied customers.

Lululemon was founded in 1998 by Chip Wilson in Kitsilano, a trendy neighbourhood in Vancouver, British Columbia, in response to the growing number of females taking up sports, especially yoga. Previously, sports had been largely male-dominated and, therefore, women were not a focus for the major athletic apparel companies. Thus, many women found themselves purchasing men's athletic clothes, which were both ill-fitting and masculine-looking. Lululemon started as a design studio surrounded by a retail store, which interestingly shared its space with a yoga studio. By putting customers at the centre of its business strategy, lululemon continued to create clothing with its clientele's feedback in mind, growing its business to twenty-eight stores across Canada, as well as stores in the U.S., Australia, and Japan.

To a true lululemon convert, the gear isn't just clothing. It's a way of life. An experience. A statement. With every pair of "Boogie Woogie Pants" it sells, lululemon creates a happy customer. And, each happy customer can't wait to tell others about their experience. Although lululemon's clothing was originally designed for athletes, Wilson notes that the clothing can be used by almost anyone for any activity. And therein perhaps lies its success— lululemon's clothes are functional, extremely comfortable, and, most of all, trendy. Its stores appeal to individuals of all ages, with customers ranging in age from 13 to 60. Further, although women were the original target, lululemon currently has an entire line of men's clothing.

Lululemon is focused on the experience that it creates, to the point where the brand is largely defined through the store experience. In fact, the brand was built almost entirely via word-of-mouth. Although lululemon is advertised in the *Yoga Journal*, and local newspaper ads are placed when a new store is opened, it is the positive shopping experience that turns customers into brand advocates who spread the word. A pretty amazing feat, especially when you consider lululemon's price-point. Indeed, lululemon gear is not cheap—the average pair of pants costs $90, and a top will cost about $50. And, yet, people flock to its stores. Why? Lululemon's combination of superior-quality garments, enticing retail stores, and a community-based philosophy is a winning formula. Lululemon goes to great lengths to reinforce its philosophy in all that it does. From developing a store ambassador system with local yoga instructors or yoga enthusiasts who informally spread the good word about lululemon, to offering employees free yoga classes and making charitable contributions to its communities, which totalled more than $300 000 in 2005, lululemon reinforces its mission of "provid[ing] components for people to live a longer healthier and more fun life." The result: customers are passionate about the brand, and they share this passion with others.

Who else could run the controversial but famous "Grin and Bare it!" store openings. Newspaper ads entice a certain number of brave souls to show up on opening day wearing only their undies. In return, they will receive a free top and bottom. Huge crowds are drawn to each and every opening. It seems that people will go to great lengths to be a part of the lululemon franchise.

Thus, lululemon does much more than just sell athletic apparel. It creates an unparalleled experience for its customers. And, these experiences have led to impressive business results. Although it has been growing rapidly since its inception, lululemon's focus on growing only as fast as it can find the right individuals to carry on its brand philosophy has ensured strong and consistent brand messaging. Thus, the future looks bright for lululemon and its many loyal customers.[1]

Clearly, athletic apparel is more than just sweatpants when lululemon sells them. This chapter begins with a deceptively simple question: *What is a product?* After answering this question, we look at ways to classify products in consumer and business markets. Then we discuss the important decisions that marketers make regarding individual products, product lines, and product mixes. Next, we look into the critically important issue of how marketers build and manage brands. Finally, we examine the characteristics and marketing requirements of a special form of product—services.

What Is a Product?

Product

Anything that can be offered to a market for attention, acquisition, use, or consumption that might satisfy a want or need.

A Sony DVD player, a Ford Taurus, a Costa Rican vacation, a Green Tea Latte at Second Cup, TD Waterhouse online investment services, and advice from your family doctor—all are products. We define a **product** as anything that can be offered to a market for attention, acquisition, use, or consumption and that might satisfy a want or need. Products include more than just tangible goods. Broadly defined, products include physical objects, services, events, persons, places, organizations, ideas, or mixes of these entities. Thus, throughout this text, we use the term *product* broadly to include any or all of these entities.

Service

Any activity or benefit that one party can offer to another that is essentially intangible and does not result in the ownership of anything.

Because of their importance in the world economy, we give special attention to services. **Services** are a form of product that consists of activities, benefits, or satisfactions offered for sale that are essentially intangible and do not result in the ownership of anything. Examples are banking services, accommodation services (hotels, motels), transportation services (airlines, rail, water), retail, tax preparation, and home repair services. We will look at services more closely later in this chapter.

Products, Services, and Experiences

The product is a key element in the *market offering*. Marketing-mix planning begins with formulating an offering that brings value to target customers. This offering becomes the basis upon which the company builds profitable relationships with customers.

A company's market offering often includes both tangible goods and intangible services. Each component can be a minor or a major part of the total offer. At one extreme, the offer may consist of a *pure tangible good*, such as soap, toothpaste, or salt—no services accompany the product. At the other extreme are *pure services,* for which the offer consists primarily of a service. Examples include a doctor's exam or financial services. Between these two extremes, however, many goods-and-services combinations are possible.

Today, as products and services become more and more commoditized, many companies are moving to a new level in creating value for their customers. To differentiate their offers, beyond simply making products and delivering services, companies are staging, marketing, and delivering memorable customer *experiences.*

Experiences have always been important in the entertainment industry—Disney has long manufactured memories through its movies and theme parks. Today, however, all kinds of firms are recasting their traditional goods and services to create experiences. For example, Starbucks patrons are paying for more than just coffee. The company treats customers to artwork on its walls, apron-clad performers behind espresso machines, and a warm but modern interior ambience that leaves them feeling more affluent and fulfilled. And you don't just shop at the Toys "R" Us store on Times Square in New York City, you *experience* it.[2]

Step into Toys "R" Us Times Square to enjoy three levels of incredible fun right on Broadway! Take a ride on a 60-foot high Ferris Wheel with cool character-themed cabs. Feel like a celebrity in our amazing two-story Barbie Dollhouse. Take a stroll through our life-size Candy Land. Gaze up in wonder at our LEGO Empire State Building. And for a classic Jurassic experience, say hello to a larger than life, 20-foot tall, T-Rex with realistic moves and a mighty roar. You really have to see it to believe it!

Companies that market experiences realize that customers are really buying much more than just products and services. They are making purchasing decisions based on what those offers will *do* for them.[3]

Levels of Product and Services

Product planners need to think about products and services on three levels. (See Figure 9.1.) Each level adds more customer value. The most basic level is the *core*

You don't just shop at the Toys "R" Us store on Times Square in New York City, you experience it.

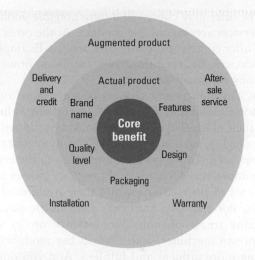

Figure 9.1 Three levels of product

benefit, which addresses the question *What problem is the buyer trying to solve?* When designing products, marketers must first define the core, problem-solving benefits or services that consumers seek. A woman buying lipstick buys more than lip colour. Charles Revson of Revlon saw this early: "In the factory, we make cosmetics; in the store, we sell hope." CIBC does more than sell financial services—it promises to give its customers "The power to do more."

At the second level, product planners must turn the core benefit into an *actual product*. They need to develop product and service features, design, a quality level, a brand name, and packaging. For example, an iPod nano MP3-player is an actual product. Its name, parts, styling, features, packaging, and other attributes have all been combined carefully to deliver the core benefit—a convenient, high-quality, very cool, and "impossibly small" way to store and listen to your favourite music.

Finally, product planners must build an *augmented product* around the core benefit and actual product by offering additional consumer services and benefits. Apple must offer more than just an MP3 player. It must provide consumers with a complete solution to their music-listening problems. Thus, when consumers buy an Apple iPod nano, Apple and its dealers also might give buyers a warranty on parts and workmanship, instructions on how to use the MP3 player, quick repair services when needed, access to iTunes and a website or toll-free telephone number to call if they have problems or questions.

Consumers see products as complex bundles of benefits that satisfy their needs. When developing products, marketers first must identify the *core* consumer needs the product will satisfy. They must then design the *actual* product and find ways to *augment* it in order to create the bundle of benefits that will provide the most satisfying customer experience.

Product and Service Classifications

Products and services fall into two broad classes based on the types of consumers that use them—*consumer products* and *industrial products*. Broadly defined, products also include other marketable entities, such as experiences, organizations, persons, places, and ideas.

Consumer Products

Consumer product
Product bought by final consumer for personal consumption.

Consumer products are products and services bought by final consumers for personal consumption. Marketers usually classify these products and services further based on how consumers go about buying them. Consumer products include *con-*

Consumers perceive this Apple iPod nano as a complex bundle of intangible features and services that deliver a core benefit—a convenient, high-quality, very cool, and "impossibly small" way to store and listen to your favourite music.

Completely remastered. The new ⌘ iPod nano

Completely remastered. The new ⌘ iPod nano

venience products, *shopping products*, *specialty products*, and *unsought products*. These products differ in the ways consumers buy them and therefore in how they are marketed. (See Table 9.1.)

TABLE 9.1 Marketing Considerations for Consumer Productions

Marketing Considerations	Type of Consumer Product			
	Convenience	Shopping	Specialty	Unsought
Customer buying behaviour	Frequent purchase, little planning, little comparison or shopping effort, low customer involvement	Less frequent purchase, much planning and shopping effort, comparison of brands on price, quality, style	Strong brand preference and loyalty, special purchase effort, little comparison of brands, low price sensitivity	Little product awareness, knowledge (or, if aware, little or even negative interest)
Price	Low price	Higher price	High price	Varies
Distribution	Widespread distribution, convenient locations	Selective distribution in fewer outlets	Exclusive distribution in only one or a few outlets per market area	Varies
Promotion	Mass promotion by the producer	Advertising and personal selling by both producer and resellers	More carefully targeted promotion by both producer and reseller	Aggressive advertising and personal selling by producer and resellers
Examples	Toothpaste, magazines, chocolate bars	Major appliances, televisions, furniture, clothing	Luxury goods, such as Rolex watches or fine crystal	Life insurance, blood donations

Convenience product
Consumer product that the customer usually buys frequently, immediately, and with a minimum of comparison and buying effort.

Shopping product
Consumer good that the customer, in the process of selection and purchase, characteristically compares on such bases as suitability, quality, price, and style.

Specialty product
Consumer product with unique characteristics or brand identification for which a significant group of buyers is willing to make a special purchase effort.

Unsought product
Consumer product that the consumer either does not know about or knows about but does not normally think of buying.

Convenience products are consumer products and services that the customer usually buys frequently, immediately, and with a minimum of comparison and buying effort. Examples include soap, candy, newspapers, and fast food. Convenience products are usually low priced, and marketers often place them in many locations to make them readily available when customers need them.

Shopping products are less frequently purchased consumer products and services that customers compare carefully on suitability, quality, price, and style. When buying shopping products and services, consumers spend much time and effort in gathering information and making comparisons. Examples include furniture, clothing, cars, major appliances, and hotel and airline services. Marketers of shopping products usually distribute their products through fewer outlets but provide deeper sales support to help customers in their comparison efforts.

Specialty products are consumer products and services with unique characteristics or brand identification for which a significant group of buyers is willing to make a special purchase effort. Examples include specific brands and types of cars, high-priced photographic equipment, designer clothes, and the services of medical or legal specialists. A Lamborghini automobile, for example, is a specialty product because buyers are usually willing to travel great distances to buy one. Buyers normally do not compare specialty products. They invest only the time needed to reach dealers carrying the wanted products.

Unsought products are consumer products that the consumer either does not know about or knows about but does not normally think of buying. Most major new innovations are unsought until the consumer becomes aware of them through advertising. Classic examples of known but unsought products and services are life insurance, preplanned funeral services, and blood donations. By their very nature, unsought products require a lot of advertising, personal selling, and other marketing efforts.

Business Products

Business product
Product bought by individuals and organizations for further processing or for use in conducting a business.

Business products are those purchased for further processing or for use in conducting a business. Thus, the distinction between a consumer product and an industrial product is based on the *purpose* for which the product is bought. If a consumer buys a lawn mower for use around home, the lawn mower is a consumer product. If the same consumer buys the same lawn mower for use in a landscaping business, the lawn mower is a business product.

The three groups of business products and services include materials and parts, capital items, and supplies and services. *Materials and parts* include raw materials and manufactured materials and parts. Raw materials consist of farm products (wheat, cotton, livestock, fruits, vegetables) and natural products (fish, lumber, crude petroleum, iron ore). Manufactured materials and parts consist of component materials (iron, yarn, cement, wires) and component parts (small motors, tires, castings). Most manufactured materials and parts are sold directly to industrial users. Price and service are the major marketing factors; branding and advertising tend to be less important.

Capital items are business products that aid in the buyer's production or operations, including installations and accessory equipment. Installations consist of major purchases, such as buildings (factories, offices) and fixed equipment (generators, drill presses, large computer systems, elevators). Accessory equipment includes portable factory equipment and tools (hand tools, lift trucks) and office equipment (computers, fax machines, desks). They have a shorter life than installations and simply aid in the production process.

Aramark offers everything from food, housekeeping, laundry, office, and equipment maintenance services to facilities and supply chain management.

The final group of business products is *supplies and services*. Supplies include operating supplies (lubricants, coal, paper, pencils) and repair and maintenance items (paint, nails, brooms). Supplies are the convenience products of the industrial field because they are usually purchased with a minimum of effort or comparison. Business services include maintenance and repair services (window cleaning, computer repair) and business advisory services (legal, management consulting, advertising). Such services are usually supplied under contract.

Organizations, Persons, Places, and Ideas

In addition to tangible products and services, in recent years marketers have broadened the concept of a product to include other market offerings—organizations, persons, places, and ideas.

Organizations often carry out activities to "sell" the organization itself. *Organization marketing* consists of activities undertaken to create, maintain, or change the attitudes and behaviour of target consumers toward an organization. Both profit and not-for-profit organizations practise organization marketing. Business firms sponsor public relations or corporate advertising campaigns to polish their images. *Corporate image advertising* is a major tool companies use to market themselves to various publics. For example, BASF ads say, "We don't make a lot of the products you buy. We make a lot of the products you buy better." And General Electric stands for "imagination at work." Similarly, not-for-profit organizations, such as universities, charities, museums, and performing arts groups, market their organizations in order to raise funds and attract members or patrons.

People can also be thought of as products. *Person marketing* consists of activities undertaken to create, maintain, or change attitudes or behaviour toward particular people. People ranging from presidents, entertainers, and sports figures to professionals, such as chiropractors, lawyers, and architects, use person marketing to build their reputations and increase business. Businesses, charities, sports teams, and other organizations also use person marketing. Creating or associating with well-known personalities often helps these organizations achieve their goals better. That's why more than a dozen different companies—including Nike, Target, Buick,

Companies use corporate image advertising to market themselves to various publics. BASF says, "We don't make a lot of the products you buy. We make a lot of the products you buy better."

American Express, Disney, Accenture, and Titleist—combine to pay more than US$70 million a year to link themselves with golf superstar Tiger Woods.[4]

The skilful use of person marketing can turn a person's name into a powerhouse brand. Wayne Gretzky has his own brand of apparel, a namesake restaurant in Toronto, a charitable foundation, and more. The brand power of Oprah Winfrey's name has made her a billionaire: Oprah-branded products include her television show; TV and feature movies; O, *The Oprah Magazine*; and Oprah's Book Club. And businessman Donald Trump has slapped his well-known name on everything from skyscrapers and casinos to bottled water, magazines, and reality TV programs:

Donald Trump has made and lost fortunes as a real estate developer. But Trump's genius is in brand building, and he is the brand. Thanks to tireless self-promotion, "The Donald" has established the Trump brand as a symbol of quality, luxury, and success. In a recent survey, Trump was named as one of two of the most recognizable names in real estate. More than twenty-five buildings and five casinos bear Donald Trump's name, and he's erecting seven new skyscrapers (including one in Toronto) and three lavish new golf courses. What's the value of the Trump brand? Plenty. In residential real estate in particular, Trump's name commands a premium. "I put my name on a building and I get $5000 a square foot," says Trump. "I put my name on a golf course, Trump National in Briarcliff Manor, and I get $300 000 per member. Other guys only get $25 000." In Chicago, Trump is planning a 90-storey condo tower downtown—the Trump International Hotel & Tower. Even before the building now on the site has been razed, Trump has sold so many units at such high prices—from US$575 000 to US$15 million—that he single-handedly raised the average condo price for the entire city by 25 percent. Based on this real estate success,

Businessman Donald Trump has put his well-known name on everything from skyscrapers and casinos to bottled water, magazines, and reality TV programs.

Trump's name now adorns everything from magazines and bottled water (Trump Ice) to beauty pageants and reality TV shows (*The Apprentice*). Trump does commercials for Verizon, was host of *Saturday Night Live*, and recently unveiled Trump Visa, which rewards cardholders with casino discounts. "He's like P.T. Barnum on steroids," says a friend. "What's his greatest asset? It's his name. He's a skillful marketing person, and what he markets is his name."[5]

Place marketing involves activities undertaken to create, maintain, or change attitudes or behaviour toward particular places. Cities, provinces, regions, and even entire countries compete to attract tourists, new residents, conventions, and company offices and factories. Newfoundland and Labrador advertises that it is the place "Where land, water and sky embrace like old friends," and Ontario declares that "There's more to discover." Canada has been investing heavily to build its brand reputation with considerable success. A 2005 survey of twenty-five countries' brand reputations placed Canada in second place, just behind Australia, in terms of brand power and being one of the world's best places in which to invest and live. We lead both Britain and the United States.[6] In a similar fashion, the Irish Development Agency has attracted more than 1200 companies to locate their plants in Ireland. At the same time, the Irish Tourist Board has built a flourishing tourism business by advertising "Live a different life: friendly, beautiful, relaxing." And the Irish Export Board has created attractive markets for Irish exports.[7]

Ideas can also be marketed. In one sense, all marketing is the marketing of an idea, whether it be the general idea of brushing your teeth or the specific idea that Crest toothpastes "create smiles every day." Here, however, we narrow our focus to the marketing of *social ideas*. This area has been called **social marketing**, defined by the Social Marketing Institute as the use of commercial marketing concepts and tools in programs designed to influence individuals' behaviour to improve their well-being and that of society.[8]

Social marketing

The design, implementation, and control of programs seeking to increase the acceptability of a social idea, cause, or practice among a target group.

Social marketing programs include public health campaigns to reduce smoking, alcoholism, drug abuse, or consumption of fat-laden foods. Other social marketing efforts include environmental campaigns to promote wilderness protection, clean air, and conservation. Still others address issues such as family planning, human rights, and racial equality. The Canadian Landmine Foundation (www.canadianlandmine.org) used a TV campaign and event marketing titled the "Night of a Thousand Dinners." During the annual one-night event, individuals host dinner parties to raise funds for the Adopt-a-Minefield program. This Canadian-led initiative is now used in more than thirty countries. Toronto-based Covenant House, Canada's largest youth shelter, brought home the message that many kids are homeless with an award-winning poster campaign (www.covenanthouse.on.ca).

But social marketing involves much more than just advertising—the Social Marketing Institute encourages the use of a broad range of marketing tools. "Social marketing goes well beyond the promotional 'P' of the marketing mix to include every other element to achieve its social change objectives," says the SMI's executive director.[9] This is what Jolanda van den Berg did when establishing her foundation, Niños Unidos Perucinos, and Niños Hotels in Cusco, Peru. (See Real Marketing 9.1.)

Product and Service Decisions

Marketers make product and services decisions at three levels: individual product and service decisions, product line decisions, and product mix decisions. We discuss each in turn.

Individual Product and Service Decisions

Figure 9.2 shows the important decisions in the development and marketing of individual products and services. We will focus on decisions about *product attributes*, *branding*, *packaging*, *labelling*, and *product support services*.

Product and Service Attributes

Developing a product or service involves defining the benefits that it will offer. These benefits are communicated and delivered by product attributes, such as *quality*, *features*, and *style and design*.

Product quality

The ability of a product to perform its functions; it includes the product's overall durability, reliability, precision, ease of operation and repair, and other valued attributes.

Product Quality **Product quality** is one of the marketer's major positioning tools. Quality has a direct impact on product or service performance; thus, it is closely linked to customer value and satisfaction. In the narrowest sense, quality can be defined as "freedom from defects." But most customer-centred companies go beyond this narrow definition. Instead, they define quality in terms of creating customer value and satisfaction. The American Society for Quality defines quality as the characteristics of a product or service that bear on its ability to satisfy stated or implied customer needs. Similarly, Siemans defines quality this way: "Quality is when our customers come back and our products don't."[10]

Figure 9.2 Individual product and service decisions

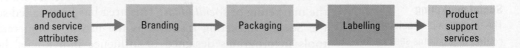

| Product and service attributes | → | Branding | → | Packaging | → | Labelling | → | Product support services |

REAL MARKETING

9.1

Social Marketing: Marketing to Achieve Social Change

In 1995, Jolanda van den Berg, an attractive young Dutch woman with a successful career in the computer industry, a home, a car, a family, and friends decided to take a vacation in Peru. She was tired and had the nagging feeling that something was missing from her life. She ended up in Cusco, the ancient Inca capital. Though she was struck by the city and the surrounding landscape, she was also captivated by the children–poor street children—swarming everywhere trying to sell fruit, sweets, postcards, and shoe-polishing services, or simply begging for money. Even when she returned home, the faces of the children stayed with her. She was haunted by the thought, "I have to do something to help these children." And that is exactly what she did.

She resolved to go back to Cusco, guided by the thought that if she could help just one child, she would make a difference. She wrote to friends and acquaintances asking them to pledge $5 per month to help aid the children. She sold everything, and four months later, on July 10 she was back in Peru—with no plan, little money, and no ability to speak the language. But she was convinced in her heart that she was doing the right thing. She spent hours in the city's central square playing with the children and getting to know them better. She offered two young boys the opportunity to come and live with her with the understanding, "If you stick by the rules, you can stay. If not, back to the streets you go." Soon two boys became eight and eventually, she had twelve children who had known nothing but hunger, violence, and neglect living with her in her small house. She had started a family with all the disagreements, conflicts, and joy such a diverse group could bring.

With twelve mouths to feed and house, Jolanda quickly realized how vulnerable the situation was. Their welfare depended on a trickle of donations, even though she had managed to increase the number of sponsors helping her cause. One day she came up with the idea of starting a hotel. Cusco was a tourist town, so this could be a viable business that would not only give her "family" some extra income but also allow the older boys to learn some new skills. The idea turned into reality when she returned to Holland for a brief visit. She met a wealthy man who was interested in her project, and he gave her $100 000 to buy a seventeenth-century colonial house that she could convert into a hotel.

Buying the property was one thing, finding the money to renovate it was another. She started sending newsletters to all her donors full of honest stories of what life was like living with twelve former street children. She shared their victories and setbacks. She solicited people to "adopt a room." In return for a donation, the donor's picture as a child would be posted outside the door. She worked with schools in Holland who raised money to help support her cause.

Jolanda wanted the hotel to be a place where she would enjoy staying:

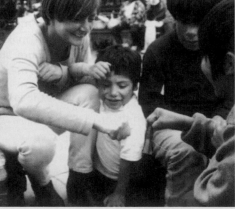

Intuitively Jolanda van den Berg used many marketing tools when launching and growing her hotel. All profits generated by the operation are devoted to helping Peru's poor children.

an affordable (US$34/night), comfortable, and pretty hotel, with no luxuries but one that was spotlessly clean, with a good breakfast and friendly service. Each room was named after one of the boys in her new family. All of the profits generated by the hotel would be devoted to helping the children. In June 1998, two years after she had returned to Peru, the hotel opened. She named it the Niños Hotel (*niños* means children in Spanish), and she and the boys lived in the back, where they still live today.

Jolanda had no money to advertise, so she wrote to the major companies, such as *Lonely Planet*, that published travel books and to major travel agencies. It wasn't long before they were listing her hotel and its unique brand promise of helping children. Despite her lack of experience, the hotel quickly booked up and word of mouth started to grow. Many guests were enthralled by the idea of all the profits going to help the children. However, the hotel itself was a selling point. Though not fancy, it provided comfort and quality.

Her cause started to generate publicity in Holland. *Libelle* (a weekly women's magazine) published a four-page article on the project and KRO (a TV/radio station) made a documentary about the family and the project. This helped generate more donations and more visitors.

During her two years in Peru, Jolanda became more and more aware of how many children were severely neglected, undernourished, or subject to violence. Teachers told her of children that would faint in school because of lack of food. They were often filthy, had lice and fleas, bronchitis, tuberculosis, and other diseases connected with extreme poverty. Yet, she couldn't take more children into her own home. The hotel was generating money, so Jolanda decided to open a children's restaurant to help address some of these problems. She hated the word "soup kitchen," thinking the very name took away the child's dignity, so she latched on the term restaurant.

She started by giving 125 young boys and girls (selected by their schools as being in the most critical cases) of primary-school age one hot meal a day. The meal was of high quality and the menu varied. The tables are child-sized and flowers grace their centre. She built an area where the children could have a hot shower several times a week. She also provided them

with medical and dental care and started getting them involved in sports to teach them anger management and cooperation. A teacher is present every day to help them with their homework since most of the children had either no home or one where doing school work was impossible. Furthermore, many of these children were behind in school because of their circumstances. Each child is given a card, so her staff can keep track of attendance.

By 2006, Jolanda's enthusiasm, vision and boundless energy had moved the project even further ahead. She has now built a second Niños hotel and she incorporated another children's restaurant into the facility, along with a larger shower facility and a large modern gymnasium. She's established two more "restaurants" in other parts of Cusco. In total, she now provides food, educational support, and dental and medical care for 500 children. She worked with two more families who have each adopted twelve children—one twelve boys, the other twelve girls. Furthermore, she employs sixty-five Peruvians. Jolanda doesn't work with volunteers—they take jobs away from Peruvians. Unemployment is a chronic problem in Peru, and by hiring Peruvians with families and improving their skills, she increases the support for even more families. Her hotels recently won the award as the best two-star hotel in Cusco and her occupancy rates are higher than other establishments in the city.

As I found out when I stayed there in 2006, there is something about waking up in the morning and hearing the laughter of children in your ears—laughter from children who once had no prospects. Perhaps a comment posted on March 26, 2006, on TripAdvisor.com, says it all: "My mother and I spent 5 nights at Los Niños, and loved it! It felt very cozy and homey. We were greeted with friendly staff and a cup of coca tea in the courtyard on our arrival.... I hope to go back someday! For the low price, it was a great deal, and to know that the money is going towards helping Cusco street children makes it a great opportunity too!" You can learn more about the hotels and the foundation that supports them at www.ninoshotel.com.

Sources: Peggy Cunningham interviewed Jolanda van den Berg April 2, 2006. Material was also drawn from "If I can help just one," *Stichting Niños Unidos Peruanos*, 2002.

Total quality management (TQM) is an approach in which all the company's people are involved in constantly improving the quality of products, services, and business processes. During the past two decades, companies large and small have credited TQM with greatly improving their market shares and profits. Recently, however, the TQM movement has drawn criticism. Too many companies viewed TQM as a magic cure-all and created token total quality programs that applied quality principles only superficially. Still others became obsessed with narrowly defined TQM principles and lost sight of broader concerns for customer value and satisfaction. As a result, many such programs failed, causing a backlash against TQM.

When applied in the context of creating customer satisfaction, however, *total quality* principles remain a requirement for success. Although many firms don't use the TQM label anymore, for most top companies customer-driven quality has become a way of doing business. Today, companies are taking a "return on quality" approach, viewing quality as an investment and holding quality efforts accountable for bottom-line results.[11]

Product quality has two dimensions—level and consistency. In developing a product, the marketer must first choose a *quality level* that will support the product's position in the target market. Here, product quality means *performance quality*—the ability of a product to perform its functions. For example, a Rolls-Royce provides higher performance quality than a Chevrolet: It has a smoother ride, handles better, and lasts longer. Companies rarely try to offer the highest possible performance quality level—few customers want or can afford the high levels of quality offered in products such as a Rolls-Royce automobile, a Sub-Zero refrigerator, or a Rolex watch. Instead, companies choose a quality level that matches target market needs and the quality levels of competing products.

Beyond quality level, high quality also can mean high levels of quality *consistency*. Here, product quality means *conformance quality*—freedom from defects and *consistency* in delivering a targeted level of performance. All companies should strive for high levels of conformance quality. In this sense, a Chevrolet can have just as much quality as a Rolls-Royce. Although a Chevy doesn't perform as well as a Rolls, it can as consistently deliver the quality that customers pay for and expect.

Many companies today have turned customer-driven quality into a potent strategic weapon. They have created customer satisfaction and value by consistently and profitably meeting customers' needs and preferences for quality.

Product Features   A product can be offered with varying features. A stripped-down model, one without any extras, is the starting point. The company can create higher-level models by adding more features. Features are a competitive tool for differentiating the company's product from competitors' products. Being the first producer to introduce a needed and valued new feature is one of the most effective ways to compete.

How can a company identify new features and decide which ones to add to its product? The company should periodically survey buyers who have used the product and ask these questions: How do you like the product? Which specific features of the product do you like most? Which features could we add to improve the product? The answers provide the company with a rich list of feature ideas. The company can then assess each feature's *value* to customers versus its *cost* to the company. Features that customers value little in relation to costs should be dropped; those that customers value highly in relation to costs should be added.

Product Style and Design   Another way to add customer value is through distinctive *product style and design*. Design is a larger concept than style. *Style* simply describes the appearance of a product. Styles can be eye-catching or yawn-producing. A sensational style may grab attention and produce pleasing aesthetics, but it does not necessarily make the product *perform* better. Unlike style, *design* is more than skin deep—it goes to the very heart of a product. Good design contributes to a product's usefulness as well as to its looks.

Good design begins with a deep understanding of customer needs. More than simply creating product or service attributes, it involves shaping the customers product or service *experience*. For example Kaiser Permanente, the U.S.'s largest health maintenance organization, has hundreds of medical offices and hospitals. It recently hired IDEO, a design firm, to help it design the next-generation medical building.

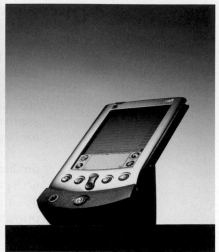

IDEO helped Kaiser Permanente design the next-generation medical facilities. It has also helped numerous other companies design products that not only look good but also reshape the customer's use, as with this shopping cart and PDA.

Thanks to IDEO's novel design process, it turned out to be a fascinating journey of self-discovery:

> For starters, Kaiser nurses, doctors, and facilities managers teamed up with IDEO's social scientists, designers, architects, and engineers and observed patients as they made their way through Kaiser medical facilities. At times, they even played the role of patient themselves. Together they came up with some surprising insights. IDEO's architects revealed that patients and family often became annoyed well before seeing a doctor, because checking in was a nightmare and waiting rooms were uncomfortable. IDEO's cognitive psychologists pointed out that many people visit doctors with a parent or friend, but that second person is often not allowed to stay with the patient, leaving the afflicted alienated and anxious. IDEO's sociologists explained that patients hated Kaiser's examination rooms because they often had to wait alone for up to twenty minutes half-naked, with nothing to do, surrounded by threatening needles. IDEO and Kaiser concluded that, even when people leave treated and cured, the patient experience can be awful.

> What to do? After working with IDEO, Kaiser realized that it didn't need lots of expensive new buildings. What it needed was to overhaul the patient *experience*. Kaiser learned that seeking medical care is much like shopping—it is a social experience shared with others. So Kaiser needed to offer more comfortable waiting rooms and a lobby with clear instructions on where to go. It needed larger exam rooms, with space for three or more people and curtains for privacy, to make patients comfortable. And it needed special corridors for medical staffers to meet and increase their efficiency. "IDEO showed us that we are designing human experiences, not buildings," says Kaiser's medical operations services manager. "[And] its recommendations didn't require big capital expenditures."[12]

> In the same way, product designers should think less about product attributes and technical specifications and more about how customers will use and benefit from the product. Good design can improve product or service performance, cut costs, and create strong competitive advantage in the target market.

Branding

Brand
A name, term, sign, symbol, or design, or a combination of these, intended to identify the goods or services of one seller or group of sellers and to differentiate them from those of competitors.

Perhaps the most distinctive skill of professional marketers is their ability to build and manage their brands. A **brand** is a name, term, sign, symbol, or design, or a combination of these, that identifies the maker or seller of a product or service.

Consumers view a brand as an important part of a product, and branding can add value to a product. For example, most consumers would perceive a bottle of Chanel Nº5 perfume as a high-quality, expensive product. But the same perfume in an unmarked bottle would likely be viewed as lower in quality, even if the fragrance were identical.

Branding has become so strong that today hardly anything goes unbranded. Salt is packaged in branded containers, common nuts and bolts are packaged with a distributor's label, and automobile parts—spark plugs, tires, filters—bear brand names that differ from those of the automakers. Even fruits, vegetables, and poultry are branded—Sunkist oranges, Dole pineapples, Chiquita bananas, Fresh Express salad greens, and Lilydale chickens.

Branding helps buyers in many ways. Brand names help consumers identify products that might benefit them. Brands also tell the buyer something about product quality. Buyers who always buy the same brand know that they will get the same features, benefits, and quality each time they buy. Branding also gives the seller several advantages. The brand name becomes the basis on which a whole story can be built about a product's special qualities. The seller's brand name and trademark provide legal protection for unique product features that otherwise might be copied by competitors. And branding helps the seller to segment markets. For example, General Mills can offer Cheerios, Wheaties, Total, Kix, Golden Grahams, Trix, and many other cereal brands, not just one general product for all consumers.

Building and managing brands is perhaps the marketer's most important task. We will discuss branding strategy in more detail later in the chapter.

Packaging

Packaging
The activities of designing and producing the container or wrapper for a product.

Packaging involves designing and producing the container or wrapper for a product. The package includes a product's primary container (the tube holding Colgate Total toothpaste). It may also include a secondary package that is thrown away when the product is about to be used (the cardboard box containing the tube of Colgate). Finally, it can include a shipping package necessary to store, identify, and ship the product (a corrugated box carrying six dozen tubes of Colgate). Labelling, printed information appearing on or with the package, is also part of packaging.

Branding has become so strong that hardly anything goes unbranded, even fruits and vegetables.

Traditionally, the primary function of the package was to contain and protect the product. In recent times, however, numerous factors have made packaging an important marketing tool. Increased competition and clutter on retail store shelves means that packages must now perform many sales tasks—from attracting attention, to describing the product, to making the sale.

Companies are realizing the power of good packaging to create instant consumer recognition of the company or brand. For example, in an average supermarket, which stocks 15 000 to 17 000 items, the typical shopper passes by some 300 items per minute, and more than 60 percent of all purchases are made on impulse. In this highly competitive environment, the package may be the seller's last chance to influence buyers. "Not long ago, the package was merely the product's receptacle, and the brand message was elsewhere—usually on TV," says a packaging expert. But changes in the marketplace environment are now "making the package itself an increasingly important selling medium."[13]

Innovative packaging can give a company an advantage over competitors. Consumer packaged-goods firms have recently upped their investments in packaging research to develop package designs that grab more shelf attention or make life easier for customers. For example, Dutch Boy recently came up with a long overdue innovation—paint in plastic containers with twist-off caps:

> How did Dutch Boy Paint stir up the paint business? It's so simple, it's scary. Imagine a paint can that's easy to carry, doesn't take a screwdriver to pry open, doesn't dribble when pouring, and doesn't take a hammer to bang closed again. It's here—in the form of Dutch Boy's new Twist and Pour paint container. Touted as "a whole new way to carry, mix, open, pour, brush, and store paint," the new container is an all-plastic gallon container with a twist-off lid, side handle, and pour spout. It's lighter weight than a can and rust-proof, too. It kind of makes you wonder: Why did it take so long to come up with an idea like this? The new containers cost a dollar or two more than traditional cans, but consumers don't seem to mind. More than 50 percent of Dutch Boy's customers are now buying the plastic containers, and new stores, like Wal-Mart, are now carrying it. "It's an amazing innovation. Worth noticing," says one observer. "Not only did the new packaging increase sales, but it also got them more distribution at a higher retail price!"[14]

In contrast, poorly designed packages can cause headaches for consumers and lost sales for the company. For example, a few years ago, Planters Lifesavers Company attempted to use innovative packaging to create an association between fresh-roasted peanuts and fresh-roasted coffee. It packaged its Fresh Roast Salted Peanuts in vacuum-packed "Brik-Pacs," similar to those used for ground coffee. Unfortunately, the coffee-like packaging worked too well: Consumers mistook the peanuts for a new brand of flavoured coffee and ran them through supermarket coffee-grinding machines, creating a gooey mess, disappointed customers, and lots of irate store managers.[15]

In recent years, product safety has also become a major packaging concern. We have all learned to deal with hard-to-open "childproof" packages. And after the rash of product tampering scares during the 1980s, most drug producers and food makers now put their products in tamper-resistant packages. In making packaging decisions, the company also must heed growing environmental concerns. Fortunately, many companies have gone "green" by reducing their packaging and using environmentally responsible packaging materials. For example, SC Johnson repackaged Agree Plus shampoo in a stand-up pouch using 80 percent less plastic. Procter & Gamble eliminated outer cartons from its Secret and Sure deodorants, saving 1.5 million kilograms of paperboard per year.

INTRODUCING THE NEW TWIST AND POUR™ PAINT CONTAINER, ONLY FROM DUTCH BOY®

THE NEAT NEW PAINT 'CAN' WITH A TWIST

Easy to hold

Easy to open

Easy to pour

Dutch Boy.

For a Twist and Pour retailer near you, call 1-800-828-5669 or visit www.dutchboy.com
* U.S. and foreign patents pending

Dutch Boy came up with a long overdue innovation—paint in plastic containers with twist-off caps. It created a paint can that's easy to carry, doesn't take a screwdriver to pry open, doesn't dribble when pouring, and doesn't take a hammer to bang closed again.

Labelling

Labels may range from simple tags attached to products to complex graphics that are part of the package. They perform several functions. At the very least, the label *identifies* the product or brand, such as the name Sunkist stamped on oranges. The label might also *describe* several things about the product—who made it, where it was made, when it was made, its contents, how it is to be used, and how to use it safely. Finally, the label might *promote* the product through attractive graphics.

There has been a long history of legal and ethical concerns about labels. Labels have the potential to mislead customers, fail to describe important ingredients, and fail to include needed safety warnings. Labelling regulations depend on the type of product being sold. Canada's *Consumer Packaging and Labelling Act,* which covers many non-food products, was passed to protect consumers from labelling or packaging that is false or misleading. The *Weights and Measures Act* deals with the units of measurement on labels. The Government of Canada's "Consumer Packaging and Labelling" page (see www.strategis.ic.gc.ca) details the requirements for the principal display panel of prepackaged, non-food consumer products.

Some important issues facing marketers when designing labels include unit pricing (stating the price per unit of standard measure), *open dating* (stating the expected shelf life of the product), and *nutritional labelling* (stating the nutritional values in the product). Further, there are strict government-enforced guidelines that dictate the use of product claims, such as "low-fat," "high-fibre," and "light." Thus, many organizations have individuals dedicated to dealing with regulatory issues surrounding packaging to ensure that their labels contain all the required information and thereby adhere to all government regulations.

Innovative labelling can help to promote a product.

Product Support Services

Customer service is another element of product strategy. A company's offer usually includes some support services, which can be a minor or a major part of the total offering. Later in the chapter, we will discuss services as products in themselves. Here, we discuss services that augment actual products.

The first step is to survey customers periodically to assess the value of current services and to obtain ideas for new ones. For example, Cadillac holds regular focus group interviews with owners and carefully watches complaints that come into its dealerships. From this careful monitoring, Cadillac has learned that buyers are very upset by repairs that are not done correctly the first time.

Once the company has assessed the value of various support services to customers, it must next assess the costs of providing these services. It can then develop a package of services that will both delight customers and yield profits to the company. Based on its consumer interviews, Cadillac has set up a system directly linking each dealership with a group of ten engineers who can help walk mechanics through difficult repairs. Such actions helped Cadillac jump, in one year, from fourteenth to seventh in independent rankings of service. For the past several years, Cadillac has rated at or near the top of its industry on the American Customer Satisfaction Index.[16]

Many companies are now using a sophisticated mix of phone, email, fax, Internet, and interactive voice and data technologies to provide support services that were not possible before. Consider the following example:

Some online merchants are watching where you surf, then opening a chat window on your screen to ask just as they would in the store if you have questions about the goods they see you eyeing. Last year, Hewlett-Packard began sending pop-up chat boxes to visitors who were shopping on HP.com's pages for digital-photography products. If a shopper loiters a few minutes over some gear, up pops a photo of an attractive woman with the words, "Hello, Need Information? An HP live chat representative is standing by to assist you." Click on "Go" and type a question, and a live sales agent responds immediately. SunTrust Banks, which has been inviting customers to chat about loan and bank products for about two years, is taking proactive chat one step further by experimenting with co-browsing. This feature essentially lets chat agents take control of a customer's computer screen, opening webpages directly on their browser to help them find what they're looking for. In the future, "call cams" will even let customers see an agent on their screen and talk directly through voice-over-Web capabilities.[17]

Product Line Decisions

Product line

A group of products that are closely related because they function in a similar manner, are sold to the same customer groups, are marketed through the same types of outlets, or fall within given price ranges.

Beyond decisions about individual products and services, product strategy also calls for building a product line. A **product line** is a group of products that are closely related because they function in a similar manner, are sold to the same customer groups, are marketed through the same types of outlets, or fall within given price ranges. For example, New Balance produces several lines of athletic shoes and apparel, Rogers produces several lines of telecommunications products, and TD Canada Trust produces several lines of financial services.

The major product line decision involves *product line length*—the number of items in the product line. The line is too short if the manager can increase profits by adding items; the line is too long if the manager can increase profits by dropping items. The company should manage its product lines carefully. Product lines tend to lengthen over time, and most companies eventually need to prune unnecessary or unprofitable items from their lines to increase overall profitability.

Product line length is influenced by company objectives and resources. For example, one objective might be to allow for upselling. Thus, BMW wants to move customers up from its 3-series models to 5- and 7-series models. Another objective might be to allow cross-selling: Hewlett-Packard sells printers as well as cartridges. Still another objective might be to protect against economic swings: Gap runs several clothing-store chains (Gap, Old Navy, Banana Republic) covering different price points.

A company can lengthen its product line in two ways: by *line stretching* or by *line filling*. *Product line stretching* occurs when a company lengthens its product line beyond its current range. The company can stretch its line downward, upward, or both ways.

Companies located at the upper end of the market can stretch their lines *downward*. A company may stretch downward to plug a market hole that otherwise would attract a new competitor or to respond to a competitor's attack on the upper end. Or it may add low-end products because it finds faster growth taking place in the low-end segments. DaimlerChrysler stretched its Mercedes line downward for all these reasons. Facing a slow-growth luxury car market and attacks by Japanese automakers on its high-end positioning, it successfully introduced its Mercedes C-Class cars. These models sell in the US$30 000 range without harming the firm's ability to sell other Mercedes for US$100 000 or more.

Companies at the lower end of a market can stretch their product lines *upward*. Sometimes, companies stretch upward in order to add prestige to their current products. Or they may be attracted by a faster growth rate or higher margins at the higher end. For example, each of the leading Japanese auto companies introduced an upmarket automobile: Toyota launched Lexus; Nissan launched Infiniti; and Honda launched Acura. They used entirely new names rather than their own names.

Companies in the middle range of the market may decide to stretch their lines in *both directions*. Marriott did this with its hotel product line. Along with regular Marriott hotels, it has added new branded hotel lines to serve both the upper and the lower ends of the market. Renaissance aims to attract and please top executives; Marriotts, upper and middle managers; Courtyards, salespeople and other "road warriors"; and Fairfield Inns, vacationers and business travellers on a tight travel

Marriott offers a full line of hotel brands, each aimed at a different target market.

budget. ExecuStay by Marriott provides temporary housing for those relocating or away on long-term assignments of thirty days or longer. Marriott's Residence Inn provides a relaxed, residential atmosphere—a home away from home for people who travel for a living. Marriott TownePlace Suites provide a comfortable atmosphere at a moderate price for extended-stay travellers.[18] The major risk with this strategy is that some travellers will trade down after finding that the lower-price hotels in the Marriott chain give them pretty much everything they want. However, Marriott would rather capture its customers who move downward than lose them to competitors.

An alternative to product line stretching is *product line filling*—adding more items within the present range of the line. There are several reasons for product line filling: reaching for extra profits, satisfying dealers, using excess capacity, being the leading full-line company, and plugging holes to keep out competitors. Sony filled its Walkman line by adding solar-powered and waterproof Walkmans, ultralight models for exercisers, the CD Discman, and the Memory Stick Walkman, which enables users to download tracks straight from the Net. However, line filling is overdone if it results in cannibalization and customer confusion. The company should ensure that new items are noticeably different from existing ones.

Product Mix Decisions

Product mix (or product assortment)
The set of all product lines and items that a particular seller offers for sale.

An organization with several product lines has a product mix. A **product mix** (or **product assortment**) consists of all the product lines and items that a particular seller offers for sale. Avon's product mix consists of five major product lines: beauty products, wellness products, jewellery and accessories, gifts, and "inspirational" products (inspiring gifts, books, music, and home accents). Each product line consists of several sublines. For example, the beauty line breaks down into makeup, skin care, bath and beauty, fragrance, and outdoor protection products. Each line and subline has many individual items. Altogether, Avon's product mix includes 1300 items. In contrast, a typical Zellers stocks 15 000 items, 3M markets more than 60 000 products, and General Electric manufactures as many as 250 000 items.

A company's product mix has four important dimensions: width, length, depth, and consistency. Product mix *width* refers to the number of different product lines the company carries. Procter & Gamble markets a fairly wide product mix consisting of 250 brands organized into five major product lines: personal and beauty, house and home, health and wellness, baby and family, and pet nutrition and care products. Product mix *length* refers to the total number of items the company carries within its product lines. P&G typically carries many brands within each line. For example, in Canada, P&G markets four laundry detergent brands, eight personal cleanser brands (body washes and soap), seven hair care brands, and two cosmetic brands.

Product line *depth* refers to the number of versions offered of each product in the line. P&G's Crest toothpaste comes in sixteen varieties, including Crest Multicare, Crest Cavity Protection, Crest Tartar Protection, Crest Sensitivity Protection, Crest Dual Action Whitening, Crest Whitening Plus Scope, Kid's Cavity Protection, and Crest Baking Soda & Peroxide Whitening formulations.[19] (Talk about niche marketing! Remember our Chapter 8 discussion?)

Finally, the *consistency* of the product mix refers to how closely related the various product lines are in end use, production requirements, distribution channels, or some other way. P&G's product lines are consistent insofar as they are consumer products that go through the same distribution channels (with the exception of its pharmaceutical division). The lines are less consistent insofar as they perform different functions for consumers.

These product mix dimensions provide the handles for defining the company's product strategy. The company can increase its business in four ways. It can add new product lines, widening its product mix. In this way, its new lines build on the company's reputation in its other lines. The company can lengthen its existing product lines to become a more full-line company. Or it can add more versions of each product and thus deepen its product mix. Finally, the company can pursue more product line consistency—or less—depending on whether it wants to have a strong reputation in a single field or in several fields.

Branding Strategy: Building Strong Brands

Some analysts see brands as *the* major enduring asset of a company, outlasting the company's specific products and facilities. John Stewart, co-founder of Quaker Oats, once said, "If this business were split up, I would give you the land and bricks and mortar, and I would keep the brands and trademarks, and I would fare better than you." A former CEO of McDonald's agrees:[20]

> A McDonald's board member who worked at Coca-Cola once talked to us about the value of our brand. He said if every asset we own, every building, and every piece of equipment were destroyed in a terrible natural disaster, we would be able to borrow all the money to replace it very quickly because of the value of our brand. And he's right. The brand is more valuable than the totality of all these assets.

Thus, brands are powerful assets that must be carefully developed and managed. In this section, we examine the key strategies for building and managing brands.

Brand Equity

Brands are more than just names and symbols. Brands represent consumers' perceptions and feelings about a product and its performance—everything that the product or service *means* to consumers. In the final analysis, brands exist in the minds of consumers. Thus, the real value of a strong brand is its power to capture consumer preference and loyalty.

Brands vary in the amount of power and value they have in the marketplace. In 2005, a national survey of Canada's best managed brands put Tim Hortons, President's Choice, Cirque du Soleil, Loblaws, Canadian Tire, WestJet, CityTV, Shoppers Drug Mart, LCBO, and Sleeman in the top ten spots. These and other brands—such as Coca-Cola, Dove, Nike, Harley-Davidson, Disney—become larger-than-life icons that maintain their power in the market for years, even generations. "These brands win competitive battles not [just] because they deliver distinctive benefits, trustworthy service, or innovative technologies," notes a branding expert. "Rather, they succeed because they forge a deep connection with the culture."[21]

Brand equity

The positive differential effect that knowing the brand name has on customer response to the product or service.

A powerful brand has high *brand equity*. **Brand equity** is the positive differential effect that knowing the brand name has on customer response to the product or service. A measure of a brand's equity is the extent to which customers are willing to pay more for the brand. One study found that 72 percent of customers would pay a 20 percent premium for their brand of choice relative to the closest competing brand; 40 percent said they would pay a 50 percent premium.[22] Tide and Heinz lovers are willing to pay a 100 percent premium. Loyal Coke drinkers will pay a 50 percent premium and Volvo buyers pay a 40 percent premium.

A brand with strong brand equity is a very valuable asset. *Brand valuation* is the process of estimating the total financial value of a brand. Measuring such value is difficult. However, according to one estimate, RBC is Canada's brand with the greatest equity at a value of $4.5 billion, followed by Loblaws at $3.3 billion, CIBC at $2.8 billion, and Petro-Canada at $1.2 billion. As large as these brand equity values are, they pale when compared with giant global brands. The brand value of Coca-Cola is almost $68 billion, Microsoft is $61 billion, and IBM is $54 billion. Other brands rating among the world's most valuable include General Electric, Intel, Nokia, Disney, McDonald's, Marlboro, and Mercedes.[23]

A strong brand is a valuable asset. How many familiar brands and brand symbols can you find in this picture?

High brand equity provides a company with many competitive advantages. A powerful brand enjoys a high level of consumer brand awareness and loyalty. Because consumers expect stores to carry the brand, the company has more leverage in bargaining with channel members, such as grocery retailers. Because the brand name carries high credibility, the company can more easily launch line and brand extensions, as when Coca-Cola used its well-known brand to introduce Vanilla Coke and Coke Zero, and when Unilever introduced Dove face-care products. A powerful brand offers the company some defence against fierce price competition.

Above all, a powerful brand forms the basis for building strong and profitable customer relationships. Therefore, the fundamental asset underlying brand equity is *customer equity*—the value of the customer relationships that the brand creates. A powerful brand is important, but what it really represents is a profitable set of loyal customers. The proper focus of marketing is building customer equity, with brand management serving as a major marketing tool.[24]

Building Strong Brands

Branding poses challenging decisions to the marketer. Figure 9.3 shows that the major brand strategy decisions involve brand positioning, brand name selection, brand sponsorship, and brand development.

Brand Positioning

Marketers need to position their brands clearly in target customers' minds. They can position brands at any of three levels.[25] At the lowest level, they can position the brand on *product attributes*. Thus, marketers of Crest toothpaste can talk about the product's innovative ingredients and good taste. However, attributes are the least desirable level for brand positioning, as competitors can easily copy attributes. More important, customers are not interested in attributes as such; they are interested in what benefits the attributes will afford them.

A brand can be better positioned by associating its name with a desirable *benefit*. Thus, Crest marketers can go beyond the brand's ingredients and talk about the resulting cavity prevention or teeth-whitening benefits. Some successful brands positioned on benefits are Volvo (safety), Hallmark (caring), Harley-Davidson (adventure), FedEx (guaranteed on-time delivery), Nike (performance), and Lexus (quality).

The strongest brands go beyond attribute or benefit positioning. They are positioned on strong *beliefs and values*. These brands pack an emotional wallop. Thus, Crest's marketers can talk not just about ingredients and cavity-prevention benefits but also about how these give customers "healthy, beautiful smiles for life." Brand expert Marc Gobe argues that successful brands must engage customers on a deeper level, touching a universal emotion.[26] His brand design agency, which has worked on such brands as Starbucks, Victoria's Secret, Godiva, Versace, and Lancôme, relies less on a product's tangible attributes and more on creating surprise, passion, and excitement surrounding a brand.

When positioning a brand, the marketer should establish a mission for the brand and a vision of what the brand must be and do. A brand is the company's promise to deliver a specific set of features, benefits, services, and experiences

Figure 9.3 Major brand strategy decisions

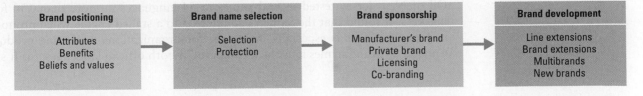

The strongest brands go beyond attribute or benefit positioning. They engage customers on a deeper level, touching universal emotions.

consistently to the target market. It can be thought of as a contract to the customer regarding how the product or service will deliver value and satisfaction. The brand contract must be simple and honest. Motel 6, for example, offers clean rooms, low prices, and good service but does not promise expensive furniture or large bathrooms. In contrast, Ritz-Carlton offers luxurious rooms and a truly memorable experience but does not promise low prices.

Brand Name Selection

A good name can add greatly to a product's success. However, finding the best brand name is a difficult task. It begins with a careful review of the product and its benefits, the target market, and proposed marketing strategies.

Desirable qualities for a brand name include the following: (1) It should suggest something about the product's benefits and qualities. Examples: Beautyrest mattresses, Craftsman tools, Snuggle fabric softener, Merry Maids cleaning service, OFF! bug spray. (2) It should be easy to pronounce, recognize, and remember. Short names help (Dove, S.O.S., Bounce). But longer ones are sometimes effective ("Love My Carpet" carpet cleaner, "I Can't Believe It's Not Butter" margarine). (3) The brand name should be distinctive (Lexus, Kodak, Oracle). (4) It should be extendable: Amazon.com began as an online bookseller but chose a name that would allow expansion into other categories. (5) The name should translate easily into foreign languages. Before spending US$100 million to change its name to Exxon, Standard Oil of New Jersey tested several names in 54 languages in more than 150 foreign markets. It found that the name Enco referred to a stalled engine when pronounced in Japanese. This is especially important for organizations marketing products in Canada as brand names must be meaningful in both official languages. (6) It should be capable of registration and legal protection. A brand name cannot be registered if it infringes on existing brand names.

Once chosen, the brand name must be protected. Many firms try to build a brand name that will eventually become identified with the product category. Brand names such as Kleenex, Levi's, Jell-O, Scotch Tape, Q-Tips, Ziploc, and Fiberglas have succeeded in this way. However, their very success may threaten the company's rights to the name. Many originally protected brand names—such as cellophane, nylon, kerosene, linoleum, yo-yo, trampoline, escalator, thermos, and shredded wheat—are now generic names that any seller can use.

Brand Sponsorship

A manufacturer has four sponsorship options. The product may be launched as a *manufacturer's brand* (or national brand), as when Kellogg and IBM sell their output under their own manufacturer's brand names. Or the manufacturer may sell to resellers who give it a *private brand* (also called a *store brand* or *distributor brand*). Although most manufacturers create their own brand names, others market *licensed brands*. Finally, two companies can join forces and *co-brand* a product.

Manufacturer's Brands Versus Private Brands   Manufacturers' brands have long dominated the retail scene. In recent times, however, an increasing number of retailers and wholesalers have created their own **private brands** (or **store brands**). And in many industries, these private brands are giving manufacturers' brands a real run for their money:

> Melanie Turner has forgotten her shopping list, but the 42-year-old pension consultant doesn't seem to mind. Entering her local Costco store, Turner knows right where she's going. In the dish detergent section, her hand goes past Procter & Gamble's Cascade to grab two 96-ounce bottles of Kirkland Signature, the in-store brand that Costco has plastered on everything from cashews to cross-trainer sneakers. Trolling for some fresh fish for dinner, she hauls in a 1-kilo

Private brand (or store brand)
A brand created and owned by a reseller of a product or service.

An increasing number of retailers have created their own store brands. Costco's Kirkland brand adorns everything from baby wipes to barbecues.

package of tilapia—it, too, emblazoned with the bold red, white, and black Kirkland logo. Then it's off to the paper aisle, where she picks up mammoth packs of Kirkland dinner napkins, Kirkland toilet paper, and ... wait, where are the Kirkland paper towels? Her eyes scan the store's maze of hulking pallets—no sign of them—before coming to rest on a 12-pack of P&G's Bounty. A moment of decision. "I'll wait on this," she says finally. And there, in microcosm, is why Melanie Turner scares the pants off Procter & Gamble, Unilever, Kraft, and just about every consumer goods company out there. Her shopping cart is headed for the checkout aisle, and there's hardly a national brand in it. An almost imperceptible tectonic shift has been reshaping the world of brands. Retailers—once the lowly peddlers of brands that were made and marketed by big, important manufacturers—are now behaving like full-fledged marketers.[27]

It seems that almost every retailer now carries its own store brands. Wal-Mart offers Sam's Choice beverages and food products; Spring Valley nutritional products; and White Cloud brand toilet tissue, diapers, detergent, and fabric softener. Loblaws markets a wide variety of products under its "President's Choice" brand. This brand has been a huge success in Canada because of its premium positioning—indeed, many consumers don't know that they are purchasing a store brand. Rather, they see President's Choice as a unique and premium brand with a variety of high-quality product offerings. This mystique is reinforced by the release of its *Insider's Report*, which features new product news, recipes, and other helpful tips. The effect is to ultimately make consumers feel that they are part of a special club—quite a feat for a store brand! At the other end of the spectrum, upscale retailer Saks Fifth Avenue carries its own Platinum clothing line, which features US$1000 jackets and US$500 cotton dress shirts.

Private-label products control almost a quarter of the Canadian grocery market and the drug store market. In some categories, private-label sales are even higher. For example, in the paper and wrap category, private-label goods account for 45.7 percent of the market. They control 36 percent of the frozen food marketplace and almost 29 percent of the pet product market.[28]

In the so-called *battle of the brands* between manufacturers' and private brands, retailers have many advantages. They control what products they stock, where they go on the shelf, what prices they charge, and which ones they will feature in local flyers. Most retailers also charge manufacturers *slotting or listing fees*—payments from the manufacturers before the retailers will accept new products and find "slots" for them on their shelves. Slotting fees have recently received much scrutiny from the Federal Trade Commission in the U.S., which worries that the fees might dampen competition by restricting retail shelf access for smaller manufacturers who can't afford them.[29] Further, the national brand–store brand battle creates an interesting dynamic for marketers as their major customers, such as Wal-Mart, Loblaws, and Shoppers Drug Mart, are suddenly among the most formidable of their competitors.

Private brands can be hard to establish and costly to stock and promote. However, they also yield higher profit margins for the reseller. And they give resellers exclusive products that cannot be bought from competitors, resulting in greater store traffic and loyalty. Retailers price their store brands lower than comparable manufacturers' brands, thereby appealing to budget-conscious shoppers, especially in difficult economic times. And most shoppers believe that store brands are often made by one of the larger manufacturers anyway.

To fend off private brands, leading brand marketers will have to invest in R&D to bring out new brands, new features, and continuous quality improvements. They must design strong advertising programs to maintain high awareness and preference. They must find ways to "partner" with major distributors in a search for distribution economies and improved joint performance.

Licensing   Most manufacturers take years and spend millions to create their own brand names. However, some companies license names or symbols previously created by other manufacturers, names of well-known celebrities, or characters from popular movies and books. For a fee, any of these can provide an instant and proven brand name.

Apparel and accessories sellers pay large royalties to adorn their products—from blouses to ties, and linens to luggage—with the names or initials of well-known fashion innovators, such as Calvin Klein, Tommy Hilfiger, Gucci, or Armani. Sellers of children's products attach an almost endless list of character names to clothing, toys, school supplies, linens, dolls, lunch boxes, cereals, and other items. Licensed character names range from classics, such as *Sesame Street*, Disney, Peanuts, Winnie the Pooh, the Muppets, Scooby Doo, and Dr. Seuss characters, to the more recent Teletubbies, Pokémon, Powerpuff Girls, Rugrats, Blue's Clues, and Harry Potter characters. Almost half of all retail toy sales come from products based on television shows and movies, such as *Scooby Doo, SpongeBob SquarePants, The Rugrats Movie, The Lion King, Batman, Spider-Man, Men in Black, Lord of the Rings,* or *Harry Potter.*

Name and character licensing has grown rapidly in recent years. Annual retail sales of licensed products in the United States and Canada have grown from only US$4 billion in 1977 to US$55 billion in 1987 and more than US$105 billion today. Licensing can be a highly profitable business for many companies. For example, Warner Brothers has turned Looney Tunes characters into one of the most sought-after licences. More than 225 licensees generate billions of dollars in retail sales of products sporting Bugs Bunny, Daffy Duck, Foghorn Leghorn, or one of the more than 100 Looney Tunes characters. Similarly, Nickelodeon has developed a stable full of hugely popular characters—such as Dora the Explorer, the Rugrats clan, and SpongeBob SquarePants. Products sporting these characters generate more than US$5 billion in annual retail sales. "When it comes to licensing its brands for consumer products, Nickelodeon has proved that it has the Midas touch," states a brand licensing expert.[30]

The fastest-growing licensing category is corporate brand licensing, as more and more for-profit and not-for-profit organizations are licensing their names to generate additional revenues and brand recognition. Coca-Cola, for example, has some

Warner Brothers has turned Looney Tunes characters into one of the world's most sought-after licences.

320 licensees in 57 countries producing more than 10 000 products, ranging from baby clothes and boxer shorts to earrings, a Coca-Cola Barbie doll, and even a fishing lure shaped like a tiny Coke can. Each year, licensees sell more than US$1 billion worth of licensed Coca-Cola products.[31]

Co-branding
The practice of using the established brand names of two different companies on the same product.

Co-Branding   Although companies have been **co-branding** products for many years, there has been a recent resurgence in co-branded products. Co-branding occurs when two established brand names of different companies are used on the same product. For example, CIBC joined forces with Air Canada to offer its CIBC Visa Aerogold card, and Nabisco joined forces with Pillsbury to create Pillsbury Oreo Bars baking mix. Ford and Eddie Bauer co-branded a sport utility vehicle—the Ford Explorer, Eddie Bauer edition. General Electric worked with Culligan to develop its Water by Culligan Profile Performance refrigerator with a built-in Culligan water filtration system. In most co-branding situations, one company licenses another company's well-known brand to use in combination with its own.

Co-branding offers many advantages. Because each brand dominates in a different category, the combined brands create broader consumer appeal and greater brand equity. Co-branding also allows a company to expand its existing brand into a category it might otherwise have difficulty entering alone. For example, by licensing its Healthy Choice brand to Kellogg, ConAgra entered the breakfast segment with a solid product. In return, Kellogg could leverage the broad awareness of the Healthy Choice name in the cereal category.

Co-branding also has limitations. Such relationships usually involve complex legal contracts and licences. Co-branding partners must carefully coordinate their advertising, sales promotion, and other marketing efforts. Finally, when co-branding, each partner must trust the other will take good care of its brand. For example, consider the marriage between Kmart and the Martha Stewart housewares brand. When Kmart declared bankruptcy, it cast a shadow on the Martha Stewart brand. In turn, when Martha Stewart was convicted of illegal financial dealings, it created negative associations for Kmart. As one Nabisco manager puts it, "Giving away your brand is a lot like giving away your child—you want to make sure everything is perfect."[32]

Brand Development

A company has four choices when it comes to developing brands. (See Figure 9.4.) It can introduce *line extensions* (existing brand names extended to new forms, sizes, and flavours of an existing product category), *brand extensions* (existing brand names extended to new product categories), *multibrands* (new brand names introduced in the same product category), or *new brands* (new brand names in new product categories).

Line extension
Using a successful brand name to introduce additional items in a given product category under the same brand name, such as new flavours, forms, colours, added ingredients, or package sizes.

Line Extensions   Line extensions occur when a company introduces additional items in a given product category under the same brand name, such as new flavours, forms, colours, ingredients, or package sizes. Thus, Danone introduced several line extensions, including new yogurt flavours, a fat-free yogurt marketed under the sub-

	Product category	
	Existing	New
Brand name Existing	Line extension	Brand extension
New	Multibrands	New brands

Figure 9.4 Brand development strategies

Pfizer Canada sells an entire line of Listerine products to its Canadian customers, meeting a wide array of their oral care needs.

brand Silhouette, a yogurt with active bacteria cultures called Activia, and large, economy-sized yogurt. And Pfizer Canada has expanded its Listerine line to include Listerine Antiseptic Mouthwash, Tartar Control Listerine Mouthwash, Cool Citrus Listerine Mouthwash, and Advanced Listerine Mouthwash. The vast majority of all new-product activity consists of line extensions.

A company might introduce line extensions as a low-cost, low-risk way to introduce new products. Or it might want to meet consumer desires for variety, to use excess capacity, or simply to command more shelf space from resellers. However, line extensions involve some risks. An overextended brand name might lose its specific meaning, or heavily extended brands can cause consumer confusion or frustration.

Another risk is that sales of an extension may come at the expense of other items in the line. For example, the original Nabisco Fig Newtons cookies have now morphed into a full line of Newtons Fruit Chewy Cookies, including Cranberry Newtons, Blueberry Newtons, and Apple Newtons. Although all are doing well, the original Fig Newton brand now seems like just another flavour. A line extension works best when it takes sales away from competing brands, not when it "cannibalizes" the company's other items.

Finally, marketers are facing unprecedented push-back from their reselling customers regarding line extensions. Shelf-space is premium real estate for retailers. Therefore, many retailers adhere to the "one-in, one-out" policy, so that if a manufacturer introduces a new product, it must remove another product (usually one of its own) from the shelf. Thus, marketers must strive to create line extensions that offer truly unique benefits to the consumer, in order to make a compelling case to have the product included in the retailer's shelf-set.

Brand extension

Using a successful brand name to launch a new or modified product in a new category.

Brand Extensions   A **brand extension** involves the use of a successful brand name to launch new or modified products in a new category. Roots, for example, has extended its brand beyond casual clothing and leather goods to categories including bedding and bath linens and accessories, camping gear and outdoor accessories, eyewear, fragrance, music, digital and wireless accessories, paper goods and pet accessories. Barbie cosmetics, Swiss Army brand sunglasses, Disney Cruise Lines, Century 21 Home Improvements, and Brinks home security systems—all are brand extensions.

A brand extension gives a new product instant recognition and faster acceptance. It also saves the high advertising costs usually required to build a new brand name. At the same time, a brand extension strategy involves some risk. Brand extensions such as Bic pantyhose, Heinz pet food, LifeSavers gum, and Clorox laundry detergent met early deaths. The extension may confuse the image of the main brand.

And if a brand extension fails, it may harm consumer attitudes toward the other products carrying the same brand name. Further, a brand name may not be appropriate to a particular new product, even if it is well made and satisfying—would you consider buying Texaco milk or Alpo chili? Companies that are tempted to transfer a brand name must research how well the brand's associations fit the new product.[33]

Multibrands   Companies often introduce additional brands in the same category. Thus, Unilever markets many different brands in many of its product categories. *Multibranding* offers a way to establish different features and appeal to different buying motives. It also allows a company to lock up more reseller shelf space.

A major drawback of multibranding is that each brand might obtain only a small market share, and none may be very profitable. The company may end up spreading its resources over many brands instead of building a few brands to a highly profitable level. These companies should reduce the number of brands they sell in a given category and set up tighter screening procedures for new brands.

New Brands   A company might believe that the power of its existing brand name is waning and a new brand name is needed. Or a company may create a new brand name when it enters a new product category for which none of the company's current brand names is appropriate. For example, Honda created the Acura brand to differentiate its luxury car from the established Honda line. Toyota created the separate Scion automobile, targeted toward GenY consumers. Japan's Matsushita uses separate names for its different families of products: Technics, Panasonic, National, and Quasar.

As with multibranding, offering too many new brands can result in a company spreading its resources too thin. And in some industries, such as consumer packaged goods, consumers and retailers have become concerned that there are already too many brands, with too few differences among them. Thus, Procter & Gamble, Frito-Lay, and other large consumer-product marketers are now pursuing *megabrand* strategies—weeding out weaker brands and focusing their marketing dollars only on brands that can achieve the number-one or number-two market share positions in their categories.

Managing Brands

Companies must manage their brands carefully. First, the brand's positioning must be continuously communicated to consumers. Major brand marketers often spend huge amounts on advertising to create brand awareness and to build preference and loyalty. For example, McDonald's spends more than US$500 million annually to promote its brand.[34]

Such advertising campaigns can help to create name recognition, brand knowledge, and maybe even some brand preference. However, the fact is that brands are not maintained by advertising but by the *brand experience*. Today, customers come to know a brand through a wide range of contacts and touchpoints. These include not only advertising but also personal experience with the brand, word of mouth, personal interactions with company people, telephone interactions, company webpages, and many others. The company must put as much care into managing these touchpoints as it does into producing its ads.

The brand's positioning will not take hold fully unless everyone in the company lives the brand. Therefore, the company needs to train its people to be consumer-centred. Even better, the company should carry on internal brand building to help employees to understand and be enthusiastic about the brand promise. Many companies go even further by training and encouraging their distributors and dealers to serve their customers well.

All of this suggests that managing a company's brand assets can no longer be left only to brand managers. Brand managers do not have enough power or scope to do all the things necessary to build and enhance their brands. Moreover, brand managers often pursue short-term results, whereas managing brands as assets calls for longer-term strategy. Thus, some companies are now setting up brand asset management teams to manage their major brands. Canada Dry and Colgate-Palmolive have appointed *brand equity managers* to maintain and protect their brands' images, associations, and quality, and to prevent short-term actions by overeager brand managers from hurting the brand. Similarly, Hewlett-Packard has appointed a senior executive in charge of the customer experience in each of its two divisions, consumer and business-to-business (B2B). Their job is to track, measure, and improve the customer relationship with Hewlett-Packard products. They report directly to the presidents of their respective divisions.

Finally, companies need to periodically audit their brands' strengths and weaknesses.[35] They should ask: Does our brand excel at delivering benefits that consumers truly value? Is the brand properly positioned? Do all of our consumer touchpoints support the brand's positioning? Do the brand's managers understand what the brand means to consumers? Does the brand receive proper, sustained support?

The brand audit may turn up brands that need to be repositioned because of changing customer preferences or new competitors. Some cases may call for completely *rebranding* a product, service, or company. The recent wave of corporate mergers and acquisitions has set off a flurry of corporate rebranding campaigns. In the fall of 2005, for example, one of the biggest rebrands in the Canadian courier and business services sector took place. The 260 business services retailers formerly known as Mail Boxes Etc., became the UPS Store. But this was nothing compared with the challenge faced by Circuit City when it acquired 874 Canadian RadioShack stores.

In March 2005, a court ruling left Circuit City Stores Inc. executives with an urgent challenge. They had just three months to develop a new brand name and identity for the chain, which was especially difficult since the court ruled that they could not link the old and new brands in future advertising. They quickly undertook market research to uncover RadioShack's brand attributes. Some they wanted to keep [friendly staff, helpful service], but others they wanted to avoid [a traditional, conservative image.] As one manager noted, "The [RadioShack] name itself sort of connotes an outdated sort of name. The idea of radios and shacks did seem a bit tired," he said. While Circuit City itself is a well-known U.S. brand, they decided not to use it in the rebranding effort because the U.S. stores are much larger than RadioShack's. After rejecting many possible names like Buzz, Live Wire, and The Verge, they settled on The Source by Circuit City. The effort has been a success and both sales and store visits are up. As Ted Matthews, known in Canada as the brand coach, says, "I think they've done a good job of coming out the door and launching a whole new fresh brand. I think they've used it as an opportunity to refresh the whole brand as well."[36]

Services Marketing

Services have grown dramatically in recent years. Service industries account for 68 percent of Canada's GDP, almost three-quarters of employment in the country, and nearly 90 percent of new job creation. Moreover, the service sector continues to grow faster than other sectors of the economy. Services are growing even faster in the world economy, making up a quarter of the value of all international trade.[37]

Service industries vary greatly. *Governments* offer services through courts, employment services, hospitals, military services, police and fire departments, postal service, and schools. *Private not-for-profit organizations* offer services through museums, charities, churches, universities, foundations, and hospitals. A large number of *business organizations* offer services—airlines, banks, hotels, insurance companies, consulting firms, medical and law practices, entertainment companies, real estate firms, retailers, and others.

Nature and Characteristics of a Service

A company must consider four special service characteristics when designing marketing programs: *intangibility*, *inseparability*, *variability*, and *perishability*. (See Figure 9.5.)

Service intangibility

A major characteristic of services—they cannot be seen, tasted, felt, heard, or smelled before they are bought.

Service intangibility means that services cannot be seen, tasted, felt, heard, or smelled before they are bought. For example, people undergoing cosmetic surgery cannot see the result before the purchase. Airline passengers have nothing but a ticket and the promise that they and their luggage will arrive safely at the intended destination, they hope at the same time. To reduce uncertainty, buyers look for "signals" of service quality. They draw conclusions about quality from the place, people, price, equipment, and communications that they can see.

Therefore, the service provider's task is to make the service tangible in one or more ways and to send the right signals about quality. One analyst calls this *evidence management*, in which the service organization presents its customers with organized, honest evidence of its capabilities. The Mayo Clinic practises good evidence management:[38]

When it comes to hospitals, it's very hard for the average patient to judge the quality of the "product." You can't try it on, you can't return it if you don't like it, and you need an advanced degree to understand it. And so, when we're considering a medical facility, most of us unconsciously turn detective, looking for evidence of competence, caring, and integrity. The world-famous Mayo Clinic doesn't leave that evidence to chance. By carefully managing a set of visual and experiential clues, Mayo offers patients and their families concrete evidence of its strengths and values. For example, staff people at the clinic are trained to act in a way that clearly signals its patient-first focus. "My doctor calls me at home to check on how I am doing," marvels one patient. "She wants to work with what is best for my schedule." Mayo's physical facilities also send the right signals. They've been carefully designed to relieve stress, offer a place of refuge, create positive distractions, convey caring and respect, signal competence, accommodate families, and make it easy to find your way around. The result? Exceptionally positive word-of-mouth and abiding customer loyalty, which have allowed Mayo Clinic to build what is arguably the most powerful brand in American health care—with very little advertising.

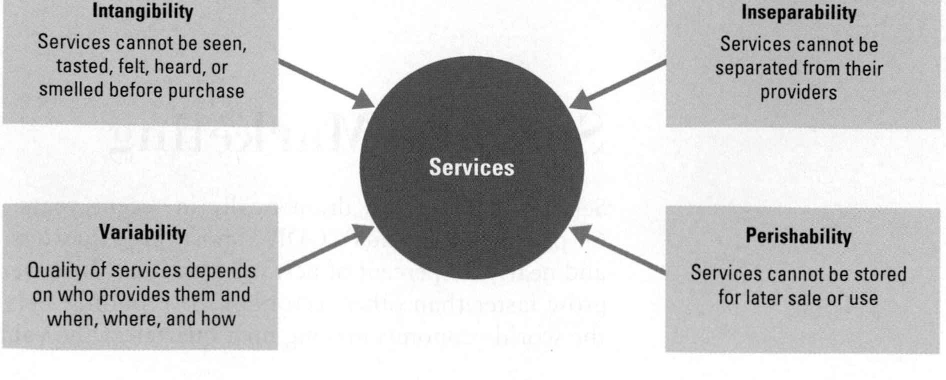

Figure 9.5 Four service characteristics

By carefully managing visual and experiential clues, Mayo Clinic offers patients concrete evidence of its strengths and values. It clearly signals that "The needs of the patient come first."

Service inseparability
A major characteristic of services—they are produced and consumed at the same time and cannot be separated from their providers.

Service variability
A major characteristic of services—their quality may vary greatly, depending on who provides them and when, where, and how.

Service perishability
A major characteristic of services—they cannot be stored for later sale or use.

Physical goods are produced, then stored, later sold, and still later consumed. In contrast, services are first sold, then produced and consumed at the same time. **Service inseparability** means that services cannot be separated from their providers, whether the providers are people or machines. If a service employee provides the service, then the employee is a part of the service. Because the customer is also present as the service is produced, *provider-customer interaction* is a special feature of services marketing. Both the provider and the customer affect the service outcome.

Service variability means that the quality of services depends on who provides them as well as when, where, and how they are provided. For example, some hotels—say, Fairmont—have reputations for providing better service than others. Still, within a given Fairmont hotel, one registration-desk employee may be cheerful and efficient, whereas another standing just a few feet away may be unpleasant and slow. Even the quality of a single Fairmont employee's service varies according to his or her energy and frame of mind at the time of each customer encounter.

Service perishability means that services cannot be stored for later sale or use. Some doctors charge patients for missed appointments because the service value existed only at that point and disappeared when the patient did not show up. The perishability of services is not a problem when demand is steady. However, when demand fluctuates, service firms often have difficult problems. For example, because of rush-hour demand, public transportation companies have to own much more equipment than they would if demand were even throughout the day. Thus, service firms often design strategies for producing a better match between demand and supply. Hotels and resorts charge lower prices in the off-season to attract more guests. And restaurants hire part-time employees to serve during peak periods.

Marketing Strategies for Service Firms

Just like manufacturing businesses, good service firms use marketing to position themselves strongly in chosen target markets. Wal-Mart promises "Always Low Prices, Always," and Home Outfitters welcomes shoppers to the "home of endless possibilities."

However, because services differ from tangible products, they often require additional marketing approaches. In a product business, products are fairly standardized and can sit on shelves waiting for customers. But in a service business, the customer and front-line service employee *interact* to create the service. Thus, service providers must interact effectively with customers to create superior value during service encounters. Effective interaction, in turn, depends on the skills of front-line service employees and on the support processes backing these employees.

The Service-Profit Chain

Service-profit chain
The chain that links service firm profits with employee and customer satisfaction.

Successful service companies focus their attention on *both* their customers and their employees. They understand the **service-profit chain**, which links service firm profits with employee and customer satisfaction. This chain consists of five links:[39]

- *Internal service quality:* superior employee selection and training, a quality work environment, and strong support for those dealing with customers, which results in …
- *Satisfied and productive service employees:* more satisfied, loyal, and hardworking employees, which results in …
- *Greater service value:* more effective and efficient customer value creation and service delivery, which results in …
- *Satisfied and loyal customers:* satisfied customers who remain loyal, repeat purchase, and refer other customers, which results in …
- *Healthy service profits and growth:* superior service firm performance.

Therefore, reaching service profits and growth goals begins with taking care of those who take care of customers. (See Real Marketing 9.2.) In fact, Starbucks CEO Howard Schultz goes so far as to say that "customers always come in second—employees matter more." The idea is that happy employees will unleash their enthusiasm on customers, creating even greater customer satisfaction. "If the battle cry of the company [is] to exceed the expectations of our customers," says Schultz, "then as managers, we [must] first exceed the expectations of our people."[40]

Internal marketing
Marketing by a service firm to train and effectively motivate its customer-contact employees and all the supporting service people to work as a team to provide customer satisfaction.

Thus, service marketing requires more than just traditional external marketing using the four Ps. Figure 9.6 shows that service marketing also requires *internal marketing* and *interactive marketing*. **Internal marketing** means that the service firm must effectively train and motivate its customer-contact employees and supporting service people to work as a *team* to provide customer satisfaction. Marketers must get everyone in the organization to be customer-centred. In fact, internal marketing must *precede* external marketing. For example, Ritz-Carlton orients its employees carefully, instils in them a sense of pride, and motivates them by recognizing and rewarding outstanding service deeds.

Interactive marketing
Marketing by a service firm that recognizes that perceived service quality depends heavily on the quality of buyer–seller interaction.

Interactive marketing means that service quality depends heavily on the quality of the buyer–seller interaction during the service encounter. In product marketing, product quality often depends little on how the product is obtained. But in services marketing, service quality depends on both the service deliverer and the quality of the delivery. Service marketers, therefore, have to master interactive marketing skills. Thus, Ritz-Carlton selects only "people who care about people" and instructs them carefully in the fine art of interacting with customers to satisfy their every need.

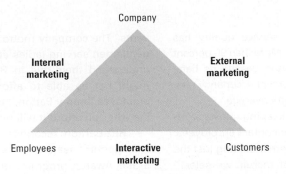

Figure 9.6 Three types of marketing in service industries

In today's marketplace, companies must know how to deliver interactions that are not only "high touch" but also "high tech." For example, customers can log on to the Charles Schwab website and access account information, investment research, real-time quotes, after-hours trading, and the Schwab learning centre. They can also participate in live online events and chat online with customer service representatives. Customers seeking more-personal interactions can contact service reps by

REAL MARKETING | 9.2

Ritz-Carlton: Taking Care of Those Who Take Care of Customers

Ritz-Carlton, a chain of luxury hotels renowned for outstanding service, caters to the top 5 percent of corporate and leisure travellers. The company's Credo sets lofty customer service goals: "The Ritz-Carlton Hotel is a place where the genuine care and comfort of our guests is our highest mission.... The Ritz-Carlton experience enlivens the senses, instils well-being, and fulfills even the unexpressed wishes and needs of our guests."

The Credo is more than just words on paper—Ritz-Carlton delivers on its promises. In surveys of departing guests, some 95 percent report that they've had a truly memorable experience. In fact, at Ritz-Carlton, exceptional service encounters have become almost commonplace. Take the experiences of Nancy and Harvey Heffner, who stayed at the Ritz-Carlton Naples, in Naples, Florida (recently rated the fourth best in the world, by *Travel & Leisure* magazine).

"The hotel is elegant and beautiful," Mrs. Heffner said, "but more important is the beauty expressed by the staff. They can't do enough to please you." When the couple's son became sick last year in Naples, the

hotel staff brought him hot tea with honey at all hours of the night, she said. When Mr. Heffner had to fly home on business for a day and his return flight was delayed, a driver for the hotel waited in the lobby most of the night.

Such personal, high-quality service has also made the Ritz-Carlton a favourite among conventioneers. "They not only treat us like kings when we hold our top-level meetings in their hotels, but we just never get any complaints," comments one convention planner. Says another, who had recently held a meeting at the Ritz-Carlton at Half Moon Bay, "The ... first-rate catering and service-oriented convention services staff [and] the Ritz-Carlton's ambiance and beauty—the elegant, Grand Dame-style lodge, nestled on a bluff between two championship golf courses overlooking the Pacific Ocean—makes a day's work there seem anything but."

Since its incorporation in 1983, Ritz-Carlton has received virtually every major award that the hospitality industry bestows. In addition, in 1992, it became the first hotel company ever to win the prestigious Malcolm Baldrige National Quality Award, which it won a *second* time in 1999. More importantly, service quality has resulted in high customer retention. More than 90 percent of Ritz-Carlton customers return. And despite its hefty room rates, the chain enjoys a 70 percent occupancy rate, almost nine points above the industry average.

Most of the responsibility for keeping guests satisfied falls to Ritz-Carlton's customer-contact employees. Thus, the hotel chain takes great care in finding just the right personnel. "We don't hire or recruit, we select," says Ritz-Carlton's director of human resources. "We want only people who care about people," notes the company's vice-president of quality. Once selected, employees are given intensive training in the art of coddling customers. New employees attend a two-day orientation, in which top management drums into them the "20 Ritz-Carlton Basics." Basic number one: "The Credo will be known, owned, and energized by all employees."

Employees are taught to do everything they can to never lose a guest. "There's no negotiating at Ritz-Carlton when it comes to solving customer problems," says the quality executive. Staff learn that *anyone* who receives a customer complaint *owns* that complaint until it's resolved (Ritz-Carlton Basic number eight). They are trained to drop whatever they're doing to help a customer—no matter what they're doing or what their department. Ritz-Carlton employees are empowered to handle problems on the spot, without consulting higher-ups. Each employee can spend up to US$2000 to redress a guest grievance. And each is allowed to break from his or her routine for as long as needed to make a guest happy. Thus, while competitors are still reading guest comment cards to learn about customer problems, Ritz-Carlton has already resolved them.

Ritz-Carlton instils a sense of pride in its employees. "You serve," they are told, "but you are not servants." The company motto states, "We are ladies and gentlemen serving ladies and gentlemen." Employees understand their role in Ritz-Carlton's success. "We might not be able to afford a hotel like this," says employee Tammy Patton, "but we can make it so people who can afford it will want to keep coming here."

Ritz-Carlton recognizes and rewards employees who perform feats of outstanding service. Under its 5-Star Awards program, outstanding performers are nominated by peers and managers, and winners receive plaques at dinners celebrating their achievements. For on-the-spot recognition, managers award Gold Standard Coupons, redeemable for items in the gift shop and free weekend stays at the hotel. Ritz-Carlton further motivates its employees with events, such as Super Sports Day, an employee talent show, and luncheons celebrating employment anniversaries and birthdays. As a result, Ritz-Carlton's employees appear to be just as satisfied as its customers. Employee turnover is less than 25 percent a year, compared with 44 percent at other luxury hotels.

Ritz-Carlton's success is based on a simple philosophy: To take care of customers, you must first take care of those who take care of customers. Satisfied employees deliver high service value, which then creates satisfied customers. Satisfied customers, in turn, create sales and profits for the company.

Sources: Quotes and other information from Duff McDonald, "Roll Out the Blue Carpet," *Business 2.0,* May 2004, pp. 53–54; Edwin McDowell, "Ritz-Carlton's Keys to Good Service," *New York Times,* March 31, 1993, p. D1; "The Ritz-Carlton, Half Moon Bay," *Successful Meetings,* November 2001, p. 40; Scott Neuman, "Relax, Put Your Feet Up," *Far Eastern Economic Review,* April 17, 2003, p. 36; Terry R. Bacon and David G. Pugh, "Ritz-Carlton and EMC: The Gold Standards in Operational Behavior," *Journal of Organizational Excellence,* Spring 2004, pp. 61–77; and the Ritz-Carlton website, www.ritzcarlton.com (accessed January 2005).

CREDO

The Ritz-Carlton Hotel is a place where the genuine care and comfort of our guests is our highest mission.
We pledge to provide the finest personal service and facilities for our guests who will always enjoy a warm, relaxed yet refined ambience.
The Ritz-Carlton experience enlivens the senses, instills well-being, and fulfills even the unexpressed wishes and needs of our guests.

THREE STEPS OF SERVICE

1
A warm and sincere greeting. Use the guest name, if and when possible.

2
Anticipation and compliance with guest needs.

3
Fond farewell. Give them a warm good-bye and use their name, if and when possible.

THE EMPLOYEE PROMISE

At The Ritz-Carlton, our Ladies and Gentlemen are the most important resource in our service commitment to our guests.
By applying the principles of trust, honesty, respect, integrity and commitment, we nurture and maximize talent to the benefit of each individual and the company.
The Ritz-Carlton fosters a work environment where diversity is valued, quality of life is enhanced, individual aspirations are fulfilled, and The Ritz-Carlton mystique is strengthened.

"We Are Ladies and Gentlemen Serving Ladies and Gentlemen"

Ritz-Carlton knows that to take care of customers, you must first take care of those who take care of customers.

phone or visit a local Schwab branch office. Thus, Schwab has mastered interactive marketing at all three levels—calls, clicks, *and* visits.

Today, as competition and costs increase, and as productivity and quality decrease, more service marketing sophistication is needed. Service companies face three major marketing tasks: They want to increase their *competitive differentiation*, *service quality*, and *productivity*.

Managing Service Differentiation

In these days of intense price competition, service marketers often complain about the difficulty of differentiating their services from those of competitors. To the extent that customers view the services of different providers as similar, they care less about the provider than the price.

The solution to price competition is to develop a differentiated offer, delivery, and image. The *offer* can include innovative features that set one company's offer apart from competitors' offers. Some hotels offer car rental, banking, and business centre services in their lobbies and high-speed Internet connections in their rooms. Airlines differentiate their offers though frequent flier reward programs and special services. For example, British Airways business- and first-class cabins offer international travellers fully flat beds and private "demi-cabins," post-flight showers, and à la carte hot breakfasts.

Service companies can differentiate their service *delivery* by having more able and reliable customer-contact people, by developing a superior physical environment in which the service product is delivered, or by designing a superior delivery process. For example, many grocery chains now offer online shopping and home delivery as a better way to shop than having to drive, park, wait in line, and tote groceries home.

Finally, service companies also can work on differentiating their *images* through symbols and branding. Royal Bank's stylized "Leo the Lion" (although you have to look hard to see it) symbolizes strength and power—desirable qualities of a large bank. Other well-known service symbols include Canadian National Railway's CN symbol, Air Canada's maple leaf, TD Canada Trust's green armchair, and Bell Canada's swirl and stylized face symbol.

British Airways offers international travellers fully flat beds and private "demi-cabins," post-flight showers, and à la carte hot breakfasts.

Managing Service Quality

One of the major ways a service firm can differentiate itself is by delivering consistently higher quality than its competitors do. Like manufacturers before them, most service industries have now joined the customer-driven quality movement. And like product marketers, service providers need to identify what target customers expect concerning service quality.

Unfortunately, service quality is harder to define and judge than is product quality. For instance, it is harder to agree on the quality of a haircut than on the quality of a hair dryer. Customer retention is perhaps the best measure of quality—a service firm's ability to hang onto its customers depends on how consistently it delivers value to them.[41]

Top service companies set high service quality standards. They watch service performance closely, both their own and that of competitors. They do not settle for merely good service; they aim for 100 percent defect-free service. A 98 percent performance standard may sound good, but using this standard, 64 000 FedEx packages would be lost each day, 10 words would be misspelled on each printed page, 400 000 prescriptions would be misfilled daily, and drinking water would be unsafe 7 days a year.[42]

Unlike product manufacturers who can adjust their machinery and inputs until everything is perfect, service quality will always vary, depending on the interactions between employees and customers. As hard as they try, even the best companies will have an occasional late delivery, burned steak, or grumpy employee. However, good *service recovery* can turn angry customers into loyal ones. In fact, good recovery can win more customer purchasing and loyalty than if things had gone well in the first place. Therefore, companies should take steps not only to provide good service every time but also to recover from service mistakes when they do occur.

The first step is to *empower* front-line service employees—to give them the authority, responsibility, and incentives they need to recognize, care about, and tend to customer needs. At Marriott, for example, well-trained employees are given the authority to do whatever it takes, on the spot, to keep guests happy. They are also expected to help management ferret out the cause of guests' problems and to inform managers of ways to improve overall hotel service and guests' comfort.

Managing Service Productivity

With their costs rising rapidly, service firms are under great pressure to increase service productivity. They can do so in several ways. They can train current employees better or hire new ones who will work harder or more skilfully. Or they can increase the quantity of their service by giving up some quality. The provider can "industrialize the service" by adding equipment and standardizing production, as in McDonald's assembly-line approach to fast-food retailing. Finally, the service provider can harness the power of technology. Although we often think of technology's power to save time and costs in manufacturing companies, it also has great—and often untapped—potential to make service workers more productive.

However, companies must avoid pushing productivity so hard that doing so reduces quality. Attempts to industrialize a service or to cut costs can make a service company more efficient in the short run. But they can also reduce its longer-run ability to innovate, maintain service quality, or respond to consumer needs and desires. In short, they can take the "service" out of service.

Additional Product Considerations

Here, we discuss two additional product policy considerations: social responsibility in product decisions and issues of international product and services marketing.

Product Decisions and Social Responsibility

Product decisions have attracted much public attention. Marketers should carefully consider public policy issues and regulations concerning acquiring or dropping products, patent protection, product quality and safety, and product warranties.

Canadian manufacturers must navigate a complex web of government departments and legislation when considering their product policies. Agriculture Canada, the Canadian Food Inspection Agency, and the Consumer Products Division of Health Canada, for example, govern food and product safety. The Competition Bureau regulates many aspects of the marketing of products. The *Competition Act*'s provisions cover pricing and advertising, not just the maintenance of a competitive marketplace. When considering a merger that would give a firm access to new products, a company has to be aware that the government may invoke the *Competition Act* if it thinks the merger would lessen competition. Companies dropping products must be aware that they have legal obligations, written or implied, to their suppliers, dealers, and customers who have a stake in the discontinued product. Companies must also obey patent laws when developing new products. A company cannot make its product illegally similar to another company's established product. Firms may also have to be aware of legislation controlled by Environment Canada and Transport Canada.

Federal statutes cover product safety (except electrical equipment), competition, labelling, and weights and measures. The *Hazardous Products Act*, for example, controls the marketing of dangerous or potentially dangerous consumer and industrial products; the *Food and Drugs Act* covers safety of cosmetics as well as food and drugs. Both acts can be found on the Department of Justice Canada website (http://canada.justice.gc.ca).[43] Provincial statutes deal with such matters as conditions of sale, guarantees, and licensing, as well as unfair business practices.

Consumers who have been injured by a defectively designed product can sue the manufacturer or dealer. The number of product liability suits has been rising, and settlements often run in the millions of dollars. This, in turn, has resulted in huge increases in the cost of product liability insurance premiums. Some companies pass these higher rates along to consumers by raising prices. Others are forced to discontinue high-risk product lines.

International Product and Services Marketing

International product and service marketers face special challenges. First, they must figure out what products and services to introduce and in which countries. Then, they must decide how much to standardize or adapt their products and services for world markets.

On the one hand, companies would like to standardize their offerings. Standardization helps a company to develop a consistent worldwide image. It also lowers manufacturing costs and eliminates duplication of research and development, advertising, and product design efforts. On the other hand, consumers around the world differ in their cultures, attitudes, and buying behaviours. And markets vary in their economic conditions, competition, legal requirements, and physical environments. Companies must usually respond to these differences by adapting their product offerings. Something as simple as an electrical outlet can create big product problems:

Those who have travelled across Europe know the frustration of electrical plugs, different voltages, and other minor annoyances of international travel.... Philips, the electrical appliance manufacturer, has to produce 12 kinds of irons to serve just its European market. The problem is that Europe does not have a universal [electrical] standard. The ends of irons bristle with different plugs for different countries. Some have three prongs, others two; prongs protrude straight or angled, round or rectangular, fat, thin, and sometimes sheathed. There are circular plug faces, squares, pentagons, and hexagons. Some are perforated and some are notched. One French plug has a niche like a keyhole. Looking for a fix? eBay.ca sells adapter plug sets for international travellers for $5 and up.[44]

Packaging also presents new challenges for international marketers. Packaging issues can be subtle. For example, names, labels, and colours may not translate easily from one country to another. A firm using yellow flowers in its logo might fare well in Canada but meet with disaster in Mexico, where a yellow flower symbolizes death or disrespect. Similarly, although Nature's Gift might be an appealing name for gourmet mushrooms in the domestic Canadian market, it would be deadly in Germany, where *gift* means poison. Packaging may also have to be tailored to meet the physical characteristics of consumers in various parts of the world. For instance, soft drinks are sold in smaller cans in Japan to fit the smaller Japanese hand better. Thus, although product and package standardization can produce benefits, companies must usually adapt their offerings to the unique needs of specific international markets.

Service marketers also face special challenges when going global. Some service industries have a long history of international operations. For example, the commercial banking industry was one of the first to grow internationally. Banks had to provide global services in order to meet the foreign exchange and credit needs of their home country clients wanting to sell overseas. In recent years, many banks have become truly global. Germany's Deutsche Bank, for example, serves more than 12 million customers in 74 countries. For its clients around the world who wish to grow globally, Deutsche Bank can raise money not only in Frankfurt but also in Zurich, London, Paris, and Tokyo.[45]

Professional and business services industries, such as accounting, management consulting, and advertising, have only recently globalized. The international growth of these firms followed the globalization of the client companies they serve. For example, as their clients began to employ worldwide marketing and advertising strategies, advertising agencies responded by globalizing their own operations. McCann-Erickson Worldwide, a large U.S. advertising agency, operates in more than 130 countries. It serves international clients such as Coca-Cola, General Motors, ExxonMobile, Microsoft, Johnson & Johnson, and Unilever in markets ranging from the United States and Canada to Korea to Kazakhstan. Moreover, McCann-Erikson is one company in the Interpublic Group of Companies, an immense, worldwide network of advertising and marketing services companies.[46]

Retailers are among the latest service businesses to go global. As their home markets become saturated, they expand into faster-growing markets abroad. Take the case of Bata, the shoe retailer, which also operates under the Athletes World Banner in Canada. It has a retail presence in more than fifty countries, operating more than 4600 retail stores. It employs more than 40 000 people and serves 1 million customers per day. It has forty production facilities across twenty-six countries and it is organized into four business units: Bata North America, located in Toronto, Bata Europe in Lausanne, Bata Asia Pacific-Africa in Singapore, and Bata Latin America, located in Mexico. Every year since 1995, Wal-Mart has entered a new country; its international division's sales grew more than 15 percent

Retailers are among the latest service businesses to go global. Here Asian shoppers buy American products in a Dutch-owned Makro store in Kuala Lumpur.

in 2003, skyrocketing to more than US$40 billion. The Japanese retailer Yaohan now operates the largest shopping centre in Asia, the twenty-one-storey Nextage Shanghai Tower in China, and Carrefour of France is the leading retailer in Brazil and Argentina.[47]

Service companies wanting to operate in other countries are not always welcomed with open arms. Whereas manufacturers usually face straightforward tariff, quota, or currency restrictions when attempting to sell their products in another country, service providers are likely to face more subtle barriers. In some cases, rules and regulations affecting international service firms reflect the host country's traditions. In others, they appear to protect the country's own fledgling service industries from large global competitors with greater resources. In still other cases, however, the restrictions seem to have little purpose other than to make entry difficult for foreign service firms.

Despite such difficulties, the trend toward growth of global service companies will continue, especially in banking, airlines, telecommunications, and professional services. Today service firms are no longer simply following their manufacturing customers. Instead, they are taking the lead in international expansion.

Reviewing the Concepts

A product is more than a simple set of tangible features. In fact, many marketing offers consist of combinations of both tangible goods and services, ranging from *pure tangible goods* at one extreme to *pure services* at the other. Each product or service offered to customers can be viewed on three levels. The *core product* consists of the core problem-solving benefits that consumers seek when they buy a product. The *actual product* exists around the core and includes the quality level, features, design, brand name, and packaging. The *augmented product* is the actual product plus the various services and benefits offered with it, such as warranty, free delivery, installation, and maintenance.

1. **Define *product* and the major classifications of products and services.**

Broadly defined, a *product* is anything that can be offered to a market for attention, acquisition, use, or consumption that might satisfy a want or need. Products include not only physical objects but also services, events, persons, places, organizations, ideas, or mixes of these entities. *Services* are products that consist of activities, benefits, or satisfactions offered for sale that are essentially intangible, such as banking, hotel, tax preparation, and home repair services.

Products and services fall into two broad classes based on the types of consumers that use them. *Consumer products*—those bought by final consumers—are usually classified according to consumer shopping habits (convenience products, shopping products, specialty products, and unsought products). *Industrial products*—purchased for further processing or for use in conducting a business—include materials and parts, capital items, and supplies and services. Other marketable entities—such as organizations, persons, places, and ideas—can also be thought of as products.

2. **Describe the decisions that companies make regarding their individual products and services, product lines, and product mixes.**

Individual product decisions involve product attributes, branding, packaging, labelling, and product support services. *Product attribute* decisions involve product quality, features, and style and design. *Branding* decisions include selecting a brand name and developing a brand strategy. *Packaging* provides many key benefits, such as protection, economy, convenience, and promotion. Package decisions often include designing *labels,* which identify, describe, and possibly promote the product. Companies also develop *product support services* that enhance customer service and satisfaction and safeguard against competitors.

Most companies produce a product line rather than a single product. A *product line* is a group of products that are related in function, customer-purchase needs, or distribution channels. *Line stretching* involves extending a line downward, upward, or in both directions to occupy a gap that might otherwise be filled by a competitor. In contrast, *line filling* involves adding items within the present range of the line. All of product lines and items offered to customers by a particular seller make up the *product mix.* The mix can be described by four dimensions: width, length, depth, and consistency. These dimensions are the tools for developing the company's product strategy.

3. **Discuss branding strategy—the decisions that companies make in building and managing their brands.**

Some analysts see brands as *the* major enduring asset of a company. Brands are more than just names and symbols—they embody everything that the product or service *means* to consumers. *Brand equity* is the positive differential effect that knowing the brand name has on customer response to the product or service. A brand with strong brand equity is a very valuable asset.

In building brands, companies need to make decisions about brand positioning, brand name selection, brand sponsorship, and brand development. The most powerful *brand positioning* builds around strong consumer beliefs and values. *Brand name selection* involves finding the best brand name based on a careful review of product benefits, the target market, and proposed marketing strategies. A manufacturer has four *brand* sponsorship options: it can launch a *manufacturer's brand* (or national brand), sell to resellers who use a *private brand*, market *licensed brands*, or join forces with another company to *co-brand* a product. A company also has four choices when it comes to developing brands. It can introduce *line extensions, brand extensions, multibrands,* or *new brands*.

Companies must build and manage their brands carefully. The brand's positioning must be continuously communicated to consumers. Advertising can help. However, brands are not maintained by advertising but by the *brand experience*. Customers come to know a brand through a wide range of contacts and interactions. The company must put as much care into managing these touchpoints as it does into producing its ads. Thus, managing a company's brand assets can no longer be left only to brand managers. Some companies are now setting up brand asset management teams to manage their major brands. Finally, companies must periodically audit their brands' strengths and weaknesses. In some cases, brands may need to be repositioned because of changing customer preferences or new competitors. Other cases may call for completely *rebranding* a product, service, or company.

4. **Identify the four characteristics that affect the marketing of a service and the additional marketing considerations that services require.**

Services are characterized by four key characteristics: they are *intangible, inseparable, variable,* and *perishable*. Each characteristic poses problems and marketing requirements. Marketers work to find ways to make the service more tangible, to increase the productivity of providers who are inseparable from their products, to standardize the quality in the face of variability, and to improve demand movements and supply capacities in the face of service perishability.

Good service companies focus attention on *both* customers and employees. They understand the *service-profit chain*, which links service firm profits with employee and customer satisfaction. Services marketing strategy calls not only for external marketing but also for *internal marketing* to motivate employees and *interactive marketing* to create service delivery skills among service providers. To succeed, service marketers must create *competitive differentiation*, offer high *service quality*, and find ways to increase *service productivity*.

5. Discuss two additional product issues: socially responsible product decisions and international product and services marketing.

Marketers must consider two additional product issues. The first is *social responsibility*. These include public policy issues and regulations involving acquiring or dropping products, patent protection, product quality and safety, and product warranties. The second involves the special challenges facing international product and service marketers. International marketers must decide how much to standardize or adapt their offerings for world markets.

Reviewing the Key Terms

Brand   340
Brand equity   348
Brand extension   355
Business product   332
Co-branding   354
Consumer product   330
Convenience product   332
Interactive marketing   360
Internal marketing   360
Line extension   354
Packaging   341
Private brand (or store brand)   351
Product   328

Product line   345
Product mix (or product assortment)   346
Product quality   336
Service   328
Service inseparability   359
Service intangibility   358
Service perishability   359
Service-profit chain   360
Service variability   359
Shopping product   332
Social marketing   335
Specialty product   332
Unsought product   332

Discussing the Concepts

1. Is Microsoft's Windows XP Professional operating software a product or a service? Describe the core, actual, and augmented levels of this software offering.

2. What is a brand? Describe the value of branding for both the buyer and seller using one of Canada's top brands, such as Air Canada, Bell Canada, Canadian Tire, Cirque de Soleil, Jean Coutu, McCain, Petro-Canada, Rona, Roots, RBC, Telus, Tim Hortons, Shoppers Drug Mart, TD Canada Trust, or WestJet.

3. Explain why brand equity is important to the seller. What is the difference between brand equity and brand value?

4. What are the three levels of brand positioning discussed in this chapter? In which level would you place the following ad headline for the Canadian Army: "One Army, One Team, One Vision"? Why?

5. Merrill Lynch (ML) is one of the world's leading financial management and advisory companies (see www.ml.com). Do ML's financial advising activities meet the four special characteristics of a service? Explain.

6. What are the five links in the service chain? Why is the service-profit concept so important to service firms?

Applying the Concepts

1. Products and services fall into two broad classifications: consumer and business-to-business. They are classified further by how customers go about buying them. Go to the five websites listed below and identify each product or service as either consumer or business-to-business and then by subtype.
   - www.electroluxusa.com
   - http://looneytunes.warnerbros.com
   - www.leoburnett.com
   - www.armee.forces.gc.ca/lf/English/6_1.asp?
   - www.google.com

2. Using the six desirable qualities that a good brand name should possess, create a brand name for a personal care product that has the following positioning statement:

   "Intended for X-Games sports participants and enthusiasts, _____ is a deodorant that combines effective odour protection with an enduring and seductive fragrance that will enhance your romantic fortunes."

3. Assume you are the marketing director for a snowboard manufacturer that holds a 45 percent share of the men's 18- to 29-year-old segment. The company is thinking about extending the brand by developing a snowboard and related sports apparel line to be targeted toward women ages 18 to 29. Argue for or against such an extension.

Focus on Ethics

As an act of social responsibility and to avoid potential problems, many companies sponsor product advisory committees. Comprising company personnel, consumer advocates, legislative and regulatory officials, and channel intermediaries, these groups meet frequently to review and comment on new products, services, and practices that their sponsoring firms are exploring. A real benefit of these meetings is that the firm often gains valuable insights into important concerns and problems before making a significant investment or market launch.

1. Are such advisory committees important for a company? What are the important advantages and drawbacks?

2. Is such an activity more appropriate for a product firm than for a service firm?

3. What sponsoring company personnel should be assigned to such a committee? What noncompany people?

Focus on Technology

According to its website, "eBay's mission is to provide a global trading platform where practically anyone can trade practically anything." Since it was founded in 1995, eBay has created the most visited Internet site in the world. On any given day, you can find millions of members reviewing, bidding on, and buying the hundreds of thousands of items listed on eBay. Members can purchase an item in an auction or at a fixed price. eBay focuses on a community of members, both buyers and sellers. It provides many features that enhance the trading experience. One of the more important ones is the eBay Feedback feature. This feature captures, in few words and symbols, the "reputation" of the members. Additional online services include convenient payment features and an assortment of tools for buyers, sellers, and developers. Go to www.ebay.com, take a tour of the site, and then respond to the following questions:

1. What is the service that eBay provides it members?

2. How has eBay differentiated itself from competitors?

3. Is the power of the eBay Feedback feature more fact or fiction?

Video Case
Mayo Clinic

Founded as the first medical clinic where doctors worked together to diagnose and treat patients, Mayo Clinic is a facility to which people travel from all over the world seeking advice and treatment. The clinic's patient-centred services ensure that every customer who walks through the door leaves feeling confident about her or his health care. As a non-profit organization, the clinic has a goal to provide the best care to every patient every day through integrated clinical practice, education, and research.

As Mayo Clinic expands into new markets, the key to maintaining the brand and building brand equity is providing the consistently high-quality, patient-focused services consumers have come to expect. The payoff is exceptionally positive word of mouth and true customer loyalty, which allow Mayo Clinic to build a powerful brand with very little advertising.

After watching the video featuring Mayo Clinic, answer the following questions about product and service strategies.

1. How does branding a service differ from branding a product? How has Mayo Clinic taken these differences into account?

2. How does the clinic manage the four service characteristics? How does the clinic manage service quality?

3. How does Mayo Clinic reinforce its brand image without advertising?

4. Mayo Clinic has licensed its name for limited uses, including branded content on various websites. In addition, the clinic has lent its name to several publications, including the *Mayo Clinic Williams-Sonoma Cookbook*. What are the risks Mayo Clinic assumes with licensing and co-branding efforts? What are the benefits?

Online Media Resources

Video Short
Log on to your Companion Website at **www.pearsoned.ca/kotler** to view the video segment related to the Video Case above.

CBC ⊕ CBC Video Case
Please refer to Appendix 2 to read a CBC Video Case for this chapter, and log on to your Companion Website at **www.pearsoned.ca/kotler** to view the corresponding video segment.

Case Pilot
Log on to your Companion Website at **www.pearsoned.ca/kotler** to sharpen your case analysis skills and take the Case Pilot Challenge!

Company Case
Converse: We Love You, Chucks!

The first Olympic basketball team wore them; the McGill University lists them as one of their key sponsors in their Corporate Partnership program; they dominated the basketball courts—amateur and professional—for more than forty years; Dr. J made them famous; Kurt Cobain died in them. What are they? Converse All Stars—more particularly the famous Chuck Taylor All Stars, known around the world as Chucks.

Compared with today's marvels of performance engineering, Chucks are very basic shoes. Rubber covered toes, high-top canvas lace-ups in black, white, navy, and red—these were the major characteristics of Chucks. But then again, compared with the high-priced modern marvels, Chucks are downright affordable—about $59.99 (see one Canadian outlet at **www.bagginsshoes.com/chucks-shop.html** for a full range of colours, styles, and prices). That should warm the hearts and pocketbooks of parents everywhere.

Converse invented basketball shoes, and by the mid-1970s, 70 to 80 percent of basketball players still wore Converse. But today the company's market share dwindled has to only about 1.35 percent of the total athletic shoe market. In fact, Converse is no longer an independent company. Nike bought it in 2003 for US$305 million. The question is: What will Nike do with Converse? Before dealing with that question, let's look at Converse's history.

Converse was founded in 1908 in North Reading, Massachusetts, by Marquis. In 1917, the company introduced a canvas high top called the All Star. By 1923, it was renamed the Chuck Taylor, after a semiprofessional basketball player from Akron, Ohio. After his basketball career ended, Charles "Chuck" Taylor became an aggressive member of the Converse sales force. He drove throughout the Midwest, stopping at playgrounds to sell the high tops to players. Some consider Taylor to be the original Phil Knight, Nike's CEO, who also started out selling his shoes at track meets from the back of his van. Throughout the '30s, '40s, '50s and '60s, Chucks were *the* shoes to have.

By the early 1980s, with a secure hold on the basketball shoe market (it thought), Converse branched out into other athletic shoe lines. It introduced a tennis shoe endorsed by Jimmy Connors and Chris Evert Lloyd. It also introduced a running shoe. In 1984, Converse was the only sporting goods company sponsoring the Olympics.

These moves appeared to be successful. Sales in 1983 increased by 21 percent to US$209 million; sales of running shoes increased by 73 percent. Market observers attributed the success to new materials and designs. For example, the top-of-the-line running shoes featured stabilizing bars designed to reduce knee injuries. In addition, the company brought out its first biomechanically designed basketball shoe, which offered better support and flexibility.

By 1986, however, Converse's fortunes had taken a turn for the worse, and it was acquired by consumer products maker and retailer Interco for approximately US$132 million. By the late 1980s, Converse had been overtaken by a host of competitors. In 1989, the top four athletic shoe companies were Nike with a 26 percent market share, Reebok with 23 percent, L.A. Gear with 13 percent, and Converse with 5 percent. Nike and Reebok had jockeyed for several years over the number-one spot, with both claiming a performance positioning. While no one was really looking, L.A. Gear

came into the market with a fashion appeal and scooped up sales. Attempting to meet the Air Jordan/Nike challenge head-on, Converse introduced The Magic line, named for L.A. Lakers guard Magic Johnson. It's strategy revolved around price. Magics were US$80, whereas some high-tech shoes sold for as much as US$175. Marketing managers at Converse thought that parents wouldn't pay that much. And kids would like the shoes because they were good enough for Magic Johnson. Strangely, while Nike was grabbing basketball shoe sales at a rapid clip, Converse was still the official shoe of the NBA, which gave it the right to use the NBA logo in its advertising.

Endorsement-wise, the '80s decade was a professional athlete's dream. Companies were signing up major stars and paying big, big bucks. Nike had the largest stable with players, including the likes of Bo Jackson, Charles Barkley, Shaquille O'Neal, and Michael Jordan. Reebok focused its ads on performance. Converse had Larry Bird (Boston Celtics), "Dr. J" Julius Irving (Philadelphia 76ers), Larry Johnson (Charlotte Hornets), and, of course, Magic. L.A. Gear also had athletic endorsers—prime among them Joe Montana (San Francisco 49ers). But there were others—Kareem Abdul-Jabar, Akeem Alajuwan, and Karl Malone.

By 1993, an ailing Converse had changed its positioning strategy. Instead of focusing on basketball and Chucks, it aimed at capitalizing on an image that was both sexy and streetwise. One ad showed a woman lying on a table while the camera panned down her body to show that she was wearing a pair of Converse shoes, with a Converse tattoo on her ankle. Another ad, entitled "Ugly," featured a mean-looking guy barking into the camera: "There are a lot more of what you call ugly people in the world than beautiful people. We don't have airbrushed bodies ... and we don't want them. We don't want to live in a beer commercial. The point is not to be beautiful ... the point is to be you!" These ads were considered edgy and provocative, and they targeted a new market segment that was more interested in fashion. Ad agency creative director Rick Herstek commented that the ads were what the target market was looking for; that they weren't supposed to appeal to the mainstream; and that their customers (Converse types?) had a higher shock threshold.

In this campaign, nothing was sacred. Even the venerable Chuck Taylor All Star shoe was dissociated from basketball shoes and given new life as a fashion statement. Initially, the All Stars didn't need advertising to become fashionable. Candy Pratts, fashion director of shoes and accessories at Vogue, said, "It's unbelievable. It's Converse's moment. It's the case of what is old is new. They work with today's fashion of loose-fitting, flowing dresses." She used high-top canvas sneakers on models in numerous layouts. The best part, according to Candy, was that this trend didn't come from advertising, but came from the kids on the street.

But Converse needed more. In 1992, it had sales of only US$215 million and a meagre 3.6 percent market share. In addition, it had a cost issue. For decades, Converse was "Made in the U.S.A." By the early 1990s, the cost of manufacturing the shoes in the United States was simply too great. Given its lower prices and higher costs, Converse's profit margins were too thin to support the brand advertising and marketing. With real sadness, Converse closed its U.S. plants and contracted for production of shoes with a sourcing firm in India. Management admitted that it had clung to the U.S. production statement for too long. It had believed for years that the U.S. claim gave it a competitive advantage over Nike and Reebok—especially when the scandals broke about labour conditions in Nike's Southeast Asian plants.

Things continued to worsen. In 1996, Converse had to restructure because of poor 1995 sales. The company cut 594 jobs from a little more than 2000 and reorganized its product into four categories: basketball, athletic-leisure, cross-training, and children's. (Notice that there are no tennis or running shoes, although Converse had once been big in those areas.) To boost its basketball shoes, Converse put the famous Chuck Taylor signature patch on a new line of performance wear—the All Star 2000 collection.

Encouraged by the successful relaunch of the All Star 2000, the company chose to launch another new line called Dr. J 2000. A remake of a '70s shoe, it was backed by heavy advertising. Dr. J was chosen because kids told Converse researchers that Dr. J was cool enough to have a shoe. The campaign tagline was "Take the Soul to the Hole," and ads consisted of a cartoon Julius Irving performing his famous moves to a Stevie Wonder soundtrack. Unfortunately, the Dr. J 2000 produced disappointing results.

At the turn of the century, nostalgia was in. Jimi Hendrix was on *Rolling Stone* and the VW bug was a hot-selling car. Consumers were looking for "retro," so companies were redesigning classic products. And no athletic shoe was more classic than Chucks. So Converse introduced an updated black shoe, the EZ Chucks.

In 2000, Converse also introduced a line of shoes for skateboarders. Street kids had begun wearing Converse because of their affordability, and Converse picked up the counterculture market segment. The company became a favourite of the antiestablishment, anticorporate crowd for continuing to make its shoes in the United States. It also appealed to the antiflash group, tired of polyester and synthetic, Michael Jordan–endorsed shoes. This segment wanted "antibrands" reflecting its antiglobalization perspective. Molly Ringwald's record-store clerk in *Pretty in Pink* wore Chucks, as did Kurt Cobain when he committed suicide.

Converse was hanging in, but only by the skin of its teeth. In 2001, the company had 180 employees and sales of US$185 million. But Converse had global brand recognition and strong brand equity in the market; it was well known. The question was, "Could the company make the products to back up its reputation?" Enter Nike and the buyout.

Initially, Nike left Converse management alone to implement its own business strategy. But Nike did help them with advertising dollars. After nearly a decade-long absence from TV advertising, Converse produced ads with the tagline "The first school." The focus was on basketball, not famous players. The ads featured a basketball being dribbled and shot, but no player. They were "narrated" by Mos Def. "Before Mr. Taylor taught the world to play. Before fibreglass. Before parquet. Before the word 'doctor' was spelled with a J. And ballrooms were ball courts where renaissance played. Before the hype and before the dunk. After the rhythm, but before the funk. Before the money and before the fame. Before new and old school. Before school had a name. There was only the ball and the soul of the game." The ad ended with shots of the Converse logo or the Chuck Taylor All Star.

So, back to the original question. What will Nike do with Converse? Some observers believe that Converse should become a second-tier brand. Nike could use Converse to sell millions and millions of shoes in Wal-Mart and Target—a sort of "Sam Walton meets Chuck Taylor" scenario. Another option would be to position Converse as a fashion statement. The old school ad is working; sales are up. This could be a golden opportunity for Nike to get into the "classics" business, where it could do special makeups in different colours and styles to continually refresh the line. People like retro shoes. A third possibility is to position Converse as a performance shoe. Nike has the technology, dollars, and market clout to try this.

But why take a classic brand with global recognition to Wal-Mart? Once there, it's not a Chuck any more. It's a discount shoe. And why take a basketball shoe and sell it short as a fashion statement? Fashions come and fashions go. Why take that chance? Finally, why would Nike create a competing in-house performance brand? Wouldn't Nike just be taking sales from itself?

What do you think Nike should do with the Converse brand?

Questions for Discussion

1. What are the core, actual, and augmented product benefits of the Converse Chuck?

2. When Converse sourced production of its shoes to India, it entered into a licensing arrangement. What are the benefits and negatives of that action? Do you think it has helped or hurt the company? The brand?

3. Converse and Chucks are great brands—known around the globe. What do these brands stand for today? What are the sources of their brand equity?

4. What should Nike do? Should it go second tier with Converse, position it as a fashion statement, develop it as a performance brand, or something else? Defend your position.

Sources: Brian Bagot, "Shoeboom!" *M&MD*, June 1990, p. 89; Kevin Goldman, "Converse Sneaker Seeks Statement of Fashion Instead of Foul Shots," *Wall Street Journal*, May 6, 1993, p. B8; Jennifer Laabs, "Converse Will Restructure and Cut Jobs," *Personnel Journal*, January 1996, p. 12; Bernhard Warner and David Gianatasio, "Erving Back on Air as Converse Rolls 'J 2000'," *Brandweek*, January 27, 1997, p. 9; Maureen Tkacik, "Leading the News: Nike to Swoosh Up Old-Line Converse for $305 Million," *Wall Street Journal*, July 10, 2003, p. A3; Lisa van der Pool and David Gianatasio, "Converse Harkens Back to Roots in New Campaign," *Adweek*, August 4, 2003, p. 10; Hilary Cassidy, "Shoe Companies Use Body and Sole to Track Down Sales," *Brandweek*, June 21, 2004, p. S.50.

CHAPTER 10

New-Product Development and Life-Cycle Strategies

The new organizer

NOKIA
6200

AFTER STUDYING THIS CHAPTER, YOU SHOULD BE ABLE TO

1. explain how companies find and develop new-product ideas

2. list and define the steps in the new-product development process

3. describe the stages of the product life cycle

4. describe how marketing strategies change during the product's life cycle

Previewing the Concepts

In the previous chapter, you learned how marketers manage individual brands and entire product mixes. In this chapter, we'll look into two additional product topics: developing new products and managing products through their life cycles. New products are the lifeblood of an organization. However, new-product development is risky, and many new products fail. So, the first part of this chapter lays out a process for finding and growing successful new products. Once introduced, marketers want their products to enjoy a long and happy life. In the second part of the chapter, you'll see that every product passes through several life-cycle stages and that each stage poses new challenges requiring different marketing strategies and tactics.

For openers, consider Nokia. Nokia's prolific new-product development process has helped it to dominate the fiercely competitive mobile communications industry. But at Nokia, new-product development isn't something that happens just in the company's R&D labs. As you'll see, innovation is a part of Nokia's very culture—something Nokia calls "renewal."

As workers quietly eat lunch in the cafeteria at Nokia House, a slide projector flips from pictures of summer cottages in Rauhalahti to snapshots of someone's favourite Finnish hound. Taken with camera phones by some of the 1500 employees who work at Nokia's headquarters in Finland, the pictures are part of an internal corporate competition that rewards staff creativity.

These photographs won't ever grace the cover of *National Geographic*. But they do illustrate Nokia's sharpest insight: creativity and innovative new products don't begin and end on an R&D lab bench. A long list of Nokia's innovative firsts came from the most unlikely of places. For example, the first user-changeable handset cover. Nokia engineer Aulis Perttula invented it after watching some of his colleagues customize their phones with car paint. Predictive text? Stephen Williams, a junior Nokia applications designer, suggested it after seeing people with disabilities make good use of it on their PCs.

Such firsts are why the venerable Scandinavian giant, founded in 1865, today has annual sales of approximately US$36 billion across 130 countries and has been way out in front for most of the mobile-phone industry's short history. Nokia sells five phones every second. Its global market share, 38 percent, is greater than that of its three nearest rivals combined. But Nokia isn't just the world's *biggest* mobile-phone company. It's also the most *innovative*. In an industry that's all about exciting new products, Nokia has created a culture where innovation is built into the way the company operates. Nokia even has a watchword for its culture of continuous innovation—renewal.

When it comes to new products, Nokia has its foot on the accelerator. It has almost tripled the launch of new products in the past four years. Why? Because peddling the same old goods to the same old customers simply doesn't work in this fast-changing, fiercely competitive business. Nokia has to keep churning out a steady stream of good new products. That means that the company's real business isn't phones, it's innovation.

At Nokia, innovation isn't an accident—it goes to the company's very core. Nokia is a company that refuses to grow big, grow old, or grow slow. Its new product development philosophy is simple: Small, nimble, creative units are much more likely to bubble up new ideas. So Nokia has organized itself into autonomous units, which are then backed with cost-effective central services. In other words, the company has built innovation into its organization.

For example, recently Nokia's Mobile Phone division splintered itself into nine smaller, independent business units, furthering its ability to explore completely new areas, such as entertainment and imaging. Each unit taps into Nokia's central research lab for basic technology and product design support and hands over end products to a shared operations and logistics group. But each independent team is a profit-and-loss centre, with the autonomy to create its own business model, conduct its own advanced R&D and marketing, and draft its own product road maps. "Big companies lose sensitivity," says a senior Nokia executive. "People need to feel that they can make a difference. And they need to have the power to make their ideas happen. [By allowing teams the space they need to dig deeper into their area of interest,] we've created a small-company soul inside a big-company body."

The end goal is innovation, and Nokia creates new products at a head-spinning pace. In part, that's a result of the extraordinary intellectual and technical resources that Nokia invests in new product development. The company boasts an annual R&D budget of US$3 billion, and 40 percent of its 52 000 employees, who work worldwide, are involved in R&D. Most Nokia business units have at least three R&D sites.

But just as important is the emphasis that Nokia puts on continuous development. "It's a combination of putting people in the right environment to generate ideas and giving them the power to make those ideas happen," says the executive. Nokia makes a healthy habit of giving its people fresh challenges in completely new areas. Job rotation is routine, even for senior managers. Lawyers have become country managers. Network engineers have moved into handset design. The goal is to bring new thinking to familiar problems associated with new product development or building market awareness.

In 1998, for example, awareness of the brand in Canada hovered around 60 percent. Through innovative campaigns, however, it grew to 90 percent by 2005. Grace Belmonte, Nokia's Canadian director of marketing, achieved this benchmark by putting products in the hands of consumers, especially youth, and getting them to interact with the products and their advertising. Recent campaigns included having people text message to vote for their favourite snowboarder during the FIS Snowboard World Championships, held in Whistler, and enabling customers to change the colour of the lights on a dazzling Christmas tree located at a busy intersection in downtown Montreal, again by text messaging.

Nokia mines outside sources as well as tapping its internal people. For example, to find fresh outside thinking, Nokia has set up Insight & Foresight teams that seek out new technologies, new business models, and promising entrepreneurs beyond Nokia's walls.

To stay atop the heap in the mobile communications industry, Nokia will need a constant flow of innovative new products that serve the needs, preferences, and lifestyles of its customers. But the Finnish company has been practising renewal for a lifetime: In its history, it has gone from manufacturing paper to making rubber boots, then raincoats, then hunting rifles, and then consumer electronics, until finally betting the farm on connecting people, whether through mobile phones or network technologies. It's all part of an ongoing emphasis on renewal.[1]

A company has to be good at developing and managing new products. Every product seems to go through a life cycle—it is born, goes through several phases, and eventually dies as newer products come along that better serve consumer needs. This product life cycle presents two major challenges: First, because all products eventually decline, a firm must be good at developing new products to replace aging ones (the challenge of *new-product development*). Second, the firm must be good at adapting its marketing strategies in the face of changing tastes, technologies, and competition as products pass through life-cycle stages (the challenge of *product life-cycle strategies*). We first look at the problem of finding and developing new products and then at the problem of managing them successfully over their life cycles.

New-Product Development Strategy

New-product development
The development of original products, product improvements, product modifications, and new brands through the firm's own R&D efforts.

Given the rapid changes in consumer tastes, technology, and competition, companies must develop a steady stream of new products and services. A firm can obtain new products in two ways. One is through *acquisition*—by buying a whole company, a patent, or a licence to produce someone else's product. The other is through **new-product development** in the company's own research-and-development department. By *new products* we mean original products, product improvements, product modifications, and new brands that the firm develops through its own research-and-development efforts. In this chapter, we concentrate on new-product development.

New-product development is the lifeblood of many firms, and Canadians have had a long history as inventors in this process. McIntosh apples, Pablum, frozen fish, and instant mashed potatoes are food products that all originated in Canada. Canadians are responsible for developing such sports and leisure activities as basketball, five-pin bowling, table hockey, Laser sail boats and Laser racing, and Trivial Pursuit. Many Canadian inventors spawned entire industries, such as is the case of Reginald Fessenden, born near Sherbrooke, Quebec, who invented amplitude modulation (AM) radio and transmitted his first broadcast in 1900. Charles Fenerty, with his ability to make paper from wood pulp, founded that industry. Modern air travel was made possible by another Canadian, Wallace Rupert Turnbull, who developed the variable-pitch propeller. Grahame Ferguson, Roman Kroitor, and Robert Kerr launched IMAX in 1968. James Gosling, currently a VP at Sun Microsystems, earned his BSc in Computer Science at the University of Calgary in 1977 and did the original design of the Java programming language. Mike Lazaridis founded Research in Motion (RIM), best known for the BlackBerry, while he was a student in 1984. Dr. Frank Gunston, of Brandon, Manitoba, may have been one of the most philanthropic inventors. After developing and building a total knee-joint replacement, he decided not to patent his invention. This made it freely available to manufacturers and allowed patients needing the joint to benefit quickly from the technology and walk without pain.

Innovation can be very risky. RCA lost more than US$580 million on its SelectaVision videodisc player; Texas Instruments lost a staggering US$660 million before withdrawing from the home computer business; and WebTV lost US$725 million before it was shut down. Other costly product failures from sophisticated companies include Roots Air (the airline that licensed the Roots brand), Eagle Snacks (Anheuser-Busch), Zap Mail electronic mail (FedEx), Polarvision instant movies (Polaroid), and Arch Deluxe sandwiches (McDonald's).[2]

New products continue to fail at a disturbing rate. One source estimates that more than 90 percent of all new products fail within two years. Another study suggested that of the staggering 25 000 new consumer food, beverage, beauty, and health care products to hit the market each year, only 40 percent will be around five years later. Moreover, failure rates for new industrial products may be as high as 30 percent.[3]

Why do so many new products fail? There are several reasons. Although an idea may be good, the market size may have been overestimated. Perhaps the actual product was not designed as well as it should have been. Or maybe it was incorrectly positioned in the market, priced too high, or advertised poorly. A high-level executive might push a favourite idea despite poor marketing research findings. Sometimes the costs of product development are higher than expected, and sometimes competitors fight back harder than expected. However, the reasons behind some new-product failures seem pretty obvious. Try the following on for size:[4]

> Strolling the aisles at Robert McMath's New Product Showcase and Learning Center is like finding yourself in some nightmare version of a supermarket. There's Gerber food for adults (puréed sweet-and-sour pork and chicken Madeira), Hot Scoop microwaveable ice cream sundaes, Premier smokeless cigarettes, and Miller Clear Beer. Most of the 80 000 products on display were abject flops. Behind each of them are squandered dollars and hopes.
>
> McMath, the genial curator of this Smithsonian of consumerism, gets lots of laughs when he asks his favourite question, "What were they thinking?" Some companies failed because the attached trusted brand names to something totally out of character. For example, when you hear the name Ben-Gay, you immediately think of the way Ben-Gay cream sears and stimulates your skin. Can you imagine swallowing Ben-Gay aspirin? Or how would you feel about quaffing a can of Exxon fruit punch or Kodak quencher? Other misbegotten attempts to stretch a good name include Cracker Jack cereal, Smucker's premium ketchup,

Visiting the New Product Showcase and Learning Center is like finding yourself in some nightmare version of a supermarket. Each product failure represents squandered dollars and hopes.

and Fruit of the Loom laundry detergent. Looking back, what *were* they thinking? You can tell that some innovative products were doomed as soon as you hear their names: Toaster Eggs. Cucumber antiperspirant spray. Health-Sea sea sausage. Look of Buttermilk shampoo. Really, what were they thinking?

So companies face a problem—they must develop new products, but the odds weigh heavily against success. In all, to create successful new products, a company must understand its consumers, markets, and competitors and develop products that deliver superior value to customers. It must carry out strong new-product planning and set up a systematic *new-product development process* for finding and growing new products. Figure 10.1 shows the eight major steps in this process.

Idea Generation

Idea generation
The systematic search for new-product ideas.

The new-product development process starts with **idea generation**. A study by two Canadian researchers at the John Molson School at Concordia University, Ulrike de

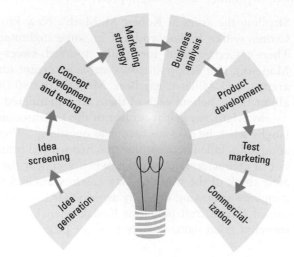

Figure 10.1 Major stages in new-product development

Bretani and Susan Reid, suggest that idea generation differs depending on whether it is an incremental new product being developed (an incremental new product is one that is similar to products that proceeded it) or a discontinuous new product being developed (a discontinuous new product is a new to the world innovation that is unlike previous products). For incremental new products, structured problems or opportunities are laid out at the organizational level and individuals are assigned to clear information-gathering tasks. With discontinuous innovations, however, individuals in boundary-spanning roles work to understand emerging trends with little or no direction from the organization. It is these individuals who act as gatekeepers, determining when and if the information will be shared with the organization.[5]

A company typically has to generate many ideas in order to find a few good ones that align its competencies and capabilities to create and launch the product. New product ideas must also fit with the strategic direction the firm wants to take and the needs of the markets it wants to serve. According to one well-known management consultant, "For every 1000 ideas, only 100 will have enough commercial promise to merit a small-scale experiment, only 10 of those will warrant substantial financial commitment, and of those, only a couple will turn out to be unqualified successes." His conclusion? "If you want to find a few ideas with the power to enthrall customers, foil competitors, and thrill investors, you must first generate hundreds and potentially thousands of unconventional strategic ideas."[6]

Major sources of new-product ideas include internal sources and external sources, such as customers, competitors, distributors and suppliers, and others.

Internal Idea Sources

Using *internal sources*, the company can find new ideas through formal research and development. It can pick the brains of its executives, scientists, engineers, manufacturing staff, and salespeople. Some companies have developed successful "intrapreneurial" programs that encourage employees to think up and develop new-product ideas. For example, 3M's well-known "15 percent rule" allows employees to spend 15 percent of their time "bootlegging"—working on projects of personal interest, whether or not those projects directly benefit the company.

Companies sometimes look for creative innovation approaches that overcome barriers to the free flow of new product ideas. For example, firms like Eureka! Ranch—a well-known "new-product hatchery"—employ both "method" and "madness" in helping companies to jumpstart their new-product idea-generation process. (See Real Marketing 10.1.)

External Idea Sources

Good new-product ideas also come from watching and listening to *customers*. The company can analyze customer questions and complaints to find new products that better solve consumer problems. Company engineers or salespeople can meet with and work alongside customers to get suggestions and ideas. The company can conduct surveys or focus groups to learn about consumer needs and wants.

Heinz did just that when its researchers approached children, who consume more than half of the ketchup sold, to find out what would make ketchup more appealing to them. The answer: change the colour. So, Heinz developed and launched EZ Squirt, green ketchup that comes in a squeezable bottle targeted at kids. Blastin' Green ketchup was a smash hit, so Heinz followed up with an entire rainbow of EZ Squirt colours, including Funky Purple, Passion Pink, Awesome Orange, Totally Teal, and Stellar Blue. The EZ Squirt bottle's special nozzle also emits a thin ketchup stream, "so tykes can autograph their burgers (or squirt someone across the table, though Heinz neglects to mention that)." In all, the new line earned the company a 5 percent increase in sales in the first year after hitting the grocery shelf.[7]

Eureka! Ranch: Method and Madness in Finding New-Product Ideas

*H*aving trouble thinking up the next hot new-product idea? Try a visit to Eureka! Ranch. For $100 000 to $150 000, you can send a dozen key marketing managers to loosen up, have some fun, and get the creative juices flowing. Located on 32 hectares, with a sand volleyball court, a water sports lake, and a three-hole golf course, Eureka! Ranch seems more like an executive resort than a new-product hatchery. But Eureka! Ranch isn't just about relaxing and having fun. Instead, it's all about the very serious business of creating new product ideas.

Founded by Doug Hall, a former Procter & Gamble "Master Marketing Inventor," and a consultant who has been featured on the CBC's *Venture* programs, the

Eureka! Ranch combines creative passion with a more systematic process and real-world data. But along with the scientific method, there's still a healthy portion of madness thrown into the brew.

ranch seems at first to be sheer madness. Consider this account:

Executives from Gardetto's, a snack foods company, stream through the doors of Eureka! Ranch. A two-man zydeco band cranks out early morning Cajun tunes. Amid the high-energy music, Doug Hall and his staff greet their visitors with laughs, handshakes, and platters of muffins, bagels, and other breakfast goodies. Hall, the opposite of Wall Street chic, in a blue Hawaiian shirt and faded jeans, soon gathers his clients in the centre of the living room and welcomes everyone. A large blanket-covered mound lurks near his bare feet. After a brief introduction, in which he notes, "Today, reality isn't relevant," Hall rips the blanket off, revealing a pile of Nerf guns. With a commando yell, he grabs a foam assault rifle and starts firing away at the momentarily shocked participants. In an instant, however, they too join the battle, blasting away at one another in a frenzy of multicoloured projectiles and screams. Let the games begin.

But there's method to the madness in Eureka! Ranch's intensive multi-day sessions. Doug Hall, once described as "a combination of Bill Gates, Ben Franklin, and Bozo the Clown," is dedicated to helping participants throw off the self-imposed constraints that too often stifle creativity in a corporate conference room. The result: breakthrough ideas and strategies for new products and services.

At Eureka! Ranch, fast-paced play and idea-generating zaniness open the flood gates for new ideas. It starts with brainstorming exercises that expand people's minds and generate new ideas around the client's problem. No idea is too far-fetched or impractical on the first day, and everything gets written down. By the time they sit down to a gourmet dinner at the ranch, clients have typically spawned some 1500 to 2000 ideas. Only after dinner do the participants start judging the fruits of their fun. For the Gardetto's team, ideas like Gar-Chia—a Chia-pet-like snack that expands in water—get tossed. But other ideas receive numerous votes of support. At 11 p.m., after the clients have retired for the night, Eureka! Ranch's tireless staff—its "trained brains"—debrief and refine the day's results.

Day two begins with a hearty breakfast and a stiff mug of Brain Brew coffee. Then the Gardetto's team gathers around a large board, to which Eureka! Ranch staffers have tacked the twelve most popular new-product ideas and the nineteen most popular new-positioning ideas from the previous day. The team reviews the concepts, adds depth and refinement to the better ones, and votes again. They spend the rest of the day assessing each surviving idea in more detail. "After the previous day's anything-that-pops-up-in-your-head brainstorming," says one observer, "today is more focused; people sense that they're discussing ideas that may evolve into a completely new line of snacks."

Yet even as the group tackles the serious issues, the atmosphere remains lighthearted. "Just the fact that a Nerf ball comes whistling at your head [during an exercise] makes you think of something different. [It's] harnessed chaos," says one participant. When the day's session ends, the Gardetto's team heads out for a relaxing dinner at a local restaurant. Meanwhile, Doug Hall and his staff prepare for the final day. They whittle down the list of ideas and write concept statements for what they think are the most viable new-product options.

The final day: Hall, dressed in a long purple robe and still barefoot, presents the results of the Gardetto's team's efforts—the best of the best. The team talks through each product idea. Some are sent packing—such as Saturday Night Snack 'Ems (featuring Charlie's skillet corn bread) and Bistro Baguettes (sweet bread with raspberry-champagne and cream cheese). But other ideas garner enthusiastic support. Gardetto's leaves satisfied, with sixteen new packaging ideas, nine new logos, and several new snack food concepts for the R&D kitchens.

Gardetto's satisfying experience is typical. *Human Resource Executive* recently named Eureka! Ranch as one of the top ten training programs in North America. Eighty-five percent of participants rate the program as the best training they've ever attended. And more than 80 percent of Eureka! Ranch sessions are repeat business from such world-class companies as Ford, Fidelity, Tenneco, Johnson & Johnson, Walt Disney, Nike, Frito-Lay, Procter & Gamble, and American Express.

In working with more than 4000 new products and 6000 front-line development groups, Eureka! Ranch has learned a good many lessons on creativity itself. Interestingly, one lesson is that zany fun is only part of the process for generating creative ideas. In fact, in recent years, Eureka! Ranch sessions are becoming more serious and less chaotic. The Ranch now tackles the tough job of being creative by balancing the "madness" with a stronger mix of "method."

There's still plenty of fast-paced action and creative brainstorming. But sessions are now supported by the heaps of qualitative and quantitative data gleaned from Eureka! Ranch's years of new-product development experience. Refined product-development tools and more methodical processes now supplement the open-ended fun of previous days. For example, Eureka! Ranch has developed its Merwyn software, a scoring system for new ideas.

What has emerged is a more effective version of Eureka! Ranch. Under Hall's notions of "capitalist creativity," new-product success "is not random. ... There are reproducible scientific lessons and laws that ... can help you win more, lose less, and make more money."

Sources: Quotes and other information from Todd Datz, "Romper Ranch," *CIO* May 15, 1999; Lori Dahm, "Pursue Passion," *Stagnito's New Products Magazine*, October 2002, p. 58; Eva Kaplan-Leiserson, "Eureka!: This Little-Ranch-That-Could Teaches You to 'Win More, Lose Less, and Make More Money,'" *T&D*, December 2001, p. 50(14); Geoff Williams, "I've Got an Idea!" *Entrepreneur*, December 2001, p. 36; Monique Reece, "Expert Shares His Ideas to Jumpstart Businesses," *Denver Business Journal*, September 28, 2001, p. 33A; Doug Hall, *Jump Start Your Business Brain* (Whitehall, VA: Betterway Publications, 2002); John Eckberg, "New Radio Host Takes on Small Biz," *The Cincinnati Enquirer,* January 13, 2003, p. 7B; and www.eurekaranch.com (accessed December 2004).

Consumers often create new products and uses on their own, and companies can benefit by putting them on the market. For example, for years customers were spreading the word that Skin-So-Soft bath oil and moisturizer were also terrific bug repellents. Whereas some consumers were content simply to bathe in water scented with the fragrant oil, others carried it in their backpacks to mosquito-infested campsites or kept a bottle on the deck of their beach houses. Avon turned the idea into a complete line of Skin-So-Soft Bug Guard PLUS IR3535® products, including the Insect Repellent Gentle Breeze Moisturizing Sunblock Lotion SPF 30, a combination moisturizer, insect repellent, and sunscreen. Eric von Hippel, a professor and head of the Innovation and Entrepreneurship Group at MIT, wrote a book titled *Democratizing Innovation*. In it he shows how companies who build strong

For years customers used Skin-So-Soft bath oil and moisturizer as a bug repellent. Avon turned the idea into a complete line of Skin-So-Soft Bug Guard PLUS IR3535® products.

relationships with user communities, such as the community of mountain bike riders, can leverage these relationships to get ideas for product improvements or for new products. Take the case of the kite-surfing community. According to von Hippel, approximately 37 percent of innovations in equipment design in the kite board industry came from users. Windsurfers were the first adopters of early designs for a combination of surfboard and parafoil. These early adopters posted sophisticated designs and CAD-generated templates through online communities, and these were downloaded by other users who then hired local talent to construct new versions. And so it went—the user community provided the ideas, testing, discussion, and refinements to manufacturers who then utilized the designs that the market had already proven.[8]

Finally, some companies even give customers the tools and resources to design their own products. For example, Bush Boake Allen (BBA), a global supplier of specialty flavours to companies like Nestlé, provides a tool kit that lets its customers develop their own flavours, which BBA then manufactures. Similarly, LSI Logic provides customers with do-it-yourself tools that let them design their own specialized chips and customized integrated circuits. Letting customers do the innovating has become a great new way to create value.[9]

Companies must be careful not to rely too heavily on customer input when developing new products. For some products, especially highly technical ones, customers may not know what they need. "Merely giving people what they want isn't always enough," says one innovation management consultant. "People want to be surprised; they want something that's better than they imagined, something that stretches them in what they like."[10]

Competitors are another good source of new-product ideas. Companies watch competitors' ads to get clues about their new products. They buy competing new products, take them apart to see how they work, analyze their sales, and decide whether they should bring out a new product of their own. *Distributors and suppliers* can also contribute many good new-product ideas. Resellers are close to the market and can pass along information about consumer problems and new-product possibilities. Suppliers can tell the company about new concepts, techniques, and materials that can be used to develop new products. Bioniche, a Canadian biotech company, with operations in Belleville, Ontario, and Montreal, Quebec, sponsors research by university professors to help it generate ideas for new drugs and cancer treatments. Other idea sources include trade magazines, shows, and seminars; government agencies; new-product consultants; advertising agencies; marketing research firms; university and commercial laboratories; and inventors.

The search for new-product ideas should be systematic rather than haphazard. Otherwise, few new ideas will surface and many good ideas will sputter and die. Top management can avoid these problems by installing an *idea management system* that directs the flow of new ideas to a central point where they can be collected, reviewed, and evaluated. In setting up such a system, the company can do any or all of the following:[11]

- Appoint a respected senior person to be the company's idea manager.
- Create a cross-functional idea management committee consisting of people from R&D, engineering, purchasing, operations, finance, and sales and marketing to meet regularly and evaluate proposed new-product and new-service ideas.
- Set up a toll-free number or website for anyone who wants to send a new idea to the idea manager.
- Encourage all company stakeholders—employees, suppliers, distributors, dealers—to send their ideas to the idea manager.
- Set up formal recognition programs to reward those who contribute the best new ideas.

The idea manager approach yields two favourable outcomes. First, it helps create an innovation-oriented company culture. It shows that top management supports, encourages, and rewards innovation. Second, it will yield a larger number of ideas, among which will be found some especially good ones. As the system matures, ideas will flow more freely. No longer will good ideas wither for the lack of a sounding board or a senior product advocate.

Idea Screening

Idea screening
Screening new-product ideas in order to spot good ideas and drop poor ones as soon as possible.

The purpose of idea generation is to create a large number of ideas. The purpose of the succeeding stages is to *reduce* that number. The first idea-reducing stage is **idea screening**, which helps spot good ideas and drop poor ones as soon as possible. Product development costs rise greatly in later stages, so the company wants to go ahead only with the product ideas that will turn into profitable products.

Many companies require their executives to write up new-product ideas on a standard form that can be reviewed by a new-product committee. The write-up describes the product, the target market, and the competition. It makes some rough estimates of market size, product price, development time and costs, manufacturing costs, and rate of return. The committee then evaluates the idea against a set of general criteria. For example, at Kao Company, the large Japanese consumer-products company, the committee asks questions such as these: Is the product truly useful to consumers and society? Is it good for our particular company? Does it mesh well with the company's objectives and strategies? Do we have the people, skills, and resources to make it succeed? Does it deliver more value to customers than do competing products? Is it easy to advertise and distribute? Many companies have well-designed systems for rating and screening new-product ideas.

Concept Development and Testing

Product concept
A detailed version of the new-product idea stated in meaningful consumer terms.

An attractive idea must be developed into a **product concept**. It is important to distinguish among a product idea, a product concept, and a product image. A *product idea* is an idea for a possible product that the company can see itself offering to the market. A *product concept* is a detailed version of the idea stated in meaningful consumer terms. A *product image* is the way consumers perceive an actual or potential product.

Concept Development

After ten years of development, DaimlerChrysler is getting ready to commercialize its experimental fuel-cell-powered electric car. This car's nonpolluting fuel-cell system runs directly on methanol, which delivers hydrogen to the fuel cell with only water as a by-product. It is highly fuel efficient (75 percent more efficient than gasoline engines) and gives the new car an environmental advantage over standard internal combustion engine cars or even today's superefficient gasoline-electric hybrid cars.

Recently DaimlerChrysler put sixty "F-Cell" cars on the road in Japan, Germany, and the United States to test their worth in everyday operation. Based on the tiny Mercedes A-Class, the car accelerates quickly, reaches speeds of 145 km per hour, and has a 450 km driving range, giving it a huge edge over battery-powered electric cars that travel only about 130 km before needing three to twelve hours of recharging. Fuel-cell systems are also being tested in buses, trucks, and other vehicles.[12]

Now DaimlerChrysler's task is to develop this new product into alternative product concepts, find out how attractive each concept is to customers, and choose the best one. It might create the following product concepts for the fuel-cell electric car:

Concept 1   A moderately priced subcompact designed as a second family car to be used around town. The car is ideal for running errands and visiting friends.

Concept 2   A medium-cost sporty compact appealing to young people.

Concept 3   An inexpensive subcompact "green" car appealing to environmentally conscious people who want practical transportation and low pollution.

Concept 4   A high-end SUV appealing to those who love the space SUVs provide but lament the poor gas mileage.

Concept Testing

Concept testing
Testing new-product concepts with a group of target consumers to find out if the concepts have strong consumer appeal.

Concept testing calls for testing new-product concepts with groups of target consumers. The concepts may be presented to consumers symbolically or physically. Here, in words, is concept 3:

An efficient, fun-to-drive, fuel-cell-powered electric subcompact car that seats four. This methanol-powered high-tech wonder provides practical and reliable transportation with virtually no pollution. It goes up to 145 km per hour and, unlike battery-powered electric cars, it never needs recharging. It's priced, fully equipped, at US$20 000.

For some concept tests, a word or picture description might be sufficient. However, a more concrete and physical presentation of the concept will increase the reliability of the concept test. Today, some marketers are finding innovative ways to make product concepts more real to consumer subjects. For example, some are using virtual reality to test product concepts. Virtual reality programs use comput-

DaimlerChrysler's task is to develop its fuel-cell-powered F-Cell car into alternative product concepts, find out how attractive each concept is to customers, and choose the best one.

ers and sensory devices (such as gloves or goggles) to simulate reality. A designer of kitchen cabinets might use a virtual reality program to help a customer "see" how his or her kitchen would look and work if remodelled with the company's products.

After being exposed to the concept, consumers then may be asked to react to it by answering questions such as those in Table 10.1. The answers will help the company decide which concept has the strongest appeal. For example, the last question asks about the consumer's intention to buy. Suppose 10 percent of the consumers said they "definitely" would buy and another 5 percent said "probably." The company could project these figures to the full population in this target group to estimate sales volume. Even then, the estimate is uncertain because people do not always carry out their stated intentions.

Many firms routinely test new-product concepts with consumers before attempting to turn them into actual new products. For example, AcuPOLL, a global brand-building research company, tests thousands of new product concepts every year. In past polls, M&M's Minis, "teeny-tiny" M&M's sold in a tube container, received a rare A1 concept rating, meaning that consumers thought it was an outstanding concept that they would try and buy. Other products, such as Glad Stand

TABLE 10.1 Questions for Fuel-Cell-Powered Electric Car Concept Test

1. Do you understand the concept of a fuel-cell-powered electric car?
2. Do you believe the claims about the car's performance?
3. What are the major benefits of the fuel-cell-powered electric car compared with a conventional car?
4. What are its advantages compared with a battery-powered electric car?
5. What improvements in the car's features would you suggest?
6. For what uses would you prefer a fuel-cell-powered electric car to a conventional car?
7. What would be a reasonable price to charge for the car?
8. Who would be involved in your decision to buy such a car? Who would drive it?
9. Would you buy such a car (definitely, probably, probably not, definitely not)?

Food, moisture, and lots of places to hide. No wonder a billion germs call your sponge home.

Don't spread germs. Kill them.

AcuPOLL tests thousands of new-product concepts every year. Its polls correctly predicted that Clorox® Wipes would be a big hit with consumers.

& Zip Bags, Clorox® Wipes, the Mead Inteli-Gear learning system, and Elmer's 3D Paint Pens were also big hits.

Other product concepts didn't fare so well. For example, Procter & Gamble's and Kimberly-Clark's moist toilet papers, tested after launch, received an F in AcuPOLL. Both companies spent millions to launch these products but have since withdrawn them from the market. Consumers saw wet toilet paper as unique but didn't find the benefit to be all that compelling. AcuPOLL has found that just being different doesn't lead to market success.[13]

Hershey does its product concept testing on the Web. It uses online test subjects to gain insight to all aspects of its product concepts. Consumers might be shown pictures of proposed candy bars or baking mixes, quizzed about flavours, and asked about potential product names. Says one Hershey researcher, "You need to test maybe 100 concepts to get one good product that might make it to market." Putting concept testing online has cut the time Hershey spends on new-product development by two-thirds.[14]

Marketing Strategy Development

Marketing strategy development

Designing an initial marketing strategy for a new product based on the product concept.

Suppose DaimlerChrysler finds that concept 3 for the fuel-cell-powered electric car is best. The next step is **marketing strategy development**, designing an initial marketing strategy for introducing this car to the market.

The *marketing strategy statement* consists of three parts. The first part describes the target market; the planned product positioning; and the sales, market share, and profit goals for the first few years. Thus:

The target market is younger, well-educated, moderate-to-high-income individuals, couples, or small families seeking practical, environmentally responsible transportation. The car will be positioned as more economical to operate, more fun to drive, and less polluting than today's internal combustion engine or hybrid cars. It is also less restrictive than battery-powered electric cars, which must be recharged regularly. The company will aim to sell 100 000 cars in the first year, at a loss of not more than US$15 million. In the second year, the company will aim for sales of 120 000 cars and a profit of US$25 million.

The second part of the marketing strategy statement outlines the product's planned price, distribution, and marketing budget for the first year:

The fuel-cell-powered electric car will be offered in three colours—red, white, and blue—and will have optional air-conditioning and power-drive features. It will sell at a retail price of US$20 000—with 15 percent off the list price to dealers. Dealers who sell more than 10 cars per month will get an additional discount of 5 percent on each car sold that month. An advertising budget of US$50 million will be split 50–50 between a national media campaign and local advertising. Advertising will emphasize the car's fun spirit and low emissions. During the first year, US$100 000 will be spent on marketing research to find out who is buying the car and their satisfaction levels.

The third part of the marketing strategy statement describes the planned long-run sales, profit goals, and marketing mix strategy:

DaimlerChrysler intends to capture a 3 percent long-run share of the total auto market and realize an after-tax return on investment of 15 percent. To achieve this, product quality will start high and be improved over time. Price will be raised in the second and third years if competition permits. The total advertising budget will be raised each year by about 10 percent. Marketing research will be reduced to US$60 000 per year after the first year.

Business Analysis

Business analysis
A review of the sales, costs, and profit projections for a new product to find out whether these factors satisfy the company's objectives.

Once management has decided on its product concept and marketing strategy, it can evaluate the business attractiveness of the proposal. **Business analysis** involves a review of the sales, costs, and profit projections for a new product to find out whether they satisfy the company's objectives. If they do, the product can move to the product development stage.

To estimate sales, the company might look at the sales history of similar products and conduct surveys of market opinion. It can then estimate minimum and maximum sales to assess the range of risk. After preparing the sales forecast, management can estimate the expected costs and profits for the product, including marketing, R&D, operations, accounting, and finance costs. The company then uses the sales and costs figures to analyze the new product's financial attractiveness.

Product Development

Product development
Developing the product concept into a physical product in order to ensure that the product idea can be turned into a workable product.

So far, for many new-product concepts, the product may have existed only as a word description, a drawing, or perhaps a crude mock-up. If the product concept passes the business test, it moves into **product development**. Here, R&D or engineering develops the product concept into a physical product. The product development step, however, now calls for a large jump in investment. It will show whether the product idea can be turned into a workable product.

The R&D department will develop and test one or more physical versions of the product concept. R&D hopes to design a prototype that will satisfy and excite consumers and that can be produced quickly and at budgeted costs. Developing a successful prototype can take days, weeks, months, or even years.

Often, products undergo rigorous tests to make sure that they perform safely and effectively, or that consumers will find value in them. Here are some examples of such product tests:[15]

At Gillette, almost everyone gets involved in new-product testing. Every working day at Gillette, 200 volunteers from various departments come to work unshaven, troop to the second floor of the company's gritty South Boston plant, and enter small booths with a sink and mirror. There they take instructions from technicians on the other side of a small window as to which razor, shaving cream, or aftershave to use. The volunteers evaluate razors for sharpness of blade, smoothness of glide, and ease of handling. In a nearby shower room, women perform the same ritual on their legs, underarms, and what the company delicately refers to as the "bikini area." "We bleed so you'll get a good shave at home," says one Gillette employee.

Thunk. Thunk. Thunk. Behind a locked door in the basement of Louis Vuitton's elegant Paris headquarters, a mechanical arm hoists a brown-and-tan handbag a half-metre off the floor—then drops it. The bag, loaded with an 3.5-km weight, will be lifted and dropped, over and over again, for four days. This is Vuitton's test laboratory, a high-tech torture chamber for its fabled luxury goods. Another piece of lab equipment bombards handbags with ultraviolet rays to test resistance to fading. Still another tests zippers by tugging them open and shutting them 5000 times. There's even a mechanized mannequin hand, with a Vuitton charm bracelet around its wrist, being shaken vigorously to make sure none of the charms falls off.

A new product must have the required functional features and also convey the intended psychological characteristics. The fuel-cell electric car, for example, should strike consumers as being well built, comfortable, and safe. Management must learn what makes consumers decide that a car is well built. To some consumers, this means that the car has "solid-sounding" doors. To others, it means that the car is able to withstand heavy impact in crash tests. Consumer tests are conducted in which consumers test-drive the car and rate its attributes.

Gillette uses employee-volunteers to test new shaving products— "We bleed so you'll get a good shave at home," says a Gillette employee.

Test Marketing

If the product passes functional and consumer tests, the next step is **test marketing**, the stage at which the product and marketing program are introduced into more realistic market settings. Test marketing gives the marketer experience with marketing the product before going to the great expense of full introduction. It lets the company test the product and its entire marketing program—positioning strategy, advertising, distribution, pricing, branding and packaging, and budget levels. Cadbury Beverages Canada, for example, uses Ontario as a test market for new Schweppes and Crush branded products that will be eventually rolled out to the entire North American market.

The amount of test marketing needed varies with each new product. Test marketing costs can be high, and it takes time that may allow competitors to gain advantages. When the costs of developing and introducing the product are low, or when management is already confident about the new product, the company may do little or no test marketing. In fact, test marketing by consumer packaged-goods firms has been declining in recent years. Companies often do not test-market simple line extensions or copies of successful competitor products. For example, P&G introduced its Folger's decaffeinated coffee crystals without test marketing.

However, when introducing a new product requires a big investment, or when management is not sure of the product or marketing program, a company may do a lot of test marketing. For instance, Unilever spent two years testing its highly successful Lever 2000 bar soap before introducing it internationally. Frito-Lay did eighteen months of testing in three markets on at least five formulations before introducing its Baked Lays line of low-fat snacks. And Nokia test-marketed its N-Gage cell phone/mobile game player extensively in London before introducing it worldwide.[16]

Although test-marketing costs can be high, they are often small when compared with the costs of making a major mistake. For example, Nabisco's launch of one new product without testing had disastrous—and soggy—results:[17]

> Nabisco hit a marketing home run with its Teddy Grahams, teddy-bear-shaped graham crackers in several different flavours. So, the company decided to extend Teddy Grahams into a new area. It introduced chocolate, cinnamon, and

Nokia test-marketed its N-Gage cell phone/mobile game player extensively before introducing it worldwide.

honey versions of Breakfast Bears Graham Cereal. When the product came out, however, consumers didn't like the taste enough, so the product developers went back to the kitchen and modified the formula. But they didn't test it. The result was a disaster. Although the cereal may have tasted better, it no longer stayed crunchy in milk, as the advertising on the box promised. Instead, it left a gooey mess of graham mush on the bottom of cereal bowls. Supermarket managers soon refused to restock the cereal, and Nabisco executives decided it was too late to reformulate the product again. So a promising new product was killed through haste to get it to market.

Still, test marketing doesn't guarantee success. For example, Procter & Gamble tested its new Fit produce rinse heavily for five years and Olay cosmetics for three years. Although market tests suggested the products would be successful, P&G had to pull the plug on both shortly after their introductions.[18]

When using test marketing, consumer products companies usually choose one of three approaches—standard test markets, controlled test markets, or simulated test markets.

Standard Test Markets

Using standard test markets, the company finds a small number of representative test cities, conducts a full marketing campaign in these cities, and uses store audits, consumer and distributor surveys, and other measures to gauge product performance. The results are used to forecast national sales and profits, discover potential product problems, and fine-tune the marketing program.

Standard test markets have some drawbacks. They can be very costly and they may take a long time—some last as long as three to five years. Moreover, competitors can monitor test market results or even interfere with them by cutting their prices in test cities, increasing their promotion, or even buying up the product being tested. Finally, test markets give competitors a look at the company's new product well before it is introduced nationally. Thus, competitors may have time to develop defensive strategies, and may even beat the company's product to the market. For example, while Clorox® was still test marketing its new detergent with bleach in selected markets, P&G launched Tide with Bleach nationally. Tide with Bleach quickly became the segment leader; Clorox® later withdrew its detergent.

Despite these disadvantages, standard test markets are still the most widely used approach for major in-market testing. However, many companies today are shifting toward quicker and cheaper controlled and simulated test marketing methods.

Controlled Test Markets

Several research firms keep controlled panels of stores that have agreed to carry new products for a fee. Controlled test marketing systems, such as ACNielsen's Scantrack and Information Resources, Inc.'s (IRI) BehaviorScan, track individual consumer behaviour for new products from the television set to the checkout counter.

In each BehaviorScan market, IRI maintains a panel of shoppers who report all of their purchases by showing an identification card at check-out in participating stores and by using a handheld scanner at home to record purchases at nonparticipating stores.[19] Within test stores, IRI controls such factors as shelf placement, price, and in-store promotions for the product being tested. IRI also measures TV viewing in each panel household and sends special commercials to panel member television sets. Direct mail promotions can also be tested.

Detailed scanner information on each consumer's purchases is fed into a central computer, where it is combined with the consumer's demographic and TV viewing information and reported daily. Thus, BehaviorScan can provide store-by-store, week-by-week reports on the sales of tested products. Such panel purchasing data

IRI's BehaviorScan system tracks individual consumer behaviour for new products from the television set to the checkout counter.

enables in-depth diagnostics not possible with retail point-of-sale data alone, including repeat purchase analysis, buyer demographics, and earlier, more accurate sales forecasts after just twelve to twenty-four weeks in market. Most importantly, the system allows companies to evaluate their specific marketing efforts.

Controlled test markets, such as BehaviorScan, usually cost less than standard test markets. Also, because retail distribution is "forced" in the first week of the test, controlled test markets can be completed much more quickly than standard test markets. As in standard test markets, controlled test markets allow competitors to get a look at the company's new product. And some companies are concerned that the limited number of controlled test markets used by the research services may not be representative of their products' markets or target consumers. However, the research firms are experienced in projecting test market results to broader markets and can usually account for biases in the test markets used.

Simulated Test Markets

Companies can also test new products in a simulated shopping environment. The company or research firm shows ads and promotions for a variety of products, including the new product being tested, to a sample of consumers. It gives consumers a small amount of money and invites them to a real or laboratory store where they may keep the money or use it to buy items. The researchers note how many consumers buy the new product and competing brands.

This simulation provides a measure of trial and the commercial's effectiveness against competing commercials. The researchers then ask consumers the reasons for their purchase or nonpurchase. Some weeks later, they interview the consumers by phone to determine product attitudes, usage, satisfaction, and repurchase intentions. Using sophisticated computer models, the researchers then project national sales from results of the simulated test market. Recently, some marketers have begun to use interesting new high-tech approaches to simulated test market research, such as virtual reality and the Internet.

Simulated test markets overcome some of the disadvantages of standard and controlled test markets. They usually cost much less, can be run in eight weeks, and keep the new product out of competitors' view. Yet, because of their small samples and simulated shopping environments, many marketers do not think that simulated test markets are as accurate or reliable as larger, real-world tests. Still, simulated test markets are used widely, often as "pretest" markets. Because they are fast and inexpensive, they can be run to quickly assess a new product or its marketing program. If the pretest results are strongly positive, the product might be introduced without further testing. If the results are very poor, the product might be dropped or substantially redesigned and retested. If the results are promising but indefinite, the product and marketing program can be tested further in controlled or standard test markets.

Commercialization

Commercialization
Introducing a new product into the market.

Test marketing gives management the information needed to make a final decision about whether to launch the new product. If the company goes ahead with **commercialization**—introducing the new product into the market—it will face high costs. The company may have to build or rent a manufacturing facility. And it may have to spend, in the case of a new consumer packaged good, between $10 million and $200 million for advertising, sales promotion, and other marketing efforts in the first year.

The company launching a new product must first decide on introduction *timing*. If DaimlerChrysler's new fuel-cell electric car will eat into the sales of the company's other cars, its introduction may be delayed. If the car can be improved further, or if the economy is down, the company may wait until the following year to launch it.

Next, the company must decide *where* to launch the new product—in a single location, a region, the national market, or the international market. Few companies have the confidence, capital, and capacity to launch new products into full national or international distribution. They will develop a planned *market rollout* over time. In particular, small companies may enter attractive cities or regions one at a time. Larger companies, however, may quickly introduce new models into several regions or into the full national market. See what happened at Kraft:

> In May 2006, Kraft Canada launched the Tassimo across the country. The Tassimo, a $199 single-cup "hot beverage system," is Kraft's first kitchen appliance entry. The launch is part of a global initiative, first launched in France in 2004, later hitting Switzerland and the U.K. before coming to Germany and the U.S. The product was developed in partnership with Germany-based Braun when the companies realized that the old way of making coffee wasn't meeting consumer needs anymore. In convenience oriented, time-pressed societies, no one wants to wait while a full pot of coffee brews. With the Tassimo, you pop discs to make coffee, cappuccino, espresso, tea or hot chocolate (produced only by Kraft) into the machine and almost instantly, you have your desired beverage.[20]

In contrast to Kraft's country-by-country roll-out, Colgate introduced its Actibrush battery-powered toothbrush into fifty countries in a year, generating US$115 million in sales. Such rapid worldwide expansion solidified the brand's market position before foreign competitors could react.[21]

Colgate introduces new products, such as its Actibrush toothbrush, in swift global assaults, solidifying the brand's market position before foreign competitors can react.

Organizing for New-Product Development

Many companies organize their new-product development process into the orderly sequence of steps shown in Figure 10.1 on page 380, starting with idea generation and ending with commercialization. Under this **sequential product development** approach, one company department works individually to complete its stage of the process before passing the new product along to the next department and stage. This orderly, step-by-step process can help bring control to complex and risky projects. But it also can be dangerously slow. In fast-changing, highly competitive markets, such slow-but-sure product development can result in product failures, lost sales and profits, and crumbling market positions. "Speed to market" and reducing new-product development cycle time have become pressing concerns to companies in all industries.

To get their new products to market more quickly, many companies are adopting a faster, team-oriented approach called **simultaneous product development** (or **team-based or collaborative product development**). Under this approach, company departments work closely together through cross-functional teams, overlapping the steps in the product development process to save time and increase effectiveness. Instead of passing the new product from department to department, the company assembles a team of people from various departments that stays with the new product from start to finish. Such teams usually include people from the marketing, finance, design, manufacturing, and legal departments, and even supplier and customer companies.

Top management gives the product development team general strategic direction but no clear-cut product idea or work plan. It challenges the team with stiff and seemingly contradictory goals—"turn out carefully planned and superior new products, but do it quickly"—and then gives the team whatever freedom and resources it needs to meet the challenge. In the sequential process, a bottleneck at one phase can seriously slow the entire project. In the simultaneous approach, if one functional area hits snags, it works to resolve them while the team moves on.

The Allen-Bradley Company, a maker of industrial controls, realized tremendous benefits by using simultaneous development. Under its old sequential approach, the company's marketing department handed off a new-product idea to designers, who worked in isolation to prepare concepts that they then passed along to product engineers. The engineers, also working by themselves, developed expensive prototypes and handed them off to manufacturing, which tried to find a way to build the new product. Finally, after many years and dozens of costly design compromises and delays, marketing was asked to sell the new product, which it often found to be too high priced or sadly out of date. Now, all of Allen-Bradley's departments work together to develop new products. The results have been astonishing. For example, the company recently developed a new electrical control in just two years; under the old system, it would have taken six years.

The simultaneous team-based approach does have some limitations. Superfast product development can be riskier and more costly than the slower, more orderly sequential approach. Moreover, it often creates increased organizational tension and confusion. And the company must take care that rushing a product to market does not adversely affect its quality—the objective is not only to create products faster, but to create them *better* and faster.

Despite these drawbacks, in rapidly changing industries facing increasingly shorter product life cycles, the rewards of fast and flexible product development far exceed the risks. Companies that get new and improved products to the market faster than competitors often gain a big competitive edge. They can respond more quickly to emerging consumer tastes and charge higher prices for more advanced designs. As one auto industry executive states, "What we want to do is get the new car approved, built, and in the consumer's hands in the shortest time possible.... Whoever gets there first gets all the marbles."[22]

Sequential product development
A new-product development approach in which one company department works to complete its stage of the process before passing the new product along to the next department and stage.

Simultaneous (or team-based) product development
An approach to developing new products in which various company departments work closely together, overlapping the steps in the product-development process to save time and increase effectiveness.

Thus, new-product success requires more than simply thinking up a few good ideas, turning them into products, and finding customers for them. It requires a systematic approach for finding new ways to create valued customer experiences, from generating and screening new-product ideas to creating and rolling out want-satisfying products to customers. More than this, successful new-product development requires a total-company commitment. At companies known for their new-product prowess—such as 3M, Gillette, Intel, and Nokia—the entire culture encourages, supports, and rewards innovation:

You see the headline in every 3M ad: "Innovation Working for You." But at 3M, innovation isn't just an advertising pitch. Throughout its history, 3M has been one of North America's most innovative companies. The company markets more than 50 000 products, ranging from sandpaper, adhesives, and hundreds of sticky tapes to contact lenses, heart-lung machines, and futuristic synthetic ligaments. Each year 3M launches more than 200 new products. But these new products don't just happen. 3M works hard to create an entrepreneurial culture that fosters innovation. For more than a century, 3M's culture has encouraged employees to take risks and try new ideas. 3M knows that it must try thousands of new-product ideas to hit one big jackpot. Trying out lots of new ideas often means making mistakes, but 3M accepts blunders and dead ends as a normal part of creativity and innovation.

In fact, "blunders" have turned into some of 3M's most successful products. Old-timers at 3M love to tell the story about 3M scientist Spencer Silver. Silver started out to develop a superstrong adhesive; instead he came up with one that didn't stick very well at all. He sent the apparently useless substance on to other 3M researchers to see whether they could find something to do with it. Nothing happened for several years. Then Arthur Fry, another 3M scientist,

At 3M, new products don't just happen. The company's entire culture encourages, supports, and rewards innovation.

had a problem—and an idea. As a choir member in a local church, Mr. Fry was having trouble marking places in his hymnal—the little scraps of paper he used kept falling out. He tried dabbing some of Mr. Silver's weak glue on one of the scraps. It stuck nicely and later peeled off without damaging the hymnal. Thus were born 3M's Post-It Notes, a product that is now one of the top-selling office supply products in the world.[23]

Product Life-Cycle Strategies

After launching the new product, management wants the product to enjoy a long and happy life. Although it does not expect the product to sell forever, the company wants to earn a decent profit to cover all the effort and risk that went into launching it. Management is aware that each product will have a life cycle, although its exact shape and length is not known in advance.

Figure 10.2 shows a typical **product life cycle (PLC)**, the course that a product's sales and profits take over its lifetime. The PLC has five distinct stages:

1. *Product development* begins when the company finds and develops a new-product idea. During product development, sales are zero and the company's investment costs mount.
2. *Introduction* is a period of slow sales growth as the product is introduced in the market. Profits are nonexistent in this stage because of the heavy expenses of product introduction.
3. *Growth* is a period of rapid market acceptance and increasing profits.
4. *Maturity* is a period of slowdown in sales growth because the product has achieved acceptance by most potential buyers. Profits level off or decline because of increased marketing outlays to defend the product against competition.
5. *Decline* is the period when sales fall off and profits drop.

Not all products follow this product life cycle. Some products are introduced and die quickly, as is the case for fads. For example, many of carbohydrate-reduced products introduced when the Atkins Diet was "hot" met an untimely demise. Other products stay in the mature stage for a long, long time. Companies and their products, such as the Hudson's Bay Company (founded in 1670), Drambui (founded in 1745), Waterford Crystal (1783), Schweppes (1798), Levi's (1850), Burberry (1856), Heineken (1864), and Campbell's (1869), have stood the test of time and continue to hold a dominant place in their categories. Some prod-

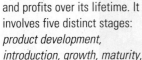
Product life cycle (PLC)
The course of a product's sales and profits over its lifetime. It involves five distinct stages: *product development, introduction, growth, maturity,* and *decline.*

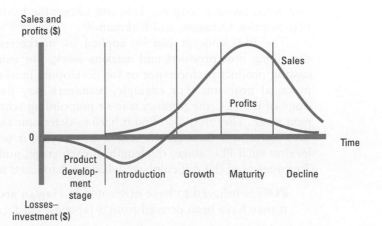
Figure 10.2 Sales and profits over the product's life from inception to demise

Some products die quickly; others stay in the mature stage for a long, long time. For more than 136 years, TABASCO® Sauce "has stood as the ultimate test of courage."

ucts enter the decline stage and are then cycled back into the growth stage through strong promotion or repositioning. In 2006, Unilever attempted to reposition its Thermasilk brand originally targeted at women over thirty-five to girls aged twenty years younger.[24] Thus, as one analyst notes, "well-managed, a brand could live forever."

The PLC concept can describe a *product class* (gasoline-powered automobiles), a *product form* (SUVs), or a *brand* (the Ford Explorer). The PLC concept applies differently in each case. Product classes have the longest life cycles—the sales of many product classes stay in the mature stage for a long time. Product forms, in contrast, tend to have the standard PLC shape. Product forms, such as "dial telephones" and "cassette tapes," passed through a regular history of introduction, rapid growth, maturity, and decline.

A specific brand's life cycle can change quickly because of changing competitive attacks and responses. For example, although laundry soaps (product class) and powdered detergents (product form) have enjoyed fairly long life cycles, the life cycles of specific brands have tended to be much shorter. Today's leading brands of powdered laundry soap are Tide and Cheer; the leading brands 75 years ago were Fels Naptha, Octagon, and Kirkman.[25]

The PLC concept can be applied by marketers as a useful framework for describing how products and markets work. But using the PLC concept for forecasting product performance or for developing marketing strategies presents some practical problems. For example, managers may have trouble identifying which stage of the PLC the product is in or pinpointing when the product moves into the next stage. They may also find it hard to determine the factors that affect the product's movement through the stages. In practice, it is difficult to forecast the sales level at each PLC stage, the length of each stage, and the shape of the PLC curve. To understand the difficulty, see what has happened to POGs:

POG is believed to have originated in Hawaii around the 1920s. Some believe it may have been derived from a Japanese card game called Menko. The name

Pet rocks, introduced one October, had sunk like a stone by the next February.

POG was derived from a brand of fruit juice made from passion fruit, orange, and guava. The caps of POG bottles were originally used to play the game. POGs became a craze with public school kids when the Canada Games Company reintroduced them to the North American public in the mid-1990s. While some thought its death knell had been sounded, they were wrong. Montreal-native Susan Spiegel, vice-president of marketing at POG licensee Funrise Toys, is working to give the game a rebirth. "Our advertising has a very simple message: POG is back," Spiegel says. While much of the strategy rests on replicating the tactics that made the game successful in the 1990s, new tactics have been added, such as a new partnership with Loblaws stores. The retailer will run a series of POG tournaments across Canada. The tactics may revitalize the brand and turn it into a craze for the current generation of children.[26]

Using the PLC concept to develop marketing strategy also can be difficult because strategy is both a cause and a result of the product's life cycle. The product's current PLC position suggests the best marketing strategies, and the resulting marketing strategies affect product performance in later life-cycle stages. Yet, when used carefully, the PLC concept can help in developing good marketing strategies for different stages of the product life cycle.

We looked at the product development stage of the product life cycle in the first part of the chapter. We now look at strategies for each of the other life-cycle stages.

Introduction Stage

Introduction stage
The product life-cycle stage in which the new product is first distributed and made available for purchase.

The **introduction stage** starts when the new product is first launched. Introduction takes time, and sales growth is apt to be slow. Well-known products, such as instant coffee and frozen orange juice, lingered for many years before they entered a stage of rapid growth.

In this stage, as compared with other stages, profits are negative or low because of the low sales and high distribution and promotion expenses. Much money is needed to attract distributors and build their inventories. Promotion spending is relatively high to inform consumers of the new product and get them to try it. Because the market is not generally ready for product refinements at this stage, the company and its few competitors produce basic versions of the product. These firms focus their selling on those buyers who are the most ready to buy.

A company, especially the *market pioneer*, must choose a launch strategy that is consistent with the intended product positioning. It should realize that the initial strategy is just the first step in a grander marketing plan for the product's entire life cycle. If the pioneer chooses its launch strategy to make a "killing," it may be sacrificing long-run revenue for the sake of short-run gain. As the pioneer moves through later stages of the life cycle, it will have to continuously formulate new pricing, promotion, and other marketing strategies. It has the best chance of building and retaining market leadership if it plays its cards correctly from the start.

Small and medium-sized enterprises form the majority of the businesses in Canada. Many of these firms were established when a market pioneer had a new product or service idea. The Running Room, for example, was launched by John Stanton, a man who developed a personal passion for running, which he shared with other Canadians who valued outdoor sports and activities to form a highly successful business. Sometimes, founders of such firms translate hobbies into successful businesses. Take the case of Domaine Pinnacle, a Quebec company that was founded in 2000:

> Domaine Pinnacle is a family-owned and -operated orchard and cidery located on a 175-hectare property on the slopes of Pinnacle Mountain near the historic village of Frelighsburg in the Eastern Townships of Quebec. (See www.icecider.com.) Susan and Charles Crawford make "ice cider," which is similar to ice wine except that it is made with apples. To found their successful business with a distinct advantage, the pair focused on distinct locational competences in their region: cold climate, many varieties of apples, access to a cider maker from France who was living in Quebec, and their own marketing expertise. In just six years, they've been able to find markets worldwide for their high-quality products. Rapid penetration of the world market for alcoholic beverages was made possible through a strategic alliance with a distribution partner—Camus Cognac—the largest independent producer of Cognac in the world. They've also won numerous prestigious awards for their products.

Growth Stage

Growth stage
The product life-cycle stage in which a product's sales start climbing quickly.

If the new product satisfies the market, it will enter a **growth stage**, in which sales will start climbing quickly. The early adopters will continue to buy, and later buyers will start following their lead, especially if they hear favourable word of mouth. Attracted by the opportunities for profit, new competitors will enter the market. They will introduce new product features, and the market will expand. The increase in competitors leads to an increase in the number of distribution outlets, and sales jump just to build reseller inventories. Prices remain where they are or fall only slightly. Companies keep their promotion spending at the same or a slightly higher level. Educating the market remains a goal, but now the company must also meet the competition.

Profits increase during the growth stage, as promotion costs are spread over a large volume and as unit manufacturing costs fall. The firm uses several strategies to sustain rapid market growth as long as possible. It improves product quality and adds new product features and models. It enters new market segments and new distribution channels. It shifts some advertising from building product awareness to building product conviction and purchase, and it lowers prices at the right time to attract more buyers.

In the growth stage, the firm faces a trade-off between high market share and high current profit. By spending a lot of money on product improvement, promotion, and distribution, the company can capture a dominant position. In doing so, however, it gives up maximum current profit, which it hopes to make up in the next stage.

Maturity Stage

Maturity stage
The stage in the product life cycle in which sales growth slows or levels off.

At some point, a product's sales growth will slow down, and the product will enter a **maturity stage**. The maturity stage normally lasts longer than the previous stages, and it poses strong challenges to marketing management.

The slowdown in sales growth results in many producers with many products to sell. In turn, this overcapacity leads to greater competition. Competitors begin marking down prices, increasing their advertising and sales promotions, and upping their R&D budgets to find better versions of the product. These steps lead to a drop in profit. Some of the weaker competitors start dropping out, and the industry eventually contains only well-established competitors.

Although many products in the mature stage appear to remain unchanged for long periods, most successful ones are actually evolving to meet changing consumer needs. (See Real Marketing 10.2.) Product managers should do more than simply

REAL MARKETING | 10.2

Age-Defying Products or Just Skilful PLC Management?

Some products are born and die quickly. Others, however, seem to defy the product life cycle, enduring for decades, or even generations. Skilful product-life-cycle management keeps them fresh, relevant, and appealing to customers. Here are examples of two long-term market winners with plenty of staying power.

Kraft Dinner

The Barenaked Ladies sing about it, FoodTV features a spa-inspired Kraft Dinner casserole, and the *Globe and Mail* refers to it as a Canadian cultural icon. University students, adults, and children across Canada wolf down an incredible 246 000 boxes of KD a day. Nine out of ten Canadian households buy the product and Canadians living overseas beg their friends to bring KD when they come to visit. Kraft Dinner is not only Kraft Canada's biggest business from a volume standpoint, but is also the country's number-one-selling grocery item, holding a 75 percent share of the market. Not bad for basic food that has been close to the hearts of Canadians since 1937. In fact, per capita, Canadians eat three times more Kraft dinner than their American counterparts.

Despite its Canadian success, KD's brand manager notes, "In an ever-changing market, you can't sit back and simply expect the brand to continue to be popular without trying to keep it relevant with consumers." The very popularity of the product presents its own challenges. How, you might ask, can you get Canadians to eat even more of the stuff? The biggest danger in trying to revitalize the brand is making changes that will alienate KD's core customers, just as Coke did when it introduced New Coke.

For a while, managers of the product had become too reliant on price to drive the KD business. Today, that is history. Kraft has put a lot of its market research muscle, new-product development skills, and advertising savvy behind revitalizing the brand. Rather than just talking to kids, as had become its habit, Kraft Canada decided it needed to reconnect with adults. Kraft Canada has a website devoted to the product (www.kraftcanada.com/en/ProductsPromotions/J-L/KraftDinner.htm) where Kraft shows parents how they can share the Kraft Dinner experience with their kids.

▶

Kraft has also been busy on other fronts. The famous blue-and yellow box was given a face-lift, giving the lettering a 3-D look. New product versions were developed, including Easy Mac Macaroni & Cheese, a microwaveable, snack-size extension. In January 2006, "Supermac & Cheese" was launched as part of Kraft's efforts to address the issue of childhood obesity. It is fortified with additional vitamins and contains whole-grain pasta. With all of this attention, it's no wonder the product continues to be a Canadian icon.

Volkswagen Beetle

The original Volkswagen Beetle first sputtered into North America in 1949. With its simple, buglike design, no-frills engineering, and economical operation, the Beetle was the antithesis of Detroit's chrome-laden gas guzzlers. During the 1960s, as young baby boomers by the thousands were buying their first cars, demand exploded and the anything-but-flashy Beetle blossomed. Bursting with personality, the understated Bug came to personify an era of rebellion against conventions. By 1968, it had become one of the most popular cars in history. By the late 1970s, however, the boomers had moved on.

Still, decades later, the mere mention of these chugging oddities evoked smiles and strong emotions.

Some products seem to defy the product life cycle. Rather than acting like a 50-year-old, the rejuvenated Volkswagen Beetle is behaving more like a frisky adolescent.

So rather than letting the old Beetle die, Volkswagen decided to rekindle the life cycle of this little car that could. In 1998, it introduced a New Beetle. Outwardly, the reborn Beetle resembles the original, tapping the strong emotions and memories of times gone by. Beneath the skin, however, the New Beetle is packed with modern features, such as a high-tech multi-speaker stereo—and options such as power windows, cruise control, and a power sunroof.

Initial advertising for the New Beetle played strongly on the car's former life, while at the same time refreshing the old Beetle heritage. "If you sold your soul in the '80s," tweaked one ad, "here's your chance to buy it back."

Volkswagen invested US$560 million to bring the Beetle back to life. But the investment paid big dividends as demand quickly outstripped supply. Rather than acting like a 50-year-old, the rejuvenated brand behaved more like a frisky adolescent. Even before the first cars reached VW showrooms, dealers across North America had long waiting lists of people who'd paid for the car without ever seeing it, let alone driving it. Even kids too young to remember the original Bug loved this new one.

Sales of the New Beetle rose quickly and it was named by *Motor Trend* as the 1999 car of the year. The New Beetle now accounts for more than a quarter of Volkswagen's North American sales and has helped VW increase sales fivefold during the past decade. Says one trend analyst, the New Beetle "is different, yet deeply familiar—a car for the times."

Sources: Quotes and information from "Kraft Dinner," Wikipedia, http://en.wikipedia.org/wiki/Kraft_Macaroni_and_Cheese (accessed April 2006); Jen Horsey, "Only in Canada You Say," www.canoe.ca/CNEWSCanadiana01/0629_food-cp.html (accessed June 29, 2000); John Heinzl, "Kraft Dinner Serves Up a New Look," *Globe and Mail,* January 13, 1999, p. B30; Lara Mills, "Kraft Builds Ads around 'KD Truths,'" *Marketing Magazine,* April 26, 1999, www.marketingmag.ca; "Easy Mac simplifies Kraft Dinner," *Marketing Magazine,* September 6, 1999, www.marketingmag.ca; Michael Cavanaugh, "The digital eye," *Marketing Magazine,* March 13, 2000, www.marketingmag.ca; Kathleen Deslauriers, "Easy Mac Stirs Up Awareness," *Strategy,* March 13, 2000, p.18; Theresa Howard, "Nostalgia Helps Beetle Score," *USA Today,* February 23, 2003, accessed online at www.usatoday.com; James R. Rosenfield, "Millennial Fever," *American Demographics,* December 1997, pp. 47–51; "A Top-Popping Good Time," *The Washington Post,* April 24, 2003, p. G18.

ride along with or defend their mature products—a good offence is the best defence. They should consider modifying the market, product, and marketing mix.

In *modifying the market,* the company tries to increase the consumption of the current product. It may look for new users and market segments, as when Johnson & Johnson targeted the adult market with its baby powder and shampoo. Or the company may reposition the brand to appeal to a larger or faster-growing segment, as Verizon did when it expanded into high-speed Internet and wireless services. The manager may also look for ways to increase usage among present customers. Amazon.com does this by sending permission-based emails to regular customers, letting them know when their favourite authors or performers publish new books or CDs. The WD-40 Company has shown a real knack for expanding the market by finding new uses for its popular substance.

In 2000, the company launched a search to uncover 2000 unique uses for WD-40. After receiving 300 000 individual submissions, it narrowed the list to the best 2000 and posted it on the company's website. Some consumers suggest simple and practical uses. One teacher uses WD-40 to clean old chalkboards in her classroom. "Amazingly, the boards started coming to life again," she reports. Others, however, report some pretty unusual applications. One man uses WD-40 to polish his glass eye; another uses it to remove a prosthetic leg. And did you hear about the nude burglary suspect who had wedged himself in a vent at a café? The fire department extracted him with a large dose of WD-40. Or how about the man who used WD-40 to repel an angry bear? Then there's the college student who wrote to say that a friend's nightly amorous activities in the next room were causing everyone in his dorm to lose sleep—he solved the problem by treating the squeaky bedsprings with WD-40.[27]

The company might also try *modifying the product*—changing characteristics such as quality, features, or style to attract new users and to inspire more usage. It might improve the product's quality and performance—its durability, reliability, speed, taste. It can improve the product's styling and attractiveness. Thus, car manufacturers restyle their cars to attract buyers who want a new look. The makers of consumer food and household products introduce new flavours, colours, ingredients, or packages to revitalize consumer buying. Or the company might add new features that expand the product's usefulness, safety, or convenience. For exam-

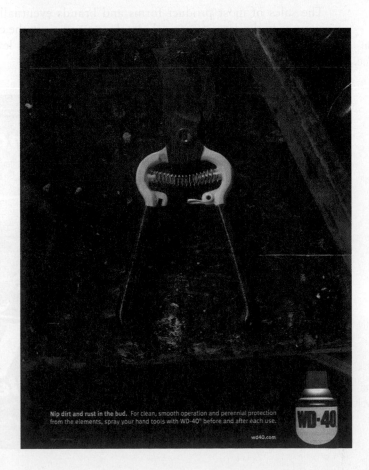

The WD-40 Company's knack for finding new uses has made this popular substance one of the truly essential survival items in most homes.

ple, Apple keeps adding new styles and features to its iPod line, and Volvo adds new safety features to its cars.

Finally, the company can try *modifying the marketing mix*—improving sales by changing one or more marketing mix elements. It can cut prices to attract new users and competitors' customers. It can launch a better advertising campaign or use aggressive sales promotions—trade deals, cents-off, premiums, and contests. Hormel, maker of Spam, recently launched a new advertising campaign and other promotions to reposition and revitalize its mature product, which has been around since the late 1930s.[28]

Joe Spam is the everyman who impresses crowds at barbecues, beach get-togethers, and breakfasts by offering basic-assembly Spam-centred recipes. The pitch is that the spicy smoked taste of Spam makes eggs, pizza—almost anything— better. And it's done with all the over the top fervour of "Monty Python's Flying Circus" famed Spam routine. In the spots, people literally eat up the stuff, and when there's none left, Joe Spam is able to clap his hands, yell out "More Spam!" and call up a Spammobile that crashes the party out of the clear blue to deliver up more of the "crazy tasty" stuff. The crowd, of course, barely notices the unusual delivery, as they only have eyes for the little tins of love. The campaign tries to capture the boldness of the brand. In one year alone, the company's three Spammobiles and their crews of SPAMbassadors doled out more than 1.5 million Spamburgers at 675 events around North America.

In addition to pricing and promotion, the company can also move into larger market channels, using mass merchandisers, if these channels are growing. Finally, the company can offer new or improved services to buyers.

Decline Stage

Decline stage
The product life-cycle stage in which a product's sales decline.

The sales of most product forms and brands eventually dip. The decline may be slow, as in the case of oatmeal cereal, or rapid, as in the case of phonograph records. Sales may plunge to zero, or they may drop to a low level where they continue for many years. This is the **decline stage**.

Hormel, maker of Spam, recently launched a new "crazy tasty" advertising and promotion campaign, complete with the SPAMMOBILE, to reposition and revitalize its mature product, which has been around since the late 1930s.

Sales decline for many reasons, including technological advances, shifts in consumer tastes, and increased competition. As sales and profits decline, some firms withdraw from the market. Those remaining may prune their product offerings. They may drop smaller market segments and marginal trade channels, or they may cut the promotion budget and reduce their prices further.

Carrying a weak product can be very costly to a firm, and not just in profit terms. There are many hidden costs. A weak product may take up too much of management's time. It often requires frequent price and inventory adjustments. It requires advertising and sales force attention that might be better used to make "healthy" products more profitable. A product's failing reputation can cause customer concerns about the company and its other products. The biggest cost may well lie in the future. Keeping weak products delays the search for replacements, creates a lopsided product mix, hurts current profits, and weakens the company's foothold on the future.

For these reasons, companies need to pay more attention to their aging products. The firm's first task is to identify those products in the decline stage by regularly reviewing sales, market shares, costs, and profit trends. Then, management must decide whether to maintain, harvest, or drop each of these declining products.

Management may decide to *maintain* its brand without change in the hope that competitors will leave the industry. For example, Procter & Gamble made good profits by remaining in the declining liquid soap business as others withdrew. Or management may decide to reposition or reformulate the brand in hopes of moving it back into the growth stage of the product life cycle. P&G did this with its Mr. Clean brand:

> Mr. Clean's share of the all-purpose household cleaner market had plunged more than 45 percent in just 10 years. But rather than abandon the 46-year-old iconic brand, P&G chose to modify and extend it. First, it reformulated

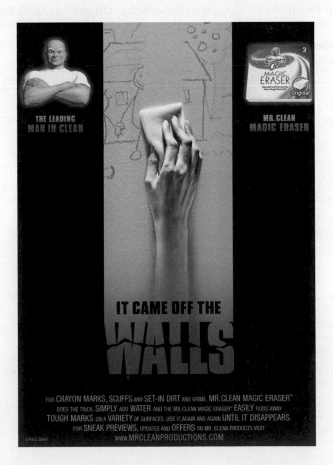

P&G revitalized the Mr. Clean brand in hopes that it can muscle its way back into a market-leading position.

the core Mr. Clean all-purpose liquid cleaner, adding antibacterial properties and several new scents. Then, it extended the brand to include two revolutionary new products. The first was Mr. Clean Magic Eraser, a soft, disposable self-cleaning pad that acts like an eraser to lift away tough dirt, including difficult scuff and crayon marks. The second was the Mr. Clean AutoDry Carwash system, which gives your car a spot-free clean and shine with no need to hand dry. P&G backed the new-product launches with US$50 million in marketing support. Now, after a decade of playing the 98-pound weakling, P&G hopes that a revitalized Mr. Clean can muscle its way back to a market-leading position.[29]

Management may decide to *harvest* the product, which means reducing various costs (plant and equipment, maintenance, R&D, advertising, sales force) and hoping that sales hold up. If successful, harvesting will increase the company's profits in the short run. Or management may decide to *drop* the product from the line. It can sell it to another firm or simply liquidate it at salvage value. In recent years, P&G has sold off a number of lesser or declining brands, such as Oxydol detergent and Jif peanut butter. If the company plans to find a buyer, it will not want to run down the product through harvesting.

Table 10.2 summarizes the key characteristics of each stage of the PLC. The table also lists the marketing objectives and strategies for each stage.[30]

TABLE 10.2 Summary of Product Life-Cycle Characteristics, Objectives, and Strategies

Characteristics	Introduction	Growth	Maturity	Decline
Sales	Low	Rapidly rising sales	Peak	Declining sales
Costs	High per customer	Average cost per customer	Low cost per customer	Low cost per customer
Profits	Negative	Rising profits	High profits	Declining profits
Customers	Innovators	Early adopters	Middle majority	Laggards
Competitors	Few	Growing number	Stable number beginning to decline	Declining number
Marketing Objectives	Create product awareness and trial	Maximize market share	Maximize profit while defending market share	Reduce expenditure and milk the brand
Strategies				
Product	Offer a basic product	Offer product extensions, service, warranty	Diversify brand and models	Phase out weak items
Price	Use cost-plus	Price to penetrate market	Price to match or best competitors	Cut price
Distribution	Build selective distribution	Build intensive distribution	Build more intensive distribution	Go selective: phase out unprofitable outlets
Advertising	Build product awareness among early adopters and dealers	Build awareness and interest in the mass market	Stress brand differences and benefits	Reduce to level needed to retain hard-core loyals
Sales promotion	Use heavy sales promotions to entice trial	Reduce to take advantage of heavy consumer demand	Increase to encourage brand switching	Reduce to minimal level

Source: Philip Kotler and Peggy Cunningham, *Marketing Management: Analysis, Planning, Implementation, and Control*, Canadian 11th ed. (Toronto: Pearson Education Canada, 2004), p. 347.

Reviewing the Concepts

A company's current products face limited life spans and must be replaced by newer products. But new products can fail—the risks of innovation are as great as the rewards. The key to successful innovation lies in a total-company effort, strong planning, and a systematic *new-product development* process.

1. Explain how companies find and develop new-product ideas.

Companies find and develop new-product ideas from a variety of sources. Many new-product ideas stem from *internal sources.* Companies conduct formal research and development, pick the brains of their employees, and brainstorm at executive meetings. Other ideas come from *external sources.* By conducting surveys and focus groups and analyzing *customer* questions and complaints, companies can generate new-product ideas that will meet specific consumer needs. Companies track *competitors'* offerings and inspect new products, dismantling them, analyzing their performance, and deciding whether to introduce a similar or improved product. *Distributors and suppliers* are close to the market and can pass along information about consumer problems and new-product possibilities.

2. List and define the steps in the new-product development process.

The new-product development process consists of eight sequential stages. The process starts with *idea generation.* Next comes *idea screening,* which reduces the number of ideas based on the company's own criteria. Ideas that pass the screening stage continue through *product concept development,* in which a detailed version of the new-product idea is stated in meaningful consumer terms. In the next stage, *concept testing,* new-product concepts are tested with a group of target consumers to determine whether the concepts have strong consumer appeal. Strong concepts proceed to *marketing strategy development,* in which an initial marketing strategy for the new product is developed from the product concept. In the *business analysis* stage, a review of the sales, costs, and profit projections for a new product is conducted to determine whether the new product is likely to satisfy the company's objectives. With positive results here, the ideas become more concrete through *product development* and *test marketing* and finally are launched during *commercialization.*

3. Describe the stages of the product life cycle.

Each product has a *life cycle* marked by a changing set of problems and opportunities. The sales of the typical product follow an S-shaped curve made up of five stages. The cycle begins with the *product development stage* when the company finds and develops a new-product idea. The *introduction stage* is marked by slow growth and low profits as the product is distributed to the market. If successful, the product enters a *growth stage,* which offers rapid sales growth and increasing profits. Next comes a *maturity stage* when sales growth slows down and profits stabilize. Finally, the product enters a *decline stage* in which sales and profits dwindle. The company's task during this stage is to recognize the decline and to decide whether it should maintain, harvest, or drop the product.

4. Describe how marketing strategies change during the product's life cycle.

In the *introduction stage*, the company must choose a launch strategy consistent with its intended product positioning. Much money is needed to attract distributors and build their inventories and to inform consumers of the new product and achieve trial. In the *growth stage,* companies continue to educate potential consumers and distributors. In addition, the company works to stay ahead of the competition and sustain rapid market growth by improving product quality, adding new product features and models, entering new market segments and distribution channels, shifting advertising from building product awareness to building product conviction and purchase, and lowering prices at the right time to attract new buyers. In the *maturity stage,* companies continue to invest in maturing products and consider modifying the market, the product, and the marketing mix. When *modifying the market,* the company attempts to increase the consumption of the current product. When *modifying the product,* the company changes some of the product's characteristics—such as quality, features, or style—to attract new users or inspire more usage. When *modifying the marketing mix,* the company works to improve sales by changing one or more of the marketing mix elements. Once the company recognizes that a product has entered the *decline stage*, management must decide whether to *maintain* the brand without change, hoping that competitors will drop out of the market; *harvest* the product, reducing costs and trying to maintain sales; or *drop* the product, selling it to another firm or liquidating it at salvage value.

Reviewing the Key Terms

Business analysis   389
Commercialization   394
Concept testing   386
Decline stage   404
Growth stage   400
Idea generation   380
Idea screening   385
Introduction stage   399
Marketing strategy development   388

Maturity stage   401
New-product development   378
Product concept   386
Product development   389
Product life cycle (PLC)   397
Sequential product development   395
Simultaneous (or team-based) product development   395
Test marketing   391

Discussing the Concepts

1. Which is a better source of new-product ideas, the company's sales force or external sources?

2. Write a 100-word, three-part marketing strategy statement for a new music CD by your favourite recording artist.

3. Under what conditions would you consider not test marketing a product? Describe a product or service that meets these no-need-to-test criteria.

4. Compare the sequential and simultaneous product development approaches. Is one approach better than the other? Explain.

5. What major commercialization plan elements must a marketer address before launching a new product?

6. The chapter states that "In the growth stage [of the product life cycle], the firm faces a trade-off between high market share and high current profit." Explain this statement.

Applying the Concepts

1. You are a new-product manager and have been asked to design an idea-screening process for your company. Prepare a five-step process for screening consumer convenience good ideas.

2. Prepare a concept test questionnaire for a new action toy figure with the following characteristics: disguised superhero, middle-aged, stout, balding man; dressed in dark grey suit, white shirt, dark tie; carries a brief case; drives a five-year-old Ford Crown Victoria; targeted to boys aged 7 to 10.

3. You are a product manager in a firm that manufactures and markets a line of branded action figure toys. The branded toy line is five years old. Annual sales and profits for this period are presented in the following chart. Prepare a one-sentence strategy for each of the four Ps based on the brand's current product life-cycle position.

Period	Sales	Profit
Year 1	$ 3 000 000	($ 100 000)
Year 2	$ 20 000 000	$ 1 500 000
Year 3	$ 50 000 000	$10 000 000
Year 4	$ 52 000 000	$ 8 000 000
Year 5	$ 31 000 000	$ 1 000 000

Focus on Technology

Many firms provide software and services to assist firms with product life-cycle management. One of the more successful companies providing these services is Agile Software Corporation. According to the company, "Agile Product Lifecycle Management (Agile™ PLM) solutions help companies accelerate revenue, reduce costs, improve quality, ensure compliance, and drive innovation throughout the product lifecycle.... Agile helps companies get the most from their products." Go to Agile's website at

www.agile.com/plm/plm_solutions.asp and review the PLM offering. Then respond to the following questions:

1. What are the PLM services that Agile provides?

2. On what portion of the product life cycle does Agile focus?

3. Based on what you have read at the Agile site, do you think Agile's PLM services would be a good or poor investment? Why?

Focus on Ethics

Concept testing is an invaluable part of the new-product development process. Time spent testing product concepts with consumers before developing them will reduce the number of false starts and conserve one of the most important resources in new-product development—money. Many companies shortcut the concept-testing stage and go direct to demand testing. They conduct what are called "dry tests." Dry testing occurs when you "test the waters" for interest in a new product by placing an ad for the product before it actually exists.

1. Do you believe that such dry testing is ethical?

2. What does the Direct Marketing Association (DMA) say about the practice? (Do a Google search on "dry testing" [in quotation marks] and DMA.) What does the Federal Trade Commission (FTC) say?

3. Would you dry test a new-product concept? Under what conditions?

Video Case
eGO Bikes

When it hit the market in 2002, the eGO was the first vehicle of its kind: an environmentally friendly, compact electric moped. Although the concept seems simple, the design and development of the new product was anything but. And, although the new concept helped create buzz and generated interest for the electric moped, it also posed some challenges for eGO's marketers. For starters, eGO struggled with how to introduce and position the new product for potential customers who are unfamiliar with the technology and unaware of the need it fills. Perhaps most important, the moped was so different from already available mopeds that there were no obvious channels for distribution.

Despite these setbacks, and with almost no advertising at all, eGO was selling nearly 1000 mopeds each month just three months after introduction, and sales

were growing rapidly. Today the company is still working to promote the product and grow sales.

After viewing the video featuring eGO vehicles, answer the following questions about new product development:

1. How did design decisions impact the development and marketing of the eGO?
2. What strategies did eGO employ to successfully launch the eGO electric moped?
3. Identify the company's target markets. What other consumers might eGO target?
4. Develop two additional concepts for the eGO Cycle. Select one concept and list three questions marketers might ask consumers to test the concept.

Online Media Resources

Video Short
Log on to your Companion Website at www.pearsoned.ca/kotler to view the video segment related to the Video Case above.

CBC ⊕ CBC Video Case
Please refer to Appendix 2 to read a CBC Video Case for this chapter, and log on to your Companion Website at www.pearsoned.ca/kotler to view the corresponding video segment.

Case Pilot
Log on to your Companion Website at www.pearsoned.ca/kotler to sharpen your case analysis skills and take the Case Pilot Challenge!

Company Case
I Want My VOIP!!!!

A $10 billion industry is up for grabs. In 2002, the Canadian Radio-television and Telecommunications Commission reported that about 95 percent of the local residential and business phone markets were controlled by former monopolies, such as Bell and Telus Corporation. Today, however, a new way to make phone calls may revolutionize the industry. Consumers and businesses alike, tired of hefty bills for local and long distance service, are starting to pay more attention to the digital telephone offers.

Take the case of Rita, a consumer annoyed with paying high long-distance charges. Rita remembered someone talking to her several years ago about making telephone calls over the Internet, but she had gotten the impression that you had to pay for each call, that sound quality was poor, and that calls were frequently interrupted. However, as she began to explore the different options, she found introductory offers for digital telephone that started at just more than $10.

So Rita set out to learn more about digital telephone. She discovered that digital telephone uses VOIP—Voice Over Internet Protocol—based on soft-switching technology. Soft switching uses a small box in the subscriber's home called an EMTA (Embedded Multimedia Terminal Adapter), which looks like a large cable modem. It brings in phone calls, converts them to digital signals, and then sends them over the coaxial cable and fibre links to the headend. There, a call is sent to either a telephone switch or a regional data service. Soft switching is a much less expensive technology than the traditional circuit switching used in the past to send cable telephone calls. It is also much less expensive to maintain.

Because VOIP converts phone calls into data, the integration of telephone, TV, and data is extensive. VOIP users will be able to access complete call lists on their PCs, send pictures from cellphones directly to set-top boxes, and easily manage computer-based telephone address books. All the regular services offered by telephone companies, such as caller ID and call waiting, can be offered with digital telephone.

The advantages do not end there. There are no long-distance charges with digital telephone. All local and long-distance calls in Canada and the United States are covered by the same basic monthly charge. Furthermore, the physical location of equipment does not matter as long as it's connected to a broadband (DSL/cable) modem. This means that a Vancouver-based consumer with a broadband connection and a VOIP phone service could carry the broadband modem abroad, plug into their European hotel's broadband connection, and call home without paying an extra penny. Because VOIP systems allow for each user to have multiple phone numbers, families with kids in university can give them each a number with a local area code and the children can call home for free. It's the number and area code that matter, not where the caller or modem is physically located.

There will be even more features in the future, features that are out of the reach of the local telephone company to develop. There could be videophones, video email, and integrating phone messages and emails on a webpage that can be retrieved from any computer with an Internet connection. Just imagine checking who's calling while you're watching TV!

What are some of the problems with digital telephone? The first is voice quality. According to one subscriber who had just switched to digital telephone, everyone she called said she sounded like she was talking underwater. The company sent technicians to work on the system and the voice quality improved, but it is still not as good as regular telephone service. Another problem is that loss of power means loss of telephone service, whereas regular telephone systems still operate when electricity is out. Companies such as Cox are working to develop batteries that provide temporary backup power, but there is nothing that would provide telephone service for extensive blackout periods.

The technology for digital telephone has been around for a couple of years but cable operators have been slow to introduce the service. They have been focusing on selling high-speed Internet service, but the growth of subscribers for that service is beginning to decline. Also, the telephone companies are taking away much of their business with satellite and DirectTV. Finally, residential telephone service is a big market—more than US$70 billion a year. For cable companies, it appears to be the next growth market.

In spite of all the current and potential advantages of digital telephone, companies are competing on the basis of cost, not services. They offer a basic package with standard features, such as call waiting and caller id, for one price. Usually the price is 30 percent less than the telephone company's price. Cable operators, such as Rogers, have found that customers want packages, not a list of services with individual prices, and they like buying their video, high-speed Internet connection, and phone service from one company. Customers want one company and one bill. According to Cox President Jim Robbins, "bundled customers are more satisfied customers—we have lots of research to support that—and bundled customers churn (turn over) less." When companies offer the triple of video, Internet, and telephone, they find that normal churn of 20 percent drops by 30 to 50 percent. Of course, companies could offer packages of different bundles of services, just like current offers for cable TV. Then, it would be up to consumers to select the package of services that they want. But in this launch period, most companies are sticking to a basic package and making their pitch on price.

Given that there are still some problems with VOIP (voice quality and others), some companies are holding off on offering VOIP until they can offer more services. Others, however, are forging ahead. Primus, an Internet service provider that also offers long-distance and some local phone packages, became first out of the gate in Canada when it offered VOIP to broadband customers in January 2004. Vonage Canada is another early mover, and it offers unlimited incoming calls, 500 outgoing minutes a month anytime to anywhere in Canada, the U.S. and Puerto Rico for only $19.99 a month. Navigata, owned by the Crown corporation Saskatchewan Telecommunications, is another player. It offers local telephone, wireless, and Internet services. It wasn't long before the television giants, Rogers Cable and Shaw Communications, jumped on board and began providing local and long-distance telephone service to their customers digitally through their cable networks. Their deep pockets and widespread infrastructure to deliver VOIP, made them a major threat to the traditional telephone companies.

The telephone companies couldn't afford to be left behind. They had already seen their markets eroded by the rise of email and low-cost competition in the cellular phone and long-distance businesses. Bell Canada launched its IP telephony service in the Toronto region and Hamilton, Ontario, in September 2005 and has since expanded the service in Ontario and Quebec as a complement to its Sympatico high-speed Internet, cellphone, and satellite TV services.

The large phone companies have been hampered from dominating this new market by recent CRTC regulations. In May 2005, the CRTC announced that Internet-based local phone service would be regulated in order to build "sustainable competition" in local telephone service. It told the big phone companies that they couldn't price their local VOIP service below cost to stifle competition. In contrast, the CRTC said that

new entrants into the Internet telephony market could set their local VOIP rates as low as they wanted.

Telus said it was "extremely disappointed" with the CRTC's decision, declaring that the decision would "restrict its ability to provide Canadians with competitively priced IP services." Bell, Telus, Aliant, and the provincially owned SaskTel appealed the CRTC decision in June 2005.

There is little doubt that Internet telephone service will change the way North Americans communicate. Consumers like Rita are living the scenario that cable companies expect. These companies realize that people like Rita aren't looking for an alternative means of making telephone calls. After all, she has a cell phone. Instead, she wants to lower cost. She wants convenience and value but would be turned off by tech-speak; hence the name, digital telephone. It communicates what the service is, and the introductory package hammered home lower price.

After finding out all about Internet telephony, Rita made a list of the pros and cons subscribing to a VOIP service. What do you think she will do?

Questions for Discussion

1. Play the role of Rita and do a search of the VOIP options in Canada. For example, go to Google.ca, and type in the search words "Internet Telephone Service Canada." Select the "pages from Canada" option. List three options you want to explore further. How do they compare in terms of what they offer?

2. If you were Rita, what do you see as the advantages and disadvantages of Internet telephone service?

3. Write the first part of a marketing strategy statement for the Vonage Canada digital telephone offer. Include the target market and planned product positioning.

4. In what stage of the product life cycle is Internet telephony? Does the answer to this question vary across companies, such as Vonage, Rogers, and Bell?

5. Why does bundling services work so well for the cable companies? What are the advantages to both the consumer and the company?

Sources: John Higgins, "A Different Kind of Price War," *Broadcasting & Cable,* July 19, 2004, p. 14; "VOIP Is Getting Very Real," *America's Network,* September 15, 2003, p. 34; Peter Grant, "Cable Giants Vie to Improve Online Phoning," *Wall Street Journal,* January 8, 2004, p. A.15; John M. Higgins, "Cox Cable Plays Defense and Offense," *Broadcasting & Cable,* February 2, 2004, p. 38; John M. Higgins, "Cable Will Eat the Phone Company's Lunch..." *Broadcasting & Cable,* May 3, 2004, p. 1; "Internet phone service: Radical technology, telecom battle," *CBC News Online,* May 10, 2006, **www.cbc.ca/news/background/voip/index.html** (accessed July 2006).

Chapter 11
Pricing

AFTER STUDYING THIS CHAPTER YOU SHOULD BE ABLE TO

1. identify and define the internal factors affecting a firm's pricing decisions

2. identify and define the external factors affecting pricing decisions, including the impact of consumer perceptions of price and value

3. contrast the two general approaches to setting prices

4. discuss how companies adjust their prices to take into account different types of customers and situations

5. discuss the key issues related to initiating and responding to price changes

Previewing the Concepts

In this chapter we look at a second major marketing mix tool—pricing. According to one pricing expert, pricing involves "harvesting your profit potential."[1] If effective product development, promotion, and distribution sow the seeds of business success, effective pricing is the harvest. Firms successful at creating customer value with the other marketing mix activities must still capture some of this value in the prices they earn. Yet, despite its importance, many firms do not handle pricing well. In this chapter we focus on the process of setting prices. We also define price, look at the internal and external factors marketers must consider when setting prices, and examine three general pricing approaches. Then we'll look at pricing strategies available to marketers—new-product pricing strategies, product line pricing strategies, price adjustment strategies, and price reaction strategies. Finally, we'll look at public policy and ethical issues related to pricing.

The headlines scream: *Name your own price! Top-flight savings on more than 8000 top-notch hotels! Last-minute deals to more than 300 destinations! Save a boatload on best-known cruise lines! Big savings on long-distance calling!* Just the usual come-ons from fly-by-night operators? Too good to be true? Not at Priceline.com, at least not according to *Yahoo! Internet Life Magazine,* which recently proclaimed Priceline as the "Best Bargain Booker" on the Web. Priceline's byline: "I Think. Therefore I Save."

In 1998, founder Jay Walker launched Priceline as a radical new Internet service. It was based on an ingeniously simple concept—empower consumers to name their own prices, then dangle their offers in front of sellers and see who bites. Such transactions, he reasoned, benefited both buyers and sellers—buyers got lower prices; sellers turned excess inventory into profits. Although simple in concept, however, such "buyer-driven commerce" represented a dramatic departure from long-held pricing practices in which sellers—not buyers—set prices. Still, the idea caught on. Priceline has now grown to become the leading name-your-own-price Internet service and one of the few profitable dot-coms.

Priceline deals primarily in travel-related products—plane tickets, hotel rooms, rental cars, cruises, and vacation packages. Here's how it works—say, for a hotel room. First, you select your destination and desired dates. You can also select the types of hotels you're willing to stay in—from one-star ("economy hotels that provide comfort with no frills") to five-star ("the best that money can buy"). Give Priceline the usual billing information and a credit card number—and decide how much you'd like to bid. Click on "Buy My Hotel Room," then sit back and wait for Priceline to broker the deal. Within fifteen minutes, Priceline emails you with the news. If no suitable hotel is willing to accept your price, you can bid again later. If Priceline finds a taker, it immediately charges your credit card—no refunds, changes, or cancellations allowed—and lets you know where you'll be staying.

The concept of setting your own prices over the Internet has real appeal to consumers. It starts with a good value proposition—getting really low prices. Beyond that, "name-your-price is a great hook," say a Priceline marketing executive. "If you get it, it's like 'I won!'" As a result, Priceline is attracting more and more customers. Its customer base has grown to 19 million users, and as many as 9 million people visit the Priceline site monthly. In April 2006, its website bragged that it had saved its customers an incredible US$5.8 billion!

Despite accepting fire-sale prices, sellers also benefit from Priceline's services. It's especially attractive to those who sell products that are time sensitive. "If airlines or hotels don't sell seats on particular flights or rooms for certain nights, those assets become worthless," comments an analyst. "Such businesses are a natural fit for Priceline."

Priceline makes its money by buying up unsold rooms, seats, or vacation packages at heavily discounted rates, marking them up, and selling them to consumers for as much as a 12 percent return. So, on a $215 plane ticket, Priceline makes about $35, compared with the $10 gross profit made by a traditional travel agent.

Along with the successes and its recent profitability, however, Priceline has encountered some formidable obstacles. For example, not all products lend themselves to Priceline's business model, and the company has met with uneven success in attempts to grow beyond travel services. Although it currently takes bids in three other categories—new cars, long distance, and home financing (home mortgages, refinancing, and home equity loans)—selling products and services that aren't time sensitive has proven difficult.

Moreover, not all customers are thrilled with their Priceline experiences. Forcing customers to commit to purchases before they know the details—such as which hotel or airline, flight times, and hotel locations—can leave some customers feeling cheated. During a recent CBC morning show from Ottawa, the presenter proclaimed, "Incidentally, I had very little luck with the infamous Priceline.com (www.priceline.com), made famous by those cheesy TV spots featuring William Shatner. ... Unfortunately, when I keyed in 'Ottawa' as my point of origin, I was given the choices of Ottawa Illinois, Kansas, and Ohio." But for every disappointed customer, Priceline has hundreds or thousands of happy ones. Some 64 percent of those who now visit Priceline to name their own prices are repeat customers.

More than just changing how people pay for travel services, Priceline is perhaps the best example of how the Internet is changing today's pricing practices. "Only through the Web could you match millions of bids with millions of products, all without a fixed price," says one analyst.[2]

Companies today face a fierce and fast-changing pricing environment. Fierce competition and powerful buyers (as is the case in Canada's grocery industry) have put many companies in a "pricing vise." One analyst sums it up this way: "They have virtually no pricing power. It's impossible to raise prices, and often the pressure to slash them continues unabated. The pricing pinch is affecting business across the spectrum of manufacturing and services—everything from chemicals and autos to hoteliers and phone services."[3] It seems that almost every company is slashing prices, and that is hurting their profits.

Yet cutting prices is often not the best answer. Reducing prices unnecessarily can lead to lost profits and damaging price wars. It can signal to customers that price is more important than brand. Instead, companies should "sell value, not price."[4] They should persuade customers that paying a higher price for the company's brand is justified by the greater value it delivers. Most customers will gladly pay a fair price in exchange for real value. The challenge is to find the price that will let the company make a fair profit by harvesting the customer value it creates.

What Is a Price?

Price
The amount of money charged for a product or service, or the sum of the values that consumers exchange for the benefits of having or using the product or service.

Price goes by many names: "You pay *rent* for your apartment, *tuition* for your education, and *fees* to your bank. In the narrowest sense, **price** is the amount of money charged for a product or service. It should be noted, however, that in Canada, prices displayed on price tags, in advertisements, on shelves, or on websites do not include taxes. These are added to the price as the sale is being made. More broadly, price is the sum of all the values that consumers exchange for the benefits of having or using the product or service. Historically, price has been the major factor affecting buyer choice. However, in recent decades, non-price factors have become more important in buyer choice behaviour.

Today's New Pricing Environment

Throughout most of history, prices were set by negotiation between buyers and sellers. *Fixed price* policies—setting one price for all buyers—is a relatively modern idea that arose with the development of large-scale retailing at the end of the nineteenth century. Now, more than a hundred years later, the Internet promises to reverse the fixed pricing trend and take us back to an era of **dynamic pricing**—charging different prices depending on individual customers and situations.

For example, think about how the Internet and companies such as Priceline.com have affected pricing. From the mostly fixed pricing practices of the past century, the Web seems now to be taking us back—into a new age of fluid pricing. "Potentially, [the Internet] could push aside sticker prices and usher in an era of dynamic pricing," says one writer, "in which a wide range of goods would be priced according to what the market will bear—instantly, constantly."[5]

Dynamic pricing offers many advantages for marketers. For example, Internet sellers, such as Amazon.com, can mine their databases to gauge a specific shopper's desires, measure his or her means, instantaneously tailor products to fit that shopper's behaviour, and price products accordingly. Catalogue retailers, such as Tilley Endurables, Veseys Seeds, or J. Crew, can change prices on the fly according to changes in demand or costs. Online music retailer MusicRebellion.com, for example, lets consumer demand set the price for downloaded songs. Each song is initially available for download at 10 cents. As demand increases, however, prices may increase to as much as $1 per song.[6]

Similarly, IBM, a B2B marketer, automatically adjusts prices on its servers based on customer demand and product life-cycle factors. As a result, customers will find that prices change dynamically when they visit the IBM website on any given day. Dell also uses dynamic online pricing. "If the price of memory or processors decreases, we pass those savings along to the customer almost in real time," says a Dell spokesperson.

Buyers also benefit from the Web and dynamic pricing. A wealth of websites—such as Froogle.com, Bizrate.com, NexTag.com, PriceGrabber.com, CompareNet.com, and PriceScan.com—give instant product and price comparisons from thousands of

Dynamic pricing
Charging different prices depending on individual customers and situations.

The challenge is to harvest the customer value the company creates. Says Panera's CEO, pictured here, "Give people something of value, and they'll happily pay for it."

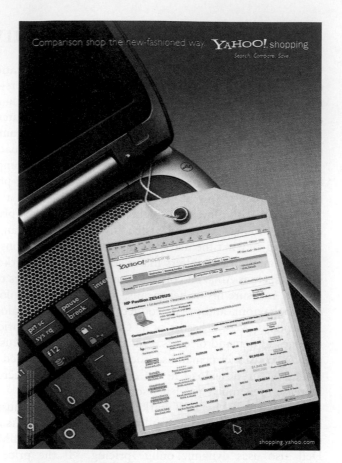

A wealth of websites—such as Yahoo! Shopping—give instant product and price comparisons from online vendors.

vendors. Yahoo! Shopping, for instance, lets shoppers browse by category or search for specific products and brands. It then searches the Web and reports links to sellers offering the best prices. In addition to simply finding the vendor with the best price, customers armed with price information can often negotiate lower prices.

Buyers can also negotiate prices at online auction sites and exchanges. Suddenly the centuries-old art of haggling is back in vogue. Want to sell that antique pickle jar that's been collecting dust for generations? Post it on eBay, the world's biggest online flea market. Want to purchase vintage baseball cards at a bargain price? Go to HeavyHitter.com.

Pricing: An Important but Difficult Decision

Price is the only element in the marketing mix that produces revenue; all other elements represent costs. Price is also one of the most flexible elements of the marketing mix. Unlike product features and channel commitments, price can be changed quickly.

At the same time, pricing and price competition is the number-one problem facing many marketing executives. Yet many companies do not handle pricing well. Companies are often too quick to reduce prices in order to get a sale rather than working to convince buyers that their products are worth the investment. Other common mistakes include pricing that is too cost oriented rather than customer-value oriented, prices that are not revised often enough to reflect market changes, pricing that does not take the rest of the marketing mix into account, and prices that are not varied enough for different products, market segments, and purchase occasions.

Paul Hunt, director of the strategic pricing division at The Advantage Group in Toronto, notes that the average company can increase its profitability by a whopping 25 to 60 percent just by improving its pricing processes. He stresses, however, that effective pricing does not mean nickel-and-diming customers; it means practising value-based pricing. When customers perceive that they are receiving superior value, they'll be willing to pay the price to get it.[7]

Factors to Consider When Setting Prices

A company's pricing decisions are affected by both internal company and external environmental factors. (See Figure 11.1.)[8]

Internal Factors Affecting Pricing Decisions

Internal factors affecting pricing include the company's *marketing objectives, marketing mix strategy, costs, product considerations*, and *organizational factors*.

Marketing Objectives

Before setting price, the company must decide on its strategy for the product. If the company has selected its target market and positioning carefully, then its marketing mix strategy, including price, will be fairly straightforward. For example, when Toyota developed its Lexus brands to compete with European luxury-performance cars in the higher-income segment, this required charging a high price. In contrast, when it introduced its "energetic but economical" Echo model, a car with "a sticker price that can really help you pursue your dreams," this positioning required charging a low price. Thus, pricing strategy is largely determined by decisions on market positioning.

At the same time, the company may seek additional general or specific objectives. General objectives include survival, current profit maximization, market share leadership, and product quality leadership. At a more specific level, a company can set prices low to prevent competition from entering the market or set prices at competitors' levels to stabilize the market. It can set prices to keep the loyalty and support of resellers or to avoid government intervention. Prices can be reduced temporarily to create excitement for a product or to draw more customers into a retail store. Or one product may be priced to help the sales of other products in the company's line. Thus, pricing may play an important role in helping to accomplish the company's objectives at many levels.

Many companies use *current profit maximization* as their pricing goal. They estimate what demand and costs will be at different prices and choose the price that will produce the maximum current profit, cash flow, or return on investment. Other

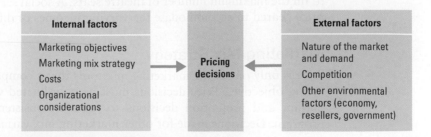

Figure 11.1 Factors affecting pricing decisions

Internal factors		External factors
Marketing objectives Marketing mix strategy Costs Organizational considerations	→ Pricing decisions ←	Nature of the market and demand Competition Other environmental factors (economy, resellers, government)

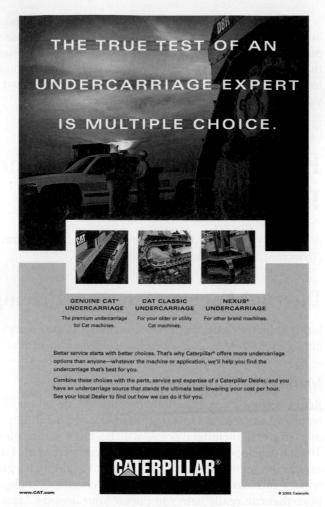

Caterpillar charges higher prices than competitors based on superior product and service quality. According to this ad, "Better service starts with better choices."

companies want to obtain *market share leadership*. To become the market share leader, these firms set prices as low as possible.

A company might decide that it wants to achieve *product quality leadership*. This normally calls for charging a high price to cover higher performance quality and the high cost of R&D. For example, Caterpillar charges 20 percent to 30 percent more than competitors for its heavy construction equipment, based on superior product and service quality. A.T. Cross doesn't sell just ballpoint pens—you can get those from Bic. Instead, it sells "fine writing instruments," with models bearing names like Classic Century, Ion, Morph, Matrix, ATX, and Radiance, selling for prices as high as US$400.

Not-for-profit and public organizations may adopt a number of other pricing objectives. A university aims for *partial cost recovery* for its public educational programs, knowing that it must rely on private gifts and public grants to cover the remaining costs, but it may aim for *full cost recovery* for its professional programs, such as MBA degrees. A not-for-profit theatre company may price its productions to fill the maximum number of theatre seats. A social service agency may set a *social price* geared to accommodate the varying incomes of different clients.

Marketing Mix Strategy

Price is only one of the marketing mix tools that a company uses to achieve its marketing objectives. Price decisions must be coordinated with product design, distribution, and promotion decisions to form a consistent and effective marketing program. Decisions made for other marketing mix variables can affect pricing decisions. For example, a decision to position the product on high-performance quality will mean that the seller must charge a higher price to cover higher costs. And producers whose resellers are expected to support and promote their products may have to build larger reseller margins into their prices.

Companies often position their products on price and then tailor other marketing mix decisions on the prices they want to charge. Here, price is a crucial product positioning factor that defines the product's market, competition, and design. Many firms support such price positioning strategies with a technique called **target costing**, a potent strategic weapon. Target costing reverses the usual process of first designing a new product, determining its cost, and then asking, "Can we sell it for that?" Instead, it starts with an ideal selling price based on customer considerations, then targets costs to ensure that the price is met.

Procter & Gamble used target costing to price and develop its highly successful Crest SpinBrush electric toothbrush:

> P&G usually prices its goods at a premium. But with Crest SpinBrush, P&G reversed its usual thinking. It started with an attractive low market price, and then found a way to make a profit at that price. SpinBrush's inventors first came up with the idea of a low-priced electric toothbrush while walking through their local Wal-Mart, where they saw Sonicare, Interplak, and other electric toothbrushes priced at more than $50. These pricy brushes held only a fraction of the overall toothbrush market. A less expensive electric toothbrush, the designers reasoned, would have huge potential. They decided on a target price of just $5, batteries included—only $1 more than the most expensive manual brushes—and set out to design a brush they could sell at that price. Every design element was carefully considered with the targeted price in mind. To meet the low price, P&G passed on the usual lavish new-product launch campaign. Instead, to give

Target costing
Pricing that starts with an ideal selling price, then targets costs that will ensure that the price is met.

Porsche proudly advertises its Cayenne as "starting at $55 900."

SpinBrush more point-of-sale impact, it relied on "Try Me" packaging that allowed consumers to turn the brush on in stores. Target cost pricing has made Crest SpinBrush one of P&G's most successful new products ever. Says brand manager Darin Yates, "It's hard for P&G's business models to conceive of a business growing as quickly as SpinBrush."[9]

Other companies de-emphasize price and use other marketing mix tools to create *non-price* positions. Often, the best strategy is not to charge the lowest price, but rather to differentiate the marketing offer to make it worth a higher price. For example, Sony builds more value into its consumer electronics products and charges a higher price than many competitors. Customers recognize Sony's higher quality and are willing to pay more to get it. Some marketers even *feature* high prices as part of their positioning. For example, Porsche proudly advertises its Cayenne as "starting at $55 900." And Steinway offers "the finest pianos in the world," with a price to match. Steinway's grand pianos can cost as much as $150 000. (See Real Marketing 11.1.)

REAL MARKETING | 11.1

Steinway: Price Is Nothing; the Steinway Experience Is Everything

A Steinway piano—any Steinway piano—costs a lot. But Steinway buyers aren't looking for bargains. In fact, it seems, the higher the prices, the better. High prices confirm that a Steinway is the very best that money can buy—the epitome of hand-crafted perfection. As important, the Steinway name is steeped in tradition. It evokes images of classical concert stages, sophisticated dinner parties, and the celebrities and performers who've owned and played Steinway pianos across more than 150 years. When it comes to Steinway, price is nothing, the Steinway experience is everything.

To be sure, Steinway & Sons makes very high-quality pianos. With 120 patents to its credit, Steinway & Sons has done more than any other manufacturer to advance the art of piano building. Steinway pioneered the development of a one-piece piano rim produced out of 17 laminations of veneer. It invented a process for bending a single 6.5 metre strip of these laminated sheets inside a massive piano-shaped vise. It's this strong frame that produces Steinway's distinctive clear tones. Steinway & Sons has continued perfecting this design, and today a Steinway piano's 243 tempered, hard-steel strings exert 32 tonnes of pressure—enough force to implode a three-bedroom house if the strings were strung between attic and cellar.

In addition to cutting-edge technology, Steinway & Sons uses only the finest materials to construct each piano. Rock maple, spruce, birch, poplar, and four

A Steinway takes you places you've never been.

A Steinway piano costs a lot, but buyers aren't looking for bargains. When it comes to Steinway, price is nothing, the Steinway experience is everything.

other species of wood each play a crucial functional role in the physical and acoustical beauty of a Steinway. Through delicate hand craftsmanship, Steinway transforms these select materials into pianos of incomparable sound quality. From start to finish, it takes 300 skilled workers more than a year to handcraft and assemble a Steinway piano from its 12 000 component parts. Thus, Steinway is anything but mass market. Each year, Steinway's factories craft only 1500 uprights and 3000 grand pianos. (By comparison, Yamaha produces 100 000 pianos per year.)

Steinway's precision quality alone would command top dollar, but Steinway buyers get much more than just a well-made piano. They also get the Steinway mystique. Owning or playing a Steinway puts you in some very good company. Fully 98 percent of piano soloists with the world's major symphony orchestras prefer playing on a Steinway. Performers of all kinds sing Steinway's praises. Singer-songwriter Randy Newman puts it this way: "I have owned and played a Steinway all my life. It's the best Beethoven piano. The best Chopin piano. And the best Ray Charles piano. I like it, too." Whereas some people want a Porsche in the garage, others prefer a Steinway in the living room—both cost about the same, and both make a statement about their owners.

Even in the worst of times, Steinway & Sons has held true to its tradition and image—and to its premium prices. Despite its very high prices—or more likely because of them—Steinway enjoys a 95 percent market share in concert halls. So, you won't find any weekend sales on Steinway pianos. Charging significantly higher prices continues to be a cornerstone of the company's "much more for much more" value proposition. And high prices have been good for Steinway & Sons.

To customers, whatever a Steinway costs, it's a small price to pay for the experience of owning one. Classical pianist Krystian Zimerman sums up his Steinway experience this way: "My friendship with the Steinway piano is one of the most important and beautiful things in my life." Who can put a price on such feelings?

Sources: Andy Serwer, "Happy Birthday Steinway," *Fortune*, March 17, 2003, p. 94; "Books and Arts: Making the Sound of Music; Piano Manufacturers," *The Economist*, June 7, 2003, p. 102; Brian T. Majeski, "The Steinway Story," *Music Trades*, September 2003, p. 18; "The Most Famous Name in Music," *Music Trades*, September 2003, p. 118–130; "Today's Steinway," *Music Trades*, September 2003, p. 140–145; Stephan Wilkinson, "High-Strung. Powerful. Very Pricey," *Popular Science*, March 1, 2003, p. 32; "Steinway Musical Instruments, Inc.," *Hoover's Company Capsules*, Austin, March 15, 2004, p. 48052; Michael Z. Wise, "Piano Versus Piano," *New York Times*, May 9, 2004; and quotes and information at www.steinway.com (accessed January 2005).

Thus, marketers must consider the total marketing mix when setting prices. If the product is positioned on non-price factors, then decisions about quality, promotion, and distribution will strongly affect price. If price is a crucial positioning factor, then price will strongly affect decisions made about the other marketing mix elements. But even when featuring price, marketers need to remember that customers rarely buy on price alone. Instead, they seek products that give them the best value in terms of benefits received for the price paid.

Costs

Costs set the floor for the price that the company can charge for its product. The company wants to charge a price that both covers all its costs for producing, distributing, and selling the product and delivers a fair rate of return for its effort and risk. A company's costs may be an important element in its pricing strategy. Many companies—such as Southwest Airlines, Wal-Mart, and Union Carbide—work to become the "low-cost producers" in their industries. Companies with lower costs can set lower prices that result in greater sales and profits.

Fixed costs
Costs that do not vary with production or sales level.

Variable costs
Costs that vary directly with the level of production.

Total costs
The sum of the fixed and variable costs for any given level of production.

Types of Costs A company's costs take two forms—fixed and variable. **Fixed costs** (also known as overhead) are costs that do not vary with production or sales level. For example, a company must pay each month's bills for rent, heat, interest, and executive salaries, whatever the company's output. **Variable costs** depend directly on the level of production. Each personal computer produced by Dell involves a cost of computer chips, wires, plastic, packaging, and other inputs. These costs tend to be the same for each unit produced. They are called *variable* because their total varies with the number of units produced. **Total costs** are the sum of the fixed and variable costs for any given level of production. Management wants to charge a price that will at least cover the total production costs. The company must watch its costs carefully: If it costs the company more than competitors to produce and sell a similar product, the company will have to charge a higher price or make less profit, putting it at a competitive disadvantage.

Costs at Different Levels of Production   To price wisely, management needs to know how its costs vary with different levels of production. For example, suppose Texas Instruments (TI) has built a plant to produce 1000 handheld calculators per day. Figure 11.2A shows the typical short-run average cost (SRAC) curve. It shows that the cost per calculator is high if TI's factory produces only a few per day. But as production moves up to 1000 calculators per day, average cost falls. This is because fixed costs are spread over more units, with each one bearing a smaller fixed cost. TI can try to produce more than 1000 calculators per day, but average costs will increase because the plant becomes inefficient. Workers have to wait for machines, the machines break down more often, and workers get in one another's way.

If TI believed it could sell 2000 calculators a day, it should consider building a larger plant. The plant would use more efficient machinery and work arrangements. Also, the unit cost of producing 2000 calculators per day would be lower than the unit cost of producing 1000 calculators per day, as shown in the long-run average cost (LRAC) curve (Figure 11.2B). In fact, a 3000-capacity plant would be even more efficient, according to Figure 11.2B. But a 4000-daily-production plant would be less efficient because of increasing diseconomies of scale—too many workers to manage, paperwork slowing things down, and so on. Figure 11.2B shows that a 3000-daily-production plant is the best size to build if demand is strong enough to support this level of production.

Costs as a Function of Production Experience   Suppose TI runs a plant that produces 3000 calculators per day. As TI gains experience in producing handheld calculators, it learns how to do it better. Workers learn shortcuts and become more familiar with their equipment. With practice, the work becomes better organized, and TI finds better equipment and production processes. With higher volume, TI becomes more efficient and gains economies of scale. As a result, average cost tends to fall with accumulated production experience. This is shown in Figure 11.3.[10] Thus, the average cost of producing the first 100 000 calculators is $10 per calculator. When the company has produced the first 200 000 calculators, the average cost has fallen to $9. After its accumulated production experience doubles again to 400 000, the average cost is $7. This drop in the average cost with accumulated production experience is called the **experience curve** (or the **learning curve**).

If a downward-sloping experience curve exists, this is highly significant for the company. Not only will the company's unit production cost fall, but it will also fall

Experience curve (learning curve)

The drop in the average per-unit production cost that comes with accumulated production experience.

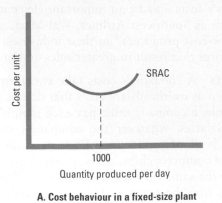

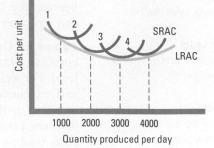

Figure 11.2 Cost per unit at different levels of production per period

A. Cost behaviour in a fixed-size plant

B. Cost behaviour over different-size plants

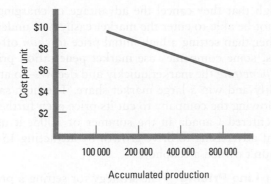

Figure 11.3 Cost per unit as a function of accumulated production: the experience curve

faster if the company makes and sells more during a given period. But the market must stand ready to buy the higher output. And to take advantage of the experience curve, TI must get a large market share early in the product's life cycle. This suggests the following pricing strategy: TI should price its calculators low; its sales will then increase, and its costs will decrease through gaining more experience, and then it can lower its prices further.

Some companies have built successful strategies around the experience curve. For example, Bausch & Lomb solidified its position in the soft contact lens market by using computerized lens design and steadily expanding its one Soflens plant. As a result, its market share climbed steadily to 65 percent. However, a single-minded focus on reducing costs and exploiting the experience curve will not always work. Experience curve pricing carries some major risks. The aggressive pricing might give the product a cheap image. The strategy also assumes that competitors are weak and not willing to fight it out by meeting the company's price cuts. Finally, while the company is building volume under one technology, a competitor may find a lower-cost technology that lets it start at lower prices than the market leader, who still operates on the old experience curve.

Product Considerations

Pricing and product line considerations are closely interrelated, especially when new products are being introduced or when marketers are working with a line of related products.

New-Product Pricing   Companies bringing out a new product face the challenge of setting prices for the first time. They can choose between two strategies: *market skimming pricing* and *market penetration pricing.*

Many companies that invent new products initially set high prices to "skim" revenues layer by layer from the market. Intel is a prime user of this strategy, called **market skimming pricing.** When Sony introduced the world's first high-definition television (HDTV) to the Japanese market in 1990, the high-tech sets cost $68 000. These televisions were purchased only by customers who could afford to pay a high price for the new technology. Sony rapidly reduced the price over the next several years to attract new buyers. By 1993 a 28-inch HDTV cost a Japanese buyer just over $9000. In 2001, a Japanese consumer could buy a 40-inch HDTV for about $3000, a price that many more customers could afford. HDTV sets now sell for about $3000 in North America, and "HDTV-ready" sets sell for about $1500. In this way, Sony skimmed the maximum amount of revenue from the various segments of the market.[11]

Market skimming makes sense only under certain conditions. First, the product's quality and image must support its higher price, and enough buyers must want the product at that price. Second, the costs of producing a smaller volume cannot

Market skimming pricing
Setting a high price for a new product to skim maximum revenues layer by layer from the segments willing to pay the high price; the company makes fewer but more profitable sales.

be so high that they cancel the advantage of charging more. Finally, competitors should not be able to enter the market easily and undercut the high price.

Rather than setting a high initial price to *skim* off small but profitable market segments, some companies use **market penetration pricing**. They set a low initial price to *penetrate* the market quickly and deeply—to attract a large number of buyers quickly and win a large market share. The high sales volume results in falling costs, allowing the company to cut its price even further. For example, when Virgin Mobile entered Canada in the summer of 2005, it used penetration pricing and irreverent advertising to drive growth by attracting 15- to 30-year-olds who previously hadn't owned a cellphone.

Market penetration pricing
Setting a low price for a new product to attract a large number of buyers and a large market share.

Product Line Pricing   The strategy for setting a product's price often has to be changed when the product is part of a product mix. Pricing is difficult because the various products have related demand and costs, and face different degrees of competition.

Companies usually develop product lines rather than single products. Toro, for example, makes many different lawn mowers, ranging from simple walk-behind versions priced at US$259.95, US$299.95, and US$399.95, to elaborate riding mowers priced at US$1000 or more. Each successive lawn mower in the line offers more features. In **product line pricing**, management must decide on the price steps to set between the various products in a line.

Product line pricing
Setting the price steps between various products in a product line based on cost differences between the products, customer evaluations of different features, and competitors' prices.

The price steps must take into account cost differences between the products in the line, customer evaluations of their different features, and competitors' prices.

In many industries, sellers use well-established *price points* for the products in their line. Thus, men's clothing stores, such as upscale Harry Rosen, may carry men's suits at three price levels: $800, $1200, $2200. The customer probably will associate good, excellent, and exceptionally high-quality suits with the three price points. Even if the three prices are raised a little, men typically will still buy suits at their own preferred price points. The seller's task is to establish perceived quality differences that support the price differences.

Organizational Considerations

Management must decide who within the organization should set prices. Companies handle pricing in a variety of ways. In small companies, prices often are set by top management rather than by the marketing or sales departments. In large companies, pricing typically is handled by divisional or product line managers. In industrial markets, salespeople may be allowed to negotiate with customers within certain price ranges. Even so, top management sets the pricing objectives and policies, and it often approves the prices proposed by lower-level management or salespeople. In industries in which pricing is a key factor (aerospace, railway, and oil companies), companies often have a pricing department to set the best prices or help others in setting them. This department reports to the marketing department or top management. Others who have an influence on pricing include sales managers, production managers, finance managers, and accountants.

External Factors Affecting Pricing Decisions

External factors that affect pricing decisions include the nature of the market and demand, competition, and other environmental elements.

The Market and Demand

Whereas costs set the lower limit of prices, the market and demand set the upper limit. Both consumer and industrial buyers balance the price of a product or service against the benefits of owning it. Thus, before setting prices, the marketer must understand the relationship between price and demand for its product. In this section, we explain how the price–demand relationship varies for different types of markets and how buyer perceptions of price affect the pricing decision. We then discuss methods for measuring the price–demand relationship.

Pricing in Different Types of Markets   The seller's pricing freedom depends on the type of market the company operates in. Economists recognize four types of markets, each presenting a different pricing challenge because markets differ in their structure and the type of competitors present in the marketplace.

Under *pure competition*, the market consists of many buyers and sellers trading in a uniform commodity, such as wheat, copper, or financial securities. No single buyer or seller has much effect on the going market price.

Under *monopolistic competition*, the market consists of many buyers and sellers who trade over a range of prices rather than at a single market price. A range of prices occurs because sellers can differentiate their offers to buyers. Either the physical product can be varied in quality, features, or style, or the accompanying services can be varied. Buyers see differences in sellers' products and will pay different prices for them. Sellers try to develop differentiated offers for different customer segments and, in addition to price, freely use branding, advertising, and personal selling to set their offers apart. Thus, Roots differentiates its lifestyle products from jeans to home furnishings through strong positioning and branding, through sponsorship of major events, and through advertising to reduce the impact of price. Because there are many competitors, each firm is less affected by competitors' marketing strategies than in oligopolistic markets.

Under *oligopolistic competition*, the market consists of a few sellers who are highly sensitive to each other's pricing and marketing strategies. The product can be uniform (steel, aluminum) or non-uniform (cars, computers). There are few sellers because it is difficult for new sellers to enter the market. Each seller is alert to competitors' strategies and moves. For example, in the summer of 2005, as the inventories of the major North American automobile manufacturers grew, General Motors

Roots avoids price competition by differentiating its lifestyle products through strong positioning and branding, sponsorship of major events, such as the Olympics, and advertising to reduce the impact of price.

decided to offer "employee discounts" to all buyers. Ford quickly followed suit, as did DailmerChrysler. Thus, an oligopolist is never sure that it will gain anything permanent through a price cut. In contrast, if an oligopolist raises its price, its competitors might not follow this lead. The oligopolist then would have to retract its price increase or risk losing customers to competitors.

In a *pure monopoly,* the market consists of one seller. The seller may be a government monopoly (Canada Post), a private regulated monopoly (Trans Alta Utilities), or a private non-regulated monopoly (Pfizer with its patent on Viagra). Pricing is handled differently in each case. A government monopoly may set a price below cost because the product is important to buyers or it may even set the price quite high to decrease consumption. Environmentalists are encouraging governments to raise prices on electric power, for example, to encourage consumers to conserve.

In a regulated monopoly, the government permits the company to set rates that will yield a "fair return." Non-regulated monopolies are free to price at what the market will bear. However, they do not always charge the full price for a number of reasons: a desire not to attract competition, a desire to penetrate the market faster with a low price, or a fear of government regulation.

Consumer Perceptions of Price and Value   In the end, the consumer will decide whether a product's price is right. Pricing decisions, like other marketing mix decisions, must be buyer oriented. When consumers buy a product, they exchange something of value (the price) to get something of value (the benefits of having or using the product). Effective, buyer-oriented pricing involves understanding how much value consumers place on the benefits they receive from the product and setting a price that fits this value.

A company often finds it hard to measure the values that customers will attach to its products. For example, calculating the cost of ingredients in a meal at a fancy restaurant is relatively easy. But assigning a value to other satisfactions such as taste, environment, relaxation, conversation, and status is very hard. And these values will vary both for different consumers and in different situations. Still, consumers will use these values to evaluate a product's price. If customers perceive that the price is greater than the product's value, they will not buy the product. If consumers perceive that the price is below the product's value, they will buy it, but the seller loses profit opportunities.

Analyzing the Price–Demand Relationship   Each price the company might charge will lead to a different level of demand. The relation between the price charged and the resulting demand level is shown in the **demand curve** in Figure 11.4. The demand curve shows the number of units the market will buy in a given time period, at different prices that might be charged. In the normal case, demand and price are inversely related: The higher the price, the lower the demand. Thus, the company would sell less if it raised its price from P_1 to P_2. Consumers with limited budgets probably will buy less of something if its price is too high.

Demand curve

A curve that shows the number of units the market will buy at different possible prices in a given time period.

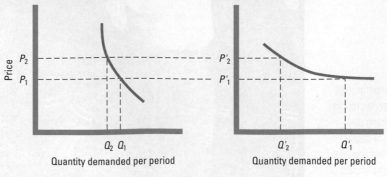

Figure 11.4 Demand curves

A. Inelastic demand   **B. Elastic demand**

In the case of prestige goods, the demand curve sometimes slopes upward. Consumers think that higher prices mean more quality. For example, Gibson Guitar Corporation recently toyed with the idea of lowering its prices to compete more effectively with Japanese rivals like Yamaha and Ibanez. To its surprise, Gibson found that its instruments didn't sell as well at lower prices. "We had an inverse [price–demand relationship]," noted Gibson's chief executive officer. "The more we charged, the more product we sold." At a time when other guitar manufacturers have chosen to build their instruments more quickly, cheaply, and in greater numbers, Gibson still promises guitars that "are made one-at-a-time, by hand. No short-cuts. No substitutions." It turns out that low prices simply aren't consistent with "Gibson's century old tradition of creating investment-quality instruments that represent the highest standards of imaginative design and masterful craftsmanship."[12] Still, if the company charges too high a price, the level of demand will be lower.

Most companies try to measure their demand curves by estimating demand at different prices. The type of market makes a difference. In a monopoly, the demand curve shows the total market demand resulting from different prices. If the company faces competition, its demand at different prices depends on whether competitors' prices stay constant or change with the company's own prices.

In measuring the price–demand relationship, the market researcher must not allow other factors affecting demand to vary. For example, if Sony increased its advertising at the same time as it lowered its television prices, we would not know how much of the increased demand was due to the lower prices and how much was due to the increased advertising. The same problem arises if the lower price is set over a holiday weekend—more gift giving over the holidays causes people to buy more televisions. Economists show the impact of non-price factors on demand through shifts in the demand curve rather than movements along it.

Price elasticity
A measure of the sensitivity of demand to changes in price.

Price Elasticity of Demand Marketers also need to know **price elasticity**—how responsive demand will be to a change in price. Consider the two demand curves in Figure 11.4. In Figure 11.4A, a price increase from P_1 to P_2 leads to a relatively small drop in demand from Q_1 to Q_2. In Figure 11.4B, however, the same price increase leads to a large drop in demand from Q'_1 to Q'_2. If demand hardly changes with a small change in price, we say the demand is *inelastic*. If demand

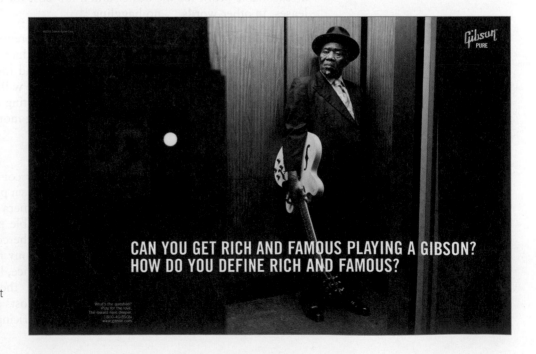

CAN YOU GET RICH AND FAMOUS PLAYING A GIBSON? HOW DO YOU DEFINE RICH AND FAMOUS?

Gibson was surprised to learn that its high-quality instruments didn't sell as well at lower prices.

changes greatly, we say the demand is *elastic*. The price elasticity of demand is given by this formula:

$$\text{Price Elasticity of Demand} = \frac{\text{\% Change in Quantity Demanded}}{\text{\% Change in Price}}$$

Suppose demand falls by 10 percent when a seller raises its price by 2 percent. Price elasticity of demand is therefore –5 (the minus sign confirms the inverse relation between price and demand) and demand is elastic. If demand falls by 2 percent with a 2 percent increase in price, then elasticity is –1. In this case, the seller's total revenue stays the same: The seller sells fewer items but at a higher price that preserves the same total revenue. If demand falls by 1 percent when price is increased by 2 percent, then elasticity is –1/2 and demand is inelastic. The less elastic the demand, the more it pays for the seller to raise the price.

What determines the price elasticity of demand? Buyers are less price sensitive when the product they are buying is unique or when it is high in quality, prestige, or exclusiveness. They are also less price sensitive when substitute products are hard to find or when they cannot easily compare the quality of substitutes. Finally, buyers are less price sensitive when the total expenditure for a product is low relative to their income or when the cost is shared by another party.[13]

If demand is elastic rather than inelastic, sellers should consider lowering their price. A lower price produces more total revenue. This practice makes sense as long as the extra costs of producing and selling more do not exceed the extra revenue. At the same time, most firms want to avoid pricing that turns their products into commodities. In recent years, deregulation and the instant price comparisons afforded by the Internet and other technologies have increased consumer price sensitivity, turning products ranging from telephones and computers to new automobiles into commodities in consumers' eyes. Here's how one group of marketers responded to this pressure:

> Seven Toyota dealers in southern Manitoba developed new pricing and sales tactics designed primarily to address the concerns of the 60 percent of car buyers who surf the Web before kicking the tires. Toyota's "product advisers" point potential customers to the Access Toyota website (www.access.toyota.ca) and explain that the price shown is the "drive-away" price for the vehicle selected—not the manufacturer's suggested retail price (MSRP), but a price that provides a reasonable profit for the dealer and a fair cost for the customer who buys or leases. In other words … no haggling.[14]

Marketers need to work harder than ever to differentiate their offerings when a dozen competitors are selling virtually the same product at a comparable or lower price. More than ever, companies need to understand the price sensitivity of their customers and prospects and the trade-offs people are willing to make between price and product characteristics. In the words of marketing consultant Kevin Clancy, those who target only the price sensitive are "leaving money on the table."[15]

Competitors' Costs, Prices, and Offers

In setting its prices, the company must also consider competitors' costs and prices and possible competitor reactions to the company's own pricing moves. A consumer who is considering the purchase of a Sony digital camera will evaluate Sony's price and value against the prices and values of comparable products made by Nikon, Kodak, Canon, Olympus, and others. In addition, the company's pricing strategy may affect the nature of the competition it faces. If Sony follows a high-price, high-margin strategy, it may attract competition. A low-price, low-margin strategy, however, may stop competitors or drive them out of the market. Sony needs to benchmark its costs and value against competitors' costs and value. It can then use these benchmarks as a starting point for its own pricing. Sleeman Breweries has adopted a two-pronged strategy for its premium and value-based brands as a result of its competitors' pricing strategies.[16]

> Sleeman Breweries Ltd., of Guelph, Ontario, and its Quebec-based subsidiary, Unibroue, is Canada's third largest brewery. In 2005, it experienced declining sales and profits in the face of a continued price war in Ontario, Quebec, and Alberta, initiated by its rivals Labatt Breweries of Canada and Molson-Coors Brewing Co. Dan Fox, Sleeman's managing director, outlines the company's response strategy when he says, "Our impetus and focus is on the premium side of business because that's where the big margins are, but the reality is you can't ignore the value segment, certainly in Ontario, given its growth in the last year or so." John Sleeman, chair and CEO of the company, echoes his words noting that "he recognizes consumers' expectations have been changed by low-priced 'value' brands.... Value pricing is here to stay." Thus Sleeman has worked hard to become a lower-cost producer, while simultaneously introducing new premium brands under its John Sleeman Presents portfolio. The company still wants more than 50 percent of its sales to come from premium brands. To better market its products, the company has developed a tiered structure for its pricing while allocating more of its marketing budget to increase awareness of its less expensive brands.

Other External Factors

When setting prices, the company also must consider other factors in its external environment. *Economic conditions* can have a strong impact on the firm's pricing strategies. Economic factors, such as boom or recession, inflation, and interest rates, influence pricing decisions because they affect both the costs of producing a product and consumer perceptions of the product's price and value. The company must also consider what impact its prices will have on other parties in its environment. How will *resellers* react to various prices? The company should set prices that give resellers a fair profit, encourage their support, and help them to sell the product effectively. The *government* is another important external influence on pricing decisions. Finally, *social concerns* may have to be considered. In setting prices, a company's short-term sales, market share, and profit goals, as well as the ability of the vulnerable to afford them, may have to be tempered by broader societal considerations.

General Pricing Approaches

The price the company charges will be somewhere between one that is too low to produce a profit and one that is too high to produce any demand. Figure 11.5 summarizes the major considerations in setting price. Product costs set a floor to the price; consumer perceptions of the product's value set the ceiling. The company must consider competitors' prices and other external and internal factors to find the best price between these two extremes.

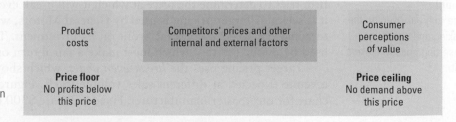

Figure 11.5 Major considerations in setting price

Companies set prices by selecting from or combining two general pricing approaches: the *cost-based approach* (cost-plus pricing, break-even analysis, and target profit pricing), and the *value-based approach* (buyer-based or perceived-value pricing).

Cost-Based Pricing

Cost-plus pricing

Adding a standard markup to the cost of the product.

The simplest pricing method is **cost-plus pricing**—adding a standard markup to the cost of the product. Construction companies, for example, submit job bids by estimating the total project cost and adding a standard markup for profit. Lawyers, accountants, and other professionals typically price by adding a standard markup to their costs. Some sellers tell their customers they charge cost plus a specified markup; for example, aerospace companies price this way to the government.

To illustrate markup pricing, suppose a toaster manufacturer had the following costs and expected sales:

Variable cost	$10
Fixed cost	$300 000
Expected unit sales	$50 000

Then the manufacturer's cost per toaster is given by:

$$\text{Unit Cost} = \text{Variable Cost} + \frac{\text{Fixed Costs}}{\text{Unit Sales}} = \$10 + \frac{\$300\ 000}{50\ 000} = \$16$$

Now suppose the manufacturer wants to earn a 20 percent markup on sales. The manufacturer's markup price is given by:[17]

$$\text{Markup Price} = \frac{\text{Unit Cost}}{(1 - \text{Desired Return on Sales})} = \frac{\$16}{1 - 0.2} = \$20$$

The manufacturer would charge dealers $20 a toaster and make a profit of $4 per unit. The dealers, in turn, will mark up the toaster. If the dealers want to earn 50 percent on sales price, they will mark up the toaster to $40 ($20 + 50% of $40). This number is equivalent to a *markup on cost* of 100 percent ($20/$20).

Does using standard markups to set prices make sense? Generally, no. Any pricing method that ignores demand and competitors' prices is not likely to lead to the best price. Suppose the toaster manufacturer charged $20 but only sold 30 000 toasters instead of 50 000. Then the unit cost would have been higher since the fixed costs are spread over fewer units, and the realized percentage markup on sales would have been lower. Markup pricing only works if that price actually brings in the expected level of sales.

Still, markup pricing remains popular for many reasons. First, sellers are more certain about costs than about demand. By tying the price to cost, sellers simplify pricing—they do not have to make frequent adjustments as demand changes. Second, when all firms in the industry use this pricing method, prices tend to be similar and price competition is thus minimized. Third, many people believe that cost-plus pricing is fairer to both buyers and sellers. Sellers earn a fair return on their investment but do not take advantage of buyers when buyers' demand becomes great.

Break-even pricing (target profit pricing)

Setting price to break even on the costs of making and marketing a product; or setting price to make a target profit.

Break-Even Analysis and Target Profit Pricing   Another cost-oriented pricing approach is **break-even pricing**, or a variation called **target profit pricing**. The firm tries to determine the price at which it will break even or make the target profit it is seeking. Target pricing is used by General Motors, which prices its automobiles to achieve a 15 to 20 percent profit on its investment. This pricing method is also used by public utilities, which must make a fair return on their investment.

Target pricing uses the *break-even chart*, which shows the total cost and total revenue expected at different sales volume levels. Figure 11.6 shows a break-even chart for our toaster manufacturer. Fixed costs are $300 000 regardless of sales vol-

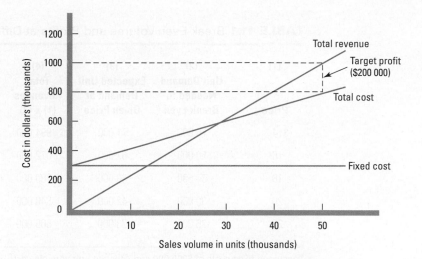

Figure 11.6 Break-even chart for determining target price

ume. Variable costs are added to fixed costs to form total costs, which rise with volume. The total revenue curve starts at zero and rises with each unit sold. The slope of the total revenue curve reflects the price of $20 per unit.

The total revenue and total cost curves cross at 30 000 units. This is the *break-even volume*. At $20, the company must sell at least 30 000 units to break even; that is, for total revenue to cover total cost. Break-even volume can be calculated with this formula:

$$\text{Break--Even Volume} = \frac{\text{Fixed Cost}}{\text{Price} - \text{Variable Cost}} = \frac{\$300\ 000}{\$20 - \$10} = 30\ 000$$

If the company wants to make a target profit, it must sell more than 30 000 units at $20 each. Suppose the toaster manufacturer has invested $1 000 000 in the business and wants to set the price to earn a 20 percent return, or $200 000. In that case, it must sell at least 50 000 units at $20 each. If the company charges a higher price, it will not need to sell as many toasters to achieve its target return; but the market may not buy even this lower volume at the higher price. Much depends on the price elasticity and competitors' prices.

The manufacturer should consider different prices and estimate break-even volumes, probable demand, and profits for each. This is done in Table 11.1. The table shows that as price increases, break-even volume drops (column 2). But as price increases, demand for the toasters also falls off (column 3). At the $14 price, because the manufacturer clears only $4 per toaster ($14 less $10 in variable costs), it must sell a very high volume to break even. Even though the low price attracts many buyers, demand still falls below the high break-even point, and the manufacturer loses money. At the other extreme, with a $22 price the manufacturer clears $12 per toaster and must sell only 25 000 units to break even. But at this high price, consumers buy too few toasters, and profits are negative. The table shows that a price of $18 yields the highest profits. Note that none of the prices produce the manufacturer's target profit of $200 000. To achieve this target return, the manufacturer will have to search for ways to lower fixed or variable costs, thus lowering the break-even volume.

Value-Based Pricing

Value-based pricing
Setting price based on buyers' perceptions of value rather than on the seller's cost.

An increasing number of companies are basing their prices on the product's perceived value. **Value-based pricing** uses buyers' perceptions of value, not the seller's cost, as the key to pricing. Value-based pricing means that the marketer cannot

TABLE 11.1 Break-Even Volume and Profits at Different Prices

(1) Price	(2) Unit Demand Needed to Break Even	(3) Expected Unit Demand at Given Price	(4) Total Revenues (1) x (3)	(5) Total costs*	(6) Profit (4) x (5)
$14	75 000	71 000	$ 994 000	$1 100 000	–$ 16 000
16	50 000	67 000	1 072 000	970 000	102 000
18	37 500	60 000	1 080 000	900 000	180 000
20	30 000	42 000	840 000	720 000	120 000
22	25 000	23 000	506 000	530 000	–24 000

*Assumed fixed costs of $300 000 and constant unit variable costs of $10.

design a product and marketing program and then set the price. Price is considered along with the other marketing mix variables *before* the marketing program is set.

Figure 11.7 compares cost-based pricing with value-based pricing. Cost-based pricing is product driven. The company designs what it considers to be a good product, determines the costs of making the product, and sets a price that covers costs plus a target profit. Marketing must then convince buyers that the product's value at that price justifies its purchase. If the price turns out to be too high, the company must settle for lower markups or lower sales, both resulting in disappointing profits.

Value-based pricing reverses this process. The company sets its target price based on customer perceptions of the product value. The targeted value and price then drive decisions about product design and what costs can be incurred. As a result, pricing begins with analyzing consumer needs and value perceptions, and the price is set to match consumers' perceived value.

A company using value-based pricing must find out what value buyers assign to different competitive offers. Measuring perceived value, however, can be difficult. Sometimes consumers are asked how much they would pay for a basic product and for each benefit added to the offer. Or a company may conduct experiments to test the perceived value of different product offers. According to an old Russian proverb, there are two fools in every market—one who asks too much and one who asks too little. If the seller charges more than the buyers' perceived value, the company's sales will suffer. If the seller charges less, its products sell very well. But they produce less revenue than they would if they were priced at the level of perceived value.

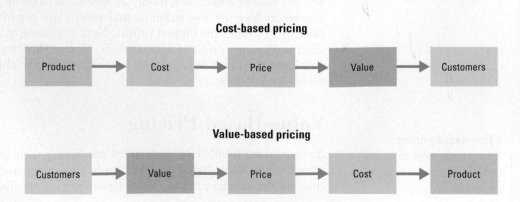

Figure 11.7 Cost-based versus value-based pricing

Source: Thomas T. Nagle and Reed K. Holden, *The Strategy and Tactics of Pricing*, 3rd ed. (Upper Saddle River, N.J.: Prentice Hall, 2002), p. 4.

Value Pricing

Value pricing
Offering just the right combination of quality and good service at a fair price.

During the past decade, marketers have noted a fundamental shift in consumer attitudes toward price and quality. Many companies have changed their pricing approaches to bring them into line with changing economic conditions and consumer price perceptions. More and more marketers have adopted **value pricing** strategies—offering just the right combination of quality and good service at a fair price. In many cases, this has involved the introduction of less expensive versions of established, brand-name products. Campbell introduced its Great Starts budget frozen-food line, Holiday Inn opened several Holiday Express budget hotels, and fast-food restaurants, such as Taco Bell and McDonald's, offered "value menus." In other cases, value pricing has involved redesigning existing brands to offer more quality for a given price or the same quality for less. In other cases, value pricing has involved redesigning existing brands to offer more quality for a given price or the same quality for less.

An important type of value pricing at the retail level is *everyday low pricing (EDLP)*. EDLP involves charging a constant, everyday low price with few or no temporary price discounts. In contrast, *high-low pricing* involves charging higher prices on an everyday basis, but running frequent promotions to temporarily lower prices on selected items below the EDLP level. In recent years, high-low pricing has given way to EDLP in retail settings ranging from Saturn car dealerships to grocery stores like Quebec's Metro chain.

Retailers adopt EDLP for many reasons, the most important of which is that constant sales and promotions are costly and have eroded consumer confidence in the credibility of everyday shelf prices. Consumers also have less time and patience for such time-honoured traditions as watching for supermarket specials and clipping coupons.

The king of EDLP is Wal-Mart, which practically defined the concept. Except for a few sale items every month, Wal-Mart promises everyday low prices on everything it sells. In contrast, Zellers' attempts to match Wal-Mart's EDLP strategy failed. To offer everyday low prices, a company must first have everyday low costs. However, because Zellers' costs are much higher than Wal-Mart's, it could not make money at the lower prices and quickly abandoned the attempt.[18] (See Real Marketing 11.2.)

A less expensive pen might write as well, but some consumers place great value on the intangibles they receive from a "fine writing instrument," such as a Montblanc.

REAL MARKETING

11.2

Pricing Power: The Value of Value-Added

When a company finds its major competitors offering a similar product at a lower price, the natural tendency is to try to match or beat that price. Though the idea of undercutting competitors' prices and watching customers flock to you is tempting, there are dangers. Successive rounds of price cutting can lead to price wars that erode the profit margins of all competitors in an industry. Or worse, discounting a product can cheapen it in the minds of customers, greatly reducing the seller's power to maintain profitable prices in the long term. "It ends up being a losing battle," notes one marketing executive. "You focus away from quality, service, prestige—the things brands are all about."

So, how can a company keep its pricing power when a competitor undercuts its price? Often, the best strategy is not to price below the competitor, but rather to price above and convince customers that the product is worth it. The company should ask, "What is the value of the product to the customer?" and then stand up for what the product is worth. In this way, the company shifts the focus from price to value.

Air Canada tried to do this with its flagship brand but was unsuccessful because of declining service quality. To counter the erosion of its market share by the discount airlines, such as WestJet, Air Canada first introduced its own discount brands: Tango and Zip. These were soon replaced by different fares: Tango, Tango Plus, Latitude, Latitude Plus, and Executive Class. In the face of a highly competitive marketplace, labour unrest, and rising fuel prices, Air Canada is still struggling with its pricing strategy. Consumers are very frustrated with the pricing of air services. Business travellers feel gouged, and leisure travellers are frustrated by the advertising of one-way fares that can't be booked and advertised prices that fail to prominently mention the many surcharges added to the price. Such frustration has been aired on the Internet, with people asking, "What if airlines sold paint?"

Customer: Hi. How much is your paint?

Clerk: Well, sir, that all depends on quite a lot of things.

Customer: Can you give me a guess? Is there an average price?

Clerk: Our lowest price is $12 a gallon, and we have 60 different prices up to $200 a gallon.

Customer: What's the difference in the paint?

Clerk: Oh, there isn't any difference; it's all the same paint.

Customer: Well, then I'd like some of that $12 paint.

Clerk: When do you intend to use the paint?

Customer: I want to paint tomorrow. It's my day off.

Clerk: Sir, the paint for tomorrow is the $200 paint.

Customer: When would I have to paint to get the $12 paint?

Clerk: You would have to start very late at night in about three weeks. But you will have to agree to start painting before Friday of that week and continue painting until at least Sunday.

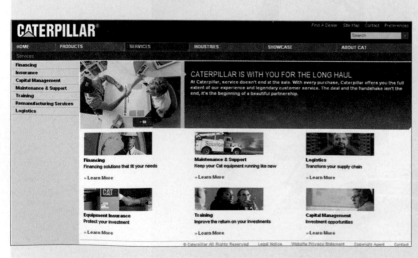

Caterpillar offers its dealers a wide range of value-added services—from guaranteed parts delivery to investment management advice and equipment training. Such added value supports a higher price.

With the increased cutting of services, airlines around the world are increasingly operating in a "commodity" business, in which the products of all competitors seem pretty much alike. In such cases, companies must find ways to "decommoditize" their products—to create superior value for customers. It can do this by developing value-added features and services that differentiate their offers and justify higher prices and margins. Here is one example of how a supplier used value-added features and services to give it a competitive edge:

> Caterpillar charges premium prices for its heavy construction and mining equipment by convincing customers that its products and service justify every additional cent—or, rather, the extra tens of thousands of dollars. Caterpillar typically reaps a 20 to 30 percent price premium over competitors—that can amount to an extra US$200 000 or more on one of those huge yellow million-dollar dump trucks.
>
> When a large potential customer says, "I can get it for less from a competitor," the Caterpillar dealer doesn't discount the price. Instead, the dealer explains that, even at the higher price, Cat offers the best value. Caterpillar equipment is designed with modular components that can be removed and repaired quickly, minimizing machine downtime. Caterpillar dealers carry an extensive parts inventory and guarantee delivery within forty-eight hours anywhere in the world, again minimizing downtime. Cat's products are designed to be rebuilt, providing a "second life" that competitors cannot match. As a result, Caterpillar used-equipment prices are often 20 percent to 30 percent higher.
>
> In all, the dealer explains, even at the higher initial price, Caterpillar equipment delivers the lowest total cost per cubic metre of earth moved, tonne of coal uncovered, or kilometre of road graded over the life of the product—guaranteed! Most customers seem to agree with Caterpillar's value proposition—the company dominates its markets, with a more than 40 percent worldwide market share.

Sources: Erin Stout, "Keep Them Coming Back for More," *Sales & Marketing Management,* February 2002, pp. 51–52; Alan H. Hess, Hess Travel, "If Airlines Sold Paint," http://etntelephone.com/stories/paint.htm, reprinted by permission of Alan H. Hess; and information at www.caterpillar.com (accessed December 2004). For other value-added pricing discussion and examples, see Stephanie N. Mehta, "How to Thrive when Prices Fall," *Fortune,* May 12, 2003, pp. 131–134; Alison Smith, "The Flip Side of Price," *Selling Power,* May 2003, pp. 28–30; and James C. Anderson and James A. Narus, *Business Market Management: Understanding, Creating, and Delivering Value* (Upper Saddle River, NJ: Prentice Hall, 2004) pp. 203–210 and elsewhere.

Price-Adjustment Strategies

Companies usually adjust their basic prices to account for various customer differences and changing situations. Here we examine the five price-adjustment strategies summarized in Table 11.2: *discount and allowance pricing, segmented pricing, psychological pricing, promotional pricing, geographical* and *international pricing.*

Discount and Allowance Pricing

Discount
A straight reduction in price on purchases during a stated period of time.

Most companies adjust their basic price to reward customers for certain responses, such as early payment of bills, volume purchases, and off-season buying. These price adjustments—called **discounts** and *allowances*—can take many forms, including a

TABLE 11.2 Price-Adjustment Strategies

Strategy	Description
Discount and allowance pricing	Reducing prices to reward customer responses such as paying early or promoting the product
Segmented pricing	Adjusting prices to allow for differences in customers, products, or locations
Psychological pricing	Adjusting prices for psychological effect
Promotional pricing	Temporarily reducing prices to increase short-run sales
Geographical and international pricing	Adjusting prices to account for the geographic location of customers and differences in international markets

cash discount, a price reduction to buyers who pay their bills promptly. For example, though a seller may demand payment within 30 days, it could provide a 2 percent discount if the bill is paid within 10 days. This type of policy improves cash flow and reduces the risk of bad debts.

A *quantity discount* is a price reduction to buyers who buy large volumes. A typical example is "$10 per unit for less than 100 units, $9 per unit for 100 or more units." Under the provisions of the *Competition Act,* quantity discounts must be offered equally to all customers and must not exceed the seller's cost savings associated with selling large quantities. These savings include lower selling, inventory, and transportation expenses. Discounts provide an incentive to the customer to buy more from one given seller, rather than from many different sources.

A *seasonal discount* is a price reduction to buyers who buy merchandise or services out of season. For example, lawn and garden equipment manufacturers offer seasonal discounts to retailers during the fall and winter months to encourage early ordering. Hotels offer bargain rates in the off-season. Seasonal discounts allow the seller to keep production steady during an entire year.

Allowances are another type of reduction from the list price. *Promotional allowances* are payments or price reductions to reward dealers for participating in advertising and sales-support programs.

Allowance
Promotional money paid by manufacturers to retailers in return for an agreement to feature the manufacturer's products in some way.

Segmented Pricing

Companies will often adjust their basic prices to allow for differences in customers, products, and locations. In **segmented pricing**, the company sells a product or service at two or more prices, even though the difference in prices is not based on differences in costs.

Segmented pricing
Selling a product or service at two or more prices, where the difference in prices is not based on differences in costs.

Segmented pricing takes several forms. Under *customer segment pricing,* different customers pay different prices for the same product or service. Museums, for example, will charge a lower admission to students and senior citizens. Under *product form pricing,* different versions of the product are priced differently, but not according to differences in their costs. For instance, Black & Decker prices its most expensive iron at US$54.98, which is US$12 more than the price of its next most expensive iron. The top model has a self-cleaning feature, yet this extra feature costs only a few more dollars to make.

Using *location pricing,* a company charges different prices for different locations, even though the cost of offering each location is the same. For instance, theatres vary their seat prices because of audience preferences for certain locations, and universities charge higher tuition to overseas students.

For segmented pricing to be an effective strategy, certain conditions must exist. The market must be segmentable, and the segments must show different degrees of demand. Members of the segment paying the lower price should not be able to turn around and resell the product to the segment paying the higher price. Competitors should not be able to undersell the firm in the segment being charged the higher price. Nor should the costs of segmenting and watching the market exceed the extra revenue obtained from the price difference. Of course, the segmented pricing must also be legal. Most importantly, segmented prices should reflect real differences in customers' perceived value. Otherwise, in the long run, the practice will lead to customer resentment and ill will.

Psychological Pricing

Price says something about the product. For example, many consumers use price to judge quality. A $100 bottle of perfume may contain only $3 worth of scent, but some people are willing to pay $100 because this price indicates something special.

Psychological pricing
A pricing approach that considers the psychology of prices and not simply the economics; the price is used to say something about the product.

In using **psychological pricing**, sellers consider the psychology of prices and not simply the economics. For example, consumers usually perceive higher-priced products as having higher quality. When consumers can judge the quality of a product by examining it or by calling on past experience with it, they use price less to judge quality. But when they cannot judge quality because they lack the information or skill, price becomes an important quality signal:

Heublein produces Smirnoff, North America's leading vodka brand. Some years ago, Smirnoff was attacked by another brand. Wolfschmidt, priced at one dollar less per bottle, claimed to have the same quality as Smirnoff. To hold on to market share, Heublein considered either lowering Smirnoff's price by one dollar or holding Smirnoff's price constant while increasing advertising and promotion expenditures. Either strategy would lead to lower profits. However, Heublein's marketers thought of a third strategy. They *raised* the price of Smirnoff by one dollar! They also introduced two "fighting" brands, Relska and Popov, respectively priced the same and lower than Wolfschmidt. This clever strategy positioned Smirnoff as the elite brand and Wolfschmidt as an ordinary brand, producing a large increase in Heublein's overall profits. The irony is that Heublein's three brands are pretty much the same in taste and manufacturing costs. Heublein knew that a product's price signals its quality. Using price as a signal, Heublein sells roughly the same product at three different quality positions.

Reference prices
Prices that buyers carry in their minds and refer to when they look at a given product.

Another aspect of psychological pricing is **reference prices**—prices that buyers carry in their minds and refer to when looking at a given product. They may form the reference price by noting current prices, remembering past prices, or assessing the buying situation. Sellers can influence or use these consumers' reference prices when setting price. For example, a company could display its product next to more expensive ones to imply that it belongs in the same class. Department stores often

What do the prices marked on this tag suggest about the product and buying situation?

sell women's clothing in separate departments differentiated by price: clothing found in the more expensive department is assumed to be of better quality. Companies also can influence consumers' reference prices by showing manufacturer's suggested prices, by indicating that the product was originally priced much higher, or by pointing to a competitor's higher price.

Even small differences in price can suggest product differences. Consider a stereo priced at $300 compared with one priced at $299.95. The actual price difference is only 5 cents, but the psychological difference can be much greater. For example, some consumers will see the $299.95 as a price in the $200 range rather than the $300 range. The $299.95 will more likely be seen as a bargain price, whereas the $300 price suggests more quality. Some psychologists argue that each digit has symbolic and visual qualities that should be considered in pricing. Thus, 8 is round and even and creates a soothing effect, whereas 7 is angular and creates a jarring effect.[19]

Promotional Pricing

Promotional pricing
Temporarily pricing products below the list price, and sometimes even below cost, to increase short-run sales.

With **promotional pricing**, companies will temporarily price their products below list price and sometimes even below cost. Promotional pricing takes several forms. Supermarkets and department stores will price a few products as *loss leaders* to attract customers to the store in the hope that they will buy other items at normal markups. For example, supermarkets often sell disposable diapers at less than cost in order to attract family buyers who make larger average purchases per trip. Sellers also use *special event pricing* in certain seasons to draw more customers. Thus, linens are promotionally priced every January to attract weary Christmas shoppers back into stores.

The frequent use of promotional pricing can also lead to industry price wars, as has been the case in the brewing industry. Such price wars usually play into the hands of only one or a few competitors—those with the most efficient operations. Until recently, the computer industry avoided price wars. When demand cooled, however, many competitors began to unload PCs at discounted prices. In response, Dell, the industry's undisputed low-cost leader, started a price war that only it could win:

In mid-2000, Dell declared a brutal price war just as the industry slipped into its worst slump ever. The result was nothing short of a rout. While Dell chalked up $US361 million in profits the following year, the rest of the industry logged $US1.1 billion in losses. Dell's edge starts with its direct-selling approach. By

Promotional pricing: Companies offer promotional prices to create buying excitement and urgency.

taking orders straight from customers and building machines to order, Dell avoids paying retailer markups, getting stuck with unsold PCs, and keeping costly inventories. This gives it a gigantic edge in a market where the price of chips, drives, and other parts typically falls 1 percent a week. Moreover, Dell has mastered supply chain management using sophisticated software that links suppliers straight into Dell's factory floor. Since launching the price war, the price of a Dell computer has dropped more than 18 percent, leaving competitors with few effective weapons. Says Michael Dell, "When we sell these products, we make money. When our competitors sell them, they lose money."[20]

Geographical and International Pricing

A company also must decide how to price its products to customers located in different parts of the country or world. Should the company risk losing the business of more distant customers by charging them higher prices to cover the higher shipping costs? Or should the company charge all customers the same prices regardless of location?

Take a northern B.C.-based paper company that sells its products to customers all over Canada. The cost of freight is high and affects the companies from whom customers buy their paper. When establishing its geographical pricing policy, it is considering how to price a $100 order to three specific customers: Customer A (Vancouver), Customer B (Winnipeg), and Customer C (Halifax). One option is for the company to ask each customer to pay the shipping cost from the factory in northern B.C. to the customer's location. All three customers would pay the same factory price of $100, with Customer A paying, say, $15 for shipping; Customer B, $25; and Customer C, $50. Called **FOB-origin pricing**, this practice means that the goods are placed *free on board* (hence, *FOB*) a carrier. At that point the title and responsibility pass to the customer, who pays the freight from the factory to the destination. Because each customer picks up its own cost, supporters of FOB pricing feel that this is the fairest way to assess freight charges. The disadvantage, however, is that the paper company's products become higher in cost for distant customers.

Uniform-delivered pricing is the opposite of FOB pricing. Here, the company charges the same price plus freight to all customers, regardless of their location. The freight charge is set at the average freight cost. Suppose this is $45. Uniform-delivered pricing therefore results in a higher charge to the Vancouver customer (who pays $45 freight instead of $15) and a lower charge to the Halifax customer (who pays $45 instead of $50). This pricing tactic may hurt the firm's chances of winning over local buyers but improve its odds of winning distant sales. Other advantages of uniform-delivered pricing are that it is fairly easy to administer and it lets the firm advertise its price nationally.

Zone pricing falls between FOB-origin pricing and uniform-delivered pricing. The company sets up two or more zones. All customers within a given zone pay a single total price; the more distant the zone, the higher the price. For example, the company might set up a Western Zone and charge $15 freight to all customers in this zone, a Central Zone in which it charges $25, and an Eastern Zone in which it charges $50.

Companies that market their products internationally must decide what prices to charge in the different countries in which they operate. In some cases, a company can set a uniform worldwide price. For example, Bombardier sells its jetliners at about the same price everywhere, whether in the United States, Europe, or a developing country. However, most companies adjust their prices to reflect local market conditions and cost considerations.

The price that a company should charge in a specific country depends on many factors, including consumer perceptions and preferences, the company's objectives,

---

FOB-origin pricing
A geographical pricing strategy in which goods are placed free on board a carrier; the customer pays the freight from the factory to the destination.

Uniform-delivered pricing
A geographical pricing strategy in which the company charges the same price plus freight to all customers, regardless of their location.

Zone pricing
A geographical pricing strategy in which the company sets up two or more zones. All customers within a zone pay the same total price; the more distant the zone, the higher the price.

economic conditions, product and shipping costs, competitive situations, laws and regulations, and development of the wholesaling and retailing system. For example, Panasonic might introduce a new product into mature markets in highly developed countries with the goal of quickly gaining mass-market share—this would call for a penetration pricing strategy. In contrast, it may enter a less-developed market by targeting smaller, less price-sensitive segments—in this case, market skimming pricing makes sense. Thus, international pricing presents some special problems and complexities. We discuss international pricing issues in more detail in Chapter 18.

Price Changes

After developing their initial pricing, companies often encounter situations in which they must initiate price changes because of changes in market conditions or to respond to price changes by competitors.

Initiating Price Changes

In some cases, the company may find it desirable to initiate either a price cut or a price increase. In both cases, it must anticipate possible buyer and competitor reactions.

Initiating Price Cuts

Several situations may lead a firm to consider cutting its price. One such circumstance is excess capacity. In this case, the firm needs more business and cannot get it through increased sales effort, product improvement, or other measures. It may drop its "follow-the-leader pricing"—charging about the same price as its leading competitor—and aggressively cut prices to boost sales. Another situation leading to price changes is falling market share in the face of strong price competition. The airline, construction equipment, fast-food, and other industries facing these dual dilemmas have learned in recent years that cutting prices in an industry loaded with excess capacity may lead to price wars, as competitors try to hold on to market share.

Another situation leading to price changes is falling market share in the face of strong price competition. Several North American industries—automobiles, consumer electronics, cameras, watches, and steel, for example—lost market share to Japanese competitors whose high-quality products carried lower prices than did their North American counterparts. In response, North American companies resorted to more-aggressive pricing action.

A company may also cut prices in a drive to dominate the market through lower costs. Either the company starts with lower costs than its competitors (as is the case with Dell), or it cuts prices in the hope of gaining market share that will further cut costs through larger volume (as is the case with Sleeman Breweries).

Initiating Price Increases

A successful price increase can greatly increase profits. For example, if the company's profit margin is 3 percent of sales, a 1 percent price increase will increase profits by 33 percent if sales volume is unaffected. A major factor in price increases is cost inflation. Rising costs squeeze profit margins and lead companies to pass cost increases along to customers. For example, with the recent dramatic rise in oil prices, 88 percent of independent business owners across Canada said energy prices were a major cause of concern.[21] Another factor leading to price increases is over-demand. When a company cannot supply all its customers' needs, it can raise its prices, ration products to customers, or both.

Companies can increase their prices in a number of ways to keep up with rising costs. Prices can be raised almost invisibly by dropping discounts and adding higher-priced units to the line. Or prices can be pushed up openly. In passing price increases on to customers, the company must avoid being perceived as a price gouger. In 2005 and 2006, oil companies recorded record profits and their pricing practices are being scrutinized by governments around the world. Customer memories are also long, and they will eventually turn away from companies or even whole industries that they perceive as charging excessive prices.

Wherever possible, the company should consider ways to meet higher costs or demand without raising prices. For example, Air Canada has worked to lower the weight of its planes by restricting everything from its passenger luggage allowance to ditching glass wine bottles in favour of lightweight containers on its Montreal-to-Paris route as it desperately struggles to save on fuel as oil prices soar.[22] Other tactics include more cost-effective ways to distribute products. A company can shrink the product instead of raising the price, as candy bar manufacturers often do. It can substitute less expensive ingredients or remove certain product features, packaging, or services. Or it can "unbundle" its products and services, removing and separately pricing elements that were formerly part of the offer. IBM, for example, now offers training and consulting as separately priced services.

Buyer Reactions to Price Changes

Whether the price is raised or lowered, the action will affect buyers, competitors, distributors, and suppliers and may interest government as well. Customers do not always interpret prices in a straightforward way. They may view a price *cut* in several ways. For example, what would you think if Joy perfume, "the costliest fragrance in the world," were to cut its price in half? You might believe that quality or status of the product has been reduced. Or you might think that the price will come down even further and that it will pay to wait and see.

Similarly, a price *increase,* which would normally lower sales, may have some positive meanings for buyers. What would you think if Joy *raised* the price of its perfume? On the one hand, you might think that the item is very "hot" and may be unobtainable unless you buy it soon. On the other hand, you might think that the company is greedy and charging what the traffic will bear.

Competitor Reactions to Price Changes

A firm considering a price change has to worry about the reactions of its competitors as well as those of its customers. Competitors are most likely to react when the number of firms involved is small, when the product is uniform, and when the buyers are well informed.

How can the firm anticipate the likely reactions of its competitors? If the firm faces one large competitor, and if the competitor tends to react in a set way to price changes, that reaction can easily be anticipated. But if the competitor treats each price change as a fresh challenge and reacts according to its self-interest, the company will have to figure out just what makes up the competitor's self-interest at the time.

The problem is complex because, like the customer, the competitor can interpret a company price cut in many ways. It might think the company is trying to grab a larger market share, that the company is doing poorly and trying to boost its sales, or that the company wants the whole industry to cut prices to increase total demand.

When there are several competitors, the company must guess each competitor's likely reaction. If all competitors behave alike, this amounts to analyzing only a typical competitor. In contrast, if the competitors do not behave alike—perhaps because of differences in size, market shares, or policies—then separate analyses are necessary. However, if some competitors will match the price change, there is good reason to expect that the rest will also match it.

Responding to Price Changes

Here we reverse the question and ask how a firm should respond to a price change by a competitor. The firm needs to consider several issues: Why did the competitor change the price? Was it to take more market share, to use excess capacity, to meet changing cost conditions, or to lead an industry-wide price change? Is the price change temporary or permanent? What will happen to the company's market share and profits if it does not respond? Are other companies going to respond? And what are the competitor's and other firms' responses to each possible reaction likely to be?

Besides these issues, the company must make a broader analysis. It must consider its own product's stage in the life cycle, the product's importance in the company's product mix, the intentions and resources of the competitor, and the possible consumer reactions to price changes. The company cannot always make an extended analysis of its alternatives at the time of a price change, however. The competitor may have spent much time preparing this decision, but the company may have to react within hours or days. About the only way to cut down reaction time is to plan ahead for both possible competitors' price changes and possible responses.

Figure 11.8 shows the ways a company might assess and respond to a competitor's price cut. Suppose the company learns that a competitor has cut its price and fears that this price cut might harm the company's sales and profits. It might simply decide to hold its current price and profit margin, or it might decide that it should wait and respond when it has more information on the effects of the competitor's price change. The argument against this holding strategy, however, is that the competitor may get stronger and more confident as its sales increase.

If the company decides that effective action can and should be taken, it might make any of four responses. First, it could *reduce its price* to match the competitor's price. It may decide that the market is price sensitive and that it would lose too

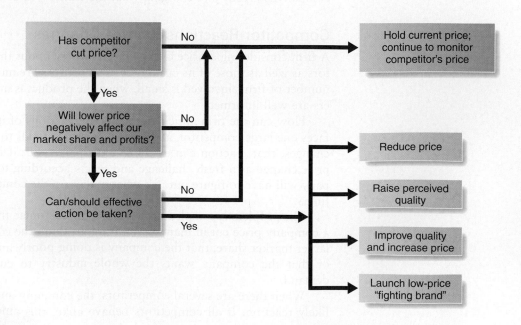

Figure 11.8 Assessing and responding to competitor's price changes

much market share to the lower-priced competitor. Or it might worry that recapturing lost market share later would be too hard. Cutting the price will reduce the company's profits in the short run. Some companies might also reduce their product quality, services, and marketing communications to retain profit margins, but this will ultimately hurt long-run market share. The company should try to maintain its quality as it cuts prices.

Alternatively, the company might maintain its price but *raise the perceived value* of its offer. It could improve its communications, stressing the relative quality of its product over that of the lower-price competitor. The firm may find it cheaper to maintain price and spend money to improve its perceived value than to cut price and operate at a lower margin.

Or the company might *improve quality and increase price*, moving its brand into a higher-price position. The higher quality justifies the higher price, which in turn preserves the company's higher margins. Or the company can hold price on the current product and introduce a new brand at a higher-price position.

Finally, the company might *launch a low-price "fighting brand"*—adding a lower-price item to the line or creating a separate lower-price brand. This is necessary if the particular market segment being lost is price sensitive and will not respond to arguments of higher quality. Thus, when challenged on price by store brands and other low-price entrants, Procter & Gamble turned a number of its brands into fighting brands, including Luvs disposable diapers, Joy dishwashing detergent, and Camay beauty soap. In turn, P&G competitor Kimberly-Clark positions its value-priced Scott Towels brand as "the Bounty killer." It advertises Scott Towels as "Common Sense on a Roll." The brand scores well on customer satisfaction measures but sells for a lower price than P&G's Bounty brand."[23]

Kimberly-Clark offers its value-priced Scott brand as "the Bounty killer." It scores well on customer satisfaction but sells for a lower price than P&G's Bounty.

Public Policy and Pricing

Pricing strategies and tactics form an important element of a company's marketing mix. In setting prices, companies must carefully consider a great many internal and external factors before choosing a price that will give them the greatest competitive advantage in selected target markets. However, companies are not usually free to charge whatever prices they wish. Several laws restrict pricing practices, and a number of ethical considerations affect pricing decisions.

Legal issues surrounding pricing are outlined in Sections 34, 36, and 38 of the *Competition Act*. Canadian pricing legislation was designed with two goals in mind: to foster a competitive environment and to protect consumers. Although pricing decisions made by firms do not generally require regulatory approval, Canadian marketers should be aware of three areas of concern: price fixing, price discrimination, and deceptive pricing (also called misleading price advertising).[24]

Price Fixing

Federal legislation on price fixing states that sellers must set prices without talking to competitors. Otherwise, price collusion is suspected. Price fixing is illegal per se—that is, the government does not accept any excuses for price fixing. Even a simple conversation between competitors can have serious consequences. The legal charge under the *Competition Act* for offences of this nature is *conspiracy*. In January 2006, for example, the Competition Bureau levied record fines of $12.5 million each against Cascades Fine Papers Group Inc., Domtar Inc., and Unisource Canada, Inc., who pleaded guilty to two counts of conspiring to lessen competition in the Ontario and Quebec carbonless sheets market (carbonless sheets are used by commercial printers in the manufacture of forms and receipts). Moreover, the judgment included the provision that key personnel involved in the conspiracy will be removed from their positions in the paper merchant business. "Conspiracies of this nature destroy competition by interfering with private markets and hurt both business and consumers," said Sheridan Scott, commissioner of competition.[25]

Bid rigging is another indictable offence under the clauses pertaining to price fixing. A number of cases in the construction industry have resulted in heavy fines being levied when competitors have been found guilty of rigging the prices of their bids. These cases have made most executives very reluctant to discuss prices in any way with competitors. In obtaining information on competitors' pricing, they rely only on openly published materials, such as trade association surveys and competitors' catalogues.

Price Discrimination

Section 34 of the *Competition Act* seeks to ensure that sellers offer the same price terms to a given level of trade. For example, every retailer is entitled to the same price terms whether the retailer is Sears or the local bicycle shop. However, price discrimination is allowed if the seller can prove that its costs are different when selling to different retailers—for example, that it costs less per unit to sell a large volume of bicycles to Sears than to sell a few bicycles to a local dealer. In other words, quantity or volume discounts are not prohibited. However, discriminatory promotional allowances (those not offered on proportional terms to all other competing customers) are illegal. Thus, large competitors cannot negotiate special discounts, rebates, and price concessions that are not made proportionally available to smaller competitors. For example, a small customer purchasing one-third as much as a larger competitor must receive a promotional allowance equal to one-third of what the large competitor was offered.

Although functional discounts (offering a larger discount to wholesalers than to retailers) are legal in the United States, they are illegal in Canada. In Canada, retailers and wholesalers are considered competing customers who must receive proportionally equal promotional allowances. Often, Canadian marketers who work for multinational firms must explain the differences in the law to their U.S. counterparts. Canadian marketers must also keep in mind that it is illegal for a buyer to knowingly benefit from any form of price discrimination. Price differentials may be used to "match competition" in "good faith," provided the firm is trying to meet competitors at its own level of competition and the price discrimination is temporary, localized, and defensive rather than offensive.

Canadian marketers are allowed to offer price breaks for one-shot deals, such as store-opening specials, anniversary specials, and stock clearance sales. However, regional price differentials that limit competition are illegal. Canadian firms cannot price products unreasonably low in one part of the country with the intent of driving out the competition.

Finally, resale price maintenance is also illegal. Canadian manufacturers can only suggest prices; it is illegal to require retailers to sell at a stipulated manufacturer's price.

Deceptive Pricing

Section 36 of the *Competition Act* covers areas where pricing and advertising practices converge. For example, firms cannot advertise a product at a low price, carry very limited stock, and then tell consumers they are out of the product so that they can entice them to switch to a higher-priced item. This "bait and switch" advertising is illegal in Canada. Firms must offer their customers "rain cheques" to avoid legal sanctions if advertised items are not stocked in sufficient quantities to cover expected demand.

Deceptive pricing occurs when a seller states prices or price savings that are not actually available to consumers. Some deceptions are difficult for consumers to discern, such as when an airline advertises a low one-way fare that is available only with the purchase of a round-trip ticket, or when a retailer sets artificially high "regular" prices, then announces "sale" prices close to its previous everyday prices.

Ethical Issues in Pricing

Compliance with the law is considered the minimum standard when judging whether pricing practices are ethical. For example, although charging inordinately high prices is not illegal, such a practice may lead to ethical concerns. Ethical criticisms have been levied when higher prices are charged for groceries in poor areas where consumers have limited access to transportation and have few choices in terms of retail outlets.

Other ethical questions centre on whether consumers can understand prices and realistically compare them. For example, consumer advocates have condemned many car-leasing contracts since the legal language used in the contracts prevents consumers from fully understanding the price they are paying for the car.

Ethical concerns about pricing also arise when consumers must negotiate prices. Often those who can least afford to pay a higher price (such as the poor, very young, elderly, or those with disabilities) have the least ability to negotiate prices. These concerns arise when prices are not fixed. This is the case when people purchase cars, houses, and professional services, or attend street markets. Many consumers are unaware that even when prices appear fixed, they may be subject to negotiation. For example, many consumers don't know that they can negotiate with their bank for more favourable terms on a consumer loan.[26]

Reviewing the Concepts

Price can be defined narrowly as the amount of money charged for a product or service, or more broadly as the sum of the values that consumers exchange for the benefits of having and using the product or service.

Despite the increased role of non-price factors in the modern marketing process, price remains an important element in the marketing mix. It is the only element in the marketing mix that produces revenue; all other elements represent costs. Price is also one of the most flexible elements of the marketing mix. Unlike product features and channel commitments, price can be raised or lowered quickly.

Even so, many companies are not good at handling pricing—pricing decisions and price competition are major problems for many marketing executives. Pricing problems often arise because prices are too cost-oriented, not revised frequently enough to reflect market changes, and not consistent with the rest of the marketing mix.

1. Identify and define the internal factors affecting a firm's pricing decisions.

Many internal factors influence the company's pricing decisions, including the firm's *marketing objectives, marketing mix strategy, costs, product-related considerations,* and *organization considerations.* The pricing strategy is largely determined by the company's target market and positioning objectives. Pricing decisions affect and are affected by product design, distribution, and promotion decisions. Therefore, pricing strategies must be carefully coordinated with the other marketing mix variables when designing the marketing program.

Costs set the floor for the company's product price—the price must cover all the costs of making and selling the product, plus a fair rate of return. Common pricing objectives include survival, current profit maximization, market share leadership, and product quality leadership.

Product and pricing decisions are closely related. In pricing innovative new products, it can follow *skimming pricing* by initially setting high prices to "skim" the maximum amount of revenue from various segments of the market. Or it can use *market penetration pricing* by setting a low initial price to penetrate the market deeply and win a large market share. When dealing with a line of products versus a single item, marketing managers must decide on the price steps to set between the various products in a line.

To coordinate pricing goals and decisions, management must decide who within the organization is responsible for setting price. In large companies, some pricing authority may be delegated to lower-level managers and salespeople, but top management usually sets pricing policies and approves proposed prices. Production, finance, and accounting managers also influence pricing decisions.

2. Identify and define the external factors affecting pricing decisions, including the impact of consumer perceptions of price and value.

External factors that influence pricing decisions include the *nature of the market and demand, competitors' prices and offers,* and other factors, such as the *economy, reseller needs,* and *government regulations.* The seller's pricing freedom varies with different types of markets. Pricing is especially challenging in markets characterized by monopolistic competition or oligopoly.

Ultimately, the consumer decides whether the company has set the right price. The consumer weighs the price against the perceived values of acquiring and using the product—if the price exceeds the sum of the values, consumers will not buy the product. The more *inelastic* the demand, the higher the company can set its price. Therefore, *demand* and *consumer value perceptions* set the ceiling for prices. Consumers differ in the values they assign to different product features, and marketers often vary their pricing strategies for different price segments. When assessing the market and demand, the company estimates the demand curve, which shows the probable quantity purchased per period at alternative price levels. Consumers also compare a product's price to the prices of *competitors'* products. As a result, a company must learn the price and quality of competitors' offers and use them as a starting point for its own pricing.

3. **Contrast the two general approaches to setting prices.**

A company can select from one or combine two general pricing approaches: the *cost-based approach* (cost-plus pricing, break-even analysis, and target profit pricing), and the *value-based approach.* Cost-based pricing sets prices based on the seller's cost structure, while value-based pricing relies on consumer perceptions of value to drive pricing decisions.

4. **Discuss how companies adjust their prices to take into account different types of customers and situations.**

Pricing is a dynamic process. Companies change their pricing structure over time and adjust it to account for different customers and situations. Pricing strategies usually change as a product passes through its life cycle. Companies apply a variety of *price-adjustment strategies* to account for differences in consumer segments and situations. One is *discount and allowance pricing,* whereby the company establishes cash or quantity discounts, or varying types of allowances. A second strategy is *segmented pricing,* whereby the company sells a product at two or more prices to accommodate different customers, product forms, locations, or times. Sometimes companies consider more than economics in their pricing decisions, using *psychological pricing* to better communicate a product's intended position. In *promotional pricing,* a company offers discounts or tem-

porarily sells a product below list price as a special event, sometimes even selling below cost as a loss leader. Another approach is *geographical pricing,* whereby the company decides how to price to distant customers, choosing from such alternatives as FOB-origin pricing, uniform-delivered pricing, or zone pricing. Finally, *international pricing* means that the company adjusts its price to meet different conditions and expectations in different world markets.

5. **Discuss the key issues related to initiating and responding to price changes.**

When a firm considers initiating a *price change,* it must consider customers' and competitors' reactions. There are different implications to *initiating price cuts* and *initiating price increases.* Buyer reactions to price changes are influenced by the meaning that customers see in the price change. Competitors' reactions flow from a set reaction policy or a fresh analysis of each situation.

There are also many factors to consider in responding to a competitor's price changes. The company that faces a price change initiated by a competitor must try to understand the competitor's intent as well as the likely duration and impact of the change. If a swift reaction is desirable, the firm should preplan its reactions to different possible price actions by competitors. When facing a competitor's price change, the company can sit tight, reduce its own price, raise perceived quality, improve quality and raise price, or launch a fighting brand.

Reviewing the Key Terms

Discussing the Concepts

1. The chapter points out that many companies do not handle pricing well. Beyond focusing too much on cost, what are some of the other difficulties that marketers have in setting prices?

2. What is target costing? For what product do you believe this approach would be most powerful?

3. Which three of the following external factors would have the greatest impact on setting the price for a 30-second commercial slot on Fox's *The OC*?
   - perceived value
   - competitors' prices
   - economic conditions
   - number of viewers
   - government
   - resellers
   - social concerns
   - viewer demographics

4. Explain why the elasticity of demand is such an important concept to marketers who market a "commodity"-type product?

5. Cost-plus pricing and target-profit pricing are two different types of cost-based pricing. Explain the differences between these two methods. Which of these methods is a better tool for marketers?

6. Go to the Air Canada website (www.aircanada.com/en/home.html). Play the role of two different decision makers: (a) a student planning a post-graduation trip to Europe that will start by going to Paris in June and will return from the same city in early August, and (b) a businessperson planning to attend a major conference in Paris that runs from Tuesday morning to Thursday evening. Both trips start from the major airport closest to your home. What fare options are open to the two travellers? How do the fares change depending on the return dates for the student and for the business traveller (hint: change the return date for the business traveller from a Friday to a Sunday and see what happens). Develop a table that outlines these options. How is Air Canada using value-based pricing to serve the different segments? What potential problems may this type of pricing cause for the airline?

Applying the Concepts

1. What can you infer about the firm's marketing objectives, mix strategy, and costs based on the following positioning statement: "No one beats our prices. We crush the competition."

2. Go to a nearby Second Cup and study its price list. Then, suppose that you are on the marketing team of Blenz The Canadian Coffee Company (see www.blenz.com). It has 35 stores in Canada, mainly in B.C. Because Second Cup is well entrenched in Canada, you see it as a major competitor as you expand. Suppose you have been asked by Blenz to summarize Second Cup's pricing strategy in a few sentences. Based on the chapter's discussion of general pricing strategies, what would you report? How would you suggest Blenz price its products in order to compete with Second Cup?

3. Given the following information, calculate the number of meals a restaurant would have to sell to break even:
   - average meal price = $10.35
   - meals sold = 8560
   - food cost = $27 653
   - food labour = $18 386
   - management = $4855
   - supplies = $3133
   - maintenance = $2213
   - marketing = $1650
   - insurance/legal = $1904
   - waste management = $988
   - utilities = $3159
   - rent = $3960

   (For an online interactive break-even model, go to http://harvardbusinessonline.hbsp.harvard.edu/b01/en/academic/edu_tk_mkt_break_even.jhtml. Register and download the application. Use it as many times as you wish, but be sure to read and observe the licence restrictions.)

4. Burst-of-Energy is a food product positioned in the extreme sports market as a performance enhancer. A distributor of the product has seen an increase in demand for the product from 1 million units to 2 million units as depicted in the following chart. The manufacturer has done nothing to generate this increased demand, but there have been reports that two popu-

lar celebrities were photographed consuming the product. How could such a demand increase have happened? Based on the demand chart at right, how would you characterize the demand for the product: Is it elastic or inelastic? Would you call this an example of fluctuating demand? Support your answers.

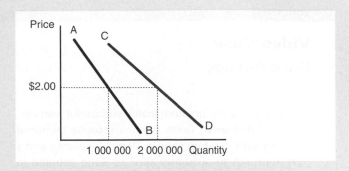

Focus on Technology

The Professional Pricing Society (PPS) is an association that supports price decision makers and price-management personnel from a wide range of industries in more than 50 countries. Typical members of the PPS include pricing, marketing, and general management executives from Fortune 1000 and mid-sized firms. The PPS provides both strategic and information resources to its members through pricing conferences and workshops, monthly and quarterly publications, consulting services, pricing workbooks, and an active Internet site. Many sponsors of the PPS are high-technology companies that provide the latest in pricing systems solution software. Setting market prices, revenue optimization, market measuring analytics, and answers designed to optimize difficult price decisions are just a few of the pricing issues tackled. Go to the PPS website at www.pricingsociety.com. This page points visitors to a number of pricing services (e.g., click on "Experts"). Read the short PPS pricing systems sponsor descriptions and answer the following questions:

1. What products or services do the sponsoring companies provide?

2. What kinds of companies would use or not use such services? Explain.

3. Do you think that products and services such as these would be useful to smaller companies as well as larger ones?

Focus on Ethics

John Wenman, merchandising manager at Goodmark's stationery store, is setting the price for Craft fountain pens. The pens cost him $5 each. The store's usual markup is 50 percent over cost, which suggests that John should set the price at $7.50. However, to make this price seem like an unusually good bargain, John begins by offering the pen at $10. He realizes that he won't sell many pens at this inflated price, but he doesn't care. John holds the price at $10 for only a few days, and then cuts it to the usual level—$7.50— and advertises: "Terrific Bargain on Craft Pens. Were $10, Now Only $7.50!"

1. If consumers perceive Craft pens to be a good value at $10, is it fair for Goodmark's to sell the pen at that price?

2. Is John's price-setting approach ethical? Is it legal? Explain.

Video Case
Song Airlines

To compete with phenomenally successful carriers, such as Southwest, Delta Airlines recently launched Song, its own low-fare service. With new planes and a new approach to customer service, Song debuted in 2003. The airline promises to take the mystery out of ticket prices by keeping one-way fares between US$79 and US$299. In addition to low fares, Song offers every passenger twenty-four channels of DISH Network Satellite TV, streaming digital radio, and video games they can play against other passengers in real time. And, rather than the typical airline food, Song provides an array of tasty, body-smart breakfast, lunch, and dinner options to choose from during a flight. By promising low fares and offering passengers perks, such as leather seating and satellite television, Song hopes to attract frequent flyers looking for more from their low-price carriers.

After viewing the video featuring Song Airlines, answer the following questions about pricing strategies:

1. What pricing strategies does Song employ to differentiate itself from other airlines?

2. Are Song's pricing strategies consistent with the rest of the airline's marketing mix?

3. Would you be interested in flying on Song Airlines? Should Song consider targeting students? Why or why not?

Online Media Resources

Video Short	**CBC ⊕ CBC Video Case**	**Case Pilot**
Log on to your Companion Website at **www.pearsoned.ca/kotler** to view the video segment related to the Video Case above.	Please refer to Appendix 2 to read a CBC Video Case for this chapter, and log on to your Companion Website at **www.pearsoned.ca/kotler** to view the corresponding video segment.	Log on to your Companion Website at **www.pearsoned.ca/kotler** to sharpen your case analysis skills and take the Case Pilot Challenge!

Company Case
Southeast Bank: Free Chequing?

Checking into Chequing

Kelly James, director of strategic planning at Southeast Bank*, looked up from her conference table as Bonnie Summers, manager of retail deposits, and Paul Bridges, retail product manager, knocked at her office door.

"Come on in," Kelly exclaimed as she waved them in. "I'm ready to hear what you've determined on the issue of whether we should start offering free chequing. I know there are a lot of pros and cons, and the issue's generated a lot of heated discussion around the bank. As you know, the executive committee's asked me to look into the issue and make a recommendation."

"Well, I've found some interesting information from a recent national study," Bonnie began. "Every six months, researchers at Bankrate.com conduct a national survey of chequing accounts, looking at things such as fees, minimum balances, service charges, and so on. It recently reported the results of its fall survey that included 1276 accounts at 350 institutions.

* The name of the bank and the names of people in this case have been disguised. Certain data on the bank's operations have also been adjusted but are indicative of reality.

"The survey found that the interest rate paid on chequing account balances fell from a 1.17 percent annual rate to 0.97 percent. The average minimum balance required to open an account and earn interest was $695, a 6 percent increase in just one year. On the other hand, to open a non-interest-bearing chequing account required just $76.30 on average, an amount that's barely changed in three years.

"To avoid monthly service fees on an interest-bearing account, you need an average minimum balance of $2434.50, up 5.6 percent in the last couple of years. The average minimum balance in non-interest-bearing accounts is just $408.16. If you don't want to keep a high balance in an interest-bearing account, the average monthly service fee is $10.85, up 4 percent per year for the last three years. The average monthly fee on non-interest-bearing accounts actually dropped to $6.19.

"About one-fourth of the chequing accounts also charge per-item fees for various transactions, such as cheque writing or deposits. The average interest-paying account allows seventeen "freebies," while the average non-interest-paying account allows twelve before fees kick in. I also found that ATM fees for non-customers who use a bank's ATM system have become almost universal and now average about $1.32 per transaction."

"Are there any true free chequing accounts with no minimum balance, no monthly service charges, and no per-item fees?" Kelly asked.

"The study showed that about 7.5 percent of the accounts surveyed were free, as you describe it, an all-time high," Bonnie answered. "I also found that the number of banks offering free non-interest chequing accounts jumped more than 15 percentage points to 45.3 percent. This move was especially true among large banks, such as Southeast."

"What about insufficient funds charges [NSFs]?" Paul asked.

"The survey showed that they were at an all-time high, also, Paul, averaging $24.85," Bonnie noted. "So, it's very expensive to bounce a cheque. Many banks offer overdraft protection—often for a fee, of course. Some banks charge an annual fee, such as $10, for overdraft protection and then add a $5 charge each time the customer uses the service."

Southeast's Situation

"That's very helpful, Bonnie. Paul, how would you summarize our situation?" Kelly asked.

"Competitors have not yet offered completely free chequing in our markets, although some are promot-ing no-fee chequing accounts that require that the account holder use direct deposit of payroll cheques. These accounts often limit access to tellers. Some banks have used free chequing as their number-one weapon in entering new markets and as a result have enjoyed significant gains in demand-deposit accounts (DDA). These banks promote their free chequing on an ongoing basis.

"From a defensive standpoint, we should be prepared for a competitor to launch a completely free chequing product in our markets. From an offensive standpoint, we have the opportunity to be the first in our markets with our own free-chequing product. I believe we could realize significant DDA share gains if we advertised the product."

"What experience have we had with these products?" Kelly asked.

"Well, we've acquired some small branches that had no-fee products, and we've experimented with some limited promotional campaigns in limited market areas," Paul replied. "Our free accounts have typically required a minimum balance of $500 or there was a $9.95 per month fee. The account holder also had to pay $0.35 per item for all cheques or debits in excess of twenty per month."

"Are these accounts profitable for the bank?" Kelly asked.

"Profitability depends on several variables," Paul answered. "First, there's the account's cash balance during the month. Then, we earn income through fees like NSF charges and ATM fees. We give certain credits to the branch that opened the account, which we treat as revenue. Then, we have allocated expenses, non-interest expenses we allocate to every account. If, however, the account has direct deposit, the allocated expenses are about 25 percent lower as it is less expensive for us to handle direct deposits. That is why so many free-chequing products require direct deposits. The savings help offset the lost fees.

"Given all that, our study shows that the free-chequing accounts we have experimented with had average balances of $1262. Our annual revenue per account from all sources was about $274 and our fully allocated expenses were about $237, giving us an annual profit of about $37. The average account had about four NSF or overdraft charges a year, producing the largest source of account revenue."

"I should add," Bonnie interjected, "that for our ten different types of chequing accounts, including accounts for students and seniors, the lower the average balance the greater the number of NSF charges, except for our student accounts. Students had *less* than one-half of the average number of overdrafts."

"Okay, what's the bottom line in terms of the impact on our revenue if we offered a free-chequing product just in our home province?" Kelly asked.

"Our analysis focused on just our home province and estimated that varying percentages of customers from each type of chequing account would move to the new product," Paul began. "If we offered the account in all 282 branches in the province for all 522 000 accounts, and if our switching estimates are correct, we could lose about $4.5 million in various fees (revenue) per year that those accounts are now paying. That is, we would lose this money as our current customers switched from fee-paying accounts to the free accounts. But, of course, we would hope that the new product would draw in new customers to offset those losses, and that those customers would also use other bank products, like home-equity loans or car loans."

"Speaking of 'drawing in,' what'll it cost us to promote this program?" Kelly asked.

"Our best estimate for an eight-week promotional program is about $127 000," Paul answered.

What to do?

"Thanks for your good work," Kelly responded. "This information is helpful. I've got to decide what to recommend to the executive committee.

"I know that free chequing is the 'in' thing now in banking, with people believing that free chequing gets people in the door. I also know that we make money on lower-income customers' accounts through fee income and on higher-income customers' accounts because of higher balances. Further, although our total dollar balance in our chequing accounts has been growing, our total number of accounts has been declining somewhat.

"One concern I have is whether or not free chequing fits the bank's positioning. We've tried to

position ourselves as a relationship bank, differentiating ourselves based on service versus price. We build and value long-term customer relationships. For that reason, we've not tried to pay the highest interest rates or charge the lowest fees because we didn't want customers who were focused only on price. I'm not sure free chequing fits our image. Further, we've not traditionally advertised products. Rather, we've used corporate advertising that focused on the bank's relationships with its customers.

"This certainly isn't as easy a decision as it might appear," Bonnie noted.

"You can say that again!" Kelly responded. "I'll just have to ponder all this information and decide what to recommend. Thanks for your help."

Questions for Discussion

1. What type of new-product pricing strategy would be involved in considering a new free-chequing product for the bank?

2. What types of product mix pricing considerations do you see in banks' pricing for chequing accounts?

3. What types of price-adjustment considerations do you see in the pricing strategies for chequing accounts?

4. What strategy would you recommend that Southeast Bank pursue on the free-chequing account issue? What options does it have? How can break-even analysis assist you in your analysis of the various options?

Sources: Officials at Southeast Bank cooperated in development of this case. See also Tim Henderson, "More ATM Fees, Free Checking," *American Banker*, June 17, 2002, p. 24; Laura Bruce, "Checking Accounts Keep Climbing in Price," Bankrate.com, posted September 28, 2001.

CHAPTER 12

Distribution Channels and Supply Chain Management

AFTER STUDYING THIS CHAPTER, YOU SHOULD BE ABLE TO

1. explain why companies use distribution channels and discuss the functions these channels perform

2. discuss how channel members interact and how they organize to perform the work of the channel

3. identify the major channel alternatives open to a company

4. explain how companies select, motivate, and evaluate channel members

5. discuss the nature and importance of marketing logistics and integrated supply chain management

CHAPTER 12
Distribution Channels and Supply Chain Management

AFTER STUDYING THIS CHAPTER, YOU SHOULD BE ABLE TO

1. explain why companies use distribution channels and discuss the functions these channels perform

2. discuss how channel members interact and how they organize to perform the work of the channel

3. identify the major channel alternatives open to a company

4. explain how companies select, motivate, and evaluate channel members

5. discuss the nature and importance of marketing logistics and integrated supply chain management

Previewing the Concepts

Let's look now at the third marketing mix tool—distribution. Firms rarely work alone in creating value for customers and building profitable customer relationships. Instead, most are only a single link in a larger supply chain and distribution channel. As such, an individual firm's success depends not only on how well *it* performs but also on how well its *entire distribution channel* competes with competitors' channels. To be good at customer relationship management, a company must also be good at partner relationship management. The first part of this chapter explores the nature of distribution channels and the marketer's channel design and management decisions. We then examine physical distribution—or logistics—an area that is growing dramatically in importance and sophistication. In the next chapter, we'll look more closely at two major intermediaries—retailers and wholesalers.

We'll start with a look at Caterpillar. You might think that Caterpillar's success, and its ability to charge premium prices, rests on the quality of the heavy construction and mining equipment that it produces. But Caterpillar sees things differently. The company's dominance, it claims, results from its unparalleled distribution and customer support system—from the strong and caring partnerships that it has built with independent Caterpillar dealers. Read on and see why.

For more than seven decades, Caterpillar has dominated the world's markets for heavy construction, mining, and logging equipment. Its familiar yellow tractors, crawlers, loaders, bulldozers, and trucks are a common sight at any construction area. Caterpillar sells more than 300 products in nearly 200 companies, generating sales of almost $30 billion annually. It captures 27 percent of the worldwide construction-equipment business, more than double that of number-two Komatsu. Its share of the North American market is more than twice that of competitors Komatsu and Deere combined. In Canada, Caterpillar distributes its products through independent dealerships, such as Finning (Canada), located in Edmonton, Alberta. Finning is one of Caterpillar's largest dealerships and aims to be Caterpillar's best global business partner, providing unrivalled services that earn customer loyalty.

Many factors contribute to Caterpillar's enduring success—high-quality products, flexible and efficient manufacturing, and a steady stream of innovative new products. Yet these are not the most important reasons for Caterpillar's dominance. Instead, Caterpillar credits its focus on customers and its corps of 220 outstanding independent dealers worldwide, who do a superb job of taking care of every customer need. According to former Caterpillar CEO Donald Fites:

After the product leaves our door, the dealers take over. They are the ones on the front line. They're the ones who live with the product for its lifetime. They're the ones customers see.... They're out there making sure that when a machine is delivered, it's in the condition it's supposed to be in. They're out there training a customer's operators. They service a product frequently throughout its life, carefully monitoring a machine's health and scheduling repairs to prevent costly downtime. The customer ... knows that there is a $[30]-billion-plus company called Caterpillar. But the dealers create the image of a company that doesn't just stand *behind* its products but *with* its products, anywhere in the world. Our dealers are the reason that our motto—Buy the Iron, Get the Company—is not an empty slogan.

"Buy the Iron, Get the Company"—that's a powerful value proposition. It means that when you buy Cat equipment, you become a member of the Caterpillar family. Caterpillar and its dealers work in close harmony to find better ways to bring value to customers. Dealers play a vital role in almost every aspect of Caterpillar's operations, from product design and delivery, to product service and support, to market intelligence and customer feedback.

In the heavy-equipment industry, in which equipment down time can mean big losses, Caterpillar's exceptional service gives it a huge advantage in winning and keeping customers. Consider Freeport-McMoRan, a Cat customer that operates one of the world's largest copper and gold mines, 24 hours a day, 365 days a year. High in the mountains of Indonesia, the mine is accessible only by aerial cableway or helicopter. Freeport-McMoRan relies on more than 500 pieces of Caterpillar mining and construction equipment—worth several hundred million dollars—including loaders, tractors, and mammoth 218-tonne, 2000-plus-horsepower trucks. Many of these machines cost more than $1.3 million apiece. When equipment breaks down, Freeport-McMoRan loses money fast. Freeport-McMoRan gladly pays a premium price for machines and service it can count on. It knows that it can count on Caterpillar and its outstanding distribution network for superb support.

The close working relationship between Caterpillar and its dealers comes down to more than just formal contracts and business agreements. The powerful partnership rests on a handful of basic principles and practices:

- *Dealer profitability:* Caterpillar's rule: "Share the gain as well as the pain." When times are good, Caterpillar shares the bounty with its dealers rather than trying to grab all the riches for itself. When times are bad, Caterpillar protects its dealers. In the mid-1980s, facing a depressed global construction-equipment market and cutthroat competition, Caterpillar sheltered its dealers by absorbing much of the economic damage. It lost almost $1.3 billion in just three years but didn't lose a single dealer. In contrast, competitors' dealers struggled and many failed. As a result, Caterpillar emerged with its distribution system intact and its competitive position stronger than ever.

- *Extraordinary dealer support:* Nowhere is this support more apparent than in the company's parts delivery system, the fastest and most reliable in the industry. Caterpillar maintains 36 distribution centres and 1500 service facilities around the world, which stock 320 000 different parts and ship 84 000 items per day, every day of the year. In turn, dealers have made huge investments in inventory, warehouses, fleets of trucks, service bays, diagnostic and service equipment, and information technology. Together, Caterpillar and its dealers guarantee parts delivery within 48 hours any-

where in the world. The company ships 80 percent of parts orders immediately and 99 percent on the same day the order is received. In contrast, it's not unusual for competitors' customers to wait four or five days for a part.

- *Communications:* Caterpillar communicates with its dealers—fully, frequently, and honestly. According to Fites, "There are no secrets between us and our dealers. We have the financial statements and key operating data of every dealer in the world.... In addition, virtually all Caterpillar and dealer employees have real-time access to continually updated databases of service information, sales trends and forecasts, customer satisfaction surveys, and other critical data."

- *Dealer performance:* Caterpillar does all it can to ensure that its dealerships are run well. It closely monitors each dealership's sales, market position, service capability, financial situation, and other performance measures. It genuinely wants each dealer to succeed, and when it sees a problem, it jumps in to help. As a result, Caterpillar dealerships, many of which are family businesses, tend to be stable and profitable.

- *Personal relationships:* In addition to more formal business ties, Cat forms close personal ties with its dealers in a kind of family relationship. One Caterpillar executive relates the following example: "When I see Chappy Chapman, a retired executive vice-president..., out on the golf course, he always asks about particular dealers or about their children, who may be running the business now. And every time I see those dealers, they inquire, 'How's Chappy?' That's the sort of relationship we have.... I consider the majority of dealers personal friends."

Thus, Caterpillar's superb distribution system serves as a major source of competitive advantage. The system is built on a firm base of mutual trust and shared dreams. Caterpillar and its dealers feel a deep pride in what they are accomplishing together. As Fites puts it, "There's a camaraderie among our dealers around the world that really makes it more than just a financial arrangement. They feel that what they're doing is good for the world because they are part of an organization that makes, sells, and tends to the machines that make the world work."[1]

Most firms cannot bring value to customers by themselves. Instead, they must work closely with other firms in a larger value delivery network.

Supply Chains and the Value Delivery Network

Producing a product or service and making it available to buyers requires building relationships not just with customers but also with key suppliers and resellers in the company's *supply chain*. This supply chain consists of "upstream" and "downstream" partners. Upstream from the company is the set of firms that supply the raw materials, components, parts, information, finances, and expertise needed to create a product or service. Marketers, however, have traditionally focused on the "downstream" side of the supply chain—on the *distribution channels* that look forward toward the customer. Downstream distribution channel partners, such as wholesalers and retailers, form a vital connection between the firm and its customers.

Both upstream and downstream partners may also be part of other firms' supply chains. But it is the unique design of each company's supply chain that enables it to deliver superior value to customers. An individual firm's success depends not only on how well *it* performs, but also on how well its entire supply chain and marketing channel competes with competitors' channels.

The term *supply chain* may be too limited—it takes a *make-and-sell* view of the business. It suggests that raw materials, productive inputs, and factory capacity should serve as the starting point for market planning. A better term would be *demand chain* because it suggests a *sense-and-respond* view of the market. Under this view, planning starts with the needs of target customers, to which the company responds by organizing a chain of resources and activities with the goal of creating customer value.

Even a demand-chain view of a business may be too limited, because it takes a step-by-step, linear view of purchase–production–consumption activities. With the advent of the Internet and other technologies, however, companies are forming more numerous and complex relationships with other firms. For example, Ford manages numerous supply chains. It also sponsors or transacts on many business-to-business (B2B) websites and online purchasing exchanges as needs arise. Like Ford, most large companies today are engaged in building and managing a continuously evolving *value-delivery network*.

Value-delivery network
The network made up of the company, suppliers, distributors, and ultimately customers who "partner" with each other to improve the performance of the entire system.

Companies today are increasingly taking a full-value-delivery-network view of their businesses. As defined in Chapter 2, a **value-delivery network** is made up of the company, suppliers, distributors, and ultimately customers. Members of the value-delivery network "partner" with each other to improve the performance of the entire system. For example, Longueuil, Quebec-based ebusiness, Mediagrif Interactive Technologies Inc., has been called the "eBay for business" because it has been so successful in building effective value-delivery networks:[2]

Mediagrif Interactive Technologies Inc. helps buyers and sellers interact more effectively and prides itself as being a world-leading operator of ebusiness networks and a provider of complete ebusiness solutions. It provides the technology behind online marketplaces, where industry buyers and suppliers can connect to do business. The company's ebusiness networks allow buyers and sellers within specific industries to source, purchase, or sell products and to exchange information over the Internet. The company operates fourteen networks, including The Broker Forum, Power Source On-Line, Telecom Finders,

Mediagrif Interactive Technologies Inc. operates fourteen networks and provides the technologies that help businesses and their suppliers connect more effectively.

Polygon and Global Wine & Spirits. It also owns and operates the MERX etendering service, the official distributor of tender documents for the Canadian federal government, and is a leading provider of government bid aggregation services and eprocurement services in the U.S. Customer service is provided twenty-four hours a day, in more than twenty languages. It serves more than 45 675 customers in sixty countries. Mediagrif was founded in 1996, and since then has grown to more than 400 employees with revenues of almost $52 million in 2005.

This chapter focuses on distribution channels—on the downstream side of the value delivery network. However, it is important to remember that this is only part of the full value network. Marketers also use communication channels to inform and relate to their customers. To bring value to customers, companies also need upstream supplier partners just as they need downstream channel partners. Increasingly, marketers are participating in and influencing their company's upstream activities as well as its downstream activities. More than marketing channel managers, they are becoming full network managers.

The chapter examines four major questions concerning distribution channels: What is the nature of distribution channels and why are they important? How do channel firms interact and organize to do the work of the channel? What problems do companies face in designing and managing their channels? What role do physical distribution and supply chain management play in attracting and satisfying customers? In Chapter 13, we will look at marketing channel issues from the viewpoint of retailers and wholesalers.

The Nature and Importance of Distribution Channels

Marketing channel (or distribution channel)
A set of interdependent organizations involved in the process of making a product or service available for use or consumption by the consumer or business user.

Few producers sell their goods directly to the final users. Instead, most use intermediaries to bring their products to market. They try to forge a **marketing channel** (or **distribution channel**)—a set of interdependent organizations involved in the process of making a product or service available for use or consumption by the consumer or business user.[3]

A company's channel decisions directly affect every other marketing decision. The company's pricing depends on whether it works with national discount chains, uses high-quality specialty stores, or sells directly to consumers via the Web. The firm's sales force and communications decisions depend on how much persuasion, training, motivation, and support its channel partners need. Whether a company develops or acquires certain new products may depend on how well those products fit the capabilities of its channel members.

Companies often pay too little attention to their distribution channels, sometimes with damaging results. In contrast, many companies have used imaginative distribution systems to *gain* a competitive advantage. It's creative and imposing distribution system has made FedEx a leader in the express delivery industry. Dell Computer revolutionized its industry by selling personal computers directly to consumers rather than through retail stores. And Amazon.com pioneered the sales of books and a wide range of other goods via the Internet.

Distribution channel decisions often involve long-term commitments to other firms. For example, companies such as Ford, IBM, or McDonald's can easily change their advertising, pricing, or promotion programs. They can scrap old prod-

FedEx's creative and imposing distribution system made it a market leader in express delivery. "Relax, it's FedEx."

ucts and introduce new ones as market tastes demand. But when they set up distribution channels through contracts with franchisees, independent dealers, or large retailers, they cannot readily replace these channels with company-owned stores or websites if conditions change. Therefore, management must design its channels carefully, with an eye on tomorrow's likely selling environment as well as today's.

How Channel Members Add Value

Why do producers give some of the selling job to channel partners? After all, doing so means giving up some control over how and to whom the products are sold. The use of intermediaries results from their greater efficiency in making goods available to target markets. Through their contacts, experience, specialization, and scale of operation, intermediaries usually offer the firm more than it can achieve on its own.

Figure 12.1 shows how using intermediaries can provide economies. Figure 12.1A shows three manufacturers, each using direct marketing, to reach three customers. This system requires nine different contacts. Figure 12.1B shows the three manufacturers working through one distributor, which contacts the three customers. This system requires only six contacts. In this way, intermediaries reduce the amount of work that must be done by both producers and consumers.

From the economic system's point of view, marketing intermediaries perform certain key *functions* that are related to transforming the assortments of products made by producers into the assortments wanted by consumers. Producers make narrow assortments of products in large quantities, but consumers want broad assortments of products in small quantities. In the distribution channels, intermediaries buy large quantities from many producers and break them down into the smaller quantities and broader assortments wanted by consumers (this function is sometimes called bulk-breaking). Thus, intermediaries play an important role in matching supply and demand. Channel members may also help with the contact function—finding and communicating with prospective buyers. They also assist with matching—shaping and fitting the offer to the buyer's needs, including activities such as manufacturing, grading, assembling, and packaging. Finally, different channel members may take on different aspects of the physical distribution function, the transporting and storing of goods.

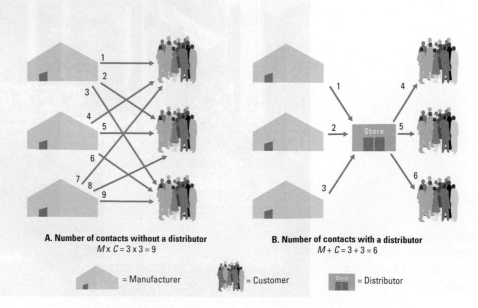

A. Number of contacts without a distributor
$M \times C = 3 \times 3 = 9$

B. Number of contacts with a distributor
$M + C = 3 + 3 = 6$

= Manufacturer   = Customer   = Distributor

Figure 12.1 How a marketing intermediary reduces the number of channel transactions

A new item has recently been added to the list of functions that has to be performed within the supply chain—*environmental sustainability*. Take the case of Ottawa-based Nortel Networks:[4]

Regulators around the world, such as the OECD, are issuing environmentally focused directives. Ranking services, such as the Dow Jones Sustainability World Index, which rates firms according to their environmental performance, are also having a powerful influence on corporate decision making. Thus, environmental sustainability is more than a nicety for Nortel—it's a competitive necessity. Furthermore, Nortel's customers—large telecom companies from around the world who have environmental targets of their own—are increasingly demanding such practices. Nortel was named to the Dow Jones Sustainability World Index in 2006 primarily because of its focus on product stewardship. Products' life cycles have to be managed for environmental sustainability from the design stage to the replacement stage and everything in between. Nortel's "design for environment" principles focus on the elimination of negative environmental impacts even before a costly product is created. Once a product has reached the end of its useful life, Nortel offers to take its customers' old telecom gear—whether it was originally from Nortel or not—and strip it down for reuse, if possible, or sold for scrap. Since Nortel outsources much of its manufacturing, it works closely with both suppliers and contract manufacturers to maintain high standards of environmental integrity. Nortel is in the business of making connections and thus it was quick to see the link between environmental sustainability and winning over customers.

In making products and services available to consumers, channel members add value by bridging the major time, place, and possession gaps that separate goods and services from those who would use them.

Members of the distribution channel also help manage different two-way flows that are essential to building customer relationships and delivering products and services. These flows include

- *Information:* Manufacturers need information about end customers and consumers just as much as customers and consumers need information about

Nortel focuses on product stewardship and works with its suppliers and manufacturers to ensure that its principles for environmental sustainability are followed.

products and services. Since wholesalers and retailers often have more direct contact with buyers and end users, they help manage the flow of information up and down the channel. The information flow may include the gathering and distributing of marketing research and intelligence about actors and forces in the marketing environment needed for planning and aiding exchange as well as the flow of promotional materials from the producer to the buyer.

- *Negotiation:* Reaching an agreement on price and other terms of the offer so that ownership or possession can be transferred from the manufacturer to the new owner.
- *Financing:* Acquiring and using funds to cover the costs of the channel work.
- *Risk taking:* Assuming the risks of carrying out the channel work.

The question is not *whether* these functions need to be performed and the flows need to be managed—they must be—but rather *who* will perform them. To the extent that the manufacturer performs these tasks, its costs go up and its prices have to be higher. When some of these responsibilities are shifted to intermediaries, the producer's costs and prices may be lower, but the intermediaries must charge more to cover the costs of their work. In dividing the work of the channel, management of the various functions and flows should be assigned to the channel members who can add the most value for the cost.

Number of Channel Levels

Channel level

A layer of intermediaries that performs some work in bringing the product and its ownership closer to the final buyer.

Companies can design their distribution channels to make products and services available to customers in different ways. Each layer of marketing intermediaries that performs some work in bringing the product and its ownership closer to the final buyer is a **channel level**. Because the producer and the final consumer both perform some work, they are part of every channel.

Direct marketing channel

A marketing channel that has no intermediary levels.

Indirect marketing channel

A channel containing one or more intermediary levels.

The *number of intermediary levels* indicates the *length* of a channel. Figure 12.2A shows several consumer distribution channels of different lengths. Channel 1, called a **direct marketing channel**, has no intermediary levels; the company sells directly to consumers. For example, Avon and Amway sell their products door-to-door, through home and office sales parties, and on the Web; Veseys located in York, Prince Edward Island, sells its plants and bulbs to gardeners across the country through mail catalogues, by telephone, and online. The remaining channels in Figure 12.2A are **indirect distribution channels**, containing one or more intermediaries.

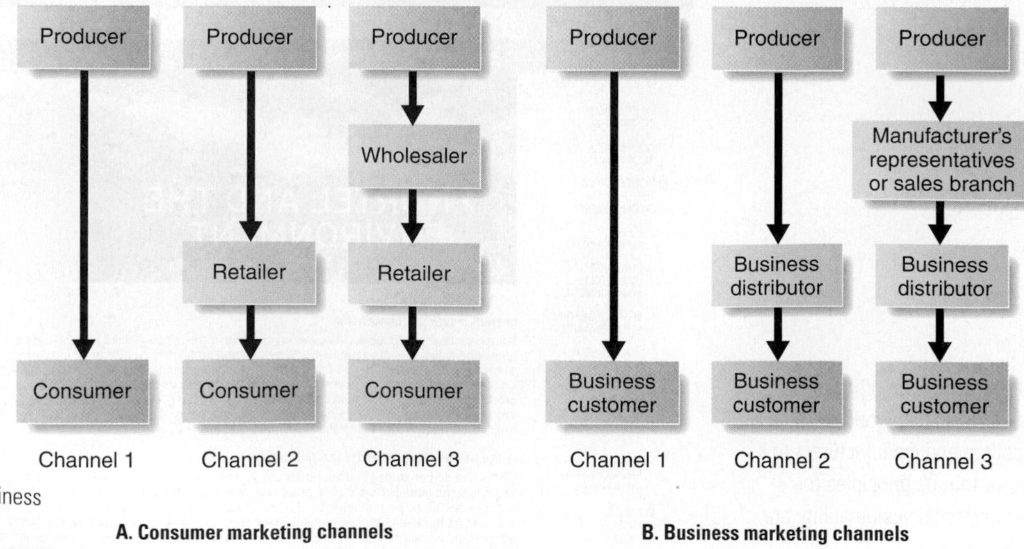

Figure 12.2 Customer and business distribution channels

A. Consumer marketing channels

B. Business marketing channels

Figure 12.2B shows some common business distribution channels. The business marketer can use its own sales force to sell directly to business customers. Or it can sell to various types of intermediaries, who in turn sell to these customers. Consumer and business distribution channels with even more levels are sometimes found, but less often. From the producer's point of view, a greater number of levels means less control and greater channel complexity. Moreover, all of the institutions in the channel are connected by several types of *flows*. These include the *physical flow* of products, the *flow of ownership*, the *payment flow*, the *information flow*, and the *promotion flow*. These flows can make even channels with only one or a few levels very complex.

Channel Behaviour and Organization

Distribution channels are more than simple collections of firms tied together by various flows. They are complex behavioural systems in which people and companies interact to accomplish individual, company, and channel goals. Some channel systems consist only of informal interactions among loosely organized firms. Others consist of formal interactions guided by strong organizational structures. Moreover, channel systems do not stand still—new types of intermediaries emerge and whole new channel systems evolve. Here we look at channel behaviour and at how members organize to do the work of the channel.

Channel Behaviour

A marketing channel consists of firms that have partnered for their common good. Each channel member depends on the others. For example, a Ford dealer depends on Ford to design cars that meet consumer needs. In turn, Ford depends on the dealer to attract consumers, persuade them to buy Ford cars, and service cars after the sale. Each Ford dealer also depends on other dealers to provide good sales and service that will uphold the brand's reputation. In fact, the success of individual Ford dealers depends on how well the entire Ford marketing channel competes with the channels of other auto manufacturers.

Each channel member plays a specialized role in the channel. For example, Sony's role is to produce consumer electronics products that consumers will like and to create demand through national advertising. Future Shop's role is to display these Sony products in convenient locations, to answer buyers' questions, and to complete sales. The channel will be most effective when each member is assigned the tasks it can do best.

Ideally, because the success of individual channel members depends on overall channel success, all channel firms should work together smoothly. They should understand and accept their roles, coordinate their activities, and cooperate to attain overall channel goals. However, individual channel members rarely take such a broad view. Cooperating to achieve overall channel goals sometimes means giving up individual company goals. Although channel members depend on one another, they often act alone in their own short-run best interests. They often disagree on who should do what and for what rewards. Such disagreements over goals, roles, and rewards generate **channel conflict**.

Horizontal conflict occurs among firms at the same level of the channel. For instance, some Ford dealers in Vancouver might complain the other dealers in the city steal sales from them by pricing too low or by advertising aggressively. Or Holiday Inn franchisees might complain about other Holiday Inn operators overcharging guests or giving poor service, hurting the overall Holiday Inn image.

Channel conflict

Disagreement among marketing channel members on goals and roles—who should do what and for what rewards.

Vertical conflict, conflicts between different levels of the same channel, is even more common. For example, office furniture maker Herman Miller created conflict with its dealers when it opened an online store—www.hmstore.com—and began selling its products directly to customers. Although Herman Miller believed that the website was reaching only smaller customers who weren't being served by current channels, dealers complained loudly. As a result, the company closed down its online sales operations. Take another case—the Great Canadian Bagel company:

> Theresa Slater-Smith celebrated Mother's Day, 2002, by stripping the Great Canadian Bagel franchise she'd bought five years previously of everything not covered by her lease. She was taking revenge on the company, believing she would never be able to recover her original $150 000 investment—let alone the hours of labour and love she had poured into the business. Slater-Smith was not alone. High rents and sagging sales have forced more than sixty Great Canadian Bagel franchisees to close down. The original business model—large in-store bakeries pumping out fresh bagels—didn't work because the margins on bagels were too slim to support the high rents on large, full-production stores. The remaining franchisees were advised to downsize or partner with other food outlets, such as pizza parlours and cafés, to share costs and cut expenses. As Calgary franchisee Todd Bilquist noted, "There is a lot of frustration out there among franchisees. The people at head office now are going in the right direction, but there's a lot of mistrust between the franchisees and the company."[5]

Some conflict in the channel takes the form of healthy competition. Such competition can be good for the channel—without it, the channel could become passive and non-innovative. But severe or prolonged conflict can disrupt channel effectiveness and cause lasting harm to channel relationships. Companies should manage channel conflict to keep it from getting out of hand.

Vertical Marketing Systems

For the channel as a whole to perform well, each channel member's role must be specified and channel conflict must be managed. The channel will perform better if

Conflict may occur between different levels of a channel, as was the case with the Great Canadian Bagel company.

it includes a firm, agency, or mechanism that provides leadership and has the power to assign roles and manage conflict.

Historically, *conventional distribution channels* have lacked such leadership and power, often resulting in damaging conflict and poor performance. One of the biggest channel developments over the years has been the emergence of *vertical marketing systems* that provide channel leadership. Figure 12.3 contrasts the two types of channel arrangements.

A **conventional distribution channel** consists of one or more independent producers, wholesalers, and retailers. Each is a separate business seeking to maximize its own profits, even at the expense of the system as a whole. No channel member has much control over the other members, and no formal means exist for assigning roles and resolving channel conflict. In contrast, a **vertical marketing system (VMS)** consists of producers, wholesalers, and retailers acting as a unified system. One channel member owns the others, has contracts with them, or wields so much power that they must all cooperate. The VMS can be dominated by the producer, wholesaler, or retailer. The Forzani Group, headquartered in Calgary, is an example of a retail-dominated VMS. It owns and operates a range of sporting goods stores including Sport Chek, Coast Mountain Sports, Sport Mart, and National Sports.

We look now at three major types of VMSs: *corporate*, *contractual*, and *administered*. Each uses a different means for setting up leadership and power in the channel.

Corporate VMS

A **corporate VMS** integrates successive stages of production and distribution under single ownership. Coordination and conflict management are attained through regular organizational channels. For example, U.S. grocery giant Kroger owns and operates 42 factories that crank out more than 4300 of the food and drink items found on its store shelves. And little-known Italian eyewear maker Luxottica produces many famous eyewear brands—including Ray-Ban, Vogue, Anne Klein, Ferragamo, and Armani. It then sells these brands through two of the world's largest optical chains, LensCrafters and Sunglass Hut, which it also owns.[6]

Controlling the entire distribution chain has turned Spanish clothing chain Zara into the world's fastest-growing fashion retailer.

The secret to Zara's success is its control over almost every aspect of the supply chain, from design and production to its own worldwide distribution network. Zara makes 40 percent of its own fabrics and produces more than half of its own clothes, rather than relying on a hodgepodge of slow-moving suppliers. New styles take

Conventional distribution channel
A channel consisting of one or more independent producers, wholesalers, and retailers, each a separate business seeking to maximize its own profits even at the expense of profits for the system as a whole.

Vertical marketing system (VMS)
A distribution channel structure in which producers, wholesalers, and retailers act as a unified system. One channel member owns the others, has contracts with them, or has so much power that they all cooperate.

Corporate VMS
A vertical marketing system that combines successive stages of production and distribution under single ownership—channel leadership is established through common ownership.

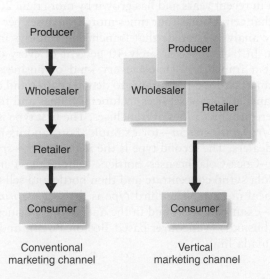

Figure 12.3 A conventional marketing channel versus a vertical marketing system

Little-known Italian eyewear maker Luxottica produces many famous eyewear brands—including Ray-Ban—then sells them through two of the world's largest optical chains, LensCrafters and Sunglass Hut, which it also owns.

shape in Zara's own design centres, supported by real-time sales data. New designs feed into Zara manufacturing centres, which ship finished products directly to 652 Zara stores in forty-eight countries, saving time, eliminating the need for warehouses, and keeping inventories low. Effective vertical integration makes Zara faster, more flexible, and more efficient than international competitors, such as Gap, Benetton, and Sweden's H&M. Its finely tuned distribution systems make Zara seem more like Dell or Wal-Mart. Zara can make a new line from start to finish in fewer than fifteen days, so a look seen on MTV can be in Zara stores within a month, versus an industry average of nine months. And Zara's low costs let it offer midmarket chic at downmarket prices. The company's stylish but affordable offerings have attracted a cult following, and the company's sales have more than doubled to $4 billion in the past five years.[7]

Contractual VMS

Contractual VMS

A vertical marketing system in which independent firms at different levels of production and distribution join together through contracts to obtain more economies or sales impact than they could achieve alone.

Franchise organization

A contractual vertical marketing system in which a channel member, called a franchiser, links several stages in the production–distribution process.

A **contractual VMS** consists of independent firms at different levels of production and distribution who join together through contracts to obtain more economies or sales impact than each could achieve alone. Coordination and conflict management are attained through contractual agreements among channel members.

The **franchise organization** is the most common type of contractual relationship—a channel member called a *franchiser* links several stages in the production–distribution process. Franchising has been the fastest-growing retailing form in Canada in recent years and has grown by more than 20 percent since 1993. It is estimated that Canada has four times more franchises per capita than the United States. Industry analysts estimate that franchising employs more than 1 million people in Canada. In fact, approximately 40 percent of every dollar spent on retail items is spent at a franchise.[8] Almost every kind of business has been franchised—from motels and fast-food restaurants to dental centres and dating services, from wedding consultants and maid services to funeral homes and fitness centres.

There are three types of franchises. The first type is the *manufacturer-sponsored retailer franchise system*—for example, Ford and its network of independent franchised dealers. The second type is the *manufacturer-sponsored wholesaler franchise system*—Coca-Cola licenses bottlers (wholesalers) in various markets who buy Coca-Cola syrup concentrate and then bottle and sell the finished product to retailers in local markets. The third type is the *service-firm-sponsored retailer franchise system*—examples are found in the auto-rental business (Hertz, Avis), the fast-food service business (Vancouver-based Boston Pizza), and the hotel business (Holiday Inn, Ramada Inn).

Boston Pizza works closely with its franchisees and has built one of the most successful chains in Canada.

Boston Pizza's on a roll, and it may be an icon of Canadian business—"a Canadian company with an American name operated by Greeks serving Italian food." First opened in Edmonton in 1964, it is now headquartered in Richmond, B.C. The name was selected for the simple reason that the fame of the Bruins and Red Sox made it easy to remember. Boston Pizza is Canada's largest casual sit-down dining chain, bigger even than Swiss Chalet. In 2006, it had 226 corporate or franchised restaurants in Canada and another 40 in the U.S. The chain's dream is to establish a Boston Pizza outlet in every country in the world. Though much of the company's success is attributed to its varied menu, reasonable prices, and carefully researched location choices, it is also because of the support and supervision that headquarters staff provides its franchises. "We go in four times a year and assess the operational performance on service levels and on food quality," says one manager. "Then we rate them and look at their overall business performance, and we see if there are ways that we can enhance their performance." Secret shoppers also drop in twelve times a year, and customers are continually surveyed to see how Boston Pizza stacks up against the competition, how often they visit and why. Guided by the company mantra, "Think like a customer, deliver outstanding food value/quality and work closely with partners," Boston Pizza has built a franchise empire.[9]

The fact that most consumers cannot tell the difference between contractual and corporate VMSs shows how successfully the contractual organizations compete with corporate chains. Chapter 13 presents a fuller discussion of the various contractual VMSs.

Administered VMS

Administered VMS
A vertical marketing system that coordinates successive stages of production and distribution, not through common ownership or contractual ties, but through the size and power of one of the parties.

In an **administered VMS**, leadership is assumed not through common ownership or contractual ties but through the size and power of one or a few dominant channel members. Manufacturers of a top brand can obtain strong trade cooperation and support from resellers. For example, General Electric, Procter & Gamble, and Kraft can command unusual cooperation from resellers regarding displays, shelf space, promotions, and price policies. Large retailers, such as Wal-Mart, Home Depot, and Chapters Indigo, can exert strong influence on the manufacturers that supply the products they sell.

Horizontal Marketing Systems

Horizontal marketing system
A channel arrangement in which two or more companies at one level join together to follow a new marketing opportunity.

Another channel development is the **horizontal marketing system,** in which two or more companies at one level join together to follow a new marketing opportunity. By working together, companies can combine their financial, production, or marketing resources to accomplish more than any one company could alone.

Companies might join forces with competitors or non-competitors. They might work with each other on a temporary or permanent basis, or they may create a separate company. For example, McDonald's now places "express" versions of its restaurants in Wal-Mart stores. McDonald's benefits from Wal-Mart's considerable store traffic, while Wal-Mart keeps hungry shoppers from having to go elsewhere to eat.

Such channel arrangements also work well globally. For example, because of its excellent coverage of international markets, Nestlé jointly sells General Mills cereal brands in 80 countries outside North America.[10] Once major competitors, Canada's two largest wineries, T.G. Bright & Co. Ltd. and Cartier & Inniskillin Vintners Inc., formed an alliance so that they could increase their economies of scale and

The perfect handful for your little handful.

Made from four healthy whole grains—corn, oats, rice and wheat—Cheerios are the perfect choice for growing families. Small and round, they make ideal finger food for toddlers too. There's a whole lot of good in those little 'o's.

Nestlé jointly sells General Mills cereal brands in markets outside North America.

resources. This was necessary because they wanted to export to the U.S. market, which is dominated by huge American vintners, such as Gallo.

Multichannel Distribution Systems

Multichannel distribution system (or hybrid marketing channel)

A distribution system in which a single firm sets up two or more distribution channels to reach one or more customer segments.

In the past, many companies used a single channel to sell to a single market or market segment. Today, with the proliferation of customer segments and channel possibilities, more and more companies such as Sport Chek, a member of the Calgary-based Forzani Group, have adopted **multichannel distribution systems**— often called **hybrid distribution channels**. Such multichannel marketing occurs when a single firm sets up two or more distribution channels to reach one or more customer segments. The use of multichannel systems has increased greatly in recent years.

Figure 12.4 shows a multichannel channel. In the figure, the producer sells directly to consumer segment 1 using direct-mail catalogues, telemarketing, and the Internet and reaches consumer segment 2 through retailers. It sells indirectly to business segment 1 through distributors and dealers and to business segment 2 through its own sales force.

These days, almost every large company and many small ones distribute through multiple channels. IBM uses multiple channels to serve dozens of segments and niches, ranging from large corporate buyers to small businesses to home office buyers. In addition to selling through its vaunted sales force, IBM also sells through a full network of distributors and value-added resellers, which sell IBM computers, systems, and services to a variety of special business segments. Final consumers can buy IBM PCs from specialty computer stores or any of several large retailers. IBM uses telemarketing to service the needs of small and medium-size business. And both business and final consumers can buy online from the company's website (www.ibm.com).

Multichannel distribution systems offer many advantages to companies facing large and complex markets. With each new channel, the company expands its sales and market coverage and gains opportunities to tailor its products and services to the specific needs of diverse customer segments. But such multichannel channel systems are harder to control, and they generate conflict as more channels compete for customers and sales. For example, when IBM began selling directly to customers through telemarketing and its own website, many of its retail dealers cried "unfair competition" and threatened to drop the IBM line or to give it less emphasis. Many outside salespeople felt that they were being undercut by the new "inside channels."

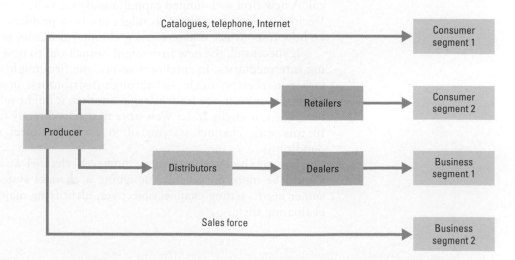

Figure 12.4 Multichannel distribution system

Changing Channel Organization

Disintermediation

The displacement of traditional resellers from a marketing channel by radical new types of intermediaries.

Changes in technology and the explosive growth of direct and online marketing are having a profound impact on the nature and design of distribution channels. One major trend is toward **disintermediation**—a big term with a clear message and important consequences. Disintermediation means that more and more, product and service producers are bypassing intermediaries and going directly to final buyers, or that radically new types of intermediaries are emerging to displace traditional ones.

Thus, in many industries, traditional intermediaries are dropping by the wayside. For example, Air Canada is selling directly to final buyers, eliminating travel agents from its distribution channels. Ecommerce is growing rapidly, taking business from traditional brick-and-mortar retailers. Consumers can buy flowers from 1-800-Flowers.com; books, CDs, videos, gift items, and other goods from Chapters.Indigo.ca; and clothes from runningroom.com or gap.com, all without ever visiting a store.

Disintermediation presents problems and opportunities for both producers and intermediaries. To avoid being swept aside, traditional intermediaries must find new ways to add value in the supply chain. (See Real Marketing 12.1.) To remain competitive, product and service producers must develop new channel opportunities, such as Internet and other direct channels. However, developing these new channels often brings them into direct competition with their established channels, resulting in conflict.

To ease this problem, companies often look for ways to make going direct a plus for both the company and its channel partners. For example, to trim costs and add business, Hewlett-Packard opened three direct-sales websites—Shopping Village (for consumers), H-P Commerce Center (for businesses buying from authorized resellers), and Electronic Solutions Now (for existing contract customers). However, to avoid conflicts with its established reseller channels, H-P forwards all its Web orders to resellers, who complete the orders, ship the products, and get the commissions. In this way, H-P gains the advantages of direct selling but also boosts business for resellers.

Channel Design Decisions

We now look at several channel decisions manufacturers face. In designing distribution channels, manufacturers struggle between what is ideal and what is practical. A new firm with limited capital usually starts by selling in a limited market area. Deciding on the best channels might not be a problem: The problem might simply be how to convince one or a few good intermediaries to handle the line.

If successful, the new firm might branch out to new markets through the existing intermediaries. In smaller markets, the firm might sell directly to retailers; in larger markets, it might sell through distributors. In one part of the country, it might grant exclusive franchises; in another, it might sell through all available outlets. Then, it might add a Web store that sells directly to hard-to-reach customers. In this way, channel systems often evolve to meet market opportunities and conditions.

For maximum effectiveness, however, channel analysis and decision making should be more purposeful. Designing a channel system calls for analyzing consumer needs, setting channel objectives, identifying major channel alternatives, and evaluating them.

Disintermediation: A Fancy Word but a Clear Message

*B*uying music can be a pretty frustrating experience. Perhaps you can identify with the following scenario:

> You whistle a happy tune as you stroll into HMV to do a little music shopping. But when you pick up *The Essential Bruce Springsteen*, your temperature starts to rise. You should be ecstatic at the discovery of twelve new releases by the Boss, but instead you're furious: You can't buy them unless you shell out $25.99 for the entire three-CD set that includes thirty "career-spanning classics" that you already own from his other hit records. You shove Bruce back into his display case and wonder, Why do they keep insisting that you buy an entire CD when you can just go online and get only the tunes you really want from iTunes or Musicmatch for ninety-nine cents each—or through Kazaa, Grokster or Limewire for free? Fed up, you walk away without buying anything.

Experiences like these, coupled with revolutionary changes in the way music is being distributed and purchased, have thrown the music industry into turmoil. Today, online music download services, such as

Online music download services, such as Apple's iTunes.com, are threatening to make traditional CD sellers obsolete.

BuyMusic.com, MusicNow.com, and Apple's iTunes.com, offer an attractive alternative to buying CDs from the limited assortments of traditional music retailers. Instead, you can go online, choose from tens of thousands of individual tracks, digitally download one or a dozen in any of several formats, burn them onto a CD or dump them into your iPod, and listen to them whenever you please.

It seems like everyone is getting into the music download business these days. Coffee chain Starbucks opened an in-store music service—Hear Music—letting customers burn downloaded tracks onto CDs while sipping their lattes. Roger's Wireless now sells MP3 phones, which allow wireless subscribers to download music directly to their phones. And fearsome competitors, such as Dell, Microsoft, and Sony, have announced their own online music stores. Even Coca-Cola launched mycokemusic.com, selling 50 000 tracks in its first week.

These new distribution options are great for consumers. But the new channel forms threaten the very existence of traditional music retailers. They're victims of *disintermediation*—the elimination of a layer of intermediaries from a marketing channel—skipping a step between the source of a product or service and its consumers.

More broadly, disintermediation includes not only the elimination of channel levels through direct marketing but also the displacement of traditional resellers by radically new types of intermediaries. For example, only a few decades ago, most recorded music was sold through independent music retailers or small chains. Many of these smaller retailers were later disintermediated by large specialty music superstores, such as HMV and Virgin Records. The superstores, in turn, have faced growing competition from broadline discount retailers, such as Wal-Mart and Best Buy. In fact, Wal-Mart is currently the world's number-one CD seller.

Now, the surge of new online music sellers is threatening to make traditional CD sellers obsolete. Retail CD sales have dropped nearly 20 percent since 1999—the year Napster (the original music download site) was launched. In 2004, Tower Records declared

▶

bankruptcy and Sam the Record Man, once a mainstay of the Canadian music scene, went bankrupt. And things will likely get worse before they get better. One study suggests that in the next five years, one-fifth to one-third of music sales will shift from CDs to digital downloads, and that eventually, "CDs, DVDs, and other forms of physical media will become obsolete." One retail consultant predicts that half of today's music stores will be out of business within five years.

How are the traditional retailers responding to the disintermediation threat? Some are following the "if you can't beat 'em, join 'em" principle by creating their own downloading services. Wal-Mart offers in-store and online downloads for only eighty-eight cents a song. HMV has partnered with Amazon and provides consumers with the opportunity to purchase new or used CDs through its online store.

Music stores still have several advantages over their online counterparts. First, the stores have a larger base of existing customers. Second, the physical store provides a shopping experience for customers that's impossible to duplicate online. Retailers can morph their stores into comfortable, sociable gathering spots were people hang out, chat with friends, listen to music, go to album signings, and perhaps attend a live performance.

But the traditional store retailers also face daunting economics. Store rents are rising while CD prices are falling. And running stores generates considerable inventory and store operating costs. Many of the new online entrants face none of those traditional distribution costs. And whereas store retailers can physically stock only a limited number of in-print titles, the music download sites can provide millions of selections and offer out-of-print songs.

Thus, disintermediation is a big word having a big impact. Disintermediation occurs only when a new channel form succeeds in serving customers better than the old channels. Marketers who continually seek new ways to create real value for customers have little to fear. However, those who fall behind in adding value risk being swept aside. Will today's specialty music retailers survive? Stay iTuned.

Sources: Opening extract adapted from Paul Keegan, "Is the Music Store Over?" *Business 2.0*, March 2004, pp. 114–118. Other quotes and information from Lorin Cipolla, "Music's on the Menu," *Promo*, May 1, 2004; Sarah E. Lockyer, "Full Steam Ahead," *Nation's Restaurant News*, May 3, 2004, p. 4; Peter Lewis, "Drop a Quarter in the Internet," *Fortune*, March 22, 2004, p. 56; and Walter Mossberg, "Boss Talk: The Music Man," *Wall Street Journal*, June 14, 2004, p. B.1; "Sam the Record Man Is a Bust," at www.chartattack.com/damn/2001/10/3106.cfm (accessed May 18, 2006); and HMV website, www.amazon.ca/exec/obidos/tg/browse/-/3238341/701-4847194-9498755 (accessed May 20, 2006).

Analyzing Consumer Needs

As noted previously, distribution channels are part of the overall *customer value delivery network*. Each channel member adds value for the customer. Thus, designing the marketing channel starts with finding out what target consumers want from the channel. Do consumers want to buy from nearby locations or are they willing to travel to more distant centralized locations? Would they rather buy in person, over the phone, through the mail, or via the Internet? Do they value breadth of assortment or do they prefer specialization? Do consumers want many add-on services (delivery, credit, repairs, installation), or will they obtain these elsewhere? The faster the delivery, the greater the assortment provided, and the more add-on services supplied, the greater the channel's service level.

Providing the fastest delivery, greatest assortment, and most services may not be possible or practical. The company and its channel members may not have the resources or skills needed to provide all the desired services. Also, providing higher levels of service results in higher costs for the channel and higher prices for consumers. The company must balance consumer needs not only against the feasibility and costs of meeting these needs but also against customer price preferences. The success of discount retailing shows that consumers will often accept lower service levels in exchange for lower prices.

Marketers must also recognize that customer needs may change over time. Take the case of VanCity Credit Union, a financial institution much like a bank that delivers services to its members (credit unions call their customers *members*). People with a preference for one channel have different needs, capabilities, and expectations than do people seeking financial services through another channel. For example, people who use online banking have a need for convenience, a "low-touch" preference, and strong technical capabilities. They prefer to serve themselves and may not want to interact with branch personnel. They often use the Internet to confirm their choices—that they are getting the best deal. They may see the credit union only as a "fulfillment" house. Other members, those who use the branches, may have the need for more advice, and have a "high-touch" preference. They value person-to-person service delivery and the social interaction it entails. If VanCity's members stuck to one channel, life would be simple, but the challenge today is that members are using multiple delivery channels. On one occasion, a member may use the Internet, on another an ATM, on a third she may telephone the customer service centre, and on a fourth she may make an appointment and visit a financial adviser.

As in the case of all services, since service production and consumption are simultaneous, the customer is frequently involved in the production and delivery of the service. For example, when interacting with her VanCity financial adviser, the customer must have a certain level of knowledge to make the interaction successful. She has to know what questions to ask and be able to understand the responses she receives from her adviser. VanCity and its service delivery personnel may have to work to educate her about the options that are available and build her knowledge base as the relationship develops. Her mood will affect the production and delivery of the service. If she is tired and upset after having a stressful day at the office before she meets with her financial adviser, her mood may affect the mood of the service provider. Thus, VanCity must train its advisers to respond with sensitivity to the moods of its members.

To further complicate the issue, members' channel preferences may change over their life cycle of financial service purchasing. Though they may be happy to transact online when they are young and use only simple products, they may value in-branch banking when the need arises for more complex products. The task for VanCity is to know the buying cycle of its members so that it can best position itself to meet these evolving needs and changes in channel preferences.

Setting Channel Objectives

Companies should state their marketing channel objectives in terms of targeted levels of customer service. Usually, a company can identify several segments wanting different levels of service. The company should decide which segments to serve and the best channels to use in each case. In each segment, the company wants to minimize the total channel cost of meeting customer service requirements.

The company's channel objectives are also influenced by the nature of the company, its products, its marketing intermediaries, its competitors, and the environment. For example, the company's size and financial situation determine which marketing functions it can handle itself and which it must give to intermediaries. Companies selling perishable products may require more direct marketing to avoid delays and too much handling.

In some cases, a company may want to compete in or near the same outlets that carry competitors' products. In other cases, producers may avoid the channels used by competitors. Mary Kay Cosmetics, for example, sells direct to customers through its corps of more than 1 million independent beauty consultants in thirty-four markets worldwide, rather than going head-to-head with other cosmetics makers for scarce positions in retail stores. And GEICO Direct markets auto and homeowner's insurance directly to consumers via the telephone and Web rather than through agents.

Finally, environmental factors, such as economic conditions and legal constraints, may affect channel objectives and design. For example, in a depressed economy, producers want to distribute their goods in the most economical way, using shorter channels and dropping unneeded services that add to the final price of the goods.

Mary Kay Cosmetics sells direct to consumers through its corps of independent beauty consultants.

Identifying Major Alternatives

When the company has defined its channel objectives, it should next identify its major channel alternatives in terms of *types* of intermediaries, the *number* of intermediaries, and the *responsibilities* of each channel member.

Types of Intermediaries

A firm should identify the types of channel members available to carry out its channel work. For example, suppose a manufacturer of test equipment has developed an audio device that detects poor mechanical connections in machines with moving parts. Company executives think this product would have a market in all industries in which electric, combustion, or steam engines are made or used. The company's current sales force is small, and the problem is how best to reach these different industries. The following channel alternatives might emerge.

Company sales force: Expand the company's direct sales force. Assign outside salespeople to territories and have them contact all prospects in the area, or develop separate company sales forces for different industries. Or add an inside telesales operation in which telephone salespeople handle small or midsize companies.

Manufacturer's agency: Hire manufacturer's agents—independent firms whose sales forces handle related products from many companies—in different regions or industries to sell the new test equipment.

Industrial distributors: Find distributors in the different regions or industries who will buy and carry the new line. Give them exclusive distribution, good margins, product training, and promotional support.

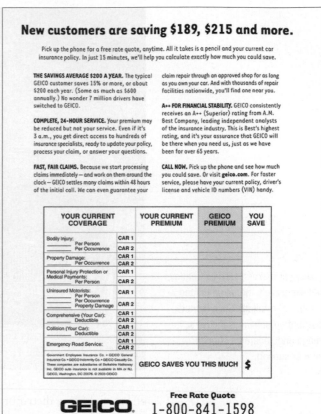

GEICO markets auto insurance via the telephone and Web for those looking to save money and do business directly with the company. "Call now," says the ad, "or visit geico.com."

Intensive distribution
Stocking the product in as many outlets as possible.

Exclusive distribution
Giving a limited number of dealers the exclusive right to distribute the company's products in their territories.

Selective distribution
The use of more than one, but fewer than all, of the intermediaries who are willing to carry the company's products.

Number of Marketing Intermediaries

Companies must also determine the number of channel members to use at each level. Three strategies are available: intensive distribution, exclusive distribution, and selective distribution. Producers of convenience products and common raw materials typically seek **intensive distribution**—a strategy in which they stock their products in as many outlets as possible. These products must be available where and when consumers want them. For example, toothpaste, candy, and other similar items are sold in millions of outlets to provide maximum brand exposure and consumer convenience. Kraft, Coca-Cola, Kimberly-Clark, and other consumer goods companies distribute their products in this way.

By contrast, some producers purposely limit the number of intermediaries handling their products. The extreme form of this practice is **exclusive distribution**, in which the producer gives only a limited number of dealers the exclusive right to distribute its products in their territories. Exclusive distribution is often found in the distribution of luxury automobiles and prestige women's clothing. For example, Bentley dealers are few and far between—even large cities may have only one dealer. By granting exclusive distribution, Bentley gains stronger distributor selling support and more control over dealer prices, promotion, credit, and services. Exclusive distribution also enhances the car's image and allows for higher markups.

Between intensive and exclusive distribution lies **selective distribution**—the use of more than one, but fewer than all, of the intermediaries who are willing to carry a company's products. Most television, furniture, and home appliance brands are distributed in this manner. For example, KitchenAid, Maytag, Whirlpool, and General Electric sell their major appliances through dealer networks and selected large retailers. By using selective distribution, they can develop good working relationships with selected channel members and expect a better-than-average selling

Luxury car makers, such as Bentley, sell exclusively through a limited number of retailers. Such limited distribution enhances the car's image and generates stronger retailer support.

effort. Selective distribution gives producers good market coverage with more control and less cost than does intensive distribution.

Responsibilities of Channel Members

The producer and intermediaries need to agree on the terms and responsibilities of each channel member. They should agree on price policies, conditions of sale, territorial rights, and specific services to be performed by each party. The producer should establish a list price and a fair set of discounts for intermediaries. It must define each channel member's territory, and it should be careful about where it places new resellers.

Mutual services and duties need to be spelled out carefully, especially in franchise and exclusive distribution channels. For example, Tim Hortons provides franchisees with promotional support, a record-keeping system, training, and general management assistance. In turn, franchisees must meet company standards for physical facilities, cooperate with new promotion programs, provide requested information, and buy specified food products.

Evaluating the Major Alternatives

Suppose a company has identified several channel alternatives and wants to select the one that will best satisfy its long-run objectives. Each alternative should be evaluated against economic, control, and adaptive criteria.

Using *economic criteria*, a company compares the likely sales, costs, and profitability of different channel alternatives. What will be the investment required by each channel alternative, and what returns will result? The company must also consider *control issues*. Using intermediaries usually means giving them some control over the marketing of the product, and some intermediaries take more control than others. Other things being equal, the company prefers to keep as much control as possible. Finally, the company must apply *adaptive criteria*. Channels often involve long-term commitments, yet the company wants to keep the channel flexible so that it can adapt to environmental changes. Thus, to be considered, a channel involving long-term commitments should be greatly superior on economic and control grounds.

Designing International Distribution Channels

International marketers face many additional complexities in designing their channels. Each country has its own unique distribution system that has evolved over time and changes very slowly. These channel systems can vary widely from country to country. Thus, global marketers must usually adapt their channel strategies to the existing structures within each country.

In some markets, the distribution system is complex and hard to penetrate, consisting of many layers and large numbers of intermediaries. Consider Japan:

The Japanese distribution system stems from the early seventeenth century when cottage industries and a [quickly growing] urban population spawned a merchant class.... Despite Japan's economic achievements, the distribution system has remained remarkably faithful to its antique pattern.... [It] encompasses a wide range of wholesalers and other agents, brokers, and retailers, differing more in number than in function from their [North] American counterparts. There are myriad tiny retail shops. An even greater number of wholesalers supplies goods to them, layered tier upon tier, many more than most [North American] executives would think necessary. For example, soap may move through three wholesalers plus a sales company after it leaves the manufacturer before it ever reaches the retail outlet. A steak goes from rancher to consumers in a process that often involves a dozen middle agents.... The distribution network ... reflects the traditionally close ties among many Japanese companies ... [and places] much greater emphasis on personal relationships with users. ... Although [these channels appear] inefficient and cumbersome, they seem to serve the Japanese customer well.... Lacking much storage space in their small homes, most Japanese homemakers shop several times a week and prefer convenient [and more personal] neighborhood shops.[11]

The Japanese distribution system has remained remarkably traditional. A profusion of tiny retail shops are supplied by an even greater number of small wholesalers.

Many Western firms have had great difficulty breaking into the closely knit, tradition-bound Japanese distribution network.

At the other extreme, distribution systems in developing countries may be scattered and inefficient, or altogether lacking. For example, China and India would appear to be huge markets, each with populations of more than 1 billion. In reality, however, these markets are much smaller than the population numbers suggest. Because of inadequate distribution systems in both countries, most companies can profitably access only a small portion of the population located in each country's most affluent cities. China's distribution system is so fragmented that logistics costs amount to 15 percent of the nation's GDP, far higher than in most other countries. After 10 years of effort, even Wal-Mart executives admit that they have been unable to assemble an efficient supply chain in China.[12]

Thus, international marketers face a wide range of channel alternatives. Designing efficient and effective channel systems between and within various country markets poses a difficult challenge. We discuss international distribution decisions further in Chapter 18.

Channel Management Decisions

Once the company has reviewed its channel alternatives and decided on the best channel design, it must implement and manage the chosen channel. Channel management calls for selecting, managing, and motivating individual channel members and evaluating their performance over time.

Selecting Channel Members

Producers vary in their ability to attract qualified marketing intermediaries. Some producers have no trouble signing up channel members. For example, when Toyota first introduced its Lexus line in North America, it had no trouble attracting new dealers. In fact, it had to turn down many would-be resellers.

At the other extreme are producers who have to work hard to line up enough qualified intermediaries. For example, in 1986 when distributors were approached about an unknown, new game called Nintendo (www.nintendo.com), many refused to carry the product: They had recently been burned by the failure of Atari. But two Canadian distributors, Larry Wasser and Morey Chaplick, owners of Beamscope, accepted the product. Not a bad move considering that within one year after that decision, their sales went from next to nothing to $24 million![13] Similarly, when the U.S. Time Company first tried to sell its inexpensive Timex watches through regular jewellery stores, most jewellery stores refused to carry them. The company then managed to get its watches into mass-merchandise outlets. This turned out to be a wise decision because of the rapid growth of mass merchandising.

When selecting intermediaries, the company should determine what characteristics distinguish the better ones. It will want to evaluate each channel member's years in business, other lines carried, growth and profit record, cooperativeness, and reputation. If the intermediaries are sales agents, the company will want to evaluate the number and character of other lines carried and the size and quality of the sales force. If the intermediary is a retail store that wants exclusive or selective distribution, the company will want to evaluate the store's customers, location, and future growth potential.

Managing and Motivating Channel Members

Once selected, channel members must be continuously managed and motivated to do their best. The company must sell not only *through* the intermediaries but *to* and *with* them. Most companies see their intermediaries as first-line customers and partners. They practise strong *partner relationship management (PRM)* to forge long-term partnerships with channel members. This creates a marketing system that meets the needs of both the company *and* its marketing partners.

In managing its channels, a company must convince distributors that they can succeed better by working together as a part of a cohesive value-delivery system.[14] For example, GE Appliances has created an alternative distribution system called CustomerNet to coordinate, support, and motivate its dealers.

GE CustomerNet gives dealers instant online access to GE Appliances' distribution and order-processing system, twenty-four hours a day, seven days a week. By logging on to the GE CustomerNet website, dealers can obtain product specifications, photos, feature lists, and side-by-side model comparisons for hundreds of GE appliance models.

They can check on product availability and prices, place orders, and review order status. They can even create custom brochures, order point-of-purchase materials, or download "advertising slicks"—professionally prepared GE appliance ads ready for insertion in local media. GE promises next-day delivery on most appliance models, so dealers need carry only display models in their stores. This greatly reduces inventory costs, making even small dealers more price competitive. GE CustomerNet also helps dealers to sell GE appliances more easily and effectively. A dealer can put a computer terminal on the showroom floor, where salespeople and customers together can use the system to dig through detailed product descriptions and check availability for GE's entire line of appliances. Perhaps the biggest benefit to GE Appliances, however, is that the system builds strong bonds between the company and its dealers and motivates dealers to put more push behind the company's products.[15]

Using GE's CustomerNet system, dealers have instant online access to GE Appliances' distribution system, twenty-four hours a day, seven days a week to check on product availability and prices, place orders, and review order status. "Simply put, it's an electronic one-stop-shopping breakthrough that can help you sell."

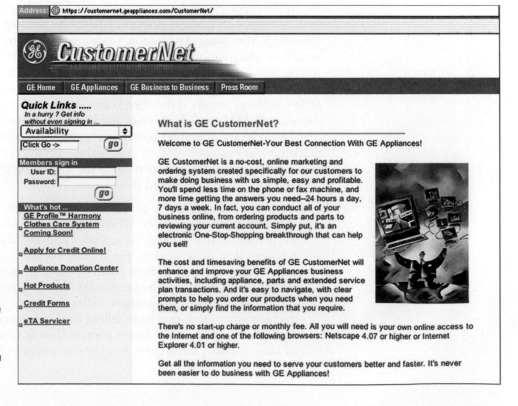

Many companies are now installing integrated high-tech partner relationship management systems to coordinate their whole-channel marketing efforts. Just as they use customer relationship management (CRM) software systems to help manage relationships with important customers, companies can now use PRM software to help recruit, train, organize, manage, motivate, and evaluate relationships with channel partners.

Evaluating Channel Members

The producer must regularly check channel member performance against standards, such as sales quotas, average inventory levels, customer delivery time, treatment of damaged and lost goods, cooperation in company promotion and training programs, and services to the customer. The company should recognize and reward intermediaries who are performing well and adding good value for consumers. Those who are performing poorly should be assisted or, as a last resort, replaced. A company may periodically "requalify" its intermediaries and prune the weaker ones.

Finally, manufacturers need to be sensitive to their dealers. Those who treat their dealers poorly risk not only losing dealer support but also causing some legal problems. The next section describes various rights and duties pertaining to manufacturers and their channel members.

Public Policy and Distribution Decisions

Supply chain management, logistics, and distribution present managers with countless ethical dilemmas—everything from what types of suppliers a company should use to the types of influence strategies that are appropriate to ensure channel members comply with channel policies. Under the heading "Fulfilment Practices," the Canadian Marketing Association Code of Ethics covers some ethical issues with regard to distribution. For example, it stipulates that goods should be shipped within thirty days of the receipt of a properly completed order (or within the time limit stated in the original offer), and notes that customers have the right to cancel orders without penalty if this time frame is not respected. The American Marketing Association (AMA) code of ethics (under which Canadian marketers also operate) focuses on issues of market power in the section dealing with distribution. Ethical marketers are advised not to manipulate product availability for purposes of exploitation and not to use coercion in the marketing channel. The AMA code puts into question practices around these issues:[16]

1. *Exclusive dealing.* Many producers and wholesalers like to develop exclusive channels for their products. When the seller allows only certain outlets to carry its products, this strategy is called *exclusive distribution*. When the seller requires that these dealers not handle competitors' products, its strategy is called *exclusive dealing*. Both parties benefit from exclusive arrangements: The seller obtains more loyal and dependable outlets, and the dealers obtain a steady source of supply and stronger seller support. But exclusive arrangements exclude other producers from selling to these dealers. They are legal as long as they do not substantially lessen competition or tend to create a monopoly and as long as both parties enter into the agreement voluntarily.

2. *Exclusive territories.* Exclusive dealing often includes exclusive territorial agreements. The producer may agree not to sell to other dealers in a given area, or the buyer may agree to sell only in its own territory. The first practice is normal under franchise systems as a way to increase dealer enthusiasm and commitment. It is also perfectly legal—a seller has no legal obligation to sell through more outlets than it wishes. The second practice, whereby the producer tries to keep a dealer from selling outside its territory, has become a major legal issue.

3. *Tying agreements.* Producers of a strong brand sometimes sell it to dealers only if the dealers will take some or all of the rest of the line—*full-line forcing.* Even though the practice isn't illegal, it causes considerable channel conflict.

4. *Dealers' rights.* Producers are free to select their dealers, but their right to terminate dealers is somewhat restricted. In general, sellers can drop dealers "for cause." But they cannot drop dealers if, for example, the dealers refuse to co-operate in a doubtful legal arrangement, such as exclusive dealing or tying agreements.

5. *Sources of supply.* As price competition increases in many industries, many firms look to overseas suppliers who can provide them with low-cost inputs. A number of ethical concerns have arisen as a result of this practice, including the loss of jobs in Canada's manufacturing sector and the use of overseas suppliers that follow questionable practices. For example, in the sporting goods market, firms have been criticized for using suppliers that pay low wages (wages far below what they pay celebrities to endorse their products) to suppliers that are reported to produce goods in *sweatshops* that use child or prison labour. Few Canadians want to think that the high-fashion apparel they wear or the sports equipment they use is made by children forced to labour instead of going to school.

Marketing Logistics and Supply Chain Management

In today's global marketplace, selling a product is sometimes easier than getting it to customers. Companies must decide on the best way to store, handle, and move their products and services so that they are available to customers in the right assortments, at the right time, and in the right place. Physical distribution and logistics effectiveness have a major impact on both customer satisfaction and company costs. Here we consider the nature and importance of logistics management in the supply chain, goals of the logistics system, major logistics functions, and the need for integrated supply chain management.

Nature and Importance of Marketing Logistics

Marketing logistics (or physical distribution)
The tasks involved in planning, implementing, and controlling the physical flow of materials, final goods, and related information from points of origin to points of consumption to meet customer requirements at a profit.

To some managers, marketing logistics means only trucks and warehouses. But modern logistics is much more than this. **Marketing logistics**—also called **physical distribution**—involves planning, implementing, and controlling the physical flow of goods, services, and related information from points of origin to points of consumption to meet customer requirements at a profit. In short, it involves getting the right product to the right customer in the right place at the right time.

In the past, physical distribution typically started with products at the plant and then tried to find low-cost solutions to get them to customers. However, today's

Supply chain management
Managing upstream and downstream value-added flows of materials, final goods, and related information among suppliers, the company, resellers, and final consumers.

marketers prefer customer-centred logistics thinking, which starts with the market-place and works backward to the factory, or even to sources of supply. Marketing logistics involves not only *outbound distribution* (moving products from the factory to resellers and ultimately to customers) but also *inbound distribution* (moving products and materials from suppliers to the factory) and *reverse distribution* (moving broken, unwanted, or excess products returned by consumers or resellers). That is, it involves entire **supply chain management**—managing upstream and downstream value-added flows of materials, final goods, and related information among suppliers, the company, resellers, and final consumers, as shown in Figure 12.5.

Thus, the logistics manager's task is to coordinate activities of suppliers, purchasing agents, marketers, channel members, and customers. These activities include forecasting, information systems, purchasing, production planning, order processing, inventory, warehousing, and transportation planning.

Companies today are placing greater emphasis on logistics for several reasons. First, companies can gain a powerful competitive advantage by using improved logistics to give customers better service or lower prices. Second, improved logistics can yield tremendous cost savings to both the company and its customers. As much as 20 percent of an average product's price is accounted for by shipping and transport alone. North American companies spend over a trillion dollars annually to wrap, bundle, load, unload, sort, reload, and transport goods. In the U.S., Ford alone has more than 450 million tonnes of finished vehicles, production parts, and aftermarket parts in transit at any given time, running up an annual logistics bill of around US$5.2 billion.[17] Shaving off even a small fraction of these costs can mean substantial savings.

Third, the explosion in product variety has created a need for improved logistics management. For example, in 1911 the typical A&P grocery store carried only 270 items. The store manager could keep track of this inventory on about 10 pages of notebook paper stuffed in a shirt pocket. Today, the average A&P carries a bewildering stock of more than 16 700 items. A Wal-Mart Supercenter store carries more than 100 000 products, 30 000 of which are grocery products.[18] Ordering, shipping, stocking, and controlling such a variety of products presents a sizable logistics challenge.

Finally, improvements in information technology have created opportunities for major gains in distribution efficiency. Today's companies are using sophisticated supply chain management software, Web-based logistics systems, point-of-sale scanners, uniform product codes, satellite tracking, and electronic transfer of order and payment data. Such technology lets them quickly and efficiently manage the flow of goods, information, and finances through the supply chain.

Goals of the Logistics System

Some companies state their logistics objective as providing maximum customer service at the least cost. Unfortunately, no logistics system can *both* maximize customer service *and* minimize distribution costs. Maximum customer service implies rapid delivery, large inventories, flexible assortments, liberal returns policies, and other services—all of which raise distribution costs. In contrast, minimum distribution

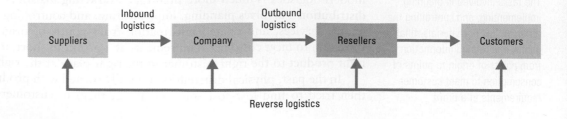

Figure 12.5 Supply chain management

At any given time, Ford has more than 450 million tonnes of finished vehicles, production parts, and aftermarket parts in transit, running up an annual logistics bill of around US$5.2 billion.

costs imply slower delivery, smaller inventories, and larger shipping lots—which represent a lower level of overall customer service.

The goal of marketing logistics should be to provide a *targeted* level of customer service at the least cost. A company must first research the importance of various distribution services to customers and then set desired service levels for each segment. The objective is to maximize *profits*, not sales. Therefore, the company must weigh the benefits of providing higher levels of service against the costs. Some companies offer less service than their competitors and charge a lower price. Other companies offer more service and charge higher prices to cover higher costs.

Major Logistics Functions

Given a set of logistics objectives, the company is ready to design a logistics system that will minimize the cost of attaining these objectives. The major logistics functions include *warehousing*, *inventory management*, *transportation*, and *logistics information management*.

Warehousing

Production and consumption cycles rarely match. So most companies must store their tangible goods while they wait to be sold. For example, Snapper, Toro, and other lawn mower manufacturers run their factories all year long and store up products for the heavy spring and summer buying seasons. The storage function overcomes differences in needed quantities and timing, ensuring that products are available when customers are ready to buy them.

Distribution centre
A large, highly automated warehouse designed to receive goods from various plants and suppliers, take orders, fill them efficiently, and deliver goods to customers as quickly as possible.

A company must decide on *how many* and *what types* of warehouses it needs and *where* they will be located. The company might use either *storage warehouses* or *distribution centres*. Storage warehouses store goods for moderate to long periods. **Distribution centres** are designed to move goods rather than just store them. They are large and highly automated warehouses designed to receive goods from various plants and suppliers, take orders, fill them efficiently, and deliver goods to customers as quickly as possible.

Wal-Mart's $55 million distribution centre in Cornwall, Ontario, serves its stores from Belleville, Ontario, to St. John's, Newfoundland. It sits on a 52-hectare site and has a 150 000-square-metre parking lot for the trucks that deliver and pick up goods. Conveyor belts and sorting equipment whisk 200 000 cartons a day through the centre. Many of these goods are cross docked, meaning that they are unloaded from one trailer and then are computer routed within eight to nine minutes to another truck that takes them to their designated stores.[19]

Like almost everything else these days, warehousing has seen dramatic changes in technology in recent years. Older, multistoreyed warehouses with outdated materials-handling methods are steadily being replaced by newer, single-storied *automated warehouses* with advanced, computer-controlled materials-handling systems requiring few employees. Computers and scanners read orders and direct lift trucks, electric hoists, or robots to gather goods, move them to loading docks, and issue invoices.

Inventory Management

Inventory management also affects customer satisfaction. Here, managers must maintain the delicate balance between carrying too little inventory and carrying too much. With too little stock, the firm risks not having products when customers want to buy. To remedy this, the firm may need costly emergency shipments or production. Carrying too much inventory results in higher-than-necessary inventory-carrying costs and stock obsolescence. Thus, in managing inventory, firms must balance the costs of carrying larger inventories against resulting sales and profits.

Many companies have greatly reduced their inventories and related costs through *just-in-time* logistics systems. With such systems, producers and retailers carry only small inventories of parts or merchandise, often only enough for a few days of operations. For example, Dell, a master just-in-time producer, carries just three to five days of inventory, whereas competitors might carry forty days or even sixty.[20] New stock arrives exactly when needed, rather than being stored in inventory until being used. Just-in-time systems require accurate forecasting along with fast, frequent, and flexible delivery so that new supplies will be available when needed. However, these systems result in substantial savings in inventory-carrying and handling costs.

Marketers are always looking for new ways to make inventory management more efficient. In the not-too-distant future, handling inventory might even become fully automated. For example, in Chapter 3, we discussed RFID or "smart tag" technology, by which small transmitter chips are embedded in products and packaging on everything from flowers and razors to tires. "Smart" products could make the entire supply chain—which accounts for nearly 75 percent of a product's cost—intelligent and automated. Companies would know, at any time, exactly where a product is located physically within the supply chain. "Smart shelves" would not only tell them when it's time to reorder but would also place the order automatically with their suppliers. Such exciting new information technology applications will revolutionize distribution as we know it.[21]

Transportation

The choice of transportation carriers affects the pricing of products, delivery performance, and condition of the goods when they arrive—all of which will affect customer satisfaction. In shipping goods to its warehouses, dealers, and customers, the company can choose among five main transportation modes: truck, rail, water, pipeline, and air, along with an alternative mode for digital products: the Internet. Rather than choosing a single carrier, **intermodal transportation** (combining two or more modes of transportation) is increasingly being used. For example, products manufactured in Alberta may be shipped first by rail in containers that are then

Intermodal transportation
Combining two or more modes of transportation.

loaded onto trucks for delivery in the Toronto area or are loaded onto ships in Montreal for transportation overseas.

Logistics Information Management

Companies manage their supply chains through information. Channel partners often link up to share information and to make better joint logistics decisions. From a logistics perspective, information flows, such as customer orders, billing, inventory levels, and even customer data, are closely linked channel performance.

Information can be shared and managed in many ways—by mail or telephone, through salespeople, via the Internet, or through *electronic data interchange (EDI)*, the computerized exchange of data between organizations. Wal-Mart, for example, maintains EDI links with 20 percent of its 91 000 suppliers.[22] The company wants to design a simple, accessible, fast, and accurate process for capturing, processing, and sharing channel information.

In some cases, suppliers might actually be asked to generate orders and arrange deliveries for their customers. Many large retailers—such as Wal-Mart and Home Depot—work closely with major suppliers, such as Procter & Gamble or Black & Decker, to set up *vendor-managed inventory* (VMI) systems or *continuous inventory replenishment* systems. Using VMI, the customer shares real-time data on sales and current inventory levels with the supplier. The supplier then takes full responsibility for managing inventories and deliveries. Some retailers even go so far as to shift inventory and delivery costs to the supplier. Such systems require close cooperation between the buyer and seller.

Cross-Functional Teamwork Inside the Company

In most companies, responsibility for various logistics activities is assigned to many different functional units—marketing, sales, finance, operations, purchasing. Too often, each function tries to optimize its own logistics performance without regard for the activities of the other functions. However, transportation, inventory, warehousing, and order-processing activities interact, often in an inverse way. Lower inventory levels reduce inventory-carrying costs. But they may also reduce customer service and increase costs from stock outs, back orders, special production runs, and costly fast-freight shipments. Because distribution activities involve strong trade-offs, decisions by different functions must be coordinated to achieve better overall logistics performance.

The goal of integrated supply chain management is to harmonize all of the company's logistics decisions. Close working relationships among functions can be achieved in several ways. Some companies have created permanent logistics committees, made up of managers responsible for different physical distribution activities. Companies can also create management positions that link the logistics activities of functional areas. For example, Procter & Gamble has created supply managers, who manage all of the supply chain activities for each of its product categories. Many companies have a vice-president of logistics with cross-functional authority. Finally, companies can employ sophisticated, systemwide supply chain management software, now available from wide range of suppliers.[23] The important thing is that the company must coordinate its logistics and marketing activities to create high market satisfaction at a reasonable cost.

Reviewing the Concepts

Distribution channel decisions are among the most important decisions that management faces. A company's channel decisions directly affect every other marketing decision. Management must make channel decisions carefully, incorporating today's needs with tomorrow's likely selling environment. Some companies pay too little attention to their distribution channels, but others have used imaginative distribution systems to gain competitive advantage.

1. Explain why companies use distribution channels, and discuss the functions these channels perform.

Most producers use intermediaries to bring their products to market. They try to forge a *distribution channel*—a set of interdependent organizations involved in the process of making a product or service available for use or consumption by the consumer or business user. Through their contacts, experience, specialization, and scale of operation, intermediaries usually offer the firm more than it can achieve on its own.

Distribution channels perform many key functions and handle key flows. Key *functions* include transforming the assortments of products made by producers into the assortments wanted by consumers and in matching supply and demand. Channel members may also help with the contact function—finding and communicating with prospective buyers. Finally, different channel members may take on different aspects of the physical distribution function—the transporting and storing of goods. Important *flows* include the information flow, which is needed for planning and aiding exchange by developing and spreading persuasive communications about an offer; by performing contact work—finding and communicating with prospective buyers; the negotiation flow required to reach an agreement on price and other terms of the offer so that ownership can be transferred; and the flow of financing associated with acquiring and using funds to cover the costs of the channel work; and the flow of risk taking associated with carrying out the channel work.

2. Discuss how channel members interact and how they organize to perform the work of the channel.

The channel will be most effective when each member is assigned the tasks it can do best. Ideally, because the success of individual channel members depends on overall channel success, all channel firms should work together smoothly. They should understand and accept their roles, coordinate their goals and activities, and cooperate to attain overall channel goals. By cooperat-

ing, they can more effectively sense, serve, and satisfy the target market. In a large company, the formal organization structure assigns roles and provides needed leadership. But in a distribution channel made up of independent firms, leadership and power are not formally set. Traditionally, distribution channels have lacked the leadership needed to assign roles and manage conflict. In recent years, however, new types of channel organizations have appeared that provide stronger leadership and improved performance.

3. Identify the major channel alternatives open to a company.

Each firm identifies alternative ways to reach its market. Available means vary from direct selling to using one, two, three, or more intermediary *channel levels*. Distribution channels face continuous and sometimes dramatic change. Three of the most important trends are the growth of *vertical*, *horizontal*, and *multichannel marketing systems*. These trends affect channel cooperation, conflict, and competition. *Channel design* begins with assessing customer channel service needs and company channel objectives and constraints. The company then identifies the major channel alternatives in terms of the *types* of intermediaries, the *number* of intermediaries, and the *channel responsibilities* of each. Each channel alternative must be evaluated according to economic, control, and adaptive criteria. Channel management calls for selecting qualified intermediaries and motivating them. Individual channel members must be evaluated regularly.

4. Explain how companies select, motivate, and evaluate channel members.

Producers vary in their ability to attract qualified marketing intermediaries. Some producers have no trouble signing up channel members. Others have to work hard to line up enough qualified intermediaries. When selecting intermediaries, the company should evaluate each channel member's qualifications and select those who best fit its channel objectives. Once selected, channel members must be continuously motivated to do their best. The company must sell not only *through* the intermediaries but *to* them. It should work to forge long-term partnerships with its channel partners to create a marketing system that meets the needs of both the manufacturer *and* the partners. The company must also regularly check channel member performance against established performance standards, rewarding intermediaries who are performing well and assisting or replacing weaker ones.

5. **Discuss the nature and importance of marketing logistics and integrated supply chain management.**

   Just as firms are giving the marketing concept increased recognition, more business firms are paying attention to *marketing logistics* (or *physical distribution*). Logistics is

an area of potentially high cost savings and improved customer satisfaction. Marketing logistics addresses not only *outbound distribution* but also *inbound distribution* and *reverse distribution*. That is, it involves entire *supply chain management*—managing value-added flows between suppliers, the company, resellers, and final users. No logistics system can both maximize customer service and minimize distribution costs. Instead, the goal of logistics management is to provide a *targeted* level of service at the least cost. The major logistics functions include *order processing, warehousing, inventory management*, and *transportation*.

   The *integrated supply chain management concept* recognizes that improved logistics requires teamwork in the form of close working relationships across functional areas inside the company and across various organizations in the supply chain.

Reviewing the Key Terms

Administered VMS   468
Channel conflict   463
Channel level   462
Contractual VMS   466
Conventional distribution channel   465
Corporate VMS   465
Direct marketing channel   462
Disintermediation   470
Distribution centre   483
Exclusive distribution   475
Franchise organization   466
Horizontal marketing system   468

Indirect marketing channel   462
Intensive distribution   475
Intermodal transportation   484
Marketing channel (or distribution channel)   459
Marketing logistics (or physical distribution)   481
Multichannel distribution system (or hybrid marketing channel)   469
Selective distribution   475
Supply chain management   482
Value-delivery network   457
Vertical marketing system (VMS)   465

Discussing the Concepts

1. Describe at least three different distribution channels a new textbook might take to get from the publisher to the student consumer.

2. The chapter cites IBM as an example of multichannel distribution. Discuss the pros and cons of choosing multichannel distribution channels.

3. Selecting channel members is often a difficult task, but once completed, the focus turns to managing and motivating the channel partner relationship. Identify the primary challenges an organization faces in managing its channel members. What are some of the methods companies use to motivate channel partners?

4. Provide three reasons why supply chain management is an important part of the value delivery network.

5. Why would a company consider outsourcing its own logistics functions?

6. What are the overall goals of integrated supply chain management? What can a company do to achieve the close working relationships necessary for effective supply chain management?

Applying the Concepts

1. Imagine you are a salesperson for an advertising media sales organization representing four noncompeting business publications. Answer the following questions asked by the marketing vice-president of a potential advertiser: "Can't I go directly to the magazine publisher's home office and get what I want? How are you going to add value in this relationship?"

2. You have been asked by Steve Saleen, president of Saleen, Inc., a speciality vehicle manufacturer with operations in the United States and Canada, to draft a short memo detailing your recommendations for expanding Saleen's distribution to Asia. Go to www.saleencanada.com/, and tour the website. Include in your recommendation the types, numbers, and responsibilities of proposed intermediaries.

3. PeopleSoft is one of the leading supply chain management software companies. Go to www.peoplesoft.com/corp/en/products/ent/scm/resource_library.jsp#demos and work your way through the four-page demo on "Supply Chain Analytics." Explain how this software would help a company better manage its supply chain.

Focus on Technology

Strathcom Media Inc., headquartered in Edmonton, Alberta, has emerged as a leading North American software development company that specializes in the automotive industry. It helps automotive dealerships use the Internet as an effective marketing and sales tool and has worked to help dealerships better manage their inventories of new and used vehicles. Go to www.strathcom.com/automotive-ucc.shtml, click on "Automotive Websites," and search the different options. Also review its inventory management page: www.strathcom.com/inventorymanagement.shtml.

1. What distribution channel functions and flows is Strathcom Media able to perform for automotive dealerships?

2. Why would a dealership be willing to outsource these important functions and flows? In other words, what it the unique set of values Strathcom Media creates for its clients?

Focus on Ethics

On March 14, 2005, the Competition Bureau announced that criminal charges have been laid against JD Marvel Products Inc., CDN MailOrder Exchange Inc. (CMOE), and their president, John Dragan. Go to www.competitionbureau.gc.ca/internet/index.cfm?itemID=189&lg=e and read the Competition Bureau's news release. Then, respond to the following questions:

1. According to the news release, what is the primary role of the Competition Bureau?

2. Why is the Competition Bureau so diligent in prosecuting such cases as the one described in this news release? (Hint: think about the effects of the practice on consumers and on other marketers and their channels of distribution.)

Video Case
Federated Direct

Planning a wedding—it's the most exciting time in a young couple's life. And it's perhaps the best opportunity for a retailer to begin a relationship with consumers that will last a lifetime. So retailers, ranging from department stores to specialty boutiques, reach out to young people who are starting their lives together by offering in-store and online wedding registries. Facing competition from a retailers as varied as Williams-Sonoma, Target, and Linens 'N Things, Federated Direct (the company that owns Macy's and Bloomingdale's) decided to lay the foundation for long-term relationships by offering a bridal registry of its own. To do so, the company worked with its supply-chain partners to offer consumers just the right assortment of products. The result? A new approach to

attracting young customers and building life-long relationships with consumers.

After viewing the video featuring Federated Direct, answer the following questions about distribution channels.

1. Does the explosion of retail channels benefit the average consumer?

2. How does Federated Direct act as a marketing intermediary?

3. List your three favourite retail stores. Are any of them department stores? If not, why not?

4. Do you think that Federated's approach will attract the target consumers the company is seeking?

Online Media Resources

Video Short
Log on to your Companion Website at **www.pearsoned.ca/kotler** to view the video segment related to the Video Case above.

Case Pilot
Log on to your Companion Website at **www.pearsoned.ca/kotler** to sharpen your case analysis skills and take the Case Pilot Challenge!

Company Case
Staples, Inc.: Revising the Strategy

Taking Over
Back in January 2002, Ronald Sargent assumed the reins of office supply superstore Staples from founder Thomas Stemberg. At that time, Sargent and Staples faced many challenges. The office supply market seemed to be maturing—industry sales in 2001 actually shrank 3 percent after years of double-digit growth. Further, although Staples had significantly more stores than its two major competitors—Office Depot and OfficeMax—it trailed Office Depot in sales revenue. (See Exhibit 1.)

There were bright spots for Staples—whereas both Office Depot's and OfficeMax's sales had declined

5.6 percent and 9.7 percent, respectively, in 2001, Staples's sales had inched up 0.7 percent; and its profits had soared from just US$59.7 million in 2000 to US$265 million in 2001. Yet, analysts noted that Staples's return on net assets (RONA) was below its weighted-average cost of capital (WACC) and argued that the firm needed to improve its profitability. Sargent knew he had his work cut out for him.

Taking Stock
Sargent began by questioning one of the company's basic strategic assumptions—build a store with lots of inventory and the lowest prices in town and customers

Exhibit 1   Office Supply Data for Fiscal 2001

Company	Number of Stores	Sales Revenue (US$B)	Net Income (US$M)	Revenue per Store (US$M)	Employees
Staples	1 400	$10.74	$265	$5.7	53 000
Office Depot	859	$11.15	$201	$6.7	48 000
OfficeMax	1 000	$4.64	($296)	$4.6	30 000

Source: Westchester County Business Journal, April 1, 2002, p. 14.

*Revenue per store does not include revenue from Internet or catalogue sales.

will beat a path to your door. Under this philosophy, Staples operated 400 more stores than OfficeMax and 541 more than Office Depot. Staples's stores typically stocked its stores from floor to ceiling, warehouse style, with all sorts of products. Yet, Staples's sales revenue per store was well below Office Depot's.

Sargent therefore decided to slow the company's store expansion. He also closed 32 underperforming stores, the largest store closing in the company's 16-year history. Moreover, the company planned to open only 115 new stores in 2002, down from 160 in 2001. It would also open most of these new stores in existing markets rather than new market areas in order to take advantage of operating efficiencies.

Further, focus groups with Staples's target market of small-business customers indicated that those customers did not like the warehouse look. Customers wanted to be able to see across a store and to determine quickly from signage where items were located. Staples responded by experimenting with a smaller store (1860 square metres versus about 2230), lower shelving, and a more open atmosphere. This meant that it had to reduce inventory. As a result, the company removed many items that it found were not necessary, such as child-oriented computer games and educational software. Based on customer feedback, it also stopped offering some business services, such as health insurance or prepaid legal services, so that it could focus on consumable products. Customers, it found, did not want to shop at Staples for these services.

The results with this new store format proved promising, with sales increasing up to 10 percent with about 10 percent less inventory. Sargent noted, "We're doing the same sales volume with two printers selling for more than [US]$100 than we did selling five printers at the different price points." As a result, Sargent decided to roll out the new format and reconfigure

280 stores in 2002 in hopes of improving both sales and inventory turnover. Staples's inventory turnover ratio was about 5.1 times as compared with Office Depot's 6.3 times.

As a second part of his strategy, Sargent turned to what the company calls its "North American Delivery" segment. This segment includes the company's Internet, catalogue, and corporate contracts operations—all of its operations that *bypass* its stores. In 2001, this segment accounted for 28 percent of sales and 40 percent of profits. Competitor Office Depot got 34 percent of its sales and 33 percent of its profits from similar operations. In a Home Furnishing Network survey of website traffic for the first four months of 2002, Office Depot had the highest number of unique website visits, more than 24 million, of the top 20 retail websites, ahead of Best Buy, Wal-Mart, Target, and others. Staples's site, www.staples.com, came in seventh, with just fewer than 14 million visits, while OfficeMax finished tenth, with just fewer than 10 million visits. *Forbes* magazine named Staples's site as the "Best of the Web Pick for Entrepreneurs" for the third year in a row, based on its ability to assist smaller businesses to run as smoothly as larger organizations.

To handle its catalogue operations, Staples has a subsidiary, Quill.com. A survey ranked Quill.com as highest in terms of its online sales conversion rate of 30.3 percent versus the average site's rate of 8 percent or lower. Quill offered 35 percent of its products as private label brands as compared with 7 percent for Staples. Sargent saw this as an opportunity for Staples to offer more of it own private-label brands that carried higher margins.

Although Staples built its business by targeting small businesses while OfficeMax had targeted household consumers, it also developed programs for businesses with more than 100 employees. Its StaplesLink program allowed companies to link their internal procurement systems with Staples's computer systems. This allowed users to place their orders directly with Staples, which then prepared the order and delivered it to the business the next day.

For both its catalogue and contract businesses, Sargent believed that Staples should beat a path to customers' doors. He ordered the doubling, to 400, of Staples's special sales force, which worked with customers to get them to order through its catalogue or its website. He also added 100 staff members to the 600-person sales force that worked exclusively with corporate and small-business accounts.

To help get small-business customers into the stores, Staples entered a test with FleetBoston Financial Corp. to open ten offices in select Staples stores in the Northeast. These 14-square-metre, in-store offices would have two Fleet staff members who would work with business owners to open specially designed business chequing accounts, get debit cards, and make small-business loan applications. The offices would not dispense cash or take deposits and would be open six or seven days a week. Fleet had more than 100 nontraditional branches, mostly in supermarkets.

Next, Sargent planned to continue Staples's international expansion. The retailer already operated 180 stores in the United Kingdom, Germany, the Netherlands, and Portugal. It planned to add 20 new stores in Europe and to open in one more country. European operations accounted for about US$796 million of sales in 2001.

Finally, Sargent focused on customer retention. He understood that getting a customer was expensive. The company estimated that a customer doing business for three years was 4.5 times more profitable than a new customer. Staples's managers estimated that the company had a 30 percent share of their customers' office supply purchases, and they wanted to increase that share.

Taking the Challenge

Sargent knew that Staples's 53 000 employees would have to execute all of these strategic moves for the company to reach its target of US$12 billion in sales and US$440 million in net income by 2003. And, he knew that competition was only going to intensify. The

struggling OfficeMax was trying to capture more of Staples's small-business customers. These customers were often willing to buy higher-margin items, thus leading to Staples's higher-than-average margins. In an industry with lots of stores, catalogues, and Internet sites offering similar merchandise at similar prices, maintaining a competitive advantage would not be easy. Further, Sargent worried about offering the same products and services to the same customers through multiple channels. Would this strategy generate channel conflict within the company?

Questions for Discussion

1. How are store, catalogue, and Internet-based distribution channels alike or different in terms of the channel functions they perform?

2. Do you see any potential for conflict among Staples's different channels? Why or why not?

3. Is the Staples/FleetBoston horizontal marketing effort a good idea? Why or why not?

4. What are the advantages of more intensive development of individual market areas versus the advantages of putting more stores in new markets?

5. How can Staples develop a competitive advantage in a commodity market? What marketing recommendations would you make to Staples?

6. Once you have answered the questions above, you can conduct research to see how Staples's multichannel distribution channel worked. You can begin your research to see how Staples had done through mid-2004 by using the *Additional Sources* cited below.

Sources: Alissa Swchmelkin, "Fleet to Open Offices in Staples," *American Banker*, July 11, 2002, p. 20; Alex Philippidis, "Wither the Warehouse Look: Can Staples, OfficeMax Raise Profits by Lowering Shelves?" *Westchester County Business Journal*, April 1, 2002, p. 14; Joseph Pereira, "Staples Inc. Pulls Back on Its Store-Expansion Plans, *The Wall Street Journal*, March 13, 2002, p. B4; A. H. Rubinson, "Staples," UBS Warburg, December 10, 2001.

Additional Sources: Frank Byrt, "Staples Posts 39% Profit Jump," *The Wall Street Journal*, August 18, 2004, p. B7; W. C. Symmonds, "Thinking Outside the Big Box," *Business Week*, August 11, 2003; Jim Bodor, "Shopping On All Channels," *Telegram & Gazette*, Worcester, Mass., December 22, 2002, p. E1.

CHAPTER 13
Retailing and Wholesaling

AFTER STUDYING THIS CHAPTER, YOU SHOULD BE ABLE TO

1. explain the roles of retailers and wholesalers in the distribution channel

2. describe the major types of retailers and give examples of each

3. identify the major types of wholesalers and give examples of each

4. explain the marketing decisions facing retailers and wholesalers

Previewing the Concepts

In the previous chapter, you learned the basics of distribution channel design and management. Now, we'll look more deeply into the two major intermediary channel functions, retailing and wholesaling. You already know something about retailing—you're served every day by retailers of all shapes and sizes. However, you probably know much less about the horde of wholesalers that work behind the scenes. In this chapter, we'll examine the characteristics of different kinds of retailers and wholesalers, the marketing decisions they make, and trends for the future.

To start, we'll look at the Forzani Group, Canada's largest specialty sports retailer. You probably know it better as Sport Chek, Coast Mountain Sports, or Sport Mart. The chain employees 9600 people and operates 511 000 square metres of retail space. Despite growing competition, it has excelled, because, as Chief Executive Officer Bob Sartor notes, "We have a focus on being the best store in town—with a passion for exceptional merchandise, superior customer service, and extensive marketing."

Only a few years ago, analysts forecast the demise of the Forzani Group Ltd. as it faced an onslaught from American big-box sporting-goods stores. However, the Calgary-based retailer refused to roll over and play dead. In fact, the Forzani Group has managed to grow in an increasingly competitive environment.

Part of this growth is due to the firm's acquisition strategy. It acquired Coast Mountain Sports in 2000 and Sport Mart in 2001. Gen-X Sports and Nevada Bob's were purchased in 2005. But acquisition alone cannot explain Forzani's success. Much of it is also due to the insight, drive, and enthusiasm of owner/founder John Forzani. One analyst describes him as "the only man at the 12-mile mark in a 26-mile marathon."

John Forzani, a former lineman with the Calgary Stampeders and now the team owner, has always loved the sporting-goods industry and has been able to spot trends and opportunities. "The beauty of this business," he says, "is that we're in an industry that is constantly growing, and has been for the past thirty years." As new technologies improve the performance of athletic equipment, demand is constantly renewed.

Unlike some of its smaller competitors, Forzani's stores sell a vast assortment of sports-related products, from athletic footwear to sports equipment. Its size allows it to achieve economies of scale in both purchasing and advertising. Forzani markets products using national brands as well as its own private labels.

The Forzani Group is structured into two segments: its corporate and its franchise operations. In the corporate segment, it owns and operates 252 stores under the banners Sport Chek, Sports Experts, Coast Mountain Sports, National Sports, and Sport Mart. The franchise segment consists of 194 stores that operate under the banners Sports Experts, Atmosphere, RnR, Intersport, Econosports, Tech Shop, and Nevada Bob's.

The company's unique structure and multi-banner concept allows its corporate stores to tailor their mix of quality products to meet the specific needs and preferences of a broad base of consumers, no matter what price point they prefer. They can respond to local interests while preventing one store from cannibalizing the sales of others in the chain. For example, Sport Chek is positioned as the athletic and lifestyle store that offers the best brands in a great store atmosphere, while Sport Mart is positioned as the place for discount sporting goods, footwear, and fashion. National Sports is the "athletic family" store with a team sport focus and grassroots marketing.

The franchise segment allows the firm to combine the economies of scale in purchasing and advertising, use of technology, and training with the enthusiasm and customer and community focus of an independent store. There are also online operations at www.sportchek.ca and www.sportmart.ca that provide consumers with tonnes of information on products available in the stores. It also features some items for online sales. No matter what retailing format is used, expert advice, value pricing, selection, and customer service are hallmarks of the Forzani shopping experience.

By the end of 2005, the Canadian sporting goods industry accounted for approximately $7.5 billion in sales, and the Forzani Group commands 16.1 percent of this marketplace. It's a highly competitive marketplace, however, and it must battle both the giants, such as Canadian Tire, Sears, and Wal-Mart, as well as small, specialized chains, such as The Running Room and lululemon.

Forzani has certainly had its ups and downs. In 1974 John Forzani and three partners opened the first Calgary store, selling just two shoe brands. The chain experienced explosive growth during the 1980s, driven by that decade's fitness boom and growing interest in professional and amateur sports. However, growth and profitability attracted U.S. superstores, such as Sports Authority, into the Canadian marketplace. Initially, their entry spelled tough times for Forzani, because its stores were much smaller than many of its American competitors'. However, as in sports, sometimes smaller, more nimble competitors win. Although the larger, standardized American stores could carry larger amounts of inventory, the flexible size and format of the Forzani stores meant they could be designed to meet the specific needs of the local marketplace. They could also locate in existing shopping malls that consumers could easily access, rather than in the fringe locations where American firms built their megastores. Finally, size and selection weren't the deciding factors in this battle, according to Forzani. Members of the Forzani chain pride themselves on their ability to provide exceptional service to their customers.

Another weapon in the chain's sports bag of tricks has been its ongoing focus on keeping costs low. Again,

John Forzani leads by example. He goes so far as to wedge his husky frame into economy-class seats when he travels. When Forzani managers travel in pairs, they must share rooms. Not only does this save money, but it also makes for effective team building, just as it does in professional sports, Forzani believes. Being able to buy in volume for the entire chain helps the firm get better deals from suppliers. Similarly, Forzani's ability to use umbrella advertising for the chain also keeps advertising costs lower than if separate ads had to be formulated for regional markets.

The years 2005 and 2006 weren't good to the chain. The hockey strike, a poor season for snow and winter sports, and the decline in popularity of some sports, such as rollerblading, dampened profits. The company also faced the challenge of the blurring of product lines. Suddenly, sports and fashion started to collide. However, the Forzani Group is out to reinvent itself again. It put savvy marketer Hubert Wat at the helm as the Forzani Group's new corporate marketing vice-president. He's taking the chain in a new direction: "We want to build ourselves to be a category killer. If a consumer goes out to buy running shoes or a bike or a snowboard, we want one of our brands to be top of mind." To accomplish this goal, he is working to establish a clear, more definitive brand identity for each of the sports retailer's three main banners. For example, it's upgrading and redesigning the stores of its biggest banner, Sport Chek. It's improving its product assortment by adding more high-end brands, such as North Face, and adding more running, outdoor, and fashion products, such as Vans, Burton, and O'Neil. For Sport Mart, Forzani is working to strengthen its image as a discount retailer that offers great value in footwear and hockey equipment. It's giving its Nevada Bob's Golf franchise a total facelift. The Forzani Group is also investing heavily in elearning technologies for its associates and is increasing training and regional knowledge. It's hired a new advertising agency and is creating new advertising and flyers that are targeted more precisely. The chains are back on track for growth and there is no doubt that the Forzani Group knows how to keep its eye on the ball.[1]

The Forzani Group Ltd. story provides many insights into the workings of one of Canada's most successful retailers. This chapter looks at *retailing* and *wholesaling*. In the first section we look at the nature and importance of retailing, major types of store and non-store retailers, the decisions retailers make, and the future of retailing in Canada and abroad. In the second section, we discuss these same topics as they relate to wholesalers.

Retailing

Retailing
All activities involved in selling goods or services directly to final consumers for their personal, nonbusiness use.

Retailer
A business whose sales come *primarily* from retailing.

What is retailing? We all know that Wal-Mart, The Bay, and Canadian Tire are retailers, but so are Avon representatives, Amazon.ca, the local Holiday Inn, your bank, and a dentist seeing patients. **Retailing** traditionally is defined as all the activities involved in selling products or services directly to final consumers for their personal, nonbusiness use. Retailing is a dynamic industry, however, and traditional boundaries between selling to end customers and selling to other businesses is blurring. Many **retailers** today, such as Costco, Home Depot, Staples, eBay, and Amazon, sell to both end consumers and business buyers. What's more, it is often difficult to classify today's retailers by the types of goods they sell. As *Strategy Magazine* recently noted, "Mac's Milk now carries M+M Meats. Canadian Tire has Mark's Work Wearhouse and Budget Rent-a-Car. Canada Post sells gifts and Loblaws sells everything—just like Wal-Mart." John Torella, a retail consultant at Toronto-based J.C. Williams Group, puts it this way, "Everybody is in everybody else's business and nobody is protected." Take the case of London Drugs, for example.[2]

> London Drugs, based in Richmond, B.C., has 63 retail stores situated across British Columbia, Alberta, Saskatchewan, and Manitoba. But if there isn't a London Drug store in your area, don't be dismayed. You can order many of its products online. As its name suggests, London Drugs offers a full-service pharmacy, but it is also one of the largest distributors of cameras and computers in western Canada. It entered the computer age early, starting to sell its own computer brand in 1984. It started to offer high-end electronics in 1992 and introduced its own brand of insurance services in 1995. London Drugs also carries a wide range of beauty products as well as many grocery items and ethnic foods. If offers its customers home décor items and appliances as varied as air conditioners, espresso machines, books, and automotive accessories. It is currently test marketing its own London Spa in its newest drugstore in New Westminster, B.C. The spa is designed to fit into 33 square metres between the makeup department and the cashiers, and it offers most typical spa services, such as manicures, facials, and massages. "London Drugs is a maverick retailer," says London Drugs president, Wynne Powell. "We get ahead of customer needs and wants, and this is just another example of us being ahead of the crowd."

Although most retailing is done in retail stores, in recent years *non-store retailing* has been growing much faster than has store retailing. Non-store retailing includes selling to final consumers through direct mail, catalogues, telephone, the Internet, TV home shopping shows, home and office parties, door-to-door contact, vending machines, and other direct selling approaches. We discuss such direct-marketing approaches in detail in Chapter 16. In this chapter, we focus on store retailing.

Types of Retailers

Retailing is an important sector in the Canadian economy. The Retail Council of Canada reports that retailing accounts for 11.78 percent of employment in the country, and as an industry it is the second-largest employer in Canada, next to manufacturing. There are 220 000 retail stores in Canada. Together, they account for more than $346 billion in operating revenues.[3]

Retail stores come in all shapes and sizes, and new retail types keep emerging. The most important types of retail stores are described in Table 13.1 and discussed in the following sections. They can be classified in terms of several characteristics, including the *amount of service* they offer, the breadth and depth of their *product lines*, the *relative prices* they charge, and how they are *organized*.

TABLE 13.1 Major Store Retailer Types

Specialty Stores: Carry a narrow product line with a deep assortment, such as apparel stores, sporting-goods stores, furniture stores, florists, and bookstores. A clothing store would be a *single-line* store, a men's clothing store would be a *limited-line store,* and a men's custom-shirt store would be a *superspecialty* store. Examples: The Body Shop, Gap, The Running Room, Abercrombie & Fitch

Department Stores: Carry several product lines—typically clothing, home furnishings, and household goods—with each line operated as a separate department managed by specialist buyers or merchandisers. Examples: Sears, The Bay

Supermarkets: A relatively large, low-cost, low-margin, high-volume, self-service operation designed to serve the consumer's total needs for food and household products. Examples: Safeway Foods, Sobeys, Loblaws, A&P, Food Basics, Loeb, Provigo

Convenience Stores: Relatively small stores located near residential areas, open long hours, seven days a week, and carrying a limited line of high-turnover convenience products at slightly higher prices. Examples: 7-Eleven, Becker's, Mac's, Couche-Tarde, Husky Market

Discount Stores: Carry standard merchandise sold at lower prices with lower margins and higher volumes. Examples: Zellers, Wal-Mart (general); Sport Mart, The Brick, Best Buy (specialty)

Off-Price Retailers: Sell merchandise bought at less-than-regular wholesale prices and sold at less than retail: often leftover goods, overruns, and irregulars obtained at reduced prices from manufacturers or other retailers. These include *factory outlets*, owned and operated by manufacturers (Examples: Mikasa, Liz Claiborne, Ralph Lauren); *independent off-price retailers*, owned and run by entrepreneurs (Example: S&R Discount Department Store in Kingston, Ontario); *off-price chains*, which are divisions of larger retail corporations (Examples: Winners, Dollarama, The Silver Dollar); and *warehouse (or wholesale) clubs*, selling a limited selection of brand-name groceries, appliances, clothing, and other goods at deep discounts to consumers who pay membership fees. Examples: Max Club, Costco, Sam's, BJ's Wholesale Club

Superstores: Very large stores traditionally aimed at meeting consumers' total needs for routinely purchased food and nonfood items. Includes *category killers*, which carry a deep assortment in a particular category and have a knowledgeable staff (Examples: Chapters-Indigo, Petsmart, Staples); *supercentres,* combined supermarket and discount stores (Examples: Wal-Mart and Loblaws Supercentres), and *hypermarkets* with up to 20 000 square metres of space, combining supermarket, discount, and warehouse retailing (Examples: Carrefour [France], Pyrca [Spain]).

Amount of Service

Different products require different amounts of service, and customer service preferences vary. Retailers may offer one of three levels of service—self-service, limited service, and full service.

Self-service retailers serve customers who are willing to perform their own "locate-compare-select" process to save money. Self-service is the basis of all discount operations and is typically used by sellers of convenience goods (such as supermarkets) and nationally branded, fast-moving shopping goods (such as Future Shop).

Limited-service retailers, such as The Bay or La Maison Simons in Quebec, provide more sales assistance because they carry more shopping goods about which customers need information. Their increased operating costs result in higher prices. In *full-service retailers*—specialty stores, such as Birks, and first-class department stores, such as Holt Renfrew—salespeople assist customers in every phase of the shopping process. Full-service stores usually carry more specialty goods for which customers like to be "waited on." They provide more services, resulting in much higher operating costs, which are passed along to customers as higher prices.

Product Line

Specialty store

A retail store that carries a narrow product line with a deep assortment within that line.

Retailers also can be classified by the length and breadth of their product assortments. Some retailers, such as **specialty stores**, carry narrow product lines with deep assortments within those lines. Today, specialty stores are flourishing. The increasing use of market segmentation, market targeting, and product specialization has resulted in a greater need for stores that focus on specific products and segments.

Department store

A retail organization that carries a wide variety of product lines— typically clothing, home furnishings, and household goods; each line is operated as a separate department managed by specialist buyers or merchandisers.

Supermarket

Large, low-cost, low-margin, high-volume, self-service store that carries a wide variety of food, laundry, and household products.

Convenience store

A small store, located near a residential area, that is open long hours, seven days a week, and carries a limited line of high-turnover convenience goods.

In contrast, **department stores** carry a wide variety of product lines. In recent years, department stores have been squeezed between more focused and flexible specialty stores on the one hand, and more efficient, lower-priced discounters on the other. In response, many have added promotional pricing to meet the discount threat. Others have stepped up the use of store brands and single-brand "designer shops" to compete with specialty stores. Still others are trying mail-order, telephone, and Web selling. Service remains the key differentiating factor. Department stores, such as Holt Renfrew and other high-end department stores, are doing well by emphasizing high-quality service.

Supermarkets are the most frequently shopped type of retail store. Today, however, they are facing slow sales growth because of slower population growth and an increase in competition from convenience stores, discount food stores, and superstores. Supermarkets also have been hit hard by the rapid growth of out-of-home eating.

Thus, most supermarkets are making improvements to attract more customers. In the battle for "share of stomachs," many large supermarkets have moved upscale, providing from-scratch bakeries, gourmet deli counters, and fresh seafood departments. Others are cutting costs, establishing more efficient operations, and lowering prices in order to compete more effectively with food discounters.

Convenience stores are small stores that carry a limited line of high-turnover convenience goods. These stores are located near residential areas and remain open long hours, seven days a week. When supermarkets won the right to open for business on Sundays, and drugstore chains and gas station boutiques began selling groceries and snack foods, convenience stores lost their monopoly on their key differentiating variable—*convenience*.

In recent years, the convenience store industry has suffered from overcapacity as its primary market of young, blue-collar men has shrunk. As a result, many chains are redesigning their stores to attract female shoppers. They are shedding the image of a "truck stop" where men go to buy beef jerky, cigarettes, and magazines, and instead offer fresh prepared foods and cleaner, safer environments. For example, Husky launched a new store format, called the Husky Market, which includes the traditional service station with a new ultra-modern retail store. The stores are bright and inviting, offer fresh products, such as sandwiches, fruit, and premium Kicking Horse Coffee, and have a distinct focus on customer service.

Although many of the "mom-and-pop" stores that once dominated the industry are closing, others are being opened by the huge chains. For example, even

Turning many of its convenience stores into destination outlets featuring branded products has enabled Couche-Tarde to achieve superior profitability.

Superstore

A store much larger than a regular supermarket that carries a large assortment of routinely purchased food products, nonfood items, and services.

though Alimentation Couche-Tarde Inc., based in Laval, Quebec, may not exactly be a household name, it is Canada's largest operator of convenience stores. Its outlets operate under the Couche-Tarde name as well as such banners as Mac's, Becker's, Mike's Mart, and Daisy Mart. The chain has been growing in both size and profitability for some time, but in October 2003, it really got a boost when it purchased the U.S.-based Circle K chain. The takeover makes Couche-Tarde North America's fourth-largest convenience store operator, with 4845 stores.[4]

Superstores are much larger than regular supermarkets and offer a large assortment of routinely purchased food products, non-food items, and services. Wal-Mart and Loblaws offer *supercentres*, combination food and discount stores that emphasize cross-merchandising. Toasters are above the fresh-baked bread, kitchen gadgets are across from produce, and infant centres carry everything from baby food to clothing. Real Canadian Super Store, which started with one SuperValu store in Saskatoon in 1979, has locations from Thunder Bay, Ontario, west to Vancouver, British Columbia, with stores in all of western Canada's major cities, including Whitehorse in the Yukon. Real Canadian Super Stores carry everything from electronics to children's apparel to fresh fruit, seafood, and housewares.

Category killer

Giant specialty store that carries a very deep assortment of a particular line and is staffed by knowledgeable employees.

Recent years have also seen the explosive growth of superstores that are actually giant specialty stores, the so-called **category killers**. They feature stores the size of airplane hangars that carry a very deep assortment of a particular line with a knowledgeable staff. Category killers are prevalent in a wide range of categories, including books, baby gear, toys, electronics, home improvement products, linens and towels, party goods, sporting goods, even pet supplies. Home Depot Canada, Chapters, Staples, and Michaels Arts and Crafts are among the many recent entrants into the Canadian marketplace. Another superstore variation, *hypermarkets*, are huge superstores, perhaps as large as *six* football fields. Although hypermarkets have been very successful in Europe and other world markets, they have met with little success in the North America.

Finally, for some retailers, the product line is actually a service. Service retailers include hotels and motels, banks, airlines, universities, movie theatres, tennis clubs, bowling alleys, restaurants, repair services, hair care shops, and dry cleaners. Service retailers in Canada are growing faster than product retailers.

Relative Prices

Retailers can also be classified according to the prices they charge (see Table 13.1 on page 496). Most retailers charge regular prices and offer normal-quality goods and customer service. Others offer higher-quality goods and service at higher prices. The retailers that feature low prices are discount stores and "off-price" retailers.

Discount store

A retail institution that sells standard merchandise at lower prices by accepting lower margins and selling at higher volume.

Discount Stores   A **discount store** sells standard merchandise at lower prices by accepting lower margins and selling higher volume. The early discount stores cut expenses by offering few services and operating in warehouse-like facilities in low-rent, heavily travelled districts. In recent years, facing intense competition from other discounters and department stores, many discount retailers have "traded up." They have improved décor, added new lines and services, and expanded regionally and nationally, leading to higher costs and prices.

Off-price retailer

Retailer that buys at less-than-regular wholesale prices and sells at less than retail. Examples are factory outlets, independents, and warehouse clubs.

Off-Price Retailers   When the major discount stores traded up, a new wave of **off-price retailers** moved in to fill the low-price, high-volume gap. Ordinary discounters buy at regular wholesale prices and accept lower margins to keep prices down. In contrast, off-price retailers buy at less-than-regular wholesale prices and charge consumers less than retail. Off-price retailers can be found in all areas, from food, clothing, and electronics to no-frills banking and discount brokerages. Off-price retailer Winners' surprising move into the high-fashion, upscale shopping district between Yonge Street and Avenue Road along Toronto's Bloor Street, where it rubs elbows with Tiffany's and Prada, marks a new trend in cross shopping:[5]

In 1982, Winners opened its first store in Toronto, Ontario with a simple idea in mind: offer Canadian consumers the surprising combination of the latest designer brand names in women's and children's fashions at unheard of savings (20% to 60% less than department or specialty stores). With more than 10 000 new items arriving in their stores every week, Canadians flocked to the stores where they experienced the "Thrill of the Find." In 1990, the chain was acquired by the TJX Companies Inc., the world's leading off-price retailer of home and apparel fashions. TJX's international sourcing, financial clout, and buying power enabled Winners stores to open across Canada and to offer a wider variety of merchandise, including menswear, home fashions, women's shoes, and jewellery. In 2006, the chain operated 170 stores across the country. The move onto Bloor street marks Winners recognition of a new trend. As Shannon Johnson, a spokesperson for Winners notes, today's Winners' shopper "is often the same person who shops both at designer boutiques and at Winners." Retailing boundaries are blurring, especially in the middle ground where there is a mixture of up- and down-scale shopping. Consumers will pick up designer items along with discount lower-price goods, mixing a little cachet in with a lot of affordability. "Twenty years ago people went down or up market. Now they cross-shop," says John Williams, a retail consultant.

The four main types of off-price retailers are **independents, factory outlets, warehouse clubs,** and **discount chains.** One of the fastest growing is the dollar store:

Stores such as The Great Canadian Dollar Store, Dollarama, Your Dollar Store, and a Buck or Two ask, "Why pay $5 if you can pay $1 and get just as nice a card?" This is the kind of question more and more shoppers are answering by going to dollar stores. In the past ten years, the lowly dollar store has moved from the fringe of retailing to become one of the hottest retail trends. As destination stores that offer a smaller-format alternative to the huge discounters like Wal-Mart, they're so respectable that they now locate in some better malls. Dollar stores are even setting the retailing agenda. Loblaw Companies Limited and A&P Canada, for example, are piloting dollar-store merchandise. "The dollar-store phenomenon is growing and consumers have accepted that," said Doug Brummer, senior vice-president of marketing at A&P. "We wanted to get

Factory outlet
An off-price retailing operation that is owned and operated by a manufacturer and that normally carries the manufacturer's surplus, discontinued, or irregular goods.

Independent off-price retailer
An off-price retailer that is either owned and run by an entrepreneur or is a division of a larger retail corporation.

Warehouse club
An off-price retailer that sells a limited selection of brand name grocery items, appliances, clothing, and a hodgepodge of other goods at deep discounts to members, who pay annual membership fees.

Off-price retailers: Shoppers at warehouse clubs, such as Costco, "trade up," getting good prices on items that make their hearts pound. At the same time, they "trade down" to private labels for things like paper towels, detergent, and vitamins.

a piece of that action. As is the case with Winners, dollar-store customers range from the budget-conscious to the well-heeled. Products that were unthinkable at only $1 twenty years ago are commonplace today. The larger chains import products directly from overseas manufacturers, trimming costs by cutting out the middleman. The chains are creating their own packaging and private labels. Some are even adding clothing and name-brand cosmetics. And the consumers just keep flocking in to grab up better and better bargains.[6]

Organizational Approach

Although many retail stores are independently owned, an increasing number are banding together under some form of corporate or contractual organization. The major types of retail organizations—*corporate chains*, *voluntary chains* and *retailer cooperatives*, *franchise organizations*, and *merchandising conglomerates*—are described in Table 13.2.

Chain stores are two or more outlets that are commonly owned and controlled. They have many advantages over independents. Their size allows them to buy in large quantities at lower prices and gain promotional economies. They can hire specialists to deal with areas such as pricing, promotion, merchandising, inventory control, and sales forecasting.

Forty percent of Canadian retailers belong to some type of chain, making retailing more concentrated in Canada than it is in the U.S., where only 20 percent of retail-

Chain store
Two or more outlets that are owned and controlled in common, have central buying and merchandising, and sell similar lines of merchandise.

TABLE 13.2 Major Types of Retail Organizations

Type	Description	Examples
Corporate chains	Two or more outlets that are commonly owned and controlled, employ central buying and merchandising, and sell similar lines of merchandise. Corporate chains appear in all types of retailing, but they are strongest in department stores, variety stores, drugstores, food stores, shoe stores, and women's clothing stores.	La Senza (lingerie), Sport Chek (sports goods), Loblaws (groceries), Pottery Barn (housewares), Reitmans (Canada's largest women's specialty retailer with 800 stores operating under eight divisions: Reitmans, Smart-Set, RW & CO., Pennington's, MXM, Thyme Maternity, Addition-Elle, and Cassis), Jacob Boutique Inc. (privately owned Canadian fashion retailer with more than 200 stores).
Voluntary chains	Wholesaler-sponsored groups of independent retailers engaged in bulk buying and common merchandising.	Independent Grocers Alliance (IGA), Western Auto, True Value Hardware
Retailer cooperatives	Groups of independent retailers that set up a central buying organization and conduct joint promotion efforts.	Calgary Group (groceries), ACE (hardware), Mountain Equipment Co-op (outdoor goods), Credit Unions
Franchise organizations	Contractual association between a franchiser (a manufacturer, wholesaler, or organization) and franchisees (independent businesspeople who buy the right to own and operate one or more units in the franchise system). Franchise organizations are normally based on some unique product, service, or method of doing business, or on a trade name or patent, or on goodwill that the franchiser has developed.	McDonald's, Subway, Pizza Hut, Jiffy Lube, 7-Eleven, Yogen Früz
Merchandising conglomerates	A free-form corporation that combines several diversified retailing lines and forms under central ownership, along with some integration of their distribution and management functions.	The Venator Group (owner of Foot Locker, Lady Foot Locker, Northern Reflections, Northern Traditions), Gap Inc.

ers are chain members. Many U.S.-based chain stores have invaded Canada, and more are on the way. For example, Old Navy (the discount division of Gap), American Eagle Outfitters, and Skechers USA Inc. (a trendy California-based shoe store) have recently entered the Canadian market.[7] Though many of these operations are welcomed by consumers, they threaten to take business away from their Canadian rivals. To fight this invasion, Canadian chains often consolidate even further.

The great success of corporate chains caused many independents to band together in one of two forms of contractual associations. One is the *voluntary chain*—a wholesaler-sponsored group of independent retailers that engages in group buying and common merchandising—which we discussed in Chapter 12. Examples include the Independent Grocers Alliance (IGA) and Western Auto. The other form of contractual association is the *retailer cooperative*—a group of independent retailers that bands together to set up a jointly owned, central wholesale operation and conducts joint merchandising and promotion efforts. True Value Hardware is an example of this contractual association. These organizations give independents the buying and promotion economies they need to meet the prices of corporate chains.

Another form of contractual retail organization is a **franchise**. The main difference between franchise organizations and other contractual systems (voluntary chains and retail cooperatives) is that franchise systems are normally based on some unique product or service; on a method of doing business; or on the trade name, goodwill, or patent that the franchiser has developed. Franchising has been prominent in fast foods, video stores, health and fitness centres, haircutting, auto rentals, motels, travel agencies, real estate, and dozens of other product and service areas. See how quickly one Ontario franchise has expanded:[8]

Founded in Southern Ontario 1993 by Fred Lopreiato, the Shoeless Joe's chain has grown from a single restaurant to 40 outlets, making it the largest sports-themed chain in Canada. Shoeless Joe's has strategically positioned itself away from the "sports bar" stereotype. Nonetheless, its restaurants burst with excitement no matter the time of day. Business professionals come in for lunch, families enjoy a casual dinner, and friends meet up to satisfy their late-night cravings. Shoeless Joe's recipe for success includes its ability to stay atop industry trends. For instance, it recently won the Award of Excellence from Eat Smart!, Ontario's healthy restaurant program, because of its innovative menu, top-notch food preparation, and the chain's steak and burger program that features only certified Angus beef. Shoeless Joe's is also committed to top-notch table service. Fred Lopreiato also attributes the company's success to giving back to the communities in which his restaurants do business. "If you donate back to the community, the community gives back to you," he says. Finally, the chain provides its franchisees with great support. Each new franchisee gets six weeks of training, covering all aspects of successful store operations, including bar service, food-handling procedures, merchandising and management controls. Since the company also provides support for site selection, design and construction of each location, the franchisees get a lot for their investment, which ranges from $600 000 to $650 000. Lopreiato lives his philosophy that any person can win a game, but it takes a team to win a championship. With this attitude, the chain is well positioned to meet its goal of being the best sports-themed restaurant in North America.

Franchises have sprung up to meet about any need. The Mad Science Group franchisees put on science programs for schools, scout troops, and birthday parties. Mr. Handyman provides repair services for homeowners, and ProForma franchisees act as sales agents for their clients, helping them select the best forms or promotional products.

Franchise
A contractual association between a manufacturer, wholesaler, or service organization (a franchiser) and independent businesspeople (franchisees) who buy the right to own and operate one or more units in the franchise system.

Franchises have sprung up to meet about any need—from familiar fast-food restaurants, such as McDonald's and Subway, to cleaning services, such as The Maids Home Services, and educational services, such as science enrichment provider Mad Science.

Once considered upstarts among independent businesses, franchises now command a hefty portion of retail sales in Canada. These days, it's nearly impossible to stroll down a city block or drive on a suburban street without seeing a McDonald's, Subway, Jiffy Lube, or Holiday Inn. One of the best-known and most successful franchisers, McDonald's, now has more than 31 000 stores in 119 countries, including more than 1375 McDonald's in Canada, employing more than 77 000 Canadians. Approximately 65 percent of all McDonald's Canadian restaurants are owned and operated by Canadian entrepreneurs.[9]

Finally, *merchandising conglomerates* are corporations that combine several different retailing forms under central ownership. An example is Gap Inc., which operates Old Navy (value-based fashion), Gap (mid-level fashion), Banana Republic (higher-end fashion), and Forth & Towne (upscale fashion for women, currently located in only five cities in the U.S.). Such diversified retailing, similar to a multibranding strategy, provides superior management systems and economies that benefit all the separate retail operations.

Retailer Marketing Decisions

Retailers are always searching for new marketing strategies to attract and hold customers. In the past, retailers attracted customers with unique products, more or better services than their competitors offered, or credit cards. Today, national-brand manufacturers, in their drive for volume, have placed their branded goods everywhere. National brands are found not only in department stores but also in mass-merchandise discount stores, off-price discount stores, and on the Web. As a result, retail assortments are looking more and more alike.

Service differentiation among retailers has also eroded. Many department stores have trimmed their services, whereas discounters have increased theirs. Customers have become smarter and more price sensitive. They see no reason to pay more for identical brands, especially when service differences are shrinking. For all these reasons, many retailers today are rethinking their marketing strategies.

As shown in Figure 13.1, retailers face major marketing decisions about their *target market and positioning*, *product assortment and services*, *price*, *promotion*, and *place*.

Target Market and Positioning Decision

Retailers first must define their target markets and then decide how they will position themselves in these markets. Should the store focus on upscale, mid-scale, or downscale shoppers? Do target shoppers want variety, depth of assort-

Figure 13.1 Retailer marketing decisions

ment, convenience, or low prices? Until they define and profile their markets, retailers cannot make consistent decisions about product assortment, services, pricing, advertising, store décor, or any of the other decisions that must support their positions.

Too many retailers fail to define their target markets and positions clearly. They try to have "something for everyone" and end up satisfying no market well. In contrast, successful retailers define their target markets well and position themselves strongly. For example, thanks to strong targeting and positioning, upscale grocer Whole Foods has become one of the most successful food retailers. (See Real Marketing 13.1.)

Even large stores, such as Wal-Mart and Sears, must define their major target markets to design effective marketing strategies. In fact, in recent years, thanks to strong targeting and positioning, Wal-Mart has become not just the world's largest retailer, but the world's largest *company*. In 2006, it operated 272 stores in Canada, and the Retail Council of Canada recently named Dave Ferguson, president and CEO of Wal-Mart Canada, as Distinguished Canadian Retailer of the Year. What are the secrets behind this spectacular success? Wal-Mart knows its customers and takes good care of them. As one analyst puts it, "The company gospel … is relatively simple: Be an agent for customers, find out what they want, and sell it to them for the lowest possible price." The company stays close to customers—for example, each top Wal-Mart executive spends at least two days a week visiting stores, talking directly with customers, and getting a first-hand look at operations. Then, Wal-Mart delivers what customers want—a broad selection of carefully selected goods at unbeatable prices. But the right merchandise at the right price isn't the only key to Wal-Mart's success. Compared with other discounters, Wal-Mart also provides the kind of service that keeps customers satisfied.

Product Assortment and Services Decision

Retailers must decide on three major product variables: *product assortment, services mix,* and *store atmosphere.*

The retailer's *product assortment* should differentiate the retailer while matching target shoppers' expectations. One strategy is to offer merchandise that no other competitor carries, such as private brands or national brands on which it holds exclusives. For example, Holt Renfrew gets exclusive rights to carry well-known designers' labels. A retailer can feature blockbuster merchandising events—Bloomingdale's is known for running spectacular shows featuring goods from a certain country, such as India or China. Or the retailer can offer surprise merchandise, as when Costco offers surprise assortments of seconds, overstocks, and close-outs. Finally, the retailer can differentiate itself by offering a highly targeted product assortment—Tall Girl carries clothing tailored exclusively for tall women; Brookstone offers an unusual assortment of gadgets in what amounts to an adult toy store.

REAL MARKETING

Whole Foods: Positioning Away from Wal-Mart

These days, Wal-Mart sells just about everything and competes ruthlessly with just about every other retailer, no matter what the product category. So, how *do* you compete with a behemoth like Wal-Mart? The best answer: You don't—at least not directly. Perhaps the worst strategy is trying to out-Wal-Mart Wal-Mart, as Zellers did when the U.S. giant entered Canada. Instead of competing head to head, smart competitors choose their turf carefully.

Take Whole Foods Market, the small, upscale grocery chain. It recently opened three outlets in Canada: in Toronto, Oakville, and West Vancouver. It has only 160 stores worldwide versus Wal-Mart's more than 5000, and its annual sales total little more than $3.9 billion, compared with Wal-Mart's $338 billion. Although it may not seem like a fair fight, Whole Foods is thriving. It succeeds through careful positioning—specifically, by positioning *away* from Wal-Mart. Rather than pursuing mass-market sales volume and razor-thin margins, Whole Foods targets a select group of upscale customers and offers them "organic, natural, and gourmet foods, all swaddled in Earth Day politics." As one analyst puts it, "While other grocers are looking over their shoulder, watching and worrying about Wal-Mart, Whole Foods is going about business as

usual. The tofu is still selling; the organic eggs are fresh in the back dairy cooler; and meats are still hormone free."

Whole Foods' strong positioning is summed up in its motto: "Whole Foods, Whole People, Whole Planet." If you have the opportunity to step into one of Canada's Whole Foods stores, you'll quickly see that it's not your typical food store. Instead of aisles of sugary mass-market colas, you'll find organic sodas and Odwalla juices. In the produce department, you'll find blue potatoes, dinner-plate-sized portabella mushrooms, taro root, and edamame (green Japanese soybeans). Natural soaps and toilet papers displace the usual national brands. Or pick up some meatless moussaka and herbal tea for your post-meditation snack. In keeping with the company's positioning, most of the store's goods carry labels proclaiming "organic," "100% natural," and "contains no additives."

The Whole Foods website, bathed in earth tones, reinforces the company's positioning. The site offers recipes for healthy eating, such as "Sweet Potato Pancakes with Creamy Dill Sauce," and "Beginner's Tips for Tofu, Tempeh, and Other Soy Foods." It bursts at the seams with information on a wide range of health and wellness issues from all you ever wanted to know about the potential medical uses of more than 100 herbs to alternative therapies such as acupuncture, reflexology, and homeopathy.

Whole Foods is more than just a shopping trip, it's an experience. And the experience is anything but what you'd find at Wal-Mart. "We create store environments that are inviting, fun, unique, informal, comfortable, attractive, nurturing, and educational," the company claims. "We want our stores to become community meeting places where our customers come to join their friends and to make new ones."

By design, Whole Foods is not for everyone—the upscale retailer caters to a carefully selected segment of consumers. Whole Foods customers are affluent, liberal, educated people living in very upscale neighbourhoods. Whole Foods customers live a health-conscious lifestyle, care about the food they eat, and worry about the environment. They tend to be social

Whole Foods Market—the small, upscale grocery chain—thrives by giving carefully targeted customers an experience that is anything but what you'd find at Wal-Mart.

do-gooders who abhor soulless corporate greed. Whole Foods doesn't really have to compete with mass merchandisers like Wal-Mart for these customers. In fact, a Whole Foods customer is more likely to boycott the local Wal-Mart than to shop at it.

Whole Foods customers like the fact that the store's commitment to quality reaches far beyond what's on its shelves. In its "Declaration of Interdependence," the company recognizes that living up to its "Whole Foods, Whole People, Whole Planet" motto means doing more than simply selling food. It means caring about all its stakeholders. Its concern for customers runs deep. "We go to extraordinary lengths to satisfy and delight our customers," says a company spokesperson. "We want to meet or exceed their expectations on every shopping trip." Whole Foods also cares about its employees—for the past seven years, it's been listed among *Fortune* magazine's "Top 100 Companies to Work for in America." Whole Foods cares about its suppliers. The Declaration of Interdependence states, "We view our trade partners as allies in serving our stakeholders. We treat them with respect, fairness, and integrity, and expect the same in return." To back this up, the company supports sustainable, environmentally friendly agriculture practices, offering organically grown foods almost exclusively. These practices are in stark contrast to Wal-Mart, who has received a great deal of negative press coverage in recent years surrounding its treatment of its employees and suppliers.

Whole Foods also cares about its communities. It provides financial support for employees doing voluntary community service. And it invests in the local environment. Perhaps most telling of Whole Foods broad community commitment: it donates 5 percent of its after-tax profits to not-for-profit organizations.

Such commitment, along with strong targeting and positioning, has made Whole Foods one of the fastest-growing and most profitable food retailers. It's now the world's number-one natural food chain. So, Whole Foods can't compete directly with the Wal-Marts of the world. It can't match Wal-Mart's massive economies of scale, incredible volume purchasing power, ultra-efficient logistics, wide selection, and hard-to-beat prices. But then again, it doesn't even try. Instead, it targets customers that Wal-Mart can't serve, offering them value that Wal-Mart can't deliver. By positioning away from Wal-Mart and other mainstream grocers, Whole Foods has found its own very profitable place in the world.

Sources: Aliya Sternstein, "Green Grocer," *Forbes*, March 31, 2003, p. 40; Michael Thuresson, "Hot Food," *Los Angeles Business Journal*, February 24, 2003, p. 4; "Whole Foods Pushing for Organic Profit Growth," *Money Digest*, February 2003, p. 14; Galina Espinoza and Alicia Dennis, "The Natural," *People Weekly*, November 4, 2002, p. 137; Vilma Barr, "Sunshine Supermarket," *Progressive Grocer*, March 1, 2003, p. 94; "Whole Foods Market Inc.," *Hoover's Company Profiles*, Austin, June 15, 2003; "Whole Foods Market, Inc," *Hoover's Company Capsules*, March 15, 2004, p. 10952; Samantha Thompson Smith, "Grocer's Success Seems Entirely Natural," *The News & Observer*, May 21, 2004, p. D1; and www.wholefoods.com (accessed May 2006).

The *services mix* can also help set one retailer apart from another. For example, some retailers invite customers to ask questions or consult service representatives in person or via phone or keyboard. Home Depot offers a diverse mix of services to do-it-yourselfers, from "how-to" classes to a proprietary credit card.

The *store's atmosphere* is another element in the reseller's product arsenal. Every store has a physical layout that makes moving around in it either hard or easy. Each store has a "feel"; one store is cluttered, another cheerful, a third plush, a fourth sombre. The store must plan an atmosphere that suits the target market and moves customers to buy.

For example, many retailers are practising "experiential retailing." At a Mountain Equipment Co-op store, consumers can try out climbing equipment on a huge wall in the store, and they can test new hiking boots by climbing up their simulated mountain slope. Similarly, Maytag is now setting up "try-before-you-buy" stores in which products are displayed in realistic home kitchen and laundry room settings, beckoning customers to test drive products before making a choice. "Potential buyers of washers and dryers can do a load of laundry," notes an analyst. "Or if the need is a new range, consumers can bake a sheet of cookies first. They can listen to a dishwasher to see whether it's really quiet."[10]

Increasingly, retailers are turning their stores into theatres that transport customers to unusual, exciting shopping environments. For example, The Rainforest Café, with outlets in Canada, the U.S., China, Mexico and Europe, bills itself as a "beast of a feast." It creates a jungle atmosphere using state-of-the-art décor and animatronics. A life-sized gorilla pounds his chest in the bushes. A trumpeting elephant rears its head. Exotic birds sing and butterflies float under a lush canopy of banyan trees and flowering vines. Cool mists float through the air, amid sounds of far-off thunder and cascading waterfalls. Huge aquariums of tropical fish add a live element. The menu supports the theme with appetizers such as Leaping Lizard Lettuce Wraps and main dishes like Rasta Pasta and Congo Catfish Plate. At the Magic Mushroom Bar, adventurers sip specialty drinks, smoothies, and coffees on the backs of carved animals.[11]

Perhaps the most dramatic conversion of stores into theatre is the West Edmonton Mall, which bills itself as the world's largest shopping and entertainment centre. It features more than 800 stores, 100 eating establishments, and 7 world-class attractions, including a golf course and a water park.[12]

All of this confirms that retail stores are much more than simply assortments of goods. They are environments to be experienced by the people who shop in them. Store atmospheres offer a powerful tool by which retailers can differentiate their stores from those of competitors.

Price Decision

A retailer's price policy must fit its target market and positioning, product and service assortment, and competition. All retailers would like to charge high markups and achieve high volume, but the two seldom go together. Most retailers seek *either* high markups on lower volume (most specialty stores) *or* low markups on higher volume (mass merchandisers and discount stores). Thus, Winnipeg-based Hanford Drewitt prices men's suits starting at $1000 and shoes at $400—it sells a low volume but makes a hefty profit on each sale. At the other extreme, Winners sells brand-name clothing at discount prices, settling for a lower margin on each sale but selling at a much higher volume.

Promotion Decision

Retailers use any or all of the promotion tools—advertising, personal selling, sales promotion, public relations, and direct marketing—to reach consumers. They advertise in newspapers, magazines, radio, television, and on the Internet. Advertising may be supported by newspaper inserts and direct mail. Personal selling requires careful training of salespeople in how to greet customers, meet their needs, and handle their complaints. Sales promotions may include in-store demonstrations, displays, contests, and visiting celebrities. Public relations activities, such as press conferences and speeches, store openings, special events, newsletters, magazines, and public service activities, are always available to retailers. Most retailers have also set up websites, offering customers information and other features and often selling merchandise directly.

Place Decision

Retailers often point to three critical factors in retailing success: *location, location,* and *location*! It's very important that retailers select locations that are accessible to the target market in areas that are consistent with the retailer's positioning. Small retailers may have to settle for whatever locations they can find or afford. Large retailers, however, usually employ specialists who select locations using advanced methods.

Most stores today cluster together to increase their customer pulling power and to give consumers the convenience of one-stop shopping. *Central business districts* were the main form of retail cluster until the 1950s. Every large city and town had a central business district with department stores, specialty stores, banks, and movie theatres. When people began to move to the suburbs, however, these central business districts, with their traffic, parking, and crime problems, began to lose business. Downtown merchants opened branches in suburban shopping centres, and the decline of the central business districts continued. In recent years, many cities have joined with merchants to try to revive downtown shopping areas by building malls and providing underground parking.

Shopping centre

A group of retail businesses planned, developed, owned, and managed as a unit.

A **shopping centre** is a group of retail businesses planned, developed, owned, and managed as a unit. A *regional shopping centre*, or *regional shopping mall,* the largest and most dramatic shopping centre, contains from 40 to more than 200 stores. It is like a covered mini-downtown and attracts customers from a wide area. A *community shopping centre* contains between 15 and 40 retail stores. It normally contains a branch of a department store or variety store, a supermarket, specialty stores, professional offices, and sometimes a bank. Most shopping centres are *neighbourhood shopping centres* or *strip malls* that generally contain between 5 and 15 stores. They are close and convenient for consumers. They usually contain a supermarket, perhaps a discount store, and several service stores—dry cleaner, self-service laundry, drugstore, video-rental outlet, barber or beauty shop, hardware store, or other stores.

A recent addition to the shopping centre scene is the so-called *power centre.* These huge unenclosed shopping centres consist of a long strip of retail stores, including large, freestanding anchors, such as Home Depot, Best Buy, Michaels, Staples, or HomeSense. Each store has its own entrance with parking directly in front for shoppers who wish to visit only one store. Power centres have increased rapidly during the past few years to challenge traditional indoor malls.

Through the past decade, on average, consumers have been going to traditional malls less often, staying a shorter period of time, and visiting fewer stores. Why are people using shopping malls less? First, with more dual-income households, people have less time to shop. "You have two workers in every family and no one has time to go to the mall for four hours anymore," observes one industry analyst. "People who used to go to the mall twenty times a year now go two or three times." Though time-pressed consumers are making fewer trips, they are buying more per trip. Second, a recent survey of British Columbia shoppers revealed that 58 percent of consumers now find shopping more of a chore than they did in the past. Listed as the top three reasons for their frustration were long line-ups at checkouts, poor service, and lack of assistance in stores.[13]

Thus, despite the recent development of many new "megamalls," such as the West Edmonton Mall, the current trend is toward value-oriented outlet malls and power centres on the one hand, and smaller malls on the other. Many shoppers now prefer to shop at "lifestyle centres," smaller malls with upscale stores, convenient locations, and expensive atmospheres.

The Future of Retailing

Retailers operate in a harsh and fast-changing environment, which offers threats as well as opportunities. For example, the industry suffers from chronic overcapacity, resulting in fierce competition for customer dollars. Consumer demographics, lifestyles, and shopping patterns are changing rapidly, as are retailing technologies. To be successful, then, retailers will have to choose target segments carefully and position themselves strongly. They will have to take the following retailing developments into account as they plan and execute their competitive strategies.

New Retail Forms and Shortening Retail Life Cycles

New retail forms continue to emerge to meet new situations and consumer needs, but the life cycle of new retail forms is getting shorter. Department stores took

The West Edmonton Mall is the largest mall in the world. Besides containing more than 800 shops and services, it features the world's largest indoor amusement park and the world's largest indoor lake.

Wheel-of-retailing concept
A concept of retailing that states that new types of retailers usually begin as low-margin, low-price, low-status operations but later evolve into higher-priced, higher-service operations, eventually becoming like the conventional retailers they replaced.

about 100 years to reach the mature stage of the life cycle; more recent forms, such as warehouse stores, reached maturity in about ten years. In such an environment, seemingly solid retail positions can crumble quickly. Of the top ten discount retailers in 1962 (the year that Wal-Mart and Kmart began), not one still exists today.

The mantra of Canadian retailing today may have been best expressed by George Heller, who was the chief executive officer of Hudson's Bay Co. (HBC). "Get good or get lost," he exclaimed in a recent speech. The ground is shifting under retailers and many of Canada's most familiar names—Eaton's, Simpson's, Woodward's, Robinson's, Bretton's, Kmart, Woolco—have disappeared over the past decade. Retailers that were unable to adapt to the fierce competition from powerhouses such as Wal-Mart, Costco, and Home Depot are gone.

Retailers can no longer sit back and rely on a once-successful formula—they must keep adapting. Many retailing innovations are partially explained by the **wheel-of-retailing concept.**[14] According to this concept, many new types of retailing forms begin as low-margin, low-price, low-status operations. They challenge established retailers that have become "fat" by letting their costs and margins increase. The new retailers' success leads them to upgrade their facilities and offer more services. In turn, their costs increase, forcing them to increase their prices. Eventually, the new retailers become like the conventional retailers they replaced. The cycle begins again when still newer types of retailers evolve with lower costs and prices. The wheel-of-retailing concept seems to explain the initial success and later troubles of department stores, supermarkets, and discount stores, and the recent success of off-price retailers.

Growth of Non-store Retailing

Most of us still make most of our purchases the old-fashioned way: We go to the store, find what we want, wait patiently in line to plunk down our cash or credit card, and bring home the goods. However, consumers now have an array of alternatives, including mail-order, television, phone, and online shopping. Canadians are increasingly avoiding the hassles and crowds at malls by doing more of their shopping by phone or computer. Although such retailing advances may threaten some traditional retailers, they offer exciting opportunities for others. Most store retailers have now developed direct retailing channels. In fact, more online retailing is conducted by "click-and-brick" retailers than by "click-only" retailers.

Online retailing is the newest form of non-store retailing. Only a few years ago, prospects for online retailing were soaring. As more and more consumers flocked to the Web, some experts even saw a day when consumers would bypass stodgy "old economy" store retailers and do almost all of their shopping via the Internet. However, the dot-com meltdown of 2000 dashed these overblown expectations. Many once-brash Web sellers, such as eToys.com and Garden.com, crashed and burned. After the shakeout, expectations reversed almost overnight. The experts began to predict that etailing was destined to be little more than a tag-on to in-store retailing.

However, although the pace has slowed, today's online retailing is alive, well, and growing. With easier-to-use websites, improved online service, and the demise of so many early competitors, business is booming for the survivors. In fact, online buying is growing at a much brisker pace than retail buying as a whole.

Although the dramatic dot-com collapses grabbed most of the headlines, some click-only retailers are now making it big on the Web. Heading this group is online auction site eBay, which has been consistently profitable since its inception. Click-only etailers account for a majority of online sales in several other categories as well, including books, music, and video; foods and beverages; and collectibles. Business is also booming for online travel companies, such as Travelocity and Expedia, which use the Web to sell airline tickets, hotel rooms, and discount travel packages to consumers.

Still, much of the anticipated growth in online sales will go to multichannel retailers—the click-and-brick marketers who can successfully merge the virtual and physical worlds. Such retailers accounted for 67 percent of total online sales last year. Consider Staples Business Depot, the $16.9 billion office-supply retailer. After just six years on the Web, Staples Business Depot captures annual online sales of more than $2.7 billion. Its online sales have averaged double-digit quarterly growth for more than three years. But it's not robbing from store sales in the process. The average yearly spending of small-business customers jumps from $780 when they shop in Staples Business Depot stores to $3640 when they shop online. As a result, although Staples Business Depot has slowed new store openings recently, it plans to keep expanding its Web presence. "We're still going whole hog," says former CEO Thomas Stemberg. "The payoffs are just very high."[15]

Today's etailing is alive, well, and growing, especially for click-and-brick competitors, such as Staples Business Depot. Its online sales have averaged double-digit quarterly growth for more than three years.

Retail Convergence

Today's retailers are increasingly selling the same products at the same prices to the same consumers in competition with a wider variety of other retailers. For example, you can buy books at outlets ranging from independent local bookstores to discount stores such as Wal-Mart, superstores such as Chapters, or Websites such as Amazon.com. And when it comes to brand-name appliances, department stores, discount stores, home improvement stores, off-price retailers, electronics superstores, and a slew of websites all compete for the same customers. So if you can't find the microwave oven you want at Sears, just step across the street and find one for a better price at Rona or The Bay—or order one online.

This merging of consumers, products, prices, and retailers is called *retail convergence*:[16]

> Retail convergence is the coming together of shoppers, goods, and prices. Customers of all income levels are shopping at the same stores, often for the same goods. Old distinctions such as discount store, specialty store, and department store are losing significance: The successful store must match a host of rivals on selection, service, and price.

> The Canadian consumer's road map for where products can be found has shifted from a segmented approach to a consolidation that is almost a throw-back to the 1800s, when a general store was the place to shop for everything from coffee to a coffeepot. In the 1900s, shoppers migrated from the Sears catalogue to the department store, and then to the shopping mall and specialty stores. A few years ago, the coffee pot customer may have gone to Williams-Sonoma or even Starbucks. Today, it could be Zellers or Wal-Mart.

> Where you go for what you want—that has created the biggest challenge facing retailers. Consider fashion. Once the exclusive of the wealthy, fashion now moves just as quickly from the runways of New York and Paris to retailers at all levels. Liz Claiborne sells in upscale department stores like Holt Renfrew as well as in discount outlets at the strip mall. Further, some designers are playing in new market segments. For example, designer Mossimo Giannuli was once only concerned with selling boarder shorts in small retail establishments. Today, his Mossimo line sells in Target in the U.S., and Zellers in Canada.

Such convergence means greater competition for retailers and greater difficulty in differentiating offerings. The competition between chain superstores and smaller, independently owned stores has become particularly heated. Because of their bulk-buying power and high sales volume, chains can buy at lower costs and thrive on smaller margins. The arrival of a superstore can quickly force nearby independents out of business. For example, the decision by electronics superstore Best Buy to sell CDs as loss leaders at rock-bottom prices pushed a number of specialty record store chains into bankruptcy. And Wal-Mart has been accused of destroying independents in countless small towns around the country.

Yet the news is not all bad for smaller companies. Many small, independent retailers are thriving. They are finding that sheer size and marketing muscle are often no match for the personal touch that small stores can provide or the specialty niches that small stores fill for a devoted customer base.

The Rise of Megaretailers

The rise of huge mass merchandisers and specialty superstores, the formation of vertical marketing systems, and a rash of retail mergers and acquisitions have created a core of superpower megaretailers. Through their superior information systems and buying power, these giant retailers can offer better merchandise selections, good service, and strong price savings to consumers. As a result, they grow even larger by squeezing out their smaller, weaker competitors.

The megaretailers are also shifting the balance of power between retailers and producers. A relative handful of retailers now controls access to enormous numbers of consumers, giving them the upper hand in their dealings with manufacturers. For example, Wal-Mart's revenues are more than six times those of Procter & Gamble, and Wal-Mart generates almost 20 percent of P&G's revenues. Wal-Mart can, and often does, use this power to wring concessions from P&G and other suppliers.[17]

Growing Importance of Retail Technology

Retail technologies are becoming critically important as competitive tools. Progressive retailers are using advanced information technology and software systems to produce better forecasts, control inventory costs, order electronically from suppliers, send email between stores, and even sell to customers within stores. They are adopting checkout scanning systems, online transaction processing, electronic data interchange, in-store television, and improved merchandise-handling systems. Here's how technology helped to unravel a mystery:[18]

> The managers of a newly renovated A&P in Hamilton, Ontario, were perplexed. Their scanner data revealed that the 5 percent of the store clientele who used frequent-buyer cards were purchasing less. A follow-up survey revealed that although most people liked the store's new look, they didn't like the new self-serve deli. As a result of this customer feedback, the store was remodelled again. Purchasing levels went back up, and A&P avoided making a chain-wide blunder.

Perhaps the most startling advances in retailing technology concern the ways in which today's retailers are connecting with customers. Many retailers now routinely use technologies, such as touch screen kiosks, electronic shelf labels and signs, hand-held shopping assistants, smart cards, self-scanning systems, and virtual reality displays. For example, in its new pilot store—Bloom—U.S. grocery chain Food Lion is using technology to make shopping easier for its customers:

> Ever stood in the wine aisle at the grocery store and felt intimidated? You think that bottle of Shiraz looks pretty good but you're not sure what it goes with. It's the sort of problem the creators of a new concept store—Bloom—thought about, and one they will use technology to solve. The store relies on technology to enhance the shopping experience and to help customers find products, get information, and check out with greater ease. A computerized kiosk in its wine section lets you scan a bottle and get serving suggestions. The kiosk, and a second one in the meat section, lets you print recipes off the screen. Eight stations with touch screens and scanners around the store let you check an item's price or locate it on the map. To make it easier to keep track of purchases and check out, you can pick up a personal hand-held scanner as you walk in the door, then scan and bag items as you shop. Checkout then is just a simple matter of paying as you leave. And if you drop off a prescription, the pharmacy can send a message to your scanner when your order is ready.[19]

Global Expansion of Major Retailers

Retailers with unique formats and strong brand positioning are increasingly moving into other countries. Many are expanding internationally to escape mature and saturated home markets. Over the years, several giant U.S. retailers—McDonald's, Gap, Toys "R" Us—have become globally prominent as a result of their great marketing prowess. Others, such as Wal-Mart, are rapidly establishing a global presence. Wal-Mart, which operated 2700 stores in 14 countries outside the US in 2006, racked up international sales of more than US$62 billion, an 11.4 percent increase over the previous year. Operating profit rose to $3.3 billion, an increase of 11.4 percent over that generated in 2005 (see http://walmartstores.com/GlobalWMStoresWeb/navigate.do?catg=369 for more information). Here's what happened when it opened two new stores in Shenzhen, China:[20]

> [Customers came] by the hundreds of thousands—up to 175 000 on Saturdays alone—to China's first Wal-Mart Supercenter and Sam's Club. They broke the display glass to snatch out chickens at one store and carted off all the big-screen TVs before the other store had been open an hour. The two outlets … were packed on Day One and have been bustling ever since.

However, North American retailers are still significantly behind Europe and Asia when it comes to global expansion. Less than 20 percent of the top North American retailers operate globally, compared with 40 percent of European retailers and 31 percent of Asian retailers. Among foreign retailers that have gone global are France's Carrefour, Britain's Marks and Spencer, Italy's Benetton, Sweden's IKEA home furnishings stores, and Japan's Yaohan supermarkets.[21]

Marks and Spencer, which started out as a penny bazaar in 1884, grew into a chain of variety stores over the decades and now has a thriving string of 150 franchised stores around the world, which sell mainly its private-label clothes, including Brooks Brothers. It also runs a major food business. IKEA's well-constructed but fairly inexpensive furniture has proven very popular in Canada, where shoppers often spend an entire day in an IKEA store. And French discount retailer Carrefour, the world's second-largest retailer after Wal-Mart, has embarked on an aggressive mission to extend its role as a leading international retailer:

> Carrefour now operates more than 9600 discount stores in 30 countries in Europe, Asia, and the Americas, including 657 hypermarkets. In the European market, it now claims retail dominance in four leading markets: France, Spain, Belgium, and Greece; it's the number two retailer in Italy. Outside Europe, in the all-important emerging markets of China, South America, and the Pacific Rim, Carrefour outpaces Wal-Mart five-to-one in actual revenue. In South America, Carrefour is the market leader in Brazil and Argentina, where it operates more than 300 stores. By comparison, Wal-Mart has only twenty-five units in those two countries. In China, Carrefour operates twenty-two hypermarkets to Wal-Mart's five supercentres and one Sam's Club. In the Pacific Rim, excluding China, Carrefour operates thirty-three hypermarkets in five countries. Wal-

Many retailers are expanding internationally to escape mature and saturated home markets. French discount retailer Carrefour, the world's second-largest retailer after Wal-Mart, has embarked on an aggressive mission to extend its role as a leading international retailer.

Mart, in contrast, recently closed down its operations in Germany and South Korea. In short, Carrefour is bounding ahead of Wal-Mart in most markets outside North America. The only question: Can the French titan hold its lead? Though no one retailer can rightly claim to be in the same league with Wal-Mart as an overall retail presence, Carrefour stands a better chance than most to dominate global retailing.[22]

Retail Stores as "Communities" or "Hangouts"

With the rise in the number of people living alone, working at home, or living in isolated and sprawling suburbs, there has been a resurgence of establishments that, regardless of the product or service they offer, also provide a place for people to get together. These places include cafes, tea shops, juice bars, bookshops, superstores, children's play spaces, brew pubs, and urban greenmarkets. Brew pubs, such as the Kingston Brew Pub, offer tastings and a place to pass the time. And today's bookstores have become part bookstore, part library, and part living room.

Welcome to today's bookstore. The one featuring not only shelves and cash registers but also cushy chairs and coffee bars. It's where backpack-toting university students come to do homework and drink coffee, where retirees thumb through the gardening books, and parents read aloud to their toddlers. If no one actually buys books, that's just fine, say bookstore owners and managers. They're offering something grander than ink and paper, anyway. They're selling comfort, relaxation, community.[23]

Retailers with physical stores are not the only ones creating community. Others have also built virtual communities on the Internet.

Sony actively builds community among its Playstation customers. Its recent Playstation.com campaign created message boards where its game players could post messages to one another. The boards are incredibly active, discussing techie topics but also providing the opportunity for members, fiercely competitive and opinionated, to vote on lifestyle issues, such as music and personal taste, no matter how trivial. Although Sony is laissez-faire about the boards and does not feed them messages, the company sees the value in having its customers' adamant conversations occur directly on its site. "Our customers are our evangelists. They are a very vocal and loyal fan base," says a Sony spokesperson. "There are things we can learn from them."[24]

Wholesaling

Wholesaling
All activities involved in selling goods and services to those buying for resale or business use.

Wholesaler
A firm engaged *primarily* in wholesaling activity.

Wholesaling includes all activities involved in selling goods and services to those buying for resale or business use. We call **wholesalers** those firms engaged *primarily* in wholesaling activity.

Wholesalers buy mostly from producers and sell mostly to retailers, industrial consumers, and other wholesalers. As a result, many of the nation's largest and most important wholesalers are largely unknown to final consumers. Vancouver-based Group Telecom (GT), for example, is a telecommunications services wholesaler that targets Canada's 2.5 million small and medium-sized businesses. These independent business firms are price sensitive and demand a high level of service from their wholesaler. This market is one GT believes has been "underserved," so it offers customized bundles of services—all on a single bill and with one customer service number to phone.[25] Despite the fact that they may be relatively unknown to end-consumers, wholesaling is a major industry in Canada, accounting for $470 billion in sales.[26]

But why are wholesalers used at all? For example, why would a producer use wholesalers rather than selling directly to retailers or consumers? Simply put, wholesalers add value by performing one or more of the following channel functions:

- *Selling and promoting:* Wholesalers' sales forces help manufacturers reach many small customers at a low cost. The wholesaler has more contacts and is often more trusted by the buyer than the distant manufacturer.

- *Buying and assortment building:* Wholesalers can select items and build assortments needed by their customers, thereby saving the consumers much work.

- *Bulk-breaking:* Wholesalers save their customers money by buying in carload lots and breaking bulk (breaking large lots into small quantities).

- *Warehousing:* Wholesalers hold inventories, thereby reducing the inventory costs and risks of suppliers and customers.

- *Transportation:* Wholesalers can provide quicker delivery to buyers because they are closer than the producers.

- *Financing:* Wholesalers finance their customers by giving credit, and they finance their suppliers by ordering early and paying bills on time.

- *Risk bearing:* Wholesalers absorb risk by taking title and bearing the cost of theft, damage, spoilage, and obsolescence.

- *Market information:* Wholesalers give information to suppliers and customers about competitors, new products, and price developments.

- *Management services and advice:* Wholesalers often help retailers train their salesclerks, improve store layouts and displays, and set up accounting and inventory control systems.

Types of Wholesalers

Merchant wholesaler
Independently owned business that takes title to the merchandise it handles.

Wholesalers fall into three major groups (see Table 13.3): *merchant wholesalers, agents and broker,* and *manufacturers' sales branches and offices.* **Merchant wholesalers** are the largest single group of wholesalers, accounting for roughly 50 percent of all wholesaling. Merchant wholesalers include two broad types: full-service wholesalers and limited-service wholesalers. *Full-service wholesalers* provide a full set of services, whereas the various *limited-service wholesalers* offer fewer services to their suppliers and customers. The several different types of limited-service wholesalers perform varied specialized functions in the distribution channel.

Broker
A wholesaler who does not take title to goods and whose function is to bring buyers and sellers together and assist in negotiation.

Brokers and *agents* differ from merchant wholesalers in two ways: They do not take title to goods, and they perform only a few functions. Like merchant wholesalers, they generally specialize by product line or customer type. A **broker** brings buyers and sellers together and assists in negotiation. **Agents** represent buyers or sellers on a more permanent basis. *Manufacturers' agents* (also called manufacturers' representatives) are the most common type of agent wholesaler. The third major type of wholesaling is that done in **manufacturers' sales branches and offices** by sellers or buyers themselves rather than through independent wholesalers.

Agent
A wholesaler who represents buyers or sellers on a relatively permanent basis, performs only a few functions, and does not take title to goods.

Manufacturers' sales branches and offices
Wholesaling by sellers or buyers themselves rather than through independent wholesalers.

Wholesaler Marketing Decisions

Wholesalers now face growing competitive pressures, more demanding customers, new technologies, and more direct-buying programs on the part of large industrial, institutional, and retail buyers. As a result, they have had to take a fresh look at their marketing strategies. As with retailers, their marketing decisions include choices of target markets, positioning, and the marketing mix—product assortments and services, price, promotion, and place (see Figure 13.2 on page 516).

TABLE 13.3 Major Types of Wholesalers

Type	Description
Merchant wholesalers	Independently owned businesses that take title to the merchandise they handle. In different trades they are called *jobbers, distributors,* or *mill supply houses.* Include full-service wholesalers and limited-service wholesalers:
Full-service wholesalers	Provide a full line of services: carrying stock, maintaining a sales force, offering credit, making deliveries, and providing management assistance. There are two types:
Wholesale merchants	Sell primarily to retailers and provide a full range of services. *General merchandise wholesalers* carry several merchandise lines, whereas *general line wholesalers* carry one or two lines in great depth. *Specialty wholesalers* specialize in carrying only part of a line. Examples: health food wholesalers, seafood wholesalers.
Industrial distributors	Sell to manufacturers rather than to retailers. Provide several services, such as carrying stock, offering credit, and providing delivery. May carry a broad range of merchandise, a general line, or a specialty line.
Limited-service wholesalers	Offer fewer services than full-service wholesalers. Limited-service wholesalers are of several types:
Cash-and-carry wholesalers	Carry a limited line of fast-moving goods and sell to small retailers for cash. Normally do not deliver. Example: A small fish store retailer may drive to a cash-and-carry fish wholesaler, buy fish for cash, and bring the merchandise back to the store.
Truck wholesalers (or truck jobbers)	Perform primarily a selling and delivery function. Carry limited line of semiperishable merchandise (such as milk, bread, snack foods), which they sell for cash as they make their rounds to supermarkets, small groceries, hospitals, restaurants, factory cafeterias, and hotels.
Drop shippers	Do not carry inventory or handle the product. On receiving an order, they select a manufacturer, who ships the merchandise directly to the customer. The drop shipper assumes title and risk from the time the order is accepted to its delivery to the customer. They operate in bulk industries, such as coal, lumber, and heavy equipment.
Rack jobbers	Serve grocery and drug retailers, mostly in nonfood items. They send delivery trucks to stores, where the delivery people set up toys, paperbacks, hardware items, health and beauty aids, or other items. They price the goods, keep them fresh, set up point-of-purchase displays, and keep inventory records. Rack jobbers retain title to the goods and bill the retailers only for the goods sold to consumers.
Producers' cooperatives	Are owned by farmer members and assemble farm produce to sell in local markets. The co-op's profits are distributed to members at the end of the year. They often attempt to improve product quality and promote a co-op brand name, such as Sun Maid raisins, Sunkist oranges, or Diamond walnuts.
Mail-order wholesalers	Send catalogues to retail, industrial, and institutional customers featuring jewellery, cosmetics, specialty foods, and other small items. Maintain no outside sales force. Main customers are businesses in small outlying areas. Orders are filled and sent by mail, truck, or other transportation.
Brokers and agents	Do not take title to goods. Main function is to facilitate buying and selling, for which they earn a commission on the selling price. Generally specialize by product line or customer type.
Brokers	Chief function is bringing buyers and sellers together and assisting in negotiation. They are paid by the party who hired them and do not carry inventory, get involved in financing, or assume risk. Examples: food brokers, real estate brokers, insurance brokers, and security brokers.
Agents	Represent either buyers or sellers on a more permanent basis than brokers do. There are several types:
Manufacturers' agents	Represent two or more manufacturers of complementary lines. A formal written agreement with each manufacturer covers pricing, territories, order-handling, delivery service and warranties, and commission rates. Often used in such lines as apparel, furniture, and electrical goods. Most manufacturers' agents are small businesses, with only a few skilled salespeople as employees. They are hired by small manufacturers who cannot afford their own field sales forces and by large manufacturers who use agents to open new territories or to cover territories that cannot support full-time salespeople.

continued

TABLE 13.3 Major Types of Wholesalers (*continued*)

Selling agents	Have contractual authority to sell a manufacturer's entire output. The manufacturer either is not interested in the selling function or feels unqualified. The selling agent serves as a sales department and has significant influence over prices, terms, and conditions of sale. Found in product areas such as textiles, industrial machinery and equipment, coal and coke, chemicals, and metals.
Purchasing agents	Generally have a long-term relationship with buyers and make purchases for them, often receiving, inspecting, warehousing, and shipping the merchandise to the buyers. They provide helpful market information to clients and help them obtain the best goods and prices available.
Commission merchants	Take physical possession of products and negotiate sales. Normally, they are not employed on a long-term basis. Used most often in agricultural marketing by farmers who do not want to sell their own output and do not belong to producers' cooperatives. The commission merchant takes a truckload of commodities to a central market, sells it for the best price, deducts a commission and expenses, and remits the balance to the producers.
Manufacturers' and retailers' branches and offices	Wholesaling operations conducted by sellers or buyers themselves rather than through independent wholesalers. Separate branches and offices can be dedicated to either sales or purchasing.
Sales branches and offices	Set up by manufacturers to improve inventory control, selling, and promotion. *Sales branches* carry inventory and are found in industries such as lumber and automotive equipment and parts. *Sales offices* do not carry inventory and are most prominent in dry-goods and notions industries.
Purchasing officers	Perform a role similar to that of brokers or agents but are part of the buyer's organization. Many retailers set up purchasing offices in major market centres such as New York and Chicago.

Target Market and Positioning Decision

Like retailers, wholesalers must define their target markets and position themselves effectively—they cannot serve everyone. They can choose a target group by size of customer (only large retailers), type of customer (convenience stores only), need for service (customers who need credit), or other factors. (See Real Marketing 13.2.) Within the target group, they can identify the more profitable customers, design stronger offers, and build better relationships with them. They can propose automatic reordering systems, set up management-training and advising systems, or even sponsor a voluntary chain. They can discourage less profitable customers by requiring larger orders or adding service charges to smaller ones.

Marketing Mix Decisions

Like retailers, wholesalers must decide on product assortment and services, prices, promotion, and place. The wholesaler's "product" is the assortment of *products and services* that it offers. Wholesalers are under great pressure to carry a full line and to stock enough for immediate delivery. But this practice can damage profits. Wholesalers today are cutting down on the number of lines they carry, choosing to

Figure 13.2 Wholesaler marketing decisions

Grainger: The Biggest Market Leader You've Never Heard Of?

*G*rainger may be the biggest market leader you've never heard of. It's a $6.1 billion business that offers more than 500 000 products and parts to more than 1.6 million customers. Its more than 575 North American branches, more than 15 000 employees, and innovative website handle more than 100 000 transactions a day. Grainger's customers include organizations ranging from factories, garages, and grocers to military bases and schools. Most North American businesses are located within twenty minutes of a Grainger branch. Customers include notables such as Abbott Laboratories, General Motors, Campbell Soup, American Airlines, Mercedes-Benz, and the U.S. Postal Service. Grainger also operates one of the highest-volume business-to-business sites on the Web.

So, how come you've never heard of Grainger? Most likely it's because Grainger is a wholesaler. And like most wholesalers, it operates behind the scenes, selling only to other businesses. Moreover, Grainger

Although you may never have heard it, Grainger is by far the world's leading wholesaler of maintenance, repair, and operating supplies.

operates in the not-so-glamorous world of maintenance, repair, and operating (MRO) supplies.

But whereas you might know little about Grainger, to its customers the company is very well known and much valued. Through its branch network, service centres, sales reps, catalogue, and website, Grainger links customers with the supplies they need to keep their facilities running smoothly—everything from light bulbs, cleaners, and display cases to nuts and bolts, motors, valves, power tools, and test equipment. Grainger is by far North America's largest MRO wholesaler. Notes one industry reporter, "If industrial America is an engine, Grainger is its lubricant."

Grainger serves as an important link between thousands of MRO supplies manufacturers on one side and millions of industrial and commercial customers on the other. It operates on a simple value proposition: to make it easier and less costly for customers to find and buy MRO supplies. It starts by acting as a one-stop shop for products to maintain facilities. Most customers will tell you that Grainger sells everything—*everything*—from the ordinary to the out-of-the-ordinary. For example, it stocks thousands of light bulbs—about every light bulb known to mankind. If you don't believe it, go to www.grainger.com and search "light bulbs"! As for the not-so-ordinary:

> Grainger sells nineteen models of floor-cleaning machines, has forty-nine catalogue pages of socket wrenches, and offers nine sizes of hydraulic service jacks, an assortment of NFL-licensed hard hats bearing team logos, and item No. 6AV22, a $36.90 dispenser rack for two 1-gallon containers of Gatorade. According to corporate legend, [Grainger] is the only place that workers on the Alaskan Pipeline have been able to find repellent to cope with arctic bears during their mating season.

Beyond making it easier for customers to find the products they need, Grainger also helps them streamline their acquisition processes. For most companies, acquiring MRO supplies is a very costly process. In fact, 40 percent of the cost of MRO supplies stems from the purchase process, including finding a supplier, negotiating the best deal, placing the order,

▶

receiving the order, and paying the invoice. Grainger constantly seeks ways to reduce the costs associated with MRO supplies acquisition, both internally and externally. Says one analyst, "Grainger will reduce your search and your process costs for items, instead of your having to order 10 things from 10 different companies, and you'll get one invoice. That's pretty powerful."

One company found that working with Grainger cut MRO requisition time by more than 60 percent; lead times went from days to hours. Its supply chain dropped from 12 000 suppliers to 560—significantly reducing expenses. Similarly, a large timber and paper-products company has come to appreciate the value of Grainger's selection and streamlined ordering process. It orders two-thirds of its supplies from Grainger's website at an annual acquisition cost of only $390 000. By comparison, for the remainder of its needs, this company deals with more than 1300 small distributors at an acquisition cost of $3.1 million each year—eight times the cost of dealing with Grainger for half of the volume. As a result, the company is now looking for ways to buy all of its MRO supplies from Grainger.

You might think that helping customers find what they need easily and efficiently would be enough to keep Grainger atop the MRO mountain. But Grainger goes even further. On a broader level, it builds lasting relationships with customers by helping them find *solutions* to their overall MRO problems. Acting as consultants, Grainger sales reps help buyers with everything from improving their supply chain management to reducing inventories and streamlining warehousing operations.

> Branches ... serve as the base for Grainger territory managers who provide on-site help to big facilities.... [Reps can] tour a factory or an office complex or even a hotel and suggest to its managers exactly what supplies they really need to keep the place up to snuff, right down to how many gallons of carpet cleaner they'll require each week. That's how Grainger knows, for example, that one Biltmore Hotel has 7000 light bulbs.... "Our reps can pretty much stand outside a building and get a general feel for what kinds of products the customer needs," [says James Ryan, Grainger's executive vice-president of marketing, sales, and service].

Grainger has launched a series of programs designed to add value to its commodity business. For example, through its "click & sell" program, Grainger uses information collected about customers, such as industry data and purchase histories, to help sales reps find solutions for customer needs. If, for example, a customer places an order for a pump to use with caustic chemicals, the Grainger rep might also suggest gloves and safety glasses. If an item is unavailable, the database identifies alternative products to get the job done.

Grainger also offers value to customers through its links to and clout with suppliers:

> Jason Eastin is facilities operations director for JRV Management, a ... company that runs community and private sports facilities in metropolitan Detroit. He relies on Grainger in part because of its clout with factory reps. When his company was opening its newest complex, he asked Chris Clemons, a Grainger territory manager, for help figuring out the number and kinds of fixtures that would be required. Clemens summoned a rep from Rubbermaid, the household-products maker, who showed up with a laptop and a software program that churned out a reasonable supply chain within twenty minutes. Similarly, Clemens worked with a General Electric salesperson who figured out how Eastin could stretch out "relamping" his facilities to every two years, instead of annually, and cut costs significantly as well by switching to a different kind of metal-halide bulb as the primary kind of illumination for his ice arenas. "To have General Electric provide that service to me at no charge would never happen," Eastin says. "But Grainger has that buying-power structure. They open up those kinds of opportunities to me."

So now you've heard of Grainger, a wholesaler that succeeds by making life easier and more efficient for commercial and industrial buyers and sellers. Although a market leader, Grainger still captures only 4 percent of the highly fragmented U.S. market for MRO goods. That leaves a lot of room for growth. But to take advantage of the opportunities, Grainger must continue to find innovative ways to add value. "Our system makes our business partners and suppliers more efficient," says Fred Loepp, vice-president of product management at Grainger, "and that benefits the entire supply chain." Says Theresa Dubiel, branch manager at Grainger's Romulus, Michigan, branch, "If we don't save [customers] time and money every time they come [to us], they won't come back."

Sources: Excerpts from Dale Buss, "The New Deal," *Sales & Marketing Management*, June 2002, pp. 25–30; and Colleen Gourley, "Redefining Distribution," *Warehousing Management*, October 2000, pp. 28–30. Also see Steve Konicki and Eileen Colkin, "Attitude Adjustment," *Informationweek*, March 25, 2002, pp. 20–22; "W.W. Grainger, Inc.," *Hoover's Company Profiles*, Austin, July 15, 2003, p. 11593; "Grainger to Add, Relocate and Expand Branches," *Industrial Distribution*, June 2004, p. 20; and information at www.grainger.com (accessed December 2004).

carry only the more profitable ones. Wholesalers are also rethinking which services count most in building strong customer relationships and which should be dropped or charged for. The key is to find the mix of services most valued by their target customers.

Price is also an important wholesaler decision. Wholesalers usually mark up the cost of goods by a standard percentage—say, 20 percent. Expenses may run 17 percent of the gross margin, leaving a profit margin of 3 percent. In grocery wholesaling, the average profit margin is often less than 2 percent. Wholesalers are trying new pricing approaches. They may cut their margin on some lines in order to win important new customers. They may ask suppliers for special price breaks when they can turn them into an increase in the supplier's sales.

Although *promotion* can be critical to wholesaler success, most wholesalers are not promotion minded. Their use of trade advertising, sales promotion, personal selling, and public relations is largely scattered and unplanned. Many are behind the times in personal selling—they still see selling as a single salesperson talking to a single customer instead of as a team effort to sell, build, and service major accounts. Wholesalers also need to adopt some of the non-personal promotion techniques used by retailers. They need to develop an overall promotion strategy and to make greater use of supplier promotion materials and programs.

Finally, *place* is important—wholesalers must choose their locations, facilities, and Web locations carefully. Wholesalers typically locate in low-rent, low-tax areas and tend to invest little money in their buildings, equipment, and systems. As a result, their materials-handling and order-processing systems are often outdated. In recent years, however, large and progressive wholesalers are reacting to rising costs by investing in automated warehouses and online ordering systems. Orders are fed from the retailer's system directly into the wholesaler's computer, and the items are picked up by mechanical devices and automatically taken to a shipping platform where they are assembled. Most large wholesalers are using technology to carry out accounting, billing, inventory control, and forecasting. Modern wholesalers are adapting their services to the needs of target customers and finding cost-reducing mehods of doing business.

Trends in Wholesaling

As the wholesaling industry moves into the twenty-first century, it faces considerable challenges. The industry remains vulnerable to one of the most enduring trends of the last decade—fierce resistance to price increases and the winnowing out of suppliers who are not adding value based on cost and quality. Progressive wholesalers constantly watch for better ways to meet the changing needs of their suppliers and target customers. They recognize that, in the long run, their only reason for existence comes from adding value by increasing the efficiency and effectiveness of the entire marketing channel. To achieve this goal, they must constantly improve their services and reduce their costs.

McKesson HBOC, North America's leading wholesaler of pharmaceuticals, health and beauty care, and home health care products, provides an example of progressive wholesaling. To survive, McKesson HBOC has to remain more cost-effective than manufacturers' sales branches. Thus, the company has built efficient, automated warehouses, established direct computer links with drug manufacturers, and set up extensive online supply management and accounts-receivable systems for customers. It offers retail pharmacists a wide range of online resources, including supply management assistance, catalogue searches, real-time order tracking, and account management systems. Retailers can even use the McKesson system to maintain medical profiles on their customers. McKesson's medical-surgical supply and equipment customers receive a rich assortment of online solutions and supply

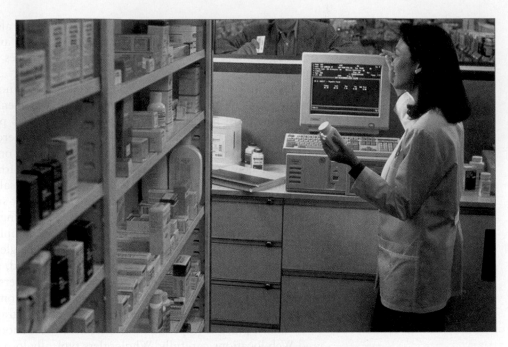

To improve efficiency and service, McKesson set up an extensive online supply management system by which customers can order, track, and manage their pharmaceutical and medical-surgical supplies. Retailers can even use the McKesson system to maintain medical profiles on their customers.

management tools, including an online order-management system and real-time information on products and pricing, inventory availability, and order status. According to McKesson, it adds value in the channel by providing "supply, information, and health care management products and services designed to reduce costs and improve quality across healthcare."[27]

The distinction between large retailers and large wholesalers continues to blur. Many retailers now operate formats, such as wholesale clubs and hypermarkets, that perform many wholesale functions. In return, many large wholesalers are setting up their own retailing operations. For example, SuperValu, North America's largest food wholesaling company, is also Canada's eleventh-largest food retailer. Almost half of the company's $26 billion in sales comes from its Bigg's, Cub Foods, Save-A-Lot, Farm Fresh, Hornbacher's, Laneco, Metro, Scott's Foods, Shop 'n Save, and Shoppers Food Warehouse stores.[28]

Wholesalers will continue to increase the services they provide to retailers—retail pricing, cooperative advertising, marketing and management information reports, accounting services, online transactions, and others. Rising costs on the one hand, and the demand for increased services on the other, will put the squeeze on wholesaler profits. Wholesalers who do not find efficient ways to deliver value to their customers will soon drop by the wayside. However, the increased use of computerized, automated, and Web-based systems will help wholesalers to contain the costs of ordering, shipping, and inventory holding, boosting their productivity.

Finally, facing slow growth in their domestic markets and such developments as the North American Free Trade Agreement, many large wholesalers are now going global. For example, in 1991, McKesson bought out its Canadian partner, Provigo. The company now receives about 3 percent of its total revenues from Canada. Its Information Solutions group operates widely throughout North America, the United Kingdom, and other European countries.

Reviewing the Concepts

In this chapter, we first looked at the nature and importance of retailing, major types of retailers, the decisions retailers make, and the future of retailing. We then examined these same topics for wholesalers. Although most retailing is conducted in retail stores, in recent years, non-store retailing has increased rapidly. In addition, although many retail stores are independently owned, an increasing number are now banding together under some form of corporate or contractual organization. Wholesalers, too, have experienced recent environmental changes, most notably mounting competitive pressures. They have faced new sources of competition, more demanding customers, new technologies, and more direct-buying programs on the part of large industrial, institutional, and retail buyers.

1. Explain the roles of retailers and wholesalers in the distribution channel.

Retailing and wholesaling consist of many organizations bringing goods and services from the point of production to the point of use. *Retailing* includes all activities involved in selling goods or services directly to final consumers for their personal, non-business use. *Wholesaling* includes all the activities involved in selling goods or services to those who are buying for the purpose of resale or for business use. Wholesalers perform many functions, including selling and promoting, buying and assortment building, bulk-breaking, warehousing, transporting, financing, risk bearing, supplying market information, and providing management services and advice.

2. Describe the major types of retailers and give examples of each.

Retailers can be classified as *store retailers* and *non-store retailers*. Although most goods and services are sold through stores, non-store retailing has been growing much faster than has store retailing. Store retailers can be further classified by the *amount of service* they provide (self-service, limited service, or full service), *product line sold* (specialty stores, department stores, supermarkets, convenience stores, superstores, and service businesses), and *relative prices* (discount stores and off-price retailers). Today, many retailers are banding together in corporate and contractual *retail organizations* (corporate chains, voluntary chains and retailer cooperatives, franchise organizations, and merchandising conglomerates).

3. Identify the major types of wholesalers and give examples of each.

Wholesalers fall into three groups. First, *merchant wholesalers* take possession of the goods. They include *full-service wholesalers* (wholesale merchants, industrial distributors) and *limited-service wholesalers* (cash-and-carry wholesalers, truck wholesalers, drop shippers, rack jobbers, producers' cooperatives, and mail-order wholesalers). Second, *brokers* and *agents* do not take possession of the goods but are paid a commission for aiding buying and selling. Finally, *manufacturers' sales branches and offices* are wholesaling operations conducted by non-wholesalers to bypass the wholesalers.

4. Explain the marketing decisions facing retailers and wholesalers.

Each retailer must make decisions about its target markets and positioning, product assortment and services, price, promotion, and place. Retailers need to choose target markets carefully and position themselves strongly. Today, wholesaling is holding its own in the economy. Progressive wholesalers are adapting their services to the needs of target customers and are seeking cost-reducing methods of doing business. Faced with slow growth in their domestic markets and developments such as the North American Free Trade Agreement, many large wholesalers are also now going global.

Reviewing the Key Terms

Agent   514
Broker   514
Category killer   498
Chain store   500
Convenience store   497
Department store   497
Discount store   498
Factory outlet   499
Franchise   501
Independent off-price retailer   499
Manufacturers' sales branches and offices   514
Merchant wholesaler   514

Off-price retailer   498
Retailer   495
Retailing   495
Shopping centre   507
Specialty store   496
Supermarket   497
Superstore   498
Warehouse club   499
Wheel-of-retailing concept   508
Wholesaler   513
Wholesaling   513

Discussing the Concepts

1. There are retailers and there are retailers. What are the four major characteristics used in the chapter to classify retailers? What are the seven major store retailer types? Give an example of each type. Why is it becoming harder to classify retailers according to the "pure" types presented in the chapter?

2. Retailing is a hotbed of entrepreneurial start-ups. Look at your local marketplace. Is there a small independent retailer that is holding its own against large national chains? Describe the things it has done well that have helped distinguish it from its larger competitors. Could this retailer itself grow into a major chain? Explain why or why not.

3. Explain why it is important for retailers to define their target markets and to decide how they will position

themselves in these markets. Give an example of a national specialty retailer who has done this well.

4. Consider this statement made by a retailing insider: "The mall represents a point in time in the evolution of retailing.... We are reaching the end of one era and entering something new." What is the "something new" that is being suggested? Where will Canadians be shopping if not at today's malls?

5. The chapter states that "the life cycle of new retail forms is getting shorter." What does this mean? Cite an example.

6. What is the primary challenge facing a wholesaler who wishes to remain a viable part of the marketing channel? Explain.

Applying the Concepts

1. Find a retail store "hangout" near campus, such as a coffee shop or bookstore, and visit it eight times (twice at 8 a.m., 12 noon, 4 p.m., and 10 p.m.) over the course of a week. On each visit record your observations regarding the number of people in the location, what they are doing, what they look like, how long they stay, and whether they are alone or with someone. Did you notice differences in patrons at different hours of the day? Did you see any repeat customers? What is the retailer doing to build community?

2. In a small group, discuss the pros and cons of locating an off-price retailer, such as Costco, in a power centre location?

3. Suppose that you are a manufacturer's agent for three lines of complementary women's apparel. Discuss what types of marketing mix decisions you will be making.

Focus on Technology

Retail site selection is a difficult job, and the consequences of a mistake can be very costly. However, new technology designed to assist marketers in retail location selection is becoming readily available. One site selection tool is MapInfo's AnySite. Its Canadian offices are located in Toronto. Says MapInfo: "Designed for both site selection analysts and executive decision makers, AnySite is the essential tool for leaders in the retail, hotel, restaurant, real estate, and financial services industries to analyze existing store locations and potential new sites. Dedicated to site selection, AnySite's features and functions are optimized to support the site selection process. [Use it to] create ring studies, drive-times, custom polygons. Analyze and report on multiple existing and potential sites. Easily create detailed, eye-opening market and demographic maps." Go to the MapInfo website (www.mapinfo.com), learn as much as you can, and answer the following questions:

1. What do you think of this technology?

2. Would this technology be helpful in making a site selection decision?

3. Is this a tool only for large retailers, or can smaller one- or two-location retailers afford and use this technology?

Focus on Ethics

Large discount stores and superstores can wield enormous power and have a significant impact on a local community. When a megaretailer, such as Wal-Mart, enters a town, especially a smaller one, it often drives nearby small retailers out of business and sends downtown business districts into a nosedive. Wal-Mart entered Canada in 1994, when it purchased 122 Woolco stores. Since that time, Wal-Mart has been the target of much criticism for its operations on issues ranging from its resistance to unionization to the contention that it drives small businesses out of operation (for example, see http://canadiandimension.com/articles/2005/05/01/26/). In contrast, a 2005 article in *Macleans* magazine noted, "Wal-Mart isn't engaged in a series of messy local zoning disputes. It's at war with a well-financed, well-organized opposition, determined to fight it on every front. From Los Angeles to the Saguenay, from Hartford, Conn., to Vancouver, a broad array of activist groups and unions have launched protests, lawsuits and ad campaigns, all aimed at discrediting Wal-Mart, halting its growth, and unionizing its workforce. Like most wars, it's about money and power, and the first casualty is truth. Because even after all the scrutiny and analysis of the Wal-Mart phenomenon, most of what we've been told—about worker abuse, destroyed small-town economies, crushed suppliers and greedy management—is wrong." You can find the full story at www.macleans.ca/topstories/business/article.jsp?content=20050725_109503_109503.

When criticized for driving small businesses out of operation, Wal-Mart's founder, Sam Walton, responded as follows: "Quite a few smaller stores have gone out of business during the time of Wal-Mart's growth. Some people have tried to turn it into this big controversy, sort of a 'Save the Small Town Merchants' deal, like they were whales or whooping cranes or something that has the right to be protected. Of all the notions I've heard about Wal-Mart, none has ever baffled me more than this idea that we are somehow the enemy of small-town America. Nothing could be further from the truth. Wal-Mart has actually kept quite a number of small towns from becoming extinct by saving literally billions of dollars for the people who live in them, as well as by creating hundreds of thousands of jobs in our stores. I believe millions of people are better off today than they would have been if Wal-Mart had never existed. I don't want to be too critical of small-town merchants, but the truth is that a lot of these folks just weren't doing a very good job of taking care of their customers. Whenever we put a Wal-Mart store into a town, customers would just flock to us from the variety stores. With our low prices, we ended an era of 45 percent markups and limited selection. We shut the door on variety-store thinking."*

1. Compare the arguments of the critics and the supporters of Wal-Mart. Which side do you support? Why?

2. When Wal-Mart entered Canada, many retail analysts predicted that many Canadian retailers would go out of business. Although some Canadian retailers, such as Zellers, have staggered, others, such as Canadian Tire and Loblaws, have prospered. Even small local retailers have often held their ground. Select a retailer from your local marketplace and describe how it has prospered despite competition from Wal-Mart.

*See www.emich.edu/public/geo/557book/c313.impactwalmart.html.

Video Case

Reebok

Today, Reebok is more than just aerobics shoes. The company sells everything from shoes and shorts to treadmills and sunglasses. To promote these products, Reebok infuses its fashions with pop culture. It's all part of an effort to position itself as an edgy, fresh company with products that appeal to young people. Reebok even developed a new brand, RBK, to better appeal to its newly defined target market. The goal? To reach young people before they establish a substantial preference for an athletic brand.

To reach these new consumers, Reebok builds programs with individual retailers, relying heavily on such partnerships to help differentiate the brand. Many of those partnerships include exclusive rights to carry particular Reebok products. So Footlocker and Sears, for example, carry different assortments of Reebok shoes and gear. As a result, Reebok and its retail part-

ners provide the continually evolving, fresh set of options that young consumers demand.

After viewing the video featuring Reebok, answer the following questions about retailing and whole-saling:

1. Visit Reebok's website and search for retailers near you. What types of retailers does Reebok rely on to sell its products? Are there any additional retailers with whom Reebok should consider working?

2. What consumers does Reebok target? How does the company reach these target consumers to build relationships?

3. Do you think that Reebok's chosen retail outlets are the most effective places to reach the company's targeted consumers?

Online Media Resources

Company Case

Sears: Visions of Grandeur?

Sears Canada, headquartered in Toronto, began its operations as Simpsons-Sears Limited, a catalogue retailer, in 1952. The company was formed as a joint venture between the Robert Simpson Company (Simpson's), an existing Canadian department store retailer, and Sears, Roebuck & Co. of the United States. By the 1970s, Sears was North America's largest retailer. Positioned as a middle-line retailer, between low-priced, discount houses and higher-end department stores, Sears was indeed where almost everyone shopped—especially for hardware and appliances.

Craftsman and Kenmore have consistently been among the most highly praised brand names in the country. North Americans still wash clothes and dishes with Kenmores, and mow lawns and drive nails with Craftsman. Reliance on the hard lines, however, has not allowed Sears to keep pace with the retailing scene.

The past thirty years have brought major changes to retailing. The most dramatic development was the explosion of Wal-Mart. Sam Walton's original idea was to rely on low prices, stand-alone stores, and locations in small towns that were underserved by the retailing system. To maintain growth, Wal-Mart eventually moved to larger towns and cities and began international operations, starting in Canada. Today, it dominates both North American and global retailing. Although Wal-Mart is a fierce competitor, it is not the primary source of Sears's market woes. Though Wal-Mart has undoubtedly siphoned off some of Sears's customers, the two retailers don't compete with each other on their individual strengths. Wal-Mart sells soft goods and Sears sells hardware. In some ways, they almost complement each other.

While Wal-Mart was gobbling up sales outside the mall, other retailers were changing their strategies within the mall. Canadian retailers, such as Reitmans and Boutique Jacob, practised careful target marketing and pinpoint product selection to meet the needs and tastes of their customers. The Bay and Zellers worked to improve customer service and product selection. U.S. retailer JC Penney, the company most closely resembling Sears in the 1970s, eliminated its hardware and appliance lines, beefed up soft goods—especially women's and children's clothing—and located *in* the mall, where 75 percent of women's clothing is sold.

Sears, in contrast, kept the appliances and hardware, tried to beef up the soft goods, and located stores both in and adjacent to malls. It also diversified into financial services. While other retailers focused on expanding their clothing lines and developing exciting in-store clothing sections, Sears spread itself too thin. From its beginnings 118 years ago, Sears always carried some women's clothing, household items, and toys at Christmas in order to make shopping a family experience. However, the predominant ambiance at Sears stores into the 1950s was that of a hardware store in which the tools and hard goods were the champs.

This image of a "hardware store" has been hard for Sears to change, and the retailer has not always shown a real willingness to do so. While saying that it would improve its clothing lines, and while signing contracts with Cheryl Tiegs and Stefani Powers, Sears left the position of women's fashion director unfilled for nine years. Even when new, more-upscale lines were introduced, they were displayed next to neon-flowered tops and stretch pants. Clothing racks were a mess—overcrowded, sloppy, and utilitarian. There was no organization within the women's clothing department. A shopper might find $20 sweaters next to $80 sweaters. If the two looked alike, guess which the consumer bought.

Not only were the clothing departments shabby and uninviting, there were not enough mirrors and dressing rooms—without which a store can't sell to women. Marketing research in the early 1990s showed that the woman who bought her clothes at Sears was almost 50, had an income of less than US$30 000, and was there to buy US$6.99 stretch pants. The company's 1990 ad slogan "You gotta be puttin' me on" admitted to the consumer that fashion had not been Sears's strength.

To change that, during the 1990s Sears threw out most of the cheap, polyester pants and brought in recognized brand lines, such as Chaus and Village. Unfortunately, all the merchandising problems persisted. Goods were jumbled together, there were not enough mirrors, and the departments were still shabby and uninviting. Ugly red signs remained in place to remind consumers that goods were "as advertised" or "on sale." The clean-up of Sears's image was not complete and the introduction of "the softer side of Sears" was not a success.

In 2002, to specifically address its fashion image shortcomings, Sears purchased Lands' End, a major U.S.-based catalogue company, for US$1.86 billion and immediately put Lands' End management in charge of Sears fashion apparel. Unfortunately, the two companies are quite dissimilar. Lands' End appealed largely to white baby boomers, and it sells mostly casual wear supplemented with some professional wear and prides itself on its "folksy" and helpful telephone operators. Contrast this with Sears's many layers of management and hodgepodge of bureaucracy. Sears executives dress for success and use the latest business jargon, while Lands' End managers ride bicycles to work and had little experience with in-store retailing. The end result was overstocks of Lands' End merchandise that had to be discounted at the end of the season.

The clash between the two groups emphasizes the difficulty that Sears faces in determining an appropriate positioning for the company. A major issue at Sears is this: Just who *is* the consumer? Not only is it difficult to determine who Sears' customers are, but it's also difficult to determine what Sears is. In the past twenty years, its financial business, especially the credit card operation, was so successful that some analysts dubbed Sears a financial company with a retail unit on the side. In late 2003, the U.S. arm of Sears sold its credit card operation to Citigroup. In 2005, Sears Canada Inc. put its credit card division up for sale, including both its Sears Card, which was the largest in-house proprietary retail credit card in Canada, and the Sears MasterCard, which boasted another 4 million accounts. The financial services division generated about $100 million in operating income in 2004, nearly two-fifths of Sears Canada's total operating profit. JPMorgan Chase Bank bought the division. The combined transactions left Sears free to concentrate on improving its retail operations and also generated some US$32 billion, which Sears can use to renovate stores. It also means that Sears *must* increase operating income from retail sales.

Sears has been working to improve on this front for more than ten years, but results have been mixed. In 1995, Sears Canada opened Sears Whole Home furniture stores located in power centres. In 1999, they were renamed Sears Furniture and Appliance stores to reflect the addition of major appliances. In 2003, the name was changed again to Sears Home stores in the hope that the brand would have broader appeal for customers seeking a one-stop experience for redoing their home décor. The stores' product lines were expanded to include floor coverings and customer drapery.

In 1998, Sears Canada's website, www.sears.ca, was activated. It featured only 500 products. By 2001, the website became Canada's most popular retail Internet destination, with more than a million orders placed that year. Today, the site gets more than 30 million visits annually, and it features more than 100 000 items, which are shipped free to 2200 pick-up locations in Canada. In 2005, Sears hired the services subsidiary of Amazon.com Inc. to provide "a more robust online shopping experience" at sears.ca. "This is a significant business initiative with aggressive growth opportunities and other long-term benefits and is planned with a substantial return on investment," according to Brent Hollister, president and CEO of Sears Canada. "It is important to us to incorporate Web features that make sears.ca as user friendly as today's technology allows," Hollister added. Sears will concentrate on its "core competencies including merchandising, marketing, fulfillment and customer service."

In 1999, Sears Canada acquired the bankrupt T. Eaton Company Limited. For the first time in its history, Sears Canada gained access to prime locations in Toronto (Eaton Centre and Yorkdale Mall), Vancouver (Pacific Centre), Victoria, Winnipeg, Ottawa, and Calgary. Despite its attempts to relaunch "eatons," the

operation was unsuccessful, and Sears converted the eatons stores to the Sears brand in 2002. Many said that the eatons stores were too upscale or too thinly scattered across the country for the mini-chain to have ever been profitable and worthwhile.

In addition to the above initiatives, Sears has also spent hundreds of millions of dollars to renovate stores. Sears may be seeing the light at the end of the tunnel. Though it continued to report operating losses in 2005, the picture looked rosier in 2006, and Sears reported stronger-than-anticipated second-quarter profit, attributed to less discounting and better cost control.

Sears knows, however, that the battle is far from over. The retail environment has changed forever, with more of the Canadian population shopping at big-box outlets or at speciality stores. This has put a squeeze on the middle market, which is the base of the traditional department store. Sears has also lost market share to Wal-Mart and category killers, such as Best Buy and Future Shop. It knows that it must find some means of competing with these retailers.

Questions for Discussion

1. List Sears's strengths and weaknesses, opportunities and threats. Then assess how well each of the changes in Sears's strategy will build on the strengths and will help it eliminate the weaknesses so that it can respond to its opportunities and threats.

2. Develop a positioning statement for the new Sears that would be broad enough to cover all the types of Sears retail operations.

3. Select a retailer you believe poses a threat to Sears Canada. Describe some tactics Sears could use to better meet the competitive challenges this retailer presents.

Sources: Michelle Halpern, "Sears to open three new retail concepts," *Marketing Magazine*, June 25, 2004; "Sears to sell off credit-card division," *Marketing Magazine*, June 14, 2005; "Sears Canada hires Amazon to redo online retail," *Marketing Magazine*, April 28, 2005; Marina Strauss, "Sears Canada shares hit 52-week high on results," *GlobeInvestor.com*, July 28, 2006; Francine Schwadel, "Fashion Statement: Its Earnings Sagging, Sears Upgrades Line of Women's Apparel," *Wall Street Journal*, May 9, 1990, p. A1; Amy Merrick, "New Outfit: Sears Orders Fashion Makeover From the Lands' End Catalog," *Wall Street Journal*, January 28, 2004, p. A1; Debbie Howell, "Retail Experiments in Cities Starting to Pay Off," *DSN Retailing Today*, August 2, 2004, p. 17–18.

CHAPTER 14
Integrated Marketing Communications Strategy

AFTER STUDYING THIS CHAPTER YOU SHOULD BE ABLE TO

1. name and define the tools of the marketing communications mix

2. discuss the process and advantages of integrated marketing communications

3. outline the steps in developing effective marketing communications

4. explain the methods for setting the marketing communications

budget and factors that affect the design of the marketing communications mix (also called the promotion mix)

Previewing the Concepts

In this and the next two chapters, we'll examine the last of the marketing mix tools—promotion. Promotion is not a single element but rather a mix of several tools. Ideally, under the concept of *integrated marketing communications,* the company will carefully coordinate these promotion elements to deliver a clear, consistent, and compelling message about the organization and its products. We'll begin by introducing you to the various promotion mix tools that marketers use to communicate with their key audiences. We'll discuss the importance of integrated marketing communications, the steps in developing marketing communication, and the promotion budgeting process. In the next two chapters, we'll visit the specific marketing communications tools.

To start, let's look at an award-winning integrated marketing communications campaign. BMW Group acquired the British-made MINI car brand in 2001, in an attempt to mimic the success of nostalgia-mobiles, such as the VW New Beetle and the PT Cruiser. However, hardly anyone in North America had even heard of the brand. It had been twenty years since it had been sold in Canada. And North America was a market apparently in love with large, powerful cars and SUVs. Thus, marketing the anything-but-ordinary car presented some big challenges for MINI and its ad agencies in both Canada and the United States. What's more, communications used in one market didn't always fit the needs of the other. But big challenges call for innovative solutions. Let's take a closer look.

The MINI was a dramatic departure from anything that North American car buyers had seen—it was potent but tiny (30 cm shorter than the new Beetle), and it had a funky two-tone, retro '60s look. To add to the challenge, BMW assigned the MINI unit a paltry marketing budget—less than half of what was used for the PT Cruiser introduction. In the face of these hurdles, how could the company get consumers interested in the quirky little MINI? The answer: with very creative integrated marketing and promotion campaigns. To help launch the new vehicle, MINI USA unit hired Crispin Porter + Bogusky (CP+B) as its ad agency. BMW Canada went with cheeky Toronto-based Taxi.

MINI USA and CP+B decided to position the diminutive MINI as an anything-but-ordinary kind of car. Rather than trying to mask the car's small size, the company featured it as a lifestyle choice, as a key part of the brand's personality. The MINI represented an alternative driving culture. "It was not just a car to get you here to there, but an experience, or a way of living," explains CP+B executive Jim Poh. The marketing team summarized the MINI brand experience under a simple campaign theme: "Let's Motor!" Whereas the major automakers typically relied on big-budget, mass-media campaigns, the MINI marketers ruled against these media from the start. Instead, they assembled a rich mix of unconventional media, carefully integrated to create personality for the car and a tremendous buzz of excitement among consumers. MINI's marketers discovered that the little car's physical presence elicits a stronger emotional reaction. They watched as people got their first glimpse of the car. "Almost always they smiled." As a result, the communications campaign focused on tactics that let consumers experience the car firsthand.

The American campaign was a huge success, developing a cult-like following for the personable little car. By the time the car was introduced in spring 2002, the buyer waiting list was approximately ten months long. Awareness jumped from 2 percent to 53 in just three years.

BMW Group Canada, based in Whitby, Ontario, is responsible for the marketing of the MINI in Canada. It carefully examined the tactics of the U.S. and European subsidiaries. It certainly learned from them. However, it was also convinced that it needed to carve out its own road with a unique campaign specifically designed for the Canadian marketplace. Neither the U.S. "Let's Motor" tagline nor the European "Is it love?" would accomplish the Canadian subsidiary's brand objectives.

Canadians tend to be serious about their cars. Research showed that they valued safety and suggested that SUVs weren't cool but that urban playthings were. However, Canadians like driving up to the cottage, for instance, and many drive on roads where snow tires are mandatory for half the year. Yet, the MINI would be the smallest vehicle on Canadian roads. Research also suggested that males would be the prime market for the car, and that they would not buy a car they perceived high in female attributes, like the VW Beetle. The MINI had to be a sexy little car that avoided the deathtrap of "cute and trendy." Could MINI cut it?

The marketing team quickly concluded that the car's performance was the main attribute to stress. Kevin Marcotte, corporate communications manager for BMW Canada noted, "The original MINI was a performance car, with the wheels at the corner and low centre of gravity and ability to handle like a go-kart. The new MINI is very much the same, but it has the BMW DNA. Moreover, the German engineering adds a degree of seriousness to the car.".

To communicate the new MINI's personality to the Canadian marketplace, BMW chose Taxi as its agency. Taxi prides itself on its creativity, results-driven integrated approach and ability to tell compelling stories across all media. The first thing MINI did in the spring of 2001 was send Taxi's creative team off to Munich to test drive the car and learn the "brand pillars" that would be the heart of the long-term brand strategy in Canada. Mini's character was seen as an individualistic, high-performance, premium vehicle that's fun to drive. The agency was also given a MINI for the boardroom. People working on the account could be intimately acquainted with the car and see other's reactions to it first hand.

In designing its integrated marketing campaign, Taxi began the MINI launch with a "teaser" campaign to prepare consumers for later messaging. Nontraditional outdoor advertising media was used. For example, people at a busy Toronto intersection saw a MINI in a zoo-like cage, labelled only with the words: "Please do not feed, tease or annoy the MINI."

Though Taxi built on ideas used in other markets, the communications it designed were edgier. It decided not to use a single tag line as had been done in the U.S. or Europe. Instead Taxi developed a series of print ads that focused on the car's performance in a quirky and off-beat way. The campaign kicked off with a 60-second movie theatre spot, called "Anthem." Showing a firecracker and a hand lighting it, a regular-size boxer who defeats a much larger opponent, and a guy eating a small hot pepper that causes him to scream, Taxi brought home the message that "Size is deceptive."

Traditional print and outdoor advertising followed next, using lines such as "Parks faster than a Ferarri," "Onramps are foreplay," and "The world is your go-kart track." The cheeky ads were placed everywhere, from washroom doors to the classified sections of local newspapers. Edgy and humorous TV spots were also used. In the now-infamous threesome spot, two amorous girls and a guy show just how much room the MINI offered. As Zak Mroueh, co-creative director at Taxi says, "The execution can be shocking, but the message is simple: MINI is a potent little package." In another award-winning spot, called "Speeding Ticket," a policeman is shown stopping a MINI and negotiating with the driver to let him drive the car. The tag line: "$24 950 before speeding tickets."

Advertising was only one component of an ongoing communications effort. Like its American counterparts, BMW Canada knew people had to see and experience the car firsthand. As a BMW Canada insider noted, "Once they sit in a MINI, performance is what they remember." Thus, a number of events were staged. "Velocity" parties featuring such Canadian recording artists as the New Deal were held in Vancouver, Montreal, and Toronto. Celebrities, buyers of the MINI Cooper launch edition, retailers, and radio promo winners were invited. An online contest was developed at www.mini.ca, where people could win a place on the guest list. MINI street teams hit the streets, stopping at clubs, restaurants, movie theatres, concerts, and sporting events to hand out Velocity promotional materials and encourage online registration. The advertising and launch parties drove an unprecedented ten-fold increase in visitors to the website.

Driving events were also featured at auto shows across the country. One allowed people to run a slalom course accompanied by a professional driver at the Winter Driving Challenge at Mount Tremblant, Quebec.

Hip, downtown dealerships were carefully selected. They were trained in a new soft-sell approach designed to appeal to clientele used to boutique shopping. Investments in showroom improvement were also made.

Product placement was another innovative tool used by MINI. The international marketing team gave the producers of the 2003 remake of *The Italian Job*, thirty MINIs to use as they liked. The result—the MINI ended up featured as the vehicle the heroes used as their getaway wheels. *The Italian Job* was also the inspiration behind a $15 million ride that opened in the spring of 2005 at Paramount Canada's Wonderland—a venue that draws more than 3 million visitors a year.

Online marketing continues to drive MINI sales. The recent "speed & safety scenario simulator" at www.mini.ca uses text-to-speech recognition software to encourage visitors to "experience" the power of the MINI. The simulator plays a MINI-driving scenario customized with the user's input. At the end of the simulation, people are encouraged to visit a dealer to experience the real thing. They can also send the simulation on to friends.

Generating publicity has also been a cost-effective and powerful tool in MINI's communication portfolio. The launch caught the eye of journalists right from the start. Today, as one MINI marketer noted, "It's still a highly sought-after car and a highly newsworthy car from a PR perspective." The annual launch of new versions of the car, such as the MINI convertible, kept the stories flowing.

Finally, word of mouth has been one of MINI's best friends. MINI owners have become brand advocates. "The MINI is unique in that it creates a sense of community," says MINI's communication manager. "To see ... parking lots filled with MINIs of all different colours and combinations and accessories and have all the owners ... together, it really showed the pride and passion that people have for their cars."

From 2001 until today, the campaign has been a huge success, both for MINI and for Taxi. Annual sales goals have been exceeded. Taxi's work not only won it major awards from Cannes to the Clios, but it also helped the agency win new business overseas.

Whether in Canada, the U.S., or other markets around the world, the MINI communications campaigns have been impressive both for what they *did do* and for what they *don't do*. First, they got a lot of mileage out of a modest budget. Second, they used a dazzling array of unconventional media and tactics to create innovative customer experiences with the MINI brand. Equally impressive, they carefully integrated this rich variety of unusual media to create a unified brand personality suited specifically to their own country market. Whether it's an outdoor ad, an airport display, or the website, each message had the same distinctive MINI look and feel. "Every consumer 'touchpoint' conveys the same message as the ad campaign," says one advertising analyst. "The campaign[s] fit the brand personality perfectly," says another.[1]

Marketing communications mix (promotion mix)
The specific mix of advertising, personal selling, sales promotion, and public relations a company uses.

Advertising
Any paid form of nonpersonal presentation and promotion of ideas, goods, or services by an identified sponsor.

Sales promotion
Short-term incentives to encourage the purchase or sale of a product or service.

Public relations
Building good relations with the company's various publics by obtaining favourable publicity, building up a good "corporate image," and handling or heading off unfavourable rumours, stories, and events.

In addition to developing a good product, pricing it attractively, and making it available to target customers, companies must also *communicate* with current and prospective customers. What they communicate should not be left to chance. All of their communications efforts must be blended into a consistent and coordinated communications program. Good communication is a crucial element in a company's efforts to build profitable customer relationships.

The Marketing Communications Mix

A company's total **marketing communications mix**—also called its **promotion mix**—consists of the specific blend of advertising, sales promotion, public relations, personal selling, and direct-marketing tools that the company uses to pursue its advertising and marketing objectives. Definitions of the five major promotion tools follow:[2]

- **Advertising:** Any paid form of nonpersonal presentation and promotion of ideas, goods, or services by an identified sponsor.
- **Sales promotion:** Short-term incentives to encourage the purchase or sale of a product or service.
- **Public relations:** Building good relations with the company's various publics by obtaining favourable publicity, building up a good corporate image, and handling or heading off unfavourable rumours, stories, and events.

Personal selling
Personal presentation by the firm's sales force for the purpose of making sales and building customer relationships.

Direct marketing
Direct communications with carefully targeted individual consumers—the use of telephone, mail, fax, email, the Internet, and other tools to communicate directly with specific consumers.

- **Personal selling:** Personal presentation by the firm's sales force for the purpose of making sales and building customer relationships.
- **Direct marketing:** Direct connections with carefully targeted individual consumers to both obtain an immediate response and cultivate lasting customer relationships—the use of telephone, mail, fax, email, the Internet, and other tools to communicate directly with specific consumers.

Each category involves specific tools. For example, advertising includes print, broadcast, Internet, outdoor, and other forms. Sales promotion includes point-of-purchase displays, premiums, discounts, coupons, specialty advertising, and demonstrations. Public relations includes press releases, sponsorships, and special events. Personal selling includes sales presentations, trade shows, and incentive programs. Direct marketing includes catalogues, telephone marketing, kiosks, the Internet, and more. Thanks to technological breakthroughs, people can now communicate through a wide variety of media, including newspapers, radio, telephone, television, fax, cellphones, and the Internet.

At the same time, communication goes beyond these specific promotion tools. The product's design, its price, the design of its package, and the stores that sell it *all* communicate something to buyers. Thus, although the promotion mix is the company's primary communication activity, the entire marketing mix—promotion *and* product, price, and place—must be coordinated for greatest communication impact.

In this chapter, we begin by examining the rapidly changing marketing communications environment, the concept of integrated marketing communications, and the marketing communication process. Next, we discuss the factors that marketers must consider in shaping an overall communication strategy. We then summarize the legal, ethical, and social responsibility issues in marketing communications. In Chapter 15, we look at *mass-communication tools*—advertising, sales promotion, and public relations. Finally, Chapter 16 examines the *sales force* and *direct marketing* as communication and promotion tools.

Integrated Marketing Communications

During the past several decades, companies around the world have perfected the art of mass marketing—selling highly standardized products to masses of consumers. In the process, they have developed effective mass-media advertising techniques to support their mass-marketing strategies. These companies routinely invest millions of dollars in the mass media, reaching tens of millions of customers with a single ad. However, as we move further into the twenty-first century, marketing managers face some new and challenging marketing communications realities.

The Changing Communications Environment

Two major factors are changing the face of today's marketing communications. First, as mass markets have fragmented, marketers are shifting away from mass marketing. More and more, they are developing focused marketing programs designed to build closer relationships with consumers in more narrowly defined micromarkets. Second, vast improvements in information technology are speeding the movement toward segmented marketing. Today's information technology helps marketers to keep closer track of consumer needs—more information about consumers at the individual and household levels is available than ever before. New technologies also provide new communications avenues for reaching smaller market segments with more-tailored messages.

The shift from mass marketing to segmented marketing has had a dramatic impact on marketing communications. Just as mass marketing gave rise to a new generation of mass-media communications, the shift toward one-to-one marketing is spawning a new generation of more specialized and highly targeted communications efforts.

Given this new communications environment, marketers must rethink the roles of various media and promotion mix tools. Mass-media advertising has long dominated the promotion mixes of consumer product companies. However, although television, magazines, and other mass media remain very important, their dominance is now declining. *Market* fragmentation has resulted in *media* fragmentation—in an explosion of more focused media that better match today's targeting strategies. Beyond the traditional mass-media channels, advertisers are making increased use of new, highly targeted media, ranging from highly focused specialty magazines and cable television channels to Internet catalogues and Web coupon promotions, from airport kiosks to floor decals in supermarket aisles. In all, companies are doing less *broadcasting* and more *narrowcasting*.

The Need for Integrated Marketing Communications

The shift from mass marketing to targeted marketing, and the corresponding use of a larger, richer mix of communication channels and promotion tools, poses a problem for marketers. Consumers don't distinguish between message sources the way marketers do. In the consumer's mind, advertising messages from different media and different promotional approaches all become part of a single message about the company or product. Conflicting messages from these different sources can result in confused images and brand positions.

The relatively few mass magazines of past decades have been replaced by thousands of magazines targeting special-interest audiences. Rogers Publishing alone publishes nine English titles, four French titles, and one specialty trade publication, ranging from *Flare* and *Lou Lou* to *Maclean's* and *Canadian Business*.

All too often, companies fail to integrate their various communications channels. The result is a hodgepodge of communications to consumers. Mass-media advertisements say one thing, while a price promotion sends a different signal, and a product label creates still another message. Company sales literature says something altogether different and the company's website seems out of sync with everything else.

The problem is that often these communications come from different company sources. Advertising messages are planned and implemented by the advertising department or advertising agency. Personal selling communications are developed by sales management. Other functional specialists may be responsible for public relations, sales promotion, direct marketing, websites, and other forms of marketing communications.

Recently, such functional separation has been a major problem for companies and their Internet communications. Many companies first organized their new Web and other digital communications operations into separate groups or divisions, isolating them from mainstream marketing activities. However, whereas some companies have compartmentalized the new communications tools, consumers won't. According to one integrated communications expert:[3]

> The truth is, most [consumers] won't compartmentalize their use of the new systems. They won't say, "Hey, I'm going off to do a bit of Web surfing. Burn my TV, throw out all my radios, cancel all my magazine subscriptions and, by the way, take out my telephone and don't deliver any mail anymore." It's not that kind of world for consumers, and it shouldn't be that kind of world for marketers either.

Thus, if treated as a special case, the Internet—or any other marketing communication tool—can be a *dis*integrating force in marketing communications. Instead, all the communication tools must be carefully integrated into the broader marketing communications mix. Today, the best bet is to wed the emotional pitch and

Today, all the marketing communication tools must be carefully integrated. For example, this Jeep print ad points consumers to the company's website, where serious car buyers build and price a model, find a dealer online, and learn more about "the Jeep life."

impact of traditional brand marketing with the interactivity and real service offered online. For example, print and television ads for Jeep build consumer preference for the brand. But the ads also point viewers to the company's website, which offers lots of help and very little hype. The site helps serious car buyers build and price a model, find a dealer online, and learn more about "the Jeep life."

In the past, in many organizations, no one person or department was responsible for thinking through the communication roles of the various promotion tools and coordinating the promotion mix. Today, however, more companies are adopting the concept of **integrated marketing communications (IMC)**. Under this concept, as illustrated in Figure 14.1, corporate brand managers carefully integrate and coordinate the many communications channels to deliver a clear, consistent, and compelling message about the organization as a whole, while individual brand managers undertake this task for each product, service, or category. For example, Bell Canada Enterprises is a corporate brand whose reputation must be carefully managed. Bell ExpressVu and Bell Mobility are service brands owned by the corporation. Not only must their images be aligned with that of the corporation, but they must also carve out a distinct position in their respective marketplaces.[4]

Whether at the corporate or product level, IMC builds brand identity and strong customer relationships by tying together all of the company's messages and images. Brand messages and positioning are coordinated across all communication activities and media. IMC means that the company's advertising and personal selling communications have the same message, look, and feel as its website. And its public relations materials say the same thing as its direct mail campaign.[5]

IMC calls for recognizing all contact points where the customer may encounter the company, its products, and its brands. Each *brand contact* will deliver a message, whether good, bad, or indifferent. The company must strive to deliver a consistent and positive message with each contact. To help implement integrated marketing communications, some companies appoint a marketing communications director who has overall responsibility for the company's communications efforts.

Integrated marketing communications produces better communications consistency and greater sales impact. It places the responsibility in someone's hands—where none may have existed before—to unify the company's image as it is shaped by thousands of company activities. It leads to a total marketing communication strategy aimed at showing how the company and its products can help consumers solve their problems.

Integrated marketing communications (IMC)

The concept under which a company carefully integrates and coordinates its many communications channels to deliver a clear, consistent, and compelling message about the organization and its products.

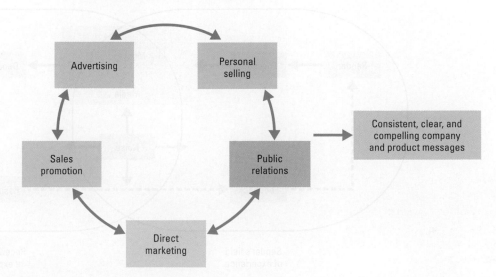

Figure 14.1 Integrated marketing communications

A View of the Communication Process

Integrated marketing communications involves identifying the target audience and shaping a well-coordinated promotional program to obtain the desired audience response. Too often, marketing communications focus on immediate awareness, image, or preference goals in the target market. But this approach to communication is too shortsighted. Today, marketers are moving toward viewing communications as *managing the customer relationship over time*.

Because consumers differ, communications programs need to be developed for specific segments, niches, and even individuals. And, given the new interactive communications technologies, companies must ask not only, "How can we reach our customers?" but also, "How can we find ways to let our customers reach us?"

Thus, the communications process should start with an audit of all the potential contacts that target customers may have with the company and its brands. For example, someone purchasing a new kitchen appliance may talk to others, see television ads, read articles and ads in newspapers and magazines, visit various websites, and check out appliances in one or more stores. The marketer needs to assess what influence each of these communications experiences will have at different stages of the buying process. This understanding will help marketers allocate their communication dollars more efficiently and effectively.

To communicate effectively, marketers need to understand how communication works. Communication involves the nine elements shown in Figure 14.2. Two of these elements are the major parties in a communication—the *sender* and the *receiver*. Another two are the major communication tools—the *message* and the *media*. Four more are major communication functions—*encoding, decoding, response,* and *feedback*. The last element is *noise* in the system. Definitions of these elements follow and are applied to an ad for a Dell Notebook computer.

- *Sender:* The *party sending the message* to another party—here, Dell.
- *Encoding:* The process of *putting thought into symbolic form*—Dell's advertising agency assembles words and illustrations into an advertisement that will convey the intended message.
- *Message:* The *set of symbols* that the sender transmits—the actual Dell Notebook ad.

Figure 14.2 Elements in the communication process

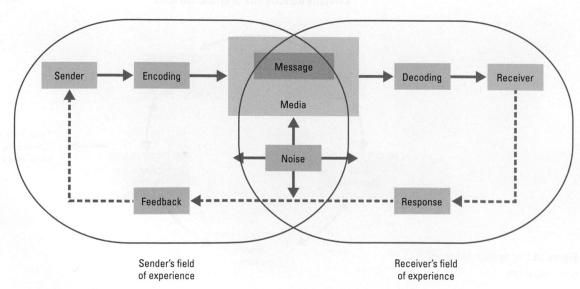

Sender's field
of experience

Receiver's field
of experience

- *Media:* The *communication channels* through which the message moves from sender to receiver—in this case, the specific magazines, TV stations, and other media that Dell selects.

- *Decoding:* The process by which the receiver *assigns meaning to the symbols* encoded by the sender—a consumer sees the Dell Notebook ad and interprets the messages it contains.

- *Receiver:* The *party receiving the message* sent by another party—the home or business customer who sees the Dell Notebook ad.

- *Response:* The *reactions of the receiver* after being exposed to the message—any of hundreds of possible responses, such as the consumer being more aware of the attributes of Dell Notebooks, actually buying a Dell Notebook, or doing nothing.

- *Feedback:* The part of the *receiver's response communicated back to the sender*—Dell's research shows that consumers are struck by and remember the ad, or consumers write or call Dell praising or criticizing the ad or Dell's products.

- *Noise:* The *unplanned static or distortion* during the communication process, which results in the receiver's getting a different message than the one the sender sent—for example, the consumer is distracted while reading the magazine and misses the Dell ad or its key points.

For a message to be effective, the sender's encoding process must mesh with the receiver's decoding process. Thus, the best messages consist of words and other symbols that are familiar to the receiver. The more the sender's field of experience overlaps with that of the receiver, the more effective the message is likely to be. Marketing communicators may not always *share* their consumers' field of experience. For example, an advertising copywriter from one social stratum might create ads for consumers from another stratum—say, wealthy business owners. However, to communicate effectively, the marketing communicator must *understand* the consumers' field of experience.

This model points out several key factors in good communication. Senders need to know what audiences they wish to reach and what responses they want. They must be good at encoding messages that take into account how the target audience decodes them. They must send messages through media that reach target audiences, and they must develop feedback channels so that they can assess the audience's response to the message.

Steps in Developing Effective Communication

We now examine the steps in developing an effective integrated communications and promotion program. The marketing communicator must do the following: *Identify the target audience, determine the communication objectives, design a message, choose the media through which to send the message, select the message source,* and *collect feedback.*

Identifying the Target Audience

A marketing communicator starts with a clear target audience in mind. The audience may be potential buyers or current users, those who make the buying decision or those who influence it. The audience may be individuals, groups, special publics, or the general public. The target audience will heavily affect the communicator's decisions on *what* will be said, *how* it will be said, *when* it will be said, *where* it will be said, and *who* will say it.

Determining the Communication Objectives

Once the target audience has been defined, the marketing communicator must decide what response is sought. Of course, in many cases, the final response is *purchase*. But purchase is the result of a long process of consumer decision making. The marketing communicator needs to know where the target audience now stands and to what stage it needs to be moved. The target audience may be in any of six **buyer-readiness stages**, the stages consumers normally pass through on their way to making a purchase. These stages include *awareness*, *knowledge*, *liking*, *preference*, *conviction*, and *purchase* (see Figure 14.3).

Buyer-readiness stages
The stages consumers normally pass through on their way to purchase, including awareness, knowledge, liking, preference, conviction, and purchase.

The marketing communicator's target market may be totally unaware of the product, know only its name, or know only a few things about it. The communicator must first build *awareness* and *knowledge*. For example, when Nissan introduced its Infiniti automobile line, it began with an extensive "teaser" advertising campaign to create name familiarity. Initial ads for the Infiniti created curiosity and awareness by showing the car's name but not the car. Later ads created knowledge by informing potential buyers of the car's high quality and its many innovative features. Chrysler recently ran similar teaser ads when introducing its new Chrysler 300 model.

Assuming that target consumers *know* about the product, how do they *feel* about it? Once potential buyers knew about the Infiniti, Nissan's marketers wanted to move them through successively stronger stages of feelings toward the car. These stages included *liking* (feeling favourable about the Infiniti), *preference* (preferring Infiniti to other car brands), and *conviction* (believing that Infiniti is the best car for them). Infiniti marketers used a combination of the promotion mix tools to create positive feelings and conviction. Advertising extolled the Infiniti's advantages over competing brands and established its "Accelerating the Future" positioning. Press releases and other public relations activities stressed the car's innovative features and performance. Dealer salespeople told buyers about options, value for the price, and after-sale service.

Finally, some members of the target market might be convinced about the product but may not quite get around to making the *purchase*. Potential Infiniti buyers might have decided to wait for more information or for the economy to improve. The communicator must lead these consumers to take the final step. Actions might include offering special promotional prices, rebates, or premiums. Salespeople might call or write to selected customers, inviting them to visit the dealership for a special showing. The Infiniti website (www.infiniti.ca) tells potential buyers that they are "Exceeding your every expectation. Always." They provide information regarding the various models, financing options, and invites them to visit a local dealer's showroom for a "Guest Drive."

Figure 14.3 Buyer-readiness stages

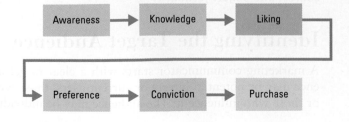

Chrysler used teaser ads to create initial curiosity and awareness for its new Chrysler 300 model.

Of course, marketing communications alone cannot create positive feelings and purchases for Infiniti. The car itself must provide superior value for the customer. In fact, outstanding marketing communications can actually speed the demise of a poor product. The more quickly potential buyers learn about the poor product, the more quickly they become aware of its faults. Thus, good marketing communication calls for "good deeds followed by good words."

Designing a Message

Having defined the desired audience response, the communicator turns to developing an effective message. Ideally, the message should get *Attention*, hold *Interest*, arouse *Desire*, and obtain *Action* (a framework known as the *AIDA model*). In practice, few messages take the consumer all the way from awareness to purchase, but the AIDA framework suggests the desirable qualities of a good message.

In putting the message together, the marketing communicator must decide what to say (*message content*) and how to say it (*message structure* and *format*).

Message Content

The communicator has to figure out an appeal or theme that will produce the desired response. There are three types of appeals: rational, emotional, and moral. *Rational appeals* relate to the audience's self-interest. They show that the product will produce the desired benefits. Examples are messages showing a product's quality, economy, value, or performance. Thus, in its ads, Mercedes offers automobiles that are "engineered like no other car in the world," stressing engineering design, performance, and safety.

Emotional appeals attempt to stir up either negative or positive emotions that can motivate purchase. Communicators may use positive emotional appeals, such as love, pride, joy, and humour. For example, advocates for humorous messages claim that they attract more attention and create more liking and belief in the sponsor. Take a recent campaign by Becel:[6]

Unilever Canada broke with tradition in 2006 when it launched its new "Win a $20 000 Heart Health Makeover" campaign for Becel margarine. Using a 30-second TV spot and a online two-minute video, the company used humour and a contest to bring home its message. For almost 30 years, Becel's main message is how Becel can help people look after their heart health. This is certainly a serious topic. However, as the new campaign's co-creative director, Nancy Vonk, noted, "We've tried to handle it in a not-too-serious way, because if you get too heavy duty, it can be a big downer and you sound like you're nagging." The new ad, called "Stuck," features two people who find themselves suddenly "trapped" on an escalator that breaks down. Crying out, they ask others for help, emphasizing in a hilarious way that some people need a "heart health makeover." Since Becel had never taken this tack before or done a contest, there was considerable discussion as to whether this approach was appropriate, says Vonk. Viewers were also encouraged to enter a contest at becel.ca to win one of three health makeovers that included consultations with a personal dietician, life coach, and trainer, free groceries for a year, a $5000 gift certificate for Fitness Depot, and a getaway for two to the Willowstream Spa at Fairmont Banff Springs Hotel. Visitors to the website are also encouraged to forward the video to friends.

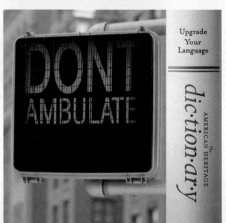

Humour in advertising: These days, it seems as though almost every company is using humour in its advertising, even the scholarly American Heritage Dictionary.

Properly used, humour can capture attention, make people feel good, and give a brand personality. However, advertisers must be careful when using humour. Used poorly, it can detract from comprehension, wear out its welcome fast, overshadow the product, or even irritate consumers. For example, many ads for breweries have been criticized for their use of sexist and "toilet bowl" humour that insulted viewers' intelligence. Critics and consumers complain that such ads showed that brands like Budweiser were "reaching for the lowest common denominator in commercials aimed at the most frequent beer drinkers—men from 21 to 25 years old—resulting in a race to the bottom to

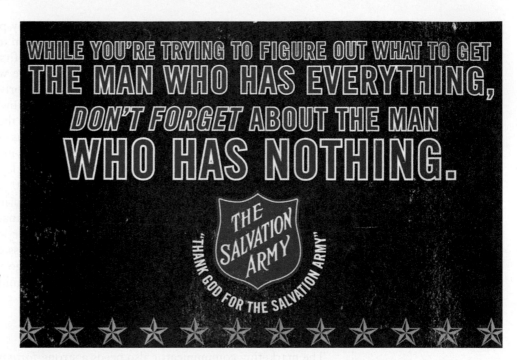

Moral appeals: The Salvation Army says "While you're trying to figure out what to get the man who has everything, don't forget the man who has nothing."

fill commercials with bathroom humor, double entendres, crude sight gags and vulgarisms."[7]

Communicators can also use negative emotional appeals, such as fear, guilt, and shame, that get people to do things they should (brush their teeth, buy new tires) or to stop doing things they shouldn't (smoke, drink too much, eat unhealthy foods). For example, a Crest ad invokes mild fear when it claims, "There are some things you just can't afford to gamble with" (cavities). And Etonic ads ask, "What would you do if you couldn't run?" They go on to note that Etonic athletic shoes are designed to avoid injuries—they're "built so you can last."

Moral appeals are directed to the audience's sense of what is "right" and "proper." They are often used to urge people to support social causes, such as a cleaner environment, better race relations, equal rights for women, and aid to the disadvantaged. An example of a moral appeal is the Salvation Army's "While you're trying to figure out what to get the man who has everything, don't forget the man who has nothing."

Message Structure

The communicator must also decide how to handle three message structure issues. The first is whether to draw a conclusion or leave it to the audience. Recent research suggests that in many cases, rather than drawing a conclusion, the advertiser is better off asking questions and letting buyers come to their own conclusions. The second message structure issue is whether to present the strongest arguments first or last. Presenting them first gets strong attention but may lead to an anticlimactic ending. The third message structure issue is whether to present a one-sided argument (mentioning only the product's strengths) or a two-sided argument (touting the product's strengths while also admitting its shortcomings). Usually, a one-sided argument is more effective in sales presentations—except when audiences are highly educated or likely to hear opposing claims, or when the communicator has a negative association to overcome. In this spirit, Heinz ran the message "Heinz Ketchup is slow good" and Buckley's Mixture built its entire business around "It tastes awful. And it works."[8]

Buckley's Mixture was first developed in 1919 by pharmacist W.K. Buckley in his Toronto drugstore. W.K. was a pioneer, not only in terms of developing a highly effective product, but also because he was one of the first to recognize the power of catchy copy. He used both print and radio at a time when advertising, especially radio advertising, was a relatively new and poorly understood phenomenon. Advertising made the product a hit, despite its taste. In fact, as the years rolled on, Buckley's advertising stuck consistently with two core themes based on the product's key characteristics: its terrible taste and its tremendous efficacy. Using these two differentiating points, Buckley's produced the award-winning advertising that made Buckley's Mixture a household name in Canada. Buckley's Mixture is the top-selling cough syrup in Canada by volume, commanding a 10 percent share of the market. The "bad taste" campaign also solidified its position in the Caribbean, Australia, New Zealand, and the United States. If, like other Canadians, you regard Buckley's as part of your Canadian heritage, you can win a role in a Buckley's advertisement in their recent "Bad Face tour." Canadians from across the country are having their faces video taped as they taste the mixture. You can go to the company's website at www.buckleys.com and vote for your favourite, winning a $1 off coupon in the process.

Message Format

The marketing communicator also needs a strong *format* for the message. In a print ad, the communicator has to decide on the headline, copy, illustration, and colour. To attract attention, advertisers can use novelty and contrast; eye-catching pictures and headlines; distinctive formats; message size and position; and colour, shape, and movement. If the message is to be carried over the radio, the communicator has to

Buckley's Mixture has won world renown by using a simple and humorous two-sided advertising message—"It tastes awful. And it works."

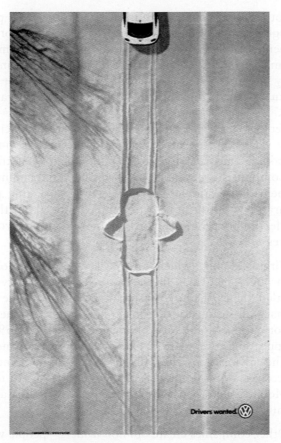

To attract attention, advertisers can use novelty and contrast, eye-catching pictures and headlines, and distinctive formats, as in this Volkswagen New Beetle ad.

choose words, sounds, and voices. The "sound" of an announcer promoting banking services should be different from one promoting quality furniture.

If the message is to be carried on television or in person, then all these elements plus body language have to be planned. Presenters plan their facial expressions, gestures, dress, posture, and hairstyles. If the message is carried on the product or its package, the communicator has to watch texture, scent, colour, size, and shape. For example, age and other demographics affect the way in which consumers perceive and react to colour. Here are examples:

> How do you sell margarine—stodgy, wholesome margarine—to today's kids? One answer: colour. "We knew we wanted to introduce a colour product. It's been a big trend with kids since the blue M&M," says a Parkay spokesperson. So Parkay tried out margarine in blue, pink, green, and purple. "When we tested four different colours in focus groups, kids had a blast." Electric blue and shocking pink margarine emerged as clear favourites.
>
> In contrast, as we get older, our eyes mature and our vision takes on a yellow cast. Colour looks less bright to older people, so they gravitate to white and other bright tones. A recent survey found 10 percent of people 55 years and older want the brightness of a white car, compared with 4 percent of 21- to 34-year-olds and 2 percent of teens. Lexus, which skews toward older buyers, makes sure that 60 percent of its cars are light in colour.[9]

Thus, in designing effective marketing communications, marketers must consider colour and other seemingly unimportant details carefully.

Choosing Media

The communicator now must select *channels of communication*. There are two broad types of communication channels—*personal* and *nonpersonal*.

Personal Communication Channels

Personal communication channels

Channels through which two or more people communicate directly with each other, including face to face, person to audience, over the telephone, or through the mail.

In **personal communication channels**, two or more people communicate directly with each other. They might communicate face to face, over the telephone, through the mail, or even through an Internet "chat." Personal communication channels are effective because they allow for personal addressing and feedback.

Some personal communication channels are controlled directly by the company. For example, company salespeople contact buyers in the target market.

Word-of-mouth influence
Personal communication about a product between target buyers and neighbours, friends, family members, and associates.

Buzz marketing
Cultivating opinion leaders and getting them to spread information about a product or service to others in their communities.

Nonpersonal communication channels
Media that carry messages without personal contact or feedback, including major media, atmospheres, and events.

But other personal communications about the product may reach buyers through channels not directly controlled by the company. These might include independent experts—consumer advocates, consumer buying guides, and others—making statements to target buyers. Or they might be neighbours, friends, family members, and associates talking to target buyers. This last channel, known as **word-of-mouth influence**, has considerable effect in many product areas.

Personal influence carries great weight for products that are expensive, risky, or highly visible. For example, buyers of automobiles and major appliances often go beyond mass-media sources to seek the opinions of knowledgeable people.

Companies can take steps to put personal communication channels to work for them. For example, they can create marketing programs that will generate favourable word-of-mouth communications about their brands. See what Virgin Mobile did to promote word of mouth among young consumers of wireless services:

Virgin Mobile, which targets 16- to 24-year-olds, stokes word of mouth through creative ad messages for its wireless service. One 30-second TV spot, titled "Share the Love" campaign, opens with the view of a car's back window that's all steamed up. In the condensation are the words: "Hello lovers: Get a hot Virgin Mobile cell phone for as low as $59." A kissing sound and the appearance of a woman's foot thrust out the window suggest backseat action. The ad mentions that anyone who gets a friend to sign up for the service receives a $20 bonus. Word of mouth is key to this campaign, suggest Virgin Mobile's chief marketing executive. "Kids this age still find out about most things through their friends," he says.[10]

Other companies create *opinion leaders*—people whose opinions are sought by others—by supplying the influencer with the product on attractive terms or by educating them so that they can inform others. **Buzz marketing** involves cultivating opinion leaders and getting them to spread information about a product or service to others in their communities (see Real Marketing 14.1).

Nonpersonal Communication Channels

Nonpersonal communication channels are media that carry messages without personal contact or feedback. They include major media, atmospheres, and events. Major *media* include print media (newspapers, magazines, direct mail), broadcast media (radio, television), display media (billboards, signs, posters), and online media (email, websites). *Atmospheres* are designed environments that create or reinforce the buyer's leanings toward buying a product. Thus, lawyers' offices and banks are designed to communicate confidence and other qualities that might be valued by their clients. *Events* are staged occurrences that communicate messages to target audiences. For example, public relations departments arrange press conferences, grand openings, shows and exhibits, public tours, and other events.

Nonpersonal communication affects buyers directly. In addition, using mass media often affects buyers indirectly by causing more personal communication. Communications first flow from television, magazines, and other mass media to opinion leaders and then from these opinion leaders to others. Thus, opinion leaders step between the mass media and their audiences and carry messages to people who are less exposed to media. This suggests that mass communicators should aim their messages directly at opinion leaders, letting them carry the message to others.

Selecting the Message Source

In either personal or nonpersonal communication, the message's impact on the target audience is also affected by how the audience views the communicator. Messages delivered by highly credible sources are more persuasive. Thus, many food companies promote to doctors, dentists, and other health care providers to motivate these professionals to recommend their products to patients. And marketers hire celebrity endorsers—well-known athletes, actors, and even cartoon characters—to deliver their messages. Tiger Woods speaks for Nike, Buick, and a dozen other brands. Don Cherry was hired by Molson to promote its "Bubba" mini-keg. As part of the promotion, some of Cherry's most outlandish suits have been reproduced on the party-sized containers and on cans of Molson Canadian. Canadian PGA champion golfer Mike Weir promotes the products of his sponsors—Bell, Kia, and Taylor Made. Hockey legend Wayne Gretzky is featured in ads for Ford. Six-time Olympic speed-skating medallist Cindy Klassen, named Canada's 2005 Female Athlete of the Year, recently signed a five-year, $1 million endorsement deal, reported to be the most lucrative corporate relationship deal ever signed by an amateur athlete in Canada, with MTS Allstream Inc., Canada's longest established coast-to-coast provider of communication solutions.[11]

REAL MARKETING | 14.1

Buzz Marketing: A Powerful New Way to Spread the Word

These days, buzz marketing is all the rage. Buzz marketing involves getting consumers themselves to spread information about a product or service to others in their communities. "In a successful buzz-marketing campaign, each carefully cultivated recipient of the brand message becomes a powerful carrier, spreading the word to yet more carriers, much as a virus rampages through a given population," says one expert.

Why the new trend? For starters, buzz marketing is cheap. It's a great way to extend brand exposure without blowing out the marketing budget. Buzz marketing's increasing popularity can also be attributed the growing ranks of skeptical consumers—such as teens and twenty-somethings—who are notoriously disdainful of mass-media advertising. Finally, word-of-mouth communications is often the way we hear about products and services. A recent online survey of 2000 English and French Canadians conducted by Arnold Worldwide, showed that we rely on each other for recommendations. When people were asked if they had liked any product or service from within a number of categories well enough to recommend it to others, at least 50 percent said they had done so during the last year, no matter what the category.

However, it is just a few people who are responsible for the majority of the buzz. Key influencers represent only 14 percent of the Canadian population. As the survey findings reveal, "They are not defined by gender, age, region, education or income. What sets them apart is attitude." People who drive buzz can be divided into two groups: Inspirationals and Connectors. Inspirationals have deep product knowledge, and they are innovative, unconventional, and intelligent. However, they may be a bit introverted. Connectors, on the other hand, are defined by their sociability and extroversion. Both groups see themselves as adventurous, socially conscious, and sophisticated. Because Connectors are at least twice as likely than any other cluster to recommend brands to seven or more friends, it is important to target them with buzz marketing initiatives. Ironically, however, you often have to go through Inspirationals, since that is where Connectors get their information.

▶

Reaching Inspirationals can be a challenge because they tend to dislike traditional advertising. They must be approached through authentic, shared-values approaches. For example, Volkswagen transformed itself through speaking to real drivers: people who love the road, who want to stand out a bit, who have a sense of fun, and who want more than the car industry was letting them have at the prices they could afford. Perhaps the single most important reason that marketers are employing buzz marketing is that it really works. Consider the following examples.

Lee Dungarees: In recent years, VF had managed to re-energize the image of its stodgy Lee jeans brand among younger target consumers—mostly young males 17 to 22. But it needed to do more to convert that cooler image into sales at teen-toxic retailers, such as traditional department stores, its biggest outlets. So VF came up with one of the most freewheeling and influential buzz-marketing campaigns to date. The campaign played on target consumers' weakness for video games and computers. First, VF developed a list of 200 000 "influential" guys from a list of Web surfers. It then zapped them a trio of grainy video clips that were hilarious in their apparent stupidity. The videos appeared to be ultra-low-budget flicks meant to draw visitors to the websites of amateur filmmakers, such as open-shirted Curry, a 23-year-old race car driver. To the young Web surfers who received them, the clips seemed like delicious examples of the oddball digital debris that litters the Web. On average, recipients forwarded them to six friends apiece. Not many of them guessed that they actually were part of a marketing campaign orchestrated by Lee. Despite virtually no advertising, some 100 000 visitors stormed the fictional filmmakers' websites the week they went live, crashing the server. Ultimately, the effort drove thousands of kids age 17 to 22 into the stores and helped propel Lee sales upward by 20 percent.

Vespa: Meaning hornet or yellow jacket in Italian, the Vespa has been ridden in Europe and elsewhere since 1946. When Vespa re-entered Canada in 2003, it had only a measly marketing budget to support sales. However, when singer Nelly Furtado snapped up one of the scooters, the idea was born to use trendy local celebs to generate word-of mouth. Jeremy Logan, VP marketing of the Canadian Scooter Corp., which distributes the brand, noted, "The best form of marketing for the Vespa is seeing people on them. [And] seeing someone really cool on it is even better." Now members of the up-and-coming band Metric, Much Music veejays, and indie singers, such as JackSoul, are spreading the word. Toronto CityTV's *BreakfastTelevision* host Liza Fromer rode a Vespa to work every day for a week and chatted up the brand on air. Even CBC had a segment on the scooter. Street teams were given scooters so they could zoom around cafés, bars, events, and other hot spots because the bike itself has an appeal all its own. People who ogle the scooters are given special brochures. Logan has shared his plan with all the 23 Vespa distributors across Canada so they can create their own buzz among 30- to 55-year-olds in their local markets. The brand has attracted a wealth of co-branders, such as HMV, Reebok, Diet Pepsi, and Snapple, which have added caché to its marketing. Timex Canada and Bell Mobility offered Vespas as the top prize in a recent contests. This combination of buzz-related tactics has helped the company double sales.

Procter & Gamble's Tremor: Gina Lavagna is the ideal pitch gal. After receiving a $2 minidisc for Sony's Net MD and six $10-off coupons, she rushed four of her chums to a mall near her home to show them the digital music player, which sells for $99 and up. "I've probably told 20 people about it," she says, adding, "At least 10 are extremely interested in getting one." Her parents got her one for Christmas.

Gina is a member of Procter & Gamble's huge stealth teenage sales force. Some 280 000 strong, all of them have been enlisted by an arm of Procter & Gamble called Tremor. Their mission is to help companies spread the word about their brands among teens, who are maddeningly difficult to reach and influence through advertising. They deliver endorsements in school cafeterias, at sleepovers, by cell-phone, and by email—and they do it for free. Initially focused only on P&G brands, Tremor's forces are now

Tremor, an arm of Procter & Gamble, has a huge stealth teenage sales force—some 280 000 strong in the U.S. Tremorites help companies spread the word about their brands among teens.

being tapped to talk up just about any brand, from Sony, Coca-Cola, and Kraft to Toyota and Valvoline motor oil.

Tremor recruits teens with a wide social circle and a gift of gab. (Tremorites have an average of 170 names on their buddy lists; a typical teen has 30.) Though P&G screens the kids it taps, it doesn't coach them beyond encouraging them to feel free to talk to friends. The kids, natural talkers, do the work without pay, not counting the coupons, product samples, and the thrill of being something of an "insider." "It's cool to know about stuff before other people," says one Tremorite. More than just talk, such buzz can give a real lift to a brand's sales. Recently, CoverGirl sent groups of Tremor gals in three cities a booklet of makeup tips in a thin round tin with some $1-off coupons. Nothing fancy, but CoverGirl wanted to see if it would give its lipstick, mascara, and foundation a boost. It did. Purchases rose 10 percent among teens in the targeted cities.

P&G's buzz-marketing effort has been so successful that the packaged-goods giant is now building a new net-work of equal or greater size, one that will focus on moms—a much bigger and more affluent target than teens. Says P&G's marketing chief: "The possibilities are almost limitless."

Though buzz marketing can be a powerful tool, it is not without its critics. Since it often occurs "below the radar screen" of consumer consciousness, it has been labelled as manipulative or deceptive by some critics. Others are concerned that it may exploit vulnerable children and young people. If not undertaken with integrity, buzz marketing may end up stinging those who misuse it.

Sources: Excerpts adapted from Lynn Fletcher, "The Buzz on 'Buzz'," *Marketing Magazine,* August 23, 2004; Gerry Khermouch and Jeff Green, "Buzz Marketing, *Business Week,* July 30, 2001, pp. 50–56; Melanie Wells, "Nabbing Teens," *Forbes,* February 2, 2004, pp. 85–88; Bob Garfield, "War & Peace and Subservient Chicken," April 26, 2004, www.adage.com; and Gregg Cebrzynski, "Burger King Says It's OK to Have Your Way with the Chicken," *Nation's Restaurant News,* May 10, 2004, p. 16; "Vespa planning new campaign by Dentsu, *Marketing Daily,* July 7, 2005, www.marketingmag.ca/; "The allure of the Vespa, *Strategy Magazine,* September 2005, p. 61.

But companies must be careful when selecting celebrities to represent their brands. Picking the wrong spokesperson can result in embarrassment and a tarnished image. Kobe Bryant lost his sponsorship contracts with McDonald's and other companies after being accused of sexual assault. Alexander Keith's beer, made by the Labatt Brewing Co., had to look for a new spokesman after child pornography charges were filed against Robert Norman Smith, the actor who plays the cantankerous, outlandish, kilt-clad Scotsman who sings the praises of a beer he called "the pride of Nova Scotia." Mr. Smith's character was the centrepiece for beer's television advertising campaign for more than three years, and the ads even made it to the Super Bowl. Some say he had become a Canadian icon. The series of advertisements was credited with pushing Alexander Keith's into the number one spot in the Canadian specialty beer market. Though Labatt's is hoping that people will stick with the beer because they love it, others believe loss of the memorable advertising will severely damage brand sales.[12]

Collecting Feedback

After sending the message, the communicator must research its effect on the target audience. This involves asking the target audience members whether they remember the message, how many times they saw it, what points they recall, how they felt about the message, and their past and present attitudes toward the product and company. The communicator would also like to measure behaviour resulting from the message—how many people bought a product, talked to others about it, or visited the store.

Feedback on marketing communications may suggest changes in the promotion program or in the product offer itself. For example, Air Canada uses in-flight, Internet, magazine, and newspaper advertising to inform consumers about the airline, its routes, and its fares. Suppose feedback research shows that 80 percent of all fliers in a particular area recall seeing the airline's ads and are aware of its flights and prices. Sixty percent of these aware fliers have flown Air Canada, but only

Marketers hire celebrity endorsers to deliver their messages. Here, Mike Weir promotes Taylor Made Golf Equipment and Bell.

20 percent of those who tried it were satisfied. These results suggest that although promotion is creating *awareness*, the airline isn't giving consumers the *satisfaction* they expect. Therefore, Air Canada needs to improve its service while staying with the successful communication program. In contrast, suppose the research shows that only 40 percent of area consumers are aware of the airline, only 30 percent of those aware have tried it, but 80 percent of those who have tried it return. In this case, Air Canada needs to strengthen its promotion program to take advantage of its power to create customer satisfaction.

Setting the Total Promotion Budget and Mix

We have looked at the steps in planning and sending communications to a target audience. But how does the company decide on the total *promotion budget* and its division among the major promotional tools to create the *promotion mix*? By what process does it blend the tools to create integrated marketing communications? We now look at these questions.

Setting the Total Promotion Budget

One of the hardest marketing decisions facing a company is how much to spend on promotion. John Wanamaker, the department store magnate, once said, "I know that half of my advertising is wasted, but I don't know which half. I spent $2 million for advertising, and I don't know if that is half enough or twice too much." Thus, it is not surprising that industries and companies vary widely in how much they spend on promotion. Promotion spending may be 20 to 30 percent of sales in the cosmetics industry and only 2 or 3 percent in the industrial machinery industry. Within a given industry, both low and high spenders can be found.[13]

How does a company decide on its promotion budget? We look at four common methods used to set the total budget for advertising: the *affordable method*, the *percentage-of-sales method*, the *competitive-parity method*, and the *objective-and-task method*.[14]

Affordable Method

Affordable method
Setting the promotion budget at the level management thinks the company can afford.

Some companies use the **affordable method**: They set the promotion budget at the level they think the company can afford. Small businesses often use this method, reasoning that the company cannot spend more on advertising than it has. They start with total revenues, deduct operating expenses and capital outlays, and then devote some portion of the remaining funds to advertising.

Unfortunately, this method of setting budgets completely ignores the effects of promotion on sales. It tends to place advertising last among spending priorities, even in situations in which advertising is critical to the firm's success. It leads to an uncertain annual promotion budget, which makes long-range market planning difficult. Although the affordable method can result in overspending on advertising, it more often results in underspending.

Percentage-of-Sales Method

Percentage-of-sales method
Setting the promotion budget at a certain percentage of current or forecasted sales or as a percentage of the unit sales price.

Other companies use the **percentage-of-sales method**, setting their promotion budget at a certain percentage of current or forecasted sales. Or they budget a percentage of the unit sales price. The percentage-of-sales method has advantages. It is simple to use and helps management think about the relationships among promotion spending, selling price, and profit per unit.

Despite these claimed advantages, however, the percentage-of-sales method has little to justify it. It wrongly views sales as the *cause* of promotion rather than as the *result*. Although studies have found a positive correlation between promotional spending and brand strength, this relationship often turns out to be effect and cause, not cause and effect. Stronger brands with higher sales can afford the biggest ad budgets.

Thus, the percentage-of-sales budget is based on availability of funds rather than on opportunities. It may prevent the increased spending sometimes needed to turn around falling sales. Because the budget varies with year-to-year sales, long-range planning is difficult. Finally, the method does not provide any basis for choosing a *specific* percentage, except what has been done in the past or what competitors are doing.

Competitive-Parity Method

Competitive-parity method
Setting the promotion budget to match competitors' outlays.

Still other companies use the **competitive-parity method**, setting their promotion budgets to match competitors' outlays. They monitor competitors' advertising or get industry promotion spending estimates from publications or trade associations, and then set their budgets based on the industry average.

Two arguments support this method. First, competitors' budgets represent the collective wisdom of the industry. Second, spending what competitors spend helps prevent promotion wars. Unfortunately, neither argument is valid. There are no grounds for believing that the competition has a better idea of what a company should be spending on promotion than does the company itself. Companies differ greatly, and each has its own special promotion needs. Finally, there is no evidence that budgets based on competitive parity prevent promotion wars.

Objective-and-Task Method

Objective-and-task method
Developing the promotion budget by (1) defining specific objectives, (2) determining the tasks that must be performed to achieve these objectives, and (3) estimating the costs of performing these tasks. The sum of these costs is the proposed promotion budget.

The most logical budget-setting method is the **objective-and-task method**, whereby the company sets its promotion budget based on what it wants to accomplish with promotion. This budgeting method entails (1) defining specific promotion objectives, (2) determining the tasks needed to achieve these objectives, and (3) estimating the costs of performing these tasks. The sum of these costs is the proposed promotion budget.

The advantage of the objective-and-task method is that it forces management to spell out its assumptions about the relationship between dollars spent and promotion results. But it is also the most difficult method to use. Often, it is hard to figure out which specific tasks will achieve stated objectives. For example, suppose Sony wants 95 percent awareness for its latest camcorder model during the six-month introductory period. What specific advertising messages and media schedules should Sony use to attain this objective? How much would these messages and media schedules cost? Sony management must consider such questions, even though they are hard to answer.

Setting the Overall Communication Mix

The concept of integrated marketing communications suggests that the company must blend the promotion tools carefully into a coordinated *promotion mix*. But how does the company determine what mix of promotion tools it will use? Companies within the same industry differ greatly in the design of their promotion mixes. For example, Avon spends most of its promotion funds on personal selling and direct marketing, whereas CoverGirl spends heavily on consumer advertising. Hewlett-Packard relies on advertising and promotion to retailers, whereas Dell Computer uses only direct marketing. We now look at factors that influence the marketer's choice of promotion tools.

Companies within the same industry may use different mixes. Avon relies heavily on personal selling and direct marketing; CoverGirl devotes significant resources to advertising.

The Nature of Each Promotion Tool

Each promotion tool has unique characteristics and costs. Marketers must understand these characteristics in selecting their mix of tools.

Advertising   Advertising can reach masses of geographically dispersed buyers at a relatively low cost per exposure, and it enables the seller to repeat a message many times. For example, television advertising can reach huge audiences. On an average day, 76 percent of Canadians view television at least once. This viewership may be split among Canadian English national networks (13 percent), French networks (30 percent), Canadian global and independents (14 percent), Canadian pay and speciality channels (14 percent), U.S. conventional and superstations (7 percent), U.S. pay and speciality channels (5 percent), and others (17 percent). More than 120 million North Americans tune in to at least part of the Super Bowl, and nearly 52 million watched the final episode of the first *Survivor* series. *Canadian Idol* drew an audience of 5.8 million viewers (or one in six Canadians) for its 2005 closing episodes, while the highest-rated Canadian program to date was the gold-medal men's hockey game at the 2002 Olympics, watched by more than 10 million devoted fans. "If you want to get to the mass audience," says a media services executive, "broadcast TV is where you have to be." He adds, "For anybody introducing anything who has to lasso an audience in a hurry—a new product, a new campaign, a new movie—the networks are still the biggest show in town."[15]

Beyond its reach, large-scale advertising says something positive about the seller's size, popularity, and success. Because of advertising's public nature, consumers tend to view advertised products as more legitimate. Advertising is also very expressive—it allows the company to dramatize its products through the artful use of visuals, print, sound, and colour. On the one hand, advertising can be used to build up a long-term image for a product (such as Coca-Cola ads). On the other hand, advertising can trigger quick sales (as when Shopper's Drug Mart advertises its weekend specials).

Advertising also has some shortcomings. Although it reaches many people quickly, advertising is impersonal and cannot be as directly persuasive as can company salespeople. For the most part, advertising can carry on only a one-way communication with the audience, and the audience does not feel that it has to pay attention or respond. In addition, advertising can be very costly. Although some advertising forms, such as newspaper and radio advertising, can be done on smaller budgets, other forms, such as network TV advertising, require very large budgets.

Personal Selling   Personal selling is the most effective tool at certain stages of the buying process, particularly in building up buyers' preferences, convictions, and actions. It involves personal interaction between two or more people, so each person can observe the other's needs and characteristics and make quick adjustments. Personal selling also allows all kinds of relationships to spring up, ranging from matter-of-fact selling relationships to personal friendships. The effective salesperson keeps the customer's interests at heart in order to build a long-term relationship. Finally, with personal selling, the buyer usually feels a greater need to listen and respond, even if the response is a polite "No thank you."

These unique qualities come at a cost, however. A sales force requires a longer-term commitment than does advertising—advertising can be turned on and off, but sales-force size is harder to change. Personal selling is also the company's most expensive promotion tool, costing companies $220 on average per sales call. In some industries, the average cost of a sales call reaches $440.[16] North American firms spend up to three times as much on personal selling as they do on advertising.

Sales Promotion   Sales promotion includes a wide assortment of tools—coupons, contests, cents-off deals, premiums, and others—all of which have many unique qualities. They attract consumer attention, offer strong incentives to purchase, and can be used to dramatize product offers and to boost sagging sales. Sales promotions invite and reward quick response—whereas advertising says, "Buy our product," sales promotion says, "Buy it now." Sales promotion effects are often short-lived, however, and often are not as effective as advertising or personal selling in building long-run brand preference.

Public Relations   Public relations is very believable—news stories, features, sponsorships, and events seem more real and believable to readers than ads do. Public relations can also reach many prospects who avoid salespeople and advertisements—the message gets to the buyers as "news" rather than as a sales-directed communication. And, as with advertising, public relations can dramatize a company or product. Marketers tend to underuse public relations or to use it as an afterthought. Yet a well-thought-out public relations campaign used with other promotion mix elements can be very effective and economical.

Direct Marketing   Although there are many forms of direct marketing—telephone marketing, direct mail, online marketing, and others—they all share four distinctive characteristics. Direct marketing is *nonpublic*: The message is normally directed to a specific person. Direct marketing is *immediate* and *customized*: Messages can be prepared very quickly and can be tailored to appeal to specific consumers. Finally, direct marketing is *interactive*: It allows a dialogue between the marketing team and the consumer, and messages can be altered depending on the consumer's response. Thus, direct marketing is well suited to highly targeted marketing efforts and to building one-to-one customer relationships.

Promotion Mix Strategies

Marketers can choose from two basic promotion mix strategies—*push* promotion or *pull* promotion. Figure 14.4 contrasts the two strategies. The relative emphasis on the specific promotion tools differs for push and pull strategies. A **push strategy** involves "pushing" the product through distribution channels to final consumers. The producer directs its marketing activities (primarily personal selling and trade promotion) toward channel members to induce them to carry the product and to promote it to final consumers.

Push strategy
A promotion strategy that calls for using the sales force and trade promotion to push the product through channels. The producer promotes the product to wholesalers, the wholesalers promote to retailers, and the retailers promote to consumers.

Figure 14.4 Push versus pull promotion strategy

Push strategy

Pull strategy

With personal selling, the customer feels a greater need to listen and respond, even if the response is a polite "No thank you."

Pull strategy

A promotion strategy that calls for spending a lot on advertising and consumer promotion to build up consumer demand. If the strategy is successful, consumers will ask their retailers for the product, the retailers will ask the wholesalers, and the wholesalers will ask the producers.

Using a **pull strategy,** the producer directs its marketing activities (primarily advertising and consumer promotion) toward final consumers to induce them to buy the product. If the pull strategy is effective, consumers will then demand the product from channel members, who will in turn demand it from producers. Thus, under a pull strategy, consumer demand "pulls" the product through the channels.

Some industrial goods companies use only push strategies; some direct-marketing companies use only pull. However, most large companies use some combination of both. For example, Kraft uses mass-media advertising and consumer promotions to pull its products and a large sales force and trade promotions to push its products through the channels. In recent years, consumer goods companies have been decreasing the pull portions of their mixes in favour of more push. This has caused concern that they may be driving short-run sales at the expense of long-term brand equity. (See Real Marketing 14.2.)

Companies consider many factors when designing their promotion mix strategies, including *type of product/market* and the *product life-cycle stage.* For example, the importance of different promotion tools varies between consumer and business markets. Business-to-consumer (B2C) companies usually "pull" more, putting more of their funds into advertising, followed by sales promotion, personal selling, and then public relations. In contrast, business-to-business (B2B) marketers tend to "push" more, putting more of their funds into personal selling, followed by sales promotion, advertising, and public relations. In general, personal selling is used more heavily with expensive and risky goods and in markets with fewer and larger sellers.

The effects of different promotion tools also vary with stages of the product life cycle. In the introduction stage, advertising and public relations are good for producing high awareness, and sales promotion is useful in promoting early trial. Personal selling must be used to get the trade to carry the product. In the growth stage, advertising and public relations continue to be powerful influences, whereas sales promotion can be reduced because fewer incentives are needed. In the mature stage, sales promotion again becomes important relative to advertising. Buyers know the brands, and advertising is needed only to remind them of the product. In the decline stage, advertising is kept at a reminder level, public relations is dropped, and salespeople give the product only a little attention. Sales promotion, however, might continue strong.

REAL MARKETING

14.2

Are Consumer Goods Companies Getting Too Pushy?

Consumer packaged-goods companies, such as Kraft, Unilever, Kellogg, General Mills, and Gillette, grew into giants by using mostly pull promotion strategies. They used massive doses of national advertising to differentiate their products, gain market share, and build brand equity and customer loyalty. But during the past few decades, these companies have gotten more "pushy," de-emphasizing national advertising and putting more of their marketing budgets into trade and consumer sales promotions.

General trade promotions (trade allowances, displays, cooperative advertising, slotting fees) now account for 49 percent of total marketing spending by consumer product companies. Another 10 percent of the marketing budget goes to the trade in the form of "account-specific" marketing expenditures—promotional spending personalized to the local needs of a specific retail chain that backs both the brand and the retailer. The total of 59 percent represents a 7-percentage-point increase in trade spending in just the past

Today's food marketers are using more and more push promotion, including consumer price promotions. But they must be careful that they don't win the battle for short-run sales at the expense of long-run brand equity.

five years. Consumer promotions (coupons, cents-off deals, premiums) account for another 17 percent of the typical marketing budget. That leaves less than 24 percent of total marketing spending for mass-media advertising, down from 42 percent 20 years ago.

Why have these companies shifted so heavily toward push strategies? One reason is that mass-media campaigns have become more expensive and less effective in recent years. Network television costs have risen sharply while audiences have fallen off, making national advertising less cost-effective. Further, new technological advances, such as TiVo and digital cable, allow consumers to "fast-forward" through advertisements, making the large sums of money spent on TV advertising much less effective in reaching target audiences. Companies have also increased their market segmentation efforts and are now tailoring their marketing programs more narrowly, making national advertising less suitable than localized retailer promotions. And in these days of brand extensions and me-too products, companies sometimes have trouble finding meaningful product differences to feature in advertising. So they have differentiated their products through price reductions, premium offers, coupons, and other push techniques.

Another factor speeding the shift from pull to push has been the growing strength of retailers. Retail giants, such as Wal-Mart, Loblaws, Safeway, and Sobeys, now have the power to demand and get what they want—and what they want is more push. Whereas national advertising bypasses them on its way to the masses, push promotion benefits them directly. Consumer promotions give retailers an immediate sales boost, and cash from trade allowances and other trade promotions pads retailer profits. Thus, producers must often use push just to obtain good shelf space and other support from important retailers.

However, many marketers are concerned that the reckless use of push will lead to fierce price competition and a never-ending spiral of price slashing and deal making. If used improperly, push promotion can mortgage a brand's future for short-term gains. Sales promotion buys short-run reseller support and consumer sales, but advertising builds long-run brand equity and consumer preference. By robbing the media advertising budget to pay for more sales promotion, companies might win the battle for short-run earnings but lose the war for long-run brand equity, consumer loyalty, and market share. In fact, some analysts blame the shift away from advertising dollars for a recent two-decade-long drop in the percentage of consumers who buy only well-known brands.

Of special concern is the overuse of price promotions. The regular use of price as a selling tool can destroy brand equity by encouraging consumers to seek value though price rather than through the benefits of the brand. In fact, studies show that almost 60 percent of consumers now go to the store to make a purchase without a specific brand in mind. Once they get to the store, shoppers are often more swayed by special prices, sales, and coupons than by brand. In cases where price is a key part of the brand's positioning, featuring price makes sense. But for brands where price does not underlie value, "price promotions are really desperate acts by brands that have their backs against the wall," says one marketing executive. "Generally speaking, it is better to stick to your guns with price and invest in advertising to drive sales."

Many consumer companies now are rethinking their promotion strategies and reversing the trend by shifting their promotion budgets back toward advertising. They have realized that it's not a question of sales promotion versus advertising, or of push versus pull. Success lies in finding the best mix of the two: consistent advertising to build long-run brand value and consumer preference, and sales promotion to create short-run trade support and consumer excitement. The company needs to blend both push and pull elements into an integrated promotion program that meets immediate consumer and retailer needs as well as long-run strategic needs.

Sources: Promotion spending statistics from *2002 Trade Promotion Spending & Merchandising Industry Study* (Cannondale Associates, Wilton, CT, May 2002), p. 13; and *Trade Promotion Spending & Merchandising 2003 Industry Study* (Wilton, CT: Cannondale Associates, 2003), p. 7. Other information from Jack Trout, "Prices: Simple Guidelines to Get Them Right," *Journal of Business Strategy*, November–December 1998, pp. 13–16; Tim Ambler, "Kicking Price Promotion Habit Is Like Getting Off Heroin—Hard," *Marketing*, May 27, 1999, p. 24; Alan Mitchell, "When Push Comes to Shove, It's All About Pull," *Marketing Week*, January 9, 2003, pp. 26–27; "Promotions and Incentives: Offers You Can't Refuse," *Marketing Week,* April 15, 2004, p. 31; and E. Craig Stacey, "Abandon TV at Your Own Risk," *Advertising Age*, June 7, 2004, p. 32.

Integrating the Promotion Mix

Having set the promotion budget and mix, the company must now take steps to see that all of the promotion mix elements are smoothly integrated. Here is a checklist for integrating the firm's marketing communications.[17]

- *Analyze trends—internal and external—that can affect the company's ability to do business.* Look for areas where communications can help the most. Determine the strengths and weaknesses of each communications function. Develop a combination of promotional tactics based on these strengths and weaknesses.

- *Audit the pockets of communications spending throughout the organization.* Itemize the communications budgets and tasks and consolidate these into a single budgeting process. Reassess all communications expenditures by product, promotional tool, stage of the life cycle, and observed effect.

- *Identify all contact points for the company and its brands.* Work to ensure that communications at each point are consistent with the overall communications strategy and that communications efforts are occurring when, where, and how *customers* want them.

- *Team up in communications planning.* Engage all communications functions in joint planning. Include customers, suppliers, and other stakeholders at every stage of communications planning.

- *Create compatible themes, tones, and quality across all communications media.* Make sure each element carries the company's unique primary messages and selling points. This consistency achieves greater impact and prevents the unnecessary duplication of work across functions.

- *Create performance measures that are shared by all communications elements.* Develop systems to evaluate the combined impact of all communications activities.
- *Appoint a director responsible for the company's persuasive communications efforts.* This move encourages efficiency by centralizing planning and creating shared performance measures.

Socially Responsible Marketing Communication

In shaping its promotion mix, a company must be aware of the large body of legal and ethical issues surrounding marketing communications. Most marketers work hard to communicate openly and honestly with consumers and resellers. Still, abuses may occur, and public policymakers have developed a substantial body of laws and regulations to govern advertising, sales promotion, personal selling, and direct-marketing activities. In this section, we discuss issues regarding advertising, sales promotion, and personal selling. Issues regarding direct marketing are addressed in Chapter 16.

Advertising and Sales Promotion

By law, companies must avoid false or deceptive advertising. Advertisers must not make false claims, such as suggesting that a product cures something when it does not. They must avoid ads that have the capacity to deceive, even though no one actually may be deceived. An automobile cannot be advertised as using seven litres per hundred kilometres unless it does so under typical conditions, and a diet bread cannot be advertised as having fewer calories simply because its slices are thinner.

Sellers must avoid bait-and-switch advertising that attracts buyers under false pretenses. For example, a large retailer advertised a sewing machine at $179. However, when consumers tried to buy the advertised machine, the seller downplayed its features, placed faulty machines on showroom floors, understated the machine's performance, and took other actions in an attempt to switch buyers to a more expensive machine. Such actions are both unethical and illegal.

The advertising industry in Canada is controlled both by the Canadian Radio-television and Telecommunications Commission (CRTC) and by voluntary industry codes administered by Advertising Standards Canada. The CRTC (www.crtc.gc.ca), which independently governs broadcast licensing, is itself governed by the *Broadcasting Act* of 1991 and the *Telecommunications Act* of 1993. The primary objective of the *Broadcasting Act* is to ensure that all Canadians have access to a wide variety of high-quality Canadian programming. The main objective of the *Telecommunications Act* is to ensure that Canadians have access to reliable telephone and other telecommunication services at affordable prices.

In addition, the CRTC has the mandate to ensure that programming in the Canadian broadcasting system reflects Canadian social values, creativity, and talent, as well as the country's linguistic duality, its multicultural diversity, and the special place of Aboriginal people within Canadian society. The CRTC regulates more than 5900 broadcasters, including television, cable distribution, AM and FM radio, pay and specialty television, direct-to-home satellite systems, multi-point distribution systems, subscription television, pay audio, and sixty-one telecommunication carriers, including major Canadian telephone companies.

Beyond simply avoiding legal pitfalls, such as deceptive or bait-and-switch advertising, companies can use advertising and other forms of promotion to encourage and promote socially responsible programs and actions. For example, Caterpillar is one of several companies and environmental groups forming the Tropical Forest Foundation, which is working to save the great Amazon rain forest. It uses advertising to promote the cause and its involvement. Similarly, KitchenAid Canada has built a successful partnership with the Canadian Breast Cancer Foundation (CBCF). The company made a commitment to raise funds for breast cancer research on an ongoing basis. For every Limited Edition Pink KithcenAid® Artisan® Stand Mixer it sells, KitchenAid Canada will donate $100 to the CBCF—and the collection of pink products continues to grow. KitchenAid Canada's commitment also goes beyond cause marketing—it has made a conscious effort to help develop ongoing grassroots support for breast cancer programs through its KitchenAid Cook for the Cure initiative. Supporters hold home parties at which guests provide donations instead of hostess gifts. By learning more about breast cancer at these gatherings, the guests become ambassadors for fundraising and the program. Online support at www.kitchenaid-cookforthecure.ca helps hosts with party hints, including food tips from Christine Cushing of the Food Network Canada and forms for online invitations and donations. At the end of 2005, more than $1.5 million had been raised through the initiative.[18]

Personal Selling

A company's salespeople must follow the rules of "fair competition." For example, salespeople may not lie to consumers or mislead them about the advantages of buying a product. To avoid bait-and-switch practices, salespeople's statements must match advertising claims.

KitchenAid Canada helps the cause of breast cancer research with its "Cook for the Cure" initiative.

Different rules apply to consumers who are visited by salespeople at home than to those who go to a store in search of a product. Because people called on at home may be taken by surprise and may be especially vulnerable to high-pressure selling techniques, most provincial governments have stipulated a *three-day cooling-off rule* to give special protection to customers who are not seeking products. Under this rule, customers who agree in their own homes to buy something have seventy-two hours in which to cancel a contract or return merchandise and get their money back, no questions asked.

Much personal selling involves business-to-business trade. In selling to businesses, salespeople may not offer bribes to purchasing agents or to others who can influence a sale. They may not obtain or use technical or trade secrets of competitors through bribery or industrial espionage. Finally, salespeople must not disparage competitors or competing products by suggesting things that are not true.[19]

Reviewing the Concepts

Modern marketing calls for more than just developing a good product, pricing it attractively, and making it available to target customers. Companies also must *communicate* with current and prospective customers, and what they communicate should not be left to chance.

1. Name and define the tools of the marketing communications mix.

A company's total *marketing communications mix*—also called its *promotion mix*—consists of the specific blend of *advertising, personal selling, sales promotion, public relations,* and *direct-marketing* tools that the company uses to pursue its advertising and marketing objectives. Advertising includes any paid form of nonpersonal presentation and promotion of ideas, goods, or services by an identified sponsor. Personal selling is any form of personal presentation by the firm's sales force for the purpose of making sales and building customer relationships. Firms use sales promotion to provide short-term incentives to encourage the purchase or sale of a product or service. Public relations focuses on building good relations with the company's various publics by obtaining favourable publicity. Finally, firms seeking immediate response from targeted individual customers use nonpersonal direct-marketing tools to communicate with customers.

2. Discuss the process and advantages of integrated marketing communications.

Recent shifts in marketing strategy from mass marketing to targeted or one-to-one marketing, coupled with advances in information technology, have had a dramatic impact on marketing communications. Although still important, the mass media are giving way to a profusion of smaller, more focused media. Companies are doing less *broadcasting* and more *narrowcasting*. As marketing communicators adopt richer but more fragmented media and promotion mixes to reach their diverse markets, they risk creating a communications hodgepodge for consumers. To prevent this, more companies are adopting the concept of *integrated marketing communications*, which calls for carefully integrating all sources of company communication to deliver a clear and consistent message to target markets.

To integrate its external communications effectively, the company must first integrate its internal communications activities. The company then works out the roles that the various promotional tools will play and the extent to which each will be used. It carefully coordinates the promotional activities and the timing of when major campaigns take place. Finally, to help implement its integrated marketing strategy, the company appoints a marketing communications director who has overall responsibility for the company's communications efforts.

3. Outline the steps in developing effective marketing communications.

In preparing marketing communications, the communicator's first task is to *identify the target audience* and its characteristics. Next, the communicator has to determine the *communication objectives* and define the response sought, whether it be *awareness, knowledge, liking, preference, conviction,* or *purchase.* Then a *mes-*

sage should be constructed with an effective content and structure. *Media* must be selected, both for personal and for nonpersonal communication. The communicator must find highly credible sources to deliver messages. Finally, the communicator must collect *feedback* by watching how much of the market becomes aware, tries the product, and is satisfied in the process.

4. **Explain the methods for setting the marketing communications budget and factors that affect the design of the marketing communications mix (also called the promotion mix).**

   The company has to decide how much to spend for promotion. The most popular approaches are to spend what the company can afford, to use a percentage of sales, to base promotion on competitors' spending, or to base it on an analysis and costing of the communication objectives and tasks.

   The company has to divide the *promotion budget* among the major tools to create the *promotion mix*. Companies can pursue a *push* or a *pull* promotional strategy, or a combination of the two. The best specific blend of promotion tools depends on the type of product/market, the buyer's readiness stage, and the product life-cycle stage.

   People at all levels of the organization must be aware of the many legal and ethical issues surrounding marketing communications. Companies must work hard and proactively at communicating openly, honestly, and agreeably with their customers and resellers.

Reviewing the Key Terms

Discussing the Concepts

1. Many companies are adopting the integrated marketing communication concept. Discuss two major problems that this marketing communications philosophy is designed to remedy.

2. Why does the marketing communicator need to know the target market's readiness stage? Give an example of an ad targeting each stage.

3. Compare and contrast personal and nonpersonal communication channels.

4. What is the major advantage of the objective-and-task method for setting the promotional budget? What is the major drawback?

5. Suppose you are an advertising coordinator and your boss asks you to recommend a message appeal for the next series of print ads for a new scanner software product directed at small clothing retailers. What would you recommendation? Explain.

Applying the Concepts

1. In your judgment who would be the best and the worst celebrity endorser for each of these products/services:
   - MADD
   - Dell
   - Canada Revenue Agency
   - Weight Watchers
   - Microsoft
   - Chatelaine
   - Lego
   - Canadian Breast Cancer Foundation
   - Lamborghini
   - Norwegian Cruise Lines

2. In a small group, prepare a chart comparing the five promotion mix tools on five different characteristics.

3. Outline a domestic Canadian promotion mix strategy for ski apparel manufacturer Spyder (www.spyder.com). Include both push and pull promotion mix strategies.

Focus on Technology

Once you have identified the target audience, determined the communication objective, designed a message, chosen media, set the budget, established the overall communication mix, and checked to see if the promotional mix is integrated properly with other marketing communication efforts, it's time to put it all into a written document. Fortunately, some software tools exist to help you with this task. Advertising Plan Pro is one such software tool. It guides you through the creation of a comprehensive integrated marketing communications document, from strategy to implementation and evaluation. First, go to www.paloalto.com/ps/ap/index.cfm, and

tour the application. Next go to www.paloalto.com/sampleplans/protected/app4/boulderstop-app.pdf, download a free sample of a complete advertising plan, and review it. Now, respond to the following.

1. Assess Advertising Plan Pro as a tool for communications professionals.

2. Does the Advertising Plan Pro tool do all of the work for an advertiser? Explain.

3. Is this a tool designed only for large companies?

Focus on Ethics

Is it puffery or is it deceptive advertising? This is a question many communication professionals can't answer. Advertising puffery is legal but deceptive advertising isn't. So how do you tell the difference? Fortunately, Advertising Standards Canada (ASC) the Canadian advertising industry self-regulatory body most responsible for consumer protection, has established standards. The ASC says an advertisement is questionable if it (1) omits relevant information, (2) contains deceptive or inaccurate claims, (3) includes disclaimers (e.g., "the small print") that contradict more prominent aspects of the advertisement, (4) has unsupport-

able claims, and (5) does not clearly identify the advertiser. Still not clear? Some practice may help. Read the advertising claims below and state whether they are most likely deceptive or just plain puffery. Explain your reasoning.

- There's a smile in every Hershey bar.
- I lost 95 pounds in just over 6 months. And I've kept the weight off for nearly 1 year!
- 93 percent Fat Free Frozen Dessert with chocolate-flavoured coating.

Sources: www.adstandards.com/en/

Video Case
Dunkin' Donuts

More than 50 years ago, the Dunkin' Donuts chain opened its first store. Five years later, the first franchise opened. Now the largest coffee and doughnut chain in the world, Dunkin' Donuts serves more than 2 million customers each day at more than 5500 restaurants in North America and abroad. Why the success? According to Dunkin' Donuts, it's all in the details. Dunkin' Donuts offers a consistent experience—the same doughnuts, the same coffee, the same store décor—each time a customer drops in.

Along with providing a consistent product and experience, Dunkin' Donuts marketers work to deliver a consistent marketing message to current and potential customers. But communicating the details of the Dunkin' Donuts experience to so many potential customers is a challenge. So, everything from print ads and television commercials to the company's website to the in-store experience work

together to engage customers and keep them coming back.

After viewing the video featuring Dunkin' Donuts, answer the following questions about integrated marketing communications:

1. How does Dunkin' Donuts ensure that consumers have a consistent experience in restaurants across North America and the world?

2. Based on your experience and the information presented in the video, which communications tools does Dunkin' Donuts use to reach consumers? Do the tools, together, consistently communicate Dunkin' Donuts product mix and benefits?

3. Visit Dunkin' Donuts website (www.dunkindonuts.com). Are the messages and images there consistent with your impressions of Dunkin' Donuts? How do they differ?

Online Media Resources

Video Short
Log on to your Companion Website at
www.pearsoned.ca/kotler to view the
video segment related to the Video Case on
page 560.

CBC ⊕ CBC Video Case
Please refer to Appendix 2 to read a
CBC Video Case for this chapter, and log
on to your Companion Website at
www.pearsoned.ca/kotler to view the
corresponding video segment.

Case Pilot
Log on to your Companion Website at
www.pearsoned.ca/kotler to sharpen
your case analysis skills and take the Case
Pilot Challenge!

Company Case
Pass the Mustard

Burger King Corporation is a large international chain of fast-food restaurants. It has operations in every Canadian province and it predominantly sells burgers, french fries, soft drinks, desserts, and various sandwiches. In early 2004, as Burger King's CEO, Brad Blum, reviewed the company's 2003 performance, he decided once again that he had to do something to spice up BK's bland performance. Industry leader McDonald's had just reported a 9 percent sales jump in 2003 to a total of US$22.1 billion, while number-two BK's U.S. sales had slipped about 5 percent to US$7.9 billion. Further, number-three Wendy's sales had spiked 11 percent to US$7.4 billion, putting it in position to overtake BK.

Blum surprised the fast-food industry by abruptly firing the firm's advertising agency, Young & Rubicam (Y&R), and awarding its global creative account to a small, upstart firm, Crispin Porter + Bogusky (CBP). The switch marked the fifth time in four years that BK had moved its account!

Ad agency Y&R had gotten the US$350 million BK account only 10 months earlier. To help revive BK's sales, it had developed a campaign with the theme "The Fire's Ready," which focused on BK's flame-broiled versus frying cooking method. However, observers found the message to be flat and uninspiring, and the sales decline sealed Y&R's fate.

Challenging Conventional Wisdom

In announcing the CPB selection, Blum indicated he had challenged the firm to develop "groundbreaking, next-level, results-oriented, and innovative advertising that strongly connects with our core customers." BK automatically became the small firm's largest customer, but CPB was not without an impressive track record.

Chuck Porter joined Crispin Advertising in 1988. A middle-aged windsurfer, he wanted to be near the water. Alex Bogusky joined the firm later as a 24-year-old art director who raced motorbikes. The Porter-Bogusky combination clicked, and CPB racked up local awards for its ad campaigns. A Sunglass Hut billboard featured a huge pair of sunglasses with the headline "What to Wear to a Nude Beach." Because its clients often had little money for advertising, CPB found inexpensive ways to gain attention. For a local homeless shelter, it placed ads on shopping carts, trash dumpsters, and park benches.

In 1997, with Bogusky serving as creative director, CPB finally got national attention with its "Truth" campaign aimed at convincing Florida teens to stop smoking. CPB started with street-level research, actually talking to teens in order to "get inside their heads." CPB found that cigarettes allowed teens to establish identities, associate with brand names, and take risks. To counter this, CPB created the "Truth" logo and turned it into a brand. It plastered the logo on everything from posters to T-shirts, developed a "Truth" website, and staged impromptu live "Truth" parties around the state. Between 1998 and 2002, teenage smoking in Florida declined 38 percent. The American Legacy Foundation picked up the "Truth" campaign and turned it into a national promotion, leading to a big-budget ad at the Super Bowl—the "Shards O'Glass Freeze Pop."

CPB followed with an award-winning, low-budget campaign for the BMW MINI Cooper. It decided to violate conventional wisdom and launch the U.S. campaign without TV advertising. It placed the MINIs inside sports stadiums as seats and on top of SUVs driving around town. It got the car included in centrefold pictures in *Playboy* and in movies, such as *The Italian Job*. It also created street props, such as a coin-operated children's ride as well as MINI games, MINI booklets, and MINI suitcases. When BMW finally introduced the MINI in spring 2002, the waiting list was ten months long.

Similar success with IKEA furniture and Virgin Atlantic Airways forged CPB's reputation as an out-of-the-box, results-oriented agency. Along the way, it developed some loose "rules." Among them were: zero in on the product, kick the TV commercial habit, find the sweet spot (the overlap between product characteristics and customer needs), surprise = buzz = exposure, don't be timid, and think of advertising as a product rather than a service.

Back to the Future

Within a month of getting BK's account, rather than recommending some kinky new idea, CPB recommended going back to the firm's "Have It Your Way" tagline, developed by BK's second advertising agency, BBDO, in 1974. CPB argued that it could take that old phrase and make it relevant to today's customers.

Uncharacteristically, CBP kicked of the new campaign with TV commercials that were a takeoff on a British comedy series, *The Office*. In the ad series, offbeat office workers compete and compare their "made my way" BK burgers, reinforcing the message that each customer can have a burger just as he or she wants it—no matter how unusual that might be. CPB planned an entire package of promotions around the new-old theme, including everything from in-store signage to messages on cups.

Then, however, the real CPB approach emerged. To promote BK's TenderCrisp chicken, CPB launched a website, www.subservientchicken.com. When people visited the site, they saw what appeared to be a Web camera focused on a somewhat seedy living room. In the room was a man dressed like a chicken (except for the lady's garter belt he is wearing). The site invited the visitor to "Get chicken just the way you like it. Type in your command here." The visitor could type in a command, such as "stand on your head" or "do jumping jacks" and the chicken would respond. If someone typed in a risqué request, the chicken would wave a wing at the camera, as if to say "no-no."

Below the chicken video area were five other icons. "SubservientTV" featured three video clips with various people "having their way" with the chicken. "Photos" presented five "glamour" shots of the chicken. The "Chicken Mask" icon produced a printable chicken mask to print, cut out, and wear. The mask's instructions were to "cut along dotted line, put on chicken face, be subservient." A fourth icon, "Tell a friend," pulled up an Outlook Express email document that invited you to send an email to a friend with the text: "Finally, somebody in a chicken costume who will do whatever you

want. Check it out: www.subservientchicken.com." Finally, an icon marked "BK TenderCrisp" took the visitor to the Burger King home page. This was the only indication of BK's sponsorship on the site, reflecting CPB's desire to avoid seeming too commercial and "uncool." Unless a visitor clicked on that last icon, he or she would have no indication that the site had anything to do with Burger King.

When CPB launched the site, it told only 20 - people —all of whom were friends of people who worked at the agency. Within the first 10 *days*, 20 million people visited the site, with the average visitor spending more than seven minutes. Many visitors apparently selected the "tell a friend" icon, sending emails flying like feathers.

Food for Thought

CPB clearly demonstrated with the subservient chicken that it was a master at viral marketing—using unusual methods to get attention and generate buzz and word of mouth. Despite its success, however, many analysts wonder if the campaign will produce increased sales for BK.

In 2005, CPB and BK launched a new website, www.coqroq.com. The site was designed to look like a heavy metal band of the same name had created it. It featured videos showing the fictional band members in chicken heads, downloadable ring tones, and photo galleries with shots of young girls with handwritten captions such as "Groupies love the Coq" and "groupies love Coq." Immediately after the launch, the bawdy captions were erased and replaced with the title "Shots From The Road." Many viewers and advertising critics were outraged by the implications of the campaign. *Advertising Age* magazine posted numerous comments including: "Just the name Coq Roq in general is offensive to families," said Aliza Pilar Sherman, an authority and author on women and the Internet and founder of cybergrrl. "I can't imagine if parents of a smaller child saw this. They'd say they don't want their child exposed to this. Where do we as responsible individuals draw the line? Of course there's freedom of speech but does that mean Burger King should be perpetuating stereotypes, negative attitudes and demeaning behavior to the market?" The site was subsequently pulled.

Burger King Canada avoided the controversy by following a different path with made-in-Canada campaigns. Take its recent "a revolution in chicken" radio and television campaign used to launch Burger King's french-fry-shaped chicken strips that come in a portable french-fry-like container with a built-in well for dipping sauce. The new product was launched because of the growing popularity of handheld chicken products, such as chicken strips. The campaign featured chickens staging revolts on farms across the country. One 30-second TV spot shows a farmer and his wife trapped in their barn as a result of rebel hens, another features tractor-driving chickens chasing two farmers through a field, and the third shows a farmer's wife waking up surrounded by chickens. Leslie Root, Canadian director of marketing at Burger King, notes, "We wanted to do something to exploit that opportunity but in a unique way, so we weren't the umpteenth to market with yet another chicken strip." The campaign was created by Bleu Blanc Rouge and is airing in English and French Canada.

Questions for Discussion

1. Who is BK's target audience and what are its communication objectives for that audience?

2. Why is viral or buzz marketing effective? Analyze the design of the subservient chicken site's message, including content, structure, and format (www.subservientchicken.com/). What can you conclude from this analysis?

3. The Coq Roq campaign generated considerable controversy and alienated some consumers. As a manager at Burger King, what guidelines would you develop to prevent viral marketing from going "too far" in an attempt to generate buzz?

4. Do the TV and viral elements of the Burger King campaign work well together? What additional elements and media might CPB add to the integrated marketing communications campaign?

5. Creating national campaigns is expensive. Some marketers believe it is more effective and efficient to generate campaigns that can be used around the world with few changes. Burger King Canada thought it was important to have a "made-in-Canada" campaign. What are the pros and cons of these two different approaches to integrated communications?

Sources: Rebecca Harris, "Burger King chickens are rising up," *Marketing Magazine*, August 15, 2005; Bob Garfield, "Garfield's Ad Review," *Advertising Age*, April 26, 2004, p. 103; Catharine P. Taylor, "Playing Chicken," *Adweek*, April 19, 2004, p. 19; Brian Steinberg and Suzanne Vranica, "Burger King Seeks Some Web Heat," *The Wall Street Journal*, April 15, 2004, p. B3; Warren Berger, "Dare-Devils: The Ad World's Most Buzzed-About Agency Is Miami's Crispin Porter & Bogusky," *Business 2.0*, April 2004, p. 110; Kate McArthur, "Burger King's Big Idea: Have It Your Way, Again," *Advertising Age*, February 16, 2004, p. 1; David Kiley, "Burger King's Coq Roq Site Stirs Pot. But Will It Sell Greasy Chicken Fries?" *Business Week*, July 27, 2005.

CHAPTER 15

Advertising, Sales Promotion, and Public Relations

AFTER READING THIS CHAPTER, YOU SHOULD BE ABLE TO

1. define the roles of advertising, sales promotion, and public relations in the promotion mix

2. describe the major decisions involved in developing an advertising program

3. explain how sales-promotion campaigns are developed and implemented

4. explain how companies use public relations to communicate with their publics

Previewing the Concepts

Now that we've looked at overall integrated marketing communications planning, let's dig more deeply into the specific marketing communications tools. In this chapter, we'll explore the mass-communications tools—advertising, sales promotion, and public relations.

At the start of the previous chapter, we examined the highly successful integrated marketing campaign for the BMW's British-made MINI automobile. To start this chapter, let's look behind the scenes at creation of an award-winning advertising campaign from the not-for-profit sector: The United Way of Greater Toronto. As it turns out, the campaign, created by Arnold Worldwide, reflects all the current trends in the fast-changing world of modern advertising.

To start, ponder this question: what is great advertising? Or, put another way, what is the best advertisement you've seen? Perhaps you're chuckling to yourself recalling some of the somewhat scandalous spots run during recent Super Bowls. Did the ad you're remembering entice you to try the product it was advertising? Did the spot make you laugh? Can you even remember what product or service was that the spot was advertising?

As the simple exercise above illustrates, we are exposed to literally thousands of advertisements every day, most of which are utterly forgettable. With each campaign, marketers and their advertising agencies are generally battling for a share of our wallets. Advertising is increasingly becoming a form of entertainment, and with large advertising budgets, companies seek to thrill, shock, or humour us into purchasing their products.

With this hostile setting in mind, consider this: How does a charitable organization break through? See what the United Way of Greater Toronto, and its advertising agency Arnold Worldwide, did as they developed a series of campaigns in support of the charity's donation drives.

In 2003, the United Way knew it was in a heated battle for what they term "share of compassion." A downturn in the economy, combined with recent government cutbacks in social services created a difficult landscape for the many charitable organizations in Canada. Literally thousands of charities appeared to be fighting for the same small percentage of donors, as 5 percent of donors in Canada account for more than 50 percent of total donations. With charities aggressively marketing themselves in an already cluttered landscape, the United Way needed a campaign that would break through the clutter and, ultimately, entice potential donors to support its many charities.

With these objectives in mind, the Arnold Worldwide team went to work. Informal focus groups with both donors and non-donors were first conducted in an effort to uncover key consumer insights. As expected, participants reaffirmed the notion that many donors give to organizations that have personal meaning to them. For example, many people who have had a loved one afflicted by cancer donate to the Canadian Cancer Society. Unexpectedly, however, the agency discovered that though people rationalized not giving to the poor by giving to other more "personal" causes, they felt an underlying guilt associated with this decision, just as most people feel a tinge of guilt when they walk past a homeless person. This sense of guilt is enhanced with feelings of conflict—what will the person do with the money if I give it to them? Do they really need it? This was a key insight for the creative team. Furthermore, during the focus groups, the team found that there was a great deal of equity within the United Way's brand imagery. People viewed the United Way logo as a "helping hand to those in need."

Thus, a strategy was born: "Giving to the United Way is the simple way to take care of those most vulnerable in the city." By giving to the United Way of Greater Toronto, donors could be assured that they were helping those in need in the best possible way, and could thus eliminate their feelings of guilt and conflict.

With a solid strategy in place, work began on execution. The United Way relies entirely on donated media space; compelling creative material was of paramount importance, as the amount of advertising space given is directly related to the media's perception of the campaign. As one analyst noted, "Good creative can often make or break pro-bono work: If you're not paying for media space, your campaign had better be interesting, or it just won't get picked up."

The final campaign used the imagery of the hand as "an icon of protection." The lead execution, which ran in both print and outdoor transit, showed a homeless man being sheltered from the rain with a hand. The campaign also featured two TV spots, three print executions, three transit posters, zoom media (in bars and restaurants), and painted GO Transit trains in the Toronto area. In 2004, the campaign continued with superboards, online banner and skyscraper ads, as well as support from major websites, including globeandmail.com, tsn.ca, Toronto.com, and chatelaine.com. As one advertising critic noted, "The hand, used properly, is a wonderful advertising device, because it evokes such warmth and unique humanity. Here, coupled with that dynamic yet quiet theme line, it is dramatic, and involving, and says precisely what The United Way wants it to say. I think I'm going to increase my gift this year, in tribute."

The campaign ran for two years, and in 2004 alone, it helped the United Way generate the equivalent of $10 million in donated editorial and promotional media. It also won two gold Cassies (Canadian Advertising Success Stories) awards. Although the campaign was certainly a success from a media perspective, the question remains: what did it do for the United Way of Greater Toronto? First, donations increased in both 2003 and 2004 despite the competitive environment. Increased donations allowed the Toronto United Way to support 200 social and community health service agencies in the Toronto area. Second, advertising awareness jumped by 10 percent in one year, with 58 percent of Torontonians recalling one or more executions of the 2003 campaign. Finally, brand image was positively affected, with almost 60 percent of those polled either agreeing or somewhat agreeing with the statement "United Way is the most effective way to deal with social issues in the community" and "United Way makes a posi-

tive and lasting different in people's lives." In fact, the "Hands" campaign was so effective that it was picked up by other United Ways across Canada.

No matter how successful a campaign has been, however, time is not its friend. Viewers grow tired of the same message and imagery. Thus, in 2005, Arnold Worldwide and the United Way changed course. The next campaign built on the foundation of the previous campaign and its theme "Without you there would be no way." However, the 2005 campaign visually demonstrated exactly what donations can do and how individual donations can make a difference—from helping the homeless get off the streets to making sure the elderly aren't isolated. The new print ads show a person in need sitting in the middle of a two-way arrow—a timeline concept used to illustrate how people's lives can move forward, toward employment, job training, or living with more dignity, or backward into depression, violence, and suffering.

The two new 30-second TV spots use dramatic special effects to show what might happen if a person didn't receive help. In one spot, a boy plays baseball, but as he swings the bat, the screen goes dark and an image emerges of him smashing a car window and running away. It then cuts back to daylight shot, showing the same boy running bases, thanks to the fact that the United Way reached him before he ran into trouble. Noting the strategy behind the two campaigns, Bill Newbery, Arnold Worldwide's co-creative director, says the "hand" campaigns were part of the United Way's attempt to show how it helps with immediate needs. In contrast, the 2005 initiative was one where "we wanted to freshen it up, as well as address the strategy that the United Way wanted to get across, which was the long-term role it plays."

The United Way, like all charities, has a limited budget that it can devote to promotions. Thus, in addition to its advertising campaign, it must use other communications techniques to "speak" to donors and build relationships with them. It must be creative and innovative since its budget is small, and it must also ensure that all elements of its communication plan are integrated so that consumers hear a single message linked by a common theme.

It's not surprising, therefore, that the United Way also relies heavily on public relations and its own website as a means of maintaining relationships and keeping the United Way top of mind. For example, part of the Toronto United Way's website is devoted to true stories—tales of people who have been able to change their lives as a result of help from the United Way. Since the person's picture accompanies each story, a human face is provided to those interested in seeing concrete results from their donations. The stories are also used as a means of generating publicity for the United Way. Some of the stories currently featured on the United Way of Greater Toronto's webpage have also been featured in articles in the *Toronto Star*.

Another tool to generate publicity was employed in 2006. As part of its 50th anniversary, the United Way of Greater Toronto challenged the city's creative community to design a special logo to complement the familiar "hand" logo. This was a win-win idea as the winning agency would gain recognition for its creative work. Finally, the United Way uses volunteers as its sales force. For its board of directors it recruits people who are well connected with others in the business community. When running its annual campaign, it relies on volunteers within firms, universities, and other organizations to head the campaign. These volunteers work tirelessly to convince their fellow workers to give generously to the United Way. The United Way, in turn, hosts a volunteer appreciation night at the end of the campaign.

As the United Way example illustrates, great advertising and a blend of other promotional tools need not be for a consumer product or service. Beginning with key consumer insights, the Arnold Worldwide team was able to create two arresting and compelling television campaigns that were nothing short of exceptional. The TV ads could be linked to other elements in the communication mix so that the United Way could have a unified voice when speaking to its key stakeholders.[1]

Whether selling products or ideas, organizations must inform consumers about their activities and carefully position benefits in consumers' minds. To do this, many skilfully use the mass-promotion tools of *advertising*, *sales promotion*, and *public relations*. In this chapter, we take a closer look at each of these tools.

Advertising

Advertising
Any paid form of nonpersonal presentation and promotion of ideas, goods, or services by an identified sponsor.

Advertising can be traced back to the very beginnings of recorded history. Archaeologists working in the countries around the Mediterranean Sea have dug up signs announcing various events and offers. The Romans painted walls to announce gladiator fights, and the Phoenicians painted pictures promoting their wares on large rocks along parade routes.

Modern advertising, however, is a far cry from these early efforts. Canadian organizations annually spend more than $11 billion on advertising, and companies aren't the only ones advertising. During the 2004–2005 fiscal year, the Government of Canada spent almost $50 million on advertising for campaigns on issues such as taking the "one tonne challenge," understanding the harm caused by secondhand smoke, and convincing Canadians to buy Canada Savings Bonds. Worldwide ad spending approaches an estimated US$498 billion.[2]

In the early 2000s, growth in media expenditures slowed significantly. This was partially due to marketplace dynamics, especially the numerous mergers and acquisitions of Canadian organizations. Furthermore, a strong sentiment existed in the marketing community that mass communications were becoming less effective. Today, mass media expenditures are on the rise again. There has, however, been a marked shift in how these dollars are spent. Marketers are panning traditional network TV stations in favour of speciality channels, such as the Food Network. Further, Internet expenditures are increasing, while radio spending has decreased.[3]

Though business is the heaviest user of advertising, not-for-profit organizations, professionals, governments, and social agencies also use advertising to speak to their various target publics. Advertising is a good way to inform and persuade, whether the purpose is to sell Coca-Cola worldwide or to get consumers in a developing nation to use birth control.

Marketing management must make four important decisions when developing an advertising program (see Figure 15.1): *setting advertising objectives, setting the advertising budget, developing advertising strategy* (*message decisions* and *media decisions*), and *evaluating advertising campaigns*.

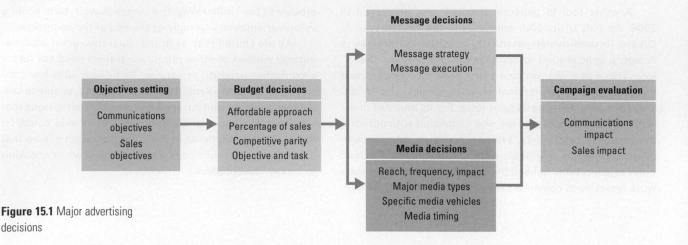

Figure 15.1 Major advertising decisions

Setting Advertising Objectives

The first step is to set *advertising objectives*. These objectives should be based on past decisions about the target market, positioning, and marketing mix, which define the job that advertising must do in the total marketing program.

Advertising objective

A specific communication *task* to be accomplished with a specific *target* audience during a specific period of *time*.

An **advertising objective** is a specific communication *task* to be accomplished with a specific *target* audience during a specific period of *time*. Advertising objectives can be classified by primary purpose—whether the aim is to *inform*, *persuade*, or *remind*. Table 15.1 lists examples of each of these objectives.

Informative advertising is used heavily when introducing a new product category. In this case, the objective is to build primary demand. Thus, early producers of DVD players first had to inform consumers of the image quality and convenience benefits of the new product. *Persuasive advertising* becomes more important as competition increases. Here, the company's objective is to build selective demand. Sony, for example, works to convince consumers that its DVD players are better quality than those of competitors.

TABLE 15.1 Possible Advertising Objectives

Informative Advertising

Telling the market about a new product	Describing available services
Suggesting new uses for a product	Correcting false impressions
Informing the market of a price change	Reducing consumers' fears
Explaining how the product works	Building a company image

Persuasive Advertising

Building brand preference	Persuading consumer to purchase now
Encouraging switching to your brand	Persuading consumer to receive a sales call
Changing consumer's perception of product attributes	

Reminder Advertising

Reminding consumer that the product may be needed in the near future	Keeping it in consumer's mind during off-seasons
Reminding consumer where to buy it	Maintaining its top-of-mind awareness

Some persuasive advertising has become *comparative advertising*, in which a company directly or indirectly compares its brand with one or more other brands. Comparative advertising has been used for products ranging from soft drinks, beer, and pain relievers to computers, batteries, car rentals, and credit cards. For example, in its classic comparative campaign, Avis positioned itself against market-leading Hertz by claiming, "We're number two, so we try harder."

More recently, Progresso ran ads showing side-by-side comparisons of its soups versus Campbell's condensed soups, inviting consumers to "Enjoy a better soup … with a more adult taste." Other examples abound: Winner's advertisements remind savvy shoppers that paying "name brand prices" isn't necessary; Tide runs spots showcasing superior performance over the competition. Advertisers should use comparative advertising with caution. All too often, such ads invite competitor responses, resulting in an advertising war that neither competitor can win.

Reminder advertising is important for mature products—it keeps consumers thinking about the product. Expensive Coca-Cola television ads primarily remind people about Coca-Cola rather than informing or persuading them.

Setting the Advertising Budget

After determining its advertising objectives, the company next sets its *advertising budget* for each product. Four commonly used methods for setting promotion budgets were discussed in Chapter 14. Here we discuss some specific factors that should be considered when setting the advertising budget.

A brand's advertising budget often depends on its *stage in the product life cycle*. For example, new products typically need large advertising budgets to build awareness and to gain consumer trial. In contrast, mature brands usually require lower

Progresso makes side-by-side comparisons of its soup versus Campbell's, inviting consumers to "Enjoy a better soup … with a more adult taste."

budgets as a ratio to sales. *Market share* also affects the amount of advertising needed: Because building the market or taking share from competitors requires larger advertising spending than does simply maintaining current share, low-share brands usually need more advertising spending as a percentage of sales. Also, brands in a market with many competitors and high advertising clutter must be advertised more heavily to be noticed above the noise in the market. L'Oréal Canada, for example, has been investing heavily in its five-year-old brand, Garnier, described as "a shining example of the big-spend-big-results school of thought." Scott Moon, director of marketing, noted that Garnier's marketing and ad spending increased by 30 percent in 2005 but that this expenditure built preference for the brand. Its hair colour line, for example, grew by 30 percent in a crowded category where other competitors experienced flat sales.[4]

Undifferentiated brands—those that closely resemble other brands in their product class (beer, soft drinks, laundry detergents)—may require heavy advertising to set them apart. When the product differs greatly from its competitors, advertising can be used to point out the differences to consumers.

No matter what method is used, setting the advertising budget is no easy task. How does a company know whether it is spending the right amount? Some critics charge that large consumer packaged-goods firms tend to spend too much on advertising and business-to-business marketers generally underspend on advertising. They claim that, on the one hand, the large consumer companies use lots of image advertising without really knowing its effects. They overspend as a form of "insurance" against not spending enough. On the other hand, business advertisers tend to rely too heavily on their sales forces to bring in orders. They underestimate the power of company and product image in pre-selling industrial customers. Thus, they do not spend enough on advertising to build customer awareness and knowledge.

Companies such as Coca-Cola and Kraft have built sophisticated statistical models to determine the relationship between promotional spending and brand sales, and to help determine the "optimal investment" across various media. Still, because so many factors affect advertising effectiveness, some controllable and others not, measuring the results of advertising spending remains an inexact science. In most cases, managers must rely on large doses of judgment along with more quantitative analysis when setting advertising budgets.[5]

Developing Advertising Strategy

Advertising strategy consists of two major elements: creating advertising *messages* and selecting advertising *media*. In the past, companies often viewed media planning as secondary to the message-creation process. The creative department first created good advertisements, and then the media department selected the best media for carrying these advertisements to desired target audiences. This often caused friction between creatives and media planners.

Today, however, media fragmentation, soaring media costs, and more-focused target marketing strategies have promoted the importance of the media-planning function. More and more, advertisers are orchestrating a closer harmony between their messages and the media that deliver them. In some cases, an advertising campaign might start with a great message idea, followed by the choice of appropriate media. In other cases, however, a campaign might begin with a good media opportunity, followed by advertisements designed to take advantage of that opportunity.

Among the more noteworthy ad campaigns based on tight media-creative partnerships is the pioneering campaign for Absolut vodka (www.absolut.com), marketed by Seagram:[6]

For years, Seagram Canada of Montreal has worked closely with more than 100 magazines, to create media-specific ads tightly targeted to audiences of the media

Absolut vodka has targeted many niche markets as part of its advertising strategy. Its ad "Absolut GLAAD" was created as part of its support for the Gay and Lesbian Alliance Against Defamation (GLAAD) awards program.

in which they appear. In all, Seagram has developed more than 500 ads for the almost two-decade-old campaign. For example, Seagram has long been an avid supporter of the gay community, and it wanted to develop ads specifically geared to gays and lesbians. For example, it worked closely with niche publication *Xtra!* magazine staff to develop the concept for the print ads "Absolut Pride," "Absolut Out" (aptly featuring a closet), and "Absolut Commitment" (showcasing two grooms on a wedding cake). A more recent ad, "Absolut GLAAD" was created for the Gay and Lesbian Alliance Against Defamation awards program. Absolut vodka made a 17-year commitment to support the Media Awards as the Founding Sponsor. The awards recognize and honour mainstream media for fair, accurate, and inclusive representations of the lesbian, gay, bisexual, and transgender community and the issues that affect their lives. When asked why she targeted the gay and lesbian community, brand manager Holly Wyatt noted, "They're young, sophisticated, somewhat upscale. And Absolut consumers do tend to swing towards the arts," she says. "It just makes sense for us."

Creating the Advertising Message

No matter how big the budget, advertising can succeed only if advertisements gain attention and communicate well. When BMO Financial Group wanted to revitalize its wealth management business and encourage people to think about saving for retirement, getting the message right for its target audience, people over 45, was an essential ingredient of success:[7]

BMO's research showed that traditional views of retirement, and in fact the word *retirement*, needed to be trashed. Its extensive study of more than 5000 Canadians revealed that more than 70 percent expect to work in retirement, so that they can stay mentally engaged, maintain social connections, and earn extra income. Caroline Dabu, vice-president and head of marketing and client strategy noted, "We wanted to really develop a marketing strategy that better reflected this new meaning. ... We wanted something more reflective of this new phase of life that people told us was going to be a period ... of personal reinvention, renewal of growth, learning new things, taking on new challenges. We wanted the advertising to portray that sense of optimism." Dabu didn't think any advertising used by banks to urge people to plan early for retirement was inspiring for younger people. Thus, Cossette Communication, the bank's advertising agency, developed the theme of "regeneration" for the new BMO campaign that integrated a TV spot, direct mail, in-branch posters and print ads, online ads that run on sites such as globeandmail.com, yahoo.ca, and nationalpost.com, and a microsite at bmo.com/regeneration. In English Canada, the ads show images of people with phrases such as "I will retire on my own terms. I will restart the clock and reclaim lost time. I will review my options. Reassess my balance sheet. Reinvest in my self. I will regenerate." In Quebec, the campaign has a slightly different focus, as attitudes toward retirement differed. Quebecers look "at retirement as continuing what they're doing, as opposed to this whole notion of personal reinvention," says Dabu.

Good advertising messages are especially important in today's costly and cluttered advertising environment. The number of television channels beamed into Canadian homes has skyrocketed from two in the 1950s to 143 commercial channels today. Add to this the growing number of American signals that are picked up by Canadians. Canadian media options also include 1998 radio stations, 108 daily newspapers, more than 1100 French and English community newspapers, and more

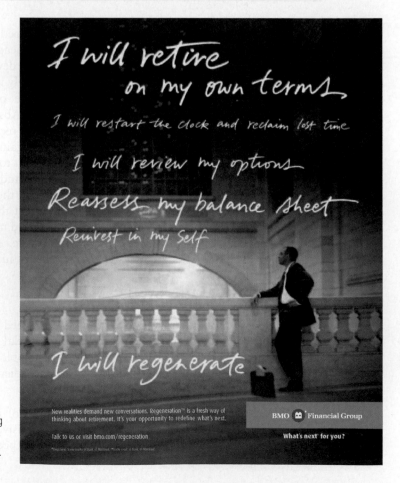

Research helped the BMO Financial Group design a powerful advertising message that inspired its target to see "retirement" in a different light.

than 1600 consumer magazines.[8] The clutter is magnified by a continuous barrage of catalogues, direct-mail and online ads, and out-of-home media.

Breaking Through the Clutter   If all this advertising clutter bothers some consumers, it also causes big problems for advertisers. Take the situation facing network television advertisers. They regularly pay US$200 000 or more for thirty seconds of advertising time during a popular prime-time program, even more if it's an especially popular program such as *ER* (US$479 000) or *Survivor* (US$412 000), or a mega-event such as the Super Bowl (as much as US$2.4 million).[9] In comparison, Canadian advertising is a bargain, but the reach is much smaller. Thirty-second spots on national networks, such as CBC and CTV, are often less than $80 000, and ads on specialty channels, such as the Discovery Channel, may be as low as $5000.

Then, sponsors' ads are sandwiched in with a clutter of other commercials, announcements, and network promotions, totalling more than fifteen minutes of non-program material per prime-time hour, more than twenty-one minutes per daytime hour. Such clutter in television and other ad media has created an increasingly hostile advertising environment. According to one recent poll, 65 percent of people say they are "constantly bombarded with too much" advertising; 61 percent say that the quantity of marketing and advertising "is out of control"; and 60 percent say that their view of advertising is "much more negative than just a few years ago."[10]

Television viewers today can avoid ads altogether by watching commercial-free cable channels. They can "zap" commercials by pushing the fast-forward button during recorded programs. A recent study found that nearly half of all television viewers now switch channels when the commercial break starts. Adding to the problem is the new wave of digital video recorders (DVRs) and personal television services—such as TiVo and ReplayTV—that have armed viewers with an arsenal of new-age commercial-avoiding weapons. A recent study of TiVo and other DVR system users found that these users skip commercials 77 percent of the time, a much higher rate than for those watching live television or using VCRs. One ad agency executive calls TiVo and Replay "electronic weedwhackers." "These machines will rock the foundation of network advertising," he declares. "In time, the number of people using them to obliterate commercials will totally erode faith in the 30-second commercial."[11]

Just to gain and hold attention, today's advertising messages must be better planned, more imaginative, more entertaining, and more rewarding to consumers. Many advertisers now see themselves as creating "advertainment"—ads that are

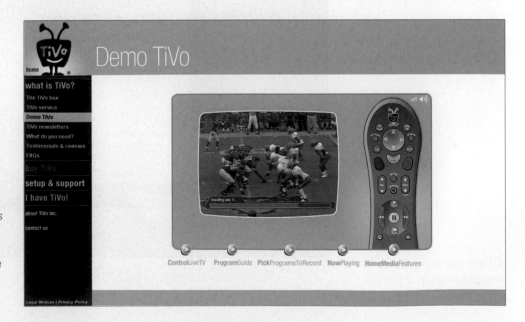

The new wave of personal video recorder services, such as TiVo, has armed viewers with an arsenal of new-age zipping and zapping weapons. One ad agency executive calls TiVo an "electronic weedwhacker."

both persuasive and entertaining. "Today we have to entertain and not just sell, because if you try to sell directly and come off as boring or obnoxious, people are going to press the remote on you," points out one advertising executive. "A commercial has to cut through the clutter and seize the viewers in one to three seconds, or they're gone," comments another.[12] When done right, even commodities can be entertaining. See what BC Dairy did with its recent milk campaign:

In an integrated, print, outdoor, cinema, television, and Internet campaign, BC Dairy imagined what would happen if prehistoric cavemen made unhealthy or healthy beverage choices. Its animated spots for cinema and TV featured a caveman so distracted by a glistening can of pop he is squashed by the foot of a sprinting T-Rex, followed by the tag line: "It's always been survival of the fittest. Drink milk." While its online campaign used a similar theme, it didn't retread the other executions. Instead, it used "Second Chance Caveman," in which it brought a caveman frozen in a block of ice into the modern world and showed what happened in a series of amusing video clips when he made the right choices and drank milk. You can view the award-winning campaign at www.drinkmilk.ca/.[13]

Some advertisers even create intentionally controversial ads to break through the clutter and gain attention for their products. (See Real Marketing 15.1.)

Many advertisers are trying to counter the TiVo trend or even turn it into an opportunity. Some companies are developing six-second ad spots that run in the time it takes a consumer to fast forward through a commercial break. Others, like Porsche, Best Buy, and Universal Music, have sponsored "advertisement showcases" on TiVo. For example, when Porsche launched its Cayenne SUV, it targeted TiVo's half million customers with an opt-in ad that allowed them to pause the pro-

It's always been survival of the fittest. Drink milk.

BC Dairy used an innovative integrated campaign to promote milk consumption.

gram and visit a branded showcase. Once there, consumers were offered additional product information, encouraged to visit the website, and given the opportunity to receive additional information.[14]

Message Strategy   The first step in creating effective advertising messages is to plan a *message strategy*—to decide what general message will be communicated to consumers. The purpose of advertising is to get consumers to think about or react to the product or company in a certain way. People will react only if they believe that they will benefit from doing so. Thus, developing an effective message strategy begins with identifying customer *benefits* that can be used as advertising appeals. Ideally, the advertising message strategy will follow directly from the company's broader positioning strategy.

REAL MARKETING   15.1

Advertising on the Edge: You Either Hate 'Em or Love 'Em

You either love 'em or you hate 'em. Today's cluttered advertising environment has spawned a new genre of "gross-out" ads that go to extremes to get attention. These irreverent, cutting-edge ads intentionally create controversy, even if it means turning off some potential customers. "It's the age-old question of breaking through the clutter," says an ad agency creative director. You turn to "anything you can to get noticed," he says.

You see these controversial ads almost everywhere. While flipping through your favourite magazine, you might encounter a Toyota ad targeting Gen Ys with the headline "Attention nose pickers." Next comes an Altoids ad in which a man peers down the front of his boxer shorts: "Shrinkage may occur," proclaims the ad's headline. "The curiously strong mints." The headline for an Altoids Sours ad screams "One bad motherpucker!" Other Altoids ads feature a women in a seductively devilish outfit, complete with horns, and headlines such as "Hot and bothered?" "Frigid?" and "Taste like hell!"

Print ads often lead a reader to microsites where the gross out continues. Take the case of Guru, a Montreal-based maker of high-end, custom-made bicycles. Headlines in print ads read, "Biking can

SHRINKAGE MAY OCCUR
THE CURIOUSLY STRONG MINTS

IS IT HOT IN HERE, OR IS IT JUST ME?

WWW.TOOHOT.COM

To be truly cutting-edge, advertising must do more than just capture attention. Altoids's irreverent ads fit the brand's "curious, strong, original" positioning and appeal to its cutting-edge target customers.

▶

teach valuable lessons about focus and perseverance. Not to mention the importance of turning your head to spit." Readers are then led to an online game in which the player is challenged to spit at other cyclists going by. (Try it out at www.gurubikes.com/devoted_to_cycling/.) The penalty for a miss is a mass of gob hitting the player's face and total destruction if you lose the contest five times. Other crude humour on the site included a vulture eating the losing cyclist's entrails. The site drew traffic because of its original retro-look graphics as well as its off-the-wall humour and it helped Guru's sales rise by 22 percent.

On television, Axe shower gel ads feature young men in a variety of risqué situations with beautiful women. The tagline calls out "New Axe Shower Gel—How Dirty Boys Get Clean." Then, there's the "They're Nuts" outdoor campaign which ran in Western Canada to promote Edmonton's K-Rock 97.3 FM. The billboards featured three nude radio announcers holding large nuts in front of their "private parts" while the tagline proclaimed "See, They're Nuts." The ads generated a huge amount of publicity, not all of it good. Numerous complaints were registered with the Advertising Standards Council, which ordered the ads to be taken down. Steve Jones, VP of programming for Nova-Scotia-based NewCap Broadcasting, owners of K-Rock, said he wasn't surprised by the complaints. But he notes, "From a PR point of view, the ads did some pretty exceptional work for us. They generated a great deal of local and national newspaper and TV coverage."

For pure gross-out value, few ads top the recent ad from Wendy's for their Spicy Chicken sandwich. The ad opens with a full clothed man in the shower, drinking the water from the shower-head. As the spot continues, people are shown drinking from progressively more disgusting locations: a sprinkler, a flower-vase, a public-pool, a waterbed, and, most appallingly, a fish tank. At the end of the ad, the announcer calmly states, "If you can't stand the heat, stay out of the chicken."

Such outrageous ads can grab attention, create word of mouth, and even win awards. However, such techniques often attract more attention to the ad itself than to the brand's selling proposition. If used improperly, controversial ads can boost viewer attention but actually *distract* from the selling message. To be effective, advertising must support and enhance the brand and its positioning.

If used properly, cutting-edge humour can help do that, as proved by Altoids and its "Curiously Strong" campaign. The campaign's irreverent, sometimes controversial ads fit the brand's "curious, strong, original" positioning. They also appeal to the tastes as well as the taste buds of Altoids' cutting-edge target consumers. "We're allowed to poke fun at people," says an Altoids executive, "so we take advantage of it when we can." As a result, in only two years, the small-budget but high-impact ad campaign propelled Altoids past long-time strong-mint market leader Tic Tac. "Altoids is now—improbably—the boss of the mint world," says an analyst. What's the power behind this cheeky campaign? The analyst confirms that "Everything links back to [the brand's] 'curiously strong' and 'original' [positioning]."

Sources: Samson Okalow, "Now That the Ad Code Is Relaxed, How Far Should You Go?" *Strategy,* June 30, 2003, p. 2; Advertising Standards Canada, "2002 Ad Complaints Report," 2003, www.adstandards.com/en/standards/complaints_report/2002ascReportEn.pdf; Melanie Wells; Rob Gerlsbeck, "2005 Digital Marketing Award Winners," *Marketing Daily,* October 31, 2005; Tim Nudd and Jack Feuer, "Everyone's an Ad Critic," *Adweek,* February 3, 2003, p. 44; Tom Kurtz, "Unsettling TV Commercials: And Now, a Gross-Out from Our Sponsor," *New York Times,* July 25, 1999, p. 7; Mae Anderson, "The Fine Print," *Adweek,* June 7, 2004, p. 24; and information at www.altoids.com (accessed January 2005).

Message strategy statements tend to be plain, straightforward outlines of benefits and positioning points that the advertiser wants to stress. The advertiser must next develop a compelling *creative concept*—or "big idea"—that will bring the message strategy to life in a distinctive and memorable way. At this stage, simple message ideas become great ad campaigns. Usually, a copywriter and art director will team up to generate many creative concepts, hoping that one of these concepts will turn out to be the big idea. The creative concept may emerge as a visualization, a phrase, or a combination of the two.

The creative concept will guide the choice of specific appeals to be used in an advertising campaign. *Advertising appeals* should have three characteristics: First, they should be *meaningful,* pointing out benefits that make the product more desirable or interesting to consumers. Second, appeals must be *believable*—consumers must believe that the product or service will deliver the promised benefits.

However, the most meaningful and believable benefits may not be the best ones to feature. Appeals should also be *distinctive*—they should tell how the product is better than the competing brands. For example, the most meaningful benefit of owning a wristwatch is that it keeps accurate time, yet few watch ads feature this benefit. Instead, based on the distinctive benefits they offer, watch advertisers might select any of a number of advertising themes. For years, Timex has been the affordable watch that "Takes a lickin' and keeps on tickin'." In contrast, Guess has featured style and fashion, whereas Rolex stresses luxury and status.

Message Execution   The advertiser now has to turn the big idea into an actual ad execution that will capture the target market's attention and interest. The creative people must find the best style, tone, words, and format for executing the message. Any message can be presented in different *execution styles*, such as the following:

- *Slice of life:* This style shows one or more "typical" people using the product in a normal setting. For example, two mothers at a picnic discuss the nutritional benefits of Kraft peanut butter.

- *Lifestyle:* This style shows how a product fits in with a particular lifestyle. For example, an ad for Mongoose mountain bikes shows a serious biker traversing remote and rugged but beautiful terrain and states, "There are places that are so awesome and so killer that you'd like to tell the whole world about them. But please, *don't.*"

- *Fantasy:* This style creates a fantasy around the product or its use. For instance, many ads are built around dream themes. The Gap even introduced a perfume named Dream. Ads show a woman sleeping blissfully and suggests that the scent is "the stuff that clouds are made of."

- *Mood or image:* This style builds a mood or image around the product, such as beauty, love, or serenity. No claim is made about the product except through suggestion. Bermuda tourism ads create such moods.

- *Musical:* This style shows one or more people or cartoon characters singing about the product. For example, one of the most famous ads in history was a Coca-Cola ad built around the song "I'd Like to Teach the World to Sing." Similarly, Oscar-Meyer has long run ads showing children singing its now famous classic "Oh, I wish I were an Oscar-Meyer wiener ..." jingle.

- *Personality symbol:* This style creates a character that represents the product. The character might be *animated* (the Jolly Green Giant, Cap'n Crunch, Garfield the Cat) or *real* ("Joe" from Molson's "I am Canadian!" campaign, Ol' Lonely the Maytag repairman, or the AFLAC duck).

- *Technical expertise:* This style shows the company's expertise in making the product. Thus, Maxwell House shows one of its buyers carefully selecting coffee beans, and Gallo tells about its many years of wine-making experience.

- *Scientific evidence:* This style presents survey or scientific evidence that the brand is better or better liked than one or more other brands. For years, Crest toothpaste has used scientific evidence to convince buyers that Crest is better than other brands at fighting cavities.

- *Testimonial evidence or endorsement:* This style features a highly believable or likable source endorsing the product. It could be ordinary people saying how much they like a given product or a celebrity presenting the product. For example, Apple recently ran ads featuring real people who'd recently switched from Microsoft Windows-based PCs to Macs. And many companies use actors or sports celebrities as product endorsers.

The advertiser also must choose a *tone* for the ad. Procter & Gamble always uses a positive tone: its ads say something very positive about its products. P&G usually avoids humour that might take attention away from the message. In contrast, many advertisers now use edgy humour to break through the commercial clutter.

Oscar Mayer has long run ads featuring its now classic "Oh, I wish I were an Oscar Mayer wiener ..." jingle.

The advertiser must use memorable and attention-getting *words* in the ad. For example, rather than claiming simply that "a BMW is a well-engineered automobile," BMW uses more creative and higher-impact phrasing: "The ultimate driving machine."

Finally, *format* elements make a difference in an ad's impact as well as in its cost. A small change in ad design can make a big difference in its effect. To understand format elements, let's look at ads in two media: print and radio. In print ads, the *illustration* is the first thing the reader notices—it must be strong enough to draw attention. Next, the *headline* must effectively entice the right people to read the copy. Finally, the *copy*—the main block of text in the ad—must be simple but strong and convincing. Moreover, these three elements must effectively work *together*. Terry O'Reilly, director of Pirate Radio in Toronto and host of the radio show *O'Reilly on Advertising* aired on CBC, believes you can do more with a radio ad than with any other medium. Since people are often doing something else when listening to the radio, ads in this medium are formatted to grab attention immediately so format is extremely important. His shows demonstrate how radio advertisers creatively use humour, music, voiceovers, and sound effects to grab listeners' attention and drive sales.

Selecting Advertising Media

The major steps in media selection are (1) deciding on *reach*, *frequency*, and *impact*; (2) choosing among major *media types*; (3) selecting specific *media vehicles*; and (4) deciding on *media* timing.

Deciding on Reach, Frequency, and Impact   To select media, the advertiser must decide on the reach and frequency needed to achieve advertising objectives. *Reach* is a measure of the *percentage* of people in the target market who are exposed to the ad campaign during a given period of time. For example, the advertiser might try to reach 70 percent of the target market during the first three months of the campaign. For newspapers and magazines, pass-along readership (where the same newspaper or magazine is read by more than one person) may increase its reach. *Frequency* is a measure of how many *times* the average person in the target market is exposed to the message. For example, the advertiser might want an average exposure frequency of three.

The advertiser also must decide on the desired *media impact*—the *qualitative value* of a message exposure through a given medium. For example, for products that need to be demonstrated, messages on television may have more impact than messages on radio because television uses sight *and* sound. The same message in one magazine (say, *Newsweek*) may be more believable than in another (say, *The National Enquirer*). In general, the more reach, frequency, and impact the advertiser seeks, the higher the advertising budget will have to be.

Choosing Among Major Media Types   The media planner has to know the reach, frequency, and impact of each of the major media types. As summarized in Table 15.2, the major media types are newspapers, television, direct mail, radio, magazines, outdoor, and the Internet. Each medium has advantages and limitations.

Media planners consider many factors when making their media choices. The *media habits of target consumers* will affect media choice—advertisers look for media that reach target consumers effectively. So will the *nature of the product*—for example, fashions are best advertised in colour magazines, and automobile performance is best demonstrated on television. Different *types of messages* may require different media. A message announcing a major sale tomorrow will require radio or newspapers; a message with a lot of technical data might require magazines, direct mailings, or an online ad and website. *Cost* is another major factor in media choice. For example, network television is very expensive, whereas news-

TABLE 15.2 Profiles of Major Media Types

Medium	Advantages	Limitations
Newspapers	Flexibility; timeliness; good local market coverage; broad acceptability; high believability	Short life; poor reproduction quality; small pass-along audience
Television	Good mass-market coverage; low cost per exposure; combines sight, sound, and motion; appealing to the senses	High absolute costs; high clutter; fleeting exposure; less audience selectivity
Direct mail	High audience selectivity; flexibility; no ad competition within the same medium; allows personalization	Relatively high cost per exposure; "junk mail" image
Radio	Good local acceptance; high geographic and demographic selectivity; low cost	Audio only; fleeting exposure; low attention ("the half-heard" medium); fragmented audiences
Magazines	High geographic and demographic selectivity; credibility and prestige; high-quality reproduction; long life and good pass-along readership	Long ad purchase lead time; high cost
Outdoor	Flexibility; high repeat exposure; low cost; low message competition; good positional selectivity	Little audience selectivity; creative limitations
Internet	High selectivity; low cost; immediacy; interactive capabilities	Small, demographically skewed audience; relatively low impact; audience controls exposure

paper or radio advertising costs much less but also reaches fewer consumers. The media planner looks both at the total cost of using a medium and at the cost per exposure of reaching specific target customers.

Media impact and cost must be re-examined regularly. For a long time, television and magazines have dominated in the media mixes of national advertisers, with other media often neglected. Recently, however, as network television costs soar and audiences shrink, many advertisers are looking for new ways to reach consumers. The move toward micromarketing strategies, focused more narrowly on specific consumer groups, has also fuelled the search for new media to replace or supplement network television. As a result, advertisers are increasingly shifting larger portions of their budgets to media that cost less and target more effectively.

Three media benefiting greatly from the shift are outdoor advertising, cable television, and digital satellite television systems. Billboards have undergone a resurgence in recent years. Gone are the ugly eyesores of the past; in their place we now see cleverly designed, colourful attention grabbers. Outdoor advertising provides an excellent way to reach important local consumer segments at a fraction of the cost per exposure of other major media. Cable television and satellite systems are also booming. Such systems allow narrow programming formats, such as all sports, all news, nutrition, arts, gardening, cooking, travel, history, and others that target select groups. Advertisers can take advantage of such "narrowcasting" to "rifle in" on special market segments rather than using the "shotgun" approach offered by network broadcasting.

Outdoor, cable, and satellite media seem to make good sense. But, increasingly, ads are popping up in far less likely places. In their efforts to find less costly and more highly targeted ways to reach consumers, advertisers have discovered a dazzling collection of "alternative media." (See Real Marketing 15.2.)

Another important trend affecting media selection is the rapid growth in the number of "media multi-taskers," people who absorb more than one medium at a time:

> It looks like people who aren't satisfied with "just watching TV" are in good company. According to a [recent] survey,... three-fourths of U.S. TV viewers read the newspaper while they watch TV, and two-thirds of them go online dur-

REAL MARKETING | 15.2

Advertisers Seek Alternative Media

These days, no matter where you go or what you do, you probably will run into some new form of advertising. Tiny billboards attached to shopping carts, ads on shopping bags, and even advertising decals on supermarket floors urge you to buy Jell-O Pudding Pops or Pampers. Signs atop parking meters hawk everything from Jeeps to Minolta cameras to Recipe dog food. You escape to the ballpark, only to find bill-

board-size video screens running Budweiser ads while a blimp with an electronic message board circles lazily overhead. How about a quiet trip in the country? Sorry—you find an enterprising farmer using his milk cows as four-legged billboards mounted with ads for Ben & Jerry's ice cream.

You pay to see a movie at your local theatre, but first have to view a series of ads, and then discover that the film itself is full of not-so-subtle promotional plugs for Molson beer, Pepsi, Domino's Pizza, MasterCard, Mercedes, Ray Ban sunglasses, or any of a dozen other products. You head home and pop in the latest video game and find that your action character is jumping into a Jeep on the way to the skateboarding park. Tired, you decide to watch a little TV only to find your favourite sitcom full of "virtual placements" of Coca-Cola, Frito Lay, or Sony products digitally inserted into the program. Toronto-based MMI Product Placement may be responsible for these placements. It pioneered product placement in Canada. Since its birth in 1985, it has been credited with more than 2000 product placements in feature films and TV episodes.

Trains and buses can be seen covered in billboards or painted with sponsors' ads. Go to the airport, you're treated to the CNN Airport Network. Shortly after your plane lifts off the runway, you look out the window and spot a 150-metre-diameter crop circle carved into a farmer's field depicting Monster.com's mascot and corporate logo. As you wait to pick up your luggage, ads for Kenneth Cole baggage roll by on the luggage carousel conveyor belt.

These days, you're likely to find ads—well, anywhere. Boats cruise along public beaches flashing advertising messages for Sundown Sunscreen as sunbathers spread their towels over ads for Snapple pressed into the sand. Ad space is being sold on video cases, parking-lot tickets, golf scorecards, delivery trucks, gas pumps, ATMs, municipal garbage cans, police cars, and church bulletins. One agency even rents space on the foreheads of college students for temporary advertising tattoos.

Some consumers resent this "ad nauseam." But for many marketers, these media can save money and provide a way to hit selected consumers where they live, shop, work, and play. Think of every place you wait in line (the average person waits in line about 30 minutes a day)—you're sure to find advertising there. "We like to call it the captive pause," says an executive of an alternative-media firm. Transit riders are one such captive audience. So, companies such as Snapple, Calvin Klein, and American Express are testing new technologies to reach captive consumers. Riders on Manhattan's subway system, for example, now see a series of light boxes speed by that create a moving commercial in the subway car's windows.

Of course, this may leave you wondering if there are any commercial-free havens remaining for ad-weary consumers. The back seat of a taxi, perhaps, or public elevators, or stalls in a public restroom? Forget it! Each has already been invaded by innovative marketers.

Sources: See Cara Beardi, "From Elevators to Gas Stations, Ads Multiplying," *Advertising Age,* November 13, 2000, pp. 40–42; Charles Pappas, "Ad Nauseam," *Advertising Age,* July 10, 2000, pp. 16–18; Wayne Friedman, "Eagle-Eye Marketers Find Right Spot," *Advertising Age,* January 22, 2001, pp. S2–S3; Stephanie Mehta, "Ads Invade Video Games," *Fortune,* May 26, 2003, p. 46; Brian Hindo, "Getting a Head," *Business Week,* January 12, 2004, p. 14; and Sam Jaffe, "Easy Riders," *American Demographics,* March 2004, pp. 20–23; Deena Waisberg, "Branded clientele," *Financial Post,* September 17, 2005.

Marketers have discovered a dazzling array of "alternative media."

ing their TV time. Of those who are waiting for downloads from the Internet, 61.8 percent watch TV, 52.1 percent listen to the radio, and 20.2 percent read the newspaper. According to the study, 70 percent of media users say they at one time or another try to absorb two or more forms of media at once.[15]

Media planners need to take such media interactions into account when selecting the types of media they will use.

Selecting Specific Media Vehicles   The media planner now must choose the best *media vehicles*—specific media within each general media type. For example, television vehicles include *This Hour Has 22 Minutes, Grey's Anatomy, The National,* and *Hockey Night in Canada.* Magazine vehicles include *Maclean's, Chatelaine,* and *Lou Lou.*

Media planners must also compute the cost per thousand persons reached by a vehicle. For example, if a full-page, four-colour advertisement in *Maclean's* costs $32 600 and *Maclean's* readership is 400 029 people, the cost of reaching each group of a thousand persons is about $81. The same advertisement in *Cottage Life* may cost only $9940 but reach only 70 351 persons—at a cost per thousand of about $142. The media planner would rank each magazine by cost per thousand and favour those magazines with the lower cost per thousand for reaching target consumers.[16]

The media planner must also consider the costs of producing ads for different media. Whereas newspaper ads may cost very little to produce, flashy television ads may cost millions. If companies want to reach the massive U.S. audience, they may have to pay anywhere from US$350 000 to US$2 million to produce a single 30-second television commercial.[17] In selecting media vehicles, the media planner must balance media cost measures against several media impact factors. First, the planner should balance costs against the media vehicle's *audience quality.* For a Huggies disposable diapers advertisement, for example, *Today's Parent* magazine would have a high exposure value; *The Hockey News* would have a low-exposure value. Second, the media planner should consider *audience attention.* Readers of *Flare,* for example, typically pay more attention to ads than do readers of *The Economist.* Third, the planner should assess the vehicle's *editorial quality*— *Maclean's* and *Canadian Business* are more believable and prestigious than *The National Enquirer.*

Deciding on Media Timing   The advertiser must also decide how to schedule the advertising over the course of a year. Suppose sales of a product peak in December and drop in March. The firm can vary its advertising to follow the seasonal pattern, to oppose the seasonal pattern, or to be the same all year. Most firms do some seasonal advertising. For example, Sears Portrait Studio advertises more heavily before major holidays, such as Christmas, and newspapers in May are full of flyers featuring Mother's Day gifts. Some marketers do *only* seasonal advertising: For example, Hallmark advertises its greeting cards only before major holidays. Some firms advertise heavily around certain events rather than seasons. Visa has been a long-time Olympic sponsor. Before the 2006 Winter Games in Torino, it ran a contest called Visa's Olympics of the Imagination children's art challenge, a program Visa first started running in the lead-up to the 1994 Lillehammer Olympic Winter Games in Norway, in which it invited children aged 9 to 13 from all over the world to take part in its "art challenge." Four winners from Canada were invited to attend the games and blog about their Olympic experience. The contest was promoted through schools and more than 6500 Canadian kids entered the contest.[18]

Finally, the advertiser has to choose the pattern of the ads. *Continuity* means scheduling ads evenly within a given period. *Pulsing* means scheduling ads unevenly over a given time period. Thus, 52 ads could either be scheduled at one

Visa's Olympics of the Imagination contest was a novel means of promoting its sponsorship of the winter games.

per week during the year or pulsed in several bursts. The idea behind pulsing is to advertise heavily for a short period to build awareness that carries over to the next advertising period. Those who favour pulsing feel that it can be used to achieve the same impact as a steady schedule but at a much lower cost. However, some media planners believe that although pulsing achieves minimal awareness, it sacrifices depth of advertising communications.

Recent advances in technology have had a substantial impact on the media planning and buying functions. Today, for example, computer software applications called *media optimizers* allow media planners to evaluate vast combinations of television programs and prices. Such programs help advertisers to make better decisions about which mix of networks, programs, and day parts will yield the highest reach per ad dollar.

Evaluating Advertising

The advertising program should evaluate both the communication effects and the sales effects of advertising regularly. Measuring the *communication effects* of an ad—*copy testing*—tells whether the ad is communicating well. Copy testing can be done before or after an ad is printed or broadcast. Before the ad is placed, the advertiser can show it to consumers, ask how they like it, and measure message recall or attitude changes resulting from it. After the ad is run, the advertiser can measure how the ad affected consumer recall or product awareness, knowledge, and preference.

But what *sales* are caused by an ad that increases brand awareness by 20 percent and brand preference by 10 percent? The *sales effects* of advertising are often harder to measure than the communication effects. Sales are affected by many factors besides advertising—such as product features, price, and availability.

One way to measure the sales effect of advertising is to compare past sales with past advertising expenditures. Another way is through experiments. For example, to test the effects of different advertising spending levels, Coca-Cola could vary the amount it spends on advertising in different market areas and measure the differences in the resulting sales levels. It could spend the normal amount in one market area, half the normal amount in another area, and twice the normal amount in a third area. If the three market areas are similar, and if all other marketing efforts in the area are the same, then differences in sales in the three areas could be related to advertising level. More complex experiments could be designed to include other variables, such as difference in the ads or media used.

Other Advertising Considerations

In developing advertising strategies and programs, the company must address two additional questions. First, how will the company organize its advertising function—who will perform which advertising tasks? Second, how will the company adapt its advertising strategies and programs to the complexities of international markets?

Organizing for Advertising

Different companies organize in different ways to handle advertising. In small companies, advertising might be handled by someone in the sales department. Large companies set up advertising departments whose job it is to set the advertising budget, work with the ad agency, and handle other advertising not done by the agency. Most large companies use outside advertising agencies because they offer several advantages.

Advertising agency
A marketing services firm that assists companies in planning, preparing, implementing, and evaluating all or portions of their advertising programs.

How does an **advertising agency** work? Advertising agencies were started in the mid-to-late 1800s by salespeople and brokers who worked for the media and received a commission for selling advertising space to companies. As time passed, the salespeople began to help customers prepare their ads. Eventually, they formed agencies and grew closer to the advertisers than to the media.

Today's agencies employ specialists who can often perform advertising tasks better than the company's own staff. Agencies also bring an outside point of view to solving the company's problems, along with lots of experience from working with different clients and situations. So, today, even companies with strong advertising departments of their own use advertising agencies.

Marketing Magazine produces an annual report that ranks advertising agencies according to their revenues. However, it should be noted that many U.S.-based agencies with Canadian branch offices (e.g., Interpublic Group of Companies, Grey Global Group, Omnicom Group, and Publics S.A.) are excluded from the list since they refuse to provide financial data. Cossette Communication Group, headquartered in Quebec City, remains the dominant player in the Canadian market. Other firms making the top five are MDC Partners, Maritz Canada, Carlson Marketing Group Canada, and Redwood Custom Communications.[19]

Having Canadian agencies with insight into our unique marketplaces is important. One survey revealed that 45 percent of English Canadians say they care a lot about whether the commercials they view on television are created in Canada. This percentage is even higher in Quebec, where 58 percent of the respondents stressed that they want commercials especially designed for them. Canadian viewers also believe that they can tell whether a commercial is Canadian made.[20]

In recent years, many agencies have grown by gobbling up other agencies, thus creating huge agency holding companies. The largest of these agency "megagroups," Omincon Group, includes several large advertising, public relations, and promotion agencies with combined worldwide revenues of US$8.6 billion.[21] Most large advertising agencies have the staff and resources to handle all phases of an advertising campaign for their clients, from creating a marketing plan to developing ad campaigns and preparing, placing, and evaluating ads.

Many agencies have sought growth by diversifying into related marketing services. These new diversified agencies offer a complete list of integrated marketing and promotion services under one roof, including advertising, sales promotion, marketing research, public relations, and direct and online marketing. Some have even added marketing consulting, television production, and sales training units in an effort to become full "marketing partners" to their clients.

However, agencies are finding that most advertisers don't want much more from them than traditional media advertising services plus direct marketing, sales promotion, and sometimes public relations. Thus, many agencies have recently limited their diversification efforts in order to focus more on traditional services. Some have even started their own "creative boutiques," smaller and more independent agencies that can develop creative campaigns for clients free of large-agency bureaucracy.

International Advertising Decisions

International advertisers face many complexities not encountered by domestic advertisers. The most basic issue concerns the degree to which global advertising should be adapted to the unique characteristics of various country markets. Some large advertisers have attempted to support their global brands with highly standardized worldwide advertising, with campaigns that work as well in Bangkok, Thailand, as they do in Battleford, Saskatchewan. For example, Jeep has created a worldwide brand image of ruggedness and reliability; Coca-Cola's Sprite brand uses standardized appeals to target the world's youth. Gillette's ads for its Gillette for Women Venus razor are almost identical worldwide, with only minor adjustments to suit the local culture.

Standardization produces many benefits—lower advertising costs, greater global advertising coordination, and a more consistent worldwide image. But it also has drawbacks. Most importantly, it ignores the fact that country markets differ greatly in their cultures, demographics, and economic conditions. Thus, most international advertisers "think globally but act locally." They develop global advertising *strategies* that make their worldwide advertising efforts more efficient and consistent. Then they adapt their advertising *programs* to make them more responsive to consumer needs and expectations within local markets. For example, Coca-Cola has a pool of different commercials that can be used in or adapted to several different international markets. Some can be used with only minor changes—such as language—in several different countries. Local and regional managers decide which commercials work best for which markets.

Global advertisers face several special problems. For instance, advertising media costs and availability differ vastly from country to country. Countries also differ in the extent to which they regulate advertising practices. Many countries have extensive systems of laws restricting how much a company can spend on advertising, the media used, the nature of advertising claims, and other aspects of the advertising program. Such restrictions often require advertisers to adapt their campaigns from country to country.

Gillette's ads for its Gillette for Women Venus razors are almost identical worldwide, with only minor adjustments to suit the local culture.

What is it about PINK that makes you feel so good?

Introducing *Passion Pink Venus*
From Gillette.

It shaves you so close, your skin stays smoother, longer.

¿Qué tiene el ROSA que te hace sentir tan bien?

Presentamos Venus de Gillette en un escandaloso nuevo color. Rosa Pasión.

Jamais le ROSE ne vous a fait autant d'effet !

Découvrez Venus Rose Passion de Gillette.

For example, alcoholic products cannot be advertised or sold in Muslim countries. In many countries, Sweden, for example, or in the province of Quebec, no TV ads may be directed at children. Moreover, Sweden is lobbying to extend that ban to all European Union countries. To play it safe, McDonald's advertises itself as a family restaurant in Sweden. Comparative ads, though acceptable and even common in the United States and Canada, are less commonly used in the United Kingdom, unacceptable in Japan, and illegal in India and Brazil. China has restrictive censorship rules for TV and radio advertising; for example, the words *the best* are banned, as are ads that "violate social customs" or present women in "improper ways." Coca-Cola's Indian subsidiary was forced to end a promotion that offered prizes, such as a trip to Hollywood, because it violated India's established trade practices by encouraging customers to buy in order to "gamble."[22]

Thus, although advertisers may develop global strategies to guide their overall advertising efforts, specific advertising programs must usually be adapted to meet local cultures and customs, media characteristics, and advertising regulations.

Sales Promotion

Sales promotion

Short-term incentives to encourage the purchase or sale of a product or service.

Advertising often works closely with another promotion tool, sales promotion. **Sales promotion** consists of short-term incentives to encourage purchase or sales of a product or service. Whereas advertising offers reasons to buy a product or service, sales promotion offers reasons to buy *now*.

Examples of sales promotions are found everywhere. A freestanding insert (FSI) in the Sunday newspaper contains a coupon offering $1 off President's Choice coffee. An email from Chapters.Indigo.ca offers iRewards members free shipping on their next purchase over $35. The end-of-the-aisle display in the local supermarket tempts impulse buyers with a wall of Coke cartons. An executive buys a new Sony laptop and gets a free carrying case, or a family buys a new Pontiac Montana and receives a factory rebate of $500. A hardware store chain receives a 10 percent discount on selected Black & Decker portable power tools if it agrees to advertise them in local newspapers. Sales promotion includes a wide variety of promotion tools designed to stimulate earlier or stronger market response.

Rapid Growth of Sales Promotion

Sales promotion tools are used by most organizations, including manufacturers, distributors, retailers, and not-for-profit institutions. They are targeted toward final buyers (*consumer promotions*), retailers and wholesalers (*trade promotions*), business customers (*business promotions*), and members of the sales force (*sales force promotions*). Today, in the average consumer packaged-goods company, sales promotion accounts for 76 percent of all marketing expenditures.[23]

Several factors have contributed to the rapid growth of sales promotion, particularly in consumer markets. First, inside the company, product managers face greater pressures to increase their current sales, and promotion is viewed as an effective short-run sales tool. Second, externally, the company faces more competition and competing brands are less differentiated. Increasingly, competitors are using sales promotion to help differentiate their offers. Third, advertising efficiency has declined because of rising costs, media clutter, and legal restraints. Finally, consumers have become more deal oriented, and ever-larger retailers are demanding more deals from manufacturers.

The growing use of sales promotion has resulted in *promotion clutter*, similar to advertising clutter. Consumers are increasingly tuning out promotions, weakening their ability to trigger immediate purchase. Manufacturers are now searching for ways to rise above the clutter, such as offering larger coupon values or creating more dramatic point-of-purchase displays.

In developing a sales promotion program, a company must first set sales promotion objectives and then select the best tools for accomplishing these objectives.

Sales Promotion Objectives

Sales promotion objectives vary widely. Sellers may use *consumer promotions* to increase short-term sales or to help build long-term market share. Objectives for *trade promotions* include getting retailers to carry new items and more inventory, getting them to advertise the product and give it more shelf space, and getting them to buy ahead. For the *sales force*, objectives include getting more sales force support for current or new products or getting salespeople to sign up new accounts. Sales promotions are usually used together with advertising, personal selling, or other promotion mix tools. Consumer promotions must usually be advertised and can add excitement and pulling power to ads. Trade and sales force promotions support the firm's personal selling process.

In general, rather than creating only short-term sales or temporary brand switching, sales promotions should help to reinforce the product's position and build long-term *customer relationships*. Increasingly, marketers attempt to avoid "quick fix," price-only promotions in favour of promotions designed to build brand equity.

Even price promotions can be designed to help build customer relationships. Examples include all of the "frequency marketing programs" and loyalty clubs that have mushroomed in recent years. For example, many supermarkets, drugstores, hotels, and airlines now offer frequent-buyer/flyer/guest programs offering discounts to regular customers. Lladró, maker of fine porcelain figurines, sponsors the Lladró Privilege Society. Members receive a subscription to the *Lladró Privilege Magazine*, access to exclusive Lladró sculptures, invitations to attend a variety of prestigious social gatherings and cultural events, as well as other relationship benefits.

The "loyalty marketing programs" that have mushroomed in recent years are other examples of sales promotions used to solidify relationships with customers. Air Miles is one of the best-known programs, but many others flourish. Shoppers Drug Market offers the Optimum card, HBC offers its own points, and Indigo has an iRewards program for book and music lovers.

Major Sales Promotion Tools

Many tools can be used to accomplish sales promotion objectives. Descriptions of the main consumer, trade, and business promotion tools follow.

Consumer Promotion Tools

The main *consumer promotion tools* include samples; coupons; cash refunds; price packs; premiums; advertising specialties; patronage rewards; point-of-purchase displays and demonstrations; and contests, sweepstakes, and games.

Sample
A small amount of a product offered to customers for trial.

Samples are offers of a trial amount of a product. Sampling is the most effective—but most expensive—way to introduce a new product. For example, to launch Vanilla Coke, Coca-Cola distributed more than 1.3 million samples of the beverage. But the soft drink marketer didn't just hand out the samples. Instead, Coke's "experiential sampling teams" stopped targeted teen consumers at hangouts like malls, skate parks, concerts, and fairs, then delivered live commercials with messages like

LLADRÓ PRIVILEGE

INNER BEAUTY

Benefits of the Lladró Privilege Society include a subscription to the *Lladró Privilege Magazine,* access to exclusive Lladró sculptures, invitations to attend a variety of prestigious social gatherings and cultural events, and other relationship benefits.

"Satisfy your curiosity, try a free Vanilla Coke." Says the president of Coca Cola's promotion agency, "We wanted to get Vanilla Coke's target audience with a memorable live experience for the brand." Based on the success of the Vanilla Coke sampling effort, Coca-Cola recently used its sampling teams to distribute more than 4 million samples of its new low-carb alternative, C2.[24]

Some samples are free; for others, the company charges a small amount to offset its cost. The sample might be delivered door to door, sent by mail, handed out in a store, attached to another product, or featured in an ad. Sometimes, samples are combined into sample packs, which can then be used to promote other products and services. The U.K. health food brand Eat Natural distributed samples via the Internet by encouraging customers to log on and send free products to their friends and families. Procter & Gamble also distributed samples via the Web:[25]

When Procter & Gamble decided to relaunch Pert Plus shampoo, it extended its $26 million ad campaign by constructing a new website (www.pertplus.com). P&G had three objectives for the website: to create awareness for reformulated Pert Plus, get consumers to try the product, and gather data about Web users. The site's first page invited visitors to place their heads against the computer screen in a mock attempt to measure the cleanliness of their hair. After "tabulating the results," the site told visitors that they "need immediate help." The solution: "How about a free sample of new Pert Plus?" Visitors obtained the sample by filling out a short demographic form. The site offered other interesting features as well. For example, clicking "get a friend in a lather" produced a template that sent an email to a friend with an invitation to visit the site and receive a free sample. How did the sampling promotion work out? Even P&G was shocked by the turnout. Within just two months of launching the site, 170 000 people visited and 83 000 requested samples. More surprising, given that the site was only ten pages deep, the average person visited the site 1.9 times and spent a total of 7.5 minutes each visit.

Sampling has grown rapidly in Canada. Recent research has shown that when given a choice between a free sample and a coupon, 92 percent of consumers prefer a sample. New parents, giddy with the excitement of a new baby, soak up marketing material like sponges and are prime targets for sampling campaigns. At Starcom Worldwide in Toronto, whose clients include baby-food manufacturer H.J. Heinz Canada, VP media director Mariam Hoosen announces, "New moms are always looking for information, so sampling and direct mail are ideal ways of reaching them." Expectant mothers who sign up for baby clubs, such as Mead Johnson's Baby Steps (through subscription forms available in pregnancy magazines and online), can expect to receive free samples of formula through the mail, together with information about baby nutrition. Sampling is also key for Gerber, whose products include bottles, pacifiers, and cups.[26]

Coupon
Certificate that gives buyers a saving when they purchase a specified product.

Coupons are certificates that give buyers a saving when they purchase specified products. Coupons can promote early trial of a new brand or stimulate sales of a mature brand. However, as a result of coupon clutter, redemption rates have been declining in recent years. Thus, most major consumer goods companies are issuing fewer coupons and targeting them more carefully.

Marketers are also cultivating new outlets for distributing coupons, such as supermarket shelf dispensers, or electronic point-of-sale coupon printers. Some companies also offer coupons on their websites or through online coupon services, such as save.ca. Last year, as a result of sites like these, the number of coupons distributed online in the U.S. more than doubled.[27]

Cash refund offer (rebate)
Offer to refund part of the purchase price of a product to consumers who send a "proof of purchase" to the manufacturer.

Cash refund offers (or **rebates**) are like coupons except that the price reduction occurs after the purchase rather than at the retail outlet. The consumer sends a "proof of purchase" to the manufacturer, who then refunds part of the purchase price by mail. For example, Toro ran a clever preseason promotion on some of its snowblower models, offering a rebate if the snowfall in the buyer's market area turned out to be below average. Competitors were not able to match this offer on such short notice, and the promotion was very successful.

Price pack (cents-off deal)
Reduced price that is marked by the producer directly on the label or package.

Price packs (also called **cents-off deals**) offer consumers savings off the regular price of a product. The reduced prices are marked by the producer directly on the label or package. Price packs can be single packages sold at a reduced price (such as two for the price of one), or two related products banded together (such as a toothbrush and toothpaste). Price packs are very effective—even more so than coupons—in stimulating short-term sales.

Premium
Good offered either free or at low cost as an incentive to buy a product.

Premiums are goods offered either free or at low cost as an incentive to buy a product, ranging from toys included with kids' products to phone cards and CDs. A premium may come inside the package (in-pack), outside the package (on-pack), or through the mail.

In a recent Canadian promotion, Coca-Cola added value to a purchase of Coke products by printing entry numbers behind the labels of Coke products and in cases. Customers enter these numbers into the icoke.ca website to see if they are instant winners of prizes such as a Sony Vega 50-inch LCD TV. Those consumers who don't win instantly still earn credits towards prizes such as unlimited movie passes, or the opportunity to star in a PlayStation commercial. Launched in May of 2005, iCoke.ca is meant to "breathe life into a place where consumers can interact with the brand" as opposed to just being a passive viewer of advertisements. The site includes the expected product plugs, but also includes value-adding content, such as the iCoke recording studio, where consumers can create their own ringtones.[28]

In an innovative Web-based promotion campaign, titled iCoke, Coca-Cola added value to its products for Canadian consumers.

Advertising specialty
Useful article imprinted with an advertiser's name, given as a gift to consumers.

Advertising specialties, also called *promotional products*, are useful articles imprinted with an advertiser's name, logo, or message that are given as gifts to consumers. Typical items include T-shirts and other apparel, pens, coffee mugs, calendars, key rings, mouse pads, matches, tote bags, coolers, golf balls, and caps. Such items can be very effective. In a recent study, 63 percent of all consumers surveyed were either carrying or wearing an ad specialty item. More than three-quarters of those who had an item could recall the advertiser's name or message before showing the item to the interviewer.[29]

Patronage reward
Cash or other award for the regular use of a certain company's products or services.

Patronage rewards are cash or other awards offered for the regular use of a certain company's products or services. For example, airlines offer frequent flier plans, awarding points for distances travelled that can be turned in for free airline trips. Hotels have adopted honoured-guest plans that award points to users of their hotels. And supermarkets issue frequent shopper cards that dole out a wealth of discounts at the checkout. For example, the Fairmont Hotel chain (operators of the Royal York in Toronto and the Banff Springs Hotel) use their President's Club to reward frequent travellers with services such as free in-room high-speed Internet access.

Point-of-purchase (POP) promotion
Display and demonstration that take place at the point of purchase or sale.

Point-of-purchase (POP) promotions include displays and demonstrations that take place at the point of purchase or sale. An example is a 1.5-metre-high cardboard display of Cap'n Crunch next to Cap'n Crunch cereal boxes. Unfortunately, many retailers do not like to handle the hundreds of displays, signs, and posters they receive from manufacturers each year. Manufacturers have responded by offering better POP materials, tying them in with television or print messages, and offering to set them up.

Contests, sweepstakes, games
Promotional events that give consumers the chance to win something—such as cash, trips, or goods—by luck or through extra effort.

Contests, sweepstakes, and games give consumers the chance to win something, such as cash, trips, or goods, by luck or through extra effort. A *contest* calls for consumers to submit an entry—a jingle, guess, suggestion—to be judged by a panel that will select the best entries. A *sweepstakes* calls for consumers to submit their names for a drawing. A *game* presents consumers with something—bingo numbers, missing letters—every time they buy, which may or may not help them win a prize. A sales contest urges dealers or the sales force to increase their efforts, with prizes going to the top performers.

Canadians love coupons—they encourage us to try new products or buy old favourites more often.

Trade Promotion Tools

Manufacturers direct more sales promotion dollars toward retailers and wholesalers (78 percent) than to consumers (22 percent). Trade promotion can persuade resellers to carry a brand, give it shelf space, promote it in advertising, and push it to consumers. Shelf space is so scarce these days that manufacturers often have to offer price-offs, allowances, buy-back guarantees, or free goods to retailers and wholesalers to get products on the shelf and, once there, to stay on it.

Manufacturers use several trade promotion tools. Many of the tools used for consumer promotions—contests, premiums, displays—can also be used as trade promotions. Or the manufacturer may offer a straight **discount** off the list price on each case purchased during a stated period of time (also called a *price-off, off-invoice,* or *off-list*). Manufacturers also may offer an **allowance** (usually so much off per case) in return for the retailer's agreement to feature the manufacturer's products in some way. An *advertising allowance* compensates retailers for advertising the product. A *display allowance* compensates them for using special displays.

Manufacturers may offer *free goods*, which are extra cases of merchandise, to resellers who buy a certain quantity or who feature a certain flavour or size. They may offer *push money*—cash or gifts to dealers or their sales forces to "push" the manufacturer's goods. Manufacturers may give retailers free *specialty advertising items* that carry the company's name, such as pens, pencils, calendars, paperweights, matchbooks, memo pads, and yardsticks.

Business Promotion Tools

Companies spend billions of dollars each year on promotion to industrial customers. These *business promotion tools* are used to generate business leads, stimulate purchases, reward customers, and motivate salespeople. Business promotion includes many of the same tools used for consumer or trade promotions. Here, we focus on two additional major business promotion tools—conventions and trade shows, and sales contests.

Many companies and trade associations organize *conventions and trade shows* to promote their products. Firms selling to the industry show their

Discount
A straight reduction in price on purchases during a stated period of time.

Allowance
Promotional money paid by manufacturers to retailers in return for an agreement to feature the manufacturer's products in some way.

Some trade shows are huge. In 2007, the International Consumer Electronics Show's 2700 exhibitors attracted more than 140 000 visitors.

products at the trade show. Vendors receive many benefits, such as opportunities to find new sales leads, contact customers, introduce new products, meet new customers, sell more to present customers, and educate customers with publications and audiovisual materials. Trade shows also help companies reach many prospects not reached through their sales forces. Some trade shows are huge. In 2007, the International Consumer Electronics Show's 2700 exhibitors attracted more than 140 000 visitors. Even more impressive, at the BAUMA mining and construction equipment trade show in Munich, Germany, some 2800 exhibitors from 47 countries presented their latest product innovations to more than 400 000 attendees from 171 countries.[30] The success of trade shows is revealed in the bottom lines of many Canadian companies. Recently, the 400 Canadian firms that displayed their wares at the 40 largest German trade fairs rang up more than $250 million in sales.

A *sales contest* is a contest for salespeople or dealers to motivate them to increase their sales performance over a given period. Sales contests motivate and recognize good company performers, who may receive trips, cash prizes, or other gifts. Some companies award points for performance, which the receiver can turn in for any of a variety of prizes. Sales contests work best when they are tied to measurable and achievable sales objectives (such as finding new accounts, reviving old accounts, or increasing account profitability).

Developing the Sales Promotion Program

The marketer must make several other decisions in order to define the full sales promotion program. First, the marketer must decide on the *size of the incentive*. A certain minimum incentive is necessary if the promotion is to succeed; a larger incentive will produce more sales response. The marketer also must set *conditions for participation*. Incentives might be offered to everyone or only to select groups.

The marketer must then decide how to *promote and distribute the promotion* program itself. A 50-cents-off coupon could be given out in a package, at the store, by mail, or in an advertisement. Each distribution method involves a different level of reach and cost. Increasingly, marketers are blending several media into a total campaign concept. The *length of the promotion* is also important. If the sales promotion period is too short, many prospects (who may not be buying during that time) will miss it. If the promotion runs too long, the deal will lose some of its "act now" force.

Evaluation is also very important. Yet many companies fail to evaluate their sales promotion programs, and others evaluate them only superficially. The most common evaluation method is to compare sales before, during, and after a promotion. Suppose a company has a 6 percent market share before the promotion, which jumps to 10 percent during the promotion, falls to 5 percent right after, and rises to 7 percent later on. The promotion seems to have attracted new users and stimulated more buying by current customers. After the promotion, sales fell as consumers used up their inventories. The long-run rise to 7 percent means that the company succeeded in converting those new users to their product, as the rise in total demand signals repurchase. If the brand's share had returned to the old level, then the promotion would have changed only the *timing* of demand rather than the *total* demand.

Consumer research would also show the kinds of people who responded to the promotion and what they did after it ended. *Surveys* can provide information on how many consumers recall the promotion, what they thought of it, how many took advantage of it, and how it affected their buying. Sales promotions also can be evaluated through *experiments* that vary factors, such as incentive value, length, and distribution method.

Clearly, sales promotion plays an important role in the total promotion mix. To use it well, the marketer must define the sales promotion objectives, select the best tools, design the sales promotion program, implement the program, and evaluate the results. Moreover, sales promotion must be coordinated carefully with other promotion mix elements within the integrated marketing communications program.

Mackenzie Investments and its agency, Lowe Roche, generated a lot of press coverage with their novel and insightful "Burn Rate" campaign.

Public Relations

Public relations

Building good relations with the company's various publics by obtaining favourable publicity, building up a good "corporate image," and handling or heading off unfavourable rumours, stories, and events.

Another major mass-promotion tool is **public relations**—building good relations with the company's various publics by obtaining favourable publicity, building up a good corporate image, and handling or heading off unfavourable rumours, stories, and events. Public relations departments may perform any or all of the following functions:[31]

- *Press relations or press agency:* Creating and placing newsworthy information in the news media to attract attention to a person, product, or service.
- *Product publicity:* Publicizing specific products.
- *Public affairs:* Building and maintaining national or local community relations.
- *Lobbying:* Building and maintaining relations with legislators and government officials to influence legislation and regulation.
- *Investor relations:* Maintaining relationships with shareholders and others in the financial community.
- *Development:* Public relations with donors or members of not-for-profit organizations to gain financial or volunteer support.

Public relations is used to promote products, people, places, ideas, activities, organizations, and even nations. Companies use public relations to build good relations with consumers, investors, the media, and their communities. Mackenzie Investments, the Toronto-based investment firm, shook up the stodgy RRSP buying season, with its campaign "Burn Rate," which combined advertising with a PR

The City of Hong Kong used public relations, print advertising, and a contest to coax Chinese Canadians back to the city after the SARS crisis.

media push. Created by ad agency Lowe Roche, their "burn rate calculator" and attention-grabbing headlines in print ads such as "Can you afford to keep your husband?" showed consumers, in a humorous fashion, just how little they had to give up to save money. Along with the ads, the agency developed multi-piece informational packages sent to the media. Combined, the campaign helped Mackenzie stand out from other advertisers in newsrooms across the country. The result—coverage by almost 100 news outlets that didn't cost Mackenzie a penny.[32] Trade associations have also used PR to rebuild interest in declining commodities, such as eggs, apples, milk, and potatoes. Nations have used public relations to attract more tourists, foreign investment, and international support, as was the case with Hong Kong in 2003 after the SARS outbreak.

The Role and Impact of Public Relations

Public relations can have a strong impact on public awareness at a much lower cost than advertising. The company does not pay for the space or time in the media. Rather, it pays for a staff to develop and circulate information and to manage events. If the company develops an interesting story, it could be picked up by several different media, having the same effect as advertising that would cost millions of dollars. And it would have more credibility than advertising.

Public relations results can sometimes be spectacular. Here's how publisher Scholastic, Inc., used public relations to turn a simple, new book introduction into a major international event, all on a very small budget:

Secret codes. A fiercely guarded text. Huddled masses lined up in funny hats at the witching hour. Welcome to one of the biggest and oddest literary events in history. As the clock crept past midnight, kids worldwide rushed to buy the next instalment of the Harry Potter series. It was the fastest-shrinking book pile in history—with all of the 915 000 Canadian copies sold in less than one week. The spellbinding plots, written by Scottish welfare-mom-turned-millionaire J. K. Rowling, captivated kids everywhere, but the hidden hand of [public relations] played a role, too. With contests, theme parties, and giveaways, conditions were hot for Harry. How do you whip up a consumer frenzy with a mere $400 000 promotion budget? The Canadian publisher, Raincoast, and their agency, Palmer Jarvis DDB, mixed in-store promotions with a few carefully placed ads [and a heap of public relations hype] to create a sense of celebration. The sense of magic was heightened by guerrilla marketing, with carefully orchestrated events in Toronto and Vancouver, where the day before the launch, kids dressed as Harry, Ron, and Hermione swarmed the stations, brandishing "tickets" for platform 9¾.[33]

Despite its potential strengths, public relations is sometimes described as a marketing stepchild because of its often limited and scattered use. The PR department is usually located at corporate headquarters. Its staff is so busy dealing with various publics—stockholders, employees, legislators, city officials—that public relations programs to support product marketing objectives may be ignored. Marketing

Public relations results can sometimes be spectacular. Raincoast and Palmer Jarvis DDB organized low-cost guerrilla campaigns and in-store promotions to whip up consumer frenzy for the fifth instalment of its Harry Potter series.

managers and public relations practitioners do not always talk the same language. Many PR practitioners see their job as simply communicating. In contrast, marketing managers tend to be much more interested in how advertising and public relations affect brand building, sales, and profits.

This situation is changing, however. Although public relations still captures only a small portion of the overall marketing budgets of most firms, PR is playing an increasingly important brand-building role. For example, Procter & Gamble used PR to launch Crest Whitestrips:

> Just before the product launch, to spread the word about Whitestrips, Procter & Gamble first identified key "influencer groups" to target: bridal consultants, salon and spa owners, and national and local sorority leaders. P&G held special conferences for these image experts to introduce them to Whitestrips. It also hired Joan and Melissa Rivers for Whitestrips launch-day celebrations. These celebrities, along with the permission slips they distributed and a giant billboard in Times Square, assured consumers that it is "Okay to Wear White after Labour Day." In all, the PR campaign brought 240 million media impressions, including broadcast coverage on the *Today* show and print coverage in *Good Housekeeping*, *Family Circle*, *Glamour*, *InStyle*, and *Elle*. One-third of Whitestrips initial sales were directly linked to public relations, and P&G now holds a substantial lead in the whitening segment of the US$500 million a year oral care market.[34]

Major Public Relations Tools

Public relations professionals use several tools. One of the major tools is *news*. PR professionals find or create favourable news about the company and its products or people. Sometimes news stories occur naturally, and sometimes the PR person can suggest events or activities that would create news. *Speeches* can also create product and company publicity. Increasingly, company executives must field questions from the media or give talks at trade associations or sales meetings, and these events can either build or hurt the company's image.

Another common PR tool is *special events*, ranging from news conferences, press tours, grand openings, and fireworks displays to laser shows, hot air balloon releases, multimedia presentations, star-studded spectaculars, or educational programs designed to reach and interest target publics. And as we discussed in Chapter 14, many marketers are now designing *buzz marketing* campaigns that create excitement and generate favourable word-of-mouth communication for their brands. Buzz marketing creates publicity by getting consumers themselves to spread the brand message.

Recently, *mobile marketing*—travelling promotional tours that bring the brand to consumers—has emerged as an effective way to build one-to-one relationships with targeted consumers.[35]

These days, it seems that almost every company is putting its show on the road. Not only are tours relatively cheap, but they also offer an irresistible opportunity to build brands while attracting additional sponsorship dollars and promotional relationships with retailers and other marketing partners. Home Depot recently brought do-it-yourself home project workshops and demonstrations to twenty-six NASCAR racetracks. Mattel's Matchbox Toys' tour hit store parking lots in twenty-five cities with events such as interactive games, historic displays, gifts, and an obstacle course for kids riding battery-powered vehicles. Nintendo of Canada uses sampling tours when introducing new products since their research shows that people like to find out about games from friends or by trying them out themselves.

Public relations people also prepare *written materials* to reach and influence their target markets. These materials include annual reports, brochures, articles, and company newsletters and magazines. *Audiovisual materials*, such as films, slide-and-sound programs, and video and audio CDs, are being used increasingly as communication tools. *Corporate identity materials* can also help create a corporate identity that the public immediately recognizes. Logos, stationery, brochures, signs, business forms, business cards, buildings, uniforms, and company cars and trucks—all become marketing tools when they are attractive, distinctive, and memorable. Finally, companies can improve public goodwill by contributing money and time to *public service activities*.

A company's website can be a good public relations vehicle. Consumers and members of other publics can visit the site for information and entertainment. Such sites can be extremely popular. For example, Butterball's site (www.butterball.com), which features cooking and carving tips, received 550 000 visitors in one day during US Thanksgiving week. The website supplements the Butterball Turkey Talk-Line (1-800-BUTTERBALL)—called by some the "granddaddy of all help lines"—staffed by 50 home economists and nutritionists who respond to more than 100 000 questions each November and December.[36]

Websites can also be ideal for handling crisis situations. For example, American Home Products quickly set up a website to distribute accurate information and advice after a model died reportedly after inhaling its Primatene Mist. The Primatene site, up less than twelve hours after the crisis broke, remains in place today (www.primatene.com). In all, notes one analyst, "Today, public relations is reshaping the Internet and the Internet, in turn, is redefining the practice of public relations." Says another, "People look to the Net for information, not salesmanship, and that's the real opportunity for public relations."[37]

As with the other promotion tools, in considering when and how to use product public relations, management should set PR objectives, choose the PR messages and vehicles, implement the PR plan, and evaluate the results. The firm's public relations should be blended smoothly with other promotion activities within the company's overall integrated marketing communications effort.

Reviewing the Concepts

Companies must do more than make good products—they have to inform consumers about product benefits and carefully position products in consumers' minds. To do this, they must master three mass-promotion tools: *advertising, sales promotion,* and *public relations.*

1. **Define the roles of advertising, sales promotion, and public relations in the promotion mix.**

Advertising—the use of paid media by a seller to inform, persuade, and remind about its products or organization—is a strong promotion tool. Canadian advertising expenditures in 2004 topped $11 billion and advertising takes many forms and has many uses. *Sales promotion* covers a wide variety of short-term incentive tools—coupons, premiums, contests, buying allowances—designed to stimulate final and business consumers, the trade, and the company's own sales force. Sales-promotion spending has been growing faster than advertising spending in recent years. *Public relations (PR)*—gaining favourable publicity and creating a favourable company image—is the least used of the major promotion tools, although it has great potential for building consumer awareness and preference.

2. **Describe the major decisions involved in developing an advertising program.**

   Advertising decision making involves decisions about the objectives, the budget, the message, the media, and, finally, the evaluation of results. Advertisers should set clear *objectives* as to whether the advertising is supposed to inform, persuade, or remind buyers. The advertising *budget* can be based on sales, on competitors' spending, or on the objectives and tasks. The *message decision* calls for planning a message strategy and executing it effectively. The *media decision* involves defining reach, frequency, and impact goals; choosing major media types; selecting media vehicles; and deciding on media timing. Message and media decisions must be closely coordinated for maximum campaign effectiveness. Finally, *evaluation* calls for evaluating the communication and sales effects of advertising before, during, and after the advertising is placed.

3. **Explain how sales promotion campaigns are developed and implemented.**

   Sales promotion campaigns call for setting sales promotions objectives (in general, sales promotions

   should be *consumer relationship building*); selecting tools; developing and implementing the sales promotion program by using trade promotion tools (*discounts, allowances, free goods, push money*) and business promotion tools (*conventions, trade shows, sales contests*) as well as deciding on such things as the size of the incentive, the conditions for participation, how to promote and distribute the promotion package, and the length of the promotion. After this process is completed, the company evaluates the results.

4. **Explain how companies use public relations to communicate with their publics.**

   Companies use public relations to communicate with their publics by setting PR objectives, choosing PR messages and vehicles, implementing the PR plan, and evaluating PR results. To accomplish these goals, PR professionals use several tools, such as *news, speeches,* and *special events.* They also prepare *written, audiovisual,* and *corporate identity materials* and contribute money and time to *public service activities.*

Reviewing the Key Terms

Discussing the Concepts

1. Discuss why it is important for an organization to set advertising objectives.

2. A number of factors make management's task of setting advertising budgets difficult. What are they?

3. What is advertising clutter and why is it a problem? How can an advertiser break through it?

4. Discuss three potential problems facing a Canadian pharmaceutical manufacturer who decides to advertise

   in Europe. Are these problems different from those the manufacturer would face when advertising in Asia?

5. Compare the major tools used in consumer sales promotion with those used in trade promotion and business promotion.

6. Public relations is sometimes referred to as a marketing stepchild. What is the basis for this comment, and what can be done to correct this problem?

Applying the Concepts

1. Prepare an advertising objective for a PC solutions provider who is entering a new business-to-business market in which the buying decision is made by a business buyer.

2. In a small group, choose three appropriate advertising media for an advertising campaign to introduce a new line of men's personal care products from Wayne Gretzky.

3. Suppose you are the marketing coordinator responsible for recommending the sales promotion plan for the market launch of a new brand of bubble tea sold in supermarkets. What promotional tools would you consider for this task? Explain.

Focus on Technology

Coupons can play a major role in promoting trials of new brands and in reviving sales of mature brands. The delivery of coupons over the Internet has increased significantly over the years. One survey found that 19 percent of all Internet users have redeemed Internet coupons. Many organizations, including save.ca, provide technology for sellers to create, post, and track coupons on the Internet. Advantages of Internet coupons for consumers include ease of use, convenience, relevance, and a targeted offer. For merchants, the advantages of using online coupon delivery over traditional mail or newspaper delivery are many. They are easy to prepare, quickly delivered, and cost effective. They can be used to target high-income and hard-to-reach markets and individuals with customized offers, and redemption is easy to track and measure. However, there are risks associated with Internet coupons. First is the risk of copying of coupons for multiple use. Second,

Internet coupons are vulnerable to alteration, increasing the redemption value or extending the time period. Finally, coupon print quality cannot be controlled, and printed coupons may not scan properly. This may lead to unhappy customers or line slow-downs.

1. Do the advantages of Internet coupons outweigh the risks? Explain.

2. Beyond the risks discussed above, are there any other disadvantages to using Internet coupons?

3. What products or categories are good candidates for Internet coupons?

4. Can Internet coupons be integrated with other promotional tools? Explain.

Sources: See www.santella.com/Internet%20Coupon%20Guidelines.pdf; and www.imediaconnection.com/news/989.asp.

Focus on Ethics

The Advertising Standards Canada (ASC) was founded in 1957 on the belief that advertising self-regulation best serves the interests of the industry and the public. The ASC is committed to fostering community confidence in advertising and to ensuring the integrity and viability of advertising in Canada. It uses a complaint-driven system to monitor advertising. If a consumer has a concern about a particular advertisement, he or she may complain by mail, email, or fax. Telephone complaints are not accepted. The person complaining must state the reason for the complaint, identify the product being advertised, the medium on which it is carried, the date the ad appeared, and the location of the ad (in the case of outdoor advertising and cinema advertising). Complaints that raise a potential violation of one of the ASC's Advertising *Codes* are reviewed by independent, volunteer body—one of the national and regional Consumer Response Councils. There are five Councils across Canada in Halifax, Montreal, Toronto, Calgary, and Vancouver. Each year, the Council publishes quarterly reports of those complaints.

Reports have two sections. The first outlines cases that have been upheld as a code violation and the advertiser is named; the second lists cases where the advertiser voluntarily dealt and appropriately with the issue and the offender is not named. You can find the reports on the ASC webpage (www.adstandards.com/ en/Standards/report.asp).

1. Do you believe that a complaint-driven system is the most effective way to deal with violations of the ASC's advertising codes?

2. Review the most recent report on the website. Click on the "Identified Cases" and the "Non-Identified Cases." What are the three most frequent types of violations reported?

3. Select an example from the "Identified Cases" list. As a manager within your selected company, what would you do to ensure that you did not appear on this list again?

Video Case
AFLAC

Quick, name a supplemental insurance company! The chances are good that you thought of AFLAC, even if you're not entirely certain what supplemental insurance is. The highly successful US$9.7 billion insurer is now by far the best-known firm in the supplemental insurance industry, which offers policies that kick in to pay expenses not covered by the standard health, life, and disability policies provided by most employers.

But AFLAC hasn't always enjoyed such high levels of recognition. Until recently, about the only people who'd ever heard of AFLAC lived either in Columbus, Georgia (where the company was founded) or in Japan (where it does more than 70 percent of its business, commands 85 percent of the supplemental insurance market, and serves 95 percent of the companies listed on the Tokyo Stock Exchange). Just a few years ago, only 13 percent of Americans even recognized the company's name. But now, thanks to an unorthodox advertising campaign—featuring an improbable squawking white duck—practically every American knows about AFLAC.

After viewing the video featuring AFLAC, answer the following questions about advertising, sales promotion, and public relations.

1. What key attributes of AFLAC's ads make them so successful? Now that the insurance company is so widely known, should it consider changing its advertising approach or stick with the spokes-duck?

2. How did the advertising media that AFLAC marketers selected for communicating with consumers affect the success of the campaign?

3. Could AFLAC supplement its advertising campaign with public relations? List two possible public relations activities that would help AFLAC publicize its products.

Online Media Resources

Video Short
Log on to your Companion Website at **www.pearsoned.ca/kotler** to view the video segment related to the Video Case above.

CBC ⊕ CBC Video Case
Please refer to Appendix 2 to read a CBC Video Case for this chapter, and log on to your Companion Website at **www.pearsoned.ca/kotler** to view the corresponding video segment.

Case Pilot
Log on to your Companion Website at **www.pearsoned.ca/kotler** to sharpen your case analysis skills and take the Case Pilot Challenge!

Company Case
Pepsi: Promoting Nothing

Water Wars
Everyone's familiar with the cola wars—the epic battles between Pepsi Cola and Coca-Cola in the soft-drink market. The war has featured numerous taste tests and mostly friendly, but sometimes not-so-friendly, television ads featuring Pepsi and Coke delivery-truck drivers, each trying to outdo the other.

The major problem that Pepsi and Coke face is that the cola market is mature and not growing very rapidly. Thus, to generate new sales and new customers, the companies have to look for new fronts.

In the early 1990s, the bottled-water market was just a drop in huge North American beverage market bucket. The Evian and Perrier brands dominated the tiny niche and helped establish bottled spring water's clean, healthy image. Pepsi took an early interest in the water market. It tried several different ways to attack this market, with both spring water and sparkling water, but each failed. Then it hit on the idea of taking advantage of a built-in resource—its existing bottlers.

Pepsi's bottlers already had their own water treatment facilities to purify municipal tap water used in making soft drinks. Municipal tap water was already pure and had to pass constant monitoring and rigorous quarterly U.S. Environmental Protection Agency (EPA) prescribed tests. Still, cola bottlers filtered it again before using it in the production process.

Pepsi decided that it would *really* filter the tap water. It experimented with a reverse osmosis process, pushing already-filtered tap water at high pressure through fibreglass membranes to remove even the tiniest particles. Then, carbon filters removed chlorine and any other particles that might give the water any taste or smell. However, all this filtering removed even good particles that killed bacteria, so Pepsi had to add ozone to the water to keep bacteria from growing. The result? Aquafina—a water with no taste or odour—that Pepsi believed could compete with the spring waters already on the market. Further, Pepsi could license its bottlers to use the Aquafina name and sell them the filtration equipment. Because the process used tap water that was relatively inexpensive, Pepsi's Aquafina would also compete well on price with the spring waters.

The marketing strategy was relatively simple. Whereas Evian and the other early entrants targeted women and high-end consumers, Pepsi wanted consumers to see Aquafina as a "unisex, mainstream" water with an everyday price. When the company launched the product in 1994, it was content just to build distribution using its established system and spend very little money on promotion. Pepsi believed that soft-drink advertising should be for soft drinks, not water.

Come On In—The Water's Fine

By 1999, what had been a minor trickle in the beverage market had turned into a geyser—bottled water had become the fastest-growing beverage category, and Pepsi had a big head start. Coca-Cola decided it was time to take the plunge. Like Pepsi, Coca-Cola realized its bottlers were already set up to handle a filtered-water process. Unlike Pepsi, however, rather than taking everything out of the tap water, it wanted to put something in.

Coca-Cola's researchers analyzed tap waters and bottled waters and concocted a combination of minerals they believed would give filtered tap water a fresh, clean taste. The formula included magnesium sulphate, potassium chloride, and salt. Coca-Cola guarded the new water formula just as it had the original Coke recipe. Thus, it could sell the formula to its bottlers, as it does Coke concentrate, and let them make the water. Like Pepsi, Coca-Cola was content initially just to get its water, which it called Dasani, into distribution.

How to Promote Water

By 2001, however, the bottled-water category had more than 800 competitors and had grown to US$3.53 billion in sales. Analysts predicted bottled water would become the second-largest beverage category by 2004.

Given the rapid market growth rate and all the competition, Pepsi and Coca-Cola decided they had better promote their water products, just as they did their soft drinks. In 2001, Pepsi launched a U$14 million campaign. John Grant, Pepsi's Mississauga, Ontario-based director of marketing, portfolio brands, noted, "The canvas was fairly clear, there wasn't a lot of advertising in the category, and we felt that there was a position there that we could really own." He added, "In the beverage market, you need to develop a strong brand connection with your consumer group, and establish brand equity with those emotional links." To accomplish this task, Pepsi first improved the distribution of Aquafina in Canada since the company wanted the product to be found in "as many places as possible," not just grocery stores, but convenience shops, hockey arenas, and gas stations. When developing advertising for the brand, Grant explained, "We tried to get across a very approachable, friendly and humorous brand character. Because consumption of water is so broad, we just wanted to have a common chord we thought would connect with an array of consumers." In one radio ad, consumers heard an older woman storytelling, while running a bath faucet. The voiceover says, "This is the water you put your naked butt into. The good stuff we put in bottles called Aquafina." Not to be outdone, Coca-Cola countered with a US$20-million campaign that targeted women and used the tagline: "Treat yourself well. Every day."

Pepsi responded by more than doubling its *promotion* budget to US$40 million in 2002. Included in the advertising was a spot featuring *Friends* star Lisa Kudrow. Lisa described how refreshing and mouth-watering Aquafina was—emphasizing that it made no promises it couldn't keep. She described Aquafina as "Pure nothing." The ads featured the tagline: "We promise nothing."

By 2003, the North American wholesale bottled-water market had surged to more than US$9 billion, up 6.7 percent from 2002. In the same period, wholesale sales of carbonated beverages inched up only 1.5 percent to US$45.7 billion. During 2003, Pepsi spent US$24 million on Aquafina's *advertising*, while Coke spent US$19 million on Dasani's. Although these two brands were number one and number two, respectively, with 17.7 and 13 percent market shares, all private-label brands combined took third place with a 10.4 percent market share.

One Aquafina 2003 ad featured black-and-white images of an artist, skier, and guitar player drinking the water and carried the tagline "Aquafina. Purity Guaranteed." In mid-2004, Pepsi introduced a new tagline, "Drink more water," to promote sales of all water. One ad showed people partying at an English pub and a German beer garden. Instead of drinking beer, however, they were chugging Aquafina. Coke also had an ad showing young people sipping Dasani at a nightclub.

Have Another Round

Pepsi, however, is not satisfied with its water advertising and plans to juice up what it sees as generally lacklustre advertising and promotion throughout the industry. A problem with the category, a Pepsi marketing officer notes, is that many consumers shop based on price. This is especially true in a product category where the products are so similar. Analysts note that such similarity makes it difficult to build a brand or brand loyalty.

Further, even in such a category, the companies keep introducing new products. Pepsi already has Aquafina Essentials on the market, a water fortified with vitamins and minerals that comes in four fruit flavours. It has also applied for a trademark for Aquafina Sparkling water and is test marketing H2Oh!, a lower-priced bottled water.

So, Pepsi and Coca-Cola have drawn new battle lines—this time for the water wars. Can Pepsi convince consumers to prefer a water that offered nothing versus Coca-Cola's water that offered something—although both products were colourless, odourless, and tasteless? Further, can Pepsi develop a promotion mix that builds brand loyalty across several products in a market characterized by price-conscious shoppers?

Questions for Discussion

1. What events have made bottled water an important market in Canada? Have marketers unduly exploited consumers' fears to sell bottled water?

2. What advertising objectives should Pepsi set for Aquafina?

3. What message strategy and message execution recommendations would you make for Aquafina?

4. What advertising media recommendations would you make for Aquafina, and how would you evaluate the effectiveness of those media and your advertising?

5. What sales promotion and public relations recommendations would you make for Aquafina?

6. What promotion recommendations would you make for Aquafina Essentials, Aquafina Sparkling Water, and H2Oh!?

Sources: , "H2O brands boost marketing," *Strategy Magazine*, September 24, 2001, p. 1; Suzanne Vranica, "Partyers Knock Back a Few … Aquafinas," *The Wall Street Journal*, July 13, 2004, p. B4; "No Slowdown In Sight for Bottled Water," *Beverage Industry*, September 2003, p. 22; Betsy McKay, "In a Water Fight, Coke and Pepsi Try Opposite Tacks," *The Wall Street Journal*, April 18, 2002, p. A1; Bob Garfield, "The Product Is Questionable, But Aquafina's Ads Hold Water," *Advertising* Age, July 9, 2001, p. 39; Kenneth Hein, "Coke, Pepsi Mull Jump Into 'Aquaceuticals'," *Brandweek*, June 25, 2001, p. 8; Betsy McKay, "Coke and Pepsi Escalate Their Water Fight, *The Wall Street Journal*, May 18, 2001, p. B8.

CHAPTER 16

Personal Selling and Direct Marketing

> **10:45 pm.** Account Manager Erin Bliss finishes Advanced Linux Volume IX. Meanwhile, husband Gary begins XP For Dummies.

CDW The Right Technology.
Right Away.®

They undergo continuous training and provide expert advice on over 1,200 leading technology brands. That's your dedicated account manager. Someone who knows technology and you.

800.800.4CDW

CDW.com

AFTER STUDYING THIS CHAPTER, YOU SHOULD BE ABLE TO

1. discuss the role of a company's salespeople in creating value for customers and building customer relationships

2. identify and explain the six major sales force management steps

3. discuss the personal selling process, distinguishing between transaction-oriented marketing and relationship marketing

4. define direct marketing and discuss its benefits to customers and companies

5. identify and discuss the major forms of direct marketing

Previewing the Concepts

In the previous two chapters, you learned about integrated marketing communication (IMC) and three specific elements of the marketing communications mix—advertising, sales promotion, and publicity. In this chapter, we'll learn about the final two IMC elements—personal selling and direct marketing. Personal selling is the interpersonal arm of marketing communications in which the sales force interacts with customers and prospects to make sales and build relationships. Direct marketing consists of direct connections with carefully targeted consumers to both obtain an immediate response and cultivate lasting customer relationships. As you read on, remember that although this chapter examines personal selling and direct marketing as separate tools, they must be carefully integrated with other elements of the marketing communications mix.

When someone says "salesperson," what image comes to mind? Or how about "direct marketing"? Perhaps you think about a stereotypical glad-hander who's out to lighten your wallet by selling you something you don't really need, or about a high-pressure telemarketing call that interrupts your dinner. Think again. Today, for most companies, personal selling and direct marketing play an important role in building profitable customer relationships. Consider CDW Corporation, whose customer-focused "clicks-and-people" direct marketing strategy has helped it grow rapidly while competitors have faltered.

*P*erhaps no industry felt the recent economic slowdown in the large North American market more than the technology sector—total information technology spending has been relatively flat for several years. But despite the slump, CDW Corporation, one of North America's largest direct marketers of multi-brand technology products and services, is thriving. The company's Canadian office, CDW Canada Inc., located in Toronto, serves business and public sector customers. Even as the tech world has collapsed, CDW has managed to increase its customer base, its sales, and its profits.

How has CDW managed to grow while other tech companies have faltered? The company owes its success to its highly effective "clicks-and-people" direct-marketing strategy. CDW's direct model combines good old-fashioned, high-touch personal selling with a modern, high-tech Web presence to build lasting one-to-one customer relationships. The strategy is fuelled by a genuine passion for solving customer problems. Under CDW's "Circle of Service" philosophy, "everything revolves around the customer."

CDW sells a complex assortment of more than 100 000 technology products and services—computers, software, accessories, and networking products—including top name brands, such as APC, Apple, Cisco, HP, IBM, Microsoft, Sony, Symantec, Toshiba, and ViewSonic. Many of CDW's competitors chase after a relative handful of very large customers. However, although CDW serves customers of all sizes, one of the company's core customer segments is small and midsize businesses (SMBs). These smaller customers often need lots of advice and support. "Many of our clients don't have IT departments," says one CDW executive, "so they look to us for expertise."

That's where the "people" part of CDW's clicks-and-people strategy comes in. The major responsibility for building and managing customer relationships falls to CDW's sales force of nearly 2000 account managers. Each customer is assigned an account manager, who helps the customer select the right products and technologies and keep them running smoothly.

Account managers do more than just sell technology products and services. They work closely with customers to find solutions to their technology problems. "This is a big deal to us," says Jim Grass, senior director of sales at CDW. "We want to go beyond fulfilling the order and become the trusted adviser for them. We [want to] talk ... about what a customer is trying to accomplish and really add value to the sale, as opposed to just sending out a box."

To become trusted advisers and effective customer-relationship builders, CDW account managers really have to know their stuff. And CDW boasts some of the most knowledgeable salespeople in the industry. New account managers complete a six-week training program followed by six months of just-in-time training, courtesy of CDW University. They receive intensive schooling in the science behind the company's products and in the art of consultative selling. But that's just the beginning—the training never ends. Tenured account managers receive ongoing training to enhance their relationship-selling skills. Each year, CDW's sales force completes a whopping 339 000 hours of sales-specific training.

To further support salespeople's customer problem-solving efforts, CDW has also created nine technology teams consisting of more than 150 certified specialists. Account managers can draw on these teams to design customer-specific solutions in technology areas such as mobility/wireless, networking, security, and storage.

Customers who want to access CDW's products and expertise without going through their account manager can do so easily at any of several CDW websites—the "clicks" side of CDW's clicks-and-people strategy. Better yet, CDW will create a free, personalized CDW@work extranet site that reflects a given customer's pricing, order status, account history, and special considerations. The extranet site serves as a 24-hour extension of the customer's account manager. CDW has set up more than 170 000 such sites, resulting in direct Web sales of more than US$1.8 billion in 2005. But even here, the ever-present account man-

agers are likely to add personal guidance. Account managers receive immediate notification of their customers' online activities. So if a blurry-eyed SMB manager makes a mistake on an emergency order placed in the middle of the night, chances are good that the account manager will find and correct the error first thing in the morning.

Beyond being knowledgeable and ever-present, CDW's account managers are energetic and passionately customer-focused. Much of the energy has passed down from CDW founder and former chairman and CEO Michael Krasny. Selling has always been a top priority for Krasny, not surprising given that he began testing his direct marketing model by selling used personal computers out of his home through classified ads. During his nearly 20-year reign as head of CDW, Krasny created a hard-working and dedicated sales force. However, Krasny's most important legacy is the "Circle of Service" culture that he created—a culture that focuses on taking care of customers and the CDW employees who serve them (he calls them "co-workers"). "Whenever he made a decision, he'd always ask two questions," says current chairman and CEO John Edwardson: "'What will the reaction of the co-workers be?' and 'What will the response of the customers be?'"

When someone says "salesperson," you may still think of the stereotypical "travelling salesman"—the fast-talking, ever-smiling peddler who travels his territory, foisting his wares on reluctant customers. Such stereotypes, however, are sadly out of date. Today, like CDW's account managers, most professional salespeople are well-educated, well-trained men and women who work to build valued customer relationships. They succeed not by taking customers in, but by helping them out—by assessing customer needs and solving customer problems.

CDW's high-touch, high-tech, clicks-and-people direct marketing strategy instils loyalty in what are traditionally very price-conscious SMB customers. The company wants to create customer satisfaction at every touchpoint."[1]

In this chapter, we examine two more marketing communication and promotion tools—*personal selling* and *direct marketing*. Both involve direct connections with customers aimed at building customer-unique value and lasting relationships

Personal Selling

Robert Louis Stevenson once noted that "everyone lives by selling something." Today, however, rather than focusing on *selling to* potential buyers, savvy marketers stress building *relationships with* potential buyers. The sales force, assisted by massive databases called customer relationship management systems (discussed in detail in Chapter 5), is at the heart of this relationship building process. Sales forces are important entities in businesses and many other kinds of organizations. For example, universities use recruiters to attract new students, and churches use membership committees to attract new members. Museums and fine arts organizations use fund-raisers to contact donors and raise money. Even governments use sales forces. For example, Agriculture Canada sends specialists into the field to convince farmers to use new agricultural methods and products. In the first part of this chapter, we examine the role of personal selling in the organization, sales force management decisions, and the personal selling process.

The Nature of Personal Selling

Selling is one of the oldest professions in the world. The people who do the selling go by many names: *salespeople, sales representatives, account executives, sales consultants, sales engineers, agents, district managers, client service representatives,* and *account development reps* to name just a few.

People hold many stereotypes of salespeople—including some unfavourable ones. "Salesman" may bring to mind the image of Arthur Miller's pitiable Willy Loman in *Death of a Salesman.* Or you might think of Robin Williams in *Cadillac Man.* These examples depict salespeople as loners, travelling their territories, trying to foist their wares on unsuspecting or unwilling buyers.

However, modern salespeople are a far cry from these unfortunate stereotypes. Today, most salespeople are well-educated, well-trained professionals who work to build and maintain long-term customer relationships. They listen to their customers, assess customer needs, and organize the company's efforts to solve customer problems. Consider Boeing, the aerospace giant competing in the rough-and-tumble worldwide commercial aircraft market. It takes more than fast talk and a warm smile to sell expensive airplanes:

> Selling high-tech aircraft at US$100 million or more a copy is complex and challenging. A single big sale can easily run into billions of dollars. Boeing salespeople head up an extensive team of company specialists—sales and service technicians, financial analysts, planners, engineers—all dedicated to finding ways to satisfy airline customer needs. The selling process is nerve-wrackingly slow—it can take two or three years from the first sales presentation to the day the sale is announced. After getting the order, salespeople

It takes more than fast talk and a warm smile to sell high-tech aircraft at US$100 million or more a copy. Success depends on building solid, long-term relationships with customers.

then must stay in almost constant touch to keep track of the account's equipment needs and to make certain the customer stays satisfied. Success depends on building solid, long-term relationships with customers, based on performance and trust. "When you buy an airplane, it is like getting married," says the head of Boeing's commercial airplane division. "It is a long-term relationship."[2]

Salesperson
An individual acting for a company by performing one or more of the following activities: prospecting, communicating, servicing, and information gathering.

The term **salesperson** covers a wide range of positions. At one extreme, a salesperson might be largely an *order taker*, such as the department store salesperson standing behind the counter or a waitperson taking an order. Today, however, even these people are expected to give sales support by making suggestions to customers about the products and services that might best meet their needs. At the other extreme are *order getters*, whose positions demand *creative selling* and *relationship building* for products and services ranging from appliances, industrial equipment, and airplanes to insurance and information technology services. Here, we focus on the more creative types of selling and on the process of building and managing an effective sales force.

The Role of the Sales Force

Personal selling is the interpersonal arm of the promotion mix. Advertising consists of one-way, nonpersonal communication with target consumer groups. In contrast, personal selling involves two-way, personal communication between salespeople and individual customers—whether face to face, by telephone, through video or Web conferences, or by other means. Personal selling can be more effective than advertising in more complex selling situations, and people are often the essential element in building strong customer relationships. Salespeople can probe customers' thoughts to learn more about their problems, then adjust the marketing offer and presentation to fit the special needs of each customer.

The role of personal selling varies from company to company. Some firms have no salespeople at all—for example, companies that sell only online or through catalogues, or companies that sell through manufacturer's reps, sales agents, or brokers. In most firms, however, the sales force plays a major role. In companies that sell business products and services, such as IBM or DuPont, the company's salespeople work directly with customers. In consumer product companies, such as Procter & Gamble and Nike, the sales force plays an important behind-the-scenes role. It works with wholesalers and retailers to gain their support and to help them be more effective in selling the company's products.

The sales force serves as a critical link between a company and its customers. In many cases, salespeople serve both masters—the seller and the buyer. First, they *represent the company to customers*. They find and develop new customers and communicate information about the company's products and services. They sell products by approaching customers, presenting their products, answering objections, negotiating prices and terms, and closing sales. In addition, salespeople provide customer service and carry out market research and intelligence work.

At the same time, salespeople *represent customers to the company*, acting inside the firm as "champions" of customers' interests and managing the buyer–seller relationship. Salespeople relay customer concerns about company products and actions back inside to those who can handle them. They learn about customer needs and work with other marketing and nonmarketing people in the company to develop greater customer value. The old view was that salespeople should worry about sales and the company should worry about profit. However, the current view holds that salespeople should be concerned with more than just producing *sales*—they should work with others in the company to produce *customer satisfaction* and *company profit*.

Managing the Sales Force

Sales force management
The analysis, planning, implementation, and control of sales force activities. It includes setting and designing sales force strategy; and recruiting, selecting, training, supervising, compensating, and evaluating the firm's salespeople.

We define **sales force management** as the analysis, planning, implementation, and control of sales force activities. It includes designing sales force strategy and structure and recruiting, selecting, training, compensating, supervising, and evaluating the firm's salespeople. These major sales force management decisions are shown in Figure 16.1 and are discussed in the following sections.

Designing Sales Force Strategy and Structure

Marketing managers face several sales force strategy and design questions. How should salespeople and their tasks be structured? How big should the sales force be? Should salespeople sell alone or work in teams with other people in the company? Should they sell in the field or by telephone? We address these issues below.

Sales Force Structure

A company can divide up sales responsibilities along any of several lines. The decision is simple if the company sells only one product line to one industry with customers in many locations. In that case the company would use a *territorial sales force structure*. However, if the company sells many products to many types of customers, it might need either a *customer sales force structure*, or a combination of the two.

Territorial sales force structure
A sales force organization that assigns each salesperson to an exclusive geographic territory in which that salesperson sells the company's full line.

Territorial Sales Force Structure   In the **territorial sales force structure**, each salesperson is assigned to an exclusive geographic area and sells the company's full line of products or services to all customers in that territory. This organization clearly defines each salesperson's job and fixes accountability. It also increases the salesperson's desire to build local business relationships that, in turn, improve selling effectiveness. Finally, because each salesperson travels within a limited geographic area, travel expenses are relatively small.

A territorial sales organization is often supported by many levels of sales management positions. For example, Campbell Soup uses a territorial structure in which each salesperson is responsible for selling all Campbell Soup products. Starting at the bottom of the organization, *sales merchandisers* report to *sales representatives*, who report to *retail supervisors*, who report to *directors of retail sales operations*, who report to one of twenty-two *regional sales managers*. Regional sales managers, in turn, report to *general sales managers*, who report to a *vice-president* and *general sales* manager.

Product sales force structure
A sales force organization under which salespeople specialize in selling only a portion of the company's products or lines.

Product Sales Force Structure   Salespeople must know their products—especially when the products are numerous and complex. This need, together with the growth of product management, has led many companies to adopt a **product sales force structure**, in which the sales force sells along product lines. For example, Kodak uses different sales forces for its film products than for its industrial products. The film products sales force deals with simple products that are distributed intensively, whereas the industrial products sales force deals with complex products that require technical understanding.

The product structure can lead to problems, however, if a single large customer buys many different company products. For example, Cardinal Health, the large North American health care products and services company, with offices in

Figure 16.1 Major steps in sales force management

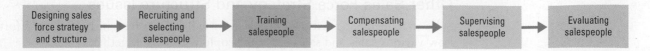

Designing sales force strategy and structure → Recruiting and selecting salespeople → Training salespeople → Compensating salespeople → Supervising salespeople → Evaluating salespeople

Toronto, has several product divisions, each with a separate sales force. Several Cardinal salespeople might end up calling on the same hospital on the same day. This means that they travel over the same routes and wait to see the same customer's purchasing agents. These extra costs must be compared with the benefits of better product knowledge and attention to individual products.

Customer sales force structure
A sales force organization under which salespeople specialize in selling only to certain customers or industries.

Customer Sales Force Structure   More and more companies are now using a **customer sales force structure,** in which they organize the sales force along customer or industry lines. Separate sales forces may be set up for different industries, for serving current customers versus finding new ones, and for major accounts versus regular accounts.

Organizing the sales force around customers can help a company build closer relationships with important customers. For example, IBM recently shifted from a product-based structure to a customer-based one. Before the shift, droves of salespeople representing different IBM software, hardware, and services divisions might call on a single large client, creating confusion and frustration. Such large customers wanted a "single face," one point of contact for all of IBM's vast array of products and services. Following the restructuring, a single IBM "client executive" works with each large customer and manages a team of IBMers who work with the customer. One client executive describes his role this way: "I am the owner of the business relationship with the client. If the client has a problem, I'm the one who pulls together software or hardware specialists or consultants." According to a sales organization expert, "This structure puts salespeople in the position of being advisers to clients, and it also allows them to offer holistic solutions to clients' business problems."[3] Such an intense focus on customers is widely credited for IBM's dramatic turnaround in recent years.

Complex Sales Force Structures   When a company sells a wide variety of products to many types of customers over a broad geographic area, it often combines several types of sales force structures. Salespeople can be specialized by customer and territory; by product and territory; by product and customer; or by territory, product, and customer. No single structure is best for all companies and situations. Each company should select a sales force structure that best serves the needs of its customers and fits its overall marketing strategy.

Sales Force Size

Once the company has set its structure, it is ready to consider *sales force size*. Sales forces may range in size from only a few salespeople to many tens of thousands. Salespeople constitute one of the company's most productive—and most expensive—assets. Therefore, increasing their number will increase both sales and costs.

Many companies use some form of *workload approach* to set sales force size. Using this approach, a company first groups accounts into different classes according to size, account status, or other factors related to the amount of effort required to maintain them. It then determines the number of salespeople needed to call on each class of accounts the desired number of times. The company might think as follows: Suppose we have 1000 Type-A accounts and 2000 Type-B accounts. Type-A accounts require 36 calls a year and Type-B accounts require 12 calls a year. In this case, the sales force's *workload*—the number of calls it must make per year—is 60 000 calls [(1000 × 36) + (2000 × 12) = 36 000 + 24 000 = 60 000]. Suppose our average salesperson can make 1000 calls a year. Thus, the company needs 60 salespeople (60 000 ÷ 1000).[4]

Other Sales Force Strategy and Structure Issues

Sales management must also decide who will be involved in the selling effort and how various sales and sales support people will work together.

Some sales forces are huge. Salespeople, therefore, constitute one of the company's most productive—and most expensive—assets.

Outside sales force (or field sales force)
Outside salespeople who travel to call on customers.

Inside sales force
Inside salespeople who conduct business from their offices via telephone or through visits from prospective buyers.

Outside and Inside Sales Forces   The company may have an **outside sales force** (or *field sales force*), an **inside sales force**, or both. Outside salespeople travel to call on customers. Inside salespeople conduct business from their offices via telephone or through visits from prospective buyers.

To reduce time demands on their outside sales forces, many companies have increased the size of their inside sales forces. Inside salespeople include technical support people, sales assistants, and telemarketers. *Technical support people* provide technical information and answers to customers' questions. *Sales assistants* provide clerical backup for outside salespeople. They call ahead and confirm appointments, conduct credit checks, follow up on deliveries, and answer customers' questions when outside salespeople cannot be reached. *Telemarketers* use the phone to find new leads and qualify prospects for the field sales force, or to sell and service accounts directly.

The inside sales force frees outside salespeople to spend more time selling to major accounts and finding major new prospects. Depending on the complexity of the product and customer, a telemarketer can make from twenty to thirty-three decision-maker contacts a day, compared with the average of four that an outside salesperson can make. And for many types of products and selling situations, telemarketing can be as effective as a personal call but much less expensive. Whereas the average business-to-business personal sales call costs about $300, a routine industrial telemarketing call costs only about $5.50 and a complex call about $25.[5] Notes a DuPont telemarketer: "I'm more effective on the phone. [When you're in the field], if some guy's not in his office, you lose an hour. On the phone, you lose 15 seconds. ... Through my phone calls, I'm in the field as much as the rep is." There are other advantages. "Customers can't throw things at you," quips the rep, "and you don't have to outrun dogs."[6]

Telephone marketing can be used successfully by both large and small companies:

IBM's traditional image has long been symbolized by the outside salesman in the blue suit, crisp white shirt, and red tie—an imposing fellow far more comfortable in corporate Canada's plush executive suites than in the cramped quarters of some fledgling entrepreneur. Small businesses were often ignored. Now, to sell its technology solutions to small businesses, IBM is boosting emphasis on

Experienced telemarketers sell complex chemical products by telephone at DuPont's Customer Telecontact Center. Quips one, "I'm more effective on the phone … and you don't have to outrun dogs."

its telemarketing effort. Stroll through the IBM call centre with its sea of cubicles, and a new image of the IBM salesperson emerges: men and women, many recent college grads, sporting golf shirts and khakis or—gasp!—blue jeans. They wear headsets and talk on the phone with customers they'll likely never meet in person. IBM's roughly 1200 phone reps now generate 30 percent of IBM's revenues from small and midsize businesses. The reps focus on specific industries and each calls on as many as 300 accounts. They nurture client relationships, pitch IBM solutions, and, when needed, refer customers to product and service specialists.[7]

Climax Portable Machine Tools has proven that a small company can use telemarketing to save money and still lavish attention on buyers. Under the old system, Climax sales engineers spent one-third of their time on the road and could make about four calls a day. Now, each of five sales engineers on Climax's telemarketing team calls about thirty prospects a day, following up on leads generated by ads and direct mail. The sales engineers update a prospect's computer file after each contact, noting the degree of commitment, requirements, next call date, and personal comments. "If anyone mentions he's going on a fishing trip, our sales engineer enters that in the computer and uses it to personalize the next phone call," says Climax's president, noting that's just one way to build good relations. Another is that the first mailing to a prospect includes the sales engineer's business card with his or her picture on it. Of course, it takes more than friendliness to sell $19 000 machine tools over the phone (special orders may run $260 000), but the telemarketing approach is working well. When Climax customers were asked, "Do you see the sales engineer often enough?" the response was overwhelmingly positive. Obviously, many people didn't realize that the only contact they'd had with Climax had been on the phone.[8]

Inside salespeople may perform a wide range of functions, from direct selling and account service to customer analysis and acting as liaisons between outside salespeople and customers. And they now have a broader range of tools at their disposal. According to one observer, "today's … representatives are just as likely to answer emails or add to their employer's Frequently Asked Questions list as they are to answer the phones."[9]

Just as telemarketing is changing the way that many companies go to market, the Internet offers explosive potential for restructuring sales forces and conducting sales operations. More and more companies are now using the Internet to support their personal selling efforts—not just for selling, but for everything from training salespeople to conducting sales meetings and servicing accounts. (See Real Marketing 16.1.)

Team Selling   As products become more complex, and as customers grow larger and more demanding, a single salesperson simply can't handle all of a large customer's needs. Instead, most companies now are using **team selling** to service large, complex accounts. Companies are finding that sales teams can unearth problems, solutions, and sales opportunities that no individual salesperson could. Such teams might include experts from any area or level of the selling firm—sales, marketing, technical and support services, R&D, engineering, operations, finance, and others. In team selling situations, the salesperson shifts from "soloist" to "orchestrator."

In many cases, the move to team selling mirrors similar changes in customers' buying organizations. "Today, we're calling on teams of buying people, and that requires more firepower on our side," says one sales vice-president. "One salesperson just can't do it all—can't be an expert in everything we're bringing to the customer. We have strategic account teams, led by customer business managers, who basically are our quarterbacks."[10]

Some companies, such as IBM, Xerox, and Procter & Gamble, have used teams for a long time. P&G sales reps are organized into "customer business development (CBD) teams." Each CBD team is assigned to a major P&G customer, such as Wal-Mart, Loblaws, or Shoppers Drug Mart. Teams consist of a customer business development manager, several account executives (each responsible for a specific category of P&G products), and specialists in marketing strategy, operations, information systems, logistics, and finance. This organization places the focus on serving the complete needs of each important customer. It lets P&G "grow business by working as a 'strategic partner' with our accounts, not just as a supplier. Our goal: to grow their business, which also results in growing ours."[11]

Team selling does have some pitfalls. For example, selling teams can confuse or overwhelm customers who are used to working with only one salesperson.

Team selling
Using teams of people from sales, marketing, engineering, finance, technical support, and even upper management to service large, complex accounts.

This Procter & Gamble "customer business development team" serves a major southeastern grocery retailer. It consists of a customer business development manager and five account executives (shown here), along with specialists from other functional areas.

REAL MARKETING | 16.1

Point, Click, and Sell: Welcome to the Web-Based Sales Force

There are few rules at Fisher Scientific International's sales training sessions. The chemical company's salespeople are allowed to show up for new workshops in their pyjamas. And no one flinches if they stroll in at midnight for their first class, take a dozen breaks to call clients, or invite the family cat to sleep in their laps while they take an exam. Sound unorthodox? It would be if Fisher's salespeople were trained in a regular classroom. But for the past few years, the company has been using the Internet to teach the majority of its salespeople in the privacy of their homes, cars, hotel rooms, or wherever else they bring their laptops.

To get updates on Fisher's pricing or refresh themselves on one of the company's highly technical products, all salespeople have to do is log on to the website and select from the lengthy index. Any time of the day or night, they can get information on a new product, take an exam, or post messages for product experts—all without ever entering a corporate classroom. Welcome to the world of the Web-based sales force.

In the past few years, sales organizations around the world have begun saving money and time by using a host of new Web approaches to train reps, hold sales meetings, and even conduct live sales presentations. Fisher Scientific's Canadian reps headquartered in Nepean, Ontario, can dial up the website at their leisure, and whereas newer reps might spend hours online going through each session in order, more seasoned sellers might just log on for a quick refresher on a specific product before a sales call. "It allows them to manage their time better, because they're only getting training when they need it, in the doses they need it in," says John Pavlik, director of the company's training department. If salespeople are spending less time on training, Pavlik says, they're able to spend more time on what they do best: selling.

The Internet can also be a handy way to hold sales strategy meetings. Consider Cisco Systems, which provides networking solutions for the Internet. Sales meetings used to take an enormous bite out of Cisco's travel budget. Now the company saves about US$1 million per month by conducting many of those sessions on the Web, using PlaceWare Web conferencing software. Whenever Cisco introduces a new product, it holds a Web meeting to update salespeople, in groups of 100 or more, on the product's marketing and sales strategy.

Usually led by the product manager or a vice-president of sales, the meetings typically begin with a 10-minute slide presentation that spells out the planned strategy. Then, salespeople spend the next 50 or so minutes asking questions via teleconference. The meeting's leader can direct attendees' browsers to competitors' websites or ask them to vote on certain issues by using the software's instant polling feature. "Our salespeople are actually meeting more online then they ever were face to face," says Mike Mitchell, Cisco's distance learning manager, adding that some salespeople who used to meet with other reps and managers only a few times a quarter are meeting online nearly every day. "That's very empowering for the sales force, because they're able to make suggestions at every step of the way about where we're going with our sales and marketing strategies."

Thus, Web-based technologies can produce big organizational benefits for sales forces. They help conserve salespeople's valuable time, save travel dollars, and give salespeople a new vehicle for selling and

Sales organizations around the world are now using a host of new Web approaches to train reps, hold sales meetings, and even conduct live sales presentations.

servicing accounts. But the technologies also have some drawbacks. For starters, they're not cheap. Setting up a Web-based system can cost up to several hundred thousand dollars. And such systems can intimidate low-tech salespeople or clients. "You must have a culture that is comfortable using computers," says one marketing communications manager. "As simple as it is, if your salespeople or clients aren't comfortable using the Web, you're wasting your money." Also, Web tools are susceptible to server crashes and other network difficulties, not a happy event when you're in the midst of an important sales meeting or presentation.

For these reasons, some high-tech experts recommend that sales executives use Web technologies for training, sales meetings, and preliminary client sales presentations, but resort to old-fashioned, face-to-face meetings when the time draws near to close the deal.

"When push comes to shove, if you've got an account worth closing, you're still going to get on that plane and see the client in person," says sales consultant Sloane. "Your client is going to want to look you in the eye before buying anything from you, and that's still one thing you just can't do online."

Sources: Portions adapted from Melinda Ligos, "Point, Click, and Sell," *Sales & Marketing Management,* May 1999, pp. 51–55; and Tom Kontzer, "Web Conferencing Embraced," *Information Week,* May 26, 2003, pp. 68–70. Also see Julia Chang, "No Instructor Required," *Sales & Marketing Management,* May 2003, p. 26; Nicole Ridgeway, "A Safer Place to Meet," *Forbes,* April 28, 2003, p. 97; Andy Cohen, "Virtual Sales Meetings on the Rise," *Sales & Marketing Management,* August 2003, p. 12; and Daniel Tynan, "Next Best Thing to Being There," *Sales & Marketing Management,* April 2004, p. 22 Also see Chad Kaydo, "You've Got Sales," *Sales & Marketing Management,* October 1999, pp. 29–39; Ginger Conlon, "Ride the Wave," *Sales & Marketing Management,* December 2000, pp. 67–74; and Tom Reilly, "Technology and the Salesperson," *Industrial Distribution,* January 2001, p. 88.

Salespeople who are used to having customers all to themselves may have trouble learning to work with and trust others on a team. Finally, difficulties in evaluating individual contributions to the team selling effort can create some sticky compensation issues.

Recruiting and Selecting Salespeople

At the heart of any successful sales force operation is the recruitment and selection of good salespeople. The performance difference between an average salesperson and a top salesperson can be substantial. In a typical sales force, the top 30 percent of the salespeople might bring in 60 percent of the sales. Thus, careful salesperson selection can greatly increase overall sales force performance. Beyond the differences in sales performance, poor selection results in costly turnover. When a salesperson quits, the costs of finding and training a new salesperson—plus the costs of lost sales—can be very high. Also, a sales force with many new people is less productive, and turnover disrupts customer relationships.

What sets great salespeople apart from all the rest? In an effort to profile top sales performers, Gallup Management Consulting Group, a division of the well-known Gallup polling organization, has interviewed as many as half a million salespeople. Its research suggests that the best salespeople possess four key talents: intrinsic motivation, a disciplined work style, the ability to close a sale, and, perhaps most important, the ability to build relationships with customers.[12]

Super salespeople are motivated from within. "Different things drive different people—pride, happiness, money, you name it," says one expert. "But all great salespeople have one thing in common: an unrelenting drive to excel." Some salespeople are driven by money, a hunger for recognition, or the satisfaction of competing and winning. Others are driven by the desire to provide service and to build relationships. The best salespeople possess some of each of these motivations. "A competitor with a strong sense of service will probably bring in a lot of business while doing a great job of taking care of customers," observes the managing director of the Gallup Management Consulting Group. "Who could ask for anything more?"

The best salespeople possess intrinsic motivation, a disciplined work style, the ability to close a sale, and, perhaps most important, the ability to build relationships with customers.

Whatever their motivations, salespeople must also have a disciplined work style. If salespeople aren't organized and focused, and if they don't work hard, they can't meet the ever-increasing demands customers make these days. Great salespeople are tenacious about laying out detailed, organized plans, then following through in a timely, disciplined way. Says one sales trainer, "Some people say it's all technique or luck. But luck happens to the best salespeople when they get up early, work late, stay up till two in the morning working on a proposal, or keep making calls when everyone is leaving at the end of the day."

Other skills mean little if a salesperson can't close the sale. So what makes for a great closer? For one thing, it takes unyielding persistence. "Great closers are like great athletes," says one sales trainer. "They're not afraid to fail, and they don't give up until they close." Great closers also have a high level of self-confidence and believe that they are doing the right thing.

Perhaps most important in today's relationship-marketing environment, top salespeople are customer problem solvers and relationship builders. They have an instinctive understanding of their customers' needs. Talk to sales executives and they'll describe top performers in these terms: empathetic, patient, caring, responsive, good listeners, honest. Top performers can put themselves on the buyer's side of the desk and see the world through their customers' eyes. They don't want just to be liked, they want to add value for their customers.

When recruiting, companies should analyze the sales job itself and the characteristics of its most successful salespeople to identify the traits needed by a successful salesperson in their industry. Then, it must recruit the right salespeople. The human resources department looks for applicants by getting names from current salespeople, using employment agencies, placing classified ads, searching the Web, and working through college and university placement services. Another way is to attract top salespeople from other companies. Proven salespeople need less training and can be immediately productive.

Recruiting will attract many applicants from whom the company must select the best. The selection procedure can vary from a single informal interview to lengthy testing and interviewing. Many companies give formal tests to sales applicants. Tests typically measure sales aptitude, analytical and organizational skills, personality traits, and other characteristics. But test scores provide only one piece of information in a set that includes personal characteristics, references, past employment history, and interviewer reactions.

Training Salespeople

New salespeople may spend anywhere from a few weeks or months to a year or more in training. Then, most companies provide continuing sales training via seminars, sales meetings, and the Web throughout the salesperson's career. Although training can be expensive, it can also yield dramatic returns. For example, one recent study showed that sales training conducted by a major telecommunications firm paid for itself in sixteen days and resulted in a six-month return on investment of 812 percent. Similarly, Nabisco analyzed the return on its two-day Professional Selling Program, which teaches sales reps how to plan for and make professional presentations. Although it cost about $1300 to put each sales rep through the program, the training resulted in additional sales of more than $160 000 per rep and yielded almost $27 000 of additional profit per rep.[13] Although some firms do their sales training in-house, others send their representatives to executive education programs or turn to the Canadian Professional Sales Association (www.cpsa.com) for help.

Training programs have several goals. Salespeople need to know and identify with the company and its products, so most training programs begin by describing the company's objectives, organization, financial structure, facilities, and chief products and markets. They also need to know about customers and competitors. So the training program teaches them about competitors' strategies and about different types of customers and their needs, buying motives, and buying habits. Finally, because salespeople must know how to sell effectively, they are also trained in the basics of the selling process.

Today, as Real Marketing 16.1 pointed out, many companies are adding Web-based training to their sales training programs. In fact, the industry for online training was expected to more than triple to $30.8 billion by 2006.[14] Such training may range from simple text-based product information to Internet-based sales exercises that build sales skills to sophisticated simulations that recreate the dynamics of real-life sales calls.

Compensating Salespeople

To attract good salespeople, a company must have an appealing compensation plan. Compensation is made up of several elements—a fixed amount, a variable amount, expenses, and fringe benefits. The fixed amount, usually a salary, gives the salesperson some stable income. The variable amount, which might be commissions or bonuses based on sales performance, rewards the salesperson for greater effort and success. Salespeople in Canada may earn $25 000 or more in commissions, but the median commission cheque is for approximately $6000.[15] Expense allowances, which repay salespeople for job-related expenses, let salespeople undertake needed and desirable selling efforts. Fringe benefits, such as paid vacations, sickness or accident benefits, pensions, company vehicles, and life insurance, provide job security and satisfaction.

Management must decide what *mix* of these compensation elements makes the most sense for each sales job. Different combinations of fixed and variable compensation give rise to four basic types of compensation plans—straight salary, straight commission, salary plus bonus, and salary plus commission. A study of sales force compensation plans showed that 70 percent of all companies surveyed use a combination of base salary and incentives. The average plan consisted of about 60 percent salary and 40 percent incentive pay.[16]

The sales force compensation plan can both motivate salespeople and direct their activities. Compensation should direct the sales force toward activities that are consistent with overall marketing objectives. For example, if the strategy is to grow rapidly and gain market share, the compensation plan might include a larger commission component coupled with a new-account bonus to encourage high sales performance and new-account development. In contrast, if the goal is to maximize current account profitability and strengthen relationships with current customers, the compensation plan might contain a larger base-salary component with additional incentives for solving customer's problems and increasing customer satisfaction.

In fact, more and more companies are moving away from high commission plans that may drive salespeople to make short-term grabs for business. They worry that a salesperson who is pushing too hard to close a deal may ruin the customer relationship. Instead, companies are designing compensation plans that reward salespeople for building customer relationships and growing the long-run value of each customer.

Supervising Salespeople

New salespeople need more than a territory, compensation, and training—they need *supervision*. Through supervision, the company *directs* and *motivates* the sales force to do a better job.

Companies vary in how closely they supervise their salespeople. Many help their salespeople in identifying customer targets and setting call norms. Some may also specify how much time the sales force should spend prospecting for new accounts and set other time management priorities. One tool is the *annual call plan,* which shows which customers and prospects to call on in which months and which activities to carry out. Activities include taking part in trade shows, attending sales meetings, and carrying out marketing research. Another tool is *time-and-duty analysis.* In addition to time spent selling, the salesperson spends time travelling, waiting, eating, taking breaks, and doing administrative chores.

Figure 16.2 shows how salespeople spend their time. On average, actual face-to-face selling time accounts for less than 30 percent of total working time! If selling time could be raised from 30 percent to 40 percent, this would be a 33 percent increase in the time spent selling. Companies always are looking for ways to save time—using phones instead of travelling, simplifying record-keeping forms, finding better call and routing plans, and supplying more and better customer information. Consider the changes GE made to support its sales force:[17]

When Jeff Immelt became General Electric's new chair, he was dismayed to find that members of the sales team were spending far more time on deskbound

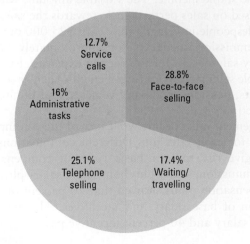

Figure 16.2 How salespeople spend their time

Source: Dartnell Corporation; *30th Sales Force Compensation Survey.* © 1999 Dartnell Corporation.

administrative chores than in face-to-face meetings with customers and prospects. "He said we needed to turn that around," recalls Venki Rao, an IT leader in global sales and marketing at GE Power Systems, a division focused on energy systems and products. "[We need] to spend four days a week in front of the customer and one day for all the admin stuff." GE Power's salespeople spent much of their time at their desks because they had to go to many sources for the information needed to sell multimillion-dollar turbines, turbine parts, and services to energy companies worldwide. To fix the problem, GE created a new sales portal, a kind of "one-stop shop" for just about everything they need. The sales portal connects the vast array of existing GE databases, providing everything from sales tracking and customer data to parts pricing and information on planned outages. GE also added external data, such as news feeds. "Before, you were randomly searching for things," says Bill Snook, a GE sales manager. Now, he says, "I have the sales portal as my home page, and I use it as the gateway to all the applications that I have." The sales portal has freed Snook and 2500 other users around the globe from once time-consuming administrative tasks, greatly increasing their face time with customers.

Many firms have adopted *sales force automation systems*, computerized sales force operations for more efficient order-entry transactions, improved customer service, and better salesperson decision-making support. Salespeople use laptops, handheld computing devices, and Web technologies, coupled with customer-contact software and customer relationship management (CRM) software, to profile customers and prospects, analyze and forecast sales, manage account relationships, schedule sales calls, make presentations, enter orders, check inventories and order status, prepare sales and expense reports, process correspondence, and carry out many other activities. Sales force automation not only lowers sales force costs and improves productivity but also improves the quality of sales management decisions. Here is an example of successful sales force automation:[18]

Owens-Corning has put its sales force online with FSA—its Field Sales Advantage system. FSA gives Owens-Corning salespeople a constant supply of information about their company and the people they're dealing with. Using

Owens-Corning's Field Sales Advantage system gives salespeople a constant supply of information about their company and the people with whom they're dealing.

laptop computers, each salesperson can access three types of programs. First, FSA gives them a set of *generic tools*, everything from word processing and fax and email transmission to creating presentations online. Second, it provides *product information*—tech bulletins, customer specifications, pricing information, and other data that can help close a sale. Finally, it offers up a wealth of *customer information*—buying history, types of products ordered, and preferred payment terms. Before FSA, reps stored such information in loose-leaf books, calendars, and account cards. Now, FSA makes working directly with customers easier than ever. Salespeople can prime themselves on backgrounds of clients; call up prewritten sales letters; transmit orders and resolve customer-service issues on the spot during customer calls; and have samples, pamphlets, brochures, and other materials sent to clients with a few keystrokes. With FSA, "salespeople automatically become more empowered," says Charley Causey, regional general manager. "They become the real managers of their own business and their own territories."

Perhaps the fastest-growing sales force technology tool is the Internet. The most common uses include gathering competitive information, monitoring customer websites, and researching industries and specific customers. As more and more companies provide their salespeople with Web access, experts expect continued growth in sales force Internet usage.[19]

Beyond directing salespeople, sales managers must also motivate them. Some salespeople will do their best without any special urging from management. To them, selling may be the most fascinating job in the world. But selling can also

Many companies offer cash, trips, or merchandise as incentives. Marriott suggests that companies reward outstanding sales performers by letting them "spread their wings and reenergize" at the fabulous Marriott resorts worldwide.

be frustrating. Salespeople often work alone and they must sometimes travel away from home. They may face aggressive competing salespeople and difficult customers. Therefore, salespeople often need special encouragement to do their best.

Management can boost sales force morale and performance through its organizational climate, sales quotas, and positive incentives. *Organizational climate* describes the feeling that salespeople have about their opportunities, value, and rewards for a good performance. Some companies treat salespeople as if they are not very important, and performance suffers accordingly. Other companies treat their salespeople as valued contributors and allow virtually unlimited opportunity for income and promotion. Not surprisingly, these companies enjoy higher sales force performance and less turnover.

Sales quota
A standard that states the amount a salesperson should sell and how sales should be divided among the company's products.

Many companies motivate their salespeople by setting **sales quotas**—standards stating the amount they should sell and how sales should be divided among the company's products. Compensation is often related to how closely salespeople meet their quotas. Companies also use various *positive incentives* to increase sales force effort. *Sales meetings* provide social occasions, breaks from routine, chances to meet and talk with "company brass," and opportunities to air feelings and to identify with a larger group. Companies also sponsor *sales contests* to spur the sales force to make a selling effort above what would normally be expected. Other incentives include honours, merchandise and cash awards, trips, and profit-sharing plans. In all, companies spend a great deal of money motivating their sales staff.

Evaluating Salespeople

We have thus far described how management communicates what salespeople should be doing and how it motivates them to do it. This process requires good feedback. And good feedback means getting regular information about salespeople to evaluate their performance.

Management gets information about its salespeople in several ways. The most important source is *sales reports,* including weekly or monthly work plans and longer-term territory marketing plans. Salespeople also write up their completed activities on *call reports* and turn in *expense reports* for which they are partly or wholly repaid. Additional information comes from personal observation, customer surveys, and talks with other salespeople.

Using various sales force reports and other information, sales management evaluates members of the sales force. It evaluates salespeople on their ability to "plan their work and work their plan." Formal evaluation forces management to develop and communicate clear standards for judging performance. It also provides salespeople with constructive feedback and motivates them to perform well.

Selling process
The steps that the salesperson follows when selling, which include prospecting and qualifying, preapproaching, approaching, presenting and demonstrating, handling objections, closing, and following up.

The Personal Selling Process

We now turn from designing and managing a sales force to the actual personal selling process. The **selling process** consists of several steps that the salesperson must master. These steps focus on the goal of getting new customers and obtaining orders from them. However, most salespeople spend much of their time maintaining existing accounts and building long-term customer *relationships*. We discuss the relationship aspect of the personal selling process in a later section.

Steps in the Selling Process

As shown in Figure 16.3, the selling process consists of seven steps: *prospecting and qualifying, preapproach, approach, presentation and demonstration, handling objections, closing,* and *follow-up.*

Prospecting and Qualifying

Prospecting
The step in the selling process in which the salesperson identifies qualified potential customers.

The first step in the selling process is **prospecting**—identifying qualified potential customers. Approaching the right potential customers is crucial to selling success. As one expert puts it: "If the sales force starts chasing anyone who is breathing and seems to have a budget, you risk accumulating a roster of expensive-to-serve, hard-to-satisfy customers who never respond to whatever value proposition you have." He continues, "The solution to this isn't rocket science. [You must] train salespeople to actively scout the right prospects. If necessary, create an incentive program to reward proper scouting." Another expert concludes: "Increasing your prospecting effectiveness is the fastest single way to boost your sales."[20]

The salesperson must often approach many prospects to get just a few sales. Although the company supplies some leads, salespeople need skill in finding their own. They can ask current customers for referrals. They can cultivate referral sources, such as suppliers, dealers, noncompeting salespeople, and bankers. They can search for prospects in directories or on the Web and track down leads using the telephone and direct mail. Or they can drop in unannounced on various offices (a practice known as "cold calling").

Salespeople also need to know how to *qualify* leads—that is, how to identify the good ones and screen out the poor ones. Prospects can be qualified by looking at their financial ability, volume of business, special needs, location, and possibilities for growth.

Preapproach

Preapproach
The step in the selling process in which the salesperson learns as much as possible about a prospective customer before making a sales call.

Before calling on a prospect, the salesperson should learn as much as possible about the organization (what it needs, who is involved in the buying) and its buyers (their characteristics and buying styles). This step is known as the **preapproach**. The salesperson can consult standard industry and online sources, acquaintances, and others to learn about the company. The salesperson should set *call objectives*, which may be to qualify the prospect, to gather information, or to make an immediate sale. Another task is to decide on the best approach, which might be a personal visit, a phone call, or a letter. The best timing should be considered carefully because many prospects are busiest at certain times. Finally, the salesperson should give thought to an overall sales strategy for the account.

Approach

Approach
The step in the selling process in which the salesperson meets the customer for the first time.

During the **approach** step, the salesperson should know how to meet and greet the buyer and get the relationship off to a good start. This step involves the sales-

Figure 16.3 Major steps in effective selling

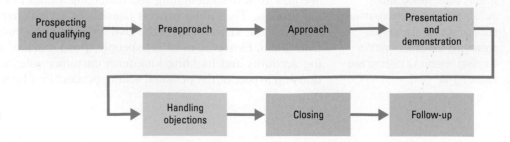

person's appearance, opening lines, and the follow-up remarks. The opening lines should be positive to build goodwill from the beginning of the relationship. This opening might be followed by some key questions to learn more about the customer's needs or by showing a display or sample to attract the buyer's attention and curiosity. As in all stages of the selling process, listening to the customer is crucial.

Presentation and Demonstration

Presentation

The step in the selling process in which the salesperson tells the "benefit story" to the buyer, highlighting the ways in which the product can meet customer needs and aspirations.

During the **presentation** step of the selling process, the salesperson tells the product "story" to the buyer, presenting customer benefits and showing how the product solves the customer's problems. The problem-solver salesperson fits better with today's marketing concept than does a hard-sell salesperson or the glad-handing extrovert. Buyers today want solutions, not smiles; results, not razzle-dazzle. They want salespeople who listen to their concerns, understand their needs, and respond with the right products and services.

This *need-satisfaction approach* calls for good listening and problem-solving skills. "I think of myself more as a ... well, psychologist," notes one experienced salesperson. "I listen to customers. I listen to their wishes and needs and problems, and I try to figure out a solution. If you're not a good listener, you're not going to get the order." Another salesperson suggests, "It's no longer enough to have a good relationship with a client. You have to understand their problems. You have to feel their pain." One sales manager suggests that salespeople need to put themselves in their customers' shoes: "Make yourself a customer and see first-hand how it feels," he says.[21]

The qualities that buyers *dislike most* in salespeople include being pushy, late, deceitful, and unprepared, or disorganized. The qualities they *value most* include empathy, good listening, honesty, dependability, thoroughness, and follow-through. Great salespeople know how to sell, but more importantly, they know how to listen and to build strong customer relationships.

Today, advanced presentation technologies allow for full multimedia presentations to only one or a few people. CDs and DVDs, online presentation technologies, and handheld and laptop computers with presentation software have replaced the flip chart. Here's an example:[22]

Only recently, Credant Technologies, a firm that sells security software programs for handhelds, used standard presentation equipment—laptops and LCD

The old-fashioned flip chart has been replaced by CDs, online presentation technologies, and handheld and laptop computers. Each member of Credant Technologies' sales team is equipped with Presenter-to-Go, a credit-card-sized device that slips into handheld PDAs or pocket PCs to make them compatible with projectors.

projectors—to showcase its products to potential clients. That's no longer the case. Each member of the company's sales team is now equipped with Presenter-to-Go, a credit card-sized device that slips into handheld PDAs or pocket PCs to make them compatible with projectors. The $260 device reads PowerPoint, Microsoft Word, and Excel files, as well as webpages, allowing salespeople to create presentations on computers, then transfer them to a PDA. It also lets reps add notes to presentations instantaneously by transmitting handwriting on their pocket PC to the screen. And it includes a wireless remote control, so sales reps can move freely throughout the presentation room, unattached to their laptop or projector-advancing button. When Credant Regional Account Executive Tom Gore met recently with an important prospect, he wowed buying executives with a feature that enabled him to type some of their comments into his PDA. Within seconds, their comments appeared on screen. "It makes each presentation more personal and interactive," Gore says.

Handling Objections

Handling objections

The step in the selling process in which the salesperson seeks out, clarifies, and overcomes customer objections to buying.

Customers almost always have objections during the presentation or when asked to place an order. The problem can be either logical or psychological, and objections are often unspoken. In **handling objections**, the salesperson should use a positive approach, seek out hidden objections, ask the buyer to clarify any objections, take objections as opportunities to provide more information, and turn the objections into reasons for buying. Every salesperson needs training in the skills of handling objections.

Closing

Closing

The step in the selling process in which the salesperson asks the customer for an order.

After handling the prospect's objections, the salesperson now tries to close the sale. Some salespeople do not get around to **closing** or do not handle it well. They may lack confidence, feel guilty about asking for the order, or fail to recognize the right moment to close the sale. Salespeople should know how to recognize closing signals from the buyer, including physical actions, comments, and questions. For example, the customer might sit forward and nod approvingly or ask about prices and credit terms. Salespeople can use one of several closing techniques: They can ask for the order, review points of agreement, offer to help write up the order, ask whether the buyer wants this model or that one, or note that the buyer will lose out if the order is not placed now. The salesperson may offer the buyer special reasons to close, such as a lower price or an extra quantity at no charge.

Follow-Up

Follow-up

The last step in the selling process in which the salesperson follows up after the sale to ensure customer satisfaction and repeat business.

The last step in the selling process—**follow-up**—is necessary if the salesperson wants to ensure customer satisfaction and repeat business. Right after closing, the salesperson should complete any details on delivery time, purchase terms, and other matters. The salesperson then should schedule a follow-up call when the initial order is received, to make sure there is proper installation, instruction, and servicing. This visit would reveal any problems, assure the buyer of the salesperson's interest, and reduce any buyer concerns that might have arisen since the sale.

Personal Selling and Customer Relationship Management

The principles of personal selling as just described are *transaction oriented*—their aim is to help salespeople close a specific sale with a customer. But in many cases,

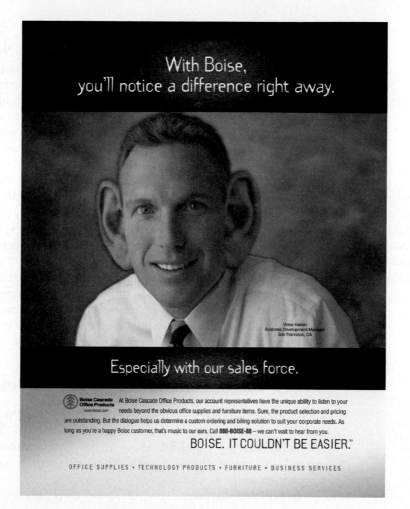

With Boise,
you'll notice a difference right away.

Vince Keelan
Business Development Manager
San Francisco, CA

Especially with our sales force.

Boise Cascade Office Products At Boise Cascade Office Products, our account representatives have the unique ability to listen to your
www.bcop.com needs beyond the obvious office supplies and furniture items. Sure, the product selection and pricing
are outstanding. But the dialogue helps us determine a custom ordering and billing solution to suit your corporate needs. As
long as you're a happy Boise customer, that's music to our ears. Call **888-BOISE-88** – we can't wait to hear from you.

BOISE. IT COULDN'T BE EASIER.™

OFFICE SUPPLIES • TECHNOLOGY PRODUCTS • FURNITURE • BUSINESS SERVICES

Smart companies listen to customers, understand their needs, and carefully coordinate the whole company's efforts toward creating customer value.

the company is not seeking simply a sale: It has targeted a major customer that it would like to win and keep. The company would like to show that it has the capabilities to serve the customer over the long haul in a mutually profitable *relationship*. The sales force usually plays an important role in building and managing profitable customer relationships. "My company is selling something intangible," says one salesperson. "What we are really selling is 'Hey, when the time comes, we'll be there.' It all comes down to trust."[23]

Today's large customers favour suppliers who can sell and deliver a coordinated set of products and services to many locations, and who can work closely with customer teams to improve products and processes. For these customers, the first sale is only the beginning of the relationship. Unfortunately, some companies ignore these new realities. They sell their products through separate sales forces, each working independently to close sales. Their technical people may not be willing to lend time to educate a customer. Their engineering, design, and manufacturing people may have the attitude that "it's our job to make good products and the salesperson's to sell them to customers." Their salespeople focus on pushing products toward customers rather than listening to customers and providing solutions. Other companies, however, recognize that winning and keeping accounts requires more than making good products and directing the sales force to close lots of sales. It requires listening to customers, understanding their needs, and carefully coordinating the whole company's efforts to create customer value and to build lasting relationships with important customers.

Direct Marketing

Many of the marketing and promotion tools that we've examined in previous chapters were developed in the context of *mass marketing:* targeting broad markets with standardized messages and offers distributed through intermediaries. Today, however, with the trend toward more narrowly targeted or one-to-one marketing, many companies are adopting *direct marketing,* either as a primary marketing approach or as a supplement to other approaches. In this section, we explore the exploding world of direct marketing.

Direct marketing

Direct communications with carefully targeted individual consumers—the use of telephone, mail, fax, email, the Internet, and other tools to communicate directly with specific consumers.

Direct marketing consists of direct connections with carefully targeted individual consumers to both obtain an immediate response and cultivate lasting customer relationships. Direct marketers communicate directly with customers, often on a one-to-one, interactive basis. Using detailed databases, they tailor their marketing offers and communications to the needs of narrowly defined segments or even individual buyers.

Beyond brand and image building, direct marketers usually seek a direct, immediate, and measurable consumer response. For example, Dell Computer interacts directly with customers, by telephone or through its website, to design built-to-order systems that meet customers' individual needs. Buyers order directly from Dell, and Dell quickly and efficiently delivers the new computers to their homes or offices.

The New Direct-Marketing Model

Early direct marketers—catalogue companies, direct mailers, and telemarketers—gathered customer names and sold goods mainly by mail and telephone. Today, however, fired by rapid advances in database technologies and new marketing media—especially the Internet—direct marketing has undergone a dramatic transformation.

In previous chapters, we've discussed direct marketing as direct distribution—as marketing channels that contain no intermediaries. We also include direct marketing as one element of the marketing communications mix—as an approach for communicating directly with consumers. In actuality, direct marketing is both of these things.

Most companies still use direct marketing as a supplementary channel or medium for marketing their goods. Thus, Lexus markets mostly through mass-media advertising and its high-quality dealer network but also supplements these channels with direct marketing. Its direct marketing includes promotional CDs and other materials mailed directly to prospective buyers and a webpage (www.lexus.ca) that provides consumers with information about various models, competitive comparisons, financing, and dealer locations. Similarly, most department stores sell the majority of their merchandise off their store shelves but also sell through direct mail and online catalogues.

However, for many companies today, direct marketing is more than just a supplementary channel or medium. For these companies, direct marketing—especially in its newest transformation, Internet marketing and ecommerce—constitutes a new and complete model for doing business. More than just another marketing channel or advertising medium, this new *direct model* is rapidly changing the way companies think about building relationships with customers.

Whereas most companies use direct marketing and the Internet as supplemental approaches, firms employing the direct model use it as the *only* approach. Some of these companies, such as Dell Computer, Amazon.com, and eBay, began as only direct marketers. Other companies—such as Cisco Systems, Canadian Tire, IBM, and many others—are rapidly transforming themselves into direct-marketing superstars. The company that perhaps best exemplifies this new direct-marketing model is Dell Computer. (See Real Marketing 16.2.) Dell has built its entire approach to the marketplace around direct marketing.

Benefits and Growth of Direct Marketing

Whether employed as a complete business model or as a supplement to a broader integrated marketing mix, direct marketing brings many benefits to both buyers and sellers. As a result, direct marketing is growing very rapidly.

For buyers, direct marketing is convenient, easy to use, and private. From the comfort of their homes or offices, they can browse mail catalogues or company websites at any time of the day or night. Direct marketing gives buyers ready access to a wealth of products and information, at home and around the globe. Finally, direct marketing is immediate and interactive—buyers can interact with sellers by phone or on the seller's website to create exactly the configuration of information, products, or services they desire, then order them on the spot.

For sellers, direct marketing is a powerful tool for building customer relationships. Using database marketing, today's marketers can target small groups or individual consumers, tailor offers to individual needs, and promote these offers through personalized communications. Direct marketing can also be timed to reach prospects at just the right moment. Because of its one-to-one, interactive nature, the Internet is an especially potent direct-marketing tool. Direct marketing also gives sellers access to buyers that they could not reach through other channels. For example, the Internet provides access to *global* markets that might otherwise be out of reach.

Finally, direct marketing can offer sellers a low-cost, efficient alternative for reaching their markets. For example, direct marketing has grown rapidly in B2B marketing, partly in response to the ever-increasing costs of marketing through the sales force. When personal sales calls cost $300 per contact, they should be made only when necessary and to high-potential customers and prospects. Lower-cost-per-contact media—such as telemarketing, direct mail, and company websites—often prove more cost effective in reaching and selling to more prospects and customers.

As a result of these advantages to both buyers and sellers, direct marketing has become the fastest growing form of marketing. Sales through traditional direct-marketing channels (telephone marketing, direct mail, catalogues, direct-response television, and others) have been growing rapidly. According to the Computer Industry Almanac, there were 21 900 000 Internet users in Canada as of December 2005. This represents 67.9 percent of the population; thus few marketers can ignore its potential as a direct sales channel. Moreover, with increases in wireless Internet usage, marketers can contact us everywhere. A Ipsos Reid poll conducted on behalf of Bell Canada and Starbucks shows that wireless Internet usage in Canada was poised to double, moving from 18 percent in 2005 to 40 percent of Internet users in 2006.[24]

Customer Databases and Direct Marketing

Customer database
An organized collection of comprehensive data about individual customers or prospects, including geographic, demographic, psychographic, and behavioural data.

Effective direct marketing begins with a good customer database. A **customer database** is an organized collection of comprehensive data about individual customers or prospects, including geographic, demographic, psychographic, and behavioural data. The database can be used to locate good potential customers, tailor products and services to the special needs of targeted consumers, and maintain long-term customer relationships. "If there's been any change in the past decade it's the knowledge we now can have about our customers," says one expert. "Strategically, the most essential tool is our customer database. A company is no better than what it knows."[25]

REAL MARKETING | 16.2

Dell: Be Direct!

*W*hen 19-year-old Michael Dell began selling personal computers out of his dorm room at the University of Texas in 1984, competitors and industry insiders scoffed at the concept of mail-order computer marketing. Yet young Michael proved the skeptics wrong—way wrong. In little more than two decades, he has turned his dorm-room mail-order business into a burgeoning, US$41-billion computer empire.

Dell sells more systems globally than any computer company. Its Canadian headquarters are located in Toronto, and it has offices in Montreal, Ottawa, and Edmonton. It has been growing rapidly in Canada. For example, at its new Customer Contact Centre, which opened in 2006, it expects to employ 1500 people. Lawrence Pentland, president of Dell Canada, notes, "This growth shows that Canadian businesses and consumers are embracing Dell's direct model, leading-edge technology, competitive pricing, and services and support." Direct buyers now account for nearly a third of all PC sales, and Dell's once-skeptical competitors are now scrambling to build their own direct-marketing systems. Moreover, Dell Canada has been working to solidify alliances formed with

Canadian colleges and universities. Under these alliance agreements, students and employees can purchase state-of-the-art Dell branded products at prices below the standard educational price. Further, many institutions are turning to Dell to be their IT solution provider. For example, the University of Toronto selected Dell as its IT vendor in 2005, equipping campuses in Toronto, Scarborough, and Mississauga with servers, desktops, and notebooks.

What's the secret to Dell's stunning success? Anyone at Dell can tell you without hesitation: It's the company's radically different business model—the *direct model*. "We have a tremendously clear business model," says Michael Dell. "There's no confusion about what the value proposition is, what the company offers, and why it's great for customers."

Dell's direct-marketing approach delivers greater customer value through an unbeatable combination of product customization, low prices, fast delivery, and award-winning customer service. A customer can talk by phone with a Dell representative or log onto www.dell.ca on Monday morning; order a fully customized, state-of-the-art PC to suit his or her special needs; and have the machine delivered to his or her doorstep or desktop by Wednesday—all at a price that's 10 to 15 percent below competitors' prices for a comparably performing PC. Dell backs its products with high-quality service and support. As a result, Dell consistently ranks among the industry leaders in product reliability and service, and its customers are routinely among the industry's most satisfied.

Dell's direct-marketing approach delivers greater customer value through an unbeatable combination of product customization, low prices, fast delivery, and award-winning customer service.

Dell customers get exactly the machines they need. Michael Dell's initial idea was to serve individual buyers by letting them customize machines with the special features they wanted at low prices. However, this one-to-one approach also appeals strongly to corporate buyers, because Dell can so easily preconfigure each computer to precise requirements. Dell routinely preloads machines with a company's own software and even undertakes tedious tasks, such as pasting inventory tags onto each machine so that computers can be delivered directly to a given employee's desk. As a result, more than 70 percent of Dell's sales now come from large corporate, government, and educational buyers.

The direct model results in more efficient selling and lower costs, which translate into lower prices for customers. "Nobody, but nobody, makes [and markets] computer hardware more efficiently than Dell," says another analyst. "No unnecessary costs: This is an all-but-sacred mandate of the famous Dell direct business model." Because Dell builds machines to order, it carries barely any inventory—less than three days' worth by some accounts. Dealing one-to-one with customers helps the company react immediately to shifts in demand, so Dell doesn't get stuck with PCs no one wants. Finally, by selling directly, Dell has no dealers to pay. As a result, on average, Dell's costs are 12 percent lower than those of its leading PC competitor.

Dell also knows that time is money, and the company is obsessed with "speed." According to one account, Dell squeezes "time out of every step in the process—from the moment an order is taken to collecting the cash. [By selling direct, manufacturing to order, and] tapping credit cards and electronic payment, Dell converts the average sale to cash in less than 24 hours." By contrast, competitors selling through dealers might take thirty-five days or longer. Such blazing speed results in more satisfied customers

and still lower costs. And because Dell doesn't order parts until an order is booked, it can take advantage of ever-falling component costs. Moreover, its parts are sixty days newer than those in competing machines.

The Internet is a perfect extension of Dell's direct-marketing model. By simply clicking the "Buy a Dell" icon at Dell's website, customers can design and price customized computer systems electronically. The direct-marketing pioneer now sells computers on some eighty country-specific websites, accounting for more than 50 percent of revenues. "The Internet is like a booster rocket on our sales and growth," proclaims Dell. "Our vision is to have *all* customers conduct *all* transactions on the Internet, globally."

As you might imagine, competitors are no longer scoffing at Michael Dell's vision of the future. It's hard to argue with success.

Sources: Quotes, performance statistics, and other information from Kathryn Jones, "The Dell Way," *Business 2.0*, February 2003, pp. 60–66; "The InternetWeek Interview—Michael Dell," *InternetWeek*, April 13, 1999, p. 8; Andy Serwer, "Dell Does Domination," *Fortune*, January 21, 2002, pp. 71–75; Mark Boslet, "PC Market Posts Fresh Growth as Dell Regains No. 1 Ranking," *Wall Street Journal*, April 18, 2003, p. B3; "Dell Computer Corporation," *Hoover's Company Profiles*, Austin, March 15, 2004, p. 13193; Telis Demos, Richard Morgan, and Christopher Tkaczyk, "40 Under 40," *Fortune*, September 20, 2004, p. 72; "Dell Triples Employment Projection at Its Ottawa Customer Contact Centre, Press Release, Ottawa, May 5, 2006, www1.ca.dell.com/content/topics/topic.aspx/ca/corporate/pressoffice/en/2006/2006_05_05_ott_000?c=ca&l=en&s=gen; Association of Canadian Community Colleges, "Association of Canadian Community Colleges/Dell Alliance" (news Release), August 28, 2002, www.accc.ca/english/services/Dell_ACCC_Alliance.cfm; ICD Canada, "Canadian Market Back in the Black, According to IDC" (press release), October 30, 2003, www.idc.ca/investigate/press/pressRelease103003.html; "University of Toronto Selects Dell as Tier 1 IT Vendor" (Dell Press Release), June 23, 2005, www1.ca.dell.com/content/topics/topic.aspx/ca/corporate/pressoffice/en/2005/2005_06_23_tor_000?c=ca&cs=CABSDT1&l=en&s=bsd (accessed May 5, 2006), and www.dell.com/us/en/gen/corporate/access_company_direct_model.htm (accessed January 2005).

Many companies confuse a customer mailing list with a customer database. A customer mailing list is simply a set of names, addresses, and telephone numbers. A customer database contains much more information. In business-to-business marketing, the salesperson's customer profile might contain the products and services the customer has bought; past volumes and prices; key contacts (and their ages, birthdays, hobbies, and favourite foods); competitive suppliers; status of current contracts; estimated customer spending for the next few years; and assessments of competitive strengths and weaknesses in selling and servicing the account.

In consumer marketing, the customer database might contain a customer's demographics (age, income, family members, birthdays), psychographics (activities, interests, and opinions), buying behaviour (past purchases, buying preferences), and other relevant information. Some of these databases are huge, as the following example shows:

The Canadian Automobile Association (CAA), with its 11 geographic-based clubs, boasts 4.2 million members from almost three million Canadian households. CAA members are loyal and 92 percent annually renew their membership. The CAA is currently working to leverage this database to encourage members to buy more than mere memberships. For example, even though it has sold property, auto, travel, medical, health, dental, and life insurance since 1974, many members were unaware of these products. Furthermore, the CAA is partnering with other firms, such as Lenscrafters, who want to access the CAA database. CAA members are mailed offers from partnering firms and win in terms of being offered valuable products and services and discount prices.[26]

Other examples abound. Internet portal Yahoo! records every click made by every visitor, adding some 400 billion bytes of data per day to its database—the equivalent of 800 000 books. And Wal-Mart's database contains more than 100 terabytes of data—that's 100 trillion bytes, equivalent to 16 000 bytes for every one of the world's 6 billion people.[27]

Armed with the information in their databases, these companies can identify small groups of customers to receive fine-tuned marketing offers and communications. Kraft Foods has amassed a list of more than 30 million users of its products who have responded to coupons or other Kraft promotions. Based on their interests, the company sends these customers tips on issues such as nutrition and exercise, as well as recipes and coupons for specific Kraft brands. FedEx uses its sophisticated database to create 100 highly targeted, customized direct-mail and telemarketing campaigns each year to its nearly 5 million customers shipping to 212 countries. By analyzing customers carefully and reaching the right customers at the right time with the right promotions, FedEx achieves response rates of 20 to 25 percent and earns an 8-to-1 return on its direct-marketing dollars.[28]

Companies use their databases in many ways. They can use a database to identify prospects and generate sales leads by advertising products or offers. Companies can use a database to deepen customer loyalty—they can build customers' interest and enthusiasm by remembering buyer preferences and sending appropriate information, gifts, or other materials. Or they can use the database to profile customers based on previous purchasing and to decide which customers should receive particular offers. For example, the Royal Canadian Mint recently used a multi-pronged effort to reposition the mint and reach Canadian coin collectors. Part of the initiative included using the names and addresses from its catalogue database to build a direct mail campaign that publicized the launch of a new coin to more than potential 300 000 collectors.[29] See how Warnaco of Canada built its database:[30]

Warnaco of Canada, which manufactures and markets bra brands such as Warner's, Olga, and Calvin Klein, used an online contest to help build an email database to promote its JLo Lingerie in the Greater Toronto Area. Contestants could bring three friends to the "Ultimate Slumber Party" which included a weekend in the three-storey penthouse loft of the Soho Metropolitan Hotel, complete with a massage, manicure, pedicure, dinner, and a $500 JLo Lingerie gift package. "In this initiative, the onus is on the consumer showing a level of interest," says Melissa Vargas, marketing manager at Warnaco. Information gathered as part of the contest entry will help the company learn more about buying behaviour and create a panel of consumers who can provide feedback about future product and branding initiatives.

Mars, a market leader in pet food as well as candy, maintains an exhaustive pet database. In Germany, the company has compiled the names of virtually every German family that owns a cat. It has obtained these names by contacting veterinarians, via its Katzen-Online.de website, and by offering the public a free booklet titled "How to Take Care of Your Cat." People who request the booklet fill out a

In Germany, Mars has compiled a database containing information on virtually every family that owns a pet. To build lasting relationships, it sends free kitten starter packs to cat owners in Germany who register online.

questionnaire, providing their cat's name, age, birthday, and other information. Mars then sends a birthday card to each cat in Germany each year, along with a cat food sample and money-saving coupons for Mars brands. The result is a lasting relationship with the cat's owner.

Like many other marketing tools, database marketing requires a special investment. Companies must invest in computer hardware, database software, analytical programs, communication links, and skilled personnel. The database system must be user-friendly and available to various marketing groups, including those in product and brand management, new-product development, advertising and promotion, direct mail, telemarketing, Web marketing, field sales, order fulfillment, and customer service. A well-managed database should lead to sales gains that will more than cover its costs.

Forms of Direct Marketing

The major forms of direct marketing—as shown in Figure 16.4—include *personal selling, telephone marketing, direct-mail marketing, catalogue marketing, direct-response television marketing, kiosk marketing,* and *online marketing.* We examined personal selling in depth earlier in this chapter and will look closely at online marketing in Chapter 17. Here, we examine the other direct-marketing forms.

Telephone Marketing

Telephone marketing
Using the telephone to sell directly to customers.

Telephone marketing—using the telephone to sell directly to consumers and business customers—has become the major direct-marketing communication tool. Telephone marketing now accounts for more than 39 percent of all direct-marketing media expenditures and 35 percent of direct-marketing sales. We're all familiar with telephone marketing directed toward consumers, but B2B marketers

Figure 16.4 Forms of direct marketing

also use telephone marketing extensively, accounting for 59 percent of all telephone marketing sales.[31]

Marketers use *outbound* telephone marketing to sell directly to consumers and businesses. *Inbound* toll-free 800 numbers are used to receive orders from television and print ads, direct mail, or catalogues. The use of 800 numbers has taken off in recent years as more and more companies have begun using them, and as current users have added new features, such as toll-free fax numbers. Residential use has also grown. To accommodate this rapid growth, new toll-free area codes, such as 888, 877, and 866, have been added. After the 800 area code was established in 1967, it took almost thirty years before its 8 million numbers were used up. In contrast, 888 area code numbers, established in 1996, were used up in only two years.[32]

Properly designed and targeted telemarketing provides many benefits, including purchasing convenience and increased product and service information. However, the explosion in unsolicited telephone marketing has annoyed many consumers, who object to the almost daily "junk phone calls" that pull them away from the dinner table or fill the answering machine. In November 2005, the federal government passed do-not-call legislation through which a registry will be established for people who do not wish to receive marketing calls. The registry will be similar to the one launched in the U.S. in 2003. Though the Canadian Marketing Association supported the legislation, it successfully lobbied for some major amendments to the bill. The new legislation recognized exemptions where there is an established relationship with the consumer and will give special consideration for calls from registered charities. The do-not-call list is expected to be up and running by the fall of 2007. The CRTC will impose hefty fines on telemarketers who break the rules: up to $1500 per offending call for individuals and up to $15 000 per offending call for corporations. Some companies in the telemarketing industry predicted dire consequences as a result of the legislation, including a reduction in the number of jobs within the industry.[33]

However, consumers support such actions on the part of governments, as U.S. humorist Dave Barry found out. In his regular newspaper column, Barry explained the U.S. do-not-call registry and noted that several telemarketing organizations had filed lawsuits to block the registry. Barry published the telephone number of one of the telemarketing organizations and suggested that readers give the organization a dose of its own medicine. They responded by the thousands.

"I've *never* touched a nerve like the one I touched when I wrote about telemarketers." The telemarketing company complained bitterly about Dave's article and the resulting phone calls, stating that it had been given no warning about what was coming. Dave just chuckled and responded that he hoped no one called them during dinner.[34]

Direct-Mail Marketing

Direct-mail marketing Sending an offer, an announcement, a reminder, or other item to a person at a particular address.

Direct-mail marketing involves sending an offer, an announcement, a reminder, or other item to a person at a particular address. Using highly selective mailing lists, direct marketers send out millions of mail pieces each year—letters, ads, brochures, samples, video- and audiotapes, CDs, and other "salespeople with wings." Direct mail accounts for nearly 24 percent of all direct-marketing media expenditures and more than 32 percent of direct-marketing sales. Together, telemarketing and direct-mail marketing account for some 64 percent of direct-marketing expenditures and 67 percent of direct-marketing sales.

Direct mail is well suited to direct, one-to-one communication. It permits high target-market selectivity, can be personalized, is flexible, and allows easy measurement of results. Although the cost per thousand people reached is higher than with mass media, such as television or magazines, the people who are reached are much better prospects. Direct mail has proved successful in promoting all kinds of products, from books, magazine subscriptions, and insurance to gift items, clothing, gourmet foods, and industrial products. Direct mail is also used heavily by charities to raise billions of dollars each year:

Toronto-based Foster Parents Plan of Canada (FPP) recently began combining market and database research. By matching survey research conducted by Market Facts to its in-house database, the not-for-profit organization has been able to better understand foster parents' commitment levels. "The early indications are that it's being quite predictive of whether or not a foster parent will continue their support or leave," says one researcher. "It gives them a chance not only to look ahead and see what kind of risk they face, but also to try and take actions that will build and retain the support of a foster parent."[35]

The direct-mail industry constantly seeks new methods and approaches. For example, CDs are now among the fastest-growing direct-mail media. America Online has mailed out CDs by the hundreds of millions in one of the most successful direct mail campaigns in history. Now other marketers, especially those in technology or ecommerce, are using CDs in their direct mail offers. Used in conjunction with the Internet, CDs offer an affordable way to drive traffic to webpages personalized for a specific market segment or a specific promotion. They can also be used to demonstrate computer-related products. For example, Sony sent out a CD that allowed PC users to demo its VAIO portable notebook on their own computers.

It wasn't long ago that all mail was paper based and handled by Canada Post, telegraphic services, or for-profit mail carriers, such as Purolator, Federal Express, DHL, UPS, or Airborne Express. Now marketers can use *fax mail, email,* or *voice mail* to announce special offers, sales, and other events. These tools can be highly effective. Today's email messages, for example, have moved far beyond the drab text-only messages of old. They use animation, interactive links, streaming video, and personalized audio messages to reach out and grab attention. However, as is the case with telemarketing, consumer resentment arises when these tools are used inappropriately. Smart marketers are using permission-based programs.

Catalogue Marketing

Advances in technology, along with the move toward personalized, one-to-one marketing have resulted in exciting changes in **catalogue marketing**. *Catalog Age* magazine used to define a *catalogue* as "a printed, bound piece of at least eight pages, selling multiple products, and offering a direct ordering mechanism." Today, only a few years later, this definition is sadly out of date.

With the stampede to the Internet, more and more catalogues are going electronic. Most print cataloguers have added Web-based catalogues to their marketing mixes, and a variety of new Web-only cataloguers have emerged. See how justwhiteshirts built its business:

In 1994, three Canadian businessmen felt trapped by the fact that they had little choice but to pay between $125–$250 for quality cotton dress shirts. Cheaper shirts were too thin, or a poly-blend, or an unappealing colour. They decided they could do better, and justwhiteshirts was born. Using the finest fabrics from around the world, the partners designed dress shirts with superior features such as buttonholes stitched 144 times to ensure non-ravel wear. They used a mail order catalogue to market their reasonably priced main product, the "Chairman's Choice" 100% cotton white dress shirts, and a small selection of silk ties and socks at reasonable prices products. In 1997, its website justwhiteshirts.com was launched, and today 40 percent of the company's gross revenues of about $5 million are generated through its online catalogue. The success of its online operations is due to the fact that the company has never lost sight of the need to focus on the needs of the customer in the various geographic markets it serves. According to its vice-president of marketing, Michael Sachter, "the Internet is like the fax machine, it changed the way people did business but it did not change business." Today, justwhiteshirts is anything but. It offers thousands of dress shirts, casual shirts, golf shirts, ties and casual accessories through its catalogues and one Toronto-based clearance store.[36]

The Internet has not yet killed off printed catalogues—far from it. Web catalogues currently generate only about 13 percent of all catalogue sales. Although the

Internet has provided a new avenue for catalogue sales, printed catalogues remain the primary medium. Like justwhiteshirts, most cataloguers use the Internet as an added sales tool to augment their printed catalogues.[37]

Catalogue marketing has grown explosively during the past 25 years. According to Canada Post Borderfree, 13 000 mail catalogue titles are circulated to American consumers generating $76.8 billion in annual sales. In sharp contrast, only 35 titles are circulated in Canada, generating $1.38 billion in annual sales, suggesting that the Canadian market is underserved.[38] It's not surprising, therefore, that some large general-merchandise retailers—such as Sears and Canadian Tire—sell a full line of merchandise through catalogues. In recent years, these giants have been challenged by thousands of specialty catalogues that serve highly specialized market niches.

Consumers can buy just about anything from a catalogue. IKEA Canada can help you furnish almost any living space with style; Harry Rosen can dress you for any occasion; and Veseys can help you create a garden oasis. Sears Canada features print and online catalogues. Though some customers get Sears' print catalogue for free, others buy it on newsstands for $6. Tilley Endurables and Mountain Equipment Co-op feature everything you would need to go hiking in the Sahara or the rain forest. Several major corporations have also developed or acquired catalogue divisions. For example, Avon now issues 10 women's fashion catalogues along with catalogues for children's and men's clothes. Walt Disney Company mails out more than 6 million catalogues each year, featuring videos, stuffed animals, and other Disney items.

Ninety-seven percent of all catalogue companies now present merchandise and take orders over the Internet. Web-based catalogues present a number of benefits over printed catalogues. They save on production, printing, and mailing costs. Whereas print-catalogue space is limited, online catalogues can offer an almost unlimited amount of merchandise. Web catalogues also allow real-time merchandising: products and features can be added or removed as needed, and prices can be adjusted instantly to match demand. Finally, online catalogues can be spiced up with interactive entertainment and promotional features, such as games, contests, and daily specials.

Along with the benefits, however, Web-based catalogues also present challenges. Whereas a print catalogue is intrusive and creates its own attention, Web catalogues

Catalogue marketing has grown explosively during the past 25 years.

are passive and must be marketed. Attracting new customers is much more difficult for a Web catalogue than for a print catalogue. Thus, even cataloguers who are sold on the Web are not likely to abandon their print catalogues.

Direct-Response Television Marketing

Direct-response television marketing takes one of two major forms. The first is *direct-response advertising*. Direct marketers air television spots, often 60 or 120 seconds long, that persuasively describe a product and give customers a toll-free number for ordering. Television viewers often encounter 30-minute advertising programs, or *infomercials*, for a single product.

Some successful direct-response ads run for years and become classics. For example, Dial Media's ads for Ginsu knives ran for seven years and sold almost 3 million sets of knives worth more than $50 million in sales; its Armourcote cookware ads generated more than twice that much. And over the past forty years, infomercial czar Ron Popeil's company, Ronco, has sold more than $1.3 billion worth of TV-marketed gadgets, including the original Veg-O-Matic, the Pocket Fisherman, Mr. Microphone, the Giant Food Dehydrator and Beef Jerky Machine, and the Showtime Rotisserie & BBQ.[39]

For years, infomercials have been associated with somewhat questionable pitches for juicers and other kitchen gadgets, get-rich-quick schemes, and nifty ways to stay in shape without working very hard at it. Traditionally, they have "almost been the Wild West of advertising, where people make rules for themselves as they go along," says Jack Kirby, chair of the Electronic Retailing Association.[40] In recent years, however, a number of large companies—GTE, Johnson & Johnson, MCA Universal, Sears, Procter & Gamble, Revlon, IBM, Pontiac, Land Rover, and Anheuser-Busch—have begun using infomercials to sell their wares over the phone, refer customers to retailers, send out coupons and product information, or attract buyers to their websites. (See Real Marketing 16.3.) According to Kirby, it's "time to really set some standards and move forward."

Direct-response TV commercials are usually cheaper to make and the media purchase is less costly. Moreover, results are easily measured. Unlike most media campaigns, direct-response ads always include a toll-free number or Web address, making it easier for marketers to measure the impact of their pitches.

Home shopping channels, another form of direct-response television marketing, are television programs or entire channels dedicated to selling goods and services. Some home shopping channels, such as The Shopping Channel (tSc), broadcast twenty-four hours a day. The program's hosts offer bargain prices on products ranging from jewellery, lamps, collectible dolls, and clothing to power tools and consumer electronics—usually obtained by the home shopping channel at closeout prices.

The Shopping Channel's savvy customer-centred marketers didn't take long to add the Web to their marketing mix. Long accustomed to providing consumers with the convenience of shopping at any time, day or night, in the medium of their choice, tSc launched its website in May 1999 (www.theshoppingchannel.com). The tSc website presents browsers with a full selection of products, spanning nine product categories—jewellery, health and beauty, fashions, fitness, at home, electronics, toys, crafts, and collectibles. The site has enabled the television retailer to break free of the limitations inherent in using TV, which can focus on only one product at a time. TV did not allow shoppers to browse through the channel's full offerings, but tSc's online customers can now have access to a full assortment of products at any time without having to wait for information to pop up on the TV show. The Shopping Channel's best customers, those with higher income and education, have naturally gravitated to the website, but, more importantly, the site has attracted a significant number of new customers. Moreover, the average order value is 27 percent higher than that of television-only users. View and click obviously makes a dynamic marketing option.[41]

REAL MARKETING

16.3

Infomercials: But Wait, There's More!

It's late at night and you can't get to sleep. So you grab the TV remote, surf channels, and chance upon a fast-talking announcer, breathlessly pitching some new must-have kitchen gadget. A grinning blonde co-announcer fawns over the gadget's every feature, and the studio audience roars its approval. After putting the gadget through its paces, the announcer asks, "How much would you expect to pay? Three hundred dollars? Two hundred? Well, think again! This amazing gadget can be yours for just four easy payments of $19.95 plus shipping and handling!" "Oooooh!" the audience screams. "But wait! There's more," declares the announcer. "If you act now, you will also receive an additional gadget, absolutely free. That's two for the price of one." With operators standing by, you don't have a minute to lose.

Ronco and Ron Popeil, with his Veg-O-Matics, food dehydrators, and electric egg scramblers, paved the way for a host of mainstream marketers who now use direct-response ads.

Sound familiar? We've all seen countless infomercials like this, hawking everything from kitchen gadgets, cleaning solutions, and exercise equipment to psychic advice and get-rich-quick schemes. Traditionally, such pitches have had a kind of fly-by-night feel about them. And in the cold light of day, such a purchase may not seem like such a good deal after all. Such is the reputation of direct-response TV advertising. Yet, behind the hype is a powerful approach to marketing that is becoming more mainstream every day. Direct TV (DRTV) generates an estimated US$2 trillion in business globally. DRTV accounted for approximately $45 million (compared with $10 million just ten years ago) of Canada's estimated $3 billion TV ad spending in 2005, according to the financial services firm TD Newcrest.

Ron Popeil pioneered direct-response product sales. Whether you realize it or not, you've probably been exposed to dozens of Popeil's inventions over the years, and his direct-marketing model has become the standard for the infomercial industry. His company, Ronco, has brought us such classics as the Veg-O-Matic, the Giant Food Dehydrator, the Showtime Rotisserie Oven, the GLH Formula Hair System, the Automatic 5-Minute Pasta and Sausage Maker, the Popeil Pocket Fisherman, the Inside the Egg Shell Electric Egg Scrambler, and the Dial-O-Matic Food Slicer.

Infomercials do work—most of you will attest to seeing the ads, and many of you have probably bought goods you've "seen on TV." Since its beginning, Ronco has sold more than $1.3 billion worth of merchandise—that's millions of easy payments of just $19.95 each. The success of Ronco and its countless imitators has not gone unnoticed among the big hitters in the corporate world. Direct-response television marketing is rapidly becoming a mainstay weapon in the marketing arsenals of even the most reputable companies.

Ronco's revenues aren't the only reason for the expansion of direct-response TV. The explosion of cable and digital channels that reach a wide range of demographically targeted markets has created a glut of airtime, which can be snapped up at attractive rates.

Changing retailer reactions to direct-response TV products have also given infomercials a boost. Mass retailers are now embracing such direct-response staples as OxiClean, Roll-A-Hose, or George Foreman's Lean Mean Grilling Machine. Whereas it used to take years to get retail distribution for "as seen on TV" products, many now make it to store shelves within a month of going on TV.

All this makes direct-response television advertising both attractive and cost-effective for an expanding range of companies and products, including the marketing heavyweights. Dell, Procter & Gamble (P&G), General Motors, Johnson & Johnson, Sears, Sharper Image, and many other mainstream marketers now use direct-response TV to peddle specific products and promotions, and to draw new customers into their other direct-to-consumer channels. Today's infomercials have evolved with the times—most now include highly professional pitches and websites to go along with the ever-present toll-free phone number.

Procter & Gamble, one of North America's premier marketing companies, now routinely uses infomercials to sell products, such as the Swiffer WetJet and Dryel. A series of infomercials helped to propel the WetJet past rival Clorox's ReadyMop when other marketing efforts alone failed to do the trick. P&G launched its Swiffer Dusters product with a campaign that included direct-response ads and a tie-in to the DVD release of the Jennifer Lopez film *Maid in Manhattan*. Consumers contacting the 800 number got coupons for both the new Swiffer Duster and the DVD.

Even retailers and marketers of durable goods and services are starting to use Direct TV and infomercials. For example, ShopTV Canada has featured programs by marketers such as The Ford Motor Company of Canada, L'Oréal, Scotiabank, Canada Savings Bonds, and Toronto tourism attraction Ontario Place. So, direct-response TV ads are no longer just the province of Ron Popeil and his Veg-O-Matics, food dehydrators, and electric egg scramblers. Although Popeil and his imitators paved the way, their success now has mainstream marketers tuning in to direct-response ads. Marketers are increasing their spending and their revenues through the use of direct-response advertising. The future certainly looks bright for this industry!

Sources: Jack Neff, "Direct Response Getting Respect," *Advertising Age*, January 20, 2003, p. 4; Paul Miller, "Sharper Image Tunes in to Infomercials," *Catalog Age*, February 2001, p. 12; Bridget McCrea, "Removing the Blemishes," *Response*, March 2003, p. 32–34; "Nearly Two-Thirds of Americans Are Exposed to Direct-Response TV," *Research Alert*, March 21, 2003, p. 9; Millie Takaki, "Now Available," *SHOOT*, April 25, 2003, p. 11; "Pharmaceutical Infomercial," *Back Stage*, April 18, 2003, p. 37; Nat Ives, "Informercials Clean Up Their Pitch," *New York Times*, April 12, 2004, p. C1; and Robert Yallen, "Marketers: DRTV Can Be Your Friend," *Brandweek*, May 10, 2004, p. 24; Chris Power, "From Flowbees to Fords," *Marketing*, April 25, 2005.

Kiosk Marketing

Some companies place information and ordering machines—called *kiosks* (in contrast to vending machines, which dispense actual products)—in stores, airports, and other locations. Hallmark uses kiosks to help customers create and purchase personalized greeting cards. Toyota Canada used kiosks to target younger buyers. The Liquor Control Board of Ontario installed interactive kiosks to run advertisements for featured products and to enhance customer service. IKEA allows UNICEF to set up fundraising kiosks in its stores. The use of such kiosks is expected to increase fivefold during the next three years and generate more than $8.4 billion in annual sales by 2006.[42]

Business marketers also use kiosks. Investment Canada placed a kiosk at an Atlanta trade show to introduce Canadian telecommunication and computer products to international buyers. Dow Plastics places kiosks at trade shows to collect sales leads and to provide information on its 700 products. The kiosk system reads customer data from encoded registration badges and produces technical data sheets that can be printed at the kiosk or faxed or mailed to the customer. The system has resulted in a 400 percent increase in qualified sales leads.[43]

Like almost everything else these days, kiosks are also going online, as many companies merge the powers of the real and virtual worlds. For example, at the local Disney Store, kiosk guests can buy merchandise online, purchase theme-park passes, and learn more about Disney vacations and entertainment products. In some of its stores, Gap has installed interactive kiosks, called Web lounges, which provide

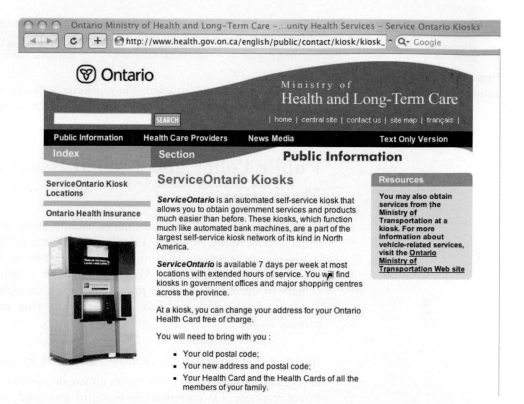

Various branches of the Ontario government, such as the Ministry of Health and Long-Term Care, use kiosks to provide citizens with information and services in locations that are easy to access. These kiosks are part of the largest self-service kiosk network in North America.

gift ideas or let customers match up outfits without trying them in dressing rooms. Kiosks in Virgin stores allow customers to download and purchase individual songs or entire albums online. Outdoor equipment retailer REI has at least four Web-enabled kiosks in each of its sixty-three stores that provide customers with product information and let them place orders online.[44]

Integrated Direct Marketing

Too often, a company's individual direct-marketing efforts are not well integrated with one another or with other elements of its marketing and promotion mixes. For example, a firm's media advertising may be handled by the advertising department working with a traditional advertising agency. Meanwhile, its direct-mail and catalogue business may be handled by direct-marketing specialists, while its website is developed and operated by an outside Internet firm. Even within a given direct-marketing campaign, too many companies use only a "one-shot" effort to reach and sell a prospect or a single vehicle in multiple stages to trigger purchases.

Integrated direct marketing
Direct-marketing campaigns that use multiple vehicles and multiple stages to improve response rates and profits.

A more powerful approach is **integrated direct marketing**, which involves using carefully coordinated multiple-media, multiple-stage campaigns. Such campaigns can greatly improve response. Whereas a direct-mail piece alone might generate a 2 percent response, adding a website and toll-free phone number might raise the response rate by 50 percent. Then, a well-designed outbound telemarketing effort might lift response by an additional 500 percent. Suddenly, a 2 percent response has grown to 15 percent or more by adding interactive marketing channels to a regular mailing.

More elaborate integrated direct-marketing campaigns can be used. Consider the multimedia, multistage campaign shown in Figure 16.5. Here, the paid ad creates product awareness and stimulates phone, mail, or Web inquiries. The company immediately sends direct mail or email responses to those who inquire. Within a few days, the company follows up with a phone call seeking an order. Some prospects will order by phone or the company's website; others might request a face-to-face

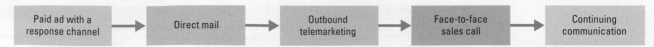

Paid ad with a response channel	→	Direct mail	→	Outbound telemarketing	→	Face-to-face sales call	→	Continuing communication

Figure 16.5 An integrated direct-marketing campaign

sales call. In such a campaign, the marketer seeks to improve response rates and profits by adding media and stages that contribute more to additional sales than to additional costs.

Public Policy and Ethical Issues in Direct Marketing

Direct marketers and their customers usually enjoy mutually rewarding relationships. Occasionally, however, a darker side emerges. The aggressive and sometimes shady tactics of a few direct marketers can bother or harm consumers, giving the entire industry a black eye. Abuses range from simple excesses that irritate consumers to instances of unfair practices or even outright deception and fraud. The direct-marketing industry has also faced growing concerns about invasion-of-privacy issues.

Irritation, Unfairness, Deception, and Fraud

Direct-marketing excesses sometimes annoy or offend consumers. Most of us dislike direct-response TV commercials that are too loud, too long, and too insistent. Especially bothersome are dinnertime or late-night phone calls. Beyond irritating consumers, some direct marketers have been accused of taking unfair advantage of impulsive or less sophisticated buyers. In early 2006, for example, the RCMP laid more than 400 charges against illicit marketers who were targeting victims in the United States. TV shopping channels and program-long "infomercials" targeting television-addicted shoppers seem to be the worst culprits. They feature smooth-talking hosts, elaborately staged demonstrations, claims of drastic price reductions, "while they last" time limitations, and unequalled ease of purchase to inflame buyers who have low sales resistance.

Worse yet, so-called heat merchants design mailers and write copy intended to mislead buyers. Even well-known direct mailers have been accused of deceiving consumers. Sweepstakes promoter Publishers Clearing House recently paid $68 million to settle accusations that its high-pressure mailings confused or misled consumers, especially the elderly, into believing that they had won prizes or would win if they bought the company's magazines.[45]

Other direct marketers pretend to be conducting research surveys when they are actually asking leading questions to screen or persuade consumers. Fraudulent schemes, such as investment scams or phony collections for charity, have also multiplied in recent years. Crooked direct marketers can be hard to catch: Direct-marketing customers often respond quickly, do not interact personally with the seller, and usually expect to wait for delivery. By the time buyers realize that they have been bilked, the thieves are usually somewhere else plotting new schemes.

Invasion of Privacy

Invasion of privacy is perhaps the toughest public policy issue now confronting the direct-marketing industry. These days, it seems that almost every time consumers enter a sweepstakes, apply for a credit card, take out a magazine subscription, or order products by mail, telephone, or the Internet, their names are entered into some company's already bulging database. Using sophisticated computer technologies, direct marketers can use these databases to "microtarget" their selling efforts.

Consumers often benefit from such database marketing—they receive more offers that are closely matched to their interests. However, many critics worry that marketers may know *too* much about consumers' lives and that they may use this knowledge to take unfair advantage of consumers. At some point, they claim, the extensive use of databases intrudes on consumer privacy.

For example, they ask, should a company such as American Express be allowed to make data on its millions of cardholders worldwide available to merchants who accept AmEx cards? Is it right for credit bureaus to compile and sell lists of people who have recently applied for credit cards—people who are considered prime direct-marketing targets because of their spending behaviour?

In their drives to build databases, companies sometimes get carried away. For example, when first introduced, Intel's Pentium III chip contained an embedded serial number that allowed the company to trace users' equipment. When privacy advocates screamed, Intel disabled the feature.

These days, it's not only the large companies that can access such private information. The explosion of information technology has put these capabilities into the hands of almost any business. For example, one bar owner discovered the power of information technology after he acquired a simple, inexpensive device to check IDs.

About 10 000 people a week go to The Rack, a bar in Boston.... One by one, they hand over their driver's licenses to a doorman, who swipes them through a sleek black machine. If a license is valid and its holder is over 21, a red light blinks and the patron is waved through. But most of the customers are not aware that it also pulls up the name, address, birth date, and other personal details from a data strip on the back of the license. Even height, eye color, and sometimes social security number are registered. "You swipe the license, and all of a sudden someone's whole life as we know it pops up in front of you," said Paul Barclay, the bar's owner. "It's almost voyeuristic." Mr. Barclay soon found that he could build a database of personal information, providing an intimate perspective on his clientele that can be useful in marketing. Now, for any given night or hour, he can break down his clientele by sex, age, ZIP code, or other characteristics. If he wanted to, he could find out how many blond women named Karen over 5 feet 2 inches came in over a weekend, or how many of his

The explosion of information technology has put sometimes frightening capabilities into the hands almost any business. One bar owner discovered the power of information technology after he acquired a simple, inexpensive device to check IDs.

customers have the middle initial M. More practically, he can build mailing lists based on all that data—and keep track of who comes back.[46]

Such access to and use of information has caused much concern and debate among companies, consumers, and public policymakers. Consumer privacy has become a major regulatory issue.

Predictably, the U.S. and Canada have responded to the whole privacy issue differently. While the U.S. opted for industry self-regulation, Canadian governments believed more controls were needed. Until recently, Quebec was the only province with legislation dealing with the privacy of personal information, but on January 1, 2004, the *Personal Information Protection and Electronic Documents Act* came into full effect. It uses a number of guiding principles to protect consumers and control how firms gather and use personal information:

- *Consumer consent.* Knowledge and consent must be obtained from consumers before a firm can collect, use, or disclose consumers' personal information.

- *Limitations.* A firm may collect only the information appropriate for the purposes for which it is being gathered. For example, if it needs to mail you something, the firm can ask for your home mailing address, but not any additional, unnecessary information beyond what it needs to address the mailing. Furthermore, a firm may use the information only for the purpose for which it was gathered. To make additional use of the information, it must get permission from the individual. Finally, a firm may not transfer the information to a third party without the permission of the individual.

- *Accuracy.* A firm must ensure that the information it gathers is recorded accurately, and it must appoint an employee to be responsible for this. For example, to comply with this portion of the legislation, Peter Cullen was recently designated as the new chief privacy strategist at Microsoft.

- *Right to access.* Individuals have the right to know what information is being held about them. They can also demand that errors in their personal information be rectified and may request that their personal information be withdrawn from a firm's database.

For full details about the *Personal Information Protection and Electronic Documents Act,* visit the Privacy Commissioner of Canada website at www.privcom.gc.ca/.

Most direct marketers want the same things that consumers want: honest and well-designed marketing offers targeted only toward consumers who will appreciate and respond to them. Direct marketing is just too expensive to waste on consumers who don't want it.

Reviewing the Concepts

Personal selling and direct marketing are both direct tools for communicating with and persuading current and prospective customers. Selling is the interpersonal arm of the communications mix. To be successful in personal selling, a company must first build and then manage an effective sales force. Firms must also be good at direct marketing, the process of forming one-to-one connections with customers. Today, many companies are turning to direct marketing in an effort to reach carefully targeted customers more efficiently and to build stronger, more personal, one-to-one relationships with them.

1. Discuss the role of a company's salespeople in creating value for customers and building customer relationships.

Most companies use salespeople, and many companies assign them an important role in the marketing mix. For companies selling business products, the firm's salespeople work directly with customers. Often, the sales force is the customer's only direct contact with the company and therefore may be viewed by customers as representing the company itself. In contrast, for consumer product companies that sell through intermediaries, consumers usually do not meet salespeople or even know about them. The sales force works behind the scenes, dealing with wholesalers and retailers to obtain their support and helping them become effective in selling the firm's products.

As an element of the promotion mix, the sales force is very effective in achieving certain marketing objectives and carrying out such activities as prospecting, communicating, selling and servicing, and information gathering. But with companies becoming more market oriented, a market-focused sales force also works to produce both *customer satisfaction* and *company profit*. To accomplish these goals, the sales force needs skills in marketing analysis and planning in addition to the traditional selling skills.

2. Identify and explain the six major sales force management steps.

High sales force costs necessitate an effective *sales management process* consisting of six steps: *designing sales force strategy and structure, recruiting and selecting, training, compensating, supervising,* and *evaluating* salespeople.

In designing a sales force, sales management must address strategy issues, such as what type of sales force structure will work best (territorial, product, customer, or complex structure); how large the sales force should be; who will be involved in the selling effort; and how its various sales and sales support people will work together (inside or outside sales forces and team selling).

To hold down the high costs of hiring the wrong people, salespeople must be *recruited* and *selected* carefully. In recruiting salespeople, a company may look to job duties and the characteristics of its most successful salespeople to suggest the traits it wants in its salespeople and then look for applicants through recommendations of current salespeople, employment agencies, classified ads, and the Internet and by contacting college and university students. In the selection process, the procedure can vary from a single informal interview to lengthy testing and interviewing. After the selection process is complete, *training* programs familiarize new salespeople not only with the art of selling but also with

the company's history, its products and policies, and the characteristics of its market and competitors.

The sales force *compensation* system helps to reward, motivate, and direct salespeople. In compensating salespeople, companies try to have an appealing plan, usually close to the going rate for the type of sales job and needed skills. In addition to compensation, all salespeople need *supervision*, and many need continuous encouragement because they must make many decisions and face many frustrations. Periodically, the company must *evaluate* their performance to help them do a better job. In evaluating salespeople, the company relies on getting regular information gathered through sales reports, personal observations, customers' letters and complaints, customer surveys, and conversations with other salespeople.

3. Discuss the personal selling process, distinguishing between transaction-oriented marketing and relationship marketing.

The art of selling involves a seven-step *selling process: prospecting and qualifying, preapproach, approach, presentation and demonstration, handling objections, closing,* and *follow-up.* These steps help marketers close a specific sale and therefore are *transaction oriented.* However, a seller's dealings with customers should be guided by the larger concept of *relationship marketing.* The company's sales force should help to orchestrate a whole-company effort to develop profitable long-term relationships with key customers based on superior customer value and satisfaction.

4. Define direct marketing and discuss its benefits to customers and companies.

Direct marketing consists of direct connections with carefully targeted individual consumers to both obtain an immediate response and cultivate lasting customer relationships. Using detailed databases, direct marketers tailor their offers and communications to the needs of narrowly defined segments or even individual buyers.

For buyers, direct marketing is convenient, easy to use, and private. It gives them ready access to a wealth of products and information, at home and around the globe. Direct marketing is also immediate and interactive, allowing buyers to create exactly the configuration of information, products, or services they desire, then order them on the spot. For sellers, direct marketing is a powerful tool for building customer relationships. Using database marketing, today's marketers can target small groups or individual consumers, tailor offers to individual needs, and promote these offers through personalized communications. It also offers them a low-cost, efficient alternative for reaching their markets. As a result of these advantages to both buyers and sellers, direct marketing has become the fastest growing form of marketing.

5. **Identify and discuss the major forms of direct marketing.**

The main forms of direct marketing include *personal selling, telephone marketing, direct-mail marketing, catalogue marketing, direct-response television marketing, kiosk marketing,* and *online marketing.* We discuss personal selling in the first part of this chapter and will examine online marketing in detail in Chapter 17.

Telephone marketing consists of using the telephone to sell directly to consumers. *Direct-mail marketing* con-

sists of the company sending an offer, announcement, reminder, or other item to a person at a specific address. Recently, three new forms of mail delivery have become popular—*fax mail, email,* and *voice mail.* Some marketers rely on *catalogue marketing,* or selling through catalogues mailed to a select list of customers or made available in stores. *Direct-response television marketing* has two forms: *direct-response advertising* or *infomercials* and *home shopping channels. Kiosks* are information and ordering machines that direct marketers place in stores, airports, and other locations. *Online marketing* involves online channels and ecommerce, which electronically link consumers with sellers.

Reviewing the Key Terms

Approach   622
Catalogue marketing   634
Closing   624
Customer database   627
Customer sales force structure   610
Direct-mail marketing   633
Direct marketing   626
Direct-response television marketing   636
Follow-up   624
Handling objections   624
Inside sales force   611
Integrated direct marketing   639

Outside sales force   611
Preapproach   622
Presentation   623
Product sales force structure   609
Prospecting   622
Sales force management   609
Sales quota   621
Salesperson   608
Selling process   621
Team selling   613
Telephone marketing   631
Territorial sales force structure   609

Discussing the Concepts

1. According to the chapter, salespeople serve two masters. What does this mean? Is it a good or bad thing?

2. The chapter states that the ability to build relationships with customers is the most important of a salesperson's key talents. Do you agree? Explain.

3. The sales force serves as a critical link between a company and its customers. Describe three tasks that a salesperson performs that are difficult to replicate with any other communications tool.

4. The text emphasizes the link between personal selling and customer relationship management. Why is this such an important concept?

5. How does direct marketing differ from personal selling?

6. Write a description of the most irritating, unfair, deceptive, or fraudulent experience you've had with a direct marketing company. Is the company still in business?

Applying the Concepts

1. Suppose your grade in one of your classes is hovering between an A and B. How would you apply the seven steps in the personal selling process to convince your professor that you deserve an A?

2. Suppose that you are a sales information technology consultant who has been asked to design a sales

automation system for the Black & Decker sales force. What hardware would you include in this system? What software? What input information would the system require and what outputs would it provide?

3. In a small group, prepare a list of the pros and cons from the seller's perspective of a "Do Not Email" list.

Focus on Technology

Database marketing has emerged as a major weapon in the marketer's arsenal. Over the past 15 years, database marketing technology has improved significantly. One of the better organizations in this area is DataFlux. In a white-paper on database marketing, the company states, "The goal of a marketing database is to provide consistent, accurate, and reliable data that can be used to build and maintain mutually rewarding customer relationships." Visit the DataFlux website at www.dataflux.com and explore some of the key pages (e.g., see the "Master Data Management" section). Then respond to the following questions:

1. What are some of the challenges cited by DataFlux that require implementation of a database marketing system?

2. What services would DataFlux be able to provide a company interested in database marketing?

3. What are the potential benefits to the buyer of implementing a database marketing system? Are these benefits realistic?

Sources: See www.dataflux.com/Resources.

Focus on Ethics

According to many privacy advocates, consumer information privacy is a growing public policy concern. One area of special concern is the sharing of consumer financial information with affiliates of the same company. Visit Canadian Tire Financial Services webpage (www.ctfs.com/english/privacy.html) and read about the retailer's privacy policy. Then respond to the following questions.

1. What are the important privacy concerns the website works to address?

2. How might the retailer use such database marketing information?

3. Would such information sharing be fair to the consumer? Explain.

Video Case
Motorola

In the midst of the thousands of marketing messages consumers receive each day, how can a company break through the clutter to reach target customers? The answer is consistent messages that convey the real value of products and services. That's how Motorola built its global brand. The company's current campaign offers consumers a simple way to identify with Motorola and its product and service offerings. The entire campaign is based on simple tagline—Moto—that Motorola hopes consumers will associate with edgy innovation.

To firmly establish the brand worldwide, Motorola adapted the campaign for each local market, changing advertising images and media to effectively convey the same brand attributes across the globe. Connecting with consumers requires Motorola to use a variety of communications tools.

After viewing the video featuring Motorola, answer the following questions about personal selling and direct marketing:

1. How did Ogilvy & Mather apply the concepts of integrated marketing communications to build Motorola's communications strategy? What was the goal of the campaign that resulted?

2. How does Motorola use direct marketing, in addition to the advertising featured in the video, to communicate and promote the new brand concept? What other forms of direct marketing could Motorola use to communicate with consumers?

Online Media Resources

Video Short
Log on to your Companion Website at www.pearsoned.ca/kotler to view the video segment related to the Video Case on page 645.

CBC ⊕ CBC Video Case
Please refer to Appendix 2 to read a CBC Video Case for this chapter, and log on to your Companion Website at www.pearsoned.ca/kotler to view the corresponding video segment.

Case Pilot
Log on to your Companion Website at www.pearsoned.ca/kotler to sharpen your case analysis skills and take the Case Pilot Challenge!

Company Case

Jefferson Pilot Financial: Growing the Sales Force

After the Meeting

On a hot Friday afternoon in July, Bob Powell and John Knowles walked across a parking lot toward Bob's car. They had just finished a two-day strategic planning meeting with other members of Jefferson Pilot Financial's (JPF) independent marketing channel at the Grandover Resort and Conference Hotel just outside Greensboro, North Carolina. The group had gathered to develop the sales goals it wanted to achieve in the next two and a half years, to identify strategic projects it needed to accomplish to meet those goals, and to assign responsibility for each project.

"Wow, it's going to be hot in your car," John noted. John served as vice-president for independent marketing and Bob was senior vice-president.

"Especially after sitting in that air-conditioned room for two days," Bob responded. "But I'm glad we're riding together. This'll give us a few minutes to talk about the sales force strategy project the group assigned us."

Jefferson Pilot Financial

Jefferson Pilot Corporation (JP), a holding company, was one of the largest shareholder-owned life insurance companies in the United States. Jefferson Pilot's life insurance and annuity businesses, known collectively as Jefferson Pilot Financial (JPF), comprised principally Jefferson Pilot Life Insurance Company, Jefferson Pilot Financial Insurance Company, and Jefferson Pilot LifeAmerica Insurance Company. JPF offered full lines of individual and group life insurance products as well as annuity and investment products. Jefferson Pilot Communications Company, which operated three network television stations and seventeen radio stations, produced and syndicated sports programming.

In the previous year, the company amassed US$3.33 billion in revenues and US$513 million in net income. JP's insurance and investment products produced about 84 percent of its net income. JP took pride in its excellent financial ratings, having earned the highest possible financial ratings from A.M. Best, Standard and Poors, and Fitch.

Historically, the company generated its individual life insurance sales using a career sales force. The company employed managers to recruit and train life insurance agents, paying the managers commissions based on the insurance premiums their agents generated and an expense allowance to cover their overhead costs. The agents became "captive" Jefferson Pilot employees who sold *only* JP's policies.

Like most life insurance companies, the company paid agents on a commission-only basis. The agent earned a commission of 50 to 60 percent of the *first-year* premium paid by the policyholder. In the following years, the agent earned a much lower commission on annual renewal premiums, usually in the range of 3 percent. In addition to paying commission, the company provided the career agents with a full range of fringe benefits, such as health insurance, vacation, and sick leave. The individual agent had to pay his or her own business expenses.

A New Strategy

In 1993, JP was a conservative, well-run company. However, the board of directors wanted the company to grow more rapidly. The board brought in a new top-management team and charged the team with speeding up the company's growth. The new team immediately examined the company's sales-force strategy. It concluded that although the career sales force had been a valuable asset, the company was not capable of meeting its growth goals using only a career force. It simply took too long to hire and train new agents and bring them up to the necessary productivity levels. Further, industry-wide, only about one of every seven or eight recruits actually succeeded in the insurance business.

In addition to career agents, JPF had used some independent agents all along. Independent agents worked for themselves or for independent companies. They, like captive agents, sold life insurance; but they could sell policies offered by a variety of companies. JPF decided to expand it sales force by focusing on the independent agents. It began to recruit these established, experienced independent salespeople, licensing them to sell JPF's policies and encouraging them to do so. Because the agents remained independent, JPF did not have to provide them with typical employee benefits. However, because the independent agents still had to cover these expenses, the company had to pay a higher percentage of first-year premiums, usually about 80 percent. The average first-year premium in the independent channel was about US$5000. Because independent agents were located throughout the United States, the company was able to expand more rapidly outside of its traditional Southeastern market area and have agents offering its policies nationwide.

The new focus was extremely successful, and by 1999, the independent channel had become JPF's primary distribution channel, although the company retained its career agents. In 1999, JPF hired Bob Powell to head the Independent Marketing channel.

JPF had begun to recruit not only individual independent agents but also so-called Independent Marketing Organizations (IMOs). An IMO was in the business of serving life insurance agents. IMOs did not produce or "manufacture" life-insurance policies; they just served independent life insurance agents. Thus, the insurance company was the "manufacturer," the IMO a "wholesaler," and the independent agent the "retailer." The IMO represented multiple insurance companies and often had a large staff that helped agents develop customized policies to serve special customer needs.

IMOs dealt with the insurance companies, talked with underwriters and medical directors, and helped secure the needed life insurance on behalf of the agent's client. This allowed the agents to sell policies without having to worry about the massive amounts of paperwork and administrative details that someone had to perform after an agent made a sale. As a result,

the IMO earned an additional fee from the insurance company on policies sold by the agents who worked through it. The insurance company was able to pay this additional fee because the IMOs performed some functions that the insurance company would have to perform if it sold directly through the agent.

By recruiting IMOs, JPF was able to bring on more agents more rapidly than it could by having to recruit individual agents. There were also some IMOs that were "recruiting only;" that is, they recruited agents but did not provide any of the administrative support for the agents.

Powell and Knowles realized that there was no way JPF could recruit and serve the thousands of IMOs in the United States from the Greensboro home office. Thus, they began to put together a field sales team. They divided the country into five multi-state regions and, with the help of an executive search firm, recruited a sales vice-president (SVP) for each region.

The SVPs JPF recruited had many years of industry experience with other insurance companies, and several had held similar sales positions with other companies. The SVPs typically spent several days a week travelling to recruit new IMOs or to provide training and support for IMOs with whom JPF had a relationship. They also worked with the IMOs to resolve policy issuance or customer service problems the IMOs might have with the home office. The SVPs were relationship builders. They saw themselves as "premium gatherers" who wanted to get more "shelf space" for JPF's products with each IMO. They wanted to get the IMOs, their staff, and agents into the JPF "culture," make them comfortable doing business with JPF, and make it convenient to do so.

Like the career agents, the SVPs were JPF employees to whom it paid a small percentage of all the first-year premium dollars generated by JPF policies sold in their territory. Even though the percentage was small, because of the size of their territories, SVPs could earn a substantial income.

Because the SVPs put more "feet on the street" for JPF, and because JPF had very competitive products, policy sales had taken off in the previous year. By the time of this mid-year sales meeting, the IMO channel was well ahead of its annual sales targets.

Back in the Car

"The problem we have," Bob Powell noted, "is that we are too successful. We are way ahead of this year's targets and you know top management is going to want us to exceed what we do this year next year. And all of us are working as hard as we can. We can't do more by working any harder. You know that means we will have to add more SVPs."

"That's right," John Knowles observed, "but you saw in the meeting how the five SVPs reacted when we brought this up. They want to protect and keep all of their territory."

"Yes, but we all know that an SVP can't possibly cover eight to twelve states and develop the kinds of IMO relationships we need," Bob answered. "I don't think an SVP can work with more than thirty or so IMOs. What are we going to do when an SVP gets a full client load? How do we bring on more SVPs without upsetting the apple cart?"

"Well," John continued, "that brings up the issue of productivity. We have three marketing coordinators now based in Greensboro who work with the SVPs. However, we don't have a formal job description for them, and the SVPs are unhappy that they don't each have their own coordinator. But you know that in these economic times the company's reluctant to add more people, more overhead."

"I can see that some of our discussions may get as hot as this July weather," Bob laughed.

"When I get home," John said, "I'm going to dig out the old Kotler/Armstrong marketing textbook I had at Auburn and look back over the chapter on personal selling to see if it'll remind me of any issues we ought to be considering."

"We have a September 30 deadline for our sales force strategy proposals, so we'd better get to work," Bob concluded.

Questions for Discussion

1. What are the advantages and disadvantages of using a career sales force versus an independent sales force?

2. What are the advantages and disadvantages of commission-only compensation versus salary-only compensation?

3. What problems do you see with JPF's sales force strategy and structure decisions?

4. What recommendations would you make to JPF to help it deal with these problems?

Source: Officials at Jefferson Pilot Financial cooperated in development of this case.

CHAPTER 17

Marketing in the Digital Age

AFTER STUDYING THIS CHAPTER, YOU SHOULD BE ABLE TO

1. identify the major forces shaping the digital age

2. explain how companies have responded to the Internet and other powerful new technologies with ebusiness

strategies, and how these strategies have resulted in benefits to both buyers and sellers

3. describe the four major ecommerce domains

4. discuss how companies go about conducting ecommerce to profitably deliver more value to customers

5. overview the promise and challenges that ecommerce presents for the future

Previewing the Concepts

In previous chapters, you've learned that the aim of marketing is to create value *for* customers in order to capture value *from* consumers in return. In the final chapters, we'll extend this concept to two special areas—marketing in the digital age and global marketing. Although we've visited these topics regularly in each previous chapter, because of their special importance, we will focus exclusively on them here.

In this chapter, we look into marketing in the digital environment. Marketing strategy and practice have undergone dramatic changes during the past decade. Major technological advances, including the explosion of the Internet, have had a major impact on buyers and the marketers who serve them. To thrive in this new digital age—even to survive—marketers must rethink their strategies and adapt them to today's new environment.

For starters, consider Canadian Tire Corporation. After at first resisting the Internet, it has transformed itself from a traditional retailer to one that has successfully combined online marketing with its traditional retail format. This transformation has propelled the company to leadership in the highly competitive and swiftly changing retail industry.

anadian Tire is a national institution and it is one of Canada's most recognized and trusted brands. The ubiquitous red and white triangle with the green maple leaf has been part of our landscape since 1922. It has a long history of innovation. It was the first retailer in the country to offer a branded MasterCard, and it has one of the industry's leading rewards program—its Canadian Tire "money"—which has achieved icon status. In 2006, there were 462 Canadian Tire stores across Canada and some 259 gas stations. The company has 50 000 employees. In 2005, it generated more than $9 billion in total retail sales and profits climbed 13.3 percent.

Canadian Tire stores offer customers a large selection of national and private label brands through three "stores" under one roof—automotive parts, accessories, and service; sports and leisure products; and home products. Canadiantire.ca, the company's online store, offers more than 15 500 products for sale via the Internet and this channel also serves as an important communication vehicle.

Thanks to its dual format, Canadian Tire is Canada's largest hard-goods retailer and most-shopped non-grocery retailer. In fact, nine out of ten adult Canadians shop at Canadian Tire at least twice a year, and 40 percent of

Canadians shop at Canadian Tire every week. Its flyer is delivered to 10 million homes every week, making its advertising the highest read in the country. Its retail outlets span the country and 85 percent of the Canadian population lives within a 15-minute drive of a Canadian Tire store.

The firm has long been applauded for its ability to move with the times. It was founded by two brothers, A. J. and John W. Billes, who took note of the rising demand for automobiles. With their combined savings of $1800, they bought a small tire garage. Within five years, their business of repairing automobiles and renting out heated parking-garage spaces grew into an incorporated business. People from across Canada began writing to the brothers requesting automotive parts. Recognizing that there was a great demand for automotive parts across Canada but a limited supply, the brothers gained a competitive advantage by introducing a Canadian Tire catalogue. By 1928, it was distributed across the country. This was the first of many instances where Canadian Tire recognized an opportunity for expansion and better customer service and developed an innovative solution.

In the early 1930s, Canadian Tire again differentiated itself from the competition by offering the first guarantee on tires it sold. Though this was a risky offer, it proved successful in promoting the business. The next great initiative from Canadian Tire became their best-known innovation. In 1958, Canadian Tire "money" was introduced. This customer loyalty program lifted Canadian Tire above the competition during a very competitive period and made it a Canadian household name.

Throughout its history, Canadian Tire has striven to be the number one retailer in Canada. When powerful American competitors Wal-Mart and Home Depot entered the market during the 1990s, Canadian Tire had to take a step back from normal day-to-day activities to understand what its customers valued about the business. It was becoming increasingly important for Canadian Tire to show Canadians that it wasn't just the closest store in which to shop, but the best store in which to shop whether they visited a physical location or shopped online. To accomplish this aim, many stores were renovated, new outlets were built, and all operations began to focus on delivering superior customer service.

Given its history of innovation, it is surprising that Canadian Tire waited until 2002 to launch Canadian Tire Online, and the company was criticized for its reluctance to enter cyberspace. However, its "wait and see" approach enabled Canadian Tire to learn from others' mistakes.

To ensure that the ecommerce initiatives continue to meet consumer needs, Canadian Tire Online is working to further develop the webstore's capabilities and service features. In 2001, a line of "Available Only Online" products was introduced. This line includes more than 1000 items and features higher-end appliances and new categories of electronic products, such as digital cameras and MP3 players, as well as licensed apparel, luggage, and an extended assortment of power tools.

Most recently, Canadiantire.ca was completely redesigned to make shopping faster, better, and easier for customers. Major enhancements include

- information about the "item of the week" and weekly specials right on the home page
- a new delivery-cost calculator, enabling customers to determine delivery costs before beginning the checkout process (delivery costs can be calculated as soon

as an item is added to the shopping cart and as additional items are selected)
- a more comprehensive list of product categories within key departments such as housewares, home care and décor, recreation, garden and patio, and automotive—making it faster and easier to browse and shop
- a gift registry, a link to its financial services arm, and an online account inquiry service
- instant access to its Debbie Travis brand collection

In addition, Canadian Tire's unique eFLYER is now fully integrated into the webstore, meaning eFLYER subscribers can shop directly from their eFLYER. Users can also sign up to receive weekly emails featuring information about weekly specials and promotions on the site. And there's a quick link to eFLYER Weekly Specials from the home page.

With this complex mix of online and retail store formats and different media choices for advertising, Canadian Tire and its media agency, MBS, wanted to get a better handle on how different vehicles worked together to drive sales. In 2005, they tested a French and English advertising campaign designed to get adults 25 to 54 to go to Canadian Tire to purchase Father's Day gifts. The campaign, which ran for two weeks, included 30-second radio spots, online display ads and flyers, as well as promotional offers on the Canadiantire.ca site itself. The research revealed that adding online advertising to Canadian Tire's heavy radio campaign increased aided advertising awareness by an additional 6 percent. Moreover, the combination of online advertising and radio was particularly effective against the female portion of the target group, whose unaided brand awareness increased by over 16 percent. Finally, the combination of online and radio resulted in the Canadian Tire website achieving the highest percentage of total unique visitors to the site in two years.

In melding its online and traditional retail worlds, Canadian Tire has created a powerful new model of retailing—a robust two-tiered system where consumers have the choice of shopping by the method they value most. The model recognizes that, most of the time, customers can visit a local store, but occasionally they will like the convenience and different selection afforded by the Web.[1]

Recent technological advances have created a new digital age. Widespread use of the Internet and other powerful new technologies are having a dramatic impact on marketers and buyers. Many standard marketing strategies and practices of the past—mass marketing, product standardization, media advertising, store retailing, and others—were well suited to the old economy. These strategies and practices will continue to be important in the new digital age. However, marketers will also have to develop new strategies and practices better suited to today's new environment.

Use of digital technologies combined with marketing using the Internet are proving to be among the most important implements in marketing's toolbox for cultivating customer relationships and building customer communities. For example, companies such as Amazon.ca use the Internet to record and analyze customers' previous purchase and search behaviour so that they can make product suggestions aligned with the customers' preferences. Other companies, such as Dell, use these tools to help better customize products to precisely meet customer needs. Dove Canada uses the Internet to gather feedback from its consumers (see www.campaign forrealbeauty.ca/share.asp?section=share) and to create a community of support for its new Self-Esteem Fund. The website encourages supporters of the Self-Esteem Fund to share information about the fund and its new advertisement with friends.

In this chapter, we first describe the key forces shaping the new digital age. Then we examine how marketing strategy and practice are changing to take advantage of today's new technologies.

Major Forces Shaping the Digital Age

Many forces are playing a major role in reshaping the world economy, including technology, globalization, environmentalism, and others. Here we discuss four specific forces that underlie the new digital age: *digitalization and connectivity, the explosion of the Internet, new types of intermediaries*, and *customization*. (See Figure 17.1.)

Digitalization and Connectivity

Many appliances and systems in the past—ranging from telephone systems, wristwatches, and musical recordings to industrial gauges and controls—operated on analog information. Analog information is continuously variable in response to physical stimuli. Today a growing number of appliances and systems operate on *digital information,* which comes as streams of zeros and ones, or *bits*. Text, data, sound, and images can be converted into *bitstreams*. A laptop computer manipulates bits in its thousands of applications. Software consists of digital content for operating systems, games, information storage, and other applications.

For bits to flow from one appliance or location to another requires *connectivity*, a telecommunications network. Much of the world's business today is carried

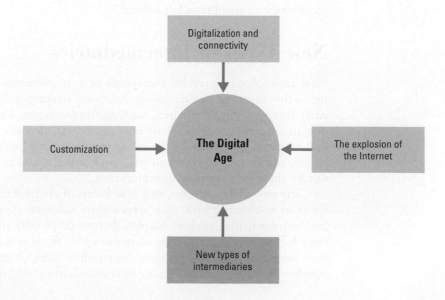

Figure 17.1 Forces shaping the digital age

Intranet
A network that connects people within a company to one another and to the company network.

Extranet
A network that connects a company with its suppliers and distributors.

Internet
A vast public web of computer networks, which connects users of all types all around the world to one another and to an amazingly large information repository.

out over networks that connect people and companies. **Intranets** are networks that connect people within a company to one another and to the company network. **Extranets** connect a company with its suppliers, distributors, and other outside partners. And the **Internet**, a vast public web of computer networks, connects users of all types all around the world to one another and to an amazingly large "information repository." The Internet makes up one big "information highway" that can dispatch bits at incredible speeds from one location to another.

The Internet Explosion

With the creation of the World Wide Web and Web browsers in 1990s, the Internet was transformed from a mere communication tool into a certifiably revolutionary technology. The Internet continues to grow explosively. According to the Canadian Media Directors Council, Internet penetration in Canada has reached 78 percent, with more than 25 million Canadians now using the Internet. Moreover, 2005 ecommerce sales volume forecast has topped $2.7 billion, a 108 percent increase over volume of $1.5 billion a year before.[2]

Although the dot-com crash in 2000 led to cutbacks in technology spending, research suggests that the growth of Internet access among the world's citizens will continue to explode, reaching 1.5 billion by 2007. Not only are more people using the Web, but they are also increasingly moving faster when they get there. A recent study found that 65 percent of Canadians now go online through high-speed broadband connections.[3]

This explosive worldwide growth in Internet usage forms the heart of the new digital age. The Internet has been *the* revolutionary technology of the new millennium, empowering consumers and businesses alike with blessings of connectivity. The Internet enables consumers and companies to access and share huge amounts of information with just a few mouse clicks.

Recent studies have shown that consumers are accessing information on the Internet before making major life decisions. One in three consumers relies heavily on the Internet to gather information about choosing a school, buying a car, finding a job, dealing with a major illness, or making investment decisions. The average Canadian family spends more than 32 hours per week online. A recent survey of Canadian online parents found that many Canadians view the Internet as an essential part of their lives, with 72 percent claiming that the Internet saves them time and enables them to spend more of their valuable time with their families. As a result, to be competitive in today's new marketplace, companies must adopt Internet technology or risk being left behind.[4]

New Types of Intermediaries

New technologies have led thousands of entrepreneurs to launch Internet companies—the so-called dot-coms—in hopes of striking gold. The amazing success of early Internet-only companies, such as Amazon.com, Expedia, Priceline, eBay, and dozens of others, struck terror into the hearts of many established manufacturers and retailers. Established store-based retailers of all kinds—from bookstores, music stores, and florists to travel agents, stockbrokers, and car dealers—feared being cut out by these new types of intermediaries.

The new intermediaries and new forms of channel relationships caused existing firms to re-examine how they served their markets. At first, the established *brick-and-mortar* firms—such as Staples, Barnes & Noble, and Merrill Lynch—dragged their feet hoping that the aggressive *pure-play* firms would falter or disappear. Then they wised up and started their own online sales channels, becoming companies *combining traditional and online operations*. Ironically, many companies combining traditional and online operations have become stronger than the pure-play competitors that pushed them reluctantly onto the Internet. Still, many pure-play competitors are surviving and even prospering in today's marketplace.

Customization

The old economy revolved around *manufacturing companies* that mainly focused on standardizing their production, products, and business processes. They invested large sums in brand building to tout the advantages of their standardized market offerings. In contrast, today's economy revolves around *information businesses*. Information has the advantages of being easy to differentiate, customize, personalize, and send at incredible speeds over networks. With rapid advances in Internet and other information technologies, companies have grown skilled in gathering information about individual customers and business partners (suppliers, distributors, retailers). In turn, they have become more adept at individualizing their products and services, messages, and media.

Customization involves more than simply taking the initiative to customize the market offering. It also means giving customers the opportunity to design their own offerings. Dell, for example, lets customers specify exactly what they want in their computers and delivers customer-designed units in only a few days. In the Web-Fit section of its pinggolf.com website, Ping enables consumers to enter in their measurements, handicap, preferred club materials, and typical flight-path trajectory (e.g., straight, hook, slice), and then provides a "static fitting" based on these needs. Consumers can then look up a custom fitter in their area to have their clubs made. Nike ID (see http://nikeid.nike.com) allows sports enthusiasts to personalize shoes.

Marketing Strategy in the Digital Age

Conducting business in the new digital age will call for a new model for marketing strategy and practice. The Internet is revolutionizing how companies create value for customers and build customer relationships. The digital age has fundamentally changed customers' notions of convenience, speed, price, product information, and service. Thus, today's marketing requires new thinking and action. Companies need to retain most of the skills and practices that have worked in the past. But they will also need to add major new competencies and practices if they hope to grow and prosper in the new environment.

Ebusiness, Ecommerce, and Emarketing in the Digital Age

Ebusiness
The use of electronic platforms—intranets, extranets, and the Internet—to conduct a company's business.

Ebusiness involves the use of electronic platforms—intranets, extranets, and the Internet—to conduct a company's business. Almost every company has set up a website to inform about and promote its products and services. Others use websites simply to build stronger customer relationships.

Most companies have also created intranets to help employees communicate with one another and to access information found in the company's computers. For example, some 14 000 employees regularly log on to P&G intranet, mNet, to receive training and to research marketing news from around the world.[5] Companies also set up extranets with their major suppliers and distributors to enable information exchange, orders, transactions, and payments.

Customization: At pinggolf.com, consumers define their club needs and are provided with a "static fitting."

Ecommerce
Buying and selling processes supported by electronic means, primarily the Internet.

Emarketing
The marketing side of ecommerce—company efforts to communicate about, promote, and sell products and services over the Internet.

Ecommerce is more specific than ebusiness. Ebusiness includes all electronics-based information exchanges within or between companies and customers. In contrast, ecommerce involves buying and selling processes supported by electronic means. Ecommerce includes such activities as electronic funds transfer, supply chain management activities, emarketing, online transaction processing, electronic data interchange, automated inventory management systems, and automated data-collection systems. It typically uses electronic communications technology, such as the Internet, extranets, email, ebooks, databases, and mobile phones. *Emarkets* are "market*spaces*," rather than physical market*places*. Sellers use emarkets to offer their products and services online. Buyers use them to search for information, identify what they want, and place orders using credit or other means of electronic payment.

Ecommerce includes *emarketing* and *epurchasing (eprocurement)*. **Emarketing** is the marketing side of ecommerce. It consists of company efforts to communicate about, promote, and sell products and services over the Internet. Companies such as Amazon and Dell use their Canadian websites (www.amazon.ca and www.dell.ca) to conduct Internet marketing in Canada. The flip side of emarketing is epurchasing, the buying side of ecommerce. It consists of companies purchasing goods, services, and information from online suppliers. In business-to-business buying, emarketers and epurchasers come together in huge ecommerce networks.

Ecommerce and the Internet bring many benefits to both buyers and sellers. Let's review some of these major benefits.

Benefits to Buyers

Internet buying benefits both final buyers and business buyers in many ways. It can be *convenient*: Customers don't have to battle traffic, find parking spaces, and trek through stores and aisles to find and examine products. They can do comparative shopping by surfing websites. Web marketers never close their doors. Buying is *easy* and *private*: Customers encounter fewer buying hassles and don't have to face sales-people or open themselves up to persuasion and emotional pitches. Business buyers can learn about and buy products and services without waiting for and tying up time with salespeople.

In addition, the Internet often provides buyers with greater *product access and selection*. Unrestrained by physical boundaries, online sellers can offer an almost unlimited selection. Compare the incredible selections offered by Web merchants, such as Chapters.Indigo (www.chapters.indigo.ca), with the more meagre assortments of their counterparts in the bricks-and-mortar world. For example, though there are approximately 3 million book titles available in print, most physical book-stores hold approximately 125 000 titles. By selling books online, Indigo can make all 3 million titles available to its customers.

Ecommerce channels also give buyers access to a wealth of comparative *information* about companies, products, and competitors. Good sites often provide more information in more useful forms than even the most solicitous salesperson can. For example, Amazon.ca offers top-10 product lists, extensive product descriptions, expert and user product reviews, and recommendations based on customers' previous purchases.

Finally, online buying is *interactive* and *immediate*. Buyers often can interact with the seller's site to create exactly the configuration of information, products, or services they desire, then order or download them on the spot. Moreover, the Internet gives consumers a greater measure of control. Like nothing else before it, the Internet has empowered consumers. These days, for example, 60 percent of car buyers bargain hunt online before visiting a dealership, arming themselves with car and cost information. This is the new reality of consumer control.[6] See how P&G used consumer empowerment, the interactive nature of the Internet and a concept called "brand democratization," to give viewers a real say in product development:

When Procter & Gamble Co. launched an online contest for Crest toothpaste recently, it turned consumer participation in Internet marketing campaigns into an outright democracy. It developed an online "election" surrounding the Crest Whitening Expressions brand. Internet users were asked to vote for their favourite potential new flavour online, and Crest promised to make a product based on the winner. "Consumers like to feel that their vote counts," says Lisa

Internet buying is easy and private. Final consumers can shop the world from home with few hassles; business buyers can learn about and obtain products and information without tying up time with salespeople.

Festa, a spokeswoman with Procter & Gamble in Toronto. As one expert notes, "It's about giving individuals the power to be in control of the brand." In the process, consumers can not only express themselves but P&G can "educate" them about a brand to encourage a deeper connection to it. Crest received more than 785 000 votes in its online election over the course of three months.[7]

Benefits to Sellers

Ecommerce also yields many benefits to sellers. First, the Internet is a powerful tool for *customer relationship building*. Because of its one-to-one, interactive nature, companies can interact online with customers to learn more about specific needs and wants. In turn, online customers can ask questions and volunteer feedback. Based on this ongoing interaction, companies can increase customer value and satisfaction through product and service refinements.

The Internet and other electronic channels can also *reduce costs* and *increase speed and efficiency*. By using the Internet to link directly to suppliers, factories, distributors, and customers, businesses can cut costs and pass savings on to customers. Emarketers avoid the expense of maintaining a store and the related costs of rent, insurance, and utilities. Because customers deal directly with sellers, online selling often results in lower costs and improved efficiencies for channel and logistics functions, such as order processing, inventory handling, delivery, and trade promotion. Finally, communicating electronically often costs less than communicating on paper through the mail. For instance, a company can produce digital catalogues for much less than the cost of printing and mailing paper ones.

Emarketing can also offer greater *flexibility*, allowing the marketer to make ongoing adjustments to its offers and programs. For example, once a paper catalogue is mailed to final consumers or business customers, the products, prices, and other catalogue features are fixed until the next catalogue is sent. However, an online catalogue can be adjusted daily or even hourly, adapting product assortments, prices, and promotions to match changing market conditions.

The Internet is a truly *global* medium. A Web surfer from Paris or Istanbul can access an online L.L. Bean catalogue as easily as someone living in Freeport, Maine, the direct retailer's hometown.

Finally, the Internet is a truly *global* medium that allows buyers and sellers to click from one country to another in seconds. A Web surfer from Paris or Istanbul can access an online L.L. Bean catalogue as easily as someone living in Freeport, Maine, the direct retailer's hometown. Even small emarketers find that they have ready access to global markets.

Emarketing Domains

The four major emarketing domains are shown in Figure 17.2 and discussed below. They include B2C (business to consumer), B2B (business to business), C2C (consumer to consumer), and C2B (consumer to business).

B2C (Business-to-Consumer)

B2C (business-to-consumer) ecommerce
The online selling of goods and services to final consumers.

The popular press has paid the most attention to **B2C (business-to-consumer) ecommerce**—the online selling of goods and services to final consumers. Despite some gloomy predictions, online consumer buying continues to grow at a healthy rate. While Statistics Canada found that 57 percent of Internet users only window shop online, more and more Canadians are starting to buy products and services online. It is projected that Canadians will double their online spending for retail goods to total $16 billion by 2009. To take advantage of this growing online market, some firms, like TD Canada Trust, have been pioneers in the online market. TD Canada Trust was one of the first banks in the world to allow its customers to conduct transactions online. Since Canadians are among the most "wired" people in the world, we have adapted to online banking much more quickly than our American counterparts. Air Canada was another leader, launching its ecommerce site in 1998. Customers can purchase tickets online with their credit cards or Aeroplan points. Air Canada also uses the Internet extensively for marketing activities—its "Websaver" email announces special last-minute fares every Wednesday to anyone who registers to receive it. The largest categories of consumer online spending include travel services, clothing, computer hardware and software, consumer electronics, books, music and video, health and beauty, home and garden, flowers and gifts, sports and fitness equipment, and toys.[8]

Online Consumers

In its early days, the Internet was populated largely by pasty-faced computer nerds or young, techy, upscale, male professionals. As the Web has matured, however, Internet demographics have changed significantly. Today, almost three-quarters of Canadians surf the Internet. As more and more people find their way onto the Web, the cyberspace population is becoming more mainstream. The Internet is an important global medium. *The Face of the Web* study,[9] conducted by Ipsos Insight in November and December 2005, surveyed a random sample of 6544 adults in urban Brazil, Canada, urban China, France, Germany, urban India, Japan, urban Mexico, urban Russia, South Korea, the U.K., and the U.S. It found that the global online

Figure 17.2 Emarketing domains

	Targeted to consumers	Targeted to businesses
Initiated by business	B2C (business to consumer)	B2B (business to business)
Initiated by consumer	C2C (consumer to consumer)	C2B (consumer to business)

population grew a modest 5 percent in 2005, well below the 20 percent growth rate observed in 2004. Japan was the main driver of overall global Internet user growth. The country is the world's number-one Internet-based economy, with 89 percent of the people sampled reporting that they had used the Internet in the past 30 days. Canada was in second place, with 72 percent of our population going online in the same period, followed by the U.S., with 71 percent of its population surfing the Web. South Korea and Germany follow, with 68 percent and 62 percent, respectively, of their populations using the Internet. Mexico (40 percent), Brazil (21 percent), Russia (19 percent) and India (15 percent) trail in terms of the proportion of their populations using the Internet during the survey period.

Growth in adoption may be slowing in North America. North Americans are more technically sophisticated Internet users, however, leading the charge in wireless Internet use on a PC as well as in awareness and usage of Wi-Fi Internet connectivity. Thus, one expert involved with the survey noted, "measuring growth of the Internet in [North America] in the coming years will be less about user volume, and more about consumers' reliance on this medium as a way of life. Whether it is checking RSS feeds, blogging, or picking up a podcast or yesterday's sitcom, consumers continue to expand and apply new depth of Internet use that we haven't seen before."

In Europe, France and Germany appear poised to drive global Internet growth in 2006, as does urban Russia, where Internet usage remains a nascent activity. In East Asia, the urban China market (50 percent reported use) is quickly evolving into one of the most dynamic Internet-based economies in the world.

Thus, increasingly, the Internet provides emarketers with access to a broad range of demographic segments. For example, another recent study found that North American consumers who have been buying online for more than six years have an average income exceeding $79 000. Thirty-four percent are women and 57 percent have university degrees. In contrast, consumers who've shopped less than one year online have an average income of $52 000. About 57 percent are women and 39 percent have university degrees.[10] These days, it seems, just about everybody is logging on, but they may not be neglecting other media. See what a recent Canadian survey revealed:

A survey undertaken by the Canadian Internet Project revealed that Canadians who spend the most time online are avid consumers of media in general. Although Internet users spend less time with television, radio, magazines, and newspapers (1.8 hours less per week) than non-users, they still spend a considerable amount of time with all four media, the study concluded. As one expert noted, the Internet is viewed as an important source of information rather than as a place to be entertained. The average Internet user is online 13.5 hours per week. Fifty-nine percent of Internet users said newspapers are an important source of information, versus 50 percent of non-users. Only television was more important to non-users, 60 percent of whom cited it as an important source of information versus 54 percent of those online. MSN was the top Internet site to access news among English-speaking Canadians (19.2%), followed by Yahoo (10.1%) and CBC (9.5%). French Canadians picked Radio Canada/SRC/RDI number one (15%), followed by MSN (13.9%) and Canoe (11.5%). Finally, the study showed that Canadians are the most experienced Internet users in the world. Sixty percent have been online five years or more, compared to 58 percent in the U.S. and 55 percent in Sweden.[11]

As the population using the Internet comes to more closely match the population in general, it continues to open new ecommerce targeting opportunities for marketers. For example, children and teens are going online more than any other age group. Sites such as the Habbo Hotel (www.habbo.ca/), managed by Toronto-based Sulake Canada, have created an international online community populated

As more and more Canadians find their way onto the Web, the online population is becoming more mainstream. The Web now offers marketers a palette of different kinds of consumers seeking different kinds of online experiences.

by teens 13 to 19 years of age, where they can play games and create their own virtual characters. The Hotel gets more than 4 million unique visitors a month. While at the site, teens are exposed to ads from companies as diverse as Petro Canada, The Kids Help Phone, and Starburst. In a recent promotion on the site, Alliance Atlantis Motion Picture Distribution, in association with Sulake and CHUM Interactive, launched a contest to promote the Antonio Banderas film *Take the Lead*.[12]

At the other end of the age spectrum, although consumers over the age of 50 make up less of the online population, more and more individuals in this demographic are getting online every day. Whereas younger groups are more likely to use the Internet for entertainment and socializing, older Websters go online for more serious matters. For example, 24 percent of people in this age group use the Internet for investment purposes, compared with only 3 percent of those 25 to 29. Thus, older Internet users make an attractive market for many Web businesses, ranging from florists and automotive retailers to travel sites and financial services providers.[13]

Internet consumers differ from traditional offline consumers in their approaches to buying and in their responses to marketing. The exchange process via the Internet has become more customer initiated and customer controlled. People who use the Internet place greater value on information and tend to respond negatively to messages aimed only at selling. Traditional marketing targets a somewhat passive audience. In contrast, emarketing targets people who actively select which websites they will visit and what marketing information they will receive about which products and under what conditions. Thus, the new world of ecommerce requires new marketing approaches.

B2C Websites

Consumers can find a website for buying almost anything. The Internet is most useful for products and services when the shopper seeks greater ordering convenience or lower costs. The Internet is also a great source of information about differences in product features and value. However, consumers find the Internet less useful when buying products that must be touched or examined in advance. Still, even here there are exceptions. For example, who would have thought that tens of thousands of people would order automobiles online each year without seeing and trying them first? Or, ten years ago, who would have thought of buying lobster online? Clearwater Seafood Company (www.clearwater.ca) of Lunenberg, Nova Scotia, sells live lobsters and various other types of seafood through its website and ships them anywhere in North America!

People now go online to order a wide range of goods—clothing from Gap or Roots, groceries from Grocery Gateway, books or electronics from Amazon.ca, furniture from Ethan Allen, major appliances from Sears Canada. Today more and more Canadian options are available for online shoppers. In fact, more than $2 of every $3 in online purchases by Canadians are now made from Canadian sites.[14] Sites such as Black's Cameras, La Vie en Rose (lingerie), HMV (music and movies), Canadian Tire, and The Body Shop offer their products to Canadians. Hundreds of small, specialty vendors, such as Added Touch and Belen Gift and Basket, have also gone online. Many of these smaller retailers partner with Yahoo! Canada or eBay to build their webstores, avoiding the trouble and expense of maintaining their own websites.

B2B (Business-to-Business)

B2B (business-to-business) ecommerce
Using B2B trading networks, auction sites, spot exchanges, online product catalogues, barter sites, and other online resources to reach new customers, serve current customers more effectively, and obtain buying efficiencies and better prices.

Open trading exchanges
Huge emarketspaces in which B2B buyers and sellers find each other online, share information, and complete transactions efficiently.

Private trading exchanges
B2B trading networks that link a particular seller with its own trading partners.

Although the popular press has given the most attention to business-to-consumer (B2C) websites, consumer goods sales via the Web are dwarfed by **B2B (business-to-business) ecommerce**. In Canada, 70 percent of all ecommerce sales are in the B2B sector, amounting to $28.3 billion.[15] These firms are using B2B trading networks, auction sites, spot exchanges, online product catalogues, barter sites, and other online resources to reach new customers, serve current customers more effectively, and obtain buying efficiencies and better prices.

Most major B2B marketers now offer product information, customer purchasing, and customer support services online. For example, corporate buyers can visit Sun Microsystems' website (www.sun.com), select detailed descriptions of Sun's products and solutions, request sales and service information, and interact with staff members. Some major companies conduct almost all of their business on the Web. Networking equipment and software maker Cisco Systems takes more than 80 percent of its orders over the Internet.

Some B2B ecommerce takes place in **open trading exchanges**—huge emarketspaces in which buyers and sellers find each other online, share information, and complete transactions efficiently. For example, PlasticsNet.com, an Internet marketplace for the plastics product industry, connects more than 90 000 monthly visitors with more than 200 suppliers. However, despite the use of such emarketspaces, one Internet research firm estimates that 93 percent of all B2B ecommerce is conducted through private sites. Increasingly, online sellers are setting up their own **private trading exchanges**. Open trading exchanges facilitate transactions between a wide range of online buyers and sellers. In contrast, a private trading exchange links a particular seller with its own trading partners.

Rather than simply completing transactions, private exchanges give sellers greater control over product presentation and allow them to build deeper relationships with buyers and sellers by providing value-added services. As an example, consider what Ontario hospitals are doing:

People now go online to order a wide range of goods and services, even home mortgages.

There probably isn't a Canadian alive who hasn't heard about the rising costs of health care, but you may not have thought about how more efficient marketing and supply chain management could help. A recent report found that Ontario hospitals spend more than $1.65 billion a year on supplies and pharmaceuticals. Costs associated with doing this purchasing exceeded $250 million. Now hospitals are starting to fight rising costs by revamping the way they buy supplies. For example, Sunnybrook Hospital and Women's College Health Sciences Centre in Toronto recently joined together to standardize their purchasing processes. To further boost these savings, Sunnybrook also adopted an electronic purchasing system. The system allows the hospital's employees to order from an online catalogue, using electronic requisitions that are relayed directly to suppliers. The new technology has not only reduced errors and eliminated paperwork, it has also freed up time. This, in turn, has enabled purchasing staff to hunt for better deals and has given doctors and nurses more time to spend with patients.[16]

C2C (Consumer-to-Consumer)

C2C (consumer-to-consumer) ecommerce
Online exchanges of goods and information between final consumers.

Much **C2C (consumer-to-consumer) ecommerce** and communication occurs on the Web between interested parties over a wide range of products and subjects. In some cases, the Internet provides an excellent means by which consumers can buy or exchange goods or information directly with one another. For example, eBay, Amazon.com Auctions, and other auction sites offer popular marketspaces for displaying and selling almost anything, from art and antiques, coins and stamps, and jewellery to computers and consumer electronics. Auto Trader (www.trader.ca) lets customers post ads to sell their cars.

In 2006, eBay's C2C online trading community of more than 203 million registered users generated billions in sales transactions. On any given day, the company's website lists more than 16 million items up for auction in more than 27 000 categories. TripAdvisor.com bills itself as the largest global travel information and advice destination on the Web. On its site it has more than 4 million reviews that provide commentary on more than 200 000 hotels and attractions

PlasticsNet.com, an Internet marketplace for the plastics product industry, connects more than 90 000 monthly visitors with more than 200 suppliers.

around the world. In early 2006, the site registered 19 million visitors worldwide. Such C2C sites give people access to much larger audiences than the local flea market, travel brochure, or newspaper classified advertisements (which, by the way, are now also going online). Interestingly, based on its huge success in the C2C market, eBay has now attracted a large number of B2C sellers, ranging from small businesses peddling their regular wares to large businesses liquidating excess inventory at auction.[17]

In other cases, C2C involves interchanges of information through Internet forums that appeal to specific special-interest groups. Such activities may be organized for commercial or noncommercial purposes. An example is Web logs, or *blogs*, which are growing in popularity and offer opportunities for individuals to exchange information on any almost topic, including their view of companies.

Not that long ago, blogs were one of those annoying buzzwords that you could safely get away with ignoring. A blog is a website where you can post daily scribblings, journal-style, about whatever you like. Bloggers usually focus their efforts on narrow topics, often rising to become de facto watchdogs and self-proclaimed experts. Blogs can be about anything: politics, sex, baseball, haiku, car repair. There are even blogs about blogs. Big whoop, right? But it turns out that some of the better blogs are drawing sizable audiences. They're free. They catch people at work, at their desks, when they're alert and thinking and making decisions. Blogs are fresh and often seem to be miles ahead of the mainstream news. Bloggers put up new stuff every day, all day, and there are thousands of them. Blogs have voice and personality. They're human. They are the voice of the little guy. In a way, blogs represent everything the Web was always supposed to be: a mass medium controlled by the masses, in which getting heard depends solely on having something to say and the moxie to say it.[18]

Many marketers are now tapping into blogs as a medium for reaching carefully targeted consumers. For example, Oxygen Media launched a blog to promote its new show *Good Girls Don't*. And Web-savvy Nike recently created an "Art of Speed" microsite on blog site Gawker.com. The Art of Speed showcases the work of fifteen innovative filmmakers who interpret the idea of speed. The showcase gave Nike high-quality exposure within a small audience. "Gawker is a very influential

Nike recently created an "Art of Speed" microsite on blog site Gawker.com, giving it high-quality exposure within a small, select audience.

site among a community that appreciates creativity, film, and interesting projects and who are going to dig deeper and find out the back story," said Nike's communications manager. "In some circles, Gawker has more authenticity than Nike," says an online communications analyst. "That's why blogs really work for advertisers, because of the credibility of the blog."[19]

C2C means that online visitors don't just consume product information—increasingly, they create it. They join Internet interest groups, such as *Chatelaine's* online book club or NHL.com, to share information, with the result that "word of Web" is joining "word of mouth" as an important buying influence. Word about good companies and products travels fast. Word about bad companies and products travels even faster. Many general sites, including ConsumerReview.com and BadDealings.com, have cropped up to provide consumers a forum in which to air complaints and share information about product and service experiences. Other sites are more specific, such as those that have specifically targeted firms such as Wal-Mart or Air Canada (for example see http://walmartwatch.com/blog, www.cs.ubc.ca/~deaton/iHateAC.html, or www.airlinequality.com/Forum/air_can.htm). Savvy marketers would be wise to monitor such sites and work to eliminate the source of complaints since these sites can damage or help build corporate reputation and brand image.

C2B (consumer-to-business) ecommerce

Online exchanges in which consumers search out sellers, learn about their offers, and initiate purchases, sometimes even driving transaction terms.

C2B (Consumer-to-Business)

The final ecommerce domain is **C2B (consumer-to-business) ecommerce**. Thanks to the Internet, today's consumers are finding it easier to communicate with companies. Most companies now invite prospects and customers to send in suggestions and questions via company websites. Beyond this, rather than waiting for an invitation, consumers can search out sellers on the Web, learn about their offers, initiate purchases, and give feedback. Using the Web, consumers can even drive transactions with businesses, rather than the other way around. For example, starting in 2000, Priceline.com announced its Name Your Own Price Hotel Service for Canada. U.S. customers travelling to Canada can set the price they are willing to pay for one- to four-star hotel rooms in all of Canada's largest cities and the most popular tourist locations, including Toronto, Montreal, Vancouver, Calgary, Ottawa, Edmonton, Niagara Falls, Winnipeg, Halifax, Quebec City, Victoria, Whistler, and others. They can also set their own price for flights to Canada using Priceline.com's Name Your Own Price Airline Service. Travellers start by visiting priceline.com's website (www.priceline.com) and selecting the cities they want to visit and the dates of their trips. Then they name the price they want to pay per night for a room and guarantee their offer with a major credit card. Priceline.com then works to find a brandname hotel willing to release a room at the traveller's price. If Priceline.com finds an even more luxurious hotel willing to accept that price, the traveller is upgraded automatically, free of charge. Priceline is also supposed to be available to Canadian consumers, but most travellers to date have had difficulties using the service.

Consumers can also use websites such as PlanetFeedback.com to ask questions, offer suggestions, lodge complaints, ask questions, or deliver compliments to companies. The site provides letter templates for consumers to use based on their moods and reasons for contacting the company. The site then forwards the letters to the customer service manager at each company and helps to obtain a response. Recently, PlanetFeedback.com forwarded 67 000 emails to 15 000 companies. "About 80 percent of the companies respond to complaints, some within an hour," says a PlanetFeedback spokesperson.[20]

Conducting Ecommerce

Companies of all types are now engaged in ecommerce. In this section, we first discuss different types of emarketers shown in Figure 17.3. Then, we examine how companies go about conducting marketing online.

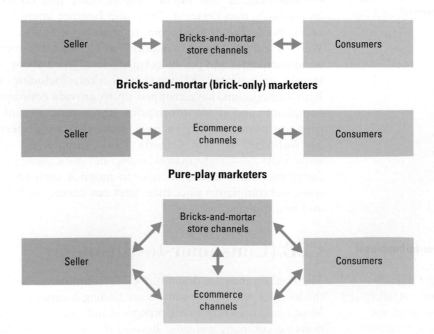

Figure 17.3 Types of emarketers

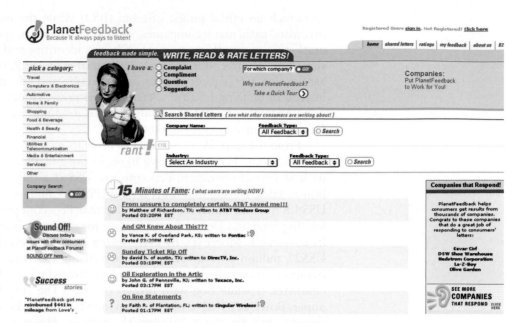

Consumers can use websites, such as PlanetFeedback.com, to ask questions, offer suggestions, lodge complaints, or deliver compliments to companies.

Pure-Play Versus Companies Combining Traditional and Online Marketing

The Internet gave birth to a new species of emarketers—what some call *pure-play* or *click-only* dot-coms—that operate only online without any bricks-and-mortar market presence. In addition, most traditional companies have transformed themselves into hybrid, or "*click-and-mortar*," competitors by becoming companies *combining traditional and online marketing*.

Pure-Play Companies

Pure-play companies

The so-called dot-coms, which operate only online without any bricks-and-mortar market presence.

Pure-play companies that transact business online come in many shapes and sizes. They include *etailers*, dot-coms that sell products and services directly to final buyers via the Internet. Familiar etailers include Amazon.ca, Expedia, and Wine.com. The pure-play group also includes s*earch engines and portals,* such as Yahoo! Canada, Sympatico, Google, and Excite, which began as search engines and later added services, such as news, weather, stock reports, entertainment, and storefronts, hoping to become the first port of entry to the Internet.

Internet service providers (ISPs), such as Bell Sympatico and Rogers High-Speed Internet, provide Internet and email connections for a fee. *Transaction sites,* such as auction site eBay.ca, take commissions for transactions conducted on their sites. Various *content sites,* such as the *Globe and Mail* (www.globeandmail.com), Canada.com, CBC.ca, and TSN.ca, provide news, financial, sports, research, and other information. Finally, *enabler sites* provide the hardware and software that enable Internet communication and commerce.

The hype surrounding such pure-play Web businesses reached astronomical levels during the "dot-com gold rush" of the late 1990s, when avid investors drove dot-com stock prices to dizzying heights. However, the investing frenzy collapsed in the year 2000, and many high-flying, overvalued dot-coms came crashing back to earth and declared bankruptcy. Survivors, such as Amazon.com and Priceline.com, saw their stock values plunge.

Pure-plays failed for many reasons. Many relied too heavily on spin and hype instead of developing sound business and marketing strategies. Some rushed into the market without proper research or planning. Often, their primary goal was simply to launch an initial public offering (IPO) while the market was hot. Flush with investors' cash, many companies, such as Chapters.ca, spent lavishly offline on mass marketing in an effort to establish brand identities and attract consumers to their sites. For example, during the fourth quarter of 1999, the average etailer spent an astounding 109 percent of sales on marketing and advertising to acquire customers instead of building loyalty.[21] Pets.com, the now defunct online pet store, provides a good example of what one analyst called a "dumb as dirt" plan combined with a failure to understand its marketplaces.

From the start, Pets.com tried to force its way to online success with unbeatable low prices and heavy marketing hype. In the end, however, neither worked. During its first year of operation, Pets.com lost US$61.8 million on a meagre US$5.8 million in sales. During that time, it paid US$13.4 million for the goods it sold for just US$5.8 million. Thus, for every dollar that Pets.com paid suppliers, such as Purina for dog food and United Parcel Service for shipping, it collected only 43 cents from its customers. Moreover, by early spring of 1999, Pets.com had burned more than US$21 million on marketing and advertising to create an identity and entice pet owners to its site. Its branding campaign centred on the wildly popular Sock Puppet character, a white dog with brown patches. The singing mascot was featured in Super Bowl ads that cost Pets.com more than US$2 million. At first, investors bought into Pet.com's "landgrab" strategy. However, even though it attracted 570 000 customers, Pets.com never did figure out how to make money in a low-margin business with high shipping costs. In early 2001, the once-bold etailer retired Sock Puppet and quietly closed its cyberdoors.[22]

At the same time, many pure-play companies are surviving and even prospering in today's marketspace. Of those that survived the crash, however, only 50 percent have achieved profitability. However, many dot-coms, including some Internet giants, need to describe to their investors how they will eventually make profits. Table 17.1 shows that a dot-com's revenues may come from any of several sources.

Companies Combining Traditional and Online Operations

At first, many established companies moved quickly to open websites providing information about their companies and products. However, many, like Canadian Tire, resisted adding ecommerce to their sites. Companies struggled

Like many other dot-coms, Pets.com never did figure out how to make money on the Web. Following the "dot-com meltdown," the once-bold etailer retired its popular Sock Puppet spokesdog and quietly closed its cyberdoors.

TABLE 17.1 Sources of Ecommerce Revenue

Product and service sales income	Many ecommerce companies draw a good portion of their revenues from markups on goods and services they sell online.
Advertising income	Sales of online ad space can provide a major source of revenue. At one point, Buy.com received so much advertising revenue that it was able to sell products at cost.
Sponsorship income	A dot-com can solicit sponsors for some of its content and collect sponsorship fees to help cover its costs.
Alliance income	Online companies can invite business partners to share costs in setting up a website and offer them free advertising on the site.
Membership and subscription income	Web marketers can charge subscription fees for use of their site. Many online newspapers (e.g., *Wall Street Journal* and *Financial Times*) require subscription fees for their online services. Auto-By-Tel receives income from selling subscriptions to auto dealers who want to receive hot car buyer leads.
Profile income	Websites that have built databases containing the profiles of particular target groups may be able to sell these profiles if they get permission first. However, ethical and legal codes govern the use and sale of such customer information.
Transaction commissions and fees	Some dot-coms charge commission fees on transactions between other parties who exchange goods on their websites. For example, eBay puts buyers in touch with sellers and takes from a 1.25 percent to a 5 percent commission on each transaction.
Market research and information fees	Companies can charge for special market information or intelligence. For example, NewsLibrary charges a dollar or two to download copies of archived news stories. LifeQuote provides insurance buyers with price comparisons from approximately 50 different life insurance companies, then collects a commission of 50 percent of the first year's premium from the company chosen by the consumer.
Referral income	Companies can collect revenue by referring customers to others. Edmunds receives a "finder's fee" every time a customer fills out an Auto-By-Tel form at its Edmunds.com website, regardless of whether a deal is completed.

with the question of how to conduct online sales without cannibalizing the sales of their own stores, resellers, or agents. They also worried about *channel conflict*—that selling their products or services online would be competing with their offline retailers and agents. For example, Hewlett-Packard feared that its retailers would drop HP's computers if the company sold the same computers directly online.

However, many companies soon realized that the risks of losing business to online competitors were even greater than the risks of angering channel partners. If they didn't cannibalize these sales, online competitors soon would. Thus, most established companies created **combined traditional and online operations**. Some call these types of firms "click-and-mortar" companies. Consider Staples, the $16 billion office-supply retailer. After just two years on the Net, Staples captured annual online sales of $768 million in 2002. However, it didn't rob store sales in the process. The average yearly spending of small-business customers jumped from $900 when they shopped in stores to $4200 when they shopped online. As a result, Staples continued to invest to expand its Net presence. "We're still going whole hog," says former CEO Thomas Stemberg. "The payoffs are just very high." Other earlier movers into the online space weren't so successful. Toronto-based Danier Leather Inc., the country's largest leather retailer, announced in May 2006 that it was shutting its online shopping business. It will retain its website as a marketing and information tool for consumers. Danier had invested heavily to build the ecommerce venture, even providing virtual shoppers with real-time feed-

Combined traditional and online operations
Traditional bricks-and-mortar companies that have added emarketing to their operations.

Staples' website now supplements its bricks-and-mortar operations. After two years on the Net, Staples captured online sales of more than $500 million.

back on products. However, the firm has been struggling and the shutdown will save the firm about $300 000 over the next year. [23]

Most marketers that have combined traditional and online formats have found ways to resolve channel conflicts. For example, Gibson Guitars found that although its dealers were outraged when it tried to sell guitars directly to consumers, the dealers didn't object to direct sales of accessories, such as guitar strings and parts. Avon worried that direct online sales might cannibalize the business of its Avon ladies, who had developed close relationships with their customers. Fortunately, Avon's research showed little overlap between existing customers and potential Web customers. Avon shared this finding with the reps and then moved into online marketing. As an added bonus for the reps, Avon also offered to help them set up their own websites.

Despite potential channel conflict issues, many companies combining traditional and online operations are now having more online success than their pure-play competitors. In fact, in one study of the top 50 retail sites, ranked by the number of unique visitors, 56 percent were companies combining traditional and online operations, whereas 44 percent were Internet-only retailers.[24]

What gives these dual-format companies an advantage? Established companies, such as Staples, Canadian Tire, Home Depot, Sears, and Gap, have known and trusted brand names and greater financial resources. They have large customer bases, deeper industry knowledge and experience, and good relationships with key suppliers. By combining online marketing and established brick-and-mortar operations, they can offer customers more options. For example, consumers can choose the convenience and assortment of twenty-four-hour-a-day online shopping, the more personal and hands-on experience of in-store shopping, or both. Customers can buy merchandise online, then easily return unwanted goods to a nearby store.

Setting Up an Emarketing Presence

Clearly all companies need to consider moving into emarketing. Companies can conduct emarketing in any of the four ways shown in Figure 17.4: *creating a website, placing ads and promotions online, creating or participating in Web communities*, or *using email and webcasting*.

Creating a Website

For most companies, the first step in conducting emarketing is to create a website. However, beyond simply creating a website, marketers must design an attractive site and find ways to get consumers to visit the site, stay around, and come back often.

Types of Websites Websites vary greatly in purpose and content. The most basic type is a **corporate website**. These sites are designed to build customer goodwill and to supplement other sales channels, rather than to sell the company's products directly. For example, you can't buy ice cream at benjerrys.com, but you can learn all about Ben & Jerry's company philosophy, products, and locations. Or you can visit the Fun Stuff area and send a free ecard to a friend, subscribe to the Chunk Mail newsletter, or while away time playing Scooper Challenge or Virtual Checkers.

Corporate websites typically offer a rich variety of information and other features in an effort to answer customer questions, build closer customer relationships, and generate excitement about the company. They generally provide information about the company's history, its mission and philosophy, and the products and services that it offers. They might also tell about current events, company personnel, financial performance, and employment opportunities. Most corporate websites also provide entertainment features to attract and hold visitors. Finally, the site might also provide opportunities for customers to ask questions or make comments through email before leaving the site.

Other companies create a **marketing website**. These sites engage consumers in an interaction that will move them closer to a direct purchase or other marketing outcome. Such sites might include a catalogue, shopping tips, and promotional features, such as coupons, sales events, or contests. For example, visitors to SonyStyle.com can search through dozens of categories of Sony products, review detailed features and specifications lists for specific items, read expert product reviews, and check out the latest hot deals. They can place an order for the desired Sony products online and pay by credit card, all with a few mouse clicks. Companies aggressively promote their marketing websites in offline print and broadcast advertising and through "banner-to-site" ads that pop up on other websites.

Toyota operates a marketing website at www.toyota.ca. Once a potential customer clicks in and indicates whether they want to use the English or French page, the carmaker wastes no time trying to turn the inquiry into a sale. The site offers plenty of useful information and a garage full of interactive selling features, such as detailed descriptions of current Toyota models and information on dealer locations and services, complete with maps and dealer Web links. Visitors who want to go

Corporate website
A website designed to build customer goodwill and to supplement other sales channels, rather than to sell the company's products directly.

Marketing website
A website that engages consumers in interactions that will move them closer to a direct purchase or other marketing outcome.

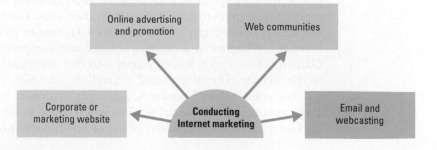

Figure 17.4 Setting up for emarketing

You can't buy ice cream at the Ben & Jerry's website, but you can learn all about Ben & Jerry's company and do lots of fun-related stuff.

further can use the Shop@Toyota feature to choose a Toyota, select equipment, and price it, then contact a dealer and even apply for credit. Or they fill out an online order form (supplying name, address, phone number, and email address) for brochures and a free, interactive CD-ROM that shows off the features of Toyota models. The chances are good that before the CD-ROM arrives, a local dealer will call to invite the prospect in for a test drive. Toyota's website has now replaced its 800 number as the number-one source of customer leads.

B2B marketers also make good use of marketing websites. For example, customers visiting GE Plastics' website can draw on more than 1500 pages of information to get answers about the company's products anytime and from anywhere in the world. FedEx's website allows customers to schedule their own shipments, request package pickup, and track their packages in transit.

Designing Effective Websites   Creating a website is one thing; getting people to *visit* the site is another. The key is to create enough value and excitement to get consumers to come to the site, stick around, and come back again. Today's Web users are quick to abandon any site that doesn't measure up. "Whether people are online for work reasons or for personal reasons," says a Web design expert, "if a website doesn't meet their expectations, two-thirds say they don't return—now or ever. They'll visit you and leave and you'll never know. We call it the Internet death penalty."[25] This means that companies must constantly update their sites to keep them current, fresh, and useful. Doing so involves time and expense, but the expense is necessary if the emarketer wishes to cut through the increasing online clutter.

As is the case with Canadian Tire, many marketers that combine traditional and online formats spend heavily on good old-fashioned advertising and other offline marketing avenues to attract visitors to their sites. For example, Mitsubishi recently ran an expensive Super Bowl ad to draw visitors to its Galant website. The ad featured a cliffhanger of a crash-avoidance test comparing the manoeuvrability of a Gallant GTS versus a Toyota Camry—to find out what happened, viewers had to go to the website. The ad attracted 1.6 million site visits.[26]

For some types of products, attracting visitors is easy. Consumers buying new cars, computers, or financial services will be open to information and marketing initiatives from sellers. Marketers of lower-involvement products, however, may face a difficult challenge in attracting website visitors. As one veteran notes, "If you're shopping for a computer and you see a banner that says, 'We've ranked the top 12 computers to purchase,' you're going to click on the banner. [But] what kind of banner could encourage any consumer to visit dentalfloss.com?"[27]

For such low-interest products, the company can create a corporate website to answer customer questions, build goodwill and excitement, supplement selling efforts through other channels, and collect customer feedback. For example, although Kraft Food's LifeSavers Candystand website doesn't sell candy, it does generate a great deal of consumer excitement and sales support:

> The highly entertaining LifeSavers Candystand.com website, teeming with free videogames, endless sweepstakes, and sampling offers, has cast a fresh face on a brand that young consumers once perceived as a stodgy adult confection. Visitors to the site—mostly children and teenagers—are not just passing through. They're clicking the mouse for an average 27-minute stay playing Foul Shot Shootout, Stingin' Red Ants Run, Arctic 3D Racer, and dozens of other arcade-style games. All the while, they're soaking in a LifeSavers aura swirling with information about products. "Our philosophy is to create an exciting online experience that reflects the fun and quality associated with the LifeSavers brands," says the company's manager of new media. "For the production cost of about two television spots we have a marketing vehicle that lives 24 hours a day, 7 days a week, 365 days a year." The buzz generated by the site makes it an ideal vehicle for offering consumers their first glimpse of a new product. LifeSavers sales reps use the site to help seal distribution deals. And the site offers LifeSavers an efficient channel for gathering customer feedback. Candystand is now the number-one consumer packaged goods website, attracting more than twice the traffic of the number-two site.[28]

A key challenge is designing a website that is attractive on first view and interesting enough to encourage repeat visits. To attract new visitors and to encourage revisits, suggests one expert, emarketers should pay close attention to the seven Cs of effective website design:[29]

- *Context:* the site's layout and design
- *Content:* the text, pictures, sound, and video that the website contains
- *Community:* the ways that the site enables user-to-user communication
- *Customization:* the site's ability to tailor itself to different users or to allow users to personalize the site
- *Communication:* the ways the site enables site-to-user, user-to-site, or two-way communication
- *Connection:* the degree to which the site is linked to other sites
- *Commerce:* the site's capabilities to enable commercial transactions

At the very least, a website should be easy to use and physically attractive. Ultimately, however, websites must also be *useful*. "The bottom line: People seek substance over style, usefulness over flash," says one analyst. "They want to get what they want quickly. Surfers should know almost immediately upon accessing your site why they should stick around, what's in it for them."[30] Thus, effective websites contain deep and useful information, interactive tools that help buyers find and evaluate products of interest, links to other related sites, changing promotional offers, and entertaining features that lend relevant excitement. For example, the McKenzie Seed Company, founded in Brandon, Manitoba, in 1896, has a great website (www.mckenzieseeds.com) that offers avid gardeners a wealth of advice. The site can be used to find local retailers, to order anything from their selection of more than 1000 flowering or vegetable plants, or as a forum to interact with other

Applying the seven Cs of effective website design, is this a good site? (See www.altoids.com.)

passionate gardeners. McKenzie Seeds is one of Canada's oldest firms, and it prides itself on its unsurpassed quality and a deep commitment to the customer.

From time to time, a company needs to reassess its website's attractiveness and usefulness. One way is to invite the opinion of site-design experts. But a better way is to have users themselves evaluate what they like and dislike about the site. For example, Otis Elevator Company's website serves 20 000 registered customers, among them architects, general contractors, building managers, and others interested in elevators. The site, offered in fifty-two countries and twenty-six languages, provides a wealth of helpful information, from modernization, maintenance, and safety information to drawings of various Otis models. To gauge user satisfaction with its complex site, Otis conducts quarterly phone surveys with 200 customers each in half the countries in which it does business. Such customer satisfaction tracking has resulted in many site improvements. For example, Otis found that some customers were finding it hard to locate a local Otis office, so the company added an Office Locator feature.[31]

Placing Ads and Promotions Online

Online advertising

Advertising that appears while consumers are surfing the Web, including fixed placement ads, banner and ticker ads, interstitials, skyscrapers, and other forms.

Emarketers can use **online advertising** to build their Internet brands or to attract visitors to their websites. Here, we discuss forms of online advertising and promotion and their future.

Forms of Online Advertising and Promotion   *Fixed-placement advertisements* are text links that are locked into a specific position, among other paid listings on the search results page. Google and Yahoo, for example, offer such fixed-placement advertising programs to some of their clients. If you go to Google.ca and type in Hotels Halifax, you will see a list of "sponsored links" on the right-hand side of the page. Each link, when clicked, takes visitors to the website of a hotel in the area. Since these ads relate directly to the item a Google user is searching for, they have proven to be more effective than other types of Web-based advertising. Companies paying fees to obtain fixed-placement advertising have the advantage of being able to lock their competitors out of the top spots on the relevant page and they have the first right to renew their spot.

Online ads pop up while Internet users are surfing online. Such ads include *banner ads* and *tickers* (banners that move across the screen). A Web user who is looking up airline schedules or fares might find a flashing banner on the screen exclaiming, "Rent a car from Enterprise and get up to 2 days free!" To attract visitors to its own website, Toyota sponsors Web banner ads on other sites, ranging from ESPN SportZone (www.espn.com) to Parent Soup (www.parentsoup.com). Advertisers pay as much as US$100 000 to post a banner ad atop ESPN.com's home page for 24 hours.[32]

Content sponsorships are another form of Internet promotion. Many companies gain name exposure on the Internet by sponsoring special content on various websites, such as news or financial information. For example, Advil sponsors ESPN SportZone's Injury Report and General Mills sponsors an area on AOL called Quick Meals for Kids. The sponsor pays for showing the content and, in turn, receives recognition as the provider of the particular service on the website. Sponsorships are best placed in carefully targeted sites where they can offer relevant information or service to the audience.

Emarketers can also go online with *microsites*, limited areas on the Web managed and paid for by an external company. For example, an insurance company might create a microsite on a car-buying site, offering insurance advice for car buyers and at the same time offering good insurance deals. Internet companies can also develop alliances and affiliate programs in which they work with other online companies to "advertise" each other. AOL has created many successful alliances with other companies and mentions their names on its site. Amazon.com has more than 350 000 affiliates who post Amazon.com banners on their websites.

Finally, online marketers use **viral marketing**, the Internet version of word-of-mouth marketing. As one observer puts it, viral marketing is "an extension of the oldest form of advertising in the world—word of mouth—on the newest platform, the Internet." Viral marketing involves creating an email message or other marketing event that is so infectious that customers will want to pass it along to their friends. Because customers pass the message or promotion along to others, viral marketing can be very inexpensive. And when the information comes from a friend, the recipient is much more likely to open and read it. "The idea is to get your customers to do your marketing for you," notes a viral marketing expert. Consider this example:[33]

Viral marketing
The Internet version of word-of-mouth marketing—email messages or other marketing events that are so infectious that customers will want to pass them along to friends.

> Gillette used viral marketing to introduce the three-bladed Venus razor for women. To reach college students, Gillette designed a truck that travelled around the Florida spring-break circuit, parking daily near a beach. Women were invited to come in and get some aromatherapy, learn about Venus, enter a "Celebrate the Goddess in You" sweepstakes, and make a digital greeting card with a picture of themselves enjoying the beach. The viral part came when they emailed the digital cards to friends. The emailed messages automatically included a chance for friends to enter the sweepstakes themselves. If email recipients entered the contest, they saw a pitch for the Venus razor. Some 20 percent of the entries came from the viral-marketing cards, greatly expanding the audience reached by the beach-site promotions.

Although viral marketing can be successful, Heather Clark, associate director of creative strategy at Henderson Bas in Toronto, who has worked on viral campaigns for ING Direct and Levi's, warns there is just as much potential for failure since chances of a commercial message being passed along using email are extremely low. A 2006 study outlines several tactics to improve success. Using humour is important, as funny messages spread the fastest. News-related items are the next most frequently forwarded types of messages. Incentives, such as an extra entry in a sweepstakes contest, also improve pass along. The "send to a friend" feature accompanied by a box where the initial recipient can personalize the message also increases the chances that it will be forwarded. A company following this advice was Virgin Mobile. Its recent Canadian campaign used humour and consumer involvement (viewers could choose different plot lines) for its highly successful "Billy the Finger" campaign that promoted new rate plans. James Powell, senior manager, brand and communications, says, "We just made the creative funny.... We made it engaging—embedding things like the phone number (for Billy the Finger) in there, embedding risqué scenes that people will find hilarious." The tactics worked. During the first two weeks of the campaign, billythefinger.com got 50 000 unique visitors a day. [34]

Viral marketing can also work well for B2B marketers and they can use similar techniques to help ensure success. For example, to improve customer relationships, Hewlett-Packard sent tailored email newsletters to business customers who registered online. The newsletters contained information about optimizing the performance of H-P products and services. The newsletters also featured a button that let customers forward the newsletters to friends or colleagues. New recipients were then asked if they'd like to receive future H-P newsletters themselves. The program allowed Hewlett-Packard to inexpensively meet its goal of driving consumers to its website and ultimately increasing sales. "For those on our original email list, the click-through rate was 10 to 15 percent," says an H-P executive. "For those who received it from a friend or colleague, it was between 25 and 40 percent." [35]

The Future of Online Advertising   Online advertising serves a useful purpose, especially as a supplement to other marketing efforts. However, the Internet will not soon rival the major television and print media. Costs are reasonable compared with those of other advertising media, but Web surfers can easily ignore such advertising and often do. As a result, Web advertising still plays only a minor role in most promotion mixes. The 2005/2006 *Media Digest* predicts that Canadian online advertising spending will total $400 million, about 4 percent of total advertising dollars. [36] Still, online advertising is playing an increasingly important role in the marketing mixes of many advertisers. Kimberly-Clark found that increasing the levels of online advertising boosted the impact of the ad campaign for its Kleenex SoftPack line. The combination of print and online advertising helped raise brand awareness for SoftPack among its target audience from 34.7 percent to 42.7 percent; brand image from 35 percent to 41.8 percent; trial intent from 43.9 percent to 55.7 percent, and purchase intent from 24.2 to 34.0 percent. [37]

Some websites, such as Google, have been very successful in creating effective online advertising processes and environments. (See Real Marketing 17.1.) Companies, themselves, are also finding more effective forms and uses for Web advertising. They are taking advantage of new technologies to create bolder, higher-impact online ads including entertaining TV-like commercials that are being shown only on the Internet:

> LOOK! Down on the PC. It's a banner ad. No, it's a pop-up ad. No, it's Web-only advertising for American Express that teams Jerry Seinfeld with Superman. In the entertaining 5-minute American Express "Webisode," Seinfeld and Superman stroll through New York talking about, well, nothing. All of a sudden a street hood steals Seinfeld's new DVD player. The Man of Steel leaps into action and nabs the crook, but damages the DVD player in the process. Luckily,

Seinfeld bought it with his Amex card so the damage is covered. The ads seek to avoid being perceived as hard-selling hucksterism while appealing to busy, educated, affluent, media-savvy consumers like—well, Jerry Seinfeld. "We're trying to reach consumers where they're going today, on the Internet," says an American Express marketing executive. "We're trying to create media content where people actually opt in to watch." And opt in they did. The creative and engaging Web ad garnered 1.1 million unique visitors in just its first two weeks.[38]

REAL MARKETING | 17.1

"We Love You, Google Users"—and Advertisers, Too!

ounded in late 1998 by Sergey Brin and Larry Page, then 25 and 29 years old, Google got its start in a rented garage, complete with a washer, dryer, and hot tub. Since then, Google has grown from three employees to more than 6800 in 2006. Whereas other dot-coms have struggled, Google has grown at a phenomenal rate. Google is now by far the world's largest search engine, powering almost half of all Web searches. Globally, more than 380 million unique visitors use Google's search engine each month. Finally, unlike many other dot-coms, Google turns a profit. In fact, Google is three times more profitable than eBay was at the same stage in its development.

What's behind this incredible success? Google's technology is an important part of the equation. The company's PageRank search technology revolutionized Internet searching. But beyond technology, Google has triumphed by focusing heavily on simply helping users search. Its website promises "a laser-like focus on finding the right answer for each and every inquiry." In fact, the name of the company is a play on the word *googol*, a mathematical term for a 1 followed by 100 zeros. Google chose the name to reflect its mission to organize and make accessible the immense amount of information available on the Web. It tailors its country sites to the needs of local users. Google.ca, for example, offers search engines in both English and French. Users rave about Google's accurate and easy-to-use, search-only home page, uncluttered with news reports or banner ads.

The best part is that Google's extraordinary services are free to users. But how, then, does Google make money? Some of Google's revenues come from contracts with corporate partners to provide search services for their own Internet and intranet sites. Today, more than 130 companies in 30

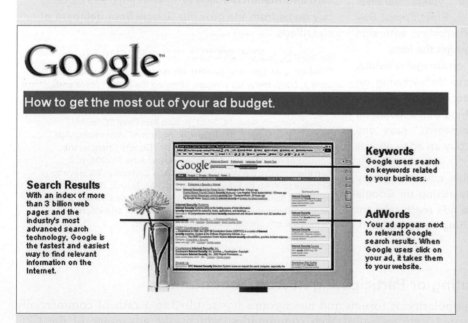

With the world's largest online search audience, Google has become a very attractive advertising medium. Its highly targeted ads reach users when they are already searching for related information.

countries rely on Google's WebSearch and SiteSearch technologies to power the search services on their websites. These partners include companies such as Cisco, Palm, Nextel, Virgin, Netscape, Sony, and Cingular Wireless.

But most of Google's revenues come from advertising sales. With its ability to attract the largest online search audience in the world, Google has made itself a very attractive advertising medium. Over the past four years, Google has billed advertisers in 65 countries more than US$11.2 billion in 48 currencies. Here's how it works. Through constant data mining, Google determines which search terms are most popular. It then approaches companies who sell in those categories and offers them space for sponsored ad messages and links for a fee. Advertisers then bid on a search term, and the highest bidder gets the highest position on the page. Then, when someone searches Google for a topic related to the sponsor's product or service, a tasteful ad box (termed a fixed placement advertisement) appears at the top or side of the Google results page, with a short ad message and links to the sponsor's website.

Try it yourself. Go to the Google site (www.google.com), search for a word or phrase, and see what advertiser messages and links appear. For example, if you search "Disneyland," you'll see ads and links in the search list for Expedia and other online travel services, promising deals on hotels and resort tickets. A search of "hockey gear" yields "Jerseys, Skates, Sticks Equipment and more. Great Prices! Buy Online!" with a link to www.sportsmart.ca, with side boxes for eight other suppliers. You get the idea.

This "contextual advertising" on Google is subtle, not like the pop-up ads that make Web-viewing on other sites like swatting flies. In fact, the ads are actually useful. Google "wants everything that appears on the page to be related to your search," says one reporter, "so a car company can't buy an ad to appear with your search for 'perfume.'"

Whereas other forms of online advertising may produce questionable results, advertising on Google delivers. Google's highly targeted ads reach relevant users when they are already searching for information.

According to a Google advertising executive, Google is reaching the person "who is actually sticking a hand up and is interested in your product or service." Moreover, Google's matching process lets advertisers tailor their ad messages or sites closely to users' search inquiries. Last year, Google added local advertising. Thus, if you are searching from a computer in Ontario, your search results and advertising messages reflect your location. As a result, "click-through" rates for the typical ad on Google average 4 to 6 percent, versus less than 0.5 percent for traditional banner ads. Google also proactively monitors ads to ensure their success. Google even lets advertisers know when their ads *aren't* working. One small-business owner was shocked when he received an email from Google suggesting that he pull his ads.

This unique approach to selling advertising space has resulted in loyalty and satisfaction among the Google clients who do stay. Online advertisers, such as Loblaws' President's Choice, Acura, Expedia, Eddie Bauer, and Bell Mobility, regularly rank Google as their top online advertising choice. This, in turn, has fuelled the company's financial success.

Google isn't about to rest on its past success. In May 2006, it launched an online payment service that may grow to rival that of PayPal and eBay. People who have registered with Gmail or other Google services, can type in a credit card number and buy videos from Google Video or T-shirts from the Google store. Once card information is added to an account, users can also buy items from the growing Google Base database of classifieds.

Sources: Quotes and other information from Mathew Ingram, "On-line payments next on Google's to-do list," *Globe and Mail*, June 1, 2006; Betsy Cummings, "Beating the Odds," *Sales and Marketing Management*, March 2002, pp. 24–28; David Kirkpatrick, "In the Hands of Geeks, Web Advertising Actually Works," *Fortune*, April 14, 2003, p. 388; Kris Oser, "Google Challenge: Growth Without Sacrificing Brand," *Advertising Age*, May 10, 2004, pp. 4–5; Michael Krauss, "Google Changes the Context of Advertising," *Marketing News*, June 1, 2004, p. 6; Ben Elgin, "Why the World's Hottest Tech Company Will Have to Struggle to Keep Its Edge," *Business Week*, May 3, 2004, pp. 82–90; Melanie Warner, "What Your Company Can Learn from Google," *Business 2.0*, June 2004, pp. 100–106; and information from www.google.com (accessed June 2006).

Creating or Participating in Web Communities

Web communities

Websites where members can congregate online and exchange views on issues of common interest.

The popularity of forums and newsgroups has resulted in a rash of commercially sponsored websites called **Web communities**, which take advantage of the C2C properties of the Internet. Such sites allow members to congregate online and exchange views on issues of common interest. They are the cyberspace equivalent to a Starbucks coffeehouse, a place where everybody knows your email address.

For example, Today's Parent (www.todaysparent.com) is an online community for parents, while Chatelaine.com gathers people interested in women's health issues, food, fashion, and family, and even offers an online book club. For hockey fans there is NHL.com. In addition to getting all the latest news and statistics on your favourite hockey team, you can play fantasy games, chat with other fans, post messages on a bulletin board, and buy tickets to games. Askmen.com is an online magazine that was founded by Concordia University graduates. It draws 5 million visitors a month and its has been recognized for its success on Nielsen//NetRatings Top 300 Largest Websites Ranking, *Time* magazine, the *LA Times*, *Forbes* magazine, and MSNBC.

Visitors to these Internet neighbourhoods develop a strong sense of community. Such communities are attractive to advertisers because they draw consumers with common interests and well-defined demographics. People who use these services visit frequently and stay online longer, increasing the chance of meaningful exposure to the advertiser's message:

> *Chatelaine* provides an ideal environment for the Web ads of companies such as Royale bathroom tissue, L'Oréal cosmetics, Crest Whitestrips, and other brands that target women consumers. Midas Muffler recently ran a comprehensive online campaign on *Chatelaine*'s website, which included a microsite with car maintenance tips for women. Many of *Chatelaine*'s advertisers choose this type of powerful, targeted advertising.

Web communities can be either social or work related. One successful work-related community is Canadagriculture Online (www.agcanada.com). The site includes agricultural discussion groups organized into topics such as "Canadian Cattleman" and "Grain News."

Using Email and Webcasting

Email has exploded onto the scene as an important emarketing tool. A 2005 study from Forrester Research suggests that 80 percent of marketers are using or planning to use email as part of their marketing tactics.[39]

Web communities: iVillage.com, a Web community for women, provides an ideal environment for Web ads of companies such as Procter & Gamble, Kimberly Clark, Avon, Hallmark, and others.

To compete effectively in this ever-more-cluttered email environment, marketers are designing "enriched" email messages—animated, interactive, and personalized messages full of streaming audio and video. Then, they are targeting these attention-grabbers more carefully to those who want them and will act upon them. Consider Nintendo, a natural for email-based marketing:

> Young computer-savvy gaming fans actually look forward to Nintendo's monthly email newsletter for gaming tips and for announcements of exciting new games. When the company launched its Star Fox Adventure game in 2002, it created an intensive email campaign in the weeks before and after the product launch. The campaign included a variety of messages targeting potential customers. "Each message has a different look and feel, and ... that builds excitement for Nintendo," notes an executive working on the account. The response? More than a third of all recipients opened the emails. And they did more than just glance at the messages: nearly two-thirds of those opening the message watched its 30-second streaming video in its entirety. Nintendo also gathered insightful customer data from the 20 percent of people who completed an embedded survey. Although the company feared that the barrage of messages might create "list fatigue" and irritate customers, the campaign received very few negative responses. The unsubscribe rate was under 1 percent.[40]

Spam
Unsolicited, unwanted commercial email messages.

As with other types of online marketing, companies must be careful that they don't cause resentment among Internet users who are already overloaded with "junk email." The recent explosion of **spam**—unsolicited, unwanted commercial email messages that clog up our emailboxes—has produced consumer frustration and anger. Fifty-five percent of Canadians receive more than 10 unsolicited emails per week, and 82 percent report they are currently using spam filters, up from 77 percent in 2005, according to Canadian Interactive Reid Report for 2006 by research firm Ipsos-Reid.[41] Email marketers walk a fine line between adding value for consumers and being intrusive. (See Real Marketing 17.2.)

Companies must beware of irritating consumers by sending unwanted email to promote their products. Marketers should ask customers for permission to email marketing pitches. They should also tell recipients how to "opt in" or "opt out" of email promotions at any time. This approach, known as permission-based marketing, has become a standard model for email marketing.

The Promise and Challenges of Ecommerce

Ecommerce continues to offer both great promise and many challenges for the future. We now look at both the promises of ecommerce and the "darker side" of the Web.

The Continuing Promise of Ecommerce

Its most ardent apostles still envision a time when the Internet and ecommerce will replace magazines, newspapers, and even stores as sources for information and buying. Most marketers, however, hold a more realistic view. To be sure, online marketing will become a successful business model for some companies, Internet firms such as Amazon.com, eBay, Expedia, and Google, and direct-marketing companies such as Dell. However, for most companies, online marketing will remain just one important approach to the marketplace that works alongside other approaches in a fully integrated marketing mix.

Eventually, as companies become more adept at integrating ecommerce with their everyday strategy and tactics, the "e" will fall away from ebusiness or emarketing. "The key question is not whether to deploy Internet technology—companies have no choice if they want to stay competitive—but how to deploy it," says business strategist Michael Porter. He continues: "We need to move away from the rhetoric about 'Internet industries,' 'e-business strategies,' and a 'new economy,' and see the Internet for what it is ... a powerful set of tools that can be used, wisely or unwisely, in almost any industry and as part of almost any strategy."[42]

The Web's Darker Side

It cannot be denied that Internet marketing continues to show considerable promise. It has to be remembered, however, that even though the Internet greatly reduced the geographical limitations associated with traditional marketing, transactions across nations through the Internet are still being limited because of duties and government restrictions. These may be removed over time, but, along with the Internet's considerable promise, there is a "darker side" to Internet marketing. Here we examine two major sets of concerns: Internet profitability and legal and ethical issues.

REAL MARKETING | 17.2

Email Marketing: The Hot New Marketing Medium? Or Pestering Millions for Profit?

*E*mail is *the* hot new marketing medium. But there's a dark side to the exploding use of email marketing. The biggest problem? *Spam*—the deluge of unsolicited, unwanted commercial messages that now clutter up our emailboxes and our lives. Various studies show that spam now accounts for an inbox-clogging 60 to 85 percent of emails sent daily throughout the world, up from only 7 percent in 2002. One recent study found that the average company employee now receives 29 spam messages per day. AOL blocks some 2 billion spam messages sent to its subscribers each day.

Despite these dismal statistics, when used properly, email can be the ultimate direct marketing medium. Large firms, such as Amazon.com, Dell, and Staples, use it regularly, but with the help of specialist email marketing firms, such as Montreal-based GOT Corporation, small firms, such as magazine publisher CanadaScope and Toronto software publisher Varicent, can use it too with great success. Email lets these marketers send highly targeted, tightly personalized, rela-tionship-building messages to consumers who actually *want* to receive them, at a cost of only a few cents per contact. According to one estimate, well-designed email campaigns typically achieve 10 percent to 15 percent click-through rates. That's pretty good when compared with the 0.5 percent to 2 percent average response rates for traditional direct mail.

In contrast, critics argue that most commercial email messages amount to little more than annoying "junk mail." There is no customization—no relationship building. Everyone gets the same messages. Moreover, too often, the spam comes from shady sources or as pitches for objectionable products—everything from thieves pretending to be legitimate banks, to Viagra and body enhancement products to pornography.

At least in part, it's email economics that are to blame for our overflowing inboxes. Sending email is so easy and so inexpensive that almost anyone can afford to do it, even at paltry response rates. For example, Data Resource Consulting, Inc., pumps out 720 million emails every year. That makes the company

▶

sound like a big-city direct marketing behemoth. But in reality, it's a home-based business run by Laura Betterly, a 41-year-old single mother who sends out as many as 60 million such messages a month. The problem, of course, it that it's far easier for Betterly to hit the "send" button on an email to a million strangers than it is for the beleaguered recipients to hit the delete key on all those messages.

Assume that the average time getting rid of the junk was 2 seconds, and that the average recipient values his or her time at the mean wage paid in Canada, which is around $20 per hour, or $0.0055 per second. This implies a total cost, incurred by uninterested recipients, of 500 000 times 2 seconds times $0.0055 per second, which gives $5500. And such dollar calculations don't begin to account for the shear frustration of having to deal with all those many junk messages.

The impact of spam on consumers and businesses is alarming. One recent study places the average yearly company cost of spam at $1934 per employee. AOL and other Internet service providers are being inundated with complaints from subscribers. And spam is ruining

YOU CAN E-MAIL.

BUT

CAN YOU BLOCK %!#@*% JUNK MAIL?

High-Speed Spam Haters MEET Premeditated Spamicide.

Add AOL. for Broadband on top of your basic high-speed Internet connection, and get a whole lot more from your online experience. AOL's advanced spam filter automatically moves junk mail into your spam folder, and helps to keep it out of your inbox. Also, e-mail anti-virus protection scans every attachment for known viruses, then automatically repairs files. So high-speed Internet users MEET

AOL FOR BROADBAND

To sign up, call 1-888-AOL-4-YOU or visit aol.com

Email can be an effective marketing medium, but there's a dark side. AOL and other companies are now offering solutions—"premeditated spamicide."

the rich potential of email for companies that want to use it as a legitimate marketing tool.

So, what's a marketer to do? Stefan Eyram, the Canadian business development manager for email specialist firm ExactTarget, says effective email marketing includes four key ingredients: permission, targeting, relevance, and deliverability. Companies can send emails only to customers who "opt in"—those who grant permission in advance. They can also let consumers specify what types of messages they'd like to receive. Financial services firms, such as TD Canada Trust, use configurable email systems that let customers choose what they want to get. Although permission-based marketing ensures that emails are sent only to customers who want them, marketers must be careful not to abuse the privilege.

Ipsos-Reid reports that Canadians today both love and hate their email. Approximately 50 percent of Canadians check their email daily, and the average number of emails received is 164 per week. One-fifth of Canadians, however, receive more than 200 emails per week. Though many Canadians find email to be a positive thing in their lives, making their working lives more efficient, many also feel that email has resulted in feelings of guilt, being overwhelmed and frustrated with trying to keep up with the sheer volume of email received.

Given these feelings, Canadians are becoming more selective about the businesses they register with to receive email marketing messages, but they are still receptive to the technique, according to the 2006 Canadian Interactive Reid Report of Internet behaviours and attitudes. Four in five Canadian Internet users surveyed register at websites to receive email, 86 percent are interested in receiving surveys and polls via email, and 76 percent are interested in receiving discounts. Among those who have registered for emails, 63 percent have gone to the advertiser's website.

Email marketing is thus a double-edged sword. It can be used with great success to build better customer relationships or, if abused, it can end relationships and anger recipients.

Sources: Excerpts and other information from Tessa Wegert, "Get help if you want customers to get the message," *Globe and Mail*, May 30, 2006; Matt Haig, Mylene Mangalindan "Spam Queen: For Bulk E-Mailer, Pestering Millions Offers Path to Profit," *Wall Street Journal*, November 13, 2002, p. A1; Nikki Swartz, "Spam Costs Businesses $13 Billion Annually," *Information Management* Journal, March/April 2003, p. 9; Lorraine Woellert, "Slamming Spam," *Business Week*, May 12, 2003, p. 40; "Spam Makes up Two-Thirds of All E-mail Worldwide," *New Media Age*, March 11, 2004, p. P.12; and "Spam Costs," *The Controller's Report*, August 2004, p. 7; Ipsos-Reid, "Canadians are Regaining Control of their Inboxes—Are You?" (press release), http://www.ipsos-ideas.com/article.cfm?id=3033&CFID=5481085&CFTOKEN=17835437 (accessed May 10, 2006).

Internet Profitability

One major concern is profitability, especially for B2C dot-coms. Surprisingly few B2C Internet companies are profitable. Of the 456 Internet companies that went public since 1994, only 11 percent are still in business and profitable. Of those still in business and not acquired by another company, only about 40 percent are profitable. One analyst calls this "the Web's pretty little secret."[43]

One problem is that, although expanding rapidly, online marketing still reaches only a limited audience. The Web audience is becoming more mainstream, but online users still tend to be somewhat more upscale and better educated than the general population. This makes the Internet ideal for marketing financial services, travel services, computer hardware and software, and certain other classes of products. However, in most product categories, users still do more window browsing and product research than actual buying.

Finally, the Internet offers millions of websites and a staggering volume of information. Thus, navigating the Internet can be frustrating, confusing, and time consuming for consumers. In this chaotic and cluttered environment, many Web ads and sites go unnoticed or unopened. Even when noticed, marketers will find it difficult to hold consumer attention. One study found that a site must capture Web surfers' attention within eight seconds or lose them to another site. That leaves very little time for marketers to promote and sell their goods.

Legal and Ethical Issues

From a broader societal viewpoint, Internet marketing practices have raised a number of ethical and legal questions. In previous sections, we've touched on some of the negatives associated with the Internet, such as unwanted email and the annoyance of pop-up ads. Here we examine concerns about consumer online privacy and security and other legal and ethical issues.

Online Privacy and Security   *Online privacy* is perhaps the number one ecommerce concern. Most online marketers have become skilled at collecting and analyzing detailed consumer information. Marketers can easily track website visitors, and many consumers who participate in website activities provide extensive personal information. This may leave consumers open to information abuse if companies make unauthorized use of the information in marketing their products or exchanging databases with other companies.

Many consumers and policymakers worry that marketers have stepped over the line and are violating consumers' right to privacy. A recent survey found that 7 out of 10 consumers are concerned about online privacy.[44]

Many consumers also worry about *online security*. They fear that unscrupulous snoopers will eavesdrop on their online transactions or intercept their credit card numbers and make unauthorized purchases. In turn, companies doing business online fear that others will use the Internet to invade their computer systems for the purposes of commercial espionage or even sabotage. There appears to be an ongoing competition between the technology of Internet security systems and the sophistication of those seeking to break them.

In response to these concerns, the Canadian government passed the *Personal Information Protection and Electronic Documents Act* in 2001.

Many companies have responded to consumer privacy and security concerns with actions of their own. Companies such as Expedia and E-Loan have conducted voluntary audits of their privacy and security policies. Other companies have taken similar and other steps, sometimes going even further.

As a company that relies on client trust to build long-term relationships, Royal Bank of Canada (RBC) has used progressive privacy practices to strengthen its client-focused strategies. As a leader in this area, the company has taken a number of internal actions (such as privacy risk self assessments and internal audit reviews of privacy protection practices) to ensure that its customers are protected, and it has used a variety of programs to show customers that it strives to meet or exceed government-mandated privacy regulations in relevant jurisdictions. The latter includes providing clients with a one-year subscription, at no cost, to security and privacy software to help them feel more comfortable with their general online experiences and to promote safe computing practices. RBC also provides its clients with relevant information about its privacy and security practices on its public website.[45]

Still others are taking a broad, industry-wide approach. Founded in 1996, TRUSTe is a non-profit, self-regulatory organization that works with a number of large corporate sponsors, including Microsoft, AT&T, and Intuit, to audit companies' privacy and security measures and help consumers navigate the Web safely. According to the company's website, "TRUSTe believes that an environment of mutual trust and openness will help make and keep the Internet a free, comfortable, and richly diverse community for everyone." To reassure consumers, the company lends it "trustmark" stamp of approval to websites that meet its privacy and security standards.[46]

Other Legal and Ethical Issues   Beyond issues of online privacy and security, consumers are also concerned about *Internet fraud*, including identity theft, investment fraud, and financial scams. There are also concerns about *segmentation and discrimination* on the Internet. Some social critics and policymakers worry about the so-called *digital divide*—the gap between those who have access to the latest Internet and information technologies and those who don't. They are concerned that in this information age, not having equal access to information can be an economic and social handicap. For example, in Canada though the percentage of Canadians having access to the Internet is high (78 percent total, 67 percent from home), Internet users skew toward a certain demographic. In English Canada, more than 50 percent of Internet users have a household income greater than $60 000, and 25- to 55-year-olds make up the largest user group. Further, 62 percent of users are located in either Ontario or Quebec, with the Atlantic provinces constituting only 7 percent of Canadian Internet users.[47] Internationally, in most African countries, less than 1 percent of the population is online. "The ideal of the Internet was to be free," says one critic. "The reality is that not everyone can afford a computer or Internet access."[48] This leaves poorer consumers less informed about products, services, and prices. Some people consider the digital divide to be a national crisis; others see it as an overstated nonissue.

A final Internet marketing concern is that of *access by vulnerable or unauthorized groups*. For example, marketers of adult-oriented materials have found it difficult to restrict access by minors. In a more specific example, some time ago, sellers using eBay.com found themselves the victims of a 14-year-old boy who'd bid on and purchased more than $3 million worth of high-priced antiques and rare artworks on the site. EBay has a strict policy against bidding by anyone under age 18 but works largely on the honour system. Unfortunately, this honour system did little to prevent the teenager from taking a cyberspace joyride.[49]

Despite these challenges, companies large and small are quickly integrating online marketing into their marketing strategies and mixes. As it continues to grow, online marketing will prove to be a powerful tool for building customer relationships, improving sales, communicating company and product information, and delivering products and services more efficiently and effectively.

Reviewing the Concepts

Recent technological advances have created a new digital age. To thrive in this new environment, marketers will have to add some Internet thinking to their strategies and tactics. This chapter introduces the forces shaping the new Internet environment and how marketers are adapting.

1. Identify the major forces shaping the digital age.

Four major forces underlie the digital age: digitalization and connectivity, the explosion of the Internet, new types of intermediaries, and customization. Much of today's business operates on digital information, which flows through connected networks. Intranets, extranets, and the Internet now connect people and companies with each other and with important information. The Internet has grown explosively to become *the* revolutionary technology of the new millennium, empowering consumers and businesses alike with the blessings of connectivity.

The Internet and other new technologies have changed the ways that companies service their markets. New Internet marketers and channel relationships have arisen to replace some types of traditional marketers. The new technologies are also helping marketers to tailor their offers effectively to targeted customers or even to help customers customize their own marketing offers. Finally, the new economy technologies are blurring the boundaries between industries, allowing companies to pursue opportunities that lie at the convergence of two or more industries.

2. Explain how companies have responded to the Internet and other powerful new technologies with ebusiness strategies, and how these strategies have resulted in benefits to both buyers and sellers.

Conducting business in the new digital age will call for a new model of marketing strategy and practice. Companies need to retain most of the skills and practices that have worked in the past. However, they must also add major new competencies and practices if they hope to grow and prosper in the digital environment. Ebusiness is the use of electronic platforms to conduct a company's business. Ecommerce involves buying and selling processes supported by electronic means, primarily the Internet. It includes emarketing (the selling side of ecommerce) and epurchasing (the buying side of ecommerce).

Ecommerce benefits both buyers and sellers. For buyers, ecommerce makes buying convenient and private, provides greater product access and selection, and makes available a wealth of product and buying information. It is interactive and immediate and gives the consumer a greater measure of control over the buying process. For sellers, ecommerce is a powerful tool for building customer relationships. It also increases the sellers' speed and efficiency, helping to reduce selling costs. Ecommerce also offers great flexibility and better access to global markets.

3. Describe the four major ecommerce domains.

Companies can practise ecommerce in any or all of four domains. B2C (business-to-consumer) ecommerce is initiated by businesses and targets final consumers. Despite recent setbacks following the "dot-com gold rush" of the late 1990s, B2C ecommerce continues to grow at a healthy rate. Although online consumers are still somewhat higher in income and more technology oriented than traditional buyers, the cyberspace population is becoming much more mainstream and diverse. This growing diversity opens up new ecommerce targeting opportunities for marketers. Today, consumers can buy almost anything on the Web.

B2B (business-to-business) ecommerce dwarfs B2C ecommerce. Most businesses today operate websites or use B2B trading networks, auction sites, spot exchanges, online product catalogues, barter sites, or other online resources to reach new customers, serve current customers more effectively, and obtain buying efficiencies and better prices. Business buyers and sellers meet in huge marketspaces—or open trading networks—to share information and complete transactions efficiently. Or they set up private trading networks that link them with their own trading partners.

Through C2C (consumer-to-consumer) ecommerce, consumers can buy or exchange goods and information directly from or with one another. Examples include online auction sites, forums, and Web logs (blogs).

Finally, through C2B (consumer-to-business) ecommerce, consumers are now finding it easier to search out sellers on the Web, learn about their products and services, and initiate purchases. Using the Web, customers can even drive transactions with business, rather than the other way around.

4. **Discuss how companies can go about conducting ecommerce to profitably deliver more value to customers.**

Companies of all types are now engaged in ecommerce. The Internet gave birth to the *pure-play* dot-coms, which operate only online. In addition, many traditional brick-and-mortar companies have now added emarketing operations, transforming themselves into companies combining traditional and online operations. Many companies combining traditional and online operations are now having more online success than their pure-play competitors.

Companies can conduct emarketing in any of the four ways: creating a website, placing ads and promotions online, setting up or participating in Web communities, or using online email or webcasting. The first step typically is to set up a website. Beyond simply setting up a site, however, companies must make their sites engaging, easy to use, and useful in order to attract visitors, hold them, and bring them back again.

Emarketers can use various forms of online advertising to build their Internet brands, or to attract visitors to their websites. Beyond online advertising, other forms of online marketing include content sponsorships,

microsites, and viral marketing, the Internet version of word-of-mouth marketing. Online marketers can also participate in Web communities, which take advantage of the C2C properties of the Web. Finally, email marketing has become a hot new emarketing tool for both B2C and B2B marketers.

5. **Overview the promise and challenges that ecommerce presents for the future.**

Ecommerce continues to offer great promise for the future. For most companies, online marketing will become an important part of a fully integrated marketing mix. For others, it will be the major means by which they serve the market. Eventually, the "e" will fall away from ebusiness or emarketing as companies become more adept at integrating ecommerce with their everyday strategy and tactics. However, ecommerce also faces many challenges. One challenge is Web profitability—surprisingly few companies are using the Web profitably. The other challenge concerns legal and ethical issues—issues of online privacy and security, Internet fraud, and the *digital divide*. Despite these challenges, companies large and small are quickly integrating online marketing into their marketing strategies and mixes.

Reviewing the Key Terms

B2B (business-to-business) ecommerce   662
B2C (business-to-consumer) ecommerce   659
C2B (consumer-to-business) ecommerce   665
C2C (consumer-to-consumer) ecommerce   663
Combined traditional and online operations   669
Corporate website   671
Ebusiness   655
Ecommerce   656
Emarketing   656
Extranet   654

Internet   654
Intranet   654
Marketing website   671
Online advertising   674
Open trading exchanges   662
Private trading exchanges   662
Pure-play companies   667
Spam   680
Viral marketing   675
Web communities   678

Discussing the Concepts

1. This chapter discusses how today's economy revolves around information businesses. Compare two new-economy information companies and how they have differentiated, customized, personalized, and delivered information to their customers over the Internet.

2. The Internet benefits both buyers and sellers in a number of ways. Using eBay as an example, describe the potential benefits gained by both the buyer and the seller.

3. What are the primary differences between private trading exchanges and public trading exchanges in B2B ecommerce? What are the advantages of each type of exchange?

4. Many traditional bricks-and-mortar companies have now become companies combining traditional and online operations. Has the reverse been true? (Can you name many pure-play companies that are now companies combining traditional and online operations?) Explain.

5. What is a blog? Are blogs usually social or work-related? How are blogs the same as or different from Web communities? Explain.

6. What are the basic Internet security fears of consumers? Are these fears usually justified? Identify five actions a consumer can take to reduce the risk of security problems?

Applying the Concepts

1. Visit two Internet sites, one you like and one you don't like. Evaluate and compare each site using the seven Cs of effective Web design. Based on the evaluation, which site is better designed?

2. Assume that you are a member of a marketing department for a pure-play provider of financial services. Your company exchanges very personal and sensitive financial information with each customer over the Internet on a weekly basis. You have been asked by your boss to come up with a security idea that will be communicated in an ad. What primary message would you like to communicate to your customers in this ad?

3. Based on all that you have read and studied about ebusiness, what would you say to a friend who wanted to start a pure-play business in a highly competitive sector of the market, such as resale of used textbooks?

Focus on Technology

Most consumers have tired of uninvited pop-up ads that interrupt their Web sessions. Many Internet users have installed the latest "pop-up blocker" software but are still not completely satisfied. But that's just one side of the story. Suppose that you are an Internet merchant who wants to run pop-up ads because you have heard they are effective and efficient. What do you do? You go to a company like Falk eSolutions. Falk is a full-service provider of interactive advertising campaigns. One of its many products is AdSolutions, a full-featured ad service offering everything a company needs to conduct interactive advertising campaigns. Visit www.falkag.com and respond to the following questions.

1. What would some of your concerns be about using this type of ad-serving technology?

2. If pop-up ads were effective and efficient, would you stop using them if your target segment disliked them? Why or why not?

3. What "rules of the road" should a pop-up advertiser observe to gain as much from this ad technique as possible?

Source: See www.cipher-sys.com/index.asp.

Focus on Ethics

In the summer of 2006, the *Globe and Mail* carried a story about Sandi Thom, a 24-year-old Scottish-born singer, who would be playing in Toronto on August 12. Thom caused a lot of debate after her cyber-savvy tactics helped her rise to the top of the U.K. singles charts with her song "I Wish I Was a Punk Rocker (with Flowers in My Hair)." In 2005, Thom was an unknown musician signed to a small independent label. In less than a year, she became a star on a major label.

What did Thom do? Tired of travelling by car from one small gig to the next, she purchased a webcam and began streaming her *21 Nights from Tooting* "tour" from the basement of her flat in Tooting, South London, on myspace.com. The concerts were webcast from February 24 to March 16, 2006. Tickets were sold for each concert, but the basement only had a capacity of "six people" ("10 including the band"). Using inexpensive props like a small model of the Eiffel Tower, she created the illusion of multi-city venues.

Thom's manager alerted various news services about Thom's online efforts to promote her music. The *Sunday Times* was the first newspaper to pick up a story on the "tour." Others quickly followed. Channel 4 reported, "On the first night seventy people logged on to watch. After two weeks that had risen to more than one hundred thousand per night. To put that in context, the new Wembley stadium will hold only ninety thousand." The publicity helped Thom's music quickly rise on the British charts and helped build her online audience from around 60 or 70 for the first performance to what was reported as 70 000 viewers for the last concert. Thom reportedly drew viewers from as far afield as Russia, the United States, and Pakistan.

Controversy arose when people began to ask how Thom could afford the broadband required to simultaneously sustain webcasts to more than 70 000 people if she was really a starving artist. Others questioned the figures reported with regard to her online audience. There were other questions about whether Thom's broadcasts had actually created buzz and word-of-mouth communication or whether they resulted from a major public relations effort. The most cynical analysts accused Sony of orchestrating the entire thing.

In response to the criticism, Thom acknowledged that a company agreed to handle the bandwidth for the webcasts free of charge, to test their systems. Figures claiming 70 000 viewers reported to have watched Thom's final *21 Nights from Tooting* concert were reduced to about 48 000.

Rather than buzz driving online viewership, it was acknowledged that it was largely media hype and the work of a public relations agency had spammed up interest in Thom and the webcasts. In her own defence, Thom noted, "Promotion—it's always been there. People have been controlling things since the fifties, ever since Elvis's manager had girls screaming at concerts."

Sources: Brad Wheeler, "Rags to riches, thanks to a webcam," *Globe and Mail*, August 12, 2006, p. R4; "Sandi Thom, Wikipedia, http://en.wikipedia.org/wiki/Sandi_Thom (accessed August 2006); "Sandi Thom interview," Channel 4 News, April 4, 2006, www.channel4.com/news/special-reports/special-reports-storypage.jsp?id=2101 (accessed August 2006);

1. Take a stand—do you think Thom is just an astute marketer, or did she cross an ethical line and use deception to build her reputation?

Video Case
iWon

Want to win US$10 000 just for surfing the Web? Visit iWon.com. There, members use iWon as a portal to search the Internet, clicking on links and browsing for news and entertainment information. But unlike other search engines, including Yahoo and Google, every time iWon members follow a sponsored link they are entered in a daily sweepstakes for a chance to win US$10 000. To date, iWon has given away almost US$61 million to more than 265 000 members.

Why the daily giveaways? iWon uses the incentive to attract a large group of loyal, responsive users. To become members, those users fill out demographic and psychographic profiles that iWon uses to attract advertisers who are interested in tailoring messages and offers to online consumers. And advertisers, from Amazon.com and Dell to Kraft and Wal-Mart, are lining up for their shot at iWon's members.

After viewing the video featuring iWon.com, answer the following questions about marketing in the digital age.

1. What product or service does iWon.com offer consumers? How does iWon.com's approach differ from that of Publishers Clearing House?

2. What edge does iWon offer advertisers? Why might a company choose to advertise with iWon rather than Google?

3. Visit the iWon website (iWon.com). How does iWon address concerns about privacy? As a consumer, would you be comfortable giving iWon the personal information required to become a member? Does the possibility of winning US $10 000 change your feelings about giving iWon such personal information?

Online Media Resources

Video Short
Log on to your Companion Website at **www.pearsoned.ca/kotler** to view the video segment related to the Video Case above.

Case Pilot
Log on to your Companion Website at **www.pearsoned.ca/kotler** to sharpen your case analysis skills and take the Case Pilot Challenge!

Company Case
EBay: Connecting Internationally

A Rare Success

Legend has it that Pierre Omidyar, a young engineer, concocted the idea for eBay in 1995 so that his girlfriend would have an easy way to meet and trade with fellow Pez dispenser collectors. Omidyar envisioned eBay's Internet site as becoming a place where a network of buyers and sellers could connect, forming a community. Bill Cobb, the company's global marketing director, calls eBay a step toward "the first worldwide economic democracy."

EBay is just a step in one sense. The company pales in comparison to Wal-Mart, the world's largest retailer based on 2005 revenue. Wal-Mart raked in about $316 billion of revenue resulting in a net income of $11.2 billion in 2005 from its network of 6628 stores located worldwide, 1.6 million workers, and countless warehouses. By comparison, eBay is the world's eleventh-largest retailer. It generated only $3.4 billion in revenue from sales fees and advertising on the $44 billion in goods. It has more than 100 million registered members from around the world who conduct millions of searches each and every day on eBay's sites. However, eBay has no stores or warehouses or inventory and accomplished its results with fewer than 12 000 employees. It uses its websites, including www.ebay.ca. Further, unlike most of the dot-coms that sprouted in the late 1990s, eBay is profitable.

EBay, however, is no flash-in-the-pan. In 2006, it reported that it accounted for 14 percent share of global ecommerce. It has set itself the goal of being the number-one ecommerce franchise and that it will outstrip growth in the ecommerce industry itself. Investors seemed to believe the predictions, as eBay's stock was trading at 33 times earnings in mid-2006. It should be noted, that this ratio is down from the astounding 94 times earnings reported in 2004.

How eBay Works

The idea for eBay's business model is simple—and old. Residents in rural and urban communities have for centuries gathered in town squares and marketplaces to buy, sell, and exchange goods and services. The modern-day "flea market" is a throwback to these markets.

EBay simply took this old idea and removed the need for a physical meeting between buyer and seller.

The Internet provided the cyberspace where the marketing exchange could take place. EBay simply created the software programs to enable the transactions. The eBay system, however, improves on the old market system in that the seller can "display" his or her items to a huge number of potential customers at the same time. Given that there may be more than one person interested in the item, the seller can hold a virtual auction, hoping that demand for the item will produce a higher price than a typical market where the number of potential buyers would be more limited or even non-existent. Obviously, the process also depends on modern transportation and payment systems that allow the buyers and sellers to arrange for the product's physical delivery as eBay plays no role in closing the transaction.

EBay charges the sellers insertion fees for listing an item, picture services fees, final value fees upon a sale, and listing upgrade fees. The following table presents the impact of the final value fee structure at various closing values:

Auction's Gross

Closing Value	Final Value Fee
Item Not Sold	No Fee
$0–$25	5.25% of the closing value
$25–$1000	5.25% of the initial $25.00 ($1.31), plus 3.00% of the remaining closing value balance ($25.01 to $1000.00)
$10 000	5.25% of the initial $25.00 ($1.31), plus 3.00% of the initial $25.00–$1000.00 ($29.25), plus 1.50% of the remaining closing value balance ($1000.01—closing value)

Source: eBay website.

Because eBay does not take title to anything sold over its system, it has a gross margin of about 81 percent! Even with eBay's projected growth, analysts predicted that its sales and marketing expense would hold at 30 percent of revenues.

EBay's average auction lasted 6.55 days as of the first quarter of 2002, and the average gross value per auction was $22.50. As of early 2002, the average seller sponsored three auctions and produced $1.72 in net revenue for eBay per auction. EBay classified its offerings into 18 000 categories, with high-priced merchandise, such as cars and computers, continuing to grow as a percentage of total sales value. In fact, eBay motors was the company's fastest-growing category. Collectibles, such as the Pez dispensers, accounted for only about one-third of eBay's items.

EBay's members, or users (never called customers), would tell you that one reason the system has been successful is that they feel like "winners" whenever they are successful at an auction. The members police themselves, providing feedback points to each other so that disreputable buyers and sellers are quickly identified. Members also communicate directly with eBay's staff to point out problems and suggest solutions. And it is very easy for members to use eBay's system.

A New CEO

In 1997, eBay recruited Meg Whitman to become the company's CEO. Whitman had worked at Disney and Hasbro but was not an Internet junkie. She had degrees from Princeton and Harvard and brought with her a marketing background built on a commitment to customer satisfaction. When Whitman took over, the company had only $49 million in merchandise sales. She helped the company go public in 1998.

Whitman has led eBay through many changes. Recently, the company instituted a "buy-it-now" pricing system that lets a seller set a fixed price at which a buyer can purchase the item without going through the traditional auction process. Whitman estimates that this type of purchase will increase from 20 percent to 33 percent of eBay's sales.

Although the company began as a way for individuals to buy and sell, many people have realized that it is a perfect vehicle for their own businesses. As a result, analysts estimate there are more than 430 000 businesses that exist only on eBay.

New Frontiers

In 2005, eBay exceeded its sales goal by 39 percent and achieved $4.552 billion in sales revenue. In 2006, eBay announced that its goal was to achieve sales in the range of $5.7 to 5.9 billion. To reach this lofty target, Whitman realizes that eBay must develop international markets—especially in light of analysts' suggestions that the company's core U.S. market growth rate is slowing and advertising revenues are down because of the economic slowdown.

EBay has already ventured into international markets. It has operations in Australia, Austria, Canada, France, Germany, Ireland, Italy, New Zealand, Switzerland, the United Kingdom and other countries. In the first quarter of 2002, international revenues

accounted for 21 percent of eBay's revenues, up from 18 percent in the last quarter of 2001; and its 2001 international revenue reached $115 million, up from $34 million a year earlier.

Despite eBay's progress in international markets, all has not gone well. Yahoo! Japan beat eBay to the punch by offering online auctions in Japan in September 1999. EBay entered Japan five months later, but those five months were critical. EBay charged a fee for each transaction, which Yahoo! did not, and required users to provide a credit card number. Many young Japanese do not use credit cards, preferring to pay by cash or bank draft. Further, although many observers thought online auctions would not work in Japan due to Japanese reluctance to buy used goods from strangers, its economic recession and the emergence of environmental awareness helped to overcome this reluctance. Plus, Yahoo! users could adopt Internet nicknames for their transactions, removing some of the stigma. Then, observers suggested, eBay was slow to adopt local touches, such as horoscopes and newsletters, that it needed to attract users. EBay compounded all this by taking a low-key approach to promotion, while Yahoo! bought billboards and opened an Internet café with Starbucks.

All these missteps, analysts argue, resulted in the "network effect." Sellers want to go where there are buyers, and buyers want to go where there is a large selection, i.e., sellers. Once this network reaches critical mass, it becomes very difficult for a competitor to succeed. Sellers and buyers flocked to Yahoo!; and by mid-2001, Yahoo! had captured 95 percent of the $1.6 billion online market—eBay had only 3 percent. By early 2002, eBay threw in the towel and announced its withdrawal from Japan.

Within weeks, however, eBay announced it had purchased 33 percent of a China Internet auction site, EachNet, for $30 million. Two young entrepreneurs who met at Harvard Business School started EachNet in 1999. Shao Yibo and Tan Haiyin studied Internet businesses as part of a class project and decided that the eBay model was the only one that would work in Asia. With support from Asian venture capitalists, they launched their site, which by 2002 had 3.5 million registered users and 50 000 items listed for sale.

Although eBay executives argue that the eBay model has universal application, the company's experience in Japan and China highlight key differences as companies move from one national market to another. In China, for example, EachNet's customers hurried to the site to trade practical items such as apparel or cellular phones, not the collectibles that fuelled growth in the U.S. market. Rather than use the postal or courier systems to make payment, as one might do in the United States, Chinese traders mostly sell within their own cities. Although transportation systems are improving, they are still creaky by U.S. standards; so shipping items is not easy or reliable. Many Chinese still don't feel comfortable doing business online, especially when they are dealing with other individuals rather than companies. Moreover, ecommerce companies have also been concerned about regulation by the Chinese government. In early 2002, the government blocked access to foreign-based news and information sites.

China represents the world's fifth-largest online economy, with 47 million Internet users. Of these, some 32 percent indicate they made purchases online in the past year. Yet 30 percent of users say they rarely visit an ecommerce site. With a population of more than 1 billion people, however, there certainly is plenty of room for growth. In recognition of this potential, eBay purchased the remainder of Eachnet.com in mid-2003, although the company was still not profitable. However, Yahoo also sees China's potential. In early 2004, it announced that it was purchasing another Chinese online auction business, Sino.com, signalling that it would battle eBay.

Moreover, in mid-2004, eBay announced that it would enter India, following a strategy similar to the one it followed in China. EBay indicated that it would acquire the country's largest online auction site, Baazee.com, Inc., for US$50 million. Even though India ranks just behind China in population, it lags far behind the U.S. and other nations in Internet usage, with only 17 million users.

Meg Whitman and eBay's other executives know that to meet their sales and revenue targets, they must be successful in international markets—especially in China and India. EBay is the world's largest person-to-person trading community. Whitman hopes that China and India, with the world's two largest populations, will be perfect fits for eBay's business model.

Questions for Discussion

1. What are the forces shaping the development of Internet businesses, such as eBay, in Canada and the United States? How are these forces similar or different in other countries, such as Japan, China, or India?

2. How do the text's terms "customization" and "customerization" apply to eBay's marketing strategy?

3. How does eBay create value for the members of its community?

4. What marketing recommendations would you make to eBay to help it be successful as it enters the Chinese and Indian markets?

Sources: Nick Wingfield, "Auctioneer to the World," *The Wall Street Journal,* August 5, 2004, p. B1; Nick Wingfield, "EBay Sets Sights On Indian Market with Acquisition," *The Wall Street Journal,* June 23, 2004, p. A3; Jerry Adler, "The eBay Way of Life," *Newsweek,* June 17, 2002, pp. 51–59; Brad Stone, "eBay in China," *China Ebusiness,* April 1, 2002, p. 4; Nick Wingfield and Connie Ling, "Unbowed by Its Failure in Japan, eBay Will Try Its Hand in China," *The Wall Street Journal,* March 18, 2002, p. B1; Ina Steiner, "eBay Regroups in Asia: Goodbye Japan, Hello China," February 27, 2002, AuctionBytes.com; Ken Belson, Rob Hoff, and Ben Elgin, "How Yahoo! Japan Beat eBay at Its Own Game, *BusinessWeek online,* June 4, 2001;"eBay Inc. Announces Second Quarter 2006 Financial Results," eBay Inc., July 19, 2006.

CHAPTER 18
The Global Marketplace

Welcome to
mccain.com

McCain Foods Limited is a privately-owned, multinational leader in the frozen food industry

McCain Foods is the world's largest producer of frozen French fries and the manufacturer of other quality food products sold in more than 110 countries.

McCain Foods Limited

- McCain Home ▷
- About Us ▷
- McCain Today ▷
- Worldwide Operations ▷
- Media Desk ▷
- Careers ▷
- Contact Us ▷

◁ Other McCain S

http://www.mccain.com – mc_home

AFTER STUDYING THIS CHAPTER, YOU SHOULD BE ABLE TO

1. discuss how the international trade system, economic, political-legal, and cultural environments affect a company's international marketing decisions

2. describe three key approaches to entering international markets

3. explain how companies adapt their marketing mixes for international markets

4. identify the three major forms of international marketing organization

Previewing the Concepts

You've now learned the fundamentals of how companies develop competitive marketing strategies to create customer value and to build lasting customer relationships. In this final chapter, we'll extend these fundamentals to another special area—global marketing. Although we visited this topic regularly in each previous chapter, because of its special importance, we will focus exclusively on it here. We'll look first at special considerations in global marketing. As we move into the twenty-first century, advances in communication, transportation, and other technologies have made the world a much smaller place. Today, almost every firm, large or small, faces international marketing issues. In this chapter, we will examine six major decisions marketers make in going global.

Our first stop is McCain Foods Limited. Read on and see how finding the right balance between global standardization and local adaptation has made McCain a world-leading brand.

McCain Foods Limited was founded in 1956 by Harrison and Wallace McCain with the support of their brothers, Andrew and Robert. Their first operation was a small factory located in Florenceville, N.B. Today, it is a global leader among food processors. No matter where in the world you travel, chances are you will be tasting a McCain french fry if you order this item off a menu or pick some up from a food stand. McCain produces about one-third of the french-fried potatoes produced internationally. McCain sells both to end consumers and to businesses, such as restaurants and institutions that have food operations (such as hospitals and schools). When selling to business buyers, the challenge for the company is to convince quick-service restaurants of the world that it has a high-quality product at the right price and service. So far, McCain has been highly successful, and today it is one of the world's largest french fry suppliers to McDonald's Restaurants and a preferred supplier to such high-demand customers as Jollibee and Burger King.

McCain Foods employs 20 000 people, generated $5.71 billion in revenues in fiscal 2005, and operates more than fifty-five production facilities on six continents. As you may suspect, the company is no longer a single-product enterprise. It is known for its appetizers, juices, pizzas, vegetables, desserts, entrées, oven-ready meals, and quality frozen foods that it sells at home and exports to more than 110 countries. McCain Foods' growth has been the result of vision, unwavering devotion to product quality, careful operations management, advanced information technology, insightful marketing, acquisition strategy, innovative product development and Canadian know-how.

McCain Foods has been named the winner of Canada's export awards two times (1983 and 1997). It ships hundreds of millions of kilograms of frozen product a year, customized for local tastes and requirements. "Global leadership cannot be qualified by merely the size factor," states Kai Bockmann, managing director, Greater China. "It's about looking beyond your backyard and, as we say at McCain, drinking the local wine and learning the local ways." Such an attitude has led McCain to great success. For example, ACNielson recently found that McCain is one of only 23 food, beverage, and confectionery brands to qualify as a Global Mega Brand.

When McCain Foods first enters a market, it often imports products from Canada, and then gradually develops its own operations within the country. Take its recent entry into China. The shoe-string fries that accompany a consumer's "Old Beijing" chicken and veggie wrap in a KFC restaurant first came from Coaldale, Alberta, the McCain Foods factory near Lethbridge that supplied much of the product sold in China. McCain used imports from Canada to built its Chinese business to the point where it supplied 25 percent of the fries sold in China by KFC, as well as 80 percent of the needs of Dicos, a major Chinese fast-food chain.

However, McCain Foods knew that to really penetrate the market, it needed in-country operations. After careful research and experimentation, McCain began making french fries from locally grown potatoes in a new state-of-the-art plant located near Harbin. Getting to this point took a lot of patience and investment. The new factory was the result of a decade of growing sales in China, six years of agricultural trials, endless lobbying to get New Brunswick seed potatoes into China, and a $53 million investment in farms as well as the factory. In addition to french fries, the plant will also produce hash browns and vegetable products.

Once these operations were established, the next challenge was to sell the themes of local production and high quality to fast-food vendors. As Dale Morrison, McCain Foods Limited's Toronto-based chief executive officer, notes, "Our challenge is to build a commercial business and we haven't demonstrated we can do that in a big way."

With the dizzying pace of Chinese urbanization, industrialization, and rural depopulation—forces driving the rising demand for prepared meals—McCain knew it had to build operations in this marketplace. More than 10 million people are leaving the countryside each year. This urbanization feeds the proliferation of U.S.-style fast-food joints and major cultural shifts that included adding potatoes into a diet once dominated by rice.

McCain had to work closely with the Chinese government. McCain is leasing 600 hectares of land to grow its Russet Burbank and Kennebec potatoes, mostly in 20- to 30-hectare fields, which are a far cry from the small plots that are common in Chinese agriculture. It had to get government permission to allow it to lease huge blocks. McCain won government officials over with its emphasis on value-added agriculture, which will improve quality and yields, and technology transfer, teaching modern planting, irrigation, spraying, and harvesting methods to local people.

McCain Foods used similar tactics when it entered India. Canadian companies exported more than $1 billion in goods and services to India in 2005 alone. McCain Foods Ltd. has been sending frozen potato products to India since 1998. However, as was the case in China, the company began planting test patches of potatoes around the country with an eye on in-country operations. McCain constructed its first Indian plant in 2006. As in China, potatoes have long been a staple food in India. The new plant will produce french fries as well as making frozen versions of traditional Indian potato-based foods, which McCain expects to become the company's biggest sellers. Customizing products for the local market is crucial to foreign success in India, says Peter Nesbitt, of Export Development Canada. "Canadian companies often think that because their product sells into the U.S. it will automatically work in India, too. That's not true."

Whether operating in India, China, or the United States, McCain Foods works to give the firm a local face and tailors its communications to local needs, attitudes, market life-cycle stage and consumers' media habits. If you look at the firm's U.S. website (see www.mccainusa.com/fs_potato/content/default.asp), you might think McCain was an American firm.

In Canada, Andrew Young, the company's former director of retail marketing, notes, "Our old model of advertising certainly is not as effective as it used to be because of all the factors that are out there—proliferation of TV channels and the time-strapped consumer who isn't watching commercials unless they're entertained," he says. So that is what McCain did. Its campaign called "Tan Lines" for Crescendo Rising Crust pizza showed people with a strip of tan across their eyes from watching the oven as their pizza cooked. It was so popular that it crossed over into popular culture and was even parodied on *This Hour Has 22 Minutes*. McCain got the last laugh as sales leaped 34 percent, winning a CASSIES award for the company.

In contrast, McCain Foods took a very different tack in Great Britain. Research showed that people didn't understand how much fat should be in their diet or what foods contained fat. Of particular concern for McCain was the fact that 52 percent of the survey respondents felt guilty serving french fries to their families, believing they were high in fat. McCain launched an information-intense advertising campaign. Ads focused on little known facts such as McCain Oven Chips contain less fat than a hard-boiled egg, a plain omelette, or macaroni and cheese. It also launched a website called "Fat or Fiction," where viewers can play a game that pairs different foods and asks consumers to guess which one is lower in fat. Players also have a chance to win a trip to a spa.

No matter where in the world McCain Foods operates, it follows its values of honesty, fairness, and integrity. So next time you are travelling and that urge for a french fry overwhelms you, rest assured that it may be a product from a world-leading Canadian company that you pop into your mouth.[1]

Canada has a long history of international trade. Our small domestic market forced companies to look beyond our borders for additional markets. Our diverse population has made us comfortable working in other countries with people from other cultures. Thus, Canada is well positioned to exploit opportunities in the global marketplace.

Global Marketing in the Twenty-First Century

The world is shrinking rapidly with the advent of faster communication, transportation, and financial flows. Products developed in one country—Gucci purses, Sony electronics, McCain french fries, Japanese sushi, German BMWs—are finding enthusiastic acceptance in other countries. We would not be surprised to hear about a Canadian businessman wearing an Italian suit meeting a Polish friend at a Japanese restaurant and later returning home to drink French wine and watch an American show on TV.

International trade is booming. Since 1969, the number of multinational corporations in the world has grown from 7000 to more than 63 000. Some of these multinationals are true giants. In fact, of the largest 100 "economies" in the world, only forty-seven are countries. The remaining fifty-three are multinational corporations. Exxon Mobil, the world's largest company, has annual revenues greater than the gross domestic product of all but the world's twenty largest countries.[2]

Because of our relatively small population, Canada has been a trading nation for most of its history. We are particularly well positioned to understand markets in other countries because of the cultural diversity of our major cities. Montreal, Toronto, and Vancouver are among the most culturally diverse cities in the world. Thus, it is not surprising that international trade now accounts for approximately 38 percent of Canada's GDP, while in the United States international trade accounts for 25 percent of its GDP. World trade now accounts for 29 percent of world GDP, a 10 percent increase from 1990.[3]

Global companies, such as Sony, Toyota, BP, Nestlé, Nokia, Nestle, and Prudential, have become household words in North America. "Already two-thirds of all industry either operates globally or is in the process of doing so," notes one analyst. "Michelin, the oh-so-French tire manufacturer, now makes 35 percent of its money in the United States, while Johnson & Johnson does 43 percent of its business abroad.... The scope of every manager is the world." This is certainly true for many Canadian companies that have long been successful at international marketing: Alcan, Bell Canada, Bombardier, Dofasco, Cirque de Soleil, Inco, Nortel, SNC Lavalin, and dozens of other Canadian firms have made the world their market. Take the case of Vincor:

In 2006, Vincor International Inc. was North America's fourth-largest producer and marketer of wines, including its world renowned ice wines, and it is the world's eighth-largest wine company by revenue. Vincor's premium brands include Inniskillin, Jackson-Triggs, R.H. Phillips, Toasted Head, Sumac Ridge, and Sawmill Creek. The global wine industry is highly fragmented. No single wine producer controls more than 1.5 percent of world sales of a market that is estimated to be US$150 billion in size. Vincor's top four competitors in Canada include Diageo, Andres, Mission Hill, and Maxxium. Together these producers have a 45 percent share of the Canadian market by volume. Vincor's Canadian sales account for an estimated 21 percent of the market. Vincor's production system is as international as its sales. It has wineries and vineyards in British Columbia, Ontario, Quebec, New Brunswick, California, Washington State, South Africa, Western Australia, and New Zealand. Vincor was born when the two Canadian founding partners bought out Labatt's Canadian wine interests. The new company became the Cartier winery. Cartier wines merged with Inniskillin, and then Inniskillin merged with T.G. Bright to form Vincor International Inc., in 1993. As is the case recently with many successful Canadian companies, it became an acquisition target. In June 2006, Constellation Brands,

Many companies have made the world their market.

the world's largest wine-maker, completed a hostile takeover of Vincor for U.S. US$1.56 billion.[4]

Global competition is intensifying. Foreign firms are expanding aggressively into new international markets, and home markets are no longer as rich in opportunity. Few industries are now safe from foreign competition. If companies delay taking steps toward internationalizing, they risk being shut out of growing markets in Western and Eastern Europe, China and the Pacific Rim, Russia, and elsewhere. Firms that stay at home to play it safe not only might lose their chances to enter other markets but also risk losing their home markets. Domestic companies that never thought about foreign competitors suddenly find these competitors in their own backyards.

Globalization—the growing integration of economies and societies around the world—has been one of the most hotly debated topics in international economics over the past few years as witnessed by the protests at many of the World Trade Organization meetings. Supporters of globalization and free trade point to the rapid economic growth and poverty reduction in developing countries, such as China and India. Those who support globalization also suggest that it leads to a more efficient allocation of resources that benefits all peoples and countries through lower prices, increased choice, higher employment, greater levels of material wealth, and higher output. Supporters claim that globalization will also lead to a greater degree of political and economic freedom in the form of democracy and capitalism. In contrast, those who criticize globalization contend that it is essentially imperialistic, and that the interests of poorer nations, the working class, and the environment have not been taken into account. Furthermore, critics claim that unrestricted free trade benefits only those people and nations with the most financial leverage (i.e., the rich) at the expense of the poor. Finally, anti-globalization activists see globalization as the promotion of a corporatist agenda at the expense of human rights. As corporations increase in wealth and power, it is also feared by those who oppose globalization that corporations will increasingly shape the political agenda of nation-states.[5]

Ironically, although the need for companies to go abroad is greater today than in the past, so are the risks. Companies that go global may face highly unstable governments and currencies, restrictive government policies and regulations, and high trade barriers. Corruption is also an increasing problem—officials in several countries often award business not to the best bidder but to the highest briber.

A **global firm** is one that, by operating in more than one country, gains marketing, production, R&D, and financial advantages that are not available to purely domestic competitors. The global company sees the world as one market. It minimizes the importance of national boundaries and develops "transnational" brands. It raises capital, obtains materials and components, and manufactures and markets its goods wherever it can do the best job. Though many global firms are large, others are miniscule, such as the world-leading firm, Cervélo Cycles:

> Cervélo Cycles Inc., a tiny Toronto-based company founded by two McGill engineering students, employs only 30 people. However, it was catapulted onto the world stage when Tyler Hamilton rode one of the firm's cycles to victory in one stage of the gruelling Tour de France bicycle race. This wasn't the first victory for Cervélo. Cyclists have ridden Cervélo bikes to victory in Ironman triathlons, world time trial championships, and numerous road-racing World Cups. Such wins helped Cervélo's sales leap to more than $11 million. The company's bikes range in price from $2000 to $10 000 and are sold to tightly defined target markets: cycling pros and committed weekend warriors. Cervélo is now ranked tenth by volume in North America specialty cycle sales, but it wants to be number one globally in road-racing bikes. Cervélo's single-minded devotion to its customers and product innovation are two keys to its success. The third is its willingness to outsource any functions that don't add high value. Since design is Cervélo's strength, that function remains in Toronto. So does assembly, because quality control is important and the company needs the flexibility to respond to rapidly changing market needs and technology. Cervélo

Global firm
A firm that, by operating in more than one country, gains R&D, production, marketing, and financial advantages in its costs and reputation that are not available to purely domestic competitors.

Cervélo Cycles has proven that even small firms can be global firms. It is well on the road to becoming the top firm in the competitive world of road-racing cycles.

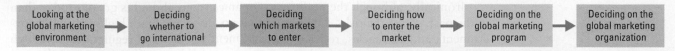

Figure 18.1 Major decisions in international marketing

sources its components from ten countries, however, including the U.S., Italy, Germany, Japan, Poland, South Korea, China, and Thailand as well as Canada.[6]

This does not mean that small and medium-size firms must operate in a dozen countries to succeed. These firms can practise global niching. But the world is becoming smaller, and every company operating in a global industry—whether large or small—must assess and establish its place in world markets.

The rapid move toward globalization means that all companies will have to answer some basic questions: What market position should we try to establish in our country, in our economic region, and globally? Who will our global competitors be, and what are their strategies and resources? Where should we produce or source our products? What strategic alliances should we form with other firms around the world?

As shown in Figure 18.1, a company faces six major decisions in international marketing. Each decision will be discussed in detail in this chapter.

Looking at the Global Marketing Environment

Before deciding whether to operate internationally, a company must understand the international marketing environment. That environment has changed a great deal in the past two decades, creating both new opportunities and new problems.

The International Trade System

Tariff
A tax levied by a government against certain imported products, designed to raise revenue or to protect domestic firms.

Quota
A limit on the amount of goods that an importing country will accept in certain product categories.

Embargo
A ban on the import of a certain product.

Exchange controls
Government limits on the amount of foreign exchange with other countries and on the exchange rate against other currencies.

Nontariff trade barriers
Nonmonetary barriers to foreign products, such as biases against a foreign company's bids or product standards that go against a foreign company's product features.

Companies looking abroad must start by understanding the international *trade system*. When selling to another country, Canadian firms face various trade restrictions. The most common is the **tariff**, a tax levied by a foreign government against certain imported products. The tariff may be designed either to raise revenue or to protect domestic firms. The exporter also may face a **quota**, which sets limits on the amount of goods the importing country will accept in certain product categories. The purpose of the quota is to conserve on foreign exchange and to protect local industry and employment. An **embargo**, or boycott, which totally bans some kinds of imports, is the strongest form of quota.

Canadian firms may face **exchange controls** that limit the amount of foreign exchange and the exchange rate against other currencies. The company also may face **nontariff trade barriers**, such as biases against foreign company bids or restrictive product standards or other rules that go against Canadian product features:

One of the cleverest ways the Japanese have found to keep foreign manufacturers out of their domestic market is to plead "uniqueness." Japanese skin is different, the government argues, so foreign cosmetics companies must test their products in Japan before selling there. The Japanese say their stomachs are small and have room for only the *mikan*, the local tangerine, so imports of U.S. oranges are limited. Now the Japanese have come up with what may be the flakiest argument yet: Their snow is different, so ski equipment should be too.[7]

At the same time, certain forces *help* trade between nations. Examples include the General Agreement on Tariffs and Trade (GATT) and various regional free trade agreements.

The World Trade Organization and GATT

The General Agreement on Tariffs and Trade (GATT) is an almost six-decade-old treaty designed to promote world trade by reducing tariffs and other international trade barriers. Since the treaty's inception in 1948, member nations (currently numbering 149) have met in eight rounds of GATT negotiations to reassess trade barriers and set new rules for international trade. The first seven rounds of negotiations reduced the average worldwide tariffs on manufactured goods from 45 percent to just 5 percent.[8]

The most recently completed GATT negotiations, dubbed the Uruguay Round, dragged on for seven long years before concluding in 1993. The benefits of the Uruguay Round will be felt for many years as the accord promotes long-term global trade growth. It reduced the world's remaining merchandise tariffs by 30 percent, boosting global merchandise trade by as much as 10 percent, or US$270 billion in current dollars, by 2002. The agreement also extended GATT to cover trade in agriculture and a wide range of services, and it toughened international protection of copyrights, patents, trademarks, and other intellectual property.[9]

Beyond reducing trade barriers and setting global standards for trade, the Uruguay Round set up the World Trade Organization (WTO) to enforce GATT rules. In general, the WTO acts as an umbrella organization, overseeing GATT, mediating global disputes, and imposing trade sanctions. The previous GATT organization never possessed such authorities. A new round of GATT negotiations, the Doha round, began in Doha, Qatar, in late 2001 with the aim of eliminating trade barriers and encouraging global commerce among developing nations. Although it was expected to conclude in January 2005, disputes have drawn out the timeframe.[10]

The General Agreement on Tariffs and Trade (GATT) promotes world trade by reducing tariffs and other international trade barriers. The WTO, which oversees GATT, began a new round of negotiations in Doha, Qatar, in late 2001.

Regional Free Trade Zones

Economic community
A group of nations organized to work toward common goals in the regulation of international trade.

Certain countries have formed *free trade zones* or **economic communities**. These are groups of nations organized to work toward common goals in the regulation of international trade. One such community is the *European Union (EU)*. Formed in 1957, the EU set out to create a single European market by reducing barriers to the free flow of products, services, finances, and labour among member countries and developing policies on trade with nonmember nations. Today, the European Union represents one of the world's single largest markets. Its current twenty-five member countries contain some 448 million consumers and account for more than 20 percent of the world's exports.[11]

European unification offers tremendous trade opportunities for Canadian firms. However, it also poses threats. As a result of increased unification, European companies will grow bigger and more competitive. Perhaps an even greater concern, however, is that lower barriers *inside* Europe will create only thicker *outside* walls. Some observers envision a "Fortress Europe" that heaps favours on firms from EU countries but hinders outsiders by imposing obstacles.

Progress toward European unification has been slow—many doubt that complete unification will ever be achieved. However, in recent years, twelve member nations have taken a significant step toward unification by adopting the euro as a common currency. Widespread adoption of the euro will decrease much of the currency risk associated with doing business in Europe, making member countries with previously weak currencies more attractive markets. See how Czechoslovakian brewers have exploited this expanded marketplace:[12]

> Though Czechoslovakians are the biggest beer-drinkers in the world, they are increasingly looking to the expanded European common market for sales. Achieving membership in the EU made exporting much easier. Robert Chrt, sales manager with the third-largest Czech brewer, Budejovicky Budvar, noted, "Countries such as Hungary, Poland and the Baltics previously had restrictively high customs duties, but with us all in the EU now there is free trade between us." The state-owned brewer exports 46 percent of its output. Neighbouring Germany is its biggest market, accounting for 40 percent of all exports, followed by Slovakia and Britain. What makes exporting even more attractive is the price Czech brewers can charge elsewhere in the EU. "The retail price of beer is two to three times higher abroad so exporting can be more profitable," Jan Vesely, head of the Czech Brewers' Association, told AFP.

Even with the adoption of the euro, it is unlikely that the EU will ever go against 2000 years of tradition and become the "United States of Europe." As one observer asks, "Can a community that speaks at least a dozen languages and has two dozen different cultures effectively come together and operate as a single unified entity?" Although economic and political boundaries may fall, social and cultural differences will remain. And companies marketing in Europe will face a daunting mass of local rules. Still, even if only partly successful, unification will make Europe a global force with which to reckon.[13]

In North America, the United States and Canada phased out trade barriers in 1989. In January 1994, the *North American Free Trade Agreement (NAFTA)* established a free trade zone among the United States, Mexico, and Canada. Today, the gross domestic product (GDP) of the three countries combined makes up about one-third of the world's GDP. The single market has a population of 434 million people who produce and consume $11 trillion worth of goods and services. NAFTA will eventually eliminate all trade barriers and investment restrictions among the three countries.

Despite some major disputes (such as the softwood lumber case), the agreement has allowed trade among the countries to flourish. The United States is Canada's largest trading partner. Canada–U.S. trade has nearly tripled since the

The European Union represents one of the world's single largest markets. Its current twenty-five member countries contain more than 448 million consumers and account for 20 percent of the world's exports.

inception of the agreement. In 2005, 84 percent of our exports were sent to the U.S. Compare this figure with our second-largest trading partner, Japan. Only 2.1 percent of our exports go there. Every day, more than $2 billion worth of goods and services cross the Canada–U.S. border, making the Canada–U.S. trade relationship the largest in the world. Spurred on by NAFTA's success, Canada has been pursuing additional trade agreements. A bilateral free trade agreement with Chile took effect in 1997, and another was signed with Costa Rica in 2003. Canada is currently negotiating agreements with El Salvador, Guatemala, Honduras, and Nicaragua. As well, Canada, Mexico, the U.S., and the other 31 democratic countries of the hemisphere are now working toward establishing a Free Trade Area of the Americas. This is an effort to unite all the economies of the Americas into a single free trade area began in 1994. Canada chaired the negotiations in the 1998–1999 period. This mammoth free trade zone would stretch from the Bering Strait to Cape Horn, with a population of 800 million, a combined gross domestic product of more than US$13 trillion, and more than US$3.4 trillion in annual world trade.[14]

Other free trade areas have formed in Latin America and South America. For example, MERCOSUR now links six members, including full members Argentina, Brazil, Paraguay, and Uruguay, and associate members Bolivia and Chile. With a population of more than 200 million and a combined economy of more than $1 trillion a year, these countries make up the largest trading bloc after NAFTA and the European Union. There is talk of a free trade agreement between the EU and MERCOSUR, and MERCOSUR's member countries are considering adopting a common currency, the merco.[15]

Although the recent trend toward free trade zones has caused great excitement and new market opportunities, some see it as a mixed blessing. Some fear that NAFTA will lead to the further exodus of manufacturing jobs to Mexico, where wage rates are much lower. Environmentalists worry that companies will relocate in Mexico, where pollution regulation has been lax.[16]

Each nation has unique features that must be understood. A nation's readiness for different products and services and its attractiveness as a market to foreign firms depend on its economic, political-legal, and cultural environments.

Economic Environment

The international marketer must study each country's economy. Two economic factors reflect the country's attractiveness as a market: the country's industrial structure and its income distribution.

The country's *industrial structure* shapes its product and service needs, income levels, and employment levels. The four types of industrial structures are as follows:

- *Subsistence economies:* In a subsistence economy, the vast majority of people engage in simple agriculture. They consume most of their output and barter the rest for simple goods and services. They offer few market opportunities.

- *Raw material exporting economies:* These economies are rich in one or more natural resources but poor in other ways. Much of their revenue comes from exporting these resources. Examples are Zaire (copper, cobalt, and coffee) and Saudi Arabia (oil). These countries are good markets for large equipment, tools and supplies, and trucks. If there are many foreign residents and a wealthy upper class, they are also a market for luxury goods.

- *Industrializing economies:* In an industrializing economy, manufacturing accounts for 10 to 20 percent of the country's economy. Examples include China, Chile, Egypt, India, and Brazil. As manufacturing increases, the country needs more imports of raw textile materials, steel, and heavy machinery, and fewer imports of finished textiles, paper products, and automobiles. Industrialization typically creates a new rich class and a small but growing middle class, both demanding new types of imported goods.

- *Industrial economies:* Industrial economies, such as those found in Europe and North America, are major exporters of manufactured goods, services, and investment funds. They trade goods among themselves and also export them to other types of economies for raw materials and semifinished goods. The varied manufacturing activities of these industrial nations and their large middle class make them rich markets for all sorts of goods.

The second economic factor is the country's *income distribution*. Countries with subsistence economies may consist mostly of households with very low family incomes. In contrast, industrialized nations may have low-, medium-, and high-income households. Still other countries may have households with only either very low or very high incomes. However, in many cases, poorer countries may have small but wealthy segments of upper-income consumers. Also, even in low-income and developing economies, people may find ways to buy products that are important to them:

Philosophy professor Nina Gladziuk thinks carefully before shelling out her hard-earned zlotys for Poland's dazzling array of consumer goods. But spend she certainly does. Although she earns just US$550 a month from two academic jobs, Gladziuk, 41, enjoys making purchases. Such purchases are changing her lifestyle after years of deprivation under communism. In the past year, she has furnished a new apartment in a popular neighbourhood near Warsaw's Kabaty Forest, splurged on foreign-made beauty products, and spent a weekend in Paris before attending a seminar financed by her university. Meet Central Europe's fast-rising consumer class. From white-collar workers such as Gladziuk and factory workers in Budapest to hip young professionals in Prague, incomes are rising and confidence is surging as their economies grow. In the region's leading economies—the Czech Republic, Hungary, and Poland—the new class of buyers is increasing not only in numbers but also in sophistication. Nearly one-third of the population of these three countries—some 17 million people—are under 30 years old, with dreams of the good life and buying habits to match.[17]

In Central Europe, companies are catering to the new class of buyers with dreams of the good life, and buying habits to match, who are eager to snap up everything from western consumer goods to high fashions and the latest cellphones.

Thus, international marketers face many challenges in understanding how the economic environment will affect decisions about which global markets to enter and how.

Political-Legal Environment

Nations differ greatly in their political-legal environments. At least four political-legal factors should be considered in deciding whether to do business in a given country: *attitudes toward international buying, government bureaucracy, political stability*, and *monetary regulations*.

In their *attitudes toward international buying*, some nations are quite receptive to foreign firms, and others are quite hostile. For example, India has complicated the operations of some foreign businesses with import quotas, currency restrictions, and limits on the percentage of the management team that can be nonnationals. Canada wants to improve trade relationships with India, especially in the field of science and technology. Thus, in 2005, it signed a Joint Declaration on Science and Technology (S&T) Cooperation. As former International Trade Minister Jim Peterson noted, "India is a true economic giant that boasts the largest emerging consumer market in the world."[18] Other nations in the region, such as Singapore, Thailand, Malaysia, and the Philippines, court foreign investors and shower them with incentives and favourable operating conditions.

A second factor is *government bureaucracy*—the extent to which the host government runs an efficient system for helping foreign companies: efficient customs handling, good market information, and other factors that aid in doing business.

Political stability is another issue. Governments change hands, sometimes violently. Even without a change, a government may decide to respond to new popular feelings. The foreign company's property may be taken, its currency holdings may be blocked, or import quotas or new duties may be set. International marketers may find it profitable to do business in an unstable country, but the unstable situation will affect how they handle business and financial matters.

Finally, companies must also consider a country's *monetary regulations*. Sellers want to take their profits in a currency of value to them. Ideally, the buyer can pay in the seller's currency or in other world currencies. Short of this, sellers might accept a blocked currency—one whose removal from the country is restricted by the buyer's government—if they can buy other goods in that country that they need themselves or can sell elsewhere for a needed currency. Besides currency limits, a changing exchange rate also creates high risks for the seller.

Other countries may not have restrictive monetary regulations, but they may have too little hard currency to pay for their purchases from other countries. They may want to pay with other items instead of cash, which has led to a growing practice called **countertrade**. Countertrade makes up an estimated 20 percent of all world trade.[19] It takes several forms: *Barter* involves the direct exchange of goods or services, as when Australian cattlemen swapped beef for Indonesian goods including beer, palm oil, and cement. Another form is *compensation* (or *buyback*), whereby the seller sells a plant, equipment, or technology to another country and agrees to take payment in the resulting products. Thus, Goodyear provided China with materials and training for a printing plant in exchange for finished labels. Another form is *counterpurchase*, in which the seller receives full payment in cash but agrees to spend some of the money in the other country. For example, Pepsi sells its cola syrup to Russia for rubles and agrees to buy Russian-made Stolichnaya vodka for sale in the United States.

Countertrade deals can be very complex. For example, a few years back, DaimlerChrysler agreed to sell 30 trucks to Romania in exchange for 150 Romanian jeeps, which it then sold to Ecuador for bananas, which were in turn sold to a German supermarket chain for German currency. Through this roundabout process, DaimlerChrysler finally obtained payment in German money.[20]

Given Canada's political stability, attitude toward free trade, and reputation for quality of life, many international firms and their employees see it as an ideal place to invest, live, and do business. In 2006, KPMG's guide to international business costs ranked Canada as the lowest-cost G7 country in which to do business. As International Trade Minister David L. Emerson noted, "In today's global marketplace, companies continue to seek out the best, most cost-competitive places in which to locate and invest." Another study, the Anholt-GMI Nation Brands Index, which surveyed 10 000 people to rank the world's nations as brands, put Canada in second place among twenty-five countries as one of the world's best places to invest and live. Canada elbowed out Britain and the United States, and it falls just behind Australia in terms of its brand power.[21]

Countertrade
International trade involving the direct or indirect exchange of goods for other goods instead of cash.

Cultural Environment

Each country has its own folkways, norms, and taboos. When designing global marketing strategies, companies must understand how culture affects consumer reactions in each of its world markets. In turn, they must also understand how their strategies affect local cultures.

The Impact of Culture on Marketing Strategy

The seller must examine the ways consumers in different countries think about and use certain products before planning a marketing program. There are often surprises. For example, while France is viewed as the spiritual home of beauty and fragrance products, French women don't wear foundation. They think it makes them look old, or even worse, look like a street walker. They prefer a glowing, clear skin look. Perhaps even more surprising is that 97 percent of Spanish men use fragrance, compared with only 94 percent of French women.[22] Despite stereotypes, the Germans and the French eat more packaged, branded spaghetti than do Italians. Italian children like to eat chocolate bars between slices of bread as a snack. Women in Tanzania will not give their children eggs for fear of making them bald or impotent.

International researchers who have studied different cultures have developed a set of dimensions that they believe differentiate people living in different countries and that these differences affect their decision-making styles. These dimensions include *power distance, uncertainty avoidance, future orientation, humane orientation, collectivism (societal and in-group), assertiveness,* and *performance orientation.*[23]

Companies that ignore such differences can make some very expensive and embarrassing mistakes. Here's an example:

McDonald's and Coca-Cola managed to offend the entire Muslim world by putting the Saudi Arabian flag on their packaging. The flag's design includes a passage from the Koran (the sacred text of Islam), and Muslims feel very strongly that their Holy Writ should never be wadded up and tossed in the garbage. Nike faced a similar situation in Arab countries when Muslims objected to a stylized "Air" logo on its shoes, which resembled "Allah" in Arabic script. Nike apologized for the mistake and pulled the shoes from distribution.[24]

Business norms and behaviour also vary from country to country. North American business executives need to be briefed on these factors before conducting business in another country. Here are some examples of different global business behaviour:[25]

- South Americans like to sit or stand very close to each other when they talk business—in fact, almost nose to nose. They also like to build relationships before talking business. The North American business executive tends to keep backing away as the South American moves closer, and rushes to get down to business before taking the time to get to know the other person. Both may end up being offended.

- Fast and tough bargaining, which works well in other parts of the world, is often inappropriate in Japan and other Asian countries. Moreover, in face-to-

Overlooking cultural differences can result in embarrassing mistakes. When Nike learned that this stylized "Air" logo resembled "Allah" in Arabic script, it apologized and pulled the shoes from distribution.

face communications, Japanese business executives rarely say no. Thus, North Americans tend to become impatient with having to spend time in polite conversation about the weather or other such topics before getting down to business. And they become frustrated when they don't know where they stand. However, when North Americans come to the point quickly, Japanese business executives may find this behaviour offensive.

- When setting up a meeting with a business person from Belgium, book an appointment at least one week in advance. Belgians expect you to arrive punctually, or you may be branded as unreliable. A handshake is the common greeting for those who don't know each other, but once a relationship has been established between men and women, three kisses directed at the air close to the cheek—left, right, left—may replace the handshake. Jackets are never removed during meetings because Belgians take pride in personal appearance. Despite the formality, first appointments will often be socially orientated, as most Belgians like to get to know someone before proceeding with business of any kind. For example, if you are scheduled to meet at 11:30 a.m., this is likely to be a luncheon appointment designed as a "get acquainted" meeting.

By the same token, companies that understand cultural nuances can use them to advantage when positioning products internationally. Consider the following example:

A television ad in India shows a mother lapsing into a daydream: Her young daughter is in a beauty contest dressed as Snow White, dancing on a stage. Her flowing gown is an immaculate white. The garments of other contestants, who dance in the background, are a tad grey. Snow White, no surprise, wins the blue ribbon. The mother awakes to the laughter of her adoring family—and glances proudly at her Whirlpool White Magic washing machine. The TV spot is the product of 14 months of research by Whirlpool into the psyche of the Indian consumer. Among other things, [Whirlpool] learned that Indian homemakers prize hygiene and purity, which they associate with white. The trouble is, white garments often get discoloured after frequent machine washing in local water. Besides appealing to this love of purity in its ads, Whirlpool custom-designed

By understanding nuances, Whirlpool has become the leading brand in India's fast-growing market for automatic washing machines. It designed machines that keep whites whiter.

Now all her whites have the magic of her hands

winning whites her whites are whitest whites

her whites are pretty whites

You & Whirlpool.
The world's best homemakers.

machines that are especially good with white fabrics. Whirlpool now is the leading brand in India's fast-growing market for fully automatic washing machines.[26]

Thus, understanding cultural traditions, preferences, and behaviours can help companies not only to avoid embarrassing mistakes but also to take advantage of cross-cultural opportunities.

The Impact of Marketing Strategy on Cultures

Whereas marketers worry about the impact of culture on their global marketing strategies, others may worry about the impact of marketing strategies on global cultures. For example, some critics argue that "globalization" really means "Americanization."

> Down in the mall, between the fast-food joint and the bagel shop, a group of young people huddles in a flurry of baggy combat pants, skateboards, and slang. They size up a woman teetering past wearing DKNY, carrying *Time* magazine in one hand and a latte in the other. She brushes past a guy in a Yankees' baseball cap who is talking on his Motorola cellphone about the Martin Scorsese film he saw last night.
>
> It's a standard American scene—only this isn't America, it's Britain. U.S. culture is so pervasive, the scene could be played out in any one of dozens of cities. Budapest or Berlin, if not Bogota or Bordeaux. Even Manila or Moscow. America exports its culture on an unprecedented scale.... Sometimes, U.S. ideals get transmitted—such as individual rights, freedom of speech, and respect for women—and local cultures are enriched. At other times, cultural imperialism is the outcome, and local traditions get crushed. As a result, Canadians struggle to keep their unique identity, as do people in France, where anti-Americanism rose to a peak in 2003 as a result of the invasion of Iraq and U.S. anti-French campaigns aggravated the problems (remember "freedom fries"?).[27]

Deciding Whether to Go International

Not all companies need to venture into international markets to survive. For example, most local businesses need to market well only in the local marketplace. Operating domestically is easier and safer. Managers don't need to learn another country's language and laws. They don't have to deal with unstable currencies, face political and legal uncertainties, or redesign their products to suit different customer expectations. However, even small companies must monitor international businesses, since only too often they find an international competitor entering the market they thought was their own backyard. Companies that do operate in global industries, where their strategic positions in specific markets are affected strongly by their overall global positions, must compete on a worldwide basis to succeed.

Any of several factors might draw a company into the international arena. Global competitors might attack the company's domestic market by offering better products or lower prices. The company might want to counterattack these competitors in their home markets to tie up their resources. Or the company's domestic market might be small, stagnant or shrinking, and foreign markets may present higher sales and profit opportunities. Or the company's customers might be expanding abroad and require international servicing.

Before going abroad, the company must weigh several risks and answer many questions about its ability to operate globally. Can the company learn to understand the preferences and buyer behaviour of consumers in other countries? Can it offer competitively attractive products? Will it be able to adapt to other countries' business cultures and deal effectively with foreign nationals? Do the company's managers have the necessary international experience? Has management considered the impact of regulations and the political environments of other countries?

Because of the difficulties of entering international markets, most companies do not act until some situation or event thrusts them into the global arena. Someone—a domestic exporter, a foreign importer, a foreign government—may ask the company to sell abroad. Or the company may be saddled with overcapacity and need to find additional markets for its goods.

Deciding Which Markets to Enter

Before going abroad, the company should try to define its international *marketing objectives and policies*. It should decide what *volume* of foreign sales it wants. Most companies start small when they go abroad. Some plan to stay small, seeing international sales as a small part of their business. Other companies have bigger plans, seeing international business as equal to or even more important than their domestic business. Consider Waterloo-based NDI. It is an industry leader in 3D motion and position measurement, and has more than 9000 of its systems installed in some twenty-five countries worldwide, in applications ranging from image-guided brain surgery to wind-tunnel testing, from biomechanics and human motion research to quality control in automotive manufacturing. Ninety-three percent of its production is destined for international markets.[28]

The company also needs to choose *how many* countries it wants to market in. Companies must be careful not to spread themselves too thin or to expand beyond their capabilities by operating in too many countries too soon. Next, the company needs to decide on the *types* of countries to enter. A country's attractiveness depends on the product, geographical factors, income and population, political climate, and other factors. The seller may prefer certain country groups or parts of the world. In recent years, many major new markets have emerged, offering both substantial opportunities and daunting challenges. Research In Motion Ltd. (RIM), headquar-

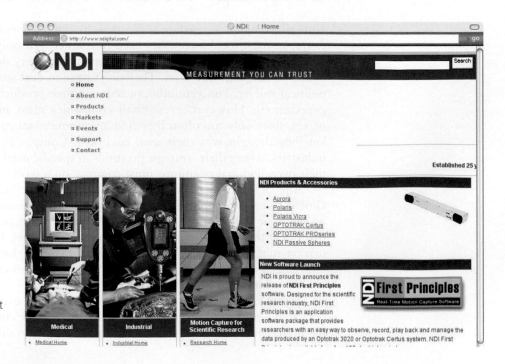

Waterloo-based NDI is an industry leader in 3D motion and position measurement. Ninety-three percent of its production is destined for international markets.

tered in Waterloo, Ontario, and maker of the famous BlackBerry, announced in May 2006 that it was taking its wireless BlackBerry service to South Korea. The move is part of its continuing efforts to diversify its international markets. There are about 5 million subscribers who use BlackBerrys around the world today, and more than 70 percent of those are in the United States and Canada.[29]

After listing possible international markets, the company must screen and rank each one. Consider the following example:

> Many mass marketers, like McCain, dream of selling to China's more than 1.3 billion people. For example, Colgate is waging a pitched battle in China, seeking control of the world's largest toothpaste market. Yet, this country of infrequent brushers offers great potential. Only 20 percent of China's rural dwellers brush daily, so Colgate and its competitors are aggressively pursuing promotional and educational programs, from massive ad campaigns to visits to local schools and sponsoring oral care research. Through such efforts in this US$350-million market, Colgate has expanded its market share from 7 percent in 1995 to 35 percent today, despite competing with a state-owned brand managed by Unilever and Procter & Gamble's Crest.[30]

Colgate's decision to enter the Chinese market seems fairly simple and straightforward: China is a huge market without much established competition. Given the low rate of brushing, this already huge market can grow even larger. Yet we still can question whether market size *alone* is reason enough for selecting China. Colgate also must consider other factors: Will Colgate be able to overcome cultural barriers and convince Chinese consumers to brush their teeth regularly? Does China provide for the needed production and distribution technologies? Can Colgate continue to compete effectively with dozens of local competitors? Will the Chinese government remain stable and supportive? Colgate's current success in China suggests that it could answer yes to all of these questions. Still, the company's future in China is filled with uncertainties.

Possible global markets should be ranked on several factors, including market size, market growth, cost of doing business, competitive advantage, and risk level. The goal is to determine the potential of each market, using indicators such as those shown in Table 18.1. Then the marketer must decide which markets offer the greatest long-run return on investment.

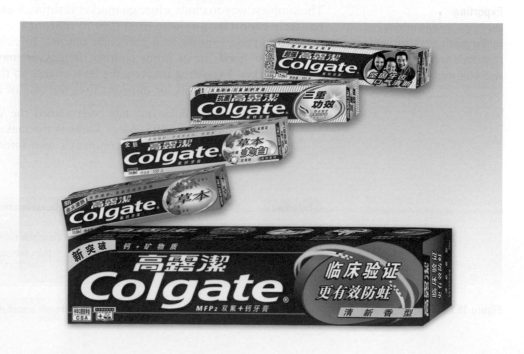

Colgate's decision to enter the huge Chinese market seems fairly straightforward. Using aggressive promotional and educational programs, Colgate has expanded its market share from 7 percent to 35 percent in less than a decade.

TABLE 18.1 Indicators of Market Potential

Demographic characteristics

Education

Population size and growth

Population age composition

Geographic characteristics

Climate

Country size

Population density—urban, rural

Transportation structure and market accessibility

Economic factors

GDP size and growth

Income distribution

Industrial infrastructure

Natural resources

Financial and human resources

Sociocultural factors

Consumer lifestyles, beliefs, and values

Business norms and approaches

Social norms

Languages

Political and legal factors

National priorities

Political stability

Government attitudes toward global trade

Government bureaucracy

Monetary and trade regulations

Deciding How to Enter the Market

Once a company has decided to sell in a foreign country, it must determine the best mode of entry. Its choices are *exporting*, *joint venturing*, and *direct investment*. Figure 18.2 shows three market entry strategies, along with the options each one offers. As the figure shows, each succeeding strategy involves more commitment and risk, but also more control and potential profits.

Exporting

Exporting

Entering a foreign market by selling goods produced in the company's home country, often with little modification.

The simplest way to enter a foreign market is through **exporting**. The company may passively export its surpluses from time to time, or it may make an active commitment to expand exports to a particular market. In either case, the company produces all its goods in its home country. It may or may not modify them for the export market. Exporting involves the least change in the company's product lines, organization, investments, or mission. Take the case of Mega Bloks:

> Montreal's Mega Bloks Inc. has been named the winner of Canada's Export Awards in 2003 and 2005. Mega Bloks is the maker of a broad range of construction toys that feature the company's own interlocking plastic blocks. The

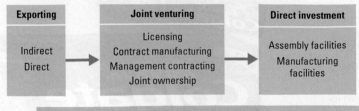

Figure 18.2 Market entry strategies

family-run business has been exporting its construction toys since the mid-1980s. Today, thousands of children in more than 100 countries enjoy playing with its products. Company President and CEO Marc Bertrand sums up the firm's winning strategy with the following words, "No matter where kids live, they love to build, create and learn." Having a global market with a common need is certainly one of the keys to Mega Bloks' success. Its products have universal appeal and are known worldwide as safe, high-quality toys designed to help children learn, discover, and have fun. Other factors contributing to the firm's success are its affordable price, dynamic and dedicated local sales teams, and a step-by-step strategic approach to international expansion. Innovative retail partnerships are also at the heart of its strategy. Today, Mega Bloks sells its toys in more than 100 countries through 11 offices located around the world. It employs approximately 1000 people, and 75 percent of the company's products are made in Montreal, using cost-efficient manufacturing technologies.[31]

Companies typically start with *indirect exporting*, working through independent international marketing intermediaries. Indirect exporting involves less investment because the firm does not require an overseas marketing organization or set of contacts. It also involves less risk. International marketing intermediaries bring know-how and services to the relationship, so the seller normally makes fewer mistakes.

Sellers may eventually move into *direct exporting*, whereby they handle their own exports. The investment and risk are somewhat greater in this strategy, but so is the potential return. A company can conduct direct exporting in several ways: It can set up a domestic export department that carries out export activities. It can set up an overseas sales branch that handles sales, distribution, and perhaps promotion. The sales branch gives the seller more presence and program control in the foreign market and often serves as a display centre and customer service centre. The company can also send home-based salespeople abroad at certain times in order to find business. Finally, the company can do its exporting either through foreign-based distributors who buy and own the goods or through foreign-based agents who sell the goods on behalf of the company.

Montreal's Mega Bloks Inc. was named the winner of Canada's Export Awards in 2003 and 2005 because of its success exporting its construction toys to more than 100 international markets.

Joint Venturing

Joint venturing
Entering foreign markets by joining with foreign companies to produce or market a product or service.

A second method of entering a foreign market is **joint venturing**—joining with foreign companies to produce or market products or services. Joint venturing differs from exporting in that the company joins with a host country partner to sell or market abroad. It differs from direct investment in that an association is formed with someone in the foreign country. There are four types of joint ventures: *licensing, contract manufacturing, management contracting,* and *joint ownership.*[32]

Licensing

Licensing
A method of entering a foreign market in which the company enters into an agreement with a licensee in the foreign market, offering the right to use a manufacturing process, trademark, patent, trade secret, or other item of value for a fee or royalty.

Licensing is a simple way for a manufacturer to enter international marketing. The company enters into an agreement with a licensee in the foreign market. For a fee or royalty, the licensee buys the right to use the company's manufacturing process, trademark, patent, trade secret, or other item of value. The company thus gains entry into the market at little risk; the licensee gains production expertise or a well-known product or name without having to start from scratch.

Coca-Cola markets internationally by licensing bottlers around the world and supplying them with the syrup needed to produce the product. In Japan, Budweiser beer flows from Kirin breweries, Lady Borden ice cream is churned out at Meiji Milk Products dairies, and Marlboro cigarettes roll off production lines at Japan Tobacco, Inc. Online brokerage E*TRADE has set up E*TRADE-branded websites under licensing agreements in several countries. And Tokyo Disneyland is owned and operated by Oriental Land Company under licence from the Walt Disney Company.[33]

Licensing has potential disadvantages, however. The firm has less control over the licensee than it would over its own production facilities. Furthermore, if the licensee is very successful, the firm has given up these profits, and if and when the contract ends, it may find it has created a competitor.

Contract Manufacturing

Contract manufacturing
A joint venture in which a company contracts with manufacturers in a foreign market to produce the product or provide its service.

Another option is **contract manufacturing**—the company contracts with manufacturers in the foreign market to produce its product or provide its service. Sears used this method in opening up department stores in Mexico and Spain, where it found qualified local manufacturers to produce many of the products it sells. The drawbacks of contract manufacturing are decreased control over the manufacturing process and loss of potential profits on manufacturing. The benefits are the chance to start faster, with less risk, and the later opportunity either to form a partnership with or to buy out the local manufacturer.

Management Contracting

Management contracting
A joint venture in which the domestic firm supplies the management know-how to a foreign company that supplies the capital; the domestic firm exports management services rather than products.

Under **management contracting**, the domestic firm supplies management know-how to a foreign company that supplies the capital. The domestic firm exports management services rather than products. Hilton uses this arrangement in managing hotels around the world.

Management contracting is a low-risk method of getting into a foreign market, and it yields income from the beginning. The arrangement is even more attractive if the contracting firm has an option to buy some share in the managed company later on. The arrangement is not sensible, however, if the company can put its scarce management talent to better uses or if it can make greater profits by undertaking the whole venture. Management contracting also prevents the company from setting up its own operations for a period of time.

Tokyo Disneyland is owned and operated by the Oriental Land Co., Ltd. (a Japanese development company), under licence from the Walt Disney company.

Joint Ownership

Joint ownership
A joint venture in which a company joins investors in a foreign market to create a local business in which the company shares joint ownership and control.

Joint ownership ventures consist of one company joining forces with foreign investors to create a local business in which they share joint ownership and control. A company may buy an interest in a local firm, or the two parties may form a new business venture. Joint ownership may be needed for economic or political reasons. The firm may lack the financial, physical, or managerial resources to undertake the venture alone. Or a foreign government may require joint ownership as a condition for entry. Waterloo, Ontario-based Sun Life Financial had to address many of these issues as it sought to gain a foothold in the Chinese marketplace using a joint partnership with the Beijing-based China Everbright Group. The China Insurance Regulatory Commission required an investment of $34 million of capital to start a life insurance joint venture company. Sun Life and the China Everbright Group split that cost. The strategy behind the joint partnership was to leverage Sun Life's Canadian expertise and build a company with local sensitivities. Two Canadians of Chinese descent, Timothy Chen and Andrew Cheung, were relocated to assume the CEO and VP marketing posts respectively, since Sun Life believed that "It is imperative that people who understand the market and the culture run the business."[34]

KFC entered Japan through a joint ownership venture with Japanese conglomerate Mitsubishi. KFC sought a good way to enter the large but difficult Japanese fast-food market. In turn, Mitsubishi, one of Japan's largest poultry producers, understood the Japanese culture and had money to invest. Together, they helped KFC succeed in the semiclosed Japanese market. Surprisingly, with Mitsubishi's guidance, KFC developed decidedly un-Japanese positioning for its Japanese restaurants:

When KFC first entered Japan, the Japanese were uncomfortable with the idea of fast food and franchising. They saw fast food as artificial and unhealthy. To build trust, KFC Japan created ads depicting the most authentic version of Colonel Sanders's beginnings possible. The ads featured the quintessential southern mother and highlighted the KFC philosophy—the southern hospitality, old American tradition, and authentic home cooking. With "My Old Kentucky Home" by Stephen Foster playing in the background, the commercial showed Colonel Sanders's mother making and feeding her grandchildren KFC chicken made with eleven secret spices. It conjured up scenes of good home

KFC entered Japan through a joint ownership venture with Japanese conglomerate Mitsubishi.

cookin' from the American South, positioning KFC as wholesome, aristocratic food. In the end, the Japanese people could not get enough of this special American chicken. The campaign was hugely successful, and in less than eight years KFC expanded its presence from 400 locations to more than 1000. Most Japanese now know "My Old Kentucky Home" by heart.[35]

Joint ownership has certain drawbacks. The partners may disagree over investment, marketing, or other policies. Whereas many North American firms like to reinvest earnings for growth, local firms often prefer to take out these earnings; and whereas North American firms emphasize the role of marketing, local investors may rely on selling.

Direct Investment

Direct investment

Entering a foreign market by developing foreign-based assembly or manufacturing facilities.

The biggest involvement in a foreign market comes through **direct investment**—the development of foreign-based assembly or manufacturing facilities. If a company has gained experience in exporting and if the foreign market is large enough, foreign production facilities offer many advantages. The firm may have lower costs in the form of cheaper labour or raw materials, foreign government investment incentives, and freight savings. The firm may improve its image in the host country because it creates jobs. Generally, a firm develops a deeper relationship with government, customers, local suppliers, and distributors, allowing it to adapt its products to the local market better. Finally, the firm keeps full control over the investment and therefore can develop manufacturing and marketing policies that serve its long-term international objectives.

The main disadvantage of direct investment is that the firm faces many risks, such as restricted or devalued currencies, falling markets, or government changes. In some cases, a firm has no choice but to accept these risks if it wants to operate in the host country.

Standardized marketing mix

An international marketing strategy for using basically the same product, advertising, distribution channels, and other elements of the marketing mix in all the company's international markets.

Deciding on the Global Marketing Program

Companies that operate in one or more foreign markets must decide how much, if at all, to adapt their marketing mixes to local conditions. At one extreme are global companies that use a **standardized marketing mix**, selling largely the same products and using the same marketing approaches worldwide. At the other extreme is an

Adapted marketing mix
An international marketing strategy for adjusting the marketing mix elements to each international target market, bearing more costs but hoping for a larger market share and return.

adapted marketing mix. In this case, the producer adjusts the marketing mix elements to each target market, bearing more costs but hoping for a larger market share and return.

The question of whether to adapt or standardize the marketing mix has been much debated in recent years. On the one hand, some global marketers believe that technology is making the world a smaller place and that consumer needs around the world are becoming more similar. This paves the way for "global brands" and standardized global marketing. Global branding and standardization, in turn, result in greater brand power and reduced costs from economies of scale.

On the other hand, the marketing concept holds that marketing programs will be more effective if tailored to the unique needs of each targeted customer group. If this concept applies within a country, it should apply even more in international markets. Despite global convergence, consumers in different countries still have widely varied cultural backgrounds. They still differ significantly in their needs and wants, spending power, product preferences, and shopping patterns. Because these differences are hard to change, most marketers adapt their products, prices, channels, and promotions to fit consumer desires in each country.

However, global standardization is not an all-or-nothing proposition but rather a matter of degree. Most international marketers suggest that companies should "think globally but act locally"—that they should seek a balance between standardization and adaptation. These marketers advocate a "glocal" strategy in which the firm standardizes certain core marketing elements and localizes others. The corporate level gives global strategic direction; local units focus on the individual consumer differences across global markets. Simon Clift, head of marketing for global consumer goods giant Unilever, puts it this way: "We're trying to strike a balance between being mindlessly global and hopelessly local."[36]

L'Oreal Paris, the highly successful international personal care products company, operates this way. It markets truly global brands but adapts them to meet the cultural nuances of each local market. (See Real Marketing 18.1.) Similarly, McDonald's uses the same basic operating formula in its restaurants around the world but adapts its menu to local tastes. It uses chili sauce instead of ketchup on its hamburgers in Mexico. In Korea, it sells roast pork on a bun with a garlicky soy sauce. In India, where cows are considered sacred, McDonald's serves chicken, fish, vegetable burgers, Pizza McPuffs, McAloo Tikki (a spiced-potato burger), and the Maharaja Mac—two all-mutton patties, special sauce, lettuce, cheese, pickles, onions on a sesame-seed bun.[37]

In India, McDonald's serves chicken, fish, and vegetable burgers, and the Maharaja Mac—two all-mutton patties, special sauce, lettuce, cheese, pickles, onions, on a sesame-seed bun.

REAL MARKETING | 18.1

L'Oréal Paris: Adapting Global Brands to Local Cultures

ow does a French company with a British CEO successfully market a Japanese version of an American lipstick in Russia? Ask L'Oréal Paris, the hugely successful international personal care products company. Headquartered in France (L'Oréal Paris's Canadian offices are located in Montreal), L'Oréal Paris sells more than 14.5 billion euros' worth of cosmetics, hair-care products, fragrances, and perfumes each year in 120 countries across the globe, making it the world's biggest cosmetics company. That's 85 products sold

L'Oréal

Official Partner of the Cannes Festival.

Laetitia Casta   Jennifer Lopez   Virginie Ledoyen   Claudia Schiffer

Andie MacDowell   Milla Jovovich   Kate Moss   Gong-Li

L'Oréal has always had a
passion for beauty, film stars
and their unforgettable faces.
Today we offer the best
in beauty to all
the women of the world.
Because they're worth it.

L'ORÉAL
PARIS
Because I'm worth it.

What's the secret to L'Oreal's amazing international success? The company markets its brands globally by understanding how they appeal to cultural nuances in specific local markets. It has become the United Nations of Beauty.

every second, accounting for 13 percent of all cosmetics purchases made around the world.

L'Oréal's broad list of global brands includes, among others, Garnier, Maybelline, Redken, Lancome, Helena Rubinstein, Kiehl's, Biotherm, Softsheen-Carson, Vichy, and Ralph Lauren, and Giorgio Armani Parfums. Impressively, L'Oréal Paris has achieved twenty straight years of double-digit international profit growth. In 2004 alone, its sales jumped nearly 70 percent in China, 40 percent in Russia, and 30 percent in India.

What's the secret to L'Oréal's amazing international success? The company markets its brands globally by understanding how they appeal to cultural nuances in specific local markets. Says one observer, "L'Oréal is French only when it wants to be. The rest of the time, it's happy being African, Asian, or anything else that sells." The giant cosmetics retailer buys local brands, tweaks them, and exports them globally, presenting a different face to each consumer around the world.

For example, in 1996, the company bought the stodgy American makeup producer Maybelline. To reinvigorate and globalize the brand, it moved the unit's headquarters from Tennessee to New York City and added "New York" to the label. The resulting urban, street-smart, Big Apple image played well with the mid-price positioning of the workaday makeup brand. The makeover earned Maybelline a 20 percent market share in its category in Western Europe. The young urban positioning also hit the mark in Asia. As one industry analyst recounts:

> It's a sunny afternoon outside Parkson's department store in Shanghai, and a marketing battle is raging for the attention of Chinese women. Tall, pouty models in beige skirts and sheer tops pass out flyers promoting Revlon's new spring colors. But their effort is drowned out by L'Oréal's eye-catching show for its Maybelline brand. To a pulsing rhythm, two gangly models in shimmering Lycra tops dance on a podium before a large backdrop depicting the New York City skyline. The music stops, and a makeup artist transforms a model's face while a Chinese saleswoman

delivers the punch line. "This brand comes from America. It's very trendy," she shouts into her microphone. "If you want to be fashionable, just choose Maybelline." Few of the women in the crowd realize that the trendy "New York" Maybelline brand belongs to French cosmetics giant L'Oréal.

L'Oréal does more than simply pitch a western ideal. Instead, it recognizes different cultural views of beauty throughout the world. In fact, the company often goes out of its way to challenge conventional preconceptions of beauty. For example, the cover of a recent annual report featured a Japanese model with red hair and purple lipstick. Ads for Garnier hair dye posted in Moscow picture bleached-blonde African and Asian models.

L'Oreal's secret to good brand management is hitting the right audience with the right product. For L'Oréal, that means finding local brands, sprucing them up, positioning them for a specific target market, and exporting them to new customers all over the globe. To support that effort, the company tailors global marketing messages to local cultures around the world.

Beyond tailored messages and promotions, L'Oréal's products themselves must suit local needs across the very diverse range of people, cultures, and climates. Toward that end, as a share of revenues, L'Oréal spends 50 percent more than the industry average on product research and development. In a single year, it may file 500 patents. For example, research centres in Japan focus on the needs of Asian skin and hair types. The L'Oréal Institute for Ethnic Hair and Skin Research studies the needs of consumers of African descent. A climate-controlled wind tunnel in France provides insights into the impact of weather on cosmetics. R&D helps L'Oréal to formulate products for use in high-temperature, high-humidity environments like India. R&D also forms the basis for L'Oréal's fastest-growing segment—so-called active cosmetics that are biomedically engineered by the company's scientists and dermatologists.

A seemingly conflicting array of words could be used to describe L'Oréal's brands: scientific and spiritual, mass-market and word-of-mouth, French sophistication and urban street smarts, conformity and uniqueness, luxury and affordability. How can a company stake a claim to all parts of the spectrum on so many different dimensions? For L'Oréal, being different things to different people means "conveying the allure of different cultures through its many products," says an industry analyst. Notes another observer:

In sharp contrast to other ... western brands such as Coca-Cola and McDonalds, which offer only a single cultural icon, L'Oréal can entice consumers from around the world with multiple cosmopolitan images. L'Oréal products are found in chic shops, beauty salons, pharmacies, department stores, and even grocery stores. The company goes where the customer is and delivers what that customer wants—Vichy Laboratories in pharmacies, Giorgio Armani in upscale shops, mid-priced Maybelline at Shoppers Drug Mart. When the CEO recently addressed a UNESCO conference, nobody batted an eyelid when he described L'Oréal as "the United Nations of Beauty."

Sources: Quotes and other information from Gail Edmondson, "The Beauty of Global Branding," *Business Week*, June 28, 1999, pp.70–75; Richard Tomlinson, "L'Oréal's Global Makeover," *Fortune*, September 30, 2002, p. 141; EuroFile Backgrounder: L'Oréal, September 11, 2001, accessed online at www.hemscott.co.uk; "Top Global Brands," *Global Cosmetic Industry*, February 2003, pp. 28–34; "History: Making Sure the Hair Creams Taste OK," online at www.iwon.com (accessed July 2003); "Consumer Products Brief: L'Oreal," *Wall Street Journal*, February 23, 2004, p. 1; Vito J. Racanelli, "Touching Up," February 16, 2004, pp. 18–19; and information at www.loreal.com and www.lorealparis.ca/ (accessed June 2006).

Product

Straight product extension
Marketing a product in a foreign market without any change.

Five strategies allow for adapting product and promotion to a global market. (See Figure 18.3.)[38] We first discuss the three product strategies and then turn to the two promotion strategies.

Straight product extension means marketing a product in a foreign market without any change. Top management tells its marketing people, "Take the product as is and find customers for it." The first step, however, should be to find out whether foreign consumers use that product and what form they prefer.

Straight extension has been successful in some cases and disastrous in others. Kellogg cereals, Gillette razors, Heineken beer, and Black & Decker tools are all sold successfully in about the same form around the world. But General Foods introduced its standard powdered Jell-O in the British market only to find that British consumers prefer a solid wafer or cake form. Likewise, Philips began to

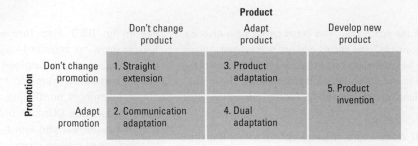

Figure 18.3 Five international product and promotion strategies

make a profit in Japan only after it reduced the size of its coffeemakers to fit into smaller Japanese kitchens and its shavers to fit smaller Japanese hands. Straight extension is tempting because it involves no additional product development costs, manufacturing changes, or new promotion. But it can be costly in the long run if products fail to satisfy foreign consumers.

Product adaptation

Adapting a product to meet local conditions or wants in foreign markets.

Product adaptation involves changing the product to meet local conditions or wants. For example, Procter & Gamble's Vidal Sassoon shampoos contain a single fragrance worldwide, but the amount of scent varies by country: more in Europe but less in Japan, where subtle scents are preferred. Gerber serves Japanese baby food fare that might turn the stomachs of many western consumers—local favourites include flounder and spinach stew, cod roe spaghetti, mugwort casserole, and sardines ground up in white radish sauce. And Finnish cellphone maker Nokia customized its 6100 series phone for every major market. Developers built in rudimentary voice recognition for Asia where keyboards are a problem and raised the ring volume so the phone could be heard on crowded Asian streets.

Product invention

Creating new products or services for foreign markets.

Product invention consists of creating something new for a specific country market. This strategy can take two forms. It might mean maintaining or reintroducing earlier product forms that happen to be well adapted to the needs of a given country. Volkswagen continued to produce and sell its old VW Beetle model in Mexico until just recently. Or a company might create a new product to meet a need in a given country. For example, Sony added the "U" model to its VAIO personal computer line to meet the unique needs of Japanese consumers, even though it wouldn't have much appeal in the United States and other world markets:

> The U may be the most "Japanese" product in the entire Sony VAIO line. The smallest laptop in the world, it is less than 7 inches wide, with a 6-inch diagonal screen, it makes an ordinary laptop look sumo sized. Sony noticed that rush-hour trains to Tokyo were simply too crowded to allow many commuters to use their laptops. "The only people in Tokyo who have the luxury of a lap are the first people on the train," says Mark Hanson, a Sony vice president. The point of the U, he explains, gripping its base with two hands and resting his thumbs on the keyboard, "is to give users the experience of what I'd call a standing computer." How would that translate into the North American? The cultural differences are daunting. Far more North Americans touch-type than do Japanese (a few Japanese characters convey a lot), and touch typists are likely to resist typing with their thumbs. And few North Americans face a Tokyo-type rush-hour commute.[39]

Promotion

Companies can either adopt the same promotion strategy they use in the home market or change it for each local market. Consider advertising messages. Some global companies use a standardized advertising theme around the world. Of course, even in highly standardized promotion campaigns, some small changes might be required to adjust for language and minor cultural differences. For example, Guy Laroche uses virtually the same ads for its Drakkar Noir fragrances in Europe as in Arab countries. However, it subtly tones down the Arab versions to meet cultural differences in attitudes toward sensuality.

Colours also are changed sometimes to avoid taboos in other countries. Purple is associated with death in most of Latin America; white is a mourning colour in Japan; and green is associated with jungle sickness in Malaysia. Even names must be changed. In Sweden, Helene Curtis changed the name of its Every Night Shampoo to Every Day because Swedes usually wash their hair in the morning. And Kellogg had to rename Bran Buds cereal in Sweden, where the name roughly translates as "burned farmer." (See Real Marketing 18.2 for more on language blunders in international marketing.)

Communication adaptation
A global communication strategy of fully adapting advertising messages to local markets.

Other companies follow a strategy of **communication adaptation**, fully adapting their advertising messages to local markets. Kellogg ads in North America promote the taste and nutrition of Kellogg's cereals versus competitors' brands. In France, where consumers drink little milk and eat little for breakfast, Kellogg's ads must convince consumers that cereals are a tasty and healthful breakfast. In India, where many consumers eat heavy, fried breakfasts, Kellogg's advertising convinces buyers to switch to a lighter, more nutritious breakfast diet.

Similarly, Coca-Cola sells its low-calorie beverage as Diet Coke in North America, the United Kingdom, and the Middle and Far East but as Light elsewhere. According to Diet Coke's global brand manager, in Spanish-speaking countries Coke Light ads position it as an object of desire, rather than as a way to feel good about yourself, as Diet Coke is positioned in North America. This "desire positioning" plays off research showing that "Coca-Cola Light is seen in other parts of world as a vibrant brand that exudes a sexy confidence."[40]

Media also need to be adapted internationally because media availability varies from country to country. TV advertising time is very limited in Europe, for instance, ranging from four hours a day in France to none in Scandinavian countries. Advertisers must buy time months in advance, and they have little control over airtimes. Magazines also vary in effectiveness. For example, magazines are a major medium in Italy and a minor one in Austria. Newspapers are national in the United Kingdom but are only local in Spain.[41]

Some companies standardize their advertising around the world, adapting only to meet cultural differences. Guy Laroche uses similar ads in Europe (left) and Arab countries (right) but tones down the sensuality in the Arab version—the man is clothed and the woman barely touches him.

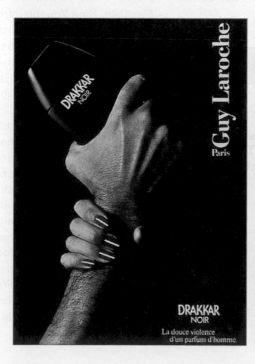

REAL MARKETING   **18.2**

Watch Your Language!

*M*any global companies have had difficulty crossing the language barrier, with results ranging from mild embarrassment to outright failure. Seemingly innocuous brand names and advertising phrases can take on unintended or hidden meanings when translated into other languages. Careless translations can make a marketer look downright foolish to foreign consumers.

We've all run across examples when buying products from other countries. Here's one from a firm in Taiwan attempting to instruct children on how to install a ramp on a garage for toy cars: "Before you play with, fix waiting plate by yourself as per below diagram. But after you once fixed it, you can play with as is and no necessary to fix off again." Many North American firms are guilty of such atrocities when marketing abroad.

The classic language blunders involve standardized brand names that do not translate well. When Coca-Cola first marketed Coke in China in the 1920s, it developed a group of Chinese characters that, when pronounced, sounded like the product name. Unfortunately, the characters actually translated to mean "bite the wax tadpole." Now, the characters on Chinese Coke bottles translate as "happiness in the mouth."

Several North American carmakers have had similar problems when their brand names crashed into the language barrier. Chevy's Nova translated into Spanish as *no va*—"it doesn't go." GM changed the name to Caribe and sales increased. Buick scrambled to rename its new LaCrosse sedan the Allure in Canada after learning that the name comes too close to a Québécois word for masturbation. And Rolls-Royce avoided the name Silver Mist in German markets, where *mist* means "manure." Sunbeam, however, entered the German market with its Mist Stick hair curling iron. As should have been expected, the Germans had little use for a "manure wand." A similar fate awaited Colgate when it introduced a toothpaste in France called Cue, the name of a notorious porno magazine.

One well-intentioned firm sold its shampoo in Brazil under the name Evitol. It soon realized it was claiming to sell a "dandruff contraceptive." An American company reportedly had trouble marketing Pet milk in French-speaking areas. It seems that the word *pet* in French means, among other things, "to break wind." Similarly, IKEA markets a children's workbench named Fartfull (the word means "speedy" in Swedish). Hunt-Wesson introduced its Big John products in Quebec as Gros Jos before learning that it means "big breasts" in French. This gaffe had no apparent effect on sales.

Interbrand of London, the firm that created household names such as Prozac and Acura, recently developed a brand-name "hall of shame" list, which contained these and other foreign brand names you're never likely to see inside the local A&P: Krapp toilet paper (Denmark), Crapsy Fruit cereal (France), Happy End toilet paper (Germany), Mukk yogurt (Italy), Zit

Some standardized brand names do not translate well globally.

lemonade (Germany), Poo curry powder (Argentina), and Pschitt lemonade (France).

Travellers often encounter well-intentioned advice from service firms that takes on meanings very different from those intended. The menu in one Swiss restaurant proudly stated, "Our wines leave you nothing to hope for." Signs in a Japanese hotel pronounced, "You are invited to take advantage of the chambermaid." At a laundry in Rome, it was, "Ladies, leave your clothes here and spend the afternoon having a good time." The brochure at a Tokyo car rental offered this sage advice: "When passenger of foot heave in sight, tootle the horn. Trumpet him melodiously at first, but if he still obstacles your passage, tootle him with vigour."

Advertising themes often lose—or gain—something in the translation. The Coors beer slogan "Get loose with Coors" in Spanish came out as "Get the runs with Coors." Coca-Cola's "Coke adds life" theme in Japanese translated into "Coke brings your ancestors back from the dead." The milk industry learned too late that its American advertising question "Got Milk?"

translated in Mexico as a more provocative "Are you lactating?" In Chinese, the KFC slogan "finger-lickin' good" came out as "Eat your fingers off." And Frank Perdue's classic line, "It takes a tough man to make a tender chicken," took on added meaning in Spanish: "It takes an aroused man to make a chicken affectionate." Even when the language is the same, word usage may differ from country to country. Thus, the British ad line for Electrolux vacuum cleaners—"Nothing sucks like an Electrolux"—would capture few customers in North America.

Sources: See David A. Ricks, "Perspectives: Translation Blunders in International Business," *Journal of Language for International Business,* 7:2, 1996, pp. 50–55; "But Will It Sell in Tulsa?" *Newsweek,* March 17, 1997, p. 8; Ken Friedenreich, "The Lingua Too Franca," *World Trade,* April 1998, p. 98; Sam Solley, "Developing a Name to Work Worldwide," *Marketing,* December 21, 2000, p. 27; Thomas T. Sermon, "Cutting Corners in Language Risky Business," *Marketing News,* April 23, 2001, p. 9; Lara L. Sowinski, "Ubersetzung, Traduzione, or Traduccion," *World Trade,* February 2002, pp. 48–49; Martin Croft, "Mind Your Language," *Marketing,* June 19, 2003, pp. 35–39; and Mark Lasswell, "Lost in Translation," *Business 2.0,* August 2004, pp. 68–70.

Price

Companies also face many problems in setting their international prices. For example, how might Black & Decker price its power tools globally? It could set a uniform price all around the world, but this amount would be too high a price in poor countries and not high enough in rich ones. It could charge what consumers in each country would bear, but this strategy ignores differences in the actual costs from country to country. Finally, the company could use a standard markup of its costs everywhere, but this approach might price Black & Decker out of the market in some countries where costs are high.

To deal with such issues, P&G adapts its pricing to local markets. For example, in Asia it has moved to a tiered pricing model.

When P&G first entered Asia, it used the approach that had made it so successful in the United States. It developed better products and charged slightly higher prices than competitors. It also charged nearly as much for a box of Tide or bottle of Pantene in Asia as it did in North America. But such high prices limited P&G's appeal in Asian markets, where most consumers earn just a few dollars a day. Two-thirds of China's population earns less than $25 per month. So in 2003 P&G adopted a tiered pricing strategy to help compete against cheaper local brands while also protecting the value of its global brands. It slashed Asian production costs, streamlined distribution channels, and reshaped its product line to create more affordable prices. For example, it introduced a 320-gram bag of Tide Clean White for 23 cents, compared with 33 cents for 350 grams of Tide Triple Action. Clean White doesn't offer such benefits as stain removal and fragrance, and it contains less advanced cleaning enzymes. But it costs less to make and outperforms every other brand at the lower price level. The results of P&G's new tiered pricing have been dramatic. Using the same approach for toothpaste, P&G now sells more Crest in China than in the United States.[42]

Twelve European Union countries have adopted the euro as a common currency, creating "pricing transparency" and forcing companies to harmonize their prices throughout Europe.

Regardless of how companies go about pricing their products, their foreign prices probably will be higher than their domestic prices for comparable products. A Gucci handbag may sell for $60 in Italy and $280 in Canada. Why? Gucci faces a *price escalation* problem. It must add the cost of transportation, tariffs, importer margin, wholesaler margin, and retailer margin to its factory price. Depending on these added costs, the product may have to sell for two to five times as much in another country to make the same profit. For example, a pair of Levi's jeans that sells for US$30 in the United States typically fetches US$63 in Tokyo and US$88 in Paris.

Another problem involves setting a price for goods that a company ships to its foreign subsidiaries. If the company charges a foreign subsidiary too much, it may end up paying higher tariff duties even while paying lower income taxes in that country. If the company charges its subsidiary too little, it can be charged with *dumping*. Dumping occurs when a company either charges less than its costs or less than it charges in its home market. For example, in 2005 a highly divisive war broke out based on accusations of dumping. On one side was the Canadian Bicycle Manufacturers Association, which represents two domestic manufacturers, Procycle Group Inc. and Raleigh Canada Ltd. In the face of rapidly rising imports, it sought substantial tariffs and import quotas applied to bikes imported into Canada (especially those from China). In the opposite trench was the Canadian Association of Specialty Bicycle Importers, which is supported by fourteen importers. It argued that such measures would be anti-competitive and would ultimately penalize Canadian consumers through higher prices. In May 2006, Jim Flaherty, Canada's Minister of Finance, and David Emerson, Minister of International Trade, jointly announced the decision not to impose the requested surcharges, saying, "After considering all of the information, it was determined that temporary protective tariffs simply wouldn't provide a competitive long-term solution.... We want to grow and strengthen our economy, and imposing these surtaxes would have increased costs for both Canadian retailers and consumers." [43]

Recent economic and technological forces have also had an impact on global pricing. For example, in the European Union, the transition to the euro is reducing the amount of price differentiation. As consumers recognize price differentiation by country, companies are being forced to harmonize prices throughout the countries that have adopted the single currency. Companies and marketers that offer the most unique or necessary products or services will be least affected by such "price transparency."

For Marie-Claude Lang, a 72-year-old retired Belgian postal worker, the euro is the best thing since bottled water—or French country sausage. Always on the prowl for bargains, Ms. Lang is now stalking the wide aisles of an Auchan hypermarket in Roncq, France, a 15-minute drive from her Wervick home. ... Ms. Lang has been coming to France every other week for years to stock up on bottled water, milk, and yogurt. But the launch of the euro ... has opened her eyes to many more products that she now sees cost less across the border. Today she sees that "saucisse de campagne," is cheaper "by about five euro cents," a savings she didn't notice when she had to calculate the difference between Belgian and French francs. At Europe's borders, the euro is turning into the coupon clipper's delight. Sure, price-conscious Europeans have long crossed into foreign territory to find everything from cheaper television sets to bargain bottles of Coca-Cola. But the new transparency is making comparisons a whole lot easier.[44]

The Internet will also make global price differences more obvious. When firms sell their wares over the Internet, customers can to see how much products sell for in different countries. They might even be able to order a given product directly from the company location or dealer offering the lowest price. This will force companies toward more standardized international pricing.

Distribution Channels

Whole-channel view
Designing international channels that take into account all the necessary links in distributing the seller's products to final buyers, including the seller's headquarters organization, channels among nations, and channels within nations.

The international company must take a **whole-channel view** of the problem of distributing products to final consumers. Figure 18.4 shows the three major links between the seller and the final buyer. The first link, the *seller's headquarters organization*, supervises the channels and is part of the channel itself. The second link, *channels between nations*, moves the products to the borders of the foreign nations. The third link, *channels within nations*, moves the products from their foreign entry point to the final consumers. Some North American manufacturers may think their job is done once the product leaves their hands, but they would do well to pay more attention to its handling within foreign countries.

Channels of distribution within countries vary greatly from nation to nation. First, there are the large differences in the *numbers and types of intermediaries* serving each foreign market. For example, a Canadian company marketing in China must operate through a frustrating maze of state-controlled wholesalers and retailers. Chinese distributors often carry competitors' products and frequently refuse to share even basic sales and marketing information with their suppliers. Hustling for sales is an alien concept to Chinese distributors, who are used to selling all they can obtain. Working with or getting around this system sometimes requires much time and investment.

Figure 18.4 Whole-channel concept for international marketing

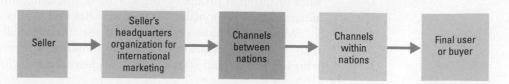

When Coke first entered China, for example, customers bicycled up to bottling plants to get their soft drinks. Many shopkeepers still don't have enough electricity to run soft drink coolers. Now, Coca-Cola has set up direct-distribution channels, investing heavily in refrigerators and trucks, and upgrading wiring so that more retailers can install coolers. The company has also built an army of more than 10 000 sales representatives that makes regular visits on resellers, often on foot or bicycle, to check on stocks and record sales. "Coke and its bottlers have been trying to map every supermarket, restaurant, barbershop, or market stall where a can of soda might be consumed," notes an industry observer. "Those data help Coke get closer to its customers, whether they are in large hypermarkets, Spartan noodle shops, or schools."[45]

Another difference lies in the *size and character of retail units* abroad. Whereas large-scale retail chains dominate the North American scene, much retailing in other countries is done by many small, independent retailers. In India, millions of retailers operate tiny shops or sell in open markets. Their markups are high, but the actual price is lowered through haggling. Supermarkets could offer lower prices, but supermarkets are difficult to build and open because of many economic and cultural barriers. Incomes are low, and people prefer to shop daily for small amounts rather than weekly for large amounts. They also lack storage and refrigeration to keep food for several days. Packaging is not well developed because it would add too much to the cost. These factors have kept large-scale retailing from spreading rapidly in developing countries.

Deciding on the Global Marketing Organization

Companies manage their international marketing activities in at least three different ways: Most companies first organize an export department, then create an international division, and finally become a global organization.

A firm normally gets into international marketing by simply shipping out its goods. If its international sales expand, the company organizes an *export department* with a sales manager and a few assistants. As sales increase, the export department can expand to include various marketing services so that it can actively go after business. If the firm moves into joint ventures or direct investment, the export department will no longer be adequate.

Many companies get involved in several international markets and ventures. A company may export to one country, license to another, have a joint ownership venture in a third, and own a subsidiary in a fourth. Sooner or later it will create *international divisions* or subsidiaries to handle all its international activity.

International divisions are organized in a variety of ways. An international division's corporate staff consists of marketing, manufacturing, research, finance, planning, and personnel specialists. It plans for and provides services to various operating units, which can be organized in one of three ways. They can be *geographical organizations*, with country managers who are responsible for salespeople, sales branches, distributors, and licensees in their respective countries. Or the operating units can be *world product groups*, each responsible for worldwide sales of different product groups. Finally, operating units can be *international subsidiaries*, each responsible for its own sales and profits.

Many firms have passed beyond the international division stage and become truly *global organizations*. They stop thinking of themselves as national marketers who sell abroad and start thinking of themselves as global marketers. The top cor-

Distribution channels vary greatly from nation to nation, as this picture from the streets of Beijing suggests.

porate management and staff plan worldwide manufacturing facilities, marketing policies, financial flows, and logistical systems. The global operating units report directly to the chief executive or executive committee of the organization, not to the head of an international division. Executives are trained in worldwide operations, not just domestic *or* international. The company recruits management from many countries, buys components and supplies where they cost the least, and invests where the expected returns are greatest.

In the twenty-first century, major companies must become more global if they hope to compete. As foreign companies successfully invade their domestic markets, companies must move more aggressively into foreign markets. They will have to change from companies that treat their international operations as secondary to companies that view the entire world as a single borderless market.

Reviewing the Concepts

Companies today, large or small, can no longer afford to pay attention only to their domestic market, regardless of its size. Many industries are global industries, and firms that operate globally achieve lower costs and higher brand awareness. At the same time, *global marketing* is risky because of variable exchange rates, unstable governments, protectionist tariffs and trade barriers, and several other factors. Given the potential gains and risks of international marketing, companies need a systematic way to make their global marketing decisions.

1. Discuss how the international trade system, economic, political-legal, and cultural environments affect a company's international marketing decisions.

A company must understand the global marketing environment, especially the international trade system. It

must assess each foreign market's economic, political-legal, and cultural characteristics. The company must then decide whether it wants to go abroad and consider the potential risks and benefits. It must decide on the volume of international sales it wants, how many countries it wants to market in, and which specific markets it wants to enter. This decision calls for weighing the probable rate of return on investment against the level of risk.

2. **Describe three key approaches to entering international markets.**

The company must decide how to enter each chosen market—whether through *exporting, joint venturing,* or *direct investment.* Many companies start as exporters, move to joint ventures, and finally make a direct investment in foreign markets. In *exporting,* the company enters a foreign market by sending and selling products through international marketing intermediaries (indirect exporting) or the company's own department, branch, or sales representative or agents (direct exporting). When establishing a *joint venture,* a company enters foreign markets by joining with foreign companies to produce or market a product or service. In *licensing,* the company enters a foreign market by contracting with a licensee in the foreign market, offering the right to use a manufacturing process, trademark, patent, trade secret, or other item of value for a fee or royalty.

3. **Explain how companies adapt their marketing mixes for international markets.**

Companies must also decide how much their products, promotion, price, and channels should be adapted for each foreign market. At one extreme, global companies use a *standardized marketing mix* worldwide. Others use an *adapted marketing mix,* in which they adjust the marketing mix to each target market, bearing more costs but hoping for a larger market share and return.

4. **Identify the three major forms of international marketing organization.**

The company must develop an effective organization for international marketing. Most firms start with an *export department* and graduate to an *international division.* A few become *global organizations,* with worldwide marketing planned and managed by the top officers of the company. Global organizations view the entire world as a single, borderless market.

Reviewing the Key Terms

Adapted marketing mix   715
Communication adaptation   719
Contract manufacturing   712
Countertrade   704
Direct investment   714
Economic community   700
Embargo   698
Exchange controls   698
Exporting   710
Global firm   697
Joint ownership   713

Joint venturing   712
Licensing   712
Management contracting   712
Nontariff trade barriers   698
Product adaptation   718
Product invention   718
Quota   698
Standardized marketing mix   714
Straight product extension   717
Tariff   698
Whole-channel view   723

Discussing the Concepts

1. Explain how the addition of the World Trade Organization as a functioning body has changed the nature of international commerce.

2. The NAFTA and EU regional free trade agreements have benefited both North America's and Europe's trading partners. But not all affected groups support these trading pacts. What are some of the concerns raised by groups opposed to such regional trade arrangements? What is your position—are you for, against, or uncertain?

3. Discuss the advantages and disadvantages of direct investment in a foreign market. Name two foreign markets where a household appliance manufacturer would be interested in investing, and two foreign markets where it would have no interest in investing. Support your answers.

4. Assume your boss has asked you for your opinion on how your company should enter the Japanese, South Korean, and Vietnamese markets with a new line of women's athletic shoes. Would you recommend enter-

ing with a standardized marketing mix or an adapted marketing mix? Explain.

5. Figure 18.4 (page 723) shows a "whole-channel view" of international distribution. Comment on why a company would or would not require the full range of international channel intermediaries discussed in the chapter.

6. The chapter discusses three forms of international marketing organizations. Identify the form for each of the following companies:

- Bank of Nova Scotia (hint: see its operations in Peru)
- General Motors
- Cervélo Cycles
- Nortel
- Alcan
- Starbucks
- Tembec

Applying the Concepts

1. Assess the joint-venture opportunities a software manufacturer would have available if it were looking to market to European Union countries.

2. Form a small group and suppose that you are members of BlockBuster's international division. Chris

Wyatt, president of the international division, wants your group to prepare a memo outlining the potential cultural, political, and economic issues facing the company if it expands directly into Lebanon. (Note: You already have a franchise dealer in Israel.)

Focus on Technology

Companies that conduct business internationally face many language skill requirements. Speaking the language of the host country is one requirement, but there are others. For example, how should the company go about converting its website and marketing literature? It's time to talk to Systran Language Translation Technologies or a similar language technology company. For a sample of what Systran does, visit www.systransoft.com/ and try the "free" translation tools on the home page. Now visit http://french.about.com/library/bl-onlinetranslators.htm and read the article on machine

translation. When you are finished with the demo and the article, respond to the following questions:

1. What are the advantages of language translation technologies like Systran's?

2. What problems might you encounter with such language translation technologies?

3. Given these advantages and problems, what can a company do to increase the chances of successfully translating its websites and marketing literature?

Focus on Ethics

Is it a gift or a bribe? North American businesses operating internationally often face this question. In addition to the Canadian *Corruption of Foreign Public Officials Act*, the American *Fair Practices Corruption Act* (FPCA), and the *International Anti-Bribery and Fair Competition Act*, there are a number of international laws designed to fight corruption and bribery in the global business community. Transparency International Canada works hard to bring the issue of corruption to the attention of Canadian businesses. Canada has been falling in Transparency International's Corruption Perceptions Index. We are now in fourteenth place. (See

ww1.transparency.org/cpi/2005/cpi2005_infocus.html#cpi, accessed September, 2006).

1. How is corruption defined by Transparency International?

2. According to Canadian legislation, when is a gift a bribe?

3. Why is bribery seen as such a negative practice? How does it harm companies? How does it harm people in countries where bribery is rampant?

Video Case
Nivea

In 1911, Nivea launched its first line of body care products, capitalizing on an innovation that created a new generation of skin cream. Today Nivea products are well known and widely used in more than 150 countries around the world. In each of those countries, the characteristic Nivea blue signifies a consistent promise—high-quality, gentle body care products. Nivea's strong, consistent brand image is one of the company's most valuable assets.

Despite Nivea's worldwide presence, a quick survey reveals that, regardless of where they live, Nivea's customers believe that the company's products are locally manufactured and marketed. Why? Because Nivea carefully adjusts the marketing mix to cater to local cultures and preferences. This globally consistent

but locally focused marketing campaign has produced phenomenal results. To date, the company has sold more than 11 billion tins of the traditional Nivea Creme.

After viewing the video featuring Nivea, answer the following questions about the company and the global marketplace.

1. Does Nivea offer a standardized marketing mix or an adapted marketing mix?

2. Visit Nivea's Website, www.nivea.com, and tour the sites for several different countries. How does Nivea market its products differently in different countries? How does the company maintain the consistency of its brand?

Online Media Resources

Video Short
Log on to your Companion Website at **www.pearsoned.ca/kotler** to view the video segment related to the Video Case above.

Case Pilot
Log on to your Companion Website at **www.pearsoned.ca/kotler** to sharpen your case analysis skills and take the Case Pilot Challenge!

Company Case
Synovate—Building a Global Business and a Global Brand

As major companies become more global in scope, their needs for market research also became more global. For example, a packaged-goods company headquartered in Toronto might need information on consumer buying habits and attitudes in Brazil, the Philippines, and South Africa. While collecting information from independent research agencies in each country is possible, it is difficult and time consuming. It requires knowledge of the reputable suppliers, an understanding of what is appropriate in terms of cultural sensitivity and sampling, and what is possible in terms of data collection methods. Even then it will be difficult to ensure data consistency and reporting that highlights both similarities and differences across markets.

Yet not very long ago, the market research industry worldwide was populated by relatively small, independent firms whose research capabilities covered their national territory or perhaps their region, but little more. It is not surprising, therefore, that the market industry began to consolidate quickly. Take the case of Market Facts. In 2000, it was a marketing research firm with operations in Canada and the United States. Although it had a fifty-year history of research excellence and considerable brand equity because of its ability to meet clients' needs with high-quality services and proprietary research products, it could provide wholly controlled research within only a limited region of the world.

Market Facts began to globalize in the 1990s by purchasing several market research companies around the world—from Canada to Latin America. It also attempted to globalize by establishing informal relationships with selected overseas research companies. This proved ineffective. Indeed it became clear that the only way to be a global research organization was to acquire or be acquired. Thus, when Aegis Group PLC, headquartered in London, U.K., came knocking with an offer to make Market Facts the first acquisition in their plan to create a new global research group, the Market Facts directors were ready to recommend the takeover to shareholders. The deal was closed in 2001. The Aegis Group was a holding a company that owned many media planning companies. Its interest in expanding and acquiring research companies was born from its need for market research to measure the success of media.

Over the next three years, Aegis Group acquired numerous companies and soon had seventy-two offices that operated in forty-three countries including Market Facts, Asia Market Intelligence, Research Fact, BAIGlobal, IMR, MarkTrend, Motoresearch, MS&P, Sample Surveys, Strategy Research Corporation, Tandem Research Associates, INNER, MEMRB, Demoscopie, Market&More, and Pegram Walters. Now Market Facts' clients had access to research all over the world. But how could Market Facts convince the client they would get the same quality research and service from the other units in the Aegis Group? Nothing about them seemed familiar, even their names. The Aegis Group had brought companies whose names were based on the founder's names, or were names that described the research agency's market locations, or were names that described what the firm did. Clearly something had to be done.

The Decision to Rebrand

It quickly became clear that if the Aegis Group of research companies was to be successful, it would need a new, compelling brand name to link all these "newly adopted children." The new brand name had to be unique so it could be legally registered and trademarked in fifty-five countries. Ideally it also needed to be something around which a meaningful identity could be created for clients and staff.

To help create a sense of ownership of the new name among the various agencies, the company initiated an internal process to develop the new brand. It started by launching a website on which staff from around the world could contribute ideas. Prizes

for the best suggestions for a new name were offered. More than 2000 submissions were received. They were vetted by a Paris legal firm to see which ones could be legally protected in key markets. The list of suggestions rapidly became shorter since many of the suggested names were being used by other companies. The new name also had to be pronounceable in all languages. Many of the more memorable suggestions were either too long or had "hard" consonants. (For example, Japanese people have trouble saying the letter L, so all names starting with L were omitted.) The new name couldn't be offensive or rude in any formal language or in common slang. The name also had to be meaningful and reflect what the company stood for both to clients and to the employees of the different agencies around the world.

It wasn't long before the list was narrowed down to fifteen alternatives. Adrian Chedore, Chief Executive Officer of the Aegis Research Division, had the daunting task of choosing the best option. One name seemed to have a lot of cachet—GIA (short for Global Intelligence and Analysis). However, a name search revealed that GIA was also the name of an Algerian terrorist group that reportedly butchered babies. Another name then rose to the top of the list—Synovate—a combination of Synergy and Innovate. As Chedore notes, "The name blends the themes of the firm's business strategy: synergy and innovation. The company looks for synergy across business units and seeks continuous innovation." As a final step, a tag line was created to accompany the name and new logo: "Research reinvented." A copy of the new brand name, logo, and tag line is presented below:

To implement the rebranding effort, a global brand team was formed. Alicia Kan, the Global Communications Director from Asia Market Intelligence headquartered in Hong Kong, was the team leader. She was joined by Kate Permut from the U.S. and other colleagues from around the world. They met frequently in person and via conference call or online when in-person meetings were impossible.

The decision to rebrand wasn't universally welcomed by all members of the Aegis family of research companies, to put it mildly! Many of the firms that had been acquired by Aegis were among the top research firms in their own country. They felt there was a lot of heritage in the individual brand names it had taken them so long to build. Despite their years of involvement in the marketing industry, many agencies expressed the opinion that the rebranding effort was a "waste" of money.

Some employees didn't like the name Synovate—they thought it sounded too much like a pharmaceutical company. Market Facts was one of the member companies that was the most resistant to the change in brand. Not only did some of the employees believe that they had built a lot of equity in the old brand name, they clearly mourned its passing. Several managers were also concerned about the pace of change that was taking place. Not only was Market Facts no longer an independent company, but its staff now had to rapidly undergo a name change too! Thus, the rebranding team knew they couldn't just tell individual agencies what their new name would be. There had to be an internal campaign to "sell it" to staff.

The timeline for the change was a tight one, as dictated by Adrian Chedore and the Aegis Group senior management team—six months from start to finish. Market Facts leaders wanted the process to slow down. They believed they needed at least a year and a half before the change could be implemented. Some believed their clients would be concerned about a new corporate name. Market research projects often have long timelines. Market Facts had some big projects with clients that were being conducted over a three-year period. Two of Market Facts's major clients were the U.S. government and the military. Selling market research contracts to these organizations often required lead times of two to three years. For government suppliers, changing names midstream might require yet-to-be-determined legalities and paperwork.

It was clear the pace of change was causing members of Market Facts and some of the other Aegis member companies a lot of emotional anxiety. There were a lot of unknowns. For example, how would global accounts be managed? By which office? How would a global bonus system be created? Although many recognized that there were significant benefits of being in a global company, some perceived that few systems had been put in place to manage such an entity.

Despite all the concerns from Market Facts and many others, global management and the branding team were determined to press ahead with an aggressive re-branding schedule. Chedore explains, "The decision was made. We were convinced it was right, but even if we were wrong, delay could only lead to more uncertainty. Our goal was a commitment to a new global structure. Commitment and delay don't go together: The process had to be swift."

Phased Rollout Campaign

Bringing so many diverse agencies under one global brand took much more than selecting a name and a new logo. It was decided, for legal purposes, that each agency had to announce the name change on the same date. Signage, phone directories, invoice forms, and business cards had to be reprinted. No one could keep the old name on budgets or paycheques because legally their old entities would cease to exist.

The most important change to be made, however, was the change to the employees' minds—this was the front on which the success of the new brand would be won or lost. Everyone in every agency around the world had to be involved. The president of each local agency had to be brought on board and made part of the change. This was one of the team's biggest challenges—often the local research agency leaders thought that they were better marketers than those in charge of the rebranding effort. Thus, internal coordination was as important as the development of communications materials to targeted clients. For example, receptionists at each office had to be fully informed and know what to say. They needed to know how to answer myriad customer questions such as "What ever happened to Market Facts?"

The team knew they had to walk a fine line. The directors of all the research agencies were very entrepreneurial, confident, and successful people who were used to making decisions themselves in their local marketplaces. Though it was important for the team to make decisions that would keep the global brand consistent, they had to avoid the impression that branding decisions were being rammed down the various agencies' throats. It was essential, therefore, to make each agency office, manager, and employee feel part of the process.

The team also had to ask, "Who are our stakeholders, and who should know about the brand change?" They had to consider the messages they were going to convey to these key people. It was quickly decided that internal staff at each agency and its clients needed different messages. For staff, the key message centred on the advantages of being part of bigger family. For clients, the promise became not "business as usual" but "business as better," multiplied by other dimensions, in other words "research reinvented."

Once the key messaging had been determined, the question became, How best to disseminate these messages? The team decided on a two-step process: (1) a period of endorsement during which the agencies would inform their clients of the upcoming name change, followed by (2) a launch stage. Using a two-stage process meant that the team would need to develop two sets of materials, which would be expensive. However, the team members were convinced the agencies needed these steps to get fully on board.

The team became unhappy with the terminology describing the phases, however. As Alicia noted, "Endorsement sounds like a celebrity promoting cornflakes, so we decided to rename the phases 'engagement' and 'marriage.'" This new terminology was much more understandable by the various employees around the world because the terms captured universal concepts. The team could ask questions such as, "It is up to you how you want to do this. Do you want to celebrate your local brand name change at the point of the 'engagement party' or on the date of the 'actual marriage'?" Some agencies put up posters with two rings, which tied in nicely with the new logo design. As the different agencies started to get on board, the complaints about rebranding lessened.

In June 2002, the name change was announced, and the "engagement" period began. The Aegis Group's staff magazine announced, "The new branding will allow all of the Aegis research companies to be united and finally dine at the global table, whilst servicing the demands of large international marketers. An increasing requirement of international clients is consistency and quality of process, both at local and global levels. One single and distinctive brand will be used throughout Aegis' market research activities to reinforce this message to worldwide markets."

The Launch

On January 6, 2003, the new brand name was officially launched. The agencies around the world held parties to announce their new name and "marriage." The effort took only four months from beginning to end. Though some agencies felt rushed, the rebranding team believed that if they made the engagement too long, they would get stuck in limbo. They knew that if the

process was too lengthy, the resistance to change would grow. Some agencies might even begin to bet that nothing would change after all. After January 6, 2003, all newly acquired research companies would go through the same process to change their names to the new global brand—Synovate.

The rebranding team used a wide variety of promotion techniques to make the message about the new brand sink in. They communicated internally through their company magazine and over a new website. Two corporate identity manuals were developed (one for the engagement period and one for the final brand launch) that outlined the requirements for logo usage in different print media, colour processes, paper sizes, etc. For external communications, extensive trade advertising, direct mail, and personal selling was undertaken. It often took face-to-face talks with agencies and clients to bring the message home.

Was the effort a success? Undoubtedly, on many fronts! Synovate is now ranked in the eighth position in world in terms of its market share in the research industry. No major clients were lost. The successful development of the new global brand was seen as the essential foundation to this growth. However, there were some employees who couldn't or wouldn't adapt to the new globally oriented brand and culture. They left the company when they found that it wasn't easy accepting the new global brand and the globalized world of marketing research.

The Keys to Success

There were several keys to the success of this major rebranding initiative. First was senior management support. The CEO, Adrian Chedore, was the chief cheerleader. Anytime he went to any office around the world, he talked about what the new brand meant and the benefits of being part of a global enterprise. As Alicia Kan exclaimed, "Adrian was behind it 150 percent. He owned the process and a lot of the communications came from him. Every employee had a letter from him."

According to Kan, Chedore handled a lot of important issues and concerns with fairness and conviction. For example, agencies came forward and said that the new brand didn't fit their market. Others, such as the agencies in Japan, didn't like the look of the new business cards. They believed they couldn't have a card that was horizontal. In Japan, cards must be vertical. Others thought the cards needed to be larger since they had to list all their offices. Another group wanted fold-over cards. To resolve this issue Adrian put all the cards on the table. There was a huge variety in all shapes and sizes. Chedore made it clear that everyone was going to have one card, and that they just had to get over their concerns. Being one company meant that there would be a single "look" to everyone's business cards worldwide.

Chedore believes that commitment to a totally unified approach is critical. "There can be no democracy in branding—you have to be single-minded and uncompromising," he says. "By all means hear everyone out, but you don't put it to a vote."

The second critical success factor was the single-minded belief from all of top management, including the chief financial officer, that proper branding principles should be applied to the business and that the brand should be global. The rebranding effort was begun during a period when people were beginning to realize that branding was as important in the business-to-business world as it was in the consumer arena. Management shared the belief that it was important to build a "branded house" versus a "house of individual brands."

Synovate's lack of a global headquarters is key to its strength but also makes branding all the more important, Chedore stresses. "Our identity doesn't emanate from a central head office but involves and reflects all of our people across the world. A unified brand and clear positioning are vital elements in building our corporate reputation and culture, both externally and internally."

Third, having a cooperative global brand team was another pivotal success factor. The team sought input from the agencies around the world right from the start. It had to listen to concerns thoughtfully and carefully, but it also had to position the value and advantage of a global brand consistently and clearly. Before trying to get the different agencies to change their mindset, the team did their homework first. They understood the brand DNA. The brand meanings were built around the core competencies of the firm.

Rather than trying to mimic the competition, the rebranding team decided the key to success was building on its own unique corporate strengths. It took more than ten rounds of questioning by the brand team before they achieved a critical insight that articulated this difference. Every suggestion as to what constituted Synovate's distinctive competence already seemed to be part of what was done by five or ten other players in the industry. Just as the team was ready to give up, it hit on the insight that the corporation's key competence lay in the capabilities and char-

acteristics of their own people. Synovate believed its people were younger, more dynamic, and more motivated than those in other firms. The more the team talked, the more these human traits were seen as a major competitive advantage. The team knew Synovate had the most "curious research people," and this was dramatically and demonstrably different from elsewhere in the research industry.

This was actually an innovative branding idea. Market researchers sometimes had a negative view of themselves, in which stereotypes, labelling researchers as "the accountants of the marketing world," had been internalized. Researchers were sometimes viewed as boring, dull, and grey, compared with the flamboyant stereotypes held for advertising creatives and other marketing jobs. The Synovate brand team knew their emerging firm was different. They did leading-edge market research that gave their clients a competitive advantage. "Curiosity in action" became the Synovate theme.

This insight gave the global branding team an authentic and credible brand story to tell. It was this story that resonated with the international offices and branches. It was also the key to the internal marketing campaign. It gave researchers in all the agencies a unique way of seeing themselves. To bring the lesson home, the team needed real examples—examples of people within the Synovate agencies who really were curious. They found a researcher in France who was tasked with studying customer satisfaction for a car dealership. He scratched his car with a screwdriver and then drove to the shop to see what the dealership would do. Now that is living the problem! Lots of similar stories emerged and it was these stories that gave people within the different agencies themselves the proof that they were different. It helped them see themselves in a new light.

Today, Synovate is truly a global company. Its global research solutions include brand tracking, business consulting, business-to-business research, concept testing, customer relationship management, employee relationship management, multiethnic marketing research, international research coordination, Internet data collection, pricing research, product testing, sales forecasting, and youth/children research.

Synovate has redefined the way a global company is run, says Chedore. "For most companies a global structure is simply about having lots of dots on a map, with control exercised from one centre and the culture based around one national identity. But we have developed a new kind of company—without a national identity, built on borderless cooperation across geographies, practices and teams. We have built a structure that makes Synovate an exciting and meaningful place to work wherever you are based and that fits the needs of global clients wherever they are based."

If you want to see how truly global the company has become, ask any member of the firm where their headquarters is located. They'll respond, "We don't have any single HQ location. ... We can work in any location. ... We have centres of excellence around the world. ... You can get the same service anywhere." It's this type of belief that has helped Synovate win leading global accounts, such as the one from Coke—itself a truly global borderless company.

Questions

1. What are the pros and cons of global branding for a company such as Synovate?

2. Why was internal marketing as important as external marketing in this case?

3. Alicia Kan continues to lead the global branding initiative. Synovate has just acquired a South African research firm. Before being acquired, the agency's website generated 22 percent of the agency's business. Local managers were upset when told that they would have to rely on the Synovate corporate website after the merger. As Alicia, how would you respond to this issue? What criteria would you use in making the decision to migrate their website to the Synovate site?

Sources: Peggy Cunningham wrote this case based on Synovate company materials and interviews with Alicia Kan, Global Head of Communication, Synovate; Kate Permut, Marketing Consultant (formerly of Synovate); and Chris Fjelddahl, Eight Partnership. She is very grateful for their time and insight. Gloria Mellinger, "Research Profile: Synovate," *WorldOpinion* Friday, April 25, 2003.

ROCKY MOUNTAIN SOAP COMPANY

Cam Baty's heart was racing as he pedalled his mountain bike toward the summit of the ridge. His thoughts were racing too. He was hoping that this long, hard ride would help him find clarity around the Rocky Mountain Soap brand. He knew the decisions he made now would be critical to the ongoing success of the company.

Rocky Mountain Soap is a small company on the verge of a major growth spurt. It produces handmade soap and other personal care products in its 370-square-metre Canmore, Alberta, factory. The company currently owns and operates three retail outlets in Alberta—one in Canmore, one in Banff, and one in the West Edmonton Mall. Cam and his wife, Karina, planned to open two more retail stores in the next few months if suitable locations can be found. These would be followed by four more outlets in 2007. In the 2008–2009 period, Cam and Karina hoped to establish seven new outlets each year.

Karina Birch and Cam Baty, founders of Rocky Mountain Soap, with their daughter, Ruby.

Company History

Cam has always loved the outdoors. He first worked as a fishing guide in the Arctic after he graduated with a Bachelor of Commerce degree from Ryerson University. This is where he met Karina. He then moved to the Canmore area but continued to manage fishing lodges in the Arctic. Karina had recently graduated from the University of Alberta with a Bachelor of Commerce degree and had started a small human resources consulting business in the Canmore area.

Cam and Karina were regular customers of the small soap company located in the town. Karina had always been interested in skin care, and she liked the company's products. When they were in the store buying Christmas presents, they found out the company was for sale. In early 1995, they scraped together the $45 000 purchase price, using $15 000 of their own money, a $15 000 loan, and a $15 000 line of credit. Karina ran the business on her own for the first year while Cam continued to manage the Arctic fishing lodges.

Rocky Mountain Soap's brand logo—a stylized drawing of the Three Sisters Peaks, mountains that can be seen rising behind Canmore, the company name, and the tagline, which appears above the drawing, "be kind, be real, be natural"—capture Cam and Karina's beliefs. First, they are kind to suppliers, customers, bankers, staff, and all other people the company has relationships with. "Be real" captures their desire not just to sell genuine products but also to achieve real growth and real profitability. "Be natural" reflects their commitment to stick to 100 percent natural ingredients in all the products the company produces and sells. The brand logo appears at left.

From its inception, the idea behind Rocky Mountain Soap was a desire to make luxurious soap by hand. The soaps would have natural scents and the healing properties associated with nature. Cam and Karina's goal has been to only use 100 percent natural ingredients. These include the finest essential oils,[1] real grains, and berries. Each soap is targeted toward a specific skin type, a specific user problem, or use situation. Take just one example from the 27 specialized soaps Rocky Mountain Soap produces: Pumpkin Patch soap. It is an unscented soap aimed at people with rough, inflamed skin, sensitive skin, dry skin, or eczema. The soap contains wheat germ, which mildly exfoliates. Pumpkin pulp protects and soothes sore rough skin and helps prevent flaking. Sweet almond oil helps to heal skin exposed to harsh climates and is extremely moisturizing. In combination, the ingredients in the soap oxygenate and repair damaged skin.

Throughout the history of the company, Cam and Karina have stayed true to their ideal of employing natural ingredients. When they discovered that some of the food, drug, and cosmetic colours they used in some of their products were not natural, they stopped using them and decided to rely on the herbs and spices used in the products to give them their distinctive hues.

The packaging used for many of the products is distinctive. When Cam and Karina bought the company, the body butters were sold in clear packages more commonly used to package men's deodorant. Though they kept the container, they knew that some consumers might be confused by the packaging. Thus, they worked on their brand logo and the labels to make it clear what the product actually is. In all their packaging, they also use recycled or recyclable containers where possible. The labelling and packaging of some of the key products is displayed in **Exhibit 1**.

In addition to their focus on natural ingredients, the couple work to be environmentally sensitive in all of their operations. They avoid excess packaging, and as there is the potential to generate considerable waste when the soap is cut, they even developed a product that incorporates the waste from other soaps—Avalanche soap. It is brightly marbled soap made from the trimmings from the other soaps. All of their soaps are produced, cut, and packaged by hand in the Canmore factory.

Rocky Mountain Soap is very much a family business rooted in its communities, and all of Rocky Mountain Soap's employees feel as if they are part of the family. Cam and Karina care about their employees, and their employees return this respect in a heartfelt fashion. For example, even though Rocky Mountain Soap is a small company, it is in the process of launching a daycare program to support its

---

1 Essential oil is oil derived from a natural substance, such as lavender or almonds, and is usually used either for its healing properties or as a perfume. Essential oils have a long history of providing a variety of therapeutic benefits, and many of these benefits have been confirmed through scientific research. The use of essential oils in a cosmetic, for example, will have an antiseptic and antimicrobial action, as well as a healing and soothing effect on the skin. Essential oils help the skin and hair detoxify, drain, heal, and regenerate. Essential oils are readily absorbed through the skin and hair follicles, and carried to all parts of the body. Their effects can last from a few hours to a few days. Essential oils are also used in some pharmaceuticals and many over-the-counter remedies. For example, cough medicines often contain one or two essential oils: camphor or eucalyptus. Essential oils are also used in the practice of aromatherapy.

EXHIBIT 1 Packaging and Labelling—Selected Products

employees. Everyone who works for the company is very devoted to it, and everyone is enthusiastic about the company's future prospects. Everyone is determined to do whatever it takes to make the company a success. Many of the employees are pictured on the company website, and the contribution each employee makes to the company is recognized. Rocky Mountain Soap is very much embedded in the local community, and Cam and Karina give a lot back to the communities in which they operate. Whenever anyone comes and asks in person, they give products and support to community organizations and causes.

Inspired by the book *The Great Game of Business*, by Jack Stack, which focuses on the concept of open-book management and the breaking down of barriers between the "we" of management and the "they" of workers, Cam and Karina wanted to ensure that their employees shared in the success of the company. Thus, they introduced profit-sharing about two years ago. They used the plan offered by WestJet as a model and adapted it to their own operations. All of the workshop staff and retailer managers benefit from the program. It is one reason the company's employees are so committed to the on-going success of the company and why everyone works to make decisions and provide the energy and service that is essential to making the company a success.

Customer Care

Rocky Mountain Soap takes pride in the fact that it stands firmly behind all its handmade products. Karina, Cam, and the other Rocky Mountain Soap employees test and use the products themselves, as do their circle of family and friends. As they note on their website, "We are committed to delivering the utmost in care and service to our valued customers. Because our products are made by hand, we know and understand every single ingredient in every single product we offer for sale. We offer an 'unconditional money-back guarantee' on everything we sell. That means that if there is part of our product that does not meet your expectations, we will cheerfully refund your money." Customers are usually highly satisfied with the company's products, however, so refunds are rarely requested. More often, customers try one product and are so impressed with its effectiveness that they then start purchasing other products from the different lines.

Rocky Mountain Soap offers products for everyone in the family—from dry to oily skin—baby skin to mature skin. Cam and Karina believe their primary purchasers are women aged 25 to 55. They purchase products for their personal use and for other family members who may have special needs. There is some doubt, however, about the true nature of their target market. Some believe the primary purchasers are women over 30; others see the stores filled with younger people, both women and men. Because of their locations, tourists of all nationalities also seem to be attracted to the stores and the products. The company is starting to build a database to better understand its purchasers.

Rocky Mountain Soap has generated two databases of its customers: one is generated for retail customers who enter contests to win gift baskets; the other is generated through the company's online operations, surveys, and shipping lists. These databases help the company better understand where its customers come from and who is buying its products. The databases are also used for customer contact and for special mailings. In the markets where there are retail stores, for example, a card is sent in the customer's birthday month and he or she is offered a free bar of soap.

Customers often become the best salespersons for Rocky Mountain Soap's products, generating word-of-mouth endorsements for the company. Many customers have also provided testimonials about the products, and some of these can be found on the company's website (www.rockymountainsoap.com/message/1036832/1000144).

Rocky Mountain Soap also works to create a customer community. It uses its *Soap Dish News*, a monthly newsletter sent electronically to all registered customers that provides the latest updates on the company's products, promotions, recipes, contests, and trends in natural products and aromatherapy. It posts an online survey on its website to solicit feedback from customers about their product needs, and it seeks information about any problems the customer may have encountered. It offers its local retail customers loyalty points, which they can redeem for products.

Because many of Rocky Mountain Soap's products serve highly specialized needs, providing customers with information to help them solve problems is also essential to Rocky Mountain Soap's success. It takes a knowledgeable, service-oriented sales staff to sell these products and explain their benefits. If you are lucky enough to be able to visit one of the company-owned retail outlets, you will find friendly, highly knowledgeable staff who can explain in detail the features of each and every product. Store managers work their way up through the company so that they become thoroughly knowledgeable about all the products the company sells. As noted earlier, store managers benefit from the company's profit-sharing plan. To further motivate staff in its retail stores to operate as a team, Cam and Karina use a sales bonus plan for the retail stores. If the store increases its sales over its target level, everyone working in the store gets an increase in their hourly wage. The increase varies in accordance with the level of sales achieved. Cam and Karina believe this is a more effective motivator than individual bonuses, which may turn some staff into overly aggressive salespeople.

New-Product Development

Everyone at Rocky Mountain Soap listens carefully to the customers and works to respond to customer needs. Karina is in charge of new-product development. She relies heavily on feedback about what is selling well from the retail store managers and the sales staff who serve the wholesale customers. When she wants to experiment to see how well a new product might sell, she will search for a competitive product and stock it in the stores. For example, Rocky Mountain Soap is thinking of adding natural candles and face creams to its product line. Thus, it first stocked products made by other firms in its retail stores to see how customers respond. If sales take off, the company will develop its own product formulation. All new products must meet the company's strict standards of using only natural ingredients and must be able to be produced at a cost that will allow them to sell profitably at prices customers can afford.

Customers are the source of many product ideas. Rather than doing formal research to support new-product development, Karina relies on customers and employees to build a strong case for the need for a new product. She then does the concept development. She works with a chemist who develops the product formulations, blends the essential oils and other ingredients, and ensures the safety of the product. Karina, Cam, and the other employees then test the product themselves and put it on trial with their store managers. The formulation may be altered many times before it is sold to consumers. For example, a new salt scrub went through seventeen versions before it was launched.

Pumpkin Patch Soap and Unscented Body Butter, two products that help people treat eczema, were developed using this process in response to customer needs. Summer Lemonade Soap was created by a Canmore grade 8 student, Rie Nakamura.

Learning from Experience—Glacier Product Line Failure

Not all product launches have been successful. In early 2003, while promoting the company's products at The Soap Maker's Guild Conference, Cam and Karina saw an opportunity for RMSC to enter the mass market. There appeared to be growing preference on the part of consumers for all-natural bath and body products. Not wanting to risk damage to its core brand and its own specialty retail operations, Rocky Mountain Soap Company launched a new brand, Glacier, aimed at the mass marketplace. The line included soaps, body butters, bath salts, and massage oils. Like the company's other products, Glacier products were 100 percent natural, handmade, and used many of the same ingredients as the Rocky product line. Glacier products had unique recipes, however, and different branding, labelling, and packaging.

Cam believed timing was critical. He wanted to launch the new product before another natural-products company saw the opportunity. Cam hoped the new products would earn $800 000 in revenues in the first year.

At first the product line seemed destined for success. Pharmasave, Save-On-Foods, and Value Drug Mart signed on to stock the products. Various health food stores also seemed interested in the products. The health food chains appeared to be an especially appealing target since they already marketed to clientele who were willing to pay for natural products, and they would not require as much education regarding the benefits of natural products. However, Cam quickly found he had to rethink his distribution model. Rather than dealing with individual sales representatives from Rocky Mountain Soap, health food stores preferred to deal with one distributor. However, such distributors, with their demands for a 4 percent advertising allowance, a 15- to 22-percent distribution fee, and a 3 percent redistribution fee, were not affordable if Rocky Mountain Soap wanted to keep its price points and profit margins. It found a compromise and subcontracted a team of sales representatives from Speyeglass Lifestyle Corporation, a company specializing in the health food industry. The new sales representatives were paid straight commission, but they generated only a total of $10 000 in sales revenue. Further complications arose when health food stores began requesting satisfaction guarantees on the Glacier product line. They also wanted the ability to return unsold product for a full refund.

It soon became clear that the launch of the new product line was not going according to plan. First-year sales were disappointing, at just under $100 000. Trying to manage the new product line was distracting Cam and Karina from their core business. They decided to exit the mass market, and the Glacier line was sold off to a liquidation centre in Ontario in February 2005.

When thinking about the reasons behind the failure, Cam noted that the company hadn't provided enough training for the inside and outside sales representatives. In addition, the company hadn't done enough research before the launch to find the optimal products to include in the line or to test the effectiveness of the packaging. The small opening on the Glacier package did not adequately showcase the natural appearance of the product or allow potential customers to appreciate the scent of the products—a key purchase motivator. Because customers could not perceive the benefits of the Glacier products, they were unwilling to purchase them over the many other lower-priced alternatives. Finally, the company didn't have the promotional budget to compete with large packaged-goods companies that operate in soap and bath products categories. Cam learned a lot from this failure, and he believes the experience the company gained during this failed launch may position it to be successful in this marketplace in the future.

Advertising and Promotion

Rocky Mountain Soap is a small company that can allocate only a limited budget to advertising and promotion. It allocates approximately 3 percent of sales to advertising and promotion. Because of its limited budget, Cam and Karina have to be creative in the tactics they use. For example, to induce trial, Rocky Mountain Soap provides hotels in their retail markets with small bars of soap. Trial is important since the benefits of the products are often perceived only when the person actually uses the product. To increase awareness of the company and trial of its products, Rocky Mountain Soap also sponsors local events.

The company relies heavily on the Internet to help promote the company, its brand, and its products as well as its retail outlets and their sales staff. As noted in the Customer Care section, Rocky Mountain Soap sends out a monthly enewsletter to its customers. It carefully follows permission-based marketing principles with this mailing. Right at the top of the letter is a box that states, "Permission Request: We respectfully request your permission to send email messages from Rocky Mountain Soap similar to the one below. If you no longer wish to receive our emails, please click the unsubscribe button at the bottom of this message. Our Removal Guarantee ensures immediate removal from our lists."

The firm is currently experimenting with addressed direct mail. Using the database generated in its retail stores, it notifies customers that a new product is coming out and it presents them with promotional offers. For example, if customers buy two of the new Bed & Body Misters, they will be sent a travel-size hand butter—a $7.99 value.

In Canmore and Banff, the company runs weekly newspaper ads. These ads show a picture of a person, and they focus on a testimonial about some aspect, such as help with eczema or foot care. In markets where it has retail operations, the company also advertises in tourist guides and publications. It prints 4" × 8" "rack cards" that are put in displays in hotel lobbies that inform travellers about the company and its products. Cam and Karina are struggling with how to build awareness in Edmonton. They tried newspaper ads in the *Edmonton Journal* but found that they were too expensive. Billboard advertising and mall posters were also tried, but they didn't prove to be successful.

Retail Operations

Rocky Mountain Soap's three company-owned retail stores sell all of the above-noted products. The stores are built in an alpine style and have a rustic, natural outdoorsy look and feel. They incorporate a lot of natural materials, such as log-work, wood, and stonework. Large signs and shelf talkers describe who the product is for (e.g., people with sensitive skin) and note the major ingredients in the product. Rocky Mountain's own products make up approximately 70 percent of the products sold in its stores. It sells products sourced from other manufacturers, such as natural sponges, soy-based candles, shaving brushes, and face creams. One of Rocky Mountain Soap's goals is to carry only its own products in its stores, just like Body Shop.

In addition to selling its products in its three company-owned retail stores, Rocky Mountain Soap sells its products online to Canadians and people around the world. To avoid conflict with its other channels of distribution (its own retail stores and its wholesale operations described below), it charges slightly higher prices for products sold over the Internet. For example, you can buy the soaps in retail outlets for $4.49, but they are priced at $4.99 on the Internet. The higher price also helps offset the costs of shipping and handling.

The Rocky Mountain Soap Company Store in the West Edmonton Mall will serve as a prototype for other stores opening in mall locations.

Wholesale Operations

Rocky Mountain Soap also has a wholesale operation. It partners with retailers from across Canada. Though it has been asked to sell through international retailers, the owners of Rocky Mountain Soap believe there is lots of growth potential in Canada for the time being and that a focus on the Canadian marketplace is the best use of their limited resources.

Rocky Mountain Soap selects its retail partners carefully because the company doesn't want to damage its image. In the early days, it was less selective about who it worked with. Today, it is working to be more selective about its retail partners that are served through the company's wholesale division. First, they have to have a store front. Rocky Mountain Soap doesn't want mass market stores. For example, because of an inability to provide customers with knowledgeable service and information about the products, and because of the inability to keep displays and products clean and well organized, the company stopped selling through Save-On-Foods. Gift stores and health food stores fit much better with the brand and present much less risk of not aligning with the brand. Rocky Mountain Soap also does not sell to gift basket companies or direct marketers that organize selling parties in people's homes.

Value-Pricing

Cam and Karina see their products as high value for their price point. They wanted people to be able to afford natural, high-quality products so that they could use them every day, rather than just on special occasions. Thus, the 110-gram bars of soap sell for $4.49 in its retail stores. Over the Internet, the new salt scrub sells for $18.99. The company's thirteen body butters sell at $11.49 to $13.99 for the 55-gram size. They offer gift packages, such as the Relaxation Indulgence Gift Set for $31.99. It contains a lavender body butter, Field and Stream handmade soap, Goat's Milk handmade soap, two Relaxation bath salts, and a Lavender bath gem. An illustrative product list along with current prices charged for Internet sales is provided in **Exhibit 2.** As noted earlier, prices charged for Internet sales are slightly higher than those in the retail stores.

Exhibit 2 Selected Products and Pricing

(This is only a partial list of products and product lines. Prices are those used for sales over the Internet in September 2006. For a complete listing of product information and product photos go to www.rockymountain soap.com/).

Product Line	Name	Size	Price
Hand Made Soaps Total: 27		110 g	
Normal Skin Soaps	Avalanche Soap		$4.99
	Mountain Spa—Avocado Facial Bar		$4.99
Oily / Combination Skin Soaps	Alpine Air Soap		$4.99
	Citrus Soother Soap		$4.99
Dry Skin Soaps	Goat's Milk Soap		$4.99
	Mountain Meadows Soap		$4.99
Specialty Soaps	Earthbound Gardener's Soap		$4.99
	Glacier Ice Shaving Soap		$4.99
Baby Soaps	Baby Bear Soap		$4.99

Body Butters Total: 17		55 g	
	Alpine Body Butter		$11.49
	Baby Body Butter		$13.49
Foot Butters	Mountain Spa Foot Butter	55 g	$12.49
	Foot Butter—Travel Size	15 g	$ 7.49
Hand Butters	Hand Butter	55 g	$14.99
	Hand Butter—Travel size	15 g	$ 7.99
Lip Butter	Coconut Lip Butter		$ 4.49
	Green Apple Lip Butter		$ 4.49
Massage Butters	Relaxation Massage Butter	70 g	$14.99
	Sensual Massage Butter		$14.99
Massage Oils	Relaxation Massage Oil	120 mL	$11.49
	Sore Muscle Massage Oil		$11.49
Bath Salts Total: 12		515 g	
	Solitude Bath Salts		$14.99
	Sore Muscle Soak		$14.99
Bath Gems Total: 6		60 g	
	Alpine Air Bath Gem		$ 4.49
	Cold & Flu Bath Gem		$ 4.49
Lotions Total: 8			
	Kogi Mango & Green Tea Hand & Body Lotion	240 mL	$16.50
	Kogi Hazelnut Hand & Body Lotion	240 mL	$16.50
Scrubs Total: 1	Detoxifying Body Facial Salt Scrub	8 oz.	$18.99
Essential Oils Total: 3	Mountain Springs Sore Muscle & Joint Ointment	2 oz.	$15.99

Competition

Although Cam and Karina are convinced that they have unique offerings, they concede that their customers may perceive their closest competitors to be other small, "craft-type" soap companies. However, they believe their closest competitors are the U.S.-based natural product maker Burt's Bees, and U.K.-based LUSH. Though larger chains, such as the Body Shop, Fruits & Passion, and Crabtree & Evelyn, may enter the competitive mix, Cam doesn't believe they are his close competitors. In particular, Cam suspects that the Body Shop isn't as popular as it once was. He notes that he never sees Body Shop gifts under anyone's Christmas tree these days.

Crabtree & Evelyn

U.S.-based Crabtree & Evelyn manufactures and sells natural skin care products in many of the same categories as Rocky Mountain Soap: facial skin care, hand care, body care, and foot care for dry, oily, and normal skin types; however, it targets the premium segment of the market. Crabtree & Evelyn is best known for its natural bath salts and soaks, soaps, shea butter hand creams, and body lotions. It uses natural ingredients, such as lavender oil, rosewater, jojoba oil, and aloe vera.

Fruits & Passion

Fruits & Passion is another company that sells personal care products with some similarities to those of Rocky Mountain Soap. It is a large company, however, that mass manufactures its products. Headquartered in Candiac, Quebec, it is a well-established Canadian brand. Founded in 1992 as a company devoted to personal care and ambiance products, Fruits & Passion creates and manufactures a line of unique products, such as its Cucina brand of hand care products for cooks. It offers diversified lines of fragrances, bath, shower, sun care, and foot care personal products. It also produces lines of gourmet food products, household care, and dog care items. It has a substantial network of boutiques in Canada and is branching out around the world. It sells through other retailers in the U.S., but uses the boutique concept in Europe, the Middle East, and Asia, and Africa. It has franchises in France, Switzerland, Korea, Hong Kong, China, Kuwait, the United Arab Emirates, and Taiwan.

Craft Companies

There are many small, independent companies located across Canada that offer handmade soap. They primarily sell handmade soap at craft markets or local craft fairs, or they may have one or more retail outlets plus an Internet sales arm. This group of competitors includes such companies as Countryrose Soap Company, located in Langley, B.C., or Essentials Handmade Soap and Cosmetics, located in Montreal. Because of their size, limited market areas, and small product lines, few of these companies pose a direct threat to Rocky Mountain Soap. There is always the possibility that they will grow into a larger player, as was the case of Escents.

Jacqui MacNeill founded Escents at the age of 23 when she chanced upon a little boutique that sold essential oils. She began custom blending her own aromas and selling handmade, quality products at a Vancouver market. Her products caught on quickly among people following the trend toward aromatherapy. Jacqui imported the finest ingredients, found the finances to maintain enough stock, and rented her first store in Park Royal in West Vancouver. She hoped the quality of the products would speak for itself, and the business started to grow, one customer at a time. Two years later, Escents had expanded to two stores and soon began to show a profit. Today, Escents comprises twenty-seven retail outlets worldwide. B.C. is home to seven outlets, five of which are in the Lower Mainland and one of which includes a spa facility. Escents also boasts eighteen retail locations in Taiwan, a new location in Korea, a wholesale division, ecommerce and mail-order distribution, and a commercial production facility.

LUSH

Cam believes that LUSH is perceived by some of his target market as the closest competitor to Rocky Mountain Soap. First founded in 1988 as Cosmetics to Go, in Poole, Dorset, U.K., it invented such products as bath bombs, shampoo bars, and massage bars that were sold through catalogue-based mail order. Despite the popularity of some of these products, the company went under, only to be born again as LUSH when two retail outlets were opened in southern England.

Today LUSH is a well-known global brand, and has more than 370 retail stores and mail-order operations around the world. LUSH produces a wide range of handmade soaps, cosmetics, bath products, hair care, skin care, fragrance, and massage products in factories located in the U.K., Italy, Canada, South America, and Japan. Having production facilities close to its retail outlets allows LUSH to promote the freshness of its products and emphasize that fresh products work better and use fewer preservatives.

LUSH is perceived as trendy, and it positions itself around its core beliefs and values. The first among these is "Fresh." LUSH strives to make effective products out of fresh organic fruit and vegetables, using the finest essential oils and safe synthetics. Second, LUSH is passionate about stopping the testing of cosmetics using animals. Its philosophy is that the only way to check that cosmetics are safe for humans is to test them on humans. So this is what it does. Third, its products are hand made. Ambience is LUSH's fourth value. LUSH believes in long candlelit baths, massage, filling the house with perfume, and in the right to make mistakes, lose everything, and start again.

Finally, LUSH believes it offers customers good value, while still making a profit. For example, LUSH's bath bombs, its most popular product, sell for $4.35 to $5.95 each. Its butter creams sell for $12.70 to $15.90, and its line of shampoos range in price from $19.95 to $37.95. Thus, some customers find LUSH products to be relatively high in price with relatively low efficacy compared with products from companies such as Rocky Mountain Soap.

Since its inception, LUSH wanted to reduce the waste associated with its products. Thus, LUSH makes many products in solid form, so they can be sold wrapped in paper or in small bags. For example, though bubble bath and shower products were traditionally sold as bottles of liquid by other manufacturers, LUSH invented solid bath bombs and solid shower bars. Products such as the popular Karma (Lush's signature fragrance) have been made into bubble bars, soap, lotion, bath bombs, dusting powder, and solid shampoo.

LUSH prides itself on its devoted customer base. There is a busy LUSH forum where customers swap tips and comments on products. Discontinued items can sell for high prices on places like eBay.

Though LUSH claims to be a natural-product company, its critics note that it uses some synthetic ingredients, most notably fragrance oils and sodium laurel sulphate. Fragrance oils are blended synthetic aroma compounds. Sodium lauryl sulphate (SLS) is commonly used in many soaps, shampoos, detergents, toothpastes. It is a very effective foaming agent. Concerns have been raised about this chemical, however, ranging from the belief that it results in skin irritations and eczema to the issue that it cannot be metabolized by the liver and even that it may be associated with some cancers.

Burt's Bees

Cam and Karina admire this company, noting that it abides by its claims and follows a natural strategy similar to the one used by Rocky Mountain Soap. Burt's Bees was founded in Maine in the 1980s by a honey producer, Burt Shavitz, and Roxanne Quimby, a divorced, unemployed mother of twins. In 1992, it moved its operations to North Carolina. Its first products were bottled honey. It soon switched from the selling of honey itself to the development of other products that used honey and beeswax as major ingredients.

In 2004, the company was acquired by a private equity group. Today Burt's Bees generates approximately US$250 million from more than 150 personal care products that are made from natural, organic, and effective ingredients, such as beeswax, therapeutic herbs, and botanical oils. Chief Executive John Replogle talks about the importance of close customer contact when thinking about where to take the company next. "We receive over a thousand phone calls and emails a week from consumers. It's through that dialogue that we know where to take our brand. For example, consumers tell us they absolutely adore products in our hand- and foot-care line. And they say, 'Can you help me by giving me a product like that that's good for all over my body?'"

Burt's Bees has been growing rapidly and has been working to exploit key trends, according to Replogle. "Health and wellness [are part of] a megatrend, and so is the greening of America. All you have to do is listen to major retailers talk about sustainability, and you see the confluence of consumer trends and retailer trends. We're right at the heart of that." The company is striving to meet consumer needs from head to toe. Burt's Bees is planning to launch a men's line and fuller range of personal cleansing products, including shampoos and conditioners. It has just launched a new body wash and is on the verge of introducing a new head-to-toe baby wash.

Burt's Bees uses a distinctive brand logo for a company selling personal care products—the face of a bearded man. This logo, combined with the distinctive yellow colour of many of its packages and displays, helps make the firm easily recognizable wherever its products are found.

Each package has a "natural bar" that states the percentage of natural ingredients contained in that particular product. Burt's Bees takes pride in the fact that it never uses potentially harmful ingredients in its products. Its website describes some of the harmful ingredients used by other companies in their personal care lines: "Things like petroleum which can be toxic. Sodium Lauryl Sulfate, which is a harsh, aggressive ingredient used in certain beauty products. And when was the last time you saw a farmer growing Propylene Glycol? Rather than loading our products up with harsh chemicals or unnecessary fillers, we offer you only the good stuff."

Its main lines are lip care (e.g., lip balm, lip shimmer), facial care (e.g., cleanser, moisturizer), and body care (e.g., soap, shampoo). As declared on its website, "To us, the word 'natural' means only one thing. It means, 'harvested from nature.' And we adhere to that definition like the strictest of school teachers." It positions itself as an "earth friendly" company.

Burt's Bees does not own any retail outlets, but it does have an online store where consumers can find excess or discontinued items at considerable price savings. Most of Burt's Bees products are sold throughout Canada, the United States, and the United Kingdom on special display racks in a wide and diverse range of outlets. In 2006, it was sold through 22 000 outlets, ranging from specialty food markets (e.g., Whole Foods Market) and stores specializing in natural foods to drug stores and Borders Books. When questioned about the danger of losing its cult brand following as it increasingly becomes a mass marketed product, Replogle notes, "[Our consumer] wants access to her favourite products at all of her favourite retailers. The authenticity of the brand shines through regardless of whether we're in 10 000 or 20 000 or even 30 000 stores."

To keep tabs on how products are selling, and which products are selling the best, Burt's Bees uses Business Intelligence software developed by BusinessObjects to manage sales data from the chain level, store level, and from their retail website (www.burtsbees.com). This system allows Burt's Bees to see the frequency in which stores and customers are ordering different products. It helps them with product planning and inventory control and allows the company to proactively manage its fast growth across many diverse distribution channels.

Moving Ahead

Today Rocky Mountain Soap has grown to become one of the largest manufacturers of 100 percent natural handmade soaps and bath products in Canada. Cam and Karina have moved beyond soap in the development of their product line. They've added body butters, hand butters, and lip butters. These higher-priced products have improved the profitability of the company. In 2 000, the year Cam and Karina bought the company, they generated $86 000 in sales revenue. By the end of 2006, they expected to generate $3.5 million in sales.

Rocky Mountain Soap's retail stores have been highly successful. Same-stores sales grow by 20 to 50 percent per year, and Cam and Karina believe there is still lots of long-term growth potential here. The Canmore store has the longest history of operations and the strongest customer base. In 2006, it generated sales of $1700 per square foot. The Banff store generated $1150 per square foot while the newest store in Edmonton generated $900 per square foot.

The three retail stores account for the majority of the company's sales. In fact, the wholesale division must sell through at least 500 independent retail accounts to generate as much sales revenue as is generated by the three company-owned retail outlets. Internet sales currently make up about $200 000 in sales revenue. Though this channel is not highly profitable at the moment, it allows customers to access products, and it helps build brand awareness. Internet sales are expected to double sales revenues annually. However, it is not surprising that Cam and Karina believe their future success lies in the opening of more company-owned retail stores.

Rocky Mountain Soap now offers complete lines of liquid soaps and bath salts. They've added massage oils, essential oils, and body misters. They're planning to add other new products, such as candles and face creams. They are also introducing more utility-type items, such as their new zit zapper. One of the company's newest products is Detoxifying Body Facial Salt Scrub, a product designed to purify the skin and remove environmental buildup.

Many Decisions

The downhill ride is certainly easier than was the climb up the mountain, but Cam's mind is still whirling. He and Karina know that they are facing some big decisions that will have a major impact on the future of their company. As they work toward expansion of their retail operations, they know that target marketing and positioning, new-product development, pricing, branding, channel management, and communication strategies will be increasingly critical to the company's success.

Sources: Much of the information in this case is based on interviews conducted by Peggy Cunningham with Cam Baty and Andre Baribeau August 24, 2006, and September 12, 2006, as well as a tour of the company facilities. The author would also like to thank Lori Armstrong, Andre Baribeau, Stefanie Crepin, Todd Kennedy, Tamara Kushnir, and David Schwarz, graduates of Queen's Accelerated MBA program 2005, for giving permission to use their Glacier Soap case. Other sources: Escents website www.escentsaromatherapy.com; "BusinessObjects XI Keeps the Information Buzzing at Burt's Bees," BusinessObjects Press Release, San Jose, California, August 23, 2005; www.businessobjects.com/news/press/press2005/ 20050823_burts_bees_cust.asp; "Sodium Lauryl Sulfate (SLS) and Sodium Laureth Sulfate (SLES). The Killers in your bathroom?" Natural Health Information Centre, www.natural-health-information-centre.com/sodium-lauryl-sulfate.html; Lush corporate website, www.lush.com/; "Lush," Wikipedia, http://en.wikipedia.org/ wiki/Lush; "Burt's Bees," Wikipedia, http://en.wikipedia.org/wiki/Burt's_Bees; Heather Riccio and Hilary Rowland, Interview with Burt's Bees founder, Roxanne Quimby, Hilary Magazine www.hilary.com/career/burtsbees.html; "Burt's Bees: Up From Craft Fairs," BusinessWeek, August 7, 2006, www.businessweek.com/magazine/content/06_32/b3996415.htm?chan=spr_magazine_brands; "Canada's Organic Industry," Agriculture and Agri-Food Canada, 2003, http://ats-sea.agr.gc.ca/supply/3313_e.htm. All websites accessed August 2006.

QUESTIONS

Capstone Question

The Rocky Mountain Soap Company case touches on many of the themes presented in this book. By the time you have finished studying the various chapters in the book, you should be able to develop a detailed marketing plan for the company for a one-year period that will guide its growth for the year. Be sure to clearly describe the company's target market(s) and how it should position and brand itself. Describe how it should build relationships with its customers and how it should communicate with them. Be sure to think about what products it should introduce or drop and what pricing changes it should make (if any). Think about its different channels of distribution and where it should place most of its investment in management time and support dollars. Below you will find questions relating to material in the various textbook chapters. Your answers to these questions may be helpful when you develop your marketing plan.

Chapter 1

What steps does Rocky Mountain Soap take to build relationships with its customers?

Chapter 2

Describe Rocky Mountain Soap's mission. The text notes that a clear mission statement acts as an "invisible hand" that guides people in the organization. Give reasons why you believe Rocky Mountain Soap's mission is effective or ineffective in accomplishing this task.

Review the product/market expansion grid shown in Figure 2.3 (page 51). Using the information in Exhibit 2 (pages A9 and A10) as well as the information in the case, use the grid to find opportunities for Rocky Mountain Soap. In particular, describe how sales for certain products might be increased by using market penetration. Where might it use market development? In what areas might it consider product development and diversification?

Chapter 3

Describe three forces from Rocky Mountain Soap's macroenvironment and three from its microenvironment that may limit or expand the company's future opportunities.

Chapter 4

Show how Rocky Mountain Soap is working to follow the principles guiding socially responsible marketing. Clearly state what things it is doing well, and make recommendations on what it could improve.

Chapter 5

Read the section of the case that describes the failure of the Glacier line. If Cam and Karina decide to re-enter the mass market, what information should they gather before re-entering this market so that they do not repeat the mistakes of the past?

Chapter 6

What type of buying behaviour typifies a consumer purchase of a Rocky Mountain Soap product?

    If Rocky Mountain Soap decides to begin (or expand) its retail operations in your province, what factors affecting consumer buying behaviour should it consider?

Chapter 7

Rocky Mountain Soap has a wholesale division. The responsibility of this division is to select and serve other independent retailers who will sell Rocky Mountain Soap products in their stores. What criteria would you recommend that Rocky Mountain Soap use when selecting potential retail partners in your area to sell its products. Using these criteria, suggest one outlet in your area that might be a good partner for Rocky Mountain Soap. If you were the manager of this retail outlet, why would you want to (or not what to) do business with the Rocky Mountain Soap company?

Chapter 8

The managers of Rocky Mountain Soap Company know they need to refine their description of the company's target market, currently described as women aged 25 to 55. What variables other than age could you use to meaningfully divide up this market? Use several of these variables to describe finer-grained market segments that Rocky Mountain Soap could focus on. Select a target market from among the subsegments you have described. Why do you think Rocky Mountain Soap should focus on this subsegment? How would you position the company to this segment (your proposed target market)?

Chapters 9 and 10

Go to Rocky Mountain Soap's website. Examine its product mix. What is the width of its product mix? Look at its line of bar soaps. What is the depth of the bar soap line? How consistent is its product mix? To make the mix more consistent, what products might the company consider developing or dropping?

    How should Rocky Mountain Soap position its corporate brand—should it refine its brand positioning based on the physical attributes of its products, on their benefits, or on the values and beliefs that underlie the company?

Chapter 11

Select a product from Rocky Mountain Soap's product mix. Compare the pricing of this product with a similar product from one or two of Rocky Mountain Soap's competitors. Based on this comparison, what recommendation would you make to Rocky Mountain Soap with regard to the pricing of your selected product?

Chapter 12

Describe the tactics the Rocky Mountain Soap company has used to manage channel conflict. As the number of retail outlets grows, will channel conflict increase or decrease?

Chapter 13

What major retailing decisions must the company make before beginning to expand the number of retail outlets? The company currently owns three retail outlets and plans to expand through wholly owned retail operations. An alternative expansion model is to franchise. What are the pros and cons of expanding through franchising?

Chapters 14 to 17

Describe the promotion mix that Rocky Mountain Soap is currently using. You have a budget of $15 000 to use to promote the opening of a new Rocky Mountain Soap store in the town or city where your university or college is located. Develop a communications plan for the store opening.

Chapter 18

One of Rocky Mountain Soap Company's competitors, Escents, began to sell its products in an international market before expanding across Canada. Why do you think it used this strategy? Select a foreign marketplace that you think might be a viable one for Rocky Mountain Soap. Describe three changes it might have to make to its marketing mix to effectively compete in this marketplace.

Please refer to Chapter 2, Table 2.2, "Contents of a Marketing Plan" on page 65, for assistance with preparing a marketing plan for this case. Log on to your Companion Website at **www.pearsoned.ca/kotler** to view a full marketing plan.

Appendix 2 CBC Video Cases

 Each video case corresponds to specific chapters. See the correlation table below for details.

Video Case 1: Chapters 1, 2, 3
Video Case 2: Chapters 4, 6, 8
Video Case 3: Chapters 4, 5, 16
Video Case 4: Chapters 8, 9
Video Case 5: Chapters 4, 11, 13
Video Case 6: Chapters 10, 16
Video Case 7: Chapter 14, 15

CBC Video Case 1

Trouble in Toyland

CBC

According to the Canadian Toy Association, the toy industry in Canada represents $1.4 billion in sales. Despite the size of the marketplace, many companies are struggling as the market becomes increasingly unpredictable. Sales of traditional toys fell by almost 3 percent in 2003, and by 5 percent in 2004 according to the NPD Group Inc. Technology is playing a bigger and bigger role in the industry. Children are increasingly sophisticated, and every day children seem to be growing older faster! Because of "age compression," toys are being put aside sooner in favour of electronic gadgets, such as cellphones, computer games, and even electronic organizers. Though some companies are struggling, others, such as Spin Master Ltd., seem to be on the road to success. Its vision is to be a company that understands kids in general versus one that manufacturers toys. Retailers, like manufacturers, are under pressure to keep pace with competition and changing tastes. On one hand, you find the giant discount retailers, such as Wal-Mart (which is now the number-one toy retailer), putting pressure on prices

and margins. On the other hand, you have small independent chains, such as Ottawa's Mrs. Tiggy Winkles, which operates only five outlets and features traditional and retro toys.

Questions

1. Identify the key trends that are affecting the toy industry and demonstrate why a player in the toy industry should be aware of these trends.

2. How can relationship marketing and market orientation help small toy retailers such as Mrs. Tiggy Winkles survive? What value can it create for its customers?

Sources: Peggy Cunningham wrote this case based on the CBC Marketplace video "Trouble in Toyland" and the following articles: "Hot Toys For The Holidays?" Canadian Toy Association press release, www.cdntoyassn.com/mnews.htm; Paul-Mark Rendon, "Campaign ushers back Irwin Toys," Marketing Magazine, January 12, 2004; "Toys 'R' Us acquired by investment group," Marketing Daily, Friday, March 18, 2005; "Toy companies expand into home décor," Marketing Daily, Tuesday, February 15, 2005, www.marketingmag.ca.

CBC Video Case 2

Buying Into Sexy

CBC ◉

Canadian children 8 to 14 years of age have lots of discretionary money. They spend $1.7 billion of their own cash on a huge range of products. Marketers are well aware of this group's buying power and it's not surprising that they are targeting this segment.

However, what children in this age group are buying and what is being marketed to them is causing some concern. Video games featuring scantily clad women and music videos with overt sexual imagery are aimed at both sexes, while "sexy" clothing and accessories are aimed particularly at very young girls. Take the case of "sex bracelets," for example. They're cheap, colourful jelly bracelets that carry sexual connotations. As one tween noted, "Pink means 'kiss,' and white means "lap dance." Some wear them because they are "fun," and tweens may not fully understand the sexual connotations.

Some analysts believe the trend towards mimicking and valuing sexual imagery starts at a very young age, as young as four years of age, with the marketing of products like the "Bratz" dolls. These toys feature skimpy clothing and heavy make-up. Marketed along with the dolls is the Bratz "Superstyling Funktivity Book," which is aimed at six-year-olds and covers topics like "luscious lip tips," "design your own sexy skirt," and "tips on being an irresistible flirt." Visit any mall, and you'll find entire chains devoted to young shoppers full of racy clothing, make-up and lingerie for girls who may not have hit puberty.

The buying and wearing of such products is sometimes causing a lot of dissention between children and their parents. While kids feel a lot of pressure to be like their friends, some parents don't want their children dressing in a sexy style or using products like video games traditionally aimed at older consumers. In other cases, parents are too busy to pay much attention to what their kids are doing, watching or accessing over the Internet.

To speak to this market, celebrities are often hired. Take a recent ad campaign for Candies shoes. It featured pop star Ashlee Simpson, who some consider a relatively "good girl" with a wholesome image. The Candies ad shows a scantily clad Simpson wearing a pair of Candies high heels. A teddy bear is tucked in the corner. Says Candies' CEO, Neil Cole, the ad shows "a young girl who's growing up."

The trend may be the result of what's called "age compression." Children are adopting the behaviours and tastes traditionally associated with older people. Instead of dolls and building blocks, children today are demanding electronic gadgets like cell phones and iPods. Nonetheless, critics are asking where we should draw the line and question if the trend towards "buying into sexy" is the result of exploiting a vulnerable market.

Questions

1. What factors in the marketing environment (technical, demographic, lifestyle, social and cultural) have contributed to the attitudes many tween girls have about buying and wearing provocative clothing? (Hint: think about what has happened to families as well as to children themselves.)

2. Big questions arise about whether marketers are responding to market demands and are just providing the services and products that this age group demands, or whether they are creating the demand with inappropriate imagery and then feeding it with products and services. Discuss how a marketer's ethical responsibility would change under these two different points of view.

Sources: "Buying into Sexy: The sexing up of tweens," CBC Marketplace, Broadcast: January 9, 2005; "Sex sells: Marketing and 'age compression'," CBC Marketplace, Broadcast: January 9, 2005.

At the heart of any good marketing practice are the concepts of market segmentation, target marketing, and positioning. Without good information about consumers' needs, attitudes, and buying behaviour, this entire process breaks down. However, many consumers believe that the gathering of information for marketing purposes violates their rights and their privacy. Accurate, timely information about consumers is especially important for the direct marketing industry. It comprises organizations that send material directed personally to you, the consumer. It may be delivered through the mail, over the Internet, by telephone, or by email. Direct marketers include companies as varied as Microsoft Canada, The Shopping Channel, Reader's Digest, and Allianz (sellers of registered education plans) as well as the many charities operating in Canada.

Many in the direct marketing industry are aware of the challenges associated with consumer resentment and the need to respect privacy. They have strict internal policies about how information will be gathered, protected, and used. Other firms, unfortunately, are abusing the goodwill of consumers and may be damaging the image of an entire industry in the process. Of particular concern are companies, such as Growing Families, that gather information and then sell it to other firms. Growing Families is a firm that goes to maternity wards to take pictures of newborns. New parents fill out forms to receive their pictures and provide a lot of personal information in the processes. Growing Families sells this information to their partner firms—companies such as Allianz and Procter & Gamble, who have products of relevance to new parents.

When it comes to the use of technology to create vast databases and target customers, marketers must ask themselves not just what they *can* do using technology to gather information and compile integrated databases, but also what they *should* do to truly create value and respect customers rights.

Question

1. Registered education savings plans are big business, and Canadians have plunked $12.8 billion into these plans to help finance the mounting cost of postsecondary education for their children. Growth in these plans has exploded. In Ontario alone, 14 firms are registered as scholarship plan dealers. The Ontario Securities Commission (OSC) recently uncovered numerous problems involving sales practices within the industry. The three largest players in the sector are Allianz Education Funds Inc., CST Consultants Inc., and USC Education Savings Plans Inc. They account for nearly $5 billion in assets and more than 600 000 plans. If the industry cannot improve its practices, regulators will soon step in. If you were a senior marketing and sales manager at Allianz, what policies would you put in place to improve the data gathering and sales practices of your firm to ensure consumer satisfaction and privacy protection?

Sources: Peggy Cunningham wrote this case based on the CBC Marketplace video "Mining Your Business" and the following articles: Rebecca Harris, "Hitting the Target," Marketing Magazine, July 4, 2005, www.marketingmag.ca; Karen Howlett And Paul Waldie, "The Ontario Securities Commission cracks down on RESP sector," Globe and Mail, July 16, 2004, http://www.vaninvestor.com/You/RESP/OSC_cracksdown_resp.htm.

The Rebirth of a Brand: Avery Wines

The American Marketing Association defines a *brand* as "a name, term, sign, symbol, or design, or a combination of them, intended to identify the goods or services of one seller or group of sellers and to differentiate them from those of competitors." Avery Wines engaged Bernie Hadley-Beauregard, owner of Brandever Strategy Inc., to rebrand and reposition their winery. When Brandever undertakes a project, it takes a broader definition of the branding and communication task than the above definition suggests. According to their website (www.brandever.com):

> Our core belief is that everything matters. Competitive advantage and marketing impact are increased significantly once a company adopts a holistic, interwoven approach to its communication [and branding] endeavours. It all begins with a thorough understanding of all touch points that a prospect, stakeholder or customer has with your company: every phone call, email, printed material, package, and web communication. Each is a vital marketing event; an opportunity to define and differentiate and advance your firm, your offerings. In essence, Brandever advocates that marketing should not be interpreted as a department, but rather a mindset. A shared frame of reference adopted throughout an organization. A powerful force.

Hadley-Beauregard had a big job ahead of him when he took on the Avery project, a family-owned winery located just west of Abbotsford in B.C.'s Fraser Valley. Avery Winery and their promise of "A'Very Fine Wine" was a play on words based on the surnames of the owners, David and Liesbeth (Liz) Avery. The winery was born in 1998. The owners had invested their life savings into the development of the vineyard and were carrying almost a million dollars in debt. Cash flow was, therefore, a big problem for them. The good news was that all of the wines were made exclusively from organically grown grapes.

Bernie had a very short timeline in which to reinvent the brand. If the project could not be completed before the important Christmas selling season, the winery would probably go into bankruptcy. The new brand name, Lotusland, was developed after a lot of thought and negotiation with the winery owners.

Questions

1. Provide clear reasons why Avery wines needed a new brand. In formulating your answer, be sure to think about the past experiences that consumers may have had with this wine.

2. Why do many firms, like Avery Wines, neglect branding?

3. Some brand researchers suggest that a brand is the totality of what is *experienced* by customers, and that brands do not have *meanings* until the product has a history and customers have experienced the brand over time. What meanings does the new Lotusland brand suggest? In formulating your answer, think about how the new brand has appropriated cultural icons as part of the branding effort and why getting adoption of the product in fine restaurants was one of the keys to success of the project.

Sources: Peggy Cunningham wrote this case based on the CBC *Marketplace* program "Avery Wines—The Brand Man," aired February 8, 2004; and the following websites; http://winesofcanada.com/bc_fraser.html and www.brandever.com

CBC Video Case 5

The Bait in Rebates

Walk into many retail stores or thumb through the advertisements in your local newspaper and it seems as if almost any product you are thinking of buying comes with the offer of a rebate. Many retailers and manufacturers love them because they tend to boost short-term sales. Rebates are featured on products as varied as automobiles, computers, stereos, and pleasure boat navigation systems. However, despite the fact that the "carrot" of a price reduction is dangled in front of consumers to get them to purchase today, many rebates are never claimed. In fact, redemption rates vary from a startling 1 to 50 percent even when a $100 rebate is offered. Today's consumers are time pressed and may not want the hassle of sending in the bar code, their original receipt, and the required photocopies.

Retailers are heavy users of mail-in rebates. In an era of growing price competition, rebates allow retailers to advertise significantly lower prices than is possible with such tactics as everyday low pricing. Such pricing gets consumers into the store and provides the retailer's sales staff with the opportunity to convince the buyer to make the purchase on the spot. Manufacturers, such as Sony, also use their own rebate programs. Manufacturers often cooperate with retailers and help pay for the costs of rebate programs either by providing lower large-order minimums or through cooperative programs. Some people wonder why they just can't get their rebate at the checkout counter. Manufacturers cling to the mail-in rebate system to obtain demographic information pertaining to the purchasers of their products and don't want to give control of this information to their retailers.

Faced with a growing mountain of complaints, some retailers and manufacturers have started to take

action. Sony and Staples, for example, have moved their rebate systems to the Internet so that the process of claiming the rebate can be streamlined. In 2005, Best Buy and Future Shop announced that they will no longer stock products that are tied to mail-in rebates.

Questions

1. What types of products are most likely to use rebates? Are rebates an effective way of adding value to a product or a service?

2. Marketers recognize that consumers often actively process price information, interpreting prices in terms of their knowledge from prior purchasing experience, formal communications (advertising, sales calls, and brochures), informal communications (friends, colleagues, or family members), and point-of-purchase or online resources. Marketers know that purchase decisions are based on how consumers perceive prices. Explain how you think rebates affect consumers' price perceptions.

3. Do you think the use of rebates is ethical and fair to all stakeholders (customers, retailers, manufacturers, competitors, the general public)? Provide clear criteria for your opinion, and clearly state the reasons why you have drawn your conclusion.

Sources: Peggy Cunningham wrote this case based on the CBC Marketplace program "The Bate in Rebates," January 2, 2005; and the following articles: Wayne Mouland, "Rebates rule!" Marketing Magazine, October 18, 2004, www.marketingmag.ca; David Menzies, "Mail-in rebates RIP," Marketing Magazine, September 12, 2005, www.marketingmag.ca.

CBC Video Case 6

Earth Energy Systems

CBC 🔘

With energy costs for cooling and heating with conventional fuels going through the roof, the time may finally be right for geothermal heating. While the technology has been available for 20 years, consumers have been skeptical about the viability of such a system.

Geothermal systems use a series of pipes buried 15 metres underground. They transfer naturally occurring heat (the heat the land absorbs from the sun) from the ground below the frost line into a building during winter, converting it into warm air and distributing it through ducts. In summer, the system is reversed to transfer heat out of the building, where it uses the cooler ground as a heat sink. The efficiency of the system is one of their major advantages. The heat obtained from the ground (via the condenser) is much greater than the electrical energy that is required to drive the various components of the system.

In an era where green house gases and global warming are becoming major concerns, geothermal heat pump systems present an attractive alternative energy source. They are one of the most environmentally friendly heating systems available. Moreover, once they are installed, these systems offer homeowners the opportunity to significantly reduce their heating costs. While geothermal systems still use electricity to run the components, they use up to 75 percent less electricity than conventional heating or cooling systems. Geothermal systems can also reduce greenhouse gas emissions by 66 percent or more, compared with conventional heating and cooling systems that use fossil fuels. Finally, the systems are misers when it comes to maintenance costs.

So what's the catch, you might ask. The systems are expensive to install and currently require a lot of land for installation. For example, a system for a relatively small house costs approximately $25 000.

Geothermal systems also have commercial applications. They can be used to heat offices, stores, hotels, schools, hospitals, and even recreational facilities. For example, the Glenboro Curling Club in southwestern Manitoba recently installed a system which not only keeps the club's dressing rooms warm, but also keeps the ice sheets cold.

Manitoba has taken the lead provincially in terms of having the highest adoption rates of geothermal systems. However, adoption rates for these alternative energy systems is still quite low compared to countries like Iceland, for example, where geothermal heating accounts for 50 percent of the country's heat development.

Questions

1. Who do you think would be the most likely early adopters of geothermal heating systems in your province?

2. Describe a marketing program you could use to target this group and build awareness about this type of system.

3. If you were a salesperson representing a company selling these systems, describe the tactics you would use to address the concerns a potential consumer might have about this type of system.

Sources: CBC Venture, "Energy: Sawdust to Bio-oil," aired January 23, 2005; "Curling club keeps cool with new geothermal heating system," CBC News, October 27, 2006; "Geothermal Power Latest News," November 9, 2006, http://www.alternative-energy-news.info/geothermal-power/; "Geothermal Energy," Manitoba Energy, Science & Technology, Energy Development Initiative, 2003, www.gov.mb.ca/est/energy/initiatives/geothermal.html; Earth Energy Society Of Canada http://www.earthenergy.ca/tech.html (all websites accessed November 9, 2006).

CBC Video Case 7

Advertising in Crisis?

In 2004, Yasmin Glanville, president of CTR Inc., a Toronto-based marketing consulting group, made a bold and controversial statement: "It's no secret that the advertising industry, as we knew it, is extinct." However, Glanville added, "the advertising industry is not dead. It is evolving and diverging into solutions relevant to the needs of our times."

Rick Shaver, a VP at The Hive Strategic Marketing in Toronto, believes that though the "rules of the game have changed forever ... a new era of infinite possibilities is upon us." New media options have not only splintered mass markets into a vast assortment of communities of common interest, but they have also created niche markets that are accessible as never before if marketers understand the new rules of consumer engagement. "Push has been replaced by permission, power is shifting to the buyer, and the advertising monologue is giving way to consumer dialogue," according to Shaver.

Advances in technology and changes in consumer behaviour are shaping a new landscape. For example, instead of TV, video games are becoming a mainstream media for young adult and teenage males. Bill Gates, chair of Microsoft, forecast that all traditional mass media will be delivered via the Internet and that "The future of advertising is the Internet." Furthermore, the Internet, along with the rapid adoption of digital video recording devices, will enable consumers to record many television programs by pressing a single button and downloading the program to their hard drive. The big concern is that they can undertake this process largely commercial free. According to Forrester Research, this may mean that exposure to advertising may be reduced by more than 50 percent.

Despite all the debate about this industry being in flux, advertising is indeed very much alive. There is no doubt that its shape and roads to success are evolving. Combining business results earned through divergent and innovative ideas will help to win the minds and hearts of increasingly empowered consumers.

Questions

1. How will marketing communications change in this era of empowered consumers?

2. Pick one of your favourite brands. State the target market for the brand. Design an innovative integrated communications program for your brand. Explain why you selected certain types of media vehicles for your campaign.

Sources: This case was written by Peggy Cunningham based on the *Venture* show "Advertising in Crisis," aired October 15, 2004, and the following articles: Yasmin Glanville, "Creativity versus performance," *Marketing Magazine*, November 22, 2004, www.marketingmag.ca; Rick Shaver, "Custom media: New rules for a new game," *Strategy*, May 31, 2004, p. 11; Michael Kanellos, "Newsmaker: Gates taking a seat in your den," CNET News.com, January 5, 2005; Jennifer Whitehead, "Gates says future of advertising lies on the Internet, *Brand Republic*, October 27, 2005; Adam Pasick, "Sorrell sees media industry 'panic' over Internet," Reuters Canada, October 27, 2005, http://ca.today.reuters.com/news/newsArticle.aspx?type=technology News&storyID=2005-10-27T161859Z_01_EIC749378_RTRIDST_0_ TECH-MEDIA-WPP-COL.XML.

One aspect of marketing not discussed within the text is marketing arithmetic. The calculation of sales, costs, and certain ratios is important for many marketing decisions. This appendix describes three major areas of marketing arithmetic: the *operating statement, analytic ratios,* and *markups and markdowns.*

Operating Statement

Balance sheet
A financial statement that shows assets, liabilities, and net worth of a company at a given time.

The operating statement and the balance sheet are the two main financial statements used by companies. The **balance sheet** shows the assets, liabilities, and net worth of a company at a given time. The **operating statement** (also called **profit-and-loss statement** or **income statement**) is the more important of the two for marketing information. It shows company sales, cost of goods sold, and expenses during a specified time. By comparing the operating statement from one time period to the next, the firm can spot favourable or unfavourable trends and take appropriate action.

Operating statement (profit-and-loss statement, income statement)
A financial statement that shows company sales, cost of goods sold, and expenses during a given time.

Table A.1 on page A26 shows the 2007 operating statement for Dale Parsons Men's Wear, a specialty store on the Prairies. This statement is for a retailer; the operating statement for a manufacturer would be somewhat different. Specifically, the section on purchases within the "cost of goods sold" area would be replaced by "cost of goods manufactured."

The outline of the operating statement follows a logical series of steps to arrive at the firm's $25 000 net profit figure:

Net sales	$300 000
Cost of goods sold	− 175 000
Gross margin	$125 000
Expenses	− 100 000
Net profit	$ 25 000

Gross sales
The total amount that a company charges during a given time for merchandise.

The first part details the amount that Parsons received for the goods sold during the year. The sales figures consist of three items: *gross sales, returns and allowances,* and *net sales.* **Gross sales** is the total amount charged to customers during the year for merchandise purchased in Parsons's store. As expected, some customers returned merchandise because of damage or a change of mind. If the customer gets a full refund or full credit on another purchase, we call this a *return.* Or the customer may decide to keep the item if Parsons will reduce the price. This is called an *allowance.* By subtracting returns and allowances from gross sales, we arrive at net sales—what Parsons earned in revenue from a year of selling merchandise:

Gross sales	$ 325 000
Returns and allowances	− 25 000
Net sales	$ 300 000

The second major part of the operating statement calculates the amount of sales revenue Dale Parsons retains after paying the costs of the merchandise. We start with the inventory in the store at the beginning of the year. During the year, Parsons bought $165 000 worth of suits, slacks, shirts, ties, jeans, and other goods. Suppliers gave the store discounts totalling $15 000, so that net purchases were $150 000. Because the store is located away from regular shipping routes, Parsons had to pay an additional $10 000 to get the products delivered, giving the firm a net cost of $160 000. Adding the beginning inventory, the cost of goods available for sale amounted to $220 000. The $45 000 ending inventory of clothes in the store on

Table A.1 Operating Statement: Dale Parsons Men's Wear, Year Ending December 31, 2007

Gross sales			$325 000
Less: Sales returns and allowances			25 000
Net sales			$300 000
Cost of goods sold			
Beginning inventory, January, at cost		$ 60 000	
Gross purchases	$165 000		
Less: Purchase discounts	15 000		
Net purchases	$150 000		
Plus: Freight-in	10 000		
Net cost of delivered purchases		$160 000	
Cost of goods available for sale		$220 000	
Less: Ending inventory, December 31, at cost		$ 45 000	
Cost of goods sold			$175 000
Gross margin			$125 000
Expenses			
Selling expenses			
Sales, salaries, and commissions	$ 40 000		
Advertising	5000		
Delivery	5000		
Total selling expenses		$ 50 000	
Administrative expenses			
Office salaries	$ 20 000		
Office supplies	5000		
Miscellaneous (outside consultant)	5000		
Total administrative expenses		$ 30 000	
General expenses			
Rent	$ 10 000		
Heat, light, telephone	5 000		
Miscellaneous (insurance, depreciation)	5000		
Total general expenses		$ 20 000	
Total expenses			$100 000
Net profit			$ 25 000

Cost of goods sold
The net cost to the company of goods sold.

December 31 is then subtracted to come up with the $175 000 **cost of goods sold.** Here again we have followed a logical series of steps to figure out the cost of goods sold:

Amount Parsons started with (beginning inventory)	$ 60 000
Net amount purchased	+150 000
Any added costs to obtain these purchases	+ 10 000
Total cost of goods Parsons had available for sale during year	$ 220 000
Amount Parsons had left over (ending inventory)	− 45 000
Cost of goods actually sold	$ 175 000

The difference between what Parsons paid for the merchandise ($175 000) and what he sold it for ($300 000) is called the **gross margin** ($125 000).

Gross margin
The difference between net sales and cost of goods sold.

In order to show the profit Parsons "cleared" at the end of the year, we must subtract from the gross margin the *expenses* incurred while doing business. *Selling expenses* included two sales employees, local newspaper and radio advertising, and the cost of delivering merchandise to customers after alterations. Selling expenses totalled $50 000 for the year. *Administrative expenses* included the salary for an office manager, office supplies such as stationery and business cards, and miscellaneous expenses including an administrative audit conducted by an outside consultant. Administrative expenses totalled $30 000 in 2007. Finally, the general expenses of rent, utilities, insurance, and depreciation came to $20 000. Total expenses were therefore $100 000 for the year. By subtracting expenses ($100 000) from the gross margin ($125 000), we arrive at the net profit of $25 000 for Parsons during 2007.

Analytic Ratios

Operating ratios
Ratios of selected operating statement items to net sales that allow marketers to compare the firm's performance in one year with that in previous years (or with industry standards and competitors in the same year).

The operating statement provides the figures needed to compute some crucial ratios. Typically these ratios are called **operating ratios**—the ratio of selected operating statement items to net sales. They let marketers compare the firm's performance in one year to that in previous years (or with industry standards and competitors in the same year). The most commonly used operating ratios are the *gross margin percentage,* the *net profit percentage,* the *operating expense percentage,* and the *returns and allowances percentage.*

Ratio	Formula	Computation from Table A.1
Gross margin percentage	$= \dfrac{\text{gross margin}}{\text{net sales}}$	$= \dfrac{\$125\ 000}{\$300\ 000} = 42\%$
Net profit percentage	$= \dfrac{\text{net profit}}{\text{net sales}}$	$= \dfrac{\$25\ 000}{\$300\ 000} = 8\%$
Operating expense percentage	$= \dfrac{\text{total expenses}}{\text{net sales}}$	$= \dfrac{\$100\ 000}{\$300\ 000} = 33\%$
Returns and allowances percentage	$= \dfrac{\text{returns and allowances}}{\text{net sales}}$	$= \dfrac{\$25\ 000}{\$300\ 000} = 8\%$

Another useful ratio is the *stockturn rate* (also called *inventory turnover rate*). The stockturn rate is the number of times an inventory turns over or is sold during a specified time period (often one year). It may be computed on a cost, selling price, or units basis. Thus the formula can be

$$\text{Stockturn rate} = \frac{\text{cost of goods sold}}{\text{average inventory at cost}}$$

or

$$\text{Stockturn rate} = \frac{\text{selling price of goods sold}}{\text{average selling price of inventory}}$$

or

$$\text{Stockturn rate} = \frac{\text{sales in units}}{\text{average inventory in units}}$$

We will use the first formula to calculate the stockturn rate for Dale Parsons Men's Wear:

$$\frac{\$175\ 000}{(\$60\ 000 + \$45\ 000) / 2} = \frac{\$175\ 000}{\$52\ 500} = 3.3$$

That is, Parsons's inventory turned over 3.3 times in 2007. Normally, the higher the stockturn rate, the higher the management efficiency and company profitability.

Return on investment (ROI)
A common measure of managerial effectiveness—the ratio of net profit to investment.

Return on investment (ROI) is frequently used to measure managerial effectiveness. It uses figures from the firm's operating statement and balance sheet. A commonly used formula for computing ROI is

$$\text{ROI} = \frac{\text{net profit}}{\text{sales}} \times \frac{\text{sales}}{\text{investment}}$$

You may have two questions about this formula: Why use a two-step process when ROI could be computed simply as net profit divided by investment? And what exactly is "investment"?

To answer these questions, let's look at how each component of the formula can affect the ROI. Suppose Dale Parsons Men's Wear has a total investment of $150 000. Then ROI can be computed as follows:

$$\text{ROI} = \frac{25\,000\,(\text{net profit})}{300\,000\,(\text{sales})} \times \frac{300\,000\,(\text{sales})}{150\,000\,(\text{investment})}$$

$$= 8.3\% \times 2 = 16.6\%$$

Now suppose that Parsons had worked to increase his share of market. He could have had the same ROI if his sales had doubled while dollar profit and investment stayed the same (accepting a lower profit ratio to get higher turnover and market share):

$$\text{ROI} = \frac{\$25\,000\,(\text{net profit})}{\$600\,000\,(\text{sales})} \times \frac{\$600\,000\,(\text{sales})}{\$150\,000\,(\text{investment})}$$

$$= 4.16\% \times 4 = 16.6\%$$

Parsons might have increased his ROI by increasing net profit through more cost cutting and more efficient marketing:

$$\text{ROI} = \frac{\$50\,000\,(\text{net profit})}{\$300\,000\,(\text{sales})} \times \frac{\$300\,000\,(\text{sales})}{\$150\,000\,(\text{investment})}$$

$$= 16.6\% \times 2 = 33.2\%$$

Another way to increase ROI is to find some way to get the same levels of sales and profits while decreasing investment (perhaps by cutting the size of Parsons's average inventory):

$$\text{ROI} = \frac{\$25\,000\,(\text{net profit})}{\$300\,000\,(\text{sales})} \times \frac{\$300\,000\,(\text{sales})}{\$75\,000\,(\text{investment})}$$

$$= 8.3\% \times 4 = 33.2\%$$

What is "investment" in the ROI formula? *Investment* is often defined as the total assets of the firm. But many analysts now use other measures of return to assess performance. These measures include *return on net assets (RONA)*, *return on stockholders' equity (ROE)*, or *return on assets managed (ROAM)*. Because investment is measured at a point in time, we usually compute ROI as the average investment between two time periods (say, January 1 and December 31 of the same year). We can also compute ROI as an "internal rate of return" by using discounted cash flow analysis (see any finance textbook for more on this technique). The objective in using any of these measures is to determine how well the company has been using its resources. As inflation, competitive pressures, and cost of capital increase, such measures become increasingly important indicators of marketing and company performance.

Markup
The percentage of the cost or price of a product added to cost in order to arrive at a selling price.

Markdown
A percentage reduction from the original selling price.

Markups and Markdowns

Retailers and wholesalers must understand the concepts of **markups** and **markdowns**. They must make a profit to stay in business, and the markup percentage affects profits. Markups and markdowns are expressed as percentages.

There are two different ways to compute markups—on *cost* or on *selling price:*

$$\text{Markup percentage on cost} = \frac{\text{dollar markup}}{\text{cost}}$$

$$\text{Markup percentage on selling price} = \frac{\text{dollar markup}}{\text{selling price}}$$

Dale Parsons must decide which formula to use. If Parsons bought shirts for $15 and wanted to mark them up $10 to a price of $25, his markup percentage on cost would be $10 ÷ $15 = 67.7%.

If Parsons based markup on selling price, the percentage would be $10 ÷ $25 = 40%. In figuring markup percentage, most retailers use the selling price rather than the cost.

Suppose Parsons knew his cost ($12) and desired markup on price (25%) for a man's tie, and wanted to compute the selling price. The formula is

$$\text{Selling price} = \frac{\text{cost}}{1 - \text{markup}}$$

$$\text{Selling price} = \frac{\$12}{0.75} = \$16$$

As a product moves through the channel of distribution, each channel member adds a markup before selling the product to the next member. This "markup chain" is shown for a suit purchased by a Parsons customer for $200:

		Dollar Amount	Percentage of Selling Price
Manufacturer	Cost	$ 108	90%
	Markup	12	10
	Selling price	120	100
Wholesaler	Cost	120	80
	Markup	30	20
	Selling price	150	100
Retailer	Cost	150	75
	Markup	50	25
	Selling price	200	100

The retailer whose markup is 25 percent does not necessarily enjoy more profit than a manufacturer whose markup is 10 percent. Profit also depends on how many items with that profit margin can be sold (stockturn rate) and on operating efficiency (expenses).

Sometimes a retailer wants to convert markups based on selling price to markups based on cost, and vice versa. The formulas are

$$\text{Markup percentage on selling price} = \frac{\text{markup percentage on cost}}{100\% + \text{markup percentage on selling cost}}$$

$$\text{Markup percentage on cost} = \frac{\text{markup percentage on selling price}}{100\% - \text{markup percentage on selling price}}$$

Suppose Parsons found that his competitor was using a markup of 30 percent based on cost and wanted to know what this would be as a percentage of selling price. The calculation would be

$$\frac{30\%}{100\% + 30\%} = \frac{30\%}{130\%} = 23\%$$

Because Parsons was using a 25 percent markup on the selling price for suits, he felt that his markup was suitable compared with that of the competitor.

Near the end of the summer, Parsons still had an inventory of summer slacks in stock. Therefore, he decided to use a *markdown,* a reduction from the original selling price. Before the summer, he had purchased 20 pairs at $10 each, and he had since sold 10 pairs at $20 each. He marked down the other pairs to $15 and sold 5 pairs. We compute his *markdown ratio* as follows:

$$\text{Markdown percentage} = \frac{\text{dollar markdown}}{\text{total net sales in dollars}}$$

The dollar markdown is $25 (5 pairs at $5 each) and total net sales are $275 (10 pairs at $20 + 5 pairs at $15). The ratio, then, is $25 ÷ $275 = 9%.

Larger retailers usually compute markdown ratios for each department rather than for individual items. The ratios provide a measure of relative marketing performance for each department and can be calculated and compared over time. Markdown ratios can also be used to compare the performance of different buyers and salespeople in a store's various departments.

Reviewing the Key Terms

Balance sheet   A25
Cost of goods sold   A26
Gross margin   A26
Gross sales   A25
Markdown   A28

Markup   A28
Operating ratios   A27
Operating statement (or profit-and-loss statement or income statement)   A25
Return on investment (ROI)   A27

References

Chapter 1

1. Quotes and other information from Mark Woods, "Readers Try to Explain Why Racin' Rocks," *The Florida Times Union*, February 16, 2003, p. C1 and NASCAR Canada's website, www.tsn.ca/auto_racing/nascar/; Paul Ferriss, "NASCAR Rides the Fast Track," *Marketing Magazine*, April 11, 2005; Marketing Daily, "Some racy new romance from Harlequin," *Marketing Magazine*, November 3, 2005; Tina Grady, "NASCAR Fan Base More Than Just Blue Collar," *Aftermarket Business*, May 2002, p. 11; George Pyne, "In His Own Words: NASCAR Sharpens Winning Strategy," *Advertising Age*, October 28, 2002, p. S6; Peter Spiegel, "Heir Gordon," *Forbes,* December 14, 1998, pp. 42–46; Tony Kontzer, "Backseat Drivers—NASCAR Puts You in the Race," *InformationWeek*, March 25, 2002, p. 83; Matthew Futterman, "What Fuels NASCAR," *The Star-Ledger*, February 16, 2003, p. 1; Rich Thomaselli, "Sponsors Sweat New NASCAR Scoring System," *Advertising Age*, February 2, 2004, p. 4; Tom Lowry, "The Prince of NASCAR," *Business Week*, February 23, 2004, pp. 91–98; Thomas Heath and Greg Sandoval, "Baseball Adding Ads to On-Field Lineup," *Washington Post,* May 6, 2004, p. A01; and www.NASCAR.com, November 2004.

2. "Top 1000 Companies," *Globe and Mail*, www.globeinvestor.com/series/top1000/tables/companies/2005/, accessed November 26, 2005.

3. Lisa M. Keefe, "Marketing Redefined," *Marketing News,* September 15, 2004, pp. 1, 16–18.

4. "Gwyn Morgan Remarks at the Launch of the EnCana Corporate Constitution on September 8, 2003," EnCana website, www.encana.com/whoweare/values/ov_remarks_gwyn_morgan.html (accessed November 27, 2005). Reprinted by permission of EnCana.

5. For an interesting discussion of creating customer value and extracting value in return, see Natalie Mizik and Robert Jacobson, "Trading Off Between Value Creation and Value Appropriation: The Financial Implications of Shifts in Strategic Emphasis," *Journal of Marketing*, January 2003, pp. 63–76.

6. Ines Colabrese, "Is bottled water safer than tap water?" CBC *Marketplace*, February 8, 2000.

7. Mark Ritson, "The Best Research Comes from Living the Life of Your Customer," *Marketing*, July 18, 2002, p. 16; June Lee Risser, "Customer Come First," *Marketing Management*, November–December 2003, pp. 22–26; Jack Neff, "Value Proposition Becomes a Priority," *Advertising Age*, February 23, 2004, p. 24; and Neff, "Q&A with Lafley: It's the Consumer, Stupid," *Advertising Age,* February 23, 2004, p. 20.

8. See Theodore Levitt's classic article, "Marketing Myopia," *Harvard Business Review*, July–August 1960, pp. 45–56. For more recent discussions, see James R. Stock, "Marketing Myopia Revisited: Lessons for Logistics," *International Journal of Physical Distribution & Logistics Management*, vol. 2, issue 1/2, 2002, pp. 12–21; and Yves Doz, Jose Santos, and Peter J. Williamson, "Marketing Myopia Re-Visited: Why Every Company Needs to Learn from the World," *Ivey Business Journal*, January–February 2004, p. 1.

9. Erika Rasmusson, "Marketing More Than a Product," *Sales & Marketing Management*, February 2000, p. 99. Also see B. Joseph Pine II and James Gilmore, "Welcome to the Experience Economy," *Harvard Business Review*, July–August 1998, p. 99; Pat Esgate, "Pine and Gilmore Stage a Fourth ThinkAbout Experience," *Strategy & Leadership*, vol. 30, issue 3, 2002, pp. 47–48; Bernd Schmitt, *Customer Experience Management: A Revolutionary Approach to Connecting with Your Customers* (New York: John Wiley & Sons, 2003); and Lawrence A. Crosby and Sheree L. Johnson, "Manufacturing Experiences," *Marketing Management,* January–February 2004, pp. 12–14.

10. See James Bandler, "Kodak Advances in Marketing Share of Digital Cameras," *Wall Street Journal*, December 21, 2001, p. B2; Bandler, "Leading the News: Kodak Posts Disappointing Net, Plans New Layoffs," January 23, 2003, p. A3; and "Kodak Changes the Picture," *Global Agenda*, January 22, 2004, p. 1.

11. See Philip Kotler, *Kotler on Marketing* (New York: Free Press, 1999), pp. 20–24; Anthony W. Ulwick, "Turn Customer Input Into Innovation," *Harvard Business Review,* January 2002, pp. 91–97; and David Kirkpatrick, "Why 'Bottom Up' Is on Its Way Up," *Fortune*, January 26, 2004, p. 54.

12. See Gail Johnson, "Changing Tastes Make a Meal of Food Guide," *Straight.com*, February 12, 2004, www.straight.com/content.cfm?id=707; Clifton Joseph, "What's the long-term impact of fast food?," CBC *Marketplace*, April 3, 2002, www.cbc.ca/consumers/market/files/food/fastfood/; Jane E. Brody, "The Widening of America, or How Size 4 Became Size 0," *New York Times*, January 20, 2004, p. F.7; and Kenneth Hein, "Salad Days to Continue for Fast-Feeders," *Brandweek*, January 5, 2004, p. 12; Wendy's corporate website, www.wendys.com/food/NutritionLanding.jsp (accessed September 2006).

13. See Neil A. Martin, "A New Ground War," *Barron's*, April 21, 2003, pp. 21–26; Kevin Kelleher, "Why FedEx Is Gaining Ground," *Business 2.0,* October 2003, p. 56; and "FedEx Corporation," Hoover's Company Capsules, http://proquest.umi.com (accessed February 2004).

14. For more on customer satisfaction, see Regina Fazio Marcuna, "Mapping the World of Customer Satisfaction, *Harvard Business Review*, May–June 2000, p. 30; Marc R. Okrant, "How to Convert '3's and '4's into '5's," *Marketing News*, October 14, 2002, pp. 14, 17; and Frederick F Reichheld, "The One Number You Need," *Harvard Business Review,* December 2003, pp. 46–54.

15. Information about the Harley Owners Group at www.hog.com (accessed September 2004).

16. See Erika Rasmusson, "Wanted: Profitable Customers," *Sales & Marketing Management*, May 1999, pp. 28–34; Chris Serres, "Banks Get Customers' Numbers," *Raleigh News & Observer*, March 19, 2002, pp. A1, A4;

"Customer Profitability," *Chief Executive,* April 2003, pp. 1–4; and Larry Selden and Geoffrey Colvin, "How to Measure the Profitability of Your Customers," *Harvard Business Review,* June 2003, p. 74.

17. See Renee Houston Zemansky and Jeff Weiner, "Just Hang On to What You Got," *Selling Power,* March 2002, pp. 60–64; and Marc R. Okrant, "How to Convert '3's and '4's into '5's," *Marketing News,* October 14, 2002, pp. 14, 17.

18. Philip Kotler, *Kotler on Marketing* (New York: Free Press, 1999), p. 20.

19. Jennifer Gilbert, "Partners in Branding," *Sales & Marketing Management,* March 2004, p. 10.

20. Thor Valdmanis, "Alliances Gain Favor over Risky Mergers," *USA Today,* February 4, 1999, p. 3B. Also see Matthew Schifrin, "Partner or Perish," *Forbes,* May 21, 2001, pp. 26–28; and Kim T. Gordan, "Strong Partnerships Build Marketing Muscle," *CRN,* February 10, 2003, p. 14A.

21. See Frederick F Reichheld, "The One Number You Need," *Harvard Business Review,* December 2003, pp. 46–54; Thomas O. Jones and W. Earl Sasser Jr. "Why Satisfied Customers Defect," *Harvard Business Review,* November–December 1995, pp. 88–99; Fred Reichheld and Christine Detrick, "Loyalty: A Prescription for Cutting Costs," *Marketing Management,* September–October, 2003, pp. 24–25; Deborah L. Vence, "Keep 'Em Coming Back for More," *Marketing News,* October 13, 2003, p. 19; and Jacquelyn S. Thomas, Robert C. Blattberg, and Edward J. Fox, "Recapturing Lost Customers," *Journal of Marketing Research,* February 2004, pp. 31–45.

22. Information from www.stew-leonards.com/html/about.cfm (accessed November 2004).

23. See Mark McMaster, "A Lifetime of Sales," *Sales & Marketing Management,* September 2001, p. 55; Lauren Keller Johnson, "The Real Value of Customer Loyalty," *MIT Sloan Management Review,* Winter 2002, pp. 14–17; and Charlotte H. Mason, "Tuscan Lifestyles: Assessing Customer Lifetime Value," *Journal of Interactive Marketing,* Autumn 2003, pp. 54–60.

24. Erin Stout, "Keep Them Coming Back for More," *Sales and Marketing Management,* February 2002, pp. 51–52; and Fiona Haley, "Fast Talk," *Fast Company,* December 2003, p. 57.

25. See Roland T. Rust, Valerie A. Zeithaml, and Katherine A. Lemon, *Driving Customer Equity* (New York Free Press 2000); Rust, Lemon, and Zeithaml, "Where Should the Next Marketing Dollar Go?" *Marketing Management,* September–October 2001, pp. 24–28; Robert C. Blattberg, Gary Getz, Jacquelyn S. Thomas, *Customer Equity* (Boston, MA: Harvard Business School Press, 2001); John E. Hogan, Katherine N. Lemon, and Roland T. Rust, "Customer Equity Management: Charting New Directions for the Future of Marketing," *Journal of Service Research,* August 2002, pp. 4–12; and Rust, Lemon, and Zeithaml, "Return on Marketing: Using Customer Equity to Focus Marketing Strategy," *Journal of Marketing,* January 2004, pp. 109–127.

26. This example is adapted from Rust, Lemon, and Zeithaml, "Where Should the Next Marketing Dollar Go?" *Marketing Management,* p. 25. For deeper discussions of how to measure customer equity, see Robert C. Blattberg, Gary Getz, Jacquelyn S. Thomas, *Customer Equity* (Boston,

MA: Harvard Business School Press, 2001); Rust, Lemon, and Zeithaml, "Return on Marketing: Using Customer Equity to Focus Marketing Strategy," *Journal of Marketing,* pp. 109–127; and James D. Lenskold, "Customer-Centered Marketing ROI," *Marketing Management,* January/February 2004, pp. 26–32.

27. Ravi Dhar and Rashi Glazer, "Hedging Customers," *Harvard Business Review,* May 2003, pp. 86–92.

28. Werner Reinartz and V. Kumar, "The Mismanagement of Customer Loyalty," *Harvard Business Review,* July 2002, pp. 86–94. For more on customer equity management, see Robert C. Blattberg, Gary Getz, Jacquelyn S. Thomas, *Customer Equity* (Boston, MA: Harvard Business School Press, 2001), chapters 3–6; Sunil Gupta and Donald R. Lehman, "Customers as Assets," *Journal of Interactive Marketing,* Winter 2003, pp. 9–24; Reinartz and Kumar, "The Impact of Customer Relationship Characteristics on Profitable Lifetime Duration," *Journal of Marketing,* January 2003, pp. 77–79; Bradley E. Hosmer, "Customer Equity: Building and Managing Relationships as Valuable Assets, *Consulting to Management,* June 2003, p. 59; Sunil Gupta, Donald R. Lehman, and Jennifer Ames Stuart, "Valuing Customers," *Journal of Marketing Research,* February 2004, pp. 7–18; and Gupta and Lehmann, *Managing Your Customers as Investments: The Strategic Value of Customer in the Long Run* (Philadelphia: Wharton School Publishing, 2005).

29. For another interesting discussion on managing the customer portfolio, see Michael D. Johnson and Fred Selnes, "Customer Portfolio Management: Toward a Dynamic Theory of Exchange Relationships." *Journal of Marketing,* April 2004, pp. 1–17.

30. "Canadian e-Commerce Statistics," Industry Canada, http://e-com.ic.gc.ca/epic/internet/inecic-ceac.nsf/en/gv00163e.html (accessed November 27, 2005); Internet World Stats, www.internetworldstats.com/stats.htm (accessed November 27, 2005); "Internet Penetration Rate Slows," *Silicon Valley/San Jose Business Journal,* February 5, 2003, http://eastbay.bizjournals.com/sanjose; "Population Explosion!" *CyberAtlas,* March 14, 2003, at www.cyberatlas.com; and information at www.internetworldstats.com (accessed February 2004).

31. Industry Canada, http://e-com.ic.gc.ca/epic/internet/inecic-ceac.nsf/en/gv00163e.html (accessed November 27, 2005); Steve Hamm, "E-Biz: Down but Hardly Out," *Business Week,* March 26, 2001, pp. 126–130; "B2B E-Commerce Headed for Trillions," March 6, 2002, www.cyberatlas.internet.com; and Mullaney, "E-biz Surprise," pp. 60–68.

32. See Ben & Jerry's full mission statement online at www.benjerry.com.

33. Caroline Riseboro, "The non-profit motive," *Marketing Magazine,* April 11, 2005.

34. "Media in Canada," *Strategy Magazine,* November 15, 2005. For other examples, and for a good review of non-profit marketing, see Philip Kotler and Alan R. Andreasen, *Strategic Marketing for Nonprofit Organizations,* 6th ed. (Upper Saddle River, NJ: Prentice Hall, 2003).

Chapter 2

1. *Walt Disney Company 2005 Annual Report*; Marc Gunther, "Mouse Hunt," *Fortune*, January 12, 2004, p. 106; "Top 50 North American Amusement/Theme Parks," *Amusement Business*, December 22, 2004, p. 18; "The Walt Disney Company," *Hoover Company Profiles,* Austin, March 15, 2004, p. 11603; David J. Jefferson and Johnnie L. Roberts, "The Magic Is Gone," March 15, 2004, p. 52; and information accessed online at www.Disney.go.com/corporate, November 2004.

2. For a more detailed discussion of corporate- and business-level strategic planning as they apply to marketing, see Philip Kotler, *Marketing Management*, 11th ed. (Upper Saddle River, NJ: Prentice Hall, 2003), Chapter 4.

3. See Forest David and Fred David, "It's Time to Redraft Your Mission Statement," *The Journal of Business Strategy*, January/February 2003, pp. 11–15; and "Crafting Mission Statements," *Association Management,* January 2004, p. 23.

4. "RBC Vision," www.rbc.com/aboutus/visionandvalues.html, accessed January 8, 2006.

5. The following discussion is based in part on information found at www.bcg.com/this_is_bcg/mission/growth_share_matrix.jsp, accessed August 2004. For more on strategic planning, see Tom Devane, "Ten Cardinal Sins of Strategic Planning," *Executive Excellence*, October 2000, p. 15; Dave Lefkowith, "Effective Strategic Planning," *Management Quarterly*, Spring 2001, pp. 7–11; Dennis Rheault, "Freshening Up Strategic Planning: More than Fill-in-the-Blanks," *The Journal of Business Strategy*, Vol. 24, Iss. 6, 2004, pp. 33–37; and Anthony Lavia, "Strategic Planning in Times of Turmoil," *Business Communications Review*, March 2004, pp. 56–60.

6. From personal knowledge of the company, plus information on Sunsilk from the Unilever.ca website (products) (accessed July 10, 2006).

7. H. Igor Ansoff, "Strategies for Diversification," *Harvard Business Review*, September–October 1957, pp. 113–124. Also see Philip Kotler, *Kotler on Marketing* (New York: Free Press, 1999), pp. 46–48; and Kevin Lane Keller, *Strategic Brand Management*, 2nd ed. (Upper Saddle River, NJ: Prentice Hall, 2003) pp. 576–578.

8. Nirmalya Kumar, "Kill a Brand, Keep a Customer," *Harvard Business Review*, December 2003, pp. 87–95.

9. Michael E. Porter, *Competitive Advantage: Creating and Sustaining Superior Performance* (New York: Free Press, 1985); and Michel E. Porter, "What Is Strategy?" *Harvard Business Review*, November–December 1996, pp. 61–78. Also see Kim B. Clark et al. *Harvard Business School on Managing the Value Chain* (Boston: Harvard Business School Press, 2000); "Buyer Value and the Value Chain," *Business Owner*, September–October 2003, p. 1; and "The Value Chain," www.quickmba.com/strategy/value-chain/, (accessed July 2004).

10. Kotler, *Kotler on Marketing*, pp. 20–22. Also see Philip Kotler, *Marketing Insights from A to Z* (Hoboken, NJ: Wiley, 2003), pp. 102–107.

11. David Stires, "Fallen Arches," *Fortune*, April 29, 2002, pp. 74–76; Sherri Day, "After Years at the Top, McDonald's Strives To Regain Ground," *New York Times*, March 3, 2003, p. A1; and McDonald's Corporation Investor Fact Sheet January 2004, www.mcdonalds.com/corp/invest/pub/2004_fact_sheet.html.

12. "Canadian Tire and NAPA Canada enter into product supply and technology agreement for select automotive hard parts," UAP Press Release, November 4, 2002, www.uapinc.com (accessed July 5, 2004).

13. Myron Magnet, "The New Golden Rule of Business," *Fortune*, February 21, 1994, pp. 60–63. For more on value network and supply chain management and strategic alliances, also see Philip Kotler, *Marketing Management,* 11th ed. (Upper Saddle River, NJ: Prentice Hall, 2003), pp. 70–71; and David A. Taylor, *Supply Chains: A Manager's Guide* (Boston: Addison-Wesley, 2004).

14. Steve MacNaull, "When life hands you apples, make juice," *Globe and Mail*, October 26, 2005, p. B9.

15. Ad Age Dataplace, www.adage.com/dataplace (accessed November 2004).

16. The four *Ps* classification was first suggested by E. Jerome McCarthy, *Basic Marketing: A Managerial Approach* (Homewood, IL: Irwin, 1960). For the 4Cs, other proposed classifications, and more discussion, see Robert Lauterborn, "New Marketing Litany: 4P's Passé; C-Words Take Over," *Advertising Age*, October 1, 1990, p. 26; Don E. Schultz, "Marketers: Bid Farewell to Strategy Based on Old 4Ps," *Marketing News*, February 12, 2001, p. 7; John Farrell, "Highlighting the 4Rs of Marketing," *Incentive*, April 2002, p. 101; and Elliott Ettenberg, "Goodbye 4Ps, Hello 4Rs," *Marketing Magazine*, April 14, 2003, p. 8.

17. Brian Dumaine, "Why Great Companies Last," *Business Week*, January 16, 1995, p. 129. See James C. Collins and Jerry I. Porras, *Built to Last: Successful Habits of Visionary Companies* (New York: HarperBusiness, 1995); Rob Goffee and Gareth Jones, *The Character of a Corporation: How Your Company's Culture Can Make or Break Your Business* (New York: HarperBusiness, 1998); Jeff Rosenthal and Mary Ann Masarech, "High-Performance Cultures: How Values Can Drive Vision," *Journal of Organizational Excellence,* Spring 2003, pp. 3–18; and Naomi Moneypenny, "Five Foundations for Developing a Corporate Culture," *The RMA Journal*, February 2004, p. 22.

18. For more on brand and product management, see Kevin Lane Keller, *Strategic Brand Management*, 2nd ed. (Upper Saddle River, NJ: Prentice Hall, 2003).

19. See Roland T. Rust, Valerie A. Zeithaml, and Katherine N. Lemon, *Driving Customer Equity: How Lifetime Customer Value Is Reshaping Corporate Strategy* (New York: Free Press, 2000); Rust, Lemon, and Zeithaml, "Where Should the Next Marketing Dollar Go?" *Marketing Management*, September–October 2001, pp. 24–28; Sunil Gupta and Donald R. Lehman, "Customers as Assets," *Journal of Interactive Marketing*, Winter 2003, pp. 9–24; Michael D. Johnson and Fred Selnes, "Customer Portfolio Management: Toward a Dynamic Theory of Exchange Relationships." *Journal of Marketing*, April 2004, pp. 1–17; and Gupta and Lehmann, *Managing Your Customer as Investment: The Strategic Value of Customers in the Long Run* (Philadelphia: Wharton School Publishing, 2005).

20. For details, see Kotler, *Marketing Management,* pp. 695–699. Also see Neil A. Morgan, Bruce H. Clark, and Rich Gooner, "Marketing Productivity, Marketing Audits, and Systems for Marketing Performance Assessment: Integrating Multiple Perspectives," *Journal of Marketing,* May 2002, pp. 363–375.

21. "Lenskold Group Announces 'Marketing ROI' Book Now Shipping," press release, July 25, 2003, www.lenskold.com/news/mroi_book.html; and Arundhati Parmar, "Barriers to Success," *Marketing News,* March 1, 2004, pp. 20–21. Also see Patrick Lapointe, "Marketing ROI: What's Next?" *B to B,* February 9, 2004, p. 11.

22. *Ibid;* and Judann Pollack, "Marketers Slap Network TV in Survey on ROI," *Advertising Age,* October 13, 2003, p. 11.

23. Mark McMaster, "ROI: More Vital than Ever," *Sales & Marketing Management,* January 2002, pp. 51–52. Also see, Jim Lenskold, "CFOs Are from Mars, CMOs Are from Venus," www.marketingpower.com/live/content17702C5226.php (accessed May 2004).

24. For a full discussion of this model and details on customer-centred measures of return on marketing, see Roland T. Rust, Katherine N. Lemon, and Valerie A. Zeithaml, "Return on Marketing: Using Customer Equity to Focus Marketing Strategy," *Journal of Marketing,* January 2004, pp. 109–127. Also see James D. Lenskold, "Customer-Centric Marketing ROI," *Marketing Management,* January–February 2004, pp. 26–32; and Sunil Gupta, Donald R. Lehmann, and Jennifer Ames Stuart, "Valuing Customers," *Journal of Marketing Research,* February 2004, pp. 7–18.

25. James D. Lenskold, "Marketing ROI: Playing to Win," *Marketing Management,* May–June 2002, pp. 30–36; Judann Pollack, "Marketers Slap Network TV in Survey on ROI," p. 1; Tim Donaldson, "Measure Returns with Process Integration," Marketing *News,* March 1, 2004, p. 23; and Michael D. Johnson and Fred Selnes, "Customer Portfolio Management: Toward a Dynamic Theory of Exchange Relationships," *Journal of Marketing,* April 2004, pp. 1–17.

Chapter 3

1. www.mcdonalds.ca/en/aboutus/mcdCanada_facts.aspx; Laura Pratt, "Sub Wars," *Marketing Magazine,* March 14, 2005; Sherri Day, "After Years at Top, McDonald's Strives To Regain Ground," *New York Times,* March 3, 2003, p. A.1; "McDonald's Real Life Choices Teaches Consumers How to Eat the McDonald's Food They Love and Stay on Track with Their Diets," McDonalds Press Release, January 6, 2004, www.McDonalds.com; Jonathan B. Cox, "From Burgers to Beans," *The News and Observer,* January 10, 2004, p. C1; Shirley Leung, "McDonald's Makeover," *Wall Street Journal,* January 28, 2004, p. B1; Steven Gray, "McDonald's Feels the Heat and Offers Some Healthier Fare," *Wall Street Journal,* April 16, 2004, p. A11; Sarah Hale Meiter, "McDonald's Bistro Gourmet Concept Spreads," *Chicago Tribune Online Edition,* May 12, 2004; David Stires, "McDonald's Keeps Right on Cookin'," *Fortune,* May 17, 2004, p. 174; "McDonald's Earnings Jump 56%," *Los Angeles Times,* April 28, 2004, p. C3; and Michael Arndt, "McDonald's: Fries with that Salad?" *Business Week,* July 5, 2004, pp. 82–84; Angela Moore,

"Tasty prospects for McDonald's: analysts," *MarketWatch,* January 19, 2006.

2. See Canadian Tire Corporate Supplier Code of Business Conduct, November 11, 2004 v2, www2.canadiantire.ca/CTenglish/pdf/Supplier_Code_of_Business_Conduct (English).pdf (accessed January 21, 2006).

3. See Sarah Lorge, "The Coke Advantage," *Sales & Marketing Management,* December 1998, p. 17; "Coca-Cola Inks New Deal with Jack in the Box Chain," *Nation's Restaurant News,* January 13, 2003, p. 52; and Chad Terhune "Coke Wins a 10-Year Contract From Subway, Ousting PepsiCo," *Wall Street Journal,* November 28, 2003, p. B.3.

4. World POPClock, U.S. Census Bureau, www.census.gov (accessed November 2004). This website provides continuously updated projections of the U.S. and world populations.

5. Adapted from Frederik Balfour, "Educating the 'Little Emperors': There's a Big Market for Products that Help China's Coddled Kids Get Ahead," *Business Week,* November 10, 2003, p. 22. Also see Clay Chandler, "Little Emperors," *Fortune,* October 4, 2004, pp. 138–150.

6. "Median Age Reaches All Time High," Statistics Canada, www12.statcan.ca/english/census01/Products/Analytic/companion/age/canada.cfm#median_age.

7. Daniel Stoffman, "Completely predictable people," *Report on Business,* November 1990, pp. 78–84; David Foot and Daniel Stoffman, *Boom, Bust and Echo* (Toronto: Macfarlane Walter & Ross, 1996), pp. 18–22.

8. Dorothy Lipovenko, "Growing old is a baby-booming business," *Globe and Mail,* April 6, 1996:A1, A4; Dorothy Lipovenko, "Rich boomers aiming to retire earlier than parents, poll says," *Globe and Mail,* October 10, 1996:B10; and Jennifer Lach, "Dateline America: May 1, 2025," *American Demographics,* p. 19.

9. See Michael Weiss, "Chasing Youth," American Demographics, October 2002, pp. 35–41; Joan Raymond, "The Joy of Empty Nesting," *American Demographics,* May 2000, pp. 49–54; David Rakoff, "The Be Generation," *Adweek,* March 5, 2001, pp. SR18–SR22; Gene Koretz, "Bless the Baby Boomers," *Business Week,* June 10, 2002, p. 30; Greg Schneider, "Rebels with Disposable Income: Aging Baby Boomers Line Up to Buy High-End Versions of Youthful Indulgences," *The Washington Post,* April 27, 2003, p. F01; and "Married Baby Boomers Heart of Cruise Market," March 31, 2004, www.hospitality.net.

10. "Mixed Success: One Who Targeted Gen X and Succeeded—Sort Of," *Journal of Financial Planning,* February 2004, p. 15.

11. See Jean Chatzky, "Gen Xers Aren't Slackers After All," *Time,* April 8, 2002, p. 87; Rebecca Ryan, "10 Questions with … Rebecca Ryan," *Journal of Financial Planning,* February 2004, pp. 12–17; "They're Not Aloof … Just Generation X," *CMA Management,* April 2004, p. 6; and "Overlooked and Under X-Ploited," *American Demographics,* May 2004, p. 48.

12. "Aritzia," Wikipedia, http://en.wikipedia.org/wiki/Aritzia (accessed September 2006); "Aritzia," Where Toronto, www.where.ca/toronto/guide_listing~listing_id~3490.htm (accessed September 2006).

13. See Ken Gronback, "Marketing to Generation Y," *DSN Retailing Today,* July 24, 2000, p. 14; and Joanna Krotz, "Tough Customers: How to Reach Gen Y," www.bcentral.com (accessed March 21, 2003).

14. Tobi Elkin, "Gen Y Quizzed about On-Demand," *Advertising Age,* February 14, 2003, p. 37. Also see Pamela Paul, "Getting Inside Gen Y," *American Demographics,* September 2001, pp. 43–49; and Rebecca Gardyn, "Born to Be Wired," *American Demographics,* April 2003, pp. 14–15; and "Teens Spent $175 Billion in 2003," press release, Teenage Research Unlimited, January 9, 2004, www.teenresearch.com/home.cfm.

15. Adapted from portions of Jean Halliday, "Automakers Mix It Up To Chase Young Buyers," *Automotive News,* April 26, 2004, p. 28B.

16. See J. Walker Smith and Ann Clurman, *Rocking the Ages* (New York: HarperBusiness, 1998); Mercedes M. Cardona, "Hilfiger's New Apparel Lines Getting Individual Efforts," *Advertising Age,* February 8, 1999, p. 24; and Alison Stein Wellner, "Generational Divide," *American Demographics,* October 2000, pp. 53–58.

17. Erin Anderssen, "Junior's at Home and Grandma's Alone," *Globe and Mail,* October 23, 2002, p. A1; Dawn Walton, "Census Reports More Canadians are Home Alone," *Globe and Mail,* October 23, 2001, p. A6; Darren Yourk, "Canadian Family Portrait Changing," *Globe and Mail,* October 23, 2002, p. A6. See also Statistics Canada, "2001 Census: Marital Status, Common-Law Status, Families, Dwellings and Households," *The Daily,* October 22, 2003, www.statcan.ca/Daily/English/021022/td022122.htm.

18. Human Resources Development Canada, Section 5.2 "Women," http://info.load-otea.hrdc-drhc.gc.ca/workplace_equity/leep/annual/2002/2002annualrep08.shtml (accessed May 5, 2003).

19. Statistics Canada, "Population Projections for 2001, 2006, 2011, 2016, 2021 and 2026, July 1," Canadian Statistics, www.statcan.ca/english/Pgdb/demo23a.htm (accessed May 5, 2003).

20. Statistics Canada, "A Profile of the Canadian Population: Where We Live," 2001 Census Release, March 12, 2002, http://geodepot.statcan.ca/Diss/Highlights/Highlights_e.cfm; and Ross Finnie, "The Effects of Inter-Provincial Mobility on Individuals' Earnings: Panel Model Estimates for Canada," Analytical Studies Branch Research Paper Series, Report 163, Catalogue No. 11F0019MIE2001163, October 2001, http://collection.nlc-bnc.ca/100/200/301/statcan/research_paper_analytical_11f0019-e/no163/11F0019MIE01163.pdf.

21. Canadian Consumer Demographics, Industry Canada, Retail Interactive, http://strategis.ic.gc.ca/SSG/ri00140e.html (accessed May 6, 2003).

22. "Who Works from Home," GDSourcing, *The Business Researcher Newsletter Archives,* Vol. 5 (3), March 22, 2002.

23. See "FedEx Rebrands Kinko's," FedEx Press Release, April 27, 2004, http://fedex.com/us/about/news/ update/officeprint.html; "Five Questions," *Sales & Marketing Management,"* July 2004, p. 13; and information found at www.fedex.com/us/officeprint/main/?link=4, November 2004.

24. Statistics Canada, "Education in Canada: School Attendance and Levels of Schooling," 2001 Census Release, March 11, 2003, www12.statcan.ca/english/census01/release/release7.cfm.

25. Hamlin Grange and Don Miller, "How to leverage diversity," *Marketing Magazine,* August 29, 2005.

26. Ibid.

27. Ashwin W. Joshi, "The visible majority," *Marketing Magazine,* August 29, 2005.

28. Statistics Canada, "Families and Household Living Arrangements," 2001 Census Release, October 22, 2003, www12.statcan.ca/english/census01/release/release3.cfm.

29. Barbara Smith, "Special Feature: Gay And Lesbian Marketing: Market Becoming More Accessible," *Strategy,* September 18, 1995, p. 35.

30. Information at Volkswagen's website, www.vw.com, and www.vsarts.org/programs/vw/ (accessed June 2004).

31. Mark MacKinnon, "High-Income Neighbourhoods," *Globe and Mail,* March 1, 1999, p. B1; Mark MacKinnon, "The Lowest Incomes in Canada Are Found on Native Reserves," *Globe and Mail,* March 1, 1999, p. B2.

32. David Leonhardt, "Two-Tier Marketing," *Business Week,* March 17, 1997, pp. 82–90. Also see "MarketLooks: The U.S. Affluent Market," a research report by Packaged Facts, January 1, 2002; and Rebecca Gardyn, "Love Richly," *American Demographics,* April 2003, pp. 16–18.

33. Statistics Canada, "Average Household Expenditures, Provinces and Territories," Canadian Statistics, www.statcan.ca/english/Pgdb/famil16a.htm (accessed March 20, 2003).

34. For more discussion, see the "Environmentalism" section in Chapter 4. "Earth in the Balance," *American Demographics,* January 2001, p. 24; Subhabrata Bobby Banerjee, "Corporate Environmentalism: The Construct and Its Measurement," *Journal of Business Research,* March 2002, pp. 177–191; Marc Gunther, "Tree Huggers, Soy Lovers, and Profits," *Fortune,* June 23, 2003, pp. 98–104; Charles Haddad, "FedEx and Brown Are Going Green," *Business Week,* August 11, 2003; "Sustainability Key to UPS's Environmental Initiatives," http://pressroom.ups.com/ (accessed June 2004); and information at www.3m.com/about3m/sustainability/policies_ehs_tradition_3p.jhtml (accessed November 2004).

35. See "Increased U.S. R&D Spending Expected in 2004," *JOM,* March 2004, p. 7.

36. "Domestic spending on research and development (GERD), funding sector, by province," Statistics Canada, December 12, 2005, www40.statcan.ca/l01/cst01/scte01a.htm.

37. OECD Countries Spend more on Research and Development, Face New Challenges, December 23, 2004, www.oecd.org/document/2/0,2340,en_2649_201185_34100162_1_1_1_1,00.html.

38. A. J. Vogl, "Does It Pay to Be Good?" *Across the Board,* January/February 2003, pp. 16–23.

39. For more on online privacy, see William M. Savino, "Protecting Online Privacy," *Marketing Management,* September–October 2002, pp. 49–51; Deborah L. Vence, "Marketers Expect to See Federal Law on Online Privacy Soon," *Marketing News,* June 24, 2002, p. 4; Eric

Goldman, "The Internet Privacy Fallacy," *Computer and Internet Lawyer*, January 2003, p. 20; and "The Spies in Your Computer," *New York Times*, February 18, 2004, p. A18.

40. For one discussion of Canadian values, see "Projecting Canadian Values And Culture," Foreign Affairs Canada, February 17, 2003; www.dfait-maeci.gc.ca/foreign_policy/cnd-world/chap5-en.asp.

41. For more on Yankelovich Monitor, see www.yankelovich.com/products/monitor.aspx.

42. Adapted from Becky Ebenkamp, "Fun/Duty Now, for the Future," *Brandweek,* January 5, 2004, p. 16.

43. Portions of this example are adapted from information in Eileen Daspin, "The End of Nesting," *Wall Street Journal,* May 16, 2003, p. W1. Also see "The Cocoon Cracks Open," *Brandweek,* April 28, 2003, pp. 32–36; and Dan Lippe, "Gimme Shelter," *Advertising Age,* special report, April 5, 2004, pp. S1–S8.

44. Michael Adams, *Better Happy Than Rich: Canadians, Money, and the Meaning of Life* (Toronto: Viking, 2000), p. 85.

45. *Ibid.* p. 150.

46. Agriculture and Agri Food Canada, "Organics Industry" (fact sheet), 2003, http://ats.agr.ca/supply/3313_e.htm (accessed September 2006). Also see Andrea Zoe Aster, "Greener pastures," *Marketing Magazine,* December 6, 2004.

47. Michael Valpy, "Religious Observance Continues To Decline," *Globe and Mail*, March 19, 2003, p. A18; and Clifford Krauss, "In God We Trust … Canadians Aren't So Sure," *New York Times*, www.nytimes.com, March 26, 2003.

48. See Philip Kotler, *Kotler on Marketing* (New York: Free Press, 1999), p. 3; and Kotler, *Marketing Insights from A to Z* (Hoboken, NJ: John Wiley & Sons, 2003), pp. 23–24.

49. Howard E. Butz Jr. and Leonard D. Goodstein, "Measuring Customer Value: Gaining the Strategic Advantage," *Organizational Dynamics*, Winter 1996, pp. 66–67.

Chapter 4

1. Information from MEC corporate website, www.mec.ca; Eve Lazarus, "MEC Facing Marketing Challenges," *Marketing Magazine*, June 19, 2000, p. 2; and Mary Lamey, "A Monument to the Environment: Focus on Recycling. Mountain Equipment Is Building First 'Green' Retail Outlet in Quebec," *Montreal Gazette,* November 22, 2002, www.canada.com/montreal/. Other information from Harriot Marsh, "Has the Body Shop Lost Its Direction for Good?" *Marketing*, May 10, 2001, p. 19; Mike Hoffman, "Ben Cohen: Ben & Jerry's Homemade, Established in 1978," *Inc*, April 30, 2001, p. 68; and Renee Volpini, "Fight Global Warming with Ice Cream, Music and Activism" (Ben & Jerry's press release), April 2, 2002, http://lib.benjerry.com/pressrel/press040202osw.html. For more on social responsibility in Canada and a listing of leading Canadian firms, see the *Corporate Knights* website, www.corporateknights.ca/, and Industry Canada, http://strategis.ic.gc.ca/; for a critique of the "values-led" practices of Ben & Jerry's and The Body Shop, see Jon

Entine, "Rain-Forest Chic," the *Globe and Mail Report on Business Magazine*, October 1995, www.jonentine.com/articles/rainforest_chic.htm.

2. Imagine website, Media: Quick Facts, www.imagine.ca/content/media/quick_facts.asp?section=media (accessed July 15, 2003).

3. Suncor website, www.suncor.com/ (accessed July 15, 2003)

4. Clifton Joseph and Virginia Smart, "What's the long-term impact of fast food?" CBC Marketplace, Broadcast: April 3, 2002, www.cbc.ca/consumers/market/files/food/fastfood/.

5. Competition Bureau News Releases, "Labatt Pleads Guilty and Pays $250,000 Fine following a Competition Bureau Investigation," November 23, 2005; "Sears deceptive tire marketing case," April 1, 2005; "Mail order companies charged for deceptive marketing practices," March 14, 2005, www.competitionbureau.gc.ca/internet/index.cfm?itemID=21&lg=e.

6. "Business Brief—Publishers Clearing House: Payment of $34 Million Set to Settle with 26 States," *Wall Street Journal,* June 27, 2001, p. B8; and "PCH Reaches $34 Million Sweepstakes Settlement with 26 States," *Direct Marketing,* September 2001, p. 6.

7. PhoneBusters, "What is deceptive telemarketing?" www.phonebusters.com/english/fraudprevention_backgrounder.html.

8. Clifton Joseph, "Fast Food," *Marketplace*, air date April 3, 2002, www.cbc.ca/consumers/market/files/food/fastfood/index.html; and "Kraft Slims Down Kids Marketing," *Marketing Magazine*, July 14/21, 2003, p. 3. See also Sandra Pesmen, "How Low Is Low? How Free Is Free?" *Advertising Age,* May 7, 1990, p. S10; and Karolyn Schuster, "The Dark Side of Nutrition," *Food Management,* June 1999, pp. 34–39.

9. David Welch, "Firestone: Is This Brand Beyond Repair?" *Business Week,* June 11, 2001, p. 48. Also see Ken Belson and Micheline Maynard, "Big Recall Behind It, Tire Maker Regains Its Footing," *New York Times,* August 10, 2002, p. 1, and CBC News, "94 000 Vehicles In Canada Affected By Ford Recall," May 30, 2001, www.cbc.ca/storyview/CBC/2001/05/24/Consumers/fordtires_010524.

10. Cliff Edwards, "Where Have All the Edsels Gone?" *Greensboro News Record,* May 24, 1999, p. B6. For a thought-provoking short case involving planned obsolescence, see James A. Heely and Roy L. Nersesian, "The Case of Planned Obsolescence," *Management Accounting,* February 1994, p. 67. Also see Joel Dryfuss, "Planned Obsolescence Is Alive and Well," *Fortune,* February 15, 1999, p. 192; and Atsuo Utaka, "Planned Obsolescence and Marketing Strategy," *Managerial and Decision Economics,* December 2000, pp. 339–344.

11. Adapted from John Markoff, "Is Planned Obsolesence Obsolete?" *New York Times*, February 17, 2002, pp. 4, 6.

12. See Judith Bell and Bonnie Maria Burlin, "In Urban Areas: Many More Still Pay More for Food," *Journal of Public Policy and Marketing,* Fall 1993, pp. 268–270; Kathryn Graddy and Diana C. Robertson, "Fairness of Pricing Decisions," *Business Ethics Quarterly,* April 1999, pp. 225–243; and Gordon Matthews, "Does Everyone Have the Right to Credit?" *USBanker,* April 2001, pp. 44–48.

13. See Brian Grow and Pallavi Gogoi, "A New Way to Squeeze the Weak?" *Business Week,* January 28, 2002, p. 92.

14. Richard W. Pollay, "The Distorted Mirror: Reflections on the Unintended Consequences of Advertising," *Journal of Marketing,* April 1986, pp. 18–36.

15. Carolyn Setlow, "Profiting from America's New Materialism," *Discount Store News,* April 17, 2000, p. 16. For interesting discussions on materialism and consumption, see Mark Rotella, Sarah F. Gould, Lynn Andriani, and Michael Scharf, "The High Price of Materialism," *Publishers Weekly,* July 1, 2002, p. 67; Lin Chiat Chang and Robert M. Arkin, "Materialism as an Attempt to Cope with Uncertainty," *Psychology & Marketing,* May 2002, pp. 389–406; John De Graaf, "The Overspent American/Luxury Fever," *Amicus Journal,* Summer 1999, pp. 41–43; and Professional Marketing Research Society, "Not Your Average Beer Drinking, Igloo-Dwelling, Hockey-Playing, 'Eh'-Sayers. Now Are We?" (press release), June 2002, www.pmrs-aprm.com/specialpr/release11.html.

16. "A No-Shopping Day," www3.sympatico.ca/dalia/buy0/index.htm.

17. James Twitchell, "Two Cheers for Materialism," *Wilson Quarterly,* Spring 1999, pp. 16–26. Also see Twitchell, *Lead Us into Temptation: The Triumph of American Materialism* (New York: Columbia University Press, 1999); and Twitchell, *Living It Up: Our Love Affair with Luxury* (New York: Columbia University Press, 2002).

18. Mark Rice-Oxley, "Britain Battles Clogged Streets," *The Christian Science Monitor,* February 18, 2003, p. 7; and Ben Walker, "Congestion Charge Is Cutting Jams, Say Chiefs," *Regeneration and Renewal,* June 13, 2003, p. 3.

19. From an advertisement for *Fact* magazine—which does not carry advertisements.

20. Greg Winter, "Hershey Is Put on the Auction Block," *New York Times,* July 26, 2002, p. 5.

21. Adapted from information found in Steve Hamm, "Microsoft's Future," *Business Week,* January 19, 1998, pp. 58–68; Dan Carney and Mike France, "The Microsoft Case: Tying It All Together," *Business Week,* December 3, 2001, pp. 68–69; and Paul Meller and Matt Richtel, "Europeans Rule Against Microsoft; Appeal Is Promised," *New York Times,* March 25, 2004, p. C.1.

22. Paul Skippen and Geoff Wallace, "Both Protests And The Summit Process Depart From Genoa's Trends," *G8 Bulletin,* Volume 5, Issue 6, June 27–30, 2002, www.g7.utoronto.ca/g8bulletin/2002/bulletin6.htm. For more on the evolution of consumerism, see Paul N. Bloom and Stephen A. Greyser, "The Maturing of Consumerism," *Harvard Business Review,* November–December 1981, pp. 130–139; Robert J. Samualson, "The Aging of Ralph Nader," *Newsweek,* December 16, 1985, p. 57; Douglas A. Harbrecht, "The Second Coming of Ralph Nader," *Business Week,* March 6, 1989, p. 28; George S. Day and David A. Aaker, "A Guide to Consumerism," *Marketing Management,* Spring 1997, pp. 44–48; Benet Middleton, "Consumerism: A Pragmatic Ideology," *Consumer Policy Review,* November/December, 1998, pp. 213–217; and Penelope Green, "Consumerism and Its Malcontents," *New York Times,* December 17, 2000, p. 9.1.

23. See Consumers' Association of Canada, "Educational Publications: Be a Wise Consumer—We'll Show You How," www.consumer.ca/educationalprograms-showyouhow.htm.

24. Government of Canada news release, "Canada Shows Continued Leadership on Protecting the Ozone Layer," December 18, 2000, www.ec.gc.ca/press/001219_n_e.htm.

25. Ken MacQueen, "Ministers Declare War on Excess Packaging," *Kingston Whig-Standard,* March 22, 1990, p. 11.

26. See the Packaging Association of Canada's web page "Half the packaging wast in two thirds the time," www.pac.ca/information/halfwaste.html.

27. Stuart L. Hart, "Beyond Greening: Strategies for a Sustainable World," *Harvard Business Review,* January–February 1997, pp. 66–76. Also see James L. Kolar, "Environmental Sustainability: Balancing Pollution Control with Economic Growth," *Environmental Quality Management,* Spring 1999, pp. 1–10; and Trevor Price and Doug Probert, "The Need for Environmentally Sustainable Developments," *International Need for Environmentally-Sustainable Developments,* 2002, pp. 1–22.

28. Sherry Noik-Bent, "The girl with the eco-touch," *Globe and Mail,* January 28, 2006.

29. Information from "Xerox Equipment Remanufacture and Parts Reuse," accessed at www.xerox.com, August 2004.

30. Adapted from Lynelle Preston, "Sustainability at Hewlett-Packard: From Theory to Practice," *California Management Review,* Spring 2001, pp. 26–36; and "Environmental Sustainability," www.hp.com/hpinfo/globalcitizenship/index.html (accessed August 2004).

31. "McGuinty Government Takes Next Step In Building Conservation Culture," Ontario Ministry of Energy News Release, 3 November, 2005, www.energy.gov.on.ca/index.cfm?fuseaction=english.news&body=yes&news_id=114

32. "About us," www.walshmobile.com/public/about_us/index.htm (accessed January 29, 2006); Linda Sutherland, "Brothers Find Focus in Waste," *Globe and Mail,* January 6, 1997, p. B8.

33. Information and quotes from Andy Milligan, "Samsung Points the Way for Asian Firms in Global Brand Race," *Media,* August 8, 2003, p. 8; Katherine Chen, Michael Jakielski, Nadia Luhr, and Joseph Mayer-Salman, "DigitAll," student paper at the University of North Carolina at Chapel Hill, Spring 2003; Gerry Khermouch, "The Best Global Brands," *Business Week,* August 5, 2002, p. 92; John Larkin, "Samsung Tries to Snatch Sony's Crown," *Far Eastern Economic Review,* October 10, 2002, pp. 36–41; Leslie P. Norton, "Value Brand," *Barron's.* September 22, 2003, p. 19; and Samsung Electronics Co. Ltd., *Hoover's Company Capsules,* Austin, March 15, 2004; and www.samsung.com/DigitAll/BrandCampaign/index.htm (accessed June 2004).

34. Mountain Equipment Co-op, "Mission and Values," undated, www.mec.ca/, accessed July 17, 2003.

35. Tim Kavander, "The Creative Eye: Canadian Hockey Association," *Marketing Magazine,* January 27, 2003, p. 16; Roy MacGregor, "Boors Under Heavy Fire in Hockey Parent Ads," *Globe and Mail,* November 28, 2003, p. A2.

36. Jacquelyn A. Ottman, "Green Marketing: Wake Up to the Truth about Green Consuming," *In Business*, May–June 2002, p. 31; Marc Gunther, "Son of Aeron," *Fortune*, May 12, 2003, p. 134; and information from www.HermanMiller.com (accessed June 2004).

37. Dan R. Dalton and Richard A. Cosier, "The Four Faces of Social Responsibility," *Business Horizons*, May–June 1982, pp. 19–27.

38. Joseph Webber, "3M's Big Cleanup," *Business Week*, June 5, 2000, pp. 96–98. Also see Kara Sissell, "3M Defends Timing of Scotchgard Phaseout," *Chemical Week*, April 11, 2001, p. 33; and Peck Hwee Sim, "Ausimont Targets Former Scotchgard Markets," *Chemical Week*, August 7, 2002, p. 32.

39. Barbara Crossette, "Russia and China Top Business Bribers," *New York Times*, May 17, 2002, p. A10.

40. John F. Magee and P. Ranganath Nayak, "Leaders' Perspectives on Business Ethics," *Prizm*, Arthur D. Little, Inc., Cambridge, MA, First Quarter, 1994, pp. 65–77. Also see Turgut Guvenli and Rajib Sanyal, "Ethical Concerns in International Business: Are Some Issues More Important than Others?" *Business and Society Review*, Summer 2002, pp. 195–206.

41. See Samuel A. DiPiazza, "Ethics in Action," *Executive Excellence*, January 2002, pp. 15–16.

42. Mark Hendricks, "Ethics in Action," *Management Review*, January 1995, pp. 53–55.

43. Kenneth Labich, "The New Crisis in Business Management," *Fortune*, April 20, 1992, pp. 167–176.

44. Samuel A. DiPiazza, "Ethics in Action," *Executive Excellence*, January 2002, p. 15.

Chapter 5

1. "Campaign for Real Beauty website (www.campaign forrealbeauty.com); Rebecca Harris, "Dove celebrates 'real beauty,'" *Marketing Magazine*, September 30, 2004; Rebecca Harris, "Keeping it real," *Marketing Magazine*, November 8, 2004; "Media Innovation Awards," *Marketing Magazine*, November 21, 2005; Samantha Yaffe, "Going Deep," *Strategy Magazine*, January 2005, p. 55; Lisa D'Innocenzo, "Braver is better," *Strategy Magazine*, November 2004; Keith McArthur, "Advertising to women gains Super yardage," *Globe and Mail*, February 7, 2006, p. B3.

2. See Christina Le Beau, "Mountains to Mine," *American Demographics*, August 2000, pp. 40–44; Diane Trommer, "Information Overload—Study Finds Intranet Users Overwhelmed with Data," *Electronic Buyers' News*, April 20, 1998, p. 98; Julie Schlosser, "Looking for Intelligence in Ice Cream," *Fortune*, March 17, 2003, pp. 114–120; Leslie Langnau, "Drowning in Data," *Material Handling Management*, December 2003, p. 22; and Rick Mullin, "Dealing with Information Overload," *Chemical and Engineering News*, March 22, 2004, p. 19.

3. Alice LaPlante, "Still Drowning!" *Computer World*, March 10, 1997, pp. 69–70; and Jennifer Jones, "Looking Inside," *InfoWorld*, January 7, 2002, pp. 22–26.

4. See Philip Kotler, *Marketing Insights from A to Z* (Hoboken, NJ: John Wiley & Sons, 2003), pp. 80–82.

5. Scott Gardiner, "A Truly Awesome Database," *Marketing Magazine*, April 29, 2002.

6. Pia Musngi, "OOH is the new DM," *Strategy*, August 2005; Sarah Dobson, "Life Beyond the TV Spot," *Marketing Magazine*, December 12. 2005; John Blasberg and Vijay Vishwanath "The keys to growing brands," *Marketing Magazine*, October 6, 2003.

7. Grant Robertson, "You can move, but can't hide, from new Rogers magazine," *Globe and Mail*, June 2, 2006.

8. Andy Serwer, "P&G's Covert Operation," *Fortune*, September 17, 2001, pp. 42–44.

9. Adapted from information in Ellen Neuborne, "Know Thy Enemy," *Sales & Marketing Management*, January 2003, pp. 29–33. Also see Gina Rollins, "Cast Deep to Sell," *Selling Power*, June 2003, pp. 26–28; and Deborah Lynne Wiley, "Super Searchers on Competitive Intelligence: The Online and Offline Secrets of Top CI Researchers," *Online*, May–June 2004, p. 62.

10. See James Curtis, "Behind Enemy Lines," *Marketing*, May 21, 2001, pp. 28–29; and Mei Fong, "The Enemy Within," *Far Eastern Economic Review*, April 22, 2004, pp. 34–38.

11. For more on research firms that supply marketing information, see Jack Honomichl, "Honomichl 50," special section, *Marketing News*, June 15, 2004, pp. H1–H55.

12. Information from www.infores.com/public/global/content/consumernetwork/householdpanel.htm and http://secure.yankelovich.com/solutions/monitor/monitor_new.asp (accessed July 2004).

13. Example adapted from Douglas McGray, "Babes in R&D Toyland," *Fast Company*, December 2002, p. 46.

14. Adapted from Linda Tischler, "Every Move You Make," *Fast Company*, April 2004, pp. 73–75.

15. "Canadian Attitudes to Survey Research: Conducted Fall 2004," Marketing Research and Intelligence Association, www.mria-arim.ca/NEWS/PDF/MRIASurveyFinal.pdf (accessed February 8, 2006).

16. Example adapted from Alison Stein Wellner, "The New Science of Focus Groups," *American Demographics*, March 2003, pp. 29–33.

17. This and other examples and quotes in this section, unless otherwise noted, are from "Market Trends: Online Research Growing," www.greenfieldcentral.com/research_solutions/rsrch_solns_main.htm, (accessed June 2003); Noah Shachtman, "Web Enhanced Market Research," *Advertising Age*, June 18, 2001, p. T18; Thomas W. Miller, "Make the Call: Online Results Are a Mixed Bag," *Marketing News*, September 24, 2001, pp. 30–35; "Cybersurveys Come of Age," *Marketing Research*, Spring 2003, pp. 32–37; and Richard Lee, "Stamford, Conn.-Based Market Research Firm Able to Reach Millions," *Knight Ridder Tribune Business News*, May 6, 2004, p. 1. Also see Catherine Arnold, "Not Done Net," *Marketing News*, April 2004, p. 17.

18. For more on Internet privacy, see James R. Hagerty and Dennis K. Berman, "Caught in the Net: New Battleground Over Web Privacy," *Wall Street Journal*, August 27, 2004,

p. A1; and "The Spies in Your Computer," *Wall Street Journal,* February 18, 2004, p. A18.

19. Adapted from examples in Gary H. Anthes, "Smile, You're on Candid Computer," *Computerworld,* December 3, 2001, p. 50; and Brandon Mercer, "Can Computers Read Your Mind?" *Techlive,* May 29, 2002, www.techtv.com/news/computing/story/0,24195,3386341,00.html.

20. For a good discussion, see Deborah L. Vence, "Better! Faster! Cheaper! Pick Any Three. That's Not a Joke," *Marketing News,* February 1, 2004, pp. 1, 31–32.

21. David Harding, David Chiefetz, Scott DeAngelo, and Elizabeth Ziegler, "CRM's Silver Lining," *Marketing Management,* March–April 2004, pp. 27–32.

22. See Sara Minoque, "Random acts of kindness," *Strategy,* August 25, 2003, p. 15; Marc L. Songini, "Fedex Expects CRM System to Deliver," *Computerworld,* November 6, 2000, p. 10. The Marks & Spencer example is adapted from "SAS Outfits Marks & Spencer with Customer Intelligence," www.sas.com/success/marksandspencer.html (accessed June 2004).

23. Darrell K. Rigby, "Avoid the Four Perils of CRM," *Harvard Business Review,* February 2002, pp. 101–109; and Karl Flinders, "CRM Set for Spending Explosion," *VNUnet.com,* March 8, 2004.

24. Michael Krauss, "At Many Firms, Technology Obscures CRM," *Marketing News,* March 18, 2002, p. 5.

25. See Robert McLuhan, "How to Reap the Benefits of CRM," *Marketing,* May 24, 2001, p. 35; Sellar, "Dust Off That Data," p. 72; Stewart Deck, "Data Mining," *Computerworld,* March 29, 1999, p. 76; "Six Changes in CRM," *Selling Power,* source book, 2003, pp. 26–30; and Jason Compton, "CRM Gets Real," *Customer Relationship Management,* May 2004, pp. 11–12.

26. Ravi Kalakota and Marcia Robinson, *E-Business: Roadmap for Success* (Reading, MA: Addison-Wesley, 1999); "Maximizing Relationships," *Chain Store Age,* August 2001, pp. 21A–23A; and Pacific Research Consulting, "Seiyu Implementing Wal-Mart's Real-Time Sales/Inventory System," *Innovative New Packaging in Japan,* February 25, 2004, p. 1.

27. Alison Stein Wellner, "Research on a Shoestring," *American Demographics,* April 2001, pp. 38–39. Also see "Bissell, Inc.," *Hoover Company Profiles,* Austin, May 15, 2004, p. 47534.

28. For some good advice on conducting market research in a small business, see "Marketing Research ... Basics 101," www.onlinewbc.gov/docs/market/mkt_res_ basics.html (accessed June 2004); and "Researching Your Market," U.S. Small Business Administration, www.sba.gov/library/pubs/mt-8.doc (accessed June 2004).

29. Jack Honomichl, "Despite Acquisitions, Firms' Revenue Dips," *Marketing News,* August 13, 2003, pp. H3–H27; and the AC Nielsen International Research website, www.acnielsen.com/services/ir/ (accessed July 2004).

30. Government of Canada, "Facts and Figures," www.investincanada.gc.ca/en/884/Facts_and_Figures.html#Computer%20and%20Internet%20Usage; other country media stats are from www.nationmaster.com (accessed December 2004).

31. Subhash C. Jain, *International Marketing Management,* 3d edition (Boston: PWS-Kent, 1990), p. 338. Also see Alvin C. Burns and Ronald F. Bush, *Marketing Research,* 3rd ed. (Upper Saddle River, NJ: Prentice Hall, 2000), pp. 317–318; and Debra L. Vence, "Leave It to the Experts," *Marketing News,* April 28, 2003, p. 37.

32. Steve Jarvis, "Status Quo = Progress," *Marketing News,* April 29, 2002, pp. 37–38; and Catherine Arnold, "Global Perspective," *Marketing News,* May 15, 2004, p. 43.

33. "Canadian Attitudes to Survey Research: Conducted Fall 2004," Marketing Research and Intelligence Association, www.mria-arim.ca/NEWS/PDF/MRIASurveyFinal.pdf (accessed February 8, 2006). Also see Canadian Survey Research Council, "Canadian Attitudes Towards Survey Research and Issues of Privacy," October 2001, www.csrc.ca/CSRC/news/ 2001CSRC.pdf.

34. Susan Vogt, "Online Privacy Laws All Over the Map," *Strategy,* September 11, 2000, p. 12.

35. Adapted from Richard Behar, "Never Heard of Acxiom? Chances Are It's Heard of You," *Fortune,* February 23, 2004, pp. 140–148.

36. See "Too Much Information?" *Marketing Management,* January–February 2004, p. 4.

37. RBC's Privacy Policy website, www.rbcroyalbank.com/privacy/, (accessed February 11, 2006).

38. Cynthia Crossen, "Studies Galore Support Products and Positions, But Are They Reliable?" *Wall Street Journal,* November 14, 1991, pp. A1, A9. Also see Allan J. Kimmel, "Deception in Marketing Research and Practice: An Introduction," *Psychology and Marketing,* July 2001, pp. 657–661.

Chapter 6

1. Quotes and other information from Elliott Ettenberg, "The church of Harley-Davidson," *Marketing Magazine,* July 28, 2003; Greg Schneider, "Rebels with Disposable Income; Aging Baby Boomers Line Up to Buy High-End Versions of Youthful Indulgences," *The Washington Post,* April 27, 2003, p. F1; Ian P. Murphy, "Aided by Research, Harley Goes Whole Hog," *Marketing News,* December 2, 1996, pp. 16, 17; Ted Bolton, "Tattooed Call Letters: The Ultimate Test of Brand Loyalty," www.boltonresearch.com (accessed April 2003); James D. Speros, "Why the Harley Brand's So Hot," *Advertising Age,* March 15, 2004, p. 26; "Harley-Davidson Reports Record Fourth Quarter and 18th Consecutive Record Year," Harley-Davidson press release, January 21, 2004, www.Harley-Davidson.com; Jay Palmer, "Vroom at the Top," *Barron's,* March 29, 2004, pp. 17–18; and the Harley-Davidson website, www.Harley-Davidson.com (accessed January 2005).

2. World POPClock, U.S. Census Bureau, www.census.gov (accessed December 2004). This website provides continuously updated projections of the U.S. and world populations.

3. Brad Weiners, "Getting Inside—Way Inside—Your Customer's Head," *Business 2.0,* April 2003, pp. 54–55.

4. Allan R. Gregg, "Strains Across the Border," *Maclean's,* December 30, 2002, www.macleans.ca/; and "Maclean's

Annual Poll," *Maclean's*, December 30, 2002, www.macleans.ca/.

5. For a deeper discussion of consumer culture theory, see Eric J. Arnould and Craig J. Thompson (2005), "Consumer Culture Theory (CCT): Twenty Years of Research," *Journal of Consumer Research*, Vol. 31 (4), pp. 868–883.

6. *The Political Voice Of Canadian Regional Identities*, The Centre for Canadian Studies, 2001, http://culturescope.ca/ ev_en.php?ID=9417_201&ID2=DO_TOPIC (accessed September 2006).

7. Sara Minogue, "Reaching new Canadians: Multicultural experts offer their best practice advice to niche marketers," *Strategy Magazine*, www.strategymag.com, September 22, 2003 (accessed July 13, 2004); Caribana Festival website, www.caribana.com (accessed July 13, 2004).

8. Statistics Canada, "Study: Canada's visible minority population in 2017," *The Daily*, March 22, 2005.

9. Hamlin Grange and Don Miller, "How to leverage diversity," *Marketing Magazine*, August 29, 2005.

10. Rebecca Harris, "Ethnic approaches," *Marketing Magazine*, March 14, 2005; Eve Lazarus, "The New Mainstream," *Marketing Magazine*, October 24, 2005; Rebecca Harris, "Embrace and prosper," *Marketing Magazine*, January 23, 2006.

11. Statistics Canada, "Study: Canada's visible minority population in 2017," *The Daily*, March 22, 2005.

12. Carey Toane, "Veering Off From the Mainstream: Marketers Are Finding Divergent Ways Beyond Traditional Advertising to Reach Ethnic Consumers," *Marketing On-Line*, June 5, 2000; and Patrick Lejtenyi, "Underlying Differences: Market Researchers Must Be Diligent About Identifying Subcultures Within Ethnic Groups," *Marketing Magazine*, June 5, 2000, www.marketingmag.ca.

13. Hamlin Grange and Don Miller, "How to leverage diversity," *Marketing Magazine*, August 29, 2005.

14. See Peter Francese, "Older and Wealthier," *American Demographics*, November 2002, pp. 40–41; Alison Stein Wellner, "The Next 25 Years," *American Demographics*, April 2003, pp. 24–27; Statistics Canada, "Profile of the Canadian population by age and sex: Canada ages," Detailed analysis of the 2001 Census population data released July 16, 2002.

15. See D. Allen Kerr, "Where There's Gray, There's Green," *Marketing News*, May 25, 1998, p. 2; "Fewer Seniors in the 1990s but Their Ranks Are Set to Explode," *Business Week*, May 28, 2001, p. 30; Laura Petrecca, "Savvy, Aging Boomers Buy into Pharma Mantra," *Advertising Age*, July 8, 2002, pp. S8–S9; Peter Francese, "Consumers Today," *American Demographics*, April 2003, pp. 28–29; and Robin Goldwyn Blumenthal, "Gray Is Good," *Barron's*, March 22, 2004, p. 37.

16. Gayle MacDonald, "The Gap Between Rich and Rich," *Globe and Mail*, July 5, 2003, pp. F4–5.

17. The Canadian Encyclopedia, "Class," http://tceplus.com /index.cfm?PgNm=TCECategories&Params=A1SUB33CAT 270 (accessed July 2006). For more on social class, see Terrell G. Williams, "Social Class Influences on Purchase Evaluation Criteria," *Journal of Consumer Marketing*, vol. 19, iss. 2/3, 2002, pp. 248–276; Michael R. Solomon, *Consumer Behavior*, 5th ed. (Upper Saddle River, NJ:

Prentice Hall, 2002), chapter 13; and Leon G. Schiffman and Leslie L. Kanuk, *Consumer Behavior*, 8th ed. (Upper Saddle River, NJ: 2004), chapter 11.

18. Ron Szekely, "L'Oréal Generates Buzz," *Marketing Magazine*, January 7, 2002, www.marketingmag.ca; Oren Yaniv and Laura Williams, "McHip-hop name-drop," *Daily News*, March 28, 2005; Pimp My Big Mac (Unfortunate Moments in Advertising), *Brand Noise*, March 29, 2005, http://brandnoise.typepad.com/ brand_noise/2005/03/pimp_my_big_mac.html (accessed July 2006).

19. Laura Mingail and Karl Moore, "Got Buzz?" *Marketing Magazine*, June 6, 2005. Reprinted by permission of Karl Moore.

20. See Darla Dernovsek, "Marketing to Women," *Credit Union Magazine*, October 2000, pp. 90–96; Sharon Goldman Edry, "No Longer Just Fun and Games," *American Demographics*, May 2001, pp. 36–38; Hillary Chura, "Marketing Messages for Women Fall Short," *Advertising Age*, September 23, 2002, pp. 4, 14–15; and Jennifer Pendleton, "Ford at 100: Targeting the Female Market," *Advertising Age*, March 31, 2003, pp. F38–F40; Lyle V. Harris, "Men Rule the Aisles," *Globe and Mail*, May 6, 1999, p. C5.

21. Information on Canadian household trends taken from Lesley Young, "Portrait of the New Family," *Marketing Magazine*, March 15, 2004; Mary Maddever, "Strategy stirs the pot. Again," Strategy, February 2006, p.6; Lisa D'Innocenzo, "Going to the Q," *Strategy*, January 2006, p. 28.

22. Tobi Elkin, "Sony Marketing Aims at Lifestyle Segments," *Advertising Age*, March 18, 2002, pp. 3, 72; and Kenneth Hein, "When Is Enough Enough?" *Brandweek*, December 2, 2002, pp. 26–28.

23. Quotes and examples from www.carhartt.com/rugged/ index.html (accessed December 2004).

24. Norma Ramage, "Mark's Super Brand Ambition," *Marketing Magazine*, March 29, 2004.

25. Natalia Williams, "Dose: The making of a youth daily," *Strategy*, January 2006, p. 35; Dose webpage www.dose.ca/ toronto/index.html (accessed July 2006).

26. www.forrester.com/Data/ConsumerTechno (accessed July 2004).

27. Jennifer Aaker, "Dimensions of Measuring Brand Personality," *Journal of Marketing Research*, August 1997, pp. 347–356. Also see Aaker, "The Malleable Self: The Role of Self Expression in Persuasion," *Journal of Marketing Research*, May 1999, pp. 45–57; and Audrey Azoulay and Jean-Noel Kapferer, "Do Brand Personality Scales Really Measure Brand Personality?" *Journal of Brand Management*, November 2003, p. 143.

28. Charles Pappas, "Ad Nauseam," *Advertising Age*, July 10, 2000, pp. 16–18.

29. Bob Garfield, "'Subliminal' Seduction and Other Urban Myths," *Advertising Age*, September 18, 2000, pp. 4, 105. Also see "We Have Ways of Making You Think," *Marketing Week*, September 25, 2003, p. 14; and Si Cantwell, "Common Sense; Scrutiny Helps Catch Catchy Ads," *Wilmington Star-News*, April 1, 2004, p. 1B.

30. Kate Fitzgerald, "Milk Tailors Effort to Teens," *Advertising Age*, February 18, 2002, p. 16; Rebecca Flass, "'Got Milk?' Takes a Serious Look Inside the Body," *Adweek*, January 27, 2003, p. 5; Katie Koppenhoefer, "MilkPEP Ads Make Big Impact with Hispanics," press release, International Dairy Foods Association, March 3, 2003, www.idfa.org/news/gotmilk/2003/miklpepads.cfm; and information from www.whymilk.com (accessed December 2004).

31. See Henry Assael, *Consumer Behavior and Marketing Action* (Boston: Kent Publishing, 1987), chapter 4. An earlier classification of three types of consumer buying behaviour—routine response behaviour, limited problem solving, and extensive problem solving—can be found in John A. Howard and Jagdish Sheth, *The Theory of Consumer Behavior* (New York: John Wiley, 1969), pp. 27–28. Also see John A. Howard, *Consumer Behavior in Marketing Strategy* (Upper Saddle River, NJ: Prentice Hall, 1989).

32. See Leon Festinger, *A Theory of Cognitive Dissonance* (Stanford, CA: Stanford University Press, 1957); Schiffman and Kanuk, *Consumer Behavior*, pp. 219–220; Jillian C. Sweeney, Douglas Hausknecht, and Geoffrey N. Soutar, "Cognitive Dissonance After Purchase: A Multidimensional Scale," *Psychology & Marketing*, May 2000, pp. 369–385; Patti Williams and Jennifer L. Aaker, "Can Mixed Emotions Peacefully Coexist?" March 2002, pp. 636–649; and Geoffrey Soutar and Jillian Sweeney, "Are There Cognitive Dissonance Segments?" *Australian Journal of Management*, December 2003, p. 227–263.

33. The following discussion draws from the work of Everett M. Rogers. See his *Diffusion of Innovations*, 5th ed. (New York: Free Press, 2003). Also see Peter J. Danaher, Bruce G. S. Hardie, and William P. Putsis, "Marketing-Mix Variables and the Diffusion of Successive Generations of a Technological Innovation," *Journal of Marketing Research*, November 2001, pp. 501–514; Eric Waarts, Yvonne M. van Everdingen, and Jos van Hillegersberg, "The Dynamics of Factors Affecting the Adoption of Innovations," *The Journal of Product Innovation Management*, November 2002, pp. 412–423; Jae H. Pae and Donald R. Lehmann, "Multigeneration Innovation Diffusion," *Academy of Marketing Science Journal*, Winter 2003, pp. 36–45; and Chaun-Fong Shih and Alladi Venkatesh, "Beyond Adoption: Development and Application of a Use-Diffusion Model," *Journal of Marketing*, January 2004, pp. 59–72.

Chapter 7

1. Quotes and other information from "Canadian Business Sweet On Multi-Million Dollar Valentine's Day Splurge," UPS Press Release, Mississauga, February 6, 2006, www.ups.com/content/ca/en/about/news/press_releases/02_06_2006_val_fr.html; Dale Buss, "Up with Brown," *Brandweek*, Jan 27, 2003 p. 16; "Business as Usual for Ads on Sunday News Shows," *B to B*, April 14, 2003 p. 30; "UPS Service Helps Companies Go Global," *Transportation & Distribution*, May 2003 p. 19; "The New Mission of Synchronizing Global Supply Chains," *Inventory Management Report*, May 2003 p. 9; Robert McGarvey, "UPS Builds Millions in Sales," *Selling Power*, June 2004, pp. 56–61; and information gathered at www.UPS.com, December 2004.

2. Eve Lazarus, "Nintendo BCAMA's Marketer of the Year," *Marketing Daily*, August 25, 2004; Michelle Halpern,

"Nintendo has fun with new positioning," *Marketing Daily*, October 20, 2004; Sarah Dobson, "Henderson Bas clicks with Nintendo," *Marketing Daily*, September 23, 2005.

3. Industry Canada, Small Business Research and Policy webpage, http://strategis.ic.gc.ca/SSG/rd00254e.html#top (accessed February 18, 2006).

4. See Kate Macarthur, "Teflon Togs Get $40 Million Ad Push," *Advertising Age*, April 8, 2002, p. 3; "Neat Pants for Sloppy People," *Consumer Reports: Publisher's Edition Including Supplemental Guides*, May 2003, p. 10; and "Sales Makes the Wearables World Go 'Round," *Wearables Business*, April 24, 2004, p. 22.

5. "How to Determine the Supplier Relationship Management Model," Supplier Selection & Management Report, July 2003, p. 4. Also see Steve Rogers, "Supply Management: Elements of Superior Design," Supply Chain Management Review, April 24, 2004, pp. 48–55; and Christopher Bouverie-Brine, "Business Relationship for Competitive Advantage," Supply Management, April 29, 2004, p. 35.

6. Patrick J. Robinson, Charles W. Faris, and Yoram Wind, *Industrial Buying Behavior and Creative Marketing* (Boston: Allyn & Bacon, 1967). Also see Erin Anderson, Weyien Chu, and Barton Weitz, "Industrial Purchasing: An Empirical Exploration of the Buyclass Framework," *Journal of Marketing*, July 1987, pp. 71–86; Michael D. Hutt and Thomas W. Speh, *Business Marketing Management*, 7th ed. (Upper Saddle River, NJ: Prentice Hall, 2001), pp. 56–66; and Junyean Moon and Surinder Tikoo, "Buying Decision Approaches of Organizational Buyers and Users," *Journal of Business Research*, April 2002, pp. 293–299.

7. See Philip Kotler, *Marketing Management*, 11th ed. (Upper Saddle River, NJ: Prentice Hall, 2003), pp. 219–220.

8. See Frederick E. Webster Jr. and Yoram Wind, *Organizational Buying Behavior* (Upper Saddle River, NJ: Prentice Hall, 1972), pp. 78–80. Also see James C. Anderson and James A. Narus, *Business Market Management: Understanding, Creating and Delivering Value* (Upper Saddle River NJ: Prentice Hall, 2004), chapter 3.

9. Frederick E. Webster, Jr., and Yoram Wind, *Organizational Buying Behavior*, pp. 33–37.

10. Patrick J. Robinson, Charles W. Faris, and Yoram Wind, *Industrial Buying Behavior and Creative Marketing* (Boston: Allyn & Bacon, 1967), p. 14.

11. Magna International Corporation website, www.magnaint.com/ (accessed February 17, 2006); Greg Keenan, "Auto Parts Maker Issues Brighter Earnings Picture for First-Quarter Results," *Globe and Mail*, February 25, 2003, www.globeandmail.com; John Buell, "The Year of Relationships," (editorial), *Constructech*, Vol. 5, No. 3, 2003, www.constructech.com/printresources/viewarticle2.asp.

12. Unless otherwise noted, quotes and spending information in this section are from Michael A. Verespej, "E-Procurement Explosion," *Industry Week*, March 2002, pp. 24–28; "E-Procurement Still Less Popular Than Paper Orders," *Supply Management*, March 13, 2003, p. 10; Jennifer Baljko, "Online Purchasing Activity on the Rise—But OEM Cost-Cutting Initiatives Are Limiting Process Changes," *EBN*, April 21, 2003, p. 6; and "Online Purchasing Still on the

Rise," *Industrial Distribution*, December 2004, p. 24; and C. Subramaniam and M. Shaw, "The Effects of Process Characteristics on the Value of B2B E-Procurement," *Information Technology and Management*, January–April, 2004, p. 161.

13. Information obtained at www.covisint.com/about/ (accessed January 2005).

14. See The RBC Financial Group's e-procurement pages www.rbc.com/sourcing/eproc_what-is.html (accessed February 19, 2006).

15. See Michael A. Verespej, "E-Procurement Explosion," *Industry Week*, March 2002, pp. 25–28; "E-Procurement: Certain Value in Changing Times," *Fortune*, April 30, 2001, pp. S2–S3.

16. Government of Canada, "The Basics of Selling to Government," November 3, 2004, http://contracts canada.gc.ca/en/how-e.htm (accessed February 19, 2006).

17. Western Economic Diversification Canada, "How to Sell (More) to Government," July 22, 2004, www.wd.gc.ca/ tools/selgov/shoyour_e.asp (accessed February 19, 2006).

Chapter 8

1. Gayle MacDonald and Val Ross, "Those Who Give—And Give Lots," *Globe and Mail*, April 15, 2006, p. E8; Sarah Hampson, "They're Young, Diverse And Brash. And They're The Last Ones With Any Cash Left To Give. But They'll Only Do It Their Way," *Globe and Mail*, April 15, 2006, p. E6; "Charitable donors, 2004," *The Daily*, Statistics Canada, November 4, 2004; Gillian Pritchett, Wah Keung Chan, Danielle Duboi, "The State of Arts Philanthropy in Canada," *La Scena Musicale*, Vol. 10, No. 4, November 29, 2004.

2. Danny Kucharsky, "Rogers Video plans up to 60 Quebec stores," *Marketing Daily*, March 5, 2004.

3. See "Home Depot Lite," *Chain Store Age*, January 2002, p. 39; "Recent Store Openings," Home Depot Canada webpage, www.homedepot.ca/webapp/wcs/stores/servlet/ DisplayTemplate?storeId=10051&catalogId=10051&lang Id=-15&display=promos_openings.

4. Eve Lazarus, "The New Mainstream," *Marketing Magazine*, October 24, 2005.

5. For these and other examples, see Patricia Sellers, "Gap's New Guy Upstairs," *Fortune*, April 24, 2003, pp. 110–116; Rob Turner, "Toothpaste for Women?" *Fortune*, March 3, 2003, p. 182; and information at www.crest.com and www.rejuvenatingeffects.com (accessed January 2005).

6. Lisa D'Innocenzo, "Is your target a man's man? Then reach out to women," *Strategy Magazine*, February 2006, p. 30. Also see www.womenandco.com (accessed July 2004); Bruce Upbin, "Merchant Princes," *Forbes*, January 20, 2003, pp. 52–56; and Debbie Howell, "Home Centers Focus on Females," *DSN Retailing Today*, May 3, 2004, p. 9.

7. Michelle Orecklin, "What Women Watch," *Time*, May 13, 2002, pp. 65–66; and information online at www.iVillage.com and www.oxygen.com (accessed December 2004).

8. Robert Berner, "Out-Discounting the Discounter," *Business Week*, May 10, 2004, pp. 78–79.

9. Lisa D'Innocenzo, "The ageless consumer," *Strategy Magazine*, March 8, 2004, p. 1.

10. "Lifestyle Marketing," *Progressive Grocer*, August 1997, pp. 107–110; and Philip Kotler, *Marketing Management: Analysis, Planning, Implementation, and Control,* 11th ed. (Upper Saddle River, NJ: Prentice Hall, 2003), pp. 291–292.

11. See Jonathon Welsh, "Transport: The Summer of the Scooter: Boomers Get a New Retro Toy," *Wall Street Journal*, April 13, 2001, p. W1; Tammy Lieber, "Vroom, Vroom: Scooter Sales Motor after Slow Start," *Indianapolis Business Journal*, December 8, 2003, pp. 39–45; and Honda's Web site at www.powersports.honda.com/scooter (accessed July 2004).

12. Information from www.kodak.com (accessed January 2005).

13. See Jennifer Ordonez, "Fast-Food Lovers, Unite!" *Newsweek*, May 24, 2004, p. 56.

14. Kendra Parker, "How Do You Like Your Beef?" *American Demographics*, January 2000, pp. 35–37.

15. Based on an example from Christine Del Valle, "They Know Where You Live—and How You Buy," *Business Week*, February 7, 1994, p. 89; and PRIZM cluster information at www.claritas.com (accessed August 2004).

16. John Fetto, American Neighborhoods' First Page," *American Demographics*, July–August 2003, p. 34.

17. For more on geodemographic segmentation, see John MacManus, "Street Wiser," *American Demographics*, July–August 2003, pp. 32–35. Information about the PRIZM segmentation system at www.clusterbigip1.claritas. com/claritas/Default.jsp?main53&submenu5seg&subcat5se gprizm (accessed August 2004).

18. Information from http://home.americanexpress.com/home/ mt_personal.shtml (accessed August, 2004).

19. For more on segmenting business markets, see Turan Senguder, "An Evaluation of Consumer and Business Segmentation Approaches," *Journal of the Academy of Business*, March 2003, pp. 618–624; and James C. Anderson and James A. Narus, *Business Market Management*, 2nd ed. (Upper Saddle River, NJ: Prentice Hall, 2004), pp. 45–52.

20. "SMART Technologies Inc.: Lifetime Achievement Award," International Trade Canada, www.infoexport.gc.ca/awards-prix/awards/2005/smart_e.htm (accessed July 2006).

21. See Arundhati Parmar, "Global Youth United," *Marketing News*, October 28, 2002, pp. 1, 49; the MTV Worldwide website, www.mtv.com/mtvinternational; "Teen Spirit," *Global Cosmetic Industry*, March 2004, p. 23; and "MTV: Music Television: The Facts," at www.viacom.com/ prodbyunit1.tin?ixBusUnit519 (accessed July 2004).

22. See Michael Porter, *Competitive Advantage* (New York: Free Press, 1985), pp. 4–8, 234–236. For more recent discussions, see Stanley Slater and Eric Olson, "A Fresh Look at Industry and Market Analysis," *Business Horizons*, January–February 2002, pp. 15–22; Kenneth Sawka and Bill Fiora, "The Four Analytical Techniques Every Analyst Must Know: 2. Porter's Five Forces Analysis," *Competitive Intelligence Magazine*, May–June 2003, p. 57; and Philip Kotler, *Marketing Management*, 11th ed. (Upper Saddle River, NJ: Prentice Hall, 2003), pp. 242–243.

23. Nina Munk, "Why Women Find Lauder Mesmerizing," *Fortune,* May 25, 1998, pp. 97–106; Christine Bittar, "New Faces, Same Name," *Brandweek,* March 11, 2002, pp. 28–34; Robin Givhan, "Estée Lauder, Sending a Message in a Bottle," *The Washington Post,* April 26, 2004, p. C.01; and information at www.elcompanies.com (accessed January 2005).

24. Peter Burrows, "How to Milk an Apple," *Business Week,* February, 3, 2003, p. 44; and Josh Quittner, "Steve Jobs," *Time,* April 26, 2004, p. 75.

25. See Gerry Khermouch, "Call It the Pepsi Blue Generation," *Business Week,* February 3, 2003, p. 96; Kathleen Sampey, "Sweet on Sierra Mist," *Adweek,* February 2, 2004, p. 20; and Nat Ives, "Mountain Dew Double-Dose for Times Square Passers-By," *New York Times,* April 8, 2004, p. C9.

26. Information online at www.ostrichesonline.com (accessed July 2004).

27. "Canadian Apparel E-Business Success Stories," Industry Canada, http://strategis.ic.gc.ca/epic/internet/inapparel-vetements.nsf/en/ap03283e.html (accessed July 6, 2005).

28. For a good discussion of mass customization and relationship building, see Don Peppers and Martha Rogers, *Managing Customers Relationships: A Strategic Framework* (Hoboken, NJ: John Wiley & Sons, 2004), chapter 10.

29. See Faith Keenan, "A Mass Market of One," *Business Week,* December 2, 2002, pp. 68–72; and information at http://shop.mms.com/customized/index.asp?UID5 (accessed August 2004).

30. Adapted from information found in Mark Tatge, "Red Bodies, Black Ink," *Forbes,* September 18, 2000. p 114; "Oshkosh Truck Corporation," *Hoover's Company Profiles,* Austin, May 15, 2004, p. 14345; and information at www.oshkoshtruck.com (accessed December 2004).

31. Sony A. Grier, "The Federal Trade Commission's Report on the Marketing of Violent Entertainment to Youths: Developing Policy-Tuned Research," *Journal of Public Policy and Marketing,* Spring 2001, pp. 123–132; Deborah L. Vence, "Marketing to Minors Still under Careful Watch," *Marketing News,* March 31, 2003, pp. 5–6; and Susan Linn, *Consuming Kids: The Hostile Takeover of Childhood* (New York: The New Press, 2004).

32. Tyler Hamilton and Robert Cribb, "Kids At Risk?" *Toronto Star,* July 9, 2005; Omar El Akkad And Tim Lai, "Cellphone Companies Reach Out To Tween Market," *Globe And Mail,* July 7, 2005, p. A1.

33. Adapted from a positioning map prepared by students Brian May, Josh Payne, Meredith Schakel, and Bryana Sterns, University of North Carolina, April 2003. SUV sales data furnished by WardsAuto.com (accessed June 2003). Price data from www.edmunds.com (accessed June 2004).

34. Lesley Young, "Plucky Branding," *Marketing Magazine Online,* www.marketingmag.ca, October 6, 2003 (accessed August 29, 2004).

35. "Raising interest: Rick White, Scotiabank," *Strategy Magazine,* March 2006, p. 16.

36. See Philip Kotler, *Kotler on Marketing* (New York: Free Press, 1999), pp. 59–63.

37. See Bobby J. Calder and Steven J. Reagan, "Brand Design," in Dawn Iacobucci, ed. *Kellogg on Marketing* (New York: John Wiley & Sons, 2001) p. 61. The Palm and Mountain Dew examples are from Alice M. Tybout and Brian Sternthal, "Brand Positioning," in Iacobucci, ed., *Kellogg on Marketing,* p. 54.

Chapter 9

1. Sources used include lululemon athletica corporate website, www.lululemon.ca (accessed March 19, 2006); Kristen Vinakmens, "Lululemon: Building the brand from the ground—yoga mat—up," *Strategy* magazine online, www.strategymag.com/articles/magazine,20040113/lululemon,html?word=lululemon, (accessed March 19, 2006).

2. Information at www.wirednewyork.com/toys_rus. htm (accessed December 2004).

3. For more on experience marketing, see B. Joseph Pine and James H. Gilmore, *The Experience Economy* (New York: Free Press, 1999); Stephen E. DeLong, "The Experience Economy," *Upside,* November 2001, p. 28; and "Brand Entertainment: Brands Play the World's Stage," *Brand Strategy,* August 2003, p. 20.

4. See Kate Fitzgerald, "Buick Rides the Tiger," *Advertising Age,* April 15, 2002, p. 41; "He Sold Fame; We Bought It," *Los Angeles Times,"* May 20, 2003, p. B14; and "The Celebrity 100," *Forbes,* www.forbes.com (accessed June 2004).

5. See Daniel Roth, "The Trophy Life," *Fortune,* April 19, 2004, p. 70; Trump, Donald, *Trump: The Art of the Comeback* (New York: Random House, 1997); Richard Linnett, "'Human Logo': Reconstructing the Trump Brand," *Advertising Age,* August 18, 2003, p. 1; Adam Lashinsky, "For Trump, Fame Is Easier Than Fortune," *Fortune,* February 23, 2004, p. 38; and Daniel Roth, "The Trophy Life," *Fortune,* April 19, 2004, pp. 70–84.

6. Caroline Alphonso, "Branding: A great place to do business—just no beacon for culture," *Globe and Mail,* August 2, 2005, p. B1; also see the tourism webpages of these provinces at www.newfoundlandandlabradortourism.com, and www.ontariotravel.net.

7. For more on marketing places, see Philip Kotler, Donald Haider, and Irving J. Rein, *Marketing Places: Attracting Investment, Industry, and Tourism to Cities, States, and Nations* (New York: Free Press, 2002). Examples include information found at www.newfoundlandandlabradortourism.com, www.ontariotravel.net, www.ireland.travel.ie, and www.ida.ie, (accessed December 2004).

8. Information at www.social-marketing.org/aboutus.html (Accessed January 2005).

9. See Alan R. Andreasen, Rob Gould, and Karen Gutierrez, "Social Marketing Has a New Champion," *Marketing News,* February 7, 2000, p. 38. Also see Philip Kotler, Ned Roberto, and Nancy Lee, *Social Marketing: Improving the Quality of Life,* 2nd ed. (Thousand Oaks, CA: Sage Publications, 2002); and www.social-marketing.org (accessed December 2004).

10. Quotes and definitions from Philip Kotler, *Kotler on Marketing* (New York: Free Press, 1999), p. 17; and www.asq.org (accessed January 2005).

11. See Roland T. Rust, Anthony J. Zahorik, and Timothy L. Keiningham, "Return on Quality (ROQ): Making Service Quality Financially Accountable," *Journal of Marketing*, April 1995, pp. 58–70; Roland T. Rust, Christine Moorman, and Peter R. Dickson, "Getting Return on Quality: Revenue Expansion, Cost Reduction, or Both?" *Journal of Marketing*, October 2002, pp. 7–24; and Roland T. Rust, Katherine N. Lemon, and Valarie A. Zeithaml, "Return on Marketing: Using Customer Equity to Focus Marketing Strategy," *Journal of Marketing*, January 2004, p. 109.

12. Example adapted from Bruce Nussbaum, "The Power of Design," *Business Week*, May 17, 2004, pp. 86–94.

13. See Kate Fitzgerald, "Packaging Is the Capper," *Advertising Age*, May 5, 2003, p. 22.

14. Adapted from examples found in Julie Dunn, "Pouring Paint, Minus a Mess," *New York Times*, October 27, 2002, p. 3.2; "Look Ma, No Drip," *Business Week*, December 16, 2002, p. 74; Seth Godin, "In Praise of the Purple Cow," *Fast Company*, February 2003, pp. 74–85; Catherine Arnold, "Way Outside the Box," *Marketing News*, June 23, 2003, pp. 13, 15; and information at www.dutchboy.com/twistandpour/index_store.asp (accessed June 2004).

15. Robert M. McMath, "Chock Full of (Pea)nuts," *American Demographics*, April 1997, p. 60. For more on packaging, see Robert L. Underwood, "The Communicative Power of Product Packaging: Creating Brand Identity via Lived and Mediate Experience," *Journal of Marketing Theory and Practice*, Winter 2003, p. 62.

16. Bro Uttal, "Companies That Serve You Best," *Fortune*, December 7, 1987, p. 116; and American Customer Satisfaction Index ratings at www.theacsi.org (accessed December 2004).

17. Example adapted from Michelle Higgins, "Pop-Up Sales Clerks: Web Sites Try the Hard Sell," *Wall Street Journal*, April 15, 2004, p. D.1.

18. Information online at www.marriott.com (accessed December 2004).

19. Information about P&G's product lines at www.pg.com/products/usa_product_facts.jhtml and www. crest.com (accessed December 2004). For more on product line strategy, see Robert Bordley, "Determining the Appropriate Depth and Breadth of a Firm's Product Portfolio," *Journal of Marketing Research*, February 2003, pp. 39–53.

20. See "McAtlas Shrugged," *Foreign Policy*, May–June 2001, pp. 26–37; and Philip Kotler, *Marketing Management*, 11th ed. (Upper Saddle River, NJ: Prentice Hall, 2003), p. 423.

21. Douglas Holt, "What Becomes an Icon Most?" *Harvard Business Review*, March 2003, pp. 43–49; John Gray, "Canadian icons," *Canadian Business*, June 2005.

22. David C. Bello and Morris. B. Holbrook, "Does an Absence of Brand Equity Generalize Across Product Classes?" *Journal of Business Research*, October 1995, p. 125; and Scott Davis, *Brand Asset Management: Driving Profitable Growth through Your Brands* (San Francisco: Jossey-Bass, 2000). Also see Kevin Lane Keller, *Building, Measuring, and Managing Brand Equity*, 2nd ed. (Upper Saddle River, NJ: Prentice Hall, 2003), chapter 2; and Kusum Ailawadi, Donald R. Lehman, and Scott A. Neslin, "Revenue Premium as an Outcome Measure of Brand Equity," *Journal of Marketing*, October 2003, pp. 1–17.

23. John Gray and Laura Bogolmony, "Brands: What's In A Brand?" *Canadian Business*, December 26, 2005; "The World's Most Valuable Brands," *Business Week*, August 2, 2004.

24. See Roland Rust, Katherine Lemon, and Valarie Zeithaml "Return on Marketing: Using Customer Equity to Focus Marketing Strategy," *Journal of Marketing*, January 2004, p. 109.

25. See Davis, *Brand Asset Management*; and Kotler, *Marketing Management*, pp. 419–420.

26. See Marc Gobe, *Emotional Branding* (New York: Allworth Press, 2001); and Jack Neff, "P&G Bets $100 Million on Crest Brand Plan," *Advertising Age*, March 22, 2004, pp. 5, 33.

27. Example adapted from Matthew Boyle, "Brand Killers," *Fortune*, August 11, 2003, pp. 89–100.

28. Peter Berlinski, "Retailers Push Premium PL," *Private Label Magazine*, May/June 2003, www.privatelabelmag.com/pdf/may2003/canada.cfm. For more reading on store brands, see David Dunne and Chakravarthi Narasimham, "The New Appeal of Private Labels," *Harvard Business Review*, May–June 1999, pp. 41–52; Kusum L. Ailawadi, Scott Neslin, and Karen Gedenk, "Pursuing the Value-Conscious Consumer: Store Brands Versus National Promotions," *Journal of Marketing*, January 2001, pp. 71–89; and Pradeep K. Chintagunta, "Investigating Category Pricing Behavior at a Retail Chain," *Journal of Marketing Research*, May 2002, pp. 141–151.

29. William Wilkie, "Marketing Research and Public Policy: The Case of Slotting Fees," *Journal of Public Policy and Marketing*, Fall 2002, pp. 275–289; Gene Epstein, "Envelope, Please," *Barron's*, November 4, 2002, p. 37; and Margaret Webb Pressler, "Shelf Game; When Stores Force Makers to Pay Them Fees, You Lose," *The Washington Post*, January 18, 2004, p. F.05.

30. Jay Sherman, "Nick Puts Muscle Behind everGirl," *TelevisionWeek*, January 5, 2004, p. 3

31. See Laura Petrecca, "'Corporate Brands' Put Licensing in the Spotlight," *Advertising Age*, June 14, 1999, p. 1; and Bob Vavra, "The Game of the Name," *Supermarket Business*, March 15, 2001, pp. 45–46.

32. Gabrielle Solomon, "Co-Branding Alliances: Arranged Marriages Made by Marketers," *Fortune*, October 12, 1998, p. 188; and "Martha Stewart, Kmart Continue Partnership," *Gourmet News*, June 2004, p. 14.

33. For more on the use of line and brand extensions and consumer attitudes toward them, see Vanitha Swaminathan, Richard J. Fox, and Srinivas K. Reddy, "The Impact of Brand Extension Introduction on Choice," *Journal of Marketing*, October 2001, pp. 1–15; Kalpesh Kaushik Desai and Kevin Lane Keller, "The Effect of Ingredient Branding Strategies on Host Brand Extendibility," *Journal of Marketing*, January 2002, pp. 73–93; Subramanian Balachander and Sanjoy Ghose, "Reciprocal Spillover Effects: A Strategic Benefit of Brand Extensions," *Journal of Marketing*, January 2003, pp. 4–13; and Eva Martinez and Leslie de Chernatony, "The Effect of Brand Extension Strategies Upon Brand Image," *The Journal of Consumer Marketing*, 2004, p. 39.

34. "Top 200 Megabrands," www.adage.com (accessed June 2004).

35. See Kevin Lane Keller, "The Brand Report Card," *Harvard Business Review,* January 2000, pp. 147–157; Kevin Lane Keller, *Strategic Brand Management,* 2nd ed. (Upper Saddle River, NJ: Prentice Hall, 2003), pp. 766–767; and David A. Aaker, "Even Brands Need Spring Cleaning," *Brandweek,* March 8, 2004, pp. 36–40.

36. Keith McArthur, "How to survive an identity crisis," *Globe and Mail,* November 14, 2005, p. B1.

37. Industry Canada, "Overview of Canada's Service Economy," http://strategis.ic.gc.ca/pics/sc/ service-eng.pdf (accessed March 2001); Ronald Henkoff, "Service Is Everybody's Business," *Fortune,* June 27, 1994, pp. 48–60; and Valerie Zeithaml and Mary Jo Bitner, *Services Marketing* (New York: McGraw-Hill, 1999), pp. 8–9.

38. Adapted from information in Leonard Berry and Neeli Bendapudi, "Clueing in Customers," *Harvard Business Review,* February 2003, pp. 100–106 and information at www.mayoclinic.org (accessed December 2004).

39. See James L. Heskett, W. Earl Sasser Jr., and Leonard A. Schlesinger, *The Service Profit Chain: How Leading Companies Link Profit and Growth to Loyalty, Satisfaction, and Value* (New York: Free Press, 1997); and Heskett, Sasser, and Schlesinger, *The Value Profit Chain: Treat Employees Like Customers and Customers Like Employees* (New York: Free Press, 2003).

40. Jeremy B. Dann, "How to Find a Hit as Big as Starbucks," *Business 2.0,* May 2004, pp. 66–68.

41. For discussions of service quality, see Valarie A. Zeithaml, A. Parasuraman, and Leonard L. Berry, *Delivering Quality Service: Balancing Customer Perceptions and Expectations* (New York: The Free Press, 1990); Zeithaml, Berry, and Parasuraman, "The Behavioral Consequences of Service Quality," *Journal of Marketing,* April 1996, pp. 31–46; Thomas J. Page Jr., "Difference Scores Versus Direct Effects in Service Quality Measurement," *Journal of Service Research,* February 2002, pp. 184–192; and Y. H. Hung, M. L. Huang, and K. S. Chen, "Service Quality Evaluation by Service Quality Performance Matrix," *Total Quality Management & Business Excellence,* January 2003, pp. 79–89.

42. See James L. Heskett, W. Earl Sasser Jr., and Christopher W. L. Hart, *Service Breakthroughs* (New York: Free Press, 1990).

43. See the *Hazardous Products Act* at http://laws.justice.gc.ca/en/H-3/index.html and the *Food and Drugs Act* at http://laws.justice.gc.ca/en/F-27/index.html.

44. See Philip Cateora, *International Marketing,* 8th ed. (Homewood, IL: Irwin, 1993), p. 270; David Fairlamb, "One Currency—But 15 Economies," *Business Week,* December 31, 2001, p. 59; and www.walkabouttravelgear.com (accessed July 200).

45. Information online at www.deutsche-bank.com (accessed July 2004).

46. Information online at www.interpublic.com and www.mccann.com (accessed December 2004).

47. See "Bata Today," www.bata.com/about_us/bata_today.php (accessed April 2006); "Wal-Mart International Operations," www.walmartstores.com (accessed July 2004); and "2004 Global Powers of Retailing," *Stores,* www.stores.org (accessed January 2004).

Chapter 10

1. Portions adapted from Patti Summerfield, "The great outdoor," *Strategy Magazine,* April 2006, p. 32; Lisa D'Innocenzo, "Dial "C" for clever: Nokia flies with snowboarders," *Strategy Magazine,* May 2005; Ian Wylie, "Calling for a Renewable Future," *Fast Company,* May 2003, pp. 4648. Also see Brad Smith, "Nokia: From Banks of Remote River Comes Innovation," *Wireless Week,* March 22, 2004, p. 26; and Andy Reinhardt, "Can Nokia Get the Wow Back?" *Business Week,* May 31, 2004, pp. 48–50.

2. For these and other examples, see Simon Romero, "Once Proudly Carried, and Now Mere Carrion," *New York Times,* November 22, 2001, p. G5; Kelly Carroll, "Satellite Telephony: Not for the Consumer," *Telephony,"* March 4, 2002, p. 17; and Eric Almquist, Martin Kon, and Wolfgang Bock, "The Science of Demand," *Marketing Management,* March–April 2004, pp. 20–26.

3. See Bruce Tait, "The Failure of Marketing 'Science,'" *Brandweek,* April 8, 2002, pp. 20–22; Alison Stein Wellner, "The New Science of Focus Groups," *American Demographics,* March 2003, p. 30; Kevin J. Clancy and Peter C. Krieg, "Surviving Innovation," *Marketing Management,* March/April 2003, pp. 14–20; and "Market Research: So What's the Big Idea?" *Marketing Week,* March 11, 2004, p. 37.

4. Information and examples from Gary Slack, "Innovations and Idiocities," *Beverage World,* November 15, 1998, p. 122; Robert M. McMath and Thom Forbes, *What Were They Thinking? Money-Saving, Time-Saving, Face-Saving Marketing Lessons You Can Learn from Products That Flopped* (New York: Times Business, 1999), various pages; Melissa Master, "Spectacular Failures," *Across the Board,* March–April 2001, p. 24; and www.newproductworks.com/product_poll/hm_index.html (accessed December 2004).

5. For a full discussion of the "Fuzzy Front End," see Susan E. Reid and Ulrike De Brentani, "The Fuzzy Front End of NPD for Discontinuous Innovation: A Theoretical Model," *Journal of Product Innovation and Management,* Vol. 21, Issue 3, 170–184.

6. Gary Hamel, "Innovation's New Math," *Fortune,* July 9, 2001, pp. 130–131

7. Paul Lukas, "Marketing: The Color of Money and Ketchup," *Fortune,* September 18, 2000, p. 38; Sonia Reyes, "Shopping List: Quick, Classic, and Cool for Kids," *Brandweek,* June 17, 2002, pp. S52–S54; "Heinz EZ Squirt Shoots for the Stars with Its Latest Creation; Stellar Blue Has Landed on Store Shelves," Heinz press release, April 7, 2003, www.heinz.com/jsp/news_f.jsp; and information accessed at www.heinz.com/jsp/new_prod.jsp (accessed July 2004).

8. Pam Weisz, "Avon's Skin-So-Soft Bugs Out," *Brandweek,* June 6, 1994, p. 4; and information at www.avon.com (accessed January 2005).

9. Stefan Thomke and Eric von Hippel, "Customers as Innovators: A New Way to Create Value," *Harvard Business Review,* April 2002, pp. 74–81; and Faith Keenan, "A Mass Market of One," *Business Week,* December 2, 2002, pp. 68–72. Eric von Hippel, *Democratizing Innovation,* 2005,

MIT Press. This book is also licensed under a Creative Commons licence and is available as a downloadable PDF document on http://web.mit.edu/evhippel/ www/democ.htm.

10. Robert Gray, "Not Invented Here," *Marketing,* May 6, 2004, pp. 34–37.

11. See Philip Kotler, *Kotler on Marketing* (New York, NY: The Free Press, 1999), pp. 43–44. For more on developing new-product ideas, see Darrell Rigby and Chris Zook, "Open-Market Innovation," *Harvard Business Review,* October 2002, pp. 80–89; and Jacob Goldenberg, Roni Horowitz, Amnon Levav, and David Mazursky, "Finding Your Innovation Sweetspot," *Harvard Business Review,* March 2003, pp. 120–129.

12. See Katherine Mieszkowski, "Fill er Up with Hydrogen," *Fast Company,* March 2003, p. 34; and "DaimlerChrysler Delivers the First Fuel Cell Cars to Customers in Berlin," June 18, 2004, www.daimlerchrysler.com.

13. Becky Ebenkamp, "The New Gold Standards," *Brandweek,* April 19, 1999, p. 34; Ebencamp, "It's Like Cheers and Jeers, Only for Brands," *Brandweek,* March 19, 2001; and Ebenkamp, "The Focus Group Has Spoken," *Brandweek,* April 23, 2001, p. 24; and discussions with Mark Sneider, General Manager, AcuPOLL, October 2004.

14. "Hershey Research Sees Net Gain," *Marketing News,* November 25, 2002, p. 17.

15. Examples adapted from those found in Linda Geil Gets Swabbed," *Wall Street Journal,* January 24, 2002, p. A1; Linda Grant, "Gillette Knows Shaving—and How to Turn Out Hot New Products," *Fortune,* October 14, 1996, pp. 207–210; and Carol Matlack, "The Vuitton Machine," *Business Week,* March 22, 2004, pp. 98–102.

16. Judann Pollack, "Baked Lays," *Advertising Age,* June 24, 1996, p. S2; Jack Neff and Suzanne Bidlake, "P&G, Unilever Aim to Take Consumers to the Cleaners," *Advertising Age,* February 12, 2001, pp. 1, 2; and Dean Takahashi, "Nokia's N-Gage Shakes Up the Gaming Market," *Electronic Business,* April 1, 2003, p. 28.

17. This and other examples can be found in Robert McMath, "To Test or Not to Test," *Advertising Age,* June 1998, p. 64; and Bret Thron, "Lessons Learned: Menu Miscues," *Nation's Restaurant News,* May 20, 2002, pp. 102–104. Also see Jerry W. Thomas, "Skipping Research a Major Error," *Marketing News,* March 4, 2002, p. 50.

18. Jack Neff, "Is Testing the Answer?" *Advertising Age,* July 9, 2001, p. 13; and Dale Buss, "P&G's Rise," *Potentials,* January 2003, pp. 26–30.

19. Information on BehaviorScan at www.infores. com (accessed December 2004).

20. Mary Maddever, "The new Kraft," *Strategy Magazine,* May 2006, p. 13.

21. Emily Nelson, "Colgate's Net Rose 10% in Period, New Products Helped Boost Sales," *Wall Street Journal,* February 2, 2001, p. B6; and "New Products Aid Colgate Net," *New York Times,* February 5, 2003, p. C.2.

22. For a good review of research on new-product development, see Rajesh Sethi, "New Product Quality and Product Development Teams," *Journal of Marketing,* April 2000, pp. 1–14; Shikhar Sarin and Vijay Mahajan, "The Effect of Reward Structures on the Performance of Cross-Functional Product Development Teams," *Journal of Marketing,* April

2001, pp. 35–54; Joseph M. Bonner, Robert W. Ruekert, and Orville C. Walker Jr. "Upper Management Control of New Product Development Projects and Project Performance," *Journal of Product Innovation Management,* May 2002, pp. 233–245; and Sandra Valle and Lucia Avella, "Cross-Functionality and Leadership of the New Product Development Teams," *European Journal of Innovation Management,* 2003, pp. 32–47. For an interesting view of an alternative new product development process, see Bruce Nussbaum, "The Power of Design," *Business Week,* May 17, 2004, pp. 86–94.

23. See Michael Arndt, "3M: A Lab for Growth," *Business Week,* January 21, 2002, pp. 50–51; Tim Studt, "3M—Where Innovation Rules," *R&D,* April 2003, pp. 20–24; Tim Stevens, "3M Reinvents Its Innovation Process," *Research Technology Management,* March/April 2004, p. 3; and "Innovation at 3M," www.3m.com/about3m/innovation/index.jhtml (accessed December 2004).

24. Natalia Williams, "Girls: PHD: Thermasilk, *Strategy Magazine,* April 2006, p. 50.

25. Laurie Freeman, "Study: Leading Brands Aren't Always Enduring," *Advertising Age,* February 28, 2000, p. 26.

26. Michelle Halpern, "POGs bounce back," *Marketing Magazine,* March 27 2006; "Pogs," Wikipedia, http://en.wikipedia.org/wiki/Pogs.

27. These and other uses found in "Always Another Use: 2000 Uses List," http://fanclub.wd40.com/Members/FanSpeak/uses.cfm (accessed July 2004).

28. Example adapted from Stephanie Thompson, "Sprucing Up Spam for New Generation," *Advertising Age,* October 28, 2002, p. 6. Additional information from "The Lighter Side of Spam," www.msn.com/id/2074884/ (accessed December 9, 2002); and information from www.spammobile.com (accessed January 2005).

29. See Jack Neff, "Mr. Clean Gets $50 Million Push," *Advertising Age,* August 18, 2003, pp. 3, 32; and information at www.homemadesimple.com/mrclean/ (accessed December 2004).

30. For a more comprehensive discussion of marketing strategies over the course of the product life cycle, see Philip Kotler, *Marketing Management,* 11th ed. (Upper Saddle River, NJ: Prentice Hall, 2003), chapter 10.

Chapter 11

1. Thomas T. Nagle and Reed K. Holden, *The Strategy and Tactics of Pricing,* 3rd ed. (Upper Saddle River, NJ: Prentice Hall, 2002), p. 1.

2. Excerpts from "Business: It Was My Idea," *The Economist,* August 15, 1998, p. 54; Karl Taro Greenfeld, "Be Your Own Barcode," *Time,* July 10, 2000, pp. 96–97; Ben Rosier, "The Price Is Right," *Marketing Magazine,* February 22, 2001, p. 26; and Priceline website, www.priceline.com (accessed July 2002, April 2006). See also Julia Angwin, "Priceline Founder Closes Online Bidding Site for Gas and Groceries," *Wall Street Journal,* October 6, 2000, p. B1; "Priceline.com Tops Forecast for Quarter, but Its Shares Fall," *New York Times,* February 5, 2002, p. C12; and "Priceline.com's Online 'Reach' Up 810% vs. a Year Ago," news release, June 7, 2002,

www.priceline.com; "Online Travel Bargains," written for CBC Ottawa's radio show, CBO Morning, www.mirror.org/lyz.kessick/radio_story7.htm (accessed April 2006).

3. Dean Foust, "Raising Prices Won't Fly," *Business Week*, June 3, 2002, p. 34.

4. Philip Kotler and Peggy Cunningham, *Marketing Management*, Canadian 11th ed. (Toronto: Pearson Education Canada, 2004), p. 479.

5. Robert D. Hof, "Going, Going, Gone," *Business Week*, April 12, 1999, pp. 30–32. Also see Mui Kung, Kent B. Monroe, and Jennifer L. Cox, "Pricing on the Internet," *The Journal of Product and Brand Management*, 2002, pp. 274–287; Charles Fishman, "Which Price is Right?" *Fast Company*, March 2003, pp. 92–102; and Faith Keenan, "The Price Is Really Right," *Business Week*, March 31, 2003, pp. 60–67.

6. "MusicRebellion: Dynamic Pricing for Music Starts with 10-Cent Tunes," *Wall Street Journal*, January 9, 2004; and "MusicRebellion, Inc." *Hoover's Company Capsules*, Austin, March 15, 2004, p. 132322.

7. Paul Hunt, "Pricing for Profit," *Marketing Magazine*, April 26, 1999, www.marketingmag.ca.

8. For an excellent discussion of factors affecting pricing decisions, nee Nagle Thomas T. Nagle and Reed K. Holden, *The Strategy and Tactics of Pricing*, 3rd ed. (Upper Saddle River, NJ: Prentice Hall, 2002, chapter 1.

9. See Robert Berner, "Why P&G's Smile Is So Bright," *Business Week*, August 12, 2002, pp. 58–60; Jack Neff, "Power Brushes a Hit at Every Level," *Advertising Age*, May 26, 2003, p. 10; and information at www.spinbrush.com (accessed December 2004).

10. Here accumulated production is drawn on a semilog scale so that equal distances represent the same percentage increase in output.

11. Philip Kotler and Peggy Cunningham, *Marketing Management*, Canadian 11th ed. (Toronto: Pearson Education Canada, 2004), p. 474; Kara Swisher, "Electronics 2001: The Essential Guide." *Wall Street Journal*, January 5, 2001; and Cliff Edwards, "HDTV: High-Anxiety Television," *Business Week*, June 10, 2002, pp. 142–146.

12. Joshua Rosenbaum, "Guitar Maker Looks for a New Key," *Wall Street Journal*, February 11, 1998, p. B1; and www.gibson.com (accessed July 2002).

13. See Thomas T. Nagle and Reed K. Holden, *The Strategy and Tactics of Pricing*, 3rd ed. (Upper Saddle River, NJ: Prentice Hall, 2002), chapter 4.

14. Judy Waytiuk, "No Haggle, No Hassle," *Marketing Magazine*, August 28, 2000, www.marketingmag.ca.

15. Kevin J. Clancy, "At What Profit Price?" *Brandweek*, June 23, 1997, pp. 24–28.

16. Canadian Press, "Sleeman hurt by price war," *Marketing Magazine*, August 11, 2005; Canadian Press, "Sleeman to increase marketing for low-price brands," *Marketing Magazine*, October 31, 2005; Sarah Dobson Sleeman stays true to premium roots," *Marketing Magazine*, Monday, November 7, 2005.

17. The arithmetic of markups and margins is discussed in Appendix 3, "Marketing Math."

18. See "Hi-Lo versus EDLP: We Want Both!" *Retail World*, August 18, 2003, p. 30; and Laura Heller, "EDLP Has Only Scratched the Surface," *DSN Retailing Today*, January 26, 2004, pp. 35–36.

19. For more reading on reference prices and psychological pricing, see Robert M. Schindler and Patrick N. Kirby, "Patterns of Right-Most Digits Used in Advertised Prices: Implications for Nine-Ending Effects," *Journal of Consumer Research*, September 1997, pp. 192–201; Dhruv Grewal, Kent B. Monroe, Chris Janiszewski, and Donald R. Lichtenstein, "A Range Theory of Price Perception," *Journal of Consumer Research*, March 1999, pp. 353–368; Tridib Mazumdar and Purushottam Papatla, "An Investigation of Reference Price Segments," *Journal of Marketing Research*, May 2000, pp. 246–258; Indrajit Sinha and Michael Smith, "Consumers' Perceptions of Promotional Framing of Price," *Psychology & Marketing*, March 2000, pp. 257–271; and Tulin Erdem, Glenn Mayhew, and Baohong Sun, "Understanding Reference-Price Shoppers: A Within- and Across-Category Analysis," *Journal of Marketing Research*, November 2001, pp. 445–457.

20. Adapted from Andrew Park and Peter Burrows, "Dell, the Conqueror," *Business Week*, September 24, 2001, pp. 92–102. See also Andy Serwer, "Dell Does Domination," *Fortune*, January 21, 2002, pp. 70–75; Gary McWilliams, "Dell Computer's Kevin Rollins Becomes a Driving Force," *Wall Street Journal*, April 4, 2002, p. B6; and David Bank, "Leading the News: Hewlett Packard Earnings Get Lift from Weak Dollar," *Wall Street Journal*, February 20, 2004, p. A.3.

21. Mary Nersessian, "Gas prices fuel concerns about entire economy," CTV.ca News, September 29, 2005, www.ctv.ca/servlet/ArticleNews/story/CTVNews/20050929/gas_pack_050929/20050929?hub=Canada (accessed April 2006).

22. Brent Jang, "Air Canada off bottle," *Globe and Mail*, April 20, 2006.

23. Jack Neff, "Kimberly-Clark Looses 'Bounty Killer,'" *Advertising Age*, April 2, 2001, p. 34; and information at www.scottbrand.com/products/towels (accessed December 2004).

24. See the *Competition Act*, Sections 34–38, http://laws.justice.gc.ca/ en/C-34/.

25. "Competition Bureau Investigation Leads to Record Fine in Domestic Conspiracy," News Release, January 9, 2006, www.competitionbureau.gc.ca/internet/index.cfm?itemID=2018&lg=e (accessed April 2006).

26. N. Craig Smith and John A. Quelch, *Ethics in Marketing* (Boston: Irwin, 1993), pp. 389–404.

Chapter 12

1. Quotes and other information from Donald V. Fites, "Make Your Dealers Your Partners," *Harvard Business Review*, March–April 1996, pp. 84–95; Sandra Ward, "The Cat Comes Back," *Barron's*, February 25, 2002, pp. 21–24; DeAnn Weimer, "A New Cat on the Hot Seat," *Business Week*, March 1998, pp. 56–62; *Hoover's Company Capsules*, March 15, 2004, p. 10304; Shirley A. Lazo, "The Cat's Meow," *Barron's*, June 14, 2004, p. 35; and information at www.caterpillar.com (accessed January 2005).

2. Raizel Robin, "Net Gains," *Canadian Business Online*, www.canadianbusiness.com, October 27, 2003 (accessed October 6, 2004); Mediagrif website, www.mediagrif.com (accessed May 2006); GlobeInvestor website, www.theglobeandmail.com, (accessed October 6, 2004).

3. For definitions and a complete discussion of distribution channel topics, see Anne T. Coughlin, Erin Anderson, Louis W. Stern, and Adel El-Ansary, *Marketing Channels*, 6th ed. (Upper Saddle River, NJ: Prentice Hall, 2001), pp. 2–3.

4. Andrew Wahl, "Clean and green: for Nortel, environmental sustainability is a competitive necessity," *Canadian Business Online*, February 22, 2006.

5. John Gray, "Sour Dough," *Canadian Business*, June 23, 2003, pp. 36–41.

6. Anne T. Coughlin, Erin Anderson, Louis W. Stern, and Adel El-Ansary, *Marketing Channels*, 6th ed. (Upper Saddle River, NJ: Prentice Hall, 2001), p. 160; Matthew Boyle, "Brand Killers," *Fortune*, August 11, 2003, pp. 89–100; and information at www.giantfood.com and www.luxottica.com/english/profilo_aziendale/index_keyfacts.html (accessed January 2005).

7. "Business Floating on Air," *The Economist*, May 19, 2001, pp. 56–57; Richard Heller, "Galician Beauty," *Forbes*, May 28, 2001, p. 98; Miguel Helft, "Fashion Fast Forward," *Business 2.0*, May 2002, p. 60; John Tagliabue, "A Rival to Gap That Operates Like Dell," *New York Times*, May 30, 2003, p. W-1; Susan Reda, "Retail's Great Race," *Stores*, March 2004, p. 36; and www.zara.com/v04/eng/home.php (accessed December 2004).

8. Industry Canada's franchising website, strategis.ic.gc.ca/SSG/dm01179e.html (accessed August 2003); "Answers to the 21 Most Commonly Asked Questions About Franchising," International Franchise Association website, www.franchise.org (accessed July 2002); and Canadian Franchise Directory, www.franchisedirectory.ca/ (accessed May 2006).

9. Rob Annandale, "Boston Pizza party," *Macleans*, September 2, 2005; Eve Lazarus, "Building the perfect franchise," *Profit* magazine, March 2006.

10. Amanda Miller, Peter Rose, and Michael Voeller, "General Mills, Inc.," Krause Fund Research, Fall 2002, at www.biz.uiowa.edu/krause/General_Mills_F02.pdf; and information at www.cerealpartners.co.uk/ (accessed January 2005).

11. See Subhash C. Jain, *International Marketing Management*, 3rd ed. (Boston: PWS-Kent Publishing, 1990), pp. 489–491. Also see Warren J. Keegan, *Global Marketing Management* (Upper Saddle River, NJ: Prentice Hall, 2002), pp. 403–404.

12. See Aruna Chandra and John K. Ryans Jr, "Why India Now?" *Marketing Management*, March–April 2002, pp. 43–45; Dana James, "Dark Clouds Should Part for International Marketers," *Marketing News*, January 7, 2002, pp. 9, 13; Russell Flannery, "Red Tape," *Forbes*, March 3, 2003, pp. 97–100; and Russell Flannery, "China: The Slow Boat," *Forbes*, April 12, 2004, p. 76.

13. Jennifer Wells, "We Can Get It for You Wholesale," *Report on Business Magazine*, March 1995, pp. 52–62.

14. For more on channel relationships, see "Supply Chain Challenges," *Harvard Business Review*, July 2003, pp. 65–73; and James C. Anderson and James A. Narus, *Business Market Management*, 2nd ed. (Upper Saddle River, NJ: Prentice Hall, 2004), chapter 9.

15. Mitch Betts, "GE Appliance Park Still an IT Innovator," *Computerworld*, January 29, 2001, pp. 20–21; and "What Is GE CustomerNet?" at www.geappliances.com/buildwithge/index_cnet.htm (accessed January 2005).

16. Marina Strauss, "Wal-Mart Supplier Was Asked for Kickbacks," *Globe and Mail*, February 2, 2000, www.globeandmail.com; P.N. Bloom, G.T. Gundlach, and J.P. Cannon, "Slotting Allowances and Fees: Schools of Thought and the Views of Practicing Managers," *Journal of Marketing*, April 2000, pp. 92–108; Andrew Stodart, "Fight for Your Rights: Marketers Are Being Far Too Passive about the Growing Concentration of Retail Power in this Country," *Marketing Magazine*, May 31, 1999, www.marketingmag.ca.

17. Martin Piszczalksi, "Logistics: A Difference Between Winning and Losing," *Automotive Manufacturing & Production*, May 2001, pp. 16–18; and Andrew D. Beadle, "Logistics Costs, Quantified," *Journal of Commerce*, June 14, 2003, p. 1.

18. Shlomo Maital, "The Last Frontier of Cost Reduction," *Across the Board*, February 1994, pp. 51–52; and "Wal-Mart to Expand Supercenters to California," *Business Journal*, May 15, 2002, http://sanjose.bizjournals.com; and information at www.walmart.com (accessed December 2004).

19. Alex Binkley, "Wal-Mart Canada Inc.," Case Study, Tibbett & Britten Group North America, www.tbgna.com/html/sub/cs_walmart.htm (accessed August 2003).

20. J. William Gurley, "Why Dell's War Isn't Dumb," *Fortune*, July 9, 2001, pp. 134–136; and Susan Kuckinskas, "Data-Based Dell," *Adweek Magazine's Technology Marketing*, September 2003, p. 20.

21. See "Business: The Best Thing Since the Bar-Code: The IT Revolution," *The Economist*, February 8, 2003, p. 57–58; Faith Keenan, "If Supermarket Shelves Could Talk," *Business Week*, March 31, 2003, pp. 66–67; Laurie Sullivan, "Reaching Down the Supply Chain," *InformationWeek*, March 22, 2004, p. 49; and information at www.autoidlabs.org (accessed August 2004).

22. Judy Strauss and Raymond Frost, *E-Marketing*, 2nd ed. (Upper Saddle River, NJ: Prentice Hall, 2001), p. 193; Jean Kinsey, "A Faster, Leaner Supply Chain: New Uses of Information Technology" *American Journal of Agricultural Economics*, November 15, 2000, pp. 11231; and Carol Sliwa, "EDI: Alive and Well After All These Years," *Computerworld*, June 14, 2004, p. 1.

23. See William C. Copacino, "Supply Chain Software Still Has Much to Offer," *Logistics Management*, May 2003, p. 76; and Martin Grossman, "The Role of Trust and Collaboration in the Internet-Enabled Supply Chain," *Journal of American Academy of Business*, September 2004, p. 391.

Chapter 13

1. The Forzani Group website and 2005 Annual Report, www.forzanigroup.com/ (accessed May 2006); and Zena

Olignyk, "At the Top of Its Game: Escaped from the Jaws of Defeat, Forzani Finds New Fans," *Canadian Business,* April 29, 2002, www.canadianbusiness.com/investing/article.jsp?content=45464; Norma Ramage, "What's up at Forzani," *Marketing,* June 13, 2005; "The Game Plan," presentation to Annual General & Special Meeting of Shareholders, June 8, 2005 www.forzanigroup.com/investors/presentations/2005/AGM_presentation_F05.pdf (accessed May 2006).

2. London Drugs webpage www.londondrugs.com (accessed August 2006); Eve Lazarus, "London Drugs puts spa right in store," *Marketing Magazine,* November 18, 2005; Sara Minoque, "Blurring the boundaries," *Strategy Magazine,* June 30, 2003, p. 13.

3. Retail Council of Canada, "Open—2004/2005 Report to Members," pp. 3, 8, www.retailcouncil.org/aboutus/ar2004_05.pdf (accessed May 27, 2006).

4. Brian Dunn, "The King of Bread, Butts and Beer," *Marketing Magazine,* October 25, 1999, p. 23; Anita Lahey, "Cornered Stores," *Marketing Magazine,* August 4, 1997, pp. 10–11; Luis Millan, "King of the Corner Store," *Canadian Business,* September 26, 1997, pp. 101–103; and Dana Flavelle, "Quebec Retailers on a Roll in U.S.," *Toronto Star,* October 12, 2003, pp. C1, C3; Natalia Williams, "Couche-Tarde: Beyond Milk, *Strategy Magazine,* November 2005.

5. Winners' website "About Us," www.winners.ca/en/about.asp (accessed May 2006); Jeff Sanford, "Retail: Let Them Shop Chic," *Canadian Business,* December 2005.

6. Marina Strauss, "The Best Bet for Your Bottom Dollar," *Globe and Mail,* August 2, 2003, p. B1; "Bucking a trend," *Marketing Magazine,* May 10, 2004.

7. Marina Strauss, "New Wave of U.S. Retailers Advance on Canada," *Globe and Mail,* January 12, 2001, p. M1.

8. Shoeless Joe's website, www.shoelessjoes.net/about.htm (accessed May 2006); "Where Every Day Is Game Day," *Canadian Business Franchise,* May 2006, www.cgb.ca/coverstory.html.

9. See David Stires, "Fallen Arches," *Fortune,* April 29, 2002, pp. 74–76; Anne Field, "Your Ticket to a New Career," *Business Week,* May 12, 2003, pp. 100–101; McDonalds Canadian website, www.mcdonalds.ca/en/aboutus/mcdCanada_facts.aspx (accessed May 2006).

10. See Lorrie Grant, "Maytag Stores Let Shoppers Try Before They Buy," *USA Today,* June 7, 2004, p. 7B.

11. Landry's Restaurants Inc., website, www.landrys restaurants.com/pages/restaurants/pg_rest_rfc.htm; and Rain Forest Café website, www.rainforestcafe.com (accessed May 2006).

12. West Edmonton Mall Website, www.westedmall.com/about/default.asp (accessed May 27, 2006).

13. See Joanna Dale, *Consumer Attitudes towards Retail in BC,* Retail Council of Canada, September 21, 2000, www.retailcouncil.org/research/bcretail/sld026.htm; and Steven Bergsman, "Slow Times at Sherman Oaks: What's Ailing the Big Malls of America?" *Barron's,* May 17, 1999, p. 39.

14. See Malcolm P. McNair and Eleanor G. May, "The Next Revolution of the Retailing Wheel," *Harvard Business Review,* September–October 1978, pp. 81–91; Stephen

Brown, "The Wheel of Retailing: Past and Future," *Journal of Retailing,* Summer 1990, pp. 143–147; Stephen Brown, "Variations on a Marketing Enigma: The Wheel of Retailing Theory," *Journal of Marketing Management,* 7, no. 2, 1991, pp. 131–155; Jennifer Negley, "Retrenching, Reinventing, and Remaining Relevant," *Discount Store News,* April 5, 1999, p. 11; and Don E. Schultz, "Another Turn of the Wheel," *Marketing Management,* March–April 2002, pp. 8–9.

15. Richard Karpinskr, "Web Delivers Big Results for Staples," *B to B,* November 11, 2002, p. 14; and Joseph Pereira, "Staples Posts Strong Earnings on High-Margin Internet Sales," *Wall Street Journal,* March 5, 2004, p. A13.

16. Excerpt adapted from Alice Z. Cuneo, "What's in Store?" *Advertising Age,* February 25, 2002, pp. 1, 30–31. Also see Robert Berner, "Dark Days in White Goods for Sears," *Business Week,* March 10, 2003, pp. 78–79.

17. See Jack Neff, "Wal-Mart Weans Suppliers," *Advertising Age,* December 1, 2003, pp. 1, 33; and "The Fortune 500," *Fortune,* April 5, 2004, p. F1.

18. David Menzies, "Retail and High-Tech," *Marketing Magazine,* August 5, 1996.

19. Adapted from information found in Christina Rexrode, "Concept Store in Bloom," *The Herald-Sun,* June 6, 2004, pp. F1, F3; and "Food Lion Opens First Bloom Concept Store," press release, May 25, 2004, www. foodlion.com/news.asp?parm5323.

20. James Cox, "Red-Letter Day as East Meets West in the Aisles," *USA Today,* September 11, 1996, p. B1; and "Wal-Mart International Operations," www.walmartstores.com (accessed July 2004).

21. Carla Rapoport, "Retailers Go Global," *Fortune,* February 20, 1995, pp. 102–108; "Global Retailing in the Connected Economy," *Chain Store Age,* December 1999, pp. 69–82; Tim Craig, "Global Retailing's Defining Moments Are Getting Lost in the Mix," *DSN Retailing Today,* April 21, 2003, p. 7; and "World's 100 Largest Retailers," www.chainstoreage.com (accessed December 2004).

22. Adapted from Tim Craig, "Carrefour: At the Intersection of Global," *DSN Retailing Today,* September 18, 2000, p. 16. Additional information from Richard Tomlinson, "Who's Afraid of Wal-Mart?" *Fortune,* June 26, 2000, pp. 186–196; "Carrefour SA," *Euroweek,* April 25, 2003, p. 1; "Carrefour SA," *Wall Street Journal,* March 5, 2004, p. C.14; and www.carrefour.com (accessed January 2005).

23. Christina Nifong, "Beyond Browsing," *Raleigh News & Observer,* May 25, 1999, p. E1. Also see Fred Brock, "Catering to the Elderly Can Pay Off," *New York Times,* February 2002, p. 3.11.

24. Kathleen Cholewka, "Standing Out Online: The Five Best E-Marketing Campaigns," *Sales & Marketing Management,* January 2001, pp. 51–58. Other information from www. playstation.com (accessed July 2004).

25. Lara Mills, "GT Pursues 'Underserved' Telco Market," *Marketing Magazine,* October 25, 1999.

26. Statistics Canada, "Wholesale Merchants' Sales by Industries," www40.statcan.ca/l01/cst01/trad20a.htm?sdi=wholesale%20trade (accessed May 27, 2006).

27. "McKesson: Raising Expectations," *Modern Materials Handling,* February 2004, p. 53; and information from

"About the Company" and "Supply Management Online," www.mckesson.com (accessed August 2004).

28. Facts from www.supervalu.com (accessed August 2004); and from "SuperValu Inc.," *Hoover's Company Capsules,* Austin, July 15, 2004, p. 11419.

Chapter 14

1. Extracts adapted from Sara Minoque, "Small but powerful," *Strategy Magazine,* July 28, 2003, p. 20; John Gaffney, "Most Innovative Campaign," *Business 2.0,* May 2002, pp. 98–99; and Warren Berger, "Dare Devils," *Business 2.0,* April 2004, pp. 111–116. Also see Joan Voight, "Mini's Wild Ride" *Adweek,* June 2, 2003, p. 24; and Joseph B. White, "Challenges Rise for BMW's Mini in U.S. Market," *Wall Street Journal,* March 24, 2004, p. 1; "BMW Mini rides with Taxi," *Marketing Daily,* February 23, 2001, www.marketingmag.ca/; "Street teams tease launch of BMW's Mini," *Marketing Daily,* March 5, 2002, www.marketingmag.ca/; "Small surprises for Taxi's debut Mini ads," *Marketing Daily,* February 1, 2002, www.marketingmag.ca/; Michelle Halpern, "Mini ride for Canada's Wonderland," *Marketing Daily,* August 17, 2004, www.marketingmag.ca/; Maya Bahar, "Exposed: Thirty seconds with a marketing maven: BMW's Hendrik von Kuenheim," *Strategy Magazine,* July 12, 2004, p. 5; Sarah Dobson, "Mini uses humour, games in new campaign," *Marketing Daily,* Sept. 23, 2005, www.marketingmag.ca/.

2. The first four of these definitions are adapted from Peter D. Bennett, *Dictionary of Marketing Terms* (Chicago: American Marketing Association, 1995). Other definitions can be found at www.marketingpower.com/live/mg-dictionary.php? (accessed August 2004).

3. Don E. Schultz, "New Media, Old Problem: Keep Marcom Integrated," *Marketing News,* March 29, 1999, p. 11. Also see Michael McLaren, "Key to Tech Marketing Is Integrated message," *B to B,* February 10, 2003, p. 16; and Claire Atkinson, "Integration Still a Pipe Dream for Many," *Advertising Age,* March 10, 2003, pp. 1, 47.

4. See Chapters 3 and 5. Also see Don E. Schultz and Philip J. Kitchen, *Communication Globally: An Integrated Marketing Approach* (New York: McGraw Hill, 2000); and Don E. Schultz and Heidi Schultz, *IMC: The Next Generation* (New York: McGraw Hill, 2004).

5. For more on integrated marketing communications, see Don E. Schultz, Stanley I. Tannenbaum, and Robert F. Lauterborn, *Integrated Marketing Communications* (Chicago, IL: NTC, 1992); Don E. Schultz and Philip J. Kitchen, *Communication Globally: An Integrated Marketing Approach* (New York: McGraw Hill, 2000); Prasad A. Naik and Kalyan Raman, "Understanding the Impact of Synergy in Multimedia Communications," *Journal of Marketing Research,* November 2003, pp. 375–388; and Don E. Schultz and Heidi Schultz, *IMC: The Next Generation* (New York: McGraw Hill, 2004).

6. Sarah Dobson, "Becel uses humour in heart-health message," *Marketing Daily,* February 8, 2006, www.marketingmag.ca/.

7. Hillary Chura, "A Creative Low Point," *Advertising Age,"* February 9, 2004, p. 49; and Stuart Elliott, "Can Beers Ads Extol Great Taste in Good Taste?" *New York Times,* April 2004, p. C2.

8. The history of Buckley's Mixture can be found online at www.buckleys.com.

9. For these and other examples, see Pamela Paul, "Color by Numbers," *American Demographics,* February 2002, pp. 31–35; and Arundhati Parmar, "Marketers Ask: Hues on First?" *Marketing News,* February 15, 2004, pp. 8–10.

10. Adapted from Sandra Yin, "Degree of Challenge," *American Demographics,* May 2003, pp. 20–22. Also see Scott Donaton, "Marketing's New Fascination, Figuring Out Word of Mouth," *Advertising Age,* November 17, 2003, p. 18; and "Word of Mouth More Influential than Ads," *Campaign,* April 23, 2004, p. 5.

11. Mark Evans, "Can Cindy Klassen Save Manitoba Tel?" February 28, 2007, http://evans.blogware.com/blog/_archives/2006/2/28/1788317.html, (accessed April 2006); Canadian Press, "Olympic hero Cindy Klassen returns home to Winnipeg," March 28, 2006, www.canada.com/globaltv/manitoba/story.html?id=1cdae7b5-5911-4abb-9b2b-877dfcd86d5e (accessed April 2006).

12. Andy Hoffman and Grand Robertson, "Beer ad's angry Scot faces porn charges," *Globe and Mail,* February 16, 2006; Oliver Moore, "Beer icon's the buzz of bars," *Globe and Mail,* February 17, 2006.

13. For more on advertising spending by company and industry, see the Advertising Age Data Center at www.adage.com.

14. For more on setting promotion budgets, see W. Ronald Lane, Karen Whitehill King, and J. Thomas Russell, *Kleppner's Advertising Procedure,* 16th ed. (Upper Saddle River, NJ: Prentice Hall, 2005), chapter 6.

15. Canadian Media Directors Council, *2003–04 Media Digest,* p. 13; Bill Carter, "After Super Bowl, 'Survivor' Is the Season's Top Hit on TV," *New York Times,* January 30, 2001, p. C8; "Canadian Idol Rocks with Star-Studded Finale as Audience Peaks at 3.8 Million Viewers, CTV, September 15, 2005, ww.ctv.ca/servlet/ArticleNews/print/CTVShows/20050915/ctv_release_20050915/20050915?hub=Corporate&subhub=PrintStory (accessed April 2006).

16. Michele Marchetti, "What a Sales Call Costs," *Sales & Marketing Management,* September 2000, p. 80; and Harry J. Abramson, "Perfect Reasons to Stop Making Cold Calls in the Eyes of a Rep," *Agency Sales,* December 2003, p. 26.

17. Based on Matthew P. Gonring, "Putting Integrated Marketing Communications to Work Today," *Public Relations Quarterly,* Fall 1994, pp. 45–48. Also see Philip Kotler, *Marketing Management,* 11th ed. (Upper Saddle River, NJ: Prentice Hall, 2003), pp. 583–584.

18. Michelle Warren, "Cause Commotion," *Marketing Magazine,* October 6/13, 2003, pp. 21–26; and KitchenAid Canada website, www.kitchenaid-cookforthecure.ca/ (accessed April 2006).

19. Advertising regulation in Canada is covered under a diverse set of federal and provincial laws and regulations. See, for example, *The Competition Act,* the *Food and Drugs Act,* the *Quebec Consumer Protection Act,* the *CRTC Code For Broadcast Advertising of Alcoholic Beverages,* the *Gaming and Liquor Act* (Alberta), and the *Copyright Act.* Also see

Eric Gross, *That's Advertainment*, (conference paper, Institute of Continuing Legal Education, 2002).

Chapter 15

1. Adapted from Cassies 2005 Cases, "United Way. The Hand Campaign," www.cassies.ca/caselibrary/ (accessed May 2, 2006); Paul-Mark Rendon, "United Way advertising focuses on long-term goals," *Marketing Daily*, September 30, 2005, www.marketingmag.ca/; Annette Bourdeau, "Outstanding new campaigns," *Strategy Magazine*, October 2005, p. 22; John Burghardt, "United Way deserves an exaggerated hand," *Strategy Magazine*, December 1, 2003, p. 15.

2. Canadian Media Directors Council—*Media Digest*, www.cmdc.ca/mediadigest.html (accessed May 2, 2006); "Renewal in Action: Annual Report on Government of Canada Advertising Activities 2004–2005," Public Works and Government Services Canada, www.pwgsc.gc.ca/advrptpub/text/ann_rpt-2004-05-ch2-e.html (accessed at May 2006). Information on international advertising spending from the Ad Age Dataplace, www.adage.com (accessed August 2004); Mercedes M. Cardona, "Ad-Spending Soothsayers Optimistic on Year Ahead," *Advertising Age*, December 15, 2003, p. 8; and "100 Leading National Advertisers," *Advertising Age*, June 28, 2004, pp. 2–5.

3. "Net Leads the Way in Spending," *Marketing Magazine*, September 25, 2000, www.marketingmag.ca; "2001: A Marketing Odyssey: Seven Association Leaders Predict the Challenges the Next Year May Bring," *Marketing Magazine*, December 18/25, 2000, www.marketingmag.ca; and Robert J. Coen, "Spending Spree," *Advertising Age Special Issue: The Advertising Century*, 1999, p. 126; Canadian Media Directors Council—Media Digest, www.cmdc.ca/mediadigest.html (accessed May 2, 2006).

4. Natalia Williams, "Shiny happy marketers!" *Strategy Magazine*, March 2005, p. 45.

5. For more on advertising budgets, see W. Ronald Lane, Karen Whitehill King, and J. Thomas Russell, *Kleppner's Advertising Procedure*, 16th ed. (Upper Saddle River, NJ: Prentice Hall, 2005), chapter 6.

6. Information from Rosalind Stefanac, "Corporate Ads in Rainbow Colours: Big Mainstream Marketers Are Crafting Innovative Advertising Strategies in a Bid to Get Closer to Gay and Lesbian Consumers," *Marketing Magazine*, May 1, 2000, www.marketingmag.ca; Gary Levin, "'Meddling' in Creative More Welcome," *Advertising Age*, April 9, 1990, pp. S4, S8; Lynne Roberts, "New Media Choice: Absolut Vodka," *Marketing Magazine*, April 9, 1998, p. 12; Eleftheria Parpis, "TBWA: Absolut," *Adweek*, November 9, 1998, p. 172; and Absolut website, Q&A section, www.absolut.com (accessed March 2000).

7. Sarah Dobson, "BMO regenerates its retirement planning," *Marketing Daily*, April 3, 2006, www.marketingmag.ca/.

8. Canadian Media Directors Council—Media Digest, www.cmdc.ca/mediadigest.html (accessed May 2, 2006), pp. 16, 32, 34, 40 and 44.

9. Richard Linnett, "Super Bowl Busts Records, *Advertising Age*, January 12, 2004, p. 1; Stuart Elliott, "NBC's 'Friends' Finale Is the Super Bowl of Sitcoms," *New York Times*, May 3, 2004, p. C.8; and Claire Atkinson, "'Idol' Tops TV Price Chart," *Advertising Age*, September 27, 2004, pp. 1, 77.

10. Gary Ruskin, "A Death Spiral of Disrespect," *Advertising Age*, April 26, 2004, p. 18; and Andrew Green, "Clutter Crisis Countdown," *Advertising Age*, April 21, 2004, p. 22.

11. Wayne Friedman, "PVR Users Skip Most Ads: Study," *Advertising Age*, July 1, 2002, pp. 4, 46; and Ronald Grover, "Can Mad Ave Make Zap-Proof Ads?" *Business Week*, February 2, 2004, pp. 36–37.

12. Edward A. Robinson, "Frogs, Bears, and Orgasms: Think Zany if You Want to Reach Today's Consumers," *Fortune*, June 9, 1997, pp. 153–156. Also see Tobi Elkin, "Courting Craftier Consumers," July 1, 2002, p. 28; and Devin Leonard, "Nightmare on Madison Avenue," *Fortune*, June 28, 2004, pp. 93–108.

13. www.drinkmilk.ca; Chris Daniels "Gold BC Dairy: 2005 Digital Marketing Award Winners," *Marketing Magazine*, October 31, 2005, www.marketingmag.ca/magazine/current/digital_mkt_rpt/article.jsp?content=20051031_71448_71448 (accessed August 2006).

14. Tobi Elkin, "Porsche, Acura Latest to Try Out TiVo Showcases," *Advertising Age*, February 24, 2003; Elkin, "Getting Viewers to Opt In, Not Tune Out," *Advertising Age*, November 4, 2002, p. 10; Jon Healey, "California; TiVo to Sell Statistics on Ads Skipped," *Los Angeles Times*, June 2, 2003, p. C2; and Joe Mandese, "Study Says DVRs, Ads Can Co-Exist," *Television Week*, June 7, 2004, p. 35.

15. "Media Multi-Taskers," *Journal of Marketing Management*, May–June 2004, p. 6.

16. *Media Digest* 05/06, Canadian Media Directors' Council, www.cmdc.ca/pdf/2006_Media_Digest.pdf (accessed May 2006).

17. See Marty Bernstein, "Why TV Commercials Are So Costly," *Automotive News*, May 10, 2004, p. 30H.

18. Annette Bourdeau, "Brilliant! Olympic Promotions," *Strategy Magazine*, February 2006, p. 8.

19. Laura Medcalf, "The Rankings—Canada's Top Marketing Communications Services Companies," *Marketing Magazine*, June 20, 2005, pp. 17–25.

20. Jim McElgunn, "Who Cares Where an Ad's Made?" *Marketing Magazine*, May 8, 1995, p. 20; and "Canada's Top Agencies," *Marketing*, July 24, 1995, p. 11.

21. Information on advertising agencies from "World's Top 25 Ad Organizations," *Advertising Age*, April 19, 2004, p. S-2.

22. See George E. Belch and Michael A. Belch, *Advertising and Promotion* (New York: McGraw-Hill/Irwin, 2004), pp. 666–668.

23. *2002 Trade Promotion Spending & Merchandising Industry Study* (Wilton, CT: Cannondale Associates, 2002), p. 13; and *Trade Promotion Spending & Merchandising 2003 Industry Study* (Wilton, CT: Cannondale Associates, 2003), p. 7. Also see "Promotions and Incentives: Offers You Can't Refuse," *Marketing Week*, April 15, 2004, p. 31; and E. Craig Stacey, "Abandon TV at Your Own Risk," *Advertising Age*, June 7, 2004, p. 32.

24. Kenneth Hein, "Coke Puts New Twist on Plain Vanilla Sampler, Summer Tours," *Brandweek*, July 1, 2002, p. 35; and "Coca-Cola Unveils U.S. Launch Plans for its New Lower-Carb, Lower-Cal Cola, Coca-Cola C2," May 24, 2004, www.coca-cola.com.

25. Debra Aho Williamson, "P&G's Reformulated Pert Plus Builds Consumer Relationships," *Advertising Age*, June 28, 1999, p. 52; and Emily Rogers, "Eat Natural Raises Awareness with Sampling Drive," *Marketing*, May 12, 2004, p. 6.

26. Lucy Saddleton, "Baby Money!" *Strategy*, October 6, 2003, p. 1.

27. See Lucia Moses, "Coupons Make Move Online," *Editor & Publisher*, February 24, 2003, p. 10; and information at www.catalinamarketing.com/manufacturer_services/products.html (accessed December 2004).

28. See www.icoke.ca.

29. See William F. Kendy, "The Great Giveaway," *Selling Power*, September 2002, pp. 98–105; and information at the Promotional Products Association International website, www.ppai.org (accessed December 2004).

30. "2007 International CES Defined by New Convergence of Broadband, Content and Consumer Electronics," Press Release, Las Vegas, Nevada, January 11, 2007 http://www.cesweb.org/press/news/rd_release_detail.asp?id= 11228 (accessed January 17, 2007); see "Nearly Half a Million Attend Bauma Trade Show," *Pit & Quarry*, May 2004, p. 16; and information found at the consumer Electronics Association website, www.cesweb.org/press/default_flash.asp (accessed December 2004).

31. Adapted from Scott Cutlip, Allen Center, and Glen Broom, *Effective Public Relations*, 8th ed. (Upper Saddle River, NJ: Prentice Hall, 2000), chapter 1. For additional definitions, see Fraser P. Seitel, *The Practice of Public Relations* (Upper Saddle River, NJ: Prentice Hall, 2004), chapter 1.

32. Annette Bourdeau, "Burning up the Headlines," *Strategy*, March 2006, p. 21.

33. Diane Brady, "Wizard of Marketing," *Business Week*, July 24, 2000, pp. 84–87. Also see Dick Lynch, "The Magic of 'Harry Potter,'" *Advertising Age*, December 10, 2001, p. 26; Stephen Brown, "Marketing for Muggles: The Harry Potter Way to Higher Profits," *Business Horizons*, January–February 2002, pp. 6–14; and "Harry Potter and the Publishing Goldmine," www.Economist.com, June 23, 2003.

34. See Kathleen Sampey, "Crest Whitestrips to Get $90M Push," *Brandweek*, June 4, 2001, p. 27; Sampey, "Breaking the Rules of PR/Fashion Results in White-Hot Campaign," *PR News*, Feb. 25, 2002; Patricia Van Arnum, "Whitening Products Help to Drive Growth in Oral Care," *Chemical Market Reporter*, May 10, 2004, p. FR10; and Molly Prior, "Whiter, Cheaper, Faster Are the Latest Buzzwords in Oral Care," *Drug Store News*, July 19, 2004, pp. 23–24.

35. Based on information from Kate Fitzgerald, "Marketing on the Move," *Advertising Age*, March 18, 2002, p. 59; Jeff St. John, "Microsoft Sends Mobile Marketing Van to Kennewick, Wash., Area," *Knight Ridder Tribune Business News*, April 28, 2004, p. 1; and Eve Lazarus, "Nintendo outsources promotions to prep for product launch," *Marketing Daily*, May 3, 2005, www.marketingmag.ca/.

36. See "Butterball Turkey Talk-Line Fact Sheet," www.butterball.com/en/files/PDF/Fact_Sheet_sheet.PDF (accessed December 2004).

37. See Mark Gleason, "Edelman Sees Niche in Web Public Relations," *Advertising Age*, January 20, 1997, p. 30; Steve Jarvis, "How the Internet Is Changing Fundamentals of Publicity," *Marketing News*, July 17, 2000, p. 6; G.A. Markin, "Why Doesn't the Press Call?" *Public Relations Quarterly*, Spring 2002, pp. 9–10; and "Best Use of the Internet 2004," *PRweek*, March 8, 2004, p. S47.

Chapter 16

1. Quotes and other information from Jeff O'Heir, "Michael Krasny—IT Sales Innovator," *Computer Reseller News*, November 18, 2002; Ed Lawler, "Integrated Campaign Winner: CDW Computer Centers," *B to B*, December 9, 2002, p. 20; "CDW Chooses Richardson to Strengthen Customer Focus," *Business Wire*, July 23, 2003, p. 5397; Mark Del Franco, Paul Miller, and Margery Weinstein, "Smooth Sailing in Choppy Waters," *Catalog Age*, March 2004, pp. 42–46; Scott Campbell, "CDW Snags Companywide Cisco Premier Status," *CRN*, April 12, 2004, p. 12; www.cdw.com (accessed July 2004); and, "CDW Ranked Among 10 Largest Online Retailers," Business Wire, June 26, 2006, www.findarticles.com/p/articles/mi_m0EIN/is_2006_June_26/ai_n16499549 (accessed January 17, 2007).

2. Quote from Laurence Zuckerman, "Selling Airplanes with a Smile," *New York Times*, February 17, 2002, p. 3.2. Also see Bill Kelley, "How to Sell Airplanes, Boeing-Style," *Sales & Marketing Management*, December 9, 1985, pp. 32–34; J. Lynn Lunsford, "Boeing Beats Out Airbus to Sell Virgin Blue $3 Billion in Jets," *Wall Street Journal*, January 16, 2003, p. B6; and Joann Muller, "7 Digital 7," *Forbes*, June 21, 2004, p. 117.

3. Quotes and other information from Geoffrey Brewer, "Love the Ones You're With," *Sales & Marketing Management*, February 1997, pp. 38–45; and Erin Stout, "Blue Skies Ahead?" *Sales & Marketing Management*, March 2003, pp. 25–29.

4. For more on this and other methods for determining sales force size, see Mark W. Johnson and Greg W. Marshall, *Churchill/Ford/Walker's Sales Force Management* (New York: McGraw-Hall Irwin, 2003), pp. 142–147; and Douglas J. Dalrymple, William L. Cron, and Thomas E. DeCarlo, *Sales Management*, 8th ed. (New York: John Wiley & Sons, 2004), pp. 112–116.

5. Michele Marchetti, "What a Sales Call Costs," *Sales & Marketing Management*, September 2000, p. 80; and "How Many Personal Sales Calls Does It Take to Close a Sale?" at www.cahnerscarr.com/5425d.htm (accessed August 2004).

6. See Martin Everett, "Selling by Telephone," *Sales & Marketing Management*, December 1993, pp. 75–79. Also see Terry Arnold, "Telemarketing Strategy," *Target Marketing*, January 2002, pp. 47–48.

7. Adapted from Geoffrey Brewer, "Lou Gerstner Has His Hands Full," *Sales & Marketing Management*, May 8, 1998, pp. 36–41. Also see Michelle Cioci, "Marketing to Small Businesses," *Sales & Marketing Management*, December 2000, pp. 94–100.

8. See "A Phone Is Better than a Face," *Sales & Marketing Management*, October 1987, p. 29. Also see "Climax Portable Machine Tools Case Study," at www.selltis.com/case_climax.html (accessed August 2004).

9. Karen J. Bannan, "Call Center's Role Evolves with CRM," *B to B*, May 5, 2003, p. 14. Also see Julia Chang, "Dialing for Dollars," *Sales & Marketing Management*, July 2003, p. 28.

10. William F. Kendy, "No More Lone Rangers," *Selling Power*, April 2004, pp. 70–74.

11. "Customer Business Development," www.pg.com/jobs/jobs_us/work_we_offer/advisor_overview.jhtml?sl5jobs_advisor_business_development (accessed August 2004).

12. Quotes and other information in this section on super salespeople from Geoffrey Brewer, "Mind Reading: What Drives Top Salespeople to Greatness?" *Sales & Marketing Management*, May 1994, pp. 82–88; Andy Cohen, "The Traits of Great Sales Forces," *Sales & Marketing Management*, October 2000, pp. 67–72; Julia Chang, "Born to Sell?" *Sales & Marketing Management*, July 2003, pp. 34–38; and Henry Canaday, "Recruiting the Right Stuff," *Selling Power*, April 2004, pp. 94–96.

13. Robert Klein, "Nabisco Sales Soar after Sales Training," *Marketing News*, January 6, 1997, p. 23; and Geoffrey James, "The Return of Sales Training," *Selling Power*, May 2004, pp. 86–91.

14. Julia Chang, "No Instructor Required," *Sales & Marketing Management*, May 2003, p. 26.

15. See Christen P. Heide, "All Levels of Sales Reps Post Impressive Earnings," press release, www.dartnell.com, May 5, 1997; "Dartnell's 30th Sales Force Compensation Survey," Dartnell Corporation, August 1999; and Christine Galea, "2002 Salary Survey," *Sales & Marketing Management*, May 2002, pp. 32–36.

16. See Christen P. Heide, "All Levels of Sales Reps Post Impressive Earnings," press release, www.dartnell.com, May 5, 1997; *Dartnell's 30th Sales Force Compensation Survey*, Dartnell Corporation, August 1999; Christine Galea, "2003 Salary Survey," *Sales & Marketing Management*, May 2003, pp. 32–41; and Galea, "2004 Salary Survey," *Sales & Marketing Management*, May 2004, pp. 28–34.

17. See Gary H. Anthes, "Portal Powers GE sales," *Computerworld*, June 2, 2003, pp. 31–32. Also see Betsy Cummings, "Increasing Face Time," *Sales & Marketing Management*, January 2004, p. 12.

18. David Prater, "The Third Time's the Charm," *Sales & Marketing Management*, September 2000, pp. 101–104. For more on sales force automation (SFA), see Cheri Speier and Viswanath Venkatesh, "The Hidden Minefields in the Adoption of Sales Force Automation Technologies," *Journal of Marketing*, July 2002, pp. 98–111; Steve Levy, "A Call to Integrate CI, Customer Relationship Management, and Sales Force Automation," *Competitive Intelligence Magazine*, March–April 2003, pp. 36–39; and Betsy Cummings, "Tools of the Trade," *Sales & Marketing Management*, October 2003, pp. 46–51.

19. Melinda Ligos, "Point, Click, and Sell," *Sales & Marketing Management*, May 1999, pp. 51–56; Tim Wilson, "Salespeople Leverage the Net," *Internetweek*, June 4, 2001, pp. PG11, PG13; Amy J. Morgan and Scott A. Inks,

"Technology and the Sales Force: Increasing Acceptance of Sales Force Automation," *Industrial Marketing Management*, July 2001, pp. 463–472; Eilene Zimmerman, "Casting the Net Wide," *Sales & Marketing Management*, April 2002, pp. 50–56; and Paul N. Romani, "The Internet and Personal Selling," *The American Salesman*, March 2003, pp. 3–10.

20. Quotes from Bob Donath, "Delivering Value Starts with Proper Prospecting," *Marketing News*, November 10, 1997, p. 5; and Bill Brooks, "Power-Packed Prospecting Pointers," *Agency Sales*, March 2004, p. 37.

21. Quotes from David Stamps, "Training for a New Sales Game," *Training*, July 1997, pp. 46–52; Erin Stout, "Throwing the Right Pitch," *Sales & Marketing Management*, April 2001, pp. 61–63; Andy Cohen, "Customers Know Best," *Sales & Marketing Management*, January 2003, p. 10; and William F. Kendy, "How to Be a Good Listener," *Selling Power*, April 2004, pp. 41–44.

22. Adapted from Betsy Cummings, "On the Cutting Edge," *Sales & Marketing Management*, June 3, 2003, pp. 39–43.

23. Renee Houston Zemanski, "Well Connected," *Selling Power*, March 2003, pp. 32–34.

24. "Wireless Internet Usage In Canada," Ipsos News Centre, October 6, 2005, www.ipsos-na.com/news/pressrelease.cfm?id=2802 (accessed May 2006).

25. Alicia Orr Suman, "Ideas You Can Take to the Bank! 10 Big Things All Direct Marketers Should Be Doing Now," *Target Marketing*, February 2003, pp. 31–33.

26. Lesley Young, "The Auto Club Takes It Slow," *Marketing Magazine*, April 29, 2002, p. MD8.

27. Dana Blakenhorn, "Marketers Hone Targeting," *Advertising Age*, June 18, 2001, p. T16; Thomas H. Davenport, "How Do They Know Their Customers So Well?" *MIT Sloan Management Review*, Winter 2001, pp. 63–73; and "The Customer Is Job 1 at Ford," www.sas.com/success/ford.html (accessed August 2003).

28. For these and other examples, see Jonathan Berry, "A Potent New Tool for Selling: Database Marketing," *Business Week*, September 4, 1994, pp. 56–62; Weld F. Royal, "Do Databases Really Work?" *Sales & Marketing Management*, October 1995, pp. 66–74; Daniel Hill, "Love My Brand," *Brandweek*, January 19, 1998, pp. 26–29; "FedEx Taps into Data Warehousing," *Advertising Age's Business Marketing*, January 1999, p. 25; and Harriet Marsh, "Dig Deeper into the Database Goldmine," *Marketing*, January 11, 2001, pp. 29–30.

29. "Royal Canadian Mint Boosts Canada Day Coin," Marketing Direct Briefs, *Marketing Magazine*, August 19, 2002, p. 7.

30. Sarah Dobson, "Sleepover contest designed to build database, *Marketing Daily*, September 28, 2005, www.marketingmag.ca/.

31. Statistics on direct media expenditures and sales throughout this section are from "Economic Impact: U.S. Direct Marketing Today," www.the-dma.org/research (accessed August 2004).

32. Matthew L. Wald, "Third Area Code Is Added in the Land of the Toll-Free," *New York Times*, April 4, 1998, p. 10; and "AT&T Offers Toll-Free Number Availability Tool Online," *Direct Marketing*, May 2001, p. 24.

33. Rebecca Harris, "Do-not-call legislation becomes law," *Marketing Daily*, November 30, 2005, www.marketingmag.ca/.

34. Excerpt from Dave Barry, "So What's Their Hang-up?" *Miami Herald*, October 5, 2003, accessed at www.miami.com/mld/miamiherald/living/columnists/dave_barry/6934584.htm?1c.

35. Marlene Milczarek, "Database Diamond Mining," *Marketing Magazine*, August 13, 2001, www.marketingmag.ca.

36. "Case Study: Just White Shirts," Industry Canada, April 20, 2006 http://strategis.ic.gc.ca/epic/internet/inee-ef.nsf/en/ee00428e.html (accessed May 2006); and http://justwhiteshirts.com.

37. Facts about the catalogue industry in this section are from "The DMA State of the Catalog Industry Report," www.the-dma.org (accessed August 2004).

38. "Snapshot spots probable Canadian catalogue buyers," Direct Marketing News, October 2005, www.dmn.ca/Articles/Articles/2005/october/borderfree.htm (accessed January 17, 2007).

39. Ron Donoho, "One-Man Show," *Sales & Marketing Management*, June 2001, pp. 36–42; and information at www.ronco.com (accessed March 2004).

40. Nat Ives, "Infomercials Clean Up Their Pitch," *New York Times*, April 12, 2004, p. C1.

41. Erika Brown, "Ooh! Aah!" *Forbes*, March 8, 1999, p. 56. Also see Shirley Leung, "Grill Sales Slow but Big Payouts Flow to Foreman," *Wall Street Journal*, February 2, 2001, p. B1; and Jane Bennett Clark, Robert Frick, Matt Popowksy, and Daniel Kohan, "As Seen on TV," *Kiplinger's Personal Finance*, July 2002, p. 99.

42. Larry Beck, "The Kiosk's Ship Has Come In," *DSN Retailing Today*, February 19, 2001, p. 14; Shayn Ferriolo, "The Key to Kiosks," *Catalog Age*, June 2003, pp. 103–108; and Charlotte Goddard, "Mobile Offers Kiosks a New Role," *Revolution*, January 2004, p. 21.

43. "Interactive: Ad Age Names Finalists," *Advertising Age*, February 27, 1995, pp. 12–14.

44. Yang, "No Web Site Is an Island," p. EB38; Matthew Haeberle, "REI Overhauls Its E-commerce," *Chain Store Age*, January 2003, p. 64; and Sarah McBride, "Virgin Group Plans New Venture to Enter Online Music Business," *Wall Street Journal*, March 8, 2004, p. B.4.

45. "Sweepstakes Groups Settles with States," *New York Times*, June 27, 2001, p. A14; and "PCH Reaches $34 Million Sweepstakes Settlement with 26 States," *Direct Marketing*, September 2001, p. 6.

46. Jennifer Lee, "Welcome to the Database Lounge," *New York Times*, March 21, 2002, p. G1.

Chapter 17

1. "Budget Sets Up Shop in Canadian Tire Stores," *Marketing Magazine, Marketing Daily*, February 21, 2003, www.marketingmag.ca; "Canadian Tire Links Catalogue to Web," *Marketing Magazine, Marketing Daily*, March 16, 2001, www.marketingmag.ca; Canadian Tire press release,

June 12, 2001, www.newswire.ca/releases/June2001/12/c3244.html; Canadian Tire press release, March 15, 2001, www.newswire.ca/releases/March2001/15/c3883.html; "Fourth CMOST Study Demonstrates Online's Ability to Influence Behavior in Short Period of Time," *IAB Canada Newsletters*, March 16, 2005; Canadian Tire website www2.canadiantire.ca/eflyer/e/index.html (accessed May 2006).

2. Canadian Media Directors Council, *Media Digest*, p. 58 www.cmdc.ca/mediadigest.html (accessed May 2, 2006); "On-line shopping expected to top $2.7 billion," *Globe and Mail*, November 24, 2005.

3. Canadian Media Directors Council, *Media Digest*, p. 60, www.cmdc.ca/mediadigest.html (accessed May 2, 2006).

4. Robyn Greenspan, "The Web as a Way of Life," www.cyberatlas.internet.com (accessed May 21, 2002); "June 2003 Internet Usage Stats," www. cyberatlas.com (accessed September, 2003); and "Internet Part of the Family in Canada," www.clickz.com/stats/sectors/geographics/article.php/964381 (accessed May 12, 2006).

5. Paola Hjelt, "Flying on the Web in a Turbulent Economy," *Business Week*, April 30, 2001, pp. 142–148.

6. Bob Parks, "Let's Remake a Dealership," *Business 2.0*, June 2004, pp. 65–67.

7. Tessa Wegert, "On-line marketing concept gives consumers a say," *Globe and Mail*, October 13, 2005, p. B13.

8. See Timothy Mullaney, "The E-Biz Surprise," *Business Week*, May 12, 2003, pp. 60–68; Patti Freeman Evans, "Market Forecast: Retail Spending Online," Jupiter Research, January 8, 2004, www.jup.com; Carrie A. Johnson, "US eCommerce Overview: 2004 to 2010," August 2, 2004, www.forrester.com/Research/Document/Excerpt/0,7211,34576,00.html; and "Canada B2C ECommerce," Research and Markets, http://www.researchandmarkets.com/reports/363343/canada_b2c_e_commerce.htm (accessed January 17, 2007).

9. "Internet Adoption Slowing—But Dependence On It Continues To Grow," Ipsos Insights Press Release, March 29, 2006, www.ipsos-na.com/news/pressrelease.cfm?id=3030 (accessed May 2006).

10. See Michael Totty, "E-Commerce (A Special Report): Selling Strategies—Demographics: The Masses Have Arrived—And E-Commerce Will Never Be the Same," *Wall Street Journal*, January 27, 2003, p. R8; and Vipul Patel, "Portrait of the Online Population," *Jupiter Research*, March 18, 2004, www.jup.com.

11. Rob Gerlsbeck, "Surfers love the web, but won't give up TV," *Marketing Daily*, November 3, 2005, www.marketingmag.ca.

12. Lisa D'Innocenzo, "Join a Community," *Strategy Magazine*, May 2006, p. 48.

13. See Joanne Cleaver, "Surfing for Seniors," *Marketing News*, July 19, 1999, pp. 1, 7; Sara Teasdale Montgomery, "Senior Surfers Grab Web Attention," *Advertising Age*, July 10, 2000, p. S4; Hassan Fattah, "Hollywood, the Internet, & Kids," *American Demographics*, May 2001, pp. 51–56; Robyn Greenspan, "Surfing with Seniors and Boomers," *CyberAtlas*, January 23, 2003, www.cyberatlas.com; and Vipul Patel, "Portrait of the

Online Population," Jupiter Research, March 18, 2004, www.jup.com.

14. Statistics Canada, "Electronic commerce households spending in Canada and in other countries, by region 2003," www40.statcan.ca/l01/cst01/comm07a.htm (accessed May 12, 2006).

15. Strategis Canada, "Canadian E-Commerce Statistics, 2004," http://e-com.ic.gc.ca/epic/Internet/inecic-ceac.nsf/en/gv00163e.html (accessed May 12, 2006).

16. Grant Buckler, "On-Line Exchanges Yield Healthy Hospital Savings," *Globe and Mail*, www.globeandmail.com (accessed March 21, 2002).

17. Facts from eBay annual reports and other information at www.ebay.com (accessed September 2004); "EBay Realizes Success in Small-Biz Arena," *Marketing News*, May 1, 2004, p. 11; and Erick Schonfeld, "Corporate America's New Outlet Mall," *Business 2.0*, April 2004, pp. 43–45.

18. Adapted from Lev Grossman, "Meet Joe Blog," *Time*, June 21, 2004, p. 65.

19. Kris Oser, "Nike Assays Blog as Marketing Tool," *Advertising Age*, June 14, 2004, p. 26.

20. Michelle Slatalla, "Toll-Free Apology Soothes Savage Beast," *New York Times*, February 12, 2004, p. G4; and information from www.planetfeedback.com/consumer (accessed August 2004).

21. Bradley Johnson, "Out-of-Sight Spending Collides with Reality," *Advertising Age*, August 7, 2000, pp. S4–S8.

22. See Ann Weintraub, "For Online Pet Stores, It's Dog-Eat-Dog," *Business Week*, March 6, 2000, pp. 78–80; "Death of a Spokespup," *Adweek*, December 11, 2000, pp. 44–46; Jacques R. Chevron, "Name Least of Pet.com's Woes," *Advertising Age*, January 22, 2001, p. 24; Norm Alster, "Initial Offerings Take a Turn to the Traditional," *New York Times*, May 19, 2002, p. 3.4; "Marketing Hits and Misses," *Sales & Marketing Management*, August 2002, p. 16; and "Dot-com Craze Sparks IPO Flameouts," *Knight Ridder Tribune Business News*, November 2, 2003, p. 1.

23. Steve Hamm, "E-Biz: Down but Hardly Out," *Business Week*, March 26, 2001, p. 127; and "Business Brief—Staples Inc.: Net Income Falls 5.2% but Its Internet Unit Posts a Pretax Profit," *Wall Street Journal*, August 22, 2001, p. B4; Marina Strauss, "Danier axes staff, stores, e-commerce," *Globe and Mail*, May 31, 2006, www.theglobeandmail.com/servlet/story/RTGAM.2006053 0.wxr-danier31/BNStory/Technology/einsider/.

24. "E-Commerce Trudges through Current Slowdown," www.cyberatlas.internet.com (accessed May 22, 2001). Also see Eyal Biyalogorsky and Prasad Naik, "Click and Mortar: The Effect of On-Line Activities on Off-Line Sales," *Marketing Letters*, February 2003, pp. 1–21.

25. Sharon Gaudin, "The Site of No Return," www.graphics-art.com/Site%20of%20no%20return.htm (accessed May 28, 2002).

26. Marty Bernstein, "Mitsubishi Super Bowl Ad Lures Viewer to Internet," *Automotive News*, March 29, 2004, p. 56B.

27. John Deighton, "The Future of Interactive Marketing," *Harvard Business Review*, November–December 1996, p. 154.

28. Don Peppers and Martha Rogers, "Opening the Door to Consumers," *Sales & Marketing Management*, October 1998, pp. 22–29; Mike Beirne, "Marketers of the Next Generation: Silvio Bonvini," *Brandweek*, November 8, 1999, p. 64; Bob Tedeschi, "Consumer Products Companies Use Web Sites to Strengthen Ties with Consumers," *New York Times*, August 25, 2003, p. C.6; and information from www.candystand.com (accessed June 2004).

29. Jeffrey F. Rayport and Bernard J. Jaworski, *e-Commerce* (New York: McGraw-Hill, 2001), p. 116. Also see Goutam Chakraborty, "What Do Customers Consider Important in B2B Websites?" *Journal of Advertising*, March 2003, p. 50; and David Sparrow, "Get 'Em to Bite," *Catalog Age*, April 1, 2003, pp. 35–36.

30. Reid Goldsborough, "Creating Web Sites for Web Surfers," *Black Issues in Higher Education*, June 17, 2004, p. 120.

31. Lisa Bertagnoli, "Getting Satisfaction," *Marketing News*, May 7, 2001, p. 11.

32. Tobi Elkin, "Size Matters; So Does Price," *Advertising Age*, January 13, 2003, p. 46.

33. For these and other examples, see William M. Bulkeley, "E-Commerce (A Special Report): Cover Story—Pass It On: Advertisers Discover They Have a Friend in 'Viral' Marketing," *Wall Street Journal*, January 14, 2002, p. R6; and Pete Snyder, "Wanted: Standards for Viral Marketing," *Brandweek*, June 28, 2004, p. 21.

34. David Chilton, "Spreading the message," *Marketing Magazine*, March 6, 2006.

35. Eilene Zimmerman, "Catch the Bug," *Sales and Marketing Management*, February 2001, pp. 78–82. Also see Ellen Neuborne, "Viral Marketing Alert," *Business Week*, March 19, 2001, p. EB8.

36. Canadian Media Directors Council—*Media Digest*, p. 10, www.cmdc.ca/mediadigest.html (accessed May 2, 2006)..

37. Tobi Elkin, "Net Advantages," *Advertising Age*, February 10, 2003, p. 29.

38. Adapted from information found in Stuart Elliott, "Seinfeld and Superman Join Forces Again in Spots for American Express, This Time on the Web," *New York Times*, March 30, 2004, p. C.5; and Michael Snider, "Internet: Watch Out for Adver-tainment," *Maclean's*, May 17, 2004, p. 54.

39. Tessa Wegert, "Get help if you want customers to get the message," *Globe and Mail*, May 30, 2006, www.theglobeandmail.com/servlet/story/LAC.20060531. SRTECHEMARK31/TPStory/?query=tessa+wegert.

40. Heidi Anderson, "Nintendo Case Study: Rules Are Made to Be Broken," *E-Mail Marketing Case Studie*s, MISSING (accessed March 6, 2003).

41. Tessa Wegert, "Get help if you want customers to get the message," *Globe and Mail*, May 30, 2006, www.theglobeandmail.com/servlet/story/LAC.20060531. SRTECHEMARK31/TPStory/?query=tessa+wegert.

42. Michael Porter, "Strategy and the Internet," *Harvard Business Review*, March 2001, pp. 614–678.

43. Timothy J. Mullaney, "Break Out the Black Ink," *Business Week*, May 13, 2002, pp. 74–76; and Timothy Mullaney, "The Web Is Finally Catching Profits," *Business Week*, February 17, 2003, p. 66.

44. See Peter Han and Angus Maclaurin, "Do Consumers Really Care About Online Privacy?" *Marketing Management,* January–February 2002, pp. 35–38; Eric Goldman, "The Internet Privacy Fallacy," *Computer and Internet Lawyer,* January 2003, p. 20; and Nancy Wong, "Getting Pragmatic about Privacy," *American Demographics,* June 2003, pp. 14–15.

45. Bob Tedeschi, "Everybody Talks about Online Privacy, but Few Do Anything about It," *New York Times,* June 3, 2002, p. C6; and Susan Johnson, "Reflecting a Global Reality," *Beyond Numbers,* April 2004, pp. 6–13.

46. Information on TRUSTe at www.truste.com (accessed September 2004).

47. Canadian Media Directors Council—*Media Digest,* pp. 58–60, www.cmdc.ca/mediadigest.html (accessed May 2, 2006).

48. Facts from Mark Warschauer, "Demystifying the Digital Divide," *Scientific American,* August 2003, p. 42; quote from Richard J. Dalton Jr., "New York Libraries Try to Close Minorities' Digital Divide," *Knight Ridder Tribune Business News,* July 4, 2004, p. 1.

49. "14-Year-Old Bids over $3M for Items in eBay Auctions," *USA Today,* April 30, 1999, p. 10B.

Chapter 18

1. Gordon Pitts, "Once a tortoise, McCain Foods is determined to be the hare," *Globe and Mail,* October 29, 2005, p. B12; Laura Ramsay, "Canada to Bombay: Want fries with that? *Globe and Mail,* June 1, 2006; Natalia Williams, "The McCain makeover," *Strategy Magazine,* January 2005, p. 15; "GB Launches Awareness Campaign," *The Star,* Vol. 38, No. 1, February 2006; "Canada Wins Cassie," *The Star,* Vol. 38, No. 1, February 2006; "2003 Export Awards," International Trade Canada, www.infoexport.gc.ca/awards-prix/awards/2003/mccain-e.htm;jsessionid=RMW5R3LSKMCT0CTHNCACFEQ (accessed June 2006).

2. George Melloan, "Feeling the Muscles of the Multi-nationals," *Wall Street Journal,* January 6, 2004, p. A19.

3. John Alden, "What in the World Drives UPS?" *International Business,* April 1998, pp. 6–7; Karen Pennar, "Two Steps Forward, One Step Back," *Business Week,* August 31, 1998, p. 116; Michelle Wirth Fellman, "A New World for Marketers," *Marketing News,* May 10, 1999, p. 13; Alan Greenspan, "International Trade: Globalization vs. Protectionism," *Vital Speeches of the Day,* April 15, 2001, pp. 386–388; and *International Trade Statistics 2002,* WTO, p. 1, www.wto.org/english/res_e/statis_e/its2002_e/its02_toc_e.htm (accessed August 2004).

4. Information on Vincor drawn from Vincor International Inc.'s website www.vincorinternational.com (accessed August 2006); "Vincor International Inc.: Good For You Too," *Share Owner,* September/October 2004, accessed at www.findarticles.com/p/articles/mi_qa4037/is_200409/ai_n 9409482; Mary Crane, "Constellation's Vincor Integration Plans," Forbes.com, July 12, 2006, www.forbes.com/2006/07/12/constellation-0712markets18.html?partner=msn, 07.12.06, (accessed August 2006). Other facts in this section drawn from Gail Edmondson, "See the World, Erase Its Borders," *Business Week,* August 28, 2000, pp. 113–114.

5. For information, video and radio segments on globalization see "Globalization," The World Bank Group, www1.worldbank.org/economicpolicy/globalization/; also refer to "Globalization," Wikipedia, http://en.wikipedia.org/wiki/Globalization#Anti-globalization_.28Global_Justice.29 (accessed August 2006).

6. Sahm Adrangi, "Tiny Toronto Bike Firms Spins Success," *Globe and Mail,* July 26, 2003, pp. B1, B4; "The amazing race: Cervélo Cycles," *Profit Magazine,* May 2006, www.canadianbusiness.com/entrepreneur/managing/article.jsp;jsessionid=MHIPHDJKDHKC?content=20060404_153018_5420 (accessed June 2006).

7. "The Unique Japanese," *Fortune,* November 24, 1986, p. 8; and James D. Southwick, "Addressing Market Access Barriers in Japan Through the WTO," *Law and Policy in International Business,* Spring 2000, pp. 923–976. For more on nontariff and other barriers, see Warren J. Keegan and Mark C. Green, *Principles of Global Marketing* (Upper Saddle River, NJ: Prentice Hall, 2000), chapter 8; and Simon P. Anderson and Nicholas Schmidt, "Nontariff Barriers and Trade Liberalization," *Economic Inquiry,* January 2003, pp. 80–98.

8. "What Is the WTO?" www.wto.org/english/thewto_e/whatis_e/whatis_e.htm (accessed September 2004).

9. See Ping Deng, "Impact of GATT Uruguay Round on Various Industries," *American Business Review,* June 1998, pp. 22–29; Helene Cooper, "U.S. Seeks a New Rounds of WTO Talks," *Wall Street Journal,* July 18, 2001, p. A12; Michael Finger, Julio J. Nogues, "The Unbalanced Uruguay Outcome: The New Areas in Future WTO Negotiations," *The World Economy,* March 2002, pp. 321–340; and *WTO Annual Report 2003,* www.wto.org/english/res_e/booksp_e/anrep_e/anrep03_e.pdf (accessed September 2004).

10. "Leaders: Deadlocked in Doha; World Trade," *The Economist,* March 29, 2003, p. 13; and Supachai Panitchpakdi, "Brave New World," *Wall Street Journal,* February 26, 2004, p. A.10.

11. Jeffrey Lewis, "The European Union," *AFP Exchange,* March/April 2003, pp. 46–50; Robert J. Samuelson, "The European Predicament," *The Washington Post,* February 4, 2004, p. A23; and "The European Union at a Glance," http://europa.eu.int (accessed December 2004).

12. "Finance and Economics: The Euro, Trade and Growth; Economic Focus," *The Economist,* July 12, 2003, p. 74; and "One Europe, United in Fiscal Misrule," *Global Agenda,* January 26, 2004, p. 1; "Czech brewers see the world as their oyster," *EUbusiness Week,* Issue 260, March 26, 2005, www.eubusiness.com/afp/050327033240.j5l4mji1.

13. For more on the European Union, see "Around Europe in 40 Years," *The Economist,* May 31, 1997, p. S4; "European Union to Begin Expansion," *New York Times,* March 30, 1998, p. A5; Joan Warner, "Mix Us Culturally? It's Impossible," *Business Week,* April 27, 1998, p. 108; Paul J. Deveney, "World Watch," *Wall Street Journal,* May 20, 1999, p. A12; and Stephen J. Dannhauser, "Can Europe Become a Global Superpower? Europe Must Have Unification," *Vital Speeches of the Day,* April 1, 2003, pp. 382–385.

14. "Canada is a Trading Nation: Canada's Major Trading Partners," www.2ontario.com/welcome/coca_401.asp (accessed June 2006); "NAFTA @ 10: A Preliminary Report," Department of Foreign Affairs and International Trade, October 7, 2003, www.dfait-maeci.gc.ca/eet/research/nafta/nafta-en.asp#message (accessed June 2006); Fay Hansen, "World Trade Update," *Business Finance,* March 2002, pp. 9–11; Daniel T Griswold, "NAFTA at 10" *World Trade,* March 2003, p. 10; Kelley Mullaney, "Importance of U.S.–Canada Trade Relationships Highlighted at Houston Partnership," January 14, 2004, www.partnershipforgrowth.org; and Michael O'Boyle, "Nafta's Birthday Party," *Business Mexico,* February 2004, pp. 28–34; Free Trade Area of the Americas (FTAA), www.ftaa-alca.org/View_e.asp (accessed August 2006).

15. Bernard Malamud and Wayne A. Label, "The Merco: A Common Currency for Mercosur and Latin America," *American Business Review,* June 2002, pp. 132–139; Terry Wade, "Latin Trade Bloc Flexes Its Muscle—New Leaders in Argentina, Brazil Give Mercosur Clout; Another Challenge for U.S." *Wall Street Journal,* June 16, 2003, p. A.13; and K D Narendranate, "Preferential Mercosur Tariffs Likely by June," *The Economic Times,* February 28, 2004, http://economictimes.indiatimes.com.

16. See Geri Smith and Cristina Lindblad "Mexico: Was NAFTA Worth It?" *Business Week,* December 22, 2003, pp. 66–72.

17. See David Woodruff, "Ready to Shop until They Drop," *Business Week,* June 22, 1998, pp. 104–108; and James MacAonghus, "Online Impact of a Growing Europe," *New Media Age,* February 12, 2004, p. 15.

18. "Canada-India Trade Relations To Intensify," News Release No. 61, Department of Foreign Affairs and International Trade, April 6, 2005.

19. See Dan West, "Countertrade," *Business Credit,* April 2001, pp. 64–67; West, "Countertrade," *Business Credit,* April 2002, pp. 48–51; and Joao Pedro Taborda, "The Use of Countertrade and Offsets as a Tool for Strategic Advantage," *Competitive Intelligence Magazine,* May–June, 2003, p. 51.

20. For this and other examples, see Louis Kraar, "How to Sell to Cashless Buyers," *Fortune,* November 7, 1988, pp. 147–154; Nathaniel Gilbert, "The Case for Countertrade," *Across the Board,* May 1992, pp. 43–45; Darren McDermott and S. Karen Witcher, "Bartering Gains Currency," *Wall Street Journal,* April 6, 1998, p. A10; Anne Millen Porter, "Global Economic Meltdown Boosts Barter Business," *Purchasing,* February 11, 1999, pp. 21–25; S. Jayasankaran, "Fire-Fighting," *Far Eastern Economic Review,* May 31, 2001, p. 52; and Dalia Marin and Monika Schnitzer, "The Economic Institution of International Barter," *Economic Journal,* April 2002, pp. 293–316.

21. "Canada tops G7 again as most competitive nation for trade," news release, Government of Canada, April 2, 2006, www.investincanada.gc.ca/en/992/News.html (accessed June 2006); and Caroline Alphonso, "A great place to do business," *Globe and Mail,* October 1, 2005.

22. "Seminars in Australia, Edouard & Co. Paris, May 2006, www.austrade.org/corporate/layout/ 0,,0_-1_-2_-3_PWB110812664-4_-5_-6_-7_DOCUMENT,00.html (accessed June 2006); Elaine Sciolino, "Skin Deep; Sans Makeup, S'il Vous Plaît," *New York Times,* May 25, 2006.

23. For a full discussion of culture see G. Hofstede, *Culture's consequences: International differences in work-related values* (Beverly Hills, CA: Sage, 1980); R. House, M. Javidan, P. Hanges, and P. Dorfman. "Understanding cultures and implicit leadership theories across the globe: and introduction to project GLOBE," *Journal of World Business,* 37, pp. 3–10.

24. Rebecca Piirto Heath, "Think Globally," *Marketing Tools,* October 1996, pp. 49–54; and "The Power of Writing," *National Geographic,* August 1999, pp. 128–129.

25. For other examples and discussion, see *Dun & Bradstreet's Guide to Doing Business Around the World* (Upper Saddle River, NJ: Prentice Hall, 2000); Betsy Cummings, "Selling Around the World," *Sales & Marketing Management,* May 2001, p. 70; James K. Sebenius, "The Hidden Challenge of Cross-Border Negotiations," *Harvard Business Review,* March 2002, pp. 76–85; Daniel Joseph, "Dangerous Assumptions," *Ceramic Industry,* January 2003, p. 120; Ellen Neuborne, "Bridging the Culture Gap," *Sales & Marketing Management,* July 2003, p. 22; and "Belgium: Language, Culture and Business Etiquette," Kwintessential Language and Culture Specialists, www.kwintessential.co.uk/resources/global-etiquette/belgium-country-profile.html (accessed October 2006).

26. Pete Engardio, Manjeet Kripalani, and Alysha Webb, "Smart Globalization," *Business Week,* August 27, 2001, pp. 132–136.

27. Adapted from Mark Rice-Oxley, "In 2,000 Years, Will the World Remember Disney or Plato?" *Christian Science Monitor,* January 15, 2004, p. 16.

28. "Notes For An Address By The Honourable Pierre Pettigrew, Minister For International Trade, At The Waterloo Export Café Luncheon, Department of Foreign Affairs and International Trade, March 5, 2003, http://w01.international.gc.ca/minpub/Publication.asp?publication_id=379894&Language=E (accessed June 2006).

29. Simon Avery, "RIM launches BlackBerry in South Korea," *Globe and Mail,* May 31, 2006.

30. See "Crest, Colgate Bare Teeth in Competition for China," *Advertising Age International,* November 1996, p. I3; and Jack Neff, "Submerged," *Advertising Age,* March 4, 2002, p. 14.

31. "Minister Pettigrew Presents Exporter Of The Year Award, Canada Export Awards Press Release No. 180, November 24, 2003, www.infoexport.gc.ca/awards-prix; Mega Bloks website www.megabloks.com; 2005 Canada Export Awards www.infoexport.gc.ca/awards-prix/mega_bloks-e_win.htm; Chris Nuttall-Smith, How To Make Mega Bucks, *Globe and Mail Report on Business,* April 2005, pp. 56–61.

32. For a good discussion of joint venturing, see James Bamford, David Ernst, and David G. Fubini, "Launching a World-Class Joint Venture," *Harvard Business Review,* February 2004, pp. 91–100.

33. Robert Neff, "In Japan, They're Goofy about Disney," *Business Week,* March 12, 1990, p. 64; "In Brief: E*Trade Licensing Deal Gives It an Israeli Link," *American Banker,* May 11, 1998; John Engen, "Going Going Global," *USBanker,* February 2000, pp. 22S–25S; "Cowboys and Samuri: The Japanizing of Universal," *Wall Street Journal,* March 22, 2001, p. B1; Chester Dawson, "Will Tokyo Embrace Another Mouse?" *Business Week,* September 10, 2001; and Bruce Orwall, "Eisner Contends Disney Is

Primed for Turnaround," *Wall Street Journal*, August 9, 2002, p. B1; and "Walt Disney Parks & Resorts," *Hoover's Company Capsules*, Austin, July 1, 2003, p. 104368.

34. "Chinese Fortunes," *Strategy Magazine*, August 2004, p. 32.

35. See Cynthia Kemper, "KFC Tradition Sold Japan on Chicken," *Denver Post*, June 7, 1998, p. J4; and Milford Prewitt, "Chains Look for Links Overseas," *Nation's Restaurant News*, February 18, 2002, pp. 1, 6.

36. For good discussions, see Laura Mazur, "Globalization Is Still Tethered to Local Variations," *Marketing*, January 22, 2004, p. 18; and Johny K. Johansson and Ilkka A. Ronkainen, "The Brand Challenge: Are Global Brands the Right Choice for Your Company?" *Marketing Management*, March/April 2004.

37. See "In India, Beef-Free Mickie D," *Business Week*, April 7, 1995, p. 52; Jeff Walters, "Have Brand Will Travel," *Brandweek*, October 6, 1997, pp. 22–26; David Barboza, "From Abroad, McDonald's Finds Value in Local Control," *New York Times*, February 12, 1999, p. 1; Suh-Kyung Yoon, "Look Who's Going Native," *Far Eastern Economic Review*, February 1, 2001, pp. 68–69; and Saritha Rai, "Tastes of India in U.S. Wrappers," *New York Times*, April 29, 2003 p. W1.

38. For more, see Warren J. Keegan, *Global Marketing Management*, 7th ed. (Upper Saddle River, NJ: Prentice Hall, 2002), pp. 346–351.

39. Adapted from Douglas McGray, "Translating Sony into English," *Fast Company*, January 2003, p. 38. Also see

Jeffrey Selingo, "Newer, Smaller, Fasters, and Not in Stores Now," *New York Times*, May 8, 2003, p. G.5.

40. Kate MacArthur, "Coca-Cola Light Employs Local Edge," *Advertising Age*, August 21, 2000, pp. 18–19; and "Case Studies: Coke Light Hottest Guy," *Advantage Marketing, msn India*, http://advantage.msn.co.in (accessed March 15, 2004).

41. See Alicia Clegg, "One Ad One World?" *Marketing Week*, June 20, 2002, pp. 51–52; and George E. Belch and Michael A. Belch, *Advertising and Promotion: An Integrated Marketing Communications Perspective*, 6th ed. (New York, NY: McGraw Hill, 2004), pp. 666–668.

42. Adapted from Normandy Madden and Jack Neff, "P&G Adapts Attitude toward Local Markets," *Advertising Age*, February 23, 2004, p. 28.

43. David Menzies, "Bicycle Brouhaha," *Canadian Business*, August 2005; Canadian Government Rejects Bicycle Surtax, *Bicycle Retailer*, May 30, 2006.

44. Sarah Ellison, "Revealing Price Discrepancies, the Euro Aids Bargain-Hunters," *Wall Street Journal*, January 30, 2002, p. A15.

45. See Patrick Powers, "Distribution in China: The End of the Beginning," *China Business Review*, July–August, 2001, pp. 8–12; Drake Weisert, "Coca-Cola in China: Quenching the Thirst of a Billion," *The China Business Review*, July–August 2001, pp. 52–55; and Gabriel Kahn, "Coke Works Harder at Being the Real Thing in Hinterland," *Wall Street Journal*, November 26, 2002, p. B1.

Name Index

Subject Index

Key terms and pages on which they're defined are indicated in bold.

Photo Credits